CSE 200: Computer Aided Problem Solving for Business/ MS Office 2003

Shelly / Cashman / Gross

THOMSON
™
COURSE TECHNOLOGY

Australia · Canada · Mexico · Singapore · Spain · United Kingdom · United States

CSE 200: Computer Aided Problem Solving for Business/ MS Office 2003
Shelly / Cashman / Gross

Executive Editors:
Michele Baird, Maureen Staudt & Michael Stranz

Project Development Manager:
Linda de Stefano

Marketing Coordinators:
Lindsay Annett and Sara Mercurio

Production/Manufacturing Supervisor:
Donna M. Brown

Pre-Media Services Supervisor:
Dan Plofchan

Rights and Permissions Specialists:
Kalina Hintz and Bahman Naraghi

Cover Image
Getty Images*

The Adaptable Courseware Program consists of products and additions to existing Thomson products that are produced from camera-ready copy. Peer review, class testing, and accuracy are primarily the responsibility of the author(s).

ISBN 1-423-96414-4

International Divisions List

Asia (Including India):
Thomson Learning
(a division of Thomson Asia Pte Ltd)
5 Shenton Way #01-01
UIC Building
Singapore 068808
Tel: (65) 6410-1200
Fax: (65) 6410-1208

Australia/New Zealand:
Thomson Learning Australia
102 Dodds Street
Southbank, Victoria 3006
Australia

Latin America:
Thomson Learning
Seneca 53
Colonia Polano
11560 Mexico, D.F., Mexico
Tel (525) 281-2906
Fax (525) 281-2656

Canada:
Thomson Nelson
1120 Birchmount Road
Toronto, Ontario
Canada M1K 5G4
Tel (416) 752-9100
Fax (416) 752-8102

UK/Europe/Middle East/Africa:
Thomson Learning
High Holborn House
50-51 Bedford Row
London, WC1R 4LS
United Kingdom
Tel 44 (020) 7067-2500
Fax 44 (020) 7067-2600

Spain (Includes Portugal):
Thomson Paraninfo
Calle Magallanes 25
28015 Madrid
España
Tel 34 (0)91 446-3350
Fax 34 (0)91 445-6218

Contents

Introduction to Computers and Windows

ESSENTIAL
Introduction to Computers

and How to Purchase a Personal Computer

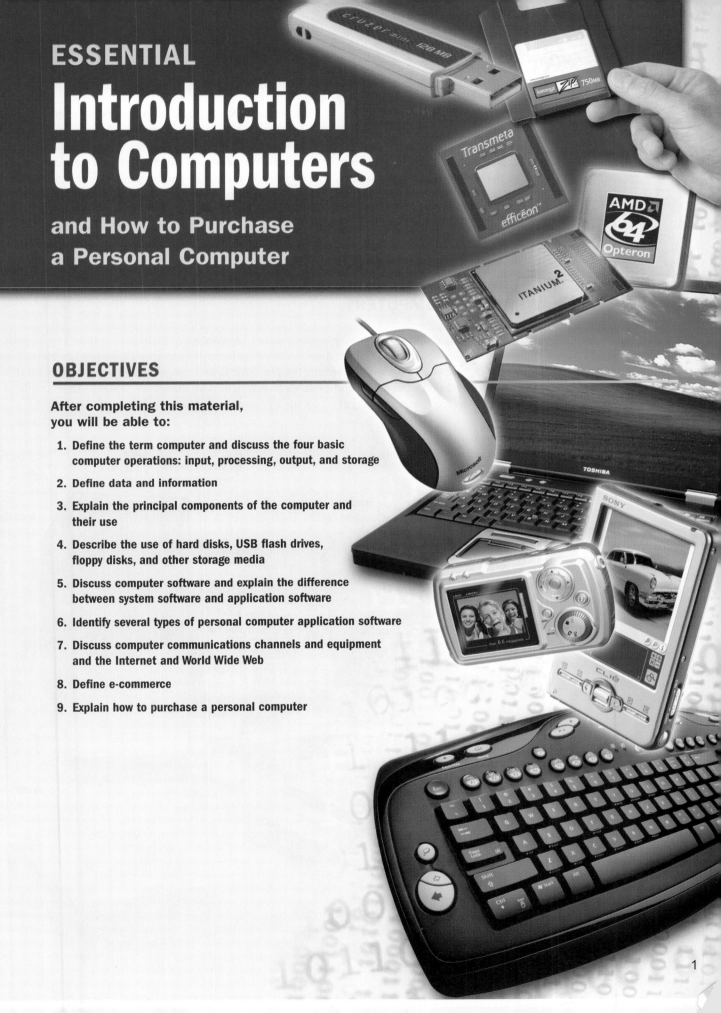

OBJECTIVES

After completing this material,
you will be able to:

1. Define the term computer and discuss the four basic computer operations: input, processing, output, and storage

2. Define data and information

3. Explain the principal components of the computer and their use

4. Describe the use of hard disks, USB flash drives, floppy disks, and other storage media

5. Discuss computer software and explain the difference between system software and application software

6. Identify several types of personal computer application software

7. Discuss computer communications channels and equipment and the Internet and World Wide Web

8. Define e-commerce

9. Explain how to purchase a personal computer

Computers are everywhere: at work, at school, and at home. In the workplace, employees use computers to create correspondence such as e-mail, memos, and letters; calculate payroll; track inventory; and generate invoices. At school, teachers use computers to assist with classroom instruction. Students complete assignments and do research on computers. At home, people spend hours of leisure time on the computer. They play games, communicate with friends and relatives using e-mail, purchase goods online, chat in chat rooms, listen to music, watch videos and movies, read books and magazines, research genealogy, compose music and videos, retouch photographs, and plan vacations. At work, at school, and at home, computers are helping people do their work faster, more accurately, and in some cases, in ways that previously would not have been possible.

WEB LINK

Computers

For more information, visit scsite.com/ic6/ weblink and then click Computers.

WHAT IS A COMPUTER?

A **computer** is an electronic device, operating under the control of instructions stored in its own memory, that can accept data (input), process the data according to specified rules (process), produce results (output), and store the results (storage) for future use. Generally, the term is used to describe a collection of hardware components that function together as a system. An example of common hardware components that make up a personal computer is shown in Figure 1.

FIGURE 1 Common computer hardware components.

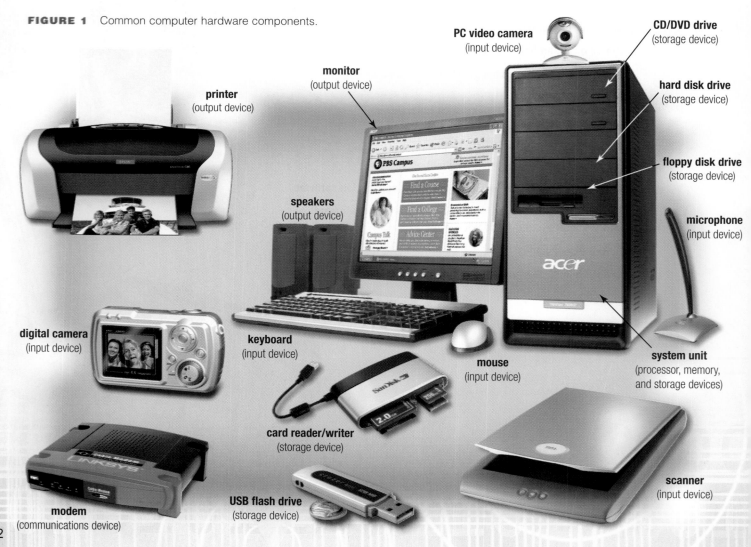

printer (output device)

monitor (output device)

PC video camera (input device)

CD/DVD drive (storage device)

hard disk drive (storage device)

floppy disk drive (storage device)

speakers (output device)

microphone (input device)

digital camera (input device)

keyboard (input device)

mouse (input device)

system unit (processor, memory, and storage devices)

card reader/writer (storage device)

scanner (input device)

modem (communications device)

USB flash drive (storage device)

WHAT DOES A COMPUTER DO?

WEB LINK

Information

For more information, visit scsite.com/ic6/ weblink and then click Information.

Computers perform four basic operations — input, process, output, and storage. These operations comprise the **information processing cycle**. Collectively, these operations change data into information and store it for future use.

All computer processing requires data. **Data** is a collection of unprocessed items, which can include text, numbers, images, audio, and video. Computers manipulate data to create information. **Information** conveys meaning and is useful to one or more people. During the output operation, the information that has been created is put into some form, such as a printed report, or it can be written on computer storage for future use. As shown in Figure 2, a computer processes several data items to produce a paycheck. Another example of information is a grade report, which is generated from data items such as a student name, course names, and course grades.

People who use the computer directly or use the information it provides are called **computer users**, **end users**, or sometimes, just **users**.

FIGURE 2 A computer processes data into information. In this example, the employee's name and address, hourly rate of pay, and hours worked all represent data. The computer processes the data to produce the payroll check (information).

DATA

Kayla Robertson
1192 Reeder Road
Hammond, IN 46323
$12.50 per hour
28 hours

PROCESSES

- Multiplies hourly pay rate by hours to determine gross pay (350.00)
- Organizes data
- Computes payroll taxes (49.00)
- Subtracts payroll taxes from gross pay to determine net pay (301.00)

678911

Date: June 17, 2006 $ 301.00
                                Dollars

Maple Construction
421 Cedar Road
Hammond, IN 46323

pay to the order of   Kayla Robertson

Three Hundred One and 00/100

Joan Smith
President

Memo _____ 006678911   :788340374934 2: 14 12 77 43 2

INFORMATION

WEB LINK

Computer Programs

For more information, visit scsite.com/ic6/ weblink and then click Computer Programs.

WHY IS A COMPUTER SO POWERFUL?

A computer derives its power from its capability to perform the information processing cycle with amazing speed, reliability (low failure rate), and accuracy; its capacity to store huge amounts of data and information; and its ability to communicate with other computers.

HOW DOES A COMPUTER KNOW WHAT TO DO?

For a computer to perform operations, it must be given a detailed set of instructions that tells it exactly what to do. These instructions are called a **computer program**, or **software**. Before processing for a specific job begins, the computer program corresponding to that job is stored in the computer. Once the program is stored, the computer can begin to operate by executing the program's first instruction. The computer executes one program instruction after another until the job is complete.

WHAT ARE THE COMPONENTS OF A COMPUTER?

To understand how computers process data into information, you need to examine the primary components of the computer. The six primary components of a computer are input devices, the processor (control unit and arithmetic/logic unit), memory, output devices, storage devices, and communications devices. The processor, memory, and storage devices are housed in a box-like case called the **system unit**. Figure 3 shows the flow of data, information, and instructions between the first five components mentioned. The following sections describe these primary components.

FIGURE 3 Most devices connected to the computer communicate with the processor to carry out a task. When a user starts a program, for example, its instructions transfer from a storage device to memory. Data needed by programs enters memory either from an input device or a storage device. The control unit interprets and executes instructions in memory and the ALU performs calculations on the data in memory. Resulting information is stored in memory, from which it can be sent to an output device or a storage device for future access, as needed.

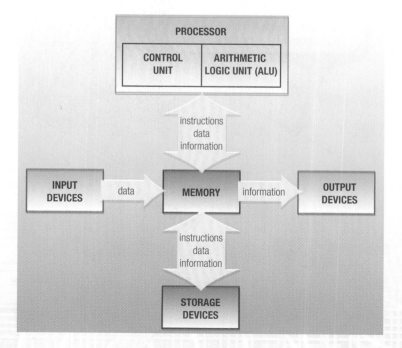

INPUT DEVICES

An **input device** is any hardware component that allows you to enter data, programs, commands, and user responses into a computer. Depending on your particular application and requirement, the input device you use may vary. Popular input devices include the keyboard, mouse, digital camera, scanner, and microphone. The two primary input devices used are the keyboard and the mouse. This section discusses both of these input devices.

WEB LINK

Input Devices

For more information, visit scsite.com/ic6/ weblink and then click Input Devices.

The Keyboard

A **keyboard** is an input device that contains keys you press to enter data into the computer. A desktop computer keyboard (Figure 4) typically has 101 to 105 keys. Keyboards for smaller computers, such as notebooks, contain fewer keys. A computer keyboard includes keys that allow you to type letters of the alphabet, numbers, spaces, punctuation marks, and other symbols such as the dollar sign ($) and asterisk (*). A keyboard also contains other keys that allow you to enter data and instructions into the computer.

FIGURE 4 On a desktop computer keyboard, you type using keys in the typing area and on the numeric keypad.

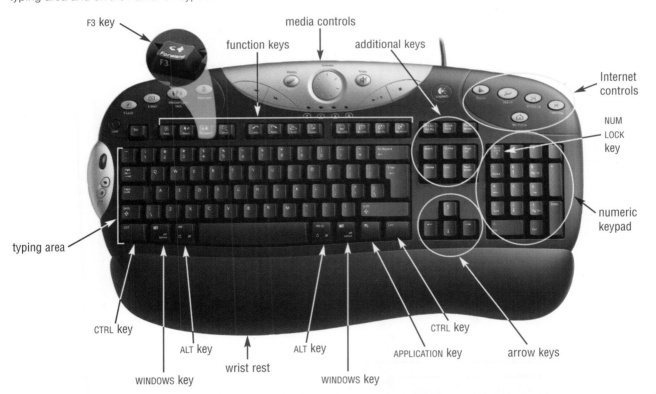

Most handheld computers, such as smart phones, PDAs, and Tablet PCs, use a variety of alternatives for entering data and instructions (Figure 5). One of the more popular handheld computer input devices is the stylus. A **stylus** is a small metal or plastic device that looks like a ballpoint pen, but uses pressure instead of ink to write, draw, or make selections.

Smart phones often include a digital camera so users can send pictures and videos to others (Figure 6).

FIGURE 5 Users enter data and instructions into a PDA using a variety of techniques.

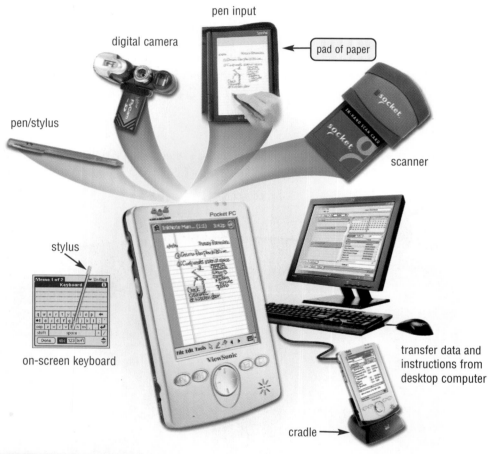

FIGURE 6 Many smart phones include a digital camera so users can send pictures and videos to others.

The Mouse

A **mouse** (Figure 7) is a pointing device that fits comfortably under the palm of your hand. With a mouse, you control the movement of the **pointer**, often called the **mouse pointer**, on the screen and make selections from the screen. A mouse has one to five buttons. The bottom of a mouse is flat and contains a mechanism (ball, optical sensor, or laser sensor) that detects movement of the mouse.

Notebook computers come with a pointing device built into the keyboard (Figure 8) so that you can select items on the screen without requiring additional desktop space. Notice in Figure 8 that the notebook computer has the keyboard built into the unit.

FIGURE 7 A mechanical mouse (a) contains a small ball. The optical mouse (b) uses an optical sensor. The laser mouse (c) uses a laser sensor. They all include a wheel you roll to scroll and zoom. The optical mouse and laser mouse contain additional buttons that enable forward and backward navigation through Web pages. The laser mouse is the most precise.

(a) mechanical mouse   (b) optical mouse   (c) laser mouse

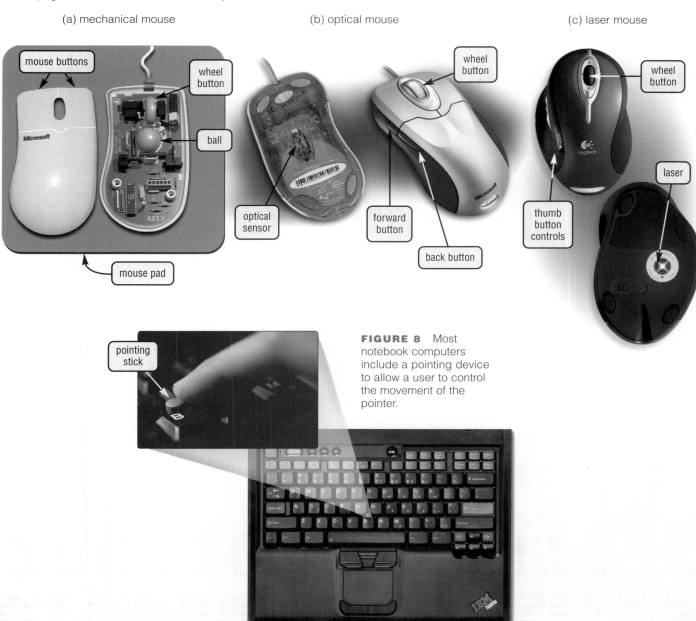

mouse buttons

wheel button

ball

Microsoft

6213

mouse pad

optical sensor

wheel button

forward button

back button

Microsoft

wheel button

laser

thumb button controls

Logitech

pointing stick

FIGURE 8 Most notebook computers include a pointing device to allow a user to control the movement of the pointer.

SYSTEM UNIT

The **system unit** (Figure 9) is a case that contains electronic components of the computer used to process the data. System units are available in a variety of shapes and sizes. The case of the system unit, also called the chassis, is made of metal or plastic and protects the internal electronic parts from damage. The **motherboard**, sometimes called a system board, is the main circuit board of the system unit. Many electronic components attach to the motherboard, such as the processor, memory, and expansion slots. The sound card and video card shown in Figure 9 are examples of adapter cards, which allow a user to enhance the computer system with add-on products.

Processor

The **processor** (top right in Figure 9), also called the **central processing unit** (**CPU**), interprets and carries out the basic instructions that operate a computer. The processor is made up of the control unit and arithmetic/logic unit (Figure 3 on page COM-4). The **control unit** interprets the instructions. The **arithmetic/logic unit** performs the logical and arithmetic processes. High-end processors contain over 100 million transistors and are capable of performing some operations 10 million times in a tenth of a second, or in the time it takes to blink your eye.

Memory

Memory, also called **random access memory**, or **RAM**, consists of electronic components that temporarily stores instructions waiting to be executed by the processor, data needed by those instructions, and the results of processed data (information). Memory consists of chips on a memory module (right side of Figure 9) that fits in a slot on the motherboard in the system unit.

The amount of memory in computers typically is measured in kilobytes, megabytes, or gigabytes. One **kilobyte** (**K or KB**) equals approximately 1,000 memory locations and one **megabyte** (**MB**) equals approximately one million memory locations. One **gigabyte** (**GB**) equals approximately one billion memory locations. A **memory location**, or **byte**, usually stores one character such as the letter A. Therefore, a computer with 512 MB of memory can store approximately 512 million characters. One megabyte can hold approximately 500 letter-size pages of text information and one gigabyte can hold approximately 500,000 letter-size pages of text information.

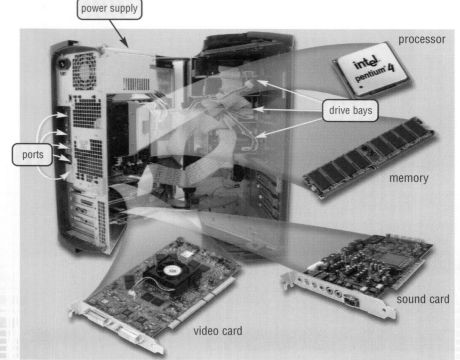

FIGURE 9 The system unit on a typical computer consists of numerous electronic components, some of which are shown in this figure. The sound card and video card are two types of adapter cards.

OUTPUT DEVICES

Output devices make the information resulting from processing available for use. The output from computers can be presented in many forms, such as a printed report or displaying it on a screen. When a computer is used for processing tasks such as word processing, spreadsheets, or database management, the two output devices more commonly used are the printer and a display device.

Printers

Printers used with computers are impact or nonimpact. An **impact printer** prints by striking an inked ribbon against the paper. One type of impact printer used with personal computers is the dot-matrix printer (Figure 10).

Nonimpact printers, such as ink-jet printers (Figure 11) and laser printers (Figure 12), form characters by means other than striking a ribbon against paper. One advantage of using a nonimpact printer is that it can print higher-quality text and graphics than an impact printer, such as the dot-matrix. Nonimpact printers also do a better job of printing different fonts, are quieter, and can print in color. The popular and affordable ink-jet printer forms a character or graphic by using a nozzle that sprays tiny drops of ink onto the page.

Ink-jet printers produce text and graphics in both black and white and color on a variety of paper types and sizes. Some ink-jet printers, called **photo printers**, produce photo-quality pictures and are ideal for home or small-business use. The speed of an ink-jet printer is measured by the number of pages per minute (ppm) it can print. Most ink-jet printers print from 3 to 19 pages per minute. Graphics and colors print at the slower rate.

A laser printer (Figure 12) is a high-speed, high-quality nonimpact printer that employs copier-machine technology. It converts data from the computer into a beam of light that is focused on a photoconductor drum, forming the images to be printed. Laser printers for personal computers can cost from a couple hundred dollars to thousands of dollars. Generally, the more expensive the laser printer, the more pages it can print per minute.

FIGURE 10
A dot-matrix printer is capable of handling wide paper and printing multipart forms. It produces printed images when tiny pins strike an inked ribbon.

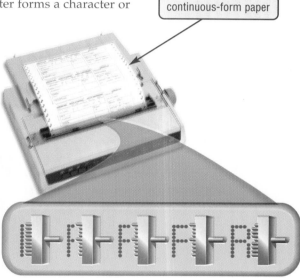

continuous-form paper

FIGURE 11 Ink-jet printers are a popular type of color printer used in the home. Many photo printers, which can produce photo-lab quality pictures, use ink-jet technology.

FIGURE 12 Laser printers, which are available in both black and white and color, are used with personal computers, as well as larger computers.

WEB LINK

Output Devices

For more information, visit scsite.com/ic6/ weblink and then click Output Devices.

Display Devices

A **display device** is an output device that visually conveys text, graphics, and video information. A **monitor** is a plastic or metal case that houses a display device. Two basic types of monitors are the LCD and CRT. The **LCD monitor**, also called a **flat panel monitor**, shown on the left in Figure 13, uses a liquid display crystal, similar to a digital watch, to produce images on the screen. The flat panel monitor, although more expensive than the CRT monitor, takes up much less desk space and has gained significant popularity over the past few years. The television-like **CRT (cathode ray tube)** monitor is shown on the right in Figure 13. The surface of the screen of either a CRT monitor or LCD monitor is composed of individual picture elements called **pixels**. A screen set to a resolution of 800 x 600 pixels has a total of 480,000 pixels. Each pixel can be illuminated to form parts of a character or graphic shape on the screen.

Mobile computers, such as notebook computers and Tablet PCs, and mobile devices, such as PDAs and smart phones, have LCD screens (Figure 14).

FIGURE 13 The LCD monitor (left), also called a flat-panel monitor, and the CRT monitor (right) are used with desktop computers. The LCD monitor is thin, lightweight, and far more popular today than the CRT monitor.

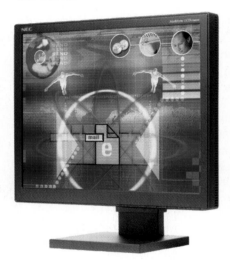

FIGURE 14 Notebook computers and Tablet PCs have color LCD screens. Some PDAs and smart phones also have color displays.

notebook computer

Tablet PC

PDA

smart phone

STORAGE DEVICES

A **storage device**, also called a **secondary storage device**, is used to store instructions, data, and information when they are not being used in memory. Four common types of storage devices are magnetic disk, optical discs, tape, and miniature mobile storage media. Figure 15 shows how different types of storage media and memory compare in terms of relative speeds and uses.

Magnetic Disks

Magnetic disks use magnetic particles to store items such as data, instructions, and information on a disk's surface. Before any data can be read from or written on a magnetic disk, the disk must be formatted. **Formatting** is the process of dividing the disk into tracks and sectors (Figure 16), so the computer can locate the data, instructions, and information on the disk. A **track** is a narrow recording band that forms a full circle on the surface of the disk. The disk's storage locations consist of pie-shaped sections, which break the tracks into small arcs called **sectors**. On a magnetic disk, a sector typically stores up to 512 bytes of data.

Three types of magnetic disks are floppy disks, Zip disks, and hard disks. Some of these disks are portable, others are not. **Portable storage medium** means you can remove the medium from one computer and carry it to another computer. The following sections discuss specific types of magnetic disks.

FIGURE 15 Comparison of different types of storage media and memory in terms of relative speed and uses. Memory is faster than storage, but is expensive and not practical for all storage requirements. Storage is less expensive but is slower than memory.

		Stores...
Primary Storage	Memory (most RAM)	Items waiting to be interpreted and executed by the processor
Secondary Storage	Hard Disk	Operating system, application software, user data and information
	CDs and DVDs	Software, backups, movies, music
	Miniature Mobile Storage Media	Digital pictures or files to be transported
	Tape	Backups
	Floppy Disk	Small files to be transported

faster transfer rates

slower transfer rates

FIGURE 16 Tracks form circles on the surface of a magnetic disk. The disk's storage locations are divided into pie-shaped sections, which break the tracks into small arcs called sectors.

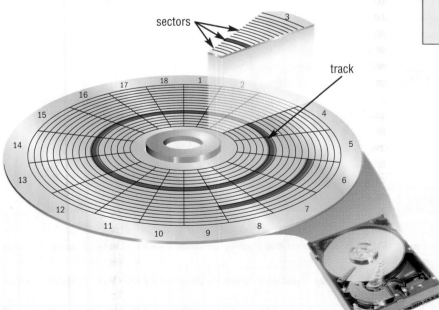

sectors

track

11

FLOPPY DISKS   A **floppy disk**, or **diskette**, is an inexpensive portable storage medium that consists of a thin, circular, flexible plastic disk with a magnetic coating enclosed in a square-shaped plastic shell (Figure 17a). The most widely used floppy disk is 3.5 inches wide and typically can store up to 1.44 megabytes of data, or 1,474,560 characters. Although the exterior of the 3.5-inch disk is not floppy, users still refer to them as floppy disks.

A **floppy disk drive** is a device that can read from and write on a floppy disk. Floppy disk drives are either built-into the system unit (Figure 17a) or are external to the system unit and connected to the computer via a cable (Figure 17b).

Data stored on a floppy disk must be retrieved and placed into memory to be processed. The time required to access and retrieve data is called the **access time**. The access time for floppy disks varies from about 175 milliseconds to approximately 300 milliseconds (one millisecond equals 1/1000 of a second). On average, data stored in a single sector on a floppy disk can be retrieved in approximately 1/15 to 1/3 of a second.

ZIP DISKS   A **Zip disk** is a type of portable storage media that can store from 100 MB to 750 MB of data. Zip disks can be built-in to the system unit or it can be external (Figure 18). The larger capacity Zip disk can hold about 500 times more than a standard floppy disk. These large capacities make it easy to transport many files or large items such as graphics, audio, or video files. Another popular use of Zip disks is to back up important data and information. A **backup** is a duplicate of a file, program, or disk that you can use in case the original is lost, damaged, or destroyed.

FIGURE 17   On a personal computer, you insert and remove a floppy disk from a floppy disk drive.

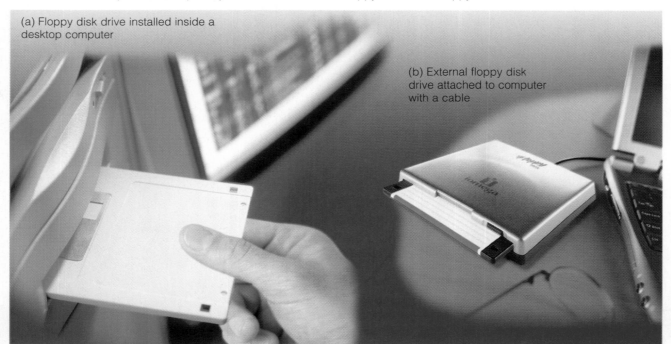

(a) Floppy disk drive installed inside a desktop computer

(b) External floppy disk drive attached to computer with a cable

HARD DISKS Another form of storage is a hard disk. A **hard disk**, also called a hard disk drive, is a storage device that contains one or more inflexible, circular patterns that magnetically store data, instructions, and information. As with floppy disks, the data on hard disks is recorded on a series of tracks located on one or more platters. The tracks are divided into sectors when the disk is formatted. Figure 19 shows how a hard disk works.

The hard disk platters spin at a high rate of speed, typically 5,400 to 7,200 revolutions per minute. When reading data from the disk, the read head senses the magnetic spots that are recorded on the disk along the various tracks and transfers that data to memory. When writing, the data is transferred from memory and is stored as magnetic spots on the tracks on the recording surface of one or more of the disk platters. When reading or writing, the read/write heads on a hard disk drive do not actually touch the surface of the disk.

The number of platters permanently mounted on the spindle of a hard disk varies. On most drives, each surface of the platter can be used to store data. Thus, if a hard disk drive uses one platter, two surfaces are available for data. If the drive uses two platters, four sets of read/write heads read and record data from the four surfaces. Storage capacities of internally mounted fixed disks for personal computers range from 10 GB to more than 200 GB.

The system unit on most desktop and notebook computers contains at least one hard disk. Although hard disks are available in removable cartridge form, most hard disks cannot be removed from the computer.

WEB LINK

Hard Disks

For more information, visit scsite.com/ic6/ weblink and then click Hard Disks.

FIGURE 18 An external Zip drive and Zip disk.

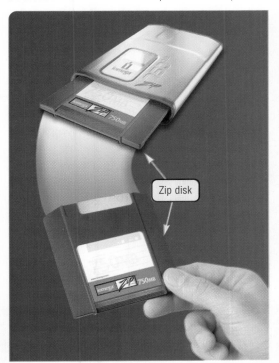

Zip disk

FIGURE 19 How a hard disk works.

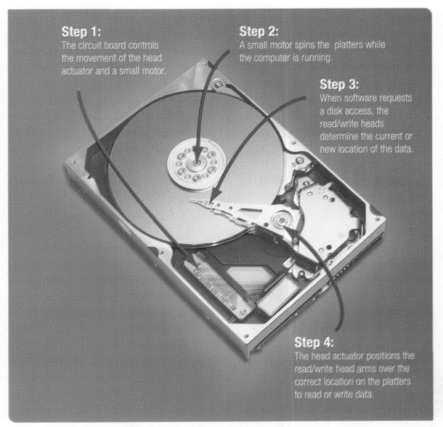

Step 1:
The circuit board controls the movement of the head actuator and a small motor.

Step 2:
A small motor spins the platters while the computer is running.

Step 3:
When software requests a disk access, the read/write heads determine the current or new location of the data.

Step 4:
The head actuator positions the read/write head arms over the correct location on the platters to read or write data.

WEB LINK

CDs

For more information, visit scsite.com/ic6/ weblink and then click CDs.

Optical Discs

An optical disc is a portable storage medium that consists of a flat, round, portable disc made of metal, plastic, and lacquer that is written and read by a laser. Optical discs used in personal computers are 4.75 inches in diameter and less than 1/20 of an inch thick. Nearly every personal computer today has some type of optical disc drive installed in a drive bay. On these drives, you push a button to slide the tray out, insert the disc, and then push the same button to close the tray (Figure 20).

Many different formats of optical discs exist today. These include CD-ROM, CD-R, CD-RW, DVD-ROM, DVD-R, DVD+R, DVD-RW, DVD+RW, and DVD+RAM. Figure 21 identifies each of these optical disc formats and specifies whether a user can read from the disc, write on the disc, and/or erase the disc.

A **CD-ROM** (compact disc read-only memory) is a type of optical disc that users can read but not write on (record) or erase — hence, the name read-only. A typical CD-ROM holds from 650 MB to 1 GB of data, instructions, and information. This is equivalent to about 450 high-density 3.5-inch floppy disks. Software manufacturers often distribute their programs using CD-ROMs.

To read a CD-ROM, insert the disc in a **CD-ROM drive** or a CD-ROM player. Because audio CDs and CD-ROMs use the same laser technology, you may be able to use a CD-ROM drive to listen to an audio CD while working on the computer. Some music companies, however, configure their CDs so the music will not play on a computer. They do this to protect themselves from customers illegally copying and sharing the music.

FIGURE 20 On optical disc drives, you push a button to slide out a tray, insert the disc, and then push the same button to close the tray.

Push the button to slide out the tray.

Insert the disc, label side up.

Push the same button to close the tray.

A **CD-R** (compact disc-recordable) is an optical disc onto which you can record your own items such as text, graphics, and audio. With a CD-R, you can write on part of the disc at one time and another part at a later time. Once you have recorded the CD-R, you can read from it as many times as you wish. You can write on each part only one time, and you cannot erase the disc's contents. Most CD-ROM drives can read a CD-R.

A **CD-RW** (compact disc-rewriteable) is an erasable optical disc you can write on multiple times. Originally called an erasable CD (CD-E), a CD-RW overcomes the major disadvantage of CD-R discs, which is that you can write on them only once. With CD-RWs, the disc acts like a floppy or hard disk, allowing you to write and rewrite data, instructions, and information onto it multiple times.

Although CDs have huge storage capacities, even a CD is not large enough for many of today's complex programs. Some software, for example, is sold on five or more CDs. To meet these tremendous storage requirements, some software companies have moved from CDs to the larger DVD — a technology that can be used to store large amounts of text and even cinema-like videos (Figure 22).

FIGURE 22 A DVD is an extremely high-capacity optical disc.

DVD

DVD drive

OPTICAL DISC FORMATS

Optical Disc	Read	Write	Erase
CD-ROM	Y	N	N
CD-R	Y	Y	N
CD-RW	Y	Y	Y
DVD-ROM	Y	N	N
DVD-R DVD+R	Y	Y	N
DVD-RW DVD+RW DVD+RAM	Y	Y	Y

FIGURE 21 Manufacturers sell CD-ROM and DVD-ROM media prerecorded (written) with audio, video, and software. Users cannot change the contents of these discs. Users, however, can purchase the other formats of CDs and DVDs as blank media and record (write) their own data, instructions, and information on these discs.

A **DVD-ROM** (digital versatile disk-read-only memory) is a very high capacity optical disc capable of storing from 4.7 GB to 17 GB — more than enough to hold a telephone book containing every resident in the United States. As with the CD-ROM format, you cannot write on an optical disc that uses the DVD-ROM format. You can only read from it. To read a DVD-ROM, you need a **DVD-ROM drive**.

DVD-R and **DVD+R** are competing DVD-recordable formats, each with up to 4.7 GB storage capacity. Both allow users to write on the disc once and read (play) it many times. **DVD-RW**, **DVD+RW**, and **DVD+RAM** are three competing DVD formats, each with storage capacities up to 4.7 GB per side, that allow users to erase and write (record) many times. To write to a DVD, you need a recordable or rewriteable DVD-ROM drive.

Tape

Tape is a magnetically coated ribbon of plastic housed in a tape cartridge (Figure 23) capable of storing large amounts of data and information at a low cost. A **tape drive** is used to read from and write on a tape. Tape is primarily used for long-term storage and backup.

Miniature Mobile Storage Media

Miniature mobile storage media are rewriteable media usually in the form of a flash memory card, USB flash drive, or a smart card. Miniature mobile storage media allow mobile users to transport digital images, music, or documents easily to and from computers and other devices (Figure 24).

FIGURE 23 A tape drive and a tape cartridge.

FIGURE 24 Many types of computers and devices use miniature mobile storage media.

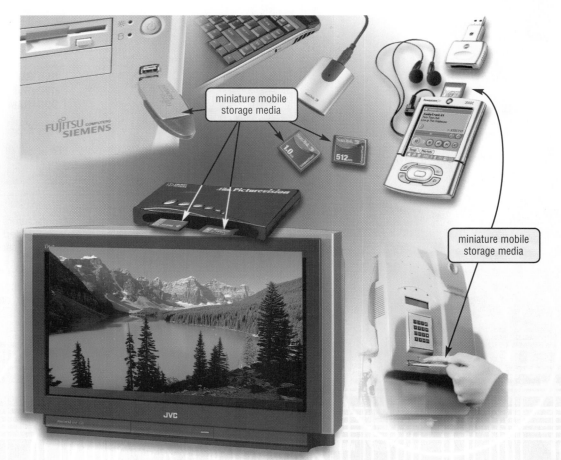

Flash memory cards are solid-state media, which means they consist entirely of electronics (chips, wires, etc.) and contain no moving parts. Common types of flash memory include CompactFlash, SmartMedia, Secure Digital, xD Picture Card, and Memory Stick (Figure 25).

A **USB flash drive** (Figure 26), sometimes called a pen drive, is a flash memory storage device that plugs into a USB port on a computer or mobile device. USB flash drives are the portable storage media of choice among users today because they are small, lightweight, and have such large storage capacities. Capacities typically range from 16 MB to 4 GB.

VARIOUS FLASH MEMORY CARDS

Media Name	Storage Capacity	Use
CompactFlash 	32 MB to 4 GB	Digital cameras, PDAs, smart phones, photo printers, music players, notebook computers, desktop computers
SmartMedia 	32 MB to 128 MB	Digital cameras, PDAs, smart phones, photo printers, music players
Secure Digital 	64 MB to 1 GB	Digital cameras, digital video cameras, PDAs, smart phones, photo printers, music players
xD Picture Card 	64 MB to 512 MB	Digital cameras, photo printers
Memory Stick 	256 MB to 2 GB	Digital cameras, digital video cameras, PDAs, photo printers, smart phones, notebook computers

FIGURE 25
A variety of flash memory cards.

FIGURE 26 A USB flash drive next to a paper clip.

A **smart card**, which is similar in size to a credit card or ATM card, stores data on a thin microprocessor embedded in the card. When you insert the smart card in a specialized card reader, the information on the card is read and, if necessary, updated (Figure 27). Use of smart cards include storing medical records, tracking customer purchases, storing a prepaid amount of money, and authenticating users, such as for Internet purchases.

COMMUNICATIONS DEVICES

A **communications device** is a hardware component that enables a computer to send (transmit) and receive data, instructions, and information to and from one or more computers. A widely used communications device is the telephone or cable modem (Figure 1 on page COM-2).

Communications occur over **transmission media** such as telephone lines, cables, cellular radio networks, and satellites. Some transmission media, such as satellites and cellular radio networks, are **wireless**, which means they have no physical lines or wires. People around the world use computers and communications devices to communicate with each other using one or more transmission media.

COMPUTER SOFTWARE

Computer software is the key to productive use of computers. With the correct software, a computer can become a valuable tool. Software can be categorized into two types: system software and application software.

System Software

System software consists of programs to control the operations of computer equipment. An important part of system software is a set of programs called the operating system. Instructions in the **operating system** tell the computer how to perform the functions of loading, storing, and executing an application program and how to transfer data. For a computer to operate, an operating system must be stored in the computer's memory. When a computer is turned on, the operating system is loaded into the computer's memory from auxiliary storage. This process is called **booting**.

Today, most computers use an operating system that has a **graphical user interface** (**GUI**) that provides visual cues such as icon symbols to help the user. Each **icon** represents an application such as word processing, or a file or document where data is stored. Microsoft Windows XP (Figure 28) is a widely used graphical operating system. Apple Macintosh computers also have a graphical user interface operating system.

WEB LINK

Operating Systems

For more information, visit scsite.com/ic6/ weblink and then click Operating Systems.

FIGURE 27 A smart card and smart card reader.

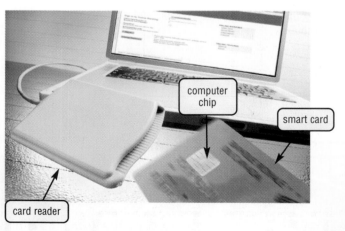

card reader

computer chip

smart card

icons

icons

FIGURE 28 A graphical user interface such as Microsoft Windows XP makes the computer easier to use. The small pictures, or symbols, on the screen are called icons. An icon represents a program or data the user can choose. A window is a rectangular area of the screen that is used to display a program, data, and/or information.

Application Software

Application software consists of programs that tell a computer how to produce information. Some widely used application software includes personal information manager, project management, accounting, computer-aided design, desktop publishing, paint/image editing, audio and video editing, multimedia authoring, Web page authoring, personal finance, legal, tax preparation, home design/landscaping, educational, reference, and entertainment (games, simulations, etc.). Often, application software is available for purchase from a Web site or store that sells computer products (Figure 29).

Personal computer users regularly use application software. Some of the more commonly used applications are word processing, electronic spreadsheet, database, and presentation graphics.

WORD PROCESSING Word processing software (Figure 30) is used to create, edit, format, and print documents. A key advantage of word processing software is that users easily can make changes in documents, such as correcting spelling; changing margins; and adding, deleting, or relocating entire paragraphs. These changes would be difficult and time consuming to make using manual methods such as a typewriter. With a word processor, documents can be printed quickly and accurately and easily stored on a disk for future use. Word processing software is oriented toward working with text, but word processing packages also support features that enable users to manipulate numeric data and utilize graphics.

SPREADSHEET Electronic spreadsheet software (Figure 31) allows the user to add, subtract, and perform user-defined calculations on rows and columns of numbers. These numbers can be changed, and the spreadsheet quickly recalculates the new results. Electronic spreadsheet software eliminates the tedious recalculations required with manual methods. Spreadsheet information frequently is converted into a graphic form, such as charts. Graphics capabilities now are included in most spreadsheet packages.

WEB LINK

Word Processing Software

For more information, visit scsite.com/ic6/ weblink and then click Word Processing Software.

WEB LINK

Spreadsheet Software

For more information, visit scsite.com/ic6/ weblink and then click Spreadsheet Software.

FIGURE 29 Stores that sell computer products have shelves stocked with software for sale.

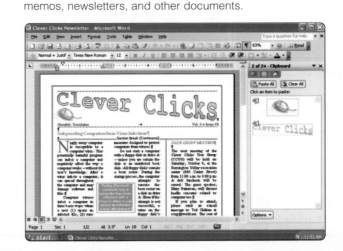

FIGURE 30 Word processing software is used to create letters, memos, newsletters, and other documents.

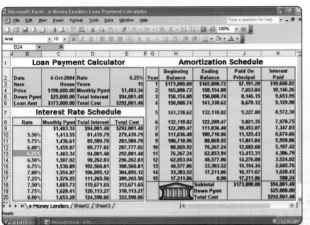

FIGURE 31 Electronic spreadsheet software frequently is used by people who work with numbers. The user enters the data and the formulas to be used on the data, and the computer calculates the results.

DATABASE Database software (Figure 32) allows the user to enter, retrieve, and update data in an organized and efficient manner. These software packages have flexible inquiry and reporting capabilities that let users access the data in different ways and create custom reports that include some or all of the information in the database.

PRESENTATION GRAPHICS Presentation graphics software (Figure 33) allows the user to create slides for use in a presentation to a group. Using special projection devices, the slides are projected directly from the computer.

NETWORKS AND THE INTERNET

A **network** is a collection of computers and devices connected via communications media and devices such as cables, telephone lines, modems, or other means.

Computers are networked together so users can share resources, such as hardware devices, software programs, data, and information. Sharing resources saves time and money. For example, instead of purchasing one printer for every computer in a company, the firm can connect a single printer and all computers via a network (Figure 34); the network enables all of the computers to access the same printer.

Most business computers are networked together. These networks can be relatively small or quite extensive. A network that connects computers in a limited geographic area, such as a school computer laboratory, office, or group of buildings, is called a **local area network** (**LAN**). A network that covers a large geographical area, such as one that connects the district offices of a national corporation, is called a **wide area network** (**WAN**) (Figure 35).

FIGURE 32 Database software allows the user to enter, retrieve, and update data in an organized and efficient manner.

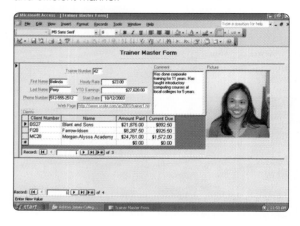

FIGURE 33 Presentation graphics software allows the user to produce professional-looking presentations.

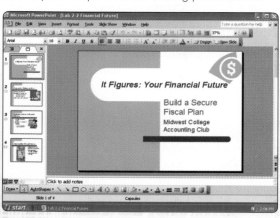

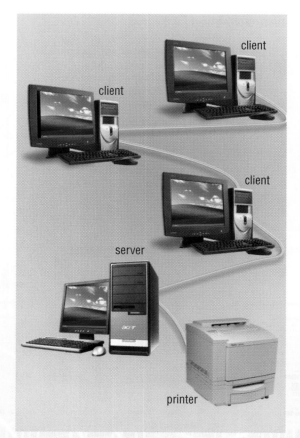

FIGURE 34 The local area network (LAN) enables two or more separate computers to share the same printer.

The Internet

The world's largest network is the **Internet**, which is a worldwide collection of networks that links together more than 200 million host computers by means of modems, telephone lines, cables, and other communications devices and media. With an abundance of resources and data accessible via the Internet, more than 1 billion users around the world are making use of the Internet for a variety of reasons. Some of these reasons include the following:

- Sending messages to other connected users (e-mail)

- Accessing a wealth of information, such as news, maps, airline schedules, and stock market data

- Shopping for goods and services

- Meeting or conversing with people around the world via chat rooms, online collaboration, and instant messaging

- Accessing sources of entertainment and leisure, such as online games, magazines, and vacation planning guides

Most users connect to the Internet in one of two ways: through an Internet service provider or through an online service provider. An **ISP** (**Internet service provider**) is an organization, such as a cable company or telephone company, that supplies connections to the Internet for a monthly fee. Like an ISP, an **online service provider** (**OSP**) provides access to the Internet, but it also provides a variety of other specialized content and services such as financial data, hardware and software guides, news, weather, legal information, and other similar commodities. For this reason, the fees for using an online service usually are slightly higher than fees for using an ISP. Two popular online services are America Online (AOL) and The Microsoft Network (MSN).

WEB LINK

World Wide Web

For more information, visit scsite.com/ic6/ weblink and then click World Wide Web.

The World Wide Web

One of the more popular segments of the Internet is the **World Wide Web**, also called the **Web**, which contains billions of documents called Web pages. A **Web page** is a document that contains text, graphics, sound, and/or video, and has built-in connections, or hyperlinks, to other Web documents. Figure 36 on the next page shows the different types of Web pages found on the World Wide Web today. Web pages are stored on computers throughout the world. A **Web site** is a related collection of Web pages. Visitors to a Web site access and view Web pages using a software program called a **Web browser**. A Web page has a unique address, called a **Uniform Resource Locator** (**URL**).

FIGURE 35   A wide area network (WAN) can be quite large and complex connecting users in district offices around the world.

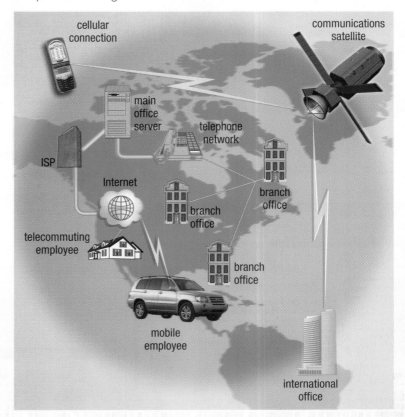

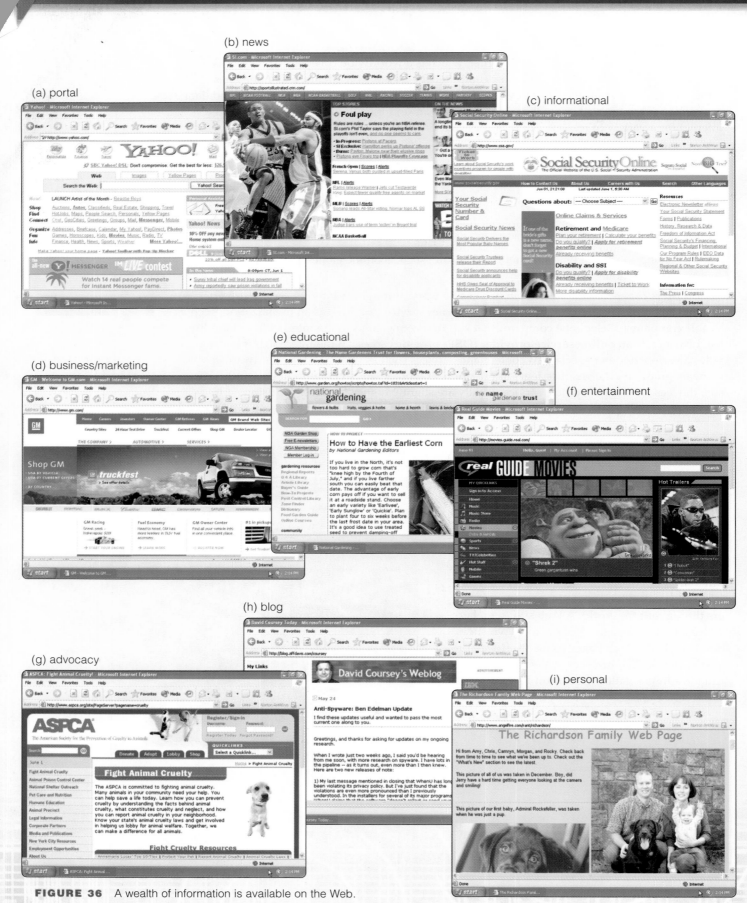

(a) portal

(b) news

(c) informational

(d) business/marketing

(e) educational

(f) entertainment

(g) advocacy

(h) blog

(i) personal

FIGURE 36 A wealth of information is available on the Web.

As shown in Figure 37, a URL consists of a protocol, a domain name, sometimes the path to a specific Web page or location in a Web page, and the Web page name. Most Web page URLs begin with **http://**, which stands for **hypertext transfer protocol**, the communications standard used to transfer pages on the Web. The domain name identifies the Web site, which is stored on a Web server. A **Web server** is a computer that delivers (serves) requested Web pages.

Electronic Commerce

When you conduct business activities online, you are participating in **electronic commerce**, also known as **e-commerce**. These commercial activities include shopping, investing, and any other venture that represents a business transaction. Today, three types of e-commerce exist: business to consumer, consumer to consumer, and business to business. **Business to consumer** (B2C) involves the sale of goods to the general public. **Consumer to consumer** (C2C) involves one consumer selling directly to another. **Business to business** (B2B) provides goods and services to other businesses.

WEB LINK

E-Commerce

For more information, visit scsite.com/ic6/ weblink and then click E-Commerce.

FIGURE 37 After entering the Web address http://www.sandiegozoo.org/wap/condor/home.html in the Address box, this Web page at the San Diego Zoo Web site is displayed. Notice the www portion of the domain name does not appear in the Address box after the Web page downloads.

How to Purchase a Personal Computer

(a) desktop computer

(b) mobile computer (notebook computer or Tablet PC)

(c) personal mobile device (smart phone or PDA)

Should I buy a desktop or mobile computer or personal mobile device?

For what purposes will I use the computer?

Should I buy a Mac or PC?

Should the computer I buy be compatible with the computers at school or work?

A t some point, perhaps while you are taking this course, you may decide to buy a personal computer. The decision is an important one and will require an investment of both time and money. Like many buyers, you may have little computer experience and find yourself unsure of how to proceed. You can get started by talking to your friends, coworkers, and instructors about their computers. What type of computers did they buy? Why? For what purposes do they use their computers? You also should answer the following four questions to help narrow your choices to a specific computer type, before reading this Buyer's Guide.

1 Do you want a desktop computer, mobile computer, or personal mobile device?

A desktop computer (Figure 38a) is designed as a stationary device that sits on or below a desk or table in a location such as a home, office, or dormitory room. A desktop computer must be plugged into an electrical outlet to operate. A mobile computer, such as a notebook computer or Tablet PC (Figure 38b), is smaller than a desktop computer, more portable, and has a battery that allows you to operate it for a period without an electrical outlet. A personal mobile device (Figure 38c) runs on a battery for a longer period of time than a notebook computer or Tablet PC and can fit in your pocket.

Desktop computers are a good option if you work mostly in one place and have plenty of space in your work area. Desktop computers generally give you more performance for your money.

Increasingly, more desktop computer users are buying mobile computers to take advantage of their portability to work in the library, at school, while traveling, and at home. The past disadvantages of mobile computers, such as lower processor speeds, poor-quality monitors, weight, short battery life, and significantly higher prices, have all but disappeared when compared with desktop computers.

FIGURE 38

If you are thinking of using a mobile computer to take notes in class or in business meetings, then consider a Tablet PC with handwriting and drawing capabilities. Typically, note-taking involves writing text notes and drawing charts, schematics, and other illustrations. By allowing you to write and draw directly on the screen with a digital pen, a Tablet PC eliminates the distracting sound of the notebook keyboard tapping and allows you to capture drawings. Some notebook computers can convert to Tablet PCs.

A personal mobile device, such as a smart phone or a PDA, is ideal if you require a pocket-size computing device as you move from place to place. Personal mobile devices provide personal organizer functions, such as a calendar, appointment book, address book, and many other applications. The small size of the processor, screen, and keyboard, however, limit a personal mobile device's capabilities when compared with a desktop or notebook computer or a Tablet PC. For this reason, most people who purchase personal mobile devices also have a desktop or notebook computer to handle heavy-duty applications.

Drawbacks of mobile computers and personal mobile devices are that they tend to have a shorter useful lifetime than desktop computers and lack the high-end capabilities. Their portability makes them susceptible to vibrations, heat or cold, and accidental drops, which can cause components such as hard disks or display devices to fail. Also, because of their size and portability, they are easy to lose and are the prime targets of thieves.

② For what purposes will you use the computer?

Having a general idea of the purposes for which you want to use your computer will help you decide on the type of computer to buy. At this point in your research, it is not necessary to know the exact application software titles or version numbers you might want to use. Knowing that you plan to use the computer primarily to create word processing, spreadsheet, database, and presentation documents, however, will point you in the direction of a desktop or notebook computer. If you want the portability of a smart phone or PDA, but you need more computing power, then a Tablet PC may be the best alternative. You also must consider that some application software runs only on a Mac, while others run only on a PC with the Windows operating system. Still

other software may run only on a PC running the UNIX or Linux operating system.

③ Should the computer be compatible with the computers at school or work?

If you plan to bring work home, telecommute, or take distance education courses, then you should purchase a computer that is compatible with those at school or work.

Compatibility is primarily a software issue. If your computer runs the same operating system version, such as Microsoft Windows XP, and the same application software, such as Microsoft Office, then your computer will be able to read documents created at school or work and vice versa. Incompatible hardware can become an issue if you plan to connect directly to a school or office network using a cable or wireless technology. You usually can obtain the minimum system requirements from the Information Technology department at your school or workplace.

④ Should the computer be a Mac or PC?

If you ask a friend, coworker, or instructor, which is better — a Mac or a PC — you may be surprised by the strong opinion expressed in the response. No other topic in the computer industry causes more heated debate. The Mac has strengths, especially in the areas of graphics, movies, photos, and music. The PC, however, has become the industry standard with 95 percent of the market share. Figure 39 compares features of the Mac and PC in several different areas.

Area	Comparison
Cost and availability	A Mac is priced slightly higher than a PC. Mac peripherals also are more expensive. The PC offers more available models from a wide range of vendors. You can custom build, upgrade, and expand a PC for less money than a Mac.
Exterior design	The Mac has a more distinct and stylish appearance than most PCs.
Free software	Although free software for the Mac is available on the Internet, significantly more free software applications are available for the PC.
Market share	The PC dominates the personal computer market. While the Mac sells well in education, publishing, Web design, graphics, and music, the PC is the overwhelming favorite of businesses.
Operating system	Users claim that Mac OS X provides a better all-around user experience than Microsoft Windows XP. Both the Mac and PC supports other operating systems, such as Linux and UNIX.
Program control	Both have simple and intuitive graphical user interfaces. The Mac relies more on the mouse and less on keyboard shortcuts than the PC. The mouse on the Mac has one button, whereas the mouse on a PC has a minimum of two buttons.
Software availability	The basic application software most users require, such as Microsoft Office, is available for both the Mac and PC. More specialized software, however, often is available only for PCs. Many programs are released for PCs long before they are released for Macs.
Speed	The PC provides faster processors than the Mac.
Viruses	Dramatically fewer viruses attack Macs. Mac viruses also generally are less infectious than PC viruses.

FIGURE 39 Comparison of Mac and PC features.

Overall, the Mac and PC have more similarities than differences, and you should consider cost, compatibility, and other factors when choosing whether to purchase a Mac or PC.

After evaluating the answers to these four questions, you should have a general idea of how you plan to use your computer and the type of computer you want to buy. Once you have decided on the type of computer you want, you can follow the guidelines presented in this Buyer's Guide to help you purchase a specific computer, along with software, peripherals, and other accessories.

Many of the desktop computer guidelines presented also apply to the purchase of a notebook computer, Tablet PC, and personal mobile device. Later in this Buyer's Guide, sections on purchasing a notebook computer or Tablet PC or personal mobile device address additional considerations specific to those computer types.

HOW TO PURCHASE A DESKTOP COMPUTER

Once you have decided that a desktop computer is most suited to your computing needs, the next step is to determine specific software, hardware, peripheral devices, and services to purchase, as well as where to buy the computer.

 Determine the specific software you want to use on your computer.

Before deciding to purchase software, be sure it contains the features necessary for the tasks you want to perform. Rely on the computer users in whom you have confidence to help you decide on the software to use. The minimum requirements of the software you select may determine the operating system (Microsoft Windows XP, Linux, UNIX, Mac OS X) you need. If you have decided to use a particular operating system that does not support software you want to use, you may be able to purchase similar software from other manufacturers.

Many Web sites and trade magazines, such as those listed in Figure 40, provide reviews of software products. These Web sites frequently have articles that rate computers and software on cost, performance, and support.

Your hardware requirements depend on the minimum requirements of the software you will run on your computer. Some software requires more memory and disk space than others, as well as additional input, output, and storage devices. For example, suppose you want to run software that can copy one CD's or DVD's contents directly to another CD or DVD, without first copying the data to your hard disk. To support that, you should consider a desktop computer or a high-end notebook computer,

Type of Computers	Web Site	Web Address
PC	CNET Shopper	shopper.cnet.com
	PC World Magazine	pcworld.com
	BYTE Magazine	byte.com
	PC Magazine	zdnet.com/reviews
	Yahoo! Computers	computers.yahoo.com
	MSN Shopping	eshop.msn.com
	Dave's Guide to Buying a Home Computer	css.msu.edu/PC-Guide
Mac	Macworld Magazine	macworld.com
	Apple	apple.com
	Switch to Mac Campaign	apple.com/switch

For an updated list of hardware and software reviews and their Web site addresses, visit scsite.com/ic6/buyers.

FIGURE 40 Hardware and software reviews.

because the computer will need two CD or DVD drives: one that reads from a CD or DVD, and one that reads from and writes on a CD or DVD. If you plan to run software that allows your computer to work as an entertainment system, then you will need a CD or DVD drive, quality speakers, and an upgraded sound card.

2 **Look for bundled software.**

When you purchase a computer, it may come bundled with software. Some sellers even let you choose which software you want. Remember, however, that bundled software has value only if you would have purchased the software even if it had not come with the computer. At the very least, you probably will want word processing software and a browser to access the Internet. If you need additional applications, such as a spreadsheet, a database, or presentation graphics, consider purchasing Microsoft Works, Microsoft Office, OpenOffice.org, or Sun StarOffice, which include several programs at a reduced price.

3 **Avoid buying the least powerful computer available.**

Once you know the application software you want to use, you then can consider the following important criteria about the computer's components: (1) processor speed, (2) size and types of memory (RAM) and storage, (3) types of input/output devices, (4) types of ports and adapter cards, and (5) types of communications devices. The information in Figures 41 and 42 can help you determine what system components are best for you. Figure 41 outlines considerations for specific hardware components. Figure 42 (on page COM-29) provides a Base Components worksheet that lists

PC recommendations for each category of user discussed in this book: Home User, Small Office/Home Office User, Mobile User, Power User, and Large Business User. In the worksheet, the Home User category is divided into two groups: Application Home User and Game Home User. The Mobile User recommendations list criteria for a notebook computer, but do not include the PDA or Tablet PC options.

Computer technology changes rapidly, meaning a computer that seems powerful enough today may not serve your computing needs in a few years. In fact, studies show that many users regret not buying a more powerful computer. To avoid this, plan to buy a computer that will last you for two to three years. You can help delay obsolescence by purchasing the fastest processor, the most memory, and the largest hard disk you can afford. If you must buy a less powerful computer, be sure you can upgrade it with additional memory, components, and peripheral devices as your computer requirements grow.

CD/DVD Drives: Most computers come with a 32X to 48X speed CD-ROM drive that can read CDs. If you plan to write music, audio files, and documents on a CD, then you should consider upgrading to a CD-RW. An even better alternative is to upgrade to a DVD+RW combination drive. It allows you to read DVDs and CDs and to write data on (burn) a DVD or CD. A DVD has a capacity of at least 4.7 GB versus the 650 MB capacity of a CD.

Card Reader/Writer: A card reader/writer is useful for transferring data directly to and from a removable flash memory card, such as the ones used in your camera or music player. Make sure the card reader/writer can read from and write to the flash memory cards that you use.

Digital Camera: Consider an inexpensive point-and-shoot digital camera. They are small enough to carry around, usually operate automatically in terms of lighting and focus, and contain storage cards for storing photographs. A 2- to 4-megapixel camera with an 8 MB or 16 MB storage card is fine for creating images for use on the Web or to send via e-mail.

Digital Video Capture Device: A digital video capture device allows you to connect your computer to a camcorder or VCR and record, edit, manage, and then write video back to a VCR tape, a CD, or a DVD. The digital video capture device can be an external device or an adapter card. To create quality video (true 30 frames per second, full-sized TV), the digital video capture device should have a USB 2.0 or FireWire port. You will find that a standard USB port is too slow to maintain video quality. You also will need sufficient storage: an hour of data on a VCR tape takes up about 5 GB of disk storage.

Floppy Disk Drive: If you plan to use a floppy disk drive, then make sure the computer you purchase has a standard 3.5", 1.44 MB floppy disk drive. A floppy disk drive is useful for backing up and transferring files.

Hard Disk: It is recommended that you buy a computer with 40 to 60 GB if your primary interests are browsing the Web and using e-mail and Office suite-type applications; 60 to 80 GB if you also want to edit digital photographs; 80 to 100 GB if you plan to edit digital video or manipulate large audio files even occasionally; and 100 to 160 GB if you will edit digital video, movies, or photography often; store audio files and music; or consider yourself to be a power user.

Joystick/Wheel: If you use your computer to play games, then you will want to purchase a joystick or a wheel. These devices, especially the more expensive ones, provide for realistic game play with force feedback, programmable buttons, and specialized levers and wheels.

Keyboard: The keyboard is one of the more important devices used to communicate with the computer. For this reason, make sure the keyboard you purchase has 101 to 105 keys, is comfortable and easy to use, and has a USB connection. A wireless keyboard should be considered, especially if you have a small desk area.

Microphone: If you plan to record audio or use speech recognition to enter text and commands, then purchase a close-talk headset with gain adjustment support.

Modem: Most computers come with a modem so that you can use your telephone line to dial out and access the Internet. Some modems also have fax capabilities. Your modem should be rated at 56 Kbps.

Monitor: The monitor is where you will view documents, read e-mail messages, and view pictures. A minimum of a 17" screen is recommended, but if you are planning to use your computer for graphic design or game playing, then you may want to purchase a 19" or 21" monitor. The LCD flat panel monitor should be considered, especially if space is an issue.

FIGURE 41 Hardware guidelines.

(continued next page)

(Figure 41 continued from previous page)

Mouse: As you work with your computer, you use the mouse constantly. For this reason, spend a few extra dollars, if necessary, and purchase a mouse with an optical sensor and USB connection. The optical sensor replaces the need for a mouse ball, which means you do not need a mouse pad. For a PC, make sure your mouse has a wheel, which acts as a third button in addition to the top two buttons on the left and right. An ergonomic design is also important because your hand is on the mouse most of the time when you are using your computer. A wireless mouse should be considered to eliminate the cord and allow you to work at short distances from your computer.

Network Card: If you plan to connect to a network or use broadband (cable or DSL) to connect to the Internet, then you will need to purchase a network card. Broadband connections require a 10/100 PCI Ethernet network card.

Printer: Your two basic printer choices are ink-jet and laser. Color ink-jet printers cost on average between $50 and $300. Laser printers cost from $200 to $2,000. In general, the cheaper the printer, the lower the resolution and speed, and the more often you are required to change the ink cartridge or toner. Laser printers print faster and with a higher quality than an ink-jet, and their toner on average costs less. If you want color, then go with a high-end ink-jet printer to ensure quality of print. Duty cycle (the number of pages you expect to print each month) also should be a determining factor. If your duty cycle is on the low end — hundreds of pages per month — then stay with a high-end ink-jet printer, rather than purchasing a laser printer. If you plan to print photographs taken with a digital camera, then you should purchase a photo printer. A photo printer is a dye-sublimation printer or an ink-jet printer with higher resolution and features that allow you to print quality photographs.

Processor: For a PC, a 2.8 GHz Intel or AMD processor is more than enough processor power for application home and small office/home office users. Game home, large business, and power users should upgrade to faster processors.

RAM: RAM plays a vital role in the speed of your computer. Make sure the computer you purchase has at least 512 MB of RAM. If you have extra money to invest in your computer, then consider increasing the RAM to 1 GB or more. The extra money for RAM will be well spent.

Scanner: The most popular scanner purchased with a computer today is the flatbed scanner. When evaluating a flatbed scanner, check the color depth and resolution. Do not buy anything less than a color depth of 48 bits and a resolution of 1200 x 2400 dpi. The higher the color depth, the more accurate the color. A higher resolution picks up the more subtle gradations of color.

Sound Card: Most sound cards today support the Sound Blaster and General MIDI standards and should be capable of recording and playing digital audio. If you plan to turn your computer into an entertainment system or are a game home user, then you will want to spend the extra money and upgrade from the standard sound card.

Speakers: Once you have a good sound card, quality speakers and a separate subwoofer that amplifies the bass frequencies of the speakers can turn your computer into a premium stereo system.

PC Video Camera: A PC video camera is a small camera used to capture and display live video (in some cases with sound), primarily on a Web page. You also can capture, edit, and share video and still photos. The camera sits on your monitor or desk. Recommended minimum specifications include 640 x 480 resolution, a video with a rate of 30 frames per second, and a USB 2.0 or FireWire connection.

USB Flash Drive: If you work on different computers and need access to the same data and information, then this portable miniature mobile storage device is ideal. USB flash drive capacity varies from 16 MB to 4 GB.

Video Graphics Card: Most standard video cards satisfy the monitor display needs of application home and small office users. If you are a game home user or a graphic designer, you will want to upgrade to a higher quality video card. The higher refresh rates will further enhance the display of games, graphics, and movies.

Wireless LAN Access Point: A Wireless LAN Access Point allows you to network several computers, so they can share files and access the Internet through a single cable modem or DSL connection. Each device that you connect requires a wireless card. A Wireless LAN Access Point can offer a range of operations up to several hundred feet, so be sure the device has a high-powered antenna.

Zip Drive: Consider purchasing a Zip disk drive to back up important files. The Zip drive, which has a capacity of up to 750 MB, is sufficient for most users. An alternative to purchasing a backup drive is to purchase a CD-RW or DVD+RW and burn backups of key files on a CD or DVD.

BASE COMPONENTS

	Application Home User	Game Home User	Small Office/Home Office User	Mobile User	Large Business User	Power User
HARDWARE						
Processor	Pentium® 4 at 2.66 GHz	Pentium® 4 at 3.0 GHz	Pentium® 4 at 3.0 GHz	Pentium® M at 2.2 GHz	Pentium® 4 at 3.0 GHz	Multiple Itanium™ at 2.8
RAM	512 MB	1 GB	512 MB	512 MB	1 GB	2 GB
Cache	256 KB L2	512 KB L2	512 KB L2	512 KB L2	512 KB L2	2 MB L3
Hard Disk	60 GB	120 GB	80 GB	80 GB	160 GB	250 GB
Monitor/LCD Flat Panel	17" or 19"	21"	19" or 21"	15.4" Wide Display	19" or 21"	23"
Video Graphics Card	256 MB	512 MB	256 MB	32 MB	128 MB	256 MB
CD/DVD Bay 1	48x CD-ROM	48x CD-RW Drive	48x CD-ROM	24X CD-RW/DVD	48x CD-RW Drive	16x DVD-ROM
CD/DVD Bay 2	8x DVD+RW	12x DVD+RW	8x DVD+RW	4x DVD+RW/+R	12x DVD+RW	8x DVD+RW
Floppy Disk Drive	3.5"	3.5"	3.5"	3.5"	3.5"	3.5"
Printer	Color Ink-Jet	Color Ink-Jet	18 ppm Laser	Portable Ink-Jet	50 ppm Laser	10 ppm Laser
PC Video Camera	Yes	Yes	Yes	Yes	Yes	Yes
Fax/Modem	Yes	Yes	Yes	Yes	Yes	Yes
Microphone	Close-Talk Headset With Gain Adjustment	Close-Talk Headset With Gain Adjustment	Close-Talk Headset With Gain Adjustment	Close-Talk Headset With Gain Adjustment	Close-Talk Headset With Gain Adjustment	Close-Talk Headset With Gain Adjustment
Speakers	Stereo	Full-Dolby Surround	Stereo	Stereo	Stereo	Full-Dolby Surround
Pointing Device	IntelliMouse or Optical Mouse	Optical Mouse and Joystick	IntelliMouse or Optical Mouse	Touchpad or Pointing Stick and Optical Mouse	IntelliMouse or Optical Mouse	IntelliMouse or Optical Mouse and Joystick
Keyboard	Yes	Yes	Yes	Built-In	Yes	Yes
Backup Disk/Tape Drive	250 MB Zip®	External or Removable Hard Disk	External or Removable Hard Disk	External or Removable Hard Disk	Tape Drive	External or Removable Hard Disk
USB Flash Drive	128 MB	256 MB	256 MB	128 MB	4 GB	1 GB
Sound Card	Sound Blaster Compatible	Sound Blaster Audigy 2	Sound Blaster Compatible	Built-In	Sound Blaster Compatible	Sound Blaster Audigy 2
Network Card	Yes	Yes	Yes	Yes	Yes	Yes
TV-Out Connector	Yes	Yes	Yes	Yes	Yes	Yes
USB Port	6	8	6	2	8	8
FireWire Port	2	2	2	1	2	2
SOFTWARE						
Operating System	Windows XP Home Edition with Service Pack 2	Windows XP Home Edition with Service Pack 2	Windows XP Professional with Service Pack 2	Windows XP Professional with Service Pack 2	Windows XP Professional with Service Pack 2	Windows XP Professional with Service Pack 2
Application Suite	Office 2003 Standard Edition	Office 2003 Standard Edition	Office 2003 Small Business Edition	Office 2003 Small Business Edition	Office 2003 Professional	Office 2003 Professional
AntiVirus	Yes, 12-Mo. Subscription	Yes, 12-Mo. Subscription	Yes, 12-Mo. Subscription	Yes, 12-Mo. Subscription	Yes, 12-Mo. Subscription	Yes, 12-Mo. Subscription
Internet Access	Cable, DSL, or Dial-up	Cable or DSL	Cable, DSL, or Dial-up	Wireless or Dial-up	LAN/WAN (T1/T3)	Cable or DSL
OTHER						
Surge Protector	Yes	Yes	Yes	Portable	Yes	Yes
Warranty	3-Year Limited, 1-Year Next Business Day On-Site Service	3-Year Limited, 1-Year Next Business Day On-Site Service	3-year On-Site Service	3-Year Limited, 1-Year Next Business Day On-Site Service	3-year On-Site Service	3-year On-Site Service
Other		Wheel	Postage Printer	Docking Station Carrying Case Fingerprint Scanner Portable Data Projector		Graphics Tablet Plotter or Large-Format Printer

Optional Components for all Categories	
802.11g Wireless Card	Graphics Tablet
Bluetooth™ Enabled	iPod Music Player
Biometric Input Device	IrDa Port
Card Reader/Writer	Mouse Pad/Wrist Rest
Digital Camera	Multifunction Peripheral
Digital Video Capture	Photo Printer
Digital Video Camera	Portable Data Projector
Dual-Monitor Support with Second Monitor	Scanner
Ergonomic Keyboard	TV/FM Tuner
External Hard Disk	Uninterruptible Power Supply

FIGURE 42 Base desktop and mobile computer components and optional components. A copy of the Base Components worksheet is on the Data Disk. To obtain a copy of the Data Disk, see the inside cover of this book for instructions.

 Consider upgrades to the mouse, keyboard, monitor, printer, microphone, and speakers.

You use these peripheral devices to interact with your computer, so you should make sure they are up to your standards. Review the peripheral devices listed in Figure 41 and then visit both local computer dealers and large retail stores to test the computers on display. Ask the salesperson what input and output devices would be best for you and whether you should upgrade beyond what comes standard. Consider purchasing a wireless keyboard and wireless mouse to eliminate bothersome wires on your desktop. A few extra dollars spent on these components when you initially purchase a computer can extend its usefulness by years.

 Determine whether you want to use telephone lines or broadband (cable or DSL) to access the Internet.

If your computer has a modem, then you can access the Internet using a standard telephone line. Ordinarily, you call a local or toll-free 800 number to connect to an ISP (see Guideline 6 on the next page). Using a dial-up Internet connection is relatively inexpensive but slow.

DSL and cable connections provide much faster Internet connections, which are ideal if you want faster file download speeds for software, digital photos, and music. As you would expect, they also are more expensive. DSL, which is available through local telephone companies, also may require that you subscribe to an ISP. Cable is available through your local cable television provider and some online service providers (OSPs). If you get cable, then you would not use a separate Internet service provider or online service provider.

6 **If you are using a dial-up or wireless connection to connect to the Internet, then select an ISP or OSP.**

You can access the Internet via telephone lines in one of two ways: an ISP or an OSP. Both provide Internet access for a monthly fee that ranges from $6 to $25. Local ISPs offer Internet access to users in a limited geographic region, through local telephone numbers. National ISPs provide access for users nationwide (including mobile users), through local and toll-free telephone numbers and cable. Because of their size, national ISPs generally offer more services and have a larger technical support staff than local ISPs. OSPs furnish Internet access as well as members-only features for users nationwide. Figure 43 lists several national ISPs and OSPs. Before you choose an ISP or OSP, compare such features as the number of access hours, monthly fees, available services (e-mail, Web page hosting, chat), and reliability.

Company	Service	Web Address
America Online	OSP	aol.com
AT&T Worldnet	ISP	www.att.net
Comcast	OSP	comcast.net
CompuServe	OSP	compuserve.com
EarthLink	ISP	earthlink.net
Juno	OSP	juno.com
NetZero	OSP	netzero.com
MSN	OSP	msn.com
SBC Prodigy	ISP/OSP	prodigy.net

For an updated list of national ISPs and OSPs and their Web site addresses, visit scsite.com/ic6/buyers.

FIGURE 43 National ISPs and OSPs.

7 **Use a worksheet to compare computers, services, and other considerations.**

You can use a separate sheet of paper to take notes on each vendor's computer and then summarize the information on a worksheet, such as the one shown in Figure 44. You can use Figure 44 to compare prices for either a PC or a MAC. Most companies advertise a price for a base computer that includes components housed in the system unit (processor, RAM, sound card, video card), disk drives (floppy disk, hard disk, CD-ROM, CD-RW, DVD-ROM, and DVD+RW), a keyboard, mouse, monitor, printer, speakers, and modem. Be aware, however, that some advertisements list prices for computers with only some of these components. Monitors and printers, for example, often are not included in a base computer's price. Depending on how you plan to use the computer, you may want to invest in additional or more powerful components. When you are comparing the prices of computers, make sure you are comparing identical or similar configurations.

PC or MAC Cost Comparison Worksheet

Dealers list prices for computers with most of these components (instead of listing individual component costs). Some dealers do not supply a monitor. Some dealers offer significant discounts, but you must subscribe to an Internet service for a specified period to receive the discounted price. To compare computers, enter overall system price at top and enter a 0 (zero) for components included in the system cost. For any additional components not covered in the system price, enter the cost in the appropriate cells.

Items to Purchase	Desired System (PC)	Desired System (Mac)	Local Dealer #1	Local Dealer #2	Online Dealer #1	Online Dealer #2	Comments
OVERALL SYSTEM							
Overall System Price	< $1,500	< $1,500					
HARDWARE							
Processor	Pentium(R) 4 at 2.8 GHz	PowerPC G4 at 800 MHz					
RAM	512 MB	512 MB					
Cache	256 KB L2	256 KB L2					
Hard Disk	80 GB	80 GB					
Monitor/LCD Flat Panel	17 Inch	17 Inch					
Video Graphics Card	128 MB	128 MB					
Floppy Disk Drive	3.5 Inch	NA					
USB Flash Drive	128 MB	128 MB					
CD/DVD Bay 1	48x CD-ROM	4x DVD+RW					
CD/DVD Bay 2	8x DVD+RW	NA					
Speakers	Stereo	Stereo					
Sound Card	Sound Blaster Compatible	Sound Blaster Compatible					
USB Ports	6	6					
FireWire Port	2	2					
Network Card	Yes	Yes					
Fax/Modem	56 Kbps	56 Kbps					
Keyboard	Standard	Apple Pro Keyboard					
Pointing Device	IntelliMouse	Intellimouse or Apple Pro Mouse					
Microphone	Close-Talk Headset with Gain Adjustment	Close-Talk Headset with Gain Adjustment					
Printer	Color Ink-Jet	Color Ink-Jet					
Backup	250 MB Zip®	250 MB Zip®					
SOFTWARE							
Operating System	Windows XP Home Edition	Mac OS X					
Application Software	Office 2003 Small Business Edition	Office 2004 for Mac					
Antivirus	Yes - 12 Mo. Subscription	Yes - 12 Mo. Subscription					
OTHER							
Card Reader							
Digital Camera	4-Megapixel	4-Megapixel					
Internet Connection	1-Year Subscription	1-Year Subscription					
Joystick	Yes	Yes					
PC Video Camera	With Microphone	With Microphone					
Scanner							
Surge Protector							
Warranty	3-Year On-Site Service	3-Year On-Site Service					
Wireless Card	Internal	Internal					
Wireless LAN Access Point	LinkSys	Apple AirPort					
Total Cost			$ -	$ -	$ -	$ -	

FIGURE 44 A worksheet is an effective tool for summarizing and comparing components and prices of different computer vendors. A copy of the Computer Cost Comparison worksheet for the PC and Mac is on the Data Disk. To obtain a copy of the Data Disk, see the inside cover of this book for instructions.

⑧ **If you are buying a new computer, you have several purchasing options: buying from your school bookstore, a local computer dealer, a local large retail store, or ordering by mail via telephone or the Web.**

Each purchasing option has certain advantages. Many college bookstores, for example, sign exclusive pricing agreements with computer manufacturers and, thus, can offer student discounts. Local dealers and local large retail stores, however, more easily can provide hands-on support. Mail-order companies that sell computers by telephone or online via the Web (Figure 45) often provide the lowest prices, but extend less personal service. Some major mail-order companies, however, have started to provide next-business-day, on-site services. A credit card usually is required to buy from a mail-order company. Figure 46 lists some of the more popular mail-order companies and their Web site addresses.

⑨ **If you are buying a used computer, stay with name brands such as Dell, Gateway, Hewlett-Packard, and Apple.**

Although brand-name equipment can cost more, most brand-name computers have longer, more comprehensive warranties, are better supported, and have more authorized centers for repair services. As with new computers, you can purchase a used computer from local computer dealers, local

large retail stores, or mail order via the telephone or the Web. Classified ads and used computer sellers offer additional outlets for purchasing used computers. Figure 47 lists several major used computer brokers and their Web site addresses.

⑩ **If you have a computer and are upgrading to a new one, then consider selling or trading in the old one.**

If you are a replacement buyer, your older computer still may have value. If you cannot sell the computer through the classified ads, via a Web site, or to a friend, then ask if the computer dealer will buy your old computer. An increasing number of companies are taking trade-ins, but do not expect too much money for your old computer. Other companies offer free disposal of your old PC.

⑪ **Be aware of hidden costs.**

Before purchasing, be sure to consider any additional costs associated with buying a computer, such as an additional telephone line, a cable or DSL modem, an uninterruptible power supply (UPS), computer furniture, a USB flash drive, paper, and computer training classes you may want to take. Depending on where you buy your computer, the seller may be willing to include some or all of these in the computer purchase price.

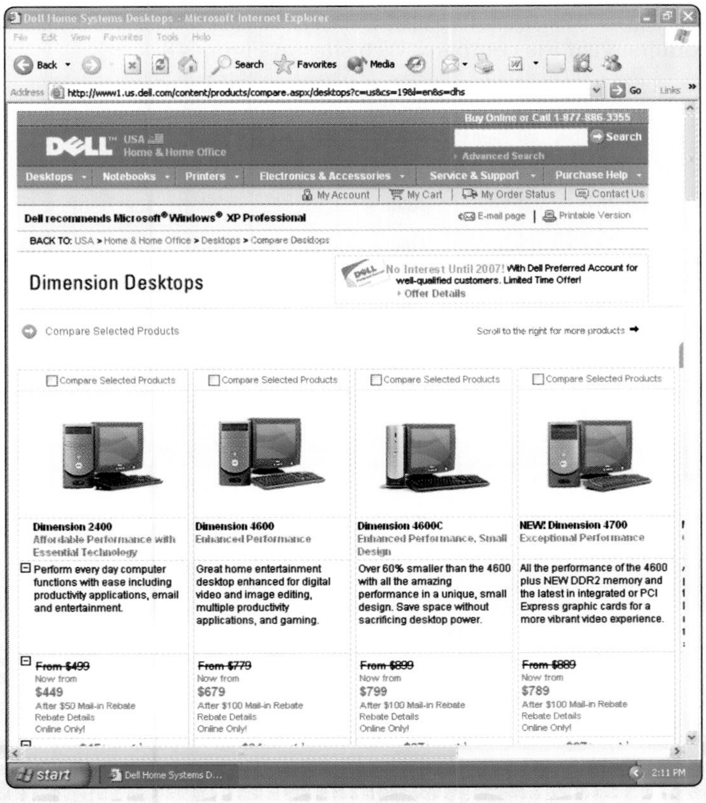

FIGURE 45 Mail-order companies, such as Dell, sell computers online.

Type of Computer	Company	Web Address
PC	CNET Shopper	shopper.cnet.com
	Hewlett-Packard	hp.com
	CompUSA	compusa.com
	Dartek	dartek.com
	Dell	dell.com
	Gateway	gateway.com
Macintosh	Apple Computer	store.apple.com
	ClubMac	clubmac.com
	MacConnection	macconnection.com
	PC & MacExchange	macx.com

For an updated list of new mail-order computer companies and their Web site addresses, visit scsite.com/ic6/buyers.

FIGURE 46 Computer mail-order companies.

Company	Web Address
Amazon.com	amazon.com
Off-Lease Computers	off-leasecomputers.com
American Computer Exchange	www.amcoex.com
U.S. Computer Exchange	usce.org
eBay	ebay.com

For an updated list of used computer mail-order companies and their Web site addresses, visit scsite.com/ic6/buyers.

FIGURE 47 Used computer mail-order companies.

31

12 **Consider more than just price.**

The lowest-cost computer may not be the best long-term buy. Consider such intangibles as the vendor's time in business, the vendor's regard for quality, and the vendor's reputation for support. If you need to upgrade your computer often, you may want to consider a leasing arrangement, in which you pay monthly lease fees, but can upgrade or add on to your computer as your equipment needs change. No matter what type of buyer you are, insist on a 30-day, no-questions-asked return policy on your computer.

13 **Avoid restocking fees.**

Some companies charge a restocking fee of 10 to 20 percent as part of their money-back return policy. In some cases, no restocking fee for hardware is applied, but it is applied for software. Ask about the existence and terms of any restocking policies before you buy.

14 **Use a credit card to purchase your new computer.**

Many credit cards offer purchase protection and extended warranty benefits that cover you in case of loss of or damage to purchased goods. Paying by credit card also gives you time to install and use the computer before you have to pay for it. Finally, if you are dissatisfied with the computer and are unable to reach an agreement with the seller, paying by credit card gives you certain rights regarding withholding payment until the dispute is resolved. Check your credit card terms for specific details.

15 **Consider purchasing an extended warranty or service plan.**

If you use your computer for business or require fast resolution to major computer problems, consider purchasing an extended warranty or a service plan through a local dealer or third-party company. Most extended warranties cover the repair and replacement of computer components beyond the standard warranty. Most service plans ensure that your technical support calls receive priority response from technicians. You also can purchase an on-site service plan that states that a technician will come to your home, work, or school within 24 hours. If your computer includes a warranty and service agreement for a year or less, think about extending the service for two or three years when you buy the computer.

CENTURY COMPUTERS
Performance Guarantee
(See reverse for terms & conditions of this contract)

Invoice #: 1984409   Effective Date: 10/12/07
Invoice Date: 10/12/07   Expiration Date: 10/12/10

Customer Name: Leon, Richard   System & Serial Numbers
Date: 10/12/07   IMB computer
Address: 1123 Roxbury   S/N: US759290C
     Sycamore, IL 60178
Day phone: (815) 555-0303
Evening Phone: (728) 555-0203

John Smith   10/12/07
Print Name of Century's Authorized Signature   Date

HOW TO PURCHASE A NOTEBOOK COMPUTER

If you need computing capability when you travel or to use in lecture or meetings, you may find a notebook computer to be an appropriate choice. The guidelines mentioned in the previous section also apply to the purchase of a notebook computer. The following are additional considerations unique to notebook computers.

1 **Purchase a notebook computer with a sufficiently large active-matrix screen.**

Active-matrix screens display high-quality color that is viewable from all angles. Less expensive, passive-matrix screens sometimes are difficult to see in low-light conditions and cannot be viewed from an angle. Notebook computers typically come with a 12.1-inch, 13.3-inch, 14.1-inch, or 15.7-inch display. For most users, a 14.1-inch display is satisfactory. If you intend to use your notebook computer as a desktop computer replacement, however, you may opt for a 15.7-inch display. Notebook computers with these larger displays weigh seven to ten pounds, however, so if you travel a lot and portability is essential, you might want a lighter computer with a smaller display. The lightest notebook computers, which weigh less than 3 pounds, are equipped with a 12.1-inch display. Regardless of size, the resolution of the display should be at least 1024 x 768 pixels. To compare the monitor size on various notebook computers, visit the company Web sites in Figure 48.

Type of Notebook	Company	Web Address
PC	Acer	global.acer.com
	Dell	dell.com
	Fujitsu	fujitsu.com
	Gateway	gateway.com
	Hewlett-Packard	hp.com
	IBM	ibm.com
	NEC	nec.com
	Sony	sony.com
	Toshiba	toshiba.com
Mac	Apple	apple.com

For an updated list of companies and their Web site addresses, visit scsite.com/ic6/buyers.

FIGURE 48 Companies that sell notebook computers.

2 **Experiment with different keyboards and pointing devices.**

Notebook computer keyboards are far less standardized than those for desktop computers. Some notebook computers, for example, have wide wrist rests, while others have none. Notebook computers also use a range of pointing devices, including pointing sticks, touchpads, and trackballs. Before you purchase a notebook computer, try various types of keyboard and pointing devices to determine which is easiest for you to use. Regardless of the pointing device you select, you also may want to purchase a regular mouse to use when you are working at a desk or other large surface.

3 **Make sure the notebook computer you purchase has a CD and/or DVD drive.**

Loading and installing software, especially large Office suites, is much faster if done from a CD-ROM, CD-RW, DVD-ROM, or DVD+RW. Today, most notebook computers come with an internal or external CD-ROM drive. Some notebook computers even come with a CD-ROM drive and a CD-RW drive or a DVD-ROM drive and a CD-RW or DVD+RW drive. Although DVD drives are slightly more expensive, they allow you to play CDs and DVD movies using your notebook computer and a headset.

4 **If necessary, upgrade the processor, memory, and disk storage at the time of purchase.**

As with a desktop computer, upgrading your notebook computer's memory and disk storage usually is less expensive at the time of initial purchase. Some disk storage is custom designed for notebook computer manufacturers, meaning an upgrade might not be available in the future. If you are purchasing a lightweight notebook computer, then it should include at least a 2.4 GHz processor, 512 MB RAM, and 80 GB of storage.

5 **The availability of built-in ports on a notebook computer is important.**

A notebook computer does not have a lot of room to add adapter cards. If you know the purpose for which you plan to use your notebook computer, then you can determine the ports you will need. Most notebooks come with common ports, such as a mouse port, IrDA port, serial port, parallel port, video port, and USB port. If you plan to connect your notebook computer to a TV, however, then you will need a PCtoTV port. If you want to connect to networks at school or in various offices, make sure the notebook computer you purchase has a built-in network card. If your notebook computer does not come with a built-in network wireless card, then you will have to purchase an external network card that slides into an expansion slot in your notebook computer, as well as a network cable. If you expect to connect an iPod portable digital music player to your notebook computer, then you will need a FireWire port.

6 **If you plan to use your notebook computer for note-taking at school or in meetings, consider a notebook computer that converts to a Tablet PC.**

Some computer manufacturers have developed convertible notebook computers that allow the screen to rotate 180 degrees on a central hinge and then fold down to cover the keyboard and become a Tablet PC (Figure 49). You then can use a stylus to enter text or drawings into the computer by writing on the screen.

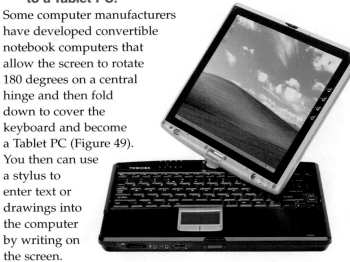

FIGURE 49 The Toshiba Protégé M200 notebook computer converts to a Tablet PC.

7 **Consider purchasing a notebook computer with a built-in wireless card to connect to your home network.**

Many users today are setting up wireless home networks. With a wireless home network, the desktop computer functions as the server, and your notebook computer can access the desktop computer from any location in the house to share files and hardware, such as a printer, and browse the Web. If your notebook computer does not come with a built-in wireless card, you can purchase an external one that slides into your notebook computer. Most home wireless networks allow connections from distances of 150 to 800 feet.

8 **If you are going to use your notebook computer for long periods without access to an electrical outlet, purchase a second battery.**

The trend among notebook computer users today is power and size over battery life, and notebook computer manufacturers have picked up on this. Many notebook computer users today are willing to give up longer battery life for a larger screen, faster processor, and more storage. In addition, some manufacturers typically sell the notebook with the lowest capacity battery. For this reason, you need to be careful in choosing a notebook computer if you plan to use it without access to electrical outlets for long periods, such as an airplane flight. You also might want to purchase a second battery as a backup. If you anticipate running your notebook computer on batteries frequently, choose a computer that uses lithium-ion batteries, which last longer than nickel cadmium or nickel hydride batteries.

9 Purchase a well-padded and well-designed carrying case.

An amply padded carrying case will protect your notebook computer from the bumps it will receive while traveling. A well-designed carrying case will have room for accessories such as spare floppy disks, CDs and DVDs, a user manual, pens, and paperwork (Figure 50).

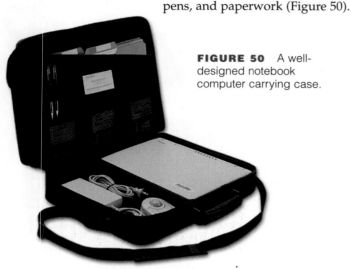

FIGURE 50 A well-designed notebook computer carrying case.

10 If you travel overseas, obtain a set of electrical and telephone adapters.

Different countries use different outlets for electrical and telephone connections. Several manufacturers sell sets of adapters that will work in most countries.

FIGURE 51 A notebook computer connected to a video projector projects the image displayed on the screen.

11 If you plan to connect your notebook computer to a video projector, make sure the notebook computer is compatible with the video projector.

You should check, for example, to be sure that your notebook computer will allow you to display an image on the computer screen and projection device at the same time (Figure 51). Also, ensure that your notebook computer has the ports required to connect to the video projector.

12 For improved security, consider a fingerprint scanner.

More than a quarter of a million notebook computers are stolen or lost each year. If you have critical information stored on your notebook computer, then consider purchasing one with a fingerprint scanner (Figure 52) to protect the data if your computer is stolen or lost. Fingerprint security offers a level of protection that extends well beyond the standard password protection.

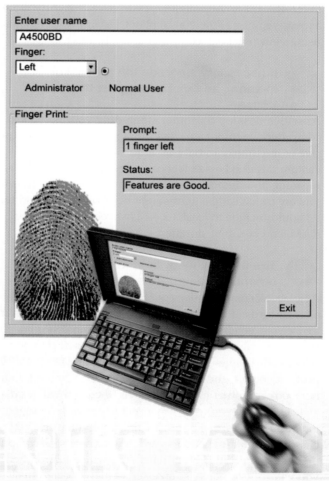

FIGURE 52 Fingerprint scanner technology offers greater security than passwords.

HOW TO PURCHASE A TABLET PC

The Tablet PC (Figure 53) combines the mobility features of a traditional notebook computer with the simplicity of pencil and paper, because you can create and save Office-type documents by writing and drawing directly on the screen with a digital pen. Tablet PCs use the Windows XP Tablet PC Edition operating system, which expands on Windows XP Professional by including digital pen and speech capabilities. A notebook computer and a Tablet PC have many similarities. For this reason, if you are considering purchasing a Tablet PC, review the guidelines for purchasing a notebook computer, as well as the guidelines below.

FIGURE 53
The lightweight Tablet PC, with its handwriting capabilities, is the latest addition to the family of mobile computers.

1 Make sure the Tablet PC fits your mobile computing needs.

The Tablet PC is not for every mobile user. If you find yourself in need of a computer in class or you are spending more time in meetings than in your office, then the Tablet PC may be the answer. Before you invest money in a Tablet PC, however, determine the programs you plan to use on it. You should not buy a Tablet PC simply because it is a new and interesting type of computer. For additional information on the Tablet PC, visit the Web sites listed in Figure 54. You may have to use the search capabilities on the home page of the companies listed to locate information about the Tablet PC.

Company	Web Address
Fujitsu	fujitsu.com
Hewlett-Packard	hp.com
Microsoft	microsoft.com/windowsxp/tabletpc
ViewSonic	viewsonic.com

For an updated list of companies and their Web site addresses, visit scsite.com/ic6/buyers.

FIGURE 54   Companies involved with Tablet PCs and their Web sites.

2 Decide whether you want a convertible or pure Tablet PC.

Convertible Tablet PCs have an attached keyboard and look like a notebook computer. You rotate the screen and lay it flat against the computer for note-taking. The pure Tablet PCs are slim and lightweight, weighing less than four pounds. They have the capability of easily docking at a desktop to gain access to a large monitor, keyboard, and mouse. If you spend a lot of time attending lectures or meetings, then the pure Tablet PC is ideal. Acceptable specifications for a Tablet PC are shown in Figure 55.

TABLET PC SPECIFICATIONS

Dimensions	12" × 9" × 1.2"
Weight	Less than 4 Pounds
Processor	Pentium III processor-M at 1.33 GHz
RAM	512 MB
Hard Disk	40 GB
Display	12.1" XGA TFT
Digitizer	Electromagnetic Digitizer
Battery	4-Cell (3-Hour)
USB	2
FireWire	1
Docking Station	Grab and Go with CD-ROM, Keyboard, and Mouse
Bluetooth Port	Yes
Wireless	802.11b/g Card
Network Card	10/100 Ethernet
Modem	56 Kbps
Speakers	Internal
Microphone	Internal
Operating System	Windows XP Tablet PC Edition
Application Software	Office Small Business Edition
Antivirus Software	Yes – 12 Month Subscription
Warranty	1-Year Limited Warranty Parts and Labor

FIGURE 55   Tablet PC specifications.

3 Be sure the weight and dimensions are conducive to portability.

The weight and dimensions of the Tablet PC are important because you carry it around like a notepad. The Tablet PC you buy should weigh four pounds or less. Its dimensions should be approximately 12 inches by 9 inches by 1.5 inches.

4 **Port availability, battery life, and durability are even more important with a Tablet PC than they are with a notebook computer.**

Make sure the Tablet PC you purchase has the ports required for the applications you plan to run. As with any mobile computer, battery life is important especially if you plan to use your Tablet PC for long periods without access to an electrical outlet. A Tablet PC must be durable because if you use it the way it was designed to be used, then you will be handling it much like you handle a pad of paper.

5 **Experiment with different models of the Tablet PC to find the digital pen that works best for you.**

The key to making use of the Tablet PC is to be comfortable with its handwriting capabilities and on-screen keyboard. Not only is the digital pen used to write on the screen (Figure 56), you also use it to make gestures to complete tasks, in a manner similar to the way you use a mouse. Figure 57 compares the standard point-and-click of a mouse unit with the gestures made with a digital pen. Other gestures with the digital pen replicate some of the commonly used keys on a keyboard.

FIGURE 56 A Tablet PC lets you handwrite notes and draw on the screen using a digital pen.

Mouse Unit	Digital Pen
Point	Point
Click	Tap
Double-click	Double-tap
Right-click	Tap and hold
Click and drag	Drag

FIGURE 57 Standard point-and-click of a mouse unit compared with the gestures made with a digital pen.

6 **Check out the comfort level of handwriting in different positions.**

You should be able to handwrite on a Tablet PC with your hand resting on the screen. You also should be able to handwrite holding the Tablet PC in one hand, as well as with it sitting in your lap.

7 **Make sure the LCD display device has a resolution high enough to take advantage of Microsoft's ClearType technologies.**

Tablet PCs use a digitizer under a standard 10.4-inch motion-sensitive LCD display to make the digital ink on the screen look like real ink on paper. To ensure you get the maximum benefits from the new ClearType technology, make sure the LCD display has a resolution of 800 × 600 in landscape mode and a 600 × 800 in portrait mode.

8 **Test the built-in Tablet PC microphone and speakers.**

With many application software packages recognizing human speech, such as Microsoft Office, it is important that the Tablet PC's built-in microphone operates at an acceptable level. If the microphone is not to your liking, you may want to purchase a close-talk headset with your Tablet PC. Increasingly more users are sending information as audio files, rather than relying solely on text. For this reason, you also should check the speakers on the Tablet PC to make sure they meet your standards.

9 **Consider a Tablet PC with a built-in PC video camera.**

A PC video camera adds streaming video and still photography capabilities to your Tablet PC, while still allowing you to take notes in lectures or meetings.

10 **Review the docking capabilities of the Tablet PC.**

The Microsoft Windows XP Tablet PC Edition operating system supports a grab-and-go form of docking, so you can pick up and take a docked Tablet PC with you, just as you would pick up a notepad on your way to a meeting (Figure 58).

FIGURE 58 A Tablet PC docked to create a desktop computer with the Tablet PC as the monitor.

11 **Wireless access to the Internet and your e-mail is essential with a Tablet PC.**

Make sure the Tablet PC has wireless networking, so you can access the Internet and your e-mail anytime and anywhere. Your Tablet PC also should include standard network connections, such as dial-up and Ethernet connections.

12 **Review available accessories to purchase with your Tablet PC.**

Tablet PC accessories include docking stations, mouse units, keyboards, security cables, additional memory and storage, protective handgrips, screen protectors, and various types of digital pens.

HOW TO PURCHASE A PERSONAL MOBILE DEVICE

Whether you choose a PDA, smart phone, or smart pager depends on where, when, and how you will use the device. If you need to stay organized when you are on the go, then a PDA may be the right choice. PDAs typically are categorized by the operating system they run. If you need to stay organized and in touch when on the go, then a smart phone or smart pager may be the right choice. Just as with PDAs, smart phones, and smart pagers are categorized by the operating system they run. The six primary operating systems for these devices are the Palm OS, Windows Mobile for Pocket PC, Windows Mobile for Smartphone, Symbian OS, Blackberry, and Embedded Linux.

This section lists guidelines you should consider when purchasing a PDA, smart phone, or smart pager. You also should visit the Web sites listed in Figure 59 on the next page to gather more information about the type of personal mobile device that best suits your computing needs.

1 **Determine the programs you plan to run on your device.**

All PDAs and most smart phones and smart pagers can handle basic organizer-type software such as a calendar, address book, and notepad. The availability of other software depends on the operating system you choose. The depth and breadth of software for the Palm OS is significant, with more than 20,000 basic programs and over 600 wireless programs. Devices that run Windows-based operating systems, such as Windows Mobile or Windows Smartphone, may have fewer programs available, but the operating system and application software are similar to those with which you are familiar, such as Word and Excel. Some Symbian-based smart phones also include the capability to read and/or edit Microsoft Office documents.

2 **Consider how much you want to pay.**

The price of a personal mobile device can range from $100 to $800, depending on its capabilities. Some Palm OS devices are at the lower end of the cost spectrum, and Windows-based devices often are at the higher end. For the latest prices, capabilities, and accessories, visit the Web sites listed in Figure 59.

3 **Determine whether you need wireless access to the Internet and e-mail or mobile telephone capabilities with your device.**

Smart pagers give you access to e-mail and other data and Internet services. Smart phones typically include these features, but also include the ability to make and receive phone calls on cellular networks. Some PDAs and smart phones include wireless networking capability to allow you to connect to the Internet wirelessly. These wireless features and

services allow personal mobile device users to access real-time information from anywhere to help make decisions while on the go.

4 **For wireless devices, determine how and where you will use the service.**

When purchasing a wireless device, you must subscribe to a wireless service. Determine if the wireless network (carrier) you choose has service in the area where you plan to use the device. Some networks have high-speed data networks only in certain areas, such as large cities or business districts. Also, a few carriers allow you to use your device in other countries.

When purchasing a smart phone, determine if you plan to use the device more as a phone, PDA, or wireless data device. Some smart phones, such as those based on the Pocket PC Phone edition or the Palm OS, are geared more for use as a PDA and have a PDA form factor. Other smart phones, such as those based on Microsoft Smartphone or Symbian operating systems, mainly are phone devices that include robust PDA functionality. RIM Blackberry-based smart phones include robust data features that are oriented to accessing e-mail and wireless data services.

5 **Make sure your device has enough memory.**

Memory (RAM) is not a major issue with low-end devices with monochrome displays and basic organizer functions. Memory is a major issue, however, for high-end devices that have color displays and wireless features. Without enough memory, the performance level of your device will drop dramatically. If you plan to purchase a high-end device running the Palm OS operating system, the device should have at least 16 MB of RAM. If you plan to purchase a high-end device running the Windows Mobile operating system, the PDA should have at least 48 MB of RAM.

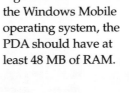

6 Practice with the touch screen, handwriting recognition, and built-in keyboard before deciding on a model.

To enter data into a PDA or smart phone, you use a pen-like stylus to handwrite on the screen or a keyboard. The keyboard either slides out or is mounted on the front of the device. With handwriting recognition, the device translates the handwriting into a computerized font. You also can use the stylus as a pointing device to select items on the screen and enter data by tapping on an on-screen keyboard. By practicing data entry before buying a device, you can learn if one device may be easier for you to use than another. You also can buy third-party software to improve a device's handwriting recognition.

7 Decide whether you want a color display.

Pocket PC devices usually come with a color display that supports as many as 65,536 colors. Palm OS devices also have a color display, but the less expensive models display in 4 to 16 shades of gray. Symbian- and Blackberry-based devices also have the option for color displays. Having a color display does result in greater on-screen detail, but it also requires more memory and uses more power. Resolution also influences the quality of the display.

8 Compare battery life.

Any mobile device is good only if it has the power required to run. For example, Palm OS devices with monochrome screens typically have a much longer battery life than Pocket PC devices with color screens. The use of wireless networking will shorten battery time considerably. To help alleviate this problem, most devices have incorporated rechargeable batteries that can be recharged by placing the device in a cradle or connecting it to a charger.

9 Seriously consider the importance of ergonomics.

Will you put the device in your pocket, a carrying case, or wear it on your belt? How does it feel in your hand? Will you use it indoors or outdoors? Many screens are unreadable outdoors. Do you need extra ruggedness, such as would be required in construction, in a plant, or in a warehouse?

10 Check out the accessories.

Determine which accessories you want for your personal mobile device. Accessories include carrying cases, portable mini- and full-sized keyboards, removable storage, modems, synchronization cradles

and cables, car chargers, wireless communications, global positioning system modules, digital camera modules, expansion cards, dashboard mounts, replacement styli, hands-free headsets, and more.

11 Decide whether you want additional functionality.

In general, off-the-shelf Microsoft operating system-based devices have broader functionality than devices with other operating systems. For example, voice-recording capability, e-book players, MP3 players, and video players are standard on most Pocket PC devices. If you are leaning towards a Palm OS device and want these additional functions, you may need to purchase additional software or expansion modules to add them later. Determine whether your employer permits devices with cameras on the premises, and if not, do not consider devices with cameras.

12 Determine whether synchronization of data with other devices or personal computers is important.

Most devices come with a cradle that connects to the USB or serial port on your computer so you can synchronize data on your device with your desktop or notebook computer. Increasingly, more devices are Bluetooth and/or wireless networking enabled, which gives them the capability of synchronizing wirelessly. Many devices today also have an infrared port that allows you to synchronize data with any device that has a similar infrared port, including desktop and notebook computers or other personal mobile devices.

Web Site	Web Address
Hewlett-Packard	hp.com
CNET Shopper	shopper.cnet.com
palmOne	palmone.com
Microsoft	windowsmobile.com pocketpc.com microsoft.com/smartphone
PDA Buyers Guide	pdabuyersguide.com
Research in Motion	rim.com
Danger	danger.com
Symbian	symbian.com
Wireless Developer Network	wirelessdevnet.com
Sharp	myzaveus.com

For an updated list of reviews and information about personal mobile devices and their Web addresses, visit scsite.com/ic6/pda.

FIGURE 59 Web site reviews and information about personal mobile devices.

Learn It Online

1 Project Reinforcement — True/False, Multiple Choice, and Short Answer

Click Project Reinforcement. Select the type of quiz and print it by clicking Print on the File menu. Answer each question. Write your first and last name at the top of each page, and then hand in the printout to your instructor.

2 Practice Test

Click Practice Test. Answer each question, enter your first and last name at the bottom of the page, and then click the Grade Test button. When the graded practice test is displayed on your screen, click Print on the File menu to print a hard copy. Continue to take practice tests until you score 80% or better. Hand in a printout of the final practice test to your instructor.

3 Who Wants To Be a Computer Genius?

Click Computer Genius. Read the instructions, enter your first and last name at the bottom of the page, and then click the PLAY button. Submit your score to your instructor.

4 Wheel of Terms

Click Wheel of Terms. Read the instructions, and then enter your first and last name and your school name. Click the PLAY button. Submit your score to your instructor.

5 Visiting Web Link Sites

Visit 10 of the 18 Web Link sites in the margins of pages COM-2 to COM-23. Print the main Web page for each of the 10 Web sites you visit and hand them in to your instructor.

6 Crossword Puzzle Challenge

Click Crossword Puzzle Challenge. Read the instructions, and then enter your first and last name. Click the PLAY button. Work the crossword puzzle. When you are finished, click the Submit button. When the crossword puzzle redisplays, click the Print button. Hand in the printout to your instructor.

7 Making Use of the Web

Click Making Use of the Web. Read 1 of the 15 areas of interest, visit each of the Web sites listed, print the first page of each Web site, and then complete the Web exercises. Hand in the printouts and your answers to the Web exercises to your instructor.

8 Scavenger Hunt

Click Scavenger Hunt. Print a copy of the Scavenger Hunt page. Use a search engine to answer the questions. Hand in your completed page to your instructor.

9 Search Sleuth

Click Search Sleuth to learn search techniques that will help make you a research expert. Hand in your completed assignment to your instructor.

10 Install and Maintain a Personal Computer

(a) Click Install Computer, visit the Ergonomics links in Figure 1, and write a brief report outlining what you learned. (b) Click Maintain Computer, choose one of the step topics. Use the Web to learn more about the topic. Write a brief report on what you learned.

Case Studies

1. Computers are ubiquitous. Watching television, driving a car, using a charge card, ordering fast food, and the more obvious activity of typing a term paper on a personal computer, all involve interaction with computers. Make a list of every computer you can recall that you encountered over the past week (be careful not to limit yourselves just to the computers you see). Consider how each computer is used. How were the tasks the computers performed done before computers existed? Write a brief report and submit it to your instructor.

2. The Internet has had a tremendous impact on business. For some businesses, that influence has not been positive. For example, surveys suggest that as a growing number of people make their own travel plans online, travel agents are seeing fewer customers. Use the Web and/or printed media to research businesses that have been affected negatively by the Internet. What effect has the Internet had? How can the business compete with the Internet? Write a brief report and submit it to your instructor.

INDEX

PHOTO CREDITS

Figure 1a, Computer, Courtesy of Acer America Corp.; Figure 1b, PC video camera, Courtesy of Logitech, Inc.; Figure 1c, Microphone, Courtesy of Logitech, Inc.; Figure 1d, Open flatbed scanner, Courtesy of Umax Systems GmbH; Figure 1e, External card reader, Courtesy of Sandisk Corporation; Figure 1f, USB flash drive, Courtesy of Sandisk Corporation; Figure 1g, External cable modem, Courtesy of Linksys, a Division of Cisco Systems Inc.; Figure 1h, digital camera, Courtesy of Umax Systems GmbH; Figure 1i, Ink-jet printer, Courtesy of Epson America, Inc.; Figure 2, payroll check, © C Squared Studios/Getty Images; Figure 4, Internet keyboard, Courtesy of Logitech; Figure 5a, PDA, Courtesy of ViewSonic® Corporation; Figure 5b, PDA scanner, Courtesy of Socket Communications, Inc.; Figure 5c, pen/stylus combination, Courtesy of Belkin Corporation; Figure 5d, stylus, Courtesy of ViewSonic® Corporation; Figure 5e, PDA digital camera, Courtesy of LifeView, Inc.; Figure 5f, pen input , Courtesy of Seiko Instruments USA Inc.; Figure 5g, PDA, Courtesy of ViewSonic® Corporation; Figure 5h, desktop computer, Courtesy of IBM; Figure 6, smart phone with picture or video on it, © Edward Bock/CORBIS; Figure 7a, mechanical mouse, Courtesy of Microsoft Corporation; Figure 7b, optical mouse, Courtesy of Microsoft Corporation; Figure 7c, laser mouse, Courtesy of Logitech; Figure 8a, laptop pointing stick, Courtesy of IBM; Figure 8b, finger using laptop mouse, © Getty Images; Figure 9a, system unit opened, © Gary Herrington; Figure 9b, Pentium 4 processor, Courtesy of Intel Corporation; Figure 9c, memory chips on a module, Courtesy of SMART Modular Technologies, Inc. © 2002; Figure 9d, sound card, Courtesy of Creative Labs, Inc. Copyright © 2003 Creative Technology Ltd. (SOUND BLASTER AUDIGY 2S). All rights reserved.; Figure 9e, video card, Courtesy of Matrox Graphics Inc.; Figure 10, dot matrix printer, Courtesy of Oki Data Americas, Inc.; Figure 11a - f, ink-jet printer with output, Courtesy of Epson America, Inc.; Figure 12, color laser printer, Courtesy of Xerox Corporation; Figure 13a, LCD monitor, Courtesy of NEC-Mitsubishi Electronics Display of America Inc.; Figure 13b, CRT monitor, Courtesy of NEC-Mitsubishi Electronics Display of America Inc.; Figure 14a, notebook computer, Courtesy of Acer America Corp.; Figure 14b, Tablet PC, Courtesy of Acer America Corp.; Figure 14c, PDA with color screen, Courtesy of Sony Electronics Inc.; Figure 14d, smart phone, Siemens press picture; Figure 17a, person inserting floppy disk into PC (tower model), © Masterfile (Royalty-Free Div.) www.masterfile.com; Figure 17b, external floppy disk drive plugged into a laptop computer, Photo Courtesy of Iomega Corporation. Copyright © 2003 Iomega Corporation. All Rights Reserved. Zip is a registered trademark in the United States and/or other countries. Iomega, the stylized "i" logo and product images are property of Iomega Corporation in the United States and/or other countries; Figure 18a, Iomega 750 MB Zip disk sticking out of a Zip drive, Photo Courtesy of Iomega Corporation; Figure 18b, product shot of a 750 MB Zip disk, Photo Courtesy of Iomega Corporation; Figure 19, SATA hard disk, Courtesy of Maxtor Corporation. © 2004 Maxtor Corporation. All Rights Reserved; Figure 20, opening CD-ROM drive, © Gary Herrington; Figure 21a, CD-ROM (with software program), Courtesy of Memorex Products, Inc.; Figure 21b, CD-R (box shot), Courtesy of Memorex Products, Inc.; Figure 21c, CD-RW box shot, Courtesy of Memorex Products, Inc.; Figure 21d, DVD-ROM, © 2004 DeLorme (www.delorme.com) Topo USA®; Figure 21e, DVD-R (box shot), Courtesy of Memorex Products, Inc.; Figure 21f, DVD+R (box shot), Courtesy of Memorex Products, Inc.; Figure 21g, DVD-RW (box shot), Courtesy of Memorex Products, Inc.; Figure 21h, DVD+RW (box shot), Courtesy of Memorex Products, Inc.; Figure 21i, DVD-RAM (box shot), Courtesy of Memorex Products, Inc.; Figure 21j, screen shot for LCD monitor, © 2004 DeLorme (www.delorme.com) Topo USA®; Figure 22, DVD software disc , © 2004 DeLorme (www.delorme.com) Topo USA®; Figure 23, tape cartridge and tape drive, Courtesy of Sony Electronics Inc.; Figure 24a, flash, Courtesy of Sandisk Corporation; Figure 24b, miniature storage media and PDA, Courtesy of palmOne, Inc.; Figure 24c, flash memory cards & USB flash drives in desktop computers, laptop computers, and mobile, Siemens Press Picture; Figure 24d, USB flash drive in desktop computer, Courtesy of Fujitsu Siemens Computers; Figure 24e, digital photo viewer with a card sticking out of it, Courtesy of Delkin Devices, Inc.; Figure 24f, JVC TV, Courtesy of JVC Company of America; Figure 24g, landscape for TV, © Digital Vision/Getty Images; Figure 24h, CompactFlash 4.0 Sandisk, Courtesy of Sandisk Corporation; Figure 25a, SmartMedia, Courtesy of Sandisk Corporation; Figure 25b, SecureDigital, Courtesy of Sandisk Corporation; Figure 25c, 1G xD-Picture Card, Courtesy of Lexar Media, Inc.; Figure 25d, memory stick, Courtesy of Sandisk Corporation; Figure 26, USB flash drive, Photo Courtesy of Iomega Corporation. Copyright (c) 2003 Iomega Corporation. All Rights Reserved. Zip is a registered trademark in the United States and/or other countries. Iomega, the stylized "i" logo and product images are property of Iomega Corporation in the United States and/or other countries; Figure 27, smart card in use, © Jean-Yves Bruel/Masterfile; Figure 29, software aisle at a computer store, ©Bonnie Kamin/Photo Edit; Figure 38a, desktop computer,Courtesy of IBM Corporation; Figure 38b1, mobile computer, Courtesy of Sony Electronics, Inc.; Figure 38b2, notebook computer\ tablet pc, Courtesy of Motion Computing; Figure 39c, personal mobile device, Courtesy of palmOne, Inc.; Figure 38c2, smart phone/PDA, Siemens press picture; Figure 38d, thinking female, © Digital Vision/Getty Images; Figure 41a, CD\ DVD drives, Courtesy of JVC; Figure 41b, Card Reader\ Writer, Courtesy of Sandisk; Figure 41c, Digital Camera, Courtesy of UMAX; Figure 41d, Digital Video Capture Device, Courtesy of Pinnacle Systems, Inc.; Figure 41f, Hard Disk, Courtesy of Seagate; Figure 41g, Joystick\ Wheel, Courtesy of Logitech; Figure 41h, keyboard, Courtesy of Microsoft; Figure 41j, Modem, Courtesy of US Robotics; Figure 41k, Monitor, Courtesy of ViewSonic Corporation; Figure 41l, Mouse, Courtesy of Microsoft; Figure 41m, Network Card, Courtesy of 3Com Corporation; Figure 41n, Printer, Courtesy of EPSON America, Inc.; Figure 41o, Processor, Courtesy of Intel Corporation; Figure 41p, RAM, Courtesy of Kingston Technology; Figure 41q, Scanner, Courtesy of UMAX; Figure 41s, Speakers, Courtesy of Logitech; Figure 41t, PC Video Camera, Courtesy of Logitech; Figure 41u, USB Flash Drive, Courtesy of Sandisk; Figure 41v, Video Graphics Card, Courtesy of 3Com Corporation; Figure 41x, Zip Drive, Courtesy of Iomega; Figure 39, notebook computer converts to a Tablet PC, Courtesy of Toshiba America; Figure 50, A well designed notebook computer carrying case, Courtesy of Toshiba America; Figure 51, a notebook computer connected to a video projector, © Britt Erlanson/Getty Images; Figure 53, light weight Tablet PC, © Thomas Barwick/PhotoDisc Collection/Getty Images; Figure 56, a Tablet PC and pen, Courtesy of ViewSonic Corporation; Figure 58, Tablet PC docked, Courtesy of Fujitsu Siemens Computers.

Developing Strategies for Managing Your Files
Management: Planning for the Growth of Bon Vivant Corporation

> *"We are the creative force of our life, and through our own decisions rather than our conditions, if we carefully learn to do certain things, we can accomplish those goals."*
> —Stephen Covey

LEARNING OBJECTIVES

Level 1

Prepare an organized computer system
Evaluate tools for managing files
Develop navigation strategies
Copy and move files

Level 2

Execute your organization plans
Use meaningful file and folder names
Work effectively with computer programs
Find stored files

Level 3

Refine your file management
Maintain your files
Exchange files
Back up your files

TOOLS COVERED IN THIS CHAPTER

Backup and Restore
My Computer
Send To command
Search Companion
Shortcuts
Windows XP Explorer
Windows XP file compression

CHAPTER INTRODUCTION

This chapter explains how to develop a strategy for organizing the folders and files you store on a hard disk and other types of disks. Whether you work on a desktop computer, a computer connected to a network, or a laptop, one of the most important tasks you face is managing folders and files so you can store and retrieve your work efficiently. To do so, you should develop a strategy for organizing files that simplifies access to your documents and improves your productivity. Level 1 explains how to prepare an organized system by exploring how Windows XP manages files and folders and how to take advantage of this system to store your files in a logical arrangement. It also examines the two tools Windows provides for managing files—My Computer and Windows Explorer. Level 2 explores skills that you will use regularly in file management, including manipulating files and folders and identifying your work with meaningful filenames. You will apply the principles you learned in Level 1 to optimize your file organization. Finally, Level 3 helps you refine your file management techniques by using shortcuts, evaluating file and folder properties, and using other tools. You will also explore how to exchange files with others and how to secure your work by archiving it and using backups.

CASE SCENARIO

Bon Vivant Corporation is a company that franchises restaurants and coffee shops, among them, Bon Vivant Cafés, neighborhood eateries that offer moderately priced cuisine designed to appeal to families who seek fresh, healthy, traditional American food with a continental accent. Alicia Fernandez is the new vice president of franchise operations for the Bon Vivant Corporation. She is in charge of managing the growth of Bon Vivant Café franchises throughout the upper Midwest, and serves as liaison between franchise managers and the Bon Vivant Corporation. She is reviewing several applications to open new franchises. Before she can consider them, she needs to analyze the performance of the 10 Bon Vivant Café franchises in Illinois, Wisconsin, Minnesota, and Michigan, and summarize the strengths and weaknesses of each franchise.

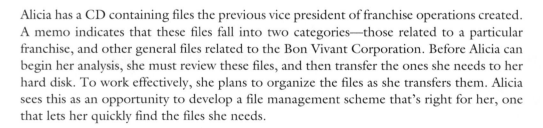

Alicia has a CD containing files the previous vice president of franchise operations created. A memo indicates that these files fall into two categories—those related to a particular franchise, and other general files related to the Bon Vivant Corporation. Before Alicia can begin her analysis, she must review these files, and then transfer the ones she needs to her hard disk. To work effectively, she plans to organize the files as she transfers them. Alicia sees this as an opportunity to develop a file management scheme that's right for her, one that lets her quickly find the files she needs.

LEVEL 1

PLANNING A WELL-ORGANIZED SCHEME FOR EFFICIENT FILE MANAGEMENT

FILE MANAGEMENT SKILLS TRAINING

- Arrange the icons in a folder in groups
- Arrange the icons in a folder by file type
- Change the view in the My Documents folder
- Close expanded folders
- Copy a file in Explorer by right-dragging
- Copy a file to a different folder
- Expand a folder using Windows Explorer
- Move multiple documents to the My Documents folder
- Move a file
- Navigate through the Windows hierarchy
- Select more than one file at a time
- Sort files in Details view
- Use Details view to examine file characteristics

PREPARING AN ORGANIZED SYSTEM

Before Alicia started working at the Bon Vivant Corporation, she was the manager of the Bon Vivant Café franchise in St. Paul, Minnesota, and used a computer primarily to process customer and vendor transactions, send and receive e-mail messages, and access the Internet. Most of the professional documents she worked with were printed copies of accounting reports and marketing material, such as advertisements, flyers, and menus. Occasionally, she prepared management reports using Microsoft Office Word 2003, and saved these electronic files on a laptop computer. Because she saved only a few files on this computer, she stored the documents in a single folder, and could find them easily when necessary.

Now that she is vice president of franchise operations for the corporation, however, she must work with many more files, including spreadsheets, reports, marketing documents, and presentations from other corporate managers and from the 10 Bon Vivant Café franchises in the upper Midwest. She anticipates that she will be creating, reading, changing, and saving dozens of electronic documents each week, and can no longer store them all in a single folder. To be productive on her new job, Alicia needs to develop an effective scheme for saving, locating, and organizing her computer files. She also wants to be able to work on her computer at home occasionally. This means that she needs to organize her home computer in a similar fashion.

The most common strategy for managing electronic files is to mimic the organization of their paper-copy counterparts. For example, Alicia can create a number of electronic folders, and then store each file in an appropriate folder. One folder might contain corporate financial data, another might contain documents for the Bon Vivant Café franchise in Ann Arbor, Michigan, and another could contain documents for the franchise in Champaign, Illinois. The two franchise folders could also contain folders to keep different types of documents separate from one another. Folders that contain other folders are called **subfolders**. See Figure 1.1.

Figure 1.1: Organizing files into folders

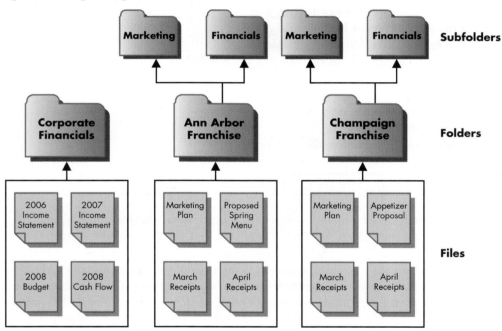

But where should Alicia store these folders? On a CD like the one her predecessor gave her? On her new desktop computer? On the corporate server? As she thinks about this, Alicia considers how computers store files in general and how Windows XP organizes its standard files and folders in particular so she can choose a logical location for her work.

Exploring How Computers Store Data

When you create and save a computer file, you store it on a disk. The disk might be a hard disk permanently attached to a computer, or a type of removable media such as a floppy disk, compact disc (CD), or flash drive. Disks vary by the amount of information they can hold, ranging from 1.44 MB of data on a floppy disk to 1 GB on a flash drive to 80 GB on a hard disk. Hard disks are the most popular type of computer storage because they can contain many gigabytes of data, allow fast access to that data, and are economical.

Best Practice

Deciding Which Computer Storage Media to Use

Compared to removable media, hard disks are larger, faster, and safer, and are therefore the preferred method for storing files. However, removable media offer advantages that hard disks do not provide. Flash drives (also called thumb drives, key drives, jump drives, and pen drives) are most often used for transferring data from one computer to another, such as from a laptop to a desktop computer, whereas CDs and tapes are used for backing up files. Flash drives are quickly becoming the most popular way to transfer files because they offer portability, reliability, convenience, and speed. You can also use Zip disks and floppy disks to transfer data, though both types of media are becoming obsolete. In fact, because floppy disks are much less reliable than other types of removable media—they can easily be damaged and lose data—you should only use them if you do not have access to a CD writer, flash drive, or USB port for the flash drive. To back up larger amounts of data, some people use portable hard disks, which blur the line between fixed disks and removable media. CDs or digital video discs (DVDs) are often the preferred media for software developers to provide when distributing software for installation. Table 1.1 compares storage media, including various types of CDs and DVDs.

Table 1.1: Removable storage media

Media	Description	Storage Capacity	Pros and Cons
Floppy disk	3.5-inch disk; inserts into a floppy disk drive	1.44 MB	Older technology becoming obsolete
Zip disk	3.5-inch disk (though thicker than a floppy disk); inserts into a Zip drive	100 MB–750 MB	Older technology becoming obsolete
Flash drive	Small device that often can be carried on a key chain; connects via a USB port	64 MB–2 GB	Inexpensive and convenient
CD-ROM (CD-read only)	Optical storage device inserts into a CD drive; often used for distributing software; cannot record new data on it	650 MB	Cannot record data on a CD-ROM
CD-R (CD-recordable); CD-RW (CD-read/write)	Similar to a CD-ROM, but can record data on CD-R once and on CD-RW many times	650 MB	Inexpensive medium; CDs can be easily damaged
DVD-ROM (DVD-read only)	Optical storage device inserts into a DVD drive; similar to a CD-ROM but with much greater storage capacity	4.7 GB (one-sided) 8.5 GB (two-sided)	Cannot record data on a DVD-ROM

Table 1.1: Removable storage media (cont.)

Media	Description	Storage Capacity	Pros and Cons
DVD-R (DVD-recordable); DVD-RAM, DVD-ER (DVD recordable and erasable); DVD +/- R/RW (DVD record and read/write)	Similar to DVD-ROM, but can record data on DVD-R once and on DVD-RAM, DVD +/- R/RW, and DVD-ER many times	4.7 GB (one-sided) 9.4 GB (two-sided)	More expensive than CDs, but much greater storage capacity; various formats are usually not compatible with each other and cannot be read in a different type of DVD drive (although this is changing)
Magnetic tape	Available in small cartridges; often used to create system backups for large corporations	2 GB–40 GB	Can store the most data, but is slower than disc technologies

To access data you store on a disk, the disk must be placed in the appropriate computer drive; for example, you insert a CD into a CD drive and a flash drive into a Universal Serial Bus (USB) port. A computer distinguishes one drive from another by assigning each a drive letter. The floppy disk drive is usually drive A. (Many new computers no longer include a floppy disk drive, as other larger and more reliable storage media become available.) The hard disk is usually assigned to drive C. The remaining drives can have any other letters, but are usually assigned in the order that the drives were installed on the computer—so your CD drive might be drive D or E.

Alicia examines her desktop computer, and notes that in addition to a hard disk, it has a floppy disk drive, a compact disc-read/write (CD-RW) drive, a DVD drive, and several USB ports. She decides to maintain her files on the hard disk, and occasionally transfer them to a flash drive that she can use on her home computer.

Exploring How Windows XP Manages Files and Folders

When the Windows XP operating system is installed on your computer, it creates thousands of files and stores them in dozens of folders on the hard disk. These are system files that Windows XP needs to display the desktop, use drives, access resources such as printers, and perform other operating system tasks. To ensure system stability and find files quickly, Windows XP organizes the folders and files in a hierarchy, or **file system**. At the top of the hierarchy, Windows XP stores folders and important files that it needs when you turn on the computer; this location is called the **root directory**, and is usually drive C (the hard disk). The term "root" refers to a common metaphor for visualizing a file system—an upside-down tree. In Figure 1.2, the root directory (the tree trunk) is the hard disk, which contains folders (branches) and files (leaves).

Figure 1.2: Windows file hierarchy

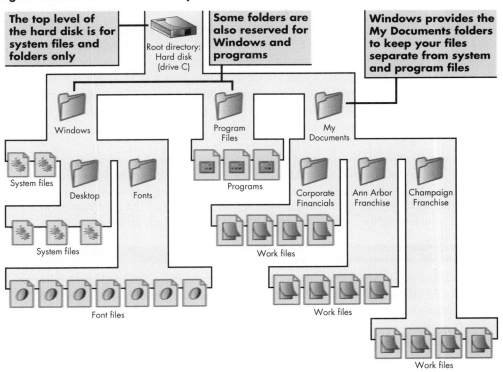

In addition to the files and folders that Windows XP created in the root directory when it was installed, some other programs also store files and folders in the root directory when they are installed.

The root directory of the hard disk is for system files and folders only; you should not store your own work here because it could interfere with Windows XP or a program. (If you are working on a network or in a computer lab, you might not even be allowed to access the root directory.)

Best Practice

Avoiding the Root Directory and Program Folders

Do not delete or move any files or folders from the root directory of the hard disk—doing so could mean that you cannot run or start the computer. In fact, you should not reorganize or change any folder that contains installed software, because Windows XP expects to find the files for specific programs within certain folders. If you reorganize or change these folders, Windows XP cannot locate and start the programs stored in that folder. Likewise, you should not make changes to the folder that contains the Windows XP operating system (usually named Windows or WINNT).

Alicia understands that because the top level of the hard disk is off-limits for her files—the ones that she creates, opens, and saves on the hard disk—she must store all her files in folders. Windows XP provides a special folder named My Documents, which is designed to contain these files. If Alicia simply stores all her files in the My Documents folder, however, she will soon have trouble finding the ones she wants. Instead, she can create folders within the My Documents folder to separate files in a way that makes sense for her. As shown earlier in Figure 1.2, this organization might require her to create folders such as Corporate Financials, Ann Arbor Franchise, and Champaign Franchise in the My Documents folder on her computer.

When Alicia transfers files from her hard disk to a flash drive or other removable media to use them on her home computer, she also needs to organize those files into folders and subfolders, preferably reflecting the organization she employs on her office computer. In both cases, she needs to plan the organization she will use to avoid the common pitfalls of creating and transferring files without knowing where they end up on a disk.

Planning an Organization for Your Files and Folders

The previous vice president of franchise operations wrote a memo to identify the files he saved on the CD he gave to Alicia. Although he did not save the files in folders on the CD, he listed them in the following categories:

- **Corporate**—Spreadsheets showing financial information, text documents such as those containing policies and procedures for franchises, sample ads, and performance reports, graphics such as logos and photographs of menu offerings, and copies of e-mail messages
- **Franchises**—Spreadsheets tracking revenue and expenses, text documents such as marketing plans, revenue reports, and menu proposals, and graphics for marketing materials for the 10 Bon Vivant Café franchises in Illinois, Michigan, Minnesota, and Wisconsin
- **Other**—Miscellaneous documents such as instructions for using the phone system, copies of the Bon Vivant electronic newsletter, stock photos of food and markets, and a calendar program

Alicia considers using three folders in her My Documents folder to arrange the files, one named Corporate, another named Franchises, and another named Other. Then she realizes that she needs to refine this organization. For example, the Corporate category is too broad for most of the files listed in that category. She can store a few general files in a Corporate folder, but by using subfolders to create subcategories, such as financial statements, corporate documents that are sent to the franchises, and ads, she can store the rest of the files according to their purpose, making them easier to find and retrieve.

Alicia also decides that she needs to use subfolders within the Franchises folder. She considers creating four subfolders, one for each state, but as she examines the list of files in the franchises category, she realizes that she will be receiving files from each franchise and needs to keep them separate from one another. She therefore needs 10 subfolders, one for each franchise.

As she considers how to organize the files currently listed in the "Other" category, she recalls learning in a time management course that containers such as physical file folders and cabinet drawers labeled "Other" or "Miscellaneous" quickly become cluttered and invite disorganization. She decides she should store the files in this category in more appropriate folders. For example, the instructions for using the phone system probably belongs with the general files in the Corporate folder.

Alicia sketches the folder organization she plans to use on her hard disk. See Figure 1.3.

Figure 1.3: Preliminary folder organization for Alicia's files

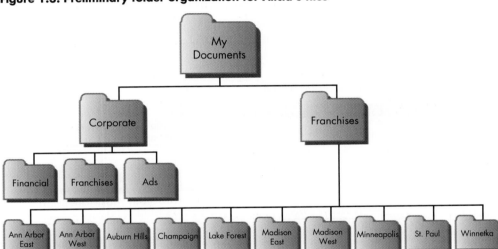

As Alicia reviews her sketch, she notices that it includes two folders named Franchises. Surely this will create confusion for her later. The Franchises subfolder in the Corporate folder is supposed to contain corporate documents that she sends to the franchises, such as forms, handbooks, and standard procedures. Instead of storing these in the Franchises subfolder of the Corporate folder, she can store them in the main Franchises folder, the one that contains a subfolder for each franchise. Then she can eliminate the Franchises subfolder in the Corporate folder. That way, she can find files she sends to franchises and those she receives from franchises in a single folder.

When she compares her sketch to the list of files on the CD, Alicia discovers a few files that don't fit into her organization: the calendar program and copies of e-mail messages. She recalls that the My Documents folder is designed to contain documents and other files that users create and save, not program files. Although the calendar program is a small program contained in a single file, she should still move this calendar program file to the Program Files folder if she decides she wants to keep it. She also wonders if she needs to keep the copies of e-mail messages on her hard disk. She'll review those and delete the ones she doesn't need.

DEVELOPING NAVIGATION STRATEGIES

The two tools that Windows XP provides for exploring the files and folders on a computer—Windows Explorer and My Computer—both display the contents of the computer, using icons to represent drives, folders, and files. However, by default, each presents a different view of your computer. To examine both views, Alicia starts her computer, opens the Windows Explorer window (she clicks the Start button, points to All Programs, points to Accessories, and then clicks Windows Explorer), and then opens the My Computer window (she clicks the Start button, and then clicks My Computer). See Figure 1.4. Windows Explorer shows the hierarchy of the files, folders, and drives on her computer, making it easy to navigate within that hierarchy. My Computer shows the drives on her computer, making it easy to perform system tasks, such as adding or removing a program.

Figure 1.4: Comparing Windows Explorer and My Computer

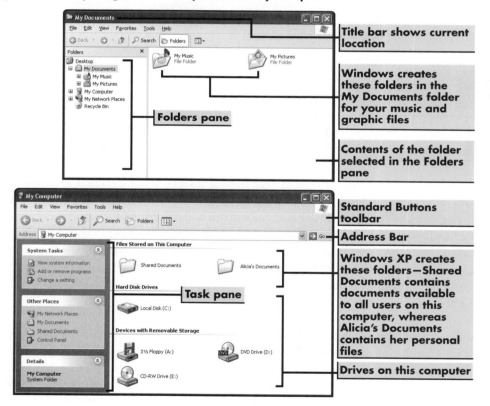

The Windows Explorer window is divided into two sections called panes. The left pane, also called the Explorer bar or Folders pane, shows the hierarchy of the folders and other locations on a computer. The right pane lists the contents of these folders and other locations. If you select a folder in the left pane, for example, the files stored in that folder appear in the right pane. The My Computer window is also divided into panes—the left pane, called the task pane, lists tasks related to the items displayed in the right pane.

Evaluating Tools for Managing Files

When you manage files, you typically first need to navigate through folders on your computer to find the files you want, and then you organize them by moving, copying, or deleting them, for example. Both My Computer and Windows Explorer help you navigate and organize. When you open My Computer (from the Start menu or by double-clicking the My Computer icon if it appears on the desktop), it displays the top level of your computer's hierarchy—the hard drive and other drives on the computer. To navigate the hierarchy, you can double-click a drive icon to display the contents of that drive. For example, you can double-click the Local Disk (C:) icon to display the next level of folders in the hierarchy. Then you can double-click a folder to display its contents, and continue opening folders as necessary until you find the file you want. In this way, you take a top-down approach to navigating your computer—you start at the top level and work your way down to a file by opening folders.

Besides using drive and folder icons, My Computer offers three other ways to navigate: the Standard Buttons toolbar, the Address Bar, and the task pane. The Standard Buttons toolbar has three buttons that let you move through the hierarchy of drives, directories, folders, subfolders, and other objects one level at a time. You click the Up button 📁 to move up one level in the hierarchy on your computer, the Back button ⬅ to move to your previous location, and the Forward button ➡ to move to the next location in your sequence of locations.

The Address Bar indicates your current location in the file hierarchy. To navigate using the Address Bar, you click its list arrow. A list of folders and drives appears, including drives for removable media, the My Documents folder, and folders containing the current folder. To open a drive or folder and display its contents in the current window, you click the drive or folder in the list. In this way, you can quickly move to an upper level of the hierarchy without navigating the intermediate levels.

The task pane lists tasks related to your current location. For example, when you are displaying the contents of the My Documents folder, the task pane lists tasks for creating a folder or displaying the top level of My Computer.

With the My Computer window open on her desktop, Alicia decides to explore the organization of her computer. She'll start by opening the My Documents folder—using the task pane seems the easiest way to do this. She clicks the My Documents link in the task pane. See Figure 1.5.

1

Level 1

Figure 1.5: Viewing the contents of the My Documents folder with My Computer

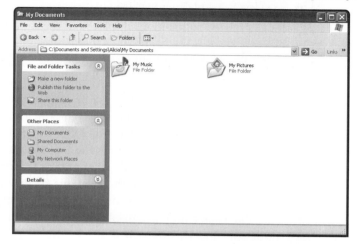

My Documents contains two built-in folders designed for storing and accessing media files: My Pictures and My Music. To view the contents of the My Music folder, Alicia double-clicks the My Music folder icon in the right pane of the My Documents window. See Figure 1.6.

Figure 1.6: Viewing the contents of the My Music folder with My Computer

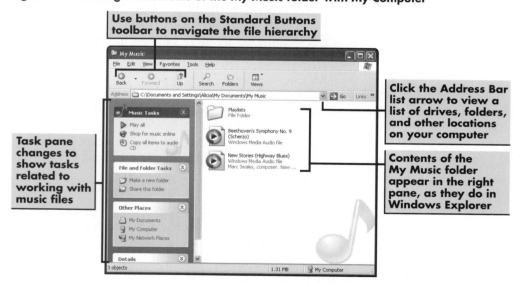

Next, Alicia examines the Windows Explorer window. Windows Explorer also lets you use the Standard Buttons toolbar and Address Bar to navigate, but most people prefer to use the Folders pane because it is faster and more direct. (The Folders pane does not appear by default in the My Computer window.)

The Folders pane shows the hierarchy of the files, folders, and drives on your computer. Recall that Windows XP creates dozens of folders when it is installed on a computer. If the Folders pane showed all the folders on a computer at once, the list of folders would be very long. The plus sign ⊞ to the left of a folder indicates that the folder contains subfolders. For example, in Figure 1.4, a plus sign ⊞ appears to the left of the My Music and My Pictures folders, indicating that these folders contain subfolders. When you click the plus sign ⊞ next to the My Music folder, the view of the My Music folder expands to show its subfolder. A minus sign ⊟ then appears next to the My Music folder; you click the minus sign ⊟ to collapse the folder. To view the files contained in the My Music folder, you click the folder icon, and the files appear in the right pane. See Figure 1.7.

Figure 1.7: Viewing the contents of the My Music folder in Windows Explorer

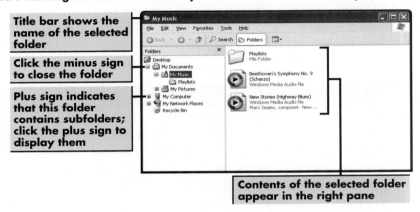

Alicia closes the My Computer window and decides to use Windows Explorer to examine the file organization on her computer. In the Folders pane, she clicks the plus sign ⊞ next to the My Computer icon. The drives and other useful locations on her computer appear under the My Computer icon. See Figure 1.8.

Figure 1.8: Viewing the contents of Alicia's computer

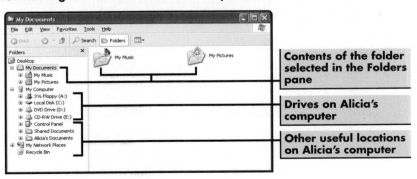

Because My Documents is the selected folder, which is the last folder she selected, its contents appear in the right pane of the window. If Alicia wanted to display the contents of My Computer in the right pane, she could click the My Computer icon itself, not its plus sign +.

To continue examining the file organization on the computer, Alicia clicks the plus sign + next to the Local Disk (C:) icon to view the contents of her hard disk. Her hard disk contains three folders: Documents and Settings, Program Files, and WINDOWS. Documents and Settings is a built-in Windows XP folder that contains a folder for each user installed on the system. The Program Files and WINDOWS folders store files that programs and Windows XP need to run.

Alicia can see that using the Folders pane helps her navigate the computer and orients her to her current location. When she begins to move, copy, delete, and perform other tasks with the files in the right pane of Windows Explorer, she can refer to the Folders pane to see how these changes affect the overall organization of the file hierarchy.

Best Practice

Using the Windows XP Standard Document Folders

To help you organize your files, Windows XP provides at least three folders for your documents: My Documents, My Pictures, and My Music. Many programs save documents to the My Documents folder by default, saving you a step when you select a drive and folder for your document file. When you open the My Pictures folder using My Computer, the task pane lists special options for working with graphic files, such as displaying images in Filmstrip view so that you can quickly locate and preview images, ordering prints online, printing a picture, and copying images to a CD. Similarly, the task pane for the My Music folder includes special options for playing the music files in the folder, shopping for music online, and copying music files to an audio CD.

Best Practice

Including Specialized Tasks in Other Folders

If you want to store certain types of files, such as music or graphics, in folders other than My Music or My Pictures, for example, you can customize those folders to display tasks appropriate for the files. For example, suppose you are working on a project team developing a new product, and you plan to keep all the project files together in one folder. You can create a subfolder named Product Graphics, and then customize it so that its task pane includes options for displaying the images in Filmstrip view or as a slide show, just as you can in the My Pictures folder. To do this, you use a folder that contains these options as a template. To create the Product Graphics folder in the example, you would use the My Pictures folder as a template. To do so, right-click the folder in which you want to display specialized tasks, and then click Properties on the shortcut menu. In the folders Properties dialog box, click the Customize tab. Click the Use this folder type as a template list arrow, click the template type you want to apply, such as Pictures (best for many files), and then click the OK button.

Figures 1.5 and 1.8 show the default views of the My Documents folder in the Windows Explorer and My Computer windows, the views you see if you do not change any window settings. These settings reflect the distinction that earlier versions of Windows made between these two tools: Windows Explorer was designed for navigating and My Computer for displaying drives and information about them. Windows XP lets you use both for navigating and for displaying system information. Choose the tool that you prefer for managing your files.

Establishing a Standard Location for Work Files

Recall that Windows XP provides the My Documents folder as a place to store the files and folders you work with regularly. This is where you can keep your data files—the memos, videos, graphics, music, and other files that you create, edit, and manipulate in various programs. However, if you are working on a network, such as your school's computer lab network, you might not be able to access the My Documents folder. On such a network, that folder quickly becomes cluttered, full of files that can occupy too much disk space, which means network administrators must empty the folder every day or restrict access to it. Instead, you might permanently store your data files on removable media or in a different folder on your computer or network. You should still establish a standard location for your files, a folder that contains only your personal files arranged in subfolders, so that you can find your files easily.

Best Practice

Creating an Alternative My Documents Folder

If you are not allowed to store files in the My Documents folder or want to use a different folder as the default folder for viewing, saving, and opening files, you can establish an alternative to the My Documents folder. To do so, create a folder, such as one named Work Files, and note its location in the Address Bar of the Windows Explorer or My Computer window, such as C:\Documents and Settings\Work Files. (If the location does not appear in your Address Bar, you can click Tools on the menu bar of My Computer or Windows Explorer, and then click Folder Options. On the View tab, click the Display the full path in the address bar check box.) Right-click the My Documents icon on the desktop, and then click Properties on the shortcut menu. The My Documents Properties dialog box opens. In the Target text box, enter the location of the alternative My Documents folder, such as C:\Documents and Settings\Work Files, and then click the OK button. When you open Windows Explorer or save or open a file, Windows displays the alternative folder, such as the Work Files folder, as the default location for your files.

Alicia is ready to copy all of the files from the CD to the My Documents folder on her hard disk. Then she can organize the files according to her plan. To do so, she inserts the CD in the appropriate drive on her computer, and a My Computer window opens to display the contents of the CD. See Figure 1.9.

Figure 1.9: Work files to copy from CD to hard disk

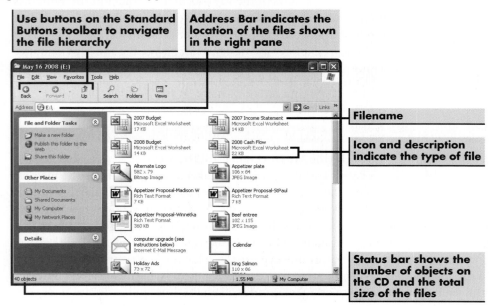

Alicia notes that the CD contains 40 files, which take up 1.55 MB of disk space, but the window shows only 14 files. To view all of the files without needing to scroll, she can change the view in the My Computer window.

Optimizing the View of Your Files

You can change your view of the files in the right pane of the My Computer or Windows Explorer windows by changing the size of the icon, displaying some file information or none, sorting the files according to a selected characteristic, and grouping them according to type. Windows XP provides five ways to view the contents of a folder—Thumbnails, Tiles, Icons, List, and Details:

- **Thumbnails view**—For graphic files, this view displays a small preview image of the graphic along with the filename. Switching to this view can be time consuming because Windows XP must first create all the preview images.
- **Tiles view**—This is the default view, and is shown in Figure 1.9 (and other figures). For each file, this view shows a large icon, title, and other information depending on how the files are sorted. If they are sorted by name or type, for example, this view shows the file type and size. The icon also provides a visual cue to the type of file. For example, in

Figure 1.9, the Appetizer plate file is displayed using an icon that contains a graphic, indicating that this is a graphic file, whereas the three Appetizer proposal files are Microsoft Word documents.

- **Icons view**—This view also displays files and folders as icons, but they are smaller than those shown in Tiles view and include only the filename (not any sort information), allowing you to display more files in a single window without scrolling.
- **List view**—This view displays the contents of a folder as a list of file or folder names with small icons. As in Icons view, you can see more files and folders at one time, which is helpful if your folder contains many files and you want to scan the list for a filename. You can sort your files and folders alphabetically in this view.
- **Details view**—This view displays the contents of a folder using the folder names and same small icons as in List view, but it also shows more information than the other three views. It provides detailed information about your files, including name, type, size, and date modified.

In addition to using these views to optimize your view of the files in a folder, you can sort and group files. You can sort files in any view by filename, size, type, or date. To do this, right-click a blank spot in the window, point to Arrange Icons By on the shortcut menu, and then select the file detail on which you want to sort. In Details view, you can sort files by clicking a column heading. In Tiles, Icons, and Details view, you can group your files by any detail of the file, such as name, size, type, or date modified. For example, if you group by file type, image files appear in one group, text files appear in another group, and spreadsheet files in another. You can also group files in Thumbnails view, but only by name (because that's the only detail shown in Thumbnails view).

Alicia decides to display the files on the CD in List view so that she can see all the files at once. She clicks the Views button ▦▾ on the Standard Buttons toolbar, and then clicks List. Now the window displays all 40 files at once. She also thinks it will be easier to copy the files from the CD to the My Documents folder using the Folders pane, so she clicks the Folders button on the Standard Buttons toolbar to open the Folders pane. See Figure 1.10.

Figure 1.10: Viewing the files in List view

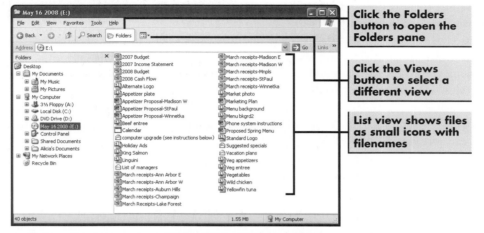

Click the Folders button to open the Folders pane

Click the Views button to select a different view

List view shows files as small icons with filenames

How To

Change the View of Your Files

1. To change the format of the file listing in the My Computer or Windows Explorer window, click the Views button 🔲 ▾ on the Standard Buttons toolbar, and then click Thumbnails, Tiles, Icons, List, or Details.
2. To sort the files, right-click a blank spot in the window, point to Arrange Icons By on the shortcut menu, and then click a sort order, such as Name, Type, Size, or Modified.
   If you are working in Details view, you can click a column heading to sort the files. For example, to sort files in ascending order by date, click the Date Modified column heading. To sort the files in descending order, click the Date Modified column heading again. To add a secondary sort, hold down the Shift key and then click another column heading. For example, you could sort files first by Type and then by Date Modified to list all the files of the same type sorted by date.
3. To group the files, right-click a blank spot in the window, point to Arrange Icons By on the shortcut menu, and then click Show in Groups.

Best Practice

Applying the Current Folder View to All Folders

After you set the view of one folder according to your preferences, you can apply the settings to all folders. To do so, click Tools on the My Computer or Windows Explorer menu bar and then click Folder Options to open the Folder Options dialog box. Click the View tab, and then click the Apply to All Folders button. If you need to reset all folders to the settings that were in effect when Windows XP was installed, open the View tab of the Folder Options dialog box again, and then click the Reset All Folders button.

Best Practice

Adding Details to Details View

By default, Details view shows the name, size, type, and date modified for each file. You can change these details to provide more or other file information. For example, you can show the date the file was created instead of modified, or display the number of pages in each file. If you are viewing music files, you can show additional details such as Album and Artist information; you can also display appropriate information for other types of media files. To add or change details shown in Details view of a My Computer or Windows Explorer window, right-click a column heading and then click a file detail you want to display. To change the arrangement of columns in Details view, drag a column heading to a different location on the column bar.

PERFORMING FILE MANAGEMENT TASKS

If you want to place a file into a folder from another location, you can either move the file or copy it. Moving a file removes it from its current location and places it in a new location you specify. Copying provides the file in both locations. Windows XP offers several techniques for moving and copying files. One way is to make sure that both the current and new location are visible on your desktop—either in a single Windows Explorer window or in two My Computer windows, for example—point to the file, hold down the right mouse button, and then drag the file from the old location to the new location. (This is called right-dragging.) A shortcut menu appears, including options to move or copy the selected file to the new location. The advantage to this technique is that it is clear whether you are moving or copying a file—when you use other techniques, such as dragging a file from a folder to a removable disk, you can inadvertently move a file when you intended to copy one.

Alicia wants to copy all of the files from the CD to the My Documents folder on her hard disk. She clicks the first file in the list—the one named 2007 Budget—holds down the Shift key, and then clicks the last file in the list—Yellowfin tuna. This selects all the files on the CD. (If she wanted to select only some files that were not adjacent to each other, she could click the first file, hold down the Ctrl key, and then click the other files she wanted to select.) With the My Documents folder visible in the Folders pane, she right-drags the selected files to the My Documents folder. When she releases the mouse button, a shortcut menu appears. See Figure 1.11.

Figure 1.11: Copying files from the CD to the My Documents folder

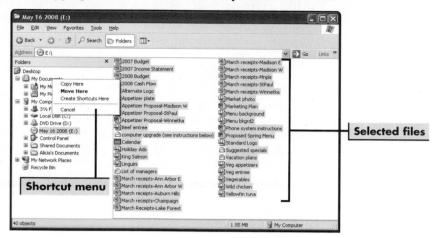

Then she clicks Copy Here on the shortcut menu and Windows copies the files to the My Documents folder.

How To

Copy and Move Files and Folders

The following steps refer to copying and moving files, but you can use the same techniques to copy and move folders.

- To copy or move files by right-dragging, select one or more files, point to the files, hold down the right mouse button, and then drag the selected files to a new location. When you release the mouse button, a shortcut menu appears. To copy the files, click Copy Here. To move the files, click Move Here.

- To move files using the drag-and-drop technique, select one or more files, and then drag the selected files to a different folder. To copy the files, hold down the Ctrl key as you drag the files. (If you drag files between drives, the files are always copied.)

- To copy files using the menu bar, select one or more files, click Edit on the menu bar, and then click Copy To Folder. Select the new location in the Copy Items dialog box and then click the Copy button. To move files, select the files, click Edit on the menu bar, and then click Move To Folder. Select the new location in the Move Items dialog box and then click the Move button.

- To copy files using the copy-and-paste technique, select one or more files, right-click the selected files, and then click Copy on the shortcut menu. Right-click the new location for the files, and then click Paste on the shortcut menu. To move the files, select the files, right-click the selected files, and then click Cut on the shortcut menu. Right-click the new location for the files, and then click Paste on the shortcut menu.

Alicia clicks the My Documents folder to view its new contents, and notices that the files she copied appear in the default Tiles view. She wants to know when the files were last modified to determine how current they are in general, so she clicks the Views button [icon] on the Standard Buttons toolbar, and then clicks Details. The file information appears in four columns—Name, Size, Type, and Date Modified. The files are sorted in alphabetic order by name, and it would be more helpful to view them listed by date, so she clicks the Date Modified column heading to sort the files. Although she can easily see the most recent file and the oldest file, it is still difficult to determine general trends from the detailed dates—she wants to know which ones were created recently, such as last week or up to a couple of months ago, which ones were created after that, and which ones were created long ago. To show this information, she can group the files. She clicks View on the menu bar, points to Arrange Icons By, and then clicks Show in Groups. Now the window displays the general date information she wants. See Figure 1.12.

Figure 1.12: Sorting and grouping files in Details view

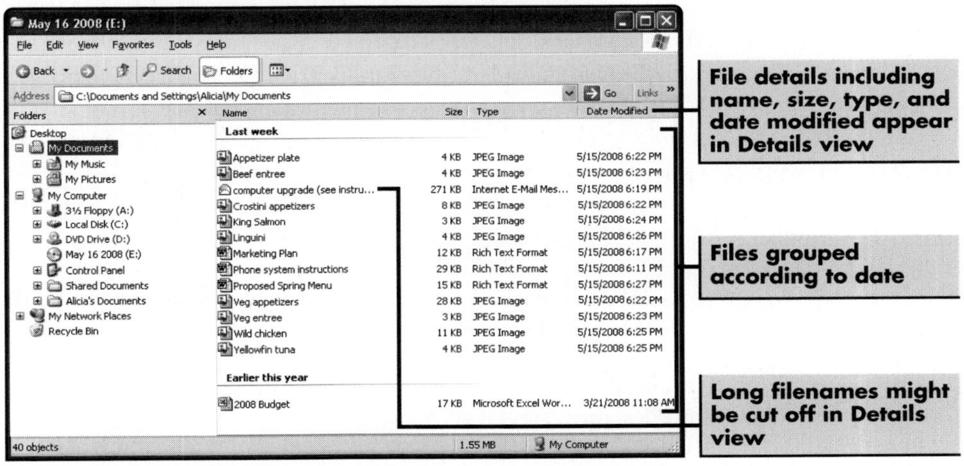

File details including name, size, type, and date modified appear in Details view

Files grouped according to date

Long filenames might be cut off in Details view

Now that Alicia has copied the files from the CD and become familiar with My Computer and Windows Explorer, she is ready to organize the files.

Steps To Success: Level 1

Alicia plans to hire an assistant, and she needs to organize files on the assistant's computer using a similar organization scheme to the one she is developing for her own computer. She asks for your help in preparing an organized system for her assistant to work with files and folders, one that will make it easy to find files when necessary. Alicia gives you files for her assistant, which fall into the following categories:

- **Management**—Reports Alicia will circulate to other managers, spreadsheets listing pricing information, and standard Bon Vivant Corporation graphics
- **Franchises**—Correspondence with the 10 Bon Vivant Café franchises in Illinois, Michigan, Minnesota, and Wisconsin, including e-mail messages
- **Marketing**—Draft of a marketing plan and a mailing list
- **Graphics**—Photos of menu offerings, logos, and a graphics viewing program

Alicia wants you to copy these files to a default location that her assistant can use, and then arrange the files logically. Alicia also asks you to prepare to show her assistant how to navigate the hard disk, emphasizing which folders she should avoid and which she should use for her files.

Complete the following:

1. Open the Communications\Chapter 1 folder and examine the files.

2. Sketch a logical file and folder organization for Alicia, similar to the one she created in Figure 1.3. Provide reasons that this system is the best one for Alicia's assistant.

3. Navigate your computer and identify other folders that should be off-limits for your files besides the Program Files and WINDOWS folders.

4. Find other built-in folders that Windows XP provides besides the My Music and My Picture folders. Identify any special features that these folders provide.

5. If you are working in Windows Explorer, open a My Computer window, then open the Communications\Chapter 1 folder. In the My Computer window, change the view so you can see all the files at once, and then open the Folders pane.

6. Copy all the files from the Communications\Chapter 1 folder to the Work Files folder.

7. Display all the files in the default location using a view, sort order, and grouping order that is logical for these files.

LEVEL 2

PUTTING FILE MANAGEMENT PLANS INTO PRACTICE

FILE MANAGEMENT SKILLS TRAINING

- **Create a folder in the My Documents folder**
- **Delete a file**
- **Delete multiple files from a folder**
- **Rename a file**
- **Save a file to a different location**
- **Search for a file by name**

ORGANIZING YOUR WORK

Now that Alicia has devised a plan for storing her files, she is ready to get organized by creating folders that will hold the files. She can start by creating two main folders in her My Documents folder—one for corporate files and one for franchise files. Then she can create the subfolders she needs according to her plan shown in Figure 1.3. (Recall, however, that she will not use a Franchises subfolder in the Corporate folder.) To create a folder, she'll give it a name, preferably one that describes its contents. A folder name can have up to 255 characters (including spaces), except / \ : * ? " < > or |. With these guidelines in mind, Alicia plans to create folders as shown in Figure 1.13.

Figure 1.13: Initial folder and file organization

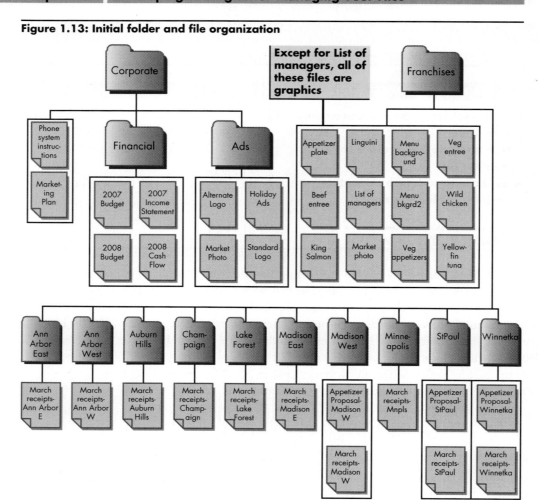

As Alicia reviews the plan, she realizes she needs to refine it again. Most of the files in the Franchises folder are graphic files that the franchises use to create ads, menus, and other marketing material. She decides to change the name of the Ads subfolder to the Marketing subfolder, and create a Graphics subfolder within it. Then she can store all these graphic files in that folder, and move the Marketing Plan file to the Marketing subfolder. Another problem is that she received files from the franchises with their location in the filename, as in March receipts-Winnetka. If she needed to send these files to anyone else, she would keep the location in the filename to clarify the contents. However, she will use these files to prepare a quarterly report, which she will circulate to other managers. Because the file-name doesn't need to identify the franchise location, she can store these files in subfolders for each franchise. She can eliminate the redundancy by renaming the files.

Viewing her file listing again (see Figure 1.10), Alicia realizes her My Documents folder contains some unnecessary files. She decides she can delete the computer upgrade instructions and Vacation plans e-mail message files—she is sure the information in these files is out of date. Alicia also realizes that she doesn't know where to store two files—Proposed Spring Menu and Suggested specials—because she doesn't know what information these files contain. She needs to learn more about their content. She will open these files in the program used to create them to discover what they contain and then determine where they belong.

Creating Folders

Alicia is ready to create the folders she needs to organize her files in the My Documents folder. She decides to use Windows Explorer to perform this task so she can easily track the folder hierarchy in the Folders pane. She right-clicks a blank spot of the My Documents window, points to New on the shortcut menu, and then clicks Folder. A folder named New Folder appears in the My Documents window, with the name selected so that Alicia can provide a more specific name. Referring to her organization plan, she types Corporate as the name of the folder, and then presses the Enter key. She uses the same technique to create a folder named Franchises in the My Documents folder. She changes to List view and turns off grouping so that she can see all the files and the two new folders she created. See Figure 1.14.

Figure 1.14: Two new folders in the My Documents folder in Windows Explorer

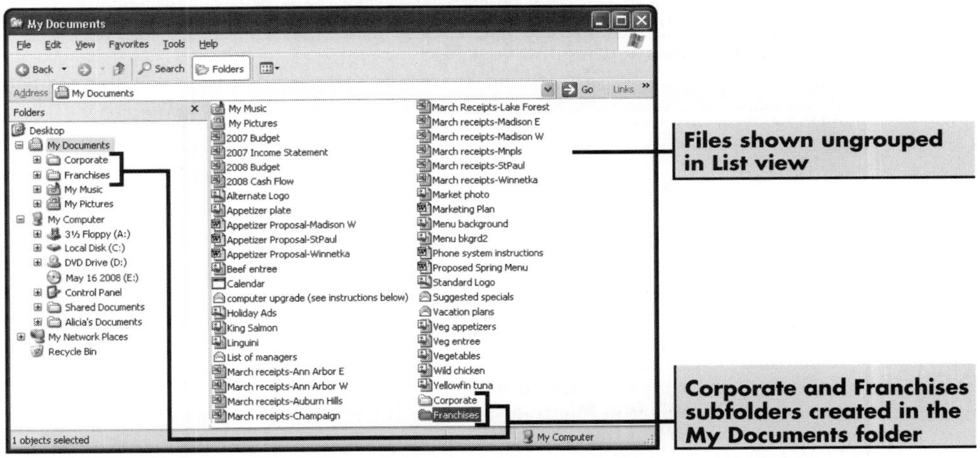

Files shown ungrouped in List view

Corporate and Franchises subfolders created in the My Documents folder

Next, Alicia opens the Corporate folder and creates two subfolders within it—Financial and Marketing. She also creates a Graphics subfolder in the Marketing folder, and then continues creating folders according to her plan. When she's finished, she expands all the folders in the My Documents folder in the Folders pane to review the organization. See Figure 1.15.

Figure 1.15: Folder organization for Alicia's files

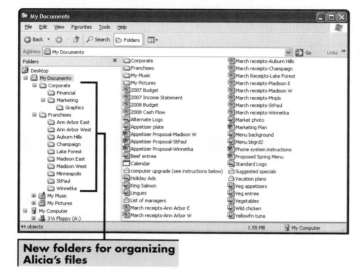

New folders for organizing Alicia's files

Alicia can finally move files from the My Documents folder to an appropriate subfolder to execute her file organization plan. For example, she moves the 2007 Budget file to the Financial subfolder, and the March receipts-Ann Arbor E file to the Ann Arbor East subfolder. When she's finished, the My Documents folder contains only a few files. See Figure 1.16.

Figure 1.16: My Documents window after moving files

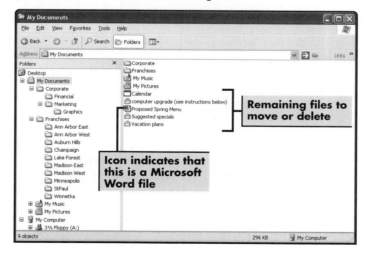

Remaining files to move or delete

Icon indicates that this is a Microsoft Word file

Alicia needs to decide what to do with these files—delete the unnecessary ones or move them to a subfolder.

Deleting Files

You should periodically delete files and folders you no longer need so that your main folders and disks don't get cluttered. However, make sure you no longer need a file before you delete it—a spreadsheet you took weeks to create might be valuable even if it is out of date. To delete a file or folder in My Computer or Windows Explorer, you delete its icon. Keep in mind that when you delete a folder, you also delete all the files it contains. When you delete a file or folder from a hard disk, Windows XP removes it from its current location, and stores it in the Recycle Bin. If you change your mind and want to retrieve a file deleted from your hard disk, you can use the Recycle Bin to recover it and return it to its original location. However, after you empty the Recycle Bin, you can no longer recover the files that were in it.

When you delete a file from a removable disk, it does not go into the Recycle Bin. Instead, it's deleted as soon as you remove its icon from the folder or disk window—and you can't recover it.

Alicia is sure that she can delete three files—Calendar, computer upgrade (see instructions below), and Vacation plans. The Calendar file is a program. Alicia has decided to use Microsoft Office Outlook 2003 as her calendar and scheduling program, so she can safely delete Calendar from the My Documents folder. If it turns out she does need it, she can copy it from the original CD. The other two files are copies of e-mails that are no longer relevant. To delete the three files, Alicia selects them in the My Documents window, and then presses the Delete key. When Windows XP asks if she's sure she wants to delete these files, Alicia clicks the Yes button.

Before she investigates the remaining two files in the My Documents window, she decides to rename other files, such as March receipts-Ann Arbor E, to eliminate redundancy.

Identifying Your Work with Meaningful File and Folder Names

Filenames provide important information about a file, including its contents and purpose. A filename such as Marketing Plan.doc has three parts:

- **Main part of the filename**—The name you provide when you create a file, and the name you associate with a file, such as Marketing Plan or Market Photo
- **Period**—The character that separates the main part of the filename and the file extension, usually referred to as "dot" as in "Marketing Plan dot doc"
- **Filename extension**—The characters (most often three) that follow the last period in the filename and identify the file type; for example, doc identifies Microsoft Word files

Like folder names, the main part of a filename can have up to 255 characters; these long filenames give you plenty of room to name your file accurately enough so that the name reflects the file contents. You can use spaces and certain punctuation symbols in your filenames; however, as with folder names, you cannot use the symbols \ / ? : * " < > | in a filename because these characters are reserved for operating system commands.

Filename extensions are not always displayed in the My Computer or Windows Explorer window. The filename extension is important to Windows XP because it identifies the file type and, in most cases, the program that you use to open and modify the file. For example, as mentioned earlier, in the filename Marketing Plan.doc, the extension "doc" identifies the file as one created by Word, a word-processing program. You might also have a file called Marketing Plan.xls—the "xls" extension identifies the file as one created in Microsoft Excel, a spreadsheet program. Though the main part of these filenames are identical, their extensions distinguish them as different file types. One special filename extension is .exe, which stands for executable. **Executable files** are programs whose contents can be loaded into memory and executed (meaning that the computer can process the instructions in the program). Table 1.2 lists common Windows XP filename extensions.

Table 1.2: Windows XP filename extensions

Extension	File Type
.bmp	Bitmap image
.doc	Microsoft Word document
.eml	E-mail message
.exe	Executable program
.htm or .html	Hypertext document
.jpg	JPEG image
.mdb	Microsoft Access database
.ppt	Microsoft PowerPoint presentation
.sys	System file
.txt	Text document
.xls	Microsoft Excel spreadsheet
.zip	Compressed file

You usually do not need to add extensions to your filenames because the program that you use to create the file adds the extension automatically.

Best Practice

Using Meaningful Filenames

Be sure to give your files and folders meaningful names that will help you remember their purpose and contents. The following list provides recommendations for naming your files and folders:

- **Use a consistent naming method**—Devise a naming scheme that is appropriate for the types of files you normally create and then use it consistently. For example, you might include the date or year as the first part of important financial files, as in 2008 Budget.
- **Keep filenames short, but not too short**—Choose filenames that are long enough to accurately reflect the file contents, but short enough to be easy to read in the My Computer or Windows Explorer window. (Refer to Figure 1.12 to see what happens to long filenames in some views.) For example, a filename such as Phone System Instructions clearly reflects its contents, whereas a name such as Instructions for New Communications Plus Phone System is too long.
- **Use folder names that also identify file contents**—Folder names that reflect the folder contents can help you name your files. For example, if you have three files named Print Logo Graphic, New Product Image, and Ad Background Graphic, you can create a folder named Graphics and store these three files in it, renamed as Print Logo, New Product, and Ad Background.
- **Include identifiers well-known in your organization or company**—To let others easily identify the files you send them and to simplify searching for files, include standard identifiers in filenames, such as model numbers, project names, or other codes your organization or company uses.

Although Windows XP keeps track of extensions, it is not set to display them by default. You can change this setting using the Folder Options dialog box so that Windows XP displays extensions for known file types. A **known file type** is a file whose extension is associated with a program on your computer. Such files are also called **registered files**. For example, when you install Word, it registers the "doc" filename extension with Windows XP, and from then on, Windows XP associates the "doc" filename extension with Word. Registered files display a custom icon, such as a W on a sheet of paper for Word (used for the Proposed Spring Menu file in Figure 1.16). Unregistered files use a generic icon.

Anticipating that she will need to open some files to view their contents, Alicia decides to display filename extensions as she works with her documents currently stored in the My Documents folder. She can then use both the file icon and extension to identify the program that will open the file. With the My Documents window open, she clicks Tools on the menu bar and then clicks Folder Options. In the Folder Options dialog box, she clicks the View tab. See Figure 1.17.

Figure 1.17: View tab in the Folder Options dialog box

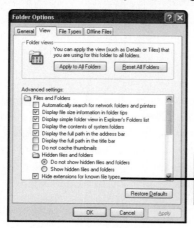

Remove the check mark from this option to display filename extensions

To display filename extensions, she clicks the Hide extensions for known file types check box to remove the check mark. Then she clicks the OK button to close the Folder Options dialog box. The My Documents window now displays extensions for all the filenames.

Now Alicia is ready to rename the files that include redundant information, such as March receipts-Ann Arbor E.xls, which she can rename to March receipts.xls. She opens the Ann Arbor East folder, right-clicks the March receipts-Ann Arbor E.xls file, and then clicks Rename on the shortcut menu. With the filename selected, Alicia types March receipts.xls as the new name and then presses the Enter key. She uses the same technique to rename the other files in the subfolders of the Franchises folder.

Best Practice

Renaming Multiple Files
Renaming each file in a folder that contains many files can be tedious. If you want to rename a collection of related files, such as digital photos you created for a new product, you can rename more than one file at the same time. Select all the files you want to rename, right-click the files, and then click Rename on the shortcut menu. Windows selects the name of one of the files. Type the new name in the following format: *filename* (1).*ext*, such as Product Photo (1).jpg. Windows uses the same name for the other selected files, but varies the number in parentheses, renaming files as Product Photo (2).jpg, Product Photo (3).jpg, and so on.

Alicia's final organization task is to determine what to do with the two files that remain in the My Documents folder—Proposed Spring Menu.doc and Suggested specials.eml.

OPENING AND SAVING FILES

As you work with your files, you often need to view or change their contents. One way to do so is to open a file in a program, usually the one used to create the file. Then you can change the contents and save the file. To update the file, you can save it with the same name and in the same location. If you want to create a new file based on the one you opened, you can save the file with a different name or in a different location.

Opening Files in Programs

Recall that Windows XP uses file extensions to reflect a file's type, which associates the file with a particular program. To open a file in the program associated with the file type, you can double-click the filename or icon. For example, when you double-click a file named Handbook.doc, Word starts and then opens the file in the program window because Windows associates the doc extension with Word. The File Types tab in the Folder Options dialog box lists the registered file types on your computer and identifies each extension and type.

You should avoid deleting or changing a file association, though you can create a new one. For example, suppose you receive a file from a colleague via e-mail that he created on a computer with a different operating system, such as a Macintosh or Linux computer, and named it Product Names.abc. He indicated that he was sending you a simple text file, but Windows doesn't recognize the abc extension. When you double-click a file with an unknown extension, Windows displays a dialog box explaining that it cannot open the file. You can then select a program from the list of programs installed on your computer, and associate the program with the extension by indicating that you always want to use this program to open this kind of file. For example, you can associate .abc files with a text editor, such as Notepad, and then double-click the file to open it in that program.

Alicia wants to examine the contents of the Suggested specials.eml and Proposed Spring Menu.doc files to determine whether to delete them or move them to a folder. First, she double-clicks the Suggested specials.eml file. Outlook Express starts and opens the file. Outlook Express is the program associated with the .eml extension on her computer. She reads the e-mail and discovers that it contains information that is more than three years old and is no longer current, so she knows that she can safely delete the file. She closes the file, and then deletes it from the My Documents folder.

When she double-clicks the Proposed Spring Menu.doc file, Word starts and opens the document. Although the menu contained in the file is a few years old and lists offerings that are more sophisticated than those served in current Bon Vivant Cafés, Alicia decides to keep the Proposed Spring Menu.doc file for future reference. She has heard that the Bon Vivant Corporation is thinking of opening a gourmet-quality restaurant in the Chicago area, and this menu could provide a starting point for discussion. She wants to add a note to this effect at the beginning of the menu. She decides to edit the document and then use the file management features in Word to save the file in the proper folder.

Saving Files in Programs

When you save a file, you give it a name and select a location for a file. Selecting a location for a file you want to save is where your knowledge of the Windows XP file system comes in handy. Programs created to run in Windows XP automatically select the My Documents folder (or another folder designated as the default) as the location for saving and opening files. You can then navigate from the My Documents folder to the subfolder in which you want to save or open the file.

To save a file using its current name and location, you click the Save button on the program's toolbar (or use the Save command on the program's File menu). If you want to save a file with a different name or in a different location, you use the Save As command on the program's File menu to open the Save As dialog box. (The Save As dialog box also opens the first time you save a newly created file.) You use this dialog box to navigate to where you want to save the file and to provide a name for the file.

Alicia wants to add a note at the beginning of the document, and then save the revised Proposed Spring Menu.doc in the Franchises subfolder. She types a note indicating that the menu contains items appropriate for the new gourmet restaurant, clicks File on the Word menu bar, and then clicks Save As. The Save As dialog box opens with the folder name of the current folder in the Save in text box at the top of the dialog box and the files and subfolders in the current folder listed below it. See Figure 1.18.

Figure 1.18: Save As dialog box

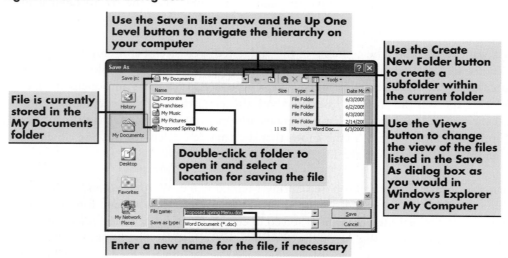

Alicia double-clicks the Franchises folder to open it and make it the current folder, types Sample Gourmet Menu as the new filename in the File name text box, and then clicks the Save button to save the document with the new name in the new location. After closing Word, she returns to the My Documents window and deletes the Proposed Spring Menu.doc file because she no longer needs it.

Expecting that other managers will meet soon to discuss the new gourmet Bon Vivant Café, Alicia wants to contact them and ask if they've tried introducing menu items considered more gourmet than their standard family fare, and if so, whether the introduction was successful. She recalls a file that lists the names of the franchise managers, and she wants to find it.

FINDING STORED FILES

After you save a file, you can use Windows Explorer or My Computer to find it. If you are using a logical organization for your folders and files, this should be fairly easy. It's also helpful to understand the **file path**, which is the standard notation that indicates a file's location on your computer. The file path leads you through the Windows file system to your file. For example, Alicia stored the Sample Gourmet Menu.doc file in the Franchises subfolder of the My Documents folder, which is a subfolder of the Documents and Settings folder on the hard disk. The path to this file is as follows:

C:\Documents and Settings\Alicia\My Documents\Franchises\Sample Gourmet Menu.doc

This path has five parts, and each part is separated by a backslash (\ ):

- **C:**—The name of the drive containing the disk, such as C: for the hard disk
- **Documents and Settings**—A top-level folder on drive C
- **Alicia**—A folder Windows created for Alicia's files
- **My Documents**—A subfolder in the Documents and Settings folder
- **Franchises**—The folder Alicia created in the My Documents folder
- **Sample Gourmet Menu.doc**—The full filename with the file extension

Basically, the full path describes the route (or path) that you (or Windows XP) navigates to locate a specific program file. If Alicia wants to remember where she stored this file, or tell someone else where to retrieve this file, she can use the file path to indicate the file's location: C:\Documents and Settings\Alicia\My Documents\Franchises\Sample Gourmet Menu.doc. The My Computer and Windows Explorer windows can display the full file path in their Address Bars so you can keep track of your current location as you navigate. (Recall that you can display the full file path in the Address Bar by clicking Tools on the menu bar of My Computer or Windows Explorer and then clicking Folder Options. On the View tab, click the Display the full path in the address bar check box.)

If you don't recall the location of a file, Windows XP provides the **Search Companion**, a tool that helps you find any kind of file, whether you know its complete name, partial name, or only other properties, such as text the file contains, file type, or date the file was created or modified. To use this tool, you click the Search button on the Standard Buttons toolbar of a My Computer or Windows Explorer window. The Search Companion pane opens in the left pane, replacing the Folders pane or the task pane. The Search Companion guides you through your search, offering options that change depending on your search strategy. For example, when you are searching for files, the Search Companion asks you questions about the file's name, contents, type, location, and date. Your responses help the Search Companion find the files you want. To find information, you respond to questions in the Search Companion pane. These responses are **search criteria**, one or more conditions that information must meet to have the Search Companion find it. For example, you could provide search criteria specifying all or part of a filename and the drive containing the file. The Search Companion then locates and displays every file that matches those criteria.

Alicia wants to find the file that lists the names of the franchise managers, but she doesn't recall where she stored it or what its filename is. With the Windows Explorer window open, she clicks the Search button on the Standard Buttons toolbar. The Search Companion pane opens on the left.

In the What do you want to search for? list in the Search Companion pane, Alicia clicks All files and folders. The Search Companion pane displays text boxes she can use to specify some or all of the filename she wants to find. The more information she provides, the more effective the search will be. You can use the options listed in Table 1.3 to specify criteria for searching for files.

Table 1.3: Search criteria

Option	Description	Search By
All or part of the filename	Search for files or folders that contain the specified text.	Filename
A word or phrase in the file	Search for files that include the specified words or phrases in their contents (not in the filename).	Keyword
Look in	Search a particular location, such as a computer, drive, or folder.	Location
When was it modified?	Search for files that were created or last modified on a particular date or within a range of dates.	Date
What size is it?	Search for files that are small, medium, large, or a specific file size.	Size
More advanced options	Search for files of a particular type and select search settings, such as whether to search subfolders or perform a case-sensitive search.	Type

Searching for a word or phrase in a file can take awhile, and Alicia is fairly sure that the name of the file she wants includes the word "managers." In the All or part of the file name text box, Alicia enters "managers." See Figure 1.19.

Figure 1.19: Searching for a file by entering a partial filename in the Search Companion pane

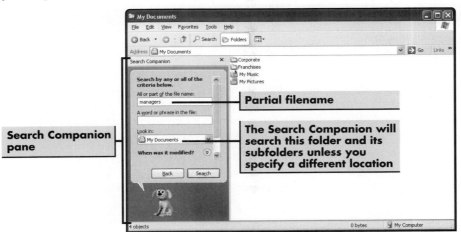

The Search Companion supplies the current folder as the file location—in this case, the My Documents folder, which includes its subfolders. Alicia does want to search the My Documents folder, so she doesn't change this entry. She could, however, click the Look in list arrow and select a different folder or drive. The filename and folder are all the criteria Alicia knows to specify now, so she clicks the Search button in the Search Companion pane. Windows XP searches for all files in the My Documents folder and its subfolders whose filenames contain "managers." Then it displays any matching files in the Search Results pane. See Figure 1.20.

Figure 1.20: Results of the search

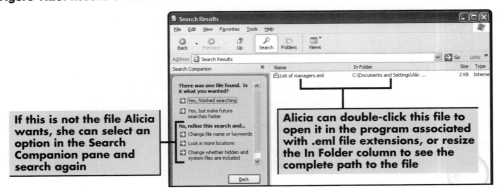

The file named List of managers.eml is the file Alicia wants—she can now double-click the file to open it directly from the Search window, or she can resize the In Folder column to see the complete path to the file and navigate to that folder. If Alicia wanted to search for a different file, she could select an option in the Search Companion pane and search again.

How To

Find a File by Name

1. In My Computer or Windows Explorer, click the Search button on the Standard Buttons toolbar. The Search Companion pane opens.
2. In the Search Companion, click All files and folders.
3. In the All or part of the file name text box, type the complete filename or a word or phrase the filename contains. You can also include an asterisk (*) to indicate any number of unknown characters or a question mark (?), where each ? indicates an unknown character.
4. Click the Look in list arrow, and then click the drive or folder you want to search, or click My Computer to select all the drives on your computer.
5. Click the Search button in the Search Companion pane. The results appear in the Search Results pane.

Alicia has finished organizing her files, and plans to follow these file management practices as she continues to receive, create, and save files. She also suspects that she can learn to work more efficiently, and wants to explore her options for refining her file management techniques.

Steps To Success: Level 2

Alicia asks you to continue helping her prepare the computer that her assistant will use. Now that you have developed a scheme for organizing the work files on the assistant's computer, she asks you to execute your plan.

Complete the following:

1. Review the files you copied from the Communications\Chapter 1 folder to the Work Files folder. Compare this to your original file organization plan and adjust the plan as necessary. Provide names for all the folders you will use. Make sure you include a folder for storing correspondence to the franchise managers and one for storing graphic files.

2. Store each file in the appropriate folder according to your plan. When you are finished, the Work Files folder should not contain any files, only folders. Delete any files you think are unnecessary.

3. Delete all the files in the Communications\Chapter 1 folder. (Copies of all the files are now stored in appropriate folders in the Work Files folder.)

4. Alicia wants her assistant to circulate two personnel memos—first one about planning for vacations and then another about the Bon Vivant policy for casual dress Fridays. She does not recall which files contain this information. Use the Search Companion to find the first file.

5. Open the file you found, examine its contents, and determine whether its filename is precise, accurate, and useful to Alicia's assistant. If necessary, save the file with a new name in a new location.

6. Use the Search Companion to find the second file about casual dress Fridays.

7. Open the file you found, add text to remind yourself to review the policy and make appropriate changes, and then save the file with a different name and in a different folder, if necessary. Make sure that the name and location are appropriate for the file. Note the path to the file.

8. Find the two original files you found by navigating the path to them. What are the paths to these files?

CHAPTER SUMMARY

This chapter presented file management skills ranging from basic to advanced to help you plan, practice, and refine a well-organized scheme for managing and maintaining your computer files and folders. In Level 1, you learned how to prepare an organized system by exploring how computers store data in general and how Windows XP manages files and folders in particular. You evaluated My Computer and Windows Explorer, the two tools Windows XP provides for managing files, and used them to develop navigation strategies, establish a standard location for your work files, optimize the view of your files, and perform file tasks. Level 2 extended the concepts from Level 1 into practice, as you learned how to perform other file management tasks, such as creating folders, deleting files, and identifying your work with meaningful file and folder names. You also learned how to manage files when working with programs and use the Search Companion to find files stored on your computer. Finally, in Level 3, you learned how to refine your file management and work with files efficiently by using shortcuts and file and folder properties. You also explored how to maintain your files on a variety of media using the Send To menu, compressed folders, and the Backup tool.

CONCEPTUAL REVIEW

1. Describe a common metaphor for organizing files on a Windows XP computer.

2. Explain the best use for the following types of storage media: hard disk, CD, and flash drive.

3. Briefly describe how Windows XP organizes files on a hard disk.

4. Where should you store your data files? Why is this location better than the root directory?

5. Explain the difference between Windows Explorer and My Computer. Name an advantage that each offers.

6. How does showing files in groups differ from sorting them in My Computer or Windows Explorer?

7. Explain what happens when you delete a folder or file from a hard disk. How does this differ from what happens when you delete a folder or file from removable media?

8. Give two recommendations for providing meaningful names for folders and files.

9. Why are file extensions important in Windows XP?

10. Under what circumstances would you save a copy of a file using a program such as Microsoft Word instead of a tool such as My Computer?

11. Assuming that your computer uses the standard location for the My Documents folder, what is the file path to a file named Business Plan.xls stored in the Corporate subfolder of the My Documents folder?

12. Under what circumstances would you use the Search Companion to find a file?

13. Explain how a shortcut to a folder differs from the folder itself.

14. What is the easiest and safest method for creating a shortcut? Why?

15. What kind of information can you learn when you examine the properties of a shortcut? Of a file? Of a disk?

16. Why might you add an option to the Send To menu? How do you do this?

17. Explain the difference between compressing and backing up a folder of documents.

18. What advantages do compressed folders offer over standard folders?

19. Explain why it is important to maintain regular backup copies of your files.

20. Why might you want to add a picture to a folder?

Microsoft
Excel

EXCEL

MICROSOFT OFFICE EXCEL

MICROSOFT OFFICE
Excel 2003

MICROSOFT OFFICE
Excel 2003

Creating a Worksheet and an Embedded Chart

PROJECT

1

CASE PERSPECTIVE

In the late 1970s, Extreme Blading pioneered the sport of inline skating as an off-season training tool for hockey players. The sport quickly caught on with fitness enthusiasts, aggressive skaters, and the population in general. Today, nearly 50 million inline skaters participate in the activity worldwide and the sport continues to grow.

The Extreme Blading product line includes a variety of skates, including inline, quad, and custom models for all age levels, as well as a complete line of protective gear and other accessories.

For years, the company sold their goods via direct mail, telesales, and company-owned outlets in major cities across the country. Thanks to the popularity of personal computers and the World Wide Web, the company added an e-commerce Web site last year. This new sales channel has given the company access to more than 600 million people worldwide and has resulted in a significant increase in sales.

Sales continued to grow during the first half of this year, thus driving senior management to ask their financial analyst, Maria Lopez, to develop a better sales tracking system. As a first step, Maria has asked you to prepare an easy-to-read worksheet that shows product sales for the second quarter by sales channel (Figure 1-1 on page EX 5). In addition, Maria has asked you to create a chart showing second quarter sales, because the president of the company likes to have a graphical representation of sales that allows her quickly to identify stronger and weaker product groups by sales channel.

As you read through this project, you will learn how to use Excel to create, save, and print a financial report that includes a 3-D Column chart.

MICROSOFT OFFICE
Excel 2003

Creating a Worksheet and an Embedded Chart

P R O J E C T

Objectives

You will have mastered the material in this project when you can:

- Start and Quit Excel
- Describe the Excel worksheet
- Enter text and numbers
- Use the AutoSum button to sum a range of cells
- Copy a cell to a range of cells using the fill handle
- Format a worksheet

- Create a 3-D Clustered column chart
- Save a workbook and print a worksheet
- Open a workbook
- Use the AutoCalculate area to determine statistics
- Correct errors on a worksheet
- Use the Excel Help system to answer questions

What Is Microsoft Office Excel 2003?

Microsoft Office Excel 2003 is a powerful spreadsheet program that allows users to organize data, complete calculations, make decisions, graph data, develop professional looking reports (Figure 1-1), publish organized data to the Web, and access real-time data from Web sites. The four major parts of Excel are:

- **Worksheets** Worksheets allow users to enter, calculate, manipulate, and analyze data such as numbers and text. The term worksheet means the same as spreadsheet.
- **Charts** Excel can draw a variety of charts.
- **Lists** Lists organize and store data. For example, once a user enters data into a worksheet, Excel can sort the data, search for specific data, and select data that satisfies defined criteria.
- **Web Support** Web support allows users to save Excel worksheets or parts of a worksheet in HTML format, so a user can view and manipulate the worksheet using a browser. Excel Web support also provides access to real-time data, such as stock quotes, using Web queries.

This latest version of Excel makes it much easier to create and manipulate lists of data. It also offers industry-standard XML support that simplifies the sharing of data within and outside an organization; improved statistical functions; smart documents that automatically fill with data; information rights management; allows two workbooks to be compared side by side; and includes the capability of searching a variety of reference information.

Excel Project 1

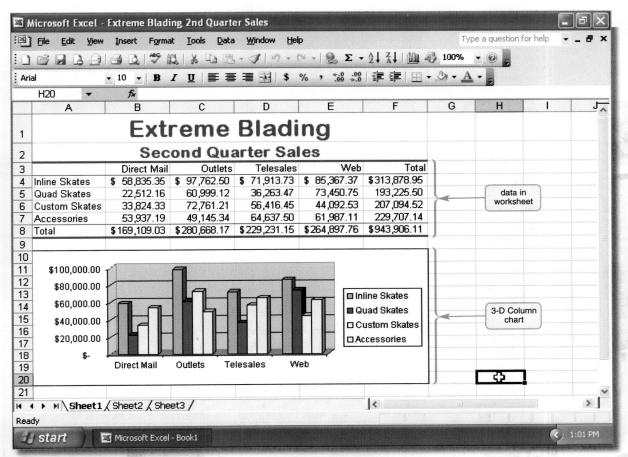

FIGURE 1-1

Project One — Extreme Blading Second Quarter Sales

The first step in creating an effective worksheet is to make sure you understand what is required. The person or persons requesting the worksheet should supply their requirements in a requirements document. A **requirements document** includes a needs statement, source of data, summary of calculations, and any other special requirements for the worksheet, such as charting and Web support. Figure 1-2 on the next page shows the requirements document for the new worksheet to be created in this project.

After carefully reviewing the requirements document, the next step is to design a solution or draw a sketch of the worksheet based on the requirements, including titles, column and row headings, location of data values, and the 3-D Column chart, as shown in Figure 1-3 on the next page. The dollar signs, 9s, and commas that you see in the sketch of the worksheet indicate formatted numeric values.

More About

Worksheet Development Cycle

Spreadsheet specialists do not sit down and start entering text, formulas, and data into a blank Excel worksheet as soon as they have a spread-sheet assignment. Instead, they follow an organized plan, or methodology, that breaks the development cycle into a series of tasks. The recom-mended methodology for creating worksheets includes (1) analyze requirements (supplied in a requirements document); (2) design solu-tion; (3) validate design; (4) implement design; (5) test solution; and (6) document solution.

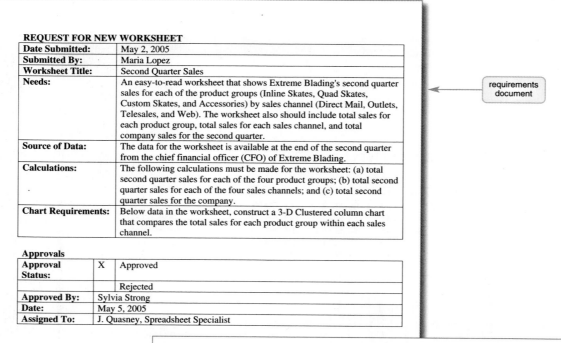

REQUEST FOR NEW WORKSHEET

Date Submitted:	May 2, 2005
Submitted By:	Maria Lopez
Worksheet Title:	Second Quarter Sales
Needs:	An easy-to-read worksheet that shows Extreme Blading's second quarter sales for each of the product groups (Inline Skates, Quad Skates, Custom Skates, and Accessories) by sales channel (Direct Mail, Outlets, Telesales, and Web). The worksheet also should include total sales for each product group, total sales for each sales channel, and total company sales for the second quarter.
Source of Data:	The data for the worksheet is available at the end of the second quarter from the chief financial officer (CFO) of Extreme Blading.
Calculations:	The following calculations must be made for the worksheet: (a) total second quarter sales for each of the four product groups; (b) total second quarter sales for each of the four sales channels; and (c) total second quarter sales for the company.
Chart Requirements:	Below data in the worksheet, construct a 3-D Clustered column chart that compares the total sales for each product group within each sales channel.

Approvals

Approval Status:	X	Approved
		Rejected
Approved By:	Sylvia Strong	
Date:	May 5, 2005	
Assigned To:	J. Quasney, Spreadsheet Specialist	

requirements document

FIGURE 1-2

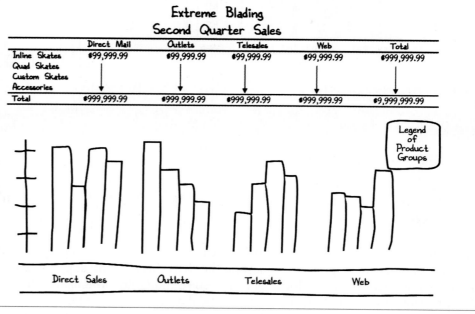

sketch of worksheet

FIGURE 1-3

With a good understanding of the requirements document and a sketch of the worksheet, the next step is to use Excel to create the worksheet and chart.

Starting and Customizing Excel

If you are stepping through this project on a computer and you want your screen to match the figures in this book, then you should change your computer's resolution to 800 × 600. For more information on how to change the resolution on your computer, see Appendix D. The following steps show how to start Excel.

To Start Excel

1

• **Click the Start button on the Windows taskbar, point to All Programs on the Start menu, point to Microsoft Office on the All Programs submenu, and then point to Microsoft Office Excel 2003 on the Microsoft Office submenu.**

Windows displays the Start menu, the All Programs submenu, and the Microsoft Office submenu (Figure 1-4).

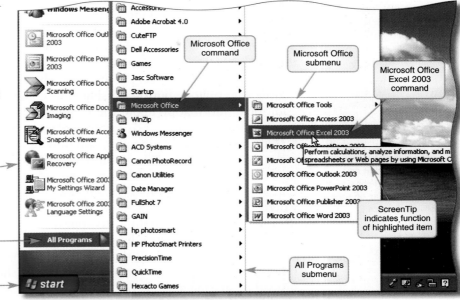

FIGURE 1-4

2

• **Click Microsoft Office Excel 2003.**

Excel starts. After several seconds, Excel displays a blank workbook titled Book1 in the Excel window (Figure 1-5).

3

• **If the Excel window is not maximized, double-click its title bar to maximize it.**

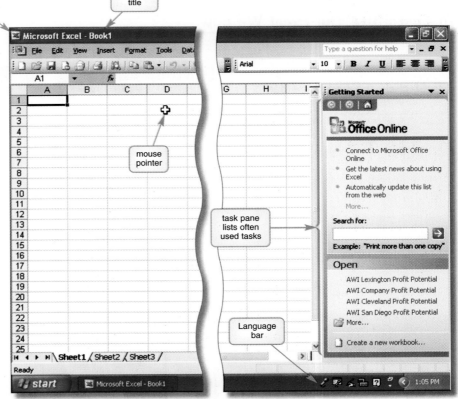

FIGURE 1-5

Other Ways

1. Double-click Excel icon on desktop
2. Click Microsoft Office Excel 2003 on Start menu
3. Click Start button, point to All Programs, click New Office Document, click General tab, double-click Blank Workbook icon

Microsoft Office
Excel 2003

The screen shown in Figure 1-5 on the previous page illustrates how the Excel window looks the first time you start Excel after installation on most computers. If the Office Speech Recognition software is installed and active on your computer, then when you start Excel, the Language bar is displayed on the screen. The **Language bar** contains buttons that allow you to speak commands and dictate text. It usually is located on the right side of the Windows taskbar next to the notification area, and it changes to include the speech recognition functions available in Excel. In this book, the Language bar is closed because it takes up computer resources and with the Language bar active, the microphone can be turned on accidentally by clicking the Microphone button causing your computer to act in an unstable manner. For additional information about the Language bar, see page EX 15 and Appendix B.

As shown in Figure 1-5, Excel displays a task pane on the right side of the screen. A **task pane** is a separate window that enables users to carry out some Excel tasks more efficiently. When you start Excel, it displays the Getting Started task pane, which is a small window that provides commonly used links and commands that allow you to open files, create new files, or search Office-related topics on the Microsoft Web site. In this book, the Getting Started task pane is hidden to allow the maximum number of columns to appear in Excel.

At startup, Excel also displays two toolbars on a single row. A **toolbar** contains buttons, boxes, and menus that allow you to perform tasks quickly. To allow for more efficient use of the buttons, the toolbars should appear on two separate rows, instead of sharing a single row. The following steps show how to close the Language bar, close the Getting Started task pane, and instruct Excel to display the toolbars on two separate rows.

More About

Task Panes

You can drag a task pane title bar to float the pane in your work area or dock it on either the left or right side of a screen, depending on your personal preference.

To Customize the Excel Window

1

• **Right-click the Language bar.**

The Language bar shortcut menu appears (Figure 1-6).

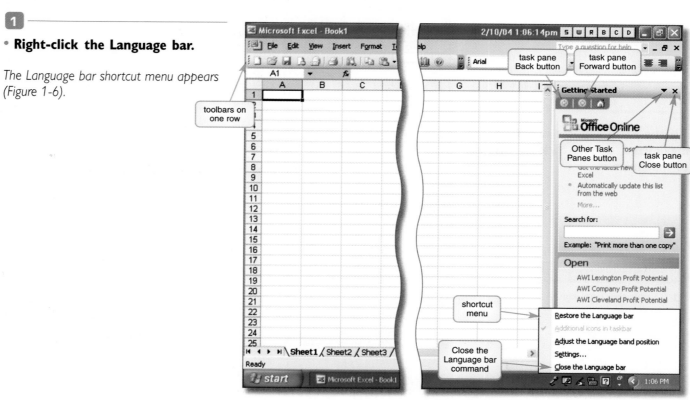

FIGURE 1-6

- **Click Close the Language bar.**

- **Click the Getting Started task pane Close button in the upper-right corner of the task pane.**

- **If the toolbars are positioned on the same row, click the Toolbar Options button.**

The Language bar disappears. Excel closes the Getting Started task pane and displays additional columns. Excel also displays the Toolbar Options list showing the buttons that do not fit on the toolbars when tool-bars appear on one row (Figure 1-7).

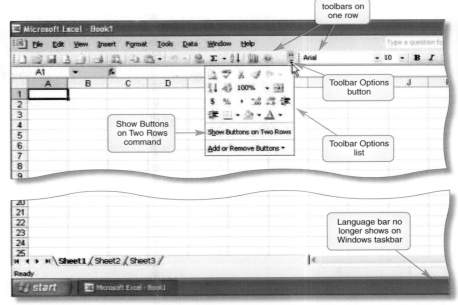

FIGURE 1-7

3

- **Click Show Buttons on Two Rows.**

Excel displays the toolbars on two separate rows (Figure 1-8). With the toolbars on two separate rows, all of the buttons fit on the two toolbars.

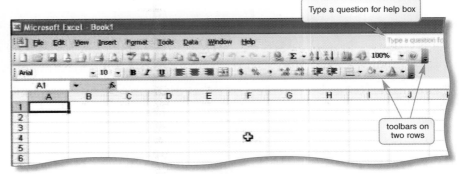

FIGURE 1-8

As you work through creating a worksheet, you will find that certain Excel operations cause Excel to display a task pane. Excel provides eleven task panes, in addition to the Getting Started task pane shown in Figure 1-6. Some of the more important ones are the Clipboard task pane, the Excel Help task pane, and the Clip Art task pane. Throughout the book, these task panes are discussed when they are used.

At any point while working with an Excel worksheet, you can open or close a task pane by clicking the Task Pane command on the View menu. You can activate additional task panes by clicking the Other Task Panes button to the left of the Close button on the task pane title bar (Figure 1-6) and then selecting a task pane in the Other Task Panes list. The Back and Forward buttons below the task pane title bar allow you to switch between task panes that you opened during a session.

The Excel Worksheet

When Excel starts, it creates a new blank workbook, called Book1. The **workbook** (Figure 1-9 on the next page) is like a notebook. Inside the workbook are sheets, each of which is called a **worksheet**. Excel opens a new workbook with three worksheets.

More About

The Excel Help System

Need Help? It is no further away than the Type a question for help box on the menu bar in the upper-right corner of the window. Click the box that contains the text, Type a question for help (Figure 1-8), type `help`, and then press the ENTER key. Excel responds with a list of topics you can click to learn about obtaining help on any Excel-related topic. To find out what is new in Excel 2003, type `what is new in Excel` in the Type a question for help box.

If necessary, you can add additional worksheets to a maximum of 255. Each worksheet has a sheet name that appears on a **sheet tab** at the bottom of the workbook. For example, Sheet1 is the name of the active worksheet displayed in the Book1 workbook. If you click the sheet tab labeled Sheet2, Excel displays the Sheet2 worksheet. This project uses only the Sheet1 worksheet.

The Worksheet

The worksheet is organized into a rectangular grid containing vertical columns and horizontal rows. A column letter above the grid, also called the **column heading**, identifies each column. A row number on the left side of the grid, also called the **row heading**, identifies each row. With the screen resolution set to 800 × 600 and the Excel window maximized, Excel displays 12 columns (A through L) and 23 rows (1 through 23) of the worksheet on the screen, as shown in Figure 1-9.

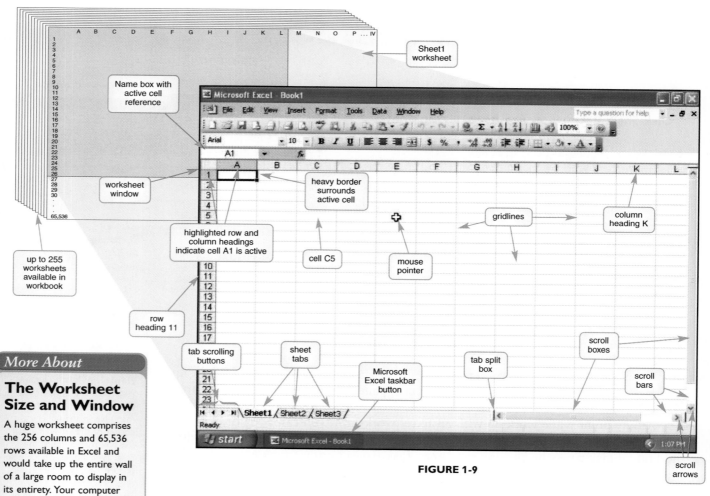

FIGURE 1-9

More About

The Worksheet Size and Window

A huge worksheet comprises the 256 columns and 65,536 rows available in Excel and would take up the entire wall of a large room to display in its entirety. Your computer screen, by comparison, is a small window that allows you to view only a minute area of the worksheet at one time. While you cannot see the entire worksheet, you can move the window over the worksheet to view any part of it.

The intersection of each column and row is a cell. A **cell** is the basic unit of a worksheet into which you enter data. Each worksheet in a workbook has 256 columns and 65,536 rows for a total of 16,777,216 cells. The column headings begin with A and end with IV. The row headings begin with 1 and end with 65,536. Only a small fraction of the active worksheet appears on the screen at one time.

A cell is referred to by its unique address, or **cell reference**, which is the coordinates of the intersection of a column and a row. To identify a cell, specify the column letter first, followed by the row number. For example, cell reference C5 refers to the cell located at the intersection of column C and row 5 (Figure 1-9).

One cell on the worksheet, designated the **active cell**, is the one into which you can enter data. The active cell in Figure 1-9 is A1. The active cell is identified in three ways. First, a heavy border surrounds the cell; second, the active cell reference shows immediately above column A in the Name box; and third, the column heading A and row heading 1 are highlighted so it is easy to see which cell is active (Figure 1-9).

The horizontal and vertical lines on the worksheet itself are called **gridlines**. Gridlines make it easier to see and identify each cell in the worksheet. If desired, you can turn the gridlines off so they do not show on the worksheet, but it is recommended that you leave them on for now.

The mouse pointer in Figure 1-9 has the shape of a block plus sign. The mouse pointer appears as a block plus sign whenever it is located in a cell on the worksheet. Another common shape of the mouse pointer is the block arrow. The mouse pointer turns into the block arrow whenever you move it outside the worksheet or when you drag cell contents between rows or columns. The other mouse pointer shapes are described when they appear on the screen.

> *More About*
>
> **The Mouse Pointer**
>
> The mouse pointer can change to one of more than 15 different shapes, such as a block arrow, cross hair, or chart symbol, depending on the task you are performing in Excel and the mouse pointer's location on the screen.

Worksheet Window

You view the portion of the worksheet displayed on the screen through a **worksheet window** (Figure 1-9). Below and to the right of the worksheet window are **scroll bars**, **scroll arrows**, and **scroll boxes** that you can use to move the worksheet window around to view different parts of the active worksheet. To the right of the sheet tabs at the bottom of the screen is the tab split box. You can drag the **tab split box** to increase or decrease the view of the sheet tabs (Figure 1-9). When you decrease the view of the sheet tabs, you increase the length of the horizontal scroll bar, and vice versa.

The menu bar, Standard toolbar, Formatting toolbar, and formula bar appear at the top of the screen, above the worksheet window and below the title bar.

Menu Bar

The **menu bar** is a special toolbar that includes the menu names as shown in Figure 1-10a on the next page. Each **menu name** represents a menu. A **menu** is a list of commands that you can use to retrieve, store, print, and manipulate data on the worksheet. When you point to a menu name on the menu bar, the area of the menu bar containing the name changes to a button. To display a menu, such as the Edit menu, click the Edit menu name on the menu bar (Figures 1-10b and 1-10c on the next page). If you point to a menu command with an arrow to its right, Excel displays a **submenu** from which you can choose a command.

> Q & A
>
> **Q:** Can the Excel window or viewing area be increased to show more of the worksheet?
>
> **A:** Yes. Two ways exist to increase what you can see in the viewing area: (1) on the View menu, click Full Screen; and (2) change to a higher resolution. See Appendix D for information about how to change to a higher resolution.

(a) Menu Bar and Toolbars

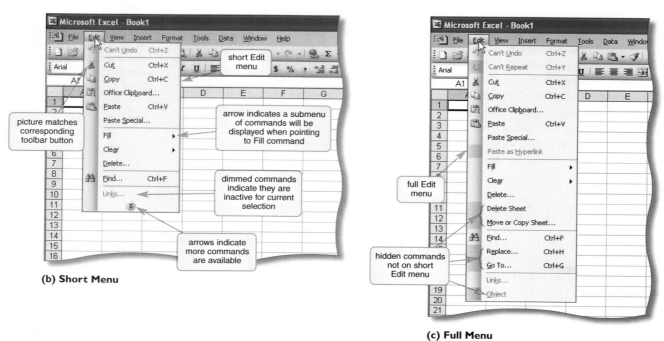

(b) Short Menu

(c) Full Menu

FIGURE 1-10

When you click a menu name on the menu bar, Excel displays a **short menu** listing the most recently used commands (Figure 1-10b). If you wait a few seconds or click the arrows at the bottom of the short menu, Excel displays the full menu. The **full menu** lists all of the commands associated with a menu (Figure 1-10c). You also can display a full menu immediately by double-clicking the menu name on the menu bar. In this book, use one of the following techniques to ensure that Excel always displays the full menu.

1. Click the menu name on the menu bar and then wait a few seconds.
2. Click the menu name on the menu bar and then click the arrows at the bottom of the short menu.
3. Click the menu name on the menu bar and then point to the arrows at the bottom of the short menu.
4. Double-click the menu name on the menu bar.

Both short and full menus display some dimmed commands. A **dimmed command** appears gray, or dimmed, instead of black, which indicates it is not available for the current selection. A command with medium blue shading to the left of it on a full menu is called a **hidden command** because it does not appear on a short menu. As you use Excel, it automatically personalizes the short menus for you based on how often you use commands. That is, as you use hidden commands, Excel *unhides* them and places them on the short menu.

The menu bar can change to include other menu names depending on the type of work you are doing in Excel. For example, if you are working with a chart sheet rather than a worksheet, Excel displays the Chart menu bar with menu names that reflect charting commands.

Standard Toolbar and Formatting Toolbar

The Standard toolbar and the Formatting toolbar (Figure 1-11) contain buttons and boxes that allow you to perform frequent tasks more quickly than when using the menu bar. For example, to print a worksheet, you click the Print button on the Standard toolbar. Each button has a picture on the button face to help you remember the button's function. Also, when you move the mouse pointer over a button or box, Excel displays the name of the button or box below it in a **ScreenTip**.

Figures 1-11a and 1-11b illustrate the Standard and Formatting toolbars and describe the functions of the buttons. Each of the buttons and boxes will be explained in detail when they are used.

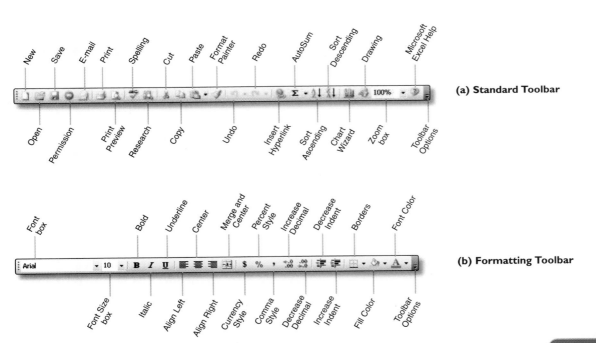

(a) Standard Toolbar

(b) Formatting Toolbar

FIGURE 1-11

When you first install Excel, both the Standard and Formatting toolbars are preset to display on the same row (Figure 1-12a on the next page), immediately below the menu bar. Unless the resolution of your display device is greater than 800 × 600, many of the buttons that belong on these toolbars are hidden. Hidden buttons appear in the Toolbar Options list (Figure 1-12b on the next page). In this mode, you also can display all the buttons on either toolbar by double-clicking the **move handle** on the left of each toolbar (Figure 1-12a).

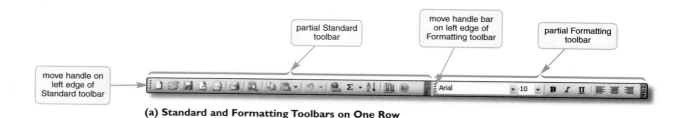

(a) Standard and Formatting Toolbars on One Row

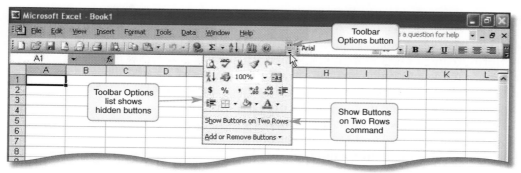

(b) Toolbar Options List

(c) Standard and Formatting Toolbars on Two Rows

FIGURE 1-12

In this book, the Standard and Formatting toolbars are shown on two rows, one below the other, so that all buttons appear on a screen with the resolution set to 800 × 600 (Figure 1-12c). You can show the two toolbars on two rows by clicking the Show Buttons on Two Rows command in the Toolbar Options list (Figure 1-12b).

Formula Bar

The formula bar appears below the Standard and Formatting toolbars (Figure 1-13). As you type, Excel displays the entry in the **formula bar**. Excel also displays the active cell reference in the Name box on the left side of the formula bar.

Status Bar

The status bar is located immediately above the Windows taskbar at the bottom of the screen (Figure 1-13). The **status bar** displays a brief description of the command selected (highlighted) on a menu, the function of the button the mouse pointer is pointing to, or the mode of Excel. **Mode indicators**, such as Enter and Ready, appear on the status bar and specify the current mode of Excel. When the mode is **Ready**, Excel is ready to accept the next command or data entry. When the mode indicator reads **Enter**, Excel is in the process of accepting data through the keyboard into the active cell.

In the middle of the status bar is the AutoCalculate area. The **AutoCalculate area** can be used in place of a calculator or formula to view the sum, average, or other types of totals of a group of numbers on the worksheet. The AutoCalculate area is discussed in detail later in this project.

Keyboard indicators, such as CAPS (Caps Lock), NUM (Num Lock), and SCRL (Scroll), show which keys are engaged. Keyboard indicators appear in the small rectangular boxes on the right side of the status bar (Figure 1-13).

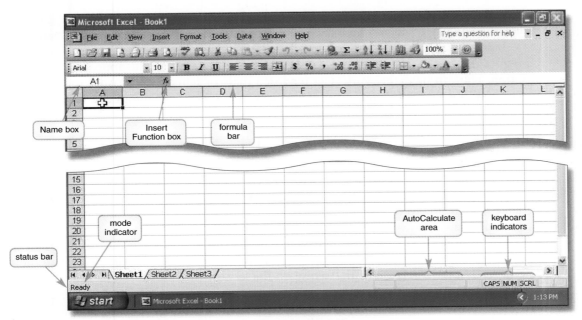

FIGURE 1-13

Speech Recognition and Speech Playback

With the **Office Speech Recognition software** installed and a microphone, you can speak the names of toolbar buttons, menus, menu commands, list items, alerts, and dialog box controls, such as OK and Cancel. You also can dictate cell entries, such as text and numbers. To indicate whether you want to speak commands or dictate cell entries, you use the Language bar. The Language bar can be in one of four states: (1) **restored**, which means it is displayed somewhere in the Excel window (Figure 1-14a); (2) **minimized**, which means it is displayed on the Windows taskbar (Figure 1-14b); (3) **hidden**, which means you do not see it on the screen but it will be displayed the next time you start your computer; (4) **closed**, which means it is hidden permanently until you enable it. If the Language bar is hidden or closed and you want it to display, then do the following:

1. Right-click an open area on the Windows taskbar at the bottom of the screen.
2. Point to Toolbars on the shortcut menu and then click Language bar on the Toolbars submenu.

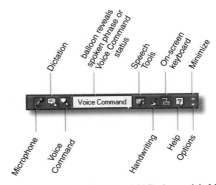

(a) Language Bar in Excel Window with Microphone Enabled

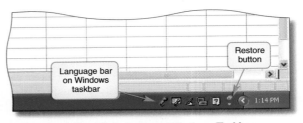

(b) Language Bar Minimized on Windows Taskbar

FIGURE 1-14

If the Language bar command is dimmed on the Toolbars submenu or if the Speech command is dimmed on the Tools menu, the Office Speech Recognition software is not installed.

In this book, the Language bar does not appear in the figures. If you want to close the Language bar so that your screen is identical to what you see in the book, right-click the Language bar and then click Close the Language bar on the shortcut menu.

If you have speakers, you can use the **speech playback** functions of Excel to instruct the computer to read a worksheet to you. By selecting the appropriate option, you can have the worksheet read in a male or female voice. Additional information about the speech recognition and speech playback capabilities of Excel is available in Appendix B.

Selecting a Cell

To enter data into a cell, you first must select it. The easiest way **to select a cell** (make it active) is to use the mouse to move the block plus sign mouse pointer to the cell and then click.

An alternative method is to use the arrow keys that are located just to the right of the typewriter keys on the keyboard. An arrow key selects the cell adjacent to the active cell in the direction of the arrow on the key.

You know a cell is selected, or active, when a heavy border surrounds the cell and the active cell reference appears in the Name box on the left side of the formula bar. Excel also changes the active cell's column heading and row heading to a gold color.

Entering Text

In Excel, any set of characters containing a letter, hyphen (as in a telephone number), or space is considered text. **Text** is used to place titles, such as worksheet titles, column titles, and row titles, on the worksheet. For example, as shown in Figure 1-15, the worksheet title, Extreme Blading, identifies the worksheet created in Project 1. The worksheet subtitle, Second Quarter Sales, identifies the type of report. The column titles in row 3 (Direct Mail, Outlets, Telesales, Web, and Total) identify the numbers in each column. The row titles in column A (Inline Skates, Quad Skates, Custom Skates, Accessories, and Total) identify the numbers in each row.

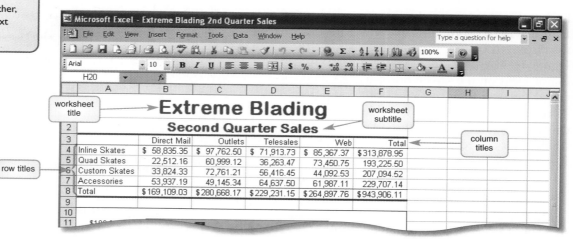

FIGURE 1-15

Entering the Worksheet Titles

The following steps show how to enter the worksheet titles in cells A1 and A2. Later in this project, the worksheet titles will be formatted so they appear as shown in Figure 1-15.

To Enter the Worksheet Titles

1

• **Click cell A1.**

Cell A1 becomes the active cell and a heavy border surrounds it (Figure 1-16).

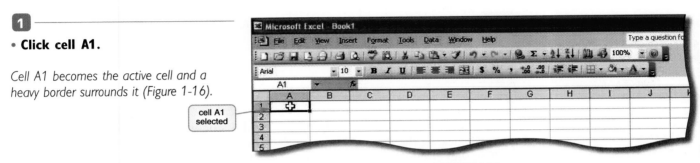

FIGURE 1-16

2

• **Type** Extreme Blading **in cell A1 and then point to the Enter box in the formula bar.**

Excel displays the title in the formula bar and in cell A1 (Figure 1-17). When you begin typing a cell entry, Excel displays two additional boxes in the formula bar: the Cancel box and the Enter box.

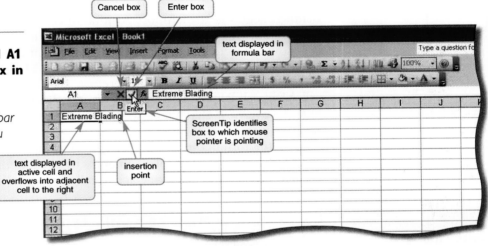

FIGURE 1-17

3

• **Click the Enter box to complete the entry.**

Excel enters the worksheet title in cell A1 (Figure 1-18).

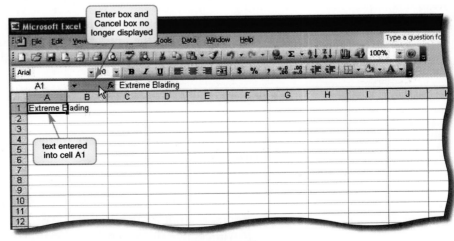

FIGURE 1-18

4

• **Click cell A2 to select it. Type** Second Quarter Sales **as the cell entry. Click the Enter box to complete the entry.**

Excel enters the worksheet subtitle in cell A2 (Figure 1-19).

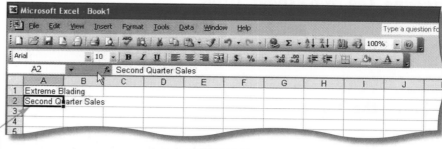

worksheet subtitle entered into cell A2

FIGURE 1-19

In Figure 1-17 on the previous page, the text in cell A1 is followed by the insertion point. The **insertion point** is a blinking vertical line that indicates where the next typed character will appear. In Steps 3 and 4, clicking the **Enter box** completes the entry. Clicking the **Cancel box** cancels the entry.

When you complete a text entry into a cell, a series of events occurs. First, Excel positions the text left-aligned in the cell. **Left-aligned** means the cell entry is positioned at the far left in the cell. Therefore, the E in the worksheet title, Extreme Blading, begins in the leftmost position of cell A1.

Second, when the text is longer than the width of a column, Excel displays the overflow characters in adjacent cells to the right as long as these adjacent cells contain no data. In Figure 1-19, the width of cell A1 is approximately 9 characters. The text consists of 15 characters. Therefore, Excel displays the overflow characters from cell A1 in cell B1, because cell B1 is empty. If cell B1 contained data, Excel would hide the overflow characters, so that only the first 9 characters in cell A1 would appear on the worksheet. Excel stores the overflow characters in cell A1 and displays them in the formula bar whenever cell A1 is the active cell.

Third, when you complete an entry by clicking the Enter box, the cell in which the text is entered remains the active cell.

Correcting a Mistake while Typing

If you type the wrong letter and notice the error before clicking the Enter box or pressing the ENTER key, use the BACKSPACE key to delete all the characters back to and including the incorrect letter. To cancel the entire entry before entering it into the cell, click the Cancel box in the formula bar or press the ESC key. If you see an error in a cell after entering the text, select the cell and retype the entry. Later in this project, additional error-correction techniques are discussed.

AutoCorrect

The **AutoCorrect feature** of Excel works behind the scenes, correcting common mistakes when you complete a text entry in a cell. AutoCorrect makes three types of corrections for you:

1. Corrects two initial capital letters by changing the second letter to lowercase.
2. Capitalizes the first letter in the names of days.
3. Replaces commonly misspelled words with their correct spelling. For example, it will change the misspelled word *recieve* to *receive* when you complete the entry. AutoCorrect will correct the spelling of hundreds of commonly misspelled words automatically.

Entering Column Titles

To enter the column titles in row 3, select the appropriate cell and then enter the text, as described in the following steps.

To Enter Column Titles

1

• **Click cell B3.**

Cell B3 becomes the active cell. The active cell reference in the Name box changes from A2 to B3 (Figure 1-20).

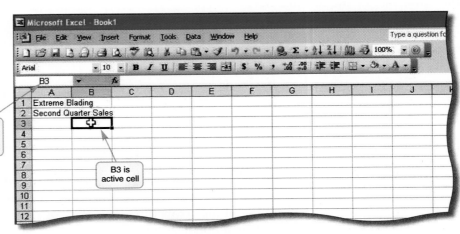

FIGURE 1-20

2

• **Type** Direct Mail **in cell B3.**

Excel displays Direct Mail in the formula bar and in cell B3 (Figure 1-21).

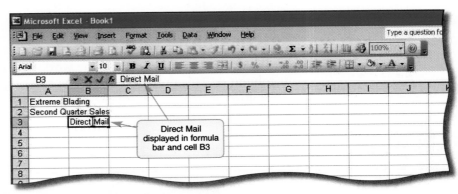

FIGURE 1-21

3

• **Press the RIGHT ARROW key.**

Excel enters the column title, Direct Mail, in cell B3 and makes cell C3 the active cell (Figure 1-22).

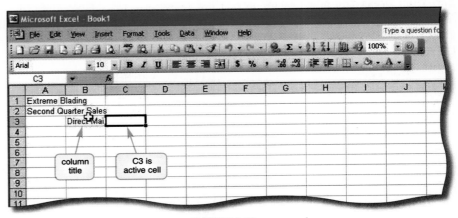

FIGURE 1-22

4

• **Repeat Steps 2 and 3 for the remaining column titles in row 3; that is, enter** Outlets **in cell C3,** Telesales **in cell D3,** Web **in cell E3, and** Total **in cell F3 (complete the last entry in cell F3 by clicking the Enter box in the formula bar).**

Excel displays the column titles left-aligned as shown in Figure 1-23.

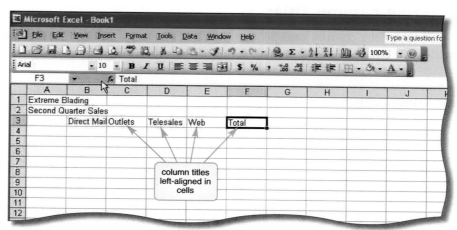

FIGURE 1-23

If the next entry is in an adjacent cell, use the arrow keys to complete the entry in a cell. When you press an arrow key to complete an entry, the adjacent cell in the direction of the arrow (up, down, left, or right) becomes the active cell. If the next entry is in a nonadjacent cell, complete an entry by clicking the next cell in which you plan to enter data. You also can click the Enter box or press the ENTER key and then click the appropriate cell for the next entry.

Entering Row Titles

The next step in developing the worksheet in Project 1 is to enter the row titles in column A. This process is similar to entering the column titles and is described in the following steps.

To Enter Row Titles

1

• **Click cell A4. Type** Inline Skates **and then press the DOWN ARROW key.**

Excel enters the row title, Inline Skates, in cell A4, and cell A5 becomes the active cell (Figure 1-24).

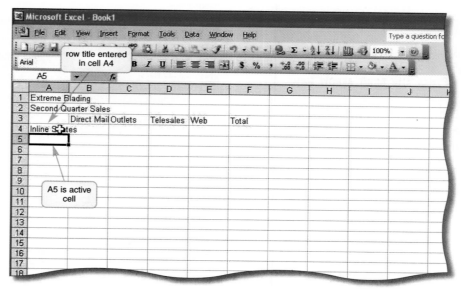

FIGURE 1-24

2

- **Repeat Step 1 for the remaining row titles in column A; that is, enter** Quad Skates **in cell A5,** Custom Skates **in cell A6,** Accessories **in cell A7, and** Total **in cell A8.**

Excel displays the row titles as shown in Figure 1-25.

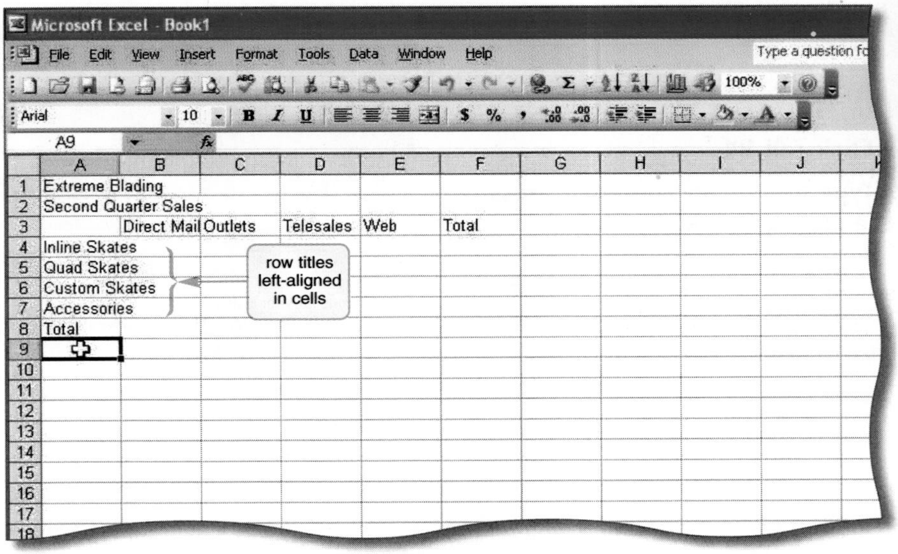

FIGURE 1-25

When you enter text, Excel automatically left-aligns the text in the cell. Excel treats any combination of numbers, spaces, and nonnumeric characters as text. For example, the following entries are text:

401AX21, 921-231, 619 321, 883XTY

You can change the text alignment in a cell by realigning it. Several alignment techniques are discussed later in the project.

Entering Numbers

In Excel, you can enter numbers into cells to represent amounts. A **number** can contain only the following characters:

0 1 2 3 4 5 6 7 8 9 + - ( ) , / . $ % E e

If a cell entry contains any other keyboard character (including spaces), Excel interprets the entry as text and treats it accordingly. The use of the special characters is explained when they are used in the project.

The Extreme Blading Second Quarter numbers used in Project 1 are summarized in Table 1-1. These numbers, which represent second quarter sales for each of the sales channels and product groups, must be entered in rows 4, 5, 6, and 7. The steps on the next page enter the numbers in Table 1-1 one row at a time.

> **More About**
>
> **Entering Numbers as Text**
>
> Sometimes, you will want Excel to treat numbers, such as Zip codes and telephone numbers, as text. To enter a number as text, start the entry with an apostrophe (').

Table 1-1 Extreme Blading Second Quarter Data				
	Direct Mail	**Outlets**	**Telesales**	**Web**
Inline Skates	58835.35	97762.50	71913.73	85367.37
Quad Skates	22512.16	60999.12	36263.47	73450.75
Custom Skates	33824.33	72761.21	56416.45	44092.53
Accessories	53937.19	49145.34	64637.50	61987.11

To Enter Numbers

1

• **Click cell B4.**

• **Type** 58835.35 **and then press the** RIGHT ARROW **key.**

Excel enters the number 58835.35 in cell B4 and changes the active cell to cell C4 (Figure 1-26).

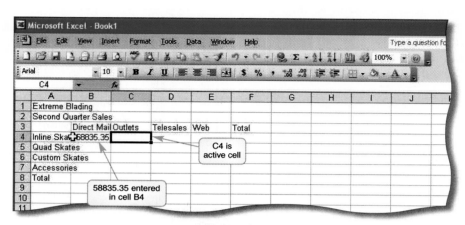

FIGURE 1-26

2

• **Enter** 97762.50 **in cell C4,** 71913.73 **in cell D4, and** 85367.37 **in cell E4.**

Row 4 now contains the second quarter sales by sales channel for the Inline Skates product group (Figure 1-27). The numbers in row 4 are right-aligned, which means Excel displays the cell entry to the far right in the cell.

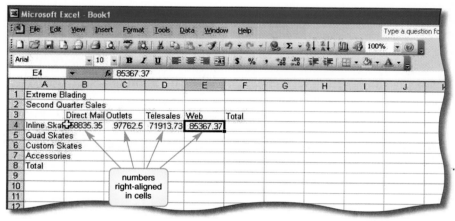

FIGURE 1-27

3

• **Click cell B5.**

• **Enter the remaining second quarter sales provided in Table 1-1 on the previous page for each of the three remaining product groups in rows 5, 6, and 7.**

Excel displays the second quarter sales as shown in Figure 1-28.

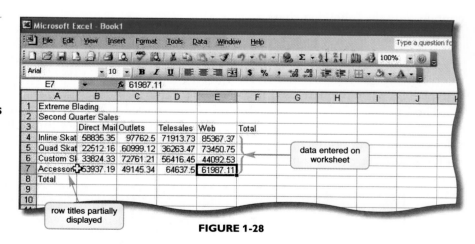

FIGURE 1-28

When the numbers are entered into the cells in column B, Excel only partially displays the row titles in column A. When the worksheet is formatted later in the project, the row titles will appear in their entirety.

Steps 1 through 3 complete the numeric entries. As shown in Figure 1-28, Excel does not display trailing zeros in cells C4 and D7. You are not required to type dollar signs, commas, or trailing zeros. When you enter a dollar value that has cents, however, you must add the decimal point and the numbers representing the cents. Later in this project, the numbers will be formatted to use dollar signs, commas, and trailing zeros to improve the appearance and readability of the numbers.

Calculating a Sum

The next step in creating the worksheet is to determine the total second quarter sales for the Direct Mail sales channel in column B. To calculate this value in cell B8, Excel must add, or sum, the numbers in cells B4, B5, B6, and B7. Excel's **SUM function**, which adds all of the numbers in a range of cells, provides a convenient means to accomplish this task.

A **range** is a series of two or more adjacent cells in a column or row or a rectangular group of cells. For example, the group of adjacent cells B4, B5, B6, and B7 is called a range. Many Excel operations, such as summing numbers, take place on a range of cells.

The following steps show how to sum the numbers in column B.

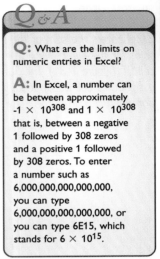

To Sum a Column of Numbers

1

• **Click cell B8.**

Cell B8 becomes the active cell (Figure 1-29).

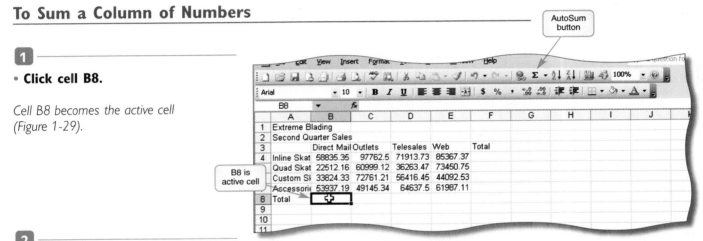

FIGURE 1-29

2

• **Click the AutoSum button on the Standard toolbar.**

*Excel responds by displaying =SUM(B4:B7) in the formula bar and in the active cell B8 (Figure 1-30). Excel displays a ScreenTip below the active cell. The B4:B7 within parentheses following the function name SUM is Excel's way of identifying that the SUM function will add the numbers in the range B4 through B7. Excel also surrounds the proposed cells to sum with a moving border, called a **marquee**.*

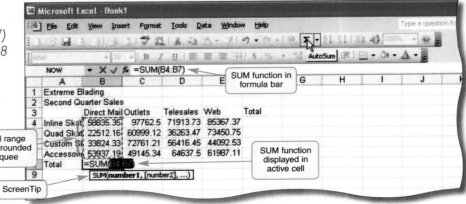

FIGURE 1-30

3

• **Click the AutoSum button a second time.**

Excel enters the sum of the second quarter sales for the Direct Mail sales channel in cell B8 (Figure 1-31). The SUM function assigned to cell B8 appears in the formula bar when cell B8 is the active cell.

SUM function assigned to active cell B8 shows in formula bar

AutoSum button arrow provides access to other often used functions

Microsoft Excel - Book1

File   Edit   View   Insert   Format   Tools   Data   Window   Help

Type a question fo

Arial   10   **B** *I* U

$ %

B8   *fx* =SUM(B4:B7)

	A	B	C	D	E	F	G	H	I	J
1	Extreme Blading									
2	Second Quarter Sales									
3		Direct Mail	Outlets	Telesales	Web	Total				
4	Inline Skat	58835.35	97762.5	71913.73	85367.37					
5	Quad Skat	22512.16	60999.12	36263.47	73450.75					
6	Custom Sl	33824.33	72761.21	56416.45	44092.53					
7	Accessorie	53937.19	49145.34	64637.5	61987.11					
8	Total	169109								
9										
10										
11										
12										
13										
14										
15										
16										
17										
18										

sum of numbers in cells B4, B5, B6, and B7

FIGURE 1-31

Other Ways

1. Click Insert Function button in formula bar, select SUM in Select a function list, click OK button, select range, click OK button
2. On Insert menu click Function, select SUM in Select a function list, click OK button, select range, click OK button
3. Press ALT+EQUAL SIGN (=) twice
4. In Voice Command mode, say "AutoSum, Sum, Enter"

When you enter the SUM function using the AutoSum button, Excel automatically selects what it considers to be your choice of the range to sum. When proposing the range to sum, Excel first looks for a range of cells with numbers above the active cell and then to the left. If Excel proposes the wrong range, you can correct it by dragging through the correct range before clicking the AutoSum button a second time. You also can enter the correct range by typing the beginning cell reference, a colon (:), and the ending cell reference.

If you click the AutoSum button arrow on the right side of the AutoSum button, Excel displays a list of often used functions from which you can choose. The list includes functions that allow you to determine the average, the minimum value, or the maximum value of a range of numbers.

Using the Fill Handle to Copy a Cell to Adjacent Cells

Excel also must calculate the totals for Outlets in cell C8, Telesales in cell D8, and for Web in cell E8. Table 1-2 illustrates the similarities between the entry in cell B8 and the entries required to sum the totals in cells C8, D8, and E8.

Table 1-2 Sum Function Entries in Row 8		
CELL	**SUM FUNCTION ENTRIES**	**REMARK**
B8	=SUM(B4:B7)	Sums cells B4, B5, B6, and B7
C8	=SUM(C4:C7)	Sums cells C4, C5, C6, and C7
D8	=SUM(D4:D7)	Sums cells D4, D5, D6, and D7
E8	=SUM(E4:E7)	Sums cells E4, E5, E6, and E7

To place the SUM functions in cells C8, D8, and E8, follow the same steps shown previously in Figures 1-29 through 1-31. A second, more efficient method is to copy the SUM function from cell B8 to the range C8:E8. The cell being copied is called the **source area** or **copy area**. The range of cells receiving the copy is called the **destination area** or **paste area**.

Although the SUM function entries in Table 1-2 are similar, they are not exact copies. The range in each SUM function entry uses cell references that are one column to the right of the previous column. When you copy cell references, Excel automatically adjusts them for each new position, resulting in the SUM function entries illustrated in Table 1-2. Each adjusted cell reference is called a **relative reference**.

The easiest way to copy the SUM formula from cell B8 to cells C8, D8, and E8 is to use the fill handle. The **fill handle** is the small black square located in the lower-right corner of the heavy border around the active cell. The following steps show how to use the fill handle to copy cell B8 to the adjacent cells C8:E8.

To Copy a Cell to Adjacent Cells in a Row

1

• **With cell B8 active, point to the fill handle.**

The mouse pointer changes to a cross hair (Figure 1-32).

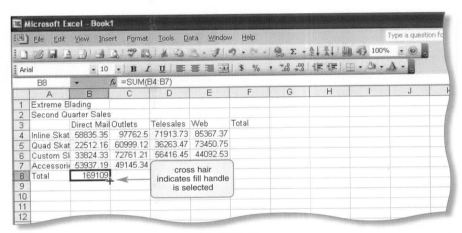

FIGURE 1-32

2

• **Drag the fill handle to select the destination area, range C8:E8. Do not release the mouse button.**

Excel displays a shaded border around the destination area, range C8:E8, and the source area, cell B8 (Figure 1-33).

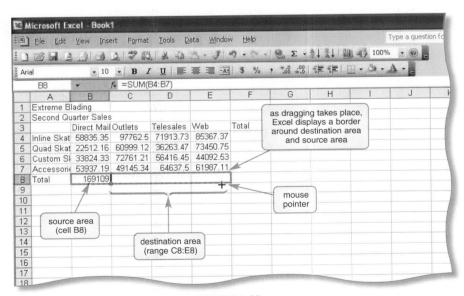

FIGURE 1-33

105

3

• **Release the mouse button.**

Excel copies the SUM function in cell B8 to the range C8:E8 (Figure 1-34). In addition, Excel calculates the sums and enters the results in cells C8, D8, and E8. The Auto Fill Options button appears to the right and below the destination area.

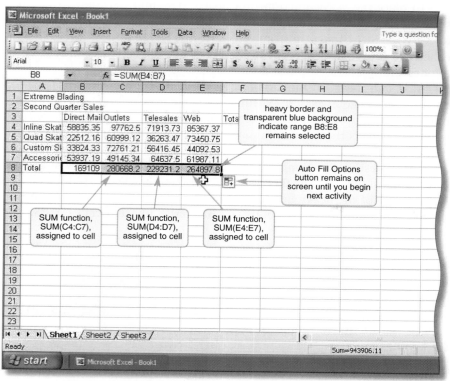

FIGURE 1-34

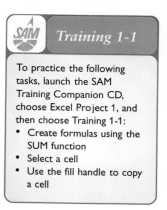

Once the copy is complete, Excel continues to display a heavy border and transparent blue background around cells B8:E8. The heavy border and transparent blue background are called **see-through view** and indicates a selected range. Excel does not display the transparent blue background around cell B8, the first cell in the range, because it is the active cell. If you click any cell, Excel will remove the heavy border and transparent blue background of the see-through view.

When you copy one range to another, Excel displays an Auto Fill Options button to the right and below the destination area (Figure 1-34). The Auto Fill Options button allows you to choose whether you want to copy the values from the source area to the destination area with formatting, without formatting, or only copy the format. To view the available fill options, click the Auto Fill Options button. The Auto Fill Options button disappears when you begin another activity.

Determining Multiple Totals at the Same Time

The next step in building the worksheet is to determine total second quarter sales for each product group and total second quarter sales for the company in column F. To calculate these totals, you can use the SUM function much as you used it to total the sales by sales channel in row 8. In this example, however, Excel will determine totals for all of the rows at the same time. The following steps illustrate this process.

To Determine Multiple Totals at the Same Time

1

• **Click cell F4.**

Cell F4 becomes the active cell (Figure 1-35).

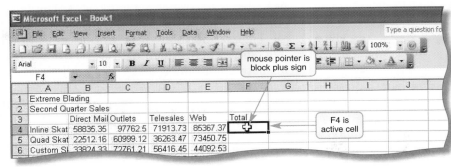

FIGURE 1-35

2

• **With the mouse pointer in cell F4 and in the shape of a block plus sign, drag the mouse pointer down to cell F8.**

Excel highlights the range F4:F8 with a see-through view (Figure 1-36).

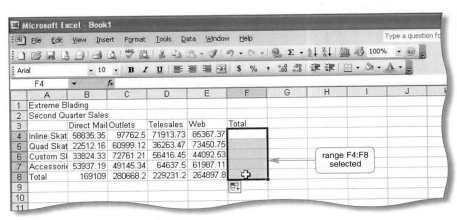

FIGURE 1-36

3

• **Click the AutoSum button on the Standard toolbar.**

Excel assigns the appropriate SUM functions to cells F4, F5, F6, F7, and F8, and then calculates and displays the sums in the respective cells (Figure 1-37).

4

• **Select cell A9 to deselect the range F4:F8.**

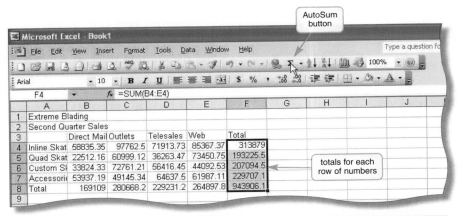

FIGURE 1-37

If each cell in a selected range is next to a row of numbers, Excel assigns the SUM function to each cell when you click the AutoSum button. Thus, as shown in the previous steps, each of the five cells in the selected range is assigned a SUM function with a different range, based on its row. This same procedure could have been used earlier to sum the columns. That is, instead of clicking cell B8, clicking the AutoSum button twice, and then copying the SUM function to the range C8:E8, the range B8:E8 could have been selected and then the AutoSum button clicked once, which would have assigned the SUM function to the entire range.

Formatting the Worksheet

The text, numeric entries, and functions for the worksheet now are complete. The next step is to format the worksheet. You **format** a worksheet to emphasize certain entries and make the worksheet easier to read and understand.

Figure 1-38a shows the worksheet before formatting. Figure 1-38b shows the worksheet after formatting. As you can see from the two figures, a worksheet that is formatted not only is easier to read, but also looks more professional.

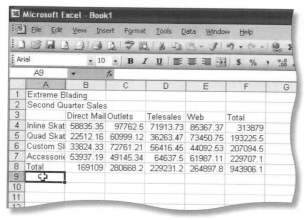

(a) Before Formatting

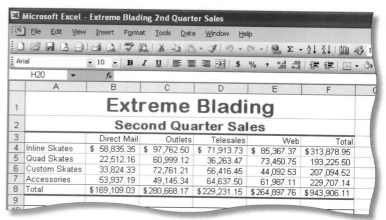

(b) After Formatting

FIGURE 1-38

To change the unformatted worksheet in Figure 1-38a to the formatted worksheet in Figure 1-38b, the following tasks must be completed:

1. Change the font type, change the font style to bold, increase the font size, and change the font color of the worksheet titles in cells A1 and A2.
2. Center the worksheet titles in cells A1 and A2 across columns A through F.
3. Format the body of the worksheet. The body of the worksheet, range A3:F8, includes the column titles, row titles, and numbers. Formatting the body of the worksheet changes the numbers to use a dollars-and-cents format, with dollar signs in the first row (row 4) and the total row (row 8); adds underlining that emphasizes portions of the worksheet; and modifies the column widths to make the text and numbers readable.

The remainder of this section explains the process required to format the worksheet. Although the format procedures are explained in the order described above, you should be aware that you can make these format changes in any order.

Font Type, Style, Size, and Color

The characters that Excel displays on the screen are a specific font type, style, size, and color. The **font type**, or font face, defines the appearance and shape of the letters, numbers, and special characters. Examples of font types include Times New Roman, Arial, and Courier. **Font style** indicates how the characters are formatted. Common font styles include regular, bold, underline, or italic. The **font size** specifies the size of the characters on the screen. Font size is gauged by a measurement system called points. A single point is about 1/72 of one inch in height. Thus, a character with a **point size** of 10 is about 10/72 of one inch in height. The **font color** defines the color of the characters. Excel can display characters in a wide variety of colors, including black, red, orange, and blue.

When Excel begins, the preset font type for the entire workbook is Arial, with a font size and font style of 10-point regular black. Excel allows you to change the font characteristics in a single cell, a range of cells, the entire worksheet, or the entire workbook.

Changing the Font Type

Different font types often are used in a worksheet to make it more appealing to the reader. The following steps show how to change the worksheet title font type from Arial to Arial Rounded MT Bold.

To Change the Font Type

1

• **Click cell A1 and then point to the Font box arrow on the Formatting toolbar.**

Cell A1 is the active cell (Figure 1-39).

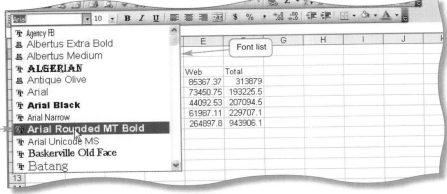

FIGURE 1-39

2

• **Click the Font box arrow and then point to Arial Rounded MT Bold.**

Excel displays the Font list with Arial Rounded MT Bold highlighted (Figure 1-40).

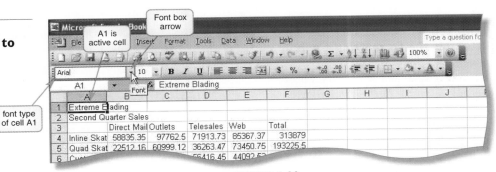

FIGURE 1-40

3

• **Click Arial Rounded MT Bold.**

Excel changes the font type of cell A1 from Arial to Arial Rounded MT Bold (Figure 1-41).

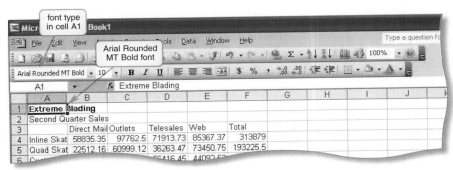

FIGURE 1-41

Because many applications supply additional font types beyond what comes with the Windows operating system, the number of font types available on your computer will depend on the applications installed. This book only uses font types that come with the Windows operating system.

Bolding a Cell

You **bold** an entry in a cell to emphasize it or make it stand out from the rest of the worksheet. The following step shows how to bold the worksheet title in cell A1.

To Bold a Cell

1

- **With cell A1 active, click the Bold button on the Formatting toolbar.**

Excel changes the font style of the worksheet title, Extreme Blading, to bold. With the mouse pointer pointing to the Bold button, Excel displays a ScreenTip immediately below the Bold button to identify the function of the button (Figure 1-42).

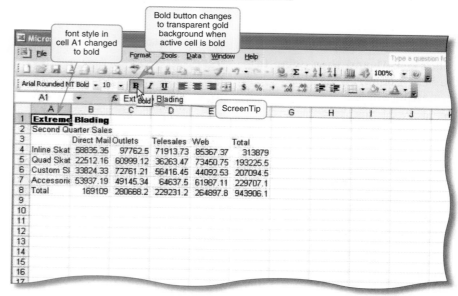

FIGURE 1-42

Other Ways

1. On Format menu click Cells, click Font tab, click Bold in Font style box, click OK button
2. Right-click cell, click Format Cells on shortcut menu, click Font tab, click Bold in Font style box, click OK button
3. Press CTRL+B
4. In Voice Command mode, say "Bold"

When the active cell is bold, Excel displays the Bold button on the Formatting toolbar with a transparent gold background (Figure 1-42). If you point to the Bold button and the active cell is already bold, then Excel displays the button with a transparent red background. Clicking the Bold button a second time removes the bold font style.

Increasing the Font Size

Increasing the font size is the next step in formatting the worksheet title. You increase the font size of a cell so the entry stands out and is easier to read. The following steps illustrate how to increase the font size of the worksheet title in cell A1.

To Increase the Font Size of a Cell Entry

1

• **With cell A1 selected, click the Font Size box arrow on the Formatting toolbar.**

Excel displays the Font Size list as shown in Figure 1-43.

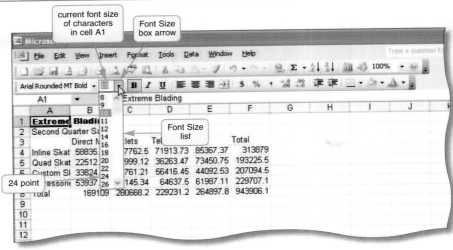

FIGURE 1-43

2

• **Click 24 in the Font Size list.**

The font size of the characters in cell A1 increase from 10 point to 24 point (Figure 1-44). The increased font size makes the worksheet title easier to read.

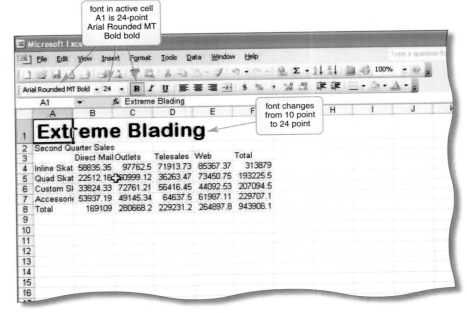

FIGURE 1-44

An alternative to clicking a font size in the Font Size list is to click the Font Size box, type the font size, and then press the ENTER key. This procedure allows you to assign a font size not available in the Font Size list to a selected cell entry. With cell A1 selected (Figure 1-44), the Font Size box shows that the new font size is 24 and the transparent gold Bold button shows that the font style is bold.

Changing the Font Color of a Cell Entry

The next step is to change the color of the font in cell A1 from black to violet. The steps on the next page show how to change the font color of a cell entry.

Other Ways

1. On Format menu click Cells, click Font tab, select font size in Size box, click OK button
2. Right-click cell, click Format Cells on shortcut menu, click Font tab, select font size in Size box, click OK button
3. In Voice Command mode, say "Font Size, [desired font size]"

To Change the Font Color of a Cell Entry

1

• **With cell A1 selected, click the Font Color button arrow on the Formatting toolbar.**

Excel displays the Font Color palette (Figure 1-45).

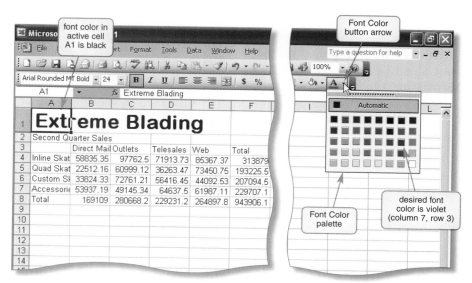

FIGURE 1-45

2

• **Click Violet (column 7, row 3) on the Font Color palette.**

The font in the worksheet title in cell A1 changes from black to violet (Figure 1-46).

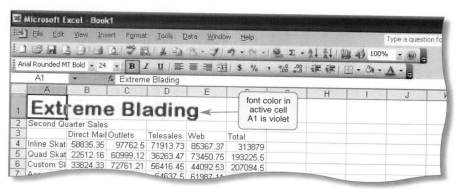

FIGURE 1-46

As shown in Figure 1-45, you can choose from 40 different font colors on the Font Color palette. Your Font Color palette may have more or fewer colors, depending on color settings of your operating system. When you choose a color on the Font Color palette, Excel changes the Font Color button on the Formatting toolbar to the chosen color. Thus, to change the font color of the cell entry in another cell to the same color, you only need to select the cell and then click the Font Color button.

Centering a Cell Entry across Columns by Merging Cells

The final step in formatting the worksheet title is to center it across columns A through F. Centering a worksheet title across the columns used in the body of the worksheet improves the worksheet's appearance. To do this, the six cells in the range A1:F1 are combined, or merged, into a single cell that is the width of the columns in the body of the worksheet. **Merging cells** involves creating a single cell by combining two or more selected cells. The following steps illustrate how to center the worksheet title across columns by merging cells.

To Center a Cell Entry across Columns by Merging Cells

1

• **With cell A1 selected, drag to cell F1.**

Excel highlights the selected cells (Figure 1-47).

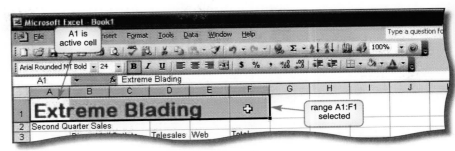

FIGURE 1-47

2

• **Click the Merge and Center button on the Formatting toolbar.**

Excel merges the cells A1 through F1 to create a new cell A1 and centers the contents of cell A1 across columns A through F (Figure 1-48). After the merge, cells B1 through F1 no longer exist on the worksheet.

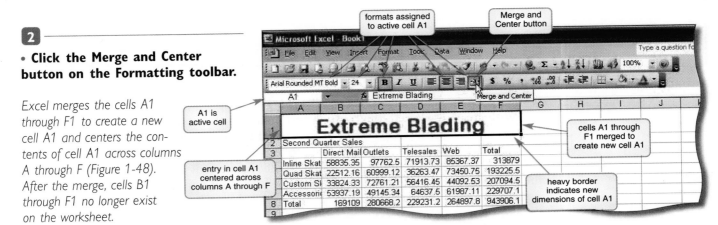

FIGURE 1-48

Excel not only centers the worksheet title across the range A1:F1, but it also merges cells A1 through F1 into one merged cell, cell A1. For the Merge and Center button to work properly, all the cells except the leftmost cell in the selected range must be empty.

The opposite of merging cells is **splitting a merged cell**. After you have merged multiple cells to create one merged cell, you can unmerge, or split, the merged cell to display the original cells on the worksheet. You split a merged cell by selecting it and clicking the Merge and Center button. For example, if you click the Merge and Center button a second time in Step 2, it will split the merged cell A1 to cells A1, B1, C1, D1, E1, and F1.

Most formats assigned to a cell will appear on the Formatting toolbar when the cell is selected. For example, with cell A1 selected in Figure 1-48, Excel displays the font type and font size of the active cell in their appropriate boxes. Transparent gold buttons on the Formatting toolbar indicate other assigned formatting. To determine if less frequently used formats are assigned to a cell, right-click the cell, click Format Cells on the shortcut menu, and then click each of the tabs in the Format Cells dialog box.

Formatting the Worksheet Subtitle

The worksheet subtitle in cell A2 is to be formatted the same as the worksheet title in cell A1, except that the font size should be 16 rather than 24. The steps on the next page show how to format the worksheet subtitle in cell A2.

Other Ways

1. On Format menu click Cells, click Alignment tab, select Center in Horizontal list, click Merge cells check box, click OK button

2. Right-click cell, click Format Cells on shortcut menu, click Alignment tab, select Center in Horizontal list, click Merge cells check box, click OK button

3. In Voice Command mode, say "Merge and Center"

To Format the Worksheet Subtitle

1 Select cell A2.

2 Click the Font box arrow on the Formatting toolbar and then click Arial Rounded MT Bold.

3 Click the Bold button on the Formatting toolbar.

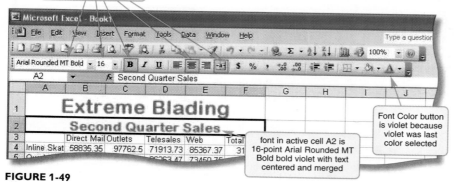

FIGURE 1-49

4 Click the Font Size box arrow on the Formatting toolbar and then click 16.

5 Click the Font Color button on the Formatting toolbar.

6 Select the range A2:F2 and then click the Merge and Center button on the Formatting toolbar.

Excel displays the worksheet subtitle in cell A2 as shown in Figure 1-49.

With cell A2 selected, the buttons and boxes on the Formatting toolbar describe the formats assigned to cell A2. The steps used to format the worksheet subtitle in cell A2 were the same as the steps used to assign the formats to the worksheet title in cell A1, except for the step that assigned violet as the font color. The step to change the font color of the worksheet subtitle in cell A2 used only the Font Color button, rather than the Font Color button arrow. Recall that, when you choose a color on the Font Color palette, Excel assigns the last font color used (in this case, violet) to the Font Color button.

Using AutoFormat to Format the Body of a Worksheet

Excel has customized autoformats that allow you to format the body of the worksheet to give it a professional look. An **autoformat** is a built-in collection of formats such as font style, font color, borders, and alignment, which you can apply to a range of cells. The following steps format the range A3:F8 using the AutoFormat command on the Format menu.

To Use AutoFormat to Format the Body of a Worksheet

1

• **Select cell A3, the upper-left corner cell of the rectangular range to format.**

• **Drag the mouse pointer to cell F8, the lower-right corner cell of the range to format.**

Excel highlights the range to format with a heavy border and transparent blue background (Figure 1-50).

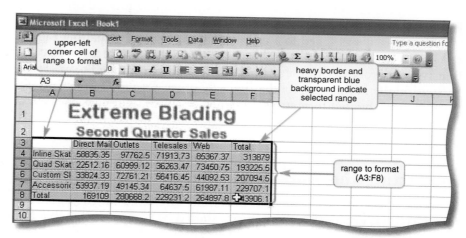

FIGURE 1-50

2

• **Click Format on the menu bar.**

Excel displays the Format menu (Figure 1-51).

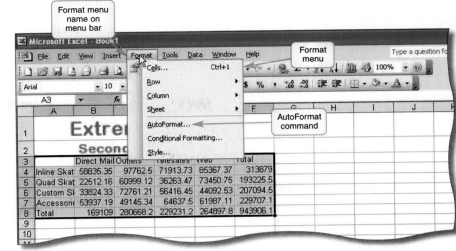

FIGURE 1-51

3

• **Click AutoFormat on the Format menu.**

• **When Excel displays the AutoFormat dialog box, click the Accounting 2 format.**

Excel displays the AutoFormat dialog box with a list of available autoformats (Figure 1-52). For each autoformat, Excel provides a sample to illustrate how the body of the worksheet will appear if that autoformat is chosen.

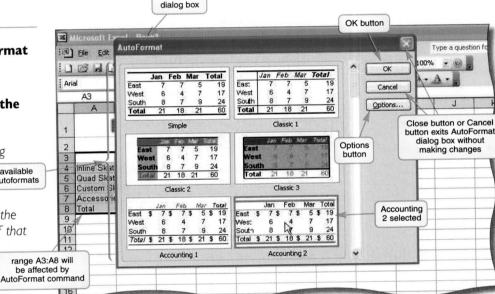

FIGURE 1-52

4

• **Click the OK button.**

• **Select cell A10 to deselect the range A3:F8.**

Excel displays the worksheet with the range A3:F8 formatted using the autoformat, Accounting 2 (Figure 1-53).

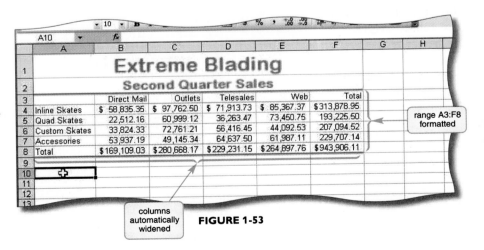

FIGURE 1-53

The formats associated with the autoformat Accounting 2 include right-aligned column titles; numbers displayed as dollars and cents with comma separators; numbers aligned on the decimal point; the first row and total row of numbers displayed with dollar signs; and top and bottom rows displayed with borders. The width of column A has been increased so the longest row title in cell A6, Custom Skates, just fits in the column. The widths of columns B through F also have been increased so that the formatted numbers will fit in the cells.

The AutoFormat dialog box shown in Figure 1-52 on the previous page includes 17 autoformats and four buttons. Use the vertical scroll bar in the dialog box to view the autoformats that are not displayed when the dialog box first opens. Each one of these autoformats offers a different look. The one you choose depends on the worksheet you are creating. The last autoformat in the list, called None, removes all formats.

The four buttons in the AutoFormat dialog box allow you to complete the entries, modify an autoformat, or cancel changes and close the dialog box. The Close button on the title bar and the Cancel button both terminate the current activity and close the AutoFormat dialog box without making changes. The Options button allows you to deselect formats, such as fonts or borders, within an autoformat.

The worksheet now is complete. The next step is to chart the second quarter sales for the four product groups by sales channel. To create the chart, you must select the cell in the upper-left corner of the range to chart (cell A3). Rather than clicking cell A3 to select it, the next section describes how to use the Name box to select the cell.

Using the Name Box to Select a Cell

As previously noted, the Name box is located on the left side of the formula bar. To select any cell, click the Name box and enter the cell reference of the cell you want to select. The following steps show how to select cell A3.

To Use the Name Box to Select a Cell

1

- **Click the Name box in the formula bar and then type** a3 **as the cell to select.**

Even though cell A10 is the active cell, Excel displays the typed cell reference a3 in the Name box (Figure 1-54).

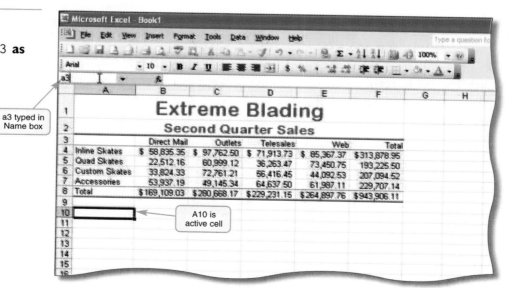

FIGURE 1-54

2

- **Press the ENTER key.**

Excel changes the active cell from cell A10 to cell A3 (Figure 1-55).

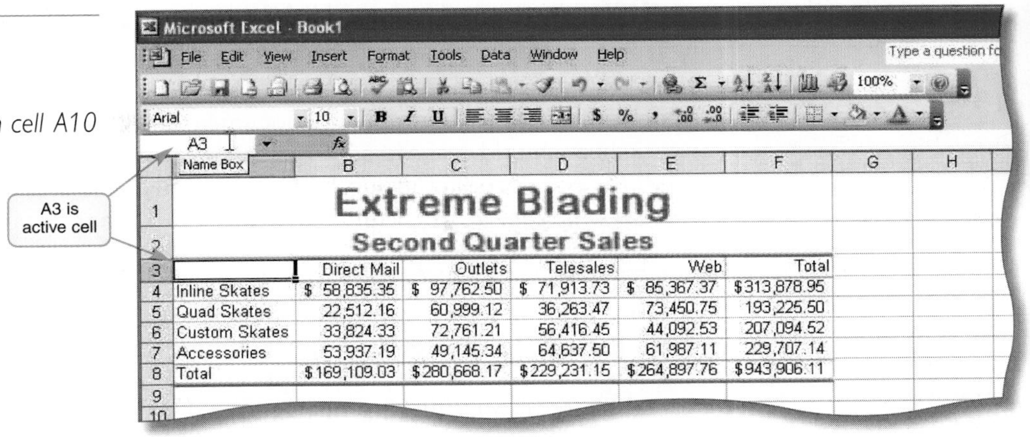

A3 is active cell

FIGURE 1-55

As you will see in later projects, in addition to using the Name box to select any cell in a worksheet, you also can use it to assign names to a cell or range of cells. Excel supports several additional ways to select a cell, as summarized in Table 1-3.

More About

Navigation

For more information about selecting cells that contain certain entries, such as constants or formulas, visit the Excel 2003 More About Web page (scsite.com/ex2003/more) and click Using Go To Special.

Table 1-3   Selecting Cells in Excel

KEY, BOX, OR COMMAND	FUNCTION
ALT+PAGE DOWN	Selects the cell one worksheet window to the right and moves the worksheet window accordingly.
ALT+PAGE UP	Selects the cell one worksheet window to the left and moves the worksheet window accordingly.
ARROW	Selects the adjacent cell in the direction of the arrow on the key.
CTRL+ARROW	Selects the border cell of the worksheet in combination with the arrow keys and moves the worksheet window accordingly. For example, to select the rightmost cell in the row that contains the active cell, press CTRL+RIGHT ARROW. You also can press the END key, release it, and then press the appropriate arrow key to accomplish the same task.
CTRL+HOME	Selects cell A1 or the cell one column and one row below and to the right of frozen titles and moves the worksheet window accordingly.
Find command on Edit menu or SHIFT+F5	Finds and selects a cell that contains specific contents that you enter in the Find dialog box. If necessary, Excel moves the worksheet window to display the cell. You also can press CTRL+F to display the Find dialog box.
Go To command on Edit menu or F5	Selects the cell that corresponds to the cell reference you enter in the Go To dialog box and moves the worksheet window accordingly. You also can press CTRL+G to display the Go To dialog box.
HOME	Selects the cell at the beginning of the row that contains the active cell and moves the worksheet window accordingly.
Name box	Selects the cell in the workbook that corresponds to the cell reference you enter in the Name box.
PAGE DOWN	Selects the cell down one worksheet window from the active cell and moves the worksheet window accordingly.
PAGE UP	Selects the cell up one worksheet window from the active cell and moves the worksheet window accordingly.

Adding a 3-D Clustered Column Chart to the Worksheet

As outlined in the requirements document in Figure 1-2 on page EX 6, the worksheet should include a 3-D Clustered column chart to graphically represent sales for each product group by sales channel. The 3-D Clustered column chart shown in Figure 1-56 is called an **embedded chart** because it is drawn on the same worksheet as the data.

The chart uses different colored columns to represent sales for different product groups. For the Direct Mail sales channel, for example, the light blue column represents the second quarter sales for the Inline Skates product group ($58,835.35); for the Outlets sales channel, the purple column represents the second quarter sales for Quad Skates ($60,999.12); for the Telesales sales channel, the light yellow column represents the second quarter sales for Custom Skates ($56,416.45); and for the Web sales channel, the turquoise column represents the second quarter sales for Accessories ($61,987.11). For the Outlets, Telesales, and Web sales channels, the columns follow the same color scheme to represent the comparable second quarter sales. The totals from the worksheet are not represented because the totals are not in the range specified for charting.

Excel derives the chart scale based the values in the worksheet and then displays the scale along the vertical axis (also called the **y-axis** or **value axis**) of the chart. For example, no value in the range B4:E7 is less than 0 or greater than $100,000.00, so the scale ranges from 0 to $100,000.00. Excel also determines the $20,000.00 increments of the scale automatically. For the numbers along the y-axis, Excel uses a format that includes representing the 0 value with a dash (Figure 1-56).

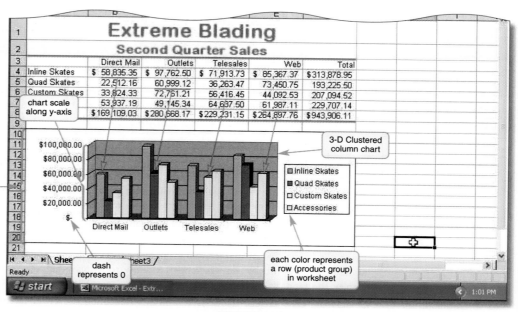

FIGURE 1-56

With the range to chart selected, you click the Chart Wizard button on the Standard toolbar to initiate drawing the chart. The area on the worksheet where the chart appears is called the **chart location**. As shown in Figure 1-56, the chart location in this worksheet is the range A10:F20, immediately below the worksheet data.

The following steps show how to draw a 3-D Clustered column chart that compares the second quarter sales by product group for the four sales channels.

To Add a 3-D Clustered Column Chart to the Worksheet

1

• **With cell A3 selected, position the block plus sign mouse pointer within the cell's border and drag the mouse pointer to the lower-right corner cell (cell E7) of the range to chart (A3:E7).**

Excel highlights the range to chart (Figure 1-57).

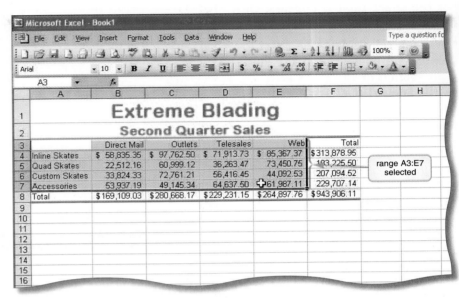

FIGURE 1-57

2

• **Click the Chart Wizard button on the Standard toolbar.**

• **When Excel displays the Chart Wizard - Step 1 of 4 - Chart Type dialog box, and with Column selected in the Chart type list, click Clustered column with a 3-D visual effect (column 1, row 2) in the Chart sub-type area.**

Excel displays the Chart Wizard - Step 1 of 4 - Chart Type dialog box as shown in Figure 1-58.

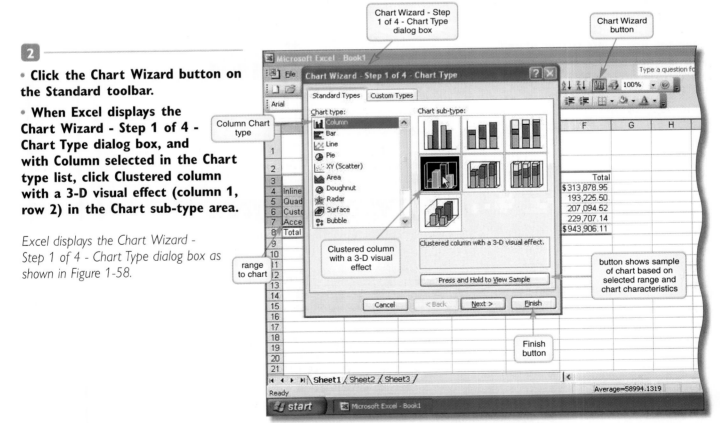

FIGURE 1-58

3

* **Click the Finish button.**

* **If the Chart toolbar appears, click its Close button.**

* **When Excel displays the chart, point to an open area in the lower-right section of the chart area so the ScreenTip, Chart Area, appears next to the mouse pointer.**

Excel draws the 3-D Clustered column chart (Figure 1-59). The chart appears in the middle of the worksheet window in a selection rectangle. The small sizing handles at the corners and along the sides of the selection rectangle indicate the chart is selected.

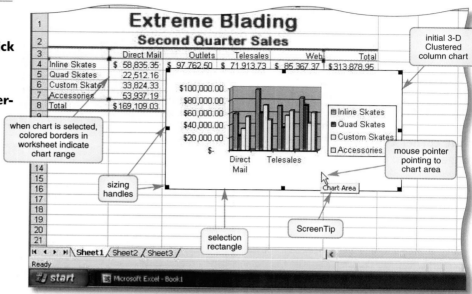

FIGURE 1-59

4

* **Drag the chart down and to the left to position the upper-left corner of the dotted line rectangle over the upper-left corner of cell A10. Do not release the mouse button (Figure 1-60).**

As you drag the selected chart, Excel displays a dotted line rectangle showing the new chart location and the mouse pointer changes to a cross hair with four arrowheads.

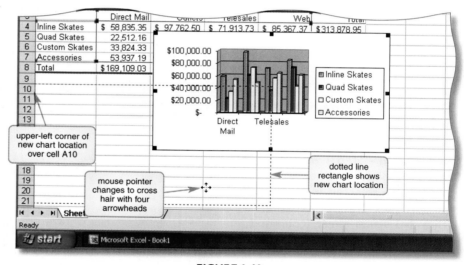

FIGURE 1-60

5

* **Release the mouse button.**

* **Point to the middle sizing handle on the right edge of the selection rectangle.**

The chart appears in a new location (Figure 1-61). The mouse pointer changes to a horizontal line with two arrowheads when it points to a sizing handle.

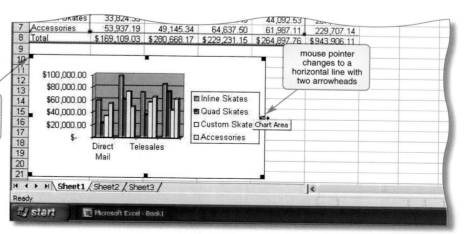

FIGURE 1-61

6

- While holding down the ALT key, drag the sizing handle to the right edge of column F.

*While you drag, the dotted line rectangle shows the new chart location (Figure 1-62). Holding down the ALT key while you drag a chart **snaps** (aligns) the edge of the chart area to the worksheet gridlines.*

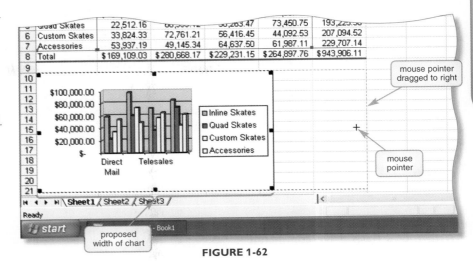

FIGURE 1-62

7

- If necessary, hold down the ALT key and drag the lower-middle sizing handle up to the bottom border of row 20.
- Click cell H20 to deselect the chart.

The new chart location extends from the top of cell A10 to the bottom of cell F20 (Figure 1-63).

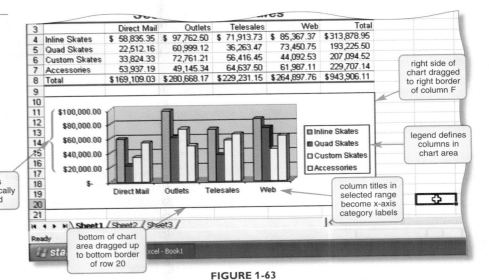

FIGURE 1-63

The embedded 3-D Clustered column chart in Figure 1-63 compares the second quarter sales for the four product groups by each sales channel. It also allows you to compare second quarter sales for the four product groups among the sales channels.

Excel automatically selects the entries in the topmost row of the chart range (row 3) as the titles for the horizontal axis (also called the **x-axis** or **category axis**) and draws a column for each of the 16 cells in the range containing numbers. The small box to the right of the column chart in Figure 1-63 contains the **legend**, which identifies the colors assigned to each bar in the chart. Excel automatically selects the entries in the leftmost column of the chart range (column A) as titles within the legend. As indicated earlier, Excel also automatically derives the chart scale on the y-axis based on the highest and lowest numbers in the chart range.

Excel offers 14 different chart types (Figure 1-58 on page EX 39). The **default chart type** is the chart Excel draws if you click the Finish button in the first Chart Wizard dialog box. When you install Excel on a computer, the default chart type is the 2-D (two-dimensional) Column chart.

Other Ways

1. On Insert menu click Chart
2. Press F11
3. In Voice Command mode, say "Chart Wizard"

More About

Printing Only the Chart

To print the embedded chart without printing the worksheet, select the chart, click File on the menu bar, click Page Setup, click the Chart tab, click the Scale to fit page in the Printed chart size area, click the Print button, and then click the OK button.

Saving a Workbook

While you are building a workbook, the computer stores it in memory. If the computer is turned off or if you lose electrical power, the workbook is lost. Hence, if you plan to use the workbook later, you must save the workbook on a USB flash drive, floppy disk, or hard disk. A saved workbook is referred to as a **file**. The following steps illustrate how to save a workbook on a USB flash drive using the Save button on the Standard toolbar.

To Save a Workbook

1

• **With a USB flash drive connected to one of the computer's USB ports, click the Save button on the Standard toolbar.**

Excel displays the Save As dialog box (Figure 1-64). The default Save in folder is Documents (your Save in folder may be different), the default file name is Book1, and the default file type is Microsoft Office Excel Workbook.

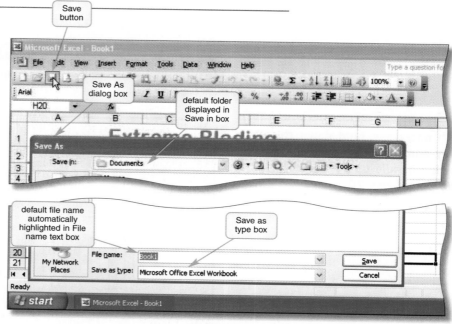

FIGURE 1-64

2

• **Type** Extreme Blading 2nd Quarter Sales **in the File name text box.**

• **Click the Save in box arrow.**

The new file name replaces Book1 in the File name text box (Figure 1-65). A file name can be up to 255 characters and can include spaces. Excel displays a list of available drives and folders.

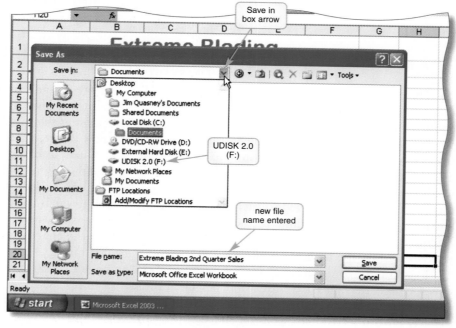

FIGURE 1-65

3

• **Click UDISK 2.0 (F:) in the Save in list. (Your USB flash drive may have a different name and letter.)**

The USB flash drive becomes the selected drive (Figure 1-66). The buttons on the top and on the side of the dialog box are used to select folders, change the appearance of file names, and complete other tasks.

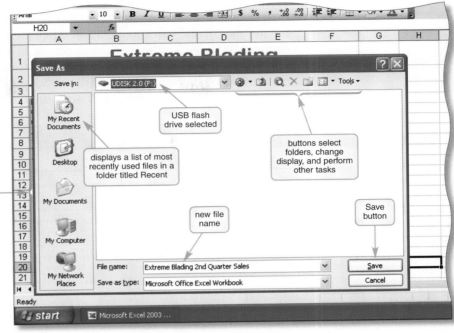

FIGURE 1-66

4

• **Click the Save button in the Save As dialog box.**

Excel saves the workbook on the USB flash drive using the file name, Extreme Blading 2nd Quarter Sales. Excel automatically appends the extension .xls to the file name you entered in Step 2, which stands for Excel workbook. Although the workbook is saved on a USB flash drive, it also remains in memory and is displayed on the screen (Figure 1-67). Excel displays the new file name on the title bar.

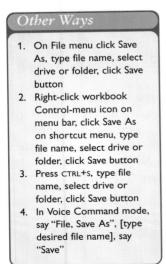

Other Ways

1. On File menu click Save As, type file name, select drive or folder, click Save button
2. Right-click workbook Control-menu icon on menu bar, click Save As on shortcut menu, type file name, select drive or folder, click Save button
3. Press CTRL+S, type file name, select drive or folder, click Save button
4. In Voice Command mode, say "File, Save As", [type desired file name], say "Save"

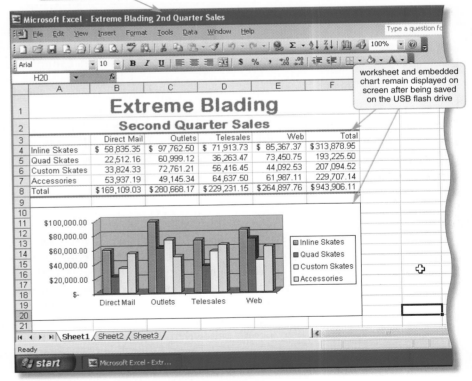

FIGURE 1-67

While Excel is saving the workbook, it momentarily changes the word Ready on the status bar to Saving. It also displays a horizontal bar on the status bar indicating the amount of the workbook saved. After the save operation is complete, Excel changes the name of the workbook on the title bar from Book1 to Extreme Blading 2nd Quarter Sales (Figure 1-67 on the previous page).

The seven buttons at the top of the Save As dialog box in Figure 1-66 on the previous page and their functions are summarized in Table 1-4.

Table 1-4	Save As Dialog Box Toolbar Buttons	
BUTTON	**BUTTON NAME**	**FUNCTION**
X	Default File Location	Displays contents of default file location
⤴	Up One Level	Displays contents of folder one level up from current folder
Q	Search the Web	Starts browser and displays search engine
X	Delete	Deletes selected file or folder
◻	Create New Folder	Creates new folder
⊞	Views	Changes view of files and folders
Tools ▾	Tools	Lists commands to print or modify file names and folders

When you click the Tools button in the Save As dialog box, Excel displays the Tools menu. The General Options command on the menu allows you to save a backup copy of the workbook, create a password to limit access to the workbook, and carry out other functions that are discussed later. Saving a **backup copy** of the workbook means that each time you save a workbook, Excel copies the current version of the workbook to a file with the same name, but with the words, Backup of, appended to the front of the file name. In the case of a power failure or some other problem, you can use the backup copy to restore your work.

You also can use the General Options command on the Tools menu to assign a password to a workbook so others cannot open it. A password is case-sensitive and can be up to 15 characters long. **Case-sensitive** means Excel can differentiate between uppercase and lowercase letters. If you assign a password and forget the password, you cannot access the workbook.

The five buttons on the left of the Save As dialog box in Figure 1-66 allow you to select frequently used folders. The My Recent Documents button displays a list of shortcuts (pointers) to the most recently used files in a folder titled Recent.

Printing a Worksheet

Once you have created the worksheet, you might want to print it. A printed version of the worksheet is called a **hard copy** or **printout**.

You might want a printout for several reasons. First, to present the worksheet and chart to someone who does not have access to a computer, it must be in printed form. A printout, for example, can be handed out in a management meeting about second quarter sales. In addition, worksheets and charts often are kept for reference by people other than those who prepare them. In many cases, worksheets and charts are printed and kept in binders for use by others. The following steps illustrate how to print the worksheet.

To Print a Worksheet

1

- **Ready the printer according to the printer instructions and then click the Print button on the Standard toolbar (Figure 1-68).**

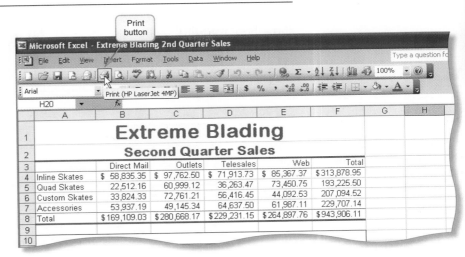

FIGURE 1-68

2

- **When the printer stops printing the worksheet and the chart, retrieve the printout.**

Excel sends the worksheet to the printer, which prints it (Figure 1-69).

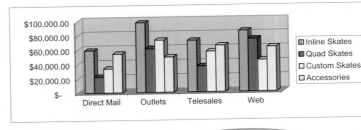

FIGURE 1-69

Other Ways

1. On File menu click Print, click OK button
2. Right-click workbook Control-menu icon on menu bar, click Print on shortcut menu, click OK button
3. Press CTRL+P, click OK button
4. In Voice Command mode, say "Print"

Prior to clicking the Print button, you can select which columns and rows in the worksheet to print. The range of cells you choose to print is called the **print area**. If you do not select a print area, as was the case in the previous set of steps, Excel automatically selects a print area on the basis of used cells. As you will see in future projects, Excel has many different print options, such as allowing you to preview the printout on the screen to see if the printout is satisfactory before sending it to the printer.

SAM Training 1-3

To practice the following tasks, launch the SAM Training Companion CD, choose Excel Project 1, and then choose Training 1-3:
- Create charts using column chart types
- Go to a specific cell
- Position a chart
- Print a chart
- Use Save
- Use Save As to store workbooks to different locations/unique names/ alternate file format

Quitting Excel

The Project 1 worksheet and embedded chart are complete. The following steps show how to quit Excel.

To Quit Excel

1

• **Point to the Close button on the right side of the title bar** (Figure 1-70).

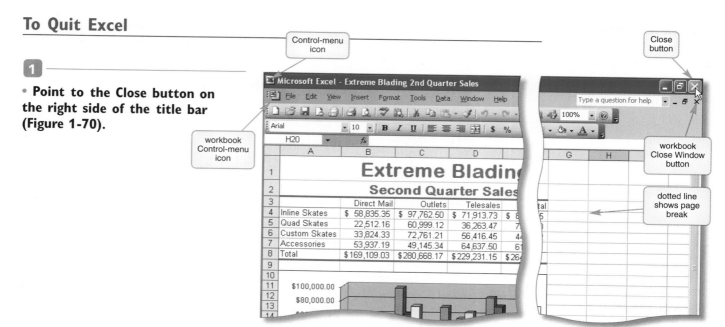

FIGURE 1-70

2

• **Click the Close button.**

If the worksheet was changed or printed, the Microsoft Excel dialog box displays the question, Do you want to save the changes you made to 'Extreme Blading 2nd Quarter Sales.xls'? (Figure 1-71). Clicking the Yes button saves the changes before quitting Excel. Clicking the No button quits Excel without saving the changes. Clicking the Cancel button closes the dialog box and returns control to the worksheet without saving the changes.

3

• **Click the No button.**

Other Ways

1. On File menu click Exit
2. Right-click Microsoft Excel button on taskbar, click Close on shortcut menu
3. Double-click Control-menu icon
4. In Voice Command mode, say "File, Exit"

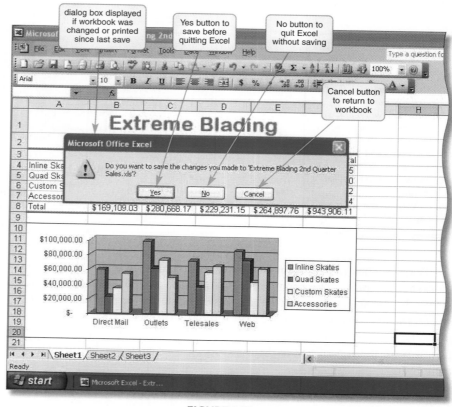

FIGURE 1-71

In Figure 1-70, you can see that the Excel window includes two Close buttons and two Control-menu icons. The Close button and Control-menu icon on the title bar can be used to quit Excel. The Close Window button and Control-menu icon on the menu bar can be used to close the workbook, but not to quit Excel.

Starting Excel and Opening a Workbook

After creating and saving a workbook, you often will have reason to retrieve it from a USB flash drive. For example, you might want to review the calculations on the worksheet and enter additional or revised data. The following steps assume Excel is not running.

To Start Excel and Open a Workbook

1

- **With your USB flash drive connected to one of the computer's USB ports, click the Start button on the Windows taskbar, point to All Programs on the Start menu, point to Microsoft Office on the All Programs submenu, and then click Microsoft Office Excel 2003 on the Microsoft Office submenu.**

Excel starts. The Getting Started task pane lists the four most recently used files in the Open area (Figure 1-72).

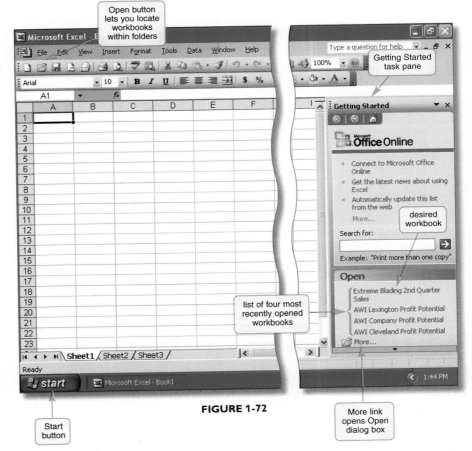

FIGURE 1-72

2

• **Click Extreme Blading 2nd Quarter Sales in the Open area in the Getting Started task pane.**

Excel opens the workbook Extreme Blading 2nd Quarter Sales (Figure 1-73). The Getting Started task pane closes.

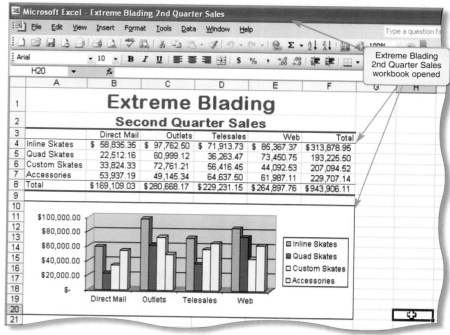

FIGURE 1-73

If you want to open a workbook other than one of the four most recently opened ones, click the Open button on the Standard toolbar or the More link in the Getting Started task pane. Clicking the Open button or the More link displays the Open dialog box, which allows you to navigate to a workbook stored on disk.

AutoCalculate

You easily can obtain a total, an average, or other information about the numbers in a range by using the **AutoCalculate area** on the status bar. First, select the range of cells containing the numbers you want to check. Next, right-click the AutoCalculate area to display the shortcut menu (Figure 1-74). The check mark to the left of the active function (Sum) indicates that the sum of the selected range is displayed in the AutoCalculate area on the status bar. The function of the commands on the AutoCalculate shortcut menu are described in Table 1-5.

The following steps show how to display the average second quarter sales for the Custom Skates product group.

Table 1-5	AutoCalculate Shortcut Menu Commands
COMMAND	**FUNCTION**
None	No value is displayed in the AutoCalculate area
Average	AutoCalculate area displays the average of the numbers in the selected range
Count	AutoCalculate area displays the number of nonblank cells in the selected range
Count Nums	AutoCalculate area displays the number of cells containing numbers in the selected range
Max	AutoCalculate area displays the highest value in the selected range
Min	AutoCalculate area displays the lowest value in the selected range
Sum	AutoCalculate area displays the sum of the numbers in the selected range

To Use the AutoCalculate Area to Determine an Average

 1

- **Select the range B6:E6 and then right-click the AutoCalculate area on the status bar.**

The sum of the numbers in the range B6:E6 is displayed (207,094.52) in the AutoCalculate area, because Sum is the active function (Figure 1-74). Excel displays a shortcut menu listing the other available functions above the AutoCalculate area. If another function is active on your shortcut menu, you may see a different value in the AutoCalculate area.

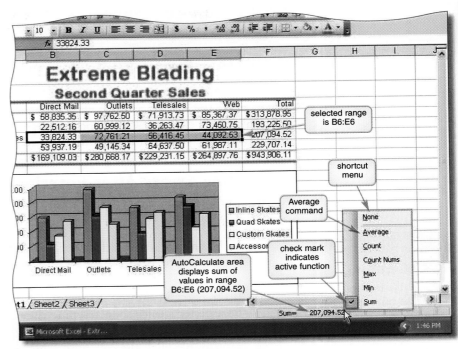

FIGURE 1-74

2

- **Click Average on the shortcut menu.**

Excel displays the average of the numbers in the range B6:E6 (51,773.63) in the AutoCalculate area (Figure 1-75).

3

- **Right-click the AutoCalculate area and then click Sum on the shortcut menu.**

The AutoCalculate area displays the sum as shown earlier in Figure 1-74.

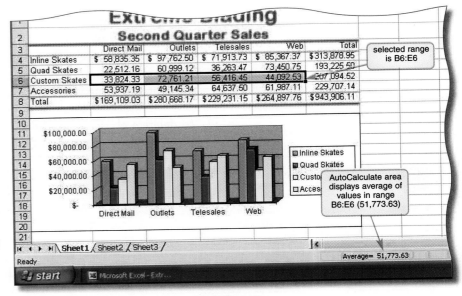

FIGURE 1-75

To change to any one of the other five functions for the range B6:E6, right-click the AutoCalculate area and then click the desired function. Clicking None at the top of the AutoCalculate shortcut menu in Figure 1-74 turns off the AutoCalculate area. Thus, if you select None, then no value will be displayed in the AutoCalculate area when you select a range.

More About

Shortcut Menus

Shortcut menus contain the most frequently used commands that relate to the object to which the mouse pointer is pointing.

Correcting Errors

You can correct errors on a worksheet using one of several methods. The method you choose will depend on the extent of the error and whether you notice it while typing the data or after you have entered the incorrect data into the cell.

Correcting Errors While You Are Typing Data into a Cell

If you notice an error while you are typing data into a cell, press the BACKSPACE key to erase the incorrect characters and then type the correct characters. If the error is a major one, click the Cancel box in the formula bar or press the ESC key to erase the entire entry and then reenter the data from the beginning.

Correcting Errors After Entering Data into a Cell

If you find an error in the worksheet after entering the data, you can correct the error in one of two ways:

1. If the entry is short, select the cell, retype the entry correctly, and then click the Enter box or press the ENTER key. The new entry will replace the old entry.

2. If the entry in the cell is long and the errors are minor, using Edit mode may be a better choice than retyping the cell entry. Use the Edit mode as described below.

   a. Double-click the cell containing the error to switch Excel to Edit mode. In **Edit mode**, Excel displays the active cell entry in the formula bar and a flashing insertion point in the active cell (Figure 1-76). With Excel in Edit mode, you can edit the contents directly in the cell — a procedure called **in-cell editing**.

   b. Make changes using in-cell editing, as indicated below.

   (1) To insert new characters between two characters, place the insertion point between the two characters and begin typing. Excel inserts the new characters at the location of the insertion point.

   (2) To delete a character in the cell, move the insertion point to the left of the character you want to delete and then press the DELETE key or place the insertion point to the right of the character you want to delete and then press the BACKSPACE key. You also can use the mouse to drag through the character or adjacent characters you want to delete and then press the DELETE key or click the Cut button on the Standard toolbar.

   (3) When you are finished editing an entry, click the Enter box or press the ENTER key.

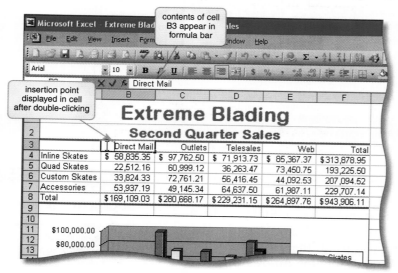

FIGURE 1-76

When Excel enters the Edit mode, the keyboard usually is in Insert mode. In **Insert mode**, as you type a character, Excel inserts the character and moves all characters to the right of the typed character one position to the right. You can change to Overtype mode by pressing the INSERT key. In **Overtype mode**, Excel overtypes, or replaces, the character to the right of the insertion point. The INSERT key toggles the keyboard between Insert mode and Overtype mode.

While in Edit mode, you may have reason to move the insertion point to various points in the cell, select portions of the data in the cell, or switch from inserting characters to overtyping characters. Table 1-6 summarizes the more common tasks used during in-cell editing.

More About

Editing the Contents of a Cell

Rather than using in-cell editing, you can select the cell and then click the formula bar to edit the contents.

Table 1-6   Summary of In-Cell Editing Tasks

	TASK	MOUSE	KEYBOARD
1	Move the insertion point to the beginning of data in a cell.	Point to the left of the first character and click.	Press HOME
2	Move the insertion point to the end of data in a cell.	Point to the right of the last character and click.	Press END
3	Move the insertion point anywhere in a cell.	Point to the appropriate position and click the character.	Press RIGHT ARROW or LEFT ARROW
4	Highlight one or more adjacent characters.	Drag the mouse pointer through adjacent characters.	Press SHIFT+RIGHT ARROW or SHIFT+LEFT ARROW
5	Select all data in a cell.	Double-click the cell with the insertion point in the cell.	
6	Delete selected characters.	Click the Cut button on the Standard toolbar.	Press DELETE
7	Delete characters to the left of the insertion point.		Press BACKSPACE
8	Toggle between Insert and Overtype modes.		Press INSERT

Undoing the Last Cell Entry

Excel provides the Undo command on the Edit menu and the Undo button on the Standard toolbar (Figure 1-77), both of which allow you to erase recent cell entries. Thus, if you enter incorrect data in a cell and notice it immediately, click the Undo command or Undo button and Excel changes the cell entry to what it was prior to the incorrect data entry.

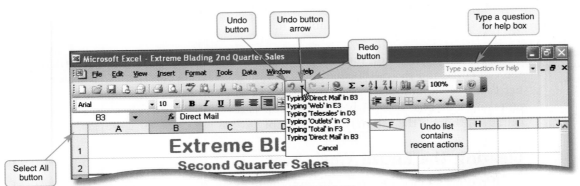

FIGURE 1-77

The Undo Button

The Undo button can undo far more complicated worksheet activities than just removing the latest entry from a cell. In fact, most commands can be undone if you click the Undo button before you make another entry or issue another command. You cannot undo a save or print, but, as a rule, the Undo button can restore the worksheet data and settings to what they were the last time Excel was in Ready mode. With Excel, you have multiple-level undo and redo capabilities.

Getting Back to Normal

If you accidentally assign unwanted formats to a range of cells, you can use the Clear command on the Edit menu to delete the formats of a selected range. Doing so changes the format to Normal style. To view the characteristics of the Normal style, click Style on the Format menu or press ALT+APOSTROPHE (').

The Quick Reference

For a table that lists how to complete the tasks covered in this book using the mouse, menu, shortcut menu, and keyboard, see the Quick Reference Summary at the back of this book, or visit the Excel 2003 Quick Reference Web page (scsite.com/ex2003/qr).

Excel remembers the last 16 actions you have completed. Thus, you can undo up to 16 previous actions by clicking the Undo button arrow to display the Undo list and then clicking the action to be undone (Figure 1-77 on the previous page). You can drag through several actions in the Undo list to undo all of them at once. If no actions are available for Excel to undo, then the Undo button is dimmed and inoperative.

The Redo button, next to the Undo button on the Standard toolbar, allows you to repeat previous actions. You also can click Redo on the Edit menu, instead of using the Redo button.

Clearing a Cell or Range of Cells

If you enter data into the wrong cell or range of cells, you can erase, or **clear**, the data using one of the first four methods listed below. The fifth method clears the formatting from the selected cells.

To Clear Cell Entries Using the Fill Handle

1. Select the cell or range of cells and then point to the fill handle so the mouse pointer changes to a cross hair.
2. Drag the fill handle back into the selected cell or range until a shadow covers the cell or cells you want to erase. Release the mouse button.

To Clear Cell Entries Using the Shortcut Menu

1. Select the cell or range of cells to be cleared.
2. Right-click the selection.
3. Click Clear Contents on the shortcut menu.

To Clear Cell Entries Using the DELETE Key

1. Select the cell or range of cells to be cleared.
2. Press the DELETE key.

To Clear Cell Entries Using the Clear Command

1. Select the cell or range of cells to be cleared.
2. Click Edit on the menu bar and then point to Clear.
3. Click All on the Clear submenu.

To Clear Formatting Using the Clear Command

1. Select the cell or range of cells that you want to remove the formatting from.
2. Click Edit on the menu bar and then point to Clear.
3. Click Formats on the Clear submenu.

The All command on the Clear submenu is the only command that clears both the cell entry and the cell formatting. As you are clearing cell entries, always remember that you should *never press the SPACEBAR to clear a cell.* Pressing the SPACEBAR enters a blank character. A blank character is text and is different from an empty cell, even though the cell may appear empty.

Clearing the Entire Worksheet

If required worksheet edits are extremely extensive, you may want to clear the entire worksheet and start over. To clear the worksheet or delete an embedded chart, use the following steps.

To Clear the Entire Worksheet

1. Click the Select All button on the worksheet (Figure 1-77 on page EX 51).
2. Press the DELETE key to delete all the entries. Click Edit on the menu bar, point to Clear, and then click All on the Clear submenu to delete both the entries and formats.

The Select All button selects the entire worksheet. Instead of clicking the Select All button, you also can press CTRL+A. To clear an unsaved workbook, click the workbook's Close Window button or click the Close command on the File menu. Click the No button if the Microsoft Excel dialog box asks if you want to save changes. To start a new, blank workbook, click the New button on the Standard toolbar or click the New command on the File menu and begin working on a new workbook.

To delete an embedded chart, complete the following steps.

To Delete an Embedded Chart

1. Click the chart to select it.
2. Press the DELETE key.

Excel Help System

At any time while you are using Excel, you can get answers to questions using the **Excel Help** system. You can activate the Excel Help system by using the Type a question for help box on the menu bar, the Microsoft Excel Help button on the Standard toolbar, or by clicking Help on the menu bar (Figure 1-78). Used properly, this form of online assistance can increase your productivity and reduce your frustrations by minimizing the time you spend learning how to use Excel.

The following section shows how to get answers to your questions using the Type a question for help box. Additional information on using the Excel Help system is available in Appendix A.

Obtaining Help Using the Type a Question for Help Box on the Menu Bar

The Type a question for help box on the right side of the menu bar (see Figure 1-77 on page EX 51) lets you type free-form questions such as, how do I save or how do I create a Web page, phrases such as save a workbook or print a worksheet, or key terms such as, copy, save, or formatting. Excel responds by displaying a list of topics related to the question or terms you entered in the Search Results task pane. The following steps show how to use the Type a question for help box to obtain information on saving a workbook.

To Obtain Help Using the Type a Question for Help Box

• **Type** save a workbook **in the Type a question for help box on the right side of the menu bar (Figure 1-78).**

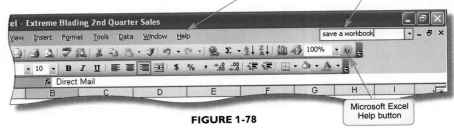

Help menu name on menu bar

Type a question for help box

Microsoft Excel Help button

FIGURE 1-78

2

- **Press the ENTER key.**

- **When Excel displays the Search Results task pane, scroll down and then click the link Save a file.**

- **If necessary, click the AutoTile button (see Figure 1-80) to tile the windows.**

Excel displays the Search Results task pane with a list of topics related to the term, save. Excel found 30 search results (Figure 1-79). When the Save a file link is clicked, Excel opens the Microsoft Excel Help window on the left side of the screen.

3

- **Click the Show All link on the right side of the Microsoft Excel Help window to expand the links in the window.**

- **Double-click the Microsoft Excel Help title bar to maximize it.**

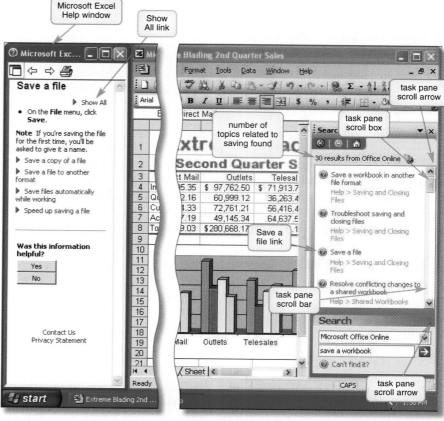

FIGURE 1-79

The links in the Microsoft Excel Help window are expanded. Excel maximizes the window that provides Help information about saving a file (Figure 1-80).

4

- **Click the Close button on the Microsoft Excel Help window title bar.**

The Microsoft Excel Help window closes and the worksheet is active.

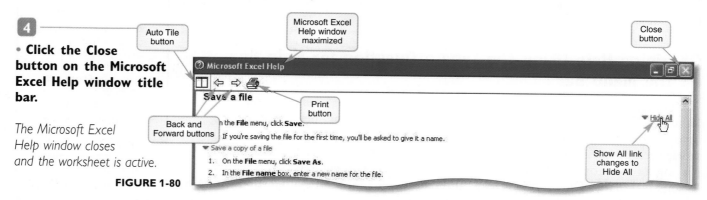

FIGURE 1-80

Use the buttons in the upper-left corner of the Microsoft Excel Help window (Figure 1-80) to navigate through the Help system, change the display, and print the contents of the window.

Quitting Excel

The following step shows how to quit Excel.

To Quit Excel

1 **Click the Close button on the right side of the title bar, and if necessary, click the No button in the Microsoft Excel dialog box.**

Project Summary

This project presented Excel basics. First, you were introduced to starting Excel. You learned about the Excel window and how to enter text and numbers to create a worksheet. You learned how to select a range and how to use the AutoSum button to sum numbers in a column or row. Using the fill handle, you learned how to copy a cell to adjacent cells. Once the worksheet was built, you learned how to format cells one at a time using buttons on the Formatting toolbar and how to format a range using the AutoFormat command. You then learned how to use the Chart Wizard to add a 3-D Clustered column chart to the worksheet. After completing the worksheet, you learned how to save the workbook, print the worksheet and chart, and then quit Excel. You also learned how to start Excel by opening an Excel document, use the AutoCalculate area, and edit data in cells. Finally, you learned how to use the Excel Help system to answer your questions.

 If your instructor has chosen to use the full online version of SAM 2003 Assessment and Training, you can go beyond the "just-in-time" training provided on the CD that accompanies this text. Simply log in to your SAM account (http://sam2003.course.com) to launch any assigned training activities or exams that relate to the skills covered in this project.

What You Should Know

Having completed this project, you should be able to perform the tasks below. The tasks are listed in the same order they were presented in this project. For a list of the buttons, menus, toolbars, and commands introduced in this project, see the Quick Reference Summary at the back of this book and refer to the Page Number column.

1. Start Excel   (EX 7)
2. Customize the Excel Window   (EX 8)
3. Enter the Worksheet Titles   (EX 17)
4. Enter Column Titles   (EX 19)
5. Enter Row Titles   (EX 20)
6. Enter Numbers   (EX 22)
7. Sum a Column of Numbers   (EX 23)
8. Copy a Cell to Adjacent Cells in a Row   (EX 25)
9. Determine Multiple Totals at the Same Time (EX 27)
10. Change the Font Type   (EX 29)
11. Bold a Cell   (EX 30)
12. Increase the Font Size of a Cell Entry   (EX 31)
13. Change the Font Color of a Cell Entry   (EX 32)
14. Center a Cell Entry across Columns by Merging Cells   (EX 33)
15. Format the Worksheet Subtitle   (EX 34)
16. Use AutoFormat to Format the Body of a Worksheet   (EX 34)
17. Use the Name Box to Select a Cell   (EX 36)
18. Add a 3-D Clustered Column Chart to the Worksheet   (EX 39)
19. Save a Workbook   (EX 42)
20. Print a Worksheet   (EX 45)
21. Quit Excel   (EX 46)
22. Start Excel and Open a Workbook   (EX 47)
23. Use the AutoCalculate Area to Determine an Average   (EX 49)
24. Clear Cell Entries Using the Fill Handle   (EX 52)
25. Clear Cell Entries Using the Shortcut Menu   (EX 52)
26. Clear Cell Entries Using the DELETE Key   (EX 52)
27. Clear Cell Entries Using the Clear Command   (EX 52)
28. Clear the Entire Worksheet   (EX 53)
29. Delete an Embedded Chart   (EX 53)
30. Obtain Help Using the Type a Question for Help Box   (EX 53)
31. Quit Excel   (EX 54)

Learn It Online

Instructions: To complete the Learn It Online exercises, start your browser, click the Address bar, and then enter the Web address scsite.com/ex2003/learn. When the Excel 2003 Learn It Online page is displayed, follow the instructions in the exercises below. Each exercise has instructions for printing your results, either for your own records or for submission to your instructor.

1 Project Reinforcement TF, MC, and SA

Below Excel Project 1, click the Project Reinforcement link. Print the quiz by clicking Print on the File menu for each page. Answer each question.

2 Flash Cards

Below Excel Project 1, click the Flash Cards link and read the instructions. Type 20 (or a number specified by your instructor) in the Number of playing cards text box, type your name in the Enter your Name text box, and then click the Flip Card button. When the flash card is displayed, read the question and then click the ANSWER box arrow to select an answer. Flip through Flash Cards. If your score is 15 (75%) correct or greater, click Print on the File menu to print your results. If your score is less than 15 (75%) correct, then redo this exercise by clicking the Replay button.

3 Practice Test

Below Excel Project 1, click the Practice Test link. Answer each question, enter your first and last name at the bottom of the page, and then click the Grade Test button. When the graded practice test is displayed on your screen, click Print on the File menu to print a hard copy. Continue to take practice tests until you score 80% or better.

4 Who Wants To Be a Computer Genius?

Below Excel Project 1, click the Computer Genius link. Read the instructions, enter your first and last name at the bottom of the page, and then click the PLAY button. When your score is displayed, click the PRINT RESULTS link to print a hard copy.

5 Wheel of Terms

Below Excel Project 1, click the Wheel of Terms link. Read the instructions, and then enter your first and last name and your school name. Click the PLAY button. When your score is displayed, right-click the score and then click Print on the shortcut menu to print a hard copy.

6 Crossword Puzzle Challenge

Below Excel Project 1, click the Crossword Puzzle Challenge link. Read the instructions, and then enter your first and last name. Click the SUBMIT button. Work the crossword puzzle. When you are finished, click the Submit button. When the crossword puzzle is redisplayed, click the Print Puzzle button to print a hard copy.

7 Tips and Tricks

Below Excel Project 1, click the Tips and Tricks link. Click a topic that pertains to Project 1. Right-click the information and then click Print on the shortcut menu. Construct a brief example of what the information relates to in Excel to confirm you understand how to use the tip or trick.

8 Newsgroups

Below Excel Project 1, click the Newsgroups link. Click a topic that pertains to Project 1. Print three comments.

9 Expanding Your Horizons

Below Excel Project 1, click the Expanding Your Horizons link. Click a topic that pertains to Project 1. Print the information. Construct a brief example of what the information relates to in Excel to confirm you understand the contents of the article.

10 Search Sleuth

Below Excel Project 1, click the Search Sleuth link. To search for a term that pertains to this project, select a term below the Project 1 title and then use the Google search engine at google.com (or any major search engine) to display and print two Web pages that present information on the term.

11 Excel Online Training

Below Excel Project 1, click the Excel Online Training link. When your browser displays the Microsoft Office Online Web page, click the Excel link. Click one of the Excel courses that covers one or more of the objectives listed at the beginning of the project on page EX 4. Print the first page of the course before stepping through it.

12 Office Marketplace

Below Excel Project 1, click the Office Marketplace link. When your browser displays the Microsoft Office Online Web page, click the Office Marketplace link. Click a topic that relates to Excel. Print the first page.

Apply Your Knowledge

1 Changing the Values in a Worksheet

Instructions: Start Excel. Open the workbook Apply 1-1 Watson's Computer Discount Annual Sales from the Data Files for Students. See the inside back cover of this book for instructions for downloading the Data Files for Students or see your instructor for information on accessing the files required in this book.

Make the changes to the worksheet described in Table 1-7 so that the worksheet appears as shown in Figure 1-81. As you edit the values in the cells containing numeric data, watch the totals in row 7, the totals in column F, and the chart change.

Change the worksheet title in cell A1 to 20-point Arial Black brown, bold font and then center it across columns A through F. Change the worksheet subtitle in cell A2 to 14-point Arial Black brown, bold font and then center it across columns A through F.

Enter your name, course, laboratory assignment number, date, and instructor name in cells A21 through A25. Save the workbook using the file name, Apply 1-1 Babbage's Computer Discount Annual Sales. Print the revised worksheet and hand in the printout to your instructor.

Table 1-7 New Worksheet Data	
CELL	**CHANGE CELL CONTENTS TO**
A1	Babbage's Computer Discount
B4	43200.75
C4	17563.52
D5	38152.43
E5	28968.78
E6	38751.49

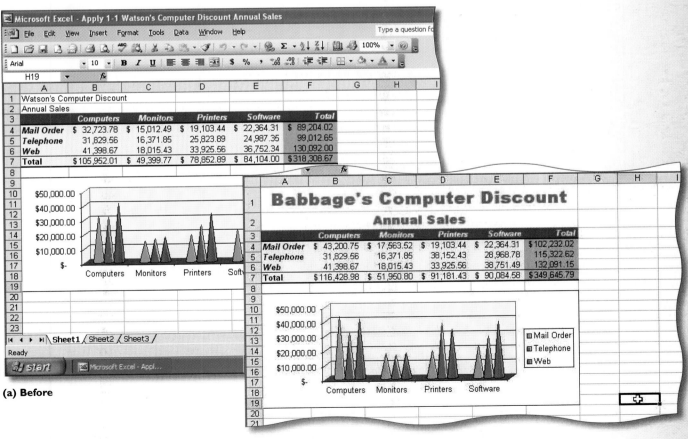

(a) Before

(b) After

FIGURE 1-81

137

1 Quarterly Sales Analysis Worksheet

Problem: You work part-time as a spreadsheet specialist for Trevor's Global Golf Outlet, one of the larger golf retail stores in the world. Your manager has asked you to develop a quarterly sales analysis worksheet similar to the one shown in Figure 1-82.

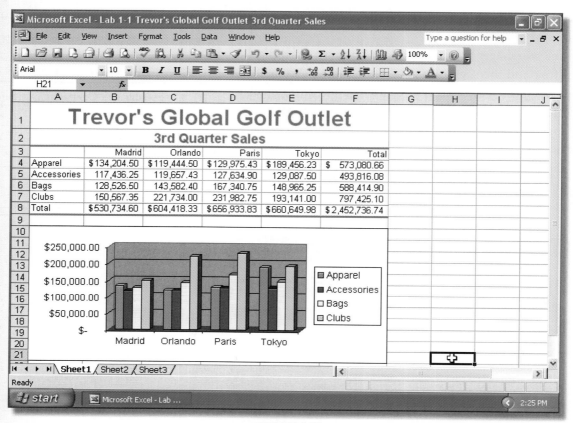

FIGURE 1-82

Instructions: Perform the following tasks.

1. Enter the worksheet title Trevor's Global Golf Outlet in cell A1 and the worksheet subtitle 3rd Quarter Sales in cell A2. Beginning in row 3, enter the sales amounts and categories shown in Table 1-8.

Table 1-8 Trevor's Global Golf Outlet 3rd Quarter Sales				
	Madrid	Orlando	Paris	Tokyo
Apparel	134204.50	119444.50	129975.43	189456.23
Accessories	117436.25	119657.43	127634.90	129087.50
Bags	128526.50	143582.40	167340.75	148965.25
Clubs	150567.35	221734.00	231982.75	193141.00

In the Lab

2. Use the SUM function to determine the totals for the cities, golf gear, and company totals.

3. Format the worksheet title to 24-point Arial plum color, bold font and center it across columns A through F. Do not be concerned if the edges of the worksheet title are not displayed.

4. Format the worksheet subtitle to 14-point Arial plum color, bold font and center it across columns A through F.

5. Format the range A3:F8 using the AutoFormat command. Select the Accounting 2 autoformat.

6. Select the range A3:E7 and then use the Chart Wizard button on the Standard toolbar to draw a Clustered column with a 3-D visual effect chart (column 1, row 2 in the Chart sub-type list). Move and resize the chart so that it appears in the range A10:F21. If the labels along the horizontal axis (x-axis) do not appear as shown in Figure 1-82, then drag the right side of the chart so that it is displayed in the range A10:H20.

7. Enter your name, course, laboratory assignment number, date, and instructor name in cells A23 through A27.

8. Save the workbook using the file name Lab 1-1 Trevor's Global Golf Outlet 3rd Quarter.

9. Print the worksheet.

10. Make the following two corrections to the sales amounts: $152,600.25 for Orlando Bag Sales (cell C6), $201,375.55 for Tokyo Apparel Sales (cell E4). After you enter the corrections, the company totals in cell F8 should equal $2,473,673.91.

11. Print the revised worksheet. Close the workbook without saving the changes.

2 Annual Business Expense Analysis Worksheet

Problem: As the chief accountant for Hitchcox Electronics, you have been asked by the vice president to create a worksheet to analyze the annual business expenses for the company by office and expense category (Figure 1-83 on the next page). The office locations and corresponding annual business expenses are shown in Table 1-9.

Table 1-9 Hitchcox Electronics Annual Business Expenses				
	Chicago	Dallas	New York	San Diego
Marketing	38895.34	34182.56	56781.60	38367.30
Rent	63925.65	77345.28	88950.45	61819.25
Supplies	21782.60	15375.00	21919.25	18374.50
Travel	7192.75	9341.57	11435.00	6819.25
Wages	72011.65	62198.10	58410.45	85357.15

Instructions: Perform the following tasks.

1. Enter the worksheet title Hitchcox Electronics in cell A1 and the worksheet subtitle Annual Business Expenses in cell A2. Beginning in row 3, enter the annual business expenses and categories shown in Table 1-9.

2. Use the SUM function to determine totals expenses for the four offices, the totals for each expense category, and the company total. Add column and row headings for the totals, as appropriate.

(continued)

Annual Business Expense Analysis Worksheet *(continued)*

3. Change the worksheet title to 28-point Arial Rounded MT Bold red, bold font, and center it across columns A through F. Format the worksheet subtitle to 18-point Arial Rounded MT Bold red, bold font, and center it across columns A through F.

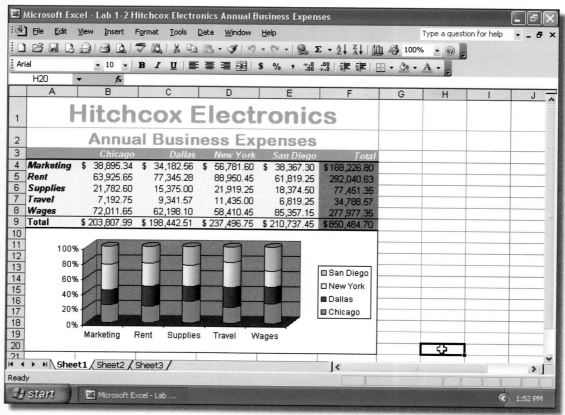

FIGURE 1-83

4. Format the range A3:F9 using the AutoFormat command on the Format menu as follows: (a) apply the autoformat Accounting 3; and (b) with the range A3:F9 still selected, apply the autoformat Colorful 2. If you make a mistake, apply the autoformat None and then apply the autoformats again. Change the background color of the range A3:F3 to red.

5. Chart the range A3:E8. Draw the 100% Stacked column with a cylindrical shape chart, as shown in Figure 1-83, by clicking the Chart Wizard button on the Standard toolbar. When Excel displays the Chart Wizard dialog box, select Cylinder in the Chart type list, and then select column 3, row 1 in the Chart sub-type list. Use the chart location A10:F20.

6. Enter your name, course, laboratory assignment number, date, and instructor name in cells A23 through A27.

7. Save the workbook using the file name, Lab 1-2 Hitchcox Electronics Annual Business Expenses. Print the worksheet.

8. Two corrections to the expenses were sent in from the accounting department. The correct expenses are $67,856.34 for the Dallas rent (cell C5) and $8,561.60 for San Diego travel expenses (cell E7). After you enter the two corrections, the company total in cell F9 should equal $842,738.11. Print the revised worksheet.

9. Use the Undo button to change the worksheet back to the original numbers in Table 1-9. Use the Redo button to change the worksheet back to the revised state.

10. Close Excel without saving the latest changes. Start Excel and open the workbook saved in step 7. Double-click cell D6 and use in-cell editing to change the New York supplies expense to $25,673.17. Write the company total in cell F9 at the top of the first printout. Click the Undo button.

11. Click cell A1 and then click the Merge and Center button to split cell A1 into cells A1, B1, C1, D1, E1, and F1. To re-merge the cells into one, select the range A1:F1 and then click the Merge and Center button.

12. Hand in the two printouts to your instructor. Close the workbook without saving the changes.

3 College Cash Flow Analysis Worksheet

Problem: Attending college is an expensive proposition and your resources are limited. To plan for your four-year college career, you have decided to organize your anticipated resources and expenses in a worksheet. The data required to prepare your worksheet is shown in Table 1-10.

Table 1-10 College Resources and Expenses				
Resources	**Freshman**	**Sophomore**	**Junior**	**Senior**
Financial Aid	6050.00	6655.00	7320.50	8052.55
Job	1650.00	1815.00	1996.50	2196.15
Parents	2800.00	3080.00	3388.00	3726.80
Savings	1300.00	1430.00	1573.00	1730.30
Other	500.00	550.00	605.00	665.50
Expenses				
Clothes	540.00	594.00	653.40	718.74
Entertainment	830.00	913.00	1004.30	1104.73
Miscellaneous	400.00	440.00	484.00	532.40
Room & Board	3880.00	4,268.00	4694.80	5164.28
Tuition & Books	6650.00	7315.00	8046.50	8851.15

Instructions Part 1: Using the numbers in Table 1-10, create the worksheet shown in columns A through F in Figure 1-84 on the next page. Format the worksheet title in cell A1 to 24-point Algerian (or a font style of your choice) green bold font. Format the worksheet subtitles in cells A2 and A10 to 18-point Algerian (or a font style of your choice) red bold font. Format the range A3:F9 using the AutoFormat command on the Format menu as follows: (a) select the range A3:F9 and then apply the autoformat Accounting 3; and (b) with the range A3:F9 still selected, apply the autoformat List 2. Use the same autoformats for the range A11:F17.

Enter your identification on the worksheet and save the workbook using the file name Lab 1-3 Part 1 College Cash Flow Analysis. Print the worksheet in landscape orientation. You print in landscape orientation by invoking the Page Setup command on the File menu and then clicking Landscape on the Page sheet in the Page Setup dialog box. Click the Save button on the Standard toolbar to save the workbook with the new print settings.

(continued)

College Cash Flow Analysis Worksheet *(continued)*

After reviewing the numbers, you realize you need to increase manually each of the Junior-year expenses in column D by $600. Manually change the Junior-year expenses to reflect this change. Manually change the financial aid for the Junior year by the amount required to cover the increase in expenses. The totals in cells F9 and F17 should equal $60,084.30. Print the worksheet. Close the workbook without saving changes. Hand in the two printouts to your instructor.

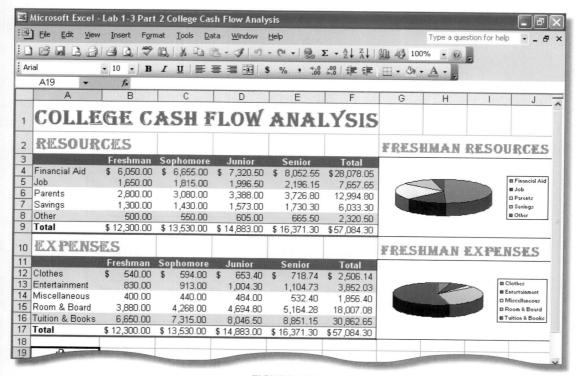

FIGURE 1-84

Instructions Part 2: Open the workbook Lab 1-3 Part 1 College Cash Flow Analysis. Draw a 3-D Pie chart in the range G3:J9 to show the contribution of each category of resources for the Freshman year. Chart the range A4:B8. Add the Pie chart title as shown in cell G2 in Figure 1-84. Draw a 3-D Pie chart in the range G11:J17 to show the contribution of each category of expenses for the Freshman year. Chart the range A12:B16. Add the Pie chart title shown in cell G10 in Figure 1-84. Save the workbook using the file name, Lab 1-3 Part 2 College Cash Flow Analysis. Print the worksheet. Hand in the printout to your instructor.

Instructions Part 3: Open the workbook Lab 1-3 Part 2 College Cash Flow Analysis. A close inspection of Table 1-10 on the previous page shows that both expenses and resources increase 10% each year. Use the Type a question for help box on the menu bar to learn how to enter the data for the last three years using a formula and the Copy command. For example, the formula to enter in cell C4 is =B4 * 1.1. Enter formulas to replace all the numbers in the range C4:E8 and C12:E16. If necessary, reformat the tables using the autoformats, as described in Part 1. The worksheet should appear as shown in Figure 1-84. Save the worksheet using the file name, Lab 1-3 Part 3 College Cash Flow Analysis. Print the worksheet. Press CTRL+ACCENT MARK(`) to display the formulas. Print the formulas version. Close the workbook without saving changes. Hand in both printouts to your instructor.

Cases and Places

The difficulty of these case studies varies:
▣ are the least difficult and ▣▣ are more difficult. The last exercise is a group exercise.

1 ▣ You are employed by the Reggae Music Company. Your manager has asked you to prepare a worksheet to help her analyze monthly sales by store and by type of reggae music (Table 1-11). Use the concepts and techniques presented in this project to create the worksheet and an embedded Clustered bar chart with a 3-D visual effect.

Table 1-11	Reggae Music Company Monthly Sales			
	Boston	**Kansas City**	**Portland**	**San Diego**
Dancehall	6734	7821	4123	7989
Dub	5423	2134	6574	3401
Dub Poetry	3495	6291	7345	7098
Lovers Rock	6789	4523	9102	7812
Ragga	8920	9812	5637	3456
Rocksteady	2134	2190	3401	2347
Ska	5462	2923	8034	5135

2 ▣ To estimate the funds you need to make it through the upcoming year, you decide to create a personal budget itemizing your expected quarterly expenses. The anticipated expenses are listed in Table 1-12. Use the concepts and techniques presented in this project to create the worksheet and an embedded 100% Stacked column chart with a conical shape that compares the quarterly cost of each expense. If necessary, reduce the size of the font in the chart so that each expense category name appears on the horizontal axis (x-axis). Use the AutoCalculate area to determine the average amount spent per quarter on each expense. Manually insert the averages with appropriate titles in an empty area on the worksheet.

Table 1-12	Quarterly Personal Budget			
	Jan – Mar	**April – June**	**July – Sept**	**Oct – Dec**
Mortgage	1500	1500	1500	1500
Food	900	950	950	1000
Car & Ins.	600	600	600	600
Clothes	567	433	200	459
Utilities	600	400	400	550
Miscellaneous	149	121	159	349

Cases and Places

3 The Magic Theater is a movie house that shows movies at weekday evening, weekend matinee, and weekend evening screenings. Three types of tickets are sold at each presentation: general admission, senior citizen, and children. The theater management has asked you to prepare a worksheet, based on the revenue from a typical week, that can be used to reevaluate its ticket structure. During an average week, weekday evening shows generate $7,250 from general admission ticket sales, $6,715 from senior citizen ticket sales, and $1,575 from children ticket sales. Weekend matinee shows make $6,723 from general admission ticket sales, $2,050 from senior citizen ticket sales, and $2,875 from children ticket sales. Weekend evening shows earn $9,415 from general admission ticket sales, $9,815 from senior citizen ticket sales, and $1,235 from children ticket sales. Use the concepts and techniques presented in this project to prepare a worksheet that includes total revenues for each type of ticket and for each presentation time, and a Clustered Bar chart illustrating ticket revenues.

4 Jasmine's Floral Shop on Michigan Avenue in Chicago sells floral arrangments to an exclusive clientele. The company is trying to decide whether it is feasible to open another boutique in the Chicago area. You have been asked to develop a worksheet totaling all the revenue received last year from customers living in the Chicago area. The revenue from customers living in the Chicago area by quarter is: Quarter 1, $221,565.56; Quarter 2, $182,704.34; Quarter 3, $334,116.31; and Quarter 4, $421,333.50. Create a Pie chart with a 3-D visual effect to illustrate Chicago-area revenue contribution by quarter. Use the AutoCalculate area to find the average, maximum, and minimum quarterly revenue and manually enter them and their corresponding identifiers in an empty area on the worksheet.

5 **Working Together** Visit the Registrar's office at your school and obtain data, such as age, gender, and resident status, for the students majoring in at least five different academic departments this semester. Have each member of your team divide the data into different categories. For example, separate the data by:

1. Age, divided into four different age groups
2. Gender, divided into male and female
3. Resident status, divided into resident and nonresident

After coordinating the data as a group, have each member independently use the concepts and techniques presented in this project to create a worksheet and appropriate chart to show the total students by characteristics by academic department. As a group, critique each worksheet and have each member re-do his or her worksheet based on the group recommendations. Hand in printouts of your original worksheet and final worksheet.

More About

Rotating Text in a Cell

In Excel, you use the Alignment sheet of the Format Cells dialog box, as shown in Figure 3-5 on the next page, to position data in a cell by centering, left-aligning, or right-aligning; indenting; aligning at the top, bottom, or center; and rotating. If you enter 90 in the Degrees box in the Orientation area, the text will appear vertically and read from bottom to top in the cell.

Rotating Text and Using the Fill Handle to Create a Series

When you first enter text, its angle is zero degrees (0°), and it reads from left to right in a cell. Text in a cell can be rotated counterclockwise by entering a number between 1° and 90° on the Alignment sheet in the Format Cells dialog box.

Projects 1 and 2 used the fill handle to copy a cell or a range of cells to adjacent cells. The fill handle also can be used to create a series of numbers, dates, or month names automatically. The following steps illustrate how to enter the month name, July, in cell B3; format cell B3 (including rotating the text); and then use the fill handle to enter the remaining month names in the range C3:G3.

To Rotate Text and Use the Fill Handle to Create a Series of Month Names

1

- **Select cell B3.**

- **Type** July **as the cell entry and then click the Enter box.**

- **Click the Font Size box arrow on the Formatting toolbar and then click 11 in the Font Size list.**

- **Click the Borders button arrow on the Formatting toolbar and then click the Bottom Border button (column 2, row 1) on the Borders palette.**

- **Right-click cell B3.**

Excel displays the text, July, in cell B3 using the assigned formats and it displays the shortcut menu (Figure 3-4).

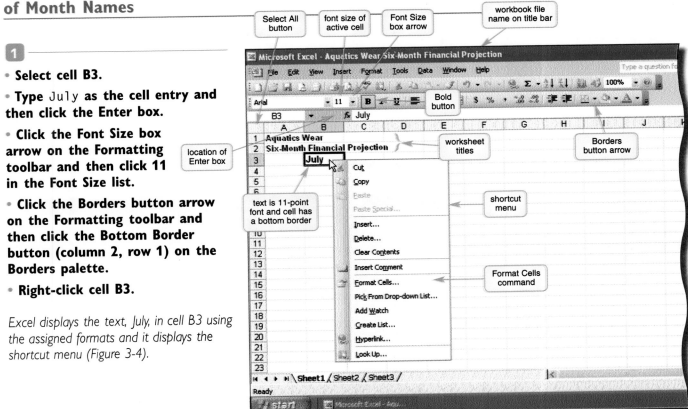

FIGURE 3-4

2

• **Click Format Cells on the shortcut menu.**

• **When the Format Cells dialog box is displayed, click the Alignment tab.**

• **Click the 45° point in the Orientation area.**

Excel displays the Alignment sheet in the Format Cells dialog box. The Text hand in the Orientation area points to the 45° point and 45 appears in the Degrees box (Figure 3-5).

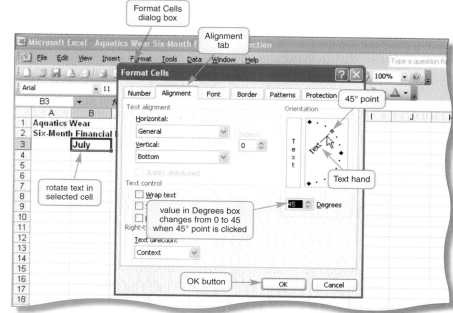

FIGURE 3-5

3

• **Click the OK button.**

• **Point to the fill handle on the lower-right corner of cell B3.**

Excel displays the text, July, in cell B3 at a 45° angle and automatically increases the height of row 3 to best fit the rotated text (Figure 3-6). The mouse pointer changes to a crosshair.

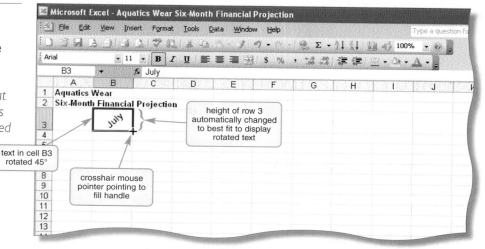

FIGURE 3-6

4

• **Drag the fill handle to the right to select the range C3:G3. Do not release the mouse button.**

Excel displays a light border that surrounds the selected range and a ScreenTip indicating the month of the last cell in the selected range (Figure 3-7).

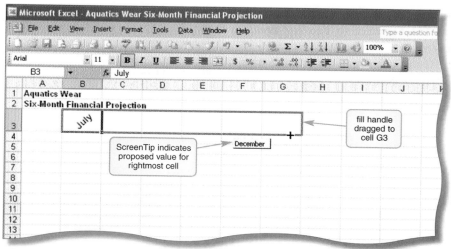

FIGURE 3-7

5

• **Release the mouse button.**

• **Click the Auto Fill Options button below the lower-right corner of the fill area.**

Using July in cell B3 as the basis, Excel creates the month name series August through December in the range C3:G3 (Figure 3-8). The formats assigned to cell B3 earlier in the previous steps (11-point font, bottom border, and text rotated 45°) also are copied to the range C3:G3. The Auto Fill Options menu shows the available fill options.

6

• **Click the Auto Fill Options button to hide the Auto Fill Options menu.**

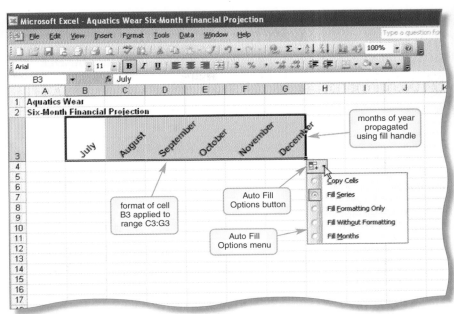

FIGURE 3-8

Other Ways

1. Enter start month in cell, right-drag fill handle in direction to fill, click Fill Months on shortcut menu
2. Select range to fill, in Voice Command mode, say "Edit, Fill, Series, AutoFill"

In addition to creating a series of values, dragging the fill handle instructs Excel to copy the format of cell B3 to the range C3:G3. With some fill operations, you may not want to copy the formats of the source cell or range to the destination cell or range. If this is the case, click the Auto Fill Options button after the range fills (Figure 3-8) and then select the option you desire on the Auto Fill Options menu. As shown in Figure 3-8, Fill Series is the default option that Excel uses to fill the area, which means it fills the destination area with a series, using the same formatting as the source area. If you choose another option on the Auto Fill Options menu, then Excel immediately changes the contents of the destination range. Following the use of the fill handle, the Auto Fill Options button remains active until you begin the next Excel operation. Table 3-2 summarizes the options on the Auto Fill Options menu.

You can use the fill handle to create a series longer than the one shown in Figure 3-8. If you drag the fill handle past cell G3 in Step 4, Excel continues to increment the months and logically will repeat July, August, and so on, if you extend the range far enough to the right.

You can create several different types of series using the fill handle. Table 3-3 on the next page illustrates several examples. Notice in examples 4 through 7 that, if you use the fill handle to create a series of numbers or non-sequential months, you must enter the first item in the series in one cell and the second item in the series in an adjacent cell. Next, select both cells and drag the fill handle through the destination area.

Table 3-2	Options Available on the Auto Fill Options Menu
AUTO FILL OPTION	**DESCRIPTION**
Copy Cells	Fill destination area with contents using format of source area. Do not create a series.
Fill Series	Fill destination area with series using format of source area. This option is the default.
Fill Formatting Only	Fill destination area using format of source area. No content is copied unless fill is series.
Fill Without Formatting	Fill destination area with contents, without the formatting of source area.
Fill Months	Fill destination area with series of months using format of source area. Same as Fill Series and shows as an option only if source area contains a month.

More About

The Mighty Fill Handle

If you drag the fill handle to the left or up, Excel will decrement the series rather than increment the series. To copy a word, such as January or Monday, which Excel might interpret as the start of a series, hold down the CTRL key while you drag the fill handle to a destination area. If you drag the fill handle back into the middle of a cell, Excel erases the contents.

Table 3-3   Examples of Series Using the Fill Handle

EXAMPLE	CONTENTS OF CELL(S) COPIED USING THE FILL HANDLE	NEXT THREE VALUES OF EXTENDED SERIES
1	2:00	3:00, 4:00, 5:00
2	Qtr3	Qtr4, Qtr1, Qtr2
3	Quarter 1	Quarter 2, Quarter 3, Quarter 4
4	5-Jan, 5-Mar	5-May, 5-Jul, 5-Sep
5	2005, 2006	2007, 2008, 2009
6	1, 2	3, 4, 5
7	430, 410	390, 370, 350
8	Sun	Mon, Tue, Wed
9	Sunday, Tuesday	Thursday, Saturday, Monday
10	4th Section	5th Section, 6th Section, 7th Section
11	-205, -208	-211, -214, -217

More About

Painting a Format to Nonadjacent Ranges

Double-click the Format Painter button on the Standard toolbar and then drag through the nonadjacent ranges to paint the formats to the ranges. Click the Format Painter button to deactivate it.

Copying a Cell's Format Using the Format Painter Button

Because the last column title, Total, is not part of the series, it must be entered separately in cell H3 and formatted to match the other column titles. Imagine how many steps it would take, however, to assign the formatting of the other column titles to this cell — first, you have to change the font to 11 point, and then add a bottom border, and finally, rotate the text 45°. Using the Format Painter button on the Standard toolbar, however, you can format a cell quickly by copying a cell's format to another cell. The following steps enter the column title, Total, in cell H3 and format the cell using the Format Painter button.

To Copy a Cell's Format Using the Format Painter Button

1

• **Click cell H3.**

• **Type** Total **and then press the LEFT ARROW key.**

• **With cell G3 selected, click the Format Painter button on the Standard toolbar.**

• **Point to cell H3.**

The mouse pointer changes to a block plus sign with a paint brush (Figure 3-9).

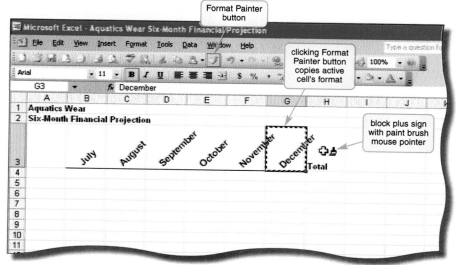

FIGURE 3-9

2

- **Click cell H3 to assign the format of cell G3 to cell H3.**
- **Click cell A4.**

Excel copies the format of cell G3 (11-point font, bottom border, text rotated 45°) to cell H3 (Figure 3-10). Cell A4 is now the active cell.

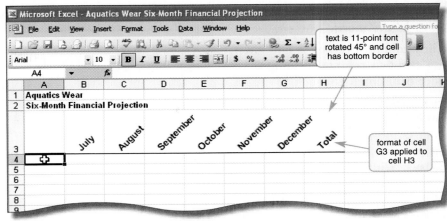

FIGURE 3-10

The Format Painter button also can be used to copy the formats of a cell to a range of cells. To copy formats to a range of cells, select the cell or range with the desired format, click the Format Painter button on the Standard toolbar, and then drag through the range to which you want to paste the formats.

Increasing the Column Widths and Indenting Row Titles

In Project 2, the column widths were increased after the values were entered into the worksheet. Sometimes, you may want to increase the column widths before you enter the values and, if necessary, adjust them later. The following steps increase the column widths and then enter the row titles in column A down to Assumptions in cell A18.

To Increase Column Widths and Enter Row Titles

1

- **Move the mouse pointer to the boundary between column heading A and column heading B so that the mouse pointer changes to a split double arrow.**

- **Drag the mouse pointer to the right until the ScreenTip displays, Width: 35.00 (250 pixels). Do not release the mouse button.**

The distance between the left edge of column A and the vertical dotted line below the mouse pointer shows the proposed column width (Figure 3-11). The ScreenTip displays the proposed width in points and pixels.

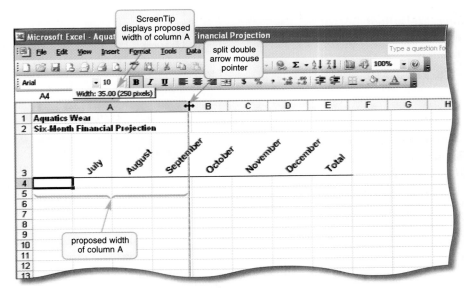

FIGURE 3-11

149

2

• **Release the mouse button.**

• **Click column heading B and then drag through column heading G to select columns B through G.**

• **Move the mouse pointer to the boundary between column headings B and C and then drag the mouse to the right until the ScreenTip displays, Width: 14.00 (103 pixels). Do not release the mouse button.**

The distance between the left edge of column B and the vertical line below the mouse pointer shows the proposed width of columns B through G (Figure 3-12). The ScreenTip displays the proposed width in points and pixels.

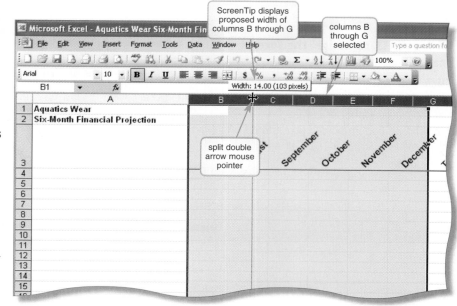

FIGURE 3-12

3

• **Release the mouse button.**

• **Use the technique described in Step 1 to increase the width of column H to 15.00.**

• **Enter the row titles in the range A4:A18 as shown in Figure 3-13, but without the indents.**

• **Click cell A5 and then click the Increase Indent button on the Formatting toolbar.**

• **Select the range A9:A13 and then click the Increase Indent button on the Formatting toolbar.**

• **Click cell A19.**

Excel displays the row titles as shown in Figure 3-13.

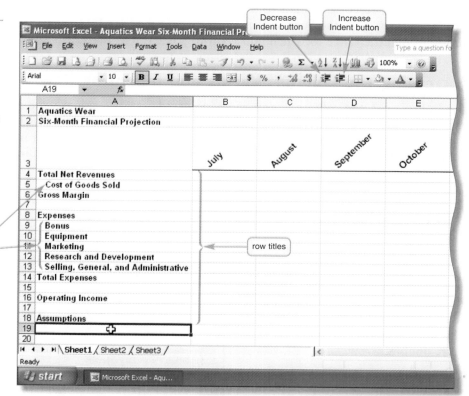

FIGURE 3-13

The Increase Indent button indents the contents of a cell to the right by three spaces each time you click it. The Decrease Indent button decreases the indent by three spaces each time you click it.

Copying a Range of Cells to a Nonadjacent Destination Area

As shown in the sketch of the worksheet (Figure 3-3a on page EX 149), the row titles in the range A9:A13 are the same as the row titles in the Assumptions table in the range A19:A25, with the exception of the two additional entries in cells A21 (Margin) and A24 (Revenue for Bonus). Hence, the Assumptions table row titles can be created by copying the range A9:A13 to the range A19:A23 and then inserting two rows for the additional entries in cells A21 and A24. The source area (range A9:A13) is not adjacent to the destination area (range A19:A23). The first two projects used the fill handle to copy a source area to an adjacent destination area. To copy a source area to a nonadjacent destination area, however, you cannot use the fill handle.

A more versatile method of copying a source area is to use the Copy button and Paste button on the Standard toolbar. You can use these two buttons to copy a source area to an adjacent or nonadjacent destination area.

The Copy button copies the contents and format of the source area to the **Office Clipboard**, a special place in the computer's memory that allows you to collect text and graphic items from an Office document and then paste them into any Office document. The Copy command on the Edit menu or shortcut menu works the same as the Copy button. The Paste button copies the item from the Office Clipboard to the destination area. The Paste command on the Edit menu or shortcut menu works the same as the Paste button.

The following steps use the Copy and Paste buttons to copy the range A9:A13 to the nonadjacent range A19:A23.

More About

Fitting Entries in a Cell

An alternative to increasing the column widths or row heights is to shrink the characters in the cell to fit the current width of the column. To shrink to fit, click Format on the menu bar, click Cells on the Format menu, click the Alignment tab, and click Shrink to fit in the Text control area. After shrinking entries to fit in a cell, consider using the Zoom box on the Standard toolbar to make the entries more readable.

Q&A

Q: Can you copy a range of cells from one workbook to another workbook?

A: Yes. You can copy a range of cells from one workbook to another by opening the source workbook, selecting the range, clicking the Copy button to place the range of cells on the Office Clipboard, activating the destination workbook, selecting the destination area, and then clicking the Paste button.

To Copy a Range of Cells to a Nonadjacent Destination Area

1

- **Select the range A9:A13 and then click the Copy button on the Standard toolbar.**

- **Click cell A19, the top cell in the destination area.**

Excel surrounds the source area A9:A13 with a marquee (Figure 3-14). Excel also copies the values and formats of the range A9:A13 to the Office Clipboard.

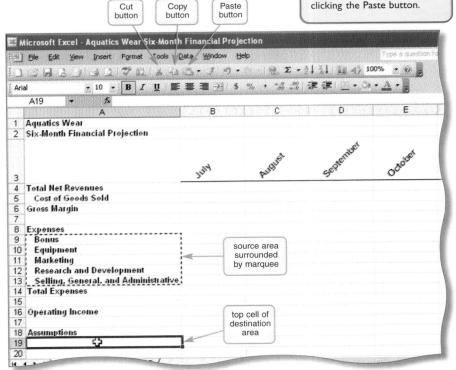

FIGURE 3-14

2

- **Click the Paste button on the Standard toolbar.**
- **Scroll down so row 5 appears at the top of the window.**

Excel copies the values and formats of the last item placed on the Office Clipboard (range A9:A13) to the destination area A19:A23 (Figure 3-15). The Paste Options button appears.

3

- **Press the ESC key.**

Excel removes the marquee from the source area and disables the Paste button on the Standard toolbar.

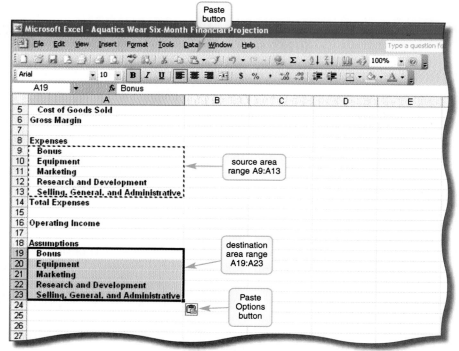

FIGURE 3-15

As shown in Step 1 and Figure 3-14 on the previous page, you are not required to select the entire destination area (range A19:A23) before clicking the Paste button. Excel only needs to know the upper-left cell of the destination area. In the case of a single column range, such as A19:A23, the top cell of the destination area (cell A19) also is the upper-left cell of the destination area.

When you complete a copy, the values and formats in the destination area are replaced with the values and formats of the source area. Any data contained in the destination area prior to the copy and paste is lost. If you accidentally delete valuable data, immediately click the Undo button on the Standard toolbar or click the Undo Paste command on the Edit menu to undo the paste.

After the Paste button is clicked, Excel immediately displays the Paste Options button, as shown in Figure 3-15. If you click the Paste Options button arrow and select an option on the Paste Options menu, Excel modifies the most recent paste operation based on your selection. Table 3-4 summarizes the options available on the Paste Options menu.

Table 3-4 Options Available on the Paste Options Menu	
PASTE OPTION	**DESCRIPTION**
Keep Source Formatting	Copy contents and format of source area. This option is the default.
Match Destination Formatting	Copy contents of source area, but not the format.
Values and Numbers Formatting	Copy contents and format of source area for numbers or formulas, but use format of destination area for text.
Keep Source Column Widths	Copy contents and format of source area. Change destination column widths to source column widths.
Formatting Only	Copy format of source area, but not the contents.
Link Cells	Copy contents and format and link cells so that a change to the cells in source area updates the corresponding cells in destination area.

The Paste button on the Standard toolbar (Figure 3-15) includes an arrow, which displays a list of advanced paste options (Formulas, Values, No Borders, Transpose, Paste Link, and Paste Special). These options will be discussed when they are used.

An alternative to clicking the Paste button is to press the ENTER key. The ENTER key completes the paste operation, removes the marquee from the source area, and disables the Paste button so that you cannot paste the copied source area to other destination areas. The ENTER key was not used in the previous set of steps so that the capabilities of the Paste Options button could be discussed. The Paste Options button does not appear on the screen when you use the ENTER key to complete the paste operation.

As previously indicated, the Office Clipboard allows you to collect text and graphic items from an Office document and then paste them into any Office document. You can use the Office Clipboard to collect up to 24 different items. To collect multiple items, you first must display the Clipboard task pane by clicking Office Clipboard on the Edit menu. If you want to paste an item on the Office Clipboard into a document, such as a spreadsheet, click the icon representing the item in the Clipboard task pane.

Using Drag and Drop to Move or Copy Cells

You also can use the mouse to move or copy cells. First, you select the source area and point to the border of the cell or range. You know you are pointing to the border of the cell or range when the mouse pointer changes to a block arrow. To move the selected cell or cells, drag the selection to the destination area. To copy a selection, hold down the CTRL key while dragging the selection to the destination area. You know Excel is in copy mode when a small plus sign appears next to the block arrow mouse pointer. Be sure to release the mouse button before you release the CTRL key. Using the mouse to move or copy cells is called **drag and drop**.

Using Cut and Paste to Move or Copy Cells

Another way to move cells is to select them, click the Cut button on the Standard toolbar (Figure 3-14 on page EX 157) to remove them from the worksheet and copy them to the Office Clipboard, select the destination area, and then click the Paste button on the Standard toolbar or press the ENTER key. You also can use the Cut command on the Edit menu or shortcut menu, instead of the Cut button.

Inserting and Deleting Cells in a Worksheet

At anytime while the worksheet is on the screen, you can insert cells to enter new data or delete cells to remove unwanted data. You can insert or delete individual cells, a range of cells, entire rows, entire columns, or entire worksheets.

Inserting Rows

The Rows command on the Insert menu or the Insert command on the shortcut menu allows you to insert rows between rows that already contain data. According to the sketch of the worksheet in Figure 3-3a on page EX 149, two rows must be inserted in the Assumptions table, one between rows 20 and 21 for the Margin assumption and another between rows 22 and 23 for the Revenue for Bonus assumption. The steps on the next page show how to accomplish the task of inserting the new rows into the worksheet.

<aside>
More About

Move It or Copy It

You may hear someone say, "move it or copy it, it's all the same." No, it is not the same! When you move a cell, the data in the original location is cleared and the format is reset to the default. When you copy a cell, the data and format of the copy area remains intact. In short, you should copy cells to duplicate entries and move cells to rearrange entries.
</aside>

<aside>

Training 3-1

To practice the following tasks, launch the SAM Training Companion CD, choose Excel Project 3, and then choose Training 3-1:
• Copy cells
• Indent text
• Move cells
• Rotate text
• Use the fill handle to create a series
</aside>

To Insert a Row

1

• **Right-click row heading 21, the row below where you want to insert a row.**

Excel highlights row 21 and displays the shortcut menu (Figure 3-16).

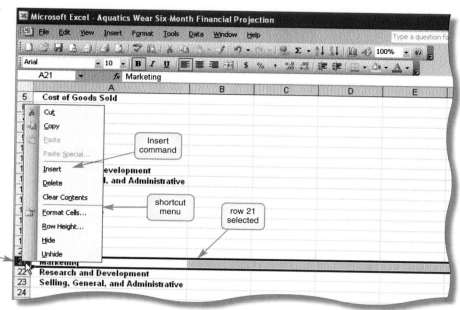

FIGURE 3-16

2

• **Click Insert on the shortcut menu.**

• **Click cell A21 in the new row and then enter** Margin **as the row title.**

Excel inserts a new row in the worksheet by shifting the selected row 21 and all rows below it down one row (Figure 3-17). Excel displays the new row title in cell A21. The cells in the new row inherit the formats of the cells in the row above them.

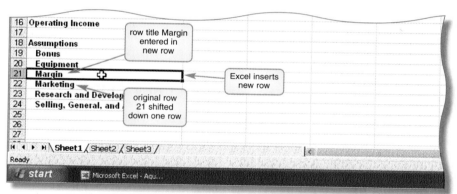

FIGURE 3-17

3

• **Right-click row heading 24 and then click Insert on the shortcut menu.**

• **Click cell A24 in the new row and then enter** Revenue for Bonus **as the row title.**

Excel inserts a new row in the worksheet and displays the new row title in cell A24 (Figure 3-18).

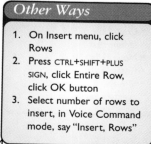

Other Ways

1. On Insert menu, click Rows
2. Press CTRL+SHIFT+PLUS SIGN, click Entire Row, click OK button
3. Select number of rows to insert, in Voice Command mode, say "Insert, Rows"

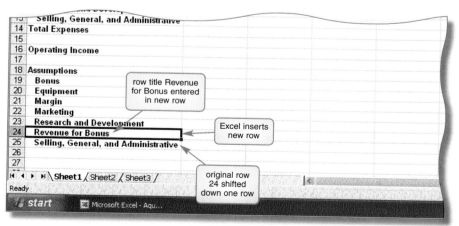

FIGURE 3-18

To insert multiple adjacent rows, first select as many rows as you want to insert by dragging through the row headings immediately below where you want the new rows inserted before invoking the Insert command.

When you insert a row, it inherits the format of the row above it. You can change this by clicking the Insert Options button that appears immediately above the inserted row. Following the insertion of a row, the Insert Options button lets you select from the following options: (1) Format Same As Above; (2) Format Same As Below; and (3) Clear Formatting. The Format Same as Above option is the default. The Insert Options button remains active until you begin the next Excel operation.

If the rows that are shifted down include cell references in formulas located in the worksheet, Excel automatically adjusts the cell references in the formulas to their new locations. Thus, in Step 2 in the previous steps, if a formula in the worksheet references a cell in row 21 before the insert, then the cell reference in the formula is adjusted to row 22 after the insert.

The primary difference between the Insert command on the shortcut menu and the Rows command on the Insert menu is that the Insert command on the shortcut menu requires that you select an entire row (or rows) in order to insert a row (or rows). The Rows command on the Insert menu requires that you select a single cell in a row to insert one row or a range of cells to insert multiple rows.

Inserting Columns

You insert columns into a worksheet in the same way you insert rows. To insert columns, select one or more columns immediately to the right of where you want Excel to insert the new column or columns. Select the number of columns you want to insert. Next, click Columns on the Insert menu or click Insert on the shortcut menu. The primary difference between these two commands is this: The Columns command on the Insert menu requires that you select a single cell in a column to insert one column or a range of cells to insert multiple columns. The Insert command on the shortcut menu, however, requires that you select an entire column (or columns) to insert a column (or columns). Following the insertion of a column, Excel displays the Insert Options button, which allows you to modify the insertion in a fashion similar to that discussed earlier when inserting rows.

Inserting Single Cells or a Range of Cells

The Insert command on the shortcut menu or the Cells command on the Insert menu allows you to insert a single cell or a range of cells. You should be aware that if you shift a single cell or a range of cells, however, it no longer may be lined up with its associated cells. To ensure that the values in the worksheet do not get out of order, it is recommended that you insert only entire rows or entire columns. When you insert a single cell or a range of cells, Excel displays the Insert Options button so that you can change the format of the inserted cell, using options similar to those for inserting rows and columns.

Deleting Columns and Rows

The Delete command on the Edit menu or shortcut menu removes cells (including the data and format) from the worksheet. Deleting cells is not the same as clearing cells. The Clear command, which was described earlier in Project 1 on page EX 52, clears the data from the cells, but the cells remain in the worksheet. The Delete command removes the cells from the worksheet and shifts the remaining

---

More About

Inserting Multiple Rows

If you want to insert multiple rows, you have two choices. First, you can insert a single row by using the Insert command on the shortcut menu and then repeatedly press F4 to keep inserting rows. Alternatively, you can select any number of existing rows before inserting new rows. For instance, if you want to insert five rows, select five existing rows in the worksheet, right-click the rows, and then click Insert on the shortcut menu.

More About

Dragging Ranges

You can move and insert a selected cell or range between existing cells by holding down the SHIFT key while you drag the selection to the gridline where you want to insert. You also can copy and insert by holding down the CTRL+SHIFT keys while you drag the selection to the desired gridline.

More About

The Insert Options Button

When you insert columns or rows, Excel only displays the Insert Options button if formats are assigned to the leftmost column or top row of the selection.

rows up (when you delete rows) or shifts the remaining columns to the left (when you delete columns). If formulas located in other cells reference cells in the deleted row or column, Excel does not adjust these cell references. Excel displays the error message **#REF!** in those cells to indicate a cell reference error. For example, if cell A7 contains the formula =A4+A5 and you delete row 5, Excel assigns the formula =A4+#REF! to cell A6 (originally cell A7) and displays the error message #REF! in cell A6. It also displays an Error Options button when you select the cell containing the error message #REF!, which allows you to select options to determine the nature of the problem.

Deleting Individual Cells or a Range of Cells

Although Excel allows you to delete an individual cell or range of cells, you should be aware that if you shift a cell or range of cells on the worksheet, it no longer may be lined up with its associated cells. For this reason, it is recommended that you delete only entire rows or entire columns.

Introduction to Problem Solving and Decision Making with Microsoft Office Excel 2003

"We are continuously faced by great opportunities brilliantly disguised as insoluble problems."
—Lee Iacocca

LEARNING OBJECTIVES

Understand concepts related to problem solving and decision making

Identify the different steps in the problem-solving process

Explain the role Excel can play in problem solving and decision making

Describe how problem solving will be presented in this text

ABOUT THIS BOOK AND MICROSOFT OFFICE EXCEL 2003

Traditional study of computer applications has mostly involved acquiring skills related to an application's features and functions. Although this approach is important in teaching the mechanics required to perform certain tasks, it does not address *when* a particular tool is most appropriate or *how* it should best be utilized in solving a specific problem.

This book focuses on learning how to solve problems using Microsoft Office Excel 2003, although the concepts and tasks presented could apply to a variety of computer applications and programming languages. Excel is widely used in business as a tool for solving problems and supporting decision making. There are two perceptions of Excel to consider: one is that Excel is the obvious extension of the desktop calculator into the personal computer; the other is that Excel is a powerful tool for the manipulation and analysis of data. Data is usually analyzed to provide support for whether or not to take some course of action—a decision. Not all decisions require a spreadsheet for analysis, but many of the complexities faced in business are made simpler and easier to understand when a tool like Excel is employed properly. This book will help you learn what kinds of problems are best solved using spreadsheets and how to solve them, but for in-depth exploration of effective decision making, further study is recommended. One of the main goals of this book is that you will "learn how to learn," becoming confident in your own ability to explore new Excel features and tools to solve problems and support your decisions.

When working with Excel, using the correct tools can greatly increase your ability to deal not only with the immediate problem presented, but also with the inevitable "what-if" analyses. One example of how an organization might perform "what-if" analysis is with a financial model of its business in a spreadsheet. The model summarizes various pieces of financial data to determine information such as assets, liabilities, sales, and profitability—creating a representation of the organization in the spreadsheet. In this example, the spreadsheet could be used to evaluate "what" would happen "if":

- The organization cut sale prices by 5%.
- The sales volume increased by 10%.
- The organization improved its inventory turnover by 8%.
- The organization issued $1,000,000 in bonds.

Using a spreadsheet allows the organization to quickly change various inputs (think of these as independent variables in a mathematical equation) and see what happens to the outputs (think of these as dependent variables in a mathematical equation). Many organizations spend hundreds of hours building models in spreadsheets. Of course, a model is limited by the detail and quality of the data used to build it.

One of the benefits of using a spreadsheet lies in the ability to quickly revise and update the data and mathematical formulas used to generate the answers or results. Consider the typewriter; it provides just as much productive value as a word-processing program until you need to revise what you are writing. Easy revision and calculation are important features of Excel, but its power as a decision-making tool is what moves it far beyond paper and pencil. "What-if" analysis is often a key element in the decision-making process, allowing decision makers to see the impact of changes to their businesses. This type of analysis is extremely valuable, because the only sure thing in business today is that nothing will stay the same.

THE RELATIONSHIP BETWEEN PROBLEM SOLVING AND DECISION MAKING

In his book, *Management Challenges for the 21st Century*, Peter Drucker states the following:

> The most important, and indeed the truly unique, contribution of management in the 20th century was the fifty-fold increase in the productivity of the "manual worker" in manufacturing. The most important contribution management needs to make in the 21st century is similarly to increase the productivity of "knowledge work" and the "knowledge worker." The most valuable assets of a 20th-century company were its production equipment. The most valuable asset of a 21st-century institution, whether business or non-business, will be its knowledge workers and their productivity.

Knowledge workers are those people who work with and develop knowledge. Data and information are their raw material. Knowledge workers use this raw material to analyze a particular situation and evaluate a course of action. As a reader of this text, you are most likely a knowledge worker or trying to become one. The rise of the knowledge worker over the last century has followed a corresponding rise in the value of information in business and society. More knowledge and information are readily available now than at any other time in history.

Information Overload

So, how much information is created every year? According to a study by Peter Lyman and Hal Varian, researchers at the University of California, Berkeley, "Print, film, magnetic, and optical storage media produced about 5 exabytes of new information in 2002. Ninety-two percent of the new information was stored on magnetic media, mostly in hard disks." This figure was roughly double the amount of information created in 1999, the first year the pair looked at this issue, and will surely continue to grow. The amount of information generated was so large that a new term, the exabyte, was coined to describe it. An exabyte is the equivalent of 1,000,000 terabytes. A terabyte is the equivalent of 1000 gigabytes. Five exabytes of information is equivalent in size to the information contained in 37,000 new libraries the size of the Library of Congress, which has the largest book collection in the world.

What is information and where does it come from? The term "information" can mean many things to different people. For the purpose of this discussion, **information** is defined as data that is organized in some meaningful way. **Data** can be words, images, numbers or even sounds. Using data to make decisions depends on an organization's ability to collect, organize, and otherwise transform data into information that can be used to support those decisions—a process more commonly referred to as **analysis**.

The amount of information available can overwhelm or overload many decision makers as they try to determine which sets of data/information are important, and which should be ignored. The result is a complex world in which decision makers can no longer rely on intuition and back-of-the-envelope calculations to make effective decisions; they need tools that support decision making and help them to solve problems.

Which Comes First: The Problem or the Decision?

You have been trained since grade school to solve problems. These problems start with simple addition and subtraction, and then move to multiplication and division. You might start by counting on your fingers, and then learn to become a "human calculator" by memorizing multiplication tables. These are skills you use everyday to solve simple problems, such as dividing the lunch bill and figuring out the tip. These problems result from the need to make a decision. Do you want to pick up the entire lunch tab? If not, you need to figure out what each person owes.

Decision making and problem solving are interrelated—two sides of the same coin. **Decision making** is simply making up your mind about something. A **problem** can be thought of in two ways: as a question to be answered, or as an obstacle or difficulty that prevents you from reaching some goal. So, which comes first; the problem or the need to make a decision? It depends. You might be presented with a decision that requires certain questions or problems be answered before the decision can be made. Or, you might encounter an obstacle or problem that requires decisions be made in order to move forward. The complexity of the situation determines the number of problems requiring solutions and decisions that have to be made. Thus, problem solving and decision making are interrelated.

The complexity of decision making in today's business world often requires that a great deal of time be spent considering the available options and what their potential outcomes will be. To do this well, you need to learn some new skills. Specifically, you need to learn how to use applications that can support your decision making. In technical terms, this type of application is referred to as a **decision support system**, or DSS. Decision making utilizing computer models is part of a larger concept of decision support systems that can encompass a variety of diverse topics, such as management science, decision theory, mathematical modeling, operations management, artificial intelligence, cognitive science, psychology, database management, and others. This text focuses on how to use Excel as a decision support tool and shows you that a spreadsheet is far more than a sophisticated calculator; it is used extensively at the highest level of decision making.

Problem solving in Excel has a numbers-oriented, or quantitative, basis. These problems can be expressed in numerical terms. Although Excel can be a powerful tool to manipulate text, especially in lists (as you will see in a later chapter), it is strongest in *quantitative* analysis. But decisions are rarely based solely on numbers. There is a more subjective, or *qualitative*, side that is hard to put into numerical terms, but which can determine the success or failure of any implementation. Consider outsourcing as an example. Outsourcing is the action of obtaining a product, component, or service from an outside supplier instead of making or doing it in-house. The quantitative basis for such a decision revolves around comparing the costs and benefits of each alternative. The qualitative factors that need to be considered include the supplier's reputation for quality and performance, as well as how much effort would be required to integrate the supplier into the organization's business processes. Regardless of the quantitative or qualitative nature of the situation, the interrelationship of problem solving and decision making will continue.

A PROBLEM-SOLVING PROCESS

Problem solving is, of course, the process used to find a solution to a given problem. But how do you know what the problem is in the first place? As mentioned earlier, a problem can be thought of as something that keeps you from achieving your goals. Usually it is the result of some sort of stoppage or obstacle—something that gets in the way of your progress, and you need to figure out a way to deal with it.

There are probably as many problem-solving approaches as there are problems. Figure 1 illustrates a general model of a problem-solving process, consisting of three main phases—Problem Recognition, Problem Statement, and Solution—with detailed analysis activities occurring to move from one phase to the next.

Figure 1: General model of a problem-solving process

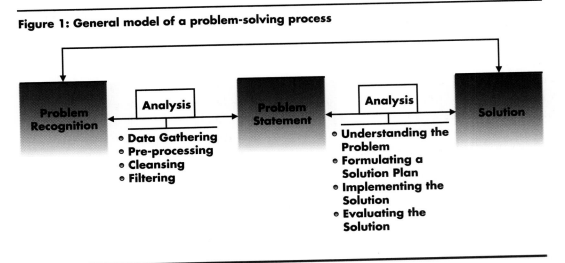

Problem Recognition

The first step in solving a problem is to recognize what the problem is or even if any problem exists. Once a problem is recognized, it needs to be described and analyzed further.

So, how do you make sense of all the information around you when faced with a problem to solve? Every day, people are presented with information that they must process in order to function in their personal and professional lives. In the morning, you might use the weather report in the paper, on the radio, or on television to guide you on how to dress for the day. Should you wear a coat, add a sweater, or even carry an umbrella? You can rely on carefully calculated weather data indicating there is a 60% chance of rain that day, or you could look at the sky and decide based on your intuition and experience that it might rain. Both are equally valid strategies. After all, what is the risk? You might get wet, but eventually you'll dry out.

Some decisions carry a bit more risk and might require more thought before acting. How do you think about making a decision and what role does gathering information play in that thought process? Using the previous example, most people have all the information they need to decide how to dress for the weather, based on past experiences. They don't need to gather raw data and take surveys. Many times in business, however, people don't have enough information to make a decision. Consider the example of an airline company that is deciding whether or not to enter a new market. The airline executives could make the decision based on intuition and experience, but the company's investors might be more comfortable if the decision could be justified based on market research and sound analysis by industry experts. Information is required to do any such analysis.

Analyzing the Problem

As shown in Figure 2, four analysis steps are required to move from the problem recognition phase to the problem statement phase.

Figure 2: Analyzing the problem

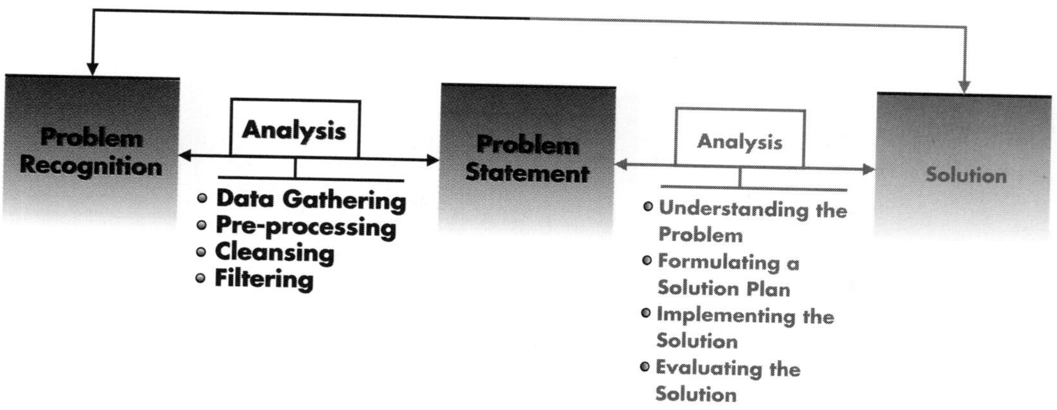

The first step in analyzing the problem is **data gathering**. Data can come from a variety of sources, such as an enterprise-wide data system or industry market analyses. Once sources have been identified, credibility, reliability and accuracy of the data should be considered. Data is rarely in exactly the right format you need and is often corrupt in some way. This brings up the next step in analysis—**pre-processing**, in which the data is manipulated into the needed format. After the format is set, you move to the **cleansing** step, in which any data corruption is identified and corrected, if possible. Corrupt data is missing some element or is incorrect in some way. Corruption can be caused by data loss due to computer problems, but is often caused by human error. The final step in analysis involves **filtering** out data that isn't useful or necessary. As you narrow your sources of data, you are beginning to transform it into information and are getting closer to being able to recognize problems that exist. Once you have firmly established the problem or problems that exist, you move to the next phase of the process: the problem statement.

Problem Statement

The problem statement can be similar to a typical math word problem found in early education. The key characteristic of any problem statement or word problem is that some missing piece of information is identified that is required to solve a problem or make a decision. Unlike many of the math word problems solved in school, today's business problems don't have the missing piece of information and the answer "in the back of the book." The problems are real, and the answers are unknown.

When you are confident that you understand the problem and can articulate the problem statement, you're ready to move toward a solution.

Solution

As illustrated in Figure 3, most problems require a minimum of four steps to move from the problem statement to a solution: understanding the problem, formulating a solution plan, implementing the solution, and evaluating the solution.

Figure 3: Analyzing the solution

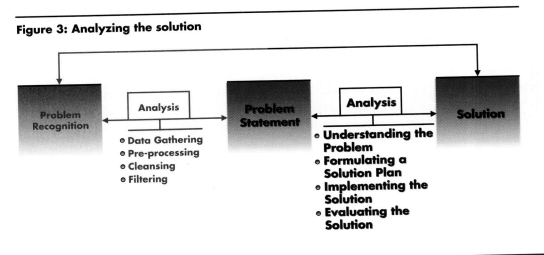

Although this process might appear to be a sequential set of tasks, it is often a reiterative process that moves back and forth through the steps. For a simple problem that you have seen many times before, these steps might require no more than a few seconds to complete, whereas more complex problems might require many hours of going back and forth formulating, implementing, and evaluating the solution.

When using Excel to solve problems, the time it takes to set up and use a spreadsheet model on the computer is often underestimated. In general, solving a problem for the first time on the computer takes at least the same amount of time as it would if you did it by hand, if not more. However, the advantage of using productivity software tools comes when dealing with more complex problems and larger amounts of data. In the same way that a lever is a tool that allows you to increase your own physical force, a spreadsheet can increase or improve your mental force. The spreadsheet can become a "thinking tool" that helps you organize and analyze data in ways that are impossible by hand. Additional benefits are gained when corrections or changes are required—and from the ability to adapt the solution to other similar problems. But in order to reap these advantages, it is important to plan your spreadsheets to take advantage of Excel's capabilities.

Understanding the Problem

Once you have recognized and defined the problem, you need to gain an understanding of what solving the problem will require. Specifically, you need to know the following:

- What data is needed and what data or information is already known?
- Is the data or information reliable and accurate?
- What is the likely range of potential solutions for the problem?
- What type of outputs are required—a single value, a table, a graph, and so on?

Consider a simple problem such as calculating the cost of a new computer system for the sales group in your company. This might take you no more than a moment to decide you need to list the price of each component and calculate a total price of the system. On the other hand, if you were asked to create a cost calculator in Excel for the sales group that would automatically retrieve the price, discount, and sales tax of a specific order, this might require hours of data gathering to determine all of the appropriate items that need to be priced, what discounts are available and how they are priced, and what sales taxes apply in which localities. You would also need to speak with the sales personnel to determine what type of output is needed—a single value or each component—and how they would use it. Would the sales personnel be able to manipulate an Excel spreadsheet, or would they need a different type of tool in which they could enter a few items and the answer would be displayed?

Formulating a Solution Plan

After you have a better understanding of the problem and its scope, you need to begin planning how you will use Excel to reach a solution. What steps will you need to take to solve the problem? Will you be performing a numerical calculation, determining if a value meets specific criteria, organizing data in a specific format, or a combination of several of these steps?

One common mistake people make is to immediately jump to a specific implementation, often worrying about how to use a particular function or tool before determining if that is the right function or tool to use. If you are unsure at all, it is always wise to ask yourself, "How would I solve this problem without a computer?" Invariably, if you think about what you need to do and define the steps you need to take, you can better surmise how to formulate a solution plan.

When considering a spreadsheet solution, you need to determine the following:

- What mathematical, logical, or organizational processes will be required?
- Will these tasks be done multiple times and, if so, will some of the calculations require looking up specific related data?
- What type of spreadsheet design will be best? How should the inputs and outputs be arranged, or "laid out"—on a single worksheet, multiple worksheets, organized by inputs and outputs, or organized by scenarios?
- What formulas and/or functions will be required to perform the necessary tasks?

Good planning can save many hours later reworking the spreadsheet. You must consider all the elements required to reach a solution and how these elements are laid out on the worksheet. An Excel worksheet can be thought of as a "smart piece of paper." You can use this paper like a scratch pad, filling it with unorganized sets of seemingly random calculations. Or, you can place your data and formulas into well-organized, easy-to-understand layouts that make it easy to evolve and refine them over time. In many ways, spreadsheet layout reflects your understanding of the problem.

As when defining a problem, formulating a solution plan can require no more than a few seconds of "unconscious" thought for a simple problem that you are familiar with, such as adding up the cost of a new computer system. But even for such a simple problem, you might develop different implementations, depending on if you are considering only one computer system or a variety of options. Creating a cost calculator for the sales group, however, might require many hours of work. First, you might consider an overall plan, and then break down the larger problem into several separate, more workable parts. For example, you might decide to break down the overall problem into the following four parts: consider the calculation of the item cost, determine how to calculate the discount, calculate the sales tax, and, finally, put together these components and create an appropriate display. Each component can then be treated as a separate sub-problem, thus breaking down what might seem like a complex task into several manageable tasks.

Implementing the Solution

At this point, you should understand the problem to be solved and how you are going to solve it. Now it's time to input the data, write the appropriate formulas, and configure the desired output. You need to know the following in order to properly implement your spreadsheet solution:

- How to correctly write formulas and functions as well as how to use the spreadsheet tools. For example, if a value is needed in several different formulas, it is best to enter the value in a cell on the spreadsheet and refer to that cell in each of the formulas. If the value changes, you can easily update the spreadsheet by changing the one cell instead of having to modify every formula that uses this value.
- How to copy repeated elements required in the solution. For example, if purchasing a computer involves the comparison of several different options, you might need to sum a single column for each option. Instead of writing a separate formula for each column, Excel provides ways for you to copy formulas that "tell" the program to use the same method of computation but change the values or to keep some values the same and change others. This is one example of the tremendous advantage a spreadsheet has over a simple calculator, where each sum operation must be done separately.

Many times during the implementation process, you might find it necessary to restructure or revise your spreadsheet. This is a necessary part of finding the optimal structure for the solution to the problem. The computational power of Excel makes it easy to revise your spreadsheet, allowing you to explore a variety of alternative solutions.

Evaluating the Solution

No matter how experienced the problem solver or how simple the task, it is always wise to check the results to ensure they are correct. You should at least estimate what the expected calculated values should be and compare them with the spreadsheet solution. With more complex spreadsheets, it's advisable to manually go through the entire series of steps to verify the answer. Something as minor as a typo in a value or an incorrect formula can result in an incorrect solution. Once it appears that the spreadsheet is correct, a good practice is to vary some of the inputs and ascertain that the results are updated correctly. And, finally, as illustrated in the original problem-solving model (Figure 1), the solution you arrive at can sometimes lead to the recognition of another problem, at which point the process loops back and begins again.

PROBLEM SOLVING IN THIS BOOK

Throughout this book, you will be presented with various problems to solve or analyses to complete using different Excel tools and features. Each chapter in this book presents three levels of problem solving with Excel. Level 1 deals with basic problems or analyses that require the application of one or more spreadsheet tools, focusing on the implementation of those tools. However, problem solving not only requires you to know *how* to use a tool, but, more importantly, *why* or *when* to use *which* tool. So, with Level 2 the problems and analyses presented increase in complexity. By the time you reach Level 3, the complexity increases further, providing you with opportunities for more advanced critical thinking and problem solving. Each level ends with a section called "Steps To Success," which provides hands-on practice of the skills and concepts presented in that level.

In the Case Problems at the end of each chapter, not only does the degree of complexity *increase*, matching how the material is presented in each level, but the structure of the problem to be solved *decreases* as well. Figure 4 illustrates this approach to problem solving in this text.

Figure 4: Pedagogical model for problem solving

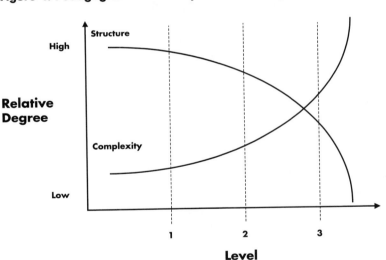

In this model, structure can be thought of as the way that various parts of a problem are held or put together. In a highly structured situation, almost all the parts of the problem are defined, and it is up to you to put the last few pieces in place to reach a solution. As the amount of structure is reduced, you need to understand more of the pieces and how they fit together to reach a solution. As structure is further reduced (more missing pieces of the puzzle) and complexity is increased (more pieces to understand), the difficulty of solving the problem increases. This difficulty can be measured in the time, number of steps, and decisions required to reach a solution. The goal is to increase your problem-solving skills while moving you toward an environment that is more like the real business world you will encounter during internships and upon graduation from college.

Skills Training

This text assumes that you are already familiar with some of the more fundamental skills in Excel, such as navigating and organizing a worksheet, entering text and values, writing simple formulas, and applying basic formatting. Depending on your skill level and working knowledge of Excel, you might want to use the Skills Training CD before you begin Chapter 1. (See the Preface section of this book or ask your instructor for more information about the Skills Training CD, powered by SAM.)

The following is a list of prerequisite skills for which Skills Training is available; your instructor might have other requirements as well:

Add borders
Add headers to worksheets
Add page numbering
Apply AutoFormats to worksheets
Apply bold, italics, underline
Change fonts
Change the font color
Change margins in Page Setup
Change Zoom settings
Check spelling in a worksheet
Clear cell contents
Clear cell formats
Close a workbook and exit Excel
Copy cells
Create folders for saving workbooks

Delete rows and columns
Delete selected cells
Edit numbers in cells
Edit text in cells
Fit a worksheet to print on one page
Go to a specific cell
Print a worksheet
Print preview a worksheet
Save a workbook
Select a cell
Use the Excel Help system
Use the Office Clipboard
Use the Research Task Pane
Use Save As to store workbooks in different locations

In addition to these prerequisite skills, additional Excel 2003 skills are listed at the beginning of each level in a chapter. These skills correspond to the material presented in that level, and give you a chance to practice the "mechanics" before you start applying the skills to solve problems. If you are using the Skills Training CD with this text, it is recommended that you check each list of Excel 2003 skills before beginning to work on a particular level. In this way, you can take advantage of the Skills Training CD to come up to speed on any of those skills and be better prepared to move forward in the chapter.

CASE SCENARIO

The problems to be solved and analyses to be performed in this text are presented within the context of a fictional large-scale sporting goods company named TheZone Sports Corporation, or simply TheZone. This case scenario is used to provide real-world, business examples to illustrate the lessons in each chapter; it is not based on real people or events. You will be guided through the solutions to realistic business problems that face various people working for this company. These "employees" represent a variety of business functions: Accounting, Finance, Human Resources, Marketing, Operations Management, and Sales. Context is an important factor to consider in problem solving. The following background on TheZone will give you perspective on the situations you will encounter throughout the book.

The Company

TheZone is an international sporting goods company that provides sports equipment, apparel, and footwear to thousands of retail locations primarily in the United States and Canada. Its corporate headquarters are located in Fort Collins, Colorado. The company is noted for its innovative product designs and quality. TheZone employs approximately 15,000 people working on three continents to provide the highest quality products and services possible.

The Brand

TheZone has paid particular attention to managing its brand image with an emphasis on associating the company's products with an athletic lifestyle that pushes individuals to be their best, while having fun. This philosophy is reflected in the company's motto:

Play Right: Get in TheZone.

Key Players

William Broadacre—Founder and Chairman of the Board

William Broadacre is chairman of the board of TheZone Sports Corporation, a position he has held since he founded the company in 1977. Prior to founding TheZone, William was the owner of the Broadacre Sporting Goods store in Fort Collins, Colorado. He holds a B.A. degree in Business from Colorado State University and an M.B.A. from Indiana University. A sports enthusiast himself, William has been able to turn a lifelong passion for athletics into a successful and rewarding business venture.

Una Baatar—President and Chief Executive Officer

Una Baatar is president and chief executive officer of TheZone, a position she has held since the company's founding in 1977. Like William, Una attended Colorado State University, from which she earned her business degree in Marketing and Finance. Una is the driving force behind TheZone's successful expansion from the original sporting goods retail store into an international supplier of sports equipment, apparel, and footwear. Una's truly innovative approach to business has allowed TheZone brand name to become an icon that represents the best in sports and athletic endeavors.

Molly Richardson—Senior Vice President and Chief Financial Officer

Molly Richardson joined TheZone in 1998 as vice president and controller. She was named senior vice president and chief financial officer in April 2001. Prior to joining TheZone, Molly was employed by Williams Corporation, a leading national advertising firm specializing in print media, as its executive vice president and chief financial officer. She earned a B.S. degree in Industrial Engineering from Cornell University, and also holds an M.B.A. from Ohio State University.

Company Goal: Expand the Product Line

TheZone's strength as a company lies in its design, marketing, and distribution capabilities. The company retains in-house manufacturing for some key products, such as certain shoes and skis, but has also been able to expand its product lines through acquisition. The company usually targets businesses that are struggling with manufacturing costs, but have strong product designs that will fit well within TheZone brand image. TheZone works with its manufacturing partners to bring the costs under control. From its humble beginnings over 25 years ago, TheZone has grown into an international sporting goods company with hundreds of products in the sports equipment, apparel, and footwear market segments of the industry.

How Is Excel Used at TheZone?

Employees of TheZone use Excel in the day-to-day management of business functions across the company. Specific examples are listed below:

- The Finance group is looking at different pricing alternatives for a new shoe being designed. This group is also using Excel to analyze projected revenues and costs/ expenses for a new swimwear product, primarily to decide whether or not to carry the new product, and if so, to help set a pricing policy for it.
- The Marketing group uses Excel to monitor and chart both industry trends and company performance for all of its product lines.
- The Accounting group monitors accounts receivable to determine what terms should be offered to the company's customers based on payment history and credit rating. This group is also using Excel to develop a projected income statement for a new sunglasses product line.

Finance

Marketing

Accounting

Operations Management

Sales

Human Resources

- The Operations Management group is using Excel to monitor quality control values in an effort to identify production problems in the ski product line. This group is also looking at ways to optimize production schedules and product distribution (transportation) for other product lines.
- The Sales group is using Excel to create a tool that will help the sales force quickly price product orders. This group, along with the Marketing group, is also analyzing different marketing plans/options for the sweatshirt category of apparel products.
- The Human Resources group is using Excel to compile and track data about the company's employees, which can then be used to create summary reports and calculate certain information based on salary data.

As you progress through the chapters in this book, you will encounter these various business functions and learn how they use Excel to analyze data, solve problems, and support decision making.

CHAPTER SUMMARY

This chapter introduced you to the focus of this text—using Excel to solve problems and to support decision making. It also described the interrelationship between problem solving and decision making, and provided a general model of the problem-solving process. The three main phases of this model—Problem Recognition, Problem Statement, and Solution—involve the completion of different analysis steps to move from one phase to another. The powerful features and capabilities of Excel enable you to apply this problem-solving process in ways that are impossible by hand, providing a "thinking tool" that helps you organize and analyze the data you need to manipulate to reach a solution.

The method of teaching problem solving in this book was also discussed. Each chapter is organized into three levels of problem solving with Excel, and the material presented increases in complexity from one level to the next. The Case Problems at the end of each chapter present problems that both increase in complexity and decrease in structure, providing more challenging problems for you to solve and analyses to perform as you move from level to level.

CONCEPTUAL REVIEW

1. Define what a "knowledge worker" is and discuss the significance of the knowledge worker in today's business world.

2. Define and differentiate between the terms "information" and "data."

3. What is the relationship between problem solving and decision making?

4. What role can Excel play in decision making?

5. Describe a time you have performed a "what-if" analysis.

6. Describe a situation in which having access to large amounts of information had a negative impact on your decision making.

7. Describe a situation in which having access to large amounts of information had a positive impact on your decision making.

8. Describe the general model of problem solving presented in the text. What are the three main phases and the different analysis steps involved?

9. Give an example of each of the following: a quantitative basis for making a decision and a qualitative basis for making a decision.

10. What should you consider before implementing or building a spreadsheet model?

Applying Fundamental Excel Skills and Tools in Problem Solving

Finance: Analyzing Costs and Projected Revenues for a New Product

LEARNING OBJECTIVES

Level 1

Define common Excel error messages

Correct basic formatting problems in a worksheet

Correct errors in simple formulas

Determine the order of precedence in formulas

Understand precision versus display for cell values

Level 2

Work with multiple worksheets

Calculate total, average, minimum, and maximum values with functions

Understand how functions work: syntax, arguments, and algorithms

Use the AutoSum feature to perform calculations quickly

Calculate the number of values using both COUNT and COUNTA

Level 3

Organize a workbook

Understand relative, absolute, and mixed cell referencing

Write formulas with different types of cell referencing

Copy formulas with different types of cell referencing

Name a cell or cell range

FUNCTIONS COVERED IN THIS CHAPTER

AVERAGE

COUNT

COUNTA

MIN

MAX

SUM

CHAPTER INTRODUCTION

Excel provides a variety of tools for designing and working with a spreadsheet, which is referred to as a **worksheet** in the Excel application. A paper spreadsheet is simply a sheet organized into columns and rows; an Excel workbook is an electronic version of this piece of paper, but with numerous features and functions that facilitate its easy and efficient use.

This chapter presents some of the fundamental skills and tools you'll encounter when working with Excel to solve problems and support decision making. You'll learn how to write formulas in cells to perform calculations, and how to design a workbook so that these calculations can be automatically updated when input values are changed. In addition, this chapter discusses some of the formatting options available that can be applied to cells and ranges of cells.

You will also learn about some of the rules that affect how information is displayed and calculations are performed in an Excel worksheet. The coverage of formulas is expanded to cover simple functions, which are shortcuts available to use for predefined tasks. And, finally, you will explore the various results of copying formulas with different kinds of cell references.

CASE SCENARIO

The product design team at TheZone has been assigned the task of bringing to market a new and significantly different athletic shoe that will combine the support of superior European footwear with the comfort and styling of American running shoes. The design team has recently created a worksheet containing the component costs for this new athletic shoe, which is called TZEdge. The team members have asked Paul Gomez, a financial analyst for the company, to review the worksheet for several reasons. First, they want to ensure that it is formatted properly and contains no errors. Also, they need Paul to perform some cost calculations to determine the value of different pricing alternatives, and to provide some preliminary budget and projected revenue information. In this way, the worksheet will become a functioning analytical tool that will help both Paul and the product design team make sound business decisions regarding the launch of the new athletic shoe.

Finance

LEVEL 1

IDENTIFYING AND CORRECTING COMMON ERRORS IN FORMATTING AND FORMULAS

EXCEL 2003 SKILLS TRAINING

- Apply number formats (currency and percent)
- Apply number formats (dates and comma)
- Center across selection
- Create formulas using the Formula Bar
- Display formula contents
- Edit a formula
- Enter formulas using Point mode
- Enter numbers with format symbols
- Insert columns and rows
- Merge cells
- Modify column widths
- Modify row height
- Set cell color
- Use the Format Painter

EXAMINING A BASIC WORKSHEET FOR ERRORS

The product design team is working with Paul and production engineers to formulate an estimate of production costs for the new TZEdge athletic shoe. Although price will not be the overriding factor in the business decision to launch this new shoe, there are still certain production cost goals that must be met to place this shoe in the correct market niche. After the designers have all the information in place, Paul needs to analyze the costs and make recommendations.

The designers started to tabulate the material costs of the TZEdge shoe. Figure 1.1 shows the Excel worksheet they have developed so far, which is contained in a workbook named "TZEdge Material Costs."

From your work with Excel, you know that cells can contain **numeric values**, such as the number "12" in cell C5; **text labels**, such as the word "Component" in cell A2; and **calculated values**, such as the total "36" shown in cell D16. As you can see, the worksheet contains the cost information in the input area, cells A2 through E8, and the results of the cost calculations in the output area, cells A11 through D16. Typically, workbooks are organized so that there are distinct areas for **inputs**, the labels and values upon which the calculations are based, and **outputs**, the calculations and their results. The input and output areas can be located on the same worksheet or on separate worksheets.

Figure 1.1: Initial worksheet for TZEdge

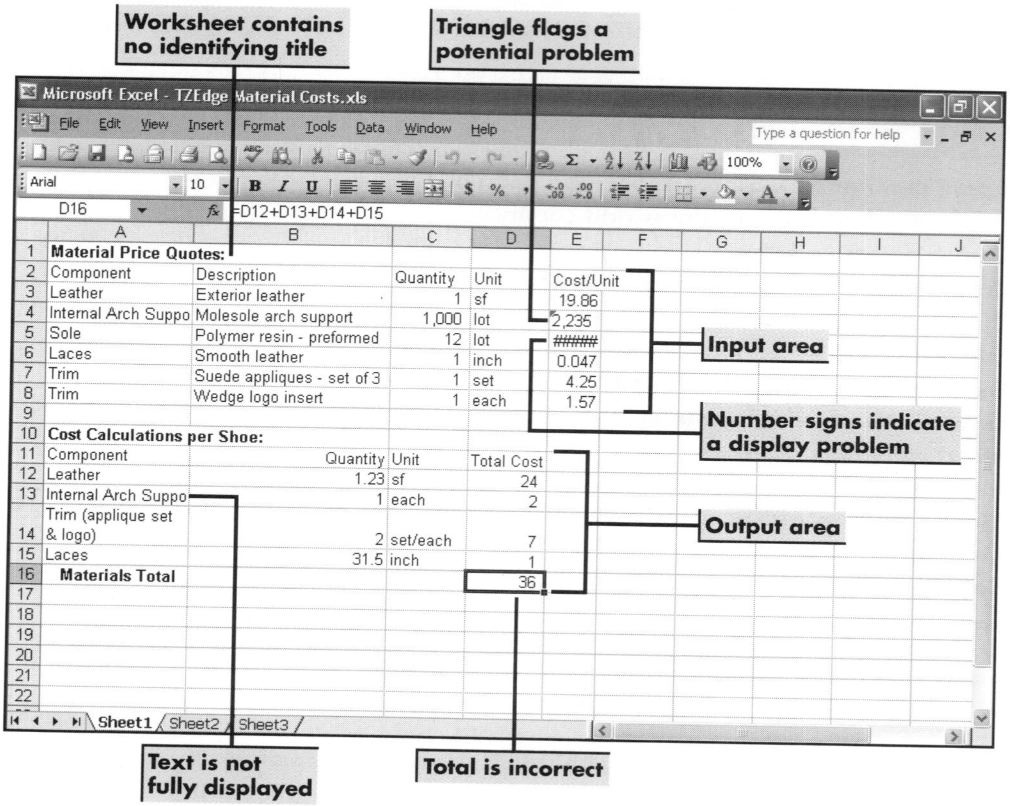

As you can also see in Figure 1.1, there are some obvious problems with the worksheet. For example, cell E5 contains a series of ### signs. Also, a quick look at the numbers reveals that the Materials Total doesn't add up to the value shown. There are other problems related to formatting and formulas as well.

Excel uses a variety of symbols to indicate specific types of errors to help you identify and resolve problems in a worksheet. Table 1.1 describes some of these error messages.

Table 1.1: Excel error messages

Error Message	Description
######	Insufficient width in cell to display data, or negative date/time
#NAME?	Unrecognized text in a formula
#N/A	No answer
#REF!	Invalid cell reference
#VALUE!	Wrong argument type or operand
#NUM!	Invalid numeric values in a formula or function
#DIV/0!	Division by zero

Because someone else has already created the spreadsheet, the focus here is on identifying the problems and testing the solution, which sometimes leads to rethinking and re-implementing various parts of the original solution. This task might involve many of the basic spreadsheet skills, including worksheet and cell formatting, as well as writing simple formulas.

CORRECTING FORMATTING PROBLEMS

In addition to the contents of a cell, individual cells, ranges of cells, and entire worksheets can be formatted to display the information in a variety of ways. After reviewing the worksheet created by the product design team, Paul determines that it needs to be formatted to make the data easier to read. The necessary changes include modifying column widths, checking error messages, formatting numbers consistently, and including a title to identify the worksheet contents. Paul decides to look at these formatting issues first before examining the worksheet formulas.

Modifying Column Width

The first problem to tackle is the ### signs in cell E5. As noted in Table 1.1, the series of number signs indicates that the column width is insufficient to display the complete value in the cell. A similar problem exists in cells A4, A13, and E2 where there is insufficient width to display the text labels within these cells. Unlike with values, if there is insufficient room to display a label, the text will either be displayed in a truncated format (A4 and A13), or spilled over into the next cell (E2) if this cell is empty.

To correct these types of problems, Paul can simply increase the column width using one of the following methods:

- Double-click the column dividing line to make the column as wide as the longest entry in the column.
- Drag the column dividing line to the desired width.
- Choose the Column option on the Format menu and then specify the column width.

Checking Error Messages

Another possible error has been flagged in cell E4. The triangle in the upper-left corner of the cell is an alert. If you select this cell, the Error Alert button ◈ appears. Clicking this button displays a drop-down menu indicating what the problem might be. In this case, the "Number stored as text" message appears. The value in cell E4 was entered with an apostrophe at the beginning of the value, causing it to be treated as a text label instead of as a numeric value. This could cause problems if this cell reference is used in formulas.

Excel is somewhat inconsistent in how it handles numbers stored as text. The formula =E4+1 would correctly return the value 2236 even though cell E4 contains text and not a numerical value. However, if E4 was included in a SUM function, the function would ignore the value entirely and not include it in the total. So, it is a good idea to correct this problem by changing numbers stored as text to numbers. There are situations when you would not want to do this, however. Consider a zip code such as 02139. In all likelihood, you would not include this zip code in any functions or formulas for calculations, and if you changed the entry from text to a number, the leading zero would be dropped and the value displayed would be 2139. In this case, you would want the number to be stored as text.

To correct the problem in cell E4, Paul can simply select the cell and retype the number 2235. Or, he can choose the Convert to Number option on the drop-down menu that appears when the Error Alert button is clicked.

Best Practice

Using Commas When Entering Values

When entering a value in a cell, you can enter the value with or without commas; for example, the entry 2,235 is equivalent to the entry 2235. However, if you plan to use this value in a formula, typing commas could be problematic. If you enter the formula =2,235+B1, Excel displays a message box asking if you want to change the formula to =2235+B1. Using commas becomes even more problematic if your formula includes functions, in which a comma indicates to Excel the beginning of the next argument. So =SUM(2,235,B1) is interpreted as =2+235+B1 instead of =2235+B1.

Some experienced Excel users recommend never typing commas with numbers, to avoid possible problems in formulas, and instead using the Comma Style button [,] on the Formatting toolbar or the options in the Format Cells dialog box, available from the Format menu, to display values in the desired manner. Other users prefer to enter values directly with commas so that the formatting is already done—particularly if they know these values will not be used in formulas or functions.

Formatting Numbers

Next, Paul considers the formatting of the input values. Consistent and appropriate formatting makes a worksheet easier to read and understand. In Figure 1.1, note that the Cost/Unit values in cells E3:E8 are displayed in various formats with different numbers of decimal places. To fix this problem, Paul can apply the predefined Currency Style to cell E3 using the Currency Style button [$] on the Formatting toolbar. The **Currency Style** is an accounting format that displays the dollar sign at the left edge of the cell, commas, and two decimal places for the numeric value, with a column of values aligned on the decimal point. For cells E4:E8, Paul can apply the Comma Style mentioned earlier, which displays values with commas and two decimal places, but no dollar signs. The dollar sign is needed only for the first unit cost; repeated dollar signs can clutter a worksheet. After applying these formats, Paul can use the Increase Decimal button [.00] on the Formatting toolbar to increase the decimal places displayed for cells E3:E8 to three places, which provides more accurate information about the unit cost for each item.

How To

Format Numbers

1. Select the cell or cells containing the numbers you want to format.
2. Click Format on the menu bar, and then click Cells to open the Format Cells dialog box.
3. Click the Number tab to display the options available for formatting numbers. See Figure 1.2.

Figure 1.2 Format Cells dialog box

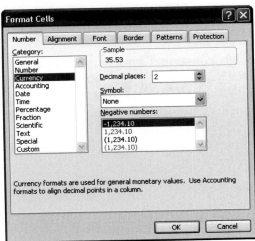

The Category box lists the available number formats. The category and other settings selected depend on which cell is active when you open the Format Cells dialog box. Note the selected Currency format in Figure 1.2; this is not to be confused with the Currency Style button on the Formatting toolbar, which applies an accounting format. The Currency format is similar to the Currency Style, except it does not align values on the decimal point, and it places the dollar sign immediately in front of the value instead of at the leftmost edge of the cell.

4. Click the number format you want, and then modify the options for the display of Decimal places, Symbol, and Negative numbers, as needed.
5. Click the OK button.

OR

1. Select the cell or cells containing the numbers you want to format.
2. Click one of the Formatting toolbar buttons to quickly apply a predefined style:

- The Currency Style button **$** formats numbers in an accounting format, with commas, two decimal places, values aligned on the decimal point, and the dollar sign displayed at the left edge of the cell.
- The Comma Style button **,** formats numbers with commas, two decimal places, and values aligned on the decimal point.
- The Percent Style button **%** formats numbers as percentages, displayed to the nearest percent, with no decimal places.

Best Practice

Formatting Dollar Values

Different disciplines or companies often have requirements for formatting dollar values in a spreadsheet. In Accounting, for example, the preferred format is to align values on the decimal point, in a column of dollar values, and to include a dollar sign only in the first entry in the column and for any grand totals. Repeated dollar signs can clutter the worksheet and are often unnecessary.

Inserting a Title

Another modification that will improve the format of the worksheet is to insert a title, such as "TZEdge Material Analysis," at the top to identify the worksheet's contents. To accomplish this, Paul can insert a row at the top of the worksheet and enter the title in the new row. Additional formatting of the title, such as centering and merging it across the columns, adding a colored background, adding a border, and bolding the text, further enhances the worksheet. To merge and center the title, Paul selects the cell containing the title and then clicks the Merge and Center button 🔳 on the Formatting toolbar.

Figure 1.3 shows the worksheet with the formatting problems corrected.

Figure 1.3: Worksheet after correcting formatting problems

Title added, and merged and centered over columns

Text fully displayed

Numbers formatted consistently

Value stored as a number

Text fully displayed

	A	B	C	D	E	F
1		TZEdge Material Analysis				
2	Material Price Quotes:					
3	Component	Description	Quantity	Unit	Cost/Unit	
4	Leather	Exterior leather	1	sf	$ 19.860	
5	Internal Arch Support	Molesole arch support	1,000	lot	2,235.000	
6	Sole	Polymer resin - preformed	12	lot	124.450	
7	Laces	Smooth leather	1	inch	0.047	
8	Trim	Suede appliques - set of 3	1	set	4.250	
9	Trim	Wedge logo insert	1	each	1.570	
10						
11	Cost Calculations per Shoe:					
12	Component		Quantity	Unit	Total Cost	
13	Leather		1.23	sf	24	
14	Internal Arch Support		1	each	2	
15	Trim (applique set & logo)		2	set/each	7	
16	Laces		31.5	inches	1	
17	Materials Total				36	
18						
19						

How To

Modify Cell Formatting

1. Select the cell or cells you want to format.

2. Click Format on the menu bar, and then click Cells to open the Format Cells dialog box.

3. Click the Alignment tab to display the options available for aligning cell contents. See Figure 1.4.

Figure 1.4: Alignment options

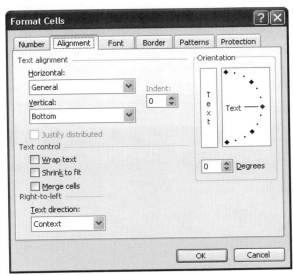

This tab provides several options for the alignment and orientation of cell contents. In particular, note the Wrap text check box; when you select this option, the text in the cell automatically wraps within the cell, and the cell height adjusts accordingly. This is a useful feature when a text entry does not fit well in a cell. Also note the Merge cells option, which allows selected adjacent cells to be treated as one cell. In addition to the Alignment tab, the Format Cells dialog box offers the following tabs: Font, Border, and Patterns. Each tab provides different settings that affect the display of cell contents, including font type, font style (bold, italic, and so on), and font size; border types, line styles, and border colors; and fill type, including colors and patterns. Note that some of the most common formatting options available in the Format Cells dialog box are also available on the Formatting toolbar.

4. Click each dialog box tab, as needed, and make the appropriate formatting changes.

5. Click the OK button.

Best Practice

Documenting a Worksheet

Frequently when working in teams, with several groups, or even with different companies, it is advisable to not only include a title on the worksheet, but also to identify the date it was created, the name of the worksheet author, and any specific information about the company and/or project. Including this information on a separate documentation worksheet usually suffices for the workbook, but not if a single worksheet will be printed separately. For example, if the current worksheet were to be printed, it would be helpful to include the following information above the "TZEdge Material Analysis" title:

TheZone: TZEdge Product Design Team
November 15, 2007
Prepared by: Paul Gomez

As an alternative to including such information on the worksheet itself, you can create a custom header when setting up the printing specifications in the Page Setup dialog box (available from the File menu). The Header dialog box, shown in Figure 1.5, allows you to customize the information that is printed in the left, center, and right sections of the page.

Figure 1.5: Header dialog box

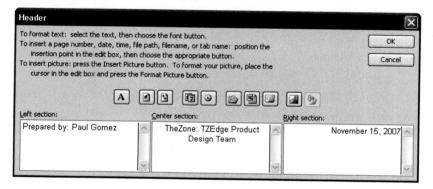

CORRECTING ERRORS IN FORMULAS

Now that the worksheet is easier to read, Paul can address any problems related to the formulas. As you know, a **formula** is an equation that performs calculations, the result of which can be either a value or a label, depending on the formula. A formula in Excel always begins with an equal sign (=) and can contain constants, cell references to previously entered values, or cell references to other calculated values. Formulas can also include one or more functions, which you'll explore later in this chapter.

One way to determine where an error might exist in a formula is to print the worksheet in two different formats: the default format, which displays the *values* in each cell, and the format that displays the *formulas* instead of the values. Figure 1.6 shows both formats for the TZEdge Material Analysis worksheet. Note that when the formulas are displayed, the worksheet column widths and formats are modified to accommodate the display.

Figure 1.6: Comparing values with their formulas

Worksheet with values displayed

	A	B	C	D	E
1		TZEdge Material Analysis			
2	Material Price Quotes:				
3	Component	Description	Quantity	Unit	Cost/Unit
4	Leather	Exterior leather	1	sf	$ 19.860
5	Internal Arch Support	Molesole arch support	1,000	lot	2,235.000
6	Sole	Polymer resin - preformed	12	lot	124.450
7	Laces	Smooth leather	1	inch	0.047
8	Trim	Suede appliques - set of 3	1	set	4.250
9	Trim	Wedge logo insert	1	each	1.570
10					
11	Cost Calculations per Shoe:				
12	Component		Quantity	Unit	Total Cost
13	Leather		1.23	sf	24
14	Internal Arch Support		1	each	2
15	Trim (applique set & logo)		2	set/each	7
16	Laces		31.5	inches	1
17	**Materials Total**				36
18					
19					

Worksheet with formulas displayed

	A	B	C	D	E
1		TZEdge Material Analysis			
2	Material Price Quot				
3	Component	Description	Quantity	Unit	Cost/Unit
4	Leather	Exterior leather	1	sf	19.86
5	Internal Arch Support	Molesole arch support	1000	lot	2235
6	Sole	Polymer resin - preformed	12	lot	124.45
7	Laces	Smooth leather	1	inch	0.047
8	Trim	Suede appliques - set of 3	1	set	4.25
9	Trim	Wedge logo insert	1	each	1.57
10					
11	Cost Calculations pe				
12	Component		Quantity	Unit	Total Cost
13	Leather	1.23		sf	=B13*E4
14	Internal Arch Support	1		each	2.235
15	Trim (applique set & logo)	2		set/each	=E8+E9*2
16	Laces	31.5		inches	=B16*E7
17	**Materials Total**				=D13+D14+D15+D16
18					
19					

The formula **=D13+D14+D15+D16** in cell D17 displays the value 36

How To

Display Formulas in a Worksheet

1. Click Tools on the menu bar, and then click Options to display the Options dialog box.

2. Click the View tab.

3. In the Window options section, click the Formulas check box to select it.

4. Click the OK button.

OR

1. Press and hold the Ctrl key while pressing ` (grave accent) to toggle between the display of formulas and the display of values.

The information in cells A4:E9 was obtained from the vendors that the product design team dealt with when making the shoe prototype. Each of the different vendors quoted prices based on varying lot sizes: per item (each), per set, per inch, or per square foot (sf). The product design team then attempted to convert this information to a per shoe basis.

Checking Simple Formulas for Accuracy

The formula in cell D13 calculates the cost of leather per shoe. Each shoe requires 1.23 sf of leather. According to the component prices, the premium leather being used is sold at $19.86 per square foot (cell E4). The formula in cell D13 should multiply the quantity times the price. In Excel syntax, this formula would be =B13*E4. So, this formula seems to be correct. Notice that Excel uses an asterisk (*) to represent multiplication, as opposed to the "x" or "." symbols frequently used in algebraic expressions. A list of the Excel arithmetic operators is provided in Table 1.2.

Table 1.2: Excel arithmetic operators

Calculation	Excel Operator	Example
Addition	+	=3+A1
Subtraction	-	=A1-A2
Multiplication	*	=A1*4
Division	/	=X4/Y4
Exponent	^	=2^8

Next, Paul looks at the formula in cell D16, which calculates the cost of laces. Laces are priced by the inch. A total of 31.5 inches is needed for each shoe. The formula =B16*E7 was entered into cell D16. This formula also appears to be correct.

Using Formulas and Cell References Instead of Values

The formula in cell D14 should calculate the cost of arch support in the shoe. The arch supports are sold in lots of 1000, for a total price of $2,235. So, the cost of *each* arch support is $2,235 divided by 1000, as represented by the arithmetic formula 2235/1000. The number of arch supports in each shoe is 1 (cell B14), so the total cost should be 1*2235/1000. However, notice that the resulting value was directly typed into cell D14. Typing a value into a cell instead of entering the formula that produced the value is not a good practice when building a spreadsheet. To correct this problem, Paul needs to replace this value with the formula =E5/C5*B14 so that any later changes to any of these cell value inputs will be automatically reflected in the costs.

Best Practice

Using Cell References in Formulas

Notice the formula in cell D13. In addition to using the correct arithmetic operator, the formula in cell D13 contains cell references pointing to the appropriate input values. Using cell references is preferable to directly inputting values into a formula. In this example, if the price of the leather changes or the quantity required to make a shoe increases, it would be easy to enter those changes. By using cell references in formulas, you can be secure in the knowledge that everywhere you have used a value in your worksheet, the calculations will be automatically updated with any changes to that value.

Determining Order of Precedence

Now look at the formula in cell D15, which calculates the cost of trim including two suede applique sets and two wedge logo inserts. The formula =E8+E9*2 was entered into cell D15. On closer inspection, this formula presents a problem. If one set of appliques costs over $4 (cell E8), certainly two would cost at least $8, plus the cost of the inserts. Yet the value displayed in cell D15 is only 7.

The problem is related to how Excel performs calculations, specifically in the order of precedence of the various operations. In this case, Excel performs the multiplication of E9 by 2 before adding the value in E8, resulting in the incorrect value of 7. To produce the correct results, the formula should first add the value in cell E8 to the value in cell E9, and then multiply that amount by 2. This would return the correct value 11.64 for the cost of trim. To fix this problem, Paul needs to enclose the addition operation in parentheses to indicate that this should be completed first, as follows: =(E8+E9)*2. Table 1.3 describes the order of precedence rules in Excel.

Table 1.3: Order of precedence rules

Order of Precedence	Example	Resulting Value	Explanation
1. Operations in parentheses	=A1*(3+5)	If A1=2, the resulting value is 2*(3+5), or 2*8, =16	Excel first performs the addition of 3+5 even though multiplication has a higher precedence than addition, because the addition operation is enclosed in parentheses.
2. Exponentiation	=3*A1^3	If A1=2, the resulting value is 3*2^3, or 3*8, =24	Excel first performs the exponential operation of cubing A1, and then performs the multiplication.
3. Multiplication and division from left to right	=A1+B2*C3	If A1=2, B2=3, and C3=10, the resulting value is 2+3*10, or 2+30, =32	Excel first multiplies B2 by C3, and then adds the result to A1.
4. Addition and subtraction from left to right	=A1-B2+C3/10	If A1=2, B2=3, and C3=10, the resulting value is 2-3+10/10, or 2-3+1, or -1+1, = 0	Excel first divides C3 by 10, then subtracts B2 from A1, and finally adds this value to the quotient.

Understanding Precision Versus Display

Paul has corrected the problems with the formulas in cells D14 and D15. Figure 1.7 shows the revised worksheet.

Figure 1.7: Worksheet after correcting formulas

	A	B	C	D	E	F
1		TZEdge Material Analysis				
2	Material Price Quotes:					
3	Component	Description	Quantity	Unit	Cost/Unit	
4	Leather	Exterior leather	1	sf	$ 19.860	
5	Internal Arch Support	Molesole arch support	1,000	lot	2,235.000	
6	Sole	Polymer resin - preformed	12	lot	124.450	
7	Laces	Smooth leather	1	inch	0.047	
8	Trim	Suede appliques - set of 3	1	set	4.250	
9	Trim	Wedge logo insert	1	each	1.570	
10						
11	Cost Calculations per Shoe:					
12	Component		Quantity	Unit	Total Cost	
13	Leather		1.23	sf	24	
14	Internal Arch Support		1	each	2	
15	Trim (applique set & logo)		2	set/each	12	
16	Laces		31.5	inches	1	
17	Materials Total				40	
18						
19						

Corrected formula for Internal Arch Support =E5/C5*B14

Corrected formula for Trim =(E8+E9)*2

Notice that the Materials Total value in cell D17 is still slightly off. If you manually add 24+2+12+1, the total is 39, not 40 as displayed in cell D17. The formula in cell D17 is =D13+D14+D15+D16, which appears to be correct. So, what is the problem?

Actually, there is no problem. The worksheet was originally set up to display the values in cells D13:D17 with no decimal places. This display does not change the precise values that are stored in the cells. So, even though cell D14 displays the value 2, you know from the calculation 1*2235/1000 entered into that cell, the actual value stored is 2.235. The discrepancy is simply the result of the display being rounded; the precise values stored in each cell are correct. To test out this theory, Paul could revise the worksheet to display five decimal places, as illustrated in Figure 1.8. By manually calculating the Materials Total cost, you can see that the result in cell D17 is correct.

Figure 1.8: Worksheet with values displaying five decimal places

	A	B	C	D	E	F
1		TZEdge Material Analysis				
2	Material Price Quotes:					
3	Component	Description	Quantity	Unit	Cost/Unit	
4	Leather	Exterior leather	1	sf	$ 19.860	
5	Internal Arch Support	Molesole arch support	1,000	lot	2,235.000	
6	Sole	Polymer resin - preformed	12	lot	124.450	
7	Laces	Smooth leather	1	inch	0.047	
8	Trim	Suede appliques - set of 3	1	set	4.250	
9	Trim	Wedge logo insert	1	each	1.570	
10						
11	Cost Calculations per Shoe:					
12	Component		Quantity	Unit	Total Cost	
13	Leather		1.23	sf	$ 24.42780	
14	Internal Arch Support		1	each	2.23500	
15	Trim (applique set & logo)		2	set/each	11.64000	
16	Laces		31.5	inches	1.48050	
17	Materials Total				$ 39.78330	
18						
19						

Values displayed with five decimal places show that there is no error in the formula

Excel can display values in several different formats without changing the precise value stored by the program. When Excel rounds the display, it does so by rounding any number *less than half* down to the next value, and any number *half or greater* up to the next value. Remember changing the display does not change the precise value stored; the stored value is the value used in any calculations. Examples of these format displays are provided in Table 1.4.

Table 1.4: Formats for displaying values

Description	Display	Actual Value Stored	Example
Display varying number of decimal places	2	2.201 (stored in cell B2)	=100*B2 results in the value 220.1
Display using percent	5%	0.05 (stored in cell B3)	=100*B3 results in the value 5
Date display	12/31/2004	38352.00 (stored in cell B4)	=B4+1 results in the value 38353 or, if formatted as a date, displays 1/1/2005

In addition to changing the number of decimal places shown, you can also display a value as a percent without having to multiply by 100. A cell formatted with the percent style displays the % symbol following the value. When entering percentages, you can do one of the following:

- Enter the decimal equivalent, such as 0.23, and then click the Percent Style button `%` on the Formatting toolbar. The value in the cell is displayed as 23%, and the precise value stored in the cell is 0.23.
- Format the cell as a percentage first, again using the Percent Style button, and then enter the value as either a whole number, such as 23, or as the decimal equivalent, such as .23. The value in the cell is displayed as 23%, and the precise value stored in the cell is 0.23.
- Type the value, such as 23, either preceded or followed by a percent sign (%23 or 23%). The value in the cell is displayed as 23%, and the precise value stored in the cell is 0.23.

Dates are also a formatting option in Excel. Just like other values, dates can be added and subtracted in formulas. Usually when you enter a date such as 12/31/06 or December 31, 2006, Excel automatically formats the entry as a date.

Best Practice

Working with Dates

Excel stores dates as sequential numbers beginning with January 1, 1900. For example, January 1, 2005 is the value 38353 representing the number of days since 1/1/1900. Excel stores times as decimal fractions. This enables you to perform numeric calculations on cells containing dates, such as adding or subtracting a specified number of days from a date to arrive at a new date, or determining the number of days between two given dates. The following are examples of date values used in formulas, assuming the date 1/10/2006 is stored in cell A1 and the date 1/20/2006 is stored in cell A2:

- =A1+10 produces the result 1/20/2006
- =A2-10 produces the result 1/10/2006
- =A2-A1 produces the result 10

Note that dates cannot be used directly in a formula because Excel interprets the date as a calculation; for example, if the formula =1/10/2006+10 was entered in a cell, Excel would interpret this as 1 divided by 10 divided by 2006 plus 10—instead of as the date January 10, 2006 plus 10.

Date inputs and values resulting from calculations with dates can be displayed in a variety of ways, including numeric values, dates shown with the format 1/1/2005, or dates written out as January 1, 2005. These formats are available on the Number tab of the Format Cells dialog box.

Depending on which version of Excel you are using and how your options are configured, Excel allows two-digit year inputs, but they might be interpreted differently. In Excel 2003, the default setting interprets the values 00 through 29 as dates after 1/1/2000, whereas two-digit values from 30 through 99 are interpreted as years prior to 1/1/2000. For example, Excel would interpret the date 3/2/88 as March 2, 1988, not as March 2, 2088. It is usually a good idea to enter the full four digits of the year to avoid any types of problems.

Checking Accuracy in Formula Updates

The worksheet includes a cost per unit (Cost/Unit) for a shoe sole in the "Material Price Quotes" section, but there is no corresponding value in the "Cost Calculations per Shoe" section. This cost was omitted in error. To complete the worksheet, Paul must insert a new row above the Materials Total to calculate the cost of the shoe sole. Then, he needs to include the formula =B17*E6/C6 in cell D17 (in the newly inserted row) to calculate the quantity times the cost. Because the preformed polymer resin soles are priced by the dozen, the cost for each is $124.45/12, and one sole per shoe is required. The updated worksheet is shown in Figure 1.9. Note that Paul also formatted the values in cells D13:D18 so that they include two decimal places, are aligned on the decimal point, and include dollar signs for only the first calculated cost and the Materials Total cost. He also included cell borders to set off the Materials Total cost.

Figure 1.9: Worksheet with inserted row for sole costs

	D18	▼	fx	=D13+D14+D15+D16		
	A	B	C	D	E	F
1		TZEdge Material Analysis				
2	**Material Price Quotes:**					
3	Component	Description	Quantity	Unit	Cost/Unit	
4	Leather	Exterior leather	1	sf	$ 19.860	
5	Internal Arch Support	Molesole arch support	1,000	lot	2,235.000	
6	Sole	Polymer resin - preformed	12	lot	124.450	
7	Laces	Smooth leather	1	inch	0.047	
8	Trim	Suede appliques - set of 3	1	set	4.250	
9	Trim	Wedge logo insert	1	each	1.570	
10						
11	**Cost Calculations per Shoe:**					
12	Component		Quantity	Unit	Total Cost	
13	Leather		1.23	sf	$ 24.43	
14	Internal Arch Support		1	each	2.24	
15	Trim (applique set & logo)		2	set/each	11.64	
16	Laces		31.5	inches	1.48	
17	Sole		1	each	10.37	
18	**Materials Total**				$ 39.78	
19						
20						

> Materials Total formula does not reflect the addition of the new row

> Inserted row with formula for the cost of sole =B17*E6/C6

Has the Materials Total been updated accordingly to reflect the addition of the sole cost? Notice that the formula in cell D18 is still =D13+D14+D15+D16. It does not include any reference to cell D17, which now contains the cost of the sole. Therefore, Paul needs to edit cell D18 manually to include the addition of cell D17 in the total, as shown in Figure 1.10.

Figure 1.10: Formula modified to include new cost

	D18	▼	fx	=D13+D14+D15+D16+D17		
	A	B	C	D	E	F
1		TZEdge Material Analysis				
2	**Material Price Quotes:**					
3	Component	Description	Quantity	Unit	Cost/Unit	
4	Leather	Exterior leather	1	sf	$ 19.860	
5	Internal Arch Support	Molesole arch support	1,000	lot	2,235.000	
6	Sole	Polymer resin - preformed	12	lot	124.450	
7	Laces	Smooth leather	1	inch	0.047	
8	Trim	Suede appliques - set of 3	1	set	4.250	
9	Trim	Wedge logo insert	1	each	1.570	
10						
11	**Cost Calculations per Shoe:**					
12	Component		Quantity	Unit	Total Cost	
13	Leather		1.23	sf	$ 24.43	
14	Internal Arch Support		1	each	2.24	
15	Trim (applique set & logo)		2	set/each	11.64	
16	Laces		31.5	inches	1.48	
17	Sole		1	each	10.37	
18	**Materials Total**				$ 50.15	
19						
20						

> Updated formula in cell D18 includes cell D17 in the calculation

This is an inefficient way to update a formula, especially if you need to add several values. There is a better method to build formulas that ensures accuracy when you update or change a formula; this method will be explored in the next level.

Steps To Success: Level 1

The product design team has prepared another worksheet with the assistance of the manufacturing group listing the labor costs involved in manufacturing the TZEdge shoe. Figure 1.11 shows this worksheet.

Figure 1.11: Initial labor costs worksheet

	A	B	C	D	E
1	Description	Production Rate	Unit	$/Hour	
2	Delivery of Boxes to Production	15	boxes/hr	10	
3	Cutting of Leather	20	shoes/hr	22.40	
4	Attachment of Appliques	30	appliques/hr	10	
5	Sewing of Logos to Leather	22.5	pieces/hr	12.5	
6	Assembly of Leather & Sole	10	shoes/hr	23	
7	Assembly of Arch Support	18.5	shoes/hr	13	
8					
9	Manufacturing Tasks Per Sho	Quantity /Shoe	Unit	Total Cost	
10	Delivery of Boxes to Production	.2	boxes/shoe	#DIV/0!	
11	Cutting of Leather	1	shoe	1	
12	Attachment of Appliques	6	appliques/sh	2	
13	Assembly of Leather & Sole	1.00	shoe	######	
14	Assembly of Arch Support	1.00	shoe	0.0043	
15	Total Labor			#DIV/0!	
16					
17					

Note the following:

- Cells A1:D7 (input area) list the different tasks that are performed in the production of the shoe and the rates at which they are performed—boxes moved per hour, pieces sewn per hour, and so on. Also listed is the labor rate to perform these tasks in dollars per hour. For example, 15 boxes can be delivered in an hour to the production line at a cost of $10 per hour.

- Cells A9:D15 (output area) show these same tasks with the specific quantities required per shoe. For example, .2 boxes will be delivered for each shoe. So, if 15 boxes can be delivered in an hour at a cost of $10, how much will it cost to deliver 0.2 boxes?

In these steps, your task is to troubleshoot this worksheet and correct any problems with formatting or formulas. Complete the following:

1. Open the workbook named **Labor.xls** located in the Chapter 1 folder, and then save it as **Labor Costs.xls**.

2. Adjust the column widths, as necessary, so that all information is fully displayed.

3. Format the values in the Production Rate and $/Hour columns with the Comma Style. In addition, format cell D2 with a dollar sign aligned at the left of the cell.

4. Address the error messages in cells B10, D10, and D15.

5. Correct the formula in cell D10 so that it accurately calculates the cost of delivering boxes for one shoe.

6. Check the formulas that were entered for each of the other manufacturing tasks to ensure they are written correctly and that the worksheet can be easily updated later if any of the inputs change (Production Rate, Unit, $/Hour, or Quantity/Shoe). Check that the formula to summarize the labor costs is correct, and modify as needed.

7. Format cells D10:D15 so that the values align on the decimal point. Also display two decimal places for all the values in column D, and include a dollar sign in rows 10 and 15.

8. Format cells B10:B14 with the Comma Style with two decimal places.

9. The labor cost of sewing logos onto the leather was accidentally omitted from the manufacturing tasks. There are two logos per shoe that need to be sewn on. Insert a new row just below the row containing the Attachment of Appliques and complete the data inputs/outputs to calculate the labor cost of sewing these logos.

10. Adjust the total labor cost accordingly.

11. Add the title "TZEdge Labor Analysis" at the top of the worksheet. Center and merge the title over the columns containing values, and format the title with a light blue background.

12. Create a custom page header to contain your name, today's date, and the name of the company.

13. Save and close the Labor Costs.xls workbook.

LEVEL 2
CALCULATING AND COMPARING DATA USING SIMPLE FUNCTIONS

EXCEL 2003 SKILLS TRAINING

- **Create formulas using the AVERAGE function**
- **Create formulas using the MAX function**
- **Create formulas using the MIN function**
- **Create formulas using the SUM function**
- **Format worksheet tabs**
- **Insert worksheets into a workbook**
- **Modify worksheet names**

WORKING WITH MULTIPLE WORKSHEETS

The product design team has been given the go-ahead to proceed with the project for the TZEdge shoe. The marketing group has just completed some testing with a small number of consumer focus groups. These focus groups have been extremely helpful in providing feedback to the design team. Most of the feedback has focused on two major areas: (1) the leather and styling, and (2) the need for more ankle support for certain customers. As a result, the team has come up with two additional design options to consider:

- Textured leather that includes only a logo, and no appliques, for trim
- A high top design similar to the original shoe

Paul needs to compile some financial information to compare the material costs for each of these options to the original design. Refinements of the designs are expected to require several additional material components for one or more of these options. So, Paul needs to plan accordingly when setting up the worksheet.

The corporate purchasing department has also supplied some information to help price the materials for these new designs. The cost of textured leather is estimated to be approximately twice the cost of the leather currently being considered. Also, the high top design requires approximately 25% more leather and twice the lace length.

Using the information calculated in the original design, Paul sets up another worksheet in the TZEdge Material Costs workbook, listing the material costs for all three options. The costs on this new worksheet for the original option are based on the worksheet previously developed. Costs for the textured leather and high top options are based on the design requirements and cost estimates specified previously. To create the worksheet, Paul simply inserts a new worksheet in the existing workbook by choosing the Worksheet command on the Insert menu. Figure 1.12 shows this new worksheet.

Figure 1.12: Worksheet with additional design options

Costs for the original option are based on previous calculations

Costs for the textured leather and high top options are adjusted from the original option costs

	A	B	C	D	E
1	TZEdge Material Analysis				
2	Component	Original Option	Textured Leather	High Top	
3	Leather	$ 24.43	$ 48.86	$ 30.53	
4	Internal Arch Support	2.24	2.24	2.24	
5	Trim (applique set & logo)	11.64	1.57	11.64	
6	Laces	1.48	1.48	2.96	
7	Sole	10.37	10.37	10.37	
8	**Materials Total**				
9					
10					

When working with multiple worksheets in a workbook, it's a good idea to rename each worksheet tab from the default labels (Sheet1, Sheet2, and so on) to assign names that better identify the worksheet contents. You can also apply color to worksheet tabs to further distinguish one worksheet from another. In this case, Paul renames the Sheet1 tab to "Original," because this worksheet contains the material analysis data for the original TZEdge shoe design; and he renames the tab for the newly inserted worksheet to "Options," because it contains the data for the three different design options.

How To

Rename and Add Color to a Worksheet Tab

1. To rename a worksheet tab, right-click the tab you want to rename, and then click Rename on the shortcut menu.

2. Type the new worksheet tab name to replace the highlighted name.

3. To add color to a worksheet tab, right-click the tab, and then click Tab Color on the shortcut menu to open the Format Tab Color dialog box.

4. Click the color you want to add to the tab, and then click the OK button.

CALCULATING TOTALS USING THE SUM FUNCTION

The next step in completing the Options worksheet is to calculate the material costs for each option. Paul could simply enter the formula =B3+B4+B5+B6+B7 in cell B8 to determine the total cost of the Original Option. However, as you saw earlier with the Original worksheet, this method does not allow additional rows to be inserted and formulas to be recalculated automatically. Because additional material components are expected later on, this method is not recommended. A better method is to use the SUM function.

In addition to writing formulas that use constants, cell references, and operands, you can also write formulas that include one or more functions. **Functions** are predefined formulas that perform calculations. For example, the **SUM** function adds a list of values and/or cell ranges. A function is always structured beginning with the function name and an open parenthesis mark. After the parenthesis, the function contains a list of inputs in a specific order, separated by commas. A closing parenthesis mark ends the function. The function inputs are referred to as **arguments**. Each function has its own **syntax**, which specifies the function name and order of the arguments. The syntax can be compared with the spelling of a word, where each word contains specific letters in a specific order. Changing the order of the letters can change the meaning of the word or render it meaningless, such as two versus tow versus wto. Similarly, changing the name of the function or the order of the arguments would change the value returned or render the formula unusable. A function always behaves in the same way, according to the rules programmed into the function. These rules are referred to as a function's **algorithm**. Later, you'll see how these rules can affect the values calculated and, therefore, how to use a particular function.

Paul needs to include a formula with a SUM function in cell B8 to total the values for the Original Option, which are located in cells B3 through B7. As is true with any formula, this formula begins with an equal sign followed by the appropriate equation—in this case, just the SUM function. So, in Excel syntax, the formula in cell B8 is =SUM(B3:B7). In a similar fashion, Paul includes the formula =SUM(C3:C7) in cell C8, and =SUM(D3:D7) in cell D8. Note the syntax used in the SUM function—two cell references separated by a colon. This is referred to as a **cell range**. Ranges can be one dimensional along a row or column, or even a two-dimensional block such as B3:D7, which includes all cells starting in B3 and going down to row 7 and then across to column D.

Functions can also be written as part of a larger formula. For example, if Paul wanted to calculate the material cost of a pair of shoes in cell B8 instead of a single shoe, he could modify the formula to the following: =2*SUM(B3:B7).

How To

Insert a Function into a Formula

1. Enter the formula up to the point where you want to insert a function.

2. Click the Insert Function button f_x to the left of the Formula Bar to open the Insert Function dialog box, shown in Figure 1.13.

Figure 1.13: Insert Function dialog box

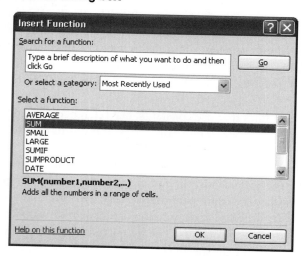

3. In the "Select a function" section, click the function you want (you might have to choose a category first to display the appropriate function list), and then click the OK button. The Function Arguments dialog box for that function opens.

4. Enter the appropriate arguments in the text boxes provided, and then click the OK button.

OR

1. Enter the formula up to the point where you want to insert a function.

2. Type the function name and each of the arguments required. When using cell references as arguments, you can either click the cell(s) to include the references, or type the cell references. This method of using a function requires you to know the syntax of the function; however, after you type the function name and the opening parenthesis, Excel automatically displays the syntax for you, as a guide. Many experienced Excel users prefer this method of entering a function because it is faster than using the Insert Function dialog box.

Calculating Quickly with AutoSum

Excel's **AutoSum** feature gives you quick access to the SUM function and other similar functions. To use this feature, you select the cell in which you want to perform the calculation, and then click the arrow for the AutoSum button **Σ** on the Standard toolbar to display a drop-down menu with a list of available functions. After you choose the function you want, Excel presents a suggested range to include in the calculation, based on rows or columns of numbers next to the current cell. It is important to verify that this is the range you require because the range chosen by Excel might not always be the one you want. If necessary, simply type the appropriate cell references to modify the range.

Table 1.5 shows the Excel functions that are similar to the SUM function and simple to use. All of these functions are available from the AutoSum drop-down menu. Unlike the functions presented later in this text, these functions contain only one type of argument—a number. A number can be represented by a constant, a cell reference where a value resides, or a range of cell references.

Table 1.5: Commonly used Excel functions

Function (arguments)	Description
SUM(number1, number2, ...)	Calculates the sum of a list of values
AVERAGE(number1, number2, ...)	Calculates the average value of a list of values
MIN(number1, number2, ...)	Calculates the minimum value in a list of values
MAX(number1, number2, ...)	Calculates the maximum value in a list of values
COUNT(number1, number2, ...)	Determines the number of values in a list

Like the SUM function, these common functions take a list of number arguments, which can include one or more of the following:

- A range along a column; for example B3:B7
- A range along a row; for example B3:D3
- A two-dimensional range (also referred to as a block of cells); for example, B3:D7
- Noncontiguous cells and/or constants; for example, B3,C4, D5:D6, 6

You can obtain more detail about each of these functions by using the Help feature in Excel. It is recommended that you look at this information when you begin working with a new Excel function.

CALCULATING AVERAGE, MINIMUM, AND MAXIMUM VALUES

In addition to totaling the material costs for each option, Paul needs to calculate the following:

- The average cost of each material component for each of the three options. This information will give the product design team a feel for the range of costs for each component.
- The lowest component cost and the highest component cost for all three options. This information was requested by the corporate purchasing department so they can get an idea of the range of cost component values, and prioritize their purchasing efforts accordingly.

Cell E3 will contain a formula that averages the cost of leather for the three options, as follows: =AVERAGE(B3:D3). Similar formulas will calculate the average costs of arch support, trim, and so on. The following formulas will determine the value of the lowest and highest cost components, respectively, for all three options: =MIN(B3:D7) and =MAX(B3:D7). Notice that the range used in these functions is two-dimensional; it includes multiple columns and rows. The revised worksheet is shown in Figure 1.14.

Figure 1.14: Worksheet revised to include average, minimum, and maximum costs

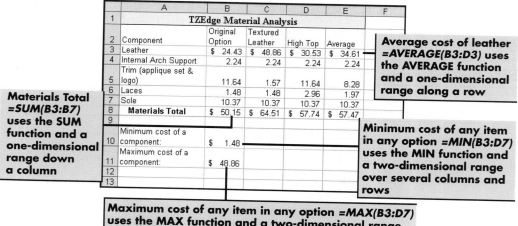

The product design team recently received some information on additional materials that will be needed to produce the shoes. For the textured leather shoe, because the material is softer than the leather in the original option, a toe support brace is needed, as well as a toe support pad to cushion it. The braces cost $1.27 each, and the cushions cost $3.29 each. A back support cushion is also required for both the textured leather shoe and the high top shoe. The back support cushions are still being designed, but the purchasing group recommends using a cost of $5.00 each for the textured leather option and $6.50 each for the high top option, although these costs could change later.

Paul needs to modify the worksheet based on this new information. He inserts three rows just above the Materials Total in row 8 to allow for the three additional components: toe support brace, toe support pad, and back support cushion. The formulas for the totals automatically update to reflect the additional costs. Excel "senses" that the new rows are part of an existing list and either automatically includes the rows in the subsequent formulas or gives you the option of including the new rows. Also, Excel extends consistent formatting to the values in the newly inserted rows.

Best Practice

Inserting Rows and the Impact on Formulas

Most often when you insert rows in a list of values that are being calculated, such as with a total, Excel includes the newly inserted values and recalculates the formulas affected. Depending on what values are in the list and how they are formatted, however, this might not always work as anticipated. If you think additional rows will be needed, you can avoid potential problems in one of two ways:

- Insert the new row or rows within the list of values instead of at the end of the list. This ensures that the newly inserted values are incorporated in any formulas. This method is acceptable if the values can be listed in any order. If you want to maintain a specific order, you would have to copy and paste and/or retype some of the data to obtain the order you want.
- Design your worksheet to include a blank row between the end of the list of values and the total formulas. The cell ranges you use in the formulas can include the blank row, and then whenever you insert rows, you can do so just above the blank row. This preserves the order of the values listed and ensures that all formulas are automatically updated. Because most of the commonly used functions ignore blank cells, the values generated should not be affected. When using this method, however, keep in mind that Excel might display an alert informing you that the formula refers to a blank cell. You can simply ignore this alert in this instance.

After inserting the rows, Paul enters labels in column A and the costs in the appropriate cells, leaving blank the cells for those options that do not include the three additional components. The revised worksheet is shown in Figure 1.15.

Figure 1.15: Values and formulas for revised worksheet

	A	B	C	D	E
1		TZEdge Material Analysis			
2	Component	Original Option	Textured Leather	High Top	Average
3	Leather	$ 24.43	$ 48.86	$ 30.53	$ 34.61
4	Internal Arch Support	2.24	2.24	2.24	2.24
5	Trim (applique set & logo)	11.64	1.57	11.64	8.28
6	Laces	1.48	1.48	2.96	1.97
7	Toe Support Brace		1.27		
8	Toe Support Pad		3.29		
9	Back Support Cushion		5.00	6.50	
10	Sole	10.37	10.37	10.37	10.37
11	**Materials Total**	$ 50.15	$ 74.07	$ 64.24	$ 62.82
12					
13	Minimum cost of a component:	$ 1.27			
14	Maximum cost of a component:	$ 48.86			
15					
16					

Worksheet displayed with updated values for SUM, MIN, and MAX functions

	A	B	C	D	E
1		TZEdge Material Analysis			
2	Component	Original Option	Textured Leather	High Top	Average
3	Leather	24.4278	=2*B3	=B3*1.25	=AVERAGE(B3:D3)
4	Internal Arch Support	2.235	=B4	=C4	=AVERAGE(B4:D4)
5	Trim (applique set & logo)	11.64	1.57	=B5	=AVERAGE(B5:D5)
6	Laces	1.4805	=B6	=2*B6	=AVERAGE(B6:D6)
7	Toe Support Brace		1.27		
8	Toe Support Pad		3.29		
9	Back Support Cushion		5	6.5	
10	Sole	10.37083333333	=B10	=B10	=AVERAGE(B10:D10)
11	**Materials Total**	=SUM(B3:B10)	=SUM(C3:C10)	=SUM(D3:D10)	=AVERAGE(B11:D11)
12					
13	Minimum cost of a component:	=MIN(B3:D10)			
14	Maximum cost of a component:	=MAX(B3:D10)			
15					
16					

Worksheet displayed with updated formulas for SUM, MIN, and MAX functions

The worksheet on the top in Figure 1.15 displays the new values. Notice that the materials totals have been updated (except the total for the original option, which does not include the new components). In addition, the minimum and maximum calculations in cells B13 and B14 have been updated as well. Because the cost of the toe support brace ($1.27) is less than any others previously entered, the value in cell B13 has been updated to show this cost.

The worksheet on the bottom in Figure 1.15 shows the new formulas. These formulas were updated automatically when the three rows were added. For example, the formula in cell C13 now reads =MIN(B3:D10); the original formula was =MIN(B3:D7). Similarly, the average calculation for the sole in cell E10 now reads =AVERAGE(B10:D10); the original formula =AVERAGE(B7:D7) was automatically updated by Excel.

The averages for the three new components must be calculated, but how should these calculations be performed? For example, to calculate the average cost of the back support cushion, should Paul average only the textured leather and high top options, because only these two options include this cushion (that is, $(5+6.50)/2$)—or should Paul also include the original option as \$0 (that is, $(0+5+6.50)/3$)? There is no one right answer to this dilemma, but it's helpful to consider how the information will be used. Because this information will only give the purchasing group a handle on the order-of-magnitude costs of these components, it would be better to average only the values where the material is being used.

What Excel formula should be written to accomplish this? To know how to proceed, you need to understand the algorithm used by the AVERAGE function. The Help feature in Excel provides the following information about the AVERAGE function: "If a reference argument contains text, logical values, or empty cells, those values are ignored; however, cells with the value zero are included." Based on this definition, the AVERAGE function in cell E9 could be written to include all three columns, as follows: =AVERAGE(B9:D9). The advantage of including cell B9 is that if, at a later date, a back support cushion is required for the original option, a value could be entered and the average would automatically be updated. This is the method Paul chooses, so he enters the appropriate formulas in column E to calculate the averages for the three new components.

Sometimes, you would want to include a blank cell in the AVERAGE calculation because it's important for the calculation to accurately reflect the number of values being averaged. In such a case, you could simply enter the value 0 in the blank cell.

CALCULATING THE NUMBER OF VALUES USING THE COUNT AND COUNTA FUNCTIONS

A final calculation needed in the current worksheet is to determine a count of the number of material components in each option. This information is needed by the production group when they plan how much storage space is required on-site and the number of hours of material handling needed during production. Paul can enter these values just below the Materials Total in row 12. In this case, blank cells must be ignored and not counted. Fortunately, like the AVERAGE function, the COUNT function also ignores blank cells and cells with text. So, in cell B12, Paul enters the formula =COUNT(B3:B10). Similar formulas will count the number of components for the textured leather and high top options, although this process is becoming repetitive. In Level 3, you'll explore more efficient ways of entering similar formulas multiple times.

In cell A12, Paul wants to display the total number of components being considered for any of the three options by simply counting the component descriptions. In this case, the COUNT function will not work, because it ignores cells with text. An alternative is to use the COUNTA function, which is similar to the COUNT function but does not ignore text cells. Paul decides to expand the formula so that it counts the number of components for each specific option as well. So, he enters the formula =COUNTA(A3:A10) in cell A12. The results, which are displayed in Figure 1.16, show that there are eight components in all; five components are used in the original option; eight components are used in the textured leather option; and six components are used in the high top option. Paul also makes the following formatting changes to improve the readability of the worksheet:

- Adds the label "count" in cell E12
- Highlights cells A12:E12 and places a border around the row
- Places borders around cells A13:B14 and around the overall worksheet cells A2:E14
- Formats the values in cells A12:E12 with centered alignment, and bold and italic styles

Figure 1.16: Final worksheet with formatting

	A	B	C	D	E	F
1	**TZEdge Material Analysis**					
2	Component	Original Option	Textured Leather	High Top	Average	
3	Leather	$ 24.43	$ 48.86	$ 30.53	$ 34.61	
4	Internal Arch Support	2.24	2.24	2.24	2.24	
5	Trim (applique set & logo)	11.64	1.57	11.64	8.28	
6	Laces	1.48	1.48	2.96	1.97	
7	Toe Support Brace		1.27		1.27	
8	Toe Support Pad		3.29		3.29	
9	Back Support Cushion		5.00	6.50	5.75	
10	Sole	10.37	10.37	10.37	10.37	
11	Materials Total	$ 50.15	$ 74.07	$ 64.24	$ 62.82	
12	***8***	***5***	***8***	***6***	***count***	
13	Minimum cost of a component:	$ 1.27				
14	Maximum cost of a component:	$ 48.86				
15						
16						

=COUNTA(A3:A10)

New formulas inserted for average costs including blank cells

=COUNT(B3:B10)

Steps To Success: Level 2

Recall that the two additional options being considered for the TZEdge shoe are as follows:

- Textured leather that includes only a logo, and no appliques, for trim
- A high top design similar to the original shoe

Now that the material analysis for the three options is in place, the labor costs must be determined. Figure 1.17 shows the labor comparison worksheet that has been developed so far; it contains the costs associated with the manufacturing tasks for one shoe produced with the original option.

Figure 1.17: Labor comparison worksheet

	A	B	C	D	E
1	TZEdge Labor Cost Comparison				
2	Manufacturing Tasks Per Shoe:	Original Option	Textured Leather	High Top	
3	Delivery of Boxes to Production Line	$ 0.14			
4	Cutting of Leather	1.12			
5	Attachment of Appliques	2.03			
6	Sewing of Logos to Leather	1.11			
7	Assembly of Leather, Sole	2.25			
8	Assembly of Arch Support	0.68			
9	Total Labor				
10					
11					

The manufacturing group has been meeting to determine how the different design options will affect the number of hours and skills required to assemble the shoe. This group has provided the following information:

Textured Leather
- The textured leather is actually easier to work with compared to the original option. The group estimates it will take about two thirds of the time to assemble the leather and sole.
- The group also estimates that it will take about two thirds of the time to assemble the arch support as compared to the original option.
- Because there are no appliques on the textured leather, there is no cost for attaching them. So, the cell calculating the attachment of appliques can be left blank.
- The cutting of the leather will take approximately the same time as for the original option.
- Only one logo needs to be sewn on, so the cost for this is approximately half the amount as that of the original option.
- The cost for delivering boxes needs to be reduced by 10% compared to the original option.

High Top
- The high top shoes require additional leather. The group estimates it will take about 15% more time to assemble the leather and sole compared to the original option.
- All other manufacturing costs remain the same as those for the original option.

Now, you need to finish the worksheet to determine the manufacturing costs of the textured leather and high top options.

Complete the following:

1. Open the workbook named **Comparison.xls** located in the Chapter 1 folder, and then save it as **Labor Comparison.xls**.

2. Complete columns C and D for the textured leather and high top options based on the data provided for the original option and the information provided by the manufacturing group.

3. Calculate the total labor cost for each option.

4. Format all the values in the worksheet with two decimal places and dollar signs displayed in the first row and total row only.

5. In row 11, below the option totals, calculate the number of tasks in each option and the number of possible tasks based on the list in column A. Format these values in bold and italic, and insert the label "# Tasks" (also in bold and italic) in cell E11.

6. In cell E3, calculate the minimum cost of the box delivery task for the three options. Label the column "Min. Cost". Then, calculate the minimum cost for each of the other manufacturing tasks and for the total labor.

7. In cell F3, calculate the maximum cost of the box delivery task for the three options. Label the column "Max. Cost". Then, calculate the maximum cost for each of the other manufacturing tasks and for the total labor.

8. Several rows below the totals, in column B, calculate the average labor cost of all manufacturing tasks for all three options combined. Blank cells should not be included in the average. Place the label "Average" to the left of the calculation.

9. The data for the toe support brace, toe support pad, and back support cushion was omitted in error from the worksheet. The manufacturing group advises to include $1.00 in labor costs to assemble these three items for the textured leather option, and to include $.75 in labor costs to assemble these three items for the high top option. Insert a row above the "Assembly of Leather, Sole" task and include the necessary values and the label "Leather Support Assembly." (Recall that the original option does not include these items.) Check all your formulas to ensure they are updated correctly based on the newly inserted values.

10. Save and close the Labor Comparison.xls workbook.

LEVEL 3

ANALYZING CELL REFERENCES WHEN WRITING AND COPYING FORMULAS

EXCEL 2003 SKILLS TRAINING

- Name a range
- Use absolute references
- Use the fill handle to copy a cell
- Use the fill handle to copy formulas
- Use a named range reference in one or more formulas
- Use relative references

CREATING A BUDGET WORKBOOK

The task of compiling material and labor costs for the TZEdge shoe is now complete. The next step for Paul is to set up a preliminary budget for each quarter of the first year of production and a combined summary. For now, Paul will produce this information for only the original option of the TZEdge shoe. He also will create budgets for three different selling price alternatives: low priced, medium priced, and high priced. The estimated sales volumes for each of these pricing alternatives in each quarter, and the associated shoe prices, are provided in Table 1.6. The expenses such as material costs and labor costs per shoe will be constant in each alternative and in each quarter, though the volumes will vary.

Table 1.6: Shoe prices and estimated sales volumes

		1stQTR	2ndQTR	3rdQTR	4thQTR
	$/Pair	#Pairs	#Pairs	#Pairs	#Pairs
Alternative:					
Low Priced	200	1,000	1,500	1,700	2,500
Medium Priced	225	750	1,000	1,100	1,600
High Priced	250	350	450	480	750

From his earlier analysis of material and labor costs, and with new information provided, Paul knows the following about the original option:

- Material costs total $50.15 per shoe.
- Labor costs total $7.33 per shoe.
- Overhead costs are calculated as 25% of the direct labor costs.
- Selling expense is calculated at $10 per pair of shoes, or $5.00 per shoe.

Organizing the Workbook

With the necessary information in hand, how should Paul organize the new budget workbook he needs to create? Consider the Options worksheet created earlier (Figure 1.16). In this worksheet, all the inputs and outputs for the three design options are displayed on the same worksheet. This layout is easy to read and implement because there are a limited number of options and relatively simple calculations. But what if each design option had a completely different set of data inputs, or the values of the inputs varied from option to option? In such a case, it might be easier to create separate worksheets for each design option, or put all the inputs together on one worksheet and the outputs together on another.

For the budget workbook, Paul needs to organize data for four quarters, with each quarter containing data for the three different pricing alternatives. If he placed all the data on one worksheet, it would contain 12 separate sets of calculations and inputs. Although this is possible, such an organization would make the worksheet cumbersome to manipulate. Figure 1.18 illustrates and compares several possible ways to organize the budget workbook.

Figure 1.18: Possible workbook designs

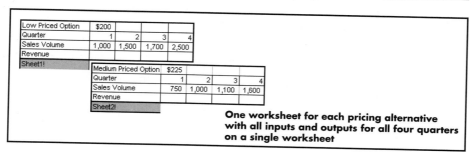

204

Note the following:

- The first organization places all the inputs on one worksheet and all the outputs on another. This is a simple organization but, again, might be difficult to work with and could cause confusion, because it would be difficult to ascertain which set of inputs are associated with a particular output.
- The second organization is by pricing alternative. The inputs and outputs are placed on a single worksheet, with each worksheet containing all four quarters for a specific pricing alternative.
- The third organization is by quarter. The inputs and outputs are placed on a single worksheet, with each worksheet containing all three pricing alternatives for a specific quarter.

Additionally, Paul could create 12 separate worksheets—one for each pricing alternative for each quarter.

Which workbook organization should Paul choose? That depends on what he wants to emphasize and compare, and what elements are most likely to change. Because management is probably most interested in the financial ramifications in each quarter, Paul decides to organize the worksheets by quarter. In this way, a single sheet will contain both the inputs and outputs associated with a specific time frame. The worksheets will be named 1stQTR, 2ndQTR, 3rdQTR, and 4thQTR. After entering the information for each of the four quarters, Paul can easily combine the data into a summary on a separate sheet named Summary.

To create the worksheets for the four quarters and the summary, Paul could select all five worksheets simultaneously by clicking the first tab and then holding down the Shift key and clicking the Summary worksheet tab. Everything he enters would be entered on all five worksheets at the same time. The values and formulas entered for the first quarter would be recorded on each selected worksheet in the identical way. So, if the cell in sheet 1stQTR!B7, for example, contained the formula =SUM(B1:B6), it would add cells B1 to B6 only on the 1stQTR worksheet. The same formula would be entered simultaneously in cell 2ndQTR!B7 and would add cells B1 to B6 on the 2ndQTR worksheet. After setting up the worksheets in this way, Paul could edit those values that are different for each quarter. Keep in mind that this method only works well on worksheets with identical structures. Furthermore, caution should be used when creating and modifying a workbook in this manner. Although this method is convenient, you could damage your workbook by inadvertently making changes, such as deleting values or formulas, to multiple selected worksheets when you intended to make the changes on only one worksheet.

Notice the syntax used for referencing cells with their worksheet names. First is the sheet name, followed by an exclamation point "!" then the usual column letter and, finally, the row number. Sheet names are only needed in formulas when the cell being referenced is on another worksheet.

Another approach would be to simply complete the first quarter worksheet with no other worksheets selected. Then, Paul could select the entire worksheet or specific ranges and copy them to the other sheets, again making the appropriate changes as needed. This is the method Paul uses. He begins by creating the 1stQTR worksheet, shown in Figure 1.19. Labels and values list the revenue and expense items down the column, and the volume values for each of the three pricing alternatives are listed across the row. Also, some of the inputs needed in all four quarters are listed at the top of the worksheet in cells B1:B2.

Figure 1.19: First quarter budget

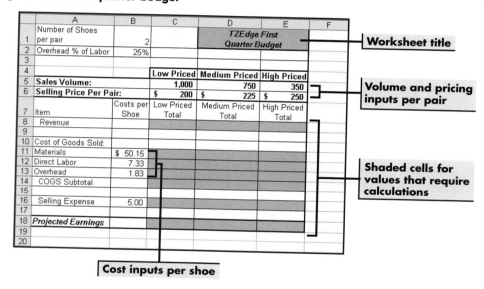

Notice cell B13, which contains the formula that calculates the unit cost (cost/shoe) of overhead for the original option. Because overhead is given as 25% of direct labor (see cell B2), the formula in cell B13 multiplies the labor expense $7.33 by 25%. In Excel syntax, this formula is =B12*B2. Note that cell B2 can be used directly in the formula because it has been formatted as a percent; the precise value stored is still 0.25. To clarify the work remaining to be done in the worksheet, the cells in which formulas need to be entered are shaded.

UNDERSTANDING RELATIVE CELL REFERENCING

Paul needs to create the necessary formulas to calculate revenues and expenses for the original option of the TZEdge shoe. The costs of material and labor on a per shoe basis are taken from the analyses done earlier. Paul will need to adjust these values later to multiply them by 2, because sales volumes are based on pairs of shoes.

Revenue can be calculated as sales volume times selling price. So, the formula =C5*C6 is entered in cell C8. Rather than create similar formulas in cells D8 and E8, wouldn't it be convenient if there was a way to tell Excel to use the same formula, but with a different set of data? In fact, Excel has the ability to change a formula *relative* to the location of the original formula. This allows you to use a "general" formula over and over again, but with a different set of numbers. To do this, you use a feature called **relative cell referencing**.

When you copy a formula from one cell to another, Excel automatically alters the new formula relative to where it is being copied. So, if you have the formula =C5*C6 in cell C8 and copy it to cell D8, a displacement of 1 column and 0 rows, the formula is rewritten adding 1 column and 0 rows to each relative cell reference. There are two of these references in this formula: the first is C5 and the second is C6. If you add 1 column to C, it becomes column D. If you add 0 rows to 5, it remains 5, resulting in the cell reference D5. In a similar manner, the cell reference C6 is changed to D6. The new formula is now =D5*D6, which is the formula needed in this case. This process is illustrated in Figure 1.20.

Figure 1.20: Copying formulas with relative cell references

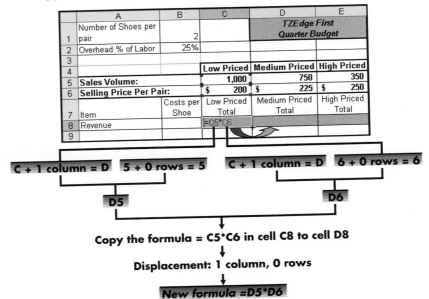

What about formulas that contain functions or constants? An example of this might be a formula to calculate the average sales volume and average selling price. If the formula =AVERAGE(C5:E5) was placed in cell F5, what would the resulting formula be if it was copied to cell F6? Here, the displacement is 0 columns and 1 row, resulting in a new formula in cell F6, =AVERAGE(C6:E6).

What happens when you copy formulas from one worksheet to another? Consider what would result if the formula =C5*C6 was copied from cell C8 on Sheet1! to cell E11 on Sheet2!. What is the displacement in this case? Because no sheet name is specified in the cell references, when the formula is copied, it would refer to cells on Sheet2! instead of Sheet1!. Which cells would it reference on Sheet2!? Here is the process:

- The displacement from C8 to E11 is 2 columns and 3 rows.
- Take the cell reference C5 and add 2 columns, 3 rows: this results in the new reference E8.
- Take the cell reference C6 and add 2 columns, 3 rows: this results in the new reference E9.
- When these elements are put together, the resulting formula is =E8*E9. Because this formula was copied to another worksheet, it now references these cells on the new sheet.

Formulas can also be copied in the opposite directions, back up columns and further to the left on rows. For example, the formula =D9*C7 could be copied from cell E9 into cell C8. In this case, the displacement is minus 2 columns and minus 1 row, resulting in the formula =B8*A6. You need to be careful that the resulting formulas contain only valid references. Copying a formula such as =A2+C3 from cell C4 to cell B3 would result in a #REF! error, because it is not possible to go minus 1 column further than column A.

Paul enters the formula =C5*C6 in cell C8 and copies it, using the fill handle, to cells D8 and E8. When copying formulas, you can use the copy/paste techniques, but it is easier to use the fill handle if you are copying to adjacent cells. The **fill handle** is a small square in the lower-right corner of a selected cell or cells that you drag to copy the contents of the selected cell or cells. The current worksheet is shown in Figure 1.21.

How To

Copy Formulas Using the Fill Handle
1. Select the cell or cells containing the formula(s) that you want to copy.
2. Place the pointer on the bottom-right corner of the selected cell(s) until it changes to the fill handle ✚.
3. Press and hold down the left mouse button, and then drag the mouse down or across, as necessary, into one or more adjacent cells. This automatically copies the formula(s) into the adjacent cells indicated.

Figure 1.21: Revenue formulas filled across

	A	B	C	D	E	F
1	Number of Shoes per pair	2		TZEdge First Quarter Budget		
2	Overhead % of Labor	25%				
3						
4			Low Priced	Medium Priced	High Priced	
5	Sales Volume:		1,000	750	350	
6	Selling Price Per Pair:		$ 200	$ 225	$ 250	
7	Item	Costs per Shoe	Low Priced Total	Medium Priced Total	High Priced Total	
8	Revenue		$ 200,000	$ 168,750	$ 87,500	
9						
10	Cost of Goods Sold:					
11	Materials	$ 50.15				
12	Labor	7.33				
13	Overhead	1.83				
14	COGS Subtotal					
15						
16	Selling Expense	5.00				
17						
18	*Projected Earnings*					
19						
20						

=C5*C6   =D5*D6   =E5*E6

UNDERSTANDING ABSOLUTE AND MIXED CELL REFERENCING

Next, Paul needs to calculate the total cost of materials. This calculation takes the number of shoes per pair, times the materials cost per shoe, times the sales volume. For the low priced alternative, this formula is entered in cell C11 as =B1*B11*C5. As with the revenue calculation, it would save time if this formula could be copied from cell C11 across row 11, varying the sales volume for each corresponding pricing alternative. In fact, it would be ideal to copy this same formula down column C, substituting the cost of labor and then the cost of overhead for the cost of materials. As currently written, if the formula =B1*B11*C5 was copied from cell C11 to cell D11, a displacement of 1 column and 0 rows, the resulting formula would be =C1*C11*C5. Not only would the cell reference for the sales volume change, but the references for the number of shoes per pair and the materials cost per shoe would change as well. This would not work; cell C1 is blank and cell C11 contains the value just calculated for the materials cost per shoe for the low priced alternative.

What you want Excel to do in such a case is to vary some of the values, but not others. For some operands, you want nothing to change; for others only the row should change; and for still others only the column should change. Can this be done? The answer is yes. In addition to relative cell references, Excel allows you to indicate that a cell reference (both column and row) or even a part of a cell reference (column or row) can remain unchanged when copying. This is called **absolute cell referencing**. The syntax used by Excel to indicate that a cell reference is absolute is a dollar sign "$" placed either before the column letter, before the row number, or both. A cell reference that has only one $ is referred to as a **mixed reference**. Mixed referencing is common when you need to copy a formula both down a column and across the row at the same time.

Paul can apply absolute and mixed cell referencing to the formula he enters in cell C11 (=B1*B11*C5) as illustrated in Figure 1.22.

Figure 1.22: Using absolute and mixed cell referencing

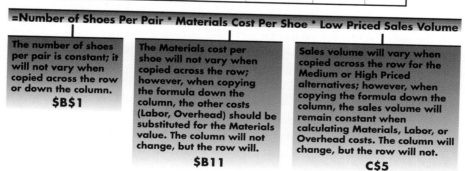

=B1*B11*C5 ⟶ $B$1*$B11*C$5

	A	B	C	D	E	F
1	Number of Shoes per pair	2		*TZEdge First*		
2	Overhead % of Labor	25%		*Quarter Budget*		
3						
4			Low Priced	Medium Priced	High Priced	
5	Sales Volume:		1,000	750	350	
6	Selling Price Per Pair:		$ 200	$ 225	$ 250	
7	Item	Costs per Shoe	Low Priced Total	Medium Priced Total	High Priced Total	
8	Revenue		$ 200,000	$ 168,750	$ 87,500	
9						
10	Cost of Goods Sold:					
11	Materials	$ 50.15	=$B$1*$B11*C$5			
12	Labor	7.33				
13	Overhead	1.83				
14	COGS Subtotal					
15						
16	Selling Expense	5.00				
17						
18	*Projected Earnings*					
19						
20						

=Number of Shoes Per Pair * Materials Cost Per Shoe * Low Priced Sales Volume

The number of shoes per pair is constant; it will not vary when copied across the row or down the column.
$B$1

The Materials cost per shoe will not vary when copied across the row; however, when copying the formula down the column, the other costs (Labor, Overhead) should be substituted for the Materials value. The column will not change, but the row will.
$B11

Sales volume will vary when copied across the row for the Medium or High Priced alternatives; however, when copying the formula down the column, the sales volume will remain constant when calculating Materials, Labor, or Overhead costs. The column will change, but the row will not.
C$5

Consider the first operand, the number of shoes per pair. Does this value change when the formula is copied down the column to calculate the total cost of labor or overhead? No, this value remains the same; specifically, you want to tell Excel, "don't change the row of the cell reference when copying the formula down." Does this value change when the formula is copied across the row to calculate the total materials cost of the medium priced alternative? Again, this value remains the same; specifically, you want to tell Excel, "don't change the column of the cell reference when copying the formula across." To convey this in Excel syntax, you write the cell reference as $B$1. The first $ indicates that the column is absolute, the second that the row is absolute.

The second operand in the formula =$B$1*B11*C5 is B11. How should this operand behave when it is copied down the column? B11 represents the cost of materials per shoe, and indeed this value should change relatively to reflect the cost of labor per shoe, and then the cost of overhead per shoe, when the formula is copied down the column. So, the row of cell reference B11 is *relative*. What about the column reference; should that vary when the cost of materials per shoe in the formulas is copied across the row for the medium priced alternative and the high priced alternative? The cost of materials does not change; it remains the same regardless of which pricing alternative is being considered. So, the reference B11 must be changed to the *mixed* reference $B11, making the column absolute but allowing the row to change relatively.

The third operand in the formula =$B$1*$B11*C5 is C5. How should this operand behave when it is copied down the column? C5 represents the sales volume for the low priced alternative. Does this volume change depending on the expense item? No, it remains the same whether you are calculating material costs, labor costs, or overhead. So, the row must be absolute. What about when this formula is copied across the row to determine the cost of materials for the medium priced and high priced alternatives? Here, the sales volume varies relative to the column. So, the reference C5 must be changed to the mixed reference to C$5.

To have the formula for the total cost of materials for the low priced alternative work correctly across all three alternatives and for each of the cost components, Paul writes the formula =$B$1*$B11*C$5 in cell C11 and uses the fill handle to copy it down the column and then across the row. Figure 1.23 shows the current worksheet values and their corresponding formulas.

Figure 1.23: First quarter budget values and formulas displayed

	A	B	C	D	E	F
1	Number of Shoes per pair	2		TZEdge First Quarter Budget		
2	Overhead % of Labor	25%				
3						
4			Low Priced	Medium Priced	High Priced	
5	Sales Volume:		1,000	750	350	
6	Selling Price Per Pair:		$ 200	$ 225	$ 250	
7	Item	Costs per Shoe	Low Priced Total	Medium Priced Total	High Priced Total	
8	Revenue		$ 200,000	$ 168,750	$ 87,500	
9						
10	Cost of Goods Sold:					
11	Materials	$ 50.15	100,300	75,225	35,105	
12	Labor	7.33	14,660	10,995	5,131	
13	Overhead	1.83	3,665	2,749	1,283	
14	COGS Subtotal					
15						
16	Selling Expense	5.00				
17						
18	Projected Earnings					
19						
20						

> **First quarter Materials cost for the Low Priced alternative (C11) is 100,300 using the formula =$B$1*$B11*C$5. This formula was copied down the column and across the row into cells C11:E13.**

	A	B	C	D	E	F
1	Number of Shoes per pair	2		TZEdge First Quarter Budget		
2	Overhead % of Labor	0.25				
3						
4			Low Priced	Medium Priced	High Priced	
5	Sales Volume:		1000	750	350	
6	Selling Price Per Pair:		200	225	250	
7	Item	Costs per Shoe	Low Priced Total	Medium Priced Total	High Priced Total	
8	Revenue		=C5*C6	=D5*D6	=E5*E6	
9						
10	Cost of Goods Sold:					
11	Materials	50.15	=$B$1*$B11*C$5	=$B$1*$B11*D$5	=$B$1*$B11*E$5	
12	Labor	7.33	=$B$1*$B12*C$5	=$B$1*$B12*D$5	=$B$1*$B12*E$5	
13	Overhead	=B2*B12	=$B$1*$B13*C$5	=$B$1*$B13*D$5	=$B$1*$B13*E$5	
14	COGS Subtotal					
15						
16	Selling Expense	5				
17						
18	Projected Earnings					
19						
20						

What would happen to the formulas if Paul needed to insert a row at the top of the worksheet to include a title? Now, the number of shoes per pair would be in cell B2 instead of cell B1. Would Paul need to rewrite the formulas, especially the ones that reference cell B1 absolutely? What happens to formulas with relative and absolute cell referencing when rows or columns are inserted into a worksheet? All references that are affected by the insertion adjust accordingly, whether they are relative or absolute. This also applies when deleting rows, columns, or cells, except when a deleted cell is directly referenced by a formula.

How To

Change a Cell Reference to an Absolute or Mixed Cell Reference
1. Type the cell reference in your formula or click the cell you want to include in the formula.
2. Type the dollar sign(s) needed to make the cell reference absolute or mixed.

OR
1. Type the cell reference in your formula or click the cell you want to include in the formula.
2. Press the F4 function key to add the dollar sign(s) needed to make the cell reference absolute or mixed. The **F4 function key** cycles through the display of dollar signs. If you press F4 once, the cell reference changes to an absolute reference, with dollar signs before both the row and column. If you press F4 twice, only the row is made absolute; and pressing F4 a third time makes only the column absolute.

Naming a Cell or Cell Range

Another technique that can be used to address a cell reference absolutely is to give that cell a name. You can name a single cell or a cell range, and then use that name directly in a formula. To name a cell or range, you first highlight the cell or cells to be named and then click the Name box, just below the toolbars. If Paul names cell B1 "pair," for example, then instead of using the cell reference $B$1 in the formula, he could write =pair*B11*C5. Note that range names, unlike text labels, are not enclosed in quotation marks when used in formulas. If you attempt to use a name that has not been defined, Excel displays the error message #NAME!.

Writing a Formula to Subtotal the Cost of Goods Sold

The next calculation Paul needs to perform is to subtotal the Cost of Goods Sold (COGS). This formula can simply be written in cell C14 as =SUM(C11:C13). Again, because this formula must be copied across the row, Paul must consider whether any absolute cell references are required. In this case, each of the cost values for each of the pricing alternatives should change, so the cell references are *relative* and no dollar signs are required.

Best Practice

Using Absolute Cell References Appropriately
When copying a formula both down a column and across a row, the placement of the $ absolute signs is critical or the wrong values will result. When copying in only one direction, either just across a row or just down a column, often the addition of extra $ absolute signs will not affect the calculated outcome, but can make for less efficient and confusing formulas. For example, you might be tempted to write the formula =SUM(C11:C13) as =SUM(C$11:C$13) because you want the column references to change, but you do not want the row references to change, when the formula is copied across the row. However, when you are only copying a formula across a row (or down a column), the row (or column) won't change. There is no displacement, which makes the $ superfluous. As a matter of good formula writing technique and to maintain the efficiency of your worksheets, you should minimize the number of $ absolute signs in your formulas and include them only when necessary.

Writing a Formula to Calculate Selling Expense

Before calculating the projected earnings, Paul needs to determine the selling expense. Again, he needs to calculate the cost per shoe—in this case by multiplying selling expense by both the number of shoes per pair and the sales volume for the associated pricing alternative. This is the same formula used for all of the COGS expenses. So, the formula can be copied from any one of the COGS expense formulas, such as the formula in cell C11, into cells C16:E16.

Writing a Formula to Calculate Projected Earnings

Now, finally, Paul is ready to determine if the original TZEdge shoe is estimated to earn any profit in the first quarter of sales. Because this worksheet is intended to provide only a rough idea of the profitability of this venture, Paul has not included any detailed accounting terminology or taken into account investment costs, which are unknown, or taxes. So, the term "projected earnings" for the purposes of this analysis is defined as revenue minus COGS minus selling expense. Paul writes the following formula in cell C18 to represent projected earnings for the low priced alternative: =C8-C14-C16. This formula can then be copied across the row into cells D18 and E18. Because each of the values changes relatively, no absolute cell referencing is required in the formula. The finished first quarter budget worksheet is shown in Figure 1.24.

Figure 1.24: Finished first quarter budget

	A	B	C	D	E	F
1	Number of Shoes per pair	2		TZEdge First Quarter Budget		
2	Overhead % of Labor	25%				
3						
4			Low Priced	Medium Priced	High Priced	
5	Sales Volume:		1,000	750	350	
6	Selling Price Per Pair:		$ 200	$ 225	$ 250	
7	Item	Costs per Shoe	Low Priced Total	Medium Priced Total	High Priced Total	
8	Revenue		$ 200,000	$ 168,750	$ 87,500	
9						
10	Cost of Goods Sold:					
11	Materials	$ 50.15	100,300	75,225	35,105	
12	Labor	7.33	14,660	10,995	5,131	
13	Overhead	1.83	3,665	2,749	1,283	
14	COGS Subtotal		118,625	88,969	41,519	
15						
16	Selling Expense	5.00	$ 10,000	$ 7,500	$ 3,500	
17						
18	Projected Earnings		$ 71,375	$ 72,281	$ 42,481	
19						
20						

Completing the Budget Workbook

To complete the budget workbook, Paul needs to create similar worksheets for the second, third, and fourth quarters, as well as a summary worksheet showing the annual budget. To do so, he simply copies the 1stQTR worksheet and pastes it on the other worksheets. Because none of the cell references used in the 1stQTR worksheet refer to a particular worksheet, the formulas adjust relative to the new worksheet when copied. Paul then substitutes the appropriate sales volumes in each of the corresponding quarters on the remaining worksheets. The revenue and expense values are updated automatically.

To create the summary worksheet, Paul can copy any one of the quarterly budgets to a separate worksheet and then name that worksheet "Summary." In each cell where he wants to aggregate the four quarter values, he can write a formula to add the corresponding values from quarter 1 + quarter 2 + quarter 3 + quarter 4. Starting in cell Summary!C8, Paul could write the formula =1stQTR!C8+2ndQTR!C8+3rdQTR!C8+4thQTR!C8, either by entering the formula directly or clicking the appropriate worksheets and cells. It is also possible to use the SUM function and then select all four worksheets simultaneously and click cell C8 in one of them. The SUM function might be more efficient if additional worksheets will be inserted within the group later on, but it could also prove problematic if a worksheet is inserted but its values were not intended to be included in the formula.

When working with multiple worksheets, as soon as one cell contains the correct formula, you can simply copy the formula into all other cells to calculate their corresponding values. When the cell references in the formula contain a sheet name, the copied cell references still refer back to the corresponding worksheets. Paul uses this method to add the sales volume values for each of the three pricing alternatives.

The final summary sheet is shown in Figure 1.25. Based on the projected earnings calculated, it appears that the low priced alternative is the best option, at least regarding profits generated for the original shoe design. The volume seems to more than make up for the lower selling price per pair of shoes.

Figure 1.25: Annual budget summary

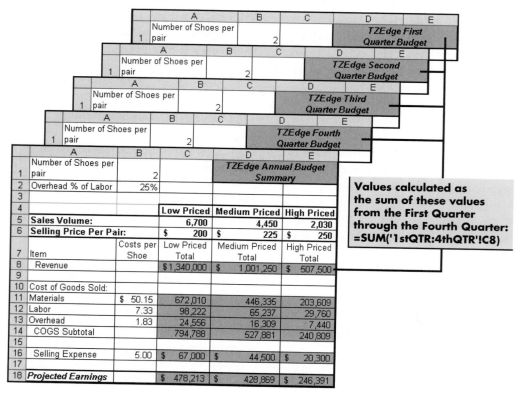

Values calculated as the sum of these values from the First Quarter through the Fourth Quarter:
=SUM('1stQTR:4thQTR'!C8)

Steps To Success: Level 3

You have learned a tremendous amount about creating the first year's budget for the original option of the new TZEdge shoe. Now you need to create quarterly budgets and a summary for the textured leather option using $74.07 per shoe as the cost of materials and $4.75 per shoe as the cost of labor.

Unlike with the original option, only two pricing alternatives are being considered for the textured leather option. Table 1.7 shows the two pricing alternatives, as well as the expected sales volume in each quarter for these alternatives. Overhead is calculated at 35% of the direct labor costs, and the selling expense is assumed to be $10 per pair, or $5 per shoe.

Table 1.7: Shoe prices and estimated sales volumes for the textured leather option

		1stQTR	2ndQTR	3rdQTR	4thQTR
Alternative:	$/Pair	#Pairs	#Pairs	#Pairs	#Pairs
Low Priced	225	660	800	1,050	1,200
High Priced	275	225	289	335	350

Complete the following:

1. Create a new workbook named **Textured Budget.xls** and save it in the Chapter 1 folder.

2. Using the finished first quarter budget worksheet for the original option as a model (see Figure 1.24), create a similar first quarter budget worksheet for the textured leather option, as follows:

   a. In cells A1:B2, enter the necessary inputs for number of shoes per pair and overhead.

   b. In cell C1, enter the title "TZEdge 1st Quarter Budget Textured Leather Option" in bold and italic; center and merge this title across cells C1:D1. Apply a gray shaded background to the title cells.

   c. In rows 4 through 6, enter the sales volume and selling price data, with the column headings "Low Priced" and "High Priced" in cells C4 and D4, respectively. Use similar formatting as shown in Figure 1.24.

   d. In cells A7:A18 and B7:D7, enter the same labels as for the original option (see Figure 1.24).

   e. In cells B11, B12, and B16, enter the costs per shoe for Materials, Labor, and Selling Expense, respectively.

   f. In cell B13, enter a formula to calculate the Overhead cost.

   g. In columns C and D, enter the necessary formulas to determine revenue, cost of goods sold, selling expense, and projected earnings for each pricing alternative. (Keep in mind that projected earnings is defined as revenue minus cost of goods sold minus selling expense.) Be sure to use the correct relative, absolute, and mixed cell referencing so that the formulas can be copied wherever it makes sense to do so, and so that the formulas will automatically update if any of the data inputs are later modified. Format the values and calculated results on your worksheet in a similar manner to those in Figure 1.24.

   h. Refer to Figure 1.24 and apply similar borders to the appropriate cells on your worksheet.

   i. Rename the Sheet1 worksheet tab as "1stQTR."

3. With the 1stQTR worksheet complete, use an appropriate method to create similar worksheets for the other three quarters. Name these worksheets "2ndQTR," "3rdQTR," and "4thQTR." Modify values and labels as necessary on these three worksheets.

4. Create a final comparison sheet named "Summary" that displays each of the budget components summarized by year for each pricing alternative. For the worksheet title in cells C1:D1, enter "TZEdge Annual Budget Textured Leather Option."

5. In cell A20, insert text to indicate which pricing alternative you would recommend, and why. Highlight this text with a yellow background.

6. Save and close the completed Textured Budget.xls workbook.

CHAPTER SUMMARY

This chapter presented some of the basic tools and concepts you need to understand when working with Excel to solve problems and support decisions. In Level 1, you learned that working with a spreadsheet created by someone else can be a challenging task—especially if the worksheet contains errors in formatting or formulas. You also learned how to locate and correct some of the more common errors to make the worksheet readable and functional. Related concepts, such as order of precedence and precision versus display, were also presented.

Level 2 covered simple functions, such as SUM and AVERAGE, and how to use these functions in formulas. You learned the syntax of these functions and their underlying algorithms, and how the AutoSum tool lets you apply these functions quickly and easily.

In Level 3, you had the opportunity to explore in greater detail the tasks of writing and copying formulas. It is clear that Excel gives you powerful tools for copying formulas using relative, absolute, and mixed cell references. Understanding the impact of these different cell references when copying formulas is critical to building successful worksheets.

CONCEPTUAL REVIEW

1. What is the meaning of each of the following error messages:

   - ######
   - #NAME?
   - #N/A
   - #REF!
   - #VALUE!
   - #NUM!
   - #DIV/0!

2. If you enter 2,806+4 in a cell exactly as shown (without an equal sign), what value would result?

3. If you enter =3+2*10 in a cell exactly as shown, what value would result?

4. List each of the following operations in order of precedence, from 1 to 4 (first to last):

   - Multiplication and division
   - Parentheses ( )
   - Addition and subtraction
   - Exponentiation

5. When writing formulas, why is it preferable to use cell references rather than typing in values?

6. In the worksheet below, cell A3 contains the formula =A1+A2. Explain the most likely reason why the value calculated appears incorrect.

	A	B	C
1	1	10%	
2	2		
3	4		
4			
5			

7. Referring to the worksheet above, if you wrote the formula =B1*120, what value would result (assuming the displayed value is the precise value)?

8. What formula would you write to do each of the following:

   a. Add a range of numbers in cells A2:Z2.
   b. Find the largest value in cells B2:B8.
   c. Find the smallest value in cells B2 through Z12.

   d. Find the average value in cells C1 through C10, assuming blank cells will be ignored.

   e. Find the total number of items listed in cells C1 through C10, including any that contain text.

9. Define the following terms: syntax, arguments, and algorithm.

10. If the formula =$B$4–SUM(A1:A5) is copied from cell A9 to cell C10, what is the resulting formula?

11. Refer to the following worksheet. What formula would you write in cell B2 that can be copied down the column and across the row to complete the multiplication table?

	A	B	C	D	E	F	G
1		1	2	3	4	5	
2	1	1	2	3	4	5	
3	2	2	4	6	8	10	
4	3	3	6	9	12	15	
5	4	4	8	12	16	20	
6	5	5	10	15	20	25	
7							
8							

12. What new formula results for each of the following if the formula is copied from cell B3 to cell D6?

   a. =A1+A2

   b. =$A$1+A2

   c. =$A1+A2

   d. =A$1+A2

13. What formula could you use to add up cell A1 from Sheet1!, Sheet 2!, and Sheet 3!?

14. Cell B1 has been given the range name "tax." How would you write a formula in cell C1 that multiplies the tax by A1? What new formula results if you copy this formula into cell C2?

CASE PROBLEMS

Level 1 – Purchasing a Computer for Grusee & Associates

Finance

You are currently employed at a small financial management firm, Grusee & Associates, as a financial analyst. Your boss has recently informed you that you can purchase a new desktop computer for your office, and has asked you to obtain three competitive bids before approving the purchase. The minimum requirements of the system you want to buy are as follows:

- 3.4 GHz Processor with 1 GB RAM
- 17" LCD monitor
- Sound system
- Optical mouse
- Keyboard

- 200 GB hard drive
- 3½" floppy drive
- CD-RW
- DVD-ROM
- Ethernet and Modem

Table 1.8 shows information for three possible computers: one from the Dell Web site, another from the Microcenter circular, and a third based on a phone quote obtained from Gateway. The data provided does not exactly match up, so you need to create a worksheet comparing all three systems and their total prices.

Table 1.8: Data for three computers

Dell	Microcenter	Gateway
Small business computer system: 3.6 GHz including 512 MB of RAM, 200 GB hard drive, keyboard, mouse, Ethernet card, CD-RW drive, speakers. Standard 1-year warranty... $979	Compaq Premier System as advertised: 3.4 GHz including 1 GB of RAM, 200 GB hard drive, keyboard, mouse, sound system, Ethernet card, CD-RW drive, 17" LCD screen monitor, DVD. Standard 90-day warranty... $1499	Gateway Premier System Computer: 3.3 GHz, 1 GB RAM, keyboard. 90-day warranty... $629
Additional items:	Additional items:	Additional items:
Upgrade to 1 GB RAM $169	3½" floppy $39.95	200 GB hard drive $219
Optical mouse $20	Free mail-in rebate for optical mouse: value $29.95	Ethernet card $19.95
LCD monitor $495	Local delivery $25	Speakers $35.99
DVD $109	Warranty extension 1 year $65	LCD 17" monitor $529
3½" floppy $45		3½" floppy drive $39.95
		CD R/W $109
Shipping and Handling $75		DVD $119
		Optical mouse $14.99
		Shipping and Handling free with orders over $700
		Warranty extension 1 year $89

Complete the following:

1. Create a new workbook named **Computer Purchase.xls** and save it in the Chapter 1 folder.

2. Create a worksheet that compares the cost of each of the listed items for the three computers. Organize the worksheet so that each component is listed separately. If an item is included in the base computer price, enter the label "Included." Be sure to include the following elements:

   a. A title formatted in Arial, size 14, bold, and italic. Center and merge the title above your worksheet and add a yellow fill.

   b. Appropriate column and row headings so that your worksheet is easily understood. If necessary, wrap the text headings into more than one row in the cell.

   c. Numbers in the first row and in any summation rows formatted with the Currency Style. All other dollar values should be formatted with the Comma Style.

3. Calculate the total cost of each system assuming all of the items on the list will be purchased.

4. Verify that your solution works even if other values are later substituted for any of the system component costs.

5. Highlight the cells in the column with the least expensive computer system in blue.

6. You learn from your boss that the corporation is planning on purchasing at least 30 similar systems. Because of this volume, the following price reductions are now available:

   • Dell has agreed to give a 10% across-the-board discount on everything but the shipping and handling fee, which remains at $75 per system.
   • Microcenter has agreed to a rebate of $100 per machine.
   • Gateway has agreed to a 15% reduction in price on the base machine and all peripherals. They have also agreed to upgrade the warranty to one year free of charge.

   Skip at least two rows at the bottom of your current data. In a separate area, calculate the total cost of a single machine using this new pricing structure. You can reference the values you have previously calculated.

7. Just below the calculation for Step 6, calculate the cost of purchasing the 30 machines with these discounts for each option.

8. Highlight the cell containing the lowest final cost for 30 machines.

9. Save and close the Computer Purchase.xls workbook.

Level 2 – Compiling Relocation Information for Devcon Finn, Inc.

Human Resources

You work in the human resources department of Devcon Finn, Inc., a computer consulting firm. An employee is considering a transfer to one of the company's other locations, and is qualified for several different positions. Your task is to help the employee choose the most appropriate position based on a number of criteria. For example, you need to determine the value of each position in terms of the disposable income the employee can expect. The position with the highest salary is located in the company's New York City office, but a studio apartment there costs about $2500 per month; however, the employee would not need a car.

You have documented each position in an Excel worksheet. On this sheet, you have recorded the positions, the annual salary, the cost of living multiplier that you obtained from a Web site, and estimates of a monthly car payment, assuming for some of these jobs the employee will need to purchase a car. You have also recorded information regarding bonuses that have been offered to the employee. Now, you need to finalize the worksheet.

Complete the following:

1. Open the workbook named **Position.xls** located in the Chapter 1 folder, and then save it as **Position Analysis.xls**.

2. In cells F2:F4, calculate the associated annual adjusted salary. This adjusted salary is the annual salary divided by the cost of living multiplier minus the expected *annual* car payments. (Note that car payments are given in $/month).

3. In cell F6, write a formula to calculate the average adjusted salary of the three positions.

4. In cell F7, write a formula to determine the value of the lowest adjusted salary. This formula should automatically update if any of the data inputs are later changed.

5. In cell F8, write a formula to determine the value of the highest adjusted salary. This formula should automatically update if any of the data inputs are later changed.

6. In cell G9, write a formula to determine the number of positions that include a bonus.

7. In cells H2:H4, calculate the value of the adjusted salary package for each position over a two-year period, including bonuses. The bonus does not need to be adjusted for location, because the employee plans on using the bonus toward a vacation. Assume that the employee will receive a 10% raise after the first year of employment in the new position.

8. Display dollar values without cents, and include a dollar sign only in the first row of columns with dollars. Format the cost of living multipliers with two decimal places displayed, and align these values on the decimal point.

9. Another position for which the employee is qualified has just become available. This

position, a Senior Consultant position, is also located in New York City, has an annual salary of $64,000, and includes a $5000 bonus. Because the position is located in New York City, assume that the employee will not be purchasing a car, and that the cost of living multiplier is 1.35. Insert the data for this new position just below the other New York position. Complete the calculations for adjusted salary and total two-year financial package. Verify that all of the other values you've calculated update correctly. Adjust the formatting of the new data, as needed, to match the formatting of the existing data.

10. Highlight in yellow the row of the position with the highest two-year financial package, and bold the text in this row.

11. Save and close the Position Analysis.xls workbook.

Level 3 – Analyzing Regional Sales Information for CKG Auto

Sales

As a regional sales manager for CKG Auto, you have just finished summarizing sales data for the first half of this year (January through June) aggregated by car model. You have started to enter data in an Excel worksheet, which lists by model the following:

- Sales Volume indicating the number of cars sold to dealers.
- Manufacturing (Mfg.) Cost per Vehicle.
- Total Cost of all vehicles sold for the model. You will need to calculate this based on the sales volume and the manufacturing costs per vehicle.
- Markup percentage, which is the percentage charged above manufacturing cost to dealers.
- Total Sales to dealers. You will need to calculate this as Total Cost plus Markup (Markup is the markup percentage times the manufacturer cost of the vehicle).
- % of Total Volume. You will need to calculate this based on volume for the model as compared to the volume of all models sold for the time period.

First, you need to complete the January through June computations based on the data contained in the worksheet and the information given above. Then, you have been asked to create a similar worksheet to estimate sales for July through December based on volume supplied by the marketing group. These volumes are based on the historical values adjusted for seasonal demand of specific car types and from market research data on car popularity.

After you have completed both the first half actual sales and second half estimated sales, you need to combine this data to determine expected yearly sales. Management is not only interested in the absolute value of those sales, but each model's contribution to the total yearly sales in each half of the year and in aggregate.

When you complete the workbook, verify that all data is correctly referenced so that your formulas will work as you copy them down the column or across the row, as necessary.

Your first task is to complete the Sales Summary for January through June by writing the necessary formulas in the cells that are highlighted in the Excel worksheet.

Complete the following:

1. Open the workbook named **Sales.xls** located in the Chapter 1 folder, and then save it as **Auto Sales.xls**. Rename the Sheet1 worksheet tab as **1st Half**.

2. In the highlighted cells, enter formulas to perform the necessary calculations. Be sure to write all formulas so that they can be copied as necessary. Note the following:

   - Display all dollar values in whole dollars and include the dollar sign in the first row and total rows only.
   - When calculating averages, do not include any models that had no sales. Display all average values (other than the percentage) with commas and no decimal places.
   - The formulas in column G need to determine the percent of total volume sales that the vehicle represents. (That is, if model A sold 100 cars and a total of 1000 cars were sold for all models, then model A would represent 10% of the total volume). Format the cells in column G to display values to the nearest tenth of a percent.

3. Your next task is to create an estimate of the July through December sales based on marketing data and the first half-year sales values. The marketing group has provided a list of all car models in identical order to the original data you received, with the expected sales volumes for each car model. This list is found in the workbook named Market.xls, which is located in the Chapter 1 folder. Manufacturing costs and markups are assumed to be the same for the second half of the year as they were for the first half. With the data and assumptions in mind, create a new worksheet named **2nd Half** in the Auto Sales.xls workbook, identical to the 1st Half worksheet. Copy and paste the sales volumes from the Market.xls workbook into your new worksheet. Verify that all the calculations in the new worksheet reflect the new data.

4. Create another new worksheet named **Summary**, and include the column headings shown in Table 1.10 on this new worksheet.

Table 1.10: Column headings for Summary worksheet

Model	Annual Volume	Jan-June Sales to Dealers	July-Dec Sales to Dealers	Total Sales to Dealers	%Total Sales to Dealers Jan-June	%Total Sales to Dealers July-Dec	%Total Sales to Dealers Annual

5. Insert the model numbers in the identical format as shown on the 1st Half and 2nd Half worksheets.

6. Insert the annual volume for each model—the combined totals of the January through June and the July through December volumes. Make sure that the values will automatically update if any of the input values are changed at a later time.

7. Insert the Jan–June sales to dealers, again ensuring that these values will automatically update if any of the input data changes.

8. Insert the July–Dec sales to dealers, again ensuring that these values will automatically update if any of the input data changes.

9. Create a combined total of sales to dealers for the entire year.

10. Calculate the total volumes and the total sales to dealers for each time period and annually in a row below the data.

11. Calculate the *percentage* of sales to dealers that each model represents, as a percent of the total sales to dealers for all models—first for the Jan–June time frame, then the July–December time frame, and finally for the annual values. *Use only one formula for this calculation* and make sure that the formula can be copied down the column to calculate the percentages for the corresponding models, and across the row to calculate the percentages for the corresponding time frames. Display the percentage values with an appropriate format and number of decimal places.

12. Format all three worksheets so that they have a professional appearance.

13. Save and close the Auto Sales.xls workbook.

Solving Problems with Statistical Analysis Tools

Manufacturing: Evaluating Quality Control Data to Perform a Cost Benefit Analysis

> *"Averages don't always reveal the most telling realities. You know Shaquille O'Neil and I have an average height of 6 feet."*
> —U.S. Labor Secretary Robert Reich (Mr. Reich is 4'10" tall, whereas the basketball star is 7'1" tall.)

LEARNING OBJECTIVES

Level 1

Understand basic concepts related to statistics
Specify the precision of values
Copy and paste information in a worksheet using Paste Special options
Calculate basic statistics: arithmetic mean, mode, median, standard deviation
Manage large worksheets by freezing panes and splitting the window

Level 2

Evaluate the rank of each value in a data set
Determine the highest and lowest values in a data set
Determine the number of items that meet specified criteria
Determine a total value for items that meet specified criteria
Include relational operators and wildcards in formulas to specify criteria

Level 3

Apply custom number formats to data
Perform what-if analyses
Perform reverse what-if analyses using the Goal Seek tool
Analyze data by category by combining functions
Simulate data to evaluate different outcomes

FUNCTIONS COVERED IN THIS CHAPTER

AVERAGE	MODE	ROUND
COUNTIF	RAND	SMALL
LARGE	RANDBETWEEN	STDEV
MEDIAN	RANK	SUMIF

CHAPTER INTRODUCTION

In this chapter, you will learn to use some data analysis tools to assist in problem solving. Excel provides a variety of predefined functions, including statistical functions that you can use to determine such values as the arithmetic mean, median, mode, and standard deviation of a set of data. These statistical values can then be compared to previously measured historical values, allowing you to determine both the differences and percent differences between the values. In addition to working with statistical functions, you will also explore other functions, such as LARGE, SMALL, and RANK, that help you to structure and analyze data in meaningful ways. The COUNTIF and SUMIF functions, which enable you to count and total data that meets specified criteria, are also covered. Using such functions can give you better insight into the values in a set of data and help you identify any patterns or trends in the data. The chapter also teaches you how to perform "what-if" analysis to examine the effects of changing specific worksheet values, and introduces Goal Seek, an Excel tool that allows you to work backward to determine the input required that will ensure a specific outcome. You will generate additional data by simulating possible outcomes with a set of inputs, which vary randomly between a certain set of values. You will also explore the use of custom formatting techniques to make your workbook easier to use and read.

CASE SCENARIO

TheZone manufactures and sells the TZBlazer line of skis, which features an innovative design that makes it one of the most popular on the market. The TZBlazer ski comes in three different styles: one designed for average skiers (A), one designed for expert skiers (E), and one designed for racing (R). Each model is available in different sizes. Due to the popularity of this ski line, the company is challenged to keep up with the demand. The manufacturing facility has been forced to add shifts in order to meet the increased sales volume. TheZone is committed to maintaining the high standards for which the company is known, but there is increasing concern that these standards will be compromised as a result of the increased production. This concern is partly due to the fact that one of the bottlenecks in the production process is Quality Control, often referred to as "QC." Here, each ski is thoroughly inspected and tested before being released for sale. Every time a ski is found to have a defect, the part is traced back to the original production line that manufactured and assembled the ski. The QC team leader, Joanna Cavallo, is responsible for coordinating quality control efforts for the ski line, including interacting with the purchasing and sales groups regarding any matters pertaining to the quality of the products. Since the increase in production, Joanna has noticed an increase in the number of TZBlazer skis being rejected by the QC group for quality defects. If this trend continues, it will directly affect the company's ability to meet the current ambitious production schedules, as well as add significant costs to the manufacturing process. Joanna needs to evaluate the new data and compare it with historical data to determine if any improvements in the manufacturing process might be required. As part of her analysis, Joanna will work with statistics.

**Operations
Management**

LEVEL 1

USING STATISTICAL FUNCTIONS TO COMPARE DATA VALUES

EXCEL 2003 SKILLS TRAINING

- **Freeze rows and columns**
- **Split a window into panes**
- **Use absolute references**
- **Use the AVERAGE function**
- **Use relative references**
- **Use the ROUND function**

UNDERSTANDING FUNDAMENTALS OF STATISTICS

Statistics is a subset of mathematics that is applied to observed data. It is widely used for explaining groups of data, also referred to as **data sets**, and how the data within a group varies. Statistical methods are also used to compare different groups or data sets. The following is a list of some common statistics terms and their definitions:

- **Mean** is the arithmetic average of a set of numbers.
- **Median** is the arithmetic value that occurs in the middle of a data set when organized from lowest to highest, where half the values are less than and half the values are greater than the median value.
- **Mode** is the arithmetic value that occurs most frequently in a data set.
- **Standard deviation** is a measure of how widely the data values are dispersed from the arithmetic mean.

For example, consider the following five values: 1, 1, 6, 7, and 10. The arithmetic mean, or average, of these values is 5, which is determined as follows: (1+1+6+7+10)/5. The median value is the "middle" value when the data is listed in ascending order; in this list of numbers, the middle value is 6, with two lower values and two higher values. The mode is the value that occurs most often; in this case, the number 1 is the mode value. And, finally, the standard deviation is 3.2. A somewhat complex formula is required to determine the standard deviation; the Help system in Excel explains this formula in detail.

Although this simple example illustrates these statistical values, to obtain meaningful statistics, you generally need to work with much larger data sets. Frequently when discussing these large sets of data, a statistician will examine the population distribution—comparing groups of values in ascending order to the frequency in which these groups of values occur. One such distribution is referred to as a **normal distribution**, which is illustrated in Figure 2.1.

Figure 2.1: Normal distribution with a mean of 5 and standard deviation of 2

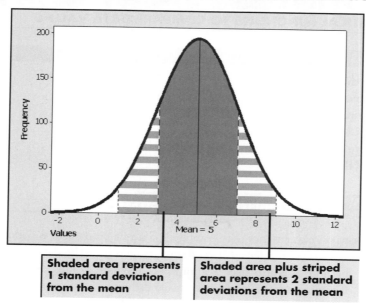

Shaded area represents 1 standard deviation from the mean

Shaded area plus striped area represents 2 standard deviations from the mean

A normal distribution exhibits equal number of occurrences of data values both below and above the arithmetic mean. The mean, median, and mode of a normal distribution are the same value. Figure 2.1 shows a normal distribution with a mean value of 5 and a standard deviation of 2.0. The shaded portions of the figure represent values included within 1 standard deviation of the mean (mean 5 +/− standard deviation 2.0 includes the range 3 to 7). The values in the shaded portion plus the values in the striped portion represent values within 2 standard deviations (mean 5 +/− standard deviation 2.0*2 represents values within the range 1 to 9). A normal distribution is characterized by the fact that approximately 95% of the values lie within plus or minus 2 standard deviations of the mean.

Figure 2.2 shows another normally distributed set of data with the same mean value of 5. Notice that these values mostly occur much closer to the mean than do the values in the data set shown in Figure 2.1. The standard deviation for the data set in Figure 2.2 is smaller, only 1.0.

Figure 2.2: Normal distribution with a mean of 5 and standard deviation of 1

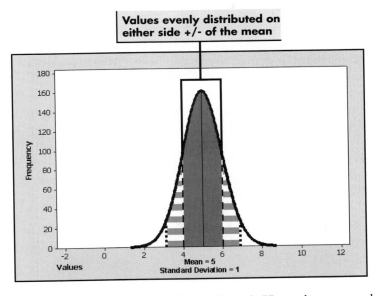

In Figure 2.3, the data set is not normally distributed. Here, the mean value is also 5, but the data has a few very high values and a large number of smaller values. In such a distribution, the arithmetic mean will not be equal to the mode or median values. Also, notice the large "tail" exhibited at one end of the distribution. The tail in this distribution indicates that a few values are at a high extreme above the median.

Figure 2.3: Non-normal distribution with a mean of 5

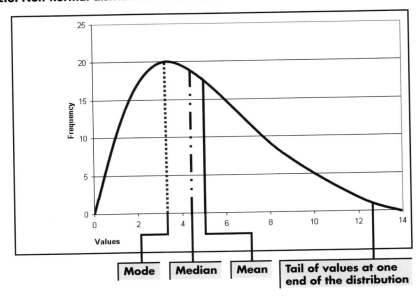

As you can see, the values of each of these statistics provide valuable information about the data set being analyzed. Whereas the mean value gives you an arithmetic average, the standard deviation tells you how closely together the values are distributed. The comparison of mean, mode, and median gives insight into the type of distribution—evenly distributed around the mean or skewed to one end or the other. Two sets of data might have the same mean but different standard deviations, indicating that the data is more or less widely distributed or even exhibits an entirely different distribution profile. Conversely, two data sets might have the same standard deviation, but the mean values in the data sets can be vastly different, indicating two dissimilar sets of data that vary in a similar manner.

In the case of the TZBlazer ski production, Joanna must analyze the recent trend in skis being rejected by the QC group for quality defects. The two most common defects being found in the TZBlazer ski models are as follows:

- High Friction Coefficient indicating poor surface finishing that can result in poor ski performance. Skis are rejected if they have a Friction Coefficient value of greater than 1.23.
- Low Torsion Strength indicating that the material strength is insufficient for the rigors of high-performance skiing, usually resulting from problems in the molding process. Skis are rejected if they have a Torsion Strength value of less than 2.0.

Joanna wants to compare the current Friction Coefficient and Torsion Strength values from the past several days to historical data to see if there has, indeed, been a significant change. She also wants to determine how many skis will be rejected due to these defects and the cost of the rejected skis to the company. This, in turn, can indicate to management the benefits that could be reaped from improving the manufacturing process. And, finally, Joanna wants to review the costs of 100% inspection of skis (the current process) and compare them to the possible costs TheZone would face if skis had to be replaced after they entered the marketplace.

Joanna has already created an Excel workbook named QC Analysis, which contains data about each ski that has been inspected. The Current worksheet, shown in Figure 2.4, includes the following information for each ski:

- Unique manufacturing identification number (Mfg ID#)
- Size
- Style
- Date manufactured
- Production line on which the ski was manufactured
- Friction Coefficient value
- Torsion Strength value

Figure 2.4: Current worksheet in the QC Analysis workbook

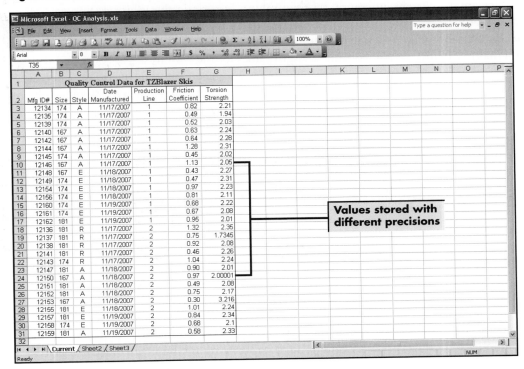

The Current worksheet includes values for only the skis Joanna is analyzing for the past several days. Joanna also has gathered the historical data, which includes the mean Friction Coefficient and Torsion Strength values for these skis, as well as the median, mode, and standard deviation values, as shown in Table 2.1.

Table 2.1: Historical values of Friction Coefficient and Torsion Strength

	Friction Coefficient	Torsion Strength
Mean	0.76	2.27
Median	0.73	2.24
Mode	0.53	2.15
Standard Deviation	0.27	0.24

Joanna wants to determine similar statistical data for the skis tested during the past several days, and then compare this information with the historical values to ascertain if there is, indeed, a problem. Therefore, she needs to calculate the values for mean, median, mode, and standard deviation for the skis shown in Figure 2.4. After calculating these values, Joanna will approach the comparison using both of the following techniques:

- Calculate the difference in values: current value – historical value
- Calculate the percent difference: (current value – historical value)/historical value

Joanna will use fairly simple statistical tests to analyze and compare the data. By examining the Friction Coefficient and Torsion Strength values for the current skis as compared with the historical values, Joanna should be able to draw some conclusions regarding whether the number of rejected skis and the distribution of these values have changed significantly. For those with a more sophisticated understanding of statistical concepts, a variety of additional tools are available that allow you to actually measure the significance of such differences by comparing the means of the current data and historical data sets. Joanna will simply be comparing the difference and percent difference to draw her conclusions.

CONTROLLING THE PRECISION OF DATA USING THE ROUND FUNCTION

In reviewing the Current worksheet (Figure 2.4), Joanna notices that the Torsion Strength values were entered with different formats and precisions. Some were entered to the nearest hundredth, some to the nearest thousandth, and so on. To be consistent in analyzing the data, Joanna first needs to round off the Torsion Strength values to a specified number of decimal places. She decides to round to the nearest hundredth.

Could Joanna use the Decrease Decimal button 🔣 on the Formatting toolbar to adjust the number of decimal places in column G? No; adjusting the number of decimal places using either the Decrease Decimal button or the Increase Decimal button 🔣 simply alters the cell display, but has *no effect on the precision* of the value stored in the cell. Excel 2003 has the capability to store 15 significant digits for each value. To specify that the Torsion Strength values in column G should be precisely stored to the nearest hundredth, Joanna needs to use the **ROUND** function. Rounding, unlike formatting, actually changes the precision of the data values stored. The syntax of the ROUND function is as follows:

$$=\texttt{ROUND(number,num\_digits)}$$

Notice that the ROUND function is somewhat different from the functions presented in Chapter 1. The ROUND function has two different types of arguments:

- The first argument, number, is a single value that can be a constant, a cell reference where the cell contains a numerical value, or another formula that results in a single number value.
- The second argument, num_digits, is the specified number of decimal places. A value of 0 for the second argument rounds to the nearest whole number. A value of 1 for the second argument rounds to the nearest tenth (0.1, 0.2, and so on). A value of 2 rounds to the nearest hundredth. Note that a value of –2 for the second argument tells Excel to round to the nearest hundred (100, 200, and so on).

Best Practice

Adhering to Function Syntax When Working with Multiple Arguments

When using a function that contains multiple arguments where each argument represents different information, you must be careful to supply the information in the exact order and format specified by the function's syntax.

Unlike the SUM, AVERAGE, MIN, and MAX functions, whose arguments all take the same type of information (values and/or cell ranges), each of the ROUND function's arguments represents different information. So, for example, to round the two values 6.25 and 3.21 to the nearest whole number, you cannot write =ROUND(6.25,3.21,0). This formula would generate an error message indicating that too many arguments have been given. Excel cannot interpret the intent to round both values, nor can it determine which value to return.

Furthermore, the order of the arguments is critical to correct usage of the ROUND function. Although =SUM(3.21,1) is equivalent to =SUM(1,3.21), the same is not true for functions, such as ROUND, that contain different types of arguments. The formula =ROUND(3.21,1) results in the value 3.2 because it takes the number 3.21 and rounds it to the nearest tenth; by contrast, the formula =ROUND(1,3.21) returns the value 1 because it takes the number 1 and attempts to round it to 3.21 decimal places. In such a case, Excel does not generate an error message indicating incorrect usage of the function; rather, it simply displays an erroneous result if your intent was to round the value 3.21 to the nearest tenth. The first value in the ROUND function is always interpreted as the value you want to round, and anything following the first comma Excel encounters is interpreted as the number of decimal places to be shown.

As with all functions, you must also use caution when entering large values. Typing in commas often causes a formula to be evaluated incorrectly. For example, the formula =ROUND(1,221.34,0) would produce an error message indicating too many arguments have been given, because Excel would assume it is rounding the value 1 not the value 1,221.34.

When you work with functions that contain multiple arguments, it's advisable to double-check the function's syntax to be certain you are using the function correctly. The Help system in Excel provides detailed information about each function's syntax, and is a good resource to check for proper function use and syntax.

The ROUND function algorithm rounds down all values of less than half the range, and rounds up values from half the range and above. For example, =ROUND(1.49,0) results in the value 1, whereas the formula =ROUND(1.50,0) results in the value 2. As with all other functions, you can use the ROUND function alone or as part of a larger formula, or even include a ROUND function inside other functions. Table 2.2 provides a few examples of the ROUND function.

Table 2.2: Examples of the ROUND function

Formula	Description	Resulting Value
=ROUND(25.449,0)	Rounds 25.449 to the nearest whole number	25
=ROUND(B2,1)	Where B2 contains the value 23.39, rounds 23.39 to the nearest tenth	23.4
=ROUND(103234,–2)	Rounds 103,234 to the nearest hundred	103,200
=ROUND(23.75%,2)	Rounds 23.75% to the nearest hundredth, which is the same as the nearest percent because the precise value is .2375	24%
=ROUND(SUM(10.33,10.44),0)	First sums 10.33 and 10.44, resulting in 20.77, then rounds this value to the nearest whole number	21

Similar functions are provided in Excel, such as ROUNDUP and ROUNDDOWN, that contain the same arguments but return a value that is always either rounded up or rounded down depending on the function used. For example, the formula =ROUNDUP(3.432,1) rounds the value 3.432 up to the next highest tenth, or 3.5. If you wanted to round the value 25.83% down to the nearest percent, you could write the formula =ROUNDDOWN (25.83%,2) resulting in the value 25%. Notice that, in this case, the num_digits argument is 2 not 0 because the precise value of 25.83% is 0.2583. Table 2.3 summarizes some of the functions you can use to change the precision of a value.

Table 2.3: Examples of functions that modify the precision of a value

Function	Description	Syntax and Example	Resulting Value
ROUND	Rounds a number to a specified number of decimal places	ROUND(number,num_digits) =ROUND(25.33%,2)	25%
ROUND-UP	Rounds a number up to the specified number of decimal places	ROUNDUP(number,num_digits) =ROUNDUP(1.002,2)	1.01
ROUNDDOWN	Rounds a number down to the specified number of decimal places	ROUNDDOWN(number,num_digits) =ROUNDDOWN(9.99,0)	9
EVEN	Rounds a number up to the next highest even integer	EVEN(number) =EVEN(2.23)	4
ODD	Rounds a number up to the next highest odd integer	ODD(number) =ODD(1.23)	3
INT	Rounds a number down to the nearest integer	INT(number) =INT(–4.3)	–5
TRUNC	Truncates a number to an integer, removing the fractional part of the number	TRUNC(number,num_digits) =TRUNC(–4.3)	–4

Rounding Values to the Nearest Hundredth

Joanna decides to use the ROUND function to alter the Torsion Strength values in column G of the Current worksheet so that they have a consistent precision. One way she can accomplish this is by calculating the rounded values in a separate column (column H) and then copying the rounded values back into the original Torsion Strength column. Could Joanna simply write the formula with the ROUND function in cell G3 and copy it down the column? No; doing so would result in a circular reference error because the values in the formula would be referencing themselves.

In cell H3, Joanna calculates the corresponding rounded value by writing the formula =ROUND(G3,2). She copies this formula down the column, relatively changing the cell reference G3 as it is copied down. Because the values in column H are formatted according to the general format, only significant digits are displayed. To display all values with two decimal places, Joanna adjusts the display using the appropriate toolbar buttons. The resulting worksheet values are shown in Figure 2.5.

Figure 2.5: Using the ROUND function to change the precision of the Torsion Strength values

Value in cell G3 is rounded to the nearest hundredth

ROUND function changes the precision of the value in cell G24 to two decimal places, so 2.00001 is now 2.00

H3   fx =ROUND(G3,2)

	A	B	C	D	E	F	G	H	I
1	Quality Control Data for TZBlazer Skis								
2	Mfg ID#	Size	Style	Date Manufactured	Production Line	Friction Coefficient	Torsion Strength		
3	12134	174	A	11/17/2007	1	0.82	2.21	2.21	
4	12135	174	A	11/17/2007	1	0.49	1.94	1.94	
5	12139	174	A	11/17/2007	1	0.52	2.03	2.03	
6	12140	167	A	11/17/2007	1	0.63	2.24	2.24	
7	12142	167	A	11/17/2007	1	0.64	2.28	2.28	
8	12144	167	A	11/17/2007	1	1.28	2.31	2.31	
9	12145	174	A	11/17/2007	1	0.45	2.02	2.02	
10	12146	167	A	11/17/2007	1	1.13	2.05	2.05	
11	12148	167	E	11/18/2007	1	0.43	2.27	2.27	
12	12149	174	E	11/18/2007	1	0.47	2.31	2.31	
13	12154	174	E	11/18/2007	1	0.97	2.23	2.23	
14	12156	174	E	11/18/2007	1	0.81	2.11	2.11	
15	12160	174	E	11/19/2007	1	0.68	2.22	2.22	
16	12161	174	E	11/19/2007	1	0.67	2.08	2.08	
17	12162	181	E	11/19/2007	1	0.95	2.01	2.01	
18	12136	181	R	11/17/2007	2	1.32	2.35	2.35	
19	12137	181	R	11/17/2007	2	0.75	1.7345	1.73	
20	12138	181	R	11/17/2007	2	0.92	2.08	2.08	
21	12141	181	R	11/17/2007	2	0.46	2.26	2.26	
22	12143	174	R	11/17/2007	2	1.04	2.24	2.24	
23	12147	181	A	11/18/2007	2	0.90	2.01	2.01	
24	12150	167	A	11/18/2007	2	0.97	2.00001	2.00	
25	12151	181	A	11/18/2007	2	0.49	2.08	2.08	
26	12152	181	A	11/18/2007	2	0.75	2.17	2.17	
27	12153	167	A	11/18/2007	2	0.30	3.216	3.22	
28	12155	181	E	11/18/2007	2	1.01	2.24	2.24	
29	12157	181	E	11/19/2007	2	0.84	2.34	2.34	
30	12158	174	E	11/19/2007	2	0.68	2.1	2.10	
31	12159	181	A	11/19/2007	2	0.58	2.33	2.33	
32									

The ROUND function in cell H3, =ROUND(G3,2), changes the precision of the value listed in cell G3 to two decimal places. For example, if the actual value in cell G3 is 2.214 and is displayed with two decimal places as 2.21, then the formula = G3*1000 results in the value 2214, not 2210. However, the formula =ROUND(G3,2)*1000 results in the value 2210 because the precise value of G3 is changed to 2.21 by the ROUND function.

Excel also provides the "Precision as displayed" option on the Calculation tab of the Options dialog box. This option allows you to set the precision globally for all values in the workbook. Selecting the "Precision as displayed" option permanently changes the values in all workbook cells from full precision (15 digits) to whatever format is displayed, including the number of decimal places. Any subsequent use of the Increase Decimal or Decrease Decimal buttons not only changes the display, but also changes the precision of the values in the selected cells. Selecting this option might result in unwanted consequences; unintentionally changing the display could instantly result in loss of data precision, so this option should be used with caution.

Now that Joanna has rounded the Torsion Strength values to the nearest hundredth, she can replace the original values in column G with these rounded values. If she tried to simply delete column G, she would receive a #REF! error in the column with the rounded numbers, because the formulas in that column would reference a column that no longer exists. A better way to handle this is to copy and paste just the rounded values—not the formulas that produced the values—into the original column G listing the Torsion Strength values. To do this, Joanna can use the Paste Special feature.

USING PASTE SPECIAL TO COPY AND PASTE DATA

A variety of methods are available to copy information from one part of a worksheet to another, to other worksheets, or even from one workbook to another. The simplest method is to first select the information you want to copy, and then use the Copy button 📋 and the Paste button 📋 on the Standard toolbar. When you use this method, Excel pastes the contents of the copied cell or range of cells, including any formatting applied to the original cell(s). You can adjust the way Excel pastes copied data by clicking the Paste button's list arrow and choosing one of the options displayed. Table 2.4 describes these additional pasting options.

Table 2.4: Options available from the Paste button list arrow

Paste Option	Description
Formulas	Pastes only the formulas from the original (copied) cell(s)
Values	Pastes only the values from the original cell(s); the formulas or any formatting are *not* pasted
No Borders	Pastes the formulas and formatting from the original cell(s), but not the format of the cell borders
Transpose	Pastes the formulas and formatting from the original range of cells, but reverses the orientation, so that the rows of the original cell range become the columns in the pasted range, and the original columns become rows
Paste Link	Pastes a connection, or link, to the original cells, including the applied formatting
Paste Special	Displays a dialog box that provides all of the preceding options plus additional paste options

You can also specify how data is pasted to a location by clicking the list arrow for the Paste Options button ![paste icon], which appears each time you paste a selection. Table 2.5 describes the options that are available from this button.

Table 2.5: Paste Options button options

Option	Description
Keep Source Formatting	Pastes the data and formulas with the same formatting as the original (copied) cell(s); this is the default option
Match Destination Formatting	Pastes the data and formulas and applies the formatting used in the cell(s) into which the data is pasted
Values Only	Pastes only the values; the formulas or any formatting from the original cell(s) are *not* pasted
Values and Numbers Formatting	Pastes values with the same number formats as those in the original cell(s)
Values and Source Formatting	Pastes values with the same formats (number, font, and style) as those in the original cell(s)
Keep Source Column Width	Pastes the data and formulas from the original cell(s), and maintains the column width of the original cell(s)
Formatting Only	Pastes just the formatting of the original cell(s)
Link Cells	Pastes a connection, or link, to the original cell(s) by inserting a formula referencing the original cell(s)

In this case, Joanna wants to copy only the values with the number formatting in column H without any of the formulas. To do so, Joanna completes the following steps: selects the range H3:H31, clicks the Copy button, clicks the upper-left cell of the range into which the values will be pasted (in this case, cell G3), clicks the Paste button's list arrow, and then selects the Paste Special option. In the Paste Special dialog box, Joanna selects the "Values and number formats" option. After moving the values from column H to column G, Joanna deletes column H by highlighting the column and pressing the Delete key. The updated worksheet is shown in Figure 2.6.

Figure 2.6: Updated Torsion Strength values displaying two decimal places

	A	B	C	D	E	F	G	H
1				Quality Control Data for TZBlazer Skis				
2	Mfg ID#	Size	Style	Date Manufactured	Production Line	Friction Coefficient	Torsion Strength	
3	12134	174	A	11/17/2007	1	0.82	2.21	
4	12135	174	A	11/17/2007	1	0.49	1.94	
5	12139	174	A	11/17/2007	1	0.52	2.03	
6	12140	167	A	11/17/2007	1	0.63	2.24	
7	12142	167	A	11/17/2007	1	0.64	2.28	
8	12144	167	A	11/17/2007	1	1.28	2.31	
9	12145	174	A	11/17/2007	1	0.45	2.02	
10	12146	167	A	11/17/2007	1	1.13	2.05	
11	12148	167	E	11/18/2007	1	0.43	2.27	
12	12149	174	E	11/18/2007	1	0.47	2.31	
13	12154	174	E	11/18/2007	1	0.97	2.23	
14	12156	174	E	11/18/2007	1	0.81	2.11	
15	12160	174	E	11/19/2007	1	0.68	2.22	
16	12161	174	E	11/19/2007	1	0.67	2.08	
17	12162	181	E	11/19/2007	1	0.95	2.01	
18	12136	181	R	11/17/2007	2	1.32	2.35	
19	12137	181	R	11/17/2007	2	0.75	1.73	
20	12138	181	R	11/17/2007	2	0.92	2.08	
21	12141	181	R	11/17/2007	2	0.46	2.26	
22	12143	174	R	11/17/2007	2	1.04	2.24	
23	12147	181	A	11/18/2007	2	0.90	2.01	
24	12150	167	A	11/18/2007	2	0.97	2.00	
25	12151	181	A	11/18/2007	2	0.49	2.08	
26	12152	181	A	11/18/2007	2	0.75	2.17	
27	12153	167	A	11/18/2007	2	0.30	3.22	
28	12155	181	E	11/18/2007	2	1.01	2.24	
29	12157	181	E	11/19/2007	2	0.84	2.34	
30	12158	174	E	11/19/2007	2	0.68	2.10	
31	12159	181	A	11/19/2007	2	0.58	2.33	
32								

Values updated with precision to two decimal places and displaying two decimal places

How To

Use Paste Special Options

1. Select the cell or range of cells to be copied, and then click the Copy button 🔲 on the Standard toolbar.

2. Select the location to which you want to copy the data by clicking the cell in the upper-left corner of the range. This cell can be on the same worksheet, another worksheet, or even in a different workbook.

3. Click the list arrow for the Paste button 🔲 on the Standard toolbar, and then click Paste Special to open the Paste Special dialog box. See Figure 2.7.

Figure 2.7: Paste Special dialog box

This dialog box contains all the options provided for pasting copied cells, including several that are not available using the other paste methods described earlier (that is, using the menu available by clicking the Paste button's list arrow or the menu available by clicking the Paste Options button's list arrow). These additional options include the following:

- Operation options, which allow you to paste values using one of four arithmetic operations—Add, Subtract, Multiply, and Divide. For example, assume that cell A2 contains the value 2 and cell B2 contains the value 4. You could copy the value in cell A2 into cell B2 using the Multiply operation to produce the result 8 in cell B2.
- The Skip Blanks option, which enables you to copy and paste a cell range that contains one or more blank cells. The cell range into which the copied cells are pasted retains its original values for any cells that correspond to the blank cells in the copied range; in other words, the blank cells are not pasted over any existing values in the range into which they are pasted. You can select the Skip blanks option in combination with any of the other pasting options.

4. After selecting the options you want in the dialog box, click the OK button.

CALCULATING THE MEAN, MEDIAN, MODE, AND STANDARD DEVIATION

Now, Joanna is ready to calculate the arithmetic mean, median, mode, and standard deviation of the Friction Coefficient and Torsion Strength values in the Current worksheet. Table 2.6 lists the Excel functions she will use to perform each of these operations. The AVERAGE function was discussed in Chapter 1. The MODE, MEDIAN, and STDEV functions work in a similar way, containing only one type of argument—a list of values. Recall that this list can contain one or more of the following: constants, cell references, a range of cells along a column, a range of cells along a row, or a two-dimensional block of cells.

Table 2.6: Excel statistical functions

Statistic	Function and Syntax	Description
Arithmetic Mean	AVERAGE(number1,number2,...)	Returns the average (arithmetic mean) of the arguments
Median	MEDIAN(number1,number2,...)	Returns the median of the given numbers, which is the number in the middle of a set of numbers; that is, half the numbers have values that are greater than the median, and half have values that are less than the median
Mode	MODE(number1,number2,...)	Returns the most frequently occurring value in a range of data
Standard Deviation	STDEV(number1,number2,...)	Estimates standard deviation, which is a measure of how widely values are dispersed from the average (mean) value, based on a sample

To calculate these statistics for the Friction Coefficient values in the Current worksheet, Joanna enters the following formulas in the cells indicated:

- Cell F33: =AVERAGE(F3:F31)
- Cell F34: =MEDIAN(F3:F31)
- Cell F35: =MODE(F3:F31)
- Cell F36: =STDEV(F3:F31)

Joanna then copies these formulas across the row into column G to calculate the respective values for the Torsion Strength data. Figure 2.8 shows the worksheet with the statistics calculated. Note that Joanna included labels in cells A33:A36 to identify each statistic.

Figure 2.8: Worksheet with statistics calculated

	A	B	C	D	E	F	G	H
11	12148	167	E	11/18/2007	1	0.43	2.27	
12	12149	174	E	11/18/2007	1	0.47	2.31	
13	12154	174	E	11/18/2007	1	0.97	2.23	
14	12156	174	E	11/18/2007	1	0.81	2.11	
15	12160	174	E	11/19/2007	1	0.68	2.22	
16	12161	174	E	11/19/2007	1	0.67	2.08	
17	12162	181	E	11/19/2007	1	0.95	2.01	
18	12136	181	R	11/17/2007	2	1.32	2.35	
19	12137	181	R	11/17/2007	2	0.75	1.73	
20	12138	181	R	11/17/2007	2	0.92	2.08	
21	12141	181	R	11/17/2007	2	0.46	2.26	
22	12143	174	R	11/17/2007	2	1.04	2.24	
23	12147	181	A	11/18/2007	2	0.90	2.01	
24	12150	167	A	11/18/2007	2	0.97	2.00	
25	12151	181	A	11/18/2007	2	0.49	2.08	
26	12152	181	A	11/18/2007	2	0.75	2.17	
27	12153	167	A	11/18/2007	2	0.30	3.22	
28	12155	181	E	11/18/2007	2	1.01	2.24	
29	12157	181	E	11/19/2007	2	0.84	2.34	
30	12158	174	E	11/19/2007	2	0.68	2.10	
31	12159	181	A	11/19/2007	2	0.58	2.33	
32								
33	Mean					0.76	2.19	
34	Median					0.75	2.21	
35	Mode					0.49	2.24	
36	Standard Deviation					0.26	0.25	
37								

Column titles and the calculations in rows 33-36 cannot be displayed simultaneously

=AVERAGE(F3:F31)
=MEDIAN(F3:F31)
=MODE(F3:F31)
=STDEV(F3:F31)

Best Practice

Working with Nested Functions

Statistical values such as mean, median, mode, and standard deviation often are computed with many decimal places. What if you wanted these values rounded to the nearest hundredth, for example? One way to do this is to write a formula in another cell referencing the value you want to round—for example, =ROUND(F33,2). A more efficient way to do this is to use a technique called *nesting* functions. When you nest a function, you include that function inside another formula or function as one of its arguments. So, you could calculate the rounded value by nesting the AVERAGE function directly inside the ROUND function, as follows: =ROUND(AVERAGE(F3:F31),2). In this formula, Excel first evaluates the nested function for the average. The result of this calculation is then used as the first argument of the ROUND function, effectively combining two distinct steps into one calculation.

Almost all the functions you use in Excel allow for functions and formulas to be nested inside each other, up to seven levels. For example, the following formula calculates the minimum value in a list: =MIN(2,3+7,AVERAGE(B2:B3)). Assuming that cells B2 and B3 contain the values 10 and 20, respectively, this formula is reduced to =MIN(2,10,15) and, ultimately, results in the value 2.

One important detail to note when nesting functions is the importance of matching parentheses. The formula must have the exact number of opening parentheses as closing parentheses, and they must be placed correctly to ensure that the formula is calculated properly. The topic of nesting functions and formulas is covered in detail in Chapter 4.

As shown in Figure 2.8, Joanna has to scroll the worksheet to view rows 33 through 36. This makes the worksheet difficult to understand because now the column titles are hidden from view. Fortunately, Excel provides several tools to help you view data on different parts of the worksheet simultaneously.

MANAGING LARGE WORKSHEETS BY FREEZING PANES AND SPLITTING THE WINDOW

To make larger worksheets more manageable, Excel provides several tools for displaying and scrolling columns and/or rows so that certain areas can be fixed, or frozen, and the remainder of the worksheet can be scrolled easily. The technique used to freeze rows 1 and 2 in Figure 2.9 is referred to as **freezing panes**. Freezing these rows keeps the titles displayed in the top pane, allowing the bottom pane to be scrolled so that both the titles and values further down the worksheet are displayed at the same time. Joanna can use this technique to freeze rows 1 and 2 so that the identifying titles are always displayed.

Figure 2.9: Freezing panes in the worksheet

Rows 1 and 2 are displayed in the frozen pane, separated by a line, and the bottom portion of the worksheet has been scrolled to begin at row 26

	A	B	C	D	E	F	G	H
1	Quality Control Data for TZBlazer Skis							
2	Mfg ID#	Size	Style	Date Manufactured	Production Line	Friction Coefficient	Torsion Strength	
26	12152	181	A	11/18/2007	2	0.75	2.17	
27	12153	167	A	11/18/2007	2	0.30	3.22	
28	12155	181	E	11/18/2007	2	1.01	2.24	
29	12157	181	E	11/19/2007	2	0.84	2.34	
30	12158	174	E	11/19/2007	2	0.68	2.10	
31	12159	181	A	11/19/2007	2	0.58	2.33	
32								
33	Mean					0.76	2.19	
34	Median					0.75	2.21	
35	Mode					0.49	2.24	
36	Standard Deviation					0.26	0.25	
37								
38								

How To

Freeze Panes

1. Arrange the worksheet showing the column(s) and/or row(s) in the location you want them to appear at all times (usually at the top of the worksheet).
2. Place the pointer in the cell that is one column to the right and one row below the columns and rows you want to freeze in place.
3. Click Window on the menu bar, and then click Freeze Panes. A black line appears below the rows that are frozen, and a black line appears to the right of the columns that are frozen.
4. To remove frozen panes, click Window on the menu bar, and then click Unfreeze Panes.

Another technique you can use to see different parts of the screen at the same time is to **split** the window by dragging either the horizontal split box or the vertical split box to create separate scrollable panes. You can also split the window by first positioning the pointer below or to the right of where you want the split, and then choose the Split command from the Window menu.

How To

Split the Window

1. To split the window vertically, drag the split box at the bottom-right corner of the worksheet to the location where you want to divide the window. The window splits into separate panes, each of which can be scrolled individually.
2. To divide the window horizontally, drag the split box at the top-right corner of the worksheet to the location where you want to divide the window. Figure 2.10 shows a worksheet that has been split both vertically and horizontally.

Figure 2.10: Splitting the window

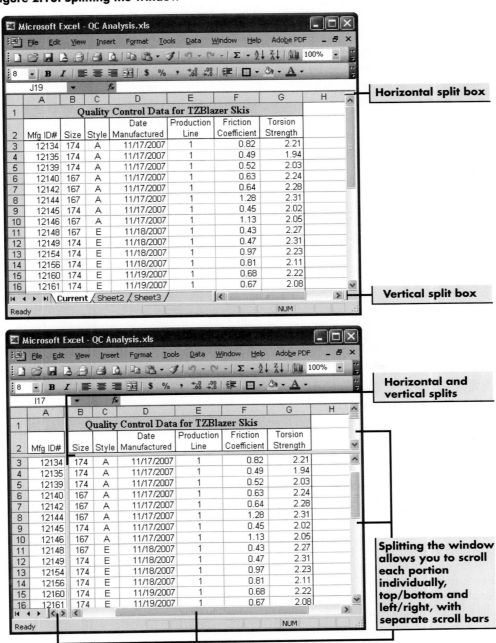

3. To remove a split window, simply drag the split line off the window, either to the side (for a vertical split) or to the top or bottom (for a horizontal split). Or, you can choose the Remove Split option from the Window menu.

COMPARING CURRENT VALUES TO HISTORICAL VALUES

The final step in Joanna's analysis is to compare the current (calculated) values with the historical values provided by QC. One way to do this is to place the current values and the historical values on a separate worksheet in the workbook, side by side, and then perform the comparisons. Joanna creates a new worksheet named Comparison to accomplish this. Figure 2.11 shows the values in this new Comparison worksheet at the top and the corresponding formulas at the bottom. Note that the formulas relate back to the calculated values on the Current worksheet. Recall from Chapter 1 that references to cells on other worksheets include the worksheet name.

Figure 2.11: Comparison worksheet values and corresponding formulas

Values

	A	B	C	D	E	F	G	H	I	J	K
1	*Analysis of Statistical Values - Current Data vs. Historical Data*										
2		Friction Coefficient					Torsion Strength				
3	Value:	Historical	Current	Difference	%Difference		Historical	Current	Difference	%Difference	
4	Mean	0.76	0.76				2.27	2.19			
5	Median	0.73	0.75				2.24	2.21			
6	Mode	0.53	0.49				2.15	2.24			
7	Standard Deviation	0.27	0.26				0.24	0.25			
8											
9											

Formulas

	A	B	C	D	E	F	G	H	I	J	K
1	*Analysis of Statistical Values - Current Data vs. Historical Data*										
2		Friction Coefficient					Torsion Strength				
3	Value:	Historical	Current	Difference	%Difference		Historical	Current	Difference	%Difference	
4	Mean	0.76	=Current!F33				2.27	=Current!G33			
5	Median	0.73	=Current!F34				2.24	=Current!G34			
6	Mode	0.53	=Current!F35				2.15	=Current!G35			
7	Standard Deviation	0.27	=Current!F36				0.24	=Current!G36			
8											
9											

The new Comparison worksheet in the QC Analysis workbook contains the following elements:

- Cells B4:B7 contain the historical values for the Friction Coefficient that were given to Joanna by the QC group for mean, median, mode, and standard deviation. These values have been entered directly into the cells.
- Cells C4:C7 contain the formulas =Current!F33, =Current!F34, and so on. These formulas simply reference the cells that contain the values previously calculated for mean, median, mode, and standard deviation for Friction Coefficient on the Current worksheet.
- Cells G4:G7 contain the historical values for the Torsion Strength that were given to Joanna by the QC group for mean, median, mode, and standard deviation. These values have been entered directly into the cells.
- Cells H4:H7 contain the formulas =Current!G33, =Current!G34, and so on. Again, these formulas simply reference the cells that contain the values previously calculated for mean, median, mode, and standard deviation for Torsion Strength on the Current worksheet.

Now that these values are side by side, Joanna can easily compare them, deriving both the difference between the current values and the historical values, as well as the percent difference between these values.

Calculating the Difference Between Two Sets of Data

To calculate the difference, Joanna needs to subtract the historical values from the current values she just calculated. A positive result indicates that the value has increased; a negative result indicates that the value has decreased. Joanna enters the formula =C4–B4 in cell D4 and copies it down the column to calculate the differences for mean, median, mode, and standard deviation, as shown in Figure 2.12. It appears, for example, that the mean of the Friction Coefficient has decreased by 0.003 (cell D4).

Figure 2.12: Calculating the difference between current and historical values

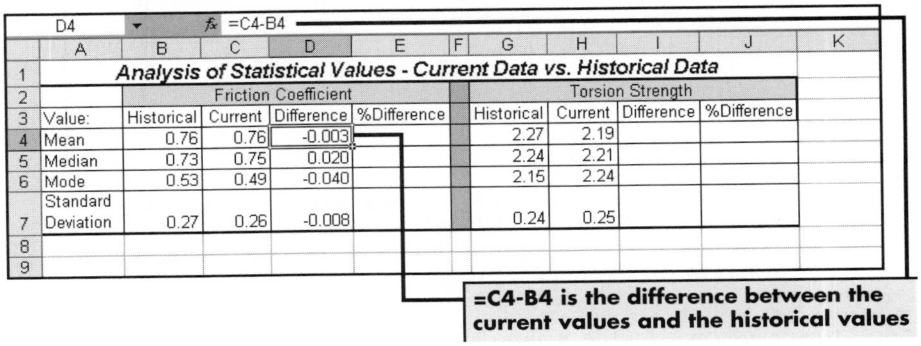

=C4-B4 is the difference between the current values and the historical values

A difference of –0.003 for the mean value between the current data and the historical data might or might not be significant, depending on the actual mean values of the data. For example, when comparing mean values such as .01 with .02, a decrease of 0.003 is significant; but, when comparing mean values such as 1000.003 with 1000.000, the same decrease is not nearly as significant. So, another way to analyze the differences between two sets of data is to look at the *percent difference* of a value in one data set compared with that value in the second data set.

Calculating the Percent Difference Between Two Sets of Data

To calculate a percent difference between two data sets, you subtract the old value from the new value and then divide the difference by the old value. The general format for this formula is as follows:

```
(New Value-Old Value)/Old Value
```

In this case, Joanna needs to write a formula that calculates (Current Value–Historical Value)/Historical Value to compare the values she just calculated from the last few days with the historical values given to her by QC. She begins with the mean values for Friction Coefficient and enters the following formula in cell E4 on the Comparison worksheet: =(C4–B4)/B4. She then copies this formula down the column to calculate the percent difference for the other statistics.

Joanna also needs to calculate these same values for Torsion Strength. Notice that columns G, H, I, and J correspond exactly to the Friction Coefficient columns B, C, D, and E. So, Joanna copies the formulas relative to the columns and rows by selecting cells D4:E7 and using the Copy and Paste buttons to copy the formulas into cells I4:J7. The final comparative analysis is shown in Figure 2.13.

Figure 2.13: Calculating the percent difference between current and historical values

	A	B	C	D	E	F	G	H	I	J	K
1	*Analysis of Statistical Values - Current Data vs. Historical Data*										
2		Friction Coefficient					Torsion Strength				
3	Value:	Historical	Current	Difference	%Difference		Historical	Current	Difference	%Difference	
4	Mean	0.76	0.76	-0.003	-0.41%		2.27	2.19	-0.082	-3.60%	
5	Median	0.73	0.75	0.020	2.74%		2.24	2.21	-0.030	-1.34%	
6	Mode	0.53	0.49	-0.040	-7.55%		2.15	2.24	0.090	4.19%	
7	Standard Deviation	0.27	0.26	-0.008	-2.95%		0.24	0.25	0.005	2.29%	
8											
9											

=(C4-B4)/B4 calculates the percent difference of current versus historical values

Formulas are copied from cells D4:E7 into cells I4:J7 to determine the difference and percent difference for the Torsion Strength values

So, what does this data show? Has the quality data changed in the last few days as compared with the historical data and, if so, for better or worse? Joanna first looks at the Friction Coefficient data and notices there is very little change in the mean value (–.41%, as shown in cell E4). The mean is slightly lower, and because a lower Friction Coefficient value is preferred, there is no indication here of any problems. Recall that Friction Coefficient values of greater than 1.23 result in rejection of the ski. The standard deviation has also decreased, as shown in cell E7, indicating the production process is more, rather than less, consistent. The only large difference appears to be for the mode value, which decreased from the historical value of .53 to .49 (cells B6:C6). Again, because a lower Friction Coefficient is better than a higher one, this change does not signal a problem.

When Joanna evaluates the data on the Torsion Strength, however, she sees a different trend. The mean seems to have decreased as well, but by a much greater percentage, as shown in cell J4. Higher Torsion Strength values are desirable, because the QC process rejects values of less than 2.0; so, a 3.6% decrease in the mean value indicates a possible problem. The standard deviation for Torsion Strength has increased, as shown in cell I7. An increase in the standard deviation indicates less consistency in the production process, and this might warrant further investigation. The median value for the current data appears to be close to that of the historical data, as indicated by the result in cell J5; so, the problem is not being caused by a large number of "tail" values at one end of the data set. The mode has increased by .09 (as shown in cell I6) indicating the most common value is now somewhat higher (better) than in the historical data set.

Joanna concludes that if there is a problem, it probably has something to do with the molding of the ski rather than the finishing. Such variations might be the result of machinery problems, modified production line procedures, changes in raw materials, or other factors. Joanna plans to share her results with the molding supervisor to try to isolate the problem quickly, before it has a major impact on production output and costs.

The statistical tools Joanna used are but a few of the most basic ones available. Excel offers a wide variety of more sophisticated statistical tools for data analysis. The Help system in Excel provides detailed information on all the statistical functions and tools available.

Steps To Success: Level 1

A separate processing line assembles the binding mechanisms for the TZBlazer skis. Recently, a new machine was installed on this line to automate the assembly for several components that had previously been done by hand. The new machine was installed about a month ago and seems to be working smoothly. The QC group wants to determine if the binding assemblies made on this new automated machine meet the same high standards as when the bindings were assembled by hand. The QC group tests ski bindings in two ways:

- Minimum pressure at which the binding mechanism will automatically unlock measured in pounds (lbs). Bindings that unlock at less than 10 lbs of pressure are rejected.
- Temperature at which the materials of construction fail, given that the cold temperatures affect the binding performance, measured in degrees Celsius (°C). The lower the failure temperature, the better the ski binding. The maximum allowable failure temperature is –60 °C. In order to not damage the ski, failure is determined at the point at which the flexibility of the materials falls below a specified level.

The QC group has provided the historical values for these quality attributes, as shown in Table 2.7, and entered the production data for the past four days in an Excel workbook named Binding1.xls on a worksheet named Binding Data.

Table 2.7: Historical data for bindings

	Pressure in Lbs.	Temperature in °C
Mean	10.305	–63.821
Median	10.221	–67.01
Mode	10	–66
Standard Deviation	0.801	2.601

In these steps, your task is to compare the mean, median, mode, and standard deviation of the current values with the historical values. Complete the following:

1. Open the workbook named **Binding1.xls** located in the Chapter 2 folder, and then save it as **QC Binding Data Analysis.xls**.

2. Modify the temperature data so that all values are precisely stored to the nearest tenth of a degree and are displayed with one decimal place.

3. In rows below the data in columns D and E, calculate the mean, median, mode, and standard deviation for the pressure and temperature values.

4. Use the Freeze Panes feature to display the column titles and the values calculated in Step 3 simultaneously.

5. On a separate worksheet named "Compare," enter the historical values for pressure and temperature (see Table 2.7), using a similar format as shown in Figure 2.13.

6. On the Compare worksheet, show the values calculated for mean, median, mode, and standard deviation by referencing the values you calculated in Step 3.

7. Calculate the difference between the current values and the historical values for pressure and temperature.

8. Calculate the percent difference between the current values and the historical values for pressure and temperature.

9. In an area below the analysis, list your conclusions about the effect of the new production machine on the quality of the bindings produced based on current temperature and pressure failure data versus historical data.

10. Format the Compare worksheet so that it is easy to read and includes a title. Use cell shading and/or colors to differentiate the pressure values from the temperature values. Format the values using appropriate numbers of decimal places to display the necessary information. Use percentage formats where indicated.

11. Save and close the QC Binding Data Analysis.xls workbook.

LEVEL 2
ORGANIZING AND EVALUATING DIFFERENT DATA GROUPINGS

EXCEL 2003 SKILLS TRAINING

- Create formulas using the COUNTIF function
- Create formulas using the SUMIF function
- Use absolute references
- Use relative references

DETERMINING A RANK FOR EACH VALUE IN A DATA SET

So far, Joanna has calculated various statistical values for the QC data and compared them with historical data. This has given her a good understanding of the average values and distributions, but no real insight into the extreme values that were obtained. Joanna now wants to look at the quality data at each of the extremes—the highest values and lowest values. She also wants to determine a rank for each data point relative to the data set. This ranking will serve as a point of reference if one of the skis is returned sometime in the future.

Joanna has slightly modified the Current worksheet, as shown in Figure 2.14, to include the component costs associated with each ski model and size. She plans to use this data later to determine some of the costs associated with rejecting a ski. But first, Joanna wants to obtain a ranking for each ski tested, by both Friction Coefficient value and Torsion Strength value, so that if any future problems arise with an individual ski she can easily see the ski's relative positions for these values compared to the other skis produced. If most of the skis coming back from retailers and consumers are at one end or another of a specific quality value, the manufacturing group will be able to quickly modify its process or quality standards for that specific variable.

Figure 2.14: Worksheet modified to include cost of skis

	A	B	C	D	E	F	G	H	I
1				Quality Control Data for TZBlazer Skis					
2	Mfg ID#	Size	Style	Date Manufactured	Production Line	Friction Coefficient	Torsion Strength	Ski Cost	
3	12134	174	A	11/17/2007	1	0.82	2.21	54.50	
4	12135	174	A	11/17/2007	1	0.49	1.94	54.50	
5	12139	174	A	11/17/2007	1	0.52	2.03	54.50	
6	12140	167	A	11/17/2007	1	0.63	2.24	45.50	
7	12142	167	A	11/17/2007	1	0.64	2.28	45.50	
8	12144	167	A	11/17/2007	1	1.28	2.31	45.50	
9	12145	174	A	11/17/2007	1	0.45	2.02	54.50	
10	12146	167	A	11/17/2007	1	1.13	2.05	45.50	
11	12148	167	E	11/18/2007	1	0.43	2.27	55.50	
12	12149	174	E	11/18/2007	1	0.47	2.31	64.50	
13	12154	174	E	11/18/2007	1	0.97	2.23	64.50	
14	12156	174	E	11/18/2007	1	0.81	2.11	64.50	
15	12160	174	E	11/19/2007	1	0.68	2.22	64.50	
16	12161	174	E	11/19/2007	1	0.67	2.08	64.50	
17	12162	181	E	11/19/2007	1	0.95	2.01	70.50	

Ski costs added

If you were to manually rank a value from a given list, you would sort the list and then count the number of entries either above or below the value in question. This can be rather tedious as the sample data sets become larger. The **RANK** function in Excel allows you to quickly and easily complete this same task. The syntax of the RANK function is as follows:

RANK(number,ref,order)

The "number" argument refers to the value to be ranked; the "ref" argument is the range of values the number is being compared with; and the "order" argument specifies the sort order. The function's algorithm defines its behavior as follows: if the "order" argument is 0 or left blank, Excel ranks the values in descending order; if the "order" argument is a positive number, Excel ranks the values in ascending order.

Joanna wants to rank both the Friction Coefficient and Torsion Strength values so that rank #1 corresponds to the "best" ski. The lower the Friction Coefficient value, the better the ski quality, so Joanna wants the rank of 1 to correspond to the lowest value. This requires the ranking to be done in ascending order. Joanna begins by ranking the first item on the Current worksheet (#12134), as compared with the items in rows 3 through 31, in ascending order by writing the following formula in cell I3:

=RANK(F3,F$3:F$31,1)

This formula finds the ranking of the value in cell F3 (0.82) as compared with the values in cells F3 through F31. The last argument, 1, specifies ascending order for the ranking. Also note that Joanna has used absolute row references in the "ref" argument so that this formula will work when copied down the column into cells I4 through I31.

To calculate the ranking for the Torsion Strength, Joanna again wants rank #1 to represent the "best" ski. In this case, the higher the Torsion Strength value, the better. To represent ranking with the highest value corresponding to rank #1, Joanna needs to specify descending order in the RANK function for Torsion Strength. Because descending order is the default order type, this argument can be omitted. Joanna writes the following formula in cell J3:

=RANK(G3,G$3:G$31)

Again, the cell range in the "ref" argument contains absolute row references so that the formula can be copied down the column into cells J4 through J31. The resulting values are shown in columns I and J of Figure 2.15.

Figure 2.15: Determining rankings for Friction Coefficient and Torsion Strength

The formula =RANK(G3,G$3:G$31) in cell J3 ranks Torsion Strength values in descending order

The formula =RANK(F3,F$3:F$31,1) in cell I3 ranks Friction Coefficient values in ascending order

	A	B	C	D	E	F	G	H	I	J	K
1				Quality Control Data for TZBlazer Skis							
2	Mfg ID#	Size	Style	Date Manufactured	Production Line	Friction Coefficient	Torsion Strength	Ski Cost	Rank Friction Coefficient	Rank Torsion Strength	
3	12134	174	A	11/17/2007	1	0.82	2.21	54.50	18	15	
4	12135	174	A	11/17/2007	1	0.49	1.94	54.50	6	28	
5	12139	174	A	11/17/2007	1	0.52	2.03	54.50	8	23	
6	12140	167	A	11/17/2007	1	0.63	2.24	45.50	10	10	
7	12142	167	A	11/17/2007	1	0.64	2.28	45.50	11	7	
8	12144	167	A	11/17/2007	1	1.28	2.31	45.50	28	5	
9	12145	174	A	11/17/2007	1	0.45	2.02	54.50	3	24	
10	12146	167	A	11/17/2007	1	1.13	2.05	45.50	27	22	
11	12148	167	E	11/18/2007	1	0.43	2.27	55.50	2	8	
12	12149	174	E	11/18/2007	1	0.47	2.31	64.50	5	5	
13	12154	174	E	11/18/2007	1	0.97	2.23	64.50	23	13	
14	12156	174	E	11/18/2007	1	0.81	2.11	64.50	17	17	
15	12160	174	E	11/19/2007	1	0.68	2.22	64.50	13	14	
16	12161	174	E	11/19/2007	1	0.67	2.08	64.50	12	19	
17	12162	181	E	11/19/2007	1	0.95	2.01	70.50	22	25	
18	12136	181	R	11/17/2007	2	1.32	2.35	82.50	29	2	
19	12137	181	R	11/17/2007	2	0.75	1.73	82.50	15	29	
20	12138	181	R	11/17/2007	2	0.92	2.08	82.50	21	19	
21	12141	181	R	11/17/2007	2	0.46	2.26	82.50	4	9	
22	12143	174	R	11/17/2007	2	1.04	2.24	76.50	26	10	
23	12147	181	A	11/18/2007	2	0.90	2.01	60.50	20	25	
24	12150	167	A	11/18/2007	2	0.97	2.00	45.50	23	27	
25	12151	181	A	11/18/2007	2	0.49	2.08	60.50	6	19	
26	12152	181	A	11/18/2007	2	0.75	2.17	60.50	15	16	
27	12153	167	A	11/18/2007	2	0.30	3.22	45.50	1	1	
28	12155	181	E	11/18/2007	2	1.01	2.24	70.50	25	10	
29	12157	181	E	11/19/2007	2	0.84	2.34	70.50	19	3	
30	12158	174	E	11/19/2007	2	0.68	2.10	64.50	13	18	
31	12159	181	A	11/19/2007	2	0.58	2.33	70.50	9	4	

Skis with the same Friction Coefficient value share the same ranking

Notice that several of the rows have duplicate ranking values. Excel ranks repeated values with an identical ranking. So, if there are two instances of the Friction Coefficient value 0.97, both are given the same rank—in this case, 23. The next rank given to the next highest Friction Coefficient value is 25. Also notice that, coincidentally, ski number 12153 has both the best Friction Coefficient value and the best Torsion Strength value.

DETERMINING THE HIGHEST AND LOWEST VALUES IN A DATA SET

With a long list, ranking the data might not highlight those elements that appear at each extreme, specifically the highest and lowest values. Although the data set Joanna is working with is relatively small, she anticipates using this analysis with larger data sets in the future and, therefore, wants to set up a separate worksheet to examine only the five highest and lowest test values for Friction Coefficient and Torsion Strength. Joanna has created a new worksheet in the QC Analysis workbook named HighLow, as shown in Figure 2.16.

Figure 2.16: HighLow worksheet

	A	B	C	D	E	F
1		Analysis of QC Data Extreme Values				
2		Top 5 (Highest)		Bottom 5 (Lowest)		
3		Friction Coefficient	Torsion Strength	Friction Coefficient	Torsion Strength	
4	1					
5	2					
6	3					
7	4					
8	5					
9						
10						

Determining the Highest Value with the LARGE Function

To obtain the value for the lowest or highest Friction Coefficient values, the MIN and MAX functions would suffice. But these functions cannot show Joanna the second or third lowest and highest values. One way to create a list of the top five (highest) Friction Coefficient values from the QC data is to manually go through the rankings and select the highest five values—again, a tedious task. The **LARGE** function determines the nth largest value in a range. The syntax of this function is as follows:

$$LARGE(array, k)$$

The "array" argument is the range of cells being evaluated. It can be a one-dimensional range along a row or a column or a two-dimensional range for a block of cells. The second argument, "k," is the desired ranking, where 1 is the largest value. The "k" argument can either be a constant or a cell reference to a cell containing a positive value. Using a 0 or negative value for "k" results in a #NUM! error. So, for example, to choose the 13th largest value from a list of values in cells A1:A1000, the formula =LARGE(A1:A1000,13) could be used.

To fill in a list of the top five (highest) Friction Coefficient values and the top five Torsion Strength values, Joanna set up the HighLow worksheet with the numbers 1 through 5 in column A and the headings for Friction Coefficient and Torsion Strength across the rows (see Figure 2.16). Now, Joanna can use the LARGE function to find the corresponding top five (highest) values for each. She needs to reference values on the Current worksheet to do so (see Figure 2.15).

What formula should Joanna write in cell HighLow!B4 which she can then copy down and across into cells HighLow!B4 through C8 to give the corresponding n^{th} highest value for the given data set? If only considering cell HighLow!B4, she could write the formula =LARGE(Current!F3:F31,A4), where Current!F3:F31 is the array argument (cell range) representing the Friction Coefficient data set, and cell A4 contains the value 1 on the HighLow worksheet, representing the 1st highest value. But will this formula work when copied down the column to obtain the second highest value or across the row to calculate the first highest value for Torsion Strength? Consider the following:

- When this formula is copied down, the array range will change from Current!F3:F31 to Current!F4:F32. Is this correct? No; Joanna wants the array ranges to remain the same as she copies the formula down. To accomplish this, she can make the rows in the range absolute. Next consider the second argument, A4. Should this reference change as she copies the formula down? Yes; this should change to determine the second highest value as represented in cell A5, the value 2. So, A4 should be copied down the column relatively.
- Now, what happens when the formula is copied across the row? Does the range Current!F3:F31 change to Current!G3:G31 corresponding to the Torsion Strength data set? Yes; this range should change when copied across, so the column address should remain relative. What about cell A4; should it change to cell B4 when copied across? In this case, Joanna still wants to reference the value 1 in cell A4, so she needs to make the column absolute for this reference. The formula needed in this case is as follows:

$$\texttt{=LARGE(Current!F\$3:F\$31,\$A4)}$$

Joanna enters this formula in cell HighLow!B4, and then copies it down the column and across the row, as shown in Figure 2.17.

Figure 2.17: Calculating the top five values

	A	B	C	D	E	F
1		Analysis of QC Data Extreme Values				
2		Top 5 (Highest)		Bottom 5 (Lowest)		
3		Friction Coefficient	Torsion Strength	Friction Coefficient	Torsion Strength	
4	1	1.32	3.22			
5	2	1.28	2.35			
6	3	1.13	2.34			
7	4	1.04	2.33			
8	5	1.01	2.31			
9						
10						

B4   *fx* =LARGE(Current!F$3:F$31,$A4)

Formula is copied down the column and across the row to calculate the five highest values for Friction Coefficient and Torsion Strength

What do the largest values represent for this data set? For the Friction Coefficient, the larger the value, the worse the ski performance; so, the largest five values represent the five worst performing skis. For the Torsion Strength, the larger the value, the better the ski performance; so, the five largest values represent the five best performing skis.

Determining the Lowest Value with the SMALL Function

Using a similar technique, Joanna can also calculate the lowest values for each data set. The **SMALL** function determines the nth smallest value in a range. The syntax of the SMALL function is identical to that of the LARGE function, with the exception of the function name:

$$SMALL(array,k)$$

The array is, again, a range of cells, and "k" is the desired ranking, where 1 is now the smallest value rather than the largest. These arguments work in the same manner as their counterparts in the LARGE function.

To create a list of the five lowest values for both Friction Coefficient and Torsion Strength, Joanna can use the identical formula that she entered to find the top five values, but substituting the function name SMALL for LARGE. Joanna enters the following formula in cell HighLow!D4:

$$=SMALL(Current!F\$3:F\$31,\$A4)$$

Note the absolute row references required in the array range and the absolute column reference required for the "k" argument. The finished worksheet is shown in Figure 2.18.

Figure 2.18: Calculating the bottom five values

	A	B	C	D	E	F
				D4	▾	fx =SMALL(Current!F$3:F$31,$A4)
1		Analysis of QC Data Extreme Values				
2		Top 5 (Highest)		Bottom 5 (Lowest)		
3		Friction Coefficient	Torsion Strength	Friction Coefficient	Torsion Strength	
4	1	1.32	3.22	0.30	1.73	
5	2	1.28	2.35	0.43	1.94	
6	3	1.13	2.34	0.45	2.00	
7	4	1.04	2.33	0.46	2.01	
8	5	1.01	2.31	0.47	2.01	
9						
10						

Formula is copied down the column and across the row to calculate the five lowest values for Friction Coefficient and Torsion Strength

What do the smallest values represent for this data set? For Friction Coefficient, the smaller the value, the better the ski performance; so, the smallest five values represent the five best performing skis. For Torsion Strength, the smaller the value, the worse the ski performance; so, the five smallest values represent the five worst performing skis.

DETERMINING THE NUMBER OF ITEMS THAT MEET SPECIFIED CRITERIA

Joanna wants to continue her analysis to determine exactly how many of the TZBlazer skis were rejected based on each of the rejection criteria and, ultimately, determine the resulting cost to the company. Recall that skis are rejected based on the following criteria:

- A Friction Coefficient value of greater than 1.23. A high Friction Coefficient value indicates poor surface finishing and results in poor ski performance.
- A Torsion Strength value of less than 2.0. A low Torsion Strength value indicates the material strength is insufficient for the rigors of high-performance skiing; this usually results from problems in the molding process.

To manually calculate the number of skis rejected based on a Friction Coefficient value that is too high, Joanna could look at this value for each ski and make a tally mark for any value greater than 1.23. After reviewing the Friction Coefficient value for all inspected skis, she could count up the number of tally marks to determine the number of skis rejected due to their Friction Coefficient being too high. For a large data set, this manual process would not be practical.

Excel provides a function that mimics this manual process. The **COUNTIF** function counts the number of items in a range that meet specified criteria. The syntax of the COUNTIF function is as follows:

$$\texttt{=COUNTIF(range,criteria)}$$

The COUNTIF function has two arguments, the cell range and the criteria:

- The range argument must be a *contiguous* set of cells down a column (A1:A100) or across a row (A1:Z1), or a block of cells (A1:Z100). If a noncontiguous range is provided with comma separators, the function interprets the second item as the criteria argument, which is not the intended interpretation.
- The criteria argument is essentially a "test" that the data must meet in order for it to be counted in the grouping. You can use various syntactical formats for this argument depending on the type of criteria test that is specified. To understand the valid methods of specifying this criteria argument, consider the worksheet shown in Figure 2.19, which is a modified version of Joanna's Current worksheet.

Figure 2.19: Examples of the COUNTIF function

	A	B	C	D	E	F	G	H	I
1	Quality Control Data for TZBlazer Skis								
2	MFG ID#	Size	Style	Date Manufactured	Production Line	Friction Coefficient	Torsion Strength	Inspector ID	Shipped
3	12134	174	A	11/17/2007	1	0.82	2.21	A313	TRUE
4	12135	174	a	11/17/2007	1	0.49	1.94	A328	FALSE
5	12139	174	A	11/17/2007	1	0.52	2.03	B224	TRUE
6	12140	167	A	11/17/2007	1	0.63	2.24	B224	TRUE
7	12142	167	A	11/17/2007	1	0.64	2.28	AA313	TRUE
8	12144	167	A	11/17/2007	1	1.28	2.31	A417	TRUE
9	12145	174	A	11/17/2007	1	0.45	2.02	A313	TRUE
10	12146	167	AA	11/17/2007	1	1.13	2.05	B313	TRUE
11	12148	167	E	11/18/2007	1	0.43	2.27	C321	TRUE
12	12149	174	E	11/18/2007	1	0.47	2.31	C321	TRUE
13	12154	174	E	11/18/2007	1	0.97	2.23	A328	FALSE
14									
15	# Style A (text)								
16	# Size 167 (numerical value)								7
17	# Shipped (Boolean value)								5
18	# Size equal to value in cell F18					167			9
19	# Friction Coefficient greater than 1								5
20	# Inspector ID starting with a								2
21	# Inspector ID starting with any letter followed by 313								6
22									3

Using text as criteria:
=COUNTIF(C3:C13,"A")

Using a numeric value as criteria:
=COUNTIF(B3:B13,167)

Using a Boolean value as criteria:
=COUNTIF(I3:I13,TRUE)

Using a cell reference as criteria:
=COUNTIF(B3:B13,F18)

Using a relational operator in criteria:
=COUNTIF(F3:F13,">1")

Using a wildcard character in criteria:
=COUNTIF(H3:H13,"?313")

Using a wildcard character in criteria:
=COUNTIF(H3:H13,"a*")

Figure 2.19 shows different types of criteria specified for the COUNTIF function, as described in the following list:

- **Criteria with a specified text value**. The formula =COUNTIF(C3:C13,"A") in cell I15 calculates the number of skis listed that have the style A. The formula finds all instances of the text string "A" in the contiguous range C3 through C13, returning the value 7. This formula does not count cells with "AA" or any other combination of letters containing "A." Note, however, that the function is not case-sensitive, so the resulting value includes the lowercase "a" in cell C4 as part of the count.

What if you wrote the formula as =COUNTIF(C3:C13,A) excluding the quotation marks around the A? The formula would return the value 0 because it would look for the value as defined in a range named A. Even if a range named A actually existed, the formula still would not return the number of values with the text string "A." So, to correctly specify a text string for the criteria argument, you must enclose the string in quotation marks.

- **Criteria with a specified numeric value**. The formula =COUNTIF(B3:B13,167) in cell I16 calculates the number of skis with the size 167. The formula finds all instances of the numerical value 167 in the range B3 through B31. Notice that the value 167 is not enclosed in quotation marks; specific numerical values do not require quotation marks when used as the criteria argument.

- **Criteria with a specified Boolean value**. The values TRUE and FALSE are referred to as Boolean values. They are distinguished from the text values "TRUE" and "FALSE" in the same way that the numerical value 1 is different from the text value "1." The formula =COUNTIF(I3:I13,TRUE) in cell I17 calculates the number of items shipped by counting the number of items with the Boolean value TRUE in column I. Note that Boolean values should *not* be enclosed in quotation marks; doing so in this example would result in counting only text strings with "TRUE" rather than counting the Boolean value TRUE. You will learn more about Boolean values in Chapter 4.

- **Criteria with a cell reference containing a specific text, numeric, or Boolean value**. The formula =COUNTIF(B3:B13,F18) in cell I18 calculates the number of skis with the size indicated in cell F18. Because cell F18 contains the value 167, the formula counts the number of instances of the value 167 in the range B3 to B13, returning the value 5. If the value in cell F18 is later changed, the value in cell I18 will be automatically updated. A cell reference works for numerical values, as shown here, and for text or Boolean values. Note that cell reference criteria should *not* be enclosed in quotation marks, or the formula will look for a text string such as "F18" rather than for the contents of cell F18. This method is extremely useful when copying formulas in which the criteria changes relative to the row and/or column.

- **Criteria that includes relational operators (>,<,>=,<=,<>)**. Relational operators are used to compare data, as described in Table 2.8. Each of these operators can be used to establish criteria, such as determining if a value is greater than a specific value, not equal to a specific value, and so on. In Figure 2.19, the formula =COUNTIF(F3:F13,">1") in cell I19 counts the occurrences of all values for the Friction Coefficient that are greater than the value 1. Note that criteria containing a relational operator must be enclosed in quotation marks in a COUNTIF function. Also note that, in its current format, criteria with a relational operator cannot contain a cell reference, only an actual text or numeric value. The use of relational operators is explored in much greater detail in Chapter 4.

Table 2.8: Relational operators used with the COUNTIF function

Relational Operator	Description	Example in a COUNTIF function
>	Greater than	=COUNTIF(F3:F13,">1") counts values greater than 1
<	Less than	=COUNTIF(C3:C13,"<E") counts values that appear alphabetically before the letter E
>=	Greater than or equal to	=COUNTIF(F3:F13,">=1") counts values greater than or equal to 1
<=	Less than or equal to	=COUNTIF(G3:G13,"<=2") counts values less than or equal to 2
=	Equal to	=COUNTIF(F3:F13,"=1") counts values equal to 1; this formula is equivalent to =COUNTIF(F3:F13,1)
<>	Not equal to	=COUNTIF(E3:E13,"<>1") counts values not equal to 1

- **Criteria that includes wildcards (*,?)**. **Wildcards** are symbols that you can use as part of the criteria to search for *text strings* in which the wildcard can be substituted for another character or set of characters. The asterisk wildcard (*) specifies that any number of characters can be substituted. The question mark wildcard (?) specifies that a single character can be substituted. Wildcards can be substituted before, within, or after the text or in combination with other wildcards. Wildcards do not work with values that are numbers or dates, only text. In Figure 2.19, the formula =COUNTIF(H3:H13,"a*") in cell I20 counts the number of values in cells H3 through H13 that begin with the letter "a" followed by any number of characters. Again, because the function is not case-sensitive, the formula counts all the Inspector ID values in column H that begin with the letter "A," returning the value 6. Additional examples of criteria using wildcards, based on the data in Figure 2.19, are provided in Table 2.9.

Table 2.9: Wildcards used with the COUNTIF function

Wildcard	Formula	Result	Description
*	=COUNTIF(H2:H13,"*3")	4	Counts all Inspector IDs that end with the text value "3".
*	=COUNTIF(H2:H13,"*1*")	7	Counts all Inspector IDs that contain the text value "1" anywhere in the value (A313, C321, B313, and so on).
?	=COUNTIF(H3:H13,"?313")	3	Counts all Inspector IDs with a single character followed by the characters "313". Notice that cell H7 is not counted because it contains two characters preceding the characters 313. This formula is illustrated in cell I21 in Figure 2.19.
?	=COUNTIF(H3:H13,"*3??")	8	Counts all Inspector IDs that have the value 3 in the third-to-last position in the text value, regardless of the number of preceding characters.

How To

Write a Formula Using the COUNTIF Function

1. Place the pointer in the cell in which you want to write the formula.
2. Type: =COUNTIF(
3. Locate the range that contains the criteria you want to test. This range must be a contiguous set of columns or rows, or a contiguous block of cells. Type the range (for example, A1:A10) into the function as the first argument followed by a comma.
4. Determine the selection criteria you want to use, applying the correct syntax for numerical values, text, Boolean values, relational operators, and/or wildcards. Enter the criteria as the second argument of the function.
5. Type the closing parenthesis mark).
6. If you intend to copy the formula, be certain to apply the appropriate relative or absolute cell referencing needed for each argument.

Joanna can now use the COUNTIF function in the Current worksheet to calculate the number of skis rejected because their Friction Coefficient value is too high, and the number of skis rejected because their Torsion Strength value is too low. Joanna enters the necessary formulas in cells F33 and G33, as shown in Figure 2.20. Cell F33 contains the formula =COUNTIF(F3:F31,">1.23"), where the contiguous range F3 through F31 represents the data to be tested and ">1.23" represents the criteria the data must meet in order to be counted—in other words, the function counts all cells in the range F3:F31 containing values greater than 1.23. Similarly, cell G33 contains the formula =COUNTIF(G3:G31,"<2"), which counts all values in the contiguous range G3 through G31 that contain values that are less than 2.

Figure 2.20: Calculating the number of rejected skis using the COUNTIF function

	A	B	C	D	E	F	G	H	I	J	K
1				Quality Control Data for TZBlazer Skis							
2	Mfg ID#	Size	Style	Date Manufactured	Production Line	Friction Coefficient	Torsion Strength	Ski Cost	Rank Friction Coefficient	Rank Torsion Strength	
8	12144	167	A	11/17/2007	1	1.28	2.31	45.50	28	5	
9	12145	174	A	11/17/2007	1	0.45	2.02	54.50	3	24	
10	12146	167	A	11/17/2007	1	1.13	2.05	45.50	27	22	
11	12148	167	E	11/18/2007	1	0.43	2.27	55.50	2	8	
12	12149	174	E	11/18/2007	1	0.47	2.31	64.50	5	5	
13	12154	174	E	11/18/2007	1	0.97	2.23	64.50	23	13	
14	12156	174	E	11/18/2007	1	0.81	2.11	64.50	17	17	
15	12160	174	E	11/19/2007	1	0.68	2.22	64.50	13	14	
16	12161	174	E	11/19/2007	1	0.67	2.08	64.50	12	19	
17	12162	181	E	11/19/2007	1	0.95	2.01	70.50	22	25	
18	12136	181	R	11/17/2007	2	1.32	2.35	82.50	29	2	
19	12137	181	R	11/17/2007	2	0.75	1.73	82.50	15	29	
20	12138	181	R	11/17/2007	2	0.92	2.08	82.50	21	19	
21	12141	181	R	11/17/2007	2	0.46	2.26	82.50	4	9	
22	12143	174	R	11/17/2007	2	1.04	2.24	76.50	26	10	
23	12147	181	A	11/18/2007	2	0.90	2.01	60.50	20	25	
24	12150	167	A	11/18/2007	2	0.97	2.00	45.50	23	27	
25	12151	181	A	11/18/2007	2	0.49	2.08	60.50	6	19	
26	12152	181	A	11/18/2007	2	0.75	2.17	60.50	15	16	
27	12153	167	A	11/18/2007	2	0.30	3.22	45.50	1	1	
28	12155	181	E	11/18/2007	2	1.01	2.24	70.50	25	10	
29	12157	181	E	11/19/2007	2	0.84	2.34	70.50	19	3	
30	12158	174	E	11/19/2007	2	0.68	2.10	64.50	13	18	
31	12159	181	A	11/19/2007	2	0.58	2.33	70.50	9	4	
32											
33	# Rejected					2	2				
34											
35											

=COUNTIF(F3:F31,">1.23") calculates the number of skis with a Friction Coefficient value greater than 1.23

=COUNTIF(G3:G31,"<2") calculates the number of skis with a Torsion Strength value less than 2

In reviewing the results of the two COUNTIF functions, would it be accurate to assume that the total number of skis rejected is equal to the sum of the two values resulting from the COUNTIF functions? In this case, two skis were rejected due to their Friction Coefficient values being too high, and two skis were rejected due to their Torsion Strength values being too low, so the sum of these two values is equal to the total number of skis rejected (4). But what if one ski had failed *both* the Friction Coefficient and Torsion Strength criteria? Then this wouldn't be an accurate way to calculate the total number of skis rejected. In later chapters, you will learn about other tools that can help to solve this seemingly simple problem.

Best Practice

Working with Noncontiguous Ranges—Divide and Conquer

One limitation of the COUNTIF function is that it can only accommodate a single contiguous range argument (a one- or two-dimensional range or a block of cells). A list of cell references and/or noncontiguous ranges cannot be interpreted by this function, because the first time it encounters the comma delimiter it assumes that what follows is the criteria—not additional ranges. For example, referring to Figure 2.20, if you wanted to eliminate ski #12137 in row 19 from a count, you could not write the formula =COUNTIF(F3:F18,F20:F31,">0"). This formula has no meaning because Excel would assume that F20:F31 is the criteria argument, which it is unable to evaluate. To solve this type of problem, you can divide the formula into parts, first counting the items that meet the criteria in the first contiguous range and adding that to a count of items that meet the criteria in the second contiguous range, as follows:

$$\texttt{=COUNTIF(F3:F18,">0")+COUNTIF(F20:F31,">0")}$$

This method works well if ranges are in nonadjacent columns or rows, or are even located on other worksheets.

DETERMINING A TOTAL VALUE FOR ITEMS THAT MEET SPECIFIED CRITERIA

Next, Joanna wants to quantify the cost TheZone incurs if a ski is rejected. Significant rejection costs could indicate to management that investing time and money in improving the production process might result in increased profits in the long run. Joanna assumes that after a ski has been rejected, it cannot be reused and, therefore, calculates the rejection cost as the cost to manufacture the ski.

For the purposes of this discussion, assume that no skis can be rejected for both too high a Friction Coefficient value and too low a Torsion Strength value. This might be handled by assuming that after a ski has failed one test it is immediately rejected and no further tests are performed. So, if a ski is first tested for Friction Coefficient and fails, it would never be tested for its Torsion Strength, and vice versa. With this technique, a rejected ski cost would never be "double counted." So, before calculating the total value of the rejected skis, to avoid any potential problems of double counting, Joanna has modified the data in the Current worksheet. For any ski that failed one test, she deleted the value for the other test for that ski. This modified worksheet is shown in Figure 2.21.

Figure 2.21: Worksheet modified to avoid double counting of failed skis

	A	B	C	D	E	F	G	H	I	J	K
1				Quality Control Data for TZBlazer Skis							
2	Mfg ID#	Size	Style	Date Manufactured	Production Line	Friction Coefficient	Torsion Strength	Ski Cost	Rank Friction Coefficient	Rank Torsion Strength	
3	12134	174	A	11/17/2007	1	0.82	2.21	54.50	16	13	
4	12135	174	A	11/17/2007	1		1.94	54.50		26	
5	12139	174	A	11/17/2007	1	0.52	2.03	54.50	7	21	
6	12140	167	A	11/17/2007	1	0.63	2.24	45.50	9	8	
7	12142	167	A	11/17/2007	1	0.64	2.28	45.50	10	5	
8	12144	167	A	11/17/2007	1	1.28		45.50	26		
9	12145	174	A	11/17/2007	1	0.45	2.02	54.50	3	22	
10	12146	167	A	11/17/2007	1	1.13	2.05	45.50	25	20	
11	12148	167	E	11/18/2007	1	0.43	2.27	55.50	2	6	
12	12149	174	E	11/18/2007	1	0.47	2.31	64.50	5	4	
13	12154	174	E	11/18/2007	1	0.97	2.23	64.50	21	11	
14	12156	174	E	11/18/2007	1	0.81	2.11	64.50	15	15	
15	12160	174	E	11/19/2007	1	0.68	2.22	64.50	12	12	
16	12161	174	E	11/19/2007	1	0.67	2.08	64.50	11	17	
17	12162	181	E	11/19/2007	1	0.95	2.01	70.50	20	23	
18	12136	181	R	11/17/2007	2	1.32		82.50	27		
19	12137	181	R	11/17/2007	2		1.73	82.50		27	
20	12138	181	R	11/17/2007	2	0.92	2.08	82.50	19	17	
21	12141	181	R	11/17/2007	2	0.46	2.26	82.50	4	7	
22	12143	174	R	11/17/2007	2	1.04	2.24	76.50	24	8	
23	12147	181	A	11/18/2007	2	0.90	2.01	60.50	18	23	
24	12150	167	A	11/18/2007	2	0.97	2.00	45.50	21	25	
25	12151	181	A	11/18/2007	2	0.49	2.08	60.50	6	17	
26	12152	181	A	11/18/2007	2	0.75	2.17	60.50	14	14	
27	12153	167	A	11/18/2007	2	0.30	3.22	45.50	1	1	
28	12155	181	E	11/18/2007	2	1.01	2.24	70.50	23	8	
29	12157	181	E	11/19/2007	2	0.84	2.34	70.50	17	2	
30	12158	174	E	11/19/2007	2	0.68	2.10	64.50	12	16	
31	12159	181	A	11/19/2007	2	0.58	2.33	70.50	8	3	

Values deleted for second test if ski fails first test

Note, for example, the ski in row 4. This ski does not meet the criteria for the Torsion Strength test (that is, its Torsion Strength value is less than 2), so Joanna manually deleted both its Friction Coefficient value from cell F4 and its Rank Friction Coefficient value from cell I4. (In later chapters, you will learn how to accomplish this automatically.)

Now, Joanna is ready to calculate the cost of all rejected skis. Ideally, she wants to calculate this cost so that if any of the Friction Coefficient or Torsion Strength values are changed later, the worksheet will be automatically updated, making it easy to reuse for future analyses. So, simply adding the values for the rejected skis directly would not work. Again, Joanna first considers what manual process she would need to complete the task before implementing a solution in Excel. She could sum the Ski Cost values (column H) for only those skis that meet specified criteria. In this case, because Joanna is considering two different rejection criteria, she needs to do the following:

1. Examine the values for Friction Coefficient (column F) to sum the Ski Cost values (column H) for skis that were rejected because their Friction Coefficient values are too high.

2. Examine the values for Torsion Strength (column G) to sum the Ski Cost values for skis that were rejected because their Torsion Strength values are too low.

3. Add the resulting values from Steps 1 and 2.

Excel provides a function that accomplishes this automatically. The **SUMIF** function adds all the values in a range that meet specified criteria. The syntax of the SUMIF function is as follows:

$$\texttt{=SUMIF(range,criteria,sum\_range)}$$

The SUMIF function has three arguments:

- The "range" argument identifies the cell range where the criteria is located.
- The "criteria" argument specifies which values should be selected.
- The "sum_range" argument identifies the corresponding cell range to sum if the specified criteria has been met in the range established by the "range" argument. If the "sum_range" argument is omitted, the function adds the values in the range indicated by the first argument.

The SUMIF function works almost identically to the COUNTIF function in that its ranges must be contiguous and the criteria can be a value, text, cell reference, or relational expression. The criteria syntax rules are identical to those in the COUNTIF function, as summarized in Table 2.10. It is also important to note that SUMIF, like the COUNTIF function, ignores blank cells, as seen in the examples shown. The examples in Table 2.10 are based on the Current worksheet (see Figure 2.21).

Table 2.10: Examples of the SUMIF function

Criteria Type	Example	Description
Single numeric or Boolean value	=SUMIF(B3:B31,174,H3:H31)	Adds all ski costs (cells H3:H31) where the corresponding ski size is 174.
Text string	=SUMIF(C3:C31,"R",H3:H31)	Adds all ski costs (cells H3:H31) where the corresponding ski style is R.
Cell reference	=SUMIF(C3:C31,C50,H3:H31)	Adds all ski costs (cells H3:H31) where the corresponding ski style is E, assuming that cell C50 contains the value "E".

Table 2.10: Examples of the SUMIF function (cont.)

Criteria Type	Example	Description
Relational operator	=SUMIF(H3:H31,">60")	Adds all ski costs (cells H3:H31) for only those skis that cost more than $60. Note that because the sum_range argument is not specified in this example, the formula uses H3:H31 as both the criteria range and the sum range.
Wildcard	=SUMIF(A3:A31,"12???",H3:H31)	Adds all ski costs (cells H3:H31) where the corresponding Mfg ID# begins with 12 and is followed by three additional characters. This formula only works if cells A3 to A31 are formatted as text values and not as numeric values.

How To

Write a Formula Using the SUMIF Function

1. Place the pointer in the cell in which you want to write the formula.
2. Type: =SUMIF(
3. Locate the range that contains the criteria you want to test. This range must be a contiguous set of columns or rows, or a contiguous block of cells. Type the range (for example, A1:A10) into the function as the first argument followed by a comma.
4. Determine the selection criteria you want to use, applying the correct syntax for numerical values, text, Boolean values, relational operators, and/or wildcards. Enter the criteria as the second argument of the function followed by a comma.
5. Locate the range that contains the values you want to sum if the criteria is met. This range must be a contiguous set of columns or rows, or a contiguous block of cells. Type the range into the function as the third argument. If the sum range is the same as the criteria range, this third argument can be omitted.
6. Type the closing parenthesis mark).
7. If you intend to copy the formula, be certain to apply the appropriate relative or absolute cell referencing needed for each argument.

To apply the SUMIF function to the problem at hand, Joanna breaks down the problem into its components, as follows:

1. Calculate the Ski Cost values (column H) for skis rejected because their Friction Coefficient values (column F) are too high.

   SUMIF(F3:F31,">1.23",H3:H31)

2. Calculate the Ski Cost values (column H) for skis rejected because their Torsion Strength values (column G) are too low.

   SUMIF(G3:G31,"<2",H3:H31)

3. Add the resulting values from Steps 1 and 2. Joanna could enter each of the preceding formulas in separate cells, or create the entire formula in one cell. She decides to enter the entire formula shown below in cell H33.

```
=SUMIF(F3:F31,">1.23",H3:H31)+SUMIF(G3:G31,"<2",H3:H31)
```

Figure 2.22 shows the resulting worksheet. Note that the panes are frozen in the work-sheet so that the column titles and the result of the SUMIF function can be viewed simultaneously.

Figure 2.22: Calculating the total value of the rejected skis using the SUMIF function

	A	B	C	D	E	F	G	H	I	J	K
	H33			fx	=SUMIF(F3:F31,">1.23",H3:H31)+SUMIF(G3:G31,"<2",H3:H31)						
1				Quality Control Data for TZBlazer Skis							
2	Mfg ID#	Size	Style	Date Manufactured	Production Line	Friction Coefficient	Torsion Strength	Ski Cost	Rank Friction Coefficient	Rank Torsion Strength	
10	12146	167	A	11/17/2007	1	1.13	2.05	45.50	25	20	
11	12148	167	E	11/18/2007	1	0.43	2.27	55.50	2	6	
12	12149	174	E	11/18/2007	1	0.47	2.31	64.50	5	4	
13	12154	174	E	11/18/2007	1	0.97	2.23	64.50	21	11	
14	12156	174	E	11/18/2007	1	0.81	2.11	64.50	15	15	
15	12160	174	E	11/19/2007	1	0.68	2.22	64.50	12	12	
16	12161	174	E	11/19/2007	1	0.67	2.08	64.50	11	17	
17	12162	181	E	11/19/2007	1	0.95	2.01	70.50	20	23	
18	12136	181	R	11/17/2007	2	1.32		82.50	27		
19	12137	181	R	11/17/2007	2		1.73	82.50		27	
20	12138	181	R	11/17/2007	2	0.92	2.08	82.50	19	17	
21	12141	181	R	11/17/2007	2	0.46	2.26	82.50	4	7	
22	12143	174	R	11/17/2007	2	1.04	2.24	76.50	24	8	
23	12147	181	A	11/18/2007	2	0.90	2.01	60.50	18	23	
24	12150	167	A	11/18/2007	2	0.97	2.00	45.50	21	25	
25	12151	181	A	11/18/2007	2	0.49	2.08	60.50	6	17	
26	12152	181	A	11/18/2007	2	0.75	2.17	60.50	14	14	
27	12153	167	A	11/18/2007	2	0.30	3.22	45.50	1	1	
28	12155	181	E	11/18/2007	2	1.01	2.24	70.50	23	8	
29	12157	181	E	11/19/2007	2	0.84	2.34	70.50	17	2	
30	12158	174	E	11/19/2007	2	0.68	2.10	64.50	12	16	
31	12159	181	A	11/19/2007	2	0.58	2.33	70.50	8	3	
32											
33	# Rejected					2	2	$ 265.00			
34											
35											

Formula first sums the value of all skis rejected due to a Friction Coefficient value that is too high, then sums the value of all skis rejected due to a Torsion Strength value that is too low, and then adds the two resulting values together

As always, it is important to check that any formulas are working properly. With the COUNTIF function, Joanna can manually count the number of skis rejected. With the SUMIF function, she needs to check if the value that is calculated in cell H33 is actually $265.00. To do this manually, Joanna adds $54.50 for ski #12135, which was rejected due to a low Torsion Strength value; $45.50 for ski #12144, which was rejected due to a high Friction Coefficient value; $82.50 for ski #12136, which was rejected due to a high Friction Coefficient value; and, finally, $82.50 for ski #12137, which was rejected due to a low Torsion Strength value. The sum of these four values is, indeed, $265.00, so the formula in cell H33 is working correctly.

When using more complex functions such as SUMIF, even an extra comma in the wrong place could result in a perfectly plausible but incorrect value. Consider the example shown in Figure 2.23. If Joanna used the formula in cell H33 instead of the correct one, the extra comma in the second SUMIF function would cause that part of the formula to return a 0, so the resulting value of the SUMIF function would be $128 instead of $265. This type of error is hard to find, because no error message is displayed; Excel simply evaluates the incorrect formula and returns a result. In Chapter 10, you will learn about several built-in tools Excel provides to help you troubleshoot formulas to find and correct such errors.

Figure 2.23: Results of using incorrect syntax in a formula

	H33		*fx* =SUMIF(F3:F31,">1.23",H3:H31)+SUMIF(G3:G31,"<,2",H3:H31)								
	A	B	C	D	E	F	G	H	I	J	K
1				Quality Control Data for TZBlazer Skis							
2	Mfg ID#	Size	Style	Date Manufactured	Production Line	Friction Coefficient	Torsion Strength	Ski Cost	Rank Friction Coefficient	Rank Torsion Strength	
10	12146	167	A	11/17/2007	1	1.13	2.05	45.50	25	20	
11	12148	167	E	11/18/2007	1	0.43	2.27	55.50	2	6	
12	12149	174	E	11/18/2007	1	0.47	2.31	64.50	5	4	
13	12154	174	E	11/18/2007	1	0.97	2.23	64.50	21	11	
14	12156	174	E	11/18/2007	1	0.81	2.11	64.50	15	15	
15	12160	174	E	11/19/2007	1	0.68	2.22	64.50	12	12	
16	12161	174	E	11/19/2007	1	0.67	2.08	64.50	11	17	
17	12162	181	E	11/19/2007	1	0.95	2.01	70.50	20	23	
18	12136	181	R	11/17/2007	2	1.32		82.50	27		
19	12137	181	R	11/17/2007	2		1.73	82.50		27	
20	12138	181	R	11/17/2007	2	0.92	2.08	82.50	19	17	
21	12141	181	R	11/17/2007	2	0.46	2.26	82.50	4	7	
22	12143	174	R	11/17/2007	2	1.04	2.24	76.50	24	8	
23	12147	181	A	11/18/2007	2	0.90	2.01	60.50	18	23	
24	12150	167	A	11/18/2007	2	0.97	2.00	45.50	21	25	
25	12151	181	A	11/18/2007	2	0.49	2.08	60.50	6	17	
26	12152	181	A	11/18/2007	2	0.75	2.17	60.50	14	14	
27	12153	167	A	11/18/2007	2	0.30	3.22	45.50	1	1	
28	12155	181	E	11/18/2007	2	1.01	2.24	70.50	23	8	
29	12157	181	E	11/19/2007	2	0.84	2.34	70.50	17	2	
30	12158	174	E	11/19/2007	2	0.68	2.10	64.50	12	16	
31	12159	181	A	11/19/2007	2	0.58	2.33	70.50	8	3	
32											
33	# Rejected						2	2	$ 128.00		
34											
35											

Extra comma in the formula results in the value $128 instead of the correct value $265

Joanna has now taken a more detailed look at the high and low values of the Friction Coefficient and Torsion Strength data, and she has also determined the quantities and ski costs associated with rejected skis—four skis totaling $265 dollars. Although this might not seem like a large sum, keep in mind that Joanna started out with a relatively small data set. The real question to consider is what the overall impact will be, such as per day or per year, for this type of rejection quantity. There might be ways of reducing the number of rejected skis, but will the cost of doing so be justified compared with the cost of the rejected skis? In the next level, Joanna will explore the cost of 100% inspection of skis versus the possible costs to the company of retailers and consumers returning these skis due to poor performance.

Steps To Success: Level 2

The QC group wants to extend the ski bindings quality control data analysis to determine the rankings, examine the tail ends of the data—both high and low values—and determine the number of bindings that will be rejected. The data being analyzed is located in a workbook named Bindings2.xls. Your task in these steps is to complete this analysis.

The criteria for rejecting bindings is based on two different quality tests, as follows:

- Minimum pressure at which the binding mechanism will automatically unlock (P) measured in pounds (lbs). Bindings that unlock at less than 10 lbs of pressure are rejected.
- Temperature at which the materials of construction fail, given that the cold temperatures affect the binding performance, measured in degrees Celsius (°C). The lower the failure temperature, the better the ski binding. The maximum allowable failure temperature is −60 °C.

Complete the following:

1. Open the workbook named **Binding2.xls** located in the Chapter 2 folder, and then save it as **QC Binding Data Analysis 2.xls**.

2. Write a formula in cell G3 that can be copied down the column to calculate the relative rankings of each data element for the pressure test. Set up your rankings so that the "best" ski is given a ranking of 1. Include an appropriate column heading in cell G2. In a similar way, set up the rankings for the Temperature test in column H so that the "best" ski is given a ranking of 1.

3. In cell D49, write a formula to determine the number of ski bindings that failed to meet the minimum pressure requirements for quality testing. Write the formula so that if any of the data inputs change later, this value will be automatically updated.

4. In cell E49, write a formula to determine the number of ski bindings that failed to meet the minimum temperature requirements for quality testing. Write the formula so that if any of the data inputs change later, this value will be automatically updated.

5. In cell F49, write a formula to determine the total value of the ski bindings that have been rejected. Assume that no binding has failed both tests. Format this cell with the Currency Style. Include the label "Rejection Summary" in cell A49.

6. Set up a separate worksheet named "Tail" in the workbook, and then create a table on the Tail worksheet listing the five highest and lowest values, as shown in Table 2.11. Be certain to include a title on this new worksheet and format the worksheet so that it is easy to read.

Table 2.11: Five highest and lowest values for binding tests

	Top 5 – Highest		Bottom 5 – Lowest	
	Pressure	Temperature	Pressure	Temperature
1				
2				
3				
4				
5				

7. Write a formula to calculate the highest pressure value so that it will be automatically updated if the binding data is later revised. Write the formula so that it can be copied down the column to determine the second highest pressure, the third highest pressure, and so on, and across the row to determine the highest temperature.

8. Write a formula to calculate the lowest pressure value so that it will be automatically updated if the binding data is later revised. Write the formula so that it can be copied down the column to determine the second lowest pressure, the third lowest pressure, and so on, and across the row to determine the lowest temperature value.

9. Save and close the QC Binding Data Analysis 2.xls workbook.

LEVEL 3

EXTENDING THE ANALYSIS WITH WHAT-IF, GOAL SEEK, AND SIMULATION

EXCEL 2003 SKILLS TRAINING

- **Create a custom number format**
- **Create formulas using the COUNTIF function**
- **Create formulas using the SUMIF function**
- **Use Goal Seek**
- **Use the ROUND function**

EVALUATING A LARGER DATA SET

In the next phase of her cost benefit analysis, Joanna needs to examine the costs of inspecting each ski and then total these values to determine the total inspection costs. Joanna also wants to calculate these values by ski style, to determine if there is a significant variable in the inspection cost per style of ski. Once the QC costs are better understood, Joanna can begin to compare the costs of doing a 100% inspection of the skis versus the cost of just paying the additional charges associated with replacing skis that fail. This, of course, does not take into account factors that can affect sales, such as customer satisfaction or the liability risk involved if ski failure results in personal injury or property damage. However, TheZone's management is responsible for weighing all the costs, benefits, and risks; Joanna's job is simply to quantify these costs.

The majority of the cost involved in ski quality testing is the cost of labor. The quality inspectors earn approximately $35 per hour, on average. To quantify the time it takes to inspect a ski, the QC group has been asked to keep a record of each test for each ski tested over a period of one hour. To make the analysis more meaningful, the QC group has expanded the data set to include 100 different skis. The time data for these 100 skis has been entered in a new worksheet named "Time," as shown in Figure 2.24. This worksheet lists the Mfg. ID# of the ski, the ski style, and the time it took to perform each of the two quality tests (Friction Coefficient and Torsion Strength) for each individual ski.

Figure 2.24: Time worksheet

	A	B	C	D	E	F
1	Time Data for Quality Control Testing - Per Ski					
2			Actual Time in Minutes			
3	MFG ID#	Style	Friction Coefficient Testing	Torsion Strength Testing		
4	2345	R	1.0	1.5		
5	2346	R	1.0	1.0		
6	2347	R	1.0	3.0		
7	2348	R	2.0	5.0		
8	2349	R	1.0	1.5		
9	2350	R	1.5	5.0		
10	2351	R				
11	2352	E	2.5	3.5		
12	2353	R	1.0	4.0		
13	2354	E	2.0	1.0		
14	2355	R	1.5	1.5		
15	2356	A	1.0	7.0		
16	2357	R	2.0	3.5		
17	2358	E	1.0	4.5		
18	2359	A	3.0	2.0		
19	2360	A	3.5	3.0		
20	2361	R	2.0	4.5		
21	2362	A	1.0	1.0		
22	2363	A	1.5	6.0		
23	2364	R	1.0	4.5		
24	2365	E	2.0	4.5		
25	2366	R	1.0	1.0		
26	2367	A	1.0	1.5		
27	2368	A	1.0	7.5		
28	2369	A	1.0	3.0		
29	2370	E	1.0	5.0		
30	2371	A	2.0	6.5		

Joanna needs to use this data to calculate the costs to quality test a ski. To accomplish this task, she can add the number of minutes spent to test a particular ski and then apply those total minutes to the cost per hour of an inspector. In theory, this should be the sum of total minutes to inspect a ski divided by the number of minutes per hour times the dollars per hour ($/hr) of labor for the inspector:

```
=SUM(minutes to inspect)/minutes per hour*$ per hour of labor
```

To calculate the cost of testing the first ski, Joanna can write the formula =SUM(C4:D4)/60*35 in cell E4. Notice the use of two constants in this formula, 60 and 35. In general, when designing a worksheet, it is important to separately list inputs, especially inputs that are likely to change or that you might want to explore with "what -if" scenarios. Because 60 (the number of minutes per hour) will not change, it can remain as a constant in the formula. The $35 hourly labor rate, however, is a number that Joanna might want to vary and, therefore, should be listed elsewhere.

If a worksheet contains a large number of data inputs, it is often best to place these inputs on a separate worksheet or in a separate area on the same worksheet. In this case, there is only one data input ($35 hourly labor rate) and it is used in a single calculation. An easy solution might be to simply list the value above the Total Cost to Inspect label, in cell E2.

However, the value $35 on its own might not convey what it represents; on the other hand, if Joanna types in the text "$35/hr-labor" the cell value cannot be used as part of the calculation for the cost per hour. One solution is to alter the format of the cell without altering the value, allowing Joanna to write the formula =SUM(C4:D4)/60*E2. She can accomplish this by creating a custom number format.

SPECIFYING A CUSTOM NUMBER FORMAT

The Format Cells dialog box, which is available from the Format menu, provides many options for changing the display of cell values. The Number tab in this dialog box lists all the available number formats in Excel and also provides an option for creating a custom number format. Here, Joanna wants to enter the more descriptive value "$35/hr-labor" in cell E2 but also use just the number 35 from this cell in the formula she needs to write.

How To

Apply Custom Number Formats to Cells

1. Select the cell or cells you want to format.

2. Click Format on the menu bar, and then click Cells to open the Format Cells dialog box.

3. Select the Number tab in the Format Cells dialog box.

4. In the Category list box, click Custom.

5. In the Type list box, enter the appropriate formatting, using quotation marks to enclose text as in the following example: $0.00"/hr-labor". See Figure 2.25.

Figure 2.25: Format Cells dialog box with Custom formatting selected

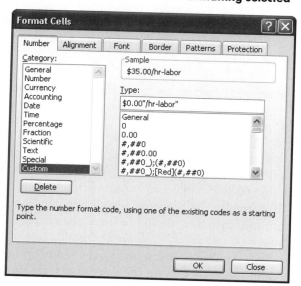

6. Click the OK button when you have finished specifying the custom format.

Joanna uses the Format Cells dialog box to specify the custom number format $0.00"/hr-labor" for cell E2 and then enters the value 35 in the cell. Now she can write the formula to calculate the costs to quality test a ski. Because Joanna does not want the cost of labor to change when she copies the formula down the column into cells E4 through E103, she needs to make the row reference for the hourly rate an absolute reference. The format of the formula is as follows:

```
=SUM(C4:D4)/60*E$2
```

Joanna enters the formula in cell E4 and copies it down the column through cell E103. Figure 2.26 shows the resulting worksheet.

Figure 2.26: Worksheet with custom number formatting applied

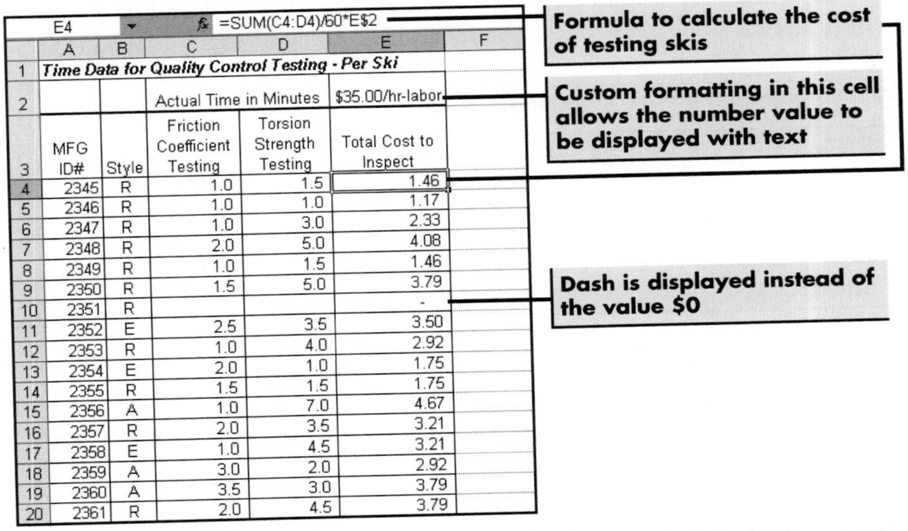

E4 =SUM(C4:D4)/60*E$2

	A	B	C	D	E	F
1	*Time Data for Quality Control Testing - Per Ski*					
2			Actual Time in Minutes		$35.00/hr-labor	
3	MFG ID#	Style	Friction Coefficient Testing	Torsion Strength Testing	Total Cost to Inspect	
4	2345	R	1.0	1.5	1.46	
5	2346	R	1.0	1.0	1.17	
6	2347	R	1.0	3.0	2.33	
7	2348	R	2.0	5.0	4.08	
8	2349	R	1.0	1.5	1.46	
9	2350	R	1.5	5.0	3.79	
10	2351	R			-	
11	2352	E	2.5	3.5	3.50	
12	2353	R	1.0	4.0	2.92	
13	2354	E	2.0	1.0	1.75	
14	2355	R	1.5	1.5	1.75	
15	2356	A	1.0	7.0	4.67	
16	2357	R	2.0	3.5	3.21	
17	2358	E	1.0	4.5	3.21	
18	2359	A	3.0	2.0	2.92	
19	2360	A	3.5	3.0	3.79	
20	2361	R	2.0	4.5	3.79	

Understanding Custom Formatting Codes

In Figure 2.26, notice that there are no values in cells C10 and D10. For some reason, this ski was not inspected for either test, even though it appears on the QC list. Notice that a dash (-) appears instead of the value $0 for the cost to inspect in cell E10. The current format of cell E10 uses the Comma Style, which by default represents values of 0 as a dash. Although this has no effect on any subsequent formulas, Joanna prefers to display a 0 in this cell for clarity. To do so, she again needs to specify a custom number format.

How can Joanna substitute a 0 for the dash in cell E10? To learn more about how custom formats work, Joanna clicks cell E10, opens the Format Cells dialog box, and selects the Custom category. The following code is displayed in the Type box:

```
_(* #,##0.00_);_(* (#,##0.00);_(* "-"??_);_(@_)
```

But what does this code mean? This is the format code currently in place for cell E10; it is the format for the Comma Style. A format code can include up to four parts, each separated by a semicolon, as follows:

```
Positive number format; Negative number format; Zero value
    format, Additional text format
```

These formats consist of combinations of symbols, such as underscores, question marks, pound signs, asterisks, and so on. Each symbol has a specific meaning that Excel translates into a specific format. Table 2.12 lists some of the common number formatting codes. Some codes display digits that are significant, and others display digits whether or not they are significant. Some codes are simply placeholders. An *insignificant* digit refers to a zero that does not change the value of the number. For example, in the number 2.030, the zero at the end of the number is insignificant because 2.03 is the same as 2.030. However, the 0 in the tenths place is significant because eliminating it would change the value.

Table 2.12: Examples of number formatting codes

Symbol	Usage	Typed Digits	Display
#	Acts as a digit placeholder that displays significant digits Example: ####.#	12.87 03.00	12.9 3
0	Acts as a digit placeholder that displays both significant and insignificant zeros Example: 0.00	.358 245	0.36 245.00
?	Acts as a digit placeholder that does not display insignificant digits but does hold a place so that decimal points will align Example: 0.00?	27.3 5.132	27.30 5.132
%	Inserts a percentage sign and automatically multiplies the value inserted by 100 for display Example: #%	.3	30%
,	Inserts a comma as a thousands separator or as a scaling operator Example as separator: #,### Example as scaling operator: ##,,	12000000 12000000	12,000,000 12
*	Indicates repetition of the following character enough times to fill the column to its complete width Example: $* 00.00 (note that the * is followed by a blank space)	1250	$ 1250.00
_	Indicates to skip the width of the next character; frequently used with ( ) to make sure positive numbers align with negative numbers displayed with ( ) Example used for positive number: _($* #,###_) Example used to align with negative number ($* #,###)	1250 –1250	$ 1,250 ($ 1,250)

Table 2.12: Examples of number formatting codes (cont.)

Symbol	Usage	Typed Digits	Display
" "	Specifies that text enclosed in quotation marks should be inserted as shown Example: 00.00 "$/hr"	43.333	43.33 $/hr
@	Indicates the location where text should be inserted in cells formatted with a custom format; if the @ is not included in the code, the text will not be displayed Example: $@	None	$None

As stated earlier, up to four different formats can be applied to a cell: one for positive numbers, one for negative numbers, one for zero values, and one for text. Each format must be separated by a semicolon. If you specify only two formats, the first is used for positive numbers and zeros, and the second is used for negative numbers. If you specify only one format, it is used for all numbers. Figure 2.27 illustrates the format code for cell E10 in the Time worksheet.

Figure 2.27: Custom number formatting codes

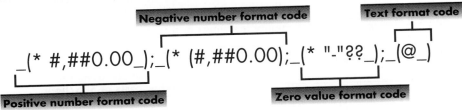

Notice that four sections are defined, so positive, negative, zero, and text values each have their own format. The positive value is defined as _(* #,##0.00_). The first underscore with an open parenthesis indicates a placeholder so that all positive values contain a space on the left side of the cell equal to the width of an open parenthesis. Next is the asterisk followed by a space, indicating to fill the cell with blank spaces in this location after all of the digits have been displayed; this also ensures that values will align on the decimal point. The #,##0.00 placeholders specify that a minimum of the ones, tenths, and hundredths digits be shown and commas be displayed for thousands. At the end, another space is reserved equivalent to the width of a closing parenthesis. In a similar manner, the negative value format can be analyzed. Here, parentheses are used to enclose the value.

The text format following the last semicolon shows that text will appear if typed into the cell. Again, blank spaces before and after the text in the width of the parentheses characters are indicated.

Joanna wants to change the format of the zero value display. This is the code following the second semicolon. She wants to modify the display from the standard Comma Style so that zero values will display the digit "0" rather than a dash. To edit the format code, Joanna simply replaces the dash "-" with a 0 in the Type box and clicks the OK button in the

Format Cells dialog box. She then copies the format into the other cells in column E using the Format Painter tool.

CONSIDERING ALTERNATIVES: WHAT-IF ANALYSIS AND GOAL SEEK

With cell E2 properly formatted to display the value 35 with the text "$/hr-labor," Joanna is now ready to do a few simple calculations to determine the total and average minutes for each test and the total and average costs to inspect the skis. She has also decided to calculate the standard deviation of the data to get an idea of its variability. To do this, she enters the following formulas in the cells indicated and copies them into columns D and E:

- C105: =SUM(C4:C103)
- C106: =AVERAGE(C4:C103)
- C107: =STDEV(C4:C103)

Figure 2.28 shows the resulting worksheet. Note that the panes are frozen in the worksheet so that the column titles and the statistics calculated can be viewed simultaneously.

Figure 2.28: Calculating statistics for quality test times and costs

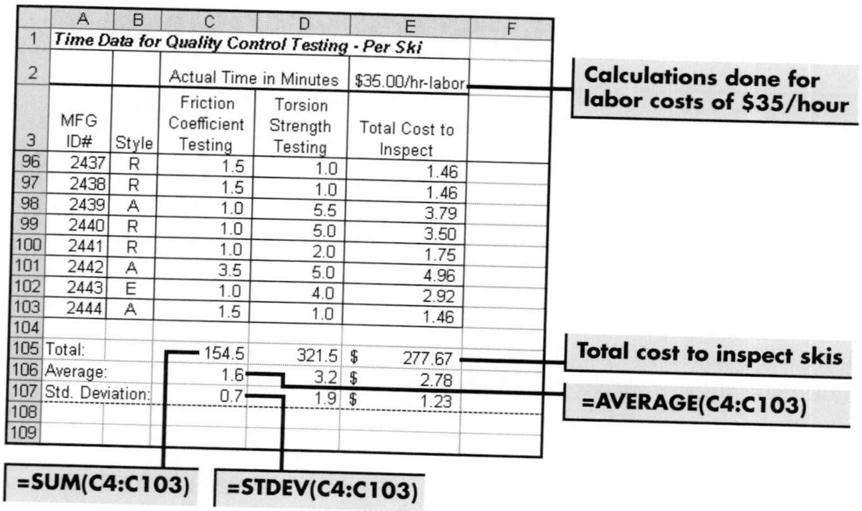

The total cost to inspect the skis is $277.67, as shown in cell E105. The average minutes and standard deviation (cells C106:D107) indicate a significant variance in the time it takes to inspect a ski. The standard deviation of 0.7 for the Friction Coefficient average of 1.6, for example, indicates for a normal distribution that over 30% of the skis tested varied by more than 50% from the average time, making it hard to predict how long it will take to inspect a given ski. Note that the average total time (cells C106 plus D106) is approximately 4.8 minutes of an inspector's time, who currently makes approximately

$35 per hour. The overall costs can now be used as a benchmark of 100% inspection. At a later time, management might choose to look into methods of reducing these costs through different testing techniques and/or improved efficiency.

Performing What-If Analysis

So, what if, after all this work, Joanna finds out that the average labor rate for a quality control inspector is $45 per hour rather than $35 per hour? Would she need to recalculate the total cost to inspect each item and then to again perform the summary calculations? Or, what if item #2444 was erroneously listed as requiring 1 minute for the Torsion Strength test but actually took 10 minutes? Would she need to recalculate all of the totals, averages, and standard deviations?

Because Joanna planned the worksheet well, updating a single cell is all that she would need to do in each of these "what-if" scenarios. Performing a **what-if analysis** means, simply, to determine the outcome of changing one or more input values and evaluate the recalculated results. In the first what-if analysis, Joanna can easily substitute the value $45 for the value $35 in cell E2 to determine the impact of a higher labor rate. All of the other values are calculated from formulas that ultimately refer back to this value. In the second what-if analysis, Joanna can simply change the Torsion Strength test time of item #2444 to 10 in cell D103. Because each of the SUM, AVERAGE, and STDEV formulas reference the range containing this value, these calculations will automatically update as well, as shown in Figure 2.29. More sophisticated techniques of varying inputs are explored in later chapters.

Figure 2.29: Performing a "what-if" analysis using $45/hour for labor

	A	B	C	D	E	F
1	*Time Data for Quality Control Testing - Per Ski*					
2			Actual Time in Minutes		$45.00/hr-labor	
3	MFG ID#	Style	Friction Coefficient Testing	Torsion Strength Testing	Total Cost to Inspect	
96	2437	R	1.5	1.0	1.88	
97	2438	R	1.5	1.0	1.88	
98	2439	A	1.0	5.5	4.88	
99	2440	R	1.0	5.0	4.50	
100	2441	R	1.0	2.0	2.25	
101	2442	A	3.5	5.0	6.38	
102	2443	E	1.0	4.0	3.75	
103	2444	A	1.5	1.0	1.88	
104						
105	Total:		154.5	321.5	$ 357.00	
106	Average:		1.6	3.2	$ 3.57	
107	Std. Deviation:		0.7	1.9	$ 1.58	
108						
109						

Total cost to inspect at $45/hour for labor equals $357 versus $277.67 at $35/hour

Using the Goal Seek Tool to Work Backward

What if Joanna wants to change an input value in order to reach a *specified output*? For example, what would the labor rate have to be for the cost of inspection to be $225 instead of the original $277.67? One possible way to solve this is to keep trying various values for labor rate, narrowing it down until the answer is reached. However, Excel provides a tool called Goal Seek that enables you to accomplish this automatically. When using **Goal Seek**, you can specify the outcome you want and which input value you want to vary, and Excel automatically calculates the solution.

To use the Goal Seek tool, Joanna needs to select options from the Goal Seek dialog box, which is available from the Tools menu. The Goal Seek dialog box is shown in Figure 2.30.

Figure 2.30: Goal Seek dialog box

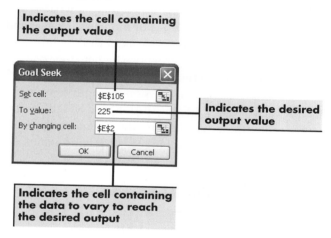

In this dialog box, you use the "Set cell" text box to specify the cell in which the output value will appear. In the "To value" text box, you enter the value you want to achieve as the output value—in other words, the goal you are seeking. In the "By changing cell" text box, you specify the cell containing the dependent data that you want to vary to achieve the desired output, or goal.

How To

Use the Goal Seek Tool

1. Click Tools on the menu bar, and then click Goal Seek to open the Goal Seek dialog box.

2. In the Set cell text box, enter the cell reference where the output value will appear.

3. In the To value text box, enter the desired outcome value.

4. In the By changing cell text box, enter the cell reference of the input you want to vary.

5. Click the OK button to close the Goal Seek dialog box and open the Goal Seek Status dialog box, which displays your target value. If the target value cannot be reached exactly, the closest value found will be listed as the current value.

6. Click the OK button to update the worksheet with these new values, or click the Cancel button to maintain the original values in the worksheet.

For Joanna's analysis, she opens the Goal Seek dialog box and specifies the following (as shown in Figure 2.30):

- Set cell: E105 (the cell containing the total cost to inspect)
- To value: 225 (the total cost to inspect that Joanna wants to achieve)
- By changing cell: E2 (the cell containing the hourly labor rate)

When Joanna clicks the OK button in the Goal Seek dialog box, the Goal Seek Status dialog box opens, as shown in Figure 2.31.

Figure 2.31: Goal Seek Status dialog box

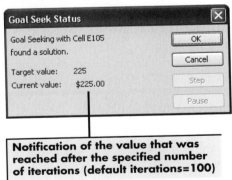

Notification of the value that was reached after the specified number of iterations (default iterations=100)

The Goal Seek Status dialog box gives the target value. If the target value cannot be reached exactly, the closest value found is listed as the current value. In this case, the target value of 225 can be reached exactly. Joanna clicks the OK button to update the worksheet, substituting these new values, as shown in Figure 2.32.

Figure 2.32: Worksheet with values updated based on the Goal Seek results

	A	B	C	D	E	F
1	*Time Data for Quality Control Testing - Per Ski*					
2			Actual Time in Minutes		$28.36/hr-labor	
3	MFG ID#	Style	Friction Coefficient Testing	Torsion Strength Testing	Total Cost to Inspect	
96	2437	R	1.5	1.0	1.18	
97	2438	R	1.5	1.0	1.18	
98	2439	A	1.0	5.5	3.07	
99	2440	R	1.0	5.0	2.84	
100	2441	R	1.0	2.0	1.42	
101	2442	A	3.5	5.0	4.02	
102	2443	E	1.0	4.0	2.36	
103	2444	A	1.5	1.0	1.18	
104						
105	Total:		154.5	321.5	$ 225.00	
106	Average:		1.6	3.2	$ 2.25	
107	Std. Deviation:		0.7	1.9	$ 0.99	
108						
109						

Goal Seek updated the labor rate to $28.36 from $35 to attain a total labor cost of $225

By using the Goal Seek tool, Excel has calculated that a labor rate of $28.36/hr results in a total cost to inspect of $225.00.

Best Practice

Testing Values with Goal Seek

The Goal Seek Status dialog box gives the target value when you use the Goal Seek tool. At this point in the process, you can click the OK button to update your worksheet with the new values based on the Goal Seek results, or you can click the Cancel button to maintain the original values. Sometimes, it's a good idea to keep both the original values and the values resulting from using Goal Seek, so that you can test various values before achieving the solution you want, while keeping your original data intact. This might be especially important if your original data is fairly complex. To do so, simply save your original workbook and then, after completing the Goal Seek, save it again with a different filename.

Goal Seek uses an iterative approach to finding the right input that achieves the desired result, or goal, in the dependent cell. Excel keeps changing values in the changing cell until it reaches the solution or finds the closest value it can. Goal Seek continues to enter values until it reaches a value that is within 0.001 of the goal or 100 iterations. You can change these defaults by using the Calculation tab of the Options dialog box (available from the Tools menu), as shown in Figure 2.33.

Figure 2.33: Modifying options related to iterations

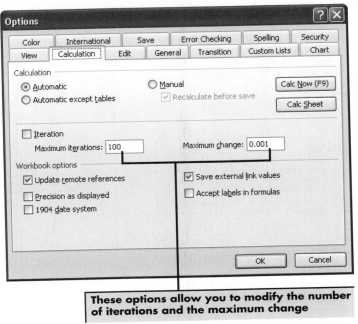

These options allow you to modify the number of iterations and the maximum change

As you can see, the Goal Seek tool enables you to explore this type of "reverse" what-if analysis quickly and easily. Although Goal Seek is simple to use, it does have limitations:

- Goal Seek allows you to vary only a single input. So, for example, Joanna could vary the labor rate or vary the number of minutes it takes to perform a single test for a single ski, but not both simultaneously.
- The input cannot be a value derived from a formula; it must be a constant value, such as 10, 100, and so on. In Joanna's case, the labor cost is in cell E2. This cell cannot contain a formula such as =30+5; it must contain the value 35. Otherwise, the warning "The cell must contain a value" will be displayed.

COMBINING COUNTIF AND SUMIF TO ANALYZE DATA IN SPECIFIC CATEGORIES

In addition to providing the number of minutes it takes to perform each test for each ski, the Time worksheet also includes information about the ski style (column B). Joanna wants to know whether the average times for each test vary based on the ski style. To determine this, Joanna needs to calculate the average times for each test by ski style. Unfortunately, there is no one function provided by Excel that averages a series of values if they meet specific criteria. However, keep in mind that an average is simply a sum divided by a count, and there are functions that sum a list of values if they meet specified criteria, and count a list of values that meet specified criteria. So, can Joanna use a SUMIF function and then divide the results by a COUNTIF function to produce the results she wants? Yes; this will work well, as shown in Figure 2.34.

Figure 2.34: Using SUMIF and COUNTIF to calculate values by category

	A	B	C	D	E	F
1	Time Data for Quality Control Testing - Per Ski					
2			Actual Time in Minutes		$35.00/hr-labor	
3	MFG ID#	Style	Friction Coefficient Testing	Torsion Strength Testing	Total Cost to Inspect	
96	2437	R	1.5	1.0	1.46	
97	2438	R	1.5	1.0	1.46	
98	2439	A	1.0	5.5	3.79	
99	2440	R	1.0	5.0	3.50	
100	2441	R	1.0	2.0	1.75	
101	2442	A	3.5	5.0	4.96	
102	2443	E	1.0	4.0	2.92	
103	2444	A	1.5	1.0	1.46	
104						
105	Total:		154.5	321.5	$ 277.67	
106	Average:		1.6	3.2	$ 2.78	
107	Std. Deviation:		0.7	1.9	$ 1.23	
108						
109						

← **Time worksheet**

`=COUNTIF(Time!B$4:B$103,A3)`

	A	B	C	D	E	F
1		Summary- By Ski Type				
2	Style	Quantity of Skis Tested	Average Friction Test Time	Average Torsion Test Time	Average Cost	
3	A	27	2.04	4.02	$ 3.53	
4	E	21	1.60	3.83	$ 3.17	
5	R	52	1.27	2.55	$ 2.23	
6						
7						
8						
9						

← **SkiType worksheet**

`=SUMIF(Time!$B$4:$B$103,$A3,Time!C$4:C$103)/$B3`

Here, Joanna has set up a new worksheet named SkiType to use in conjunction with the original Time worksheet, which contains the data provided by the QC group. In the SkiType worksheet, Joanna has set up a table with ski type categories listed as individual rows and the following data headings as individual columns: Quantity of Skis Tested, Average Friction Test Time, Average Torsion Test Time, and Average Cost.

In cell SkiType!B3, Joanna calculates the total number of items tested by style using the following formula:

`=COUNTIF(Time!B$4:B$103,A3)`

In this COUNTIF function, the criteria range is the cell range B4:B103 on the Time worksheet; this range contains the ski style information. Because this range remains constant regardless of which style is being counted—style A, E, or R—the range rows are absolute. This formula will be copied down the column, but not across rows, so only the row references need to be absolute. The criteria used is the ski style being counted, as specified in cell A3 of the SkiType worksheet. By using the cell reference A3, which contains the value "A" for ski style A, the criteria will vary when the formula is copied down the column into rows 4 and 5. Note that the sheet name is not required in the A3 cell reference because this cell is on the same worksheet as the active cell where the formula is being entered.

Columns C through E on the SkiType worksheet contain the averages for each of the test times and for the cost. To calculate the average test time for ski style A, Joanna needs to write a SUMIF function divided by the results of the COUNTIF function she wrote in cell B3. Starting in cell C3, Joanna sums all the friction test times for style A using a SUMIF function. Then, she divides this value by the count of the number of style A skis. Because Joanna has already counted the number of items tested by style in column B, she can simply reference these values directly in her formula without needing to recount them. Joanna writes the following formula in cell C3 and then copies it down the column into rows 4 and 5 and across into columns D and E:

$$\texttt{=SUMIF(Time!\$B\$4:\$B\$103,\$A3,Time!C\$4:C\$103)/\$B3}$$

Notice the relative and absolute cell referencing used in this formula:

- The range containing the criteria for the SUMIF function remains the same whether the formula is copied down the column or across the row. Column B on the Time worksheet is always used to find the criteria and, therefore, must be referenced absolutely both in terms of rows and columns (Time!$B$4:$B$103).
- The criteria argument of the SUMIF function (the ski style) changes as the formula is copied down the column, but remains the same when copied across the row for each corresponding test and the total cost. So, the column of the criteria argument must be referenced absolutely ($A3).
- The sum_range argument of the SUMIF function does not change when copied down the column as the styles change, but it does change when copied across the row to calculate each test and then the total cost. So, if values are being summed for either the friction test or the torsion test, the rows of the range containing the data will remain the same, whereas the columns will vary depending on the values being summed. To indicate this, the rows of the range must be absolute (Time!C$4:C$103).

Based on the information Joanna has derived from the data, there are indeed significant time and cost differences associated with each of the different ski styles, as shown in the SkiType worksheet. For example, Style A costs roughly 34% more to test than Style R. The reason for this is not immediately obvious to Joanna, but will be an important factor to explore further if management decides to reevaluate the quality tests themselves.

ANALYZING DATA THROUGH SIMULATION

Joanna knows the cost of 100% quality testing of skis (277.77) and now wants to compare this to the option of not doing 100% quality testing. The actual defective ski cost does not change whether the defect is found at QC testing or by a customer, but an additional cost of shipping and handling is incurred if the ski actually goes to a customer and needs to be returned. Again, these costs do not take into account customer satisfaction or liability. Also, remember that the costs of producing 100% defective-free skis might be too prohibitive; it is management's job to balance the risks the company is willing to incur versus the costs.

Joanna needs to determine the cost of not inspecting, specifically the costs of handling and returning the defective ski and getting a new ski to the customer. At this point, Joanna knows that replacement costs vary between $25 to $200 dollars, depending on the area of the country, and that the expected failure rates for all ski types is between 3% and 5%. She could just take the average replacement cost and multiply that by the average failure rate times the number of skis. For the number of skis, Joanna will use 100 to match the QC test costs previously calculated when she first started working with the larger data set of 100 skis. The average cost of forgoing testing of 100 skis would, therefore, be = (.03+.05)/2*(25+200)/2*100, which results in 450. To calculate the cost by ski type, Joanna can divide this value by 3 because there are three different ski styles. The average cost of not inspecting according to this calculation is about $450 dollars, which is more than the total cost of inspecting the skis, 277.77. But, as demonstrated earlier, the average value doesn't necessarily tell the whole story.

Another possible method of determining the costs involved with returning defective skis is to simulate these costs on a worksheet model. **Simulation** is an analytical method that creates artificially generated data to imitate real data. The advantage of a simulation is that it can be easily calculated and recalculated to show some of the different possible outcomes as opposed to the most probable outcome or even the extreme limits. A simulation that is based on randomly generating specific values that have an equal chance of appearing, such as numbers on a set of dice, is often referred to as a "Monte Carlo" simulation. Joanna will use a similar technique to generate the number of defective skis that might be returned and the costs to return them. More sophisticated simulation techniques are covered in a later chapter.

Joanna begins her simulation by setting up a worksheet named Simulation, as shown in Figure 2.35.

Figure 2.35: Simulation worksheet

	A	B	C	D	E	F	G	H	I
1		*Ski Return Cost Simulation*				*Costs for 100 Skis*			
2	Style	Return Costs	Probability of Failure	Probable Cost				*Average Cost of Returned Skis* 450	
3							Style	*Simulated Probable Costs*	
4							1 A	0	
5							2 E	0	
6							3 R	0	
7								$ -	
8									
9									
10									

Data area for simulation   **Summary area**

First, in column A, Joanna will randomly assign a ski style to each of 100 rows to obtain a sample size similar to the one provided by the QC group, where 1 represents ski style A, 2 ski style E, and 3 ski style R. In column B, she will calculate a random value for the return costs varying between $25 and $200, and in column C the probability that this ski will be defective. Joanna has been directed to use a failure rate varying randomly from 3% to 5%. The probable cost of a ski being returned can be calculated as this failure rate times the cost of returning the ski (column D). The costs will then be aggregated by type and in total in the area set up in cells F1:H8. Note that the calculation for the average costs of returning defective skis for a group size of 100 has been placed in cell H3.

Randomly Assigning a Number Between Two Values Using the RANDBETWEEN Function

Skis are always of style A, E, or R, as represented by 1, 2, and 3. To randomly assign one of these values to a cell, the most convenient method is to use a RANDBETWEEN function. The **RANDBETWEEN** function randomly assigns a number between two specified values. The syntax of the function is as follows:

$$\text{RANDBETWEEN(bottom,top)}$$

This function randomly returns an *integer* between the top and bottom values, including the values listed. So, the formula =RANDBETWEEN(1,3) randomly returns a 1, 2, or 3. This formula can then be copied down column A of the Simulation worksheet to generate 100 random occurrences of the values 1, 2, and 3.

Note that the RANDBETWEEN function is not automatically provided with Excel by default. It can be added, however, by using the Add-in Analysis ToolPak. Excel provides several different add-in programs that offer optional commands and features. These supplemental tools are available when you install Excel or can be added later on. If the Analysis ToolPak has not already been enabled, and you attempt to enter a RANDBETWEEN function, you will receive the #NAME? error message.

How To

Install Excel Add-Ins from the Analysis ToolPak

1. Click Tools on the menu bar, and then click Add-Ins.

2. In the Add-Ins dialog box, click the check box next to the add-in(s) you want to install. See Figure 2.36.

Figure 2.36: Add-Ins dialog box

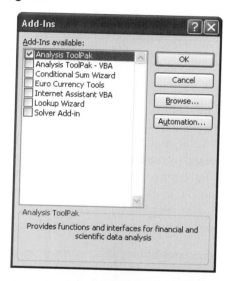

3. To install the RANDBETWEEN function and other data analysis tools, select the Analysis ToolPak check box. (Note: if this option is already checked, and you continue to receive the #NAME? error, uncheck the Analysis ToolPak, click the OK button, and then repeat the procedure to reinstall it.)

4. Click the OK button.

Note: if a full install of Microsoft Excel was not originally completed, and the Analysis ToolPak is not available, you will need your original CDs to run a custom installation to add this feature.

Assigning a Random Value Using the RAND Function

Now, Joanna needs to estimate the cost of a returned ski as a random value between $25 and $200 dollars. Because this value does not need to be an integer, she can use another function to create a value. The **RAND()** function returns a random value between 0 and 1. Notice that it has no arguments, but the syntax requires the parentheses be included when using the function. To arrive at a value between 25 and 200, Joanna could do the following:

- Start with the minimum value of 25.
- Calculate a random value between 0 and 175 because 175 is the difference between the minimum and maximum value (200–25). If RAND() gives a random number between 0 and 1, then multiplying RAND() by 175 should give a random number between 0 and 175.
- Add the minimum value of 25 to this random value.
- The resulting formula is =RAND()*175+25.

Joanna writes this formula in cell B3 of the Simulation worksheet and copies it down the column to generate a total of 100 random values between 25 and 200.

In a similar way, Joanna can estimate the probability of failure. To accomplish this, she can again start with the minimum value (3%) and then randomly generate a value from 0 to the difference between the lowest and highest limits, in this case 2% (5%–3%). To randomly calculate a value between 0 and .02, she could simply multiply the random value (a number between 0 and 1) by .02. The resulting formula is =0.03+RAND()*.02. Joanna enters this formula in cell C3 of the Simulation worksheet and copies it down the column to generate a total of 100 random values between .03 and .05.

Calculating Probable Costs Using a ROUND Function

After each of the component values have been simulated, Joanna can combine them to arrive at a probable cost. Return cost times the probability of failure results in the expected failure cost for each item. Joanna enters the formula =ROUND(B2*C2, 2) in cell D2 and copies it down the column. Including a ROUND function here allows Joanna to arrive at a specified number of dollars and cents. It is best to round off these values after all of the random values have been calculated and combined to minimize the effect of rounding errors. Figure 2.37 illustrates the use of these formulas in Joanna's Simulation worksheet.

Figure 2.37: Simulated data and summary of ski return costs

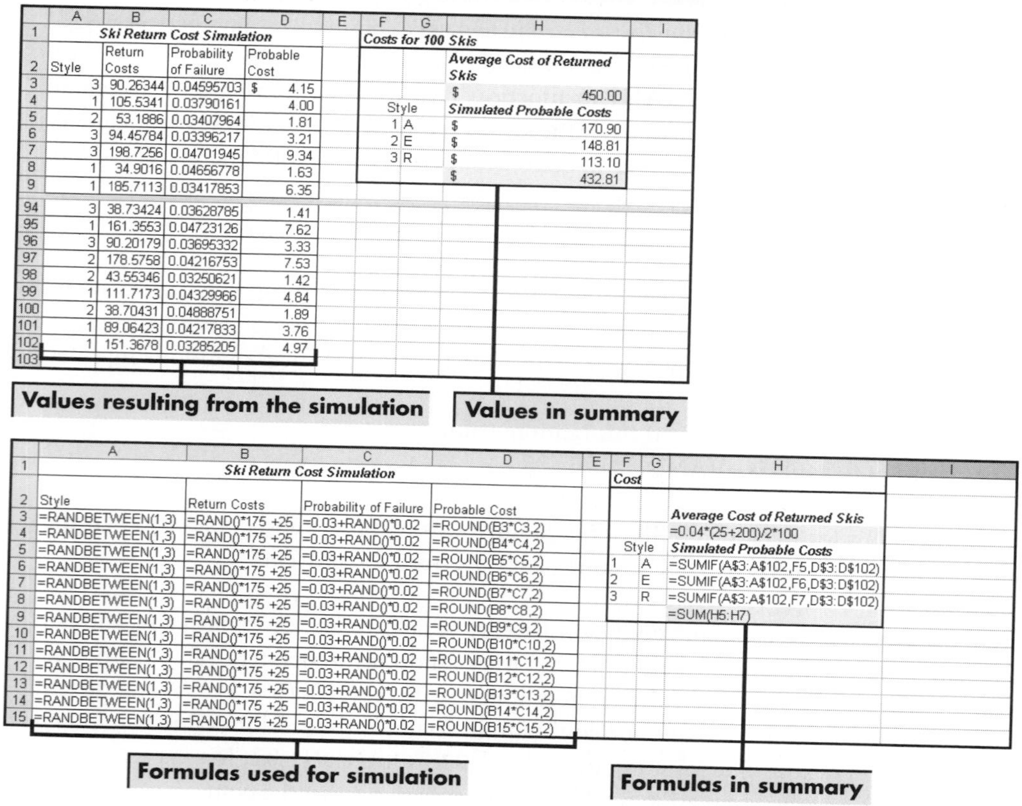

Values resulting from the simulation   Values in summary

Formulas used for simulation   Formulas in summary

The final component of the worksheet is the calculation that totals the simulated probable costs for this 100 ski sample by adding up the values in column D. Joanna has done this by ski style and in total, as shown in cells H5:H7. To total by ski style, she used the formula =SUMIF(A$3:A$102,F5,D$3:D$102) in cell H5 and copied it into cells H6 and H7. Cell H8 contains the formula =SUM(H5:H7).

When working with the RAND and RANDBETWEEN functions, an interesting result occurs. Every time you enter another value or formula in a cell anywhere on the worksheet, the random values automatically change. This is because every time a value or formula is entered in a cell, the entire worksheet is recalculated, including these random value functions, thereby generating new random values. Automatic calculation can be turned off in the Options dialog box, available from the Tools menu.

How To

Turn Off Automatic Calculation

1. Click Tools on the menu bar, and then click Options. The Options dialog box opens.

2. Click the Calculation tab to display the options related to calculations. See Figure 2.38.

Figure 2.38: Modifying options related to automatic calculation

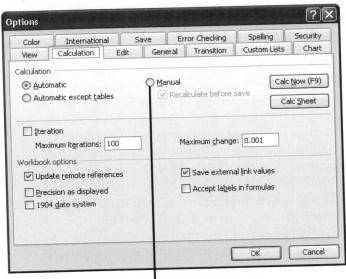

Select Manual to change the default
calculation (Automatic) to Manual

3. Click the Manual option button to change from automatic (the default) to manual calculation.

4. Click the OK button.

You can also recalculate a worksheet by pressing the F9 function key. Doing so allows you to observe different results obtained by entering different values and then pressing F9. When you press F9, the worksheet is automatically recalculated, altering the values in cells containing the RAND and RANDBETWEEN functions.

Completing the Cost Benefit Analysis

Joanna can now complete her cost benefit analysis comparing the costs of doing 100% quality testing on 100 skis versus allowing the skis to be sold, and having defective skis returned and replaced. The values generated as the cost to return defective skis ($409–$472) are all significantly above the cost of 100% quality testing each ski ($277); so, testing each ski is probably not only the "right" thing to do from the standpoint of customer satisfaction, but also appears to be the most cost-effective process. After completing her analysis, Joanna now considers the following questions:

- Can the quality testing itself be improved, given the large variance in time between not only ski styles but skis in general?
- Given that the rejection rate is estimated at 3%–5%, are there cost-effective ways of improving production to reduce this rate?

Joanna plans to raise these questions with management for further study to arrive at the best solution.

Steps To Success: Level 3

Now, you will conduct a cost benefit analysis to quantify the cost of inspecting the ski bindings versus the additional costs of not inspecting bindings and having skis returned from customers. As with the ski itself, the majority of the inspection cost with bindings is the labor. The average labor rate for the binding inspectors is $38 per hour. Historical data has shown that, on average, 1%–3% of ski bindings fail. The additional costs incurred if a ski binding fails after purchase are approximately $20–$75. Based on this information, complete the following:

1. Open the workbook named **Binding3.xls** located in the Chapter 2 folder, and then save it as **QC Binding Data Analysis 3.xls**. The worksheet named Inspection Costs contains two hours of inspection data from the QC inspectors detailing the amount of time spent testing the bindings for each of the two different tests performed: Pressure and Temperature.

2. Calculate the cost to test each ski binding and the total costs for all bindings over this two-hour period. Insert the labor cost per hour above the column heading and display the cell to include "$/hour–labor" following the value. If an error message regarding omitting adjacent cells is generated, instruct Excel to ignore this error.

3. Several rows below the data, calculate the mean, median, and standard deviation of these inspection costs (pressure, temperature) rounded to the nearest cent. Label the rows appropriately. Format these values in the Currency Style.

4. On a separate worksheet named "Type Summary," summarize these values by binding type (1–5), including both a count of the number of bindings inspected of that type and the averages for bindings of that type, as listed in Table 2.13. Be certain to use formulas that will be automatically updated if any of the binding types, values, or cost data are later updated. The formula for average pressure should work when copied down the column to determine pressure for each corresponding binding type, and across the row to determine the average temperature and average costs for each type. Format the table appropriately. Also include a value for the total number of bindings tested and the total cost of all bindings tested.

Table 2.13: Setup for binding cost analysis

Type	#Bindings Tested	Average Pressure	Average Temperature	Average Costs
1				
2				
3				
4				
5				
Total				

5. On a third worksheet named "Simulate," simulate the cost of not inspecting the bindings for a sample of 100 skis as follows. Use the headings as indicated in Table 2.14.

Table 2.14: Setup for binding simulation

Ski Binding Return Cost Simulation			
Binding Type	Return Costs	Probability of Failure	Probable Cost

- In the first column, simulate a ski binding type assuming bindings are equally likely to be any of the types 1 through 5. (Remember, you want a list of 100 simulated values.)
- In the second column, simulate the return costs based on the historical range given, assuming equal probability of any value within this range.
- In the third column, simulate the probability that this binding will fail, based on the range provided historically. Again, assume equal probability of any value within the range.
- In the fourth column, combine this information to calculate the expected cost of this ski failing, rounded to the nearest cent.

6. In an adjacent area of the worksheet, set up a small table summarizing the expected costs by binding type and in total. Recalculate the data five times and record the total cost values obtained in cells below the summary, labeled accordingly. Highlight these values in pink.

7. In a cell below this data, highlighted in yellow, enter text to describe (in a few words) which is the more expensive option for the company—100% inspection of bindings or return of defective bindings—and why.

8. Assume that the labor rates for inspection have decreased to $30 per hour. What is the revised cost to inspect, and will that affect your cost benefit analysis? Place this value in a cell below your first analysis, and highlight it in light green. Modify the worksheet to contain the original hourly labor rate.

9. Calculate the hourly labor cost that would be needed if total costs of inspection were $100. Record this value in a third cell below the other two analyses, highlighted in light blue. Do not save the worksheet with this value. (*Hint:* to be able to view the new labor rate easily without having to accept the changes, start your analysis from the Inspection Costs worksheet.)

10. Save and close the QC Binding Data Analysis 3.xls workbook.

CHAPTER SUMMARY

In Level 1 of this chapter, you applied problem-solving skills to a variety of data sets, analyzing their statistical values such as mean, mode, median, and standard deviation. Then, using these statistics, different data sets were compared to assess absolute as well as percentage changes. The ROUND function was used to modify the precision of the values in data sets.

Level 2 focused on expanding the analysis to better understand the tail values—the highest and lowest five elements of each data set—and the relative rankings of the values. The analyses were then summarized by counting the number of items that met specific criteria and summing items that met specific criteria. You also learned how to include relational operators and wildcards in functions and formulas.

In Level 3, you learned how to perform a cost benefit analysis using a larger data set. The level started with an explanation of how to specify a custom number format. Then, the topics of performing what-if analysis and using the Goal Seek tool were presented as ways of considering alternatives for the data set. You saw how to combine the COUNTIF and SUMIF functions to analyze data in categories. Finally, you learned how to analyze data through simulation using the RAND and RANDBETWEEN functions.

CONCEPTUAL REVIEW

1. What formula could you write to calculate the mean of the following data set: 2, 5, 4, 3, 1, 2, 7? (Note that a resulting value is not required.)

2. What is the median value of the data set given in Question 1?

3. What is the mode of the data set given in Question 1?

4. The data set given in Question 1 has a standard deviation of 1.58 as compared with another data set that has the same mean but a standard deviation of 2.5. What general differences would you expect to find between the two sets of data?

5. In the chapter, the original labor rate for inspectors was given as $35 per hour. However, due to a contract renegotiation, this value is now $37.50. What algebraic expression could you use to determine the percent increase in labor costs? (Note that a resulting value is not required.)

6. When using the Increase Decimal button on the toolbar, the precise value in the cell is modified. True or False?

7. The formula =ROUND(345.43,0) results in what precise value?

8. Write a formula to round up 63.54% to the nearest percent.

9. What is the symbol for the greater than or equal to relational operator in Excel?

10. What is the symbol for the not equal to relational operator in Excel?

11. Review the following worksheet, and then use the COUNTIF function to write a formula that determines the number of GM cars on this list.

	A	B	C
1	Make	Price	
2	Ford	$ 15,837	
3	GM	$ 12,883	
4	GM	$ 21,210	
5	Ford	$ 27,837	
6	Honda	$ 20,432	
7	Ford	$ 24,552	
8	Toyota	$ 21,553	
9	Lexus	$ 32,412	
10	Nissan	$ 23,134	
11	total	$ 199,850	
12			
13			

12. Using the worksheet shown in Question 11, write a formula to determine the number of cars that cost less than $20,000.

13. Using the worksheet shown in Question 11, write a formula to determine the total value of all Ford cars.

14. Explain the difference between a "what-if" analysis and Goal Seek by giving an example based on the worksheet shown in Question 11.

15. Using the worksheet shown in Question 11, write a formula to determine the value of the third most expensive car.

16. If each car shown in Question 11 is marked up between $50 and $250 in dollar increments, what function could be used to randomly assign the amount to be added to this car price in this formula: =B2+ _____?

17. The formula =RAND()gives what result?

18. What formula could you write to average the values in cells A10 through A20 excluding blank cells, rounded to the nearest 10?

19. Write a formula to determine the average price of only Ford vehicles using the worksheet in Question 11.

20. Write a formula to generate a random integer value between 10 and 20.

CASE PROBLEMS

Level 1 – Analyzing Sales for Crèmes Ice Cream

Sales

Judd Hemming is the eastern regional marketing manager for Crèmes Ice Cream. Each quarter, he completes two separate analyses: an analysis comparing ice cream flavor sales volumes from all regional locations with the same quarter sales volumes from the previous year; and an analysis comparing total sales in dollars, including mean, median, mode, and standard deviation, of sales by store.

The first analysis, sales by flavor, compares the total quantities sold in gallons. The data collected lists for each flavor the number of pints, gallons, and 10-gallon tubs sold for all stores. Pints and gallons are sold directly to the public, whereas 10-gallon tubs are used for in-store sales of cones, cups, and specialty items, such as sundaes and banana splits. To eliminate any impact of pricing changes or special promotions, Judd simply uses the ice cream volumes in gallons to compare sales by flavor. Judd has asked for your help this quarter in completing this analysis. Judd created two workbook files: Creme.xls, which contains the *current* quarter's sales on a worksheet named "Flavors," and HCreme.xls, which contains the corresponding *historical* quarterly data for the previous year on a worksheet named "HFlavors." For ease of data handling, the flavors in both data sets are in identical order except for two new flavors introduced this year, which appear at the bottom of the current data set. Keep in mind the following conversions when analyzing this data:

- There are 8 pints per gallon.
- Each tub holds 10 gallons.

Also, when calculating values for 10-gallon tubs, Judd has asked you to use the convention of rounding down the values to the nearest whole tub. In addition, you need to organize the data in the following categories:

Flavor	#Pints Sold Current Qtr	#Gallons Sold Current Qtr	# Tubs Used Current Qtr	Total Sold Current Qtr in Gallons	Total Sold Same Qtr Last Year in Gallons

The second analysis you need to complete is to summarize sales in dollars by store and compare the result with the previous year's sales. The Stores worksheet in the same workbook contains the individual store sales for the current quarter in dollars rounded to the nearest thousand dollars; this data is for the analysis by store. You need to calculate some basic statistics for store sales. In the same quarter of the previous year, these values were as follows:

- Mean: $8,817
- Median: $8,000
- Mode: $5,500
- Standard Deviation: $6,920

Throughout the steps, when writing formulas, be certain to use the most efficient method, including the use of functions and relative and absolute cell referencing.

Complete the following:

1. Open the workbook named **Creme.xls** located in the Chapter 2 folder, and then save it as **Creme Current Sales Analysis.xls**.

2. On the Flavors worksheet, for the current quarter, calculate for each flavor the total number of gallons sold. List the conversion values used at the top of the worksheet in a separate area. Remember to round down the tub quantities to the nearest whole tub when completing the calculation.

3. Copy the values for total amount of ice cream sold for the corresponding flavor from the HCreme.xls workbook, found in the Chapter 2 folder, into the Current Sales worksheet.

4. Calculate the overall total and mean number of gallons sold for all flavors for this quarter and for this quarter last year.

5. Calculate for each flavor the percent of total gallons this flavor represents compared with total sales for the current quarter of all flavors. Copy this formula to the adjacent column to calculate the percent of total gallons this flavor represents compared with historical total sales.

6. In the two adjacent columns, calculate for each flavor and for the totals the difference and percent difference in sales, assuming a positive value represents an increase in sales. Flavors without sales in both years should be left blank (these cells should be completely empty).

7. Switch to the Stores worksheet. Calculate the mean, median, mode, and standard deviation for this data set. Label the cells so that they can be easily identified.

8. On the same worksheet, set up a table to analyze the change and percent change of each of these statistical values as compared with the historical values given in the

problem description. Based on the changes, explain on the worksheet (just below your analysis), whether you feel stores are doing better this year and if sales in stores are more or less likely to vary from mean sales than they did last year.

9. Based on sales to all stores and total gallons sold for the current quarter, what is the price of a gallon of ice cream on average? Write a formula to determine this value and place it below the statistical analysis on the Stores worksheet.

10. Add appropriate worksheet titles and formatting to make the worksheets easy to read.

11. Save and close the Creme Current Sales Analysis.xls workbook.

Level 2 – Analyzing Demographic Data for La Rosa Restaurant

Marketing

You have recently decided to test your entrepreneurial skills by opening a restaurant that you plan to name La Rosa. In your restaurant, you plan to feature specialty desserts, along with fine cuisine. One critical decision you have to make is where to locate the restaurant. Right now, you are considering two different locations—one near a large retail area on the fringe of several affluent suburbs (site X), and the other in the downtown district (site Y). Before making the decision, you have hired a local market research firm to provide you with some demographics of the areas and the specific dining habits of the local population that frequent other restaurants in these areas. The raw results of this research have been placed on several worksheets in the LaRosa.xls workbook.

Each worksheet (SiteX and SiteY) contains the detailed responses of each of the participants of the study, including questions about their age, income, and the number of meals and desserts they eat outside of their homes per month.

The market research firm used the following age categories. Respondents were also asked to choose the income level closest to their own from the following list.

Age Categories	Income Levels
18 to 21	$5,000
22 to 25	$10,000
26 to 30	$20,000
31 to 35	$30,000
over 35	$40,000
	$50,000
	$75,000
	$100,000

Complete the following:

1. Open the workbook named **LaRosa.xls** located in the Chapter 2 folder, and then save it as **La Rosa Demographic Analysis.xls**.

2. On the SiteX and Site Y worksheets, rank each respondent by the number of meals they eat out per month and the number of desserts they eat out per month, respectively—ranking from most meals and desserts out to the least. Freeze the panes of the window on each worksheet to make the category headings at the top visible at all times.

3. On a separate worksheet named "Compare," display and compare the mean and standard deviation for the data sets (X and Y) for the number of meals and number of desserts per month obtained. On the same worksheet, set up a table to list the four highest number of desserts per month from each data set (X and Y) and the 10 lowest number of meals eaten out by respondents for each of the data sets (X and Y). Below the data, discuss how these values differ between the data sets and recommend either X or Y for further analysis, highlighted in pink.

4. On a separate worksheet named "Summary," determine the following for the location you think should be selected:

   - The total number of respondents
   - The total number of respondents with incomes at or above $75,000
   - The total number of respondents who eat less than five desserts out each month
   - The total number of meals eaten out per month reported by respondents who earn below $75,000
   - The total number of desserts per month reported by respondents who are in the 30–35 age category or in the 26–30 age category

5. Include appropriate titles, labels, and formatting so that the worksheets are easy to read. Be certain to double-check that your values are correct.

6. Save and close the La Rosa Demographic Analysis.xls workbook.

Level 3 – Determining Inventory Levels for CKG Auto

Operations Management

Another profitable facet of CKG Auto's business is supplying parts for auto repairs. The most critical component of the parts supply business is having enough of the right parts on hand so that repair shops can receive same-day delivery. The key to profits is minimizing the number of parts that need to be warehoused while also ensuring that sufficient parts are on hand to meet orders. Because each warehouse distribution center serves a different set of customers with different needs, each center must be considered separately.

Distribution centers have a five-day lead time for ordering of parts; this must be taken into consideration when determining target inventory levels.

The costs involved in warehousing the parts include the working capital tied up in the inventory itself (cost of each part), as well as the space to store the part. These costs can be substantial. On the other hand, alternative "generic" parts are often available from rival suppliers, and keeping the auto repair centers supplied and customers satisfied is critical.

One of the most problematic items to supply and store are bearings. This part is both high volume and relatively large, taking up considerable warehousing space. A bearing is also relatively expensive. So, analyzing bearing needs is a good place for CKG to start, specifically in one of its largest distribution centers such as Central New Jersey, which serves 10 major customers. You have been asked to analyze the bearing inventory level requirements for this center, including simulating demand levels based on 30-day historical extremes, calculating a target inventory level based on this simulation, and then comparing simulated values to actual values from the past five days from the targeted warehouse.

Complete the following:

1. Open the workbook named **Parts.xls** located in the Chapter 2 folder, and then save it as **CKG Parts Analysis.xls**.

2. Modify the format of the data on the Bearing Data worksheet so that zero values are displayed with a 0 instead of the default dash, aligned in the 1's column.

3. On the Bearing Data worksheet, take the existing 30-day data for these bearings for each customer to calculate the high and low limits of the bearing demand by customer.

4. On a new worksheet named "Simulation," use the high/low limits you just calculated to simulate daily requirements for each customer to obtain a combined daily requirement. Assume that the daily requirements will vary for each customer randomly between the high/low limits you have calculated from the existing 30-day data for that customer. Generate the data for approximately 100 instances, and then copy the results *as values* to a new worksheet in the workbook, keeping the original analysis intact on the Simulation worksheet so that it can be used again later. Name the new worksheet "Simulation Data 1."

5. On the Simulation Data 1 worksheet, use the daily demand total data to calculate the daily mean, mode, median, and standard deviation for the combined requirements of all 10 customers.

6. Extend your analysis (on the same worksheet) to include a ranking of the data (1 to 100) so that the day with the least total demand has the lowest ranking (rank 1).

7. To the right of the data on this same worksheet, create a listing of the top and bottom five daily combined demands from the 100 simulated instances. Clearly identify this listing using borders and shading.

8. Recommend a target inventory level needed for a five-day period based on the following; to be on the cautious side, assume each day's supply will be equal to the average daily demand for all locations combined, plus two standard deviations:

   - Because the mean and standard deviations might not already be integers, round the daily demand up to the nearest whole number.
   - Use the daily demand to calculate demand over a five-day period.

   Place this recommendation just below the top/bottom analysis, again clearly identifying it. Add the label "Bearing Recommended" to identify the cell containing the actual value.

9. The warehouse manager has tracked a total of five different parts over the past five days, recording for each shipment the value of the part and the number of days it was in storage. One of these tracked parts is the bearing you have just analyzed. The data has been compiled in a workbook named Demand.xls. Each line item represents a single shipment of one item. Copy the data from the Demand.xls workbook, located in the Chapter 2 folder, to your workbook and place it on a sheet named "Actual Demand."

10. On the same worksheet, summarize the data to determine the number shipped by part, the total values of those shipments by part, and the average number of days that part was stored, using the format shown in Table 2.15.

Table 2.15: Setup for parts data summary

Item Description	#Items Shipped	Total Dollar Value of Items Shipped	Average #Days Held in Inventory
Bearings			
Timing Belts			
Air Filters			
Fan Belt			
Electronic Board			

In the #Items Shipped column, write the necessary formula to determine the number of bearings shipped. Write the formula so that it can be copied down the column to automatically determine the number of timing belts shipped, the number of air filters shipped, and so on. In the Total Dollar Value of Items Shipped column, write the necessary formula to determine the value of all bearings shipped. Again, write the formula so that it can be copied down the column to automatically determine the value of timing belts, air filters, and so on. In the Average #Days Held in Inventory column, write the necessary formula to determine the average number of days bearings shipped were held in inventory; again write the formula so that it can be copied down the column. Be certain that these formulas will work even if the data is updated in the future.

11. Based on the recommended inventory level you previously calculated for bearings, would you have had enough bearings in the warehouse to cover these orders? Place your answer in a cell below your analysis on the Actual Demand worksheet. Clearly identify this answer and highlight it in yellow.

12. Double-check all values and formulas for correct implementation. Be certain that you included sufficient formatting and titles to clearly identify the worksheet elements.

13. Save and close the CKG Parts Analysis.xls workbook.

Determining Effective Data Display with Charts
Marketing: Analyzing Trends in the Sporting Goods Industry

"Information is a source of learning. But unless it is organized, processed, and available to the right people in a format for decision making, it is a burden, not a benefit."
—William Pollard

LEARNING OBJECTIVES

Level 1

Understand the principles of effective data display
Analyze various Excel chart types
Determine appropriate uses for different chart types
Modify the chart type and the chart source data
Specify chart options, including chart and axes titles, legends, and data labels

Level 2

Examine the effectiveness of different chart sub-types
Evaluate the stacked and 100% stacked sub-types
Explore the Pie of Pie and Bar of Pie sub-types
Create various stock charts to display financial data
Clarify data with trendlines and moving averages

Level 3

Understand and evaluate radar charts
Understand and evaluate bubble charts
Compare a bubble chart with a 3-D column chart
Create and customize a doughnut chart
Explore and customize a dashboard chart

CHART TYPES COVERED IN THIS CHAPTER

Area
Bubble
Column
Doughnut
Line
Pie
Radar
Stock
XY (Scatter)

3

CHAPTER INTRODUCTION

This chapter teaches you how to use Excel charts to provide a visual illustration of quantitative information, giving the viewer an overall picture of a set of data. In many ways, charts are easier to interpret than large amounts of tabular data. This chapter presents some guiding principles you can follow to create effective charts that show quantitative information clearly, precisely, and efficiently. The numerous chart types included in Excel provide great flexibility in presenting data for visual analysis.

The chapter begins with the basics of creating and modifying line and column charts while discussing how the choice of chart type can influence a viewer's perception of the information presented. Each chart type presents information in different ways that can affect the viewer's interpretation of the data. The chapter covers some basic principles to follow when creating charts and provides examples of how charts can be used in specific situations. Coverage of chart sub-types, including different types of stock charts, is also provided. Radar and bubble charts are then used to illustrate some advanced chart techniques. Finally, the last part of the chapter presents techniques for building a management dashboard by combining different chart types within the same chart.

CASE SCENARIO

Michelle Kim is an analyst in the marketing department at TheZone's corporate headquarters in Colorado. Michelle monitors company performance and assists the president and CEO to gather the data necessary for management of the company. Michelle works with counterparts in each of the company's three divisions—Equipment, Footwear, and Apparel—to monitor how well the company implements its corporate strategy. Una Baatar, president and chief executive officer of TheZone, has asked Michelle for a report and presentation on the company's performance compared with other industry competitors. The presentation will cover industry trends and the company's overall performance with specific information from each of the divisions. The performance of the company's stock in the market will also be discussed. Una is particularly interested in the Footwear division's work in bringing the new TZEdge athletic shoe line to market. Michelle will use Excel to create the necessary charts for the report and presentation.

Marketing

ANALYZING BASIC CHART TYPES

EXCEL 2003 SKILLS TRAINING

- Create charts using the pie chart types
- Create charts using column chart types
- Edit a chart
- Format charts
- Position a chart
- Print a chart
- Rotate and tilt a 3-D pie chart

SAM

VISUALIZING DATA

If a picture is worth a thousand words, can a chart be worth a thousand data points? Figure 3.1 shows one example from Edward R. Tufte's groundbreaking book, *The Visual Display of Quantitative Information*:

> This New York City Weather summary for 1980 depicts 2,220 numbers. The daily high and low temperatures are shown in relation to the long range average. The path of the normal temperatures also provides a forecast of expected change over the year; in the middle of February, for instance, New York City residents can look forward to warming at the rate of about 1.5 degrees per week all the way to July, the yearly peak. This distinguished graphic successfully organizes a large collection of numbers, makes comparisons between different parts of the data, and tells a story.

Figure 3.1: Chart of New York City weather in 1980

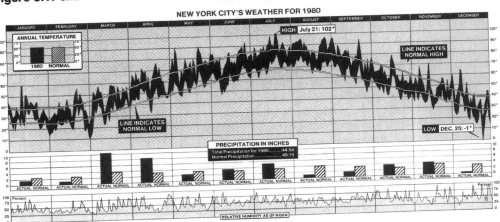

Tufte's book is concerned with the design of statistical graphics—the combined use of points, lines, numbers, words, shading, and color to present quantitative information. Tufte believes that graphical excellence depends on clarity, precision, and efficiency. Excellent graphics give the viewer "the greatest number of ideas in the shortest time with the least ink in the smallest space," according to Tufte. The "ink" here refers to everything that prints on paper. In the case of an Excel chart, the ink is the combination of data, labels, and chart effects. Tufte presents five data graphics principles related to "ink" in *The Visual Display of Quantitative Information*:

- Above all else show the data.
- Maximize the data-ink ratio, within reason.
- Erase non-data-ink, within reason.
- Erase redundant data ink, within reason.
- Revise and edit.

The first principle, "Above all else show the data," is a reminder not to clutter a chart by adding unneeded illustration or decoration. The second principle, "Maximize the data-ink ratio," refers to the portion of the ink that is devoted to displaying the data versus the portion of a graphic that can be removed without losing the data. Everything on a chart needs to have a reason for being there. The excessive use of gridlines and data labels in the chart in Figure 3.2 is an example of what Tufte refers to as "chart junk," which results in a chart with a very low data-ink ratio—in other words, lots of ink used to display a small amount of data. "Chart junk" can make charts difficult to read, use, and interpret.

The third and fourth data principles, "Erase non-data-ink" and "Erase redundant data ink," are somewhat related to maximizing the data-ink ratio. Non-data-ink is a part of the chart that decorates more than informs. Redundant data ink is ink that repeats information. For example, the use of a data table and labels on each point in the chart in Figure 3.2 is redundant.

3

Level 1

Figure 3.2: An example of "chart junk"

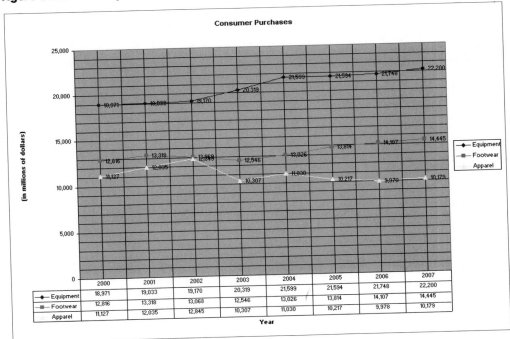

The fifth and final principle is "Revise and edit." Charts can be improved much in the same way that writing is improved by revision and editing. Feedback on a chart's usefulness and clarity should be sought wherever possible, and the chart should be adjusted accordingly. The intended message of the chart must be considered. A positive feature in one chart type might become negative if it doesn't support what the chart creator is trying to illustrate. Often, the best way to choose a chart is through trial and error. Once a chart is found to be useful, it should be saved as a template or working model for future use.

In business, charts are typically used to summarize information so it can be presented easily to others. The numerous charting options that Excel offers, however, can sometimes lead to "chart junk"—in this case, the embellishment of charts with a lot of chart effects (ink) that don't tell the viewer anything new. The purpose of formatting is to make a chart easier for the viewer to understand. Too little formatting can leave a chart ambiguous; too much formatting can cause viewers to notice the formatting, not the data. With this in mind, Figure 3.3 shows a much improved chart compared to Figure 3.2.

Figure 3.3: "Chart junk" removed

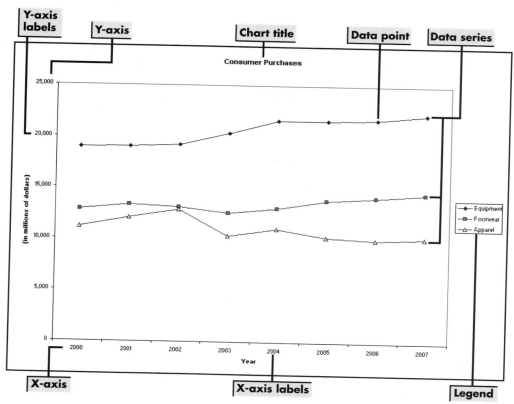

The chart in Figure 3.3 shows consumer purchase data for TheZone's three divisions—Equipment, Footwear, and Apparel—over an eight-year period beginning in the year 2000. As you can see in the figure, the chart contains the following elements:

- **Chart title**—The descriptive text that identifies the chart's contents
- **Y-axis**—The vertical axis where data values are plotted
- **Y-axis labels**—The labels that identify the data values plotted on the Y-axis
- **X-axis**—The horizontal axis where categories are plotted
- **X-axis labels**—The labels that identify the categories plotted on the X-axis
- **Data series**—The related data points that are plotted on the chart; each data series on a chart has a unique color or pattern and is identified in the chart legend
- **Data points**—The points in a data series at which the X-axis and Y-axis values intersect
- **Legend**—A box that identifies the patterns or colors assigned to the data series in a chart

As noted earlier, Michelle Kim is a marketing analyst for TheZone and is responsible for monitoring how well the company implements its corporate strategy. She has been analyzing industry trends for the company's three divisions, and has just started to put together a chart showing the sporting goods industry's last eight years of consumer purchase data by equipment, footwear, and apparel. Michelle is using Excel to organize and analyze the various sets of data shown in Figure 3.4, looking for potential problems that could disrupt the company's strategic plans. She will make extensive use of charts to summarize and present the data visually for further analysis.

Figure 3.4: Worksheet of consumer purchase data

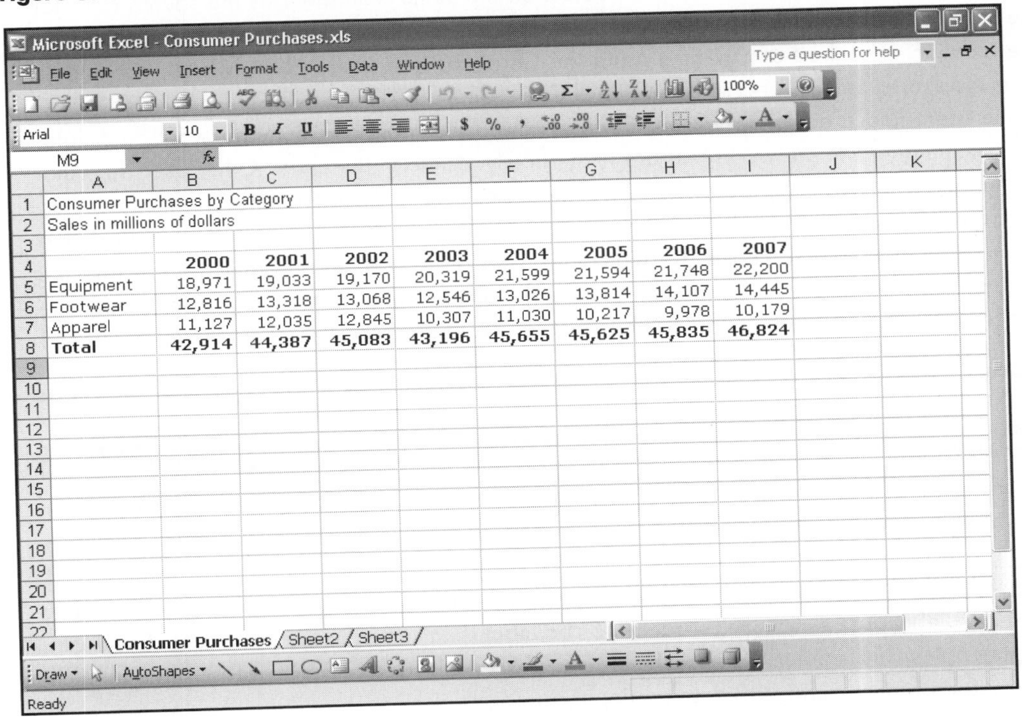

The information contained in spreadsheets is stored as tabular data arranged in rows, columns, and worksheets. This allows you to organize and analyze a large amount of data effectively, but can you see what the data means? You turn raw data into information by organizing it into something meaningful. You make information useful and give it a purpose by using it to make decisions—decisions that you couldn't have made as well without the knowledge gained from your analysis. Presenting data visually, in the form of a chart, for example, gives a global view that allows you to effectively convey the meaning hidden in a large data set, compare sets of data, and perhaps uncover a critical relationship or trend that would be hard to reveal with tabular data alone.

EFFECTIVE CHARTING IN EXCEL

To create a chart in Excel, you first select the data you want to display in the chart, and then click the Chart Wizard button 📊 on the toolbar. The Chart Wizard walks you through the steps for selecting the chart type, confirming the source data for the chart, modifying various chart options, and selecting the location for the chart—either on a new worksheet or on the same worksheet as the source data.

Best Practice

Choosing a Chart Location

Charts can either be embedded as an object on the same worksheet as the source data for the chart or placed on a separate worksheet referred to as a "chart sheet." You can modify the location of a chart at any time using the Chart Location dialog box, which is available from the shortcut menu for a selected chart. Chart location is a matter of personal preference. Some users find it easier to work with charts that are embedded with the worksheet data, because changes to the worksheet are immediately visible in the chart. Other users find that placing the chart on a separate chart sheet makes editing and printing the chart much easier. As a general rule, you should place charts that are developed for presentation and printing on a chart sheet. These charts are typically based on a specific reporting period and the source data usually doesn't change significantly. If the source data is dynamic, seeing the effect of the changes in the chart can be very handy. In this case, the chart should be placed on the worksheet with the data.

Determining the Appropriate Chart Type and Chart Options

Excel provides 14 standard chart types, with 75 sub-types that can be used to present information graphically. This doesn't include the 20 built-in custom types or the ability to combine different chart types within the same chart. Charts can display a combination of numeric and category data. An Excel chart requires at least one numeric data series and at least one label data series. Excel refers to the label data series as category data. Excel can display up to 255 numeric data series in one chart with up to 32,000 data points in each series, for a limit of 256,000 data points in one chart.

The chart type you choose depends on what you are trying to illustrate with the data. Table 3.1 identifies and describes the chart types available in Excel.

Table 3.1: Excel chart types

Chart Type	Icon	Description
Column		Compares values across categories in a vertical orientation. Values are indicated by the height of the columns.
Bar		Compares values across categories in a horizontal orientation. Values are indicated by the length of the bars.
Line		Displays trends over time or by category. Values are indicated by the height of the lines.
Area		Displays trends over time or by category. Values are indicated by the filled areas below the lines.

Table 3.1: Excel chart types (cont.)

Chart Type	Icon	Description
Pie		Compares the contribution each value in a single numeric data series makes to the whole, or 100%. Values are indicated by the size of the pie slices.
Doughnut		Compares the contribution each value in multiple numeric data series makes to the whole, or 100%. Values are indicated by the size of the doughnut segments.
XY (Scatter)		Compares pairs of numeric values on the X- and Y-axes, with the data points plotted proportionally to the values on the X-axis; can also be used to display a functional relationship, such as y=mx+b. Values are indicated by the position of the data points.
Stock		Displays stock price and volume trends over time. Plotted values can include volume, opening price, highest price, lowest price, and closing price.
Radar		Compares values across categories in a circular orientation. Values are indicated by the distance from a center point.
Bubble		Compares sets of three values. Values are indicated by the size of the bubbles (filled circles).
Surface		Displays value trends in three dimensions. Values are indicated by areas with colors or patterns on the surface of the chart.
Cylinder, Cone, Pyramid	, , and	Compare values across categories, similar to column and bar charts, using 3-D shapes of cylinders, cones, or pyramids in the chart (respectively) in place of columns or bars. Values are indicated by the size of the cylinders, cones, or pyramids.

Understanding Line and Column Charts

As noted in Table 3.1, a **line chart** displays trends over time or by category, and a **column chart** compares values across categories in a vertical orientation. Michelle has already created a line chart based on the consumer purchase data, with markers displayed at each data value (see Figure 3.5). This line chart is useful if the overall trend of the data needs to be emphasized. The vertical Y-axis shows the total sales (numeric values) and the horizontal X-axis shows the years (categories). Each line represents the trend in sales of the equipment, footwear, and apparel categories over an eight-year period. In this case, Michelle wants to compare the values in each category more than the overall trend over time, making a column chart the best choice. The two charts shown in Figure 3.5 are based on the same data series; the differences are due to the type of chart chosen. The line chart emphasizes the trend in each category over time, whereas the column chart makes it easier to compare the contribution each category made in a particular year. Note that the column chart in Figure 3.5 is displayed in the default column chart sub-type, the clustered sub-type.

Figure 3.5: Line chart versus column chart

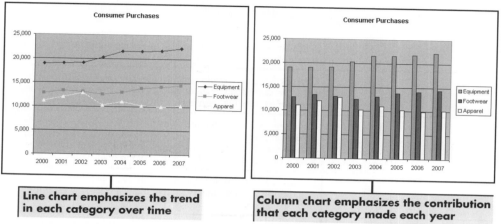

Line chart emphasizes the trend in each category over time

Column chart emphasizes the contribution that each category made each year

3

Level 1

How To

Change the Chart Type
1. Right-click the chart to display the shortcut menu.
2. Click Chart Type on the menu to open the Chart Type dialog box. This dialog box provides the same options available in the Chart Wizard dialog box for selecting the chart type.
3. Click the chart type you want to change to, and then click the sub-type (if necessary).
4. Click the OK button.

Comparing Line and XY (Scatter) Charts

There can be confusion about when to use a line chart and when to use an XY (Scatter) chart. The data used to plot an XY (Scatter) chart is different from the data used to create a line chart (or column or bar chart). An XY (Scatter) chart plots numeric values on *both* the X- and Y-axes based on the value of the data, whereas a line chart plots numeric values on one axis and category labels equidistantly on the other axis. Consider what happens if the order of the consumer purchase data is switched, as shown in Figure 3.6. The years in the worksheet are listed in descending order, from 2007 to 2000. Figure 3.6 shows this same data plotted as both a line chart and an XY (Scatter) chart.

Figure 3.6: Line chart versus XY (Scatter) chart

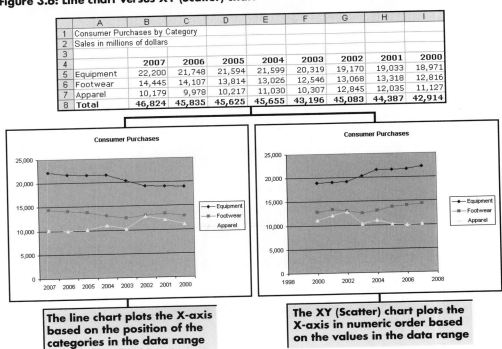

	A	B	C	D	E	F	G	H	I
1	Consumer Purchases by Category								
2	Sales in millions of dollars								
3									
4		2007	2006	2005	2004	2003	2002	2001	2000
5	Equipment	22,200	21,748	21,594	21,599	20,319	19,170	19,033	18,971
6	Footwear	14,445	14,107	13,814	13,026	12,546	13,068	13,318	12,816
7	Apparel	10,179	9,978	10,217	11,030	10,307	12,845	12,035	11,127
8	Total	46,824	45,835	45,625	45,655	43,196	45,083	44,387	42,914

The line chart plots the X-axis based on the position of the categories in the data range

The XY (Scatter) chart plots the X-axis in numeric order based on the values in the data range

As you can see in the figure, the line chart plots the data points along the Y-axis based on the value (sales volume), but the X-axis is based on position because this axis contains categories (years). The line chart's X-axis treats the year data as a category and plots based on position, beginning with 2007. By comparison, the XY (Scatter) chart plots both the Y- and X-axes data as numeric values. So, its X-axis treats the year data as numeric values and plots them from lowest to highest, based on the year number. Note that the XY (Scatter) chart is formatted with lines connecting the points; other formats are available for this chart type as well. Also note that the XY (Scatter) chart automatically generates an X-axis that applies a buffer at both ends, so the years shown on this axis range from 1998-2008. An XY (Scatter) chart should be used instead of a line chart when comparing sets of numerical data on both the X-axis and the Y-axis.

Changing the Chart Source Data

After changing the line chart to a column chart, Michelle decides that the chart is too busy and should show data from only the last five years instead of eight. The Source Data dialog box, which is available from the shortcut menu for a selected chart, provides options for modifying the values used to generate a chart. Refer back to Figure 3.4; notice that the categories and numeric data are not in a continuous range of cells. So, Michelle uses the Ctrl key to select both the categories (Equipment, Footwear, and Apparel) and the data for the years 2003–2007. The data source range changes from A4:I7 to A5:A7;E4:I7.

How To

Change the Source Data

1. Right-click the chart to display the shortcut menu.

2. Click Source Data on the menu to open the Source Data dialog box. See Figure 3.7. This dialog box provides the same options available in the Chart Wizard dialog box for choosing the data source.

Figure 3.7: Source Data dialog box

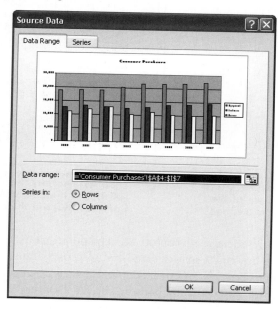

3. In the Data range box, modify the current range of values or select a new range as the source of data for the chart. In the case of a chart with multiple data series, you can change individual data series using the options on the Series tab of the Source Data dialog box.

4. Click the OK button after changing the source data.

Notice the "Series in" option on the Data Range tab of the Source Data dialog box (see Figure 3.7). This option provides settings for displaying the data series by rows or by columns. What would the impact be of changing this option in the current chart? Choosing to display the data by either rows or columns can illustrate different trends and force a different comparison of the data. Refer to Figure 3.8. When plotted by columns, the chart compares the amount of each year's sales for each of the three categories (Equipment, Footwear, Apparel). When plotted by rows, the chart emphasizes the contribution that each category made to each year's performance.

Figure 3.8: Displaying the data series by columns or by rows

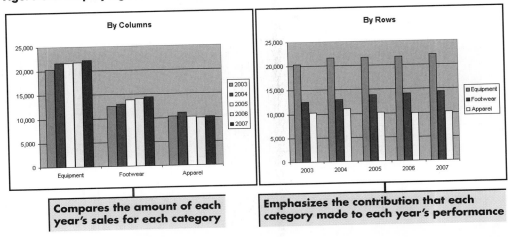

Compares the amount of each year's sales for each category

Emphasizes the contribution that each category made to each year's performance

Michelle is more interested in the amount of each year's sales of equipment, footwear, and apparel, so she chooses to plot the data by columns. She simply selects the Columns setting for the "Series in" option of the Source Data dialog box. Plotting the data by columns makes it easier to see that sales for the Equipment and Footwear categories Appear to be increasing from year to year, while sales for the Apparel category are leveling off somewhat.

Specifying Chart Options

Excel offers many formatting and display options for chart elements, including chart and axes titles, the X-axis and Y-axis, gridlines, legends, data labels, and data tables. The Chart Options dialog box, which is available from the shortcut menu for a selected chart, provides a tab for each of these chart elements and options you can set for each.

Now that Michelle has selected the chart type and determined how to display the source data, she decides to add axes titles that better describe the data on the chart. Many of the Chart Options settings can cause problems with generating excessive "ink" that obscures the information in the chart. As an illustration of this issue, Figure 3.9 shows the chart that results when too many options are selected, compared to Michelle's final chart, which contains only the elements needed to best describe the data, not overwhelm it.

Figure 3.9: Selecting the right number of chart options

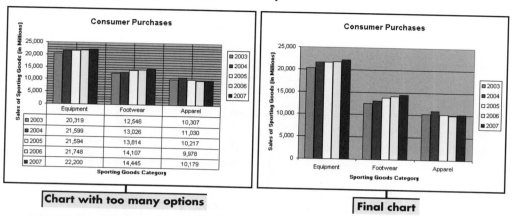

Chart with too many options

Final chart

How To

Specify Chart Options

1. Right-click the chart to display the shortcut menu.

2. Click Chart Options on the menu to open the Chart Options dialog box. See Figure 3.10.

Figure 3.10: Chart Options dialog box

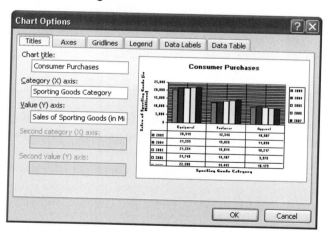

This dialog box provides six tabs for specifying chart options:

- **Titles**—Use the options on this tab to specify the chart title or the axes titles.
- **Axes**—Use the options on this tab to specify whether the X- and Y-axes are displayed. You can also choose to display the X-axis as a category or a time series axis. The Time-scale setting shows evenly spaced tick marks across the X-axis, based on the major and minor units of time.
- **Gridlines**—Use the options on this tab to modify the display of gridlines in the chart plot area. You can also modify the display of major and minor gridlines for each axis.

- **Legend**—The options on this tab control the display and placement of the chart legend. The legend shows the name of each data series along with the appropriate data marker. You can choose to display the legend in a variety of positions around the plot area.
- **Data Labels**—The options on this tab allow you to add and control the display of labels for the data points on the chart. Display options include the value of each data point, as well as the series and category to which each data point belongs. Percentages can also be displayed, if appropriate to the chart type. The selections on this tab display labels for each data point, which can become visually overwhelming. You can control the display of individual labels by selecting them on the plot area.
- **Data Table**—Use the options on this tab to display a table of values for each data series in a grid below the chart.

3. After specifying all the necessary chart options, click the OK button.

Understanding Area and Pie Charts

An **area chart** combines the features of a line chart with a bar or column chart by filling in the area below the line, and displaying the trend of values over time or categories. A **pie chart** is used to display the percentage contribution that each category makes to the whole, or 100%. The sum of the value of the categories must total 100% to use a pie chart. The highlighted numeric data range used in a pie chart is assumed to identify the individual components of some total. Excel calculates the percentage that each cell in the range contributes to the total.

Percentages are used every day in business to summarize and compare sets of data. For example, comparing the amount of labor used to create products with different overall prices can be made easier if the labor amount is expressed as a percentage of the total cost. Comparing salary rates and pay increases across various departments in a company is much clearer if the pay increases are expressed in percentages instead of actual amounts. Use a pie chart when it's most important to show relative percentages rather than values. Graphing these percentages can allow a viewer to make a quick visual comparison.

Earlier, Michelle chose a column chart over a line chart to compare the amount of each year's sales for each category rather than emphasize the trend in each category over time. How would an area chart display that same data? Figure 3.11 compares a column chart with an area chart of the consumer purchase data for all eight years (2000–2007). As you can see, the area chart does a better job of illustrating the sales trend in the equipment, footwear, and apparel categories over the longer time period (eight years), while still emphasizing the contribution that each category made to a particular year's performance. The area chart is somewhat easier to grasp than the column chart, because the large number of columns makes the column chart more difficult to interpret.

Figure 3.11: Column chart versus area chart

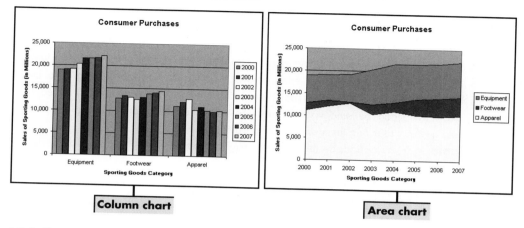

Michelle now wants to examine the contribution that the equipment, footwear, and apparel categories made to the 2007 sales as a percentage. She first creates a new worksheet, named "Consumer Purchases – 2007," and places the consumer purchase data on this worksheet. She decides to use a 3-D pie chart type to produce a more appealing visual effect compared with a flat pie chart. Because the category labels in cells A5:A7 are separated from the data in cells I5:I7, Michelle must use the Ctrl key to select the two ranges as the data source. An alternative method is to select cells I5:I7 as the data source, create a pie chart with the Chart Wizard, and then add the range containing the category labels (A5:A7) in the Series tab of the Source Data dialog box, as shown in Figure 3.12. Care must be taken to not select the total in cell I8 as part of the source data for the pie chart. Doing so would result in a pie chart that has one slice equal to half the pie, and all the other slices together making up the other half of the pie.

Figure 3.12: Selecting the pie chart source data

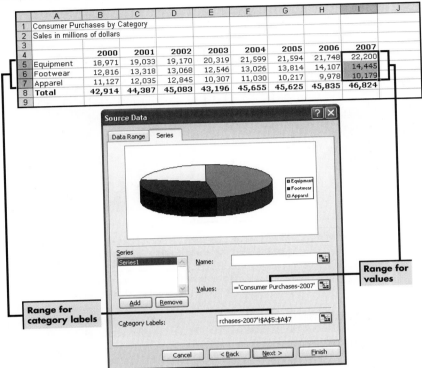

	A	B	C	D	E	F	G	H	I	J
1	Consumer Purchases by Category									
2	Sales in millions of dollars									
3										
4		2000	2001	2002	2003	2004	2005	2006	2007	
5	Equipment	18,971	19,033	19,170	20,319	21,599	21,594	21,748	22,200	
6	Footwear	12,816	13,318	13,068	12,546	13,026	13,814	14,107	14,445	
7	Apparel	11,127	12,035	12,845	10,307	11,030	10,217	9,978	10,179	
8	Total	42,914	44,387	45,083	43,196	45,655	45,625	45,835	46,824	
9										

The chart shown on the left in Figure 3.13 is the default 3-D pie chart produced by the Chart Wizard. To improve the appearance of the default chart, Michelle makes the following modifications to produce the final version of the chart, which is shown on the right in Figure 3.13:

- Removes the chart legend
- Includes category names and percentages as data labels on the pie slices
- Formats the data labels in a larger bold font to make them more visible
- Increases the elevation angle of the chart from 15 degrees to 40 degrees to provide more space on the pie slices for displaying the data labels and percentages
- Enlarges the chart overall by dragging one of its resizing handles on the plot area
- Removes the chart border to reduce clutter
- Explodes the pie slice for the Footwear category, for emphasis, by dragging it away from the other pie slices, because Una is particularly interested in the status of the new TZEdge athletic shoe line

Figure 3.13: Default pie chart and modified pie chart

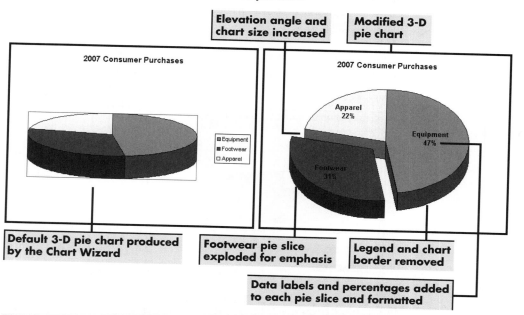

Elevation angle and chart size increased

Modified 3-D pie chart

Default 3-D pie chart produced by the Chart Wizard

Footwear pie slice exploded for emphasis

Legend and chart border removed

Data labels and percentages added to each pie slice and formatted

How To

Change the Elevation Angle

1. Right-click the chart to display the shortcut menu.

2. Click 3-D View on the menu to open the 3-D View dialog box. See Figure 3.14.

Figure 3.14: 3-D View dialog box

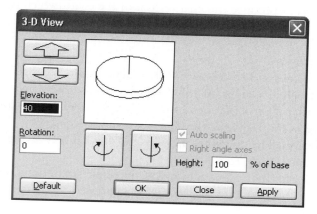

3. To increase the elevation angle, enter a higher number in the Elevation box or click the large up arrow. To decrease the elevation angle, enter a lower number in the Elevation box or click the large down arrow. Figure 3.14 shows the 3-D View dialog box with the elevation angle increased to 40 degrees.

4. Click the OK button.

How To

Format Data Labels

1. Click any data label on the chart to select the entire series of data labels; or, to select a single data label, click the label again after first selecting the entire series. The second click selects only the data label clicked.

2. With either all the labels for a series or a single label selected, right-click the selection to display the shortcut menu.

3. Click Format Data Labels on the menu to open the Format Data Labels dialog box. See Figure 3.15.

Figure 3.15: Format Data Labels dialog box

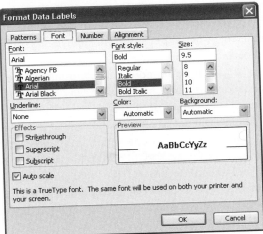

This dialog box provides four tabs for formatting data labels:

- **Patterns**—This tab provides options for changing the border and background area of the data labels.
- **Font**—Use the options on this tab to modify the font characteristics of the data labels.

- **Number**—This tab provides options for changing the appearance of numbers in the data labels.
- **Alignment**—Use the options on this tab to specify the alignment (horizontal or vertical), orientation, position, and direction of the data labels.

4. After specifying all the necessary formatting options, click the OK button.

3

Level 1

How To

Remove the Chart Border
1. Right-click the plot area surrounding the chart to display the shortcut menu.
2. Click Format Plot Area on the menu to display the Format Plot Area dialog box.
3. Click the None option button in the Border section of the dialog box.
4. Click the OK button.

Best Practice

Working with 3-D Charts
A 3-D pie chart can be much more visually appealing than a flat pie chart. Most of the chart types have 3-D options, but these should be used with caution. Although the use of 3-D can add visual interest, it might be at the expense of the data being presented. Figure 3.16 compares regular line and column charts with their 3-D equivalents. The 3-D charts are more attractive and interesting, but they are also more difficult to interpret. In the 3-D line chart, the relationship between the apparel and footwear in any particular year is difficult to determine because the lines are no longer on the same axis. The 3-D column chart does a better job of showing this, but it is still not as clear as the regular 2-D line and column charts. Additional care must be taken to ensure that one series isn't hidden behind the other. The data series order can be changed as necessary to adjust this, but if the data points are very close or cross, often this is not enough to prevent one data series from hiding a portion of another. Because 3-D charts are more visually appealing than 2-D charts in many instances, they are a good choice for presentations and reports, provided that the above interpretation issues are taken into consideration.

Figure 3.16: Regular charts versus 3-D charts

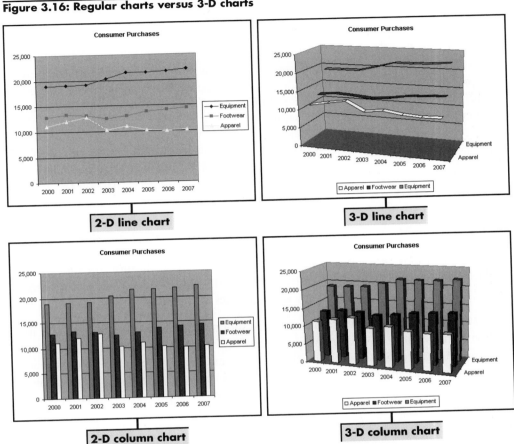

Steps To Success: Level 1

In these steps, you need to prepare some charts showing trends in the sporting goods industry. A workbook containing a variety of information on industry-wide trends has already been created. You will begin with data showing the number of people who participate in a variety of sports and activities.

Complete the following:

1. Open the workbook named **Trends.xls** located in the Chapter 3 folder, and then save it as **Industry Trends.xls**. Review the data sets on the four worksheets. You need to determine the most important information in each worksheet and select the best method for displaying that information in a chart. Remember that charts can be used to display single data series, compare multiple data series, show trends, and compare the percentage contribution to the whole.

2. The 2007 Participation worksheet contains participation data for a variety of sports, ranked in descending order by the values in the Total column. Create one column chart, one bar chart, and one line chart from the data. Place each chart on the same worksheet as the source data. In a cell below each chart, explain what the chart type emphasizes about the data. Select which chart is the best choice for comparing each sport's participation level. Place this chart on a separate chart sheet named "2007 Participation Chart" as the first worksheet in the Industry Trends workbook, and add appropriate Y-axis and chart titles to finalize this chart. Return to the 2007 Participation worksheet and, in a cell below the chart you selected to place on the chart sheet, explain the advantages and any disadvantages of this chart.

3. The 10-Year Participation worksheet contains sports participation data over a 10-year period, with values shown for every other year, for a variety of sports. Create an appropriate chart to illustrate the participation changes in each sport over the 10-year period. Place this chart on the same worksheet as the source data. Add appropriate titles and a legend to finalize the chart. In a cell below the chart, explain the advantages and any disadvantages of the chart type you chose.

4. The Female Sports Participation worksheet shows the changes in female sports participation between 2002 and 2007. Create an appropriate chart that shows the changing trends in the percentage of female participation in each sport. Place this chart on the same worksheet as the source data. Add appropriate titles to finalize the chart. In a cell below the chart, explain the advantages and any disadvantages of the chart type you chose.

5. The Purchases By Sport worksheet shows the dollar amount of consumer equipment purchases for 2005, 2006, and 2007. Create an appropriate chart to compare the contribution of each sport and illustrate the changes in consumer purchases from year to year. Place this chart on the same worksheet as the source data. Add appropriate titles and a legend to finalize the chart. In a cell below the chart, explain the advantages and any disadvantages of the chart type you chose.

6. Save and close the Industry Trends.xls workbook.

LEVEL 2
EVALUATING CHART SUB-TYPES

EXCEL 2003 SKILLS TRAINING

- **Create charts using the pie chart types**
- **Create charts using column chart types**
- **Create a trendline**
- **Edit a chart**
- **Format charts**

EXAMINING SUB-TYPES FOR VARIOUS CHART TYPES

As discussed earlier, the chart type you choose depends on what you are trying to illustrate. Charts can compare values across categories (bar and column); display trends over time or category (line and area); and compare the contribution each value in a single data series makes to the whole, or 100% (pie). Some of the chart sub-types available for the basic chart types enable you to sum or stack the values in each category, giving a slightly different perspective on the contribution that each category makes to the sum or the whole. Another option is to create a 100% stacked chart, in which the plotted values are converted into percentages of the total amount within each category. A 100% stacked chart is similar to a pie except that the pieces are in a column instead of a circle.

After reviewing the sample charts she has prepared for TheZone, Michelle is pleased with how the visual display of data makes it easier to compare the data across categories. Now she wants to modify the consumer purchases chart, which is currently an area chart, to show the total sales in each year and how much each category contributes to that total. The current chart shows the sales amount for each category, but does not show the total sales amount for each year.

Adding Things Up: Stacked Chart Options

Stacked charts do a good job of illustrating the cumulative effects of data in categories. Line, bar, column, and area charts all have a stacked chart sub-type. Figure 3.17 shows the current consumer purchases area chart compared with three stacked charts of the same data.

Figure 3.17: Area chart compared with stacked charts

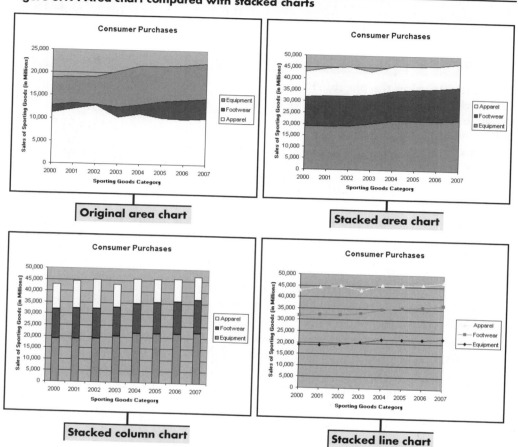

Michelle decides that the stacked column chart is the one that most clearly shows the totals for each category (in this case, each year). The stacked area and stacked line charts don't clearly show that the lines represent the cumulative total of each year. These charts can give the impression that each line represents the actual values in the data series, and not the cumulative amounts for each category. This could lead to some misinterpretation and require too much explanation of the chart to make the meaning clear.

How To

Change the Chart Sub-Type

1. Right-click the chart to display the shortcut menu.
2. Click Chart Type on the menu to open the Chart Type dialog box. The chart type for the current chart is already selected in the Chart type list box.
3. Click the icon for the chart sub-type you want in the Chart sub-type section. If necessary, click the Press and Hold to View Sample button to see an example of the selected sub-type.
4. Click the OK button.

Summing to 100%: Alternatives to Pie Charts

Another option for illustrating the cumulative contribution for each category is to express this contribution as a percentage. As was the case with the stacked sub-type, line, bar, column, and area charts offer a 100% stacked sub-type as well. Showing the cumulative contribution for each category as a percentage can reduce confusion over whether the line on the chart represents the *individual* or *cumulative* contribution to the whole. These charts combine the features of a pie chart with the features of line, column, or area charts. Figure 3.18 compares the original area chart of consumer purchase data with 100% stacked versions of the same data. Although each of these charts clearly shows the cumulative contribution each of the three divisions—Apparel, Footwear, and Equipment—makes to the whole, or 100%, for each year, Michelle chooses to use the 100% stacked column chart. She feels that displaying each year in a column makes the percentage contribution that each of the three divisions made in each year more obvious. In a way, this 100% stacked column chart is the equivalent of eight pie charts—one for each year. Each column presents the same information that would exist in a pie chart for that year; the only difference is the shape.

Figure 3.18: Comparison of 100% stacked charts

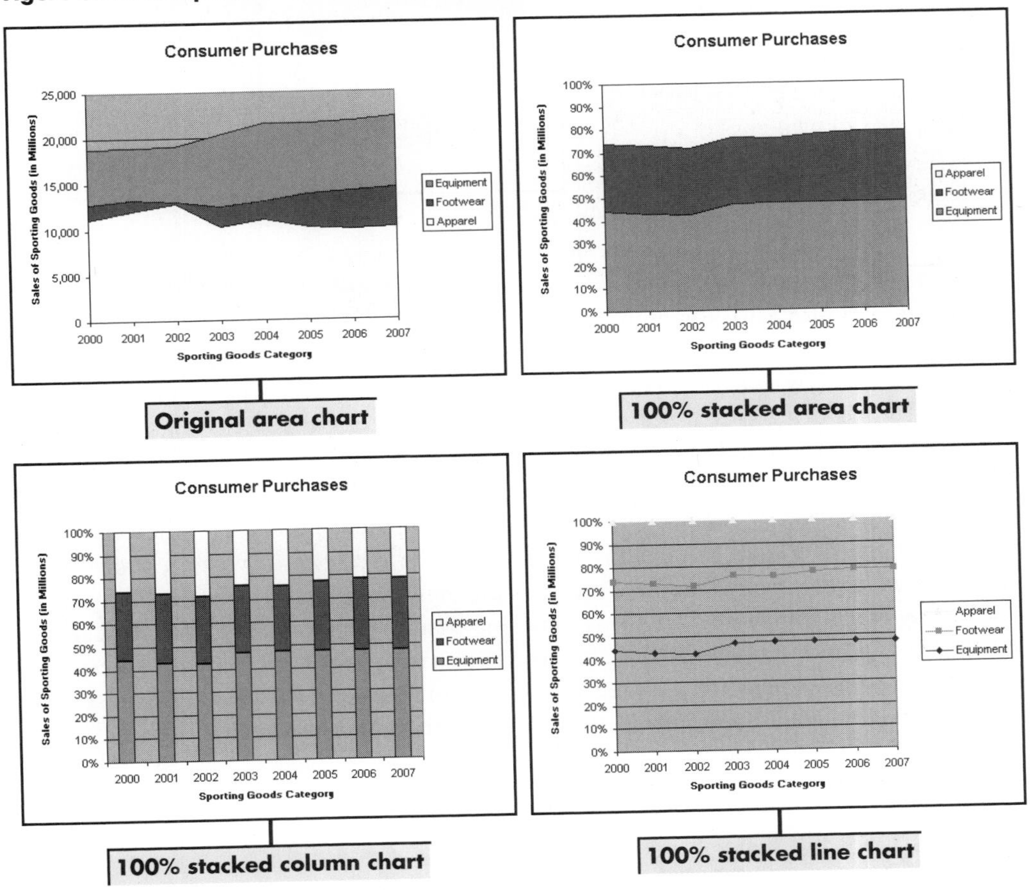

Original area chart

100% stacked area chart

100% stacked column chart

100% stacked line chart

Slicing the Pie Too Thin: Summarizing Too Much Detail in Pie Charts

Having too many categories can be a problem with pie charts. If you have an excessive number of pie slices, the chart can become very cluttered and confusing. For example, the data in Figure 3.19 shows consumer equipment purchases by sport in both worksheet format and a corresponding pie chart, which Michelle created based on some industry trend data. She wants to analyze which sports generate the most equipment purchases every year, opting to display the data in a pie chart format to show the percent contribution of each sport for the year 2007.

Figure 3.19: Consumer equipment purchases

	A	B
1	Consumer Equipment Purchases by Sport (in millions)	
2		**2007**
3	Archery	$382.77
4	Baseball & Softball	$415.17
5	Basketball	$427.05
6	Billiards & Indoor Games	$678.69
7	Bowling	$267.21
8	Camping	$1,649.61
9	Exercise	$4,992.21
10	Fishing Tackle	$2,265.21
11	Football	$167.85
12	Golf	$3,716.73
13	Hockey & Ice Skates	$258.57
14	Optics	$992.97
15	Racquetball	$105.21
16	Skin Diving & Scuba Gear	$438.93
17	Skiing, Downhill	$657.09
18	Skiing, Cross-Country	$116.01
19	Skiing, Snowboards	$347.13
20	Soccer Balls	$146.25
21	Tennis	$508.05
22	Volleyball & Badminton Sets	$110.61
23	Water Skis	$139.77
24	Wheel Sports & Pogo Sticks	$581.49
25	Team Goods	$2,835.45
26		
27	**Total**	**$22,200.00**
28		

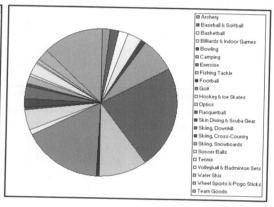

As illustrated in Figure 3.19, the number of categories makes the pie chart confusing and difficult to interpret. The data is currently sorted alphabetically by category. As a result, the chart is arranged by category. The first category (Archery) starts at the 12:00 position, and the remaining categories are placed in an alphabetical clockwise rotation. The sort order is contributing to the disarray and confusion in the chart.

Michelle decides to sort the data by the size of the equipment purchases in descending order, so that the data goes from highest to lowest. She creates a new chart, shown in Figure 3.20, using the data sorted in this order. The new chart appears more orderly and less confusing when compared with the original pie chart (see Figure 3.19). Michelle still isn't satisfied with the results, however, because the chart continues to have an excessive number of segments. There are 23 categories shown in the pie chart which, of course, is too great a number, resulting in many small, indistinguishable pie segments.

Figure 3.20: Re-sorted pie chart

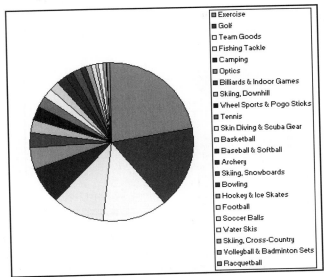

- ⊡ Exercise
- ▣ Golf
- ☐ Team Goods
- ☐ Fishing Tackle
- ■ Camping
- ⊡ Optics
- ■ Billiards & Indoor Games
- ☐ Skiing, Downhill
- ■ Wheel Sports & Pogo Sticks
- ⊡ Tennis
- ☐ Skin Diving & Scuba Gear
- ☐ Basketball
- ■ Baseball & Softball
- ■ Archery
- ■ Skiing, Snowboards
- ■ Bowling
- ⊡ Hockey & Ice Skates
- ☐ Football
- ☐ Soccer Balls
- ☐ Water Skis
- ⊡ Skiing, Cross-Country
- ⊡ Volleyball & Badminton Sets
- ⊡ Racquetball

Exploring the Pie of Pie and Bar of Pie Chart Sub-Types

How can Michelle modify the pie chart to address the problem of too many segments? One way would be to choose a different sub-type for the chart. Excel offers two interesting pie chart sub-types that can be used to combine many smaller segments of a pie chart into an "Other" category, which can then be shown as a smaller pie chart or as a single vertical bar chart next to the original pie chart. The two chart sub-types, Pie of Pie and Bar of Pie, are similar, with the exception of the chart type of the second plot in the chart. Michelle wants to emphasize the categories with the largest purchases. Either chart sub-type would do this well, but she chooses the Pie of Pie sub-type, because she feels that the Bar of Pie sub-type could cause confusion over whether or not the bar represents percentages or values. The resulting chart, shown in Figure 3.21, does decrease the number of pie segments to improve the visual display of data, but still needs formatting enhancements to meet Michelle's needs.

Figure 3.21: Pie of Pie sub-type applied to the chart

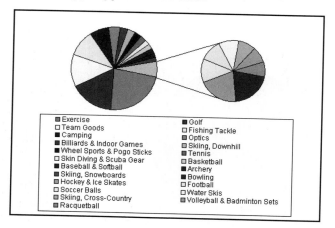

After adding the chart title "Consumer Purchases by Sport" and removing the legend from the chart, to make the pie segments larger, Michelle considers how to format the data series to make the chart easier to interpret. The series is currently split by position, with the last eight values displayed in the second, smaller pie chart, or plot. The total of the values in the second plot is represented by the pie segment on the main pie chart to which the smaller plot is connected. There are four options for splitting the data series:

- **Position**—Splitting by position assigns a specific number of values to the second plot. In the current chart, the last eight values in the data range are assigned to the second plot.
- **Value**—This option allows you to select a cut-off point that assigns all the values below that point to the second plot.
- **Percent Value**—This option allows you to select a cut-off point by percentage, rather than value, and assign all the percentages below that point to the second plot.
- **Custom**—With this option, you can drag individual pie segments between the two charts so you can include exactly the segments you want in the main pie chart and the second plot.

The Format Data Series dialog box, which is available on the shortcut menu for a selected chart, provides the option for changing how the series is split, as well as other options affecting the data series display. Michelle decides to make the following changes to the current chart to improve its appearance:

- Split the series by position, with the last 13 values assigned to the second plot.
- Emphasize the information in the main pie chart by reducing the overall size of the second plot and increasing the gap width between the two pie charts.

Figure 3.22 shows the Format Data Series dialog box settings that will implement these formatting changes.

Figure 3.22: Changing the format of the Pie of Pie chart

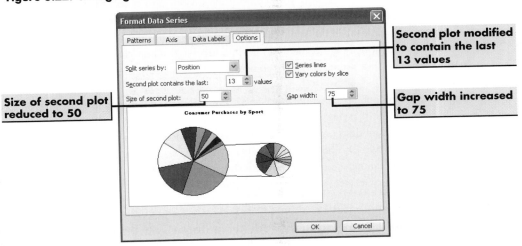

Size of second plot reduced to 50

Second plot modified to contain the last 13 values

Gap width increased to 75

As an additional enhancement, Michelle adds category name data labels. The resulting chart is shown in Figure 3.23. Notice the label "Other," which identifies the pie slice that represents the total of all the slices in the smaller pie plot. You will make some further formatting changes to this chart, which is still too "busy," in the steps section at the end of Level 2.

Figure 3.23: Pie of Pie chart with formatting changes

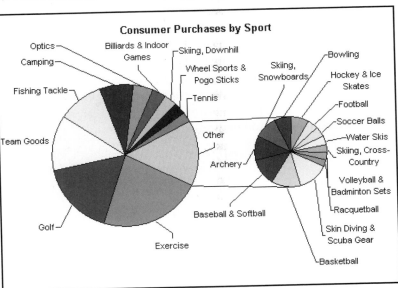

How To

Format Data Series in a Pie of Pie Chart

1. Double-click either of the pie charts to open the Format Data Series dialog box (see Figure 3.22).

2. On the Patterns tab, specify the settings you want for the border and area of the entire data series. Changes to the border style affect all of the pie slice borders. Any changes to the area color or fill effects settings result in the same appearance for all of the pie slices.

3. On the Data Labels tab, specify the content of the data labels. You can choose to display the series name, category name, value, and/or percentage. This tab also provides options for the legend display.

4. On the Options tab, you can select which data points are included in the second pie chart, or plot. The split between the first and second pie chart can be made by the position, value, or percentage of the individual data points on the worksheet. A custom setting allows pie slices to be dragged between the two pie charts. You can also modify the size of the second plot as well as the distance between the main pie chart and the second plot.

5. After making the necessary formatting changes, click the OK button.

From Pies to Doughnuts: Showing Individual Percentages with Multiple Series

Although doughnut charts are not a chart sub-type, they are related to 100% stacked charts and pie charts because of the type of data displayed. One of the limitations—or advantages, depending on your perspective—of 100% stacked charts is that they show cumulative rather than individual percentages. That is, the value for the second data point is the sum of the first and second values. Pie charts can show individual percentages, but only for one data series. Doughnut charts are a way to show the information contained in a pie chart for more than one series.

Michelle wants to show how the percentages of consumer purchases for the three divisions (Apparel, Equipment, and Footwear) have changed from year to year. She has prepared two sample doughnut charts, shown in Figure 3.24, from the same consumer purchase data she has been working with. One of the problems with doughnut charts is that they can easily become confusing if too many data series are charted at once. Michelle decides that even if she charted only two numeric data series, the doughnut charts would be difficult to understand. She thinks that multiple pie charts—one for each year, for example—would be much easier for decision makers to interpret.

Figure 3.24: Two sample doughnut charts

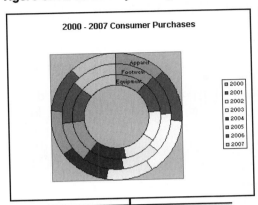

Doughnut chart showing the relative contribution that each year made to the three categories

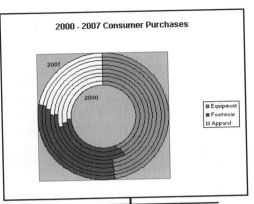

Doughnut chart showing the relative contribution that each category made to each year

Monitoring a Business with Stock Charts

On a regular basis, Michelle compares TheZone's performance in the stock market with that of other competitors in the sporting goods industry. Probably the most important investor data in business can be found in the financial sections of newspapers around the world. The international stock market is the life-blood of business. Information about the daily variations in a company's value is tracked by everyone from day traders, to investment bankers, to individual investors, and to the companies themselves. Commonly reported stock information also includes the opening and closing prices as well as the highest and lowest prices achieved. The volume of stock sales in a particular period is also commonly reported.

Excel line charts can be used to track changes in the prices of stocks at the end of each period, but they are not ideal because each of the values mentioned previously requires a single line representing one data series on the chart. A single line representing the closing prices for the time period would be the easiest to understand, but the range of values that a stock has during the reported period can be as significant as the ending price to many investors. Each of the commonly reported items of stock information can be of importance to investors. Excel can be used to create a form of "candlestick" plot, which is commonly used in financial stock reporting, to show all of this information in a compact chart. The candlestick plot is a modification of the Box and Whisker plot, which is common in statistics. All of the stock reporting charts available in Excel are somewhat based on the candlestick plot format, taking pieces of it as appropriate to report specific data.

Michelle needs to create a chart that summarizes the company's stock prices for the last year. She has a worksheet containing the daily stock price and volume information for the last several years, and now must choose one of the four available stock chart sub-types to display the data. The different sub-types display varying combinations of the high and low stock prices that are achieved for a day, as well as the day's opening and closing stock prices. Some sub-types add the volume or number of shares traded in a day to the chart. All of these chart sub-types require that the data in the worksheet be arranged in a specific order.

Creating a Chart with the High-Low-Close Sub-Type

First, Michelle considers the High-Low-Close chart sub-type. With this sub-type, the data to be plotted must be placed by column in this order: high stock value for the day, low stock value, and finally the closing stock value, as shown in Figure 3.25. The range of lowest to highest stock prices for each time period is shown by a vertical line. The horizontal dash represents the closing price for the time period.

Figure 3.25: Worksheet and sample High-Low-Close chart

Vertical line represents the range of lowest to highest stock prices for the time period

Horizontal dash represents the closing price for the time period

Date	High	Low	Close
2-Apr-07	25.36	24.14	25.35
3-Apr-07	26.47	25.15	25.94
4-Apr-07	26.05	25.72	25.80
5-Apr-07	26.03	25.68	25.91
6-Apr-07	26.46	25.55	25.95
9-Apr-07	26.15	25.62	25.63
10-Apr-07	26.05	25.68	25.86
11-Apr-07	25.90	24.96	24.96
12-Apr-07	25.05	24.77	25.00
13-Apr-07	25.03	24.54	24.64
16-Apr-07	25.20	24.55	25.20
17-Apr-07	25.64	25.12	25.55
18-Apr-07	25.72	24.51	24.52
19-Apr-07	24.73	24.01	24.70
20-Apr-07	24.90	24.06	24.41
23-Apr-07	24.64	23.95	24.47

The data must be in the same order as the name of the chart type: High-Low-Close

Creating a Chart with the Open-High-Low-Close Sub-Type

The Open-High-Low-Close chart sub-type adds information on the opening price of the stock for the time period. This chart sub-type also requires the data to be in a specific order in the worksheet. The order matches the name of the chart sub-type; in this case, the data must be listed in Open-High-Low-Close order to plot the chart properly. After adding the opening stock price to the data series, Michelle creates a chart with the Open-High-Low-Close sub-type, shown in Figure 3.26. The range of lowest to highest stock prices is still represented by a vertical line for each time period. A box is included to show the opening and closing prices. The bottom of the box represents the lower of the opening or closing values, while the top of the box represents the higher. Color is used to show if the stock closed at a higher or lower price than its opening price. If the box is white, the stock increased in value for the time period. The white box is referred to as the "up bar." If the box is black, the stock lost value for the time period. The black box is referred to as the "down bar."

Figure 3.26: Sample Open-High-Low-Close chart

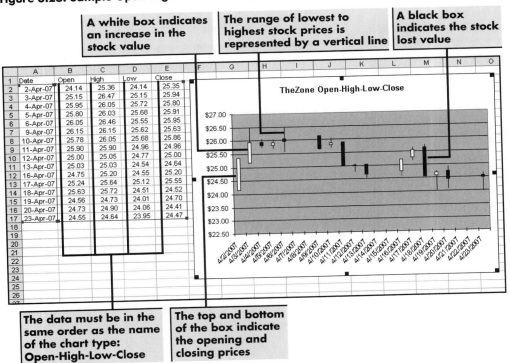

A white box indicates an increase in the stock value

The range of lowest to highest stock prices is represented by a vertical line

A black box indicates the stock lost value

The data must be in the same order as the name of the chart type: Open-High-Low-Close

The top and bottom of the box indicate the opening and closing prices

---

Best Practice

Changing the Default Colors for Excel Stock Charts

Many analysts dislike the default colors that Excel uses to indicate if a stock closed lower or higher than its opening price. Most business people consider "in the black" to be positive for a company, but the default Excel stock charts in candlestick format use a black bar to indicate that the stock closed down. One option is to change the color of the "up" bars to green, and the "down" bars to red, so that the colors better reflect the positive or negative aspect of the bars.

How To

Format Up and Down Bars in Stock Charts

1. Right-click either an up bar or a down bar in the stock chart to display the shortcut menu.

2. Click either the Format Up Bars option or the Format Down Bars option on the shortcut menu, depending on which type of bar you right-clicked, to display the appropriate dialog box.

3. On the Patterns tab, specify the color and/or pattern you want to apply to the border and area of the bars

4. Click the OK button.

Adding Volume to Stock Charts

Volume information showing how many shares of stocks were traded in the time period can be added using the Volume-High-Low-Close chart sub-type or the Volume-Open-High-Low-Close chart sub-type. These two chart sub-types shift the stock price scale to the right-side axis, or secondary Y-axis. Columns are used to indicate the stock volume for each time period. The primary Y-axis shows the stock volume on the left, and the columns representing the share volume are compared to it. The secondary Y-axis is on the right, and the stock prices shown by the lines/bars/boxes are measured against it. Using the secondary axis in a chart is a common way to include widely differing sets of data from the same time period. These types of stock charts also require the data to be arranged in a specific order in the worksheet. After moving the column containing the volume to the correct location, Michelle creates the chart shown in Figure 3.27.

Figure 3.27: Sample Volume-High-Low-Close chart

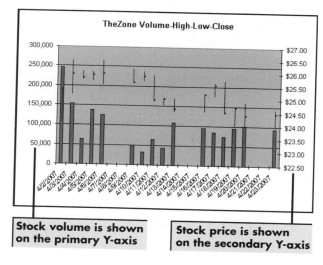

The default color setting on the column portion of the chart can obscure the High-Low line for time periods with exceptional volume. One option is to format the column data series with a different color that allows the High-Low lines to be displayed, as illustrated in Figure 3.28. Notice that the first volume column is in the same space as the stock price data for that time period. A dark column color would make the stock price information very difficult to interpret.

Figure 3.28: Modified Volume-High-Low-Close chart

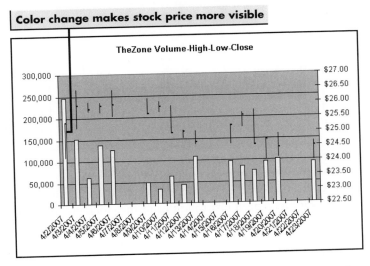

What would the impact be if the chart showed all the price and stock information for the previous year, as opposed to showing the information for only April 2007 as it does now? The Volume-Open-High-Low-Close chart sub-type combines all of the available information into one chart: lines for the high-low price range, boxes showing the open and closing prices, and columns indicating the time period volumes. This information looks great with a small data set, but when all the daily stock information for an entire year is charted, as shown in Figure 3.29, the chart becomes almost illegible. This chart is, essentially, a cluttered line chart superimposed over a column chart. This format won't work at all for the analysis of annual stock information.

Figure 3.29: Volume-Open-High-Low-Close chart showing data for one year

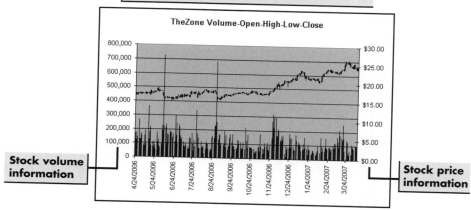

Because this chart shows a year's worth of stock price data, the differences between the open, high, low, and closing prices can't be determined

Stock volume information

Stock price information

Adding Trendlines and Moving Averages

Michelle can use a line chart to show the overall trend in the closing price of the stock for the past year, combined with a column chart indicating the stock volume. Or, she could summarize the daily stock prices by month, retaining all the information in the chart. Michelle chooses the first alternative and decides to do the following:

- Create a line chart from the closing prices for each day and place it directly above the original chart.
- Add a linear trendline and a 30-day moving average to smooth out the day-to-day variations in the data.
- Change the source data in the original chart to the stock volume only.
- Change the chart type of the original chart to column.
- Remove the title from the new volume chart and make the plot area shorter.

The resulting chart is shown in Figure 3.30.

Figure 3.30: Alternative line and column chart combination

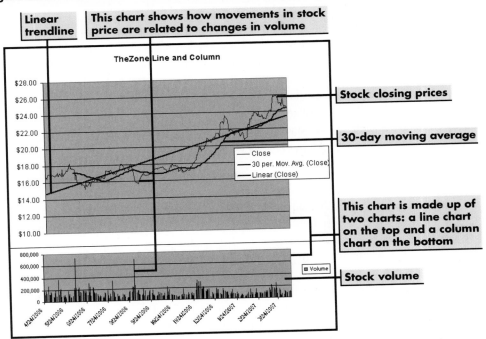

This chart is similar to those used by many financial publications to illustrate trends in a company's stock prices and the volume of stock sold in a given period. The purpose of a chart like the one in Figure 3.30 is to show overall trends, not to show the price or volume of a stock for a particular day. Notice that the chart shows that some spikes in the volume of stock sold have occurred at the same time that the stock price has reduced dramatically. This usually indicates that investors have sold off the stock in response to particularly bad news about the company's financial strength or future prospects. The linear trendline shows a definite upward trend in the stock price. **Trendlines** graphically illustrate trends in the data using a statistical technique known as regression. More advanced uses of trendlines include forecasting forward or backward in the data set, but these topics are best left to those with a strong background in regression to avoid misapplying the tool. The 30-day **moving average** line is used to smooth out the data, making it easier to spot trends. Each point on the 30-day moving average line represents an average of the stock closing prices for the last 30 days. The term "moving average" is used because the average is calculated each day for the last 30 days—moving the average along the chart. Varying degrees of smoothing are achieved by changing the length of the moving average. The longer the time period, the less sensitive the line is to day-to-day variability in the price. Generally when a stock price moves above the moving average line, it is a good indicator of an upward trend.

Add Trendlines and Moving Averages to a Chart

1. Right-click the data series to which you want to add a trendline or moving average.

2. Click Add Trendline in the shortcut menu to open the Add Trendline dialog box.

3. On the Type tab, select the Trend/Regression type you want to apply to the data series. The choices are a variety of trendlines including linear, logarithmic, polynomial, and others. The moving average selection is also available on this tab.

4. If you select the Moving Average option, you then need to specify the number of periods over which you want to calculate the average.

5. On the Options tab, set the forecast parameters for the trendline, as necessary.

6. Click the OK button.

Michelle is pleased with the results, but still wants to explore how to show annual stock data using a Volume-Open-High-Low-Close stock chart. She copies the worksheet and begins to consider how to summarize the data. The stock volume is simple; she needs to add up the stock traded during the month and can use a SUM function to do so. MAX and MIN functions can be used to take care of the highest and lowest stock price for each month. The open and close prices for each time period present more of a problem. How do you select a value that corresponds to the first and last day of the month from a range of values? Michelle decides that the quickest way to do this is to simply select these cells in the worksheet. She creates a summary table of the monthly stock prices and volumes, shown in Figure 3.31.

Figure 3.31: Worksheet with summary table

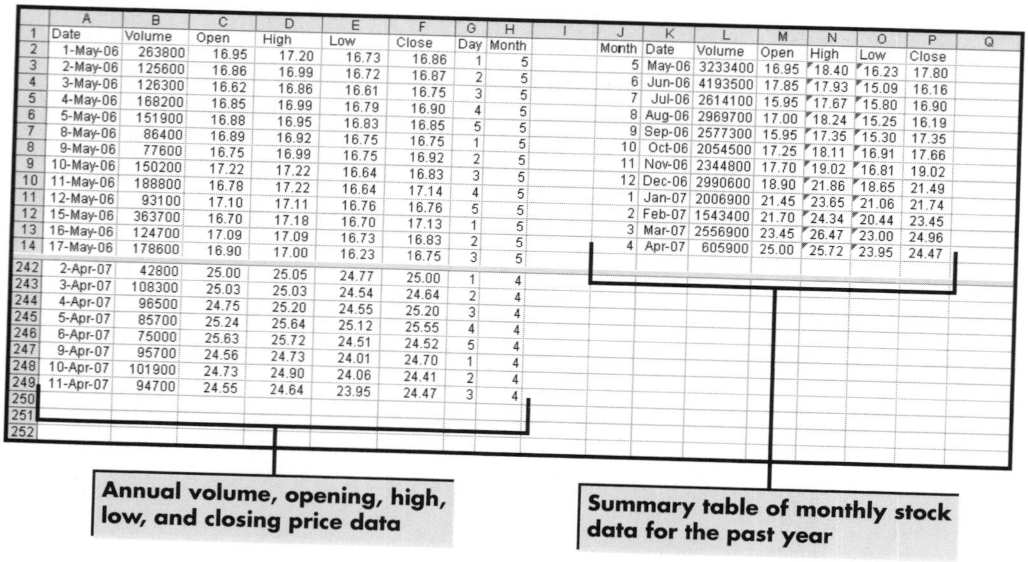

Annual volume, opening, high, low, and closing price data

Summary table of monthly stock data for the past year

The resulting Volume-Open-High-Low-Close stock chart is shown in Figure 3.32. Notice that the primary Y-axis scale showing stock volumes has been increased to keep the stock volume columns from interfering with the stock price information.

Figure 3.32: Annual Volume-Open-High-Low-Close stock chart

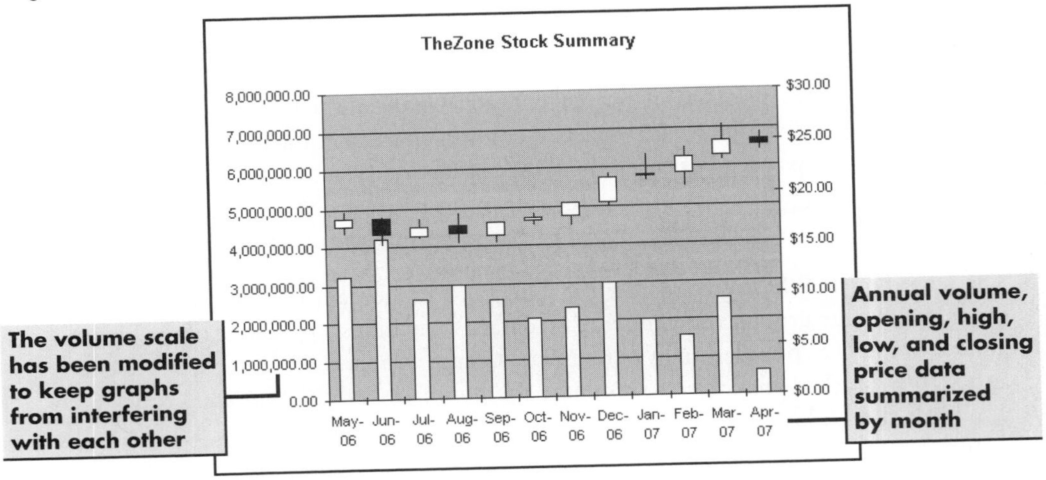

Steps To Success: Level 2

In these steps, you will work with the same consumer equipment purchasing data used to complete the Pie of Pie chart that Michelle worked on earlier. This data and the Pie of Pie chart are contained in the Excel workbook named Purchase.xls. You'll use this data to create a Bar of Pie chart. This same workbook contains detailed purchasing data broken out by age and gender for the following: footwear, camping, fitness, and golf. You'll use this data to create charts that illustrate the relationship between age and gender. The goal is to apply Tufte's principles to effectively present this quantitative information.

Complete the following:

1. Open the workbook named **Purchase.xls** in the Chapter 3 folder, and then save it as **Consumer Purchases.xls**. Review the data sets on the six worksheets. You need to determine how the chart sub-types covered in Level 2 can be used to illustrate the most important information in each worksheet.

2. The Pie of Pie worksheet contains the consumer purchase data organized by sport that Michelle used to create the Pie of Pie chart earlier. Use this data to create a Pie of Pie chart for the 2006 data. Place this chart on the same worksheet as the source data. Format the chart to look like the chart shown in Figure 3.23. Include the chart title "2006 Consumer Purchases by Sport" on your chart.

3. Use the data found on the Purchases by Sport worksheet to create a Bar of Pie chart that illustrates the percentage contribution by each sport to the total purchase amount. Create one Bar of Pie chart for each year. Place the three charts on the same worksheet as the source data. Include a chart title for each chart that is similar to the chart title you included in the Pie of Pie chart in Step 2.

4. The Footwear Purchases worksheet contains percentage data for footwear purchases organized by age groups and gender. The data also includes a breakout of the age and gender of the U.S. population by percentage. Create a clustered column chart, a stacked column chart, and a 100% stacked column chart to compare the purchases by different age groups each year with the U.S. population. Place the three charts on the same worksheet as the source data. Include appropriate titles and a legend in each chart. In a cell below each chart, explain what you think the chart illustrates.

5. The Camping Purchases worksheet contains percentage data for camping purchases organized by age groups and gender. The data also includes a breakout of the age and gender of the U.S. population by percentage. Create an area chart, a stacked area chart, and a 100% stacked area chart to compare the purchases by different age groups each year with the U.S. population. Place the three charts on the same worksheet as the source data. Include appropriate titles and a legend in each chart. In a cell below each chart, explain what you think the chart illustrates.

6. The Fitness Purchases worksheet contains percentage data for fitness purchases organized by age groups and gender. The data also includes a breakout of the age and gender of the U.S. population by percentage. Create a line chart, a stacked line chart, and a 100% stacked line chart to compare the purchases by different age groups each year with the U.S. population. Place the three charts on the same worksheet as the source data. Include appropriate titles and a legend in each chart. In a cell below each chart, explain what you think the chart illustrates.

7. The Golf Purchases worksheet contains percentage data for golf purchases organized by age groups and gender. The data also includes a breakout of the age and gender of the U.S. population by percentage. Create a doughnut chart and one other chart of your choice to compare the purchases by gender each year with the U.S. population. Place the two charts on the same worksheet as the source data. Include appropriate titles and a legend in each chart. In a cell below each chart, explain what you think the chart illustrates.

8. Save and close the Consumer Purchases.xls workbook.

LEVEL 3
EXPLORING MORE ADVANCED CHART TYPES

EXCEL 2003 SKILLS TRAINING

- **Edit a chart**
- **Format charts**

EVALUATING THE EFFECTIVENESS OF RADAR, BUBBLE, AND DASHBOARD CHARTS

Michelle is very pleased with the progress that she has made using Excel to chart and visually analyze data. However, after further reviewing both the Pie of Pie and Bar of Pie charts showing consumer purchase data, she doesn't feel that these charts adequately convey the information. She decides to look into radar charts as an alternative way to chart the consumer purchase data. Another data set she is working with has three data points for each category. Charting on three axes can be very challenging. Some options for handling this type of data include a 3-D column chart or a bubble chart. In addition, Michelle wants to set up a "management dashboard" that shows a visual summary of various performance data she uses on a regular basis.

Understanding Radar Charts

Excel has many advanced chart features and types that can be used to present data in a variety of ways. One of the more advanced chart types is the radar chart. **Radar charts** are named for their resemblance to the plots on radar screens as they scan a 360-degree circle. Values radiate from the center of the chart in a way that can be compared to radar screen plots, showing the distance of an object from the radar in the center. The categories are represented by lines that radiate out from the center. Although radar charts somewhat resemble pie charts, each segment in a radar chart is always the same size as the other segments. The number of categories determines the number of segments in the chart. The radar chart is also similar in structure to a spider web, with each "web strand" that roughly forms a circle representing the data values. The area under the curves in a radar chart can be shaded, similar to an area chart. Radar charts are like area charts in that they both allow you to compare the contributions of different categories. Whereas area charts emphasize the amount of the contribution, radar charts emphasize the relative comparison of the categories. Radar charts combine the comparison features across categories that area charts provide, with the comparison of the relative contribution to the whole that pie charts provide.

As she continues to analyze the data set of consumer equipment purchases by sport, Michelle wants to show which sports generate the most equipment purchases every year. The Pie of Pie chart created earlier shows the percentage contribution of each sport to the industry. Now, Michelle decides to try a radar chart to show the numerical value that each sport contributed to the industry. The worksheet data is sorted alphabetically by category with data for the three-year period 2005–2007. Michelle selects the 2007 data and produces the chart shown in Figure 3.33. The bold values next to each "web strand" represent the values of the data.

Figure 3.33: Consumer equipment purchase data plotted as a radar chart

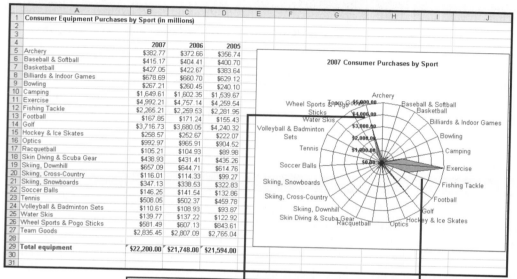

	A	B	C	D
1	Consumer Equipment Purchases by Sport (in millions)			
2				
3				
4		2007	2006	2005
5	Archery	$382.77	$372.66	$356.74
6	Baseball & Softball	$415.17	$404.41	$400.70
7	Basketball	$427.05	$422.67	$383.64
8	Billiards & Indoor Games	$678.69	$660.70	$629.12
9	Bowling	$267.21	$260.45	$240.10
10	Camping	$1,649.61	$1,602.35	$1,539.67
11	Exercise	$4,992.21	$4,757.14	$4,259.54
12	Fishing Tackle	$2,265.21	$2,259.53	$2,281.95
13	Football	$167.85	$171.24	$155.43
14	Golf	$3,716.73	$3,680.05	$4,240.32
15	Hockey & Ice Skates	$258.57	$252.67	$222.07
16	Optics	$992.97	$965.91	$904.52
17	Racquetball	$105.21	$104.93	$89.98
18	Skin Diving & Scuba Gear	$438.93	$431.41	$435.26
19	Skiing, Downhill	$657.09	$644.71	$614.76
20	Skiing, Cross-Country	$116.01	$114.33	$99.27
21	Skiing, Snowboards	$347.13	$338.53	$322.83
22	Soccer Balls	$146.25	$141.54	$132.86
23	Tennis	$508.05	$502.37	$459.78
24	Volleyball & Badminton Sets	$110.61	$108.93	$93.87
25	Water Skis	$139.77	$137.22	$122.92
26	Wheel Sports & Pogo Sticks	$581.49	$607.13	$843.61
27	Team Goods	$2,835.45	$2,807.09	$2,765.04
28				
29	Total equipment	$22,200.00	$21,748.00	$21,594.00
30				
31				

The circular lines that radiate out from the center represent the axis values for this chart—in this case, the $4,000 value

The straight lines that radiate out from the center represent categories—in this case, the Fishing Tackle category

This chart isn't very informative. The large range of values in the data set results in large jumps in the chart, as evidenced by the wide variances in the shaded areas representing the data values. Viewing the chart, you can pick out only the largest contributors to industry purchases, such as Exercise and Fishing Tackle, with little idea of the values contributed by the rest. Sorting the data in descending order by purchases in 2007 would reorganize the information presented in the radar chart. The resulting chart would only do a slightly better job of showing the dollar amount contributed by each sport category and allowing you to see the relative contribution from each sport category.

One of the problems is the range of values present in the data. There are too many insignificant data points that add more clutter than information to the chart. One option is to reduce the range of data charted to those categories that are more significant. Michelle is most interested in those categories that have over $300 million in consumer purchases in 2007. There are 15 equipment categories that meet the criteria, as shown in the radar chart in Figure 3.34. Note that the shaded area moves in a circular fashion around the chart, going up and down as necessary to indicate the data values. For example, the Exercise category data value is $4,992.21, so the shaded area for this category appears very close to the circular line representing $5,000. By contrast, the Fishing Tackle category data value is $2,265.21, so the shaded area moves down for this category and appears close to the circular line representing $2,000. How could you show the categories with the smaller values? If needed, a second chart could be created with the smaller values. Care would have to be taken that the difference in values for the two charts is obvious or a problem with interpreting the data could result. A note describing this would have to be added to the second chart.

Figure 3.34: Revised radar chart limited to purchases over $300 million

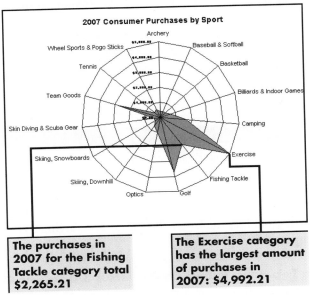

The purchases in 2007 for the Fishing Tackle category total $2,265.21

The Exercise category has the largest amount of purchases in 2007: $4,992.21

Radar charts can display more than one series, but displaying too much information on the chart can cause problems. For example, Figure 3.35 shows the consumer purchase information from three years in the chart on the left, which is labeled as a filled radar chart. The series overlap in many values, making it very difficult to determine the values represented by the chart. Changing the chart type from a filled radar to a nonfilled (standard) radar chart, shown on the right in Figure 3.35, doesn't help much because the values are so close.

Figure 3.35: Radar charts with multiple data series

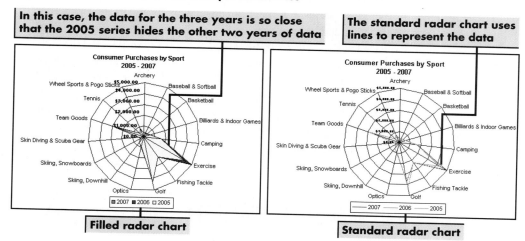

Radar charts offer a powerful method of displaying and comparing data across categories. As with all of the charts in Excel, the intended message of the chart must be considered. A positive feature in one chart type might become negative if it doesn't support what the chart creator is trying to illustrate. Often, the best way to choose a chart is through trial and error.

Understanding Bubble Charts

Bubble charts allow three-dimensional data to be plotted in 2-D on two axes. A bubble chart is similar to an XY (Scatter) chart. The X and Y axes are numeric rather than having one axis containing categories, as in bar and column charts. The third dimension is also numeric and is represented by varying the size of the data point that intersects with the X- and Y-axis—the larger the bubble, the larger the value. The varying sized data points, or bubbles, give this chart its name.

Plotting 3-D Data in Two Axes: Bubble Charts Versus 3-D Column Charts

Michelle has been working with some market share data for the Footwear division and wants to display the relationship between the number of styles offered, sales, and market share. A 3-D column chart has three axes and should, therefore, work for this data. Figure 3.36 shows the 3-D column chart; in this chart, the plot area was rotated to better show each data series. The great difference in scale for the number of styles, sales, and market share make this chart less than useful.

Figure 3.36: 3-D column chart of Footwear division market share

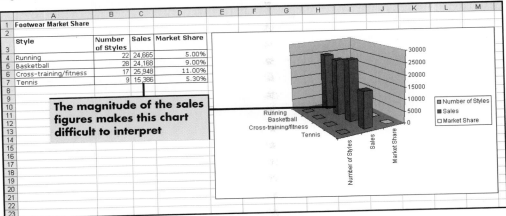

Michelle decides to try a bubble chart to display this set of data. She also removes the legend from the right-hand side of the chart and adds a title. The resulting chart is shown in Figure 3.37.

Figure 3.37: Bubble chart of Footwear division market share

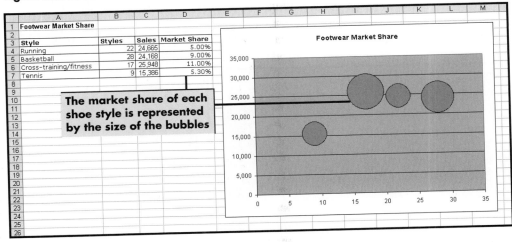

The bubble chart displays the number of styles on the X-axis and the sales on the Y-axis; the market share is represented by the size of each bubble on the chart. Now, the chart needs some descriptions to clarify the data on the chart. Michelle runs into a slight problem when attempting to add the shoe style categories to the chart. Adding the series name as a data label to the chart results in the problem shown in Figure 3.38. The series name has no meaning because all the data is in one series.

Figure 3.38: Adding a series name to the bubble chart

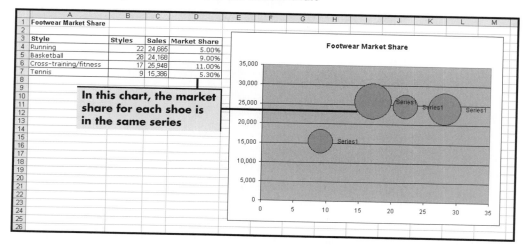

The shoe category names can be assigned to the bubble chart by selecting the Index tab of the Data Source dialog box and then adding each shoe type as an individual series. Adding the series requires the individual entry of the name, x-value, y-value, and the bubble size. Michelle adds the X- and Y-axis titles and selects the series name as a data label to create the final chart shown in Figure 3.39.

Figure 3.39: Final bubble chart showing Footwear division market share versus sales versus number of styles

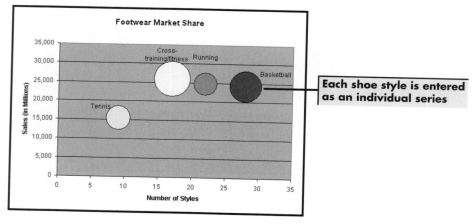

Solving Bubble Chart Problems

Bubble charts can be temperamental to work with. The source data must be selected without including labels. Figure 3.40 shows what happens if the row and column labels are selected along with the source data. The Chart Wizard is "confused" by the addition of what appears to be category data and attempts to assign numerical values to it, thereby rendering the chart useless.

Figure 3.40: Range selection problems with bubble charts

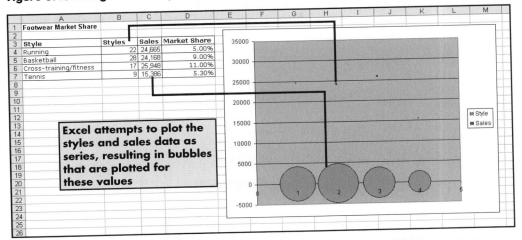

Adding Category Labels to Bubble Charts Without Using Multiple Series

There is a way to "trick" Excel into displaying category labels without having to go to the trouble of entering individual name, x-value, y-value, and bubble size values for each item. The value data label displays the cell contents for the range of cells identified as the data source for the bubble size, as shown in Figure 3.41.

Figure 3.41: Bubble chart "tricks"

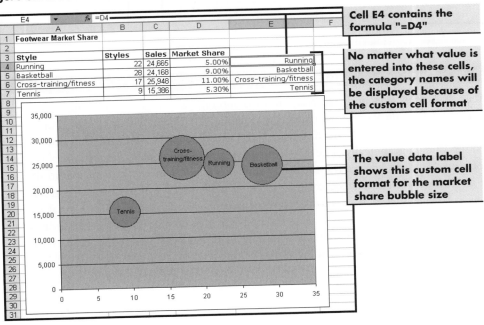

To create a custom cell format, display the Number tab of the Format Cells dialog box; then enter the category text within quotation marks, as shown in Figure 3.42. The category name becomes the displayed contents of the cell. The actual cell contents are hidden behind the text string and are used for any calculations.

Figure 3.42: Custom cell formats

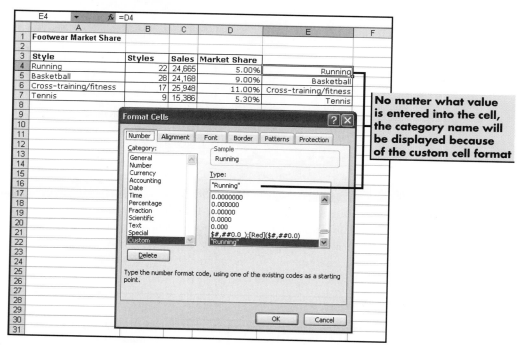

No matter what value is entered into the cell, the category name will be displayed because of the custom cell format

Creating a Management Dashboard

Michelle has been reviewing several business intelligence software packages featuring "dashboards" that display performance indicators in a fashion similar to the instrument panel in a car's dashboard. These dashboards usually feature a set of charts that summarize several sets of data graphically. The most intriguing ones feature charts that resemble actual dashboards. Michelle prefers the flexibility that using Excel gives her, but would like to add a dashboard worksheet to provide a quick, visual summary of performance indicators such as customer satisfaction, customer returns, on-time deliveries, monthly sales, and other accounting measures. She decides the first step is to create a chart that duplicates the gauges found on many of the software packages she has been reviewing. The chart will illustrate the average customer purchases per year for TheZone's top customers.

Building a Dashboard Chart

Michelle builds the dashboard chart shown in Figure 3.43. This chart is a doughnut chart with some of the data segments hidden to create the 180-degree circular band. Doughnut charts assign the relative size of each segment according to the segment's contribution to the total. For example, in a two-segment doughnut chart, each with the same value, each segment takes up one half of the doughnut. Three equal segments each take up one third, four segments each take up one fourth, and so on. Because a doughnut chart is a really a circle, Michelle can use the properties of a circle to fit the values into her dashboard chart.

Figure 3.43: Final dashboard chart

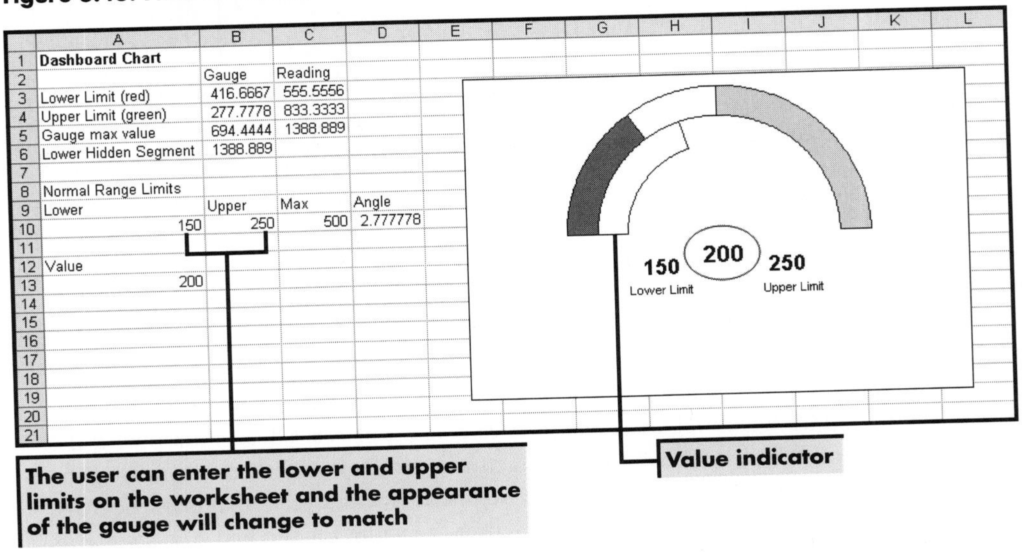

The user can enter the lower and upper limits on the worksheet and the appearance of the gauge will change to match

Value indicator

Defining the Normal Operating Range

The chart shows three segments in the top arch: the leftmost section for values below the normal operating range limit, the normal operating range section, and the rightmost section for values above the upper limit. A fourth segment of the doughnut chart takes up one half of the chart and is hidden at the lower part of the chart. Because there are 360 degrees in a circle, the easiest thing to do is to convert all values into degrees. The dashboard chart needs to display only one-half of the circle, so the lower hidden segment will always have a value of 180 degrees. Michelle wants to be able to dynamically adjust the normal operating range limits on the chart by typing values into the worksheet that define the lower and upper limits. The worksheet in Figure 3.44 is used to accomplish this.

Figure 3.44: Dashboard chart setup

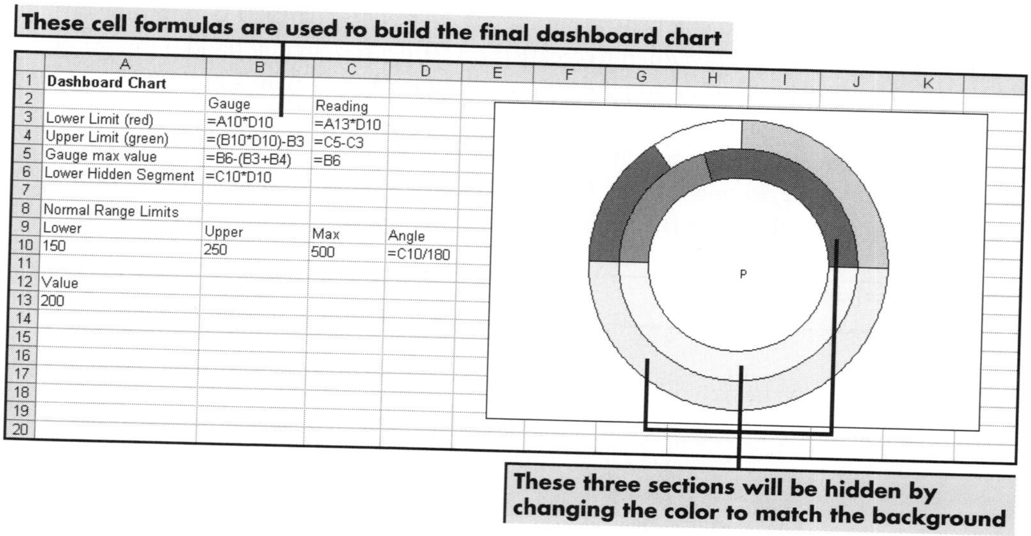

These cell formulas are used to build the final dashboard chart

	A	B	C	D	E	F	G	H	I	J	K
1	Dashboard Chart										
2		Gauge	Reading								
3	Lower Limit (red)	=A10*D10	=A13*D10								
4	Upper Limit (green)	=(B10*D10)-B3	=C5-C3								
5	Gauge max value	=B6-(B3+B4)	=B6								
6	Lower Hidden Segment	=C10*D10									
7											
8	Normal Range Limits										
9	Lower	Upper	Max	Angle							
10	150	250	500	=C10/180							
11											
12	Value										
13	200										
14											
15											
16											
17											
18											
19											
20											

These three sections will be hidden by changing the color to match the background

Michelle enters the lower limit, upper limit, and maximum (max) value of the gauge into the cells in row 10 of the worksheet. The max value will always occur at the 180-degree position of this chart, so it is divided by 180 degrees, in cell D10, to get a conversion value to use for the other values. The chart source data for the first gauge segment is created in cell B3 by multiplying the lower limit value in cell A10 by cell D10, converting the lower limit into degrees. The second chart segment is calculated in cell B4 by multiplying the upper limit value in cell B10 by the conversion factor in cell D10 and then subtracting the value for the first segment in cell B3. The third segment is whatever remains in the 180-degree arc; this is calculated in cell B5 by subtracting the value for the first two segments from the value of the lower hidden segment in cell B6.

Creating the Value Indicator

The value indicator is the portion of the doughnut chart that is below the main arch of the dashboard chart (see Figure 3.43). The value indicator only requires three segments for its doughnut chart instead of the four needed for the gauge. The first segment is calculated in cell C3 by multiplying the value entered into cell A13 by the angular conversion factor in cell D10. The value of the second segment is calculated in cell C4 by subtracting the value of the third and final segment in cell C5 from the first segment in cell C3. The third segment is the portion of the doughnut that will be hidden at the bottom of the chart and is equal in value to the normal operating range fourth segment that is to be hidden in the same way.

Creating the Doughnut Chart

Michelle uses the Chart Wizard to create the doughnut chart shown in Figure 3.44. She uses the Ctrl key to select the range B3:B6;C3:C5. The default doughnut chart starts the angle of the first slice at the 12 o'clock position, or 0 degrees. Michelle right-clicks the data series and opens the Format Data Series dialog box. The angle of the first segment setting is located on the Options tab. Michelle sets the angle to 270 degrees to have the chart start the gauge at the 9 o'clock position. This hides the bottom half of the doughnut chart.

Michelle hides the lower segments of the chart by selecting each segment and opening the Format Data Point dialog box, shown in Figure 3.45. She sets the Border and Area options to None, making these segments seem to disappear. The second segment of the value doughnut can also be hidden in this manner.

Figure 3.45: Format Data Point dialog box

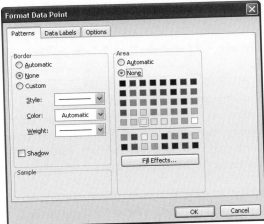

Adding Digital Values to the Chart

The lower and upper normal operating range limits and the plotted value can be added to the chart to improve the information that the chart provides. The Drawing toolbar contains a variety of autoshapes that can be added to the chart. The plotted value digital display is an oval object found on the toolbar. Michelle selects the chart, clicks the Oval button on the Drawing toolbar, and then draws the oval in the middle of the chart (see Figure 3.43). To display the value in the oval, she clicks the oval on the chart, types "=" in the Formula Bar, and then selects the cell containing the value she wants to link to this shape. For the plotted value, this is cell A13. Michelle then formats the text with bold and a larger font size to improve clarity. She creates text boxes, again using the Drawing toolbar, to display the upper and lower limits in the dashboard chart. These can be linked to cell values in the same way that the oval autoshape was.

With the dashboard chart complete, Michelle tests it by entering different numbers for the normal operating range lower and upper limits, the max gauge value, and the value to be plotted. She ensures that the chart responds properly to these changes.

Michelle is pleased with her work on this dashboard style chart. She will use this chart as a template for the other dashboard style charts she is planning to use to monitor performance indicators or metrics for the company.

Steps To Success: Level 3

In these steps, you will create charts to illustrate and analyze consumer purchase data for the Footwear division of TheZone.

Complete the following:

1. Open the workbook named **Footwear.xls** in the Chapter 3 folder, and then save it as **Footwear Analysis.xls**.

2. Use the Footwear Purchases by Price worksheet in the workbook to produce charts that compare the average price for each category of footwear. Create a radar chart and an appropriate version of a bar chart to see which one best illustrates the information. Place the two charts on the same worksheet as the source data. Include appropriate titles and a legend in each chart. Determine which chart does the best job of illustrating the relative contribution of each category to the purchase amount, and which one is best for emphasizing the year-to-year trend for each category. In a cell below each chart, explain what you think the chart illustrates.

3. Michelle has been working on sport participation data by gender and equipment sales. She built a worksheet by combining data from the 2007 overall and 2007 women's participation in sports data with the equipment purchases by sport data. Use the data in the Participants and Equipment worksheet to create a bubble chart that shows the number of women and the number of men participating in sports, as well as the amount of equipment sales that each sport generates. Place the chart on the same worksheet as the source data. Include appropriate titles and category labels in the chart.

4. Save and close the Footwear Analysis.xls workbook.

CHAPTER SUMMARY

This chapter presented many of the ways that charts can be used to illustrate quantitative information. Charts offer the opportunity to add visual analysis to problem solving. Tufte's guiding principles on the creation of graphics can be applied in Excel to create excellent charts that present quantitative information clearly, precisely, and efficiently. In Level 1, you learned how the choice of chart type can influence a viewer's perception of the information presented. Differences between the main chart types—line, column, bar, area, pie, and XY (Scatter)—were examined, as these charts were used to summarize and present a variety of data. Many of the chart types can be used on the same types of data resulting in different interpretations of that data.

Level 2 moved into coverage of chart sub-types, such as stacked and 100% stacked, for line, column, and area charts. These sub-types further summarize the data being presented, allowing a comparison of the contribution of a particular data series to a greater whole. The Pie of Pie and Bar of Pie chart sub-types were introduced to show how particular elements of pie charts can be summarized in another format. The different sub-types of stock charts were covered in some detail, showing the strengths and weaknesses of the various ways that Excel presents stock price and volume information. You also learned how trendlines and moving averages can help to clarify the data in stock charts.

In Level 3, the discussion was expanded to include more advanced chart types, such as radar and bubble charts. You also saw how to combine chart types within the same chart to build a management dashboard. This management dashboard consists of "speedometer-like" gauges that can be used to monitor various business metrics at a glance, allowing the viewer to see if any particular areas of a business require more investigation.

Table 3.2 summarizes the chart types and sub-types presented in this chapter.

Table 3.2: Summary of Excel chart types and sub-types

Chart Type	Description
Column	
Clustered Column	Compares values across categories
Stacked Column	Compares the contribution of each value to a total across categories
100% Stacked Column	Compares the percentage each value contributes to a total across categories
3-D Column	Compares values across categories and across series
Bar	
Clustered Bar	Compares values across categories
Stacked Bar	Compares the contribution of each value to a total across categories
100% Stacked Bar	Compares the percentage each value contributes to a total across categories

Table 3.2: Summary of Excel chart types and sub-types (cont.)

Chart Type	Description
Line	
Line	Displays a trend over time or categories
Stacked Line	Displays the trend of the contribution of each value over time or categories
100% Stacked Line	Displays the trend of the percentage each value contributes over time or categories
3-D Line	Displays a line with a 3-D visual effect
Pie	
Pie	Displays the contribution of each value to a total
3-D Pie	Displays the contribution of each value to a total with a 3-D visual effect
Pie of Pie	Displays a main pie chart with user-defined values extracted and combined into a second pie plot
Exploded Pie	Displays the contribution of each value to a total value while emphasizing individual values
Bar of Pie	Displays a main pie chart with user-defined values extracted and combined into a stacked bar as the second plot
XY (Scatter)	Compares pairs of values; display options include Scatter with data points connected by lines; Scatter with data points connected by smoothed lines without markers; and Scatter with data points connected by lines without markers
Area	
Area	Displays the trend of values over time or categories
Stacked Area	Displays the trend of the contribution of each value over time or categories
100% Stacked Area	Displays the trend of the percentage each value contributes over time or categories
Doughnut	
Doughnut	Displays the contribution of each value to a total (similar to a pie chart), but can contain multiple series
Exploded Doughnut	Displays the contribution of each value to a total value while emphasizing individual values (similar to an exploded pie chart), but can contain multiple series
Radar	Displays changes in values relative to a center point
Bubble	Compares sets of three values; similar to a scatter chart with the third value displayed as the size of a bubble marker
Stock	
High-Low-Close	Requires three series of values in this order
Open-High-Low-Close	Requires four series of values in this order
Volume-High-Low-Close	Requires four series of values in this order
Volume-Open-High-Low-Close	Requires five series of values in this order

3

Chapter Exercises

CONCEPTUAL REVIEW

1. List and describe the significance of each of Tufte's five data graphics principles.

2. What are the four steps involved in using the Chart Wizard?

3. Give an example of a low data-ink ratio in a chart.

4. How do you change the chart type of an existing chart?

5. What charting limits does Excel have in terms of data points and series?

6. How many standard chart types and sub-types are available in Excel?

7. What are the differences and similarities between a line chart and an XY (Scatter) chart? When should you use each one?

8. Explain the difference between the data points in a line chart and an XY (Scatter) chart.

9. What are the differences between a bar chart and a column chart? Give an example of when you would use each one.

10. What are the differences between a column chart and an area chart? Give an example of when you would use each one.

11. How do pie charts differ from doughnut charts?

12. When should you use a stacked line, column, or area chart? How do the stacked charts differ from regular charts?

13. When should you use a 100% stacked line, column, or area chart? How do the 100% stacked charts differ from stacked charts?

14. What chart sub-types are available for the stock chart in Excel? Explain how you interpret the data markers on each of the sub-types.

15. How does a radar chart differ from other charts? Give an example of when you would consider using a radar chart.

16. Define a bubble chart and explain what type of data is suitable for plotting on a bubble chart.

17. What is a dashboard chart used for?

CASE PROBLEMS

Level 1 – Illustrating Travel Data for the Indiana Department of Tourism

Marketing

As a travel industry consultant, you have been working for the state of Indiana Department of Tourism. The department manager has asked you to present a report on where Indiana residents travel to and where Indiana visitors come from. The modes of transportation must also be presented. You will also include some information from a survey that your firm has recently completed. The travel survey is located in the workbook named Indiana.xls.

Complete the following:

1. Open the workbook named **Indiana.xls** in the Chapter 3 folder, and then save it as **Indiana Travel.xls**.

2. Create a bar chart to illustrate the differences among the travel characteristics of the average Indiana resident, the average U.S. resident, and the average Indiana visitor.

3. Create a bar chart to illustrate a state-by-state comparison of the number of residents from the rest of the nation that visit Indiana to the number of Indiana residents that visit other states. Rank the information in this chart by the states with the most visitors to Indiana.

4. The Indiana Department of Tourism is very interested in learning more about how people travel in Indiana. They want to use this information to better target advertising to specific demographic groups and methods of travel. Use the appropriate chart or series of charts to illustrate how people travel; the purpose of their travel; and their income levels, age, and gender. This information should be presented for people who live within the state and those visiting the state with a comparison between the two groups.

5. Save and close the Indiana Travel.xls workbook.

Level 2 – Analyzing Stock Performance for Universal Investments

Finance

As an analyst at the Universal Investments financial company, you regularly monitor the performance of your clients' investments. You are preparing for a meeting with one of your investors to discuss how their stocks have performed over the last year and changes they should make to their portfolio. Your client has asked for information on four companies: Intel, AMD, Time Warner, and Wal-Mart. You will find daily stock price and volume information contained in the Invest.xls workbook.

Complete the following:

1. Open the workbook named **Invest.xls** located in the Chapter 3 folder, and then save it as **Investment Performance.xls**.

2. Create a chart for each company using the appropriate stock chart sub-type. Be certain to use each chart sub-type only once.

3. Summarize the data in order to clearly show some of the data markers in the charts.

4. Place each chart on a new sheet in the workbook.

5. Use the appropriate chart to compare the change in stock price for each company over the last year.

6. Using the information on the Portfolio worksheet, prepare the appropriate chart to display the relative contribution of each stock to the value of the portfolio.

7. Save and close the Investment Performance.xls workbook.

Level 3 – Illustrating Patterns in Gas Prices for CKG Auto

Sales

You have been assigned to CKG Auto's sales department as an analyst. The marketing team for the new Safari Wildebeest Sport Utility Vehicle has become concerned that the rising cost of gas will negatively affect vehicle sales. They are considering introducing limited rebates at times when gas prices are especially high. The company might also increase its marketing of the Safari Meer Cat, the new compact, sporty SUV the company introduced late last year. Your supervisor has asked you to put together a report and presentation showing the price per gallon of gas by region and large metropolitan areas. The company is interested to see if there are any patterns in the data that can be used to better time the rebate promotions. The Safari.xls file contains data on gas prices for various regions and metropolitan areas around the country.

Complete the following:

1. Open the workbook named **Safari.xls** located in the Chapter 3 folder, and then save it as **Safari Analysis.xls**.

2. Create a series of charts that compare gas prices by time of the year and by location. The time can be in quarters, months, or week of the month, as you deem appropriate. The location should be charted separately by region, by state, and by city.

3. For each location—region, state, and city—determine if a particular location has higher gas prices than the others. Add a comment near each chart to explain your findings.

4. Determine if a particular time of year has higher gas prices than the other times of the year. Add a comment near each chart to explain your findings.

5. Create a bubble chart to illustrate the number of weeks that each city's gas price is above the gas price for the entire U.S.; the number of weeks that it is below the gas price for the entire U.S.; and the average gas price in dollars per gallon for the year. Add appropriate titles, labels, and a legend to the chart.

6. Save and close the Safari Analysis.xls workbook.

Applying Logic in Decision Making
Accounting: Establishing a Credit Approval Process for Accounts Receivable

"No, no, you're not thinking; you're just being logical."
—Niels Bohr

Level 1

Understand the Boolean logical values TRUE and FALSE

Build formulas with relational operators

Evaluate criteria using the Boolean logical functions AND, OR, and NOT

Apply conditional formatting to highlight key information in a worksheet

Level 2

Understand how to build formulas with nested functions

Write IF functions to evaluate TRUE/FALSE values and perform calculations

Nest functions within an IF statement

Construct a simple nested IF function

Level 3

Combine sets of criteria in an IF function

Create a "none of" construct to perform a logical test

Create an "only" construct to perform a logical test

Solve more complex problems using nested IFs and Boolean logical functions

FUNCTIONS COVERED IN THIS CHAPTER

AND

IF

NOT

OR

CHAPTER INTRODUCTION

So far in this text, you have used arithmetic operators and functions to produce a numeric result. But what if you want to evaluate the statement, "The company sold more skis last year than this year." The result of this statement is not a numeric value, but rather the response "true" or "false." **TRUE** and **FALSE** are referred to as **Boolean logical values**. In this chapter, you will take data analysis to the next level, exploring tools that allow you to compare data as well as analyze sets of data using multiple criteria. Analyzing data in this way enables you to determine if the data meets *all* of the criteria, or *at least one* of the criteria, or even *none* of the criteria—resulting in a TRUE or FALSE Boolean value. In addition, you will use the Boolean logical functions AND, OR, and NOT. You will also learn how to specify different cell formats based on whether a set of criteria is met. In later sections of the chapter, you will take the results of logical tests and apply different outcomes to those that are TRUE versus those that are FALSE. Finally, you will learn to combine these tools together, further enhancing your ability to analyze more complex data and make decisions based on the results.

CASE SCENARIO

As an international sporting goods company, TheZone does maintain some of its own retail outlets. However, the most significant part of the company's sales are derived from selling large amounts of sporting goods equipment and apparel to other retailers and to large organizations, such as school systems and athletic teams. Most companies like TheZone have processes in place to determine the creditworthiness of potential customers before entering into business relationships with them, thereby ensuring that TheZone's accounts receivable group is able to collect payments from customers in a timely manner. The accounts receivables group at TheZone performs many vital tasks that affect the success of the company. The data provided by this group in the credit approval process has a direct impact on the cash flow and financial stability of the company. This process includes both obtaining financial data for new and existing customers, and determining the current credit status of each customer's account. These tasks are ongoing and can be challenging due to customers' changing status and the variability of economic conditions.

Accounting

Eric Carter is an accountant working in the accounts receivable group at TheZone. He has recently been asked to develop a formal system to streamline and automate the credit approval process. Eventually, the information compiled will be handed off to the finance group for final analysis and approval. The finance group is responsible for making the ultimate decisions, factoring in the effects that these decisions will have on corporate profitability, customer relations, adherence to government regulations, and so on.

LEVEL 1

ANALYZING DATA USING RELATIONAL OPERATORS AND BOOLEAN LOGICAL FUNCTIONS

EXCEL 2003 SKILLS TRAINING

- Apply conditional formatting
- Use logical functions (AND)
- Use logical functions (NOT)

REVIEWING FINANCIAL CRITERIA RELATED TO CREDIT

Before Eric can evaluate a customer's account for credit availability, he must first assemble the financial information required to make the credit decisions. The internal data, such as a customer's purchasing and payment history with TheZone, is available from TheZone's corporate accounting system. In addition, Eric plans to utilize information on each customer as compiled by Dun & Bradstreet. **Dun & Bradstreet® (D&B)** is one of the most widely used financial reporting services that provides, among other products, financial information about corporations and institutions and extensive analyses on each company's creditworthiness and payment history. The values supplied by D&B on the companies that TheZone does business with will be updated on a quarterly basis by one of the clerical staff in TheZone's accounts receivable group. Specifically, Eric plans to use D&B's services to obtain values on the net worth of companies requesting credit, a company's credit rating, and a company's payment record as follows:

- The net worth of a company is based on the assets and liabilities listed on its balance sheet.
- The credit rating consists of two parts, as listed in Table 4.1. The first is a classification ranging from 5A to HH indicating the net worth category of the company. The second is a value from 1 to 4 indicating a composite credit appraisal score, where 1 is the best and 4 is the worst. The score represents D&B's determination of the company's risk factors that affect its ability to pay its bills.

Table 4.1: D&B credit rating system*

Rating Classification		Composite Credit Appraisal			
Based on Worth from Interim or Fiscal Balance Sheet		High	Good	Fair	Limited
5A	50,000,000 and over	1	2	3	4
4A	10,000,000 to 49,999,999	1	2	3	4
3A	1,000,000 to 9,999,999	1	2	3	4

Table 4.1: D&B credit rating system* (cont.)

Rating Classification		Composite Credit Appraisal			
Based on Worth from Interim or Fiscal Balance Sheet		High	Good	Fair	Limited
2A	750,000 999,999	1	2	3	4
1A	500,000 to 749,999	1	2	3	4
BA	300,000 to 499,999	1	2	3	4
BB	200,000 to 299,999	1	2	3	4
CB	125,000 to 199,999	1	2	3	4
CC	75,000 to 124,999	1	2	3	4
DC	50,000 to 74,999	1	2	3	4
DD	35,000 to 49,999	1	2	3	4
EE	20,000 to 34,999	1	2	3	4
FF	10,000 to 19,999	1	2	3	4
GG	5,000 to 9,999	1	2	3	4
HH	Up to 4,999	1	2	3	4

*Based on information available at *www.dnb.com*

- The PAYDEX® index is an indicator of the payment habits of the company, as listed in Table 4.2. The index provides a score from 1 to 100, with 1 representing the worst payment record and 100 representing the best.

Table 4.2: D&B PAYDEX score*

Score	Payment
100	Payments received prior to date of invoice (Anticipate)
90	Payments received within trade discount period (Discount)
80	Payments received within terms granted (Prompt)
70	15 days beyond terms
60	22 days beyond terms
50	30 days beyond terms
40	60 days beyond terms
30	90 days beyond terms
20	120 days beyond terms
UN	Unavailable

*Based on information available at *www.dnb.com*

- The financial stress risk class is a rating from 1 to 5 indicating the risk of a company in financial distress, where 1 represents businesses with the lowest probability of risk, as detailed in Table 4.3.

Table 4.3: D&B financial stress risk class*

Class	% of Businesses Within This Class	Financial Stress Percentile	Financial Stress Score
1	80%	21–100	1377–1875
2	10%	11–20	1353–1376
3	6%	5–10	1303–1352
4	3%	2–4	1225–1302
5	1%	1	1001–1224

*Based on information available at www.dnb.com

Eric's first task is to develop a worksheet that will list these data elements for each of TheZone's customers. He will start with a small, selected customer list and develop the necessary formulas. Later he will expand the list to include all credit customers. He begins by entering data for each customer into a worksheet named CreditData in a workbook named Customer Credit and Payment History.xls, as shown in Figure 4.1. This worksheet includes the following information:

- Customer name (column A)
- Current credit limit (column B)
- Total sales to the customer from the previous fiscal year (column C)
- Current fiscal year's total sales to date (column D)
- Value of the customer's past due balance, which is for any unpaid invoices over 30 days (column E)
- Net worth of the company according to its D&B report in thousands of dollars (column F)
- D&B credit rating classification value (column G)
- D&B composite credit appraisal value (column H)
- D&B PAYDEX score (column I)
- D&B financial stress risk class (column J)

Figure 4.1: CreditData worksheet in the Customer Credit and Payment History workbook*

TheZone's Accounts Receivable data   D&B data

	Current Credit Limit	Previous Year's Sales	Current Year's Sales	Past Due Balance	Net Worth in (000)	D&B Credit Rating Class	D&B Composite Credit Appraisal (1 Best)	D&B PAYDEX (100 Best)	D&B Stress Risk Class (1 Best)
Athletic Gear Corp.	$ 9,000	$15,382	$11,952	$ 0	$ 450	BA	4	15	3
Baltimore O's	39,000	10,033	7,789	0	1,950	3A	1	51	1
Baseball & More	75,000	60,009	55,342	13,892	37,500	4A	2	70	1
Canadian Ski Club	33,000	35,039	50,921	495	1,650	BA	2	43	1
Concord Pro Shop					10,000	4A	1	91	1
Everything Golf	25,000	15,221	9,483	2,899	1,250	3A	3	76	1
Lake Pro Shops	42,000	80,498	81,126	0	2,100	3A	2	87	1
Mars Dept. Store	27,000	35,354	20,666	0	213	BB	3	94	1
RG Bradley	46,000	90,970	18,343	0	2,300	3A	1	21	1
RX for Sports	15,000	5,663	3,014	0	750	2A	1	59	1
School Sports Supply	45,000	50,278	32,338	0	2,250	3A	3	91	1
Ski World	26,000	25,864	28,154	0	300	BA	2	82	1
Sneaker Kingdom	45,000	40,157	25,379	0	2,250	3A	2	71	1
Sports & Stuff	15,000	15,898	14,732	14,383	450	BA	1	67	1
Toy Kingdom	22,000	10,073	1,047	0	1,100	3A	3	14	1
Under the Sea	45,000	95,411	64,418	0	150	CB	4	79	2
US Olympic Team	20,000	5,621	6,171	0	1,000	3A	1	87	1
WWW Sports Inc.	100,000	60,009	60,354	0	500,000	5A	2	97	1
Zip & Sons	10,000	15,490	22,760	0	620	1A	2	96	1

New customer with no previous account history

*Please note that companies used in this example are fictitious, but the text uses the investment ratings of the Dun & Bradstreet ® credit rating system.

Eric needs to develop the formulas that will allow him and other accounts receivable staff members to automatically reauthorize and approve new credit applications based on a set of criteria. The first step in this process is to apply several credit approval indicator rules to each customer's data. Each of these rules presents criteria that suggest credit approval might be warranted. Later, Eric will take the results of these indicator rules and combine them to make final credit recommendations. But first he needs to create the required formulas, which must be based on TheZone's credit determination rules, as follows:

Rule #1: *Accept* a customer who has a past due balance that is less than 10% of this year's total sales. This is not calculated for new customers. A customer who has a past due balance of 10% or more of this year's sales, regardless of its financial stability, has failed to consistently pay its previous bills with TheZone and, therefore, has not demonstrated a satisfactory business relationship. A customer without such a past due balance demonstrates creditworthiness.

Rule #2:   *Accept* a customer who has either a composite credit appraisal value of 1 or a PAYDEX score over 90. These values indicate a strong, financially stable enterprise with an outstanding reputation for paying its bills on time.

Rule #3:   *Accept* a customer who has all of the following: a net worth of at least $500,000; a composite credit appraisal value of 2 or lower; a PAYDEX score over 70; and a stress risk class of 1. These values indicate that the customer has a good overall financial position, a reasonable level of risk, and a reputation for paying its creditors.

What does it mean if a customer does *not* meet the criteria for a specific rule? Does this mean that credit should be rejected? Not necessarily. Consider the example of a college that might automatically accept an applicant if that applicant's SAT scores are above 1500. It cannot be assumed that if the applicant's scores are below this threshold, the school will automatically reject the applicant for admission—only that further evaluation is required. Similarly, in the case of TheZone, the three rules suggest a customer's creditworthiness, but failure to meet the criteria for any single rule does not translate to automatic denial of credit.

Evaluation of these rules is the first step in making Eric's worksheet operational. Additional information will be forthcoming from management to determine what combinations of results for these rules will cause a customer to be accepted automatically to a specific credit level or rejected outright. Automating this process in Excel will leave a greater amount of time for the accounts receivable staff to further analyze the more problematic accounts, such as customers with very large orders and less than perfect credit or smaller companies with limited assets.

USING RELATIONAL OPERATORS TO COMPARE TWO VALUES

Eric needs to determine if a company listed on the CreditData worksheet meets the specific conditions set forth in each of the three rules noted previously. Consider the first rule: *"Accept a customer who has a past due balance that is less than 10% of this year's total sales. This is not calculated for new customers."* A customer that meets the criteria has, for the most part, paid its bills. To manually determine if this condition is TRUE, Eric would need to calculate the past due percentage and determine if it is lower than 10%.

In Excel, you can use relational operators to compare two values to determine if the relational expression is TRUE or FALSE. Relational operators were first introduced in Chapter 2, when the problem in that chapter required creating criteria for the COUNTIF and SUMIF functions. Here, relational operators are used to compare two values, as shown in Table 4.4.

Table 4.4: Relational operators used in comparing two values

Description	Operator	Example	Resulting Value
Equal to	=	=3+5=8	TRUE
Not equal to	<>	=SUM(3,7)<>10	FALSE
Greater than	>	=100>MAX(5,10,20)	TRUE
Less than	<	=B3<C3 where cell B3=5 and cell C3=4	FALSE
Greater than or equal to	>=	=B3>=C3 where cell B3 contains the date 1/1/2007 and cell C3 contains the date 12/31/2006	TRUE
Less than or equal to	<=	=C1<=D1 where cell C1 contains the label "AA" and cell D1 contains the label "BB"	TRUE

For example, if you want to compare the value 3 to the value 5 to see if 3 is greater than 5, you would enter the following formula: =3>5. The resulting value displayed in the cell would be FALSE. It is important to note the order of precedence in which these relational expressions are evaluated. Relational operators are evaluated *after* arithmetic operators, exponents, and parentheses. So, the formula =(1+2)/3<>10 is evaluated as follows:

- First, Excel evaluates 1+2 in the parentheses to produce the value 3.
- Next, Excel evaluates 3 divided by 3, resulting in the value 1.
- After completing all of the arithmetic operations, Excel evaluates the <> not equal relational operator, 1<>10, resulting in a TRUE value.

Notice that like all other formulas, relational expressions begin with an equal sign. In the formula =B2=C2, Excel evaluates this expression to see if the value in cell B2 equals the value in cell C2. The first equal sign (=) indicates the beginning of a formula; the second equal sign is interpreted as a relational operator.

Relational operators can also be used to evaluate text labels. For example, you can test to see if a cell contains a specific label, such as =C2="Hello". If C2 contains the label "Hello", then the value TRUE is returned. The >, >=, <, and <= operators also work with text, where a greater value is one that appears later in the alphabet. For example, ="Goodbye">"Hello" returns the value FALSE because "Goodbye" comes alphabetically before "Hello." What is the result of the formula =Goodbye>Hello, which is written without the quotation marks around each label? Excel looks for a range named Goodbye and a range named Hello in the worksheet. If these had not been previously set up as valid range names corresponding to cell addresses, Excel would return the error message #NAME?. On the other hand, if the range named Goodbye contained the value 5 and the range named Hello contained the value 3, the value TRUE would be returned. Note that relational expressions are not case-sensitive, so any combination of lowercase and uppercase letters does not affect the outcome.

Relational operators can also be used to evaluate dates. Recall that dates are stored as sequential numbers, but can be formatted in the month/day/year format or even written out, such as January 1, 2007. You can use dates in both relational and arithmetic expressions; however, you cannot enter a date, such as 1/1/07, directly into a formula because Excel interprets the entry as a numerical expression. So, for example, assuming that cell D4 contains the date 12/31/06 and cell D1 contains the date 1/1/07, you could write the formula =D4>=D1. The result would be FALSE because 12/31/06 is before 1/1/07.

Using relational operators, Eric can easily set up a formula to test if the condition specified in Rule #1 is TRUE: "A customer has a past due balance that is less than 10% of this year's total sales." If the resulting value is TRUE, the customer's request for credit will be recommended for approval. If the resulting value is FALSE, the customer might be rejected for credit for failing to meet the credit approval criteria specified in this rule.

Eric begins by setting up a new column in the CreditData worksheet, column K, with the heading "Rule #1" in cell K2. To obtain the percentage of past due balance versus this year's total sales for the first company listed in the CreditData worksheet, Athletic Gear Corp., Eric writes a formula in cell K3 that divides the past due balance in cell E3 ($0) by the current year's sales value in cell D3 ($11,952). The result is 0, which is less than the benchmark of 10% specified in Rule #1—so, the value TRUE is displayed in cell K3. Because Eric wants to copy this formula relatively down the column, he creates the formula in cell K3 using cell references, as follows:

```
=E3/D3<0.1
```

Because all of the operands copy relatively, no absolute references are required. The resulting values are displayed in cells K3:K21 on the worksheet, as shown in Figure 4.2. Notice the value TRUE in cell K3, which indicates that the customer Athletic Gear Corp. could be granted credit approval because it meets the criteria established in Rule #1.

Figure 4.2: Applying Rule #1 using a relational operator

`=E3/D3<0.1`

	A	B	C	D	E	F	G	H	I	J	K	L
1	Accounts Receivable Department - Customer Credit Analysis											
2	Customer Name	Current Credit Limit	Previous Year's Sales	Current Year's Sales	Past Due Balance	Net Worth in (000)	D&B Credit Rating Class	D&B Composite Credit Appraisal (1 Best)	D&B PAYDEX (100 Best)	D&B Stress Risk Class (1 Best)	Rule #1	
3	Athletic Gear Corp.	$ 9,000	$ 15,382	$ 11,952	$ 0	$ 450	BA	4	15	3	TRUE	
4	Baltimore O's	39,000	10,033	7,789	0	1,950	3A	1	51	1	TRUE	
5	Baseball & More	75,000	60,009	55,342	13,892	37,500	4A	2	70	1	FALSE	
6	Canadian Ski Club	33,000	35,039	50,921	495	1,650	BA	2	43	1	TRUE	
7	Concord Pro Shop					10,000	4A	1	91	1		
8	Everything Golf	25,000	15,221	9,483	2,899	1,250	3A	3	76	1	FALSE	
9	Lake Pro Shops	42,000	80,498	81,126	0	2,100	3A	2	87	1	TRUE	
10	Mars Dept. Store	27,000	35,354	20,666	0	213	BB	3	94	1	TRUE	
11	RG Bradley	46,000	90,970	18,343	0	2,300	3A	1	21	1	TRUE	
12	RX for Sports	15,000	5,663	3,014	0	750	2A	1	59	1	TRUE	
13	School Sports Supply	45,000	50,278	32,338	0	2,250	3A	3	91	1	TRUE	
14	Ski World	26,000	25,864	28,154	0	300	BA	2	82	1	TRUE	
15	Sneaker Kingdom	45,000	40,157	25,379	0	2,250	3A	2	71	1	TRUE	
16	Sports & Stuff	15,000	15,898	14,732	14,383	450	BA	1	67	1	FALSE	
17	Toy Kingdom	22,000	10,073	1,047	0	1,100	3A	3	14	1	TRUE	
18	Under the Sea	45,000	95,411	64,418	0	150	CB	4	79	2	TRUE	
19	US Olympic Team	20,000	5,621	6,171	0	1,000	3A	1	87	1	TRUE	
20	WWW Sports Inc.	100,000	60,009	60,354	0	500,000	5A	2	97	1	TRUE	
21	Zip & Sons	10,000	15,490	22,760	0	620	1A	2	96	1	TRUE	
22												
23												

A FALSE value indicates that the customer does not meet the criteria for credit approval for Rule #1

Notice row 7, which contains the data for Concord Pro Shop. There are no values for past due balance or this year's total sales for this customer, so the formula in cell K7 has been deleted in order to avoid a DIV!# error message in the cell. A better method of dealing with this type of situation is explored later in this chapter. Based on the results displayed in column K, it appears that three customers—Baseball & More, Everything Golf, and Sports & Stuff—might be rejected due to poor payment history with TheZone.

USING BOOLEAN LOGICAL FUNCTIONS TO EVALUATE A LIST OF VALUES AND DETERMINE A SINGLE TRUE OR FALSE VALUE

So far, Eric has compared two different values using relational operators in an expression to determine if that expression is TRUE or FALSE. To evaluate Rule #2, *"Accept a customer who has either a composite credit appraisal value of 1 or a PAYDEX score over 90,"* he can individually test to see if a customer's composite credit appraisal value equals 1, and then test to see if the customer's PAYDEX score is over 90. Doing so would result in two separate TRUE/FALSE values. However, Eric wants to display only a single TRUE or FALSE value in column L of the worksheet to evaluate this rule.

So, how can Eric determine if *at least one item* meets the specified criteria? At some point, he might also need to consider if *all* the items in a group meet specified criteria, or if an item does *not* meet specified criteria. A list of Boolean values can be evaluated using the Excel functions AND, OR, and NOT. These Excel functions are described below:

- The **AND function** evaluates a list of logical arguments to determine if all of the arguments are TRUE. An AND function returns a value of TRUE if all arguments in the function are TRUE.
- The **OR function** evaluates a list of logical arguments to determine if at least one argument is TRUE. The OR function returns a value of FALSE only if all of the arguments in the function are FALSE.
- The **NOT function** evaluates only one logical argument to determine if it is FALSE. The NOT function essentially changes the value TRUE to FALSE or the value FALSE to TRUE.

Figure 4.3 lists the outcomes for the AND function using two inputs, Condition #1 and Condition #2, in a format commonly referred to as a "Truth Table."

Figure 4.3: AND Truth Table

	If Condition #1 is	
AND Condition #2 is	**TRUE**	**FALSE**
TRUE	TRUE	FALSE
FALSE	FALSE	FALSE
An AND function only results in a TRUE value if both Condition #1 and Condition #2 are TRUE. An AND function results in a FALSE value if either Condition #1 or Condition #2 is FALSE.		

Figure 4.4 lists the outcomes for the OR function using two inputs, Condition #1 and Condition #2.

Figure 4.4: OR Truth Table

	If Condition #1 is	
OR Condition #2 is	**TRUE**	**FALSE**
TRUE	TRUE	TRUE
FALSE	TRUE	FALSE
An OR function results in a TRUE value if either Condition #1 or Condition #2 is TRUE. An OR function only results in a FALSE value if both Condition #1 and Condition #2 are FALSE.		

Figure 4.5 lists the outcomes of the NOT function which, unlike the AND and OR functions, evaluates only a single input, Condition.

Figure 4.5: NOT Truth Table

	If Condition is	
	TRUE	**FALSE**
Resulting value is	FALSE	TRUE
A NOT function results in a TRUE value if the Condition is FALSE. A NOT function results in a FALSE value if the Condition is TRUE.		

Using the OR Function to Evaluate Criteria

Which Boolean operator does Eric need to evaluate the second rule for determining creditworthiness? The rule states: *"Accept a customer who has **either** a composite credit appraisal value of 1 (column H) **or** a PAYDEX score over 90 (column I)."* The key words in this case are "either" and "or." If either condition is met, then credit should be approved, which indicates the need for an OR function.

The OR function evaluates a list of logical arguments to determine if *at least one argument is TRUE*. The arguments can consist of any combination of cell references, values, or ranges that each individually reduce to a TRUE or FALSE value. The syntax of the OR function is as follows: OR(logical1,logical2,....). An OR function is FALSE only if all arguments are FALSE. Consider the following Excel formulas that use the OR function:

- =OR(I3>90,I4>90,I5>90,I6>90) returns a FALSE value if the values in cells I3, I4, I5, and I6 all contain values of 90 or less.
- =OR(K3:K21) returns a TRUE value if any of the values in K3 through K21 contain the value TRUE. When using a range in a Boolean function, the range must contain only TRUE and FALSE values.
- =OR(25<24,MIN(1,10)<2,3<=2+1) returns a TRUE value. This formula begins by evaluating the expression 25<24, which is FALSE; then evaluates the expression MIN(1,10)<2, or 1<2, which is TRUE; and finally evaluates the expression 3<=2+1, which is also TRUE. So, the formula reduces to =OR(FALSE,TRUE,TRUE), resulting in the final value of TRUE because at least one of the arguments is TRUE.

Eric can use the OR function to determine if the first customer listed in the CreditData worksheet, Athletic Gear Corp., should be granted credit approval based on Rule #2. To do this, he first needs to evaluate each individual criterion and then combine them with the OR Boolean function to calculate a single TRUE or FALSE result to be placed in column L, as follows:

- Determine if the composite credit appraisal value in column H equals 1 using the relational expression H3=1.
- Determine if the PAYDEX score given in column I is greater than 90 using the relational expression I3>90.
- Determine if either of the preceding statements is TRUE using the OR function, and then display the resulting TRUE or FALSE value.

Eric enters the formula =OR(H3=1,I3>90) in cell L3 and then copies the formula down the column to determine the results for each of the other customers. Because both cell H3 and cell I3 need to copy relatively, no absolute references are required. The resulting TRUE and FALSE values are displayed in column L, as shown in Figure 4.6.

Figure 4.6: Applying Rule #2 using an OR function

`=OR(H3=1,I3>90)`

	A	B	C	D	E	F	G	H	I	J	K	L	M
1	Accounts Receivable Department - Customer Credit Analysis												
2	Customer Name	Current Credit Limit	Previous Year's Sales	Current Year's Sales	Past Due Balance	Net Worth in (000)	D&B Credit Rating Class	D&B Composite Credit Appraisal (1 Best)	D&B PAYDEX (100 Best)	D&B Stress Risk Class (1 Best)	Rule #1	Rule #2	
3	Athletic Gear Corp.	$ 9,000	$ 15,382	$11,952	$ 0	$ 450	BA	4	15	3	TRUE	FALSE	
4	Baltimore O's	39,000	10,033	7,789	0	1,950	3A	1	51	1	TRUE	TRUE	
5	Baseball & More	75,000	60,009	55,342	13,892	37,500	4A	2	70	1	FALSE	FALSE	
6	Canadian Ski Club	33,000	35,039	50,921	495	1,650	BA	2	43	1	TRUE	FALSE	
7	Concord Pro Shop					10,000	4A	1	91	1		TRUE	
8	Everything Golf	25,000	15,221	9,483	2,899	1,250	3A	3	76	1	FALSE	FALSE	
9	Lake Pro Shops	42,000	80,498	81,126	0	2,100	3A	2	87	1	TRUE	FALSE	
10	Mars Dept. Store	27,000	35,354	20,666	0	213	BB	3	94	1	TRUE	TRUE	
11	RG Bradley	46,000	90,970	18,343	0	2,300	3A	1	21	1	TRUE	TRUE	
12	RX for Sports	15,000	5,663	3,014	0	750	2A	1	59	1	TRUE	TRUE	
13	School Sports Supply	45,000	50,278	32,338	0	2,250	3A	3	91	1	TRUE	TRUE	
14	Ski World	26,000	25,864	28,154	0	300	BA	2	82	1	TRUE	TRUE	
15	Sneaker Kingdom	45,000	40,157	25,379	0	2,250	3A	2	71	1	TRUE	FALSE	
16	Sports & Stuff	15,000	15,898	14,732	14,383	450	BA	1	67	1	FALSE	TRUE	
17	Toy Kingdom	22,000	10,073	1,047	0	1,100	3A	3	14	1	TRUE	FALSE	
18	Under the Sea	45,000	95,411	64,418	0	150	CB	4	79	2	TRUE	FALSE	
19	US Olympic Team	20,000	5,621	6,171	0	1,000	3A	1	87	1	TRUE	FALSE	
20	WWW Sports Inc.	100,000	60,009	60,354	0	500,000	5A	2	97	1	TRUE	TRUE	
21	Zip & Sons	10,000	15,490	22,760	0	620	1A	2	96	1	TRUE	TRUE	
22													
23													

4

Level 1

Substituting the values in the cells corresponding to the first customer listed in the worksheet, Athletic Gear Corp., the formula can be interpreted as follows:

- First substitute the values corresponding to the cell references, =OR(4=1,15>90).
- Analyze the first logical argument. Because 4 does not equal 1, this argument evaluates to the value FALSE.
- Analyze the second logical argument. Because 15 is not greater than 90, this argument also evaluates to the value FALSE.
- The resulting expression is, therefore, =OR(FALSE,FALSE). For an OR function to be TRUE, at least one of its arguments must be TRUE, which is not the case here. So, the value resulting from this formula for Athletic Gear Corp. is the value FALSE, which is displayed in cell L3. This customer does not meet the criteria established in Rule #2 and, therefore, is not recommended for credit approval based on this measurement.

Best Practice

Comparing a Long List of Elements to the Same Value

Referring to the worksheet in Figure 4.6, consider the following question: "Do any customers have a PAYDEX score over 90?" To find the answer to this question, you could write an expression such as =OR(I3>90,I4>90,I5>90I6>90......I21>90), listing every cell in column I from cell I3 all the way to cell I21. However, this is a cumbersome way to evaluate a list of elements, especially given that the relational expression is essentially the same in each case. Could you write the formula as =OR(I3:I21>90)? No; this is not a legitimate syntactical use of the function. Indeed, a FALSE value will be returned and not an error message, even though

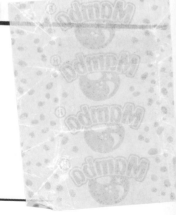

cell I7 contains a PAYDEX score of 91. This formula would perform the relational operation with cell I3 only.

In situations where you have a long list and want each element to be compared to the same value, an effective, two-step approach is to first create a separate column, such as column M shown in Figure 4.7, in which you calculate the relationship for each individual element. The formula =I3>90 can be written in cell M3 and then copied down the column, resulting in a TRUE or FALSE value for each element. Then, in a separate cell (cell M23 in Figure 4.7), you can write the formula =OR(M3:M21) to determine if any of the elements are TRUE. Because column M contains only TRUE or FALSE values, you can use a range in the formula for this OR function. In Figure 4.7, the final result is TRUE (cell M23), indicating that at least one customer has a PAYDEX score greater than 90.

Figure 4.7: Two-step approach to calculate a PAYDEX score > 90

The formula =I3>90 has been entered in cell M3 and copied down the column

	A	B	C	D	E	F	G	H	I	J	K	L	M	N
1	Accounts Receivable Department - Customer Credit Analysis													
2	Customer Name	Current Credit Limit	Previous Year's Sales	Current Year's Sales	Past Due Balance	Net Worth in (000)	D&B Credit Rating Class	D&B Composite Credit Appraisal (1 Best)	D&B PAYDEX (100 Best)	D&B Stress Risk Class (1 Best)	Rule #1	Rule #2	PAYDEX > 90	
3	Athletic Gear Corp.	$ 9,000	$15,382	$11,952	$ 0	$ 450	BA	4	15	3	TRUE	FALSE	FALSE	
4	Baltimore O's	39,000	10,033	7,789	0	1,950	3A	1	51	1	TRUE	TRUE	FALSE	
5	Baseball & More	75,000	60,009	55,342	13,892	37,500	4A	2	70	1	FALSE	FALSE	FALSE	
6	Canadian Ski Club	33,000	35,039	50,921	495	1,650	BA	2	43	1	TRUE	FALSE	FALSE	
7	Concord Pro Shop					10,000	4A	1	91	1		TRUE	TRUE	
8	Everything Golf	25,000	15,221	9,483	2,899	1,250	3A	3	76	1	FALSE	FALSE	FALSE	
9	Lake Pro Shops	42,000	80,498	81,126	0	2,100	3A	2	87	1	TRUE	FALSE	FALSE	
10	Mars Dept. Store	27,000	35,354	20,666	0	213	BB	3	94	1	TRUE	TRUE	FALSE	
11	RG Bradley	46,000	90,970	18,343	0	2,300	3A	1	21	1	TRUE	TRUE	FALSE	
12	RX for Sports	15,000	5,663	3,014	0	750	2A	1	59	1	TRUE	TRUE	TRUE	
13	School Sports Supply	45,000	50,278	32,338	0	2,250	3A	3	91	1	TRUE	FALSE	FALSE	
14	Ski World	26,000	25,864	28,154	0	300	BA	2	82	1	TRUE	FALSE	FALSE	
15	Sneaker Kingdom	45,000	40,157	25,379	0	2,250	3A	2	71	1	FALSE	TRUE	FALSE	
16	Sports & Stuff	15,000	15,898	14,732	14,383	450	BA	1	14	3	TRUE	FALSE	FALSE	
17	Toy Kingdom	22,000	10,073	1,047	0	1,100	3A	3	79	2	TRUE	FALSE	FALSE	
18	Under the Sea	45,000	95,411	64,418	0	150	CB	4	87	1	TRUE	TRUE	FALSE	
19	US Olympic Team	20,000	5,621	6,171	0	1,000	3A	1	97	1	TRUE	TRUE	TRUE	
20	WWW Sports Inc.	100,000	60,009	60,354	0	500,000	5A	2	96	1	TRUE	TRUE	TRUE	
21	Zip & Sons	10,000	15,490	22,760	0	620	1A	2						
22											At least 1 PAYDEX score >90		TRUE	
23														
24														
25														
26														

The formula =OR(M3:M21) determines if *any* PAYDEX score is greater than 90

Using the AND Function to Evaluate Criteria

Next, Eric needs to consider Rule #3, *"Accept a customer who has **all** of the following: a net worth of at least $500,000; a composite credit appraisal value of 2 or lower; a PAYDEX score over 70; and a stress risk class of 1."* The key word in this case is "all." Because each one of the four criteria must be met for the rule to be TRUE, an AND function is required.

The AND function is used to evaluate a list of logical arguments to determine if *all of the arguments are TRUE.* As with the OR function, each argument can consist of any of the following: cell references or a range of cells containing Boolean logical values, relational expressions, and functions that reduce to a single TRUE or FALSE value. The syntax of the AND function is as follows: AND(logical1,logical2,....). An AND function is TRUE only if all its arguments are TRUE.

Eric can use the AND function to evaluate the data in the CreditData worksheet to determine which customers of TheZone meet *all* the criteria in Rule #3. He can first evaluate each individual criterion and then combine them with the AND function to calculate a single TRUE or FALSE result, as follows:

- Determine if the net worth of the customer given in column F is at least $500,000 using the relational expression F3*1000>=500000 (for the first customer listed, Athletic Gear Corp.). Note that the net worth is listed in column F of the worksheet in thousands of dollars, not by the actual value; therefore, the expression must multiply the net worth by 1000 so that the resulting value can be compared with 500,000. Other algebraic equivalents of this expression that could also be used are F3>=500000/1000 or F3>=500.
- Determine if the composite credit appraisal value given in column H is 2 or lower using the relational expression H3<=2.
- Determine if the PAYDEX score given in column I is over 70 using the relational expression I3>70.
- Determine if the stress risk class given in column J is equal to 1 using the relational expression J3=1.
- Determine if *all* of the preceding statements are TRUE using the AND function, and then display the resulting TRUE or FALSE value.

Eric enters the formula =AND(F3*1000>=500000,H3<=2,I3>70,J3=1) in cell M3 and copies it down column M. The resulting TRUE and FALSE values are displayed, as shown in Figure 4.8.

Figure 4.8: Applying Rule #3 using an AND function

=AND(F3*1000>=500000,H3<=2,I3>70,J3=1)

	A	B	C	D	E	F	G	H	I	J	K	L	M	N
1	Accounts Receivable Department - Customer Credit Analysis													
2	Customer Name	Current Credit Limit	Previous Year's Sales	Current Year's Sales	Past Due Balance	Net Worth in (000)	D&B Credit Rating Class	D&B Composite Credit Appraisal (1 Best)	D&B PAYDEX (100 Best)	D&B Stress Risk Class (1 Best)	Rule #1	Rule #2	Rule #3	
3	Athletic Gear Corp.	$ 9,000	$ 15,382	$ 11,952	$ 0	$ 450	BA	4	15	3	TRUE	FALSE	FALSE	
4	Baltimore O's	39,000	10,033	7,789	0	1,950	3A	1	51	1	TRUE	TRUE	FALSE	
5	Baseball & More	75,000	60,009	55,342	13,892	37,500	4A	2	70	1	FALSE	FALSE	FALSE	
6	Canadian Ski Club	33,000	35,039	50,921	495	1,650	BA	2	43	1	TRUE	FALSE	FALSE	
7	Concord Pro Shop					10,000	4A	1	91	1		TRUE	TRUE	
8	Everything Golf	25,000	15,221	9,483	2,899	1,250	3A	3	76	1	FALSE	FALSE	FALSE	
9	Lake Pro Shops	42,000	80,498	81,126	0	2,100	3A	2	87	1	TRUE	FALSE	TRUE	
10	Mars Dept. Store	27,000	35,354	20,666	0	213	BB	3	94	1	TRUE	TRUE	FALSE	
11	RG Bradley	46,000	90,970	18,343	0	2,300	3A	1	21	1	TRUE	TRUE	FALSE	
12	RX for Sports	15,000	5,663	3,014	0	750	2A	1	59	1	TRUE	TRUE	FALSE	
13	School Sports Supply	45,000	50,278	32,338	0	2,250	3A	3	91	1	TRUE	FALSE	FALSE	
14	Ski World	26,000	25,864	28,154	0	300	BA	2	82	1	TRUE	FALSE	TRUE	
15	Sneaker Kingdom	45,000	40,157	25,379	0	2,250	3A	2	71	1	TRUE	FALSE	FALSE	
16	Sports & Stuff	15,000	15,898	14,732	14,383	450	BA	1	67	1	FALSE	TRUE	FALSE	
17	Toy Kingdom	22,000	10,073	1,047	0	1,100	3A	3	14	1	TRUE	FALSE	FALSE	
18	Under the Sea	45,000	95,411	64,418	0	150	CB	4	79	2	TRUE	FALSE	FALSE	
19	US Olympic Team	20,000	5,621	6,171	0	1,000	3A	1	87	1	TRUE	TRUE	TRUE	
20	WWW Sports Inc.	100,000	60,009	60,354	0	500,000	5A	2	97	1	TRUE	TRUE	TRUE	
21	Zip & Sons	10,000	15,490	22,760	0	620	1A	2	96	1	TRUE	TRUE	TRUE	
22														
23														

Substituting the values in the cells corresponding to the first customer listed in the worksheet, Athletic Gear Corp., the formula can be interpreted as follows:

- First substitute the values corresponding to the cell references in the formula, =AND(450*1000>=500000,4<=2,15>70,3=1).
- Analyze the first logical argument. Because 450*1000 is not greater than or equal to 500000, this argument evaluates to the value FALSE.
- Analyze the second logical argument. Because 4 is not less than or equal to 2, this argument also evaluates to the value FALSE.
- Analyze the third logical argument. Because 15 is not greater than 70, this argument also evaluates to the value FALSE.
- Analyze the fourth logical argument. Because 3 does not equal 1, this argument also evaluates to the value FALSE.
- The resulting expression is, therefore, =AND(FALSE,FALSE,FALSE,FALSE). For an AND function to be TRUE, *all* of its arguments must be TRUE, which is not the case here. So, the value resulting from this formula for Athletic Gear Corp. is the value FALSE, which is displayed in cell M3. This customer does not meet the criteria established in Rule #3 and, therefore, is not recommended for credit approval based on this measurement.

Figure 4.9 illustrates this analysis.

Figure 4.9: Analyzing the resulting value in cell M3

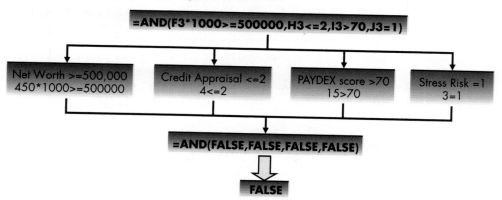

With the formulas for the three rules in place, Eric now wants to determine if the following statement is TRUE: "At least one company is recommended for credit approval based on a TRUE value for Rule #1 (K3:K21)." In reviewing the worksheet at this point (Figure 4.8), notice that there are many TRUE values in column K, so the statement is TRUE. But what if the list of customers was significantly longer with few, if any, TRUE values, and scanning the list was not practical? Eric could write a formula using an OR function to determine if the statement is TRUE. In the example shown in Figure 4.10, Eric writes the formula =OR(K3:K21) in cell K23 and copies it across the row into cells L23 and M23 to determine if at least one customer meets Rule #2 and Rule #3, respectively. Because all of the cell references change relatively, no absolute references are required in the formula.

Figure 4.10: Determining if at least one customer meets each rule

	A	B	C	D	E	F	G	H	I	J	K	L	M	N
1	*Accounts Receivable Department - Customer Credit Analysis*													
2	Customer Name	Current Credit Limit	Previous Year's Sales	Current Year's Sales	Past Due Balance	Net Worth in (000)	D&B Credit Rating Class	D&B Composite Credit Appraisal (1 Best)	D&B PAYDEX (100 Best)	D&B Stress Risk Class (1 Best)	Rule #1	Rule #2	Rule #3	
3	Athletic Gear Corp.	$ 9,000	$15,382	$11,952	$ 0	$ 450	BA	4	15	3	TRUE	FALSE	FALSE	
4	Baltimore O's	39,000	10,033	7,789	0	1,950	3A	1	51	1	TRUE	TRUE	FALSE	
5	Baseball & More	75,000	60,009	55,342	13,892	37,500	4A	2	70	1	FALSE	FALSE	FALSE	
6	Canadian Ski Club	33,000	35,039	50,921	495	1,650	BA	2	43	1	TRUE	FALSE	FALSE	
7	Concord Pro Shop					10,000	4A	1	91	1		TRUE	TRUE	
8	Everything Golf	25,000	15,221	9,483	2,899	1,250	3A	3	76	1	FALSE	FALSE	FALSE	
9	Lake Pro Shops	42,000	80,498	81,126	0	2,100	3A	2	87	1	TRUE	FALSE	TRUE	
10	Mars Dept. Store	27,000	35,354	20,666	0	213	BB	3	94	1	TRUE	TRUE	FALSE	
11	RG Bradley	46,000	90,970	18,343	0	2,300	3A	1	21	1	TRUE	TRUE	FALSE	
12	RX for Sports	15,000	5,663	3,014	0	750	2A	1	59	1	TRUE	TRUE	FALSE	
13	School Sports Supply	45,000	50,278	32,338	0	2,250	3A	3	91	1	TRUE	TRUE	FALSE	
14	Ski World	26,000	25,864	28,154	0	300	BA	2	82	1	TRUE	FALSE	FALSE	
15	Sneaker Kingdom	45,000	40,157	25,379	0	2,250	3A	2	71	1	TRUE	FALSE	TRUE	
16	Sports & Stuff	15,000	15,898	14,732	14,383	450	BA	1	67	1	FALSE	TRUE	FALSE	
17	Toy Kingdom	22,000	10,073	1,047	0	1,100	3A	3	14	1	TRUE	FALSE	FALSE	
18	Under the Sea	45,000	95,411	64,418	0	150	CB	4	79	2	TRUE	FALSE	FALSE	
19	US Olympic Team	20,000	5,621	6,171	0	1,000	3A	1	87	1	TRUE	TRUE	FALSE	
20	WWW Sports Inc.	100,000	60,009	60,354	0	500,000	5A	2	97	1	TRUE	TRUE	TRUE	
21	Zip & Sons	10,000	15,490	22,760	0	620	1A	2	96	1	TRUE	TRUE	TRUE	
22														
23														
24								Do any meet the rule?			TRUE	TRUE	TRUE	
25														

=OR(K3:K21)

As noted earlier, a range can be used in a Boolean logical AND or OR function if the range refers to cells containing only TRUE or FALSE values. Excel ignores empty cells, such as cell K7 in Figure 4.10, although it might display a warning message in such a case.

Using the NOT Function to Evaluate Criteria

How could Eric determine if *none* of the customers meet the criteria for Rule #1? In this case, Eric simply wants the opposite value that was calculated in cell K23:

- Because at least one customer meets the criteria for Rule #1, cell K23 contains the value TRUE. So, the statement "None of the customers meet Rule #1" is FALSE.
- If no customers met the criteria for Rule #1, the resulting value in cell K23 would be FALSE, and the statement "None of the customers meet Rule #1" would be TRUE.

How do you change a TRUE value to FALSE or a FALSE value to TRUE? Eric accomplishes this using the NOT function with the formula =NOT(K23). He enters this formula in cell K24 and copies it to cells L24:M24, as shown in Figure 4.11.

Figure 4.11: Determining if no customers meet each rule

	A	B	C	D	E	F	G	H	I	J	K	L	M	N
1	Accounts Receivable Department - Customer Credit Analysis													
2	Customer Name	Current Credit Limit	Previous Year's Sales	Current Year's Sales	Past Due Balance	Net Worth in (000)	D&B Credit Rating Class	D&B Composite Credit Appraisal (1 Best)	D&B PAYDEX (100 Best)	D&B Stress Risk Class (1 Best)	Rule #1	Rule #2	Rule #3	
3	Athletic Gear Corp.	$ 9,000	$ 15,382	$11,952	$ 0	$ 450	BA	4	15	3	TRUE	FALSE	FALSE	
4	Baltimore O's	39,000	10,033	7,789	0	1,950	3A	1	51	1	TRUE	TRUE	FALSE	
5	Baseball & More	75,000	60,009	55,342	13,892	37,500	4A	2	70	1	FALSE	FALSE	FALSE	
6	Canadian Ski Club	33,000	35,039	50,921	495	1,650	BA	2	43	1	TRUE	FALSE	FALSE	
7	Concord Pro Shop					10,000	4A	1	91	1		TRUE	TRUE	
8	Everything Golf	25,000	15,221	9,483	2,899	1,250	3A	3	76	1	FALSE	FALSE	FALSE	
9	Lake Pro Shops	42,000	80,498	81,126	0	2,100	3A	2	87	1	TRUE	FALSE	TRUE	
10	Mars Dept. Store	27,000	35,354	20,666	0	213	BB	3	94	1	TRUE	TRUE	FALSE	
11	RG Bradley	46,000	90,970	18,343	0	2,300	3A	1	21	1	TRUE	TRUE	FALSE	
12	RX for Sports	15,000	5,663	3,014	0	750	2A	1	59	1	TRUE	TRUE	FALSE	
13	School Sports Supply	45,000	50,278	32,338	0	2,250	3A	3	91	1	TRUE	TRUE	FALSE	
14	Ski World	26,000	25,864	28,154	0	300	BA	2	82	1	TRUE	FALSE	FALSE	
15	Sneaker Kingdom	45,000	40,157	25,379	0	2,250	3A	2	71	1	TRUE	FALSE	TRUE	
16	Sports & Stuff	15,000	15,898	14,732	14,383	450	BA	1	67	1	FALSE	TRUE	FALSE	
17	Toy Kingdom	22,000	10,073	1,047	0	1,100	3A	3	14	1	TRUE	FALSE	FALSE	
18	Under the Sea	45,000	95,411	64,418	0	150	CB	4	79	2	TRUE	FALSE	FALSE	
19	US Olympic Team	20,000	5,621	6,171	0	1,000	3A	1	87	1	TRUE	TRUE	TRUE	
20	WWW Sports Inc.	100,000	60,009	60,354	0	500,000	5A	2	97	1	TRUE	TRUE	TRUE	
21	Zip & Sons	10,000	15,490	22,760	0	620	1A	2	96	1	TRUE	TRUE	TRUE	
22									Do any meet the rule?		TRUE	TRUE	TRUE	
23									Do none meet the rule?		FALSE	FALSE	FALSE	
24														
25														

`=NOT(K23)`

Could Eric also have written this formula as =NOT(K3:K21)? No; unlike the AND and OR functions, the NOT function takes *only one argument* and essentially changes a single TRUE value to FALSE or a single FALSE value to TRUE. The logical argument can consist of a single cell reference that contains a Boolean value or an expression that will reduce to a TRUE or FALSE value. The syntax of the NOT function is as follows: NOT(logical1).

The following are some examples of the NOT function used in formulas:

- NOT(TRUE) returns the value FALSE.
- NOT(FALSE) returns the value TRUE.
- NOT(7<10) returns the value FALSE, because 7 is less than 10.
- NOT(H2=2) returns the value TRUE assuming that cell H2 contains any value other than 2.

More information and analysis are required before decisions can be made regarding whether the accounts receivable staff should recommend credit for a specific customer. For some customers, the rules clearly indicate whether to recommend accepting or rejecting a credit application, whereas for other customers, such as Sports & Stuff, the rules have returned contradictory results—to both reject credit (cells K16 and M16) and to accept credit (cell L16). Eric will revisit this worksheet later, with further input from management, to resolve these types of issues and make a final recommendation.

APPLYING CONDITIONAL FORMATTING TO A WORKSHEET

Before completing the worksheet, Eric wants to include formatting to highlight the results that were obtained. When a worksheet contains a large set of data, highlighting specific values in a different format from the rest of the worksheet data can make those values stand out or help the reader recognize trends in data. As you learned in Chapter 1, you can change the formatting of a cell quite easily using the Formatting toolbar or the options on the Format menu. However, the disadvantage of formatting in this way is that if a value changes, you might need to manually reformat the cells affected.

Excel provides a tool called **conditional formatting** that you can use to identify a set of conditions and specify the formatting of a cell if those conditions are met. If a cell value is later updated, the formatting will be updated automatically according to the specified criteria. This tool allows you to specify up to three conditions and modify the format based on whether these conditions are met. If the conditions are not mutually exclusive, resulting in more than one specified condition being TRUE, only the formatting of the first condition is applied. With conditional formatting, you can specify criteria in one of two ways: either based on the value in the cell being formatted, or based on the results of a specified formula that returns a Boolean value.

Applying Conditional Formatting Based on Cell Value

To apply conditional formatting to a worksheet based on the value in the cell(s) being formatted, you first select the cell or cell range to which you want to apply conditional formatting, and then open the Conditional Formatting dialog box from the Format menu. Figure 4.12 shows this dialog box with the "Cell Value Is" condition type selected; this is the option you need to choose if you want to apply conditional formatting based on the value in the cell or cells being formatted.

Figure 4.12: Conditional Formatting dialog box

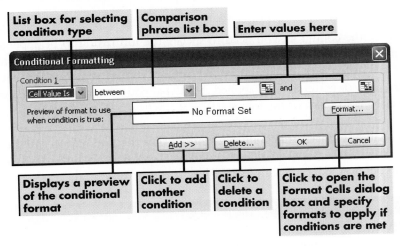

In this dialog box, you specify the condition expression for the formatting by first selecting a comparison phrase from the comparison phrase list box. Table 4.5 lists and defines the available comparison phrases.

Table 4.5: Comparison phrases for conditional formatting

Comparison Phrase	Use To
Between	Set lower and upper limits inclusive
Not between	Identify values outside of lower and upper limits
Equal to	Identify values equal to the specified value
Not equal to	Identify values not equal to the specified value
Greater than	Identify values greater than the specified value
Less than	Identify values less than the specified value
Greater than or equal to	Identify values greater than or equal to the specified value
Less than or equal to	Identify values less than or equal to the specified value

Depending on the comparison phrase you select, one or two additional boxes become available in which you specify the value or values to be compared. You can specify the following types of values:

- Arithmetic values (1, 2, 3, and so on).
- Boolean values (TRUE, FALSE).

- Text values (Accept, Reject, and so on). Note that quotation marks are not required because the conditional formatting tool adds them automatically.
- References to other cells containing arithmetic, Boolean, or text values. Note that a named range does not work with conditional formatting and cannot be used instead of a cell reference.

After establishing the condition, you need to specify the formatting to be applied if the condition is met. To do so, you click the Format button for the selected condition to open the Format Cells dialog box. Then choose the settings you want for the font style and color, borders, and/or patterns to be applied. Note that you cannot change the font type (such as Times New Roman) or the font size.

To select a second or even a third condition, you can click the Add button and the dialog box will be extended to show additional condition specification boxes. Up to three conditions can be specified, each with its own unique formatting.

How To

Apply "Cell Value Is" Conditional Formatting

1. Select the cell or cells to which you want to apply conditional formatting.
2. Click Format on the menu bar, and then click Conditional Formatting to open the Conditional Formatting dialog box.
3. Click the Condition 1 list box arrow, and then click Cell Value Is (if necessary).
4. Click the comparison phrase list box arrow, and then select the comparison phrase you want from the list. Depending on the selected comparison phrase, enter the appropriate value in the available box or boxes to complete the condition expression.
5. Click the Format button to display the Format Cells dialog box, and then specify the formatting to be applied if the condition is met.
6. To specify one or two additional conditions, click the Add button and then repeat the preceding steps for each condition.
7. Click the OK button.

Eric wants to apply conditional formatting in the CreditData worksheet so that all TRUE values in the range K3:M21 appear in a bold, italicized format. This will make it easier for him and other accounts receivable staff members to see which customers might be granted credit approval because the value TRUE appears for one or more of the three rules. In the Conditional Formatting dialog box, he selects the "Cell Value Is" option and the "equal to" comparison phrase, and enters the value TRUE, as shown in Figure 4.13, to specify the condition to apply.

Figure 4.13: Applying a "Cell Value Is" condition

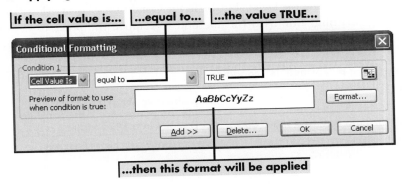

If the cell value is... ...equal to... ...the value TRUE...

...then this format will be applied

The resulting worksheet is shown in Figure 4.14.

Figure 4.14: Worksheet with conditional formatting based on the cell value

TRUE values in cells K3:M21 are displayed in bold and italic

	Customer Name	Current Credit Limit	Previous Year's Sales	Current Year's Sales	Past Due Balance	Net Worth in (000)	D&B Credit Rating Class	D&B Composite Credit Appraisal (1 Best)	D&B PAYDEX (100 Best)	D&B Stress Risk Class (1 Best)	Rule #1	Rule #2	Rule #3	
1	*Accounts Receivable Department - Customer Credit Analysis*													
3	Athletic Gear Corp.	$ 9,000	$15,382	$11,952	$ 0	$ 450	BA	4	15	3	*TRUE*	FALSE	FALSE	
4	Baltimore O's	39,000	10,033	7,789	0	1,950	3A	1	51	1	*TRUE*	*TRUE*	FALSE	
5	Baseball & More	75,000	60,009	55,342	13,892	37,500	4A	2	70	1	*TRUE*	FALSE	FALSE	
6	Canadian Ski Club	33,000	35,039	50,921	495	1,650	BA	2	43	1		*TRUE*	*TRUE*	
7	Concord Pro Shop					10,000	4A	1	91	1				
8	Everything Golf	25,000	15,221	9,483	2,899	1,250	3A	3	76	1	FALSE	FALSE	FALSE	
9	Lake Pro Shops	42,000	80,498	81,126	0	2,100	3A	2	87	1	*TRUE*	FALSE	*TRUE*	
10	Mars Dept. Store	27,000	35,354	20,666	0	213	BB	3	94	1	*TRUE*	*TRUE*	FALSE	
11	RG Bradley	46,000	90,970	18,343	0	2,300	3A	1	21	1	*TRUE*	*TRUE*	FALSE	
12	RX for Sports	15,000	5,663	3,014	0	750	2A	1	59	1	*TRUE*	*TRUE*	FALSE	
13	School Sports Supply	45,000	50,278	32,338	0	2,250	3A	3	91	1	*TRUE*	*TRUE*	FALSE	
14	Ski World	26,000	25,864	28,154	0	300	BA	2	82	1	*TRUE*	FALSE	FALSE	
15	Sneaker Kingdom	45,000	40,157	25,379	0	2,250	3A	2	71	1	*TRUE*	FALSE	*TRUE*	
16	Sports & Stuff	15,000	15,898	14,732	14,383	450	BA	1	67	1	FALSE	*TRUE*	FALSE	
17	Toy Kingdom	22,000	10,073	1,047	0	1,100	3A	3	14	1	*TRUE*	FALSE	FALSE	
18	Under the Sea	45,000	95,411	64,418	0	150	CB	4	79	2	*TRUE*	FALSE	FALSE	
19	US Olympic Team	20,000	5,621	6,171	0	1,000	3A	1	87	1	*TRUE*	*TRUE*	*TRUE*	
20	WWW Sports Inc.	100,000	60,009	60,354	0	500,000	5A	2	97	1	*TRUE*	*TRUE*	*TRUE*	
21	Zip & Sons	10,000	15,490	22,760	0	620	1A	2	96	1	*TRUE*	*TRUE*	*TRUE*	
22							Do any meet the rule?				TRUE	TRUE	TRUE	
23							Do none meet the rule?				FALSE	FALSE	FALSE	

Applying Conditional Formatting Based on the Results of a Formula

What if Eric wants to apply conditional formatting by shading an entire row if a customer's net worth is less than $1 million, and shading with a polka dot pattern an entire row if a company's net worth is above $10 million? He can again use conditional formatting, this time based on the results of a formula. He first needs to highlight a single row as the range (in this case, he highlights row 3), and then specify two separate conditions based on two different formulas, as shown in Figure 4.15. Note that when you specify a conditional format, if a previous conditional format had already been set for the same cells, that format would still be applied as well unless you modify the formatting. You can remove a previous conditional format by clicking the Delete button in the Conditional Formatting dialog box for the selected formatting. Eric used this method to remove the previous conditional formatting before applying the new conditional formats shown in Figure 4.15.

Figure 4.15: Applying a "Formula Is" condition

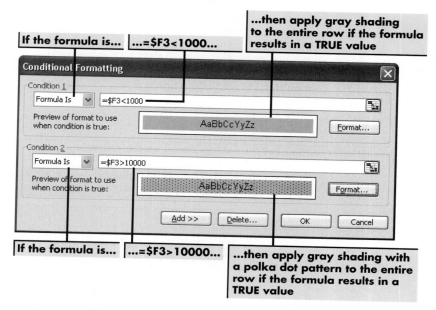

The first condition is based on the formula =$F3<1000. Because Eric needs to copy this conditional formatting down the column, he needs to ensure that the cell reference in the formula has a relative row reference (the default for conditional formatting is an absolute cell reference). The second condition is based on the formula =$F3>10000, which again has an absolute reference to the column and a relative reference to the row. Could Eric simply use one expression, such as =OR($F3<1000,$F3>10000)? Yes; this is a valid conditional formatting formula. However, this approach allows only one format to be applied, as opposed to the two different formats Eric wants.

After establishing the conditional formatting in one row, Eric uses the Format Painter tool to copy the formatting down the column to the remaining rows. The resulting worksheet is shown is Figure 4.16.

Figure 4.16: Worksheet with conditional formatting based on formulas

Because F3<1000 (Condition 1), gray shading is applied to this row

Because F5>10000 (Condition 2), gray shading with polka dots is applied to this row

	A Customer Name	B Current Credit Limit	C Previous Year's Sales	D Current Year's Sales	E Past Due Balance	F Net Worth in (000)	G D&B Credit Rating Class	H D&B Composite Credit Appraisal (1 Best)	I D&B PAYDEX (100 Best)	J D&B Stress Risk Class (1 Best)	K Rule #1	L Rule #2	M Rule #3	N
1	Accounts Receivable Department - Customer Credit Analysis													
2											TRUE	FALSE	FALSE	
3	Athletic Gear Corp.	$ 9,000	$15,382	$11,952	$ 0	$ 450	BA	4	15	3	TRUE	TRUE	FALSE	
4	Baltimore O's	$ 39,000	$10,033	$ 7,789	$ 0	$ 1,950	3A	1	51	1	FALSE	FALSE	FALSE	
5	Baseball & More	$ 75,000	$60,009	$55,342	$13,892	$ 37,500	4A	2	78	1	TRUE	FALSE	FALSE	
6	Canadian Ski Club	$ 33,000	$35,039	$50,921	$ 495	$ 1,650	BA	2	43	1		TRUE	TRUE	
7	Concord Pro Shop					$ 10,000	4A	1	91	1	FALSE	FALSE	FALSE	
8	Everything Golf	$ 25,000	$15,221	$ 9,483	$ 2,899	$ 1,250	3A	3	76	1	TRUE	FALSE	TRUE	
9	Lake Pro Shops	$ 42,000	$80,498	$81,126	$ 0	$ 2,100	3A	2	87	1	TRUE	TRUE	FALSE	
10	Mars Dept. Store	$ 27,000	$35,354	$20,666	$ 0	$ 213	BB	3	94	1	TRUE	TRUE	FALSE	
11	RG Bradley	$ 46,000	$90,970	$18,343	$ 0	$ 2,300	3A	1	21	1	TRUE	TRUE	FALSE	
12	RX for Sports	$ 15,000	$ 5,663	$ 3,014	$ 0	$ 750	2A	1	59	1	TRUE	TRUE	FALSE	
13	School Sports Supply	$ 45,000	$50,278	$32,338	$ 0	$ 2,250	3A	3	91	1	TRUE	FALSE	FALSE	
14	Ski World	$ 26,000	$25,864	$28,154	$ 0	$ 300	BA	2	82	1	TRUE	FALSE	TRUE	
15	Sneaker Kingdom	$ 45,000	$40,157	$25,379	$ 0	$ 2,250	3A	2	71	1	FALSE	TRUE	FALSE	
16	Sports & Stuff	$ 15,000	$15,898	$14,732	$14,383	$ 450	BA	1	67	1	TRUE	FALSE	FALSE	
17	Toy Kingdom	$ 22,000	$10,073	$ 1,047	$ 0	$ 1,100	3A	3	14	1	TRUE	FALSE	FALSE	
18	Under the Sea	$ 45,000	$95,411	$64,418	$ 0	$ 150	CB	4	79	2	TRUE	TRUE	TRUE	
19	US Olympic Team	$ 20,000	$ 5,621	$ 6,171	$ 0	$ 1,000	3A	1	87	1	TRUE	TRUE	TRUE	
20	WWW Sports Inc.	$100,000	$80,009	$60,354	$ 0	$500,000	5A	2	97	1	TRUE	TRUE	TRUE	
21	Zip & Sons	$ 10,000	$15,490	$22,760	$ 0	$ 620	1A	2	96					
22							Do any meet the rule?				TRUE	TRUE	TRUE	
23							Do none meet the rule?				FALSE	FALSE	FALSE	
24														
25														

Because F19 meets neither condition, the formatting remains unchanged for this row

How To

Apply "Formula Is" Conditional Formatting

1. Select the cell or cells to which you want to apply conditional formatting.
2. Click Format on the menu bar, and then click Conditional Formatting to open the Conditional Formatting dialog box.
3. Click the Condition 1 list box arrow, and then click Formula Is.
4. In the text box to the right, type the formula (beginning with an equal sign) that specifies the criteria to be evaluated. The formula *must* result in a TRUE or FALSE value using any of the relational operators or Boolean functions provided by Excel.
5. Click the Format button to display the Format Cells dialog box, and then specify the formatting to be applied if the condition is met.
6. To specify one or two additional conditions, click the Add button and then repeat the preceding steps for each condition.
7. Click the OK button.

Eric will determine which, if any, conditional formatting he will maintain in the CreditData worksheet, based on the data he wants to emphasize. In the next section, he will continue to work with payment data for TheZone's customers to streamline some of the accounts receivable tasks.

Steps To Success: Level 1

The accounting group routinely collects and analyzes credit data on the suppliers with which TheZone does business. Management is always concerned about entering into business relationships with suppliers who are financially unstable and might not be able to meet their commitments. So, before any major new contract is awarded, the accounting group collects both D&B data and previous experience data on each bidder (supplier) and makes recommendations to the purchasing department regarding the financial stability of each bidder.

Currently, the purchasing department is bidding out a contract (PO #527) for supplying a new computer-based warehousing system to all warehousing facilities. The contract includes computer equipment, software, installation, and ongoing maintenance and technical support. The contract is expected to be in the $1 to $2 million range. A list of companies bidding on this contract, together with their financial data, has been compiled in the Bidder worksheet (Figure 4.17) in a workbook named PO527.xls.

Figure 4.17: Bidder credit analysis worksheet

	A	B	C	D	E	F	G
1	PO 527 Bidder List Financial Evaluation						
2	Bidder List	Previous Experience Grade	Net Worth (Dollars)	D&B Composite Credit Appraisal (1 Best)	D&B PAYDEX (100 Best)	D&B Stress Risk Class (1 Best)	
3	Logistic SB Inc.	None	$ 2,500,000	2	85	1	
4	XBE Corporation	Satisfactory	237,000,000	1	90	1	
5	Software Solutions	Satisfactory	1,823,000	3	55	2	
6	Exceed RW	Unsatisfactory	75,000	2	38	1	
7	Roberts Wise Inc.	Satisfactory	680,000	3	43	1	
8							
9							

In these steps, you will help complete the credit analysis by applying the following set of rules:

Rule #1: Consider a bidder if its D&B stress risk class is equal to 1.

Rule #2: Consider a bidder if *all* of the following criteria are met:

- The company's D&B PAYDEX score is greater than 60.
- The company's D&B composite credit appraisal is less than or equal to 2.
- The company's net worth is greater than $1,000,000. (Net worth values are listed in dollars on the worksheet.)

Rule#3: Consider a bidder if *any* of the following criteria are met:

- The company's PAYDEX score is greater than or equal to 85.
- The company's previous experience grade is Satisfactory.

Complete the following:

1. Open the workbook named **PO527.xls** located in the Chapter 4 folder, and then save it as **PO527 Credit Analysis.xls**.

2. In a column adjacent to the data, calculate whether or not (TRUE/FALSE) the first company listed meets the criteria for Rule #1. Place an appropriate heading at the top of the column. Copy this formula down the column to analyze this rule for each of the other bidders.

3. In the next column, calculate whether or not (TRUE/FALSE) the first company listed meets the criteria for Rule #2. Place an appropriate heading at the top of the column. Copy this formula down the column to analyze this rule for each of the other bidders.

4. In the next column, calculate whether or not (TRUE/FALSE) the first company listed meets the criteria for Rule #3. Place an appropriate heading at the top of the column. Copy this formula down the column to analyze this rule for each of the other bidders.

5. In cell G9, write a formula to determine if any of the bidders has a TRUE value for Rule #1. Copy the formula across the row to determine if any bidders have a TRUE value for Rule #2, and then for Rule #3. In cell A9, enter an appropriate label for this row.

6. In cell G10, write a formula to determine if none of the bidders has a TRUE value for Rule #1. Copy this formula across the row to determine this for Rules #2 and #3. In cell A10, enter an appropriate label for this row.

7. Using conditional formatting, highlight the cells in the range G3:I7 that contain a value of FALSE with yellow shading, and highlight all the cells that contain a value of TRUE with light green shading.

8. Using conditional formatting, format in italic the name of any bidder (column A) whose previous experience grade is Unsatisfactory.

9. Save and close the PO527 Credit Analysis.xls workbook.

LEVEL 2

ANALYZING DATA USING IF FUNCTIONS AND NESTED FUNCTIONS

EXCEL 2003 SKILLS TRAINING

- Create formulas using the IF function
- Use logical functions (AND)
- Use logical functions (NOT)

4

Level 2

INTRODUCTION TO IF FUNCTIONS AND NESTED FUNCTIONS

As you learned in Level 1, you can use relational operators and Boolean functions to evaluate sets of conditions resulting in TRUE or FALSE values. Often, the goal is not just to determine if a value is TRUE or FALSE, however, but to use that information to perform another action. In Level 1, Eric used conditional formatting to change the display of worksheet data if a specified condition is met. But so far, he has not used this information to make changes to cell values, either by displaying any information other than TRUE or FALSE or by performing a calculation based on the outcome of the logical expression. Both of these tasks can be accomplished using an IF function. An **IF function** is a Boolean logical function that returns one value if a specified condition evaluates to TRUE and another value if the specified condition evaluates to FALSE.

In this level, the logical operations presented in Level 1 are combined with IF functions to specify different tasks depending on whether the value is TRUE or FALSE. For example, if an account is past due, Eric might want to calculate finance charges and add them to the previous balance, whereas accounts that are not past due would not incur finance charges.

Like other Excel functions, the IF function allows you to nest additional formulas and functions within each of its arguments. The term **nested** means that a function contains additional formulas and/or functions as one or more of its arguments. For example, if you want to calculate the average of cells B1 through B10 rounded to the nearest whole number, you could write the formula =ROUND(AVERAGE(B1:B10),0). Here, the AVERAGE function is "nested" inside of the ROUND function. Excel first calculates the average and then uses that value as the first argument of the ROUND function. This level explores some simple examples of nesting functions inside of the IF function arguments, including nesting of additional IF statements. This technique gives you the flexibility of choosing between not only two different sets of criteria, but also up to seven different levels of logical tests.

WRITING SIMPLE IF FUNCTIONS

Recall that part of Eric's task is to develop a way to track a customer's credit and payment status with TheZone—information such as when a customer's credit was last evaluated, if the customer has been approved or denied credit, and the customer's current balance. In the Customer Credit and Payment History workbook, Eric has created a second worksheet named "Status," which is shown in Figure 4.18. This worksheet is similar to a standard Accounts Receivable Ageing Schedule, except that Eric will be using the data for his analysis.

Figure 4.18: Status worksheet

	A	B	C	D	E	F	G	H	I
1	\
TheZone Customer Accounts - Credit & Payment Status								
2	Customer Name	Customer Type	Current Balance Due	30-Days Past Due	60-Days Past Due	90-Days Past Due	Total Past Due Balance	Current Credit Status	
3	Athletic Gear Corp.	A	$8,612	$ 0	$ 0	$ 0	$ 0	TRUE	
4	Baltimore O's	B	0	0	0	0	0	TRUE	
5	Baseball & More	A	2,345	3,473	5,557	4,862	13,892	TRUE	
6	Canadian Ski Club	C	0	345	0	150	495	TRUE	
7	Everything Golf	A	0	0	2,000	899	2,899	FALSE	
8	Sports & Stuff	A	0	14,000	383	0	14,383	FALSE	
9									
10									

The Status worksheet contains the following information:

- Customer name (column A).
- Customer type, which is a designation of the type of business the customer is engaged in (column B).
- Current balance, which is the value of unpaid purchases made within the past 30 days (column C).
- The 30-days past due balance, which is the value of unpaid purchases made more than 30 days ago but within the last 60 days (column D).
- The 60-days past due balance, which is the value of unpaid purchases made more than 60 days ago but within the last 90 days (column E).
- The 90-days past due balance, which is the value of unpaid purchases made more than 90 days ago (column F).
- Total past due balance, which is the value of all 30-, 60-, and 90-days past due balances (column G).
- Current credit status as indicated by the Boolean value TRUE if the accounting group has previously approved or renewed credit for the customer, or by the Boolean value FALSE if credit has been denied (column H). In some cases, a customer might still have a past due balance with a credit status of FALSE, indicating that the customer was recently denied credit but has not yet paid its outstanding balance. These values are the results of the previous manual credit approval process that Eric is endeavoring to automate.

One critical element of this worksheet is the current credit status (column H). The value TRUE could be confusing to staff members trying to interpret the data; does the value TRUE indicate that credit was approved or denied? The status of each customer's credit would be clearer if another column was added that explicitly states whether credit has been approved or denied. So, if the value in cell H3 is TRUE, Eric wants to display the text "credit approved" in cell I3; otherwise, he wants to display the text "credit denied" in cell I3. To accomplish this, Eric can use an IF function, which evaluates a logical test and then applies one solution if the value is TRUE and another solution if the value is FALSE. The syntax of the IF function is as follows:

$$\texttt{=IF(logical\_test,value\_if\_true,value\_if\_false)}$$

The first argument of the IF function is the **logical_test**. This is the hypothesis to be tested, which results in a TRUE or FALSE value. This argument can consist of any of the following:

- The value TRUE or FALSE
- A reference to a cell containing a TRUE or FALSE value
- A relational expression resulting in a single TRUE or FALSE value
- A Boolean logical function (AND, OR, NOT) resulting in a single TRUE or FALSE value
- Any other formula that results in a TRUE or FALSE value

The second argument of the IF function is the **value_if_true**. This value is applied only if the condition in the first argument is evaluated as TRUE. This argument can simply be a text string to display a label, which is what Eric wants to do, or it can contain a cell reference or even formulas containing operators and/or nested functions. If you want the argument to display a text label, you must enclose the text within quotation marks; otherwise, Excel interprets the text as a named range.

The third argument of the IF function is the **value_if_false**. This value is applied only if the condition in the first argument is evaluated as FALSE. Again, this argument can simply be a text label to be displayed or it can contain cell references, formulas, operators, and/ or nested functions. This third argument is considered to be optional. If it is omitted from the function, a FALSE value is displayed if the IF statement is evaluated to be FALSE, although this is not the recommended way to structure an IF function. To return a blank cell in an IF function, you can include an empty text string " ".

How To

Write a Simple IF Function

1. Select the cell in which you want to write the IF function.

2. Type =IF(to begin the function.

3. Enter the first argument for the function, the logical test, followed by a comma.

4. Enter the second argument for the function, the value if the logical test results in a TRUE value, followed by a comma.

5. Enter the third argument for the function, the value if the logical test results in a FALSE value.

6. Type a closing parenthesis,), to end the function.

Writing an IF Function with a Logical Test That Evaluates TRUE/FALSE Values

To perform the task of displaying "credit approved" or "credit denied" based on the corresponding Boolean value in column H, Eric can write a formula in cell I3 containing an IF function, as follows:

`=IF(H3,"credit approved","credit denied")`

The first argument, the logical test, simply references a cell that contains a Boolean value. So, this first argument tests whether cell H3 contains the value TRUE or the value FALSE. The value_if_true and value_if_false arguments are the text strings that will be displayed if the logical test is TRUE or FALSE, respectively. So, if cell H3 contains the value TRUE, then the text string "credit approved" will be displayed in cell I3; otherwise, the text string "credit denied" will be displayed in cell I3. Eric copies this formula down the column relatively, to determine if each customer was approved or denied credit, as shown in Figure 4.19.

Figure 4.19: Using the IF function to identify the credit decision

IF function displays a text label indicating the current credit approval status

	fx =IF(H3, "credit approved", "credit denied")

	A	B	C	D	E	F	G	H	I	J
1	TheZone Customer Accounts - Credit & Payment Status									
2	Customer Name	Customer Type	Current Balance Due	30-Days Past Due	60-Days Past Due	90-Days Past Due	Total Past Due Balance	Current Credit Status	Current Credit Status Detail	
3	Athletic Gear Corp.	A	$8,612	$ 0	$ 0	$ 0	$ 0	TRUE	credit approved	
4	Baltimore O's	B	0	0	0	0	0	TRUE	credit approved	
5	Baseball & More	A	2,345	3,473	5,557	4,862	13,892	TRUE	credit approved	
6	Canadian Ski Club	C	0	345	0	150	495	TRUE	credit approved	
7	Everything Golf	A	0	0	2,000	899	2,899	FALSE	credit denied	
8	Sports & Stuff	A	0	14,000	383	0	14,383	FALSE	credit denied	
9										
10										

Writing an IF Function with a Logical Test That Performs a Simple Calculation

Next, Eric wants to look at several schemes of applying penalties to those accounts with past due balances. TheZone is considering several alternatives in an effort to discourage late payments and cut down on interest expenses. At the same time, the alternative must be chosen carefully, taking into consideration how it could affect sales and customer relations.

The first alternative being considered is a flat fee of $25 charged against all past due accounts. Columns C through G of the Status worksheet (Figure 4.19) list the balances due on each customer's account, and how many days past due each amount is. To evaluate the effect of the first alternative, a flat fee of $25 as a finance charge, Eric needs to calculate a total balance including this finance charge using the following criteria:

- For customers who have no total past due balance (column G), the total balance including the finance charge will be equal to the customer's current balance (column C).
- For customers who have a total past due balance greater than 0 (column G), the total balance including the finance charge will be equal to the customer's current balance (column C), plus the customer's total past due balance (column G), plus the $25 finance charge.

How can Eric apply this logic in the worksheet? In this situation, he wants to determine if the total past due balance is equal to 0 and, if it is, he wants to simply display the current balance. If the total past due balance is not equal to 0, then he wants Excel to complete the following calculation: current balance + total past due balance + 25. So, instead of simply displaying a TRUE or FALSE value, Eric wants Excel to complete one action if the formula evaluates to TRUE and another if it evaluates to FALSE. Consequently, Eric needs to use an IF function that performs a calculation.

Figure 4.20 shows a decision tree Eric created to help illustrate this logic. In a decision tree, a logical test is represented by a diamond shape. Stemming from the logical test is one action to take if the test is TRUE and another action to take if it is FALSE; these actions are presented in rectangles.

Figure 4.20: Decision tree to evaluate new total balance

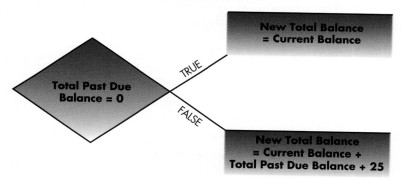

What will the first argument of the IF function be for this problem? The logical test is whether the past due balance is 0, which can be expressed as the relational expression G3=0 (for the first customer in the worksheet). The second argument is the result to be displayed if the test is TRUE; in this case, the current balance, which is in cell C3, should be displayed. The third argument is the result to be displayed if the test is FALSE, which is represented by the numerical expression C3+G3+25 (current balance + past due balance + 25). In Excel syntax, the formula is constructed as follows:

```
=IF(G3=0,C3,C3+G3+25)
```

This formula will work quite well as is; however, Eric knows that the finance charge value (currently $25) is subject to change. So, he decides to insert several rows at the top of the Status worksheet to explicitly list this input value, as shown in Figure 4.21. He also updates the formula, which is now located in cell J6, to the following:

$$\text{=IF(G6=0,C6,C6+G6+B\$2)}$$

Because each cell reference for a balance changes relatively when the formula is copied down the column, no absolute referencing is required for them. However, the value in cell B2 (penalty fee representing the finance charge) should not change when copied down column J. Therefore, the row in this cell reference must be absolute, because the formula is copied only down the column and not across rows. The results are shown in Figure 4.21.

Figure 4.21: Using an IF function to calculate the total balance including finance charge

IF function determines if the total past duebalance = 0; if true, the current balance due is displayed; if false, the result of the calculation is displayed

	A	B	C	D	E	F	G	H	I	J	K
			fx	=IF(G6=0,C6,C6+G6+B$2)							
1	Data Inputs:										
2	Base Penalty Fee	$ 25									
3											
4	TheZone Customer Accounts - Credit & Payment Status										
5	Customer Name	Customer Type	Current Balance Due	30-Days Past Due	60-Days Past Due	90-Days Past Due	Total Past Due Balance	Current Credit Status	Current Credit Status Detail	Total Balance including Finance Charge	
6	Athletic Gear Corp.	A	$8,612	$ 0	$ 0	$ 0	$ 0	TRUE	credit approved	$ 8,612	
7	Baltimore O's	B	0	0	0	0	0	TRUE	credit approved	0	
8	Baseball & More	A	2,345	3,473	5,557	4,862	13,892	TRUE	credit approved	16,262	
9	Canadian Ski Club	C	0	345	0	150	495	TRUE	credit approved	520	
10	Everything Golf	A	0	0	2,000	899	2,899	FALSE	credit denied	2,924	
11	Sports & Stuff	A	0	14,000	383	0	14,383	FALSE	credit denied	14,408	
12											

Could Eric have written the expression =IF(G6<>0,C6+G6+B$2,C6) instead? This formula is logically equivalent to the formula shown in Figure 4.21. The only difference is that this alternative formula uses a logical test to determine if the total past due balance is *not equal to 0* instead of testing to determine if it is *equal to 0*. Consequently, the value_if_true and value_if_false arguments are switched. What if a total past due value was negative? If this was a possibility, the logical test would need to be written as G6>0 instead of G6<>0. As you can see, there are often several ways of implementing a set of criteria with an IF function.

Best Practice

Using the IF Function Appropriately
Sometimes, users are tempted to include an IF function in a formula even when it is not required. When you are only comparing two values and require only a TRUE or FALSE result, an IF function is not needed. For example, if you simply want to determine if the total past due balance is greater than 0, you only need to write the formula =G6>0 to produce a TRUE or FALSE result. The formula =IF(G6>0,TRUE,FALSE) produces the same result, but is a more complicated expression and, therefore, is not recommended.

WRITING IF FUNCTIONS WITH NESTED FUNCTIONS

As Eric continues to develop the Status worksheet to assess and apply penalties, the managers in the accounts receivable group have determined that a simple finance charge of $25 might not be sufficient to deter customers from not paying their bills, especially those bills that are over 90 days past due. Furthermore, this charge might not always be sufficient to cover the interest expense TheZone incurs from not having collected funds. An additional penalty surcharge has been suggested under certain circumstances, as follows:

- If the 90-days past due amount is greater than $200, then an additional surcharge will be imposed of either $100 or 10% of the 90-days past due balance, whichever is higher.
- If the 90-days past due amount is not greater than $200, then no additional surcharge will be imposed, and a value of $0 should be displayed.

Eric needs to calculate this additional penalty as a separate value on the worksheet. Because the criteria might need to be modified depending on the outcomes, he again inserts additional rows at the top of the worksheet to list these input values, as shown in Figure 4.22.

Figure 4.22: Additional rows with new data inputs

New input values added

	A	B	C	D	E	F	G	H	I	J	K
1	Data Inputs:										
2	Base Penalty Fee	$ 25									
3	Minimum 90-Day Balance for Surcharge	$ 200									
4	Minimum Surcharge	$ 100									
5	Surcharge Percentage	10%									
6											
7	TheZone Customer Accounts - Credit & Payment Status										
8	Customer Name	Customer Type	Current Balance Due	30-Days Past Due	60-Days Past Due	90-Days Past Due	Total Past Due Balance	Current Credit Status	Current Credit Status Detail	Total Balance including Finance Charge	
9	Athletic Gear Corp.	A	$ 8,612	$ 0	$ 0	$ 0	$ 0	TRUE	credit approved	$ 8,612	
10	Baltimore O's	B	0	0	0	0	0	TRUE	credit approved	0	
11	Baseball & More	A	2,345	3,473	5,557	4,862	13,892	TRUE	credit approved	16,262	
12	Canadian Ski Club	C	0	345	0	150	495	TRUE	credit approved	520	
13	Everything Golf	A	0	0	2,000	899	2,899	FALSE	credit denied	2,924	
14	Sports & Stuff	A	0	14,000	383	0	14,383	FALSE	credit denied	14,408	
15											

The new inputs are as follows:

- Minimum 90-day past due balance before applying the surcharge—$200 (cell B3)
- Minimum surcharge value—$100 (cell B4)
- Surcharge percentage—10% (cell B5)

Again, Eric uses an IF function because the problem requires him to make a decision and then generate different values depending on whether the logical test results in a TRUE or FALSE value. So far, Eric has used an IF function where the resulting values are generated either by displaying a simple text message or the results of a simple arithmetic formula. In this case, the problem requires him to use a nested function to calculate the necessary values. One method of solving the problem is to use the MAX function to select the higher value of $100 or 10% of the 90-days past due amount. Consider each of the three arguments of this IF function:

- **Logical_test**—This test must determine if the 90-days past due amount is greater than $200. In this case, the logical test requires the following relational expression: 90-days past due amount > 200.
- **Value_if_true**—If the logical test results in a TRUE value, the worksheet needs to display either the value $100 or 10% of the 90-days past due amount, whichever is larger. Recall that the MAX function can select the highest value from a list of values, in this case MAX(100, .1*90-Days Past Due Amount). This MAX function must be nested inside the IF function as the value_if_true argument. If the logical test evaluates to a TRUE value, then Excel will calculate the value of this nested expression.
- **Value_if_false**—If the logical test results in a FALSE value, the worksheet needs to display the value $0.

Now these elements can be translated into Excel syntax to create the following formula, which Eric will enter in cell K9 of the Status worksheet:

$$IF(F9>B3,MAX(B4,B5*F9),0)$$

Because this formula must be copied down the column, Eric needs to consider which of the cell references copy relatively and which copy absolutely. Each of the input values (cells B3, B4, and B5) must remain the same as the formula is copied down the column, so each must contain an absolute row reference. Figure 4.23 illustrates the formula and describes its arguments.

Figure 4.23: IF function with nested function for value_if_true

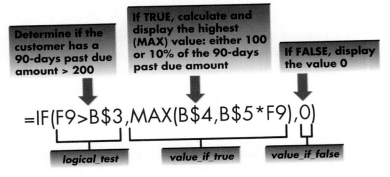

Eric enters the formula in cell K9 and copies it down the column. The resulting values are displayed in the worksheet, as shown in Figure 4.24.

Figure 4.24: Results of the 90-days past due surcharge calculation

IF function determines if the 90-days past due amount > 200; if true, the MAX of 100 or 10% of 90-days past due amount is displayed; if false, 0 is displayed

K9	▼	f_x	=IF(F9>B$3, MAX(B$4, B$5*F9),0)								

	A	B	C	D	E	F	G	H	I	J	K	L
1	Data Inputs:											
2	Base Penalty Fee	$ 25										
3	Minimum 90-Day Balance for Surcharge	$ 200										
4	Minimum Surcharge	$ 100										
5	Surcharge Percentage	10%										
6												
7	TheZone Customer Accounts - Credit & Payment Status											
8	Customer Name	Customer Type	Current Balance Due	30-Days Past Due	60-Days Past Due	90-Days Past Due	Total Past Due Balance	Current Credit Status	Current Credit Status Detail	Total Balance including Finance Charge	90-Day Past Due Surcharge	
9	Athletic Gear Corp.	A	$ 8,612	$ 0	$ 0	$ 0	$ 0	TRUE	credit approved	$ 8,612	$ 0	
10	Baltimore O's	B	0	0	0	0	0	TRUE	credit approved	0	0	
11	Baseball & More	A	2,345	3,473	5,557	4,862	13,892	TRUE	credit approved	16,262	486	
12	Canadian Ski Club	C	0	345	0	150	495	TRUE	credit approved	520	0	
13	Everything Golf	A	0	0	2,000	899	2,899	FALSE	credit denied	2,924	100	
14	Sports & Stuff	A	0	14,000	383	0	14,383	FALSE	credit denied	14,408	0	
15												

CONSTRUCTING A SIMPLE NESTED IF FUNCTION

Another alternative penalty scheme under consideration to discourage customers from being delinquent in paying their bills is to charge a different monthly penalty depending on how late the payments are. This could be used instead of the across-the-board $25 penalty or the previously calculated surcharge. This alternative penalty would work as follows:

- Customers who have balances of 90-days past due would be charged a $100 flat fee.
- Customers who have no 90-days past due balance but have a 60-days past due balance would be charged a $50 flat fee.
- Customers who have only a 30-days past due balance would be charged a $25 flat fee.
- Customers who have no past due balance would not be charged a penalty fee.

As you have seen, an IF function can be used to evaluate a logical test, such as determining if the 90-days past due balance is greater than 0, with only two resulting values: a value_if_true and a value_if_false. In this case, however, if the logical test results in a FALSE value, another calculation is needed to determine if the value of the 60-days past due balance is greater than 0—and, if that results in a FALSE value, perform yet another calculation.

How can Eric write a formula to ask a question, then another question depending on the outcome of the first question, and so on? In the previous formula, Eric nested the MAX function so that its resulting value was one component of the IF function. He can use a similar technique of nesting IF functions, one inside the other.

Before trying to solve this directly, it might be easier to first understand the logic by constructing a decision tree to illustrate the process, as shown in Figure 4.25.

Figure 4.25: Decision tree with nested IF

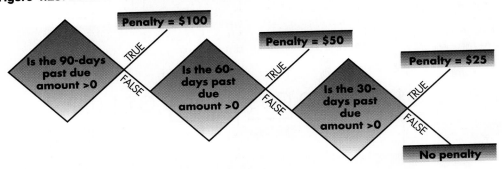

Using this logic, Eric can establish what his formula will look like for the first customer listed, Athletic Gear Corp., using a sort of a pseudocode, which is a kind of shorthand formula showing the structure of the formula without the syntactical details. After doing so, Eric can easily substitute the appropriate cell references. The following is the pseudocode for Eric's formula:

```
IF(Athletic Gear Corp.'s 90-days past due amount >0, then
    the penalty is $100, otherwise
      IF(Athletic Gear Corp.'s 60-days past due amount is >0,
         then the penalty is $50, otherwise
           IF(Athletic Gear Corp.'s 30-days past due balance
              is >0, then the penalty is $25, otherwise no
                 penalty, or $0)
```

Eric sets up an additional input area on the Status worksheet in cells D1:G4 and plans to use column L to calculate this alternative penalty scheme, converting his pseudocode into a formula in Excel syntax. The values in the cells containing the penalty amounts (cells G2:G4) should not change when the formula is copied down the column, so these cell references must have an absolute row reference. The resulting formula is illustrated in Figure 4.26.

Figure 4.26: Nested IF function for the alternative penalty scheme

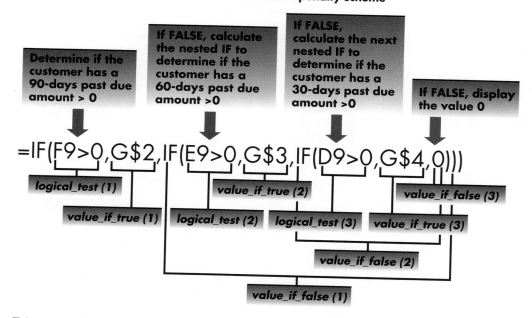

Eric enters the formula in cell L9 and copies it down the column. The resulting worksheet is shown in Figure 4.27.

Figure 4.27: Results of the nested IF for the alternative penalty scheme

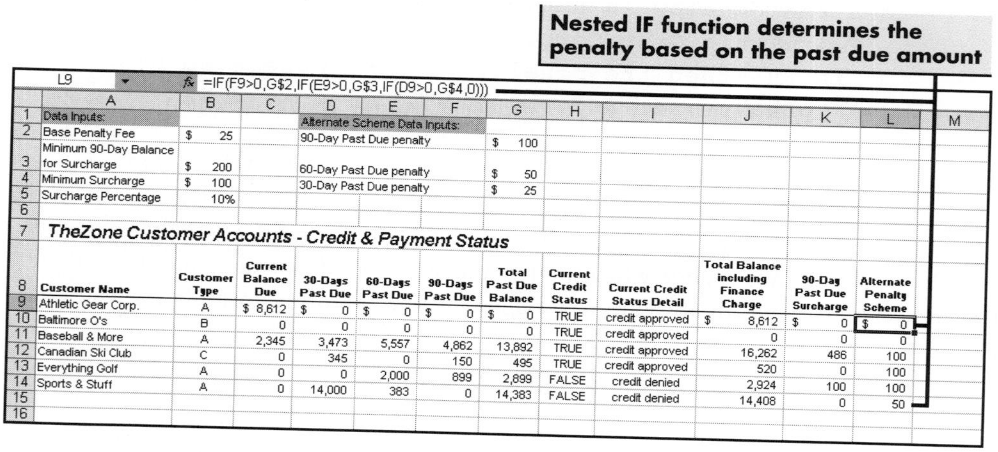

Nested IF function determines the penalty based on the past due amount

	A	B	C	D	E	F	G	H	I	J	K	L	M
	L9			fx	=IF(F9>0,G$2,IF(E9>0,G$3,IF(D9>0,G$4,0)))								
1	Data Inputs:			Alternate Scheme Data Inputs:									
2	Base Penalty Fee	$ 25		90-Day Past Due penalty			$ 100						
3	Minimum 90-Day Balance for Surcharge	$ 200		60-Day Past Due penalty			$ 50						
4	Minimum Surcharge	$ 100		30-Day Past Due penalty			$ 25						
5	Surcharge Percentage	10%											
6													
7	TheZone Customer Accounts - Credit & Payment Status												
8	Customer Name	Customer Type	Current Balance Due	30-Days Past Due	60-Days Past Due	90-Days Past Due	Total Past Due Balance	Current Credit Status	Current Credit Status Detail	Total Balance including Finance Charge	90-Day Past Due Surcharge	Alternate Penalty Scheme	
9	Athletic Gear Corp.	A	$ 8,612	$ 0	$ 0	$ 0	$ 0	TRUE	credit approved	$ 8,612	$ 0	$ 0	
10	Baltimore O's	B	0	0	0	0	0	TRUE	credit approved	0	0	0	
11	Baseball & More	A	2,345	3,473	5,557	4,862	13,892	TRUE	credit approved	16,262	486	100	
12	Canadian Ski Club	C	0	345	0	150	495	TRUE	credit approved	520	0	100	
13	Everything Golf	A	0	0	2,000	899	2,899	FALSE	credit denied	2,924	100	100	
14	Sports & Stuff	A	0	14,000	383	0	14,383	FALSE	credit denied	14,408	0	50	
15													
16													

How are the formula arguments evaluated? Excel begins by evaluating the first IF function. If logical_test results in a TRUE value, Excel evaluates the value_if_true argument; otherwise, it evaluates the value_if_false argument. In a nested IF function, the second argument (value_if_true) and/or the third argument (value_if_false) can contain another

IF function. Excel allows seven levels of nesting in this manner. In Eric's formula, both the first and second IF functions have nested IFs for the third argument (value_if_false).

In this case, if the customer has a 90-days past due amount greater than 0, *logical_test (1)*, Excel returns the *value_if_true (1)* result of $100 and the evaluation ends. None of the other arguments are evaluated once the formula encounters a condition that is met. Because Athletic Gear Corp. does not have a 90-days past due amount greater than 0 (its amount is equal to 0), Excel evaluates the *value_if_false (1)* argument, which, in turn, is another IF function.

Now, Excel evaluates the second IF function, or *logical_test (2)*, which determines if the customer has a 60-days past due amount greater than 0. If this test results in a TRUE value, Excel returns the *value_if_true (2)* result of $50 and the evaluation ends. In Figure 4.27, note that the customer Sports & Stuff meets this condition—a 60-days past due amount greater than 0 (cell E14), so the result of the nested IF function for this customer is $50 (cell L14). However, the customer Athletic Gear Corp. again does not meet the condition, so in this case, Excel next evaluates the *value_if_false (2)* argument—which, in turn, is yet another IF function. The customer Athletic Gear Corp. does not meet this condition either (a 30-days past due amount greater than 0); in fact, this customer has no past due amount at all. So, the amount $0 is returned and displayed in cell L9, which is the result of the *value_if_false (3)* argument of the last nested IF function.

In Figure 4.27, note that cells L11, L12, and L13 each display the amount $100. Each of these customers met the condition of a 90-days past due amount greater than 0 (cells F11, F12, and F13, respectively), so these customers would be assessed the highest penalty under this alternative penalty scheme.

The Order of Logical Tests for Non-Mutually Exclusive Criteria

Eric's formula first determines if an amount is past due in the 90-days category before testing for 60-days or 30-days past due amounts. Does it matter which condition is tested for first? If each customer falls into only one category (90-days, 60-days, or 30-days), it does not matter which condition is tested for first. This is not the case here, however, because a given customer can have a 30-days past due amount greater than 0 *and* also have a 90-days past due amount greater than 0. If the formula first tested for the 30-days past due amount, then the $25 penalty would be applied before the formula ever determined if the customer had a 90-days past due amount.

Consider, for example, the customer Baseball & More, which has past due amounts in all three categories. The formula as written first tests the 90-days past due amount, resulting in the value $100 in cell L11 (see Figure 4.27). What would happen if the formula was written with the order of logical arguments switched, testing the 30-days past due amount first, as follows:

```
=IF(D9>0,G$4,IF(E9>0,G$3,IF(F9>0,G$2,0)))
```

This formula would result in an incorrect value of $25 for the customer Baseball & More. This formula first tests to see if the 30-days past due amount is greater than 0 (D9>0). Because this results in a TRUE value, the value_if_true argument (G$4) is returned. In this formula, once the function evaluates an argument to be TRUE, the evaluation ends; consequently, this formula would never test to determine if the customer has a 90-days past due amount greater than 0. So, when writing a formula with nested IF functions to determine non-mutually exclusive criteria, the order in which the logical tests are placed must match the established criteria.

The Order of Logical Tests for Mutually Exclusive Criteria

In other situations, the criteria is mutually exclusive, where one data element cannot fall into more than one category. The following is an example of mutually exclusive criteria:

- If the customer is a Customer Type A, apply a $50 penalty.
- If the customer is a Customer Type B, apply a $100 penalty.
- For all other customer types, apply a $150 penalty.

Because each customer is assigned to a single type category, as listed in column B on the Status worksheet, the criteria is mutually exclusive and only one TRUE value can result. Consider the following formula:

$$=IF(B9="A",50,IF(B9="B",100,150))$$

With this formula, the customer Athletic Gear Corp. would be charged a $50 penalty because it is identified as a Customer Type A. No matter what order the logical tests are in, the penalty applied will be $50 for this customer because it is a type A (cell B9). So, the formula =IF(B9="B",100,IF(B9="A",50,150)) would produce the same results, because the criteria is mutually exclusive. Therefore, when writing a formula with nested IF functions to determine mutually exclusive criteria, the logical tests can be placed in any order.

The Order of Logical Tests for Criteria Between a Range of Values

In cases where you want to test criteria between a range of values, placing the logical tests in a specific order—either from highest to lowest or lowest to highest—can save a considerable amount of work. Consider the following criteria for applying a penalty based on the total past due balance:

- If the total past due balance is less than $1000, then the penalty is $25.
- If the total past due balance is at least $1000 but less than $5000, then the penalty is $50.
- If the total past due balance is $5000 or greater, then the penalty is $100.

In this case, could you test to see if the total past due amount is at least $1000 but less than $5000 first, and then test to see if the amount is less than $1000? The logical test would have to first determine that the amount is both greater than or equal to $1000 *and* less than $5000, as follows:

```
=IF(AND(G9>=1000,G9<5000),50,IF(G9<1000,25,100))
```

This formula requires nesting an AND function in the logical test argument of the IF function. On the other hand, if the formula first tested either the lowest value and went up in order, or first tested the highest value and went down in order, the logical tests could be simplified. Using ascending order, you could write the following formula:

```
=IF(G9<1000,25,IF(G9<5000,50,100))
```

Using descending order, you could write the following formula:

```
=IF(G9>=5000,100,IF(G9>=1000,50,100))
```

With the ascending order formula, if a customer has a total past due balance of $2,899, Excel first determines if $2,899 is less than 1000. This results in a FALSE value, so Excel next evaluates the value_if_false argument—which is the logical test of the second IF function. This test determines if $2,899 is less than $5000; it does not also have to determine if the value is at least 1000, because the first logical test (G9<1000) takes care of this. If the value was less than 1000 (in other words, it was not at least 1000), Excel executes the value_if_true argument and returns a value of $25. Therefore, the second logical test would never be executed.

So, by evaluating the conditions in a specific order, you can simplify the task. This technique works well when evaluating problems with three or four range categories, up to the maximum of seven levels of nesting in a formula. In a later chapter, you'll learn a technique that is much more effective when a large number of ranges must be considered.

As you have seen, formulas that contain IF functions and nested functions can be powerful tools for data analysis. In the next level, Eric will revisit the customer credit evaluation developed in Level 1, expanding and combining these tools to further automate the decision-making process.

Steps To Success: Level 2

TheZone accounts payable group can sometimes be delinquent in paying TheZone's vendors in a timely manner. In some cases, this is a deliberate effort to hold off payment as long as possible; in others, it is simply an oversight. The accounts payable group has developed a worksheet listing some of the vendors to which TheZone owes past due balances, organized by past due categories of 30-days past due, 60-days past due, and 90-days past due. Figure 4.28 shows this worksheet.

Figure 4.28: TheZone's accounts payable analysis

	A	B	C	D	E	F	G	H	I	J	K	L
1	Fixed Fee & 90 Day Penalties			Graduated Penalties - Range				Penalty		Category Penalties		
2	Fixed Fee Penalty	$ 50		Graduated penalty <			$ 1,000	$ 0		Utilities	10%	
3	90-day min amt for penalty	$ 100		Graduated penalty >1000 but <			5,000	100		Labor	15%	
4	90-day penalty percentage	10%		Graduated penalty >=			5,000	200		Other	5%	
5												
6												
7	TheZone Accounts Payable - Outstanding Balance Report											
8	Vendor Name	Category	Applies Fixed Penalty	30-Days Past Due	60-Days Past Due	90-Days Past Due	Total Past Due Balance	Fixed Penalty	90-Day Penalty	Graduated Penalty	Category Penalty	
9	RTF Electric	Utilities	TRUE	$ 16,254	$ 0	$ 0	$ 16,254					
10	Ross County Water & Sewer	Utilities	FALSE	1,435	0	0	1,435					
11	YNC Trucking	Transportation	TRUE	0	0	3,300	3,300					
12	Italian Leather Group Ltd.	Raw Materials	TRUE	6,756	0	5,674	12,430					
13	Union Plastics	Raw Materials	TRUE	0	436	0	436					
14	Freight to Go	Transportation	FALSE	0	0	873	873					
15	Temps R'Us	Labor	FALSE	2,700	0	0	2,700					
16	Notworth Telephone	Telephone	TRUE	0	0	2,345	2,345					
17												
18												

Recently, some vendors have started to apply different penalty and discount schemes to overdue accounts, similar to those being proposed by TheZone's accounts receivables group. As a preemptive measure, you have been asked to help calculate some of these possible penalty scenarios that TheZone might incur based on its current outstanding balances. A list of these past due balances is provided in the workbook named Unpaid.xls. This file also contains the data input values that you need to calculate the penalties in the top portion of the worksheet (see Figure 4.28). Keep in mind that you should use cell references in your formulas wherever possible.

Complete the following:

1. Open the workbook named **Unpaid.xls** located in the Chapter 4 folder, and then save it as **Unpaid Invoice Penalties.xls**.

2. Some vendors have agreed on an industry standard penalty of $50 on all past due accounts regardless of the past due amount or number of days past due. These vendors are identified by the value TRUE in the corresponding row of column C. Write a formula in column H, which can be copied down the column, listing the penalty for the corresponding account: $50 for vendors who are participating in this standard penalty and $0 for all other vendors. Only vendors who are owed past due balances are listed on this sheet.

3. Calculate another possible penalty whereby only those accounts with 90-days past due balances are owed a fee. In column I, write a formula that can be copied down the column to calculate the penalty based on the following criteria:

- For accounts with a 90-days past due balance of $100 or more, apply a fee of 10% of the 90-days past due balance.
- For all other accounts, no penalty is applied.

4. Another penalty scheme being used by vendors is a graduated method based on the total past due balances (column G). In column J, write a formula that can be copied down the column to calculate the penalty based on the following criteria:

   - For accounts with a total past due balance of less than $1000, do not apply a penalty.
   - For accounts with a past due balance of greater than or equal to $1000 but less than $5000, apply a penalty of $100.
   - For accounts with a past due balance of $5000 or more, apply a penalty of $200.

5. Penalties can sometimes be specific to vendor category. In column K, write a formula that can be copied down the column to calculate the penalty based on the following criteria:

   - For vendors in the Utilities category, apply a fee of 10% of the total past due balance (column G).
   - For vendors in the Labor category, apply a fee of 15% of the total past due balance.
   - For vendors in all other categories, apply a fee of 5% of the total past due balance.

6. Format columns H through K to match column G.

7. Save and close the Unpaid Invoice Penalties.xls workbook.

LEVEL 3
CREATING COMPLEX LOGICAL CONSTRUCTS FOR SOLVING PROBLEMS

EXCEL 2003 SKILLS TRAINING

- **Create formulas using the IF function**
- **Use logical functions (NOT)**
- **Use logical functions (OR)**

EVALUATING MORE COMPLEX CRITERIA

The previous level explored relational expressions in formulas and nested functions. This level presents similar techniques to create more complex logical constructs—combinations of multiple logical operations—to determine if *none of* the criteria are TRUE for a list of items, and even if *only certain* criteria are TRUE for a list of items.

In addition to working with logical constructs that require nesting AND, OR, and NOT functions, this level also covers, in more depth, the techniques of nesting IF functions to solve more complex problems.

Eric is now ready to go back to the CreditData worksheet in the Customer Credit and Payment History workbook to come up with a single recommendation regarding credit approval, which he can then provide to the accounts receivable manager and the finance group for final analysis and approval. He will use the information already generated based on customer accounts plus additional guidelines from management to determine the recommendation.

Recall that in Level 1, Eric created formulas using relational operators and Boolean logical functions (AND, OR, and NOT) to evaluate TheZone's credit approval rules, as follows:

Rule #1: *Accept* a customer who has a past due balance that is less than 10% of this year's total sales. This is not calculated for new customers.

Rule #2: *Accept* a customer who has either a composite credit appraisal value of 1 or a PAYDEX score over 90.

Rule #3: *Accept* a customer who has all of the following: a net worth of at least $500,000; a composite credit appraisal value of 2 or lower; a PAYDEX score over 70; and a stress risk class of 1.

Figure 4.29 shows the current CreditData worksheet. Notice that Eric chose to apply the conditional formatting so that all TRUE values in the range K3:M21 appear in a bold, italic font.

Figure 4.29: Customer credit analysis revisited

	A	B	C	D	E	F	G	H	I	J	K	L	M	N
1	Accounts Receivable Department - Customer Credit Analysis													
2	Customer Name	Current Credit Limit	Previous Year's Sales	Current Year's Sales	Past Due Balance	Net Worth in (000)	D&B Credit Rating Class	D&B Composite Credit Appraisal (1 Best)	D&B PAYDEX (100 Best)	D&B Stress Risk Class (1 Best)	Rule #1	Rule #2	Rule #3	
3	Athletic Gear Corp.	$ 9,000	$15,382	$11,952	$ 0	$ 450	BA	4	15	3	TRUE	FALSE	FALSE	
4	Baltimore O's	39,000	10,033	7,789	0	1,950	3A	1	51	1	TRUE	TRUE	FALSE	
5	Baseball & More	75,000	60,009	55,342	13,892	37,500	4A	2	70	1	FALSE	FALSE	FALSE	
6	Canadian Ski Club	33,000	35,039	50,921	495	1,650	BA	2	43	1	TRUE	FALSE	FALSE	
7	Concord Pro Shop					10,000	4A	1	91	1		TRUE	TRUE	
8	Everything Golf	25,000	15,221	9,483	2,899	1,250	3A	3	76	1	FALSE	FALSE	FALSE	
9	Lake Pro Shops	42,000	80,498	81,126	0	2,100	3A	2	87	1	TRUE	FALSE	TRUE	
10	Mars Dept. Store	27,000	35,354	20,666	0	213	BB	3	94	1	TRUE	TRUE	FALSE	
11	RG Bradley	46,000	90,970	18,343	0	2,300	3A	1	21	1	TRUE	TRUE	FALSE	
12	RX for Sports	15,000	5,663	3,014	0	750	2A	1	59	1	TRUE	TRUE	FALSE	
13	School Sports Supply	45,000	50,278	32,338	0	2,250	3A	3	91	1	TRUE	TRUE	FALSE	
14	Ski World	26,000	25,864	28,154	0	300	BA	2	82	1	TRUE	FALSE	FALSE	
15	Sneaker Kingdom	45,000	40,157	25,379	0	2,250	3A	2	71	1	TRUE	FALSE	TRUE	
16	Sports & Stuff	15,000	15,898	14,732	14,383	450	BA	1	67	1	FALSE	TRUE	FALSE	
17	Toy Kingdom	22,000	10,073	1,047	0	1,100	3A	3	14	1	TRUE	FALSE	FALSE	
18	Under the Sea	45,000	95,411	64,418	0	150	CB	4	79	2	TRUE	FALSE	FALSE	
19	US Olympic Team	20,000	5,621	6,171	0	1,000	3A	1	87	1	TRUE	TRUE	TRUE	
20	WWW Sports Inc.	100,000	60,009	60,354	0	500,000	5A	2	97	1	TRUE	TRUE	TRUE	
21	Zip & Sons	10,000	15,490	22,760	0	620	1A	2	96	1	TRUE	TRUE	TRUE	
22														
23														
24							Do any meet the rule?				TRUE	TRUE	TRUE	
25							Do none meet the rule?				FALSE	FALSE	FALSE	
26														

Reviewing the worksheet, it is not always clear how to proceed in finalizing the credit approval for a particular customer. The determination is fairly straightforward for those customers who have a TRUE value for all three rules and for those who have a FALSE value for all three rules. But what about those customers with combinations of TRUE and FALSE values? Management has provided Eric with the following directions regarding credit approval decisions:

- Automatically **reject** credit if a customer meets *none of* the approval rules. Such customers have demonstrated none of the desired attributes—either financially through their D&B credit information or through their past dealings with TheZone.
- Recommend **further evaluation** if a customer meets either of the following sets of critieria:

  - The customer has a TRUE value for *only* Rule #1 (that is, has less than a 10% past due balance). While such a customer has a satisfactory payment history with TheZone, its D&B financial data indicates possible problems in its future ability to pay.
  - The customer has a TRUE value for *only* Rule #2 and/or Rule #3 and has a FALSE value for Rule #1. While such a customer has satisfactory D&B financial indicators, its previous payment history with TheZone is less than satisfactory.

  Customer accounts identified for further evaluation will be handled manually by an experienced accountant, requiring additional financial information and consideration of this customer's current business relationship with TheZone.
- Automatically **accept** for credit those customers who have a TRUE value for Rule #1 and a TRUE value for either Rule #2 and/or Rule#3. These customers have demonstrated both financial stability and a satisfactory payment history with TheZone.

Eric now needs to assess the customer data against this final set of criteria and return one of the following results for each customer: "Reject," "Further Evaluate," or "Accept." How can he analyze criteria and return a value other than TRUE or FALSE? Recall that the IF function can evaluate a set of criteria and return one value if it is TRUE and another value if it is FALSE. By nesting levels of IF functions, multiple sets of criteria can be sequentially analyzed until a final value is returned.

USING AN IF FUNCTION TO COMBINE SETS OF CRITERIA

Before Eric can formulate a specific implementation of the rules, he must explore several aspects of the problem. For example, are the different criteria mutually exclusive, or can a customer fall into more than one category? In fact, the different criteria are mutually exclusive; a customer can fall into only one of the three categories (Accept, Further Evaluate, Reject). So, the order in which the different criteria are analyzed should not matter, except perhaps to make the analysis easier to interpret. In this case, Eric decides to follow the guidelines in the order presented earlier. First, he will determine if a company meets none of the rules (Reject); then if only Rule #1 is met or if only Rules #2 or #3 are met (Further Evaluate); and, finally, if the customer meets the approval criteria (Accept).

Another question to be answered before proposing an implementation is the following: can it be assumed if a customer is neither rejected nor identified for further evaluation that the customer, by default, will fall into the Accept category? Consider the Truth Table shown in Figure 4.30.

Figure 4.30: Truth Table showing all possible combinations of values for Rules 1 through 3

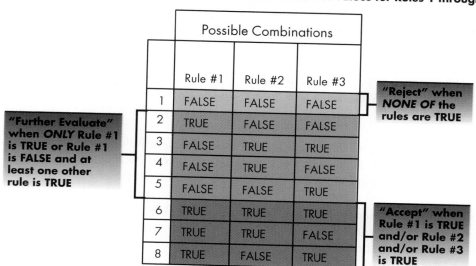

This table lists all possible combinations of values for Rules 1 through 3. There are two possible results for each rule (TRUE or FALSE), resulting in 2^3 ($2*2*2$), or 8 possible outcomes. Outcome 1 at the top of the Truth Table in Figure 4.30 results in a customer's credit being rejected. Outcomes 2 through 5 represent the results for customers who require further evaluation. This leaves outcomes 6 through 8. Do these three remaining outcomes all meet the criteria of a TRUE value for Rule #1 and a TRUE value for either Rule #2 and/or Rule #3, indicating that the customer should be accepted for credit? Yes; each of these three possible combinations contains a TRUE value for Rule #1 and a TRUE value for either Rule #2 or Rule #3, or both. So, a third IF statement is not required. Once the criteria for Reject and Further Evaluate are complete, the only other possible outcome is Accept.

The best way to proceed is to take the information and represent this process schematically in a decision tree, as illustrated in Figure 4.31. First, the rejection criteria will be analyzed, then the further evaluation criteria. And, finally, if a customer is neither rejected nor identified for further evaluation, the customer will automatically be accepted for credit.

Figure 4.31: Decision tree to determine the category: Reject, Further Evaluate, or Accept

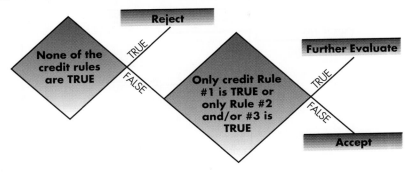

This process can also be represented in pseudocode, as follows:

```
IF(none of the rules are TRUE, "Reject",
   IF(OR(only Rule #1 is TRUE, only Rule #2 and/or Rule #3
      is TRUE), "Further Evaluate", otherwise "Accept")))
```

To implement this formula, Eric will consider each of the components separately and then combine them in cell N3. After building the formula in cell N3, he will copy it down the column. As shown in the pseudocode, this formula requires nested levels of IF statements and Boolean logical constructs within the arguments of the IF statements.

USING THE NONE OF CONSTRUCT

The first step Eric takes is to evaluate if *none of* the credit rules are met. Eric has not yet tested for a "none of" criteria directly. However, recall that he entered the formula =OR(K3:K21) in cell K23 (see Figure 4.32), which determines whether any customer meets the criteria for Rule #1. Then the question "Do none meet the rule?" is asked, with the answer value placed in cell K24. Eric simply flipped the "any" to "none of" by turning the TRUE value to a FALSE. He implemented this by writing the formula =NOT(K23) in cell K24. Note that Eric froze panes in the worksheet so that he could focus more easily on the customers and the three credit rules.

Figure 4.32: Customer credit analysis with "none of" construct

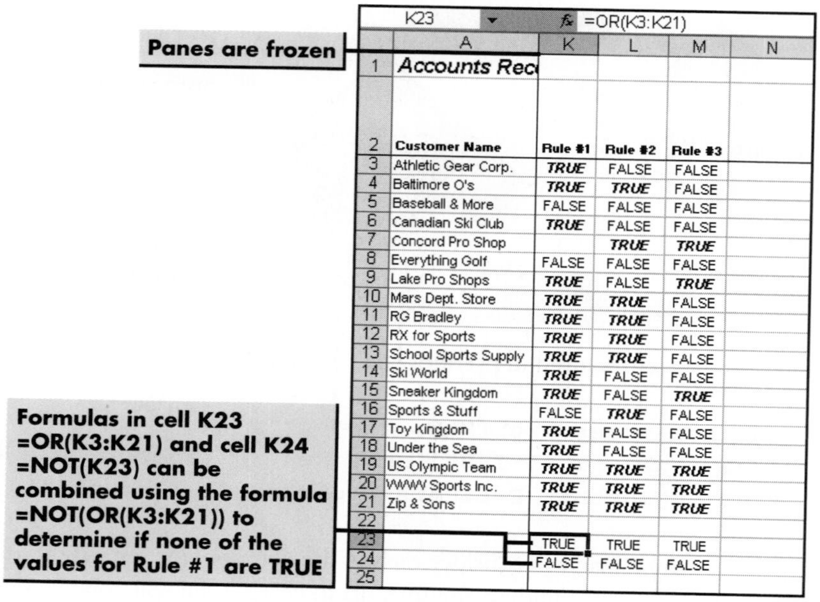

The two steps Eric took can be combined into one by nesting the formula as follows: =NOT(OR(K3:K21)). This formula directly determines (TRUE or FALSE) if none of the customers meet the criteria for Rule #1. The formula essentially finds that, if even one customer meets the criteria, then the statement "none of the customers meet the criteria" is FALSE.

Now, Eric considers how to determine if a customer meets the criteria for *none of* the rules—neither Rule #1, Rule #2, nor Rule #3—as listed in columns K through M of the worksheet. He can use a similar technique by first testing to see if *any* of the rules are TRUE for a specific customer, and then flip the result with a NOT function. The following is the logical test he uses in his formula for the first customer listed, Athletic Gear Corp.:

```
NOT(OR(K3:M3))
```

Eric substitutes this as the logical_test of the first IF statement in the pseudocode, as follows:

```
IF(NOT(OR(K3:M3)), "Reject",
   IF(OR(only Rule #1 is TRUE, only Rule #2 and/or Rule #3
     is TRUE), "Further Evaluate", otherwise "Accept")))
```

To better illustrate which customers will be affected by the Reject criteria, they have been highlighted on the worksheet in Figure 4.33. As you can see, two customers, Baseball & More and Everything Golf, both have all FALSE values for Rules 1 through 3.

Figure 4.33: Customers who will be automatically rejected

	A	K	L	M	N
1	*Accounts Rec*				
2	**Customer Name**	**Rule #1**	**Rule #2**	**Rule #3**	
3	Athletic Gear Corp.	TRUE	FALSE	FALSE	
4	Baltimore O's	TRUE	TRUE	FALSE	
5	Baseball & More	FALSE	FALSE	FALSE	
6	Canadian Ski Club	TRUE	FALSE	FALSE	
7	Concord Pro Shop		TRUE	TRUE	
8	Everything Golf	FALSE	FALSE	FALSE	
9	Lake Pro Shops	TRUE	FALSE	TRUE	
10	Mars Dept. Store	TRUE	TRUE	FALSE	
11	RG Bradley	TRUE	TRUE	FALSE	
12	RX for Sports	TRUE	TRUE	FALSE	
13	School Sports Supply	TRUE	TRUE	FALSE	
14	Ski World	TRUE	FALSE	FALSE	
15	Sneaker Kingdom	TRUE	FALSE	TRUE	
16	Sports & Stuff	FALSE	TRUE	FALSE	
17	Toy Kingdom	TRUE	FALSE	FALSE	
18	Under the Sea	TRUE	FALSE	FALSE	
19	US Olympic Team	TRUE	TRUE	TRUE	
20	WWW Sports Inc.	TRUE	TRUE	TRUE	
21	Zip & Sons	TRUE	TRUE	TRUE	
22					
23		TRUE	TRUE	TRUE	
24		FALSE	FALSE	FALSE	
25					

Customers shaded in gray will be automatically rejected based on the criteria used in the IF function

Best Practice

Implementing the "None Of" Construct Most Efficiently

Another approach to determining if *none of* the rules are TRUE for a specific customer is to figure out if each rule results in a FALSE value. So, if Rule #1, Rule #2, and Rule #3 all result in the value FALSE for a customer, then the statement "None of the rules are true" is TRUE. You can accomplish this by "flipping" the value of each rule with a NOT function to obtain a TRUE value if the rule had a FALSE value, and then combine all values with an AND function to test whether all of the rules are FALSE. The following logical construct is used in this case:

$$=AND(NOT(K3),NOT(L3),NOT(M3))$$

No matter how long the list of values to be checked is, each cell in the range needs to be listed separately using this type of construct. Clearly this method, although useable, is much more cumbersome to execute than the NOT(OR(K3:M3)) construct and, consequently, is not recommended, especially with large lists.

Could you simply write the expression NOT(K3:M3)? No; recall that the syntax of the NOT function evaluates only a single TRUE or FALSE value, not a range of values. This expression is not valid, and cannot be interpreted as either "all the items are FALSE" or as "at least one item is FALSE."

USING THE ONLY CONSTRUCT

The next step in constructing the formula is to determine if *only* Rule #1 evaluates to TRUE and, if so, to recommend further evaluation; *OR* if *only* Rule #2 and/or Rule #3 evaluates to TRUE and not Rule #1, as represented by the following pseudocode:

```
OR(only Rule #1 is TRUE, only Rule #2 and/or Rule #3 is TRUE)
```

How can Eric determine if a customer has *only* a TRUE value for Rule #1 but for neither of the other two rules? Breaking down this part of the problem into smaller logical tasks makes the process clearer. To prove this "only" construct, Eric must prove that *both* of the following statements are TRUE:

- Rule #1 has a TRUE value.

AND

- None of the other rules have a TRUE value (in this instance, both Rule #2 and Rule #3 are FALSE).

Note that an "only" construct always has a positive condition to be evaluated AND a negative condition to be evaluated. An OR function is required for either the positive condition or the negative condition if more than one item being evaluated falls in that category.

To evaluate if either Rule #2 or Rule #3 is TRUE or if both are TRUE, and that Rule #1 is not TRUE, Eric can similarly explain this as follows:

- Rule #2 OR Rule #3 has a TRUE value.

AND

- Rule #1 does not have a TRUE value (it is FALSE).

The diagram in Figure 4.34 illustrates this logic.

Figure 4.34: Defining the Further Evaluate criteria using "only" constructs

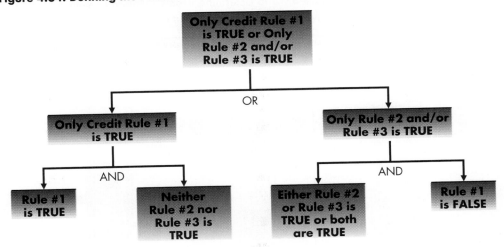

The pseudocode for the Further Evaluate criteria can now be detailed as follows:

```
OR(AND(Rule#1 is TRUE, neither Rule #2 nor Rule #3 is
    TRUE), AND(OR(Rule #2 and/or Rule #3 is TRUE), Rule #1
    is FALSE)))
```

Now Eric needs to translate the statement "This customer *only* has a TRUE value for Rule #1" into Excel syntax. To test if K3 is TRUE, Eric only needs to list the cell reference inside the AND statement. To test if neither L3 nor M3 is TRUE (both are FALSE), Eric can use the *none of* construct he used earlier. Substituting in the appropriate cell references results in the following expression:

```
AND(K3,NOT(OR(L3:M3)))
```

This expression tests that both K3 is TRUE (Rule #1) and that *none of* the other values are TRUE by using an AND function and nesting a "none of" construct inside it as the second argument.

How To

Build an "Only" Construct with Multiple Positive and Negative Items

Consider the example shown in Figure 4.35 to determine if only companies with a current credit limit of more than $50,000 have a TRUE value for Rule #1.

Figure 4.35: Example of an "only" construct containing multiple items in each category

	A	B	K	L	M
1	*Accounts Receivable*				
2	**Customer Name**	**Current Credit Limit**	**Rule #1**	**Rule #2**	**Rule #3**
3	Athletic Gear Corp.	$ 9,000	TRUE	FALSE	FALSE
4	Baltimore O's	39,000	TRUE	TRUE	FALSE
5	Baseball & More	75,000	FALSE	FALSE	FALSE
6	Canadian Ski Club	33,000	TRUE	FALSE	FALSE
7	Concord Pro Shop			TRUE	TRUE
8	Everything Golf	25,000	FALSE	FALSE	FALSE
9	Lake Pro Shops	42,000	TRUE	FALSE	TRUE
10	Mars Dept. Store	27,000	TRUE	TRUE	FALSE
11	RG Bradley	46,000	TRUE	TRUE	FALSE
12	RX for Sports	15,000	TRUE	TRUE	FALSE
13	School Sports Supply	45,000	TRUE	TRUE	FALSE
14	Ski World	26,000	TRUE	FALSE	FALSE
15	Sneaker Kingdom	45,000	TRUE	FALSE	TRUE
16	Sports & Stuff	15,000	FALSE	TRUE	FALSE
17	Toy Kingdom	22,000	TRUE	FALSE	FALSE
18	Under the Sea	45,000	TRUE	FALSE	FALSE
19	US Olympic Team	20,000	TRUE	TRUE	TRUE
20	WWW Sports Inc.	100,000	TRUE	TRUE	TRUE
21	Zip & Sons	10,000	TRUE	TRUE	TRUE
22					

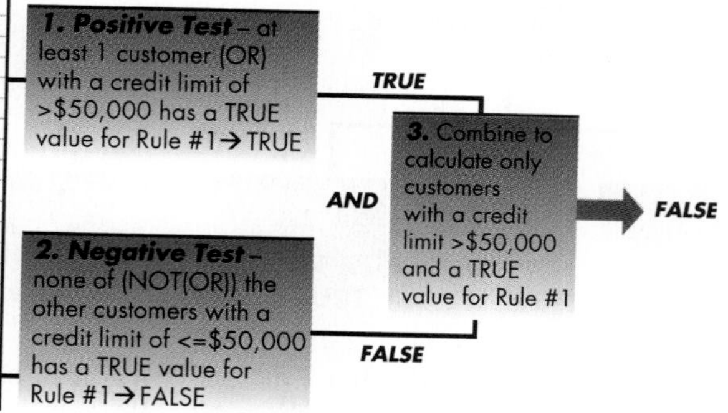

1. Complete the **Positive Test**: Evaluate if *any* of the customers with a credit limit of more than $50,000 have a TRUE value for Rule #1. In this case, Baseball & More (cell B5) and WWW Sports Inc. (cell B20) both have credit limits exceeding $50,000. To consider if either of these companies has a TRUE value for Rule #1, you can write the following:

```
OR(K5,K20)
```

2. Complete the **Negative Test**: Evaluate if *none of* the other customers have a TRUE value for Rule #1. To evaluate all customers except Baseball & More and WWW Sports Inc., you can write the following "none of" construct:

```
=NOT(OR(K3:K4,K6:K19,K21))
```

3. Combine both the Positive Test and the Negative Test to determine if both sets of criteria are met:

```
=AND(OR(K5,K20),NOT(OR(K3:K4,K6:K19,K21)))
```

Note that this formula does not automatically determine which customers have a credit limit of over $50,000, but instead these cells are directly referenced manually in the formula. Much more sophisticated techniques would be required to do this automatically.

4

Level 3

Nesting Boolean Logical Operators to Analyze Criteria

Eric now evaluates the second part of the Further Evaluate criteria. Here, he needs to prove that both of the following statements are TRUE:

- Either Rule #2 or Rule #3 is TRUE or both are TRUE.
- Rule #1 is FALSE.

Logically, this can be expressed as AND(OR(Rule #2 is TRUE, Rule #3 is TRUE), Rule #1 is FALSE). Substituting the appropriate cell references results in the following expression:

```
AND(OR(L3,M3),NOT(K3))
```

Eric has now evaluated both parts of the Further Evaluate criteria using the following two expressions:

```
AND(K3,NOT(OR(L3:M3)))
```

```
AND(OR(L3,M3),NOT(K3))
```

The guidelines management provided to Eric require that only one of these statements be TRUE for a customer to be identified for further evaluation. So, the statements must be combined using an OR operation, as follows:

```
OR(AND(K3,NOT(OR(L3:M3))),AND(OR(L3,M3),NOT(K3)))
```

Eric can substitute this expression as the second logical test of the pseudocode, as follows:

```
IF(NOT(OR(K3:M3)),"Reject",
   IF(OR(AND(K3,NOT(OR(L3:M3))),AND(OR(L3,M3),NOT(K3))),
      "Further Evaluate", otherwise "Accept"))
```

Again, to better illustrate which customers will be affected by the "Further Evaluate" criteria, these rows have been highlighted in Figure 4.36.

Figure 4.36: Customers who will be recommended for further evaluation

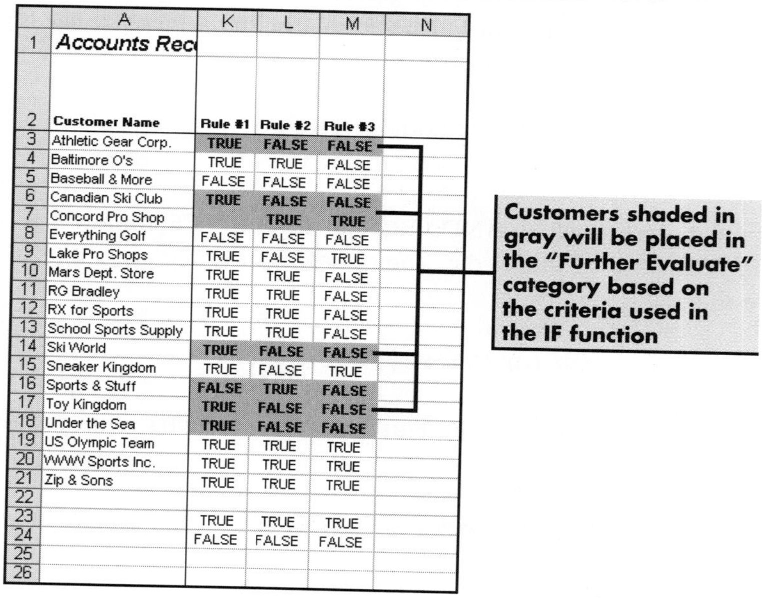

	A	K	L	M	N
1	*Accounts Rec*				
2	**Customer Name**	**Rule #1**	**Rule #2**	**Rule #3**	
3	Athletic Gear Corp.	TRUE	FALSE	FALSE	
4	Baltimore O's	TRUE	TRUE	FALSE	
5	Baseball & More	FALSE	FALSE	FALSE	
6	Canadian Ski Club	TRUE	FALSE	FALSE	
7	Concord Pro Shop		TRUE	TRUE	
8	Everything Golf	FALSE	FALSE	FALSE	
9	Lake Pro Shops	TRUE	FALSE	TRUE	
10	Mars Dept. Store	TRUE	TRUE	FALSE	
11	RG Bradley	TRUE	TRUE	FALSE	
12	RX for Sports	TRUE	TRUE	FALSE	
13	School Sports Supply	TRUE	TRUE	FALSE	
14	Ski World	TRUE	FALSE	FALSE	
15	Sneaker Kingdom	TRUE	FALSE	TRUE	
16	Sports & Stuff	FALSE	TRUE	FALSE	
17	Toy Kingdom	TRUE	FALSE	FALSE	
18	Under the Sea	TRUE	FALSE	FALSE	
19	US Olympic Team	TRUE	TRUE	TRUE	
20	WWW Sports Inc.	TRUE	TRUE	TRUE	
21	Zip & Sons	TRUE	TRUE	TRUE	
22					
23		TRUE	TRUE	TRUE	
24		FALSE	FALSE	FALSE	
25					
26					

Customers shaded in gray will be placed in the "Further Evaluate" category based on the criteria used in the IF function

As shown in Figure 4.36, it appears that seven customers will require further evaluation. For example, Athletic Gear Corp. meets the criteria that only Rule #1 is TRUE, while Sports & Stuff meets the criteria that either Rule #2 or Rule #3 is TRUE and Rule #1 is FALSE.

COMPLETING THE COMPLEX NESTED IF FORMULA

The last step is to determine the Accept criteria. However, as previously demonstrated, this requires no analysis because, if a customer is neither rejected nor identified for further evaluation, there is no other choice but to accept that customer for credit. Modifying the remainder of the pseudocode results in the following formula:

```
IF(NOT(OR(K3:M3)),"Reject",
  IF(OR(AND(K3,NOT(OR(L3:M3))),AND(OR(L3:M3),NOT(K3))),
    "Further Evaluate", "Accept"))
```

Again, to better illustrate which customers will result in a TRUE value for the "Accept" criteria, their rows have been highlighted in Figure 4.37.

Figure 4.37: Customers who will be accepted automatically

	A	K	L	M	N
1	Accounts Rec				
2	Customer Name	Rule #1	Rule #2	Rule #3	
3	Athletic Gear Corp.	TRUE	FALSE	FALSE	
4	Baltimore O's	TRUE	TRUE	FALSE	
5	Baseball & More	FALSE	FALSE	FALSE	
6	Canadian Ski Club	TRUE	FALSE	FALSE	
7	Concord Pro Shop		TRUE	TRUE	
8	Everything Golf	FALSE	FALSE	FALSE	
9	Lake Pro Shops	TRUE	FALSE	TRUE	
10	Mars Dept. Store	TRUE	TRUE	FALSE	
11	RG Bradley	TRUE	TRUE	FALSE	
12	RX for Sports	TRUE	TRUE	FALSE	
13	School Sports Supply	TRUE	TRUE	FALSE	
14	Ski World	TRUE	FALSE	FALSE	
15	Sneaker Kingdom	TRUE	FALSE	TRUE	
16	Sports & Stuff	FALSE	TRUE	FALSE	
17	Toy Kingdom	TRUE	FALSE	FALSE	
18	Under the Sea	TRUE	FALSE	FALSE	
19	US Olympic Team	TRUE	TRUE	TRUE	
20	WWW Sports Inc.	TRUE	TRUE	TRUE	
21	Zip & Sons	TRUE	TRUE	TRUE	
22					
23		TRUE	TRUE	TRUE	
24		FALSE	FALSE	FALSE	
25					
26					

> Customers shaded in gray will be accepted for credit based on the criteria used in the IF function

As shown in Figure 4.37, it appears that 11 customers will be accepted for credit. Note that the Concord Pro Shop, which has no prior sales history with TheZone, is highlighted for both the Further Evaluate criteria (see Figure 4.36) and for the Accept criteria, as seen in Figure 4.37. This happens because cell K7 is blank, and blank cells are ignored. However, because the Further Evaluate criteria is evaluated in the formula before the Accept criteria is evaluated, the result for Concord Pro Shop will be "Further Evaluate," which is appropriate for most new customers.

All that is left for Eric to do is build this carefully constructed IF formula in cell N3 and copy it down the column. Because each of the cell references changes relative to the row being evaluated, no absolute references are required. The final formula is detailed in Figure 4.38.

Figure 4.38: Final complex nested IF formula to determine credit status

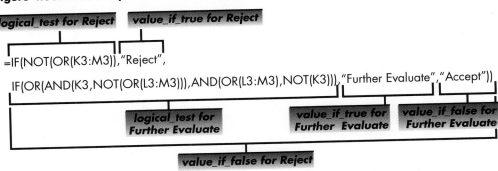

Eric copies this formula into cells N3:N21. The resulting worksheet is shown in Figure 4.39.

Figure 4.39: CreditData worksheet with final recommendations

Final complex nested IF formula

	N3			fx	=IF(NOT(OR(K3:M3)), "Reject",IF(OR(AND(K3,NOT(OR(L3:M3))),AND(OR(L3:M3),NOT(K3))),"Further Evaluate","Accept"))									

	A	B	C	D	E	F	G	H	I	J	K	L	M	N	O
1	Accounts Receivable Department - Customer Credit Analysis														
2	Customer Name	Current Credit Limit	Previous Year's Sales	Current Year's Sales	Past Due Balance	Net Worth in (000)	D&B Credit Rating Class	D&B Composite Credit Appraisal (1 Best)	D&B PAYDEX (100 Best)	D&B Stress Risk Class (1 Best)	Rule #1	Rule #2	Rule #3	Final Recommendation	
3	Athletic Gear Corp.	$ 9,000	$15,382	$11,952	$ 0	$ 450	BA	4	15	3	TRUE	FALSE	FALSE	Further Evaluate	
4	Baltimore O's	39,000	10,033	7,789	0	1,950	3A	1	51	1	TRUE	TRUE	FALSE	Accept	
5	Baseball & More	75,000	60,009	55,342	13,892	37,500	4A	2	70	1	FALSE	FALSE	FALSE	Reject	
6	Canadian Ski Club	33,000	35,039	50,921	495	1,650	BA	2	43	1	TRUE	FALSE	FALSE	Further Evaluate	
7	Concord Pro Shop					10,000	4A	1	91	1		TRUE	TRUE	Further Evaluate	
8	Everything Golf	25,000	15,221	9,483	2,899	1,250	3A	3	76	1	FALSE	FALSE	FALSE	Reject	
9	Lake Pro Shops	42,000	80,498	81,126	0	2,100	3A	2	87	1	TRUE	FALSE	TRUE	Accept	
10	Mars Dept. Store	27,000	35,354	20,666	0	213	BB	3	94	1	TRUE	TRUE	FALSE	Accept	
11	RG Bradley	46,000	90,970	18,343	0	2,300	3A	1	21	1	TRUE	TRUE	FALSE	Accept	
12	RX for Sports	15,000	5,663	3,014	0	750	2A	1	59	1	TRUE	TRUE	FALSE	Accept	
13	School Sports Supply	45,000	50,278	32,338	0	2,250	3A	3	91	1	TRUE	TRUE	FALSE	Accept	
14	Ski World	26,000	25,864	28,154	0	300	BA	2	82	1	TRUE	FALSE	FALSE	Further Evaluate	
15	Sneaker Kingdom	45,000	40,157	25,379	0	2,250	3A	2	71	1	TRUE	FALSE	TRUE	Accept	
16	Sports & Stuff	15,000	15,898	14,732	14,383	450	BA	1	67	1	FALSE	TRUE	FALSE	Further Evaluate	
17	Toy Kingdom	22,000	10,073	1,047	0	1,100	3A	3	14	1	TRUE	FALSE	FALSE	Further Evaluate	
18	Under the Sea	45,000	95,411	64,418	0	150	CB	4	79	2	TRUE	FALSE	FALSE	Further Evaluate	
19	US Olympic Team	20,000	5,621	6,171	0	1,000	3A	1	87	1	TRUE	TRUE	TRUE	Accept	
20	WWW Sports Inc.	100,000	60,009	60,354	0	500,000	5A	2	97	1	TRUE	TRUE	TRUE	Accept	
21	Zip & Sons	10,000	15,490	22,760	0	620	1A	2	96	1	TRUE	TRUE	TRUE	Accept	
22															
23															
24							Do any meet the rule?				TRUE	TRUE	TRUE		
25							Do none meet the rule?				FALSE	FALSE	FALSE		
26															

Eric now has a clear, easy-to-read set of final recommendations to pass along to management in the accounts receivable group and to the finance group. Of course, further evaluation will be needed for some of the customers listed, and many of the decisions ultimately made for those customers will depend on risk assessment versus the profit potential from a specific customer. TheZone might be willing to take a risk to foster a relationship with a customer believed to have the potential for large sales, but might be less willing to take the same risk for a customer that has little potential.

Steps To Success: Level 3

TheZone is considering different bids for the supply of plastic resins used to manufacture skis and needs to determine which bidder should be awarded the contract (PO #611). TheZone's accounts payable group has asked you to make some determinations regarding whether specific bidders should be rejected based on their lack of financial stability. Part of the analysis has already been completed, as shown in Figure 4.40.

Figure 4.40 : Bidder List Financial Evaluation worksheet

	A	B	C	D	E	F	G	H	I	J
1	PO 611 Bidder List Financial Evaluation									
2	Customer Name	Net Worth (Dollars)	D&B CCAR (1 Best)	D&B PAYDEX (100 Best)	D&B Stress Risk Class (1 Best)	Rule #1	Rule #2	Rule #3	Final Recommendation	
3	BFF Industries	$ 157,795	1	90	1	FALSE	TRUE	FALSE		
4	NRKK	387,000	4	83	3	FALSE	FALSE	FALSE		
5	Pergo Molding	775,961	2	98	1	TRUE	FALSE	TRUE		
6	Allma	17,043,973	3	55	2	TRUE	FALSE	FALSE		
7	JF & Sons	35,446,678	1	32	1	TRUE	TRUE	FALSE		
8	Argree Inc.	63,545,102	3	0	1	TRUE	FALSE	FALSE		
9	RGM Plastics	64,831,692	2	85	1	TRUE	FALSE	FALSE		
10	Soto Services	182,686,331	1	73	1	TRUE	TRUE	FALSE		
11	NE Plastic	239,227,375	2	79	2	TRUE	FALSE	FALSE		
12	SPDM	487,215,654	2	97	1	TRUE	FALSE	TRUE		
13										
14										

This worksheet contains the names of the bidders, their D&B ratings, and the results of the following analysis:

- Column F contains the results of applying Rule #1: Allow to bid if the bidder's net worth is greater than $500,000.
- Column G contains the results of applying Rule #2: The bidder has a CCAR of 1 and a stress risk class of 1.
- Column H contains the results of applying Rule #3: Allow to bid if the bidder's PAYDEX score is over 90.

Complete the following:

1. Open the workbook named **PO611.xls** in the Chapter 4 folder, and then save it as **PO611 Credit Analysis.xls**.

2. Write a formula in column I that can be copied down the column to make a final determination of "Allow to bid," "Exclude," or "Get more data" based on the following criteria:

   - Recommend to "Exclude" if *none* of the rules are TRUE.
   - Recommend to "Get more data" if only Rule #1 is TRUE or only Rule #2 is TRUE.
   - Recommend to "Allow to bid" if the bidder is neither recommended to "Exclude" nor to "Get more data."

3. To make the worksheet easier to view, split the window to show the titles in rows 1 and 2 and the row headings in column A.

4. Save and close the PO611 Credit Analysis.xls workbook.

CHAPTER SUMMARY

Level 1 of this chapter explored several tools that allow you to evaluate and compare both text and numeric data. These tools include relational operators (>, <, >=, <=, =, <>) and the Boolean logical functions AND, OR, and NOT. Both relational operators and Boolean functions return a Boolean logical value, TRUE or FALSE. Using these tools, you were able to determine if a specific data element or set of data elements met the required criteria. You also applied relational operators and Boolean logic using the Conditional Formatting tool.

In Level 2, you gained additional flexibility by applying Boolean logic within an IF statement. The IF function allows you to not only determine if an expression is TRUE or FALSE, but to also return a value other than TRUE or FALSE, such as text or numeric values depending on the outcome of a logical test. Both additional IF statements as well as other Excel functions can be nested within an IF function to complete more complicated tasks.

In Level 3, you learned about more complex logical constructs, specifically the "none of" construct and the "only" construct. You also combined the concepts presented in Levels 1 and 2 to solve more complex logical tasks, nesting IF functions, relational operators, and Boolean functions within the same formula. Table 4.6 provides a summary of commonly used logical constructs.

Table 4.6: Common logical constructs

Logical Construct	Description
Assuming cells A1:A4 contain TRUE/FALSE values	*Use this logical construct:*
AND(A1:A4)	When all items must be TRUE to return a TRUE value
OR(A1:A4)	When only one item must be TRUE to return a TRUE value
NOT(A1)	To change a single TRUE to FALSE or a single FALSE to TRUE
NOT(OR(A1:A4))	To return a TRUE if none of the items are TRUE (equivalent to all of the items are FALSE)
AND(NOT(A1),NOT(A2),NOT(A3),NOT(A4))	To return a TRUE if all of the items are FALSE (equivalent to none of the items are TRUE)
NOT(AND(A1:A4))	To return a FALSE if all of the items are TRUE (equivalent to returning a TRUE if even one item is FALSE)
OR(NOT(A1),NOT(A2),NOT(A3),NOT(A4))	To return a TRUE if even one item is FALSE (equivalent to returning a FALSE if all items are TRUE)
AND(A1,NOT(OR(A1:A4)))	To return a TRUE if only A1 is TRUE and none of the other values are TRUE
AND(OR(A1,A2),NOT(OR(A3:A4)))	To return a TRUE if only A1 or A2 is TRUE and none of the other values are TRUE

IF(OR(A1:A4),"This is true","This is false")
 	
IF(A1,25,IF(A2,50,0))
	To return any value, text or numeric, depending on if the logical test is evaluated as TRUE or FALSE. A logical test can be any expression that reduces to a TRUE or FALSE value. Additional logical tests can be performed within the same expression by nesting IFs up to seven levels.

CONCEPTUAL REVIEW

1. Evaluate the following expressions:

   a. =AND(TRUE,TRUE,TRUE)

   b. =OR(3>5,FALSE)

   c. =NOT(OR(FALSE,FALSE,FALSE))

   d. =AND(A2>6,NOT(FALSE)) where A2 contains the value 25

2. Describe how you would format a cell so that if the value is greater than 25 it would be automatically bolded.

Answer Questions 3-15 using the worksheet shown below. Assume that all of your answers will be placed in cells on the same worksheet.

	A	B	C	D	E	F
1			Sales Meeting in NY			
2	Item	Optional/ Required	Budget	Actual	Within Budget	
3	Food	R	$ 250	$ 185	TRUE	
4	Hotel	R	500	525	FALSE	
5	Transportation	R	100	40	TRUE	
6	Theater Tickets	O	100	125	FALSE	
7	Airfare	R	225	199	TRUE	
8	Tour Package	O	50	40	TRUE	
9	Total		$1,225	$1,114		
10						

3. What formula is used in cell E3, which can be copied down the column to determine (TRUE or FALSE) if this item is within budget?

4. Write a formula to determine if at least one item is within budget.

5. Write a formula to determine if all of the items are within budget.

6. Write a formula in cell F3 that can be copied down the column to determine if this food item is not within budget.

7. What formula would you write to set a conditional format for cell A3 so that the item name would be shaded in yellow if this item has a budget over 200?

8. Write a formula to determine if none of the items are within budget.

9. Write a formula to determine if (TRUE or FALSE) only the optional trips (O) are within budget. Note that this formula does not have to work if the optional/required categories are later modified.

10. Are the following two Boolean expressions equivalent? Why or why not?
=NOT(OR(E3:E8))
=AND(NOT(E3),NOT(E4),NOT(E5),NOT(E6),NOT(E7),NOT(E8))

11. Is the following formula valid? Why or why not?
=NOT(E3:E8)

12. What value would the following formula return?
=IF(D3<=C3,"within budget","over budget")

13. What value would the following formula return?
=IF(SUM(D6,D8)<150,"go to both",IF(SUM(D6,D8)>250,"go to neither", "choose one"))

14. Write a formula in cell G3 that can be copied down the column to return the following:

- If this item has an actual cost of less than $200, then return the text "Minor Component Cost".
- If this item has an actual cost of $200 or more, then return the text "Major Component Cost".

15. Write a formula in cell H3 that can be copied down the column to calculate the cost of this component for a larger sales meeting based on the following:

- If this item is optional, as indicated in column B, then the cost will be equal to the original budgeted amount.
- If this item is required, as indicated in column B, then the cost will be 3 times the original budgeted amount.

CASE PROBLEMS

Level 1 – Evaluating Job Applicants for Winston, Winston & Coombs

Human Resources

You work in the human resources department for the accounting firm, Winston, Winston & Coombs. The firm has recently increased its client base and decided to hire several university graduates into entry-level positions. The human resources manager has established a formal process for evaluating job applicants. This process takes into account not only the applicant's academic performance, but also his or her work experience and impression made during the personal interview. In addition, all applicants are given a separate skills-based exam to determine their proficiency in spreadsheet and database applications. Because some of the applicants are not business majors, but might be otherwise qualified for a position, the exam also covers some basic business concepts in accounting, finance, and marketing. You have been asked to evaluate the information on the candidates being considered.

Each job application provides the following information:

- College GPA (valid scores range from 1.5 to 4.0)
- Standardized universal Major Code indicating the applicant's undergraduate major; for example, Engineering=1, Business=2, Economics=3, Physical Science=4, and so on (valid codes for majors are 1 through 250)
- The total number of references submitted by the applicant
- A personal interview rating
- If the applicant has previous work experience (TRUE or FALSE)
- The Employment Exam score (valid scores are between 200-800)
- The undergraduate school ranking (compared with all colleges across the country)

The human resources manager has established criteria to determine if an applicant will be automatically disqualified or automatically hired, or if no decision is made. The criteria, which are applied in order, are described below.

An applicant is **automatically disqualified** if *any* of the following criteria are TRUE:

- The applicant has submitted an invalid GPA score, Employment Exam score, or Major Code.
- The applicant has a GPA less than 2.5.
- The applicant provided fewer than 3 references.
- The applicant has an Employment Exam score below 600.
- The applicant has a personal interview rating of less than 3.

An applicant is **automatically hired** if *all* of the following criteria are TRUE:

- The applicant has a GPA score over 3.5.
- The applicant has a Major Code between 1-20 (inclusive).
- The applicant graduated from one of the top 25 schools (ranking of 25 or less).
- The applicant has an Employment Exam score above 700.
- The applicant has a personal interview rating of 4 or higher.
- The applicant has prior work experience.

If an applicant is neither automatically disqualified nor automatically hired, that applicant's status is "undecided."

Complete the following:

1. Open the workbook named **Hiring.xls** located in the Chapter 4 folder, and then save it as **WWC Hiring Analysis.xls**.

2. Write a formula in cell I4 that can be copied down the column to determine if (TRUE or FALSE) *any* of the following scores/codes listed for this applicant are invalid: GPA, Major Code, Employment Exam.

3. Write a formula in cell J4 that can be copied down the column to determine if (TRUE or FALSE) the applicant should be automatically disqualified based on the criteria given.

4. In cell K4, write a formula that can be copied down the column to determine if (TRUE or FALSE) the candidate should be automatically hired based on the criteria given. (*Hint:* For criteria between two values, test that the value is both >= the lower limit and <= the higher limit.)

5. Write a formula in cell L4 to determine if this candidate is *not* automatically disqualified. Write the formula so that it can be copied down the column and across the row (into column M) to calculate if this candidate is *not* automatically hired. (*Hint:* Use the results determined in Steps 3 and 4.)

6. Write a formula in cell N4 to determine if no decision is made on this applicant. Recall that no decision is made if the applicant is *both* not automatically disqualified (L) or automatically hired (M). (*Hint:* Use the results of Step 5.)

7. Write a formula in cell I14 that can be copied across the row (through column N) to determine if all of the applicants have invalid scores.

8. Write a formula in cell I15 that can be copied across the row (through column N) to determine if any of the applicants have invalid scores.

9. To summarize the results, write a formula in cell I16 that displays the total number of applicants who have invalid scores. Copy this formula across the row (through column N). This formula should automatically update if any of the scores or criteria are later modified.

10. Apply conditional formatting to highlight the important points, as follows.

    a. Highlight all of the TRUE values obtained for the Automatically Disqualified column (J4:J12) in a green, bold text format.

    b. Highlight all of the TRUE values obtained for the Automatically Hire column (K4:K12) in a red, bold text format.

    c. Highlight the name of any applicant with a school rank of less than 10 using a yellow background.

11. Save and close the WWC Hiring Analysis.xls workbook.

Level 2 – Estimating Painting Job Costs for RJ Construction

For the past year, you have been working with a medium-size painting contractor, RJ Construction, doing everything from running errands to cutting the weekly paychecks and filing the appropriate quarterly employment withholding forms with the IRS. Given your knowledge of spreadsheets, your boss has asked you to create an Excel worksheet for estimating painting jobs that are done by a subgroup of the construction firm, as either part of larger jobs or as standalone projects. Your boss would like the worksheet to contain some basic input information and automatically calculate an estimated price, so that a customer can quickly know the cost of the work. The variables to be considered are as follows:

$ Finance

4

Chapter Exercises

- The dimensions of each room—length, width, and height
- The condition of the walls, where 1 represents excellent, 2 represents reasonable but has some peeling and/or old paint, and 3 represents poor condition with major holes, peeling, and/or very old paint
- Whether or not the requested new color is lighter than the existing wall color (TRUE or FALSE)
- Grade of paint being requested—premium, superior, or economy

Complete the following.

1. Open a new workbook and save it as **Painting Estimator.xls** in the Chapter 4 folder. Create a worksheet with the columns and data shown in Table 4.7. Also include a meaningful title at the top of your worksheet. Ultimately this worksheet will be used as a template and filled out on sight by the painter. List all other inputs that are needed for subsequent calculations on a separate worksheet in the workbook.

Table 4.7: Worksheet data for painting estimator

Room	Length in Feet	Width in Feet	Height in Feet	Square Feet (SF) of Wall/ Ceiling	Wall Condition	New Color Lighter	Paint Quality
Kitchen	20	15	8		2	TRUE	Premium
Bedroom1	16	12	8		1	FALSE	Economy
Bedroom2	10	12	8		1	FALSE	Superior
Bath	8	6	8		3	FALSE	Superior

Fill the costs by room. Write all formulas so that they can be copied down the column. Remember, your formulas will need to work when new quantities are substituted into the data entry area.

2. Calculate the total square footage (SF) of walls and ceiling. If a room is 10 feet by 12 feet with an 8-foot ceiling height, it would have two walls that are 10' × 8' (total of 160 SF) and two walls that are 12' × 8' (total of 192 SF), and a ceiling of 10' × 12' (120 SF) for a total of 472 SF. Do not subtract any area for windows, doors, and so on.

3. To the right of the Paint Quality column, calculate the cost of wall repairs and primer. Only walls with a wall condition of poor (3) will require wall repair and primer. This cost is estimated as $0.50 per SF. If no primer is required, a value of 0 should be entered.

4. In an adjacent column, calculate the cost of the first coat of paint. If the condition of the wall is 1, the cost of paint is $0.45 per SF; if the condition of the wall is 2, the cost of paint is $0.50 per SF; otherwise, the cost is $0.60 per SF.

5. In an adjacent column, calculate the cost of the second coat of paint based on the following criteria:

   - If the condition of the wall is 3, a second coat of paint will be required at $0.35 per SF.
   - If the new wall color is lighter than the existing color, a second coat of paint will be required at $.30 per SF.
   - Otherwise, no second coat will be required, and a value of $0 should be entered.

6. In an adjacent column, calculate the cost adjustment for paint quality based on the following criteria:

   - If premium paint is used, add $.15 per SF.
   - If economy paint is used, deduct $.10 per SF.

7. In an adjacent column, calculate the total cost to paint this room (primer, first coat, second coat).

8. In an adjacent column, determine if (TRUE or FALSE) this is a high-priced room. A high-priced room is one that is estimated to cost more than $450.

9. Create a row below the data that totals the costs of each item (primer, first coat, and so on) and then a grand total of all items for all rooms.

10. Because larger jobs have certain economies of scale in setup and cleanup, a discount is given based on these estimated values to jobs based on their total size. Just below the grand total, determine the *total discounted price* of the job based on the following:

- If the total cost of the painting job is less then $1000, then there is no discount.
- If the total cost of the painting job is at least $1000 but less than $2500, then a 10% discount will be given (discount is calculated based on the grand total cost for all items and all rooms).
- If the total cost of the painting job is at least $2500 but less than $5000, then a 12% discount will be given.
- If the total cost of the painting job is $5000 or more, then a 15% discount will be given.

11. Format your worksheets so that they are easy to read and information is clearly identifiable.

12. Save and close the Painting Estimator.xls workbook.

Level 3 – Analyzing Dealership Promotions for CKG Auto

CKG Auto runs several promotions each year to reward dealerships for their sales efforts, sometimes on specific car models and other times for overall sales. CKG Auto is running three different promotions for large dealerships, based on performance over this past calendar year. Small and medium-sized dealerships have similar promotions but based on different expected volumes and rebate percentages. The promotions are as follows:

Marketing

- A rebate on shipping expenses based on exceeding expected quarterly volumes. These are savings CKG Auto realizes from its trucking carriers and has decided to pass along as a reward to dealerships that have exceeded expectations. Rebates for each quarter were set by management as follows: 1st quarter, $75 per car sold (actual volume); 2nd quarter, $109 per car sold; 3rd quarter, $88 per car sold; and 4th quarter, $122 per car sold. Dealerships are awarded the rebate on a quarter-by-quarter basis, only for quarters where their actual sales exceeded expected volumes for that quarter. Expected sales volumes for large dealerships for each quarter are as follows:

  - 1st Quarter, 300
  - 2nd Quarter, 425
  - 3rd Quarter, 410
  - 4th Quarter, 320

- An overall sales volume bonus based on exceeding expected annual volumes. Dealerships that exceeded the expected annual sales volume by at least 10% are awarded a $15,000 bonus. Dealerships that exceeded the expected annual sales volume by less than 10% are awarded a $5,000 bonus. Otherwise, no bonus is awarded ($0).
- A "Best in Class" bonus of $20,000 awarded to the one dealership with the highest overall sales volume in its class.

You have been asked to set up a worksheet to record the dealer information for the past year and apply the appropriate promotions to each dealership. The actual dealership quarterly sales volumes have already been entered in a worksheet. Now, you will finalize the analysis.

Complete the following:

1. Open the workbook named **CKGPromo.xls** located in the Chapter 4 folder, and then save it as **Promotion Analysis Large Dealerships.xls**. This past year's quarterly sales volumes and expected sales volumes for large dealerships have already been entered into this workbook. Complete the analysis using any additional columns and/ or rows as you deem necessary. All formulas should work when copied either across or down, as needed. Include titles in each column and/or row to identify the corresponding data. Add any appropriate formatting to make the worksheet easy to read.

2. Insert rows at the top of the worksheet to create an input area where you can list the inputs such as bonus amounts, shipping rebates, and so on. List the inputs explicitly and use only one worksheet for this task, so that any inputs can be easily displayed for management and then later copied and modified to calculate the promotions for both the medium and small dealership classes. Insert rows as needed, and be sure to clearly label each input so that the data can be interpreted and modified easily next year. Wrap text and format the data as needed.

3. Calculate the value of the shipping rebate for each dealer for each quarter (use four new columns). This should require only one formula that can be copied down the column and across the row. Be sure your inputs are set up so that this can be easily accomplished. Remember, dealers will only receive rebates in quarters where their actual quarterly sales volumes exceeded expected sales volumes. In an adjacent column, determine the total value of the shipping rebate for all four quarters by dealership. In a row below the quarterly shipping rebate values, summarize the quarterly rebates for all dealers.

4. Analyze the quality of these volume estimates by categorizing the quality of the *annual volume estimate* versus the *actual annual volumes* for each dealership into the following categories:

- Display "Excellent" if the estimate is within 5% higher or lower of the actual sales volume. (*Hint:* As an example, if you wanted to determine if the value 26 is within +/- 25% of 40, you would need to test this value to make sure that *both* 26>=40-.25*40 and 26<=40+.25*40.)
- Display "Good" if the estimate is greater than 5% higher or lower, but within 10% higher or lower of the actual volume.
- Display "Poor" if the estimate is greater than 10% higher or lower.

5. In an adjacent column or columns, calculate the value of the annual sales volume bonus for each dealership.

6. In an adjacent column, calculate the value of the "Best in Class" bonus for each dealership. (Only the dealership with the highest annual sales volume will receive this; all others will receive $0.)

7. In an adjacent column, determine if (TRUE or FALSE) this company received *none of* the three promotions.

8. In an adjacent column, determine if (TRUE or FALSE) this company received *only* the shipping rebate bonus.

9. In a row below the data, determine for each bonus the number of dealerships receiving this bonus and the average value of the bonus (include dealerships that did not earn a bonus in the average calculation).

10. Save and close the Promotion Analysis Large Dealerships.xls workbook.

Retrieving Data for Computation, Analysis, and Reference
Sales: Creating Product Order Forms for Equipment Purchases

"I believe completely in the ability of people to get up every day and overcome barriers to success."
—Carly Fiorina

LEARNING OBJECTIVES

Level 1

Organize and evaluate data in vertical and horizontal lookup tables
Understand the VLOOKUP and HLOOKUP algorithms
Retrieve data from a vertical lookup table
Retrieve data from a horizontal lookup table

Level 2

Analyze and retrieve data from multiple worksheets
Look up data in a one-row or one-column range
Use named range references in formulas
Retrieve data from multidimensional tables

Level 3

Prevent errors in data retrieval
Nest lookup and reference functions to perform more complex calculations
Choose a value or a range of values for analysis
Retrieve data by matching the relative position of an item in a list

FUNCTIONS COVERED IN THIS CHAPTER

CHOOSE
HLOOKUP
INDEX
ISBLANK
LOOKUP
MATCH
VLOOKUP

CHAPTER INTRODUCTION

In previous chapters, you learned how to create formulas with IF and nested IF functions to make decisions based on specified criteria. However, these formulas are not adequate in some circumstances, such as selecting a particular value from a long list of values. Instead of using nested IF statements, you can use a group of Excel functions known as the **Reference and Lookup functions**. These functions expand your ability to vary values based on criteria and find an input value that produces a specific result. In this chapter, you will use Reference and Lookup functions to retrieve data stored in the same or a different worksheet, and then use that data in formulas or reference it in another location. Data is often stored in a list format on a worksheet. A data list that categorizes values you want to retrieve is called a **lookup table**. You can use the data in a lookup table to create worksheets that list items, such as products ordered and their corresponding prices, and then perform calculations. The Reference and Lookup functions enable you to retrieve the appropriate data from a lookup table for use in such calculations.

In this chapter, you will learn how to create an automated order form that uses the Reference and Lookup functions to provide prices, shipping, and other order information. Level 1 begins with VLOOKUP and HLOOKUP, the most common of these functions, which look up data based on its location in a table, and then retrieve a corresponding value that matches specified criteria. In Level 2, the LOOKUP function is used to retrieve a value in a column or a row, and the INDEX function is used to look up a value in a range. Level 3 shows how to nest various Reference and Lookup functions, including CHOOSE and MATCH, to perform more complex calculations.

CASE SCENARIO

Vijay Patel is a sales representative in TheZone's Equipment division, and calls on large and small sporting goods stores to promote TheZone's products and assist customers with their orders. Although he can provide the full line of TheZone's sporting goods to his customers, Vijay concentrates on racket sports and golf equipment. One important part of Vijay's job is maintaining up-to-date product specifications and pricing information that he can quickly retrieve to answer customer questions. Vijay and the other sales representatives have a large binder that contains lists of each product line, from helmets to soccer balls. Vijay refers to this binder when customers ask questions such as, "What would a case of golf balls cost?" or "What volume discounts are available for tennis rackets?" To answer such questions, Vijay must find the right page in his binder, match the number of the item the customer has selected with the corresponding data, and then calculate the cost or discount using a pocket calculator. He now wants to automate this process by creating order forms in Excel. These forms will serve as templates that Vijay and the other sales representatives can use to easily look up the necessary data and perform calculations, such as determining unit and total product pricing, more efficiently.

Sales

LEVEL 1

PERFORMING BASIC LOOKUPS TO CALCULATE AND EVALUATE DATA

EXCEL 2003 SKILLS TRAINING

- Use HLOOKUP
- Use lookup tables
- Use VLOOKUP

WORKING WITH LOOKUP TABLES

When working with customers, Vijay looks up item numbers, descriptions, discount amounts, and shipping amounts, and then calculates unit and total prices. Now he wants to automate this process by creating a form (template) in Excel. He begins by creating a workbook named Tennis Orders in which he wants to develop a Tennis Balls worksheet that contains a unit pricing lookup table. TheZone sells tennis balls in bulk, priced per canister, so Vijay uses a canister as the unit to calculate prices. Unit prices are based on the total quantity being ordered, as listed in Table 5.1.

Table 5.1: Unit prices for tennis balls

Quantity (in units)	Price Each
Under 60	$2.45
60–119	$2.27
120–239	$2.12
240 or more	$2.00

Vijay also wants to add a shipping costs lookup table to the worksheet. When calculating order amounts, he has to account for shipping charges, which depend on the transportation method. Table 5.2 shows the shipping charges.

Table 5.2: Shipping charges for tennis balls

Shipping Method	Charge Per Unit
Truck	$0.25
Rail	$0.20
Ship	$0.15
Customer arranges for shipping	$0.00

Vijay can then include an order table that lists the order information and calculates the total price. Vijay creates the Tennis Balls worksheet, shown in Figure 5.1, and begins to add data from recent orders.

Figure 5.1: Tennis Balls worksheet

First column contains the data to be looked up (the key data)

Unit Pricing lookup table

Shipping Costs lookup table

VLOOKUP will look up the unit price based on the quantity entered in cell D14

VLOOKUP formula will be entered in cell E14

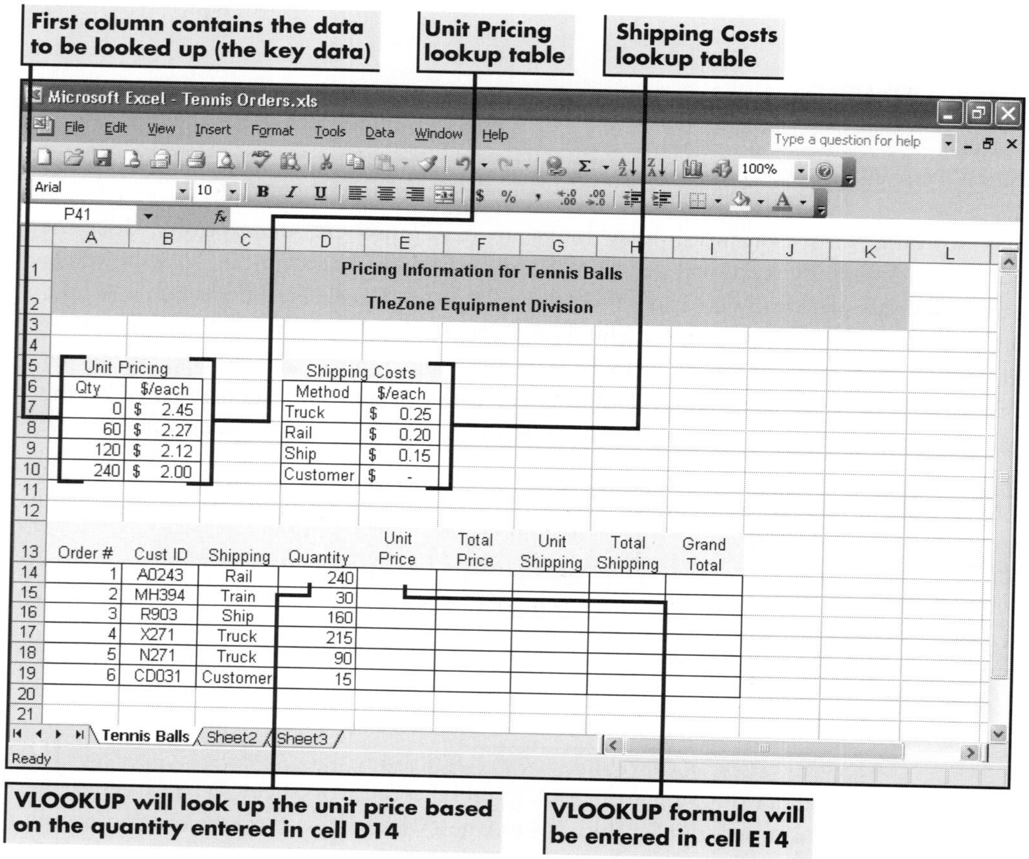

Vijay entered the order number, customer ID, shipping method, and quantity ordered. He wants to insert the unit price based on the values stored in the Unit Pricing table (cells A7:B10), and the unit shipping charge based on the values stored in the Shipping Costs table (cells D7:E10). Then, he can calculate the totals for price and shipping, and sum those to calculate the grand total.

Vijay briefly considers using an IF function to insert the unit prices and unit shipping charges. He could use nested IF logic that says, if the quantity ordered is less than 60, charge $2.45 per unit; if the quantity ordered is greater than or equal to 60 but less than 120, charge $2.27 per unit; if the quantity ordered is greater than or equal to 120 but less than 240, charge $2.12 per unit; and if the quantity ordered is greater than or equal to 240, charge $2.00 per unit. He could construct a similar nested IF formula to calculate the unit shipping charges. However, that would require two long nested IF formulas. Furthermore, Vijay thinks that the unit prices and shipping methods will be expanded to include more prices and methods, so using the IF function is not practical for this worksheet.

Instead, he can use the VLOOKUP function to look up a unit price based on quantity, and look up a shipping charge based on method.

RETRIEVING DATA FROM A VERTICAL LOOKUP TABLE

When you organize data in a **vertical lookup table**, a lookup table in which the data to be searched is organized in columns, the most effective and flexible way to retrieve data is to use the **VLOOKUP function**. (The "V" in VLOOKUP stands for vertical.) This function searches a specified part of a worksheet for data. It starts by searching for data in the first column. When it finds the required data, it retrieves the value in a specified column that is in the same row as the data found by the lookup. You use VLOOKUP when the first column of the lookup table contains the data you are looking up, also called the **key data**, and the corresponding information you want to find is in one of the columns to the right of the key data column, as shown earlier in Figure 5.1.

The VLOOKUP function is appropriate for finding the correct unit price in Vijay's Unit Pricing table and inserting it in cell E14, and for finding the correct unit shipping charge in the Shipping Costs table and inserting it in cell G14. As shown in Figure 5.1, the first column of the Unit Pricing table contains the quantities, which is what Vijay will look up. The information he wants to find—the unit price—is included in the column to the right of the Qty column. Similarly, the first column of the Shipping Costs table contains the shipping methods, which Vijay will look up, and the second column lists the corresponding unit charges, which is the information he wants to find.

When you write a VLOOKUP formula, you indicate the value you want to look up in a table. VLOOKUP searches for a matching value in the leftmost column of the table, and then retrieves the value in the same row but in another column that you specify. Vijay plans to enter a VLOOKUP formula in cell E14 to look up the unit price based on the quantity entered in cell D14.

The syntax of the VLOOKUP function is shown below and its arguments are described in Table 5.3.

```
=VLOOKUP(lookup_value,table_array,col_index_num,range_lookup)
```

Table 5.3: VLOOKUP function arguments

Argument	Description
lookup_value	The data you want to look up. This value can be a number, text, a logical value, or a name or cell reference that refers to a value.
table_array	The range containing the data that you want to search to find the lookup value. This range must start in the column with the lookup values and extend at least as far as the column containing the data to be returned.
col_index_num	The number of the column containing the data you want to retrieve. The number 1 indicates the first column of the lookup table, 2 indicates the second column, and so on.
range_lookup	The type of lookup you want to perform—TRUE or FALSE. With a **TRUE type** (the default), the VLOOKUP function finds the greatest value that does not exceed the lookup_value. When the lookup type is TRUE, the values in the first column of the lookup table must be sorted in ascending sort order; otherwise, VLOOKUP might not retrieve the correct value. With a **FALSE type**, the VLOOKUP function looks only for an exact match of the lookup_value. If it does not find an exact match, the text #N/A is displayed in the cell.

How To

Write a VLOOKUP Formula

1. Type: =VLOOKUP(

2. Enter the value you want to match, such as a cell reference, text, or number.

3. Enter the range that contains the data you want to look up, where the first column lists the matching values, or key data.

4. Enter the number of the column that contains the data you want to find.

5. Enter the type of lookup you want to perform—TRUE to search sorted data for the greatest value that meets your criteria, or FALSE to find an exact match.

6. Type a closing parenthesis), and then press the Enter key.

In this case, the function must look up the quantity ordered to find the unit price, so the lookup_value is cell D14. Cells A7:B10 contain the unit pricing data; these are the cells the function will search (table_array). In the Unit Pricing lookup table, column 2 lists the unit prices, so the col_index_num argument is 2. The range_lookup argument requires the TRUE type, because the function must look for the greatest value in the first column of the Unit Pricing table that is not greater than 240, the value specified in cell D14. With a FALSE type, the function would look only for the exact value 240 in the first column of the Unit Pricing table. Because customers might order amounts of cans of tennis balls that do not match exactly the amounts in the Unit Pricing table, the TRUE type is needed in this case. To insert the correct unit price in cell E14, Vijay enters the following formula:

=VLOOKUP(D14,A7:B10,2,TRUE)

This formula considers the value in cell D14 (240), and tries to match it in the first column of the range A7:B10. When it finds 240 (cell A10), it looks in column 2 for the data to retrieve, which is $2.00, and places this result in cell E14.

Vijay's next step is to copy the VLOOKUP formula from cell E14 to cells E15:E19 to include the unit prices for the other orders in the order table. He considers each argument of the VLOOKUP function in cell E14. If he copies the formula from cell E14 to E15, should the lookup_value change from D14 to D15? Yes, the second order in row 15 should calculate unit price according to the quantity stored in D15. Therefore, the cell reference in the first argument should be relative. Should the table_array A7:B10 become A8:B11? No, the formula should reference the Unit Pricing table and, therefore, requires absolute row references. (The column references will stay the same when the formula is copied; only absolute row references are needed.) The col_index_num and range_lookup are constants and will remain the same. Vijay changes the formula in cell E14 to use absolute row references in the second argument, as follows:

```
=VLOOKUP(D14,A$7:B$10,2,TRUE)
```

He copies the formula from cell E14 to E15:E19. Next, Vijay wants to calculate the total order value by multiplying quantity by price. In cell F14, he enters the formula =D14*E14, and then copies this formula to cells F15:F19, as shown in Figure 5.2.

Figure 5.2: Calculating the units prices and total price

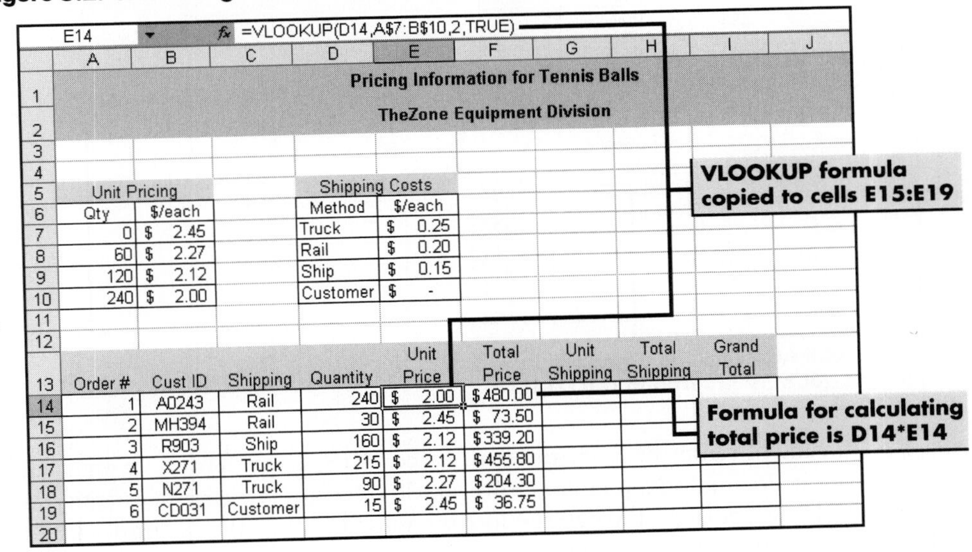

	A	B	C	D	E	F	G	H	I
5	Unit Pricing			Shipping Costs					
6	Qty	$/each		Method	$/each				
7	0	$ 2.45		Truck	$ 0.25				
8	60	$ 2.27		Rail	$ 0.20				
9	120	$ 2.12		Ship	$ 0.15				
10	240	$ 2.00		Customer	$ -				
13	Order #	Cust ID	Shipping	Quantity	Unit Price	Total Price	Unit Shipping	Total Shipping	Grand Total
14	1	A0243	Rail	240	$ 2.00	$480.00			
15	2	MH394	Rail	30	$ 2.45	$ 73.50			
16	3	R903	Ship	160	$ 2.12	$339.20			
17	4	X271	Truck	215	$ 2.12	$455.80			
18	5	N271	Truck	90	$ 2.27	$204.30			
19	6	CD031	Customer	15	$ 2.45	$ 36.75			

Vijay also wants to use a VLOOKUP formula in cell G14 to retrieve the appropriate unit shipping charges from the Shipping Costs table. Should this formula perform a TRUE type of lookup or a FALSE type?

Examining the VLOOKUP Algorithm

To understand the algorithm that the VLOOKUP function uses, you can examine the steps Excel performs to solve the VLOOKUP formula. In the Tennis Balls worksheet, you can easily follow the steps Excel performs to match the specified value of 240 in the Unit Pricing lookup table. Order #2, however, has a quantity of 30, which is not listed in the Unit Pricing table. How does Excel determine the unit price for Order #2 using the VLOOKUP formula shown in Figure 5.3?

Figure 5.3: Examining the VLOOKUP formula for Order #2

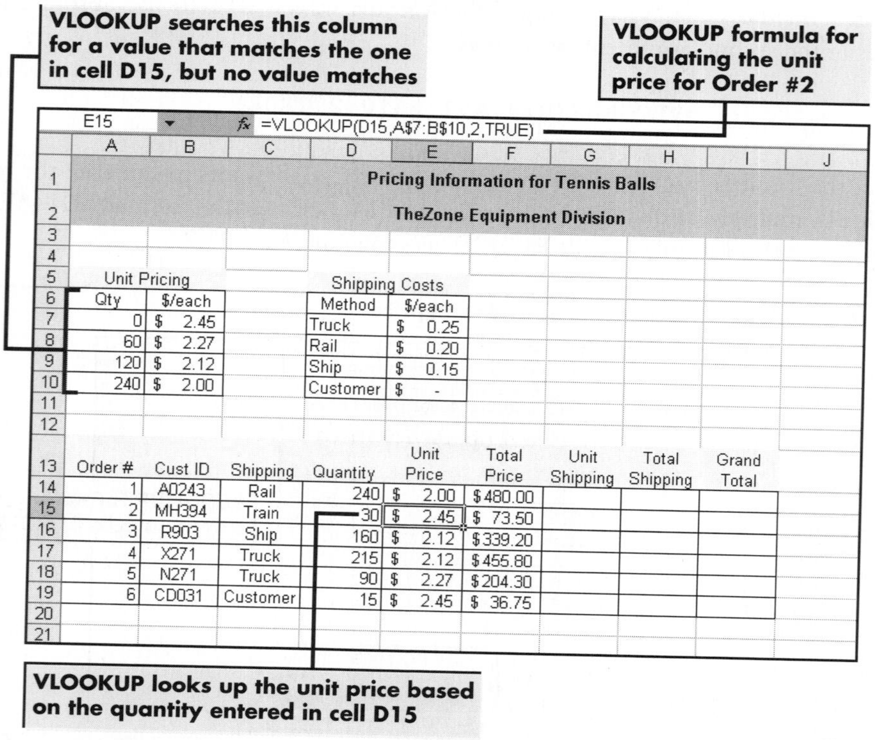

VLOOKUP searches this column for a value that matches the one in cell D15, but no value matches

VLOOKUP formula for calculating the unit price for Order #2

E15   =VLOOKUP(D15,A$7:B$10,2,TRUE)

VLOOKUP looks up the unit price based on the quantity entered in cell D15

In Order #2, 30 cans of tennis balls are ordered. In cell E15, Excel retrieves a value of $2.45 from the Unit Pricing lookup table. However, 30 does not appear as a quantity in the lookup table. How does Excel match the lookup_value of 30 to the quantities listed in cells A7:A10? To answer this question, you need to trace each step of the VLOOKUP type TRUE algorithm. (Recall that when the lookup type is TRUE, VLOOKUP finds the greatest value that does not exceed the lookup_value.) One way to better understand the process is to consider a possible model algorithm and go through each step to determine a result, as shown on the following page. This model algorithm, like the actual one, requires that the first column of the lookup_range be in ascending order for a correct answer to be guaranteed. Although it is not certain this model algorithm provides the precise method used by Excel or provides the exact result, it should give insight into how a result is determined and how the order of the first column might affect this result.

1. **Look for an exact match.** First, the VLOOKUP function tries to match the lookup_value to the first entry in the specified range (the lookup table). If it does not find a match, the function continues to check the lookup_value against each value in the lookup table. If it finds an exact match, the function retrieves the corresponding value from the lookup table. The VLOOKUP formula calculation is complete at that point. If the lookup table contains a second match, the function ignores it. If an exact match is not found, the VLOOKUP function continues with step 2 of its algorithm.

   When solving the formula in cell E15 of the Tennis Balls worksheet, the function starts by trying to match the quantity of 30 to the values listed in the first column of the Unit Pricing table in cells A7:B10. Because it does not find 30 in the Unit Pricing table, the function proceeds to step 2.

2. **Check the first value in the lookup table.** In the second step of the VLOOKUP algorithm, the function compares the lookup_value to the first value in the lookup table. If the lookup_value is smaller than the first value in the lookup table, the function displays the text #N/A and the VLOOKUP calculation is complete. If the lookup_value is greater than the first value in the lookup table, the function continues to step 3.

   The first value in the Unit Pricing table is 0. Because 30 is greater than 0, the function proceeds to step 3.

3. **Check the next value in the lookup table.** In the third step of the VLOOKUP algorithm, the function compares the lookup_value to the next value in the lookup table. If the lookup_value is less than the next value in the lookup table, the function retrieves the value that corresponds to the previous entry in the lookup table, and the VLOOKUP formula calculation is complete. If the lookup_value is greater than the next value in the lookup table, the function continues to step 4.

   In the Unit Pricing table, Excel compares 30 to 60, which is the next value in the Qty column. Because 30 is less than 60, Excel retrieves the unit price for the *previous quantity* in the Unit Pricing table—$2.45.

4. **Check the last value in the lookup table.** In the fourth step of the VLOOKUP algorithm, the function checks to see if the next value in the lookup table is the last value. If the next value is the last value in the table, the function retrieves the last value in the lookup table. If the next value is not the last value in the lookup table, the function repeats step 3, comparing the lookup_value to the next value in the lookup table.

The four steps of this model VLOOKUP type TRUE algorithm are summarized in Figure 5.4.

Figure 5.4: Steps to solve the VLOOKUP formula with the TRUE lookup type

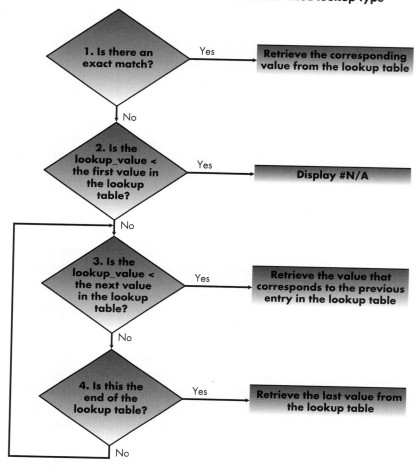

In steps 2, 3, and 4, the function compares the values in the lookup table to the lookup_value in order. Therefore, the values in the lookup table must be sorted in ascending order so that the function can make accurate comparisons.

Best Practice

Creating an Effective Vertical Lookup Table

To find and retrieve data from a vertical lookup table in the most efficient way, create a simple worksheet that contains related data, and organize this data in columns to form the vertical lookup table. Include a heading at the top of each column to easily identify the information. List the key values in the first column, and sort the data in ascending order by the values in that column. Key values are those pieces of data that you know, such as customer names or product descriptions. The remaining columns should contain values that you want to look up, such as customer numbers or product codes. You can use Excel lookup functions to find data when it's organized in a different way, but vertical lookup tables reflect the way you find information manually—by scanning the left column until you find the value for which you need information, and then looking to the right for the column containing the detail you need.

A lookup table can have only one value in each cell of its first column. For example, you can list 0, 60, 120, and 240 in the first column, but not 0–59, 60–119, and 120–239. When creating a vertical lookup table with the TRUE type, be certain to start with the lowest possible value, such as 0, so that the table covers all the possible data. For example, you might be tempted to start the Unit Pricing table with 60 because it's the first quantity associated with a unit price. However, if you need to look up a quantity such as 30, the function will display the text #N/A because 30 is less than the first value in the lookup table—instead of correctly displaying the unit price of $2.45.

Vijay decides to use the same type of formula to calculate the unit shipping value in cell G14. He uses the formula =VLOOKUP(C14,D$7:E$10,2,TRUE) to calculate the unit shipping charges, and then copies the formula to cells G15:G19. However, the results are correct only for orders 1 and 3. Vijay checks the cell references and the syntax of the formula, and realizes he should use FALSE instead of TRUE as the lookup type.

Retrieving an Exact Match

When you use a lookup type of FALSE, the VLOOKUP function looks only for an exact match of the lookup value. In this case, the values in the lookup table do not need to be sorted in ascending order, as they do with the TRUE type. If the function does not find an exact match, it displays #N/A in the cell.

When Vijay uses a lookup type of TRUE to calculate unit shipping charges, it causes a number of problems because the table is not sorted in ascending order. Furthermore, he wants an exact match to find "Rail," for example, and not the closest value. The lookup type for this formula should, therefore, be FALSE. Vijay changes the formula in cell G14 so that it uses a lookup type of FALSE, as follows:

```
=VLOOKUP(C14,D$7:E$10,2,FALSE)
```

To solve this formula, the function considers the value in cell C14 (Rail). Because the lookup type is FALSE, the function looks only for an exact match to "Rail" in the first column of the D7:E10 range, which is the Shipping Costs table. When it finds an exact match, it retrieves the corresponding value—$0.20—from the second column in the specified range.

Vijay copies the formula from cell G14 to cells G15:G19. Figure 5.5 shows the resulting worksheet.

Figure 5.5: VLOOKUP function with a FALSE lookup type

G14	▼	*fx*	=VLOOKUP(C14,D$7:E$10,2,FALSE)								
	A	B	C	D	E	F	G	H	I	J
1				Pricing Information for Tennis Balls						
2				TheZone Equipment Division						
3										
4										
5	Unit Pricing			Shipping Costs						
6	Qty	$/each		Method	$/each					
7	0	$ 2.45		Truck	$ 0.25					
8	60	$ 2.27		Rail	$ 0.20					
9	120	$ 2.12		Ship	$ 0.15					
10	240	$ 2.00		Customer	$ -					
11										
12										
13	Order #	Cust ID	Shipping	Quantity	Unit Price	Total Price	Unit Shipping	Total Shipping	Grand Total	
14	1	A0243	Rail	240	$ 2.00	$480.00	$ 0.20			
15	2	MH394	Train	30	$ 2.45	$ 73.50	#N/A			
16	3	R903	Ship	160	$ 2.12	$339.20	$ 0.15			
17	4	X271	Truck	215	$ 2.12	$455.80	$ 0.25			
18	5	N271	Truck	90	$ 2.27	$204.30	$ 0.25			
19	6	CD031	Customer	15	$ 2.45	$ 36.75	$ -			
20										
21										

Formula with the FALSE lookup type retrieves the correct values for unit shipping except in cell G15

With the FALSE lookup type, the VLOOKUP function retrieves the correct values for all of the Unit Shipping cells except G15. It retrieves values for G14 and G16:G19 because it looks for an exact match of the lookup value, which is the Shipping value in cells C14:C19. The function retrieves the values even though the list is unsorted. The text #N/A is displayed in cell G15 because the function cannot find an exact match to the value in C15, which is "Train." This is a data-entry error that Vijay can correct by changing "Train" in cell C15 to "Rail," as shown in Figure 5.6.

Figure 5.6: Completing the Unit Shipping information

	A	B	C	D	E	F	G	H	I	J
13	Order #	Cust ID	Shipping	Quantity	Unit Price	Total Price	Unit Shipping	Total Shipping	Grand Total	
14	1	A0243	Rail	240	$ 2.00	$480.00	$ 0.20			
15	2	MH394	Rail	30	$ 2.45	$ 73.50	$ 0.20			
16	3	R903	Ship	160	$ 2.12	$339.20	$ 0.15			
17	4	X271	Truck	215	$ 2.12	$455.80	$ 0.25			
18	5	N271	Truck	90	$ 2.27	$204.30	$ 0.25			
19	6	CD031	Customer	15	$ 2.45	$ 36.75	$ -			
20										
21										

After "Train" is changed to "Rail" in cell C15, the function retrieves the correct shipping cost and displays it in cell G15

Sorting a Vertical Lookup Table

To analyze the type of error an unsorted lookup table causes when you use the VLOOKUP function with a TRUE lookup type, refer to Figure 5.7. This figure shows the Unit Pricing table when it is not sorted in ascending order.

Figure 5.7: Using an unsorted lookup table

The first column of the lookup table is not sorted in ascending order

	Unit Pricing			Shipping Costs						
4										
5	Qty	$/each		Method	$/each					
6										
7	0	$ 2.45		Truck	$ 0.25					
8	240	$ 2.27		Rail	$ 0.20					
9	60	$ 2.12		Ship	$ 0.15					
10	120	$ 2.00		Customer	$ -					
11										

	Order #	Cust ID	Shipping	Quantity	Unit Price	Total Price	Unit Shipping	Total Shipping	Grand Total
12									
13									
14	1	A0243	Rail	240	$ 2.27	$544.80	$ 0.20		
15	2	MH394	Rail	30	$ 2.45	$ 73.50	$ 0.20		
16	3	R903	Ship	160	$ 2.45	$392.00	$ 0.15		
17	4	X271	Truck	215	$ 2.45	$526.75	$ 0.25		
18	5	N271	Truck	90	$ 2.45	$220.50	$ 0.25		
19	6	CD031	Customer	15	$ 2.45	$ 36.75	$ -		
20									
21									

These unit prices are incorrect

Why does the function retrieve the correct unit price for the first two orders, but not for the next four? To answer this question, you can follow the steps of the VLOOKUP algorithm. Start with the first incorrect value in cell E16. Excel retrieves the $2.45 unit price for a quantity of 160 by performing the following steps:

1. Does 160 match any value in the lookup table? No; continue to the next step.
2. Is 160 < 0? No; continue to the next lookup value.
3. Is 160 < 240? Yes; retrieve the value that corresponds to the previous entry in the lookup table, which is $2.45.

Because a VLOOKUP formula with a TRUE lookup type compares values based on their position in the lookup table, the values in the first column must be sorted in ascending order. Note that when you sort a lookup table containing text in alphabetical order, Excel considers uppercase and lowercase text as equivalent (that is, "A" is the same as "a").

Before writing a VLOOKUP formula with a TRUE type, double-check your vertical lookup table to ensure that the values in the first column are sorted in ascending order.

Now that Vijay has set up the VLOOKUP formulas in cells E14:E19 and G14:G19, he calculates the total shipping cost by multiplying the unit shipping charge by the quantity ordered, as shown in Figure 5.8.

Figure 5.8: Calculating the total shipping charge

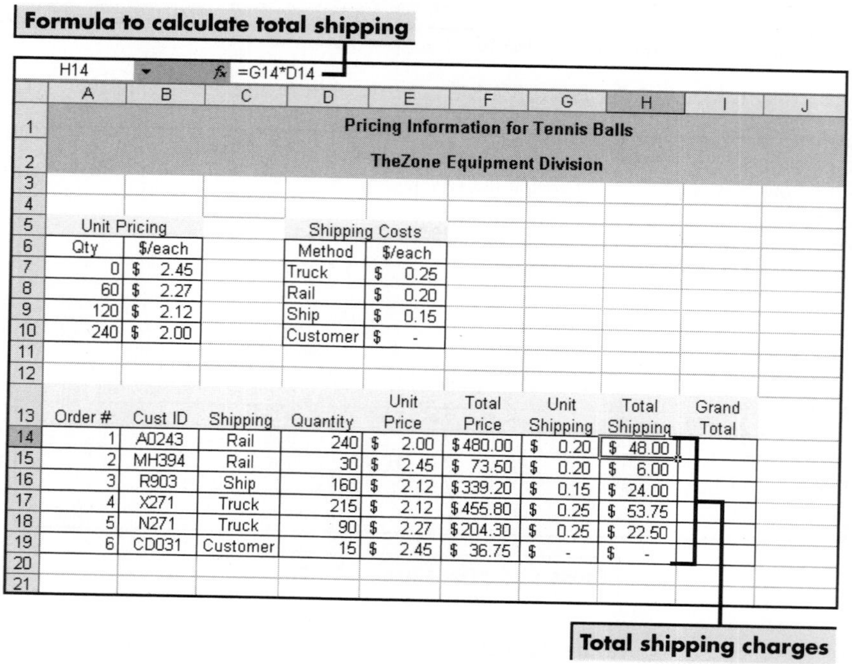

Formula to calculate total shipping

	A	B	C	D	E	F	G	H	I	J
	H14	▾		ƒx	=G14*D14					
1				Pricing Information for Tennis Balls						
2				TheZone Equipment Division						
3										
4										
5	Unit Pricing			Shipping Costs						
6	Qty	$/each		Method	$/each					
7	0	$ 2.45		Truck	$ 0.25					
8	60	$ 2.27		Rail	$ 0.20					
9	120	$ 2.12		Ship	$ 0.15					
10	240	$ 2.00		Customer	$ -					
11										
12										
13	Order #	Cust ID	Shipping	Quantity	Unit Price	Total Price	Unit Shipping	Total Shipping	Grand Total	
14	1	A0243	Rail	240	$ 2.00	$480.00	$ 0.20	$ 48.00		
15	2	MH394	Rail	30	$ 2.45	$ 73.50	$ 0.20	$ 6.00		
16	3	R903	Ship	160	$ 2.12	$339.20	$ 0.15	$ 24.00		
17	4	X271	Truck	215	$ 2.12	$455.80	$ 0.25	$ 53.75		
18	5	N271	Truck	90	$ 2.27	$204.30	$ 0.25	$ 22.50		
19	6	CD031	Customer	15	$ 2.45	$ 36.75	$ -	$ -		
20										
21										

Total shipping charges

RETRIEVING DATA FROM A HORIZONTAL LOOKUP TABLE

TheZone is considering offering customers a discount on shipping, depending on the total price of the customer's tennis ball order. Table 5.4 shows the two possible shipping discounts under consideration.

Table 5.4: Shipping discounts

Shipping Discount			
Total Price:	0	300	1000
Shipping Discount 1	0%	15%	25%
Shipping Discount 2	0%	10%	15%

For example, with Shipping Discount 1, a customer with an order totaling $350 would receive a 15% discount on the shipping costs. With Shipping Discount 2, this same order would receive a 10% discount.

Vijay now needs to evaluate the effect of this potential shipping discount on the overall total order. He begins by inserting the Shipping Discount lookup table as well as a new column labeled Shipping Discount in the Tennis Balls worksheet, as shown in Figure 5.9.

Figure 5.9: Worksheet with shipping discount data entered

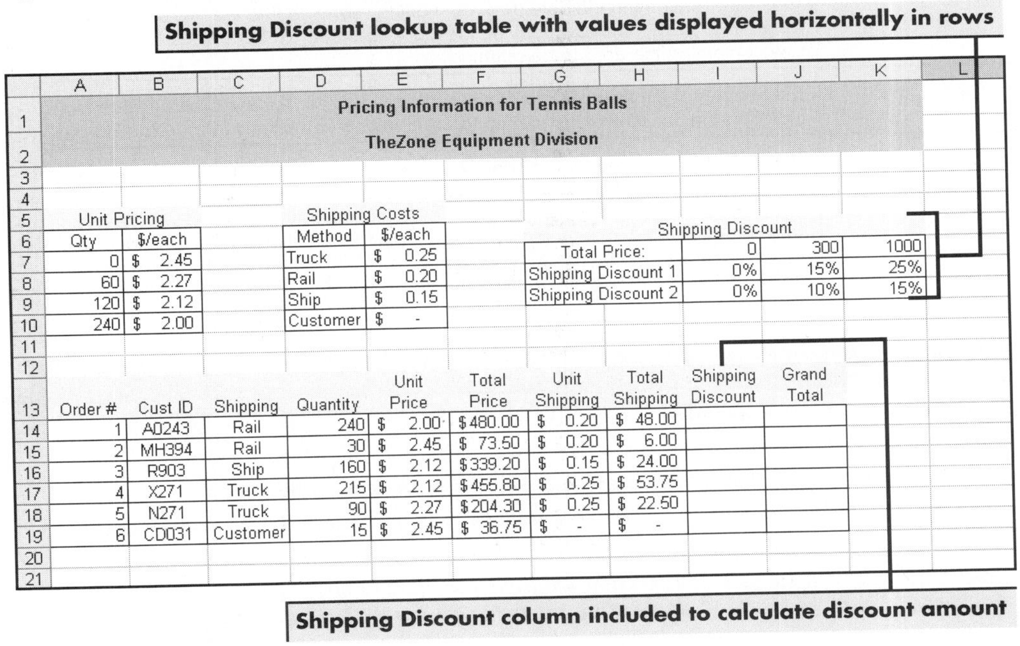

Shipping Discount lookup table with values displayed horizontally in rows

	A	B	C	D	E	F	G	H	I	J	K	L
1				Pricing Information for Tennis Balls								
2				TheZone Equipment Division								
3												
4												
5	Unit Pricing			Shipping Costs					Shipping Discount			
6	Qty	$/each		Method	$/each		Total Price:		0	300	1000	
7	0	$ 2.45		Truck	$ 0.25		Shipping Discount 1		0%	15%	25%	
8	60	$ 2.27		Rail	$ 0.20		Shipping Discount 2		0%	10%	15%	
9	120	$ 2.12		Ship	$ 0.15							
10	240	$ 2.00		Customer	$ -							
11												
12					Unit	Total	Unit	Total	Shipping	Grand		
13	Order #	Cust ID	Shipping	Quantity	Price	Price	Shipping	Shipping	Discount	Total		
14	1	A0243	Rail	240	$ 2.00	$480.00	$ 0.20	$ 48.00				
15	2	MH394	Rail	30	$ 2.45	$ 73.50	$ 0.20	$ 6.00				
16	3	R903	Ship	160	$ 2.12	$339.20	$ 0.15	$ 24.00				
17	4	X271	Truck	215	$ 2.12	$455.80	$ 0.25	$ 53.75				
18	5	N271	Truck	90	$ 2.27	$204.30	$ 0.25	$ 22.50				
19	6	CD031	Customer	15	$ 2.45	$ 36.75	$ -	$ -				
20												
21												

Shipping Discount column included to calculate discount amount

Notice that the shipping discounts are presented in a horizontal format, so Vijay cannot use the VLOOKUP function to retrieve the correct discount amount and display it in the Shipping Discount column. Instead, he can use a similar function, called **HLOOKUP**. (The "H" in HLOOKUP stands for horizontal.) When solving an HLOOKUP formula, Excel looks up a value by testing for a criterion across a row, instead of down a column. The syntax of the HLOOKUP function is as follows:

```
HLOOKUP(lookup_value,table_array,row_index_num,range_lookup)
```

The HLOOKUP function is similar to the VLOOKUP function, except that it searches a horizontal lookup table, in which data is stored in rows instead of columns. When you use the HLOOKUP function, you specify the row_index_num instead of col_index_num. Excel then searches for the lookup_value in the first row of the table_array, or lookup table, and returns the value in the specified row. The row_index_num is counted from the first row in the lookup table, not the worksheet, so the first row in the lookup table is row 1, and the second is row 2, even if the lookup table occupies other rows in the worksheet. Table 5.5 describes the four arguments in the HLOOKUP function.

Table 5.5: HLOOKUP function arguments

Argument	Description
lookup_value	The data you want to look up. This value can be a number, text, a logical value, or a name or cell reference that refers to a value.
table_array	The range containing the data that you want to search to find the lookup value. This range must start in the row with the lookup values and extend at least as far as the row containing the data to be returned.
row_index_num	The number of the row containing the data you want to retrieve. The number 1 indicates the first row of the lookup table, 2 indicates the second row, and so on.
range_lookup	The type of lookup you want to perform—TRUE or FALSE. With a TRUE type (the default), the HLOOKUP function finds the greatest value that does not exceed the lookup_value. When the lookup type is TRUE, the values in the first row of the lookup table must be sorted in ascending sort order; otherwise, HLOOKUP might not retrieve the correct value. With a FALSE type, the HLOOKUP function looks only for an exact match of the lookup_value. If it does not find an exact match, the text #N/A is displayed in the cell.

How To

Write an HLOOKUP Formula

1. Type: =HLOOKUP(
2. Enter the value you want to match, such as a cell reference, text, or number.
3. Enter the range that contains the data you want to look up, where the first row includes the matching values, or key data.
4. Enter the number of the row that contains the data you want to find.
5. Enter the type of lookup you want to perform—TRUE to search sorted data for the greatest value that meets your criteria, or FALSE to find an exact match.
6. Type a closing parenthesis), and then press the Enter key.

Vijay believes the company is more likely to go with Shipping Discount 2, which offers lower percentages as the discounts, so he decides to examine this discount first. For the formula he needs to enter in cell I14, the function must look up the total price given in cell F14 and find the corresponding discount. The lookup range (table_array argument) is the Shipping Discount lookup table in cells I7:K9. This range must start in the row with the lookup values and extend at least as far down to the row containing the data to be returned. Because Vijay wants to evaluate Shipping Discount 2, the function must retrieve data from row 3 of the lookup table (row_index_num argument). Finally, the function must use the TRUE type so that it will look for the greatest value in the first row of the lookup table that is not greater than the value in cell I14 ($480). The FALSE type, which would look for an exact match only, is not appropriate in this case.

Note that the algorithm for an HLOOKUP function with a TRUE lookup type works in the same way as for a VLOOKUP function, except that values are tested across the first row instead of down the first column. Therefore, the first row of the lookup table must be sorted in ascending order to use an HLOOKUP function with a TRUE lookup type.

Vijay is now ready to use the HLOOKUP function to calculate the shipping discount value. The discount will be the shipping discount percentage multiplied by the shipping costs. He enters the following formula in cell I14:

```
=-HLOOKUP(F14,I$7:K$9,3,TRUE)*H14
```

In this formula, the percentage retrieved from the lookup table is multiplied by the total shipping cost given in column H. The formula is preceded by a negative sign so that the resulting value will be negative, because the discount reduces the order cost. In the HLOOKUP function, the lookup_value is the total price (cell F14) because discounts are determined by this value. The table_array begins in cell I7 and extends to cell K9. The first row contains the values that the lookup_value is compared with, and the range extends at least as far down as the row containing the values to be returned. Because the percentages for Shipping Discount 2 are two rows below, the table_array must extend through row K. The value to be returned is in the third row of the range, so the row_index_num is 3. And because the function should find the greatest value that does not exceed the lookup value, the TRUE type is used. Note that the table_array argument must contain absolute cell references so that the row values will not change when the formula is copied down the column.

Vijay's final calculation is to determine the grand total (column J). To do so, he sums the following: total price (column F) plus total shipping (column H) plus shipping discount (column I). Because the shipping discount values are negative, the formula he enters will actually subtract this discount amount from the total. Vijay enters the formula =F14+H14+I14 in cell J14. The final Tennis Balls worksheet is shown in Figure 5.10.

Figure 5.10: Calculating the shipping discount and grand total

For Order #1, totaling $480, the Shipping Discount 2 corresponds to a 10% discount

Pricing Information for Tennis Balls

TheZone Equipment Division

Unit Pricing

Qty	$/each
0	$ 2.45
60	$ 2.27
120	$ 2.12
240	$ 2.00

Shipping Costs

Method	$/each
Truck	$ 0.25
Rail	$ 0.20
Ship	$ 0.15
Customer	$ -

Shipping Discount

Total Price:	0	300	1000
Shipping Discount 1	0%	15%	25%
Shipping Discount 2	0%	10%	15%

Order #	Cust ID	Shipping	Quantity	Unit Price	Total Price	Unit Shipping	Total Shipping	Shipping Discount	Grand Total
1	A0243	Rail	240	$ 2.00	$480.00	$ 0.20	$ 48.00	$ (4.80)	$ 523.20
2	MH394	Rail	30	$ 2.45	$ 73.50	$ 0.20	$ 6.00	$ -	$ 79.50
3	R903	Ship	160	$ 2.12	$339.20	$ 0.15	$ 24.00	$ (2.40)	$ 360.80
4	X271	Truck	215	$ 2.12	$455.80	$ 0.25	$ 53.75	$ (5.38)	$ 504.18
5	N271	Truck	90	$ 2.27	$204.30	$ 0.25	$ 22.50	$ -	$ 226.80
6	CD031	Customer	15	$ 2.45	$ 36.75	$ -	$ -	$ -	$ 36.75

Formula to calculate the shipping discount: =-HLOOKUP(F14,I$7:K$9,3,TRUE)*H14

Formula to calculate the grand total: =F14+H14+I14

Consider Order #1, which totals $480. The HLOOKUP function searched the Shipping Discount 2 row in the lookup table and retrieved the corresponding discount of 10%. This discount was then multiplied by the total shipping charge (cell H14) to produce the correct shipping discount of $4.80 (cell I14).

Now that Vijay has completed the pricing calculations for tennis balls, he can create the order form for all tennis products, which he will do in the next section.

Steps To Success: Level 1

In addition to creating an order form for tennis balls, Vijay also needs to create an order form for golf balls. TheZone sells golf balls in various packages, such as a box of a dozen balls, but prices them per unit. The shipping charges for golf balls are slightly different from those for tennis balls. Table 5.6 shows the unit prices and shipping charges for golf balls.

Table 5.6: Unit prices and shipping charges for golf balls

Quantity (in units)	Price Each	Shipping Method	Charge Per Unit
Under 48	$2.85	Truck	$0.20
48–107	$2.63	Rail	$0.18
108–215	$2.27	Ship	$0.12
216 or more	$2.00	Customer arranges shipping	$0.00

Vijay has already created a Golf workbook containing lookup tables and an order form in a worksheet named Pricing. See Figure 5.11.

Figure 5.11: Pricing worksheet in the Golf workbook

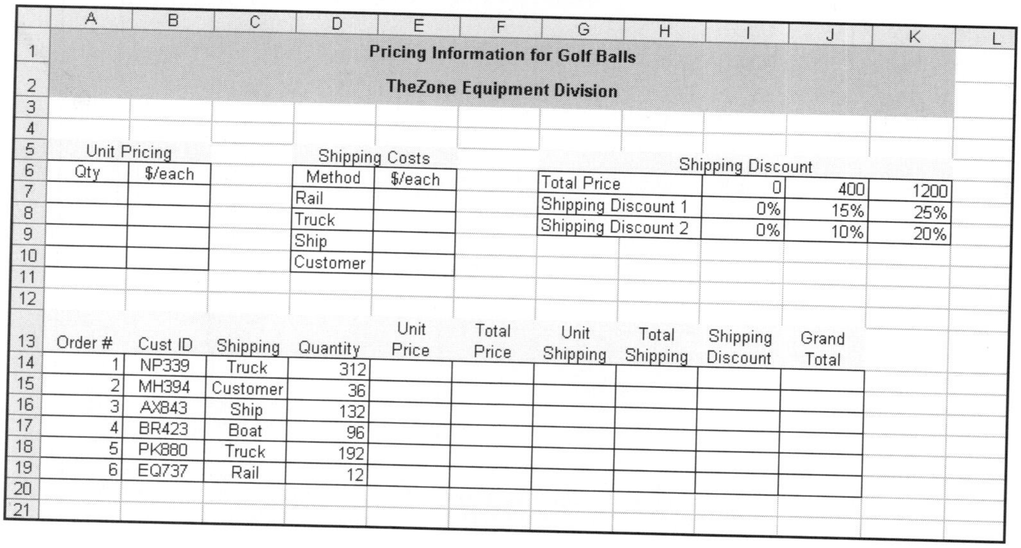

Pricing Information for Golf Balls

TheZone Equipment Division

Unit Pricing

Qty	$/each

Shipping Costs

Method	$/each
Rail	
Truck	
Ship	
Customer	

Shipping Discount

Total Price	0	400	1200
Shipping Discount 1	0%	15%	25%
Shipping Discount 2	0%	10%	20%

Order #	Cust ID	Shipping	Quantity	Unit Price	Total Price	Unit Shipping	Total Shipping	Shipping Discount	Grand Total
1	NP339	Truck	312						
2	MH394	Customer	36						
3	AX843	Ship	132						
4	BR423	Boat	96						
5	PK880	Truck	192						
6	EQ737	Rail	12						

5

Level 1

In these steps, you need to complete this worksheet using the appropriate lookup functions to calculate the total prices, total shipping charges, and grand totals. Complete the following:

1. Open the workbook named **Golf.xls** located in the Chapter 5 folder, and then save it as **Golf Orders.xls**.

2. In the Pricing worksheet, complete the Unit Pricing lookup table to include the units and corresponding prices that TheZone charges for golf balls.

3. Complete the Shipping Costs table to list the appropriate unit shipping charges.

4. In cell E14, use the appropriate lookup function to calculate the unit price for this order based on the quantity ordered. Write the formula so that it can be copied down the column, and then copy the formula into cells E15:E19.

5. In cell F14, calculate the total price of this order (excluding shipping). Write the formula so that it can be copied down the column, and then copy the formula into cells F15:F19.

6. In cell G14, calculate the unit shipping charge based on the shipping method. Write the formula so that it can be copied down the column, and then copy the formula into cells G15:G19. Correct data-entry errors, as necessary.

7. In cell H14, calculate the total shipping cost. Write the formula so that it can be copied down the column, and then copy the formula into cells H15:H19. Ignore any inconsistent formula errors.

8. In cell I14, calculate the shipping discount, using Shipping Discount 2, based on the total price. Write the formula so that it can be copied down the column, and then copy the formula into cells I15:I19.

9. In cell J14, calculate the grand total for this item. Write the formula so that it can be copied down the column, and then copy the formula into cells J15:J19.

10. Save and close the Golf Orders.xls workbook.

LEVEL 2

PERFORMING MORE COMPLEX LOOKUPS INVOLVING MULTIPLE WORKSHEETS AND MULTIDIMENSIONAL TABLES

EXCEL 2003 SKILLS TRAINING

- **Use lookup tables**
- **Use a named range reference in one or more formulas**
- **Use VLOOKUP**

RETRIEVING DATA FROM MULTIPLE WORKSHEETS

As you learned in Level 1, you can use a VLOOKUP formula and an HLOOKUP formula to retrieve data stored in lookup tables on the same worksheet. You can also use VLOOKUP and HLOOKUP to retrieve data stored in lookup tables on other worksheets. This is especially useful when lookup tables are long, such as those that contain products and prices, or when you need to retrieve data from more than one lookup table.

Now that Vijay has completed the Tennis Balls worksheet and order form, which calculates the cost of an item based on quantity ordered, he is ready to develop a worksheet for other types of tennis equipment, such as rackets and bags, which are based on a fixed price per unit. This worksheet must accommodate orders for products that have fixed prices per unit, and include many products in a single order. Vijay decides to develop this worksheet for now without including bulk tennis balls, which are priced based on quantity ordered. Later, he will explore creating an order form that can handle both fixed and variable prices per unit.

Vijay begins by adding a worksheet named "Costs" to the Tennis Orders workbook. This worksheet is a partial list of the tennis equipment TheZone sells for a fixed price. The list includes a product description and its associated unit cost.

Vijay also adds a worksheet named Orders to the Tennis Orders workbook that will serve as an order form, or template. This worksheet will include the data for a single customer's order, which can contain one or more items. Vijay's idea is that salespeople will enter an item number and quantity, and formulas will retrieve or calculate the item description and item total price. Formulas will also calculate the subtotal of all items, discounts, shipping charges, and a grand total. Figure 5.12 shows how the Costs and Orders worksheets will be used together to achieve the desired results.

Figure 5.12: Orders worksheet with calculations to be based on the Costs worksheet

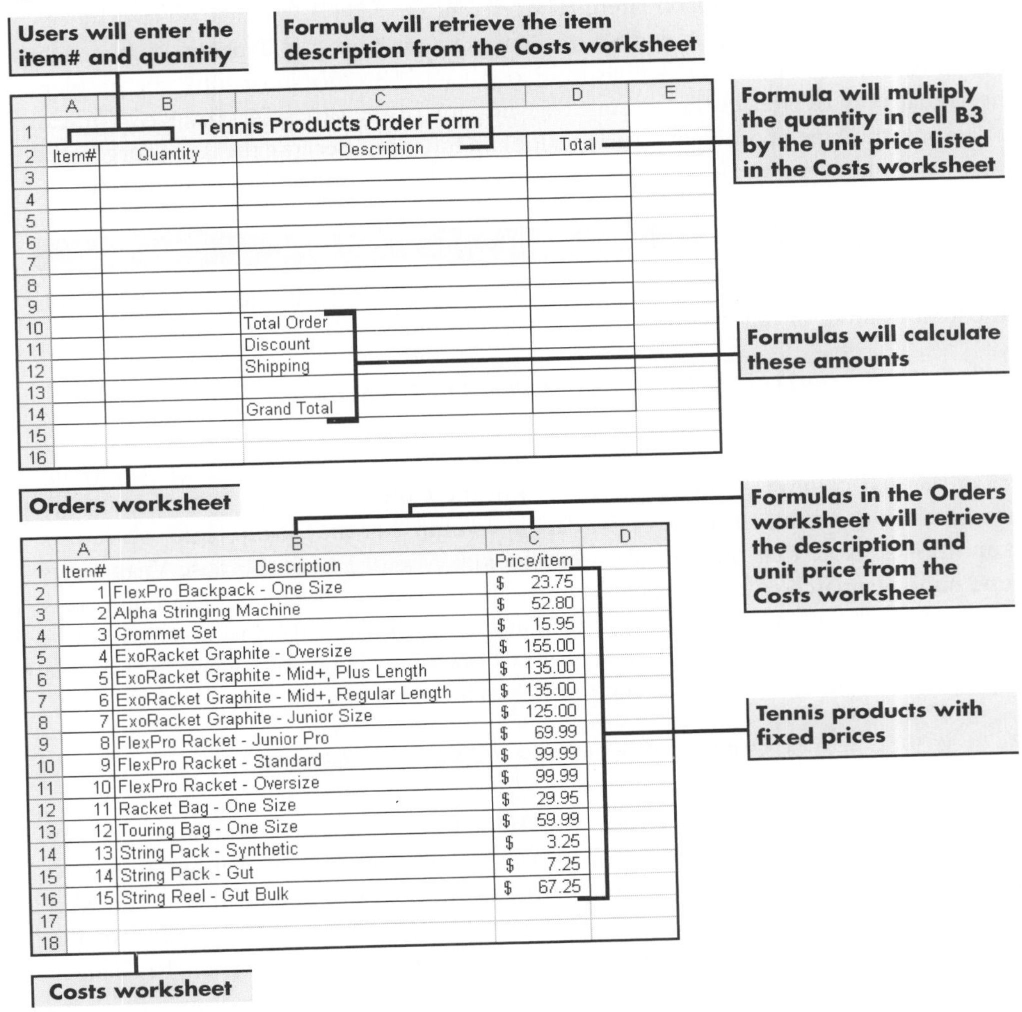

The first product ordered has the item number 12 (Touring Bag - One Size) and a quantity of 10. To create the formula that multiplies the quantity ordered by the product's unit price, Vijay considers writing the following formula in cell D3 of the Orders worksheet:

```
=Costs!C13*B3
```

This formula multiplies the value in cell C13 of the Costs worksheet by the value in cell B3 of the current worksheet. (Cell C13 contains the unit price of item number 12.) This formula would calculate the correct result—$599.90—for the first item. However, Vijay cannot copy this formula to cells D4:D8 to calculate the total price for other items. For example, if the formula =Costs!C13*B3 is copied to cell D4, it becomes =Costs!C14*B4. The reference to cell B4 is correct because that cell will contain the quantity ordered for the second item. The reference to cell C14 in the Costs worksheet, however, might or might not contain the correct unit price—it depends on the item ordered. An absolute cell reference, as in =Costs!C$13*B4, does not solve the problem either—that only references the touring bag, not any of the other 14 products. You can usually solve this type of problem by using a lookup function. Because the data is organized on the Costs sheet in a vertical format, the VLOOKUP function will work in this case.

Using VLOOKUP with Multiple Worksheets

Vijay will use the VLOOKUP function in cell D3 to retrieve the unit price that corresponds to the item number in cell A3, as in the following formula:

$$\text{=VLOOKUP(A3,Costs!A2:C16,3,FALSE)*B3}$$

To solve this formula, the function looks for the item number value in cell A3 (12, in this case) in the first column of the range A2:C16 in the Costs worksheet. When it finds an exact match to that value, it retrieves the data in column 3 of the lookup table, which lists the unit prices. Note that the formula uses a lookup type of FALSE because Vijay wants to find an exact match to the data entered in cell A3. What will happen when he copies this formula to the other cells in the column? Although cells A3 and B3 will vary relatively, the lookup range (A2:C16) needs to be absolute because it will not vary when the formula is copied. Therefore, Vijay modifies the formula as follows:

$$\text{=VLOOKUP(A3,Costs!A$2:C$16,3,FALSE)*B3}$$

Vijay plans to provide the Tennis Orders workbook to other sales representatives so they can adapt it for their primary products, and he wants to make his calculations as easy to understand as possible. One way to simplify the formula and be certain that the lookup range remains the same is to use a named range for the table_array Costs!A2:C16. He switches to the Costs worksheet and names the A2:C16 range "Pricing." Then, he changes the VLOOKUP formula in cell D3 of the Orders worksheet to the following:

$$\text{=VLOOKUP(A3,Pricing,3,FALSE)*B3}$$

Because range names copy absolutely, Vijay can copy this formula to cells D4:D8 and change only the references to cells A3 and B3, as appropriate.

Vijay can use a similar formula to insert the correct item description in cells C3:C8 of the Orders worksheet:

$$\text{=VLOOKUP(A3,Pricing,2,FALSE)}$$

To solve this formula, the function looks for the item number value in cell A3 (12, in this case) in the first column of the Pricing range in the Costs worksheet. When it finds an exact match to that value, it retrieves the data in column 2 of the table, which lists the item descriptions. Vijay enters the item number (12) and quantity (10) for the first product ordered in the Orders worksheet. He also enters both VLOOKUP formulas in the appropriate cells, as shown in Figure 5.13.

Figure 5.13: VLOOKUP formulas in the Orders worksheet

VLOOKUP formula calculates the total cost of item 12

VLOOKUP formula retrieves the description for item 12 from the Costs worksheet

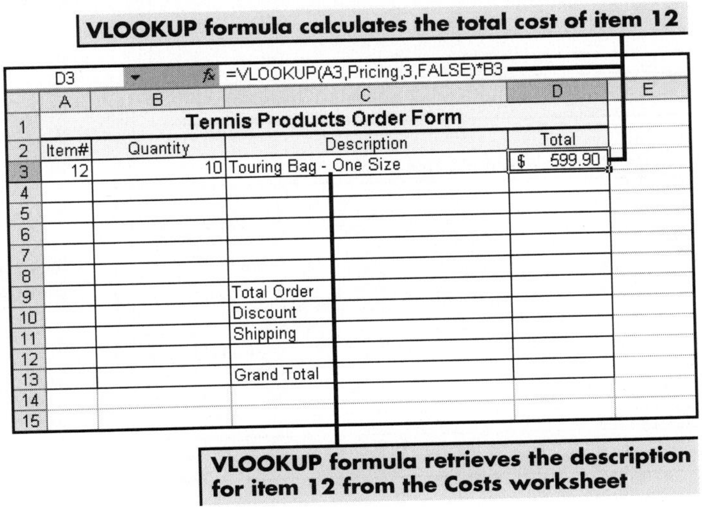

Vijay enters four more items for this order by entering item numbers in cells A4:A7 and the quantities ordered in cells B4:B7. Then, he copies the VLOOKUP formula in cell C3 to cells C4:C7 to insert the appropriate item descriptions. He also copies the VLOOKUP formula in cell D3 to cells D4:D7 to calculate the correct order totals. Then, he calculates the total order amount by summing the prices in cells D3:D7. Figure 5.14 shows the Orders worksheet with both values and formulas displayed.

Figure 5.14: Complete Orders worksheet values and formulas

	A	B	C	D	E
1			Tennis Products Order Form		
2	Item#	Quantity	Description	Total	
3	12	10	Touring Bag - One Size	$ 599.90	
4	4	50	ExoRacket Graphite - Oversize	$ 7,750.00	
5	8	25	FlexPro Racket - Junior Pro	$ 1,749.75	
6	10	25	FlexPro Racket - Oversize	$ 2,499.75	
7	13	100	String Pack - Synthetic	$ 325.00	
8					
9			Total Order	$12,924.40	
10			Discount		
11			Shipping		
12					
13			Grand Total		
14					
15					

Values resulting from calculations

	A	B	C	D	E
1			Tennis Products Order Form		
2	Item#	Quantity	Description	Total	
3	12	10	=VLOOKUP(A3,Pricing,2,FALSE)	=VLOOKUP(A3,Pricing,3,FALSE)*B3	
4	4	50	=VLOOKUP(A4,Pricing,2,FALSE)	=VLOOKUP(A4,Pricing,3,FALSE)*B4	
5	8	25	=VLOOKUP(A5,Pricing,2,FALSE)	=VLOOKUP(A5,Pricing,3,FALSE)*B5	
6	10	25	=VLOOKUP(A6,Pricing,2,FALSE)	=VLOOKUP(A6,Pricing,3,FALSE)*B6	
7	13	100	=VLOOKUP(A7,Pricing,2,FALSE)	=VLOOKUP(A7,Pricing,3,FALSE)*B7	
8					
9			Total Order	=SUM(D3:D8)	
10			Discount		
11			Shipping		
12					
13			Grand Total		
14					
15					

Corresponding formulas

LOOKING UP DATA IN A ONE-ROW OR ONE-COLUMN RANGE

Vijay's next task is to calculate the value of the discount being offered to large volume customers. TheZone offers a $150 discount on all tennis equipment orders of $5,000 or more, a $400 discount on orders of $10,000 or more, and a $1,000 discount on orders of $25,000 or more. Vijay's sales manager has already created a workbook containing this discount information on a worksheet named "Discount." Vijay copies this worksheet into his Tennis Orders workbook, as shown in Figure 5.15.

Figure 5.15: Discount worksheet

	A	B	C	D
1	Discount	Total Order Value	Description	
2	0	0	Less than $5000, no discount	
3	$ 150	$ 5,000	At least $5000 but less than $10,000, $150 discount	
4	$ 400	$ 10,000	At least $10,000 but less than $25,000, $400 discount	
5	$ 1,000	$ 25,000	$25,000 or more, $1000 discount	
6				

The total order values in this worksheet are based on the order subtotal before shipping. Vijay examines the Discount worksheet to see if he can use a VLOOKUP function to retrieve the appropriate discounts. The values he wants to look up are in column B and the values to retrieve are in column A, which means he cannot use the VLOOKUP function. One possible solution is to reconfigure the table. However, the Discount worksheet will be updated periodically by Vijay's sales manager. This means Vijay would have to reconfigure the worksheet every time he receives an updated one. Another possibility is to use the LOOKUP function. Unlike VLOOKUP, the **LOOKUP function** looks up the greatest value that does not exceed a specified value anywhere in a table or range. It can retrieve data from a lookup table with a vertical or horizontal orientation. LOOKUP also uses only a TRUE lookup type, so the column or row containing the lookup values must be in ascending order. The syntax of the LOOKUP function is as follows:

$$\text{LOOKUP(lookup\_value,lookup\_vector,result\_vector)}$$

Table 5.7 describes the three arguments of the LOOKUP function.

Table 5.7: LOOKUP function arguments

Argument	Description
lookup_value	The data you want to look up. This value can be a number, text, a logical value, or a name or cell reference that refers to a value.
lookup_vector	The location of the data you want to look up. This location is a range of only one row or column that contains the value you want to look up.
result_vector	The location of the data you want to retrieve. This location is a range of only one row or column that contains the data you want to retrieve. This range must be the same size as the lookup_vector; for example, if there are 10 values in the lookup_vector, there must be 10 corresponding values in the result_vector.

How To

Write a LOOKUP Formula

1. Type: =LOOKUP(
2. Enter the value you want to look up, such as a cell reference, text, or number.
3. Enter the range that contains the data you want to look up.
4. Enter the range that contains the data you want to retrieve.
5. Type a closing parenthesis), and then press the Enter key.

You can often use a LOOKUP function instead of a VLOOKUP or HLOOKUP function with a TRUE lookup type. You can only use a LOOKUP function when you want to retrieve a value that is stored to the left of a key data column in a vertical lookup table or above a key data row in a horizontal lookup table. Figure 5.16 illustrates this fact using data for some of TheZone's customers.

Figure 5.16: Vertical and horizontal lookup tables that work only with LOOKUP

Customer names are stored to the left of the customer numbers

	A	B	C	D	E	F	G
1	Customer Name	Number	Street	City	State	Zip	
2	A-line Athletic Goods	100-2	1366 W. Treeline Rd.	Denver	CO	80202	
3	AllBest Sporting Goods	100-3	72 S. Boyd St.	Denver	CO	80214	
4	BBK Athletics	100-4	8232 W. Rockies	Aurora	CO	80013	
5	CC Sports Supply	100-5	5378 Airport Blvd.	Denver	CO	80224	
6	First Western Sports	100-6	55 N. Cougar Way	Boulder	CO	80306	
7	Full Spectrum Sporting Goods	100-7	11285 National Rd.	Boulder	CO	80329	
8	Milton Athletic Supply	100-8	313 N. Dowler St.	Aurora	CO	80013	
9	Northern Sporting Goods	100-9	2574 Churchill Rd.	Denver	CO	80221	
10	Stedco Athletic Gear	100-10	2215 W. Jefferson	Fort Collins	CO	80525	
11							
12							

This a vertical lookup table, but if you want to look up a customer number to find the correct name, you can't use VLOOKUP—you must use LOOKUP

Customer names are stored in the row above the customer numbers

	A	B	C	D	E
1	Customer name	A-line Athletic Goods	AllBest Sporting Goods	BBK Athletics	
2	Number	100-2	100-3	100-4	
3	Zip	80202	80214	80013	
4					
5					

This a horizontal lookup table, but if you want to look up a customer number to find the correct name, you can't use HLOOKUP—you must use LOOKUP

Note that when you use the LOOKUP function, the data in the lookup table must be sorted in ascending order. As with the VLOOKUP and HLOOKUP functions with the TRUE lookup type, the LOOKUP function looks for a value that matches the criterion by comparing values based on their position in the lookup table. The function looks in the first cell in the lookup_vector for an exact match, and then looks for a value in the next cell to find the greatest value that does not exceed the lookup_value. It can only make these comparisons correctly if the values are sorted in ascending order. Also, if the lookup_value is less than the smallest value in the lookup_vector, LOOKUP displays the text #N/A, just as VLOOKUP and HLOOKUP do. The horizontal lookup table in Figure 5.16 could cause problems when you are looking for an exact match. For example, if you are looking up number 100-3, but it does not appear in the list, LOOKUP would return the value for 100-2. Because LOOKUP does not have a FALSE lookup type, it might not be the best choice in such a situation.

In this case, because Vijay wants to look up the total order amount to insert the discount amount in the Orders worksheet, he must use a lookup_value of D9, which is the cell in the Orders worksheet that stores the total order amount. In the Discount worksheet

(Figure 5.15), cells B2:B5 contain the total order amounts, so this cell range will constitute the lookup_vector. Also in the Discount worksheet, cells A2:A5 contain the discount amounts, so this cell range will constitute the result_vector.

To simplify the LOOKUP formula, Vijay names the range B2:B5 in the Discount worksheet "Totals." Then, he can use "Totals" as the second argument, the lookup_vector, in the LOOKUP formula. He also names the range A2:A5 in the Discount worksheet "Discounts" so he can use "Discounts" as the third argument, the result_vector. In the Orders worksheet, Vijay enters the following formula in cell D11:

$$=-\text{LOOKUP(D9,Totals,Discounts)}$$

The negative sign at the beginning of the formula indicates that Excel should display the results as a negative value—Vijay wants to deduct the discount amount from the order amount. To solve the rest of the formula, Excel looks for the total order amount in cell D9 ($12,924.40) in the range named Totals (cells B2:B5 in the Discount worksheet). When it finds the greatest value that does not exceed $12,924.40, it retrieves the corresponding data from the range named Discounts (cells A2:A5 in the Discount worksheet), as shown in Figure 5.17.

Figure 5.17: Using a LOOKUP function to calculate the discount

D10		fx =-LOOKUP(D9,Totals,Discounts)		
	A	B	C	D
1		Tennis Products Order Form		
2	Item#	Quantity	Description	Total
3	12	10	Touring Bag - One Size	$ 599.90
4	4	50	ExoRacket Graphite - Oversize	$ 7,750.00
5	8	25	FlexPro Racket - Junior Pro	$ 1,749.75
6	10	25	FlexPro Racket - Oversize	$ 2,499.75
7	13	100	String Pack - Synthetic	$ 325.00
8				
9			Total Order	$12,924.40
10			Discount	$ (400.00)
11			Shipping	
12				
13			Grand Total	
14				
15				

The LOOKUP function looks in the range named Totals for the greatest value that does not exceed the total order amount in cell D9 ($12,924.40), and then retrieves the corresponding data (400) from the range named Discounts

	A	B	C	D
1	Discount	Total Order Value	Description	
2	$ -		Less than $5000, no discount	
3	$ 150	$ 5,000	At least $5000 but less than $10,000, $150 discount	
4	$ 400	$ 10,000	At least $10,000 but less than $25,000, $400 discount	
5	$ 1,000	$ 25,000	$25,000 or more, $1000 discount	
6				
7				

Discounts range | Totals range

Vijay learns that TheZone's shipping procedures are changing. Before he can complete the Orders worksheet, he needs to determine the appropriate shipping charges, based on the new information.

RETRIEVING DATA FROM MULTIDIMENSIONAL TABLES

TheZone has contracted with an outside company to handle all of its shipping. This means Vijay must change his method of calculating shipping charges. Instead of basing the charge only on the shipping method or order value, he must now determine the charge according to the weight of the order in pounds. The price per pound is based on two variables—the shipping method and the shipping destination. The shipping company has segmented the United States into regions 1 through 5 (Northeast, Southeast, Midwest, Southwest, and West). Shipments outside of the United States must be priced separately. The shipping company also prices according to four shipping methods: (1) Truck, (2) Rail, (3) Air, and (4) Boat.

So far, Vijay has used different lookup functions to find only one value, such as quantity, to determine a result, such as price. Vijay now needs to vary both the destination region and the shipment method to calculate the shipping price in dollars per pound. To make this calculation, Vijay can use the **INDEX function**, which allows you to retrieve data from multidimensional tables.

Vijay adds a new worksheet named "Shipping by Region," which lists prices per pound, to the Tennis Orders workbook. Figure 5.18 shows this worksheet. If a shipping method is not available to a specific region, the worksheet displays the value NA. Prices for Air and Boat include local hauling to and from the freight terminal.

Figure 5.18: Shipping by Region worksheet

	A	B	C	D	E	F
1		Shipping Method - Standard				
2	Region	1	2	3	4	
3	1	$ 0.10	$ 0.11	$ 1.50	NA	
4	2	$ 0.18	$ 0.12	$ 2.00	NA	
5	3	$ 0.24	$ 0.14	$ 2.10	$ 0.20	
6	4	$ 0.28	$ 0.16	$ 2.25	$ 0.20	
7	5	$ 0.45	$ 0.40	$ 3.50	$ 0.35	
8						
9						

Price per pound depends on two variables—region and shipping method

This lookup table is a **two-dimensional table**. In a one-dimensional table, Excel can search a row or column to find key data, and then use that data to locate the correct value. To find a value in a two-dimensional table, Excel searches one dimension, such as the columns, and then searches another dimension, such as the rows, to find the value at the intersection of a single row and column.

The order in the Orders worksheet has a total shipping weight of 100 pounds, and it is being shipped to Region 3 via truck (Shipping Method 1). Vijay modifies the Orders worksheet to include this shipping information at the top, as shown in Figure 5.19. Because this order form will be used as a template, these data inputs must be included so that they can be changed, as needed, based on the specific order.

Figure 5.19: Modified Orders worksheet

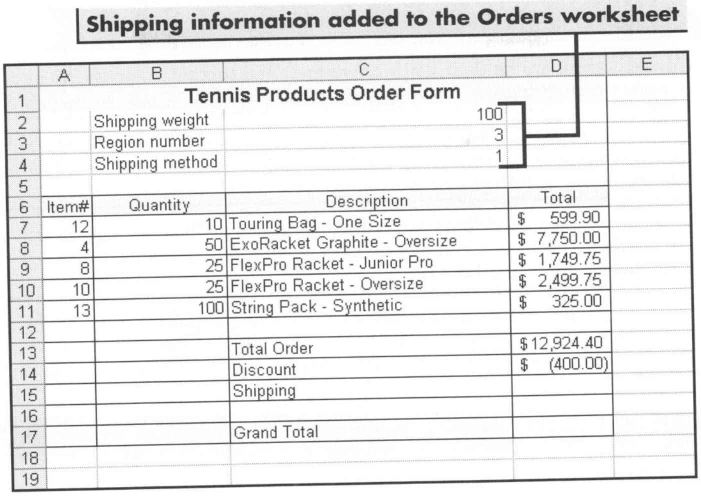

Shipping information added to the Orders worksheet

	A	B	C	D	E
1			Tennis Products Order Form		
2		Shipping weight		100	
3		Region number		3	
4		Shipping method		1	
5					
6	Item#	Quantity	Description	Total	
7	12	10	Touring Bag - One Size	$ 599.90	
8	4	50	ExoRacket Graphite - Oversize	$ 7,750.00	
9	8	25	FlexPro Racket - Junior Pro	$ 1,749.75	
10	10	25	FlexPro Racket - Oversize	$ 2,499.75	
11	13	100	String Pack - Synthetic	$ 325.00	
12					
13			Total Order	$ 12,924.40	
14			Discount	$ (400.00)	
15			Shipping		
16					
17			Grand Total		
18					
19					

So, what is the total shipping charge for this order? To determine this, Vijay needs to find the correct price per pound for the associated region and shipping method. He could do this manually by searching column A in the Shipping by Region worksheet to find Region 3, which is stored in cell A5. Then, he could search row 5 for Shipping Method 1, which appears in column B. He finds that the price per pound to ship to Region 3 via Shipping Method 1 is $0.24 per pound, shown in cell B5. So, the total cost of shipping the 100-pound shipment is 100*$0.24, or $24. However, Vijay wants to automate this process using the INDEX function.

Using the INDEX Function with a Two-Dimensional Table

To calculate the shipping charge in cell D15 of the Orders worksheet, Vijay must now account for three variables: shipping weight, region number, and shipping method. He wants to look up the region number and shipping method in the two-dimensional table stored in the Shipping by Region worksheet (Figure 5.18). He cannot use the VLOOKUP, HLOOKUP, or LOOKUP functions with a two-dimensional table. Instead, he must use the INDEX function, which returns the value in a table based on the row and column numbers that you specify. Excel provides several forms of the INDEX function. The one that Vijay will use has the following syntax and is described in Table 5.8:

```
=INDEX(reference,row_num,column_num,area_num)
```

Table 5.8: INDEX function arguments

Argument	Description
reference	The range containing the data you want to find. The range can be a continuous range or a set of nonadjacent ranges.
row_num	The number of the row in the range referenced in the first argument. You number the rows within the range, not the worksheet, so the first row of the range is row 1, even if it is stored in a different row in the worksheet.
col_num	The column in the range referenced in the first argument. You number the columns within the range, not the worksheet, so the first column of the range is column 1, even if it is stored in a different column in the worksheet.
area_num	The part of a nonadjacent range referenced in the first argument. You use this argument only if you specified a nonadjacent range in the first argument. Use an area_num of 1 to indicate the first part of a nonadjacent range, 2 to indicate the second part, and so on.

How To

Write an INDEX Formula

1. Type: =INDEX(

2. Enter the range containing the data you want to retrieve.

3. Enter the number of the row in which the data is stored.

4. Enter the number of the column in which the data is stored.

5. If the cells containing the data include nonadjacent ranges, enter the number of the area in which the data is stored.

6. Type a closing parenthesis), and then press the Enter key.

To facilitate creating the necessary formula, Vijay first names the cell range B3:E7 in the Shipping by Region worksheet "ShipByRegion."

Vijay wants to find values stored in the ShipByRegion range, which contains the per pound charges for shipments according to region and shipping method. So, the ShipByRegion range will be the reference argument in the formula. In the ShipByRegion range, rows 1–5 contain the region numbers. The region number for the order is stored in cell C3 of the Orders worksheet, so Vijay can use C3 as the second argument (row_num) when he creates the INDEX formula. In the ShipByRegion range, columns 1–4 contain the Shipping Method numbers. The shipping method for the order is stored in cell C4 of the Orders worksheet, so Vijay can use C4 as the third argument (col_num) in the INDEX formula. Finally, because ShipByRegion is a continuous range, Vijay does not need to specify the area_num argument.

Vijay wants to insert the INDEX function in cell D15 of the Orders worksheet to calculate the shipping charge according to TheZone's new policy. He enters the following formula in cell D15:

```
=INDEX(ShipByRegion,C3,C4)
```

To solve this formula, the function refers to the data stored in the ShipByRegion range. It retrieves the value at the intersection of the row specified in cell C3 (row 3) and the column specified in cell C4 (column 1).

The formula only returns the shipping charge per pound. Vijay also must multiply the results of the INDEX formula by the shipping weight, which is stored in cell C2. He modifies the formula as follows:

$$=\text{INDEX(ShipByRegion,C3,C4)*C2}$$

Figure 5.20 shows the resulting worksheet.

Figure 5.20: Using an INDEX function to calculate the shipping charge

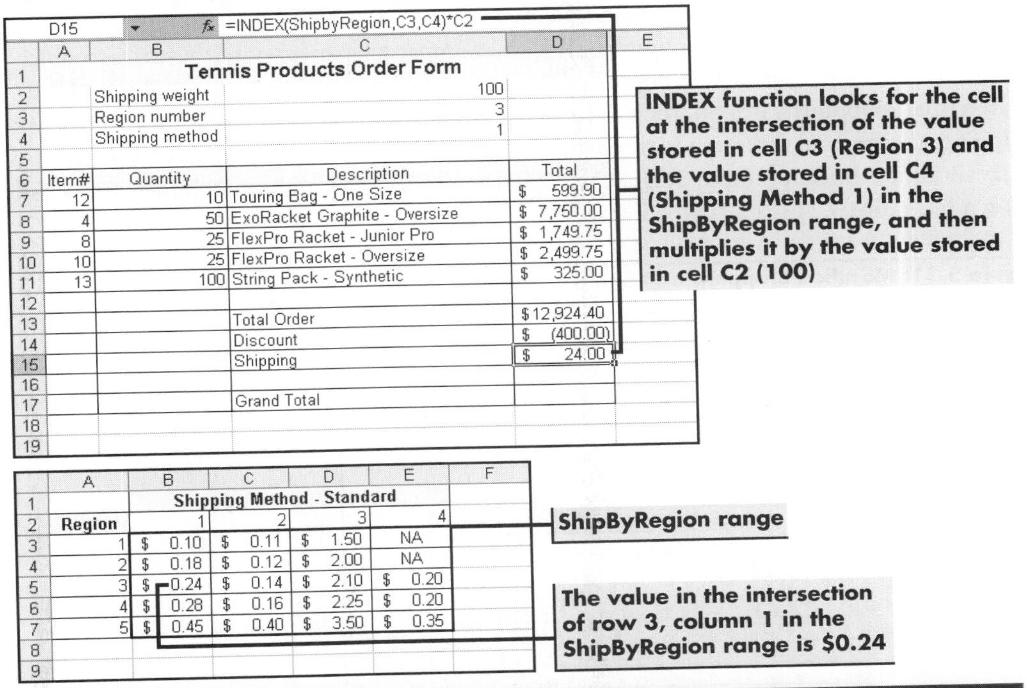

INDEX function looks for the cell at the intersection of the value stored in cell C3 (Region 3) and the value stored in cell C4 (Shipping Method 1) in the ShipByRegion range, and then multiplies it by the value stored in cell C2 (100)

ShipByRegion range

The value in the intersection of row 3, column 1 in the ShipByRegion range is $0.24

Best Practice

Nesting Functions to Set a Minimum or Maximum Value

The formula =INDEX(ShipByRegion,C3,C4)*C2 results in a value of $24 for the order shown in Figure 5.20. What if there was a minimum charge for shipping and handling set at $25 per order? How could this minimum charge be incorporated into the calculation?

To set a minimum price, you need the formula to take the higher of two prices—in this case, $25 or the result of the formula =INDEX(ShipByRegion,C3,C4)*C2. One simple way to do this is to nest the INDEX function inside a MAX function, as follows:

$$=\text{MAX(25,INDEX(ShipByRegion,C3,C4)*C2)}$$

If this formula were substituted in cell D15, the resulting value would be $25 instead of $24.

Using a similar technique, a maximum value for the cost of shipping could be set at $1000. The formula =MIN(1000,INDEX(ShipByRegion,C3,C4)*C2) would return the smaller of the two values. In this case, the value $24 would be returned because 24 (which results from the nested INDEX function) is lower than 1000.

Consider using such nested functions when you want to both retrieve data and compare it to a minimum or maximum value to determine the appropriate value to use in a calculation.

Using the INDEX Function with a Three-Dimensional Table

Vijay learns from his sales manager that, because TheZone does substantial business with certain customers on some shipping routes, the company has negotiated more favorable freight rates with their new shipping company. TheZone wants to pass along these preferential shipping rates to their large customers. So, TheZone will now calculate shipping charges for three types of customers: standard, preferred, and most preferred. Vijay modifies the Shipping by Region worksheet to reflect this additional information, as shown in Figure 5.21.

Figure 5.21: Modified Shipping by Region worksheet

	A	B	C	D	E	F	
1		Shipping Method - Standard					Schedule 1
2	Region	1	2	3	4		
3	1	$ 0.10	$ 0.11	$ 1.50	NA		
4	2	$ 0.18	$ 0.12	$ 2.00	NA		
5	3	$ 0.24	$ 0.14	$ 2.10	$ 0.20		
6	4	$ 0.28	$ 0.16	$ 2.25	$ 0.20		
7	5	$ 0.45	$ 0.40	$ 3.50	$ 0.35		
8							
9		Shipping Method - Preferred					Schedule 2
10	Region	1	2	3	4		
11	1	$ 0.09	$ 0.10	$ 1.35	NA		
12	2	$ 0.16	$ 0.11	$ 1.80	NA		
13	3	$ 0.22	$ 0.13	$ 1.89	$ 0.18		
14	4	$ 0.25	$ 0.14	$ 2.03	$ 0.18		
15	5	$ 0.41	$ 0.36	$ 3.15	$ 0.32		
16							
17		Shipping Method - Most Preferred					Schedule 3
18	Region	1	2	3	4		
19	1	$ 0.08	$ 0.09	$ 1.22	NA		
20	2	$ 0.15	$ 0.10	$ 1.62	NA		
21	3	$ 0.19	$ 0.11	$ 1.70	$ 0.16		
22	4	$ 0.23	$ 0.13	$ 1.82	$ 0.16		
23	5	$ 0.36	$ 0.32	$ 2.84	$ 0.28		

To retrieve the shipping charges in dollars per pound for an order, Vijay must now work with three different variables: shipping region, shipping method, and customer type (as given by the three different shipping schedules). The INDEX function allows you to specify a list of nonadjacent ranges as the reference argument, and then specify which of these ranges to use in the area_num argument. This means the INDEX function can solve for two or more variables. Vijay can use the INDEX function to find the shipping charge per pound, but must now include the ranges for the three schedules in the first argument. The following statement shows the logic Vijay can use in the INDEX formula:

```
=INDEX ((range for schedule 1, range for schedule 2, range
    for schedule 3), row number of the ship region, column
        number of the shipping method, range number of the
            selected shipping schedule)
```

Before entering the formula, Vijay names each range in the Shipping by Region worksheet, using the names Schedule1, Schedule2, and Schedule3. He also adds a new item to the Orders worksheet for entering the appropriate shipping schedule according to customer type, as shown in Figure 5.22.

Figure 5.22: Customer type data input added to the Orders worksheet

Order form now includes the customer type, as determined by the schedules on the Shipping by Region worksheet

	A	B	C	D	E
1			Tennis Products Order Form		
2		Shipping weight	100		
3		Region number	3		
4		Shipping method	1		
5		Customer type	2		
6	Item#	Quantity	Description	Total	
7	12	10	Touring Bag - One Size	$ 599.90	
8	4	50	ExoRacket Graphite - Oversize	$ 7,750.00	
9	8	25	FlexPro Racket - Junior Pro	$ 1,749.75	
10	10	25	FlexPro Racket - Oversize	$ 2,499.75	
11	13	100	String Pack - Synthetic	$ 325.00	
12					
13			Total Order	$12,924.40	
14			Discount	$ (400.00)	
15			Shipping	$ 24.00	
16					
17			Grand Total		
18					
19					

In the Orders worksheet, Vijay enters the following formula in cell D15 to calculate the shipping charge:

```
=INDEX((Schedule1,Schedule2,Schedule3),C3,C4,C5)*C2
```

To solve this formula, the function refers to three named ranges: Schedule1, which contains the shipping charges for standard customers; Schedule2, which contains the shipping charges for preferred customers; and Schedule3, which contains the shipping charges for most preferred customers. The function retrieves the value at the intersection of the row specified in cell C3 (3) and the column number specified in cell C4 (1) in the area specified in cell C5 (2, for Schedule2). Then, it multiplies the result by the value in cell C2 (100). Figure 5.23 shows the resulting worksheet.

Figure 5.23: Calculating the shipping charge by region, shipping method, and customer type

	A	B	C	D	E
	D15		fx =INDEX((Schedule1,Schedule2,Schedule3),C3,C4,C5)*C2		
1			Tennis Products Order Form		
2		Shipping weight	100		
3		Region number	3		
4		Shipping method	1		
5		Customer type	2		
6	Item#	Quantity	Description	Total	
7	12	10	Touring Bag - One Size	$ 599.90	
8	4	50	ExoRacket Graphite - Oversize	$ 7,750.00	
9	8	25	FlexPro Racket - Junior Pro	$ 1,749.75	
10	10	25	FlexPro Racket - Oversize	$ 2,499.75	
11	13	100	String Pack - Synthetic	$ 325.00	
12					
13			Total Order	$12,924.40	
14			Discount	$ (400.00)	
15			Shipping	$ 22.00	
16					
17			Grand Total		
18					
19					

INDEX function refers to three ranges and uses three variables to determine the shipping charge

Shipping charge is $0.22 per pound, for a total of $22.00

	A	B	C	D	E	F
1		Shipping Method - Standard				
2	Region	1	2	3	4	
3	1	$ 0.10	$ 0.11	$ 1.50	NA	
4	2	$ 0.18	$ 0.12	$ 2.00	NA	
5	3	$ 0.24	$ 0.14	$ 2.10	$ 0.20	
6	4	$ 0.28	$ 0.16	$ 2.25	$ 0.20	
7	5	$ 0.45	$ 0.40	$ 3.50	$ 0.35	
8						
9		Shipping Method - Preferred				
10	Region	1	2	3	4	
11	1	$ 0.09	$ 0.10	$ 1.35	NA	
12	2	$ 0.16	$ 0.11	$ 1.80	NA	
13	3	$ 0.22	$ 0.13	$ 1.89	$ 0.18	
14	4	$ 0.25	$ 0.14	$ 2.03	$ 0.18	
15	5	$ 0.41	$ 0.36	$ 3.15	$ 0.32	
16						

Cell B13 in the Shipping by Region worksheet is in row 3, column 1, area 2 (Schedule 2) of the specified range, and contains the value $0.22

When you use the INDEX function, keep in mind the following guidelines:

- If you are using a noncontinuous range, you must enclose the entire reference in parentheses, as in (A1:B3,A7:B9,A15:B17). In this range reference, A1:B3 is area 1, A7:B9 is area 2, and A15:B17 is area 3.
- If you specify only one continuous range, you can omit the area_num argument.
- You can use the INDEX function to look up data stored in a single row, such as B3:E3, or a single column, such as B3:B7. In this case, you enter the range as the first argument, and then enter only the row_num or the column_num, as appropriate.
- If you enter a row_num, column_num, or area_num outside of the range you referenced in the first argument, Excel displays the #REF! error.
- You can use a row_num of 0 to retrieve all the values in a specified column. Similarly, you can use a col_num of 0 to retrieve all the values in a specified row.
- If you want to use the INDEX function to retrieve data stored in more than one range, be certain to store all the lookup ranges on the same worksheet. The INDEX function can refer to ranges that are stored on a worksheet different from the one containing the

formula, but it expects to find the ranges on the same worksheet, even if you use named ranges. If you do use an INDEX formula that refers to ranges on separate worksheets, Excel displays the #VALUE error.

Vijay's final step to complete the order form in the Orders worksheet is to calculate the grand total in cell D17 with the formula =SUM(D13:D15). Figure 5.24 shows the finished order form.

Figure 5.24: Final tennis products order form

Vijay takes some time to review his work in the Tennis Orders workbook, concentrating on the Orders worksheet. He would like this order form to be more flexible and streamlined. For example, this form cannot accommodate items with variable unit pricing, such as tennis balls. He also wants to list the price per unit directly on the order form. Entering codes such as 1 or 3 for shipping method and region is awkward—Vijay usually thinks of region by state abbreviation, such as CO, and shipping method by its name, such as "Rail." He will continue to refine the order form in the next section.

Steps To Success: Level 2

Now that Vijay has completed the order form for tennis products, he needs to work on the one for golf equipment. As with tennis products, Vijay must include shipping charges and a discount for orders according to their total amount. In addition, he must add a handling charge because most golf equipment must be packed by hand. TheZone calculates handling costs for golf equipment as shown in Table 5.9.

Table 5.9: Handling charges for golf equipment

Order Amount	Handling Charge
Under $2,500	2% of the total order amount
$2,500–$5,000	3% of the total order amount
$5,000–$7,500	4% of the total order amount
$7,500–$10,000	5% of the total order amount
$10,500–$12,500	6% of the total order amount
$12,500 and over	7% of the total order amount
All orders	A minimum handling charge of $25 is applied to all orders

Vijay has updated the Golf workbook and renamed it Golf2. He consolidated the order information on a worksheet named Orders, and added worksheets for pricing information, handling charges, discounts, and shipping charges. Figure 5.25 shows the Orders worksheet.

Figure 5.25: Orders worksheet in the Golf2 workbook

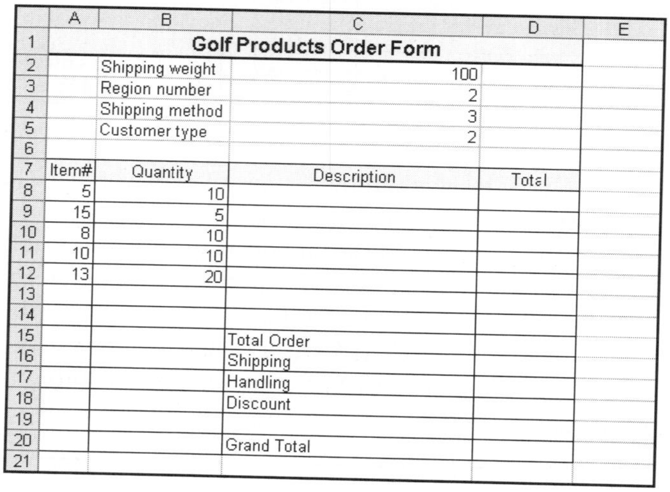

	A	B	C	D	E
1	Golf Products Order Form				
2		Shipping weight		100	
3		Region number		2	
4		Shipping method		3	
5		Customer type		2	
6					
7	Item#	Quantity	Description	Total	
8	5	10			
9	15	5			
10	8	10			
11	10	10			
12	13	20			
13					
14					
15			Total Order		
16			Shipping		
17			Handling		
18			Discount		
19					
20			Grand Total		
21					

In these steps, you need to complete the Orders worksheet using lookup functions to display the product description, and to calculate the order total and shipping, handling, and discount charges. Complete the following:

1. Open the workbook named **Golf2.xls** located in the Chapter 5 folder, and then save it as **Golf Orders2.xls**.

2. Examine the contents of each worksheet, and name ranges as indicated in Table 5.10.

Table 5.10: Naming ranges in the Golf Orders2 workbook

Range Name	Worksheet	Cells
Prices	Pricing	A5:C20
Handle	Handling	B2:G3
Disc	Discounts	A2:A5
Total_Order	Discounts	B2:B5
Schedule1	Shipping	B3:E7
Schedule2	Shipping	B11:E15
Schedule3	Shipping	B19:E23

3. In cell C8 of the Orders worksheet, write a formula that displays the product description for the first item in the order. Copy the formula into cells C9:C12.

4. In cell D8 of the Orders worksheet, calculate the price of the item. Copy the formula into cells D9:D12.

5. In cell D15 of the Orders worksheet, calculate the total cost of the order.

6. In cell D17 of the Orders worksheet, calculate the handling cost. Be certain to account for the minimum handling charge.

7. In cell D18 of the Orders worksheet, calculate the discount. Be certain to write the formula so that the discount is deducted from the total amount.

8. In cell D16 of the Orders worksheet, calculate the shipping charge based only on the shipping rates for standard customers. Save the workbook, and print a copy of the Orders worksheet.

9. Change the formula in cell D16 of the Orders worksheet to calculate the shipping charge based on three variables: the customer type (standard, preferred, or most preferred), the region being shipped to, and the method of shipping.

10. In cell D20 of the Orders worksheet, calculate the grand total for the order.

11. Save and close the Golf Orders2.xls workbook.

LEVEL 3

NESTING LOOKUP AND REFERENCE FUNCTIONS TO RETRIEVE AND CALCULATE DATA

EXCEL 2003 SKILLS TRAINING

- Use HLOOKUP
- Use lookup tables
- Use VLOOKUP

REFINING THE ORDER FORM

Vijay reviews the current order form for tennis products and decides that the form should be more professional looking and flexible so that other sales representatives can use it easily. He plans to reformat the Orders worksheet to make it easier to find and use the cells in which users enter data. He also wants to modify the worksheet to include products with variable and fixed unit pricing, and to list the price per unit.

To meet these goals, Vijay will change the Tennis Orders workbook as follows:

- Redesign the order form to incorporate the new state and shipping method entries and to list shipping weight and unit prices.
- Accommodate fixed and variable unit pricing by assigning a price schedule code to each item: 1 for fixed unit priced items and 2 for tennis balls. Based on the price schedule, Vijay can look up the unit price.
- Add two worksheets, one for each price schedule. Pricing Schedule 1 will list fixed unit prices for tennis equipment, and Pricing Schedule 2 will list variable prices for tennis balls. If TheZone adds other products with variable prices, Vijay can create other pricing schedule worksheets and related price codes.
- Support the redesigned state entry by adding a worksheet that lists each U.S. state abbreviation and its corresponding region number. Users can then enter a state directly and Excel will calculate shipping based on the region.

Vijay begins by updating the Costs and Orders worksheets, renaming Costs as "Products." He also names the range in the Products worksheet in which he will be looking up data, and he adds a Price Schedule column and a Ship Weight column to the Products worksheet. He plans to use the Discount worksheet without any changes. Figure 5.26 shows these three worksheets.

Figure 5.26: Updated Products and Orders worksheets, and Discount worksheet

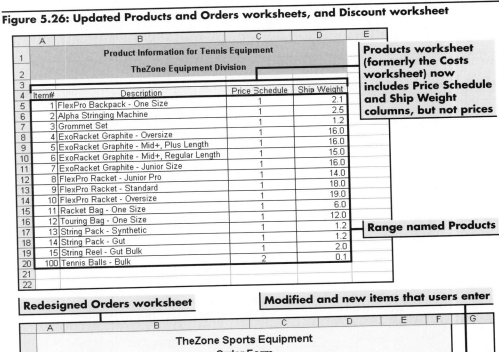

Products worksheet (formerly the Costs worksheet) now includes Price Schedule and Ship Weight columns, but not prices

	A	B	C	D	E
1		Product Information for Tennis Equipment			
2		TheZone Equipment Division			
3					
4	Item#	Description	Price Schedule	Ship Weight	
5	1	FlexPro Backpack - One Size	1	2.1	
6	2	Alpha Stringing Machine	1	2.5	
7	3	Grommet Set	1	1.2	
8	4	ExoRacket Graphite - Oversize	1	16.0	
9	5	ExoRacket Graphite - Mid+, Plus Length	1	16.0	
10	6	ExoRacket Graphite - Mid+, Regular Length	1	15.0	
11	7	ExoRacket Graphite - Junior Size	1	16.0	
12	8	FlexPro Racket - Junior Pro	1	14.0	
13	9	FlexPro Racket - Standard	1	18.0	
14	10	FlexPro Racket - Oversize	1	19.0	
15	11	Racket Bag - One Size	1	6.0	
16	12	Touring Bag - One Size	1	12.0	
17	13	String Pack - Synthetic	1	1.2	
18	14	String Pack - Gut	1	1.2	
19	15	String Reel - Gut Bulk	1	2.0	
20	100	Tennis Balls - Bulk	2	0.1	
21					
22					

Range named Products

Redesigned Orders worksheet   **Modified and new items that users enter**

	A	B	C	D	E	F	G
1		TheZone Sports Equipment Order Form					
2	Customer Name:						
3							
4	Ship to State Abbreviation						
5	Shipping Method (truck, rail, air, boat)						
6	Freight Customer Type (regular, preferred, most preferred)						
7							
8	Item#	Description	Quantity	Ship Wt. (lbs.)	Unit Price	Total	
9							
10							
11							
12							
13							
14							
15							
16			Total Order				
17			Discount				
18			Shipping				
19							
20			Grand Total				

Users also enter the item number and quantity ordered

Discount worksheet

	A	B	C	D
1	Discount	Total Order Value	Description	
2	$ -	$ -	Less than $5000, no discount	
3	$ 150	$ 5,000	At least $5000 but less than $10,000, $150 discount	
4	$ 400	$ 10,000	At least $10000 but less than $25,000, $400 discount	
5	$ 1,000	$ 25,000	$25,000 or more, $1000 discount	
6				
7				

Range named Discounts   **Range named Totals**

Vijay also adds the Pricing Schedule 1, Pricing Schedule 2, and States worksheets, and modifies the Shipping worksheet. Figure 5.27 shows these four worksheets.

Figure 5.27: Pricing Schedule 1, Pricing Schedule 2, Shipping, and States worksheets

Items and prices for fixed-price products

	A	B	C	D
1	Price List for Tennis Products Fixed-Price Items			
2				
3	Item#	$/each		
4	1	$ 23.75		
5	2	$ 52.80		
6	3	$ 15.95		
7	4	$ 135.00		
8	5	$ 135.00		
9	6	$ 139.99		
10	7	$ 142.50		
11	8	$ 69.99		
12	9	$ 99.99		
13	10	$ 99.99		
14	11	$ 29.95		
15	12	$ 59.99		
16	13	$ 3.25		
17	14	$ 7.25		
18				
19				

Pricing Schedule 1 worksheet

Quantities and unit prices for tennis balls

	A	B	C	D
1	Price List for Tennis Balls Variable-Priced Items			
2				
3	Qty	$/each		
4	0	$ 2.45		
5	60	$ 2.27		
6	120	$ 2.12		
7	240	$ 2.00		
8				
9				

Pricing Schedule 2 worksheet

	A	B	C	D	E	F
3		Shipping Method - Standard				
4	Region	Truck	Rail	Air	Boat	
5	1	$ 0.10	$ 0.11	$ 1.50	NA	
6	2	$ 0.18	$ 0.12	$ 2.00	NA	
7	3	$ 0.24	$ 0.14	$ 2.10	$ 0.20	
8	4	$ 0.28	$ 0.16	$ 2.25	$ 0.20	
9	5	$ 0.45	$ 0.40	$ 3.50	$ 0.35	
10						
11		Shipping Method - Preferred				
12	Region	Truck	Rail	Air	Boat	
13	1	$ 0.09	$ 0.10	$ 1.35	NA	
14	2	$ 0.16	$ 0.11	$ 1.80	NA	
15	3	$ 0.22	$ 0.13	$ 1.89	$ 0.18	
16	4	$ 0.25	$ 0.14	$ 2.03	$ 0.18	
17	5	$ 0.41	$ 0.36	$ 3.15	$ 0.32	
18						
19		Shipping Method - Most Preferred				
20	Region	Truck	Rail	Air	Boat	
21	1	$ 0.08	$ 0.09	$ 1.22	NA	
22	2	$ 0.15	$ 0.10	$ 1.62	NA	
23	3	$ 0.19	$ 0.11	$ 1.70	$ 0.16	
24	4	$ 0.23	$ 0.13	$ 1.82	$ 0.16	
25	5	$ 0.36	$ 0.32	$ 2.84	$ 0.28	

Shipping worksheet

Three shipping tables depend on customer type

States by name, abbreviation, region name, and region number

	A	B	C	D	E
1	Name	Abbreviation	Region	Region#	
2	Alabama	AL	SE	2	
3	Alaska	AK	W	5	
4	Arizona	AZ	SW	4	
5	Arkansas	AR	SE	2	
6	California	CA	W	5	
7	Colorado	CO	W	5	
8	Connecticut	CT	NE	1	
9	Delaware	DE	NE	1	
10	District of Columbia	DC	NE	1	
11	Florida	FL	SE	2	
12	Georgia	GA	SE	2	
13	Hawaii	HI	W	5	
14	Idaho	ID	W	5	
15	Illinois	IL	MW	3	
16	Indiana	IN	MW	3	
17	Iowa	IA	MW	3	
18	Kansas	KS	MW	3	
19	Kentucky	KY	SE	2	
20	Louisiana	LA	SE	2	

States worksheet

To complete the order form on the Orders worksheet, Vijay needs to set up the following calculations:

- Look up the item description in the Products range.
- Look up the shipping weight for each item in the Products range.
- Look up the unit price for each item by referring to the tables in the Pricing Schedule 1 or Pricing Schedule 2 worksheet, which also requires looking up the unit price for the item in the Products range.

- Calculate the total for each item by multiplying price by quantity.
- Calculate the total order amount by summing the item totals.
- Calculate the total shipping weight by summing the weight for each item.
- Look up the appropriate discount in the Discounts range, as in the original order form.
- Look up the associated shipping charge per pound in the Shipping worksheet, which also requires looking up the region number associated with the state entered.
- Calculate the shipping charge by multiplying the shipping weight by the charge per pound.
- Calculate the grand total, including discounts and shipping.

Figure 5.28 shows the lookup calculations required to complete all of these tasks.

Figure 5.28: Lookup calculations to be made in the Orders worksheet

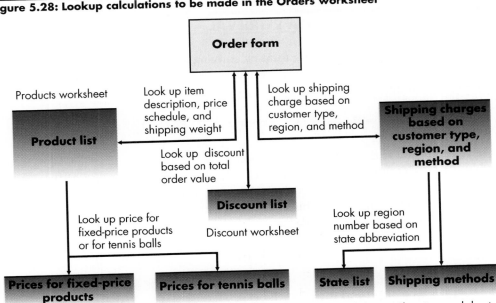

Vijay has already performed some of these calculations in the original order form, such as looking up the item description and the appropriate discount, so he only needs to repeat those formulas in the modified order form. Retrieving the unit price for each item and finding the correct shipping charge, however, require more complex formulas that nest one or more functions.

To test the order form as he enters the formulas, Vijay plans to use the sample order information shown in Table 5.11.

Table 5.11: Sample order information

Item Number	Product	Quantity
5	ExoRacket Graphite - Mid+, Plus Length	60
6	ExoRacket Graphite - Mid+, Regular Length	15
12	Touring Bag - One Size	100
100	Tennis Balls - Bulk	300

Now, Vijay is ready to create the complex lookup formulas he needs to complete the order form. He'll nest Reference and Lookup functions within IF, IS, and other Reference and Lookup functions to develop a powerful, automated order form.

PREVENTING ERRORS IN DATA RETRIEVAL

Vijay starts developing the new order form by entering a VLOOKUP formula in cell B9 of the Orders worksheet to retrieve the product description for the first item. He enters the following formula:

=VLOOKUP(A9,Products,2,FALSE)

To solve this formula, the VLOOKUP function scans the lookup range named Products for an exact match to the value specified in cell A9, which is 5. When it finds that value, it retrieves the corresponding data in column 2 of the lookup range, which contains the description for item 5. Vijay copies this VLOOKUP formula from cell B9 to cells B10:B14. Figure 5.29 shows the resulting worksheet.

Figure 5.29: Retrieving the item description using a VLOOKUP formula

In the Products range, the function looks for the value that matches the one in cell A9 (5), and then retrieves the corresponding data in column 2

	A	B	C	D	E	F	G
	B9	fx =VLOOKUP(A9,Products,2,FALSE)					
1		TheZone Sports Equipment Order Form					
2	Customer Name:						
3							
4	Ship to State Abbreviation						
5	Shipping Method (truck, rail, air, boat)						
6	Freight Customer Type (regular, preferred, most preferred)						
7							
8	Item#	Description	Quantity	Ship Wt. (lbs.)	Unit Price	Total	
9	5	ExoRacket Graphite - Mid+, Plus Length	60				
10	6	ExoRacket Graphite - Mid+, Regular Length	15				
11	12	Touring Bag - One Size	100				
12	100	Tennis Balls - Bulk	300				
13		#N/A					
14		#N/A					
15							

Formula copied to cells B10:B14, resulting in two error messages

	A	B	C	D	E
1		Product Information for Tennis Equipment			
2		TheZone Equipment Division			
3					
4	Item#	Description	Price Schedule	Ship Weight	
5	1	FlexPro Backpack - One Size	1	2.1	
6	2	Alpha Stringing Machine	1	2.5	
7	3	Grommet Set	1	1.2	
8	4	ExoRacket Graphite - Oversize	1	16.0	
9	5	ExoRacket Graphite - Mid+, Plus Length	1	16.0	
10	6	ExoRacket Graphite - Mid+, Regular Length	1	15.0	
11	7	ExoRacket Graphite - Junior Size	1	16.0	
12	8	FlexPro Racket - Junior Pro	1	14.0	
13	9	FlexPro Racket - Standard	1	18.0	
14	10	FlexPro Racket - Oversize	1	19.0	
15	11	Racket Bag - One Size	1	6.0	
16	12	Touring Bag - One Size	1	12.0	
17	13	String Pack - Synthetic	1	1.2	
18	14	String Pack - Gut	1	1.2	
19	15	String Reel - Gut Bulk	1	2.0	
20	100	Tennis Balls - Bulk	2	0.1	
21					
22					

Products range is A5:D20

Value exactly matches the one in cell A9 of the Orders worksheet; column 2 contains the item description

Cells B13 and B14 display the error #N/A because Vijay has provided item numbers for four products, but the form has room for six. The formula in B13 refers to the empty cell A13, and the formula in B14 refers to the empty cell A14. Vijay could respond to the #N/A error by deleting the VLOOKUP formulas in cells B13 and B14, but if he receives an order of more than four items, he would have to enter the formulas again. Instead, he can use the ISBLANK function to prevent the #N/A error.

Using the ISBLANK Function

Excel provides nine functions, called the **IS functions**, that test a value or cell reference, and then return a TRUE or FALSE value depending on the results. For example, you can use the ISBLANK function to test a cell reference. If the cell is blank, or empty, the function returns the value TRUE. You can specify what Excel should do in this case, such as display a dash or "n/a" in the cell.

The IS functions are often used in formulas to test the outcome of a calculation. If you combine them with the IF function, they help you locate data-entry errors. For example, you could write a formula using the ISTEXT function to check whether cell A5 contains text, such as a customer name. If a user committed a data-entry error by entering a number in cell A5 instead of text, you could display a message such as "Cell A5 must contain text." Table 5.12 lists and describes the nine IS functions, which all check for a condition and then return a TRUE or FALSE value.

Table 5.12: IS functions

IS Function	Description
ISBLANK	Value refers to an empty cell
ISERR	Value refers to any error value except #N/A
ISERROR	Value refers to any error value (#N/A, #VALUE!, #REF!, #DIV/0!, #NUM!, #NAME?, or #NULL!)
ISLOGICAL	Value refers to a logical value
ISNA	Value refers to the #N/A (value not available) error value
ISNONTEXT	Value refers to any item that is not text (this function returns TRUE if the value refers to a blank cell)
ISNUMBER	Value refers to a number
ISREF	Value refers to a reference
ISTEXT	Value refers to text

The ISBLANK function checks whether a specified value refers to an empty cell. The syntax of this function is as follows:

$$=ISBLANK(value)$$

In the Orders worksheet, the formula =ISBLANK(A13) returns the value TRUE because cell A13 is empty. Vijay can combine this ISBLANK formula with an IF function to determine if cell A13 is blank, and if it is, modify the contents of cell B13. Vijay revises the formula in cell B9 as follows:

$$=IF(ISBLANK(A9)," ",VLOOKUP(A9,Products,2,FALSE))$$

Level 3

To solve this formula, Excel first checks to see if cell A9 is blank. If it is, Excel displays a string of empty characters, the " " in the formula. If cell A9 contains a value, VLOOKUP returns the corresponding item description, as it did originally.

Vijay copies this formula from cell B9 to cells B10:B14. In a similar manner, Vijay can nest the IF, ISBLANK, and VLOOKUP functions to calculate the shipping weight in cell D9, as in the following formula:

```
=IF(ISBLANK(A9)," ",VLOOKUP(A9,Products,4,FALSE)*C9)
```

To solve this formula, Excel checks to see if cell A9 is blank. If it is, Excel displays a string of empty characters. If cell A9 contains a value, Excel performs the VLOOKUP part of the formula. In the Products range, it looks for an exact match to the value in cell A9, which is 5, the item number. When it finds an exact match, it retrieves the value in column 4, which is the shipping weight of 16 pounds. It then multiplies 16 by the value in C9, which is the quantity of 60, and displays the results of 960. Vijay copies this formula from cell D9 to cells D10:D14. Figure 5.30 shows the resulting worksheet.

Figure 5.30: Using IF, ISBLANK, and VLOOKUP to calculate the shipping weight

Excel checks to see if cell A9 is blank, and displays a string of empty characters if it is; if not, it solves the VLOOKUP function

Formula in cell B9 is
=IF(ISBLANK(A9)," ",VLOOKUP(A9,Products,2,FALSE))

Cells A13 and A14 are blank, so cells D13 and D14 contain a string of empty characters and are blank

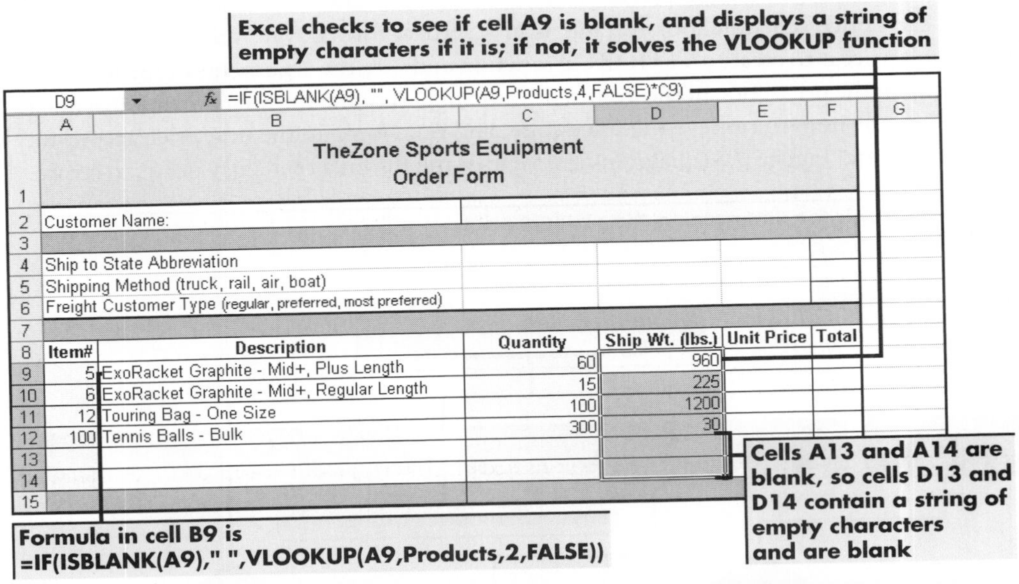

How To

Write an ISBLANK Formula
1. Type: =ISBLANK(
2. Enter the reference of the cell you want to check to determine if it is blank.
3. Type a closing parenthesis), and then press the Enter key.

Now, Vijay can turn to a complicated part of the worksheet—calculating the unit prices.

NESTING LOOKUP FUNCTIONS TO CALCULATE THE PRICE PER UNIT

In the first version of the order form that Vijay created, the price per unit was based on the quantity ordered. Because he was only considering tennis balls, Vijay could use a basic VLOOKUP formula to find the appropriate unit price. In the next version of his order form, the price per unit was based on the item ordered, and he used a VLOOKUP formula to retrieve the fixed price of a tennis product based on its item number. Now, he wants to combine these two capabilities. As TheZone expands its tennis line, Vijay might also need to accommodate other fixed- and variable-priced items. Vijay has, therefore, included a Price Schedule column in the Products worksheet. Price code 1 in this column refers to fixed-price products, and price code 2 refers to tennis balls, which are based on prices that vary by quantity. If TheZone expands its tennis products to include other fixed-price items, Vijay can include the items in the Pricing Schedule 1 worksheet and assign price code 1 to these products. If TheZone adds other types of variable-priced products, he can create additional worksheets, such as Pricing Schedule 3 and Pricing Schedule 4, and assign price codes 3 and 4 to these items in the Products worksheet.

Because each price schedule lookup table is in a vertical format, one way to look up the correct unit price is to create a VLOOKUP function and vary the arguments of the function depending on the price code of the item. The difficult part of the formula is that Excel must first look up the item to retrieve the price code, and then look up the unit price according to the price code. Figure 5.31 diagrams the logic of the formula that Vijay needs to create.

Figure 5.31: Logic for determining the product prices

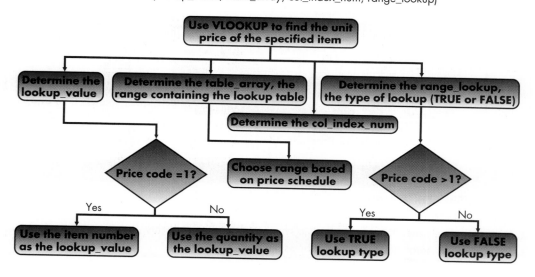

According to Figure 5.31, Vijay will choose the four arguments for the VLOOKUP function by performing the following steps:

1. Choose the lookup_value, the value he wants Excel to match in the lookup table. If that value is associated with price code 1, use the item number as the lookup_value. If the price code is not 1, use the quantity as the lookup_value.

2. Choose the table_array, the range containing the lookup table, according to the price schedule code. If the price code is 1, use the lookup table in the Pricing Schedule 1 worksheet. If the price code is 2, use the lookup table in the Pricing Schedule 2 worksheet.

3. Choose the col_index_num depending on which column contains the prices. For both lookup tables, this is column 2.

4. Choose a TRUE or FALSE lookup type according to the price code. If the price code is greater than 1, use TRUE; if the price code is 1, use FALSE.

For example, if a customer orders item 5, a graphite tennis racket, the VLOOKUP function can look up item 5 and retrieve its price schedule code, which is 1. For a product with this price code, a second VLOOKUP function uses the *item number* to look up the unit price in the Pricing Schedule 1 worksheet. Because item 5 uses price code 1, the second VLOOKUP function uses 5 as its first argument. Excel looks up item 5 in the Pricing Schedule 1 worksheet, and retrieves the unit price of $135.00.

If a customer orders 50 canisters of item 100, bulk tennis balls, the VLOOKUP function can look up item 100 and retrieve its price schedule code, which is 2. For a product with this price code, the second VLOOKUP function uses the *quantity ordered* to look up the unit price in the Pricing Schedule 2 worksheet. Because item 100 uses price code 2, the second VLOOKUP function will use 50—the quantity ordered—as its first argument. Excel looks up a quantity of 50 in the Pricing Schedule 2 worksheet, and retrieves the unit price of $2.45.

The following sections discuss how to translate these steps into the arguments of the VLOOKUP function.

Nesting VLOOKUP in an IF Function to Determine the lookup_value

The lookup_value in the VLOOKUP function is the item number Vijay wants Excel to match in the Products table. Vijay will use the following expression in a longer formula in cell E9 of the Orders worksheet:

```
IF(VLOOKUP(A9,Products,3,FALSE)=1,A9,C9)
```

To solve this expression, Excel looks up the price schedule code in the Products range for the item whose number matches the one in A9 exactly. If that price schedule code is 1, Excel returns the value in A9 (the item number); otherwise, it returns the value in C9 (the quantity ordered). This formula only returns the item number or the quantity, and doesn't provide the unit price, so it must be nested within another formula that performs that calculation.

The partial formula in cell E9 is shown in Figure 5.32. To solve this part of the formula, Excel determines whether it should match the item number or the quantity in a lookup table.

Figure 5.32: First part of the formula in cell E9 to calculate the unit price

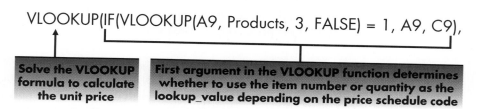

VLOOKUP(**lookup_value**, table_array, col_index_num, range_lookup)

VLOOKUP(IF(VLOOKUP(A9, Products, 3, FALSE) = 1, A9, C9),

Solve the VLOOKUP formula to calculate the unit price

First argument in the VLOOKUP function determines whether to use the item number or quantity as the lookup_value depending on the price schedule code

Using the CHOOSE Function to Determine the table_array

Next, Vijay must specify the range that contains the appropriate lookup table, which is determined by the price schedule code. He uses "Price1" as the name of the range A4:B17 in the Pricing Schedule 1 worksheet, the range containing the item numbers and unit prices for fixed-price products. He uses "Price2" as the name of the range A4:B7 in the Pricing Schedule 2 worksheet, the range containing the quantity and unit prices for tennis balls.

If the price schedule code is 1, Excel uses the Price1 range. If the price schedule code is 2, Excel uses the Price2 range. In short, Vijay wants to look up the value 1 or 2, and return the range Price1 or Price2. But how can he look up a value and return a range?

None of the Reference and Lookup functions he has used would solve the problem of returning a range and not a single value. One way to accomplish this might be to use another VLOOKUP function nested within an IF function. However, TheZone might add more pricing schedules, which would require an unnecessarily complex formula with many levels of nesting. Instead, Vijay considers using the **CHOOSE function**, another Reference and Lookup function that can return a value *or a range* for up to 29 different values. The syntax of the CHOOSE function is as follows:

=CHOOSE(index_num,value1,value2,...)

The index_num argument specifies which value to select from the list that follows. Index_num must be a number between 1 and 29, a formula, or a reference to a cell containing a number between 1 and 29. The list of values (value1, value2, and so on) can be numbers, text, cell references, or even ranges. For example, in the formula =CHOOSE(2,A2,B2,C2,D2), the first argument (2) means that Excel should choose the second value, the one stored in cell B2, from the list of four values.

Keep in mind the following conditions when specifying the index_num argument:

- If the index_num is 1, the function returns the first value from the list. If the index_num is 2, the function returns the second value from the list, and so on.
- If the index_num is less than 1 or greater than the last value in the list, the function displays the error #VALUE!.
- If the index_num is a fraction, it is truncated to the lowest integer before being used.

How To

Write a CHOOSE Formula
1. Type: =CHOOSE(
2. Enter a number that specifies which value to select from the list that follows. The number can be the result of a formula or a cell reference.
3. Enter the list of values, which can be numbers, text, cell references, or ranges.
4. Type a closing parenthesis), and then press the Enter key.

Vijay can use the CHOOSE function to determine the table_array. He can write this part of the VLOOKUP formula so that the CHOOSE function returns the Price1 range or the Price2 range, depending on the price schedule code used for the specified item number.

To create the CHOOSE function, he first considers what to use for the index_num argument. He wants to choose the appropriate price schedule—1 or 2. The price schedule code, however, is determined by the item number. For example, item 5 uses price schedule code 1. Vijay can write a formula that uses a VLOOKUP function as the index_num argument of the CHOOSE function. The resulting value determines which range to choose—Price1 or Price2. The value1 and value2 arguments are the ranges associated with price schedule 1 (Price1) and price schedule 2 (Price2). To select the appropriate price schedule for the first item, Vijay can use the following expression in the VLOOKUP formula in cell E9 of the Orders worksheet:

```
CHOOSE(VLOOKUP(A9,Products,3,FALSE),Price1,Price2)
```

To solve this expression, Excel chooses the price schedule as determined by the VLOOKUP function. In the Products range, it looks for the item number referenced in cell A9 (5), and retrieves an exact match to the value in column 3, which is 1. Then, the CHOOSE function uses that value as the index_num, selecting the first value in the list, which is the Price1 range.

Figure 5.33 shows the second part of the formula in cell E9 for calculating the unit price.

Figure 5.33: Second part of the formula in cell E9 to calculate the unit price

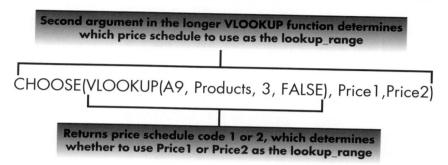

VLOOKUP(lookup_value, **table_array**, col_index_num, range_lookup)

Second argument in the longer VLOOKUP function determines which price schedule to use as the lookup_range

CHOOSE(VLOOKUP(A9, Products, 3, FALSE), Price1,Price2)

Returns price schedule code 1 or 2, which determines whether to use Price1 or Price2 as the lookup_range

Excel begins to solve the VLOOKUP function by determining whether it should match the item number or the quantity in a lookup table. It chooses which lookup table to use by looking in the Products range for the item number referenced in cell A9 (5), and then retrieving an exact match to the value in column 3, which is 1. Then, it chooses the Price1 range (value 1) as the lookup table.

Determining the col_index_num

Vijay designed the pricing schedules to list the lookup values in column 1 and the prices in column 2. He can, therefore, use the value 2 as the col_index_num, because both lookup tables list prices in column 2.

Combining the col_index_num argument with the other two parts of the formula, the partial formula in cell E9 now looks like the one shown in Figure 5.34.

Figure 5.34: Third part of the formula in cell E9 to calculate the unit price

VLOOKUP(lookup_value, table_array, **col_index_num**, range_lookup)

VLOOKUP(IF(VLOOKUP(A9, Products, 3, FALSE) = 1, A9, C9),
CHOOSE(VLOOKUP(A9, Products, 3, FALSE), Price1,Price2), 2

Third argument in the VLOOKUP function specifies from which column in the pricing schedule to retrieve a value

Determining the range_lookup

The final argument of the VLOOKUP function is the range_lookup type, which can be TRUE or FALSE. Like the lookup_value, this argument varies depending on the associated pricing schedule. If Excel uses pricing schedule 1, the Price1 range, it looks up the item number exactly, meaning Vijay should use a FALSE lookup type when the CHOOSE function chooses the Price1 range. If Excel uses any other variable pricing schedule, such as 2 for the tennis balls, it looks up the quantity, which might not exactly match the values in the lookup table and, therefore, requires a TRUE lookup type.

To determine the correct range_lookup, Vijay again needs to determine which price schedule is associated with the specified item number. Similar to how he found the price schedule in the first argument, he can use another VLOOKUP function. If the price schedule is equal to 1, this argument should be FALSE; otherwise, it should be TRUE.

To select the appropriate lookup type, Vijay can use the following expression in the VLOOKUP formula in cell E9 of the Orders worksheet:

```
VLOOKUP(A9,Products,3,FALSE)>1
```

To solve this expression, Excel looks for an exact match to the value stored in cell A9 (5), and then retrieves the corresponding value from the third column of the Products table, which lists the price schedule associated with this item. If that price schedule code is greater than 1, Excel returns a TRUE value.

After combining the range_lookup argument with the other parts of the formula, the complete VLOOKUP function to be entered in cell E9 now looks like the one shown in Figure 5.35.

Figure 5.35: Final part of the formula in cell E9 to calculate the unit price

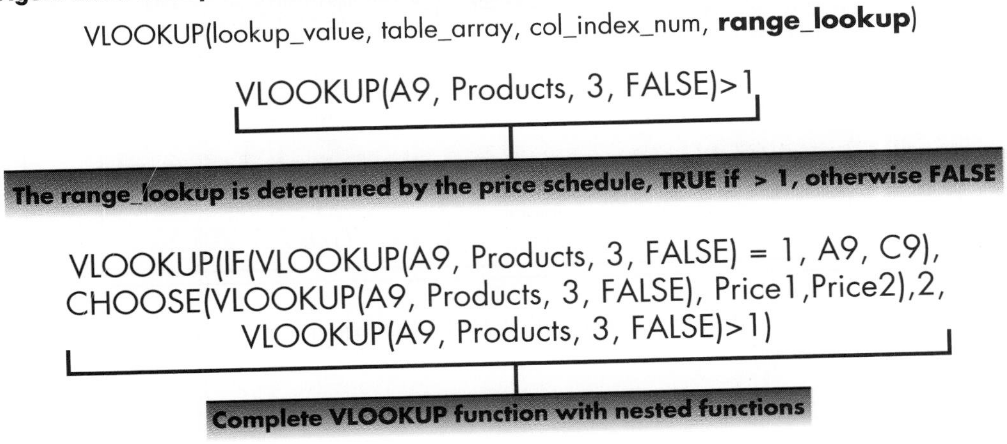

VLOOKUP(lookup_value, table_array, col_index_num, **range_lookup**)

VLOOKUP(A9, Products, 3, FALSE)>1

The range_lookup is determined by the price schedule, TRUE if > 1, otherwise FALSE

VLOOKUP(IF(VLOOKUP(A9, Products, 3, FALSE) = 1, A9, C9),
CHOOSE(VLOOKUP(A9, Products, 3, FALSE), Price1,Price2),2,
VLOOKUP(A9, Products, 3, FALSE)>1)

Complete VLOOKUP function with nested functions

Creating the Nested VLOOKUP Formula

Vijay has now determined each of the four arguments of the VLOOKUP formula that will find the unit price. He also wants to avoid displaying the error #N/A!, so he will use the IF and ISBLANK functions as he did before to display a blank cell in cell E9 if no item number is entered in cell A9. He enters the following formula in cell E9. (Note that each part of the formula is shown on a separate line for readability here; Vijay enters the entire formula on one line in Excel.)

```
=IF(ISBLANK(A9), " ",
VLOOKUP(
IF(VLOOKUP(A9,Products,3,FALSE)=1,A9,C9),
CHOOSE(VLOOKUP(A9,Products,3,FALSE),Price1,Price2),
2,
VLOOKUP(A9,Products,3,FALSE)>1))
```

Note the final parenthesis that completes the IF part of the formula. The completed formula and result are shown in Figure 5.36.

Figure 5.36: Completed formula and result

Formula for calculating unit price

	E9	▾	*fx*	=IF(ISBLANK(A9),"",VLOOKUP(IF(VLOOKUP(A9, Products, 3, FALSE) = 1, A9, C9),CHOOSE(VLOOKUP(A9, Products, 3, FALSE), Price1,Price2),2,VLOOKUP(A9, Products, 3, FALSE)>1))

	A					
	TheZone Sports Equipment					
1	**Order Form**					
2	Customer Name:					
3						
4	Ship to State Abbreviation					
5	Shipping Method (truck, rail, air, boat)					
6	Freight Customer Type (regular, preferred, most preferred)					
7						
8	Item#	**Description**	**Quantity**	**Ship Wt. (lbs.)**	**Unit Price**	**Total**
9	5	ExoRacket Graphite - Mid+, Plus Length	60	960	$ 135.00	
10	6	ExoRacket Graphite - Mid+, Regular Length	15	225		
11	12	Touring Bag - One Size	100	1200		
12	100	Tennis Balls - Bulk	300	30		
13						
14						
15						
16			Total Order			
17			Discount			
18			Shipping			
19						
20			Grand Total			

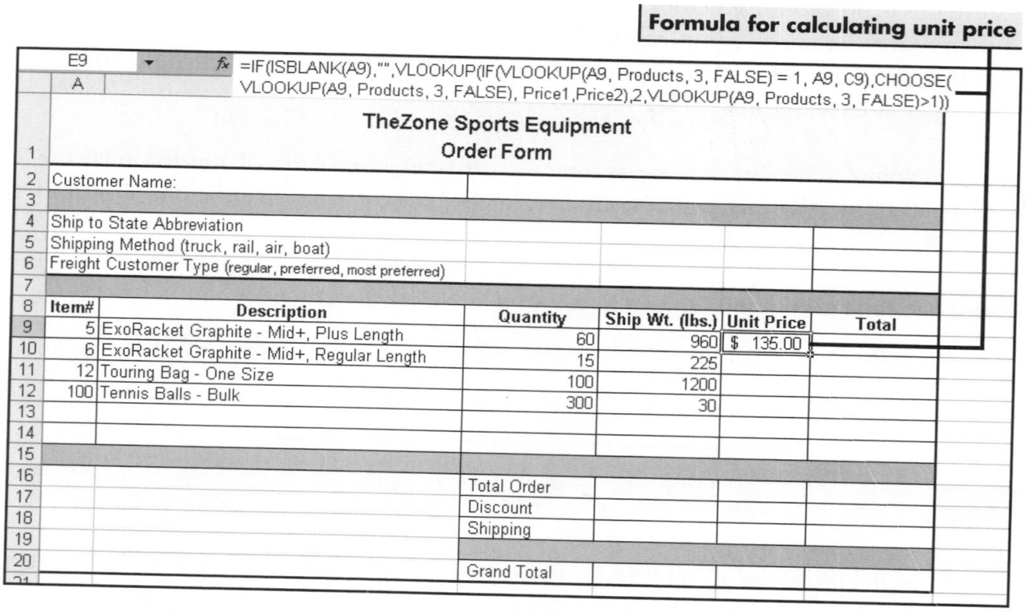

Vijay copies this formula from cell E9 to cells E10:E14 to provide the unit prices for the other items in the order.

Planning for Future Changes: The Limitations of Using Nested IF Functions

Can you solve Vijay's problem using a different type of formula? Yes; many people would use a series of nested IF functions according to the following logic:

- If the price schedule is 1, look up the price based on the item number in Pricing Schedule 1.
- If the price schedule is 2, look up the price based on the quantity in Pricing Schedule 2.

Although this technique would work equally well to solve Vijay's problem, it limits the order form to using eight pricing schedules, which would require seven levels of nesting. This might not be flexible enough to accommodate products that expand to use more than eight pricing schedules. The solution that Vijay used works for up to 29 pricing structures. If a product or company has more than 29 pricing structures, a relational database, such as Microsoft Access, might be a better choice than using a spreadsheet program. When designing a workbook, designers need to consider how the workbook will be used and what types of modifications are likely in the future.

CALCULATING TOTALS

Now that Vijay has solved the complex problem of unit pricing, he can turn to an easier task: calculating the total cost of each item and the total cost of the order. In cell F9, he can calculate the total price by multiplying the unit price by the quantity. He enters the formula =C9*E9 in cell F9. Then, he copies this formula to cells F10:F14.

Next, he can calculate the total order amount in cell F16 by using the following formula:

=SUM(F9:F14)

Finally, in cell D16, he enters the following formula to calculate the total weight of the order:

=SUM(D9:D14)

Figure 5.37 shows the Orders worksheet with totals calculated.

Figure 5.37: Totals calculated on the Orders worksheet

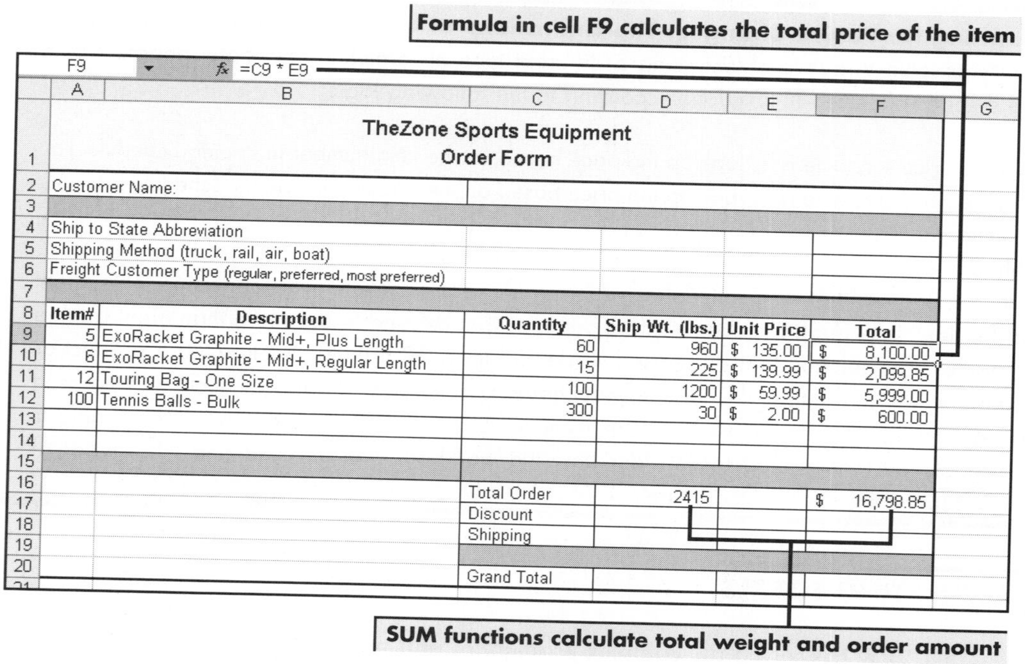

Formula in cell F9 calculates the total price of the item

	A	B		C	D	E	F	G
	F9	▼	fx =C9 * E9					
1		TheZone Sports Equipment Order Form						
2	Customer Name:							
3								
4	Ship to State Abbreviation							
5	Shipping Method (truck, rail, air, boat)							
6	Freight Customer Type (regular, preferred, most preferred)							
7								
8	Item#	Description		Quantity	Ship Wt. (lbs.)	Unit Price	Total	
9	5	ExoRacket Graphite - Mid+, Plus Length		60	960	$ 135.00	$ 8,100.00	
10	6	ExoRacket Graphite - Mid+, Regular Length		15	225	$ 139.99	$ 2,099.85	
11	12	Touring Bag - One Size		100	1200	$ 59.99	$ 5,999.00	
12	100	Tennis Balls - Bulk		300	30	$ 2.00	$ 600.00	
13								
14								
15								
16								
17				Total Order	2415		$ 16,798.85	
18				Discount				
19				Shipping				
20								
21				Grand Total				

SUM functions calculate total weight and order amount

CALCULATING THE DISCOUNT AMOUNT

Vijay decides to simplify the Discount worksheet so that it contains a basic horizontal lookup table. He names the range of values "Discounts," as shown in Figure 5.38. According to this table, all orders of $5,000 or more qualify for a discount based on a sliding scale.

Figure 5.38: Horizontal lookup table in the modified Discount worksheet

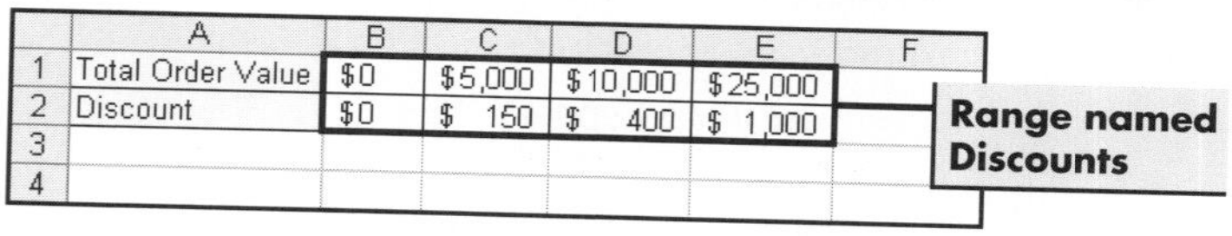

	A	B	C	D	E	F
1	Total Order Value	$0	$5,000	$10,000	$25,000	
2	Discount	$0	$ 150	$ 400	$ 1,000	
3						
4						

Range named Discounts

Vijay can use a basic HLOOKUP formula in cell F17 in the Orders worksheet to calculate the discount:

$$=-\text{HLOOKUP}(F16,\text{Discounts},2,\text{TRUE})$$

Excel solves this formula by looking up the value stored in cell F16 (the order total, $16,798.85) in the Discounts table, and retrieving the value in the second row. The formula uses the TRUE lookup type because it does not need to exactly match the specified value, and includes a negative sign at the beginning so that Excel returns a negative value. Figure 5.39 shows the Orders worksheet with this formula entered.

Figure 5.39: HLOOKUP formula added to the Orders worksheet

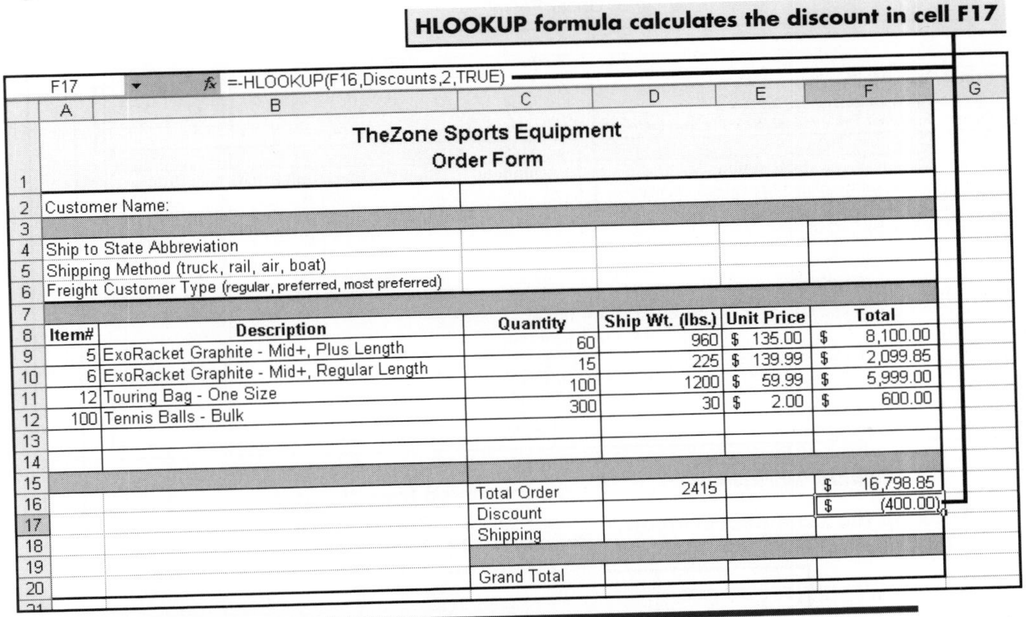

HLOOKUP formula calculates the discount in cell F17

F17   fx =-HLOOKUP(F16,Discounts,2,TRUE)

	A	B	C	D	E	F	G
1		TheZone Sports Equipment Order Form					
2	Customer Name:						
3							
4	Ship to State Abbreviation						
5	Shipping Method (truck, rail, air, boat)						
6	Freight Customer Type (regular, preferred, most preferred)						
7			Quantity	Ship Wt. (lbs.)	Unit Price	Total	
8	Item#	Description					
9	5	ExoRacket Graphite - Mid+, Plus Length	60	960	$ 135.00	$ 8,100.00	
10	6	ExoRacket Graphite - Mid+, Regular Length	15	225	$ 139.99	$ 2,099.85	
11	12	Touring Bag - One Size	100	1200	$ 59.99	$ 5,999.00	
12	100	Tennis Balls - Bulk	300	30	$ 2.00	$ 600.00	
13							
14							
15			Total Order	2415		$ 16,798.85	
16			Discount			$ (400.00)	
17			Shipping				
18							
19							
20			Grand Total				

CALCULATING THE SHIPPING COSTS USING MATCH AND INDEX FUNCTIONS

Although Vijay is using the same format for the shipping schedules as he did originally, he needs to change the formula for calculating shipping costs to let users enter the destination state, shipping method, and customer type as text. These text entries will replace the numeric codes used for region, shipping method, and customer type. In addition, Vijay will calculate the weight for the shipping charges by subtotaling the weights of the individual line items.

Vijay is now basing shipping charges on the following input variables, which are also shown in Figure 5.40.

- **State abbreviation**—The destination region is determined from the two-character state abbreviation that users enter in cell F4. Excel will look up the region number based on the state abbreviation.
- **Shipping method**—Users enter truck, rail, air, or boat as the shipping method. Excel will look up the shipping method number based on this entry.
- **Freight customer type**—Users enter regular, preferred, or most preferred as the customer type. Excel will look up the customer type number based on this entry.

Figure 5.40: Shipping charged based on three variables

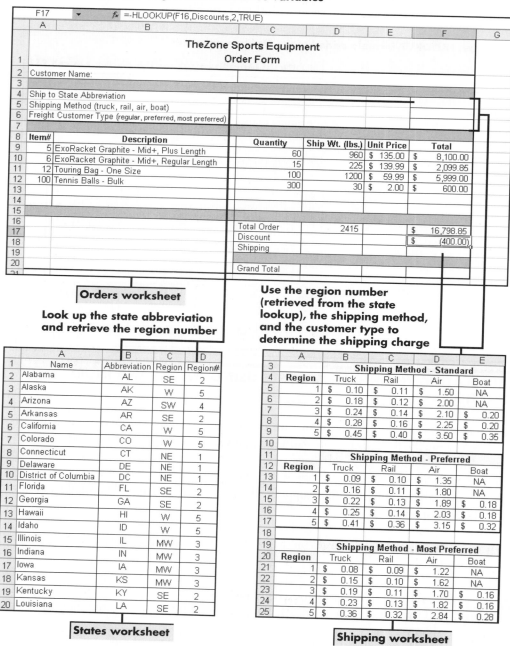

One possible way to perform these tasks is to use the INDEX function, as Vijay did in an earlier version of the order form. However, for this formula, each argument in the INDEX function might require an additional nested lookup function. Recall that the syntax of the INDEX function is as follows:

$$\texttt{=INDEX(reference,row\_num,column\_num,area\_num)}$$

Figure 5.41 illustrates this complex logic for determining the shipping charges.

Figure 5.41: Logic for determining the shipping charges

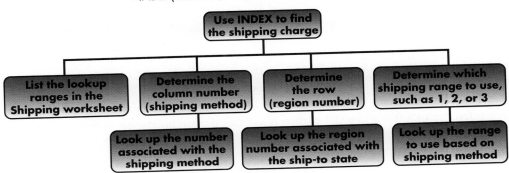

Vijay prepares the worksheets for the INDEX function. To retrieve the shipping charge per pound, he will use the state abbreviation that users enter to first retrieve the appropriate region number listed in the range B2:D52 on the States worksheet. He names this range "States" to make it easier to reference in the Orders worksheet.

He also will use the shipping method users enter to select the appropriate charge in one of the three ranges on the Shipping worksheet. He names the range B5:E9 "Shipping1," the range B13:E17 "Shipping2," and the range B21:E25 "Shipping3."

Vijay will use the customer type users enter to determine which range to use on the Shipping worksheet: Shipping1, Shipping2, or Shipping3. When he finds the shipping charge per pound, he will multiply that value by the total order weight in cell D16.

Vijay returns to the syntax of the INDEX function to analyze how he will structure this formula. The first argument, the reference, is a list of three noncontiguous areas: Shipping1, Shipping2, and Shipping3, which contain the shipping charges for each customer type. The row_num is determined by the region number, which must be determined by the ship-to state entered in cell F4 of the Orders worksheet. The column_num is determined by the shipping method. Vijay needs to find the shipping method column (1, 2, 3, or 4) that corresponds to the shipping method description, which is entered in cell F5 of the Orders worksheet. The last argument, the area_num, determines which noncontiguous range is used for this lookup. Because this must be a number, Vijay must connect the freight customer type description to a corresponding number.

Each step in creating this INDEX function is described in the following sections.

Determining the reference Argument of the INDEX Function

The first argument in the INDEX function is a list of the three ranges that contain the values Vijay wants to look up. These range names should be enclosed in parentheses. Vijay can begin the INDEX function as follows, which is similar to the INDEX function he used earlier:

$$=INDEX((Shipping1,Shipping2,Shipping3)$$

Determining the row_num of the INDEX Function

Vijay organized the shipping tables in the Shipping worksheet with rows listing the regions. Before he can look up the region number in the shipping tables, he must find the region number corresponding to the state abbreviation that users enter. The States range is a vertical lookup table, with the region number listed in the third column. Instead of using a cell reference or value as he did earlier, Vijay can use the following expression in the INDEX function to determine the row_num:

$$VLOOKUP(F4,States,3,FALSE)$$

To solve this expression, Excel looks in the States range for the value that exactly matches the one in F4 (the state abbreviation), and then retrieves the region number from the third column of that table.

Determining the col_num of the INDEX Function by Using the MATCH Function

In the shipping tables, the shipping methods are organized in columns. To determine the column number to use, Vijay must match the shipping method description entered in cell F5 of the Orders worksheet to the column number in the appropriate shipping table.

One way to do this is to set up a separate lookup table, as Vijay did for the States range, which lists states and region numbers. However, because each shipping description is listed in one column, creating a one-to-one correspondence of shipping descriptions and numbers, a simpler technique is to use a MATCH function.

The **MATCH function** is designed to return the relative position (such as 1, 2, or 3) of an item in a list. Although the LOOKUP function returns a corresponding value in a list, the MATCH function returns the relative position number of the lookup_value in a list. The syntax of the MATCH function is as follows and is described in Table 5.13.

$$=MATCH(lookup\_value,lookup\_array,match\_type)$$

Table 5.13: MATCH function arguments

Argument	Description
lookup_value	The value you want to match in the list, which can be a constant value such as 4, a text value such as "Tony", the value FALSE, or a formula that returns a numerical, textual, or Boolean value
lookup_array	A one-dimensional horizontal or vertical list, which can be a range or a list of values enclosed in curly braces { }
match_type	One of three match types, with 1 as the default: • Type 0 requires the function to find an exact match or display the error #N/A. • Type 1 finds a match that returns the greatest value that is less than or equal to the lookup value. • Type –1 finds a match that returns the smallest value that is greater than or equal to the lookup_value.

Keep in mind the following guidelines when you use the MATCH function:

- The MATCH function returns the relative position of an item in a list, and can be used instead of LOOKUP, VLOOKUP, or HLOOKUP when you need the position of an item in a range instead of the item itself. For example, the formula =MATCH("jones",A1:A5,0) returns a 3 if "jones" is stored in cell A3. The formula =MATCH("b",{"a","b","c"},0) returns 2, the relative position of "b" within the {"a","b","c"} list.
- The MATCH function does not distinguish between uppercase and lowercase letters when matching text values.
- If you use a match_type of 0 (exact match), you can use the asterisk (*) and question mark (?) wildcards in the lookup_value. An asterisk matches any sequence of characters, and a question mark matches any single character.
- If you use a match_type of 1, the function finds the largest value that is less than or equal to the lookup_value. With a 1 match type, the lookup_array must be sorted in ascending order.
- If you use a match_type of –1, the function finds the smallest value that is greater than or equal to the lookup_value. With a –1 match type, the lookup_array must be sorted in descending order.

In this case, Vijay wants to match the value entered in cell F5 in the Orders worksheet, the shipping method text, so this value will be the lookup_value. In the Shipping worksheet, cells B4:E4 list the shipping method text as column headings; this range constitutes the lookup_array. Vijay wants to find an exact match to the shipping method text entered in cell F5, so he will use a match_type of 0. So, Vijay can use the following expression as the col_num argument in the INDEX function:

```
MATCH(F5,Shipping!B4:E4,0)
```

For the MATCH function to work correctly, the shipping methods must be listed using the same text and in the same order in all three of the shipping tables.

Best Practice

Using the MATCH Function

Suppose you are working with the simple table of values shown in Figure 5.42.

Figure 5.42: Sample values for the MATCH function

	A	B	C	D	E
1	0	25	50	100	1000

The following formulas show how you can use the MATCH function:

- =MATCH(32,A1:E1,1) returns the value 2 because the greatest value that does not exceed 32 is 25, which is in the second position. The values in cells A1:E1 must be in ascending order to use this match type.
- =MATCH(32,A1:E1,−1) returns the value 3 because the smallest value that is greater than 32 is 50, which is in the third position. The values in cells A1:E1 must be in descending order to use this match type.
- =MATCH("HELP",{"Jones","help",10,9,8},0) returns the value 2 because Excel finds an exact match in the second position. Note that Excel considers HELP and help as equivalent when solving this formula.
- =MATCH("HELP",A1:E1,0) returns the error #N/A because the function cannot find an exact match to HELP in the list.

When using the MATCH function, carefully consider how items should be ordered in the list so that the correct values will be returned.

Determining the area_num of the INDEX Function

To complete the INDEX function, Vijay needs to specify the area_num value, which represents the range that contains the value he wants to retrieve—area 1, 2, or 3. He has already listed the reference ranges as Shipping1, Shipping2, and Shipping3. To determine which range to use, Vijay compares the range name to the freight customer type, where Shipping1 is for regular customers, Shipping2 is for preferred customers, and Shipping3 is for most preferred customers.

In cell F6 of the Orders worksheet, users will enter regular, preferred, or most preferred as text. Because there is a one-to-one correspondence between freight customer type descriptions and freight customer type ranges, Vijay can use a MATCH function to determine the area_num, just as he used a MATCH function to determine the col_num. Vijay can list these descriptions in the appropriate order within the function, as follows:

```
MATCH(F6,{"regular","preferred","most preferred"},0)
```

To solve this expression, Excel exactly matches the value entered in cell F6 to a description in the list, and then returns the position of that description in the list.

Creating the Complex INDEX Formula and Completing the Worksheet

Vijay has defined each argument in the INDEX function to retrieve the appropriate shipping rate. Now, he can multiply that value by the total number of pounds to create the complete formula, as follows:

```
=INDEX((Shipping1,Shipping2,Shipping3),VLOOKUP(F4,States,
    3,FALSE),MATCH(F5,Shipping!B4:E4,0),MATCH(F6,
        {"regular","preferred","most preferred"},0))*D16
```

When using the MATCH function, the lookup_array must be enclosed in curly braces if the values are not continuous. The formula is described in detail in Figure 5.43.

Figure 5.43: Calculating shipping charges with a complex nested INDEX function

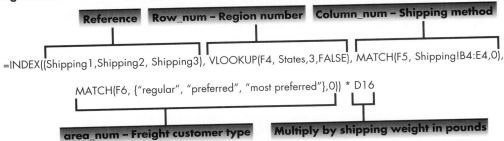

Finally, Vijay can calculate the grand total of the order by summing the discount, order amount, and shipping charge. He enters the following formula in cell F20:

```
=SUM(F16:F18)
```

Figure 5.44 shows the completed order form with sample data.

Figure 5.44: Completed order form

| F18 | ▼ | fx | =INDEX((Shipping1,Shipping2,Shipping3),VLOOKUP(F4,States,3,FALSE),MATCH(F5,ShippingIB4:E4,0), MATCH(F6,{"regular","preferred","most preferred"},0))*D16 |

	A						
		TheZone Sports Equipment Order Form				
1						
2	Customer Name:					
3						
4	Ship to State Abbreviation					CO
5	Shipping Method (truck, rail, air, boat)					Truck
6	Freight Customer Type (regular, preferred, most preferred)					Preferred
7						
8	Item#	Description	Quantity	Ship Wt. (lbs.)	Unit Price	Total
9	5	ExoRacket Graphite - Mid+, Plus Length	60	960	$ 135.00	$ 8,100.00
10	6	ExoRacket Graphite - Mid+, Regular Length	15	225	$ 139.99	$ 2,099.85
11	12	Touring Bag - One Size	100	1200	$ 59.99	$ 5,999.00
12	100	Tennis Balls - Bulk	300	30	$ 2.00	$ 600.00
13						
14						
15						
16			Total Order	2415		$ 16,798.85
17			Discount			$ (400.00)
18			Shipping			$ 990.15
19						
20			Grand Total			$ 17,389.00
21						

Nested INDEX function for calculating shipping charge

5

Level 3

Best Practice

Creating a Testing Plan to Verify Accuracy

After you enter the final formula in a worksheet, especially one as complex as the Orders worksheet presented in this level, you should take the time to verify that the formulas result in correct values. One effective way to do so is to create an order with one set of entries, and then systematically vary each entry to test each formula and cell that contains a value. This includes checking that the formulas you copied from one cell to a range are also displaying correct values.

You could use the following testing plan to verify the accuracy of the Orders worksheet:

1. Verify that the values retrieved for each line item—description, weight, and unit cost—have been correctly calculated for items from pricing schedules 1 and 2.
2. Verify that the total order amount in cell F16 is correct.
3. Test several total values in cell F16 to see if the discount in cell F17 is correctly updated.
4. Enter several state abbreviations in cell F4 in at least two regions to see if the shipping cost is correctly updated.
5. Enter each type of shipping method using the same freight customer type and shipping region to see if the costs are correctly updated.
6. Enter each freight customer type with the same shipping region and shipping mode.

When testing a worksheet, it's best to use round numbers for testing. For example, it's easier to verify 100 items * 16 pounds per item than 123 items * 16 pounds. It is also advisable to check values that represent category divisions, such as discounts at $5,000 and $10,000.

Steps To Success: Level 3

Vijay has been asked to develop an order form for fishing equipment. He has already created a workbook named Fishing.xls, which contains the worksheets described in Table 5.14.

Table 5.14: Worksheets in the Fishing workbook

Worksheet	Description
Orders	Contains an order form for fishing products.
Item List	Lists items sold by the Fishing division, including the item number, description, shipping volume in cubic feet (CF), and corresponding price schedule.
Sched1	Lists fixed unit prices based on item number.
Sched2	Lists variable unit prices for bulk soft bait.
Discount	Lists discounts based on the total value of an order. For example, orders under $5,000 receive no discount, and orders of at least $5,000 but less than $10,000 receive a 2% discount.
States	Lists all the U.S. states and their corresponding regions.
Ship	Contains shipping data. Shipping costs are based on the shipping method—Truck, Rail, or Air—the destination region, and the volume of the order. The prices given are dollars per cubic foot (CF). Regions vary by state. Regular customers are charged at the rates listed in the first shipping table, and rates for preferred customers are in the second shipping table.

In these steps, you will complete the order form, creating the formulas so that new items can be added easily to the item list. You'll need to design the order form on the Orders worksheet so that it works as follows:

- The unit price of an item is based on the price schedule code included in the Item List worksheet. Prices for fixed-price items are listed in the Sched1 worksheet, and prices for variable-price items (in this case, only soft bait) are listed in the Sched2 worksheet.
- Shipping costs are based on the freight customer type, destination region, shipping method, and total shipping volume. Users enter the freight customer type text and state abbreviation. You need to use this information to retrieve the freight customer type *number* and region *number*. Calculate the shipping volume based on the volumes listed by item number in the Item List worksheet.
- Discounts are calculated as a percentage of the total order value as listed in the Discounts worksheet. For example, orders of less than $5,000 receive no discount, and orders of at least $5,000 but less than $10,000 receive a 3% discount.

As you complete the Orders worksheet, select functions that are flexible enough to allow for additional items or up to 23 pricing schedules. Use range names to make the form easy to use and troubleshoot. If the item number field is blank, be certain your form displays a blank cell for the resulting unit price and total. Test that your workbook calculates the correct values. Where appropriate, formulas should work when copied down the column or across the row.

Complete the following:

1. Open the workbook named **Fishing.xls** located in the Chapter 5 folder, and then save it as **Fishing Orders.xls**.

2. In the Orders worksheet, use the following test data:

   - Orders: Item #208 (100 items), Item #218 (300 items)
   - Shipped by rail to Colorado to a preferred customer

3. In cell B9 of the Orders worksheet, write a formula that enters the item description. Copy the formula to cells B10:B13.

4. In cell D9 of the Orders worksheet, write a formula that calculates the total volume of the first line item (quantity * volume per item). Copy the formula to cells D10:D13.

5. In cell E9 of the Orders worksheet, write a formula that calculates the unit price. Copy the formula to cells E10:E13.

6. In cell F9 of the Orders worksheet, write a formula that calculates the total value of this line item. Copy the formula to cells F10:F13.

7. In cell F16 of the Orders worksheet, write a formula that calculates the total for all items, excluding discounts and shipping.

8. In cell D16 of the Orders worksheet, write a formula that calculates the total shipping volume of this order.

9. In cell F17 of the Orders worksheet, write a formula that calculates the discount, if any, on this order.

10. In cell F18 of the Orders worksheet, write a formula that calculates the shipping costs directly from the state and ship method (truck, rail, or air).

11. In cell F20 of the Orders worksheet, write a formula that calculates the grand total of this order.

12. Double-check your formulas to be certain that different test data produces valid results.

13. Save and close the Fishing Orders.xls workbook.

CHAPTER SUMMARY

In this chapter, you learned how using the Excel Reference and Lookup functions VLOOKUP, HLOOKUP, LOOKUP, INDEX, CHOOSE, and MATCH, can transform a multistep task that required users to enter many values more than once to a well-designed worksheet in which users enter only a few items to perform sophisticated calculations.

When you organize data in a vertical lookup table, the most effective and flexible way to retrieve the data is to use the VLOOKUP function. Use VLOOKUP when the first column of the lookup table contains the key data, and the information you want to retrieve is in one of the columns to the right of the key data column. HLOOKUP works in a similar way, except that it retrieves data stored in horizontal lookup tables. Use HLOOKUP when the first row of the lookup table contains the key data, and the information you want to retrieve is in a row below the key data row. Unlike VLOOKUP and HLOOKUP, the LOOKUP function looks up the greatest value that does not exceed a specified value anywhere in a table or range. It can retrieve data from a lookup table with a vertical or horizontal orientation.

To solve more complex problems, such as those involving multiple worksheets, you can nest the Reference and Lookup functions using the IF, IS, INDEX, CHOOSE, and MATCH functions. The ISBLANK function is one of the nine IS functions, which all check for a condition and then return a TRUE or FALSE value. ISBLANK checks whether a specified value refers to an empty cell. Use the INDEX function to return the value in a table based on the row and column numbers that you specify. Use the CHOOSE function to return a value or a range for up to 29 corresponding values. The MATCH function returns the relative position (such as 1, 2, or 3) of an item in a list. Whereas the LOOKUP function returns a corresponding value, the MATCH function returns the relative position number of the lookup value in a list.

Completing complex tasks that require several levels of lookups, as demonstrated in Level 3, might indicate that you should use a tool other than Excel. Relational databases such as Microsoft Access are designed to handle large quantities of information, especially those that involve multiple sets of related data. However, Excel does provide the capability to complete such tasks through the use of more complex formulas containing multiple nested functions.

CONCEPTUAL REVIEW

Answer Questions 1–10 as True or False.

1. _____ The lookup_value of a VLOOKUP function can be a continuous cell range.

2. _____ In a VLOOKUP formula with a FALSE lookup type, the lookup table referenced must be in ascending order to retrieve the correct value.

3. _____ The result_vector of a LOOKUP function must be sorted in descending order.

4. _____ Reference and Lookup functions cannot contain nested arguments.

5. _____ The default range_lookup type for the VLOOKUP and HLOOKUP functions is TRUE.

6. _____ Excel matches the lookup_value "JANE" with the entry "jane" in a lookup table.

7. _____ The row and column arguments in the INDEX function can be numeric values, Boolean values, or text.

8. _____ The expression =INDEX((B2:D7,B12:D17,B22:D17),2,3,2) returns the value in cell C14.

9. _____ The expression =AVERAGE(CHOOSE(2,B12:D17,B22:D17)) averages the values in cells B12 to D17.

10. _____ The expression =MATCH(40,{10,30,50,90},–1) returns the value 3.

Answer the following questions.

11. What happens when Excel is solving a VLOOKUP formula with a TRUE lookup type and does not find an exact match in the lookup table?

12. What is the difference between the LOOKUP function and the VLOOKUP or HLOOKUP function?

13. Which Excel function should you use when you want to look up a value and return a range?

14. How does the INDEX function retrieve a value from a two-dimensional table?

15. What is the difference between the LOOKUP function and the MATCH function?

Base your answers for Questions 16–18 on the Pricing and Delivery worksheets shown below.

	A	B	C	D
1	Number of copies	Price per copy		
2	1	0.07		
3	10	0.06		
4	100	0.05		
5	200	0.04		
6	500	0.03		
7	1000	0.02		
8				
9				
10				
11	Copies made:	Total cost:	Delivery cost	
12				
13	3			
14	10			
15	200			
16	1001			
17				

Pricing worksheet

	A	B	C	D	E
1		Delivery charges			
2					
3					
4					
5					
6					
7					
8					
9					
10					
11					
12					
13					
14					
15					
16					
17					

Delivery worksheet

16. Write a formula in cell B13 in the Pricing worksheet to determine the total cost of making copies for this order. Column A lists the number of copies made. Write the formula so that it works when copied into cells B14:B16.

17. The delivery charges used in the Delivery worksheet are as follows:

    - For orders under $5, there is a $5 delivery fee.
    - Orders of at least $5 but less than $20 have a $7 delivery fee.
    - Orders over $20 are delivered free of charge.

    Create a lookup table for the Delivery worksheet so that you can use a lookup function to calculate the delivery cost for each order. Organize the table in a horizontal format.

18. Write a formula in cell C13 in the Pricing worksheet to look up the correct delivery cost using the lookup table you created in Question 17. Write the formula so that it can be copied down the column.

Base your answers for Questions 19–20 on the Scores and Grades worksheets shown below.

	A	B	C	D
1	Name	Score	Final Grade	
2	Mary	930		
3	Davide	450		
4	Tang	880		
5	Bindu	750		
6	Thomas	320		
7	Rebecca	850		
8	Mallory	970		
9				
10				

Scores worksheet

	A	B	C	D	E	F
1	900	800	700	600	0	
2	A	B	C	D	F	
3						
4						
5	0	600	700	800	900	
6	F	D	C	B	A	
7						
8						
9						
10						

Grades worksheet

19. As shown in the Grades worksheet, final grades are determined using the following grading scheme:

- Students earning over 900 points receive an A.
- Students earning less than 900 points but at least 800 points receive a B.
- Students earning less than 800 points but at least 700 points receive a C.
- Students earning less than 700 points but at least 600 points receive a D.
- Students earning less than 600 points receive an F.

Write a formula in cell C2 in the Scores worksheet that determines the final grade for the first student based on the grading scheme. Use the appropriate Reference and Lookup function and write the formula so that it can be copied down the column.

20. Explain the difference between the lookup table in cells A1:E2 of the Grades worksheet and the lookup table in cells A5:E6 in the same worksheet.

CASE PROBLEMS

Level 1 – Evaluating Tax Rates for the Arlington Group

Note: The information in this Case Problem does not reflect any actual tax rates, tax rate calculation methodologies, or IRS policies, and should not be constituted as tax advice.

Accounting

The Arlington Group is a "think tank" in Washington, D.C. that provides research data to lobbyists and members of the federal government. As a tax analyst for the Arlington Group, your job is to report how tax policies affect federal, state, and local revenues. A lobbyist asks you to study how alternate flat tax rate proposals could affect the total taxes owed and residual amount of taxes owed on April 15, based on a list of sample individual tax return information. A flat tax rate is a rate applied to the total income earned. For example, a flat tax rate of 10% on $20,000 in income is $2,000. The current graduated system applies different percentages to ranges of income for each taxpayer. For example, a graduated tax on a $20,000 income might be as follows: 0% of the first $5,000, 10% of the amounts between $5,001 and $10,000, and $15% of the amounts over $10,000.

A worksheet in an Excel workbook named Taxes.xls has been set up listing sample tax return data and the actual amount of taxes owed based on the current tax rates. The worksheet also includes schedules for the proposed tax rates, penalties, and state allowances.

To complete this study, your task is to analyze the total taxes owed based on two new flat rate tax alternates. In addition, you will compare the residual amount owed and penalties applied to that residual amount for each alternate. The residual amount owed on April 15 is calculated as follows: Total tax owed − (Current withholding taxes paid + estimated taxes paid).

Withholding taxes are those amounts withheld from an employee's paycheck each pay period and remitted to the IRS by the employer. Estimated taxes are direct tax payments made by taxpayers to the IRS each quarter. Depending on the amount owed, penalties might be applied to the residual amount owed. Complete the following:

1. Open the workbook named **Taxes.xls** located in the Chapter 5 folder, and then save it as **Tax Analysis.xls**.

2. In cell G12, write a formula that uses the Alternate 1 flat tax rate to determine the total dollar value of the tax for the income in cell B12. As detailed in the Flat Tax Rate table (cells A1:F4), this tax scheme calculates taxes by multiplying the total income by the corresponding rate. For example, incomes below $15,000 pay no tax; incomes of at least $15,000 but less than $32,000 pay 3% of the income in taxes; and incomes of at least $32,000 but less than $72,000 pay 10% of the income in taxes. Write the formula so that it can be copied down the column, and then copy it to cells G13:G21.

3. In cell H12, write a formula that uses the Alternate 2 flat tax rate to determine the total dollar value of the tax for the income in cell B12. As detailed in the Flat Tax Rate table (cells A1:F4), this tax scheme also calculates taxes by multiplying the total income by the corresponding rate. For example, incomes below $15,000 pay no tax; incomes of at least $15,000 but less than $32,000 pay 5% of the income in taxes; and incomes of at least $32,000 but less than $72,000 pay 7% of the income in taxes. Write the formula so that it can be copied down the column, and then copy it to cells H13:H21.

4. In cell I12, write a formula that calculates the amount of taxes the first taxpayer still owes on April 15. The unpaid taxes are based on the actual amount of taxes owed and the actual withholding and estimated taxes paid. Write the formula so that it can be copied down the column to calculate this amount for each taxpayer. Also write the formula so that it can be copied across the row to determine the unpaid amount based on the taxes owed for the Alternate 1 and Alternate 2 tax calculations. (Assume the same withholding and estimated taxes paid.) Copy the formula to cells I13:I21 and to cells J12:K21.

5. In cell L12, write a formula that determines the actual penalty owed based on the penalty schedule. For example, unpaid tax balances of less than $100 owe no penalty, and unpaid tax balances of at least $100 but less than $1,000 are charged a penalty of 5% of the unpaid tax amount. The range H3:I8 is named "Penalty." (*Hint*: Use an IF function to determine if the unpaid tax amount is negative, indicating that the IRS owes the taxpayer a refund and, therefore, no penalties apply.) Copy this formula both down the column to calculate the penalty for the corresponding ID# and across the row to determine the penalties based on each alternate tax scheme.

6. In row 23, calculate the total values for each category (actual, Alternate 1, Alternate 2) for all 10 tax returns.

7. As part of the flat rate tax, one possible scheme would include a state allowance to balance the high and low cost of living. The amount of the allowance is listed by state in cells A7:B9. If the list does not contain the appropriate state, the error message #N/A should be displayed. In cell O12, write a formula that determines the state allowance for this taxpayer. Write the formula so that it can be copied down the column, and then copy it to cells O13:O21.

8. Highlight in yellow the column of the tax scheme that is most favorable to very low income taxpayers (actual, Alternate 1, or Alternate 2).

9. Format the worksheet to make it easy to read and understand.

10. Save and close the Tax Analysis.xls workbook.

Level 2 – Calculating Travel Costs at America Travels

As a new sales associate at America Travels travel agency, you assist travel agents in finding the best fares for corporate customers. As a high-volume travel agency, America Travels has negotiated several premium discounts with airlines, which you pass along to your large customers. Compared to standard business fares, these discounts can amount to a substantial savings, and do not have minimum stay requirements.

Texto, Inc. is a large customer with a travel department that prices its own fares online, and then contacts America Travels to see if they can provide a better rate. They e-mail an Excel workbook containing a list of proposed trips to America Travels each day by 10 a.m., and request price quotes for these trips by noon. Texto has corporate offices in New York, San Francisco, and London, which is where most of their travel originates. When the Texto workbook arrives, America Travels sales associates must work hard to enter the information that Texto requests and return the workbook to the company on time. For several months, America Travels has been working on a more automated method of replying to these inquiries. Another sales associate compiled fare data by flight number and researched airport fees. This information has been set up on separate worksheets in an Excel workbook. Your task is to complete the last piece of the project, which is to use the information on the customer's fare request sheet and automatically calculate the best fares. For this project, assume that all flight numbers are included on the flights list.

The following worksheets have already been created in an Excel workbook named Travels.xls:

- **Requests**—This worksheet contains a sample request form from Texto, including the traveler's name, date, flight number, and corporate-rate fare.
- **Flights**—This worksheet contains a list sorted by flight number of the base fare, departing city, and arrival city.

- **Fees**—This worksheet contains a table listing fare categories, ticket prices, and associated airport fees that will be added to a ticket. For example, fares of less than $200 have a $15 airport fee, and fares from $200 to $299.99 have a $25 airport fee.
- **Discounts**—This worksheet contains a two-dimensional table of discount categories based on the fare category and weekday of the ticket.

Your task is to include formulas in the Requests worksheet to provide fare information. All formulas must work when copied down the column to determine the requested information for each travel request. Complete the following:

1. Open the workbook named **Travels.xls** located in the Chapter 5 folder, and then save it as **America Travels Quotes.xls**.

2. In cell E3 of the Requests worksheet, write a formula that retrieves the name of the departure city for this flight. Copy the formula to cells E4:E6.

3. In cell F3, write a formula that retrieves the name of the arrival city for this flight. Copy the formula to cells F4:F6.

4. In cell G3, write a formula that retrieves the base fare for this flight based on the data given on the Flights worksheet. Copy the formula to cells G4:G6.

5. In cell H3, write a formula that determines the day of the week (1 through 7) of this flight using the WEEKDAY(date) function. The WEEKDAY function returns 1 for Sunday, 2 for Monday, and so on. (Refer to the Microsoft Office Excel Help feature for more details on using the WEEKDAY function.) Copy this formula to cells H4:H6.

6. Airline tickets are assigned a fare category based on the base fare ticket price (column G) and the categories listed on the Fees worksheet. In cell I3, write a formula that determines the fare category for this ticket. Copy the formula to cells I4:I6.

7. The Discounts worksheet contains a two-dimensional table that has been set up to find the discount category of a ticket based on the weekday of travel and the fare category. In cell J3, write a formula that determines the discount category for this ticket. Copy the formula to cells J4:J6.

8. In a separate area of the Discounts worksheet, create a horizontal lookup table based on the following discount information:

   - Fare discount category Z: 65% discount of the published base fare
   - Fare discount category Y: 55% discount of the published base fare
   - Fare discount category X: 40% discount of the published base fare

9. In cell K3 of the Requests worksheet, write a formula that determines the discounted fare price (base fare – discount) of this flight using the table you created in the Discounts worksheet. Fares should be rounded to the nearest dollar. (Do not use an IF function.) Copy this formula to cells K4:K6.

10. In cell L3, calculate the airport fee based on the fee schedule in the Fees worksheet. Note that the airport fee is based on the discounted fare. Copy this formula to cells L4:L6.

11. In cell M3, calculate the total ticket price that America Travels can obtain (discounted fare + airport fees). Copy this formula to cells M4:M6.

12. In cell N3, compare the America Travels total ticket price to the corporate fare that Texto found. Return a TRUE value if the America Travels price is less than the corporate fare Texto was offered. Copy this formula to cells N4:N6.

13. Format your worksheet so that it is easy to read and understand.

14. Save and close the America Travels Quotes.xls workbook.

Level 3 – Creating a Cost Estimate Form for CKG Auto

As part of its product line, CKG Auto has nine basic models, each with different options and features. Although many car buyers are concerned about the initial cost of a car, customers are also becoming increasingly curious about the yearly operating expenses they can expect. They frequently want to compare two or more purchase options to see how much a car costs to run each year. Although they might be willing to spend an extra $5,000 to purchase a sports utility vehicle or luxury car with many options, customers might reconsider when they calculate the annual cost of gas and insurance.

Fuel economy information posted on each car's window is usually stated within a range of 5 to 10 miles per gallon. For example, CKG Auto's compact car, the Pony, lists 23–27 miles per gallon in the city and 26–32 miles per gallon on the highway. This and other car sticker information is difficult to translate into annual costs for gasoline, maintenance, insurance, and other operating costs. Many CKG Auto dealerships have asked for an easy way to provide operating cost information to their customers, much the same way they can give them base car costs and option prices.

To this end, CKG Auto has decided to develop an Excel workbook that can calculate costs associated with the first three years of operating a new car, including gas expenses, maintenance, and insurance premiums. Although these costs are estimates, they will give customers a good understanding of what to expect.

5

Chapter Exercises

Sales

Your task is to work with the Costs.xls workbook, which is located in the Chapter 5 folder (save this workbook as "CKG Operating Costs.xls"), and develop a worksheet named "Estimate Form" that salespeople can complete to help their customers calculate annual operating costs for a selected vehicle. CKG Auto completed a preliminary analysis summarizing the data required from the salespeople, the information needed for the calculations, and the desired data outputs. The estimate form should compare the operating costs of the selected vehicles. When this form is complete, it should display the data inputs and outputs, and provide space to compare up to five vehicles. In the Estimate Form worksheet, users should enter the following data about the vehicle:

- Vehicle model number
- Number of cylinders (4, 6, 8 or turbo)

Users should enter the following data about the customer:

- Expected number of driving miles per year.
- Type of driving: Highway (speeds of 55 mph and over), Mixed (balance of highway and city driving), or City (speeds of 45 mph and below).
- State of residence.
- Residential status: City, Suburban, Rural.
- Driving safety record: Excellent, Average, or Poor.
- Gas price adjustment percentage, which is a multiplier that accounts for major changes in gas prices. A multiplier of 1 is based on $2 per gallon in the northeast. This assumes prices change proportionally throughout the country. A multiplier of greater than 1 increases the price, and a multiplier of less than 1 reduces the price.

Lookup tables created by the marketing and engineering departments are included in the Costs.xls workbook on the following worksheets:

- **Models**—This worksheet lists available car models including description, available engines, weight class, and expected maintenance base costs for the first three years. To the base maintenance cost, add $25 per oil change for each 3,000 miles driven and $17 to change the air filter for each 6,000 miles driven.
- **Mileage**—This worksheet includes the gas mileage schedules for each driving usage type. Each schedule lists the gas mileage in miles per gallon based on the weight class and engine.
- **States**—This worksheet lists states and their associated regions.
- **Gas Prices**—This worksheet includes regional average gas prices based on $2 per gallon in the northeast. This value should be adjusted based on the multiplier supplied as part of the user inputs. (Estimated $/gallon = $/gallon per table * multiplier.)
- **Insurance**—This worksheet lists regional insurance rate estimates for new cars. These base prices can then be adjusted based on driver safety records and residential status.

The Estimate Form worksheet should include the following outputs for up to five selected cars:

- Car model.
- Estimated annual cost of gas based on the selected type of driving, car weight class, annual miles traveled, gas price, and engine type.
- Estimated annual insurance premium based on the owner's region of residence, driving record, and residential status. (*Hint*: Include a calculation in the upper part of the form that looks up the region associated with the state of residence, and then refer to the cell that contains this result in the insurance formula.)
- Estimated average annual maintenance cost for the first three years of operation, based on the selected car model and annual miles traveled.
- Estimated total cost of operation per year.

Make sure the formulas you enter can be copied to other cells in the same column as needed for each model selected. Your formulas should also be flexible enough to easily accommodate anticipated changes to this data. If the model number is blank, leave the description field blank. You can create additional worksheets and intermediate calculations, as needed, to develop this form. Use named ranges to simplify your formulas. Be sure to test your data to verify that the Estimate Form works for different combinations of buyer profiles and cars. Use the following test data when setting up your worksheet:

Buyer's Profile

- Expected number of driving miles per year: 20,000
- Type of driving: Mixed
- Purchaser's state: ME
- Purchaser's residential status: Rural
- Purchaser's driving safety record: Excellent
- Gas price adjustment percentage: 1.1

Cars

- Model 1: 4 cylinders
- Model 2: 6 cylinders
- Model 9: turbo
- Model 4: 8 cylinders
- Model 5: turbo

Be certain your Estimate Form is easy to read and use. Highlight the data inputs so it is clear what the user needs to complete on the form. Save and close the CKG Operating Costs.xls workbook when you are finished.

Evaluating the Financial Impact of Loans and Investments
Finance: Forecasting Cash Flows for a Capital Project Analysis

> *"To succeed in business, to reach the top, an individual must know all it is possible to know about that business."*
> —J. Paul Getty

LEARNING OBJECTIVES

Level 1

Understand how compound interest and simple interest are calculated

Determine the value of a loan payment

Analyze positive and negative cash flows

Determine the future value and the present value of a financial transaction

Determine the interest rate and the number of periods of a financial transaction

Level 2

Set up an amortization table to evaluate a loan

Calculate principal and interest payments

Calculate cumulative principal and interest payments

Set up named ranges for a list

Calculate depreciation and taxes

Level 3

Set up a worksheet to analyze profitability

Calculate the net present value

Calculate the internal rate of return

Calculate the return on investment

Determine the payback period

FUNCTIONS COVERED IN THIS CHAPTER

CUMIPMT	IRR	PPMT
CUMPRINC	ISNUMBER	PV
FV	NPER	RATE
IPMT	PMT	SLN

CHAPTER INTRODUCTION

Business decisions are often greatly influenced by financial considerations, such as how much something will cost and how funding will be obtained. Money is usually not the only component in a business decision; companies must also consider long-term market ramifications, jobs, environmental and social issues, or even technical feasibility. However, ultimately when financing a corporate project or determining where to best invest funds, the issues of money, return on investment, rate of return, and so on, are central to the decision-making process.

As you will see in this chapter, keeping track of loans and investments requires more than simply multiplying the payments made or interest earned over a period of time. Level 1 explores some fundamental financial calculations to evaluate different financing options. In Level 2, these basic concepts are expanded upon to develop an amortization table—a listing by period of the cash inflows and outflows. You also learn about Excel tools for calculating depreciation, a technique used to allocate the costs of an asset over its useful life. Finally, in Level 3, you will explore the ramifications of these cash flows, using a variety of tools to analyze the financial viability of a project.

CASE SCENARIO

As you recall, TheZone is planning to bring to market a new athletic shoe called TZEdge. Previously, the project team's financial analyst compiled a list of labor and material costs to manufacture these shoes, and formulated an initial budget including overhead and selling expenses. One critical element that remains to be analyzed is the capital investment required to manufacture the TZEdge shoe. This capital investment is the money needed to purchase and install the manufacturing equipment necessary to produce the shoe.

Because the cost of this equipment will ultimately affect the profitability of the venture, TheZone needs to quantify the costs and determine how funds will be obtained before making a final decision to proceed with this project. Approximately $1 million will be needed to purchase and install the equipment to manufacture TZEdge shoes. These funds include modifications to an existing manufacturing facility, the required electrical upgrades, and the costs to purchase and install new state-of-the-art cutting and sewing machines.

Ryan Whittier, an analyst in the finance group, must use this information to explore a variety of funding options and to generate cash flow projections. Ultimately, he will use this data to compile the financial information needed by management—information that will be a critical piece in the decision-making process of whether or not to fund this project.

Finance

LEVEL 1
CALCULATING VALUES FOR SIMPLE FINANCIAL TRANSACTIONS

EXCEL 2003 SKILLS TRAINING

- **Create formulas using the FV function**
- **Create formulas using the PMT function**
- **Create formulas using the PV function**

UNDERSTANDING HOW INTEREST IS CALCULATED

When you borrow money from a bank to make a purchase, for example to buy a car, you must pay back the amount borrowed plus an additional amount known as **interest**. This interest is like a user fee, because you are paying to "use" the bank's money. The amount of interest charged by the lender depends on many variables, including the following:

- *How long do you want to borrow the money for?* In general, having $1 in hand today is preferable to having $1 in hand three years from now. When borrowing money, you need to consider the cost to you for borrowing it. How much would you be willing to pay back in the future in order to have $10,000 today, for example? This concept is often referred to as the "time value of money."
- *What level of risk is the lender assuming in lending the money?* Although a bank might be quite willing to lend a home buyer the necessary amount to purchase a house, the same bank would probably be much less willing to lend a large sum of money to a corporation for investing in an unproven product or service.
- *What are the current monetary policies and levels of supply and demand to borrow versus lend money?* An investment might be of short duration and very sound, but few lending institutions might be willing to lend money while many are seeking to borrow. Often, the fiscal policy of the Federal Reserve Bank or other monetary policies set by governmental agencies directly affect the supply and demand for funds and, ultimately, the interest rate.

These are just some of the factors that can affect the interest to be paid on an investment or charged to borrow funds. Interest is usually calculated as a percentage of the principal for a specified period of time. The **principal** is the value of the loan or investment. Interest can be accounted for in two ways: simple interest or compound interest.

Calculating Simple Interest

Interest that is paid solely on the amount of the original principal value is called **simple interest**. The computation of simple interest is based on the following formula:

```
Simple interest = Principal * Interest rate per time period *
                  Number of time periods
```

Consider the following example: you have deposited $10,000 in a two-year certificate of deposit (CD) that pays simple interest of 4% per year for a period of two years. At the end of the two years, your $10,000 plus the interest owed to you will be returned. How much interest will be owed to you at the end of two years?

```
Year 1: $10,000 [principal] * .04 [interest rate] = $400
Year 2: $10,000 [principal] * .04 [interest rate] = $400
           Total interest at the end of two years: = $800
```

In this example, the principal is $10,000, and the interest is applied yearly at the rate of 4% for a total of two years. This can be represented mathematically as the formula =$10,000*.04*2. Notice that the principal never changes, and the additional $400 of interest earned in year 1 plays no role in the calculation of interest in year 2.

Calculating Compound Interest

Most often in financial transactions, you want to take into account the interest paid in the previous period. In the example of the CD, the value of the CD increases each year by the amount of the previous interest paid. How would this affect the total interest paid if the CD earned interest on this additional amount each period?

Adding interest earned each period to the principal for purposes of computing interest for the next period is known as **compound interest**. As you will see from the examples that follow, the total value of interest payments using compound interest is greater than those using simple interest at the same percentage. Most financial instruments use compound interest; these include bank accounts, CDs, loans, and so on. Using the previous example, consider how much money you will have at the end of the two years, but this time assume that the interest (4%) will be earned on the interest accrued in the previous periods.

```
Year 1: $10,000 [principal] * .04 [interest rate] = $400
  Year 2: $10,400 [principal of $10,000 + accrued
          interest of $400] * .04 [interest rate] = $416
          Total interest at the end of two years: = $816
```

Notice that the principal changes in the second year to include the interest paid in the previous year. After two years, an additional $16 will be earned with compound interest as compared to simple interest.

Consider another example: assume you have deposited $10,000 in a credit union, which pays interest at 4% per year *compounded quarterly*. Here, interest is added to the principal each quarter. To determine the amount of money you will have at the end of one year (four quarters), you would calculate the interest as follows:

```
1st Qtr: $10,000 [principal] * .04/4 [interest rate] = $100.00
    2nd Qtr: $10,100 [principal of $10,000 + accrued
            interest of $100] * .04/4 [interest rate] = $101.00
    3rd Qtr: $10,201 [principal of $10,100 + accrued
            interest of $101) * .04/4 [interest rate] = $102.01
4th Qtr: $10,303.01 [principal of $10,201 + accrued
        interest of $102.01) * .04/4 [interest rate] = $103.03
            Total interest at the end of one year: = $406.04
```

Notice that if the annual interest is 4%, the quarterly interest is 4% divided by 4 quarters per year, or 1% per quarter. The total interest paid at the end of one year is $406.04. This amount results in $6.04 more interest paid than if this same interest rate was applied only once in the year.

Financial institutions often use the term **annual percentage yield**, or **APY**. This is the equivalent yearly simple interest rate, taking into account compounding. In the previous example, the interest rate was 4% per year compounded quarterly. The APY would be 4.0604% because, at the end of the first four quarters, a total of $406.04 would have been paid out on the initial deposit of $10,000. Often, financial institutions advertise their loan interest rates in what is referred to as an **annual percentage rate**, or **APR**. This rate reflects the interest being paid on the actual amount borrowed. Because loans often have fees associated with them, the actual amount borrowed is the face value of the loan minus any fees charged. For example, if a $100,000 mortgage requires a $1000 application fee, the amount borrowed would actually be $99,000 because the borrower had to pay $1000 to obtain the mortgage. However, the borrower still must pay back the entire mortgage amount of $100,000. This effectively makes the interest rate higher than the stated interest rate. APRs can often be problematic, because different banks calculate the APR in various ways, including or excluding certain fees. You can use the Excel tools presented in this chapter to better understand and compare these types of financial transactions.

Although the method presented in this section for calculating compound interest is effective, it is certainly not efficient, requiring multiple steps of multiplying and adding values. Consider that for a 30-year mortgage compounded monthly, you would need to perform this calculation 360 times (30 *12 periods)! Fortunately, Excel provides a wide variety of functions that perform these steps automatically.

REVIEWING ALTERNATIVE FINANCING OPTIONS

The first task Ryan faces is to analyze several possible financing options for the TZEdge shoe project. The options being considered by TheZone to raise funds for this project are as follows:

(1) Funding the entire project using a line of credit at CtrBank. CtrBank currently charges a fixed rate of 8% annual interest compounded quarterly. For this type of project, payments are scheduled out quarterly over a five-year period.

(2) Funding the project by cashing in a money market account that was set up as an emergency fund. The fund started with an initial deposit of $900,000 and paid 3.5% annual interest compounded monthly. The account was originally set up two years ago.

(3) Funding the project from an initial investment and current profits. This option requires the project to be delayed by 1½ years, investing a portion of TheZone's expected profits ($50,000 per month each month), plus an initial cash outlay to be determined. A money market account will be used to hold these funds. The current money market rates pay 4% annual interest compounded monthly.

(4) Funding the entire project through NWN Bank, an institution that has not previously done business with TheZone. In an effort to win TheZone's business, NWN Bank is offering several different options for funding, as follows:

  (a) A loan to be paid back over the next four years, with equal semiannual payments (compounded semiannually) of $150,000

  (b) A loan with a fixed interest rate of 6.5% per year compounded quarterly, and fixed quarterly payments of $95,000

Each of the options being considered involves applying compound interest over a specific time period and a constant rate of interest. However, not all of the variables have been identified. Ryan needs to examine each financing method and calculate any of the missing pieces of data. In some cases, this will require determining the periodic payments; in others, the specified loan duration; and in still others, the value of an existing financial asset. To use the manual, step-by-step method of calculating compound interest over multiple periods would be a long and tedious process. Consequently, Ryan will use some of the financial functions that are built into Excel.

USING THE PMT FUNCTION TO DETERMINE A LOAN PAYMENT

Recall that the first financing option under consideration is to fund the entire project using a line of credit at CtrBank. CtrBank currently charges a fixed rate of 8% annual interest compounded quarterly. For this type of project, payments are scheduled out quarterly over a five-year period.

What is known about this financial transaction? Ryan knows that $1 million will be given to TheZone when the loan is initiated. In exchange, each quarter for the next five years, TheZone will pay back an unspecified amount of money—paying back both the accrued interest and a portion of the principal each period. Because the loan is compounded quarterly, interest will be calculated each quarter based on the remaining principal. The rate per period (quarter) is the annual rate (8%) divided by the number of periods per year (4), in this case 2% per quarter. At the end of the loan duration (five years), the original loan amount and all of the accrued interest will be completely paid off. A timeline of this transaction is shown in Figure 6.1.

Figure 6.1: Timeline of the financial transaction for a $1 million loan

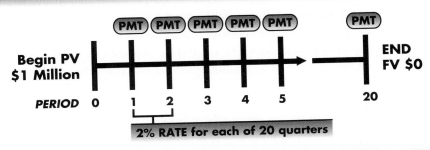

A critical element of this transaction is the unknown quarterly payment. This cannot be calculated by simply dividing $1,000,000 by 20 total quarters, because interest will be charged in each quarter based on the remaining principal. Furthermore, in each quarter, the remaining principal will be reduced based on the value of this payment less the accrued interest. To determine the quarterly payment, Ryan will use the PMT financial function. The **PMT function** finds the value of the payment per period, assuming that there are constant payments and a constant interest rate for the duration of the loan. The syntax of the PMT function is as follows:

```
PMT(rate,nper,pv,fv,type)
```

The Arguments of the PMT Function

As with any Excel functions, to use the PMT function you need to supply the correct values for each of the arguments and adhere to any specified rules. The five arguments of the PMT function are defined as follows:

- The **rate** argument is the interest rate per compounding period.
- The **nper** argument is the number of compounding periods.
- The **pv** argument is the present value, also referred to as the original principal value at the beginning of the financial transaction.

- The **fv** argument is the future value (compounded amount), also referred to as the value at the end of the financial transaction.
- The **type** argument designates when payments are made. Type 0, the default type, indicates that payments are made at the end of the period. Type 1 indicates that payments are made at the beginning of the period.

The Help system in Excel provides more detail on how the PMT function and its arguments work.

Understanding Cash Flow (Inputs and Outputs)

The fv and pv arguments, as well as the result of the PMT function, are all cash amounts that are either received or paid out during the course of the financial transaction. These inputs and outputs are often referred to as **cash flow**. For the PMT function to work properly, it must recognize which amounts are flowing to the borrower and which amounts the borrower is paying out. The convention used here is that when cash is *received* it is considered **positive cash flow**, and when cash is *paid out* it is considered **negative cash flow**. These concepts of cash received and cash paid out do not necessarily correspond to who owns the money, but rather reflect where the money is physically going, as illustrated in Figure 6.2.

Figure 6.2: Positive and negative cash flows

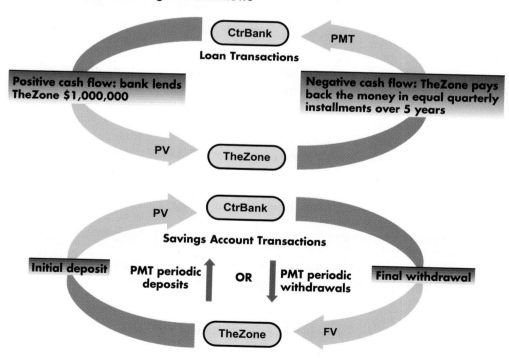

In the loan diagram in Figure 6.2, for example, the present value (pv) is a positive cash flow from the bank to TheZone. The company can subsequently take this loan to buy the new equipment needed to make shoes, but because the bank has given the money to the company, it is a positive cash flow for TheZone. Each of TheZone's payments back to the bank is a negative cash flow from the company to the bank.

The savings account transaction diagram in Figure 6.2 shows an initial deposit, which is a negative present value (pv) reflecting a transfer of funds to the bank from the company. This deposit is, therefore, a negative cash flow. This diagram also shows a final withdrawal, which is a positive future value (fv) reflecting a transfer of funds back to the company from the bank. Periodic deposits can be made either into the account (negative cash flow) or withdrawals can be taken from the account (positive cash flow) as determined by the PMT function.

Specifying Consistent Units of Time

It is also necessary when using Excel financial functions to pay close attention to the compounding period being used. The financial functions apply the *interest rate per period* and the *payment per period* to the principal value over a *specified number of periods*. It does not matter if the compounding period is months, days, quarters, and so on; the function simply applies the appropriate rate and payments the specified number of times. If the rate and nper arguments, and the results of the PMT function, are not all consistent or do not reflect the compounding period, the wrong values will be calculated. As noted previously, $10,000 compounded 1 time at 4% per period is different from $10,000 compounded 4 times at 1% per period; the latter resulted in a higher value.

In the original loan being offered by CtrBank, the interest rate per year is 8% over a period of 5 years. Because the compounding period is quarterly, a rate of 2% per quarter (8% per year ÷ 4 quarters/year) is applied over 20 separate periods (5 years * 4 quarters per year). The value that Ryan is calculating with the PMT function is the payment per quarter.

Determining the Value of the Loan Payment

To calculate the payment per quarter, Ryan can substitute the appropriate values for each of the arguments of the PMT function in an Excel worksheet. This formula is detailed in Figure 6.3. Note that commas cannot be used when typing in the value for one million. A comma is interpreted as the beginning of a new argument: =PMT(.08/4,5*4,1,000,000) is interpreted as having a pv of 1. Also note that because the fv and type arguments are both 0 and occur at the end of the function argument list, they can be omitted: =PMT(.08/4,5*4,1000000). The resulting calculated value is –$61,156.72. This value is negative because it represents the payment that will be made to the bank (cash flow out of TheZone) each quarter.

Figure 6.3: Applying the PMT function

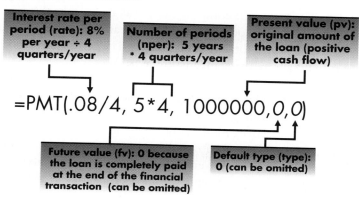

6

Level 1

Each payment goes partly to pay off the interest accrued each quarter and partly to reduce the principal (Beginning Principal + Interest − Payment). At the beginning of the transaction, when the interest expenses are high, most of the payment is used to pay off the interest. As the principal amount is slowly lowered, more and more of the payment amount is applied to reducing the principal debt.

Using a Financial Function with Cell Referencing

The calculations done so far can be easily performed using most calculators equipped with business functions. However, the power of using a spreadsheet lies in explicitly listing inputs so that values can be easily updated to perform what-if analyses, goal seeks, and so on. Ryan creates a new workbook named Financing.xls to list these inputs and outputs on a worksheet named Options. The format he uses provides an easy way to compare these values as each of the different financing options are analyzed, as shown in Figure 6.4.

Figure 6.4: Options worksheet with financial function data inputs and outputs

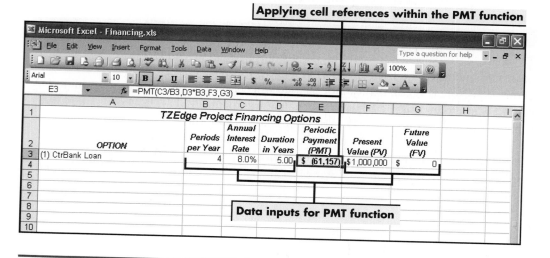

The columns list each of the relevant variables. Row 3 contains the inputs for the first financing option (CtrBank). In cell E3, note that Ryan entered the formula =PMT(C3/B3,D3*B3,F3,G3) substituting the cell references for the rate, nper, pv, and fv arguments of the PMT function. Ryan omitted the type argument because he is assuming that the default payment type is being applied for all options. Recall that the default payment type (type 0) specifies that payments are made at the end of the period. Also note that the result of the PMT function (cell E3) is displayed in parentheses to indicate it is a negative number.

USING THE RATE, NPER, PV, AND FV FUNCTIONS

In the same way Ryan just solved the problem to determine the value of the periodic payment on the loan, he could have solved for any one of the other variables. In fact, each argument of the PMT function (rate, nper, pv, and fv) is also an Excel function in itself. Each of these functions, in turn, is dependent on the other four, as described in Table 6.1.

Table 6.1: Basic financial functions

Function Syntax	Description
RATE(nper,pmt,pv,fv,type)	Solves for the interest rate per period
NPER(rate,pmt,pv,fv,type)	Solves for the number of periods
PMT(rate,nper,pv,fv,type)	Solves for the value of the payment per period
PV(rate,nper,pmt,fv,type)	Solves for the initial value, the amount in or out at the beginning of the financial transaction
FV(rate,nper,pmt,pv,type)	Solves for the final value, the amount in or out at the end of the financial transaction

How To

Write a Basic Financial Function

1. Determine which element of the financial transaction you need to calculate.

2. Type an equal sign followed by the function name: RATE, NPER, PMT, PV, or FV.

3. Fill in each of the remaining variables, excluding the one you are solving for:

- Specify the rate per period **(rate)**. If necessary, divide the annual rate by the number of compounding periods per year to arrive at the rate per period.
- Specify the number of periods **(nper)**. If necessary, multiply the number of years by the number of periods per year.
- Specify the payment per period **(pmt)**. Payments that are inflows should be positive, and payments that are outflows should be negative.
- Specify the present value of the transaction **(pv)**. This value is the amount in or out at the beginning of the transaction.

- Specify the future value of the transaction **(fv)**. This value is the amount in or out at the end of the transaction. A loan that is completely paid off would have an fv of 0; a bank account would have an fv equal to the pv plus any accrued interest, plus or minus any payments into or out of the account.
- Specify the transaction type, if necessary. The default type (0) indicates payments are made at the end of each period (this can be omitted). Use type 1 if payments are made at the beginning of each period.

Determining the Future Value of a Financial Transaction

The second financing option being considered is to fund the TZEdge project using some current liquid assets of the company, in this case, a money market account that was set up by TheZone to handle any liquidity cash flow problems that might arise. Fortunately, the funds were never needed, so now this is a possible source being considered to fund the project. The original investment placed in the money market account two years ago was $900,000. The terms of the account include a fixed annual interest rate of 3.5% compounded monthly. What is not known is the current value of this account and whether this value will be sufficient to cover the capital investment required for the project. Note that the current value in this case is actually the *future value*, because the transaction was initiated two years ago.

Because Ryan requires the value at the end of this financial transaction, he needs to use the FV function. The syntax of the FV function is: FV(rate,nper,pmt,pv,type). Ryan substitutes the appropriate arguments into the FV function, as follows:

- The rate is 3.5% per year. Because the investment is compounded each month, and there are 12 months per year, the rate per period is 3.5% divided by 12 (.035/12). It is not necessary to separately perform this calculation; it can be nested inside the function argument. Note that with this option, the interest rate is how much interest TheZone will earn on its investment; in the first option, the loan from CtrBank, the interest rate shown is the rate TheZone would have to pay on the loan.
- The nper is the duration the principal has been accruing interest, which is two years. So, the number of periods equals 2 years * 12 months per year, or 24 periods.
- No periodic payments into or out of the account have been mentioned, so the pmt argument can be assumed to be $0. Can this argument be left out of the FV function? Because this 0 does not appear at the end of the function argument list, it cannot be left out; otherwise, Excel would interpret the next value after the nper argument as the payment, even if it should be the pv argument. So, this FV function must include a 0 for the pmt argument followed by a comma or at least a comma (,) to hold the place of the pmt argument.
- The initial value of the investment (pv) is $900,000. Because this money was taken out of TheZone and placed into the money market account, it is considered a negative cash flow, so the $900,000 will be negative.
- The type argument is assumed to be the default 0. Because this is the last argument and the value is 0, it can be omitted.

The resulting formula is =FV(.035/12,2*12,0,–900000). Ryan enters the inputs for the second financing option in the Options worksheet, as shown in Figure 6.5. The formula Ryan enters in cell G4, using the appropriate cell references, is as follows:

$$=FV(C4/B4,D4*B4,E4,F4)$$

Figure 6.5: Calculating the future value of the money market account

	A	B	C	D	E	F	G	H
G4		fx =FV(C4/B4,D4*B4,E4,F4)						
1		TZEdge Project Financing Options						
2	OPTION	Periods per Year	Annual Interest Rate	Duration in Years	Periodic Payment (PMT)	Present Value (PV)	Future Value (FV)	
3	(1) CtrBank Loan	4	8.0%	5.00	$ (61,157)	$1,000,000	$ 0	
4	(2) Emergency Fund	12	3.5%	2.00	$ 0	$ (900,000)	$ 965,159	
5								
6								

Using FV to calculate the ending value of a financial transaction

At the end of the two years, the final value of the fund is $965,159. Is this amount sufficient to fund the project, which requires $1 million? By simply looking at the value in the worksheet, it is apparent that the amount is not sufficient. On a more complex worksheet, you could also create a relational expression, such as G4>=1000000. In fact, the entire financial function could be used as part of a relational expression similar to the following:

$$=FV(C4/B4,D4*B4,E4,F4)>=1000000$$

Based on the results of the FV function, there are insufficient funds in the money market account to completely fund the TZEdge project. Either another funding method will be required entirely, or this method could perhaps be used in conjunction with some other transaction.

Best Practice

Working with Positive and Negative Cash Flows
When writing formulas with financial functions, you need to be certain that the functions have the appropriate positive and negative cash flows. The present value (pv), payment (pmt), and future value (fv) are all cash flows of a financial transaction.

- If you are calculating payments to a bank (a negative cash flow), your formula requires at least one positive cash flow—either a positive present value (pv) or a positive future value (fv), or both.
- If you are calculating a positive future value (money being withdrawn from a bank, which is a positive cash flow), your formula requires at least one negative cash flow—either a negative present value (pv) or a negative payment (pmt), or both.

- If you are calculating an interest rate (using the RATE function) or a loan duration (using the NPER function), the transaction, such as a loan, requires both cash into and out of the transaction—combinations of positive and negative pv, pmt, and fv values. A typical loan has a positive cash flow at the beginning of the transaction and a negative cash flow for periodic payments.

Before constructing a formula with a financial function, it's a good idea to determine the timeline of the financial transaction, similar to the timeline shown in Figure 6.1. Doing so helps you to figure out which cash flows are positive and which are negative, and helps to ensure that the formula you create works properly.

Determining the Present Value of a Financial Transaction

The third financing option under consideration is to fund the TZEdge project from an initial investment and current profits. This option requires the project to be delayed by 1½ years, investing a portion of TheZone's expected profits ($50,000 per month each month), plus an initial cash outlay to be determined. A money market account will be used to hold these funds. The current money market rates pay 4% annual interest compounded monthly.

What is still unknown for this option is the amount of money that must be invested now, so that at the end of a year and a half, at least $1 million will be available. The elements that are already known are the interest rate, loan duration, periodic payments, and ending value. So, Ryan needs to calculate the initial outlay, or the present value, which is the amount at the *beginning* of the transaction. The syntax of the PV function is as follows:

$$PV(rate,nper,pmt,fv,type)$$

Ryan substitutes the appropriate arguments into the PV function, as follows:

- The rate per year is 4%. Because the account is compounded monthly, the corresponding rate per month is .04/12. As with the second option, this interest rate is the amount of interest TheZone would earn on this investment.
- The nper is the duration of the time delay, which is 1.5 years. Because the units of time must be consistent in the function, the nper must be expressed as months: 1.5*12 (months), or 18 periods.
- The payment (pmt) each month is –$50,000. This is a negative cash flow from TheZone into the account.
- The future value (fv) is the ending value desired of $1,000,000. Because these funds will be taken out of the account and given to TheZone, this is a positive cash flow for the company, so the fv will be positive.
- The type argument is assumed to be the default 0. Because this is the last argument and the value is 0, it can be omitted.

Substituting these values into the function results in the following formula:

$$=PV(.04/12,1.5*12,-50000,1000000)$$

Using the appropriate cell references, Ryan enters the following formula in cell F5: =PV(C5/B5,D5*B5,E5,G5). Figure 6.6 shows the results in the worksheet.

Figure 6.6: Calculating the present value of an investment

	F5	▾	*fx* =PV(C5/B5,D5*B5,E5,G5)						H
	A		B	C	D	E	F	G	
1		TZEdge Project Financing Options							
2	OPTION		Periods per Year	Annual Interest Rate	Duration in Years	Periodic Payment (PMT)	Present Value (PV)	Future Value (FV)	
3	(1) CtrBank Loan		4	8.0%	5.00	$ (61,157)	$1,000,000	$ 0	
4	(2) Emergency Fund		12	3.5%	2.00	$ 0	$ (900,000)	$ 965,159	
5	(3) Delay Project & Use Profits		12	4.0%	1.50	$ (50,000)	$ (69,736)	$1,000,000	
6									
7									

Using PV to calculate the beginning value of a financial transaction

The resulting payment value is –69,736.10; this is the amount that TheZone would need to invest in a money market account now in order to have $1 million at the end of one-and-a-half years (assuming periodic payments of $50,000 as well). The major issues that management must evaluate in this case are whether the company has this amount of money to set aside now and the long-term effects of delaying the project, both in terms of lost revenues and changes in the marketplace.

Determining the Interest Rate of a Financial Transaction

In an effort to secure TheZone's business, NWN Bank is offering two options for funding the TZEdge project, the first of which is the following:

A loan for the entire $1,000,000 to be paid back over the next four years, with equal semiannual payments of $150,000 (compounded semiannually).

Although the value of the loan and the payments are known, it would be helpful to know the interest rate being charged. Knowing the rate will give Ryan a good comparison point when he tries to determine which funding option is most favorable. To calculate the rate, Ryan can use the RATE function. The RATE function syntax is as follows:

$$RATE(nper,pmt,pv,fv,type)$$

Ryan substitutes the appropriate arguments into the RATE function, as follows:

- The nper is the duration of the loan, 4 years. Because the loan is compounded semi-annually (twice a year), the number of periods is 8 (4*2).
- The payment (pmt) per period is –$150,000. This is a negative cash flow for TheZone.

- The present value (pv) is $1,000,000 (the amount of the initial transaction). This is a positive cash flow for TheZone.
- The future value (fv) is assumed to be $0, because no mention is made of any residual amounts owed at the end of the loan.
- The type argument is assumed to be the default 0. Because this is the last argument and the value is 0, it can be omitted.

The resulting formula is =RATE(4*2,–150000,1000000). But, is this the information Ryan is seeking? This formula determines the *rate per period*—in this case, a semiannual rate. The comparative value Ryan wants to calculate is the *annual rate*. So, the formula must be multiplied by the number of periods per year (2), as follows:

=RATE(4*2,-150000,1000000)*2

Ryan enters this formula in cell C6 using the appropriate cell references. The resulting formula is =RATE(D6*B6,E6,F6,G6)*B6, as shown in Figure 6.7. The interest rate calculated is 8.5%, which is higher than the 8.0% interest rate on the loan offered by CtrBank.

Figure 6.7: Calculating the annual interest rate of a loan

Using RATE to calculate the annual interest rate of a financial transaction

Determining the Number of Periods of a Financial Transaction

The final financing option being considered by TheZone is NWN Bank's "option b," which is the following:

A loan for the entire $1,000,000 with a fixed interest rate of 6.5% per year compounded quarterly, and fixed quarterly payments of $95,000.

Although the interest rate on this loan seems favorable, the payments are quite high as compared with some of the other options. Exactly how many years will it take to pay off this loan is not specifically stated. To calculate the duration of the loan, Ryan needs to use the NPER function. The syntax of the NPER function is as follows:

NPER(rate,pmt,pv,fv,type)

Ryan substitutes the appropriate arguments into the NPER function, as follows:

- The rate per year is 6.5% compounded quarterly. So, the rate per period is 6.5%/4.
- The payment (pmt) is –$95,000 per quarter. This is a negative cash flow for TheZone.
- The present value (pv) is $1,000,000, because the bank has offered to fund all of the capital required for the project. This value is a positive cash flow for TheZone.
- The future value (fv) is assumed to be $0, because no mention is made of any residual amounts owed at the end of the loan.
- The type argument is assumed to be the default 0. Because this is the last argument and the value is 0, it can be omitted.

Remember that Ryan needs to calculate NPER in terms of the number of compounding periods, in this case the number of quarters. To calculate the loan duration in years, he must divide the number of periods (NPER) by the number of quarters per year, which produces the following formula:

$$=NPER(6.5\%/4,-95000,1000000)/4$$

Ryan enters the following formula in cell D7, as shown in Figure 6.8:

$$=NPER(C7/B7,E7,F7,G7)/B7$$

Figure 6.8: Calculating the number of periods for a loan

D7		f_x =NPER(C7/B7,E7,F7,G7)/B7						
	A	B	C	D	E	F	G	H
1		TZEdge Project Financing Options						
2	OPTION	Periods per Year	Annual Interest Rate	Duration in Years	Periodic Payment (PMT)	Present Value (PV)	Future Value (FV)	
3	(1) CtrBank Loan	4	8.0%	5.00	$ (61,157)	$1,000,000	$ 0	
4	(2) Emergency Fund	12	3.5%	2.00	$ 0	$ (900,000)	$ 965,159	
5	(3) Delay Project & Use Profits	12	4.0%	1.50	$ (50,000)	$ (69,736)	$1,000,000	
6	(4a) NWN Bank w/$150,000 Payments	2	8.5%	4.00	$(150,000)	$1,000,000	$ 0	
7	(4b) NWN Bank Loan at 6.5% Rate	4	6.5%	2.91	$ (95,000)	$1,000,000	$ 0	
8								
9								

Using NPER to calculate the number of periods of a financial transaction

As shown by the results of the NPER function, the number of years it will take to pay off this loan is 2.91 years. This is a considerably shorter time than the duration for the other two loan options being considered, but requires a much higher annual cash outlay.

Best Practice

Accounting for Loan Options

In addition to the loan elements previously discussed—principal, interest rate, payment periods, and so on—some loans include additional options that must be taken into account. The following are some tips for writing formulas to account for these other loan options:

- To account for a financial transaction that includes a **down payment**, which is money required from the borrower toward the purchase of an asset, you must adjust the present value (pv) to reflect the exact value of the loan. For example, a house that costs $200,000 and requires a 10% down payment would have an original loan value (pv) of $180,000 ($200,000−.1*200,000).

- To account for a **balloon payment**, which is additional money owed at the end of a loan, you must specify a negative future value (fv). For example, a 3-year car loan totaling $15,000 at 3% annual interest can be paid off in equal monthly installments of $436.22. This can be calculated using the formula =PMT(0.03/12,12*3,15000). Instead of completely paying off the loan, if a balloon payment of $2000 is built into the loan terms, the monthly payment would be reduced to $383.06 using the formula =PMT(0.03/12,12*3,15000,−2000).

- To account for mortgage **fees** such as points, loan origination fees, or any other fee that the borrower must pay up front, do the following:

  - Adjust the present value (pv) of the loan by subtracting these fees from the loan amount. Unlike a down payment, these fees do not change the actual face value (amount to be paid back) of the loan.
  - To determine the actual percentage rate being paid, recalculate the interest rate using the same payments and loan periods, but with the new pv amount. Banks in the United States are required to inform borrowers of this "adjusted" percentage rate; however, which fees are charged can vary from bank to bank.

For example, a bank lending a borrower $200,000 for 15 years with monthly payments of $1580.59 has a nominal interest rate of 5%. However, if this loan required a 2-point fee, 2% of the loan paid in advance, the actual amount being borrowed would only be $196,000. To calculate the actual interest rate being charged, use the formula =RATE(15*12,-1580.59,196000). The resulting interest rate is 5.31%.

SELECTING A FINANCING OPTION

With the Options worksheet complete, Ryan must now select the most favorable financing option to recommend to management. Which option should he recommend? The answer is, "that depends." Options 2 and 3 use existing funds, which will certainly avoid any additional debt to be incurred by the company. Usually, a lower amount of debt is a desirable attribute on a company's balance sheet, yet this must be weighed against the tax advantages of writing off the interest on a loan. Going with option 2 also means using emergency liquid assets, and depending on fluctuations in the market, this might have certain risk consequences. Option 3 requires delaying the project while funds are secured from current profits. Again, this has consequences beyond the scope of this analysis, because delays will also affect potential profits.

If a loan is selected as the vehicle to raise capital, a lower interest rate is generally preferable to a higher rate, all else being equal. However, not only do the rates vary for the three loans, but the durations and payments vary as well. To better compare these options, Ryan modifies the worksheet to include, in column H, the total annual payment for the three loan options—the periodic payment (values in column E) times the number of periods per year (values in column B). Figure 6.9 shows the modified worksheet.

Figure 6.9: Comparing annual payments for each of the loan options

H3		*fx* =E3*B3							
	A	B	C	D	E	F	G	H	I
1			TZEdge Project Financing Options						
2	OPTION	Periods per Year	Annual Interest Rate	Duration in Years	Periodic Payment (PMT)	Present Value (PV)	Future Value (FV)	Annual Loan Payments	
3	(1) CtrBank Loan	4	8.0%	5.00	$ (61,157)	$ 1,000,000	$ 0	$ (244,627)	
4	(2) Emergency Fund	12	3.5%	2.00	$ 0	$ (900,000)	$ 965,159		
5	(3) Delay Project & Use Profits	12	4.0%	1.50	$ (50,000)	$ (69,736)	$ 1,000,000		
6	(4a) NWN Bank w/$150,000 Payments	2	8.5%	4.00	$ (150,000)	$ 1,000,000	$ 0	$ (300,000)	
7	(4b) NWN Bank Loan at 6.5% Rate	4	6.5%	2.91	$ (95,000)	$ 1,000,000	$ 0	$ (380,000)	
8									
9									

Total value of the annual loan payment (payment per period * number of periods) for the three loan options

The lowest interest rate is for NWN Bank's option 4b at 6.5%, but this option requires annual loan payments of $380,000. CtrBank's loan with an 8% interest rate requires annual payments of only $244,627, and NWN Bank's first option at 8.5% interest requires annual payments of $300,000. If the cash flow generated in the early years of the project is minimal, it might be difficult to meet the annual loan payments—especially for NWN Bank's 6.5% loan. So, depending on the circumstances, option 1 with a higher interest rate but a longer duration and lower annual payments might be a better choice.

So, which option should Ryan recommend? Before he can select one of the financing options, Ryan needs to evaluate a few more factors. For example, he needs to understand the projected cash flows from this venture and the possible tax implications. He will explore these factors in the next section.

Steps To Success: Level 1

To promote the new TZEdge line of athletic shoes, the marketing group has decided to purchase advertising in selected print media, including leading health and fitness magazines, and brochures to upscale sport outlets. Although the cost of this advertising has been worked into the selling expense, this money will actually be needed now, in year 0, rather than in years 1 and 2, so that the advertising agencies can begin designing a promotion and arranging for publication. The finance group at TheZone will discuss financing options directly with the advertising agencies, who are willing to accept a variety of different payment terms. Your task in these steps is to set up a worksheet to analyze each of the advertising agency options.

Complete the following:

1. Open a new workbook and save it as **Advertising.xls** in the Chapter 6 folder.

2. Create a worksheet with the following column headings:

   - Option Number
   - Number Of Compounding Periods Per Year
   - Annual Interest Rate
   - Loan Duration In Years
   - Payment Per Period
   - Present Value
   - Future Value

3. Include the title "TZEdge Advertising Options" on your worksheet, merged and centered over the data.

4. Fill in the appropriate data inputs and calculations for each option (across the row) so that all information is listed. For all options, assume that the payment period duration will be used as the compounding period and that payments are made at the end of each period.

   - **Option 1**—ADshow Inc. has proposed a campaign costing $35,000. This agency will accept full payment over the next two years in equal monthly installments of $1,600. For this option, you need to calculate the annual interest rate.
   - **Option 2**—Bradshaw & Hicks has designed a campaign for $45,000 and indicated that they will charge a 7% annual rate of interest on this amount, with fixed quarterly payments paid out over the next 18 months. For this option, you need to calculate periodic payments.

- **Option 3**—Johnson, Bellview & Associates has shown the marketing team an excellent campaign that will cost $1200 a month for the next two years. This agency's payment terms are based on an annual interest rate of 5%. For this option, you need to calculate the initial value of this advertising campaign.
- **Option 4**—AdWest Inc. has proposed the most modestly priced campaign, costing $25,000. This agency is willing to accept monthly payments of $1400 until the campaign is completely paid off. AdWest Inc. will charge a 6.5% annual interest rate. For this option, you need to calculate the duration in years that will be required to pay off this debt.

5. In an adjacent column, calculate the total yearly payments required for each option.

6. Format your worksheet so that it is easy to read. Be certain that dollars and percentages are included where appropriate, and that columns display consistent numbers of decimal places. Wrap text, as necessary, to format the column headings within reasonable column widths. Highlight cells with the data outputs.

7. Save and close the Advertising.xls workbook.

LEVEL 2
CREATING A PROJECTED CASH FLOW ESTIMATE AND AMORTIZATION TABLE

EXCEL 2003 SKILLS TRAINING

- **Name a range**
- **Use a named range reference in one or more formulas**

DESIGNING THE CASH FLOW ESTIMATE WORKSHEET

The finance group is specifically interested in how the TZEdge project will affect the **cash flow** of the company—the amount of money coming in or out of the company each year. This information is important so that TheZone can ensure it has the funds needed for day-to-day operations. To estimate the cash flow generated from the TZEdge project, the finance group needs to combine the revenues and expenses associated with the shoe manufacturing with the effects of the required capital investment and financing. If the project is financed using a loan, this estimate must reflect the periodic payments that will be made to service the loan. In addition, corporate taxes allow companies to both allocate portions of the capital investment as an expense and to deduct interest associated with a loan, thereby reducing the amount of taxes owed. These are also factors that need to be taken into consideration.

The next task for Ryan is to develop a projected five-year cash flow estimate and a detailed schedule of payments for the selected financing option. Ryan has been directed to assume that TheZone will fund the project using the loan from CtrBank (option 1), requiring quarterly payments of $61,157 over a five-year period. Ryan will also use the revenues and expenses developed previously by the marketing group when evaluating the TZEdge shoe project, and the group's five-year sales projections for the shoe.

Ryan begins by creating a new workbook named "TZEdge Cash Flow Estimate." In this workbook, he establishes a worksheet named "Cashflow" that lists each of the different cash flow elements down the first column and each year across the row. He enters the data provided by the marketing group for the first five years of operation, as shown in cells B4:G12 of Figure 6.10.

Figure 6.10: Worksheet for projected 5-year cash flow estimate

	A	B	C	D	E	F	G	H
1			TZEdge Projected 5-Year Cash Flow Estimate					
2								
3		Year:	1	2	3	4	5	
4	Sales Volume		4450	25000	50000	65000	70000	
5	Selling Price Per Pair of Shoes		$ 225	$ 225	$ 225	$ 225	$ 225	
6								
7	Revenue		$ 1,001,250	$ 5,625,000	$11,250,000	$ 14,625,000	$ 15,750,000	
8		$/shoe						
9	Cost of Goods Sold	$(177.90)	$ (791,655)	$(4,447,500)	$ (8,895,000)	$(11,563,500)	$(12,453,000)	
10	Selling Expense	$ (10.00)	$ (44,500)	$ (250,000)	$ (500,000)	$ (650,000)	$ (700,000)	
11								
12	Operating Income		$ 165,095	$ 927,500	$ 1,855,000	$ 2,411,500	$ 2,597,000	
13								
14								
15								
16								
17								
18								
19								
20								
21								
22								
23								
24	Cash Flow							
25								
26								

Calculations for revenue, cost of goods sold, and selling expense based on projected yearly sales volumes

Ryan has decided to express all revenues as positive values and all costs as negative values. So far, the Cashflow worksheet includes the following information:

- Project annual sales volume (pairs sold)
- Selling price per pair of shoes
- A calculation for sales revenue—sales volume multiplied by selling price using the formula =C4*C5 in cell C7

- A calculation for cost of goods sold based on a cost of $177.90 per pair, using the formula =C$4*$B9 in cell C9, assuming a constant cost per pair for all five years
- A calculation for the selling expense per pair based on a cost to manufacture of $10 per pair—the number of pairs sold multiplied by the selling expense per pair—using the formula =C$4*$B10 in cell C10
- A calculation for operating income—summing all positive and negative cash flows using the formula =SUM(C7,C9:C10) in cell C12

Identifying the Missing Data Elements

Ryan now needs to account for the missing data elements of his projected cash flow estimate—those items associated with the loan payments and taxes. Doing so can be somewhat tricky because taxes are calculated based on "taxable income," which excludes certain elements that are cash flows and includes other non-cash flow items.

When calculating taxes in the United States, a company can expense (subtract from income) only the *interest portion* of a loan payment, and not the portion that goes toward paying off the principal. The principal payment of a loan is not directly tax deductible. So, Ryan needs to determine the interest portion of the loan payments for the corresponding year to estimate taxable income and taxes for that year. After taxes have been calculated, the principal portion of each payment then needs to be subtracted from the cash flow.

What about the $1 million that TheZone will spend on capital equipment; is that considered a taxable expense? Corporations cannot deduct the cost of capital equipment in the same way they can the cost of materials (such as shoe leather) or labor. Corporations must allocate a portion of this expense over the useful life of the equipment using a method known as depreciation. **Depreciation** is the process by which a company spreads the expense of an asset over its useful life. In other words, each year only a portion of the money spent initially on capital equipment can be used to reduce income. Depreciation needs to be subtracted from the cash flow in each year to calculate taxes for that year, but then must be added back in because it is not actually a cash flow in that year. There are several methods a company can consider for calculating depreciation, as defined in the tax codes. Ryan will estimate depreciation using a straight line method over a period of five years (this method is discussed in detail later in this section). Although this method will not produce the amount of depreciation allowed by the Internal Revenue Service (IRS), it will serve Ryan's purposes for the cash flow estimate.

After the interest expense and depreciation have been deducted, taxes can be calculated. The taxes owed will then be subtracted from the cash flow. To complete the cash flow calculation, Ryan must add back in the depreciation (which is not a cash flow) and subtract the value of the principal payments on the loan. The process Ryan will use is illustrated in Figure 6.11.

Figure 6.11: Process for calculating cash flow

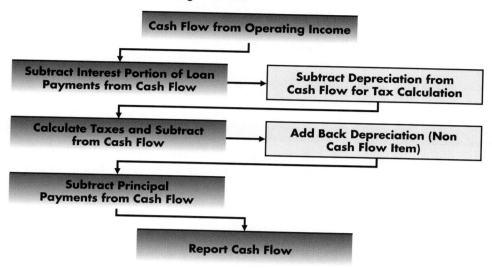

To implement this process, Ryan has expanded his worksheet to include the appropriate labels, as shown in Figure 6.12.

Figure 6.12: Additional cash flow elements included in the worksheet

	A	B	C	D	E	F	G	H
1			TZEdge Projected 5-Year Cash Flow Estimate					
2								
3	Year:		1	2	3	4	5	
4	Sales Volume		4450	25000	50000	65000	70000	
5	Selling Price Per Pair of Shoes		$ 225	$ 225	$ 225	$ 225	$ 225	
6								
7	Revenue		$ 1,001,250	$ 5,625,000	$11,250,000	$ 14,625,000	$ 15,750,000	
8		$/shoe						
9	Cost of Goods Sold	$(177.90)	$ (791,655)	$(4,447,500)	$ (8,895,000)	$(11,563,500)	$(12,453,000)	
10	Selling Expense	$ (10.00)	$ (44,500)	$ (250,000)	$ (500,000)	$ (650,000)	$ (700,000)	
11								
12	Operating Income		$ 165,095	$ 927,500	$ 1,855,000	$ 2,411,500	$ 2,597,000	
13								
14	Interest Expense							
15	Depreciation							
16	Taxable Income							
17								
18	Taxes							
19	Income After Taxes							
20								
21	Add Back Depreciation							
22	Subtract Principal Payments							
23								
24	Cash Flow							
25								
26								

Additional elements required to estimate cash flow

SETTING UP AN AMORTIZATION TABLE

Now Ryan needs to enter the necessary calculations in the worksheet. The first value that he requires is the interest portion of the loan for each year. This amount will change from year to year as the principal value of the loan is paid off. A standard method of detailing a loan transaction is to set up what is known as an **amortization table** (or schedule). This table lists, for each specific loan period, the remaining principal and the value of the payments being apportioned to interest expense and to principal pay down. Ryan will set up this amortization table according to the terms of CtrBank's option 1 loan, as follows:

> *Funding the entire project using a line of credit at CtrBank. CtrBank currently charges a fixed rate of 8% annual interest compounded quarterly. For this type of project, payments are scheduled out quarterly over a five-year period.*

To accomplish this, Ryan sets up a separate worksheet named Loan in the TZEdge Cash Flow Estimate workbook. He first lists the data inputs (loan value, interest rate, compounding periods, and so on), and then details for each period the corresponding interest and principal payment values, as shown in Figure 6.13.

Figure 6.13: Setting up a loan amortization table

	B8	▾	*fx* =PMT(B3/B5,B5*B4,B2)				Calculation for loan payment based on the given data inputs
	A	B	C	D	E		
1	Amortization Table for Loan Option (1)						
2	Original Loan	$1,000,000					Data inputs for loan
3	Annual Interest Rate	8%					
4	Loan Duration in Years	5					
5	Number of Periods per Year	4					
6	Ending Value of Loan	0					
7							
8	Quarterly Payment	($61,156.72)					
9			Remaining				
10		Period	Principal	Interest Payment	Principal Payment		
11		1					
12		2					
13		3					Data output area for periods listing remaining principal, interest payments, and principal payments
14		4					
15		5					
16		6					
17		7					
18		8					
19		9					
20		10					
21		11					
22		12					
23		13					
24		14					
25		15					
26		16					
27		17					
28		18					
29		19					
30		20					
31	Ending Balance						
32							

Previously, Ryan used the formula =PMT(.08/4,5*4,1000000,0) to calculate the payments. Here, he has substituted the appropriate cell references for these values as follows: =PMT(B3/B5,B5*B4,B2). He enters this formula in cell B8; the resulting payment value is –$61,156.72. (Note that this value is formatted to display two decimal places on this worksheet.) But how much of the $61,156.72 goes toward paying off the accrued interest for the period, and how much toward paying down the principal? Ryan could go through the calculation for each quarter, calculating the interest per quarter by multiplying the remaining principal by the interest rate and then subtracting this interest from the payment to obtain the principal payment, and finally subtracting the principal payment from the remaining principal. Although this is possible, it would be very time-consuming and tedious. Excel provides a more efficient method to accomplish this task.

Calculating Principal and Interest Payments

One method of calculating principal and interest payments is to use the PPMT and IPMT functions. The **PPMT function** calculates the value of the principal payment for a specified period, and the **IPMT function** calculates the value of the interest payment for a specified period. The syntax for each of these functions is as follows:

```
PPMT(rate,per,nper,pv,fv,type)
IPMT(rate,per,nper,pv,fv,type)
```

In both of the functions, the arguments are defined as follows:

- The **rate** argument represents the interest rate per period.
- The **per** argument is the period for which the interest or principal amount will be calculated. Valid periods begin at 1 and end at the last payment period, which equals nper.
- The **nper** argument is the total number of periods in the financial transaction.
- The **pv** argument is the value at the beginning of the financial transaction.
- The **fv** argument is the value at the end of the financial transaction.
- The **type** argument is the payment type of 0 or 1, where 0 represents payments made at the end of each period, and 1 represents payments made at the beginning of each period.

So, if Ryan wants to calculate the interest expense for period 15 of this $1 million loan compounded quarterly over a five-year period at an 8% annual rate, the formula would be =IPMT(.08/4,15,5*4,1000000,0,0). The resulting value is an interest payment of –$6,851.30.

To fill in the values on his amortization table, first Ryan enters the original principal value for period 1 in cell B11 by using the formula =B2. He then applies the IPMT function in cell C11 to write a formula that calculates the interest payment for period 1. Substituting the appropriate cell references, Ryan writes the following formula:

```
=IPMT(B$3/B$5,A11,B$4*B$5,B$2,B$6,0)
```

Because Ryan needs to copy this formula down the column, absolute row references must be applied to values that do not change. The values B2, B3, B4, B5, and B6 will all remain constant regardless of the period for which interest is being calculated. The period number (per) is the only argument that will vary. The results of the formula are shown in Figure 6.14.

Figure 6.14: Calculating the interest portion of each payment for the corresponding period

	C11	▼	*fx* =IPMT(B$3/B$5,A11,B$4*B$5,B$2,B$6,0)			Calculation for the interest portion of the loan payment for period 1, based on rate, nper, pv, and fv

	A	B	C	D	E
1	Amortization Table for Loan Option (1)				
2	Original Loan	$1,000,000			
3	Annual Interest Rate	8%			
4	Loan Duration in Years	5			
5	Number of Periods per Year	4			
6	Ending Value of Loan	0			
7					
8	Quarterly Payment	($61,156.72)			
9					
10		Period	Remaining Principal	Interest Payment	Principal Payment	
11		1	$1,000,000	($20,000.00)		
12		2		(19,176.87)		
13		3		(18,337.27)		
14		4		(17,480.88)		
15		5		(16,607.36)		
16		6		(15,716.38)		
17		7		(14,807.57)		
18		8		(13,880.59)		
19		9		(12,935.06)		
20		10		(11,970.63)		
21		11		(10,986.91)		
22		12		(9,983.51)		
23		13		(8,960.05)		
24		14		(7,916.11)		
25		15		(6,851.30)		
26		16		(5,765.19)		
27		17		(4,657.36)		
28		18		(3,527.38)		
29		19		(2,374.79)		
30		20		(1,199.15)		
31	Ending Balance				
32					

Period 1's remaining principal is equal to the original amount of the loan

The following is a description of the function arguments used in this formula:

- The rate is 8% per year divided by 4 quarters per year (B$3/B$5).
- The per argument is the period number the interest payment is being calculated for, in this case period 1 (A11). Note that this value changes relatively as each subsequent interest amount is calculated for periods 2 through 20.
- The nper argument is the total number of pay periods, in this case 5 years times 4 quarters per year (B$4*B$5).
- The pv is the present value of the loan, $1,000,000 (B$2).
- The fv is the future value of the loan, which is assumed to be 0 (B$6).
- The type argument is the default 0 because no information is given regarding payments.

The resulting value for the interest portion of this payment in period 1 is –$20,000, which is equal to $1,000,000*.08/4.

In a similar manner, Ryan calculates the value of each of the principal payments by quarter by placing the following formula in cell D11:

$$=\mathtt{PPMT(B\$3/B\$5,A11,B\$4*B\$5,B\$2,B\$6,0)}$$

Ryan copies this formula down the column into cells D12:D30. To complete the amortization table, Ryan wants to have a running total of the remaining principal value of the loan in column B. Because the payment is expressed as a negative number, this can be accomplished by taking the previous period's principal value and adding it to the previous period's principal payment. Ryan writes the formula =B11+D11 in cell B12 and copies this formula down the column. The completed amortization table is shown in Figure 6.15.

Figure 6.15: Completed amortization table

	A	B	C	D	E
1	Amortization Table for Loan Option (1)				
2	Original Loan	$1,000,000			
3	Annual Interest Rate	8%			
4	Loan Duration in Years	5			
5	Number of Periods per Year	4			
6	Ending Value of Loan	0			
7					
8	Quarterly Payment	($61,156.72)			
9					
10		Period	Remaining Principal	Interest Payment	Principal Payment
11		1	$1,000,000	($20,000.00)	($41,156.72)
12		2	958,843.28	(19,176.87)	(41,979.85)
13		3	916,863.43	(18,337.27)	(42,819.45)
14		4	874,043.98	(17,480.88)	(43,675.84)
15		5	830,368.14	(16,607.36)	(44,549.36)
16		6	785,818.79	(15,716.38)	(45,440.34)
17		7	740,378.44	(14,807.57)	(46,349.15)
18		8	694,029.29	(13,880.59)	(47,276.13)
19		9	646,753.16	(12,935.06)	(48,221.65)
20		10	598,531.51	(11,970.63)	(49,186.09)
21		11	549,345.42	(10,986.91)	(50,169.81)
22		12	499,175.61	(9,983.51)	(51,173.21)
23		13	448,002.40	(8,960.05)	(52,196.67)
24		14	395,805.73	(7,916.11)	(53,240.60)
25		15	342,565.13	(6,851.30)	(54,305.42)
26		16	288,259.71	(5,765.19)	(55,391.52)
27		17	232,868.19	(4,657.36)	(56,499.35)
28		18	176,368.84	(3,527.38)	(57,629.34)
29		19	118,739.50	(2,374.79)	(58,781.93)
30		20	59,957.57	(1,199.15)	(59,957.57)
31	Ending Balance	$ 0.00			
32					

Calculation for the principal portion of the loan payment for period 1, based on rate, nper, pv, and fv

Remaining principal calculated for each period

Calculating Principal and Interest Payments Between Two Periods

The amortization table includes the interest and principal payments by period, in this case quarters. However, the projected cash flow estimate that is being prepared requires *yearly* payments. Because each year consists of four periods, Ryan needs to summarize these values in groups of four. If Ryan assumes that the fiscal year coincides with the beginning of the loan, then year 1 consists of periods 1 through 4. He can use several different methods to aggregate the interest and principal values in yearly increments.

One method is to use the **CUMIPMT** and **CUMPRINC** functions. These functions automatically calculate the interest values between two periods and the principal values between two periods, respectively. The functions are defined as follows:

- CUMIPMT(rate,nper,pv,start_period,end_period,type) returns the cumulative interest paid on a loan between start_period and end_period.
- CUMPRINC(rate,nper,pv,start_period,end_period,type) returns the cumulative principal paid on a loan between start_period and end_period.

Ryan can enter these functions on his Cashflow worksheet, referencing the appropriate input data on the Loan worksheet. Again, consider the Projected 5-Year Cash Flow Estimate shown in Figure 6.16. Ryan needs to write a formula to calculate the interest portion of the payments for year 1 in cell C14, and the principal portion of the payments in cell C22.

Figure 6.16: Cashflow worksheet with areas for cumulative interest and principal payments

Cumulative interest payments for the corresponding year will be calculated in this row

	A	B	C	D	E	F	G	H
1			TZEdge Projected 5-Year Cash Flow Estimate					
2								
3	Year:		1	2	3	4	5	
4	Sales Volume		4450	25000	50000	65000	70000	
5	Selling Price Per Pair of Shoes		$ 225	$ 225	$ 225	$ 225	$ 225	
6								
7	Revenue		$ 1,001,250	$ 5,625,000	$ 11,250,000	$ 14,625,000	$ 15,750,000	
8		$/shoe						
9	Cost of Goods Sold	$(177.90)	$ (791,655)	$ (4,447,500)	$ (8,895,000)	$ (11,563,500)	$ (12,453,000)	
10	Selling Expense	$ (10.00)	$ (44,500)	$ (250,000)	$ (500,000)	$ (650,000)	$ (700,000)	
11								
12	Operating Income		$ 165,095	$ 927,500	$ 1,855,000	$ 2,411,500	$ 2,597,000	
13								
14	Interest Expense							
15	Depreciation							
16	Taxable Income							
17								
18	Taxes							
19	Income After Taxes							
20								
21	Add Back Depreciation							
22	Subtract Principal Payments							
23								
24	Cash Flow							
25								
26								

Cumulative principal payments for the corresponding year will be calculated in this row

Ryan begins to enter the cumulative interest formula by inputting the arguments for rate, nper, pv (located on the Loan worksheet), and starting and ending periods, as follows:

```
=CUMIPMT(Loan!B3/Loan!B5,Loan!B4*Loan!B5,Loan!B2,1,4,0)
```

This formula works fine in cell C14, but can it be copied across the row to calculate the cumulative interest payments for years two through five? The cell references for rate, nper, and pv can all be modified to make the column absolute so that these values remain constant. But what will happen to the start_period and end_period arguments when copied across? Here, Ryan uses constants, the values 1 and 4, which will not change when the formula is copied. Ryan either needs to write four additional formulas, instead of copying the formula in cell C14, or he needs to nest an expression inside the CUMIPMT function to automatically calculate the starting period and ending period values from the information he has in the workbook.

If Ryan directly references the year (cell Cashflow!C3) as the start_period, this would also not work when the formula is copied across, because the cell reference C3 would become D3 for the year 2 calculation. But, year 2 begins with quarter 5, not quarter 2. Instead, Ryan decides to write the algebraic expression C3*4–3 for the starting period—multiplying the number of years by 4 and then subtracting 3. For year 1, this results in 1*4–3, or 1; for year 2, this results in 2*4–3, or 5; for year 3, this results in 3*4–3, or 9. This approach will work when copied across the row to determine the starting period for each of the five years.

In a similar way, Ryan can construct an algebraic formula to calculate the ending period; this is simply C3*4 (the year number multiplied by 4 quarters). Ryan substitutes these expressions as the start_period and end_period arguments. His formula now looks like the one shown in Figure 6.17.

Figure 6.17: Formula to determine the cumulative interest payment for year 1

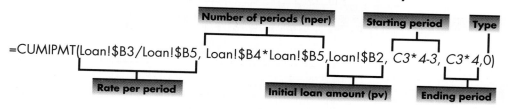

Ryan enters this formula in cell C14 and copies it across the row into cells D14 through G14.

Using the same technique, Ryan can also calculate the principal payments that must be accounted for in the Projected 5-Year Cash Flow Estimate, after taxes. He enters the following formula in cell C22 and copies it across the column:

```
=CUMPRINC(Loan!$B3/Loan!$B5,Loan!$B4*Loan!$B5,Loan!$B2,
          C3*4-3,C3*4,0)
```

Keep in mind that the principal payments represent negative cash flows—money that the company pays out. So, Ryan displays these as negative values in his analysis. The resulting worksheet is shown in Figure 6.18.

Figure 6.18: Entering the cumulative interest and principal payments

Cumulative interest payments for year 1:
=CUMIPMT(Loan!$B3/Loan!$B5,Loan!$B4*Loan!$B5,Loan!$B2,C3*4-3,C3*4,0)

	A	B	C	D	E	F	G	H
1			TZEdge Projected 5-Year Cash Flow Estimate					
2								
3		Year:	1	2	3	4	5	
4	Sales Volume		4450	25000	50000	65000	70000	
5	Selling Price Per Pair of Shoes		$ 225	$ 225	$ 225	$ 225	$ 225	
6								
7	Revenue		$ 1,001,250	$ 5,625,000	$11,250,000	$ 14,625,000	$ 15,750,000	
8		$/shoe						
9	Cost of Goods Sold	$(177.90)	$ (791,655)	$ (4,447,500)	$ (8,895,000)	$ (11,563,500)	$ (12,453,000)	
10	Selling Expense	$ (10.00)	$ (44,500)	$ (250,000)	$ (500,000)	$ (650,000)	$ (700,000)	
11								
12	Operating Income		$ 165,095	$ 927,500	$ 1,855,000	$ 2,411,500	$ 2,597,000	
13								
14	Interest Expense		$ (74,995)	$ (61,012)	$ (45,876)	$ (29,493)	$ (11,759)	
15	Depreciation							
16	Taxable Income							
17								
18	Taxes							
19	Income After Taxes							
20								
21	Add Back Depreciation							
22	Subtract Principal Payments		$ (169,632)	$ (183,615)	$ (198,751)	$ (215,134)	$ (232,868)	
23								
24	**Cash Flow**							
25								
26								

Cumulative principal payments for year 1:
=CUMPRINC(Loan!$B3/Loan!$B5,Loan!$B4*Loan!$B5,Loan!$B2,C3*4-3,C3*4,0)

CALCULATING DEPRECIATION USING THE SLN FUNCTION

The next item to be determined is the depreciation amount for each of the five years related to the $1 million TheZone will spend on equipment to manufacture the TZEdge shoe. Recall that depreciation is the process by which a company spreads the expense of an asset over its useful life. Each year, a portion of the $1,000,000 capital investment will be deducted from income for the purposes of calculating taxes. Ryan will use the straight line depreciation method, which is only an approximation of the actual depreciation allowed by the tax code. The actual depreciation is far too complex to calculate here, and will be left to the corporate accountants if the project goes forward.

Straight line depreciation basically allocates the value of an asset evenly throughout the life of the asset. So, a $12,000 piece of equipment depreciated over 10 years with a salvage value at the end of those 10 years of $2000 has an annual depreciation value of $1000. Algebraically, this can be expressed as follows:

```
(Cost of the asset - salvage value)/Life of the asset
```

Excel provides the SLN function to automatically calculate straight line depreciation. The syntax of this function is as follows:

=SLN(cost,salvage,life)

- The **cost** argument is the initial cost of the asset.
- The **salvage** argument is the value at the end of the depreciation, often referred to as the salvage value.
- The **life** argument is the number of periods over which the asset is depreciated.

The cost of the asset has already been determined as $1 million. Both the salvage value and life of the asset are unknown. The accounting group has recommended that, for planning purposes, a 10-year life is appropriate for the useful life with a salvage value of $25,000. Note that the asset life is different from the period being considered for the cash flow of the TZEdge shoe (five years). If, at the end of the five years, this product line is discontinued, the reuse or tax write-off of the equipment will be dealt with outside of this analysis. Ryan can now calculate yearly depreciation as follows:

=-SLN(1000000,25000,10)

Notice that Ryan includes a minus sign preceding the function so that the resulting value will be negative, reducing cash flow for the purposes of calculating taxable income. The resulting yearly depreciation is –$97,500.00. Best practices dictate that these input values be explicitly listed elsewhere in the workbook. Therefore, Ryan sets up a separate worksheet named Depreciation, as shown in Figure 6.19.

Figure 6.19: Depreciation worksheet

	A	B	C
1	Depreciation Values		
2			
3	Capital	$1,000,000	
4	Salvage	$ 25,000	
5	Life	10	
6			
7			

A technique Ryan can use to simplify his formula is to take this list of depreciation values and apply a range name to each, naming cell B3 "Capital," cell B4 "Salvage," and cell B5 "Life." This can be accomplished using the Create Names dialog box.

How To

Create a List of Named Ranges That Correspond to Descriptions

1. Select the cells containing both the descriptions (labels) and their corresponding values to be named. In Figure 6.19, cells A3:B5 would be selected.

2. Click Insert on the menu bar, point to Name, and then click Create. The Create Names dialog box opens. See Figure 6.20.

Figure 6.20: Naming ranges from a list

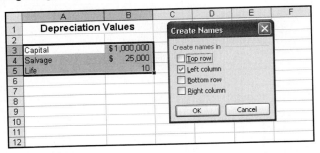

3. Click the "Create names in" check box corresponding to the relative location of the range names you want to use; in Figure 6.20, the option selected is "Left column" because the labels to be used as the range names appear to the left of their corresponding values.

4. Click the OK button.

The cells containing values can now be referenced using these assigned names. Note that symbols such as $ and # are not included in the named ranges.

Ryan creates the three named ranges for the depreciation value and uses them to write the following formula in cell C15 on the Cashflow worksheet: =–SLN(Capital,Salvage,Life). He copies the formula across the row without any further modifications, because range names copy absolutely.

Next, Ryan calculates taxable income in cell C16 as the sum of the values for operating income, interest expense, and depreciation, and copies this formula across the row. Figure 6.21 shows the resulting worksheet. Note that Ryan can sum these three values because the interest expense and depreciation values are expressed as negative values; therefore, the sum calculation actually subtracts these two values from the operating income to determine the taxable income.

Figure 6.21: Calculating straight line depreciation and taxable income

Straight line depreciation calculation includes named ranges in formula: =−SLN(Capital,Salvage,Life)

	A	B	C	D	E	F	G	H
1			TZEdge Projected 5-Year Cash Flow Estimate					
2								
3		Year:	1	2	3	4	5	
4	Sales Volume		4450	25000	50000	65000	70000	
5	Selling Price Per Pair of Shoes	$ 225	$ 225	$ 225	$ 225	$ 225		
6								
7	Revenue		$ 1,001,250	$ 5,625,000	$11,250,000	$ 14,625,000	$ 15,750,000	
8		$/shoe						
9	Cost of Goods Sold	$(177.90)	$ (791,655)	$ (4,447,500)	$ (8,895,000)	$(11,563,500)	$(12,453,000)	
10	Selling Expense	$ (10.00)	$ (44,500)	$ (250,000)	$ (500,000)	$ (650,000)	$ (700,000)	
11								
12	Operating Income		$ 165,095	$ 927,500	$ 1,855,000	$ 2,411,500	$ 2,597,000	
13								
14	Interest Expense		$ (74,995)	$ (61,012)	$ (45,876)	$ (29,493)	$ (11,759)	
15	Depreciation		$ (97,500)	$ (97,500)	$ (97,500)	$ (97,500)	$ (97,500)	
16	Taxable Income		$ (7,400)	$ 768,988	$ 1,711,624	$ 2,284,507	$ 2,487,741	
17								
18	Taxes							
19	Income After Taxes							
20								
21	Add Back Depreciation							
22	Subtract Principal Payments		$ (169,632)	$ (183,615)	$ (198,751)	$ (215,134)	$ (232,868)	
23								
24	**Cash Flow**							
25								
26								

Calculating taxable income based on operating income, interest expense, and depreciation for year 1: =C12+C14+C15

Alternative Depreciation Options Provided in Excel

In addition to straight line depreciation, Excel provides a variety of other functions that calculate depreciation. These alternative approaches also do not correspond exactly to the tax codes, which are complex and ever changing. However, they are frequently used to estimate depreciation for income reporting. These functions are described in detail in the Excel online Help system. Some of the available functions are described in the following list:

- **Double-Declining Balance**—DDB(cost,salvage,life,period,factor)

The double-declining balance method computes depreciation at an accelerated rate. Depreciation is highest in the first period and decreases in successive periods. The DDB function uses the following formula to calculate depreciation for a period:

```
((cost - salvage) - total depreciation from prior periods) *
                    (factor/life)
```

- **Sum Of The Years Digits**—SYD(cost,salvage,life,per)

  In this method, depreciation is apportioned based on a declining fractional amount of the asset's life. This fraction is calculated as follows:

  1. The denominator is determined by taking each digit of the number of years of the asset's life and adding them together. So, an asset with 3 years depreciable life takes the sum of the digits from 1 to 3 (1+2+3). In this example, the sum equals 6.

  2. The numerator of the fraction starts with the number of years in the life of an asset for year 1 and descends by 1 for each succeeding year. For an asset with a useful life of 3 years, the fraction is 3/6 for year 1, 2/6 for year 2, and 1/6 for year 3.

- **Fixed-Declining Balance**—DB(cost,salvage,life,period,month)

  This method returns the depreciation of an asset for a specified period using the fixed-declining balance method. The DB function uses the following formula to calculate depreciation for a period: (cost − total depreciation from prior periods) * rate.

- **Variable-Declining Balance**
  —VDB(cost,salvage,life,start_period,end_period,factor,no_switch)

  This method returns the depreciation of an asset for any period you specify, including partial periods, using the double-declining balance method or some other method you specify.

CALCULATING TAXES

Ryan has one last step to complete the Projected 5-Year Cash Flow Estimate: calculating the estimated value of taxes for each year. Keep in mind that these are taxes against income derived from the projected sales of the TZEdge shoe. For purposes of this analysis, TheZone's corporate taxes will be calculated based on the marginal rate paid last year; in addition, corporate tax rates are assumed to be based on a graduated income scale varying from approximately 15% to 35% of taxable income. TheZone is a large corporation with sales domestically and internationally far exceeding the maximum tax rate range of $18 million in income. So, any additional income sources should be assumed to be taxed at this highest rate of 35%.

Ryan enters the tax rate of 35% in the workbook as a range named "Taxrate" without first entering the value itself in the workbook. In Excel, you can give a value a range name without actually entering the value in a specific cell. To do so, you use the Define Name dialog box.

How To

Define a Range Name for a Value Not Listed in the Worksheet

1. Click Insert on the menu bar, point to Name, and then click Define. The Define Name dialog box opens. See Figure 6.22.

Figure 6.22: Define Name dialog box

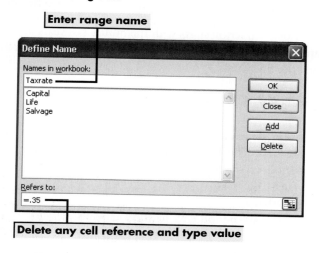

2. In the "Names in workbook" text box, enter the name you want to assign to the value.

3. In the "Refers to" text box, enter the value for which you are defining a range name. If necessary, delete any cell reference from the text box first, and then type the value.

4. Click the OK button.

This value can now be referenced anywhere in the workbook using its range name.

Ryan also assumes that the actual taxes owed will be rounded to the nearest dollar. Using this information, he enters the following formula in cell C18 to calculate the taxes:

$$\texttt{=-ROUND(Taxrate*C16,0)}$$

Note that the formula is preceded by a negative sign because this value needs to be deducted from the cash flow. Ryan also calculates the projected income after taxes in cell C19 using the formula =C18+C16. Figure 6.23 shows the resulting worksheet.

Figure 6.23: Calculating taxes and income after taxes

Calculating taxes rounded to the nearest dollar
using the named range: =-ROUND(Taxrate*C16,0)

	A	B	C	D	E	F	G	H
1			TZEdge Projected 5-Year Cash Flow Estimate					
2			1	2	3	4	5	
3		Year:						
4	Sales Volume		4450	25000	50000	65000	70000	
5	Selling Price Per Pair of Shoes		$ 225	$ 225	$ 225	$ 225	$ 225	
6								
7	Revenue		$ 1,001,250	$ 5,625,000	$11,250,000	$ 14,625,000	$ 15,750,000	
8		$/shoe						
9	Cost of Goods Sold	$(177.90)	$ (791,655)	$ (4,447,500)	$ (8,895,000)	$(11,563,500)	$(12,453,000)	
10	Selling Expense	$ (10.00)	$ (44,500)	$ (250,000)	$ (500,000)	$ (650,000)	$ (700,000)	
11								
12	Operating Income		$ 165,095	$ 927,500	$ 1,855,000	$ 2,411,500	$ 2,597,000	
13								
14	Interest Expense		$ (74,995)	$ (61,012)	$ (45,876)	$ (29,493)	$ (11,759)	
15	Depreciation		$ (97,500)	$ (97,500)	$ (97,500)	$ (97,500)	$ (97,500)	
16	Taxable Income		$ (7,400)	$ 768,988	$ 1,711,624	$ 2,284,507	$ 2,487,741	
17								
18	Taxes		$ 2,590	$ (269,146)	$ (599,068)	$ (799,578)	$ (870,709)	
19	Income After Taxes		$ (4,810)	$ 499,842	$ 1,112,556	$ 1,484,929	$ 1,617,032	
20								
21	Add Back Depreciation							
22	Subtract Principal Payments		$ (169,632)	$ (183,615)	$ (198,751)	$ (215,134)	$ (232,868)	
23								
24	**Cash Flow**							
25								
26								

Calculating income after taxes: =C18+C16

Completing the Analysis

The last two steps required for Ryan to complete the Projected 5-Year Cash Flow Estimate
are as follows:

- Add back the depreciation because this is not actually a cash flow. In this case, Ryan
  enters the formula =-C15 in cell C21 and copies it across the row. Cell C15 contains
  the depreciable amount represented as a negative value; because the value must be added
  back in, and the value is already a negative, the formula must change the sign for this
  value to a positive.
- Total the values of taxable income, depreciation added back to the cash flow, and
  principal payments deducted from the cash flow (already a negative value) to determine
  the projected cash flow. Ryan enters the following formula in cell C24 and copies it
  across the row: =SUM(C19,C21,C22).

Ryan's finished worksheet to calculate the projected cash flow estimate is shown in
Figure 6.24.

Figure 6.24: Final worksheet for the Projected 5-Year Cash Flow Estimate

Adding back depreciation: =-C15

	A	B	C	D	E	F	G	H
1			TZEdge Projected 5-Year Cash Flow Estimate					
2								
3		Year:	1	2	3	4	5	
4	Sales Volume		4450	25000	50000	65000	70000	
5	Selling Price Per Pair of Shoes		$ 225	$ 225	$ 225	$ 225	$ 225	
6								
7	Revenue		$ 1,001,250	$ 5,625,000	$11,250,000	$ 14,625,000	$ 15,750,000	
8		$/shoe						
9	Cost of Goods Sold	$(177.90)	$ (791,655)	$ (4,447,500)	$ (8,895,000)	$ (11,563,500)	$ (12,453,000)	
10	Selling Expense	$ (10.00)	$ (44,500)	$ (250,000)	$ (500,000)	$ (650,000)	$ (700,000)	
11								
12	Operating Income		$ 165,095	$ 927,500	$ 1,855,000	$ 2,411,500	$ 2,597,000	
13								
14	Interest Expense		$ (74,995)	$ (61,012)	$ (45,876)	$ (29,493)	$ (11,759)	
15	Depreciation		$ (97,500)	$ (97,500)	$ (97,500)	$ (97,500)	$ (97,500)	
16	Taxable Income		$ (7,400)	$ 768,988	$ 1,711,624	$ 2,284,507	$ 2,487,741	
17								
18	Taxes		$ 2,590	$ (269,146)	$ (599,068)	$ (799,578)	$ (870,709)	
19	Income After Taxes		$ (4,810)	$ 499,842	$ 1,112,556	$ 1,484,929	$ 1,617,032	
20								
21	Add Back Depreciation		$ 97,500	$ 97,500	$ 97,500	$ 97,500	$ 97,500	
22	Subtract Principal Payments		$ (169,632)	$ (183,615)	$ (198,751)	$ (215,134)	$ (232,868)	
23								
24	Cash Flow		$ (76,942)	$ 413,727	$ 1,011,305	$ 1,367,295	$ 1,481,664	
25								
26								

Calculating the projected cash flow estimate for year 1: =SUM(C19,C21,C22)

The projected cash flow estimate shows a moderate negative cash flow in year 1. In all subsequent years, the sales projections predict a positive cash flow, so that by year 5 the TZEdge project is generating $1.48 million in cash. The results of this analysis raise several questions. Will the original CtrBank loan be feasible for financing this project? Certainly over the course of the first five years there is enough cash generated to pay off the loan. However, if TheZone relies solely on cash flows to pay back the loan, then insufficient funds will be generated in year 1 to service the debt. Approximately $245,000 (payment of $61,000*4) is needed each year to make the loan payments. In fact, because there is no positive cash flow generated in year 1, some other type of financial arrangement might be needed, unless TheZone is willing to cover the debt from funds generated from other corporate enterprises. But even before the financing issues are resolved, the main question is should TheZone go ahead with this project? Or, as an alternative, would the company reap more profits through another means, such as buying treasury bills? If the company wants to continue with the project, can it be modified so that less capital is required, even if additional labor will be needed? These questions will be explored further in the next section.

Best Practice

Nesting Basic Financial Functions to Calculate Variable Periodic Payments

Excel provides other, more complex financial functions that allow for variable payments, interest rates, and so on. However, using only the basic functions, you can often easily solve this type of financial transaction by nesting functions within each other. Consider the example of CtrBank modifying its loan so that it would lend TheZone $1 million at 8.5% interest compounded quarterly over the next 6 years, but no payments would be expected for the first year. How would you calculate the payments for such a loan? One way would be to calculate the money owed after year 1, $1 million plus the accrued interest (future value), and then use that amount as the present value of a 5-year payment stream. The formula to accomplish this is shown in Figure 6.25.

Figure 6.25: Calculating a loan payment where payments begin after one year of accruing interest

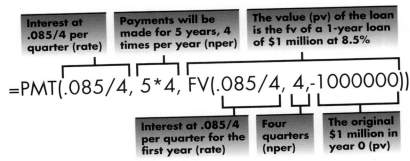

By nesting one financial function inside another—in this case, the FV function inside the PMT function—you can obtain the same results provided by more complex functions. This might be a preferred method, depending on your knowledge of and experience with building formulas with more complicated financial functions.

Steps To Success: Level 2

The Equipment division at TheZone is looking into a new piece of equipment that was developed in Europe to mold skis more precisely and less expensively than the current technology being used at TheZone. The cost of the machine plus installation is estimated to be $1,635,000. The projected cost savings are expected to be $8.50 per pair of skis. You have been asked to estimate a projected cash flow savings (if any) that will be generated by this proposed project over the next four years.

Complete the following:

1. Open the workbook named **Ski.xls** in the Chapter 6 folder, and then save it as **Ski Molder Cash Flow Estimate.xls**. The structure for the projected cash flow estimate is provided on Sheet1, as shown in Figure 6.26.

Figure 6.26: Worksheet for ski molder projected cash flow estimate

	A	B	C	D	E	F	G
1	Year		1	2	3	4	
2	Sales Volume						
3	Cost Savings Per Pair						
4							
5	Cost Savings						
6							
7	Interest Expense						
8	Depreciation						
9	Net Cost Savings						
10							
11	Additional Tax Owed						
12	Savings After Taxes						
13							
14	Add Back Depreciation						
15	Subtract Principal Payments						
16							
17	Projected Cash Flow Estimate						
18							
19							

2. Rename the Sheet1 worksheet as "Cashflow." Insert the following title at the top of the worksheet, merged and centered: "Ski Molding Project – Projected 4–Year Cash Flow Estimate."

3. Enter the sales volume for each year, assuming sales in year 1 of 160,000 pairs. The sales volume for each successive year is assumed to be 5% more than the previous year.

4. Enter the cost savings as $8.50 per pair. This will not change in subsequent years.

5. Calculate the cost savings as the number of pairs of skis sold times the cost savings per ski.

6. On a separate worksheet named "Loan" (similar to the Loan worksheet shown in Figure 6.15), create an amortization table listing the principal and interest payments and remaining principal in each monthly period, assuming TheZone will borrow the money under the following terms:

   Funding will be arranged for the entire cost of this investment at 4.5% interest compounded monthly, paid out in full in equal monthly installments over this same four-year period.

7. On the Cashflow worksheet, calculate the cumulative interest expense for year 1 (the interest portion of the loan payments for the corresponding year). You can reference cells on the Loan worksheet as needed. Assume the loan will start at the beginning of year 1. Write your formula so that it can be copied across the row to automatically calculate these values for years 2 through 4.

8. Calculate the depreciation for this equipment using the straight line depreciation method. The equipment is assumed to have a 10-year life with a salvage value of $75,000 at the end of that period. Set up a separate worksheet named "Depreciation" to store these values, and use named ranges in your formula.

9. Calculate the net cost savings—the cost savings less the interest expense and depreciation.

10. Calculate the additional tax that would be owed assuming TheZone is taxed at a 35% rate. Use a named range to store this value.

11. Calculate the savings after taxes.

12. Complete the worksheet, adding back in the depreciation that was deducted and adding in the cumulative principal payments for the corresponding year, to arrive at a final projected cash flow estimate for each of the four years. Use the correct absolute and relative cell referencing so that your formulas will work for each of the cash flow years.

13. Format your worksheet as appropriate, to make it easy to read and understand.

14. Save and close the Ski Molder Cash Flow Estimate.xls workbook.

LEVEL 3
EVALUATING THE FINANCIAL VIABILITY OF ALTERNATIVE PROJECT OPTIONS

EXCEL 2003 SKILLS TRAINING

- Edit a chart
- Position a chart

SETTING UP A WORKSHEET TO ANALYZE PROFITABILITY

Ryan has now estimated the cash flow for the manufacture of the TZEdge shoe according to the terms of option 1, which requires $1,000,000 in capital funded through a loan from CtrBank at 8% interest compounded quarterly. The engineering group has also proposed a less capital-intensive solution that requires additional labor instead of the $1 million in upfront capital equipment. This option would be less automated, replacing what a machine can do with manual labor, requiring a $250,000 capital investment and additional labor costs of $20 per pair of shoes. As he did with the original estimate, Ryan has calculated the income after taxes for this low capital alternative, assuming that it will be entirely funded from existing cash assets; therefore, no loan will be required. He has also assumed for this alternative that the equipment is depreciated using straight line depreciation over a 10-year period with a salvage value of $5000.

Ryan's next task is to analyze the profitability of each of these options. To facilitate this analysis, Ryan copies his earlier projected cash flow worksheet to a new workbook named "Profitability," and then modifies the worksheet to include all of the relevant data inputs for loan values and depreciation. Specifically, he makes the following modifications:

- Names the new worksheet "High" for the high capital option
- Inputs data for the loan, depreciation, and taxes at the top of the worksheet
- Inputs data for the interest rate (or hurdle rate, as defined later) and tax rate
- Deletes the rows below the Income After Taxes row from his original worksheet
- Modifies the formulas to reflect these changes, referencing the corresponding new data input locations

The resulting worksheet is shown in Figure 6.27.

Figure 6.27: High worksheet

Data inputs for loan, depreciation, and hurdle rates

	A	B	C	D	E	F	G	H
1	OPTION	Annual Rate	Duration in Years	Compounding Periods/Year	PV	FV	PMT	
2	(1) CtrBank Loan	8.0%	5	4	$ 1,000,000	$ 0	$ (61,157)	
3								
4	Depreciation Method		Asset Value	Salvage Value	Life			
5	SLN		1000000	25000	10			
6								
7	Hurdle Rate	25.0%		Tax Rate	35.0%			
8								
9		Projected 5-Year Income after Taxes - High Capital Option (Original)						
10	Year	0	1	2	3	4	5	
11	Sales Volume		4,450	25,000	50,000	65,000	70,000	
12	Selling Price (per pair)		$ 225	$ 225	$ 225	$ 225	$ 225	
13	Cost of Goods Sold (per pair)		$ 177.90	$ 177.90	$ 177.90	$ 177.90	$ 177.90	
14	Selling Expense (per pair)		$ 10	$ 10	$ 10	$ 10	$ 10	
15								
16	Revenue		$ 1,001,250	$ 5,625,000	$ 11,250,000	$ 14,625,000	$ 15,750,000	
17	Cost of Goods Sold		$ (791,655)	$ (4,447,500)	$ (8,895,000)	$ (11,563,500)	$ (12,453,000)	
18	Selling Expense		$ (44,500)	$ (250,000)	$ (500,000)	$ (650,000)	$ (700,000)	
19								
20	Operating Income		$ 165,095	$ 927,500	$ 1,855,000	$ 2,411,500	$ 2,597,000	
21								
22	Interest Expense		$ (74,995)	$ (61,012)	$ (45,876)	$ (29,493)	$ (11,759)	
23	Depreciation		$ (97,500)	$ (97,500)	$ (97,500)	$ (97,500)	$ (97,500)	
24	Taxable Income		$ (7,400)	$ 768,988	$ 1,711,624	$ 2,284,507	$ 2,487,741	
25								
26	Taxes		2,590	(269,146)	(599,068)	(799,578)	(870,709)	
27	Income After Taxes	(1,000,000)	(4,810)	499,842	1,112,556	1,484,930	1,617,032	
28								
29								

Cashflow worksheet copied from Sales Volume through Income After Taxes

The formulas for the High worksheet are shown in Figure 6.28.

Figure 6.28: High worksheet with formulas displayed

Cumulative interest referencing RATE, PV, and NPER from row 2

	A	B		C
1	OPTION	Annual Rate		Duration in Years
2	(1) CtrBank Loan	0.08	5	
3				
4	Depreciation Method		Asset Value	
5	SLN		1000000	
6				
7	Hurdle Rate	0.25		
8				Projected 5-Year Income
9				
10	Year	0	1	
11	Sales Volume		4450	
12	Selling Price (per pair)		225	
13	Cost of Goods Sold (per pair)		177.9	
14	Selling Expense (per pair)		10	
15				
16	Revenue		=C$11*C12	
17	Cost of Goods Sold		=-C13*C11	
18	Selling Expense		=-C11*C14	
19				
20	Operating Income		=SUM(C16:C18)	
21				
22	Interest Expense		=CUMIPMT($B$2/$D$2,$C$2*$D$2,$E$2,C10*4-3,C10*4,0)	
23	Depreciation		=-SLN($C5,$D5,$E5)	
24	Taxable Income		=SUM(C20,C22:C23)	
25				
26	Taxes		=-$E7*C24	
27	Income After Taxes	=-E2	=C26+C24	
28				
29				

Straight line depreciation referencing inputs from row 5

Now Ryan is ready to analyze the data. Companies can use numerous methods to analyze whether to proceed with a project, or to choose among alternatives based on their profitability. Ryan will look at several common methods such as *Net Present Value* and *Internal Rate of Return* in conjunction with calculations for *Return on Investment* and *Payback*. Ryan will proceed with his analysis using the projected income after taxes to measure theses values. Here, TheZone is not focusing on the cash in and out of the company, but rather on income earned, or profits.

Ultimately, the decision of whether or not to proceed will depend not only on these specific values for the TZEdge project, but also on other projects the company is considering for different uses of capital, such as expanding the tennis racket line, for example, or building a new corporate office. The decision must also factor in TheZone's ability to fund the project, the level of risk the company is willing to assume, and the company's overall corporate strategies for growth.

CALCULATING NET PRESENT VALUE

The High worksheet includes all the necessary elements to analyze the profitability of the CtrBank loan option. The formulas correctly calculate the yearly net income after taxes for the given inputs. Ryan can now begin to complete the financial analysis. The first method he will use is Net Present Value (NPV). **NPV** is preferred by most financial theorists because it uses the expected cash flows—in this case, income after taxes—and applies a minimum *rate of return* to *discount* these cash flows into current (present) value dollars, essentially finding the present value for each year's income. In other words, NPV enables you to see what the current worth is of the projected cash flows, which helps you to determine the profitability of the venture.

The **rate of return**, often referred to as the **hurdle rate** or **discount rate**, is an interest rate chosen to reflect not only the time value of money, but the desired returns the company expects for the level of risk being taken. Projects with positive NPVs at a given hurdle rate are considered to be ones that will add wealth to the corporation—the more positive the value, the greater the expected returns. Selecting a hurdle rate can be quite controversial because different analysts or managers might not all agree on the hurdle rate to choose. So, NPV is often calculated at several alternative hurdle rates to determine the sensitivity of the project to the various rates of return.

Ryan has been instructed to use a hurdle rate of 25% for the high capital option. So, if the NPV is greater than 0 for this minimum rate of return, TheZone should go ahead with the TZEdge project. Projects with positive cash flows indicate that the project will be profitable; the higher the NPV, the more profitable the project.

Entering the NPV Function

To analyze the net present value manually, Ryan would have to systematically calculate the present value based on each year's income after taxes and compound the hurdle rate over a one-year period for year 1's cash flow; compound the hurdle rate over a two-year period for year 2's cash flow, and so on. The NPV function performs these calculations automatically. This function takes the hurdle rate and the series of cash flow values and automatically calculates the discounted value. The syntax of the NPV function is as follows:

$$\text{NPV(rate,value1,value2,...)}$$

The NPV function has the following requirements:

- The hurdle (discount) rate must match the period duration, so that a yearly cash flow would apply to a yearly (annual) discount rate, for example.
- Value1, value2, value3, and so on, must be equally spaced in time and occur at the end of each period.

Level 3

6

- Because NPV uses the order of value1, value2, value3, and so on, to determine the number of periods to discount each value, cash flows must be entered in the correct sequence from earliest to latest (year 1, year 2…year n).
- Text values and error messages are ignored.

Best Practice

Avoiding Problems of Year 0 Cash Flows when Using the NPV Function

The NPV function in Excel takes the cash flow from year 0, which is referred to as value 1, and discounts the value by one year. So, essentially, the first cash flow in or out of the financial transaction is assumed to be one year from now. The function then takes value 2 and discounts it back two years at the given discount rate. So, if the actual first cash flow is now (year 0), and you include this in the NPV function, the result would be that the entire cash flow would be discounted an extra year—which is not the intended result.

This problem can be easily corrected. Consider the example of cash flows from year 0 to 4, as follows: –1000, +400, +400, +400, + 400. Assuming a 20% hurdle rate, the formula you would write is: =NPV(20%,–1000,400,400,400,400). This formula results in the value 29.58; but, as noted earlier, this formula does not take into account the fact that the first cash flow is now (year 0)—not one year from now. To work around this problem and accurately calculate the cash flow using the NPV function, again assuming a 20% hurdle rate, you could calculate the NPV by adding the value in year 0 to the discounted cash flows in years 1 to n, as follows: value1+NPV(discount rate, value2, value3…value n). In this example, the resulting formula is =–1000+NPV(20%,400,400,400,400). The result of this formula is 35.49, which accurately reflects when the cash flows actually occur.

Setting Up a Table of Hurdle Rates

Using the NPV function, Ryan can write the formula to determine the net present value of the income flows for this project, including the initial investment, as follows: –Initial investment + NPV(25%, income year 1, income year 2.....income year 5). However, Ryan decides to create a small table that calculates the NPV for several values above and below the 25% hurdle rate to give him a better idea of the sensitivity of this project to hurdle rates both above and below the target rate provided by management. For a hurdle rate of 25%, Ryan wants to calculate the NPV starting with a rate of 21% and going up to 29%, as follows:

- Target hurdle rate –4%
- Target hurdle rate –3%
- Target hurdle rate –2%
- Target hurdle rate –1%
- Target hurdle rate
- Target hurdle rate +1%
- Target hurdle rate +2%
- Target hurdle rate +3%
- Target hurdle rate +4%

To create a table that automatically updates if the hurdle rate is modified, Ryan needs to relate this range of values to the hurdle rate input value, as shown in Figure 6.29.

Figure 6.29: Setting up an NPV table for +/- 4% of a given hurdle rate

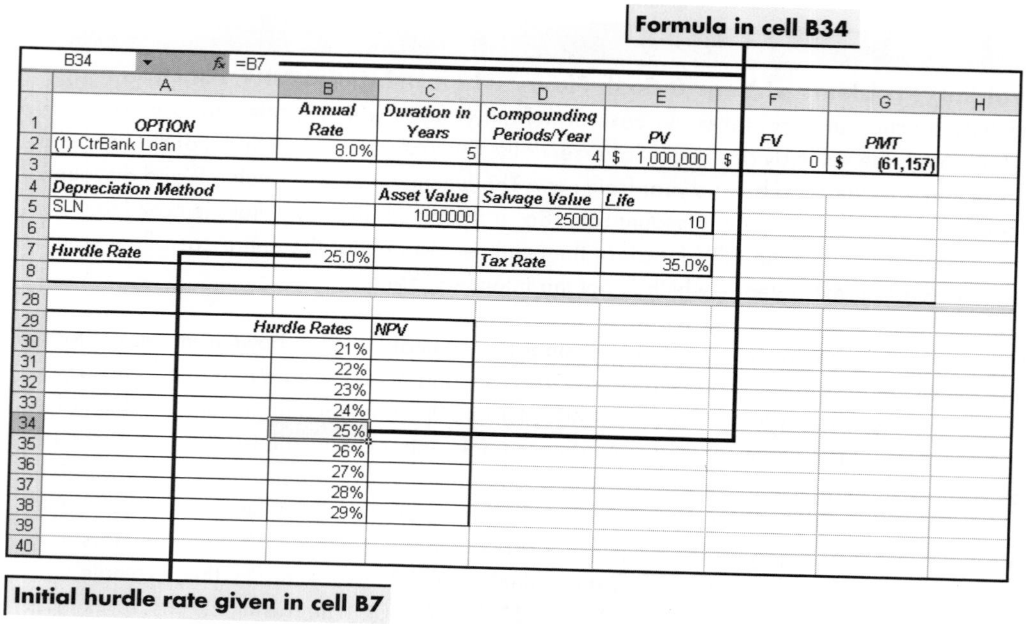

Formula in cell B34

	B34	▾	*fx* =B7						
	A	B	C	D	E	F	G	H
1	OPTION	Annual Rate	Duration in Years	Compounding Periods/Year	PV	FV	PMT	
2	(1) CtrBank Loan	8.0%	5	4	$ 1,000,000	$		
3						0	$ (61,157)	
4	Depreciation Method		Asset Value	Salvage Value	Life			
5	SLN		1000000	25000	10			
6								
7	Hurdle Rate	25.0%		Tax Rate	35.0%			
8								
28								
29			Hurdle Rates	NPV				
30			21%					
31			22%					
32			23%					
33			24%					
34			25%					
35			26%					
36			27%					
37			28%					
38			29%					
39								
40								

Initial hurdle rate given in cell B7

The process Ryan followed is described below:

- Start in the center of the hurdle rate column of the table (cell B34) and directly reference the hurdle rate from the inputs at the top of the worksheet by writing the formula =B7.
- Calculate the values below the hurdle rate by writing the formula =B34−0.01 in cell B33, and then copy this formula into the top half of the table (cells B30:B32).
- Calculate the values above the hurdle rate by writing the formula =B34+0.01 in cell B35, and then copy this formula into the bottom half of the table (cells B36:B38).

With the hurdle rates established, Ryan can now write the NPV formula in cell C30 and copy it down the column to cell C38, as follows:

$$=B\$27+NPV(B30,C\$27:G\$27)$$

Cell B$27 contains the initial capital investment of −$1,000,000 made in year 0; cell B30 contains the corresponding hurdle rate; and the range C$27:G$27 contains the cash flows from years 1 through 5. Only the hurdle rate will copy relatively; the values for the initial investment and cash flow range will remain fixed. Figure 6.30 shows the resulting worksheet. Note that all the resulting values are positive, indicating that this project, if completed, would benefit the company.

Figure 6.30: Results for NPV at different hurdle rates

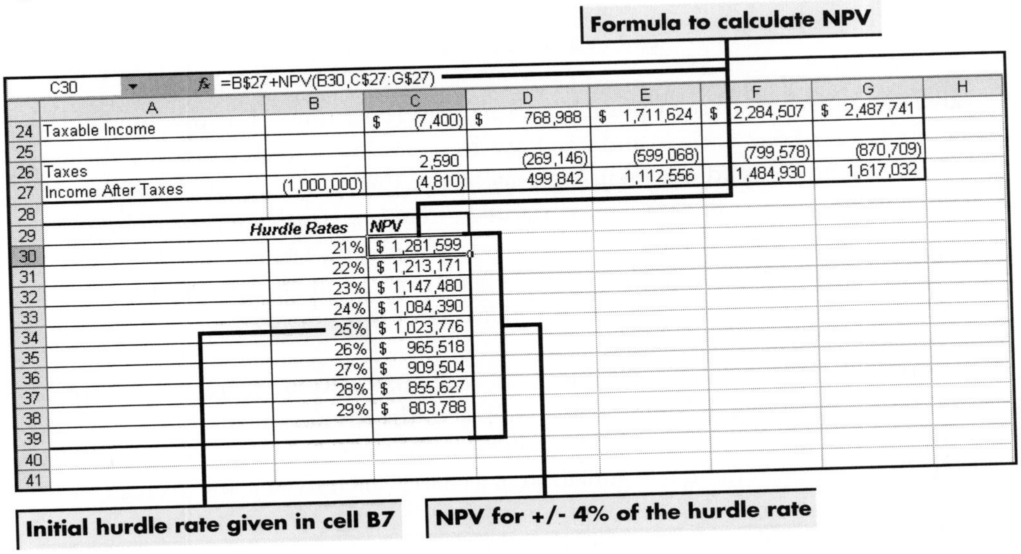

Formula to calculate NPV

C30   =B$27+NPV(B30,C$27:G$27)

	A	B	C	D	E	F	G	H
24	Taxable Income		$ (7,400)	$ 768,988	$ 1,711,624	$ 2,284,507	$ 2,487,741	
25								
26	Taxes		2,590	(269,146)	(599,068)	(799,578)	(870,709)	
27	Income After Taxes	(1,000,000)	(4,810)	499,842	1,112,556	1,484,930	1,617,032	
28								
29		Hurdle Rates	NPV					
30		21%	$ 1,281,599					
31		22%	$ 1,213,171					
32		23%	$ 1,147,480					
33		24%	$ 1,084,390					
34		25%	$ 1,023,776					
35		26%	$ 965,518					
36		27%	$ 909,504					
37		28%	$ 855,627					
38		29%	$ 803,788					
39								
40								
41								

Initial hurdle rate given in cell B7   **NPV for +/- 4% of the hurdle rate**

CALCULATING THE INTERNAL RATE OF RETURN

The second analysis Ryan will undertake is to calculate the internal rate of return (IRR) for the TZEdge project. The **internal rate of return (IRR)** method of evaluating profitability takes a similar approach to that of NPV in that it considers the cash flows and discounts them back to the present value. The difference is that the IRR method calculates the *rate at which these discounted cash flows in and out are equal*, essentially where the NPV is $0. The company can then determine if the IRR is sufficient to make it worthwhile to go ahead with a project. Usually, projects with higher IRRs are preferable to projects with lower IRRs, given that all discount rates below the IRR result in positive cash flows to the company.

In traditional projects with large capital expenditures in the early years followed by positive cash flows in later years, the two analytical methods of NPV and IRR usually (but not always) lead to similar decisions. In projects where cash flows are negative at both the beginning and end of the project life, the results are often contradictory.

To calculate the IRR manually, you would need to guess an IRR value and substitute it as the discount rate in the NPV formula. Depending on the value returned, this process would be repeated with a second guess, and then a third guess, and so on, refining the estimate until a value of 0 is reached. Like all other trial-and-error manual tasks, this would be a laborious process. Fortunately, Excel can do this work automatically with the IRR function.

The syntax of the IRR function is as follows:

$$IRR (values, guess)$$

The **values** argument is a list of positive and negative cash flows. For this function to work, a minimum of one positive and one negative cash flow must be listed. Cash flows are taken in the order listed assuming each successive one is one period later. As with the NPV function, the cash flows must occur at regular, equal intervals. The **guess** argument is optional and should not be needed, but can be used if the 20 iterations that are automatically performed by Excel do not result in an accurate value (within .00001 percent). If this happens, a #NUM! error is returned.

Applying this function to the worksheet in cell B39, Ryan writes the formula =IRR(B27:G27), as shown in Figure 6.31. He places the formula at the bottom of the table containing the hurdle rate and NPV values, and enters the value 0% in the NPV column (C39). This facilitates the formulation of a chart, which Ryan plans to create next.

Figure 6.31: Calculating the internal rate of return

Formula to calculate IRR: =IRR(B27:G27)

The calculation results in an IRR of 52%. At a discount rate of 52%, the NPV of these cash flows is 0. Using this method alone, TheZone management would accept this project only if they considered a 52% rate of return a sufficient profit for the risks involved.

Creating a Chart Showing the Hurdle Rate Versus NPV

Ryan wants to graphically depict the sensitivity of the NPV to the hurdle rates, as well as the IRR. Because he wants to show a functional relationship—in this case, hurdle rate versus NPV—the best type of chart to use is an XY plot, with scattered data points and smooth lines. Ryan creates this chart easily using the Chart Wizard and the data range $B$30:$C$39. He places the resulting chart on the worksheet and resizes it so that it fits next to the hurdle rate table, as shown in Figure 6.32.

Figure 6.32: XY Scatter plot of NPV versus hurdle rates

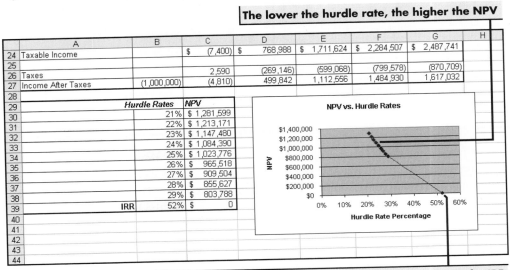

The chart clearly illustrates that all hurdle rates below 52% (IRR) result in a positive NPV—the lower the hurdle rate, the higher the NPV.

CALCULATING THE RETURN ON INVESTMENT

The third value to be calculated in Ryan's analysis is the return on investment, or ROI. **ROI** is the sum of the cash flows, excluding the initial investment, divided by the investment value. Stockholders often look at the ROI as a quick measure of how attractive a company's stock is versus other stocks within the industry. Because ROI is easy to calculate, it is often used in addition to more sophisticated measures.

For the high capital case, the ROI is the sum of the income values in years 1 through 5 divided by $1,000,000. In Excel syntax, this is =SUM(C27:G27)/C5. Ryan enters this formula in cell B41 of the worksheet. The resulting value for the high capital option is 471%, as shown in Figure 6.33.

Figure 6.33: Calculating return on investment

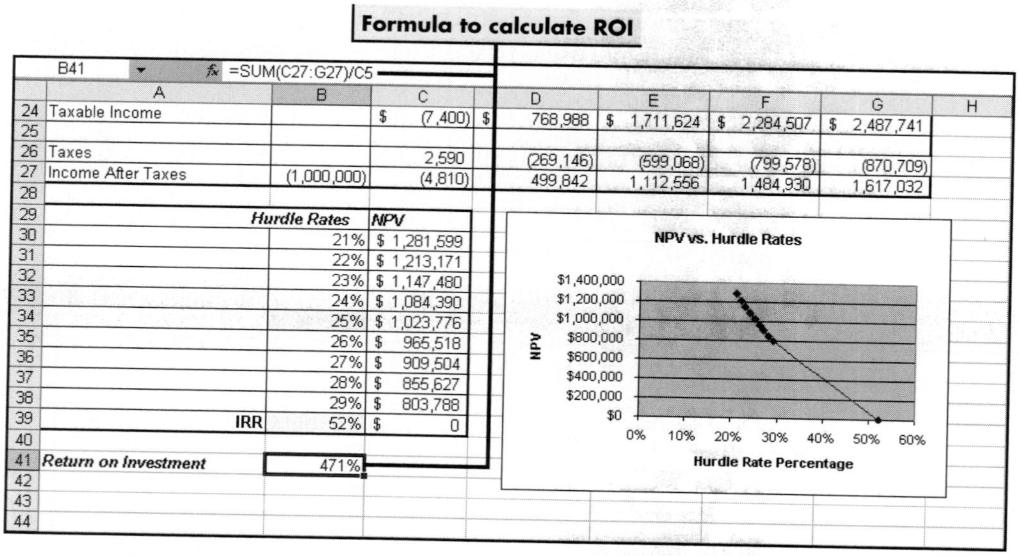

Formula to calculate ROI

	B41	▼	fx =SUM(C27:G27)/C5					
	A	B	C	D	E	F	G	H
24	Taxable Income		$ (7,400)	$ 768,988	$ 1,711,624	$ 2,284,507	$ 2,487,741	
25								
26	Taxes		2,590	(269,146)	(599,068)	(799,578)	(870,709)	
27	Income After Taxes	(1,000,000)	(4,810)	499,842	1,112,556	1,484,930	1,617,032	
28								
29		Hurdle Rates	NPV					
30		21%	$ 1,281,599					
31		22%	$ 1,213,171					
32		23%	$ 1,147,480					
33		24%	$ 1,084,390					
34		25%	$ 1,023,776					
35		26%	$ 965,518					
36		27%	$ 909,504					
37		28%	$ 855,627					
38		29%	$ 803,788					
39	IRR	52%	$ 0					
40								
41	Return on Investment	471%						
42								
43								
44								

Keep in mind that the ROI does not take into account the time value of money. In aggregate, over the entire five-year period, this project would yield $4.71 per dollar of investment. The timing of the money is not taken into account. This 471% would be the same if all of the money was earned in the first period or all in the last. However, despite the lack of accounting for timing, the value clearly shows that over this period the company would recoup its investment more than fourfold. Over a five-year period, depending on the risk, this might be a reasonable investment.

DETERMINING THE PAYBACK PERIOD

The final piece of data Ryan needs to determine is the **payback period**, which is the time it will take to earn sufficient profits so that the loan can be paid back. Projects that are paid back early are preferred. Over the long term, calculating the payback period does not always give the most realistic view of the most profitable venture. Again, this factor is only one of many to consider when making the final decision.

The payback year is the year in which the *cumulative* total cash flow is greater than or equal to $0. To determine this manually, you would need to add the cash flows together, starting with year 0 (negative value for the initial investment) and continuing with each successive year until the value reaches $0 or greater. In the case of Ryan's analysis, the cumulative total cash flow is determined as follows: B27+C27+D27+E27 (−1,000,000 + −4,810 + 499,842 + 1,112,556) to achieve a number greater than or equal to 0 (in this case, the result is 607,588). So, it is some time during the third year of operation (cell E27) that the original investment would be recouped.

Here, Ryan simply enters the value 3 in cell B42 to indicate year 3 for the payback period, as shown in Figure 6.34.

Figure 6.34: Determining the payback period

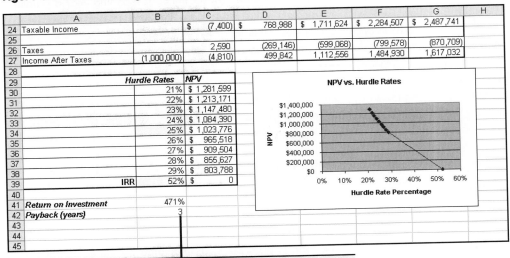

	A	B	C	D	E	F	G	H
24	Taxable Income		$ (7,400)	$ 768,988	$ 1,711,624	$ 2,284,507	$ 2,487,741	
25								
26	Taxes		2,590	(269,146)	(599,068)	(799,578)	(870,709)	
27	Income After Taxes	(1,000,000)	(4,810)	499,842	1,112,556	1,484,930	1,617,032	
28								
29		*Hurdle Rates*	*NPV*					
30		21%	$ 1,281,599					
31		22%	$ 1,213,171					
32		23%	$ 1,147,480					
33		24%	$ 1,084,390					
34		25%	$ 1,023,776					
35		26%	$ 965,518					
36		27%	$ 909,504					
37		28%	$ 855,627					
38		29%	$ 803,788					
39	IRR	52%	$ 0					
40								
41	*Return on Investment*	471%						
42	*Payback (years)*	3						
43								
44								
45								

Payback period specifies the first year in which the cumulative cash flows (0–payback year) are greater than $0

Ryan has calculated a payback of three years. It will take TheZone three years before the company earns enough money to cover its initial investment costs. Again, this method does not discount cash flows; the same value would be returned if the cash flows for years 1 and 2 were $0 and in year 3 the cash flow was any amount over $1 million. Nor does this method take into account the profitability of the venture versus the risk. In this case, if the TZEdge shoes are expected to sell for only a five-year period, almost half the life-cycle of the project would be over before any profits would be realized.

Excel does provide a method to automatically calculate the payback period, but it is a somewhat complex process that involves using the MATCH reference function and calculating a cumulative total. The following steps outline this process.

How To

Automate the Payback Calculation

1. In a row below the data being analyzed (refer to Figure 6.34 for the purposes of this discussion), write a formula to determine if the cumulative cash flow for the corresponding year is greater than $0, as follows: =SUM($B27:B27)>0 in cell B44. Copy this formula across the row to produce a row of TRUE and FALSE values. Note that by adding an absolute cell reference to only the beginning cell column reference of the sum range, copying this formula across will change only the end range reference.

2. Determine the relative position (1,2,3) of the first TRUE value using the formula =MATCH(TRUE,B44:G44,0). Recall that the MATCH function syntax requires a lookup_value, lookup_array, and match type as inputs. In this case, the lookup_value is TRUE to be found in the lookup_array B44:G44; and, because an exact match is required, the match type is 0.

3. Modify the MATCH formula to subtract 1, as follows =MATCH(TRUE,B44:G44,0)–1. Because these flows correspond to years 0, 1, 2, and so on, instead of 1, 2, 3, you need to subtract 1 to get the correct number of years in which the amount is paid back.

An implementation of this technique is shown in Figure 6.35. Again, the results show that year 3 is the year in which the loan is paid back, as indicated by the value TRUE in cell E44.

Figure 6.35: Automating the payback calculation

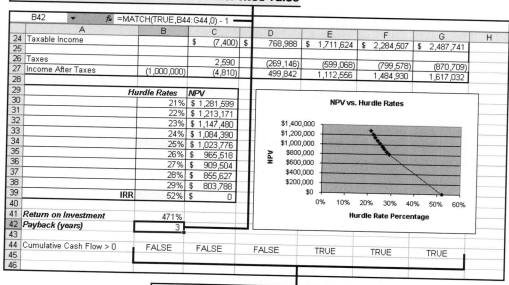

SETTING UP THE WORKSHEET FOR THE LOW CAPITAL OPTION

Recall that another option is being considered to fund the TZEdge project, one with lower capital investment requirements and higher labor costs. To set up the worksheet for this option, Ryan copies the High worksheet to create a new worksheet named "Low" and enters the new input values and headings. Figure 6.36 shows the Low worksheet.

Figure 6.36: Calculating the profitability of the low capital option

Loan information and interest calculations removed

	A	B	C	D	E	F	G	H	I
		Annual Rate	Duration in Years	Compounding Periods/Year	PV	FV	PMT		
1	OPTION								
2	(1) CtrBank Loan				$ 250,000				
3									
4	Depreciation Method		Asset Value	Salvage Value	Life				
5	SLN		$ 250,000	5000	10				
6									
7	Hurdle Rate	25.0%		Tax Rate	35.0%				
8									
9	Projected 5-Year Income after Taxes - Low Capital Option								
10	Year		0	1	2	3	4	5	
11	Sales Volume			4,450	25,000	50,000	65,000	70,000	
12	Selling Price (per pair)		$ 225	$ 225	$ 225	$ 225	$ 225	$ 225	
13	Cost of Goods Sold (per pair)		$ 197.90	$ 197.90	$ 197.90	$ 197.90	$ 197.90	$ 197.90	
14	Selling Expense (per pair)		$ 10	$ 10	$ 10	$ 10	$ 10	$ 10	
15									
16	Revenue			$ 1,001,250	$ 5,625,000	$ 11,250,000	$ 14,625,000	$ 15,750,000	
17	Cost of Goods Sold			$ (880,655)	$ (4,947,500)	$ (9,895,000)	$ (12,863,500)	$ (13,853,000)	
18	Selling Expense			$ (44,500)	$ (250,000)	$ (500,000)	$ (650,000)	$ (700,000)	
19									
20	Operating Income			$ 76,095	$ 427,500	$ 855,000	$ 1,111,500	$ 1,197,000	
21									
22	Interest Expense								
23	Depreciation			($24,500)	($24,500)	($24,500)	($24,500)	($24,500)	
24	Taxable Income			$ 51,595	$ 403,000	$ 830,500	$ 1,087,000	$ 1,172,500	
25									
26	Taxes			(18,058)	(141,050)	(290,675)	(380,450)	(410,375)	
27	Income After Taxes		(250,000)	33,537	261,950	539,825	706,550	762,125	
28									
29			Hurdle Rates	NPV					
30			21%	$ 884,792					
31			22%	$ 851,691					
32			23%	$ 819,901					
33			24%	$ 789,359					
34			25%	$ 760,004					
35			26%	$ 731,779					
36			27%	$ 704,631					
37			28%	$ 678,509					
38			29%	$ 653,364					
39			IRR	91%	$ 0				
40									
41	Return on Investment	922%							
42	Payback (years)	2							

NPV vs. Hurdle Rates — chart plotting NPV against Hurdle Rate Percentage (0% to 100%).

Updated cost of goods sold

Chart with updated data range

Depreciation values updated

To create the Low worksheet, Ryan did the following:

- Modified the title
- Removed the loan values from row 2, because this option does not involve a loan, leaving only the PV of $250,000, which is the cost of the lower capital investment

- Modified the cost of goods sold per pair of shoes from $177.90 to 197.90 (+$20/pair) and copied this value across the row (C13:G13)
- Modified the depreciation input values in row 5 to account for the new asset value of $250,000 and the new salvage value of $5000

The only element that did not copy relatively to the new Low worksheet is the chart. Chart ranges include both sheet names and absolute cell references. This happens automatically when you highlight a range in the Chart Wizard. This means that when Ryan copied the High worksheet to create the Low worksheet, the chart did not automatically update. So, Ryan had to manually edit the data range to match that of the new sheet's chart input area, essentially just changing the sheet name of the range.

The values obtained for the low capital option case show positive NPVs for all hurdle rates below 91% (IRR). The return on investment is 922%, and this project would be paid for within the first two years of operation.

6

Level 3

Best Practice

Using an ISNUMBER Function to Avoid Displaying an Error Message

In the Low worksheet (Figure 6.36), notice that the yearly interest payments are blank in cells C22:G22. These cells were manually adjusted to remove the formula =CUMIPMT($B$2/$D$2,$C$2*$D$2,$E$2,C10*4−3,C10*4,0), which automatically calculated the cumulative interest paid between the corresponding payment periods. In the low capital option, because there is no loan involved and, therefore, no values in row 2, if this formula had not been removed manually, the error message #DIV/0! would have been displayed. This would happen because the function would try to divide by D2, which contains the value 0.

If this type of worksheet were to be used again and again by the company as a template for these types of capital project analyses, it would be more efficient if this payment value could be automatically "corrected" without manually having to remove the formulas—especially if the worksheet was used for further what-if analyses that did include some type of loan funding. This can be accomplished using the ISNUMBER (presented in Chapter 5) nested inside an IF function. Recall that the ISNUMBER function tests to see if the result of the formula is a number.

In the Low worksheet, the following expression could be written in cell C22 to test to see if the cumulative value of the interest payments results in a number; if so, the results of the cumulative interest function would be displayed; otherwise, the value 0 would be displayed.

```
=IF(ISNUMBER(CUMIPMT($B2/$D2,$C2*$D2,$E2,C11*4−3,C11*4,0)),
    CUMIPMT($B2/$D2,$C2*$D2,$E2,C11*4−3,C11*4,0),0)
```

Again, using this technique is a good idea if you plan to use the worksheet as a template to perform further analyses, both with and without the values associated with a loan.

EVALUATING THE RESULTS OF THE ANALYSIS

So, which of the two options—the high capital option or the low capital option—should Ryan recommend? Or, is neither option worthwhile to pursue? Table 6.2 lists a summary of the key values.

Table 6.2: Comparison of investment values

	High Capital Option	Low Capital Option
NPV	$1,023,776	$760,004
IRR	52%	91%
ROI	471%	922%
Payback Period	3	2

If Ryan considers only the NPV measure, both options are over $0, but clearly the high capital option returns a higher value, indicating greater profits. On the other hand, the IRR is higher for the low capital option. Neither of these methods has taken into account the difference in risks, such as a possible increased risk due to labor uncertainties. Perhaps the hurdle rates themselves for the low capital option should be revisited. Consider the ROI and Payback Period indicators; these clearly also favor the low capital option, even though the subsequent cash flows are lower. So, what is the correct answer? There is no clearcut correct answer in this case; the analyses that Ryan has performed will help TheZone management choose the most viable option, taking into consideration many other factors not included in these analyses. The results of these analyses provide useful tools to guide the decision-making process toward an ultimate solution.

Steps To Success: Level 3

The Equipment division is considering starting its own line of specialty tennis shops in selected areas of the country. The endeavor would require significant upfront capital, but according to the marketing group could reap substantial rewards. Two options are under consideration, as follows:

- **Option 1**—Build three new shops on empty lots in three different locations, all of which are close to tennis facilities.
- **Option 2**—Establish three shops located in existing tennis club facilities.

Table 6.3 summarizes the projected income after taxes for the two options over a six-year period.

Table 6.3: Options for tennis shops

Year	Option 1 Income After Taxes	Option 2 Income After Taxes
Initial Investment – Year 0	$ (10,000,000)	$ (5,500,000)
1	920,743	593,091
2	2,708,380	1,710,509
3	4,120,929	2,452,864
4	5,795,889	2,595,157
5	6,158,256	2,662,386
6	6,333,029	2,729,549

The investment for the first option is the most significant, requiring the construction of new buildings, but has the lowest operating costs because it involves no significant rent or royalty sharing agreements, as does the second option. Your task in these steps is to complete the financial analysis for each option. Complete the following:

1. Open the workbook named **Tennis.xls** located in the Chapter 6 folder, and then save it as **Tennis Option Analysis.xls**.

2. Create a hurdle rate sensitivity table in cells A15:C25 that calculates the NPV for each option between +/– 5% of the hurdle rate. Be certain that if the hurdle rate in cell B13 is modified, the sensitivity table will automatically update to reflect the changed rate.

3. In cells B26:C26, calculate the corresponding internal rate of return for each option. Format the cells as percentages.

4. Calculate the return on investment for each option in cells B28:C28. Format the cells as percentages.

5. In cells D2:D9, calculate the cumulative income (including the initial investment) for each year in option 1 (example: year 1 would include –10,000,000 + 920,743 for option 1). Write the formula so that it can be copied both down the column and across the row to calculate the cumulative income for option 2.

6. In cells B29:C29, enter the payback period (year number) for each option. (*Optional challenge*: write a formula to automatically calculate the year number in which the cumulative total income exceeds $0.)

7. Highlight in yellow the income data for the option you would recommend.

8. Create an XY Scatter chart for your selected option that displays the functional relationship of the hurdle rates to the NPV values. Size the chart and place it next to the hurdle rate analysis. Give the chart an appropriate title and name the axes accordingly.

9. Save and close the Tennis Option Analysis.xls workbook.

CHAPTER SUMMARY

Although business decisions are not made solely on the basis of money, financial considerations play a significant role in the decision-making process and, therefore, must be analyzed carefully. As you learned in this chapter, Excel provides a host of tools to help in this process. In Level 1, you learned about some of the basic functions used to calculate the elements of a loan, including PMT, RATE, NPER, PV, and FV, and how they affect the positive and negative cash flows of the financial transaction.

In Level 2, a projected cash flow estimate was presented, including an amortization table, to evaluate how a proposed financial endeavor would affect the cash flow of a company. This analysis involved calculating the principal and interest payments with PPMT and IPMT; calculating the cumulative principal and interest payments with CUMPRINC and CUMIPMT; calculating depreciation using the straight line method; and calculating taxes. Level 3 extended the analysis to explore the profitability of a financial venture by calculating the NPV and IRR, and determining the ROI and payback period.

The financial functions explored in this chapter are only a small subset of the many available in Excel. Some examples are the financial functions that allow you to calculate values based on variable interest rates or uneven compounding periods. You can use the Help system in Excel to explore the different types of financial functions available.

CONCEPTUAL REVIEW

Match the following lettered items with Questions 1 through 16.

A. Compound Interest	E. IPMT	I. Payback Period	M. RATE
B. Type	F. IRR	J. PMT	N. ROI
C. CUMPRINC	G. NPER	K. PPMT	O. Simple Interest
D. FV	H. NPV	L. PV	P. SLN

1. _____ Interest calculated based on original principal regardless of the previous interest earned

2. _____ Interest calculated based on previous interest earned and principal

3. _____Function to calculate the interest percentage per period of a financial transaction

4. _____Function to calculate the value at the beginning of a financial transaction

5. _____Function to calculate value of the end of a financial transaction

6. _____Function to calculate periodic payments in or out of a financial transaction

7. _____When 0, indicates that payments will be made at the end of each compounding period

8. _____Function to calculate the number of compounding periods

9. _____Function to calculate straight line depreciation based on the initial capital investment, number of years to be depreciated, and salvage value

10. _____Function to calculate the amount of a periodic payment that is interest in a given period

11. _____Function to calculate the amount of a specific periodic payment that is principal in a given period

12. _____Function to calculate the cumulative principal paid between two periods

13. _____Function to determine the value of a variable set of cash flows discounted to its present value

14. _____Function to determine the rate of return, where the net present value of the cash flows is 0

15. _____The calculation of total cash flows excluding the initial investment divided by the initial investment

16. _____ The number of years it will take to recoup the initial investment

17. Assume that you are investing $5000 in a savings plan today and will make additional contributions of $100 per quarter. The plan pays 6% interest per year compounded quarterly. Write a formula to determine how much your savings will be worth in five years.

18. Write a formula to determine the yearly interest rate being charged by the bank on a $175,000, 30-year mortgage. You make a monthly mortgage payment of $2000 and the value of the loan at the end of 30 years is 0. Interest is compounded monthly.

19. Assume that you are buying a car for $23,500 with a $2000 down payment, and you are borrowing the rest from a bank at 6.5% annual interest compounded monthly. Your monthly payment is $350. Write a formula to determine the number of years it will take you to pay off this loan.

20. Consider a $100,000 mortgage at 6% annual interest compounded monthly, to be paid back over the next 20 years. The loan will have a $10,000 balloon payment due at the end of the loan. Write a formula to determine the payment that must be made each month on this loan.

21. Assume that you have been left an inheritance and want to save part of it toward the purchase of a car upon graduation, which is three years from now. Write a formula to determine the amount of money you need to invest now to have $15,000 at the end of the three-year period. Assume that you will place this money in a CD that pays 3% interest compounded quarterly and that you will be making no additional deposits into this account.

22. Write a formula to determine the amount of money that can be depreciated each year, using straight line depreciation, for a new packaging machine purchased by your company. The machine originally cost $100,000 and has a useful life of 7 years and an estimated salvage value of $7800.

CASE PROBLEMS

Level 1 – Evaluating Loan Options for Flowers By Diana

Finance

Diana Bullard currently rents space for her small florist business. As her business continues to grow, Diana has decided to purchase her own building. She has selected a site and now requires financing. After meeting with several banks to discuss financing options for a mortgage, Diana has the data she needs to analyze her options. She lists the purchase price of the building and the different values for each of the loan variables together with the other data inputs in an Excel workbook named Loan.xls. Her analysis must also take into account the following:

- **Down payment**—The amount of money Diana will pay at the time she purchases the building. The difference between the sale price and the down payment is the loan value—the face value of the loan.
- **Points**—The additional charges banks sometimes require when lending a mortgage. Banks usually offer mortgage loans in a variety of interest rate and point combinations. Frequently, loans with higher points have lower interest rates. One point equals one percent of the loan value, so 1 point on a $7500 loan is $75.
- **Fees**—The additional amounts banks sometimes charge when lending a mortgage. These amounts vary by bank and loan type. Typical charges include application fees, appraisal fees, credit report fees, and so on.

Your task is to complete the Loan worksheet for Diana, using cell references whenever possible. The formulas in cells G8 through K8 should be written so that they can be copied down the column to calculate values for each of the options listed. These formulas should also automatically update if the mortgage value is updated. Loan options 1–7 are all compounded monthly.

Complete the following:

1. Open the workbook named **Loan.xls** in the Chapter 6 folder, and then save it as **Loan Analysis.xls**.

2. In the Loan Value column, calculate the face value of this mortgage.

3. In the Monthly Payment column, calculate the monthly mortgage payment for this loan amount based on the loan value you just calculated. Use the corresponding loan duration and nominal interest rate indicated.

4. In the Actual Amount Borrowed column, calculate the actual amount Diana will borrow, subtracting the points and fees from the loan value.

5. To take these fees into account, the lender is required by law to disclose the APR of the loan—the *annual percentage rate of interest being charged*. However, different banks calculate APR in different ways, including or excluding different fees. So, you will calculate the APR based on the actual amount borrowed, which you just calculated. Use this amount as the present value of the loan, the monthly payment you calculated in Step 3, and the corresponding loan duration to calculate an actual annual interest rate being charged on this loan (APR).

6. In the Payment with Balloon column, use the nominal interest rate and loan value (column G) to determine the monthly loan payment if you altered the loan to include a $10,000 balloon payment at the end of the loan.

7. The building seller has also offered Diana a private loan for 80% of the value of the building. In return, Diana must pay $8000 per quarter for the next 10 years. Determine the annual interest rate being charged (cell E17). Inputs do not have to be explicitly listed elsewhere.

8. Diana is negotiating with the seller and is willing to pay $5000 *per quarter* at 7.5% interest per year compounded quarterly. She will borrow everything but a 5% down payment. Determine how many years it will take to pay off the loan (cell E18). Inputs do not have to be explicitly listed elsewhere.

9. Eight years ago, Diana invested in a bank CD worth $10,000. The CD has earned 4.25% annual interest compounded yearly. Determine (True/False) if Diana has sufficient funds from this CD for Option #1's down payment (E19).

10. Diana has decided that she prefers a bank loan and, given cash flow issues, wants the loan with the smallest payment. Highlight in light turquoise the cell containing the payment of the loan Diana should select.

11. Save and close the Loan Analysis.xls workbook.

Level 2 – Creating a Mortgage Calculator for TriState Savings & Loan

Finance

You have been working as a loan officer at TriState Savings & Loan for just over six months. Most of the work you do involves dealing with mortgages for home buyers and small business owners. Frequently, prospective buyers come in seeking information about payments for a particular size mortgage and/or the maximum size mortgage they can obtain for a particular payment. They also frequently require information on the tax implications of their selected mortgages, including cumulative yearly interest and depreciation. The answers to these questions vary based on the interest rates currently being offered and the terms the potential buyer is seeking, such as loan duration, balloon payments, and so on.

Although you have found some excellent Web sites that perform the necessary calculations, relying on the Web is sometimes problematic. You can just as easily construct this type of mortgage calculator in Excel, which is what you will do in these steps.

Complete the following:

1. Open a new workbook and save it as **Mortgage Calculator.xls** in the Chapter 6 folder. Rename Sheet1 as "Calculator" and include the following elements:

   - First, construct a small mortgage calculator in which you can fill in the data inputs for the value of the mortgage, annual rate, loan duration, balloon payment, and number of payment periods per year. Then, using this data, calculate the payment for the mortgage. Assume the payment is rounded to the nearest cent. The calculator should be easy to read with data inputs and outputs clearly defined (labeled); use formatting options to make the worksheet easy to read and use.
   - Below the mortgage calculator on the same worksheet, create an amortization table for the loan, organized as follows:

Period Number	Remaining Principal	Interest Payment	Principal Payment

   The table should be able to accommodate a maximum mortgage duration of 30 years, assuming monthly payments. The remaining principal should start out by referencing the calculator's principal value, and thereafter reflect the previous remaining principal value and principal payment. The interest and principal payment formulas should be written so that if any of the calculator elements change, these amounts will be automatically updated. They should also be written so that they can be copied down the column for each corresponding period.

   Challenge: To avoid #NUM! errors in periods past the end of the loan, nest your principal and interest payment formulas inside an IF statement to return a 0 if no further interest or principal payments are required.

2. To test the calculator, use the following customer inputs: determine the monthly payment for Zach Jones, who wants a 15-year $150,000 mortgage. The current annual interest rate is 6.5% compounded quarterly. Assume no additional points or fees.

3. On a separate worksheet named "Tax," create a table listing years 1–30 and calculate the following:

- Cumulative interest payments for each year. Write a formula that automatically calculates this value for the corresponding periods so that it can be copied down for each year. Assume that the loans all begin in January so that no "partial" years need to be calculated. Note that in order to accommodate variable periods (months, quarters, and so on), the beginning and ending periods must be formulas that reference the number of periods per year on your mortgage calculator. (*Hint*: to automatically determine the starting period, take the year number multiplied by the number of periods per year, and then subtract one less than the number of periods per year.)
- In three adjacent columns, calculate the value of the expected tax deduction for tax rates of 15%, 28%, and 32% for the corresponding year (interest payments * tax rate). Your formula should copy both down the column and across the row. Enter the tax rate in a row above the corresponding column.
- For sample data, use the values from the loan for Zach Jones.

4. In some cases, the mortgages being applied for are by small business owners who want to buy the properties for their business endeavors. For these customers, it would also be helpful to provide them with depreciation estimates. Create a separate worksheet named "Depreciation" to calculate the depreciation. Include the following:

- At the top of the table, list the inputs that will be required: asset value (which will differ from mortgage to mortgage, so it needs to be entered directly), salvage value, and asset life (1–20).
- Just below the input area, calculate the yearly depreciable value using straight line depreciation.
- Next, create a table below the straight line depreciation to calculate the depreciation for each year (1–20) based on the double-declining balance method (DDB). For more details on how to use the DDB function, refer to the Excel Help system. Assume the default factor will be used and, therefore, can be omitted. Your table should include the year and the depreciable amount as follows:

Year:	DDB

- Enter the following test data: asset value of $170,000 with a 15-year life and a salvage value of $5000.

5. Save the changes to your Mortgage Calculator.xls workbook. Then use the Save As option to create a copy of the entire workbook named **Mortgage Calculator2.xls**. Modify your inputs and formulas on the Calculator worksheet so that you can enter a known monthly payment, duration, and interest rate to calculate the associated mortgage value as output. Double-check that all of your other formulas work: amortization table, taxes, and depreciation. Use the following example for your test data: Kelly Hamilton wants to buy a building she plans to use as rental property. If she can make monthly payments of $850 per month for the next 30 years, and then make a balloon payment of $10,000, how large a mortgage can she take, assuming that the current interest rate on a 30-year mortgage is 6% per year compounded monthly? For depreciation, assume an asset value of 95% of the loan value, a salvage value of $0, and a depreciable life of 20 years.

6. Save and close both the Mortgage Calculator.xls workbook and the Mortgage Calculator2.xls workbook.

Level 3 – Analyzing Purchasing Versus Leasing Options for CKG Auto

**Operations
Management**

CKG Auto compact car manufacturing assembly plants rely on parts from multiple outside vendors and internal subassembly plants. Currently, these parts are all transported via independent trucking firms for negotiated fees based on actual tons shipped and miles. The operations management group has been dissatisfied lately with the service levels provided by these outside trucking companies, as well as with the rising costs of roughly 7% per year for the last two years. These costs are expected to rise in the foreseeable future at similar rates, according to industry analysts. So, the operations management group is beginning a study to determine if purchasing or leasing a fleet of trucks would be a more cost-effective solution over the next seven years. To do so, the group has compiled some of the costs for each transport option, as follows:

(1) Trucking by others—Using several different trucking carriers, the CKG Auto compact car manufacturing group currently pays $4,000,000 annually in trucking fees. Again, these costs are expected to rise at an annual rate of 7%. All costs are considered expenses, which can be used to reduce income for purposes of calculating taxes.

(2) Buying trucks—If CKG Auto purchased a fleet of 20 trucks, the cost of such a purchase would be based on the following:

- The model of truck being considered with trailers has been estimated at $125,000 per truck. This amount will be spent in year 0 (now).
- This purchase would be funded using a bank loan. The bank is willing to lend the money at a 5¾% annual interest rate compounded quarterly over the next four years. A 5% down payment will be required, which can be funded from current assets.

- The operations management group has been directed to assume that if CKG Auto purchases this fleet, it would be depreciated using straight line depreciation over the full seven-year period, assuming a salvage value of 10% of the original purchase price.
- Operating costs for year 1 are estimated at $1.25 per mile; this includes driver wages, gas, insurance, maintenance, fees, and licenses. It is also assumed that each truck will average 100,000 miles per year. For next year (year 1) and all subsequent years, assume a cost increase of 5% per year.
- For the calculation of taxes, CKG Auto can deduct from each year's income the following: operating costs, the interest portion of the loan payments, and depreciation.

(3) Leasing trucks—If CKG Auto leases a fleet of 20 trucks, the cost of such a lease would be based on the following:

- There will be an upfront signing fee of $12,500 per truck due at signing (year 0). These fees will be paid directly out of cash assets and no additional financing will be required. These fees can be used to reduce income in year 0 for tax purposes.
- Each year, the lease cost will be a flat fee of $25,000 per truck for each of the next seven years. This fee is fixed for the duration of the lease based on a 100,000 per mile limit per year per truck.
- Operating costs for year 1 are estimated at $1.25 per mile; this includes driver wages, gas, insurance, maintenance, fees, and licenses. It is assumed that each truck will average 100,000 miles per year. For next year (year 1) and all subsequent years, assume a cost increase of 5% per year.
- Because this is an operating lease, there is no depreciation. The entire cost of the lease is considered an expense and can be used to reduce income for purposes of calculating taxes.

Your task is to analyze the various options for CKG Auto to determine which is the most viable. Complete the following:

1. Open a new workbook and save it as **Lease vs Buy.xls** in the Chapter 6 folder. Begin by setting up three separate worksheets, one for each option, with appropriate sheet names and titles.

2. For each option, calculate the net costs after taxes for each year, starting with year 0 through year 7, as follows:

- For year 0, list any capital expenditures (purchase option) and/or upfront fees (lease option).
- For years 1–7, list the costs including any operating expenses, leasing or trucking fees paid in that year, any associated depreciation, and interest (purchase option). Remember that the $4 million for trucking costs will go up by 7% in year 1 for the first option.

- Multiply all costs (except capital expenditures) by the marginal tax rate of 25%.
- Then subtract this tax savings from the costs to arrive at the net costs after taxes. For year 0, only consider monies paid toward leases and/or purchases—not the current costs of trucking—and keep in mind that only fees, not purchases, will result in tax savings.

3. Insert a fourth worksheet named "Comparison" and include the following on this worksheet:

- List the net cost after taxes for each year for each option in three sequential rows, referencing the original worksheets so that any subsequent changes will be automatically reflected on this sheet.
- Skip several rows and then begin a row to calculate the cost savings between using the current trucking method (by others) and purchasing a fleet; and then in the next row, the costs savings between the current trucking method and leasing. Your Comparison worksheet should have a format similar to the one in Table 6.4.

Table 6.4: Comparison worksheet

Net Costs after Taxes:	Year 0	Year 1	Year 2	Year 3	Year 4	Year 5	Year 6	Year 7
Trucking by Others								
Purchasing								
Leasing								
Cost Savings Comparisons	Year 0	Year 1	Year 2	Year 3	Year 4	Year 5	Year 6	Year 7
Trucking by Others vs. Purchasing								
Trucking by Others vs. Leasing								

- Regardless of which signs you've used in your analysis so far, express a cost savings as a positive number. (For example, if costs for shipping by others for year 1 is $10,000 after taxes, and the costs for shipping with purchased trucks in year 1 is $6000 after taxes, express the cost savings as a positive $4000.)

4. Determine the net present value of the cost savings cash flows (if any) between trucking by others versus purchasing trucks for years 0 through 7, for hurdles rates between 10% and 20%. In a similar way, determine the net present value of the costs savings cash flows between trucking by others versus leasing trucks.

5. Calculate the internal rate of return for the cost savings cash flows (trucking by others versus purchasing, and trucking by others versus leasing).

6. Calculate the return on investment and payback period for the purchasing option.

7. Make a recommendation of which method to use for trucking (by others, purchasing, or leasing). Highlight in yellow the row containing the net cost savings of the option you recommend. In a separate area on the worksheet, highlighted in yellow, explain the reason for your choice.

8. Save and close the Lease vs Buy.xls workbook.

Organizing Data for Effective Analysis
Marketing: Transforming Raw Data into Various Formats

> *"There is no such thing as too much planning and tracking."*
> —Indra Nooyi

LEARNING OBJECTIVES

Level 1

Import text data into a worksheet
Concatenate values and extract characters from a text string
Parse text using the Convert Text to Columns Wizard
Analyze data by creating subtotals
Create, sort, and filter an Excel list

Level 2

Import data stored in a database into Excel
Use dates and times in calculations
Analyze data using a PivotTable report
Create a PivotChart report
Import information from the Web into Excel using a Web query

Level 3

Understand markup languages and XML
Import XML data into Excel as an XML list
Add an XML map to a workbook
Export XML data from Excel into an XML document
Map elements in an XML document to a workbook

FUNCTIONS COVERED IN THIS CHAPTER

CONCATENATE
FIND
LEFT
RIGHT
SEARCH
TODAY
TRIM
YEARFRAC

CHAPTER INTRODUCTION

In this book, you have used Excel to analyze data in a variety of ways. You can enter data into a worksheet in several ways—you might type data into cells, import data into a worksheet, or link data to another document or file. The data contained in most spreadsheets is numeric, but a significant amount of text is often used to describe that numeric data. Excel has many functions and tools that you can use to manage and analyze nonnumeric data, such as text, dates, and times. You can also use another tool, called a PivotTable report, to analyze data from a variety of perspectives.

This chapter's main focus is on working with data, especially large amounts of it. You can import data stored in a text file, a database, and an XML document into a worksheet. XML, which stands for Extensible Markup Language, was developed as a method to share data and a description of that data in an open, nonproprietary format for a variety of purposes and for use by different programs. Imported data, especially nonnumeric data, is rarely in the desired format, so it is important for you to know how to manipulate imported data into the format you need for analysis. In this chapter, you will look at ways to manage large amounts of data by using lists, a PivotTable report, and XML.

CASE SCENARIO

Marketing

TheZone just received some contact information from a distributor that recently went out of business. TheZone needs to contact the retailers serviced by this distributor to ensure that they will still carry TheZone products. The data is for the Pacific sales region, which includes the states of Alaska, California, Hawaii, Oregon, and Washington. Barbara Jones has been assigned the task of importing data about the retailers that ordered sporting goods and sports apparel from TheZone into a format that will make it easy to sort and arrange the data in ways to help the marketing department contact these retailers. Barbara wants to import this data into Excel so she can analyze it. She plans to organize this data so she can determine how long each retailer has ordered TheZone products and identify the top retailers in each state and city. Barbara will use the tools in Excel to manage, organize, and analyze the data she obtained from the distributor.

LEVEL 1
IMPORTING AND STRUCTURING TEXT DATA IN EXCEL WORKSHEETS

EXCEL 2003 SKILLS TRAINING

- **Add records with a data form**
- **Add subtotals to worksheets**
- **Bring information into Excel from external sources**
- **Create and apply custom filters**
- **Delete records with a data form**
- **Filter lists using AutoFilter**
- **Find records with a data form**
- **Import text files into an existing worksheet**
- **Remove subtotals**
- **Sort a list on multiple fields**
- **Sort a list on one field**
- **Use the List button and Toggle Row button on the List toolbar**

WORKING WITH TEXT DATA

A common way of storing data so that it is usable in other programs is to save it in a **comma-delimited file**. Because this format separates the values in each record with commas, data stored in this way is also called **comma-separated values**, or **CSV**. Excel can convert data stored in a comma-delimited file so that each value in a record appears in a separate cell of the worksheet into which you import it. A paragraph mark identifies the end of each record in a comma-delimited file.

The data that Barbara received from the distributor is not stored in a comma-delimited file, so her job is a challenging one. The data for the retailers in Alaska, shown in Figure 7.1, shows that each company's name, address, city, state, zip code, and phone number appear on separate lines in the text file.

Figure 7.1: Sporting goods retailers in Alaska

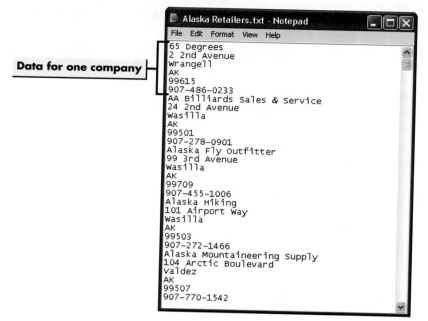

Data for one company

```
Alaska Retailers.txt - Notepad
File  Edit  Format  View  Help
65 Degrees
2 2nd Avenue
Wrangell
AK
99615
907-486-0233
AA Billiards Sales & Service
24 2nd Avenue
Wasilla
AK
99501
907-278-0901
Alaska Fly Outfitter
99 3rd Avenue
Wasilla
AK
99709
907-455-1006
Alaska Hiking
101 Airport Way
Wasilla
AK
99503
907-272-1466
Alaska Mountaineering Supply
104 Arctic Boulevard
Valdez
AK
99507
907-770-1542
```

The first goal when working with unstructured data is to determine the format you need so you can find the best way to change the unstructured data into structured data. Because the data for the sporting goods retailers in Alaska is not stored in a comma-delimited file, Barbara cannot import the data into Excel in the format she needs. She decides to copy the data from the text file and paste it into a new workbook. After completing this task, each line in the text file appears in a separate row in the worksheet. Barbara's goal for the unstructured data she received is to be able to change its format so that she can list the retailers by city, state, and zip code. To help the marketing department plan for its staff to contact these retailers, Barbara also needs to count the number of retailers by city. She needs to change the data into a format so that the company name, street address, city, state, zip code, and phone number appear in different cells, and so that the complete information for each company appears in a separate row. After she changes the data into comma-separated values, she can use the sorting and list tools in Excel to generate the list of retailers in various ways as requested by the marketing department.

Barbara's new workbook, Alaska Retailers.xls, contains all of the data from the text file. Notice that the data for each company appears in six rows in the worksheet, as shown in Figure 7.2.

Figure 7.2: Data pasted into Excel

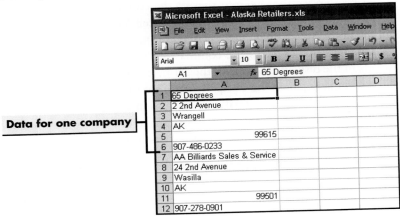

Data for one company

Barbara could move each cell containing a particular company's data into one row, but this work would be very labor intensive and might result in errors. Barbara instead decides to use a text function to combine or **concatenate** the information from multiple cells into one cell. To change the data into comma-separated values so it is in a format that makes the data easy to use in the future, she decides to insert commas between each value in a record at the same time.

Combining Text Using the CONCATENATE Function

By concatenating the data in the six cells that make up one company's information, Barbara can change the data into the desired format in which the name, address, city, state, zip code, and phone number for each company appear in one row in the worksheet. The **CONCATENATE** function combines the values in a range of cells into one text item in a new cell. The values can be text strings, numbers, or references to single cells.

The syntax for the CONCATENATE function is as follows:

```
=CONCATENATE(text1,text2,...)
```

In the CONCATENATE function, text1 and text2 are the text, number, or cell reference that contains the characters you want to join into a single text item in a new cell. Another method of concatenating text is to use the concatenation operator (&) instead of the CONCATENATE function. In this case, the formula syntax is =text1 & text2... Barbara enters the following CONCATENATE function into cell B1 to make this change and also to insert commas between the values in each row:

```
=CONCATENATE(A1,",",A2,",",A3,",",A4,",",A5,",",A6)
```

This CONCATENATE function combines the information in cells A1 through A6 as a new value in cell B1. Notice the different uses of the commas in the function. The first comma in the function, which follows the reference to cell A1, separates the first argument in the function from the second one. The second comma in the function, which appears inside the quotation marks, encloses the comma that will appear between the first and second arguments in the displayed results of the formula. The commas in quotation marks in the rest of the formula separate the company data into individual fields, as shown in cell B1 in Figure 7.3. Notice that the original data remains in cells A1:A6. If you deleted the data in cells A1:A6, the displayed results of the formula in cell B1 would contain only the commas that appear within the quotation marks because the function refers to these cells.

Figure 7.3: Results of the CONCATENATE function

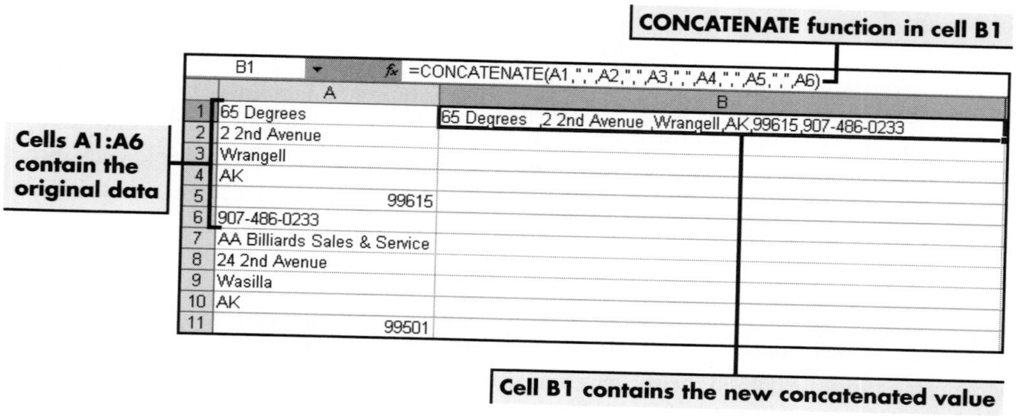

CONCATENATE function in cell B1

Cells A1:A6 contain the original data

Cell B1 contains the new concatenated value

Barbara copies the formula in cell B1 to all the cells in column B that have an entry in column A by double-clicking the fill handle in cell B1. The way that Excel copies cells with relative cell references creates a problem with the information in column B. The formula in cell B2 concatenates cells A2, A3, A4, A5, A6, and A7 together, resulting in an entry that incorrectly combines the data from two companies. The structure of the data in groups of six rows in column A means that the information in column B is correct in every sixth row. Barbara could delete all the incorrectly concatenated rows, but there are 606 rows in this worksheet. Manually deleting the incorrect rows would take a lot of time and might result in some unintentional errors. She needs a more consistent way to remove the incorrect entries.

One method is to look for a unique feature that separates the rows of data she wants (the correct rows) from the incorrect rows. Barbara notices that each cell in column B that contains the information in the order she needs ends with a phone number. She can use the phone number to select the correct rows (containing the information for one company and in the proper order) from the incorrect rows. Each correct row in column B ends with a phone number that is displayed as -#### (a dash followed by four numbers). She decides to use this format to extract the correct rows of data.

Extracting Characters from a Text String

Barbara decides to use the RIGHT function to extract the last five characters of the text strings in column B. The **RIGHT** function returns the last character or characters in a text string, based on the number of characters specified. The syntax for the RIGHT function is as follows:

$$=RIGHT(text,num\_chars)$$

In this function, text is the text string or cell reference that contains the characters you want to extract, and num_chars specifies the number of characters that you want the RIGHT function to extract.

The RIGHT function lets Barbara determine that the dash character, which indicates that the cell contains a correct row of data, is located in the correct position in the text string. The RIGHT function extracts the specified number of characters from the end or "right side" of a text string. The counterpart to this function is the **LEFT** function, which extracts characters from the beginning or "left side" of a text string. The dash character is located five positions from the end of the text string when it appears in a correct row. Barbara enters the following function into cell C1:

$$=RIGHT(B1,5)$$

The RIGHT function appears in Figure 7.4. Notice that the function returns a value of 233 in cell C1.

Figure 7.4: Results of the RIGHT function

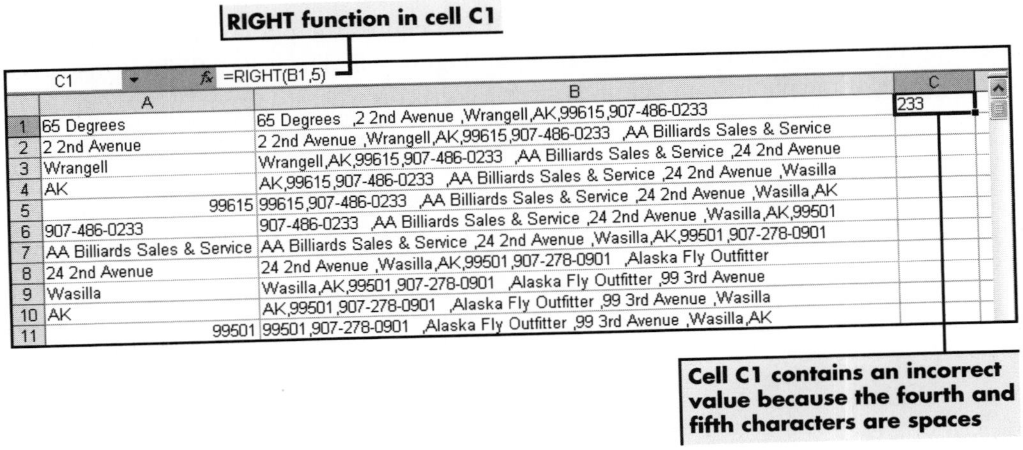

RIGHT function in cell C1

	A	B	C
	C1	▾ ƒ× =RIGHT(B1,5)	
	A	B	233
1	65 Degrees	65 Degrees ,2 2nd Avenue ,Wrangell,AK,99615,907-486-0233	
2	2 2nd Avenue	2 2nd Avenue ,Wrangell,AK,99615,907-486-0233 ,AA Billiards Sales & Service	
3	Wrangell	Wrangell,AK,99615,907-486-0233 ,AA Billiards Sales & Service ,24 2nd Avenue	
4	AK	AK,99615,907-486-0233 ,AA Billiards Sales & Service ,24 2nd Avenue ,Wasilla	
5	99615	99615,907-486-0233 ,AA Billiards Sales & Service ,24 2nd Avenue ,Wasilla,AK	
6	907-486-0233	907-486-0233 ,AA Billiards Sales & Service ,24 2nd Avenue ,Wasilla,AK,99501	
7	AA Billiards Sales & Service	AA Billiards Sales & Service ,24 2nd Avenue ,Wasilla,AK,99501,907-278-0901	
8	24 2nd Avenue	24 2nd Avenue ,Wasilla,AK,99501,907-278-0901 ,Alaska Fly Outfitter	
9	Wasilla	Wasilla,AK,99501,907-278-0901 ,Alaska Fly Outfitter ,99 3rd Avenue	
10	AK	AK,99501,907-278-0901 ,Alaska Fly Outfitter ,99 3rd Avenue ,Wasilla	
11	99501	99501,907-278-0901 ,Alaska Fly Outfitter ,99 3rd Avenue ,Wasilla,AK	

Cell C1 contains an incorrect value because the fourth and fifth characters are spaces

Removing Spaces from a Text String

The RIGHT function returns the value 233 in cell C1 instead of extracting a dash followed by four numbers as Barbara anticipated. Barbara examines the data in cell B1 and confirms that it is a correct row that includes the company's name, address, city, state, zip code, and phone number. Often, data that you copy and paste from another source contains space characters at the end of the values. Because these spaces can cause errors in Excel formulas, Barbara decides to examine the data more carefully to determine if extra spaces are causing the error. Barbara selects cell A6, which is the source of the phone number in cell B1, and then clicks the Formula Bar. She notices that there are two blank spaces at the end of the phone number. (The blank spaces can be "seen" by using the right arrow key to move to the rightmost position of the cell contents in the Formula Bar.) Barbara could use the LEN function to determine the number of characters in the text string, but because she already knows that there are blank spaces at the end of the phone number, she decides to use another text function to remove the extra spaces. The **TRIM** function removes all spaces in a text string except for the single spaces between words. This function can be very useful when importing data from another data source in which the data might contain spaces at the end of values. The syntax for the TRIM function is as follows:

```
=TRIM(text)
```

In the TRIM function, text is the text string or cell reference that contains the space(s) that you want to remove. Barbara changes the formula in cell B1 by nesting it within a TRIM function. In this formula, the CONCATENATE function produces the text to be trimmed. The new formula in cell B1 is as follows:

```
=TRIM(CONCATENATE(A1,",",A2,",",A3,",",A4,",",A5,",",A6))
```

Barbara's TRIM function removes the spaces at the end of the phone number and the value -0233 now appears in cell C1, as shown in Figure 7.5. The value -0233 is the last five characters of the phone number, indicating a correct row.

Figure 7.5: Results of the TRIM function

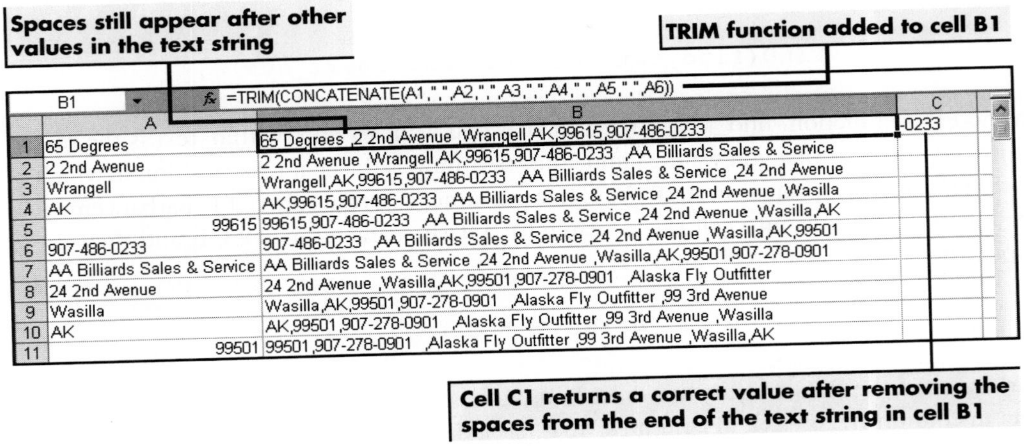

Spaces still appear after other values in the text string

TRIM function added to cell B1

	B1	▼	ƒx	=TRIM(CONCATENATE(A1,",",A2,",",A3,",",A4,",",A5,",",A6))		C
	A			B		-0233
1	65 Degrees		65 Degrees ,2 2nd Avenue ,Wrangell,AK,99615,907-486-0233		
2	2 2nd Avenue		2 2nd Avenue ,Wrangell,AK,99615,907-486-0233 ,AA Billiards Sales & Service		
3	Wrangell		Wrangell ,AK,99615,907-486-0233 ,AA Billiards Sales & Service ,24 2nd Avenue		
4	AK		AK,99615,907-486-0233 ,AA Billiards Sales & Service ,24 2nd Avenue ,Wasilla,AK		
5		99615	99615,907-486-0233 ,AA Billiards Sales & Service ,24 2nd Avenue ,Wasilla,AK,99501		
6	907-486-0233		907-486-0233 ,AA Billiards Sales & Service ,24 2nd Avenue ,Wasilla,AK,99501,907-278-0901		
7	AA Billiards Sales & Service		AA Billiards Sales & Service ,24 2nd Avenue ,Wasilla,AK,99501,907-278-0901 ,Alaska Fly Outfitter		
8	24 2nd Avenue		24 2nd Avenue ,Wasilla,AK,99501,907-278-0901 ,Alaska Fly Outfitter ,99 3rd Avenue		
9	Wasilla		Wasilla,AK,99501,907-278-0901 ,Alaska Fly Outfitter ,99 3rd Avenue ,Wasilla		
10	AK		AK,99501,907-278-0901 ,Alaska Fly Outfitter ,99 3rd Avenue ,Wasilla,AK		
11		99501	99501,907-278-0901 ,Alaska Fly Outfitter ,99 3rd Avenue ,Wasilla,AK		

Cell C1 returns a correct value after removing the spaces from the end of the text string in cell B1

Barbara notices that the TRIM function removed the spaces only at the end of the concatenated value displayed in cell B1. She can see that there are also spaces at the end of the value in A1 and at the end of other values as well by examining the spaces between the values separated by commas in cell B1 and in other cells in column B. She changes the formula in cell B1 to trim each value, which removes all extra spaces in the concatenated text string, to the following:

```
=CONCATENATE(TRIM(A1),",",TRIM(A2),",",TRIM(A3),",",
       TRIM(A4),",",TRIM(A5),",",TRIM(A6))
```

Barbara's new formula correctly returns the value -0233 in cell C1 and also trims the values in cells A1:A6 so that the concatenated value in cell B1 does not contain any spaces, other than the ones between words. Barbara copies the new formula to other cells in column B, and then copies the formula in cell C1 to other cells in column C.

Determining the Position of a Character Within a Text String

Because every correct row in column B includes a phone number as the last text string, valid rows of data in column B have cells in column C that begin with a dash character in the first position, followed by four digits. Incorrect rows of data will display something other than a dash character followed by four digits in column C. Barbara could look for the dash character manually, but decides instead to use another text function to locate the position of the dash character in row C. The **FIND** function returns the starting position of one text value within another text value. The FIND function is case sensitive, so searching for "d" returns a different result than searching for "D." The **SEARCH** function does the same thing as the FIND function, but the SEARCH function is not case sensitive. The syntax for the FIND function is as follows:

$$=FIND(find\_text,within\_text,start\_num)$$

In the FIND function, find_text is the text that you want to find, within_text is the text containing the text that you want to find, and start_num is the character position in which to start the search. If you omit start_num, Excel assumes a start number of 1. Barbara enters the following formula into cell D1 to search for a dash character in cell C1, and then she copies the formula down column D:

$$=FIND("-",C1)$$

Barbara used the RIGHT function in column C to extract the last five characters of the data in column B. Any cell in column C that has a dash character in the first position is a correct row, in which case the FIND function in column D returns a value of 1 to indicate that the dash character appears as the first character in the string. A dash located in any other position (second, third, fourth, or fifth) returns another value (2, 3, 4, or 5). If a value in column C does not contain a dash, a "#VALUE!" message is returned, as shown in Figure 7.6.

Figure 7.6: Results of the FIND function

	B	C	D	E	F
1	65 Degrees,2 2nd Avenue,Wrangell,AK,99615,907-486-0233	-0233	1		
2	2 2nd Avenue,Wrangell,AK,99615,907-486-0233,AA Billiards Sales & Service	rvice	#VALUE!		
3	Wrangell,AK,99615,907-486-0233,AA Billiards Sales & Service,24 2nd Avenue	venue	#VALUE!		
4	AK,99615,907-486-0233,AA Billiards Sales & Service,24 2nd Avenue,Wasilla	silla	#VALUE!		
5	99615,907-486-0233,AA Billiards Sales & Service,24 2nd Avenue,Wasilla,AK	la,AK	#VALUE!		
6	907-486-0233,AA Billiards Sales & Service,24 2nd Avenue,Wasilla,AK,99501	99501	#VALUE!		
7	AA Billiards Sales & Service,24 2nd Avenue,Wasilla,AK,99501,907-278-0901	-0901	1		
8	24 2nd Avenue,Wasilla,AK,99501,907-278-0901,Alaska Fly Outfitter	itter	#VALUE!		
9	Wasilla,AK,99501,907-278-0901,Alaska Fly Outfitter,99 3rd Avenue	venue	#VALUE!		
10	AK,99501,907-278-0901,Alaska Fly Outfitter,99 3rd Avenue,Wasilla	silla	#VALUE!		
11	99501,907-278-0901,Alaska Fly Outfitter,99 3rd Avenue,Wasilla,AK	la,AK	#VALUE!		
12	907-278-0901,Alaska Fly Outfitter,99 3rd Avenue,Wasilla,AK,99709	99709	#VALUE!		
13	Alaska Fly Outfitter,99 3rd Avenue,Wasilla,AK,99709,907-455-1006	-1006	1		

Callouts: **Extra spaces are removed from the end of all values** — **FIND function in cell D1** — **"1" indicates a valid row** — **Error message indicates an invalid row**

Cell reference: D1 f_x =FIND("-",C1)

Sorting and Removing Invalid Data

Now that Barbara has created a method to determine which rows contain valid information, she needs to remove the rows that contain invalid data. To preserve her imported data and the work she has done, she renames this worksheet "Imported Data," and then uses the Paste Special command on the Edit menu and the Values option button in the Paste Special dialog box to copy the contents of the Imported Data worksheet into a new worksheet named CSV and to lock the values of each cell in the CSV worksheet. This action preserves the original data and eliminates the potential problem of automatically updating formulas as she modifies the data. Barbara needs to sort the data in the CSV worksheet to separate the valid rows from the invalid rows. She selects the entire CSV worksheet to select all the data it contains, and then she uses the Sort command on the Data menu to open the Sort dialog box. She selects column D as the sort field, as shown in Figure 7.7.

Figure 7.7: Sort dialog box

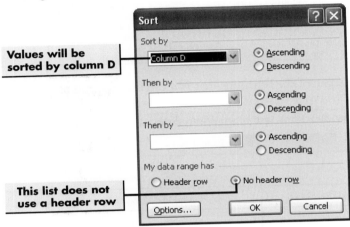

The data is sorted in ascending order on column D, which places the rows with valid entries (those with a "1" in column D) at the top of the document, as shown in Figure 7.8.

Figure 7.8: Data sorted on column D

Barbara then deletes the rows with a "#VALUE!" message in column D and deletes everything except the data in column B. Now, the data in column B is in a comma-delimited form—a single cell of data with commas separating the company name, street address, city, state, zip code, and phone number for each retailer, as shown in Figure 7.9.

Figure 7.9: Comma-delimited data

	A	B
1	65 Degrees,2 2nd Avenue,Wrangell,AK,99615,907-486-0233	
2	AA Billiards Sales & Service,24 2nd Avenue,Wasilla,AK,99501,907-278-0901	
3	Alaska Fly Outfitter,99 3rd Avenue,Wasilla,AK,99709,907-455-1006	
4	Alaska Hiking,101 Airport Way,Wasilla,AK,99503,907-272-1466	
5	Alaska Mountaineering Supply,104 Arctic Boulevard,Valdez,AK,99507,907-770-1542	
6	Alaska Outfitting Rentals,117 Arctic Boulevard,Valdez,AK,99901,907-225-1600	
7	Alaska SportMart,101 6th Avenue,Wasilla,AK,99507,907-346-1244	
8	Alaskan Experience Inc,139 Arena Avenue,Valdez,AK,99901,907-225-1750	
9	Alaskan Outfitters,171 Avenue Mall,Valdez,AK,99701,907-452-1811	
10	Anglerman's Inc,239 Business Boulevard,Soldotna,AK,99929,907-874-2229	
11	Anvil Outfitters,250 College Road,Soldotna,AK,99559,907-543-2290	
12	Apoc Design Inc,261 College Road,Soldotna,AK,99701,907-451-2300	

Table 7.1 shows some of the functions that you can use to manipulate data in Excel.

Table 7.1: Common functions that manipulate data

Function (Arguments)	Description
CLEAN(text)	Removes all nonprintable characters from a text string. Useful when importing data from an external data source.
CONCATENATE(text1,text2,...)	Joins two or more text strings into a single text string.
DOLLAR(number,decimals)	Converts a number to text in currency format with a dollar sign and the specified number of decimal places.
EXACT(text1,text2)	Compares two text strings to determine if they are identical (case sensitive).
FIND(find_text,within_text,start_num)	Finds one text string within another text string (case sensitive) using the start_num character as a starting point.
FIXED(number,decimals,no_commas)	Rounds a number to a specified number of decimals and returns the number as text with commas and a period.
LEFT(text,num_chars)	Returns the leftmost characters in a text string using num_chars as the starting point.
LEN(text)	Returns the number of characters in a text string.
LOWER(text)	Converts uppercase letters in a text string to lowercase.
MID(text,start_num,num_chars)	Returns a specific number of characters in a text string using start_num as the starting point.
PROPER(text)	Capitalizes the first letter in each word in a text string and converts all other letters to lowercase. Very useful when data has been improperly stored as uppercase characters.

Table 7.1: Common functions that manipulate data (cont.)

Function (Arguments)	Description
REPLACE(old_text,start_num,num_chars,new_text)	Replaces part of a text string with a new text string based on the number of characters specified in num_chars.
REPT(text,number_times)	Repeats a text string a specified number of times.
RIGHT(text,num_chars)	Returns the rightmost characters in a text string using num_chars as the starting point.
SEARCH(find_text,within_text,start_num)	Finds one text string within another text string (not case sensitive).
SUBSTITUTE(text,old_text,new_text,instance_num)	Substitutes new text for old text in a text string.
TEXT(value,format_text)	Converts a value to text in the specified number format.
TRIM(text)	Removes spaces from a text string, except for spaces between words. Useful when importing data from an external data source.
UPPER(text)	Converts lowercase letters in a text string to uppercase.
VALUE(text)	Converts a text string that represents a number (a number, date, or time) to a number.

WORKING WITH NONNUMERIC DATA

Now that Barbara has formatted the unstructured data into a list of comma-separated values, she can turn her attention to sorting the data for the marketing department. Each row in the worksheet contains the name, address, and phone number for each company that the marketing department needs to contact. Each cell containing data is a field. To sort the data in various ways, Barbara needs to separate the data so that each field appears in a separate column in the worksheet. She uses the Convert Text to Columns Wizard to separate the data into columns. As the name suggests, this wizard separates the values in a text string into columns or fields. You can determine how to divide (or parse) the text into columns in two ways. The first way is to identify the character that delimits (separates) the data. In Barbara's comma-delimited file, commas separate the data, so a comma is the delimiter. Another common delimiter is the tab character. The second way to parse data is to set field widths to identify the breaks between data that appears in columns. You use the fixed-width method when the data to parse does not include a consistent character to separate the field values. For example, you might have a line of data in which the first field occupies characters 1 through 10, the next field occupies characters 11 through 15, and so on. In this case, you could create a column break between characters 10 and 11, and then another column break between characters 15 and 16 to parse the data into columns.

How To

Use the Text to Columns Wizard to Parse Data

1. Select the column that contains the data to be converted from text to columns.

2. Click Data on the menu bar, and then click Text to Columns.

3. In Step 1, select the Delimited option button, and then click the Next button.

4. In Step 2, click the check box for the delimiter used in the data. See Figure 7.10.

Figure 7.10: Convert Text to Columns Wizard

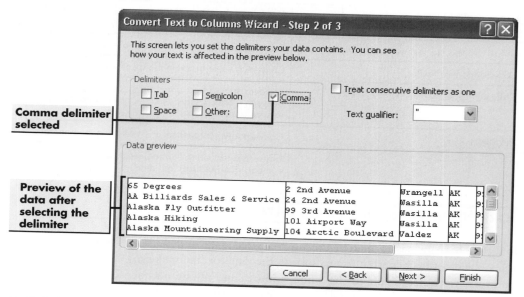

5. Click the Next button.

6. In Step 3, select the column data format for each column.

7. Click the Finish button.

Barbara uses the Convert Text to Columns Wizard to convert the comma-separated values to columns, as shown in Figure 7.11. Now, the data for each field appears in a separate column in the worksheet.

Figure 7.11: Comma-delimited data converted to columns

Each row contains data for one company

Each column contains data for one category

	A	B	C	D	E	F
1	65 Degrees	2 2nd Avenue	Wrangell	AK	99615	907-486-0233
2	AA Billiards Sales & Service	24 2nd Avenue	Wasilla	AK	99501	907-278-0901
3	Alaska Fly Outfitter	99 3rd Avenue	Wasilla	AK	99709	907-455-1006
4	Alaska Hiking	101 Airport Way	Wasilla	AK	99503	907-272-1466
5	Alaska Mountaineering Supply	104 Arctic Boulevard	Valdez	AK	99507	907-770-1542
6	Alaska Outfitting Rentals	117 Arctic Boulevard	Valdez	AK	99901	907-225-1600
7	Alaska SportMart	101 6th Avenue	Wasilla	AK	99507	907-346-1244
8	Alaskan Experience Inc	139 Arena Avenue	Valdez	AK	99901	907-225-1750
9	Alaskan Outfitters	171 Avenue Mall	Valdez	AK	99701	907-452-1811
10	Anglerman's Inc	239 Business Boulevard	Soldotna	AK	99929	907-874-2229
11	Anvil Outfitters	250 College Road	Soldotna	AK	99559	907-543-2290
12	Apoc Design Inc	261 College Road	Soldotna	AK	99701	907-451-2300

Labeling and Sorting Data

Now that the data is organized correctly, Barbara adds a row at the top of the worksheet (called a **header row**) and types labels that identify the data contained in each column. After she completes this task, Barbara needs to sort the data as requested by the marketing department; that is, first to sort the data by city, and then by zip code, and then by company name. Because she needs to sort the data by more than one column, she uses the Sort dialog box. She clicks Data on the menu bar, and then clicks Sort. Figure 7.12 shows the Sort dialog box with the City, Zip Code, and Company Name columns selected. Because Barbara added a header row to the worksheet, Excel automatically selects the Header row option button so that the header row is not included in the sort.

Figure 7.12: Sorting on three columns

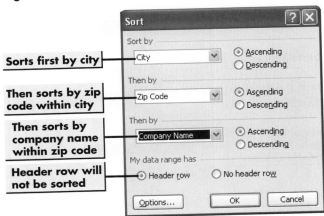

Sorts first by city

Then sorts by zip code within city

Then sorts by company name within zip code

Header row will not be sorted

After clicking the OK button, Barbara's worksheet looks like Figure 7.13. The rows are sorted in ascending order, first by city, then by zip code, and finally, by company name.

Figure 7.13: Data sorted by city, then by zip code, then by company name

Header row is not sorted

	A	B	C	D	E	F
1	Company Name	Address	City	State	Zip Code	Phone
2	Blue Sports Marketing	9209 Tongass Avenue	Anchorage	AK	99501	907-279-7272
3	Fifth Avenue Outfitters	300A University Avenue South	Anchorage	AK	99501	907-276-7335
4	Raven Sports	Upper Omalley Road	Anchorage	AK	99501	907-274-7372
5	Sunshine Outfitters	West Northern Boulevard	Anchorage	AK	99501	907-929-7867
6	Northerner Sport Shop	West 4th Avenue	Anchorage	AK	99503	907-272-7555
7	Play It Over Sports	7900 Spenard Road	Anchorage	AK	99503	907-278-7057
8	Snow Sports LLC	West 6th Avenue	Anchorage	AK	99503	907-272-7755
9	Suburban Outfitters	Richardson	Anchorage	AK	99504	907-333-8600
10	Glenn Ski & Sports	6330 South Cushman Street	Anchorage	AK	99507	907-349-6881
11	Travers Realty	Yenlo Street	Anchorage	AK	99507	907-346-8438
12	Southern Sports Authority	West Parks Highway	Anchorage	AK	99515	907-349-7665

Analyzing Data by Creating Subtotals

Barbara remembers that the marketing department needs a count of the number of retailers in each city and zip code, so she needs to be able to collapse and expand the data set. The **Subtotal tool** creates summary reports that quickly organize data into categories with subtotal calculations and lets you collapse and expand the level of detail in the report.

How To

Use the Subtotal Tool

1. Select the column that you want to summarize.
2. Click Data on the menu bar, and then click Subtotals to open the Subtotal dialog box. See Figure 7.14.

Figure 7.14: Subtotal dialog box

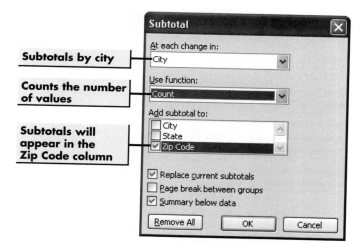

Subtotals by city

Counts the number of values

Subtotals will appear in the Zip Code column

3. Use the At each change in list box to select the category by which to group the data.
4. Use the Use function list box to select the aggregate function to use in the summary.
5. Use the Add subtotal to list box to select the column in which to place the subtotal.
6. Add check marks to the Replace current subtotals, Page break between groups, and Summary below data check boxes as necessary to replace any existing subtotals in the worksheet, print groups on separate pages, and create summaries as necessary.

Barbara uses the Subtotal tool to create a subtotal. The Subtotal tool creates an outline in the upper-left corner of the worksheet that you can use to expand or collapse the data by a specific category, in this case by city. Clicking the 1 button collapses the data set so that only the totals are shown, clicking the 2 button expands the data set to display only the subtotals (see Figure 7.15), and clicking the 3 button expands the data set to show each row included in the subtotals. Her worksheet now includes a summary row for each group of cities that calculates the number of retailers in each city. She prints this information for the marketing department so it can easily identify areas of the state in which the most retailers are located.

Figure 7.15: Subtotals by city

One limitation of the Subtotal tool is that it only works with one category and one subtotal calculation at a time. However, you can change the category by opening the Subtotal dialog box again and changing the At each change in, Use function, and Add subtotal to values. The data is grouped by common elements within the chosen category and you can expand or collapse individual groups by clicking the plus or minus boxes to the left of the row numbers shown in Figure 7.15. You can select entire hierarchy levels using the numbers in the upper-left corner of the worksheet.

To remove the subtotals from a worksheet, click Data on the menu bar, click Subtotals, and then click the Remove All button in the Subtotal dialog box.

CREATING AND WORKING WITH AN EXCEL LIST

Barbara's worksheet data is stored in a list structure in which the rows are independent and contain data organized into fields. Barbara's worksheet includes labels in the first row, and each retailer's information appears in a single row. Each column contains the same category of information in each row. For example, in column A, all values are company names. Barbara's worksheet is really just a simple database of information about retailers of sporting goods that are located in a specific geographic area. This arrangement of data is sometimes called a **flat-file database** because the data is stored in one table (or in this case, the data is stored in one worksheet). When working with data in a list structure, you can move cells of data to other areas in the worksheet without affecting the row in which the cell appears. This flexibility often causes problems when sorting and filtering data because you risk omitting a column or row from the selection and compromising the integrity of the data. For example, if you select the first five columns of data (company name, address, city, state, and zip code) and sort these rows, the values in the phone number column wouldn't be sorted with the rest of the data. The result would be a data set in which the phone numbers do not match the company name and address information.

When you are working in a worksheet that contains a list of information, as is the case with Barbara's worksheet, you can use the Excel List tools to work with all of the data in the list as a *unit* instead of as a *collection of individual cells*. An **Excel list** is a range of cells that you formalize as a single unit of data. When working with an Excel list, you should insert empty columns and rows around the list to segregate it from any other data in the work-sheet. (The exception is a list that begins in column A; in this case, you do not need to insert a blank column to the left of the first column of data.) When you sort or filter data in an Excel list, the data in the columns of each row automatically remains intact, thereby protecting the integrity of the data.

Best Practice

Deciding When to Use an Excel List

When you consider the enormous calculating power that Excel offers, it might surprise you to know that many users rely on Excel for list management. Many of the lists created in Excel would work equally well or better if they were managed using a database, but often users are more familiar with spreadsheets than databases. The flexibility of Excel lets the user "play" with the data and work out an organizational structure and supporting calculations that would require an expert's level of understanding to accomplish in a database. Creating an Excel

7

Level 1

list often bridges the gap between spreadsheets and simple databases. The database features of the Excel list protect the structure of the data, preventing the accidental deletion of rows or columns. The Excel list also adds many features that aren't available in an unstructured list, such as validation, sorting, and filtering, all of which can help you manage any set of related data. It is a good idea to use an Excel list to manage large amounts of data when your database skills are not sufficient to use a database to manage the same data.

Creating an Excel list lets you add some simple database functionality to a worksheet, but an Excel list has two important limitations that you should understand. First, the maximum number of rows and columns in a worksheet limits the number of records and fields you can have in your list to 65,536 rows and 256 columns. The second limitation is the fact that Excel must load the entire workbook into memory when you open it, which can lead to performance problems with very large lists.

Barbara decides to change the data in her worksheet to an Excel list. She selects any cell in the worksheet and then opens the Create List dialog box. Excel automatically detects the list range in the worksheet, which is why it is useful to separate the list from other data in the spreadsheet.

How To

Create an Excel List

1. Click any cell in the data that you want to format as an Excel list.
2. Click Data on the menu bar, point to List, and then click Create List. The Create List dialog box opens, as shown in Figure 7.16. Be certain that the correct data set appears in the dialog box. If the list contains a header row, be certain that the My list has headers check box contains a check mark.

Figure 7.16: Create List dialog box

Range for the Excel list

3. Click the OK button.

Barbara created the Excel list shown in Figure 7.17. An Excel list is enclosed with a dark blue line and list arrows appear in each cell in the header row.

Figure 7.17: Excel list

List arrows are added to the cells in the header row

	A	B	C	D	E	F
1	Company Name	Address	City	State	Zip Code	Phone
2	Blue Sports Marketing	9209 Tongass Avenue	Anchorage	AK	99501	907-279-7272
3	Fifth Avenue Outfitters	300A University Avenue South	Anchorage	AK	99501	907-276-7335
4	Raven Sports	Upper Omalley Road	Anchorage	AK	99501	907-274-7372
5	Sunshine Outfitters	West Northern Boulevard	Anchorage	AK	99501	907-929-7867
6	Northerner Sport Shop	West 4th Avenue	Anchorage	AK	99503	907-272-7555
7	Play It Over Sports	7900 Spenard Road	Anchorage	AK	99503	907-278-7057
8	Snow Sports LLC	West 6th Avenue	Anchorage	AK	99503	907-272-7755
9	Suburban Outfitters	Richardson	Anchorage	AK	99504	907-333-8600
10	Glenn Ski & Sports	6330 South Cushman Street	Anchorage	AK	99507	907-349-6881
11	Travers Realty	Yenlo Street	Anchorage	AK	99507	907-346-8438
12	Southern Sports Authority	West Parks Highway	Anchorage	AK	99515	907-349-7665
13	Bill's Total Sports	West 27th Avenue	Anchorage	AK	99518	907-522-8288
14	Travel of Alaska	4301 River Loop Road	Anchorage	AK	99577	907-694-6664
15	Palmer's Hardware	Alyeska Highway	Anchorage	AK	99603	907-235-8594
16	Skier's Edge	5th Upper Omalley Road	Anchorage	AK	99615	907-486-7335

Dark (blue) line encloses the Excel list when it is selected

Sorting an Excel List

Sorting is done differently when your data is stored in an Excel list. When data is not in an Excel list, you simply highlight the data you want to sort, and then click the Sort Ascending [A↓] or Sort Descending [A↓] button on the Standard toolbar or use the Sort command on the Data menu to sort the selected data. If data is stored in an Excel list, you only need to select one cell in the column you want to sort and Excel automatically determines the borders of the data set and sorts the list accordingly, keeping the integrity of each row as it sorts.

To sort the list by a specific column, you click the list arrow in the header row for that column. (You could also use the Sort Ascending or Sort Descending buttons on the Standard toolbar.) If you want to sort by more than one column, you can use the Sort dialog box to sort by up to three columns.

Lists are a great way to keep data organized in record sets by row. As long as all of your cells refer to other cells in the same row, sorting has no impact on your formulas. If your formulas refer to cells in other rows, however, you might lose the cell references when you change the order of the data. If you use absolute cell referencing, however, there is no impact.

Filtering an Excel List

When you create an Excel list, list arrows appear in the header row for each column when the AutoFilter feature is enabled. (This feature is on by default; if you need to enable it, click Data on the menu bar, point to Filter, and then click AutoFilter.) The AutoFilter feature lets you display data based on criteria you specify. When you click a list arrow in the header row, you can sort the records in ascending or descending order, display all records, display the top 10 records, display records containing a specific value that appears in the column, or create a custom filter. Barbara needs to display the retailers for each city. Barbara already sorted the list using the City column and could scroll the worksheet to find all retailers located in a certain city, such as Fairbanks. Instead, she clicks the list arrow for the City column, and then selects Fairbanks as the filter in the menu that opens. Figure 7.18 shows the worksheet after filtering the data to display only those rows with the value Fairbanks in the City column. Notice that the row numbers for the selected records remain the same and that Excel displays only the filtered data. The row numbers and the list arrow for the City column change color from black to blue to indicate that the data has been filtered.

Figure 7.18: Filtered data

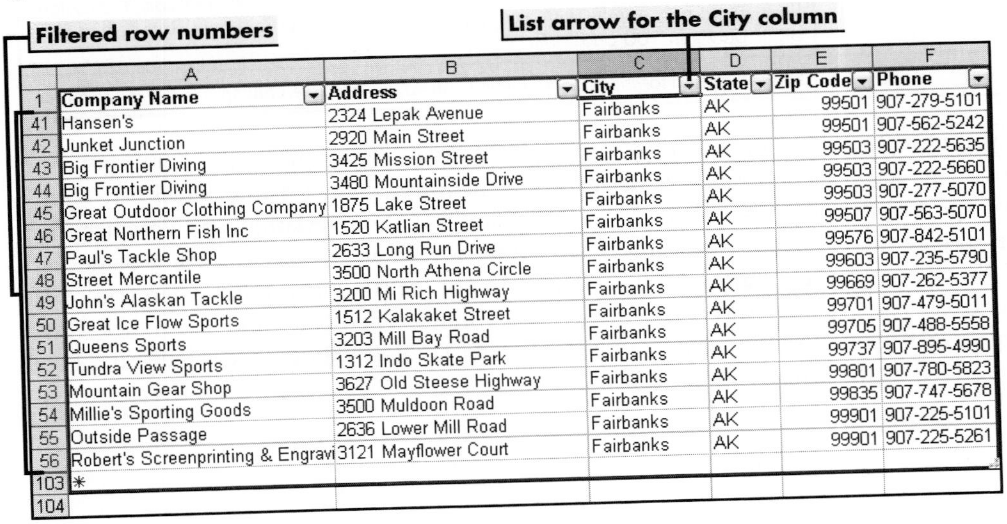

Filtered row numbers   **List arrow for the City column**

	A	B	C	D	E	F
1	Company Name ▼	Address ▼	City ▼	State ▼	Zip Code ▼	Phone ▼
41	Hansen's	2324 Lepak Avenue	Fairbanks	AK	99501	907-279-5101
42	Junket Junction	2920 Main Street	Fairbanks	AK	99501	907-562-5242
43	Big Frontier Diving	3425 Mission Street	Fairbanks	AK	99503	907-222-5635
44	Big Frontier Diving	3480 Mountainside Drive	Fairbanks	AK	99503	907-222-5660
45	Great Outdoor Clothing Company	1875 Lake Street	Fairbanks	AK	99503	907-277-5070
46	Great Northern Fish Inc	1520 Katlian Street	Fairbanks	AK	99507	907-563-5070
47	Paul's Tackle Shop	2633 Long Run Drive	Fairbanks	AK	99576	907-842-5101
48	Street Mercantile	3500 North Athena Circle	Fairbanks	AK	99603	907-235-5790
49	John's Alaskan Tackle	3200 Mi Rich Highway	Fairbanks	AK	99669	907-262-5377
50	Great Ice Flow Sports	1512 Kalakaket Street	Fairbanks	AK	99701	907-479-5011
51	Queens Sports	3203 Mill Bay Road	Fairbanks	AK	99705	907-488-5558
52	Tundra View Sports	1312 Indo Skate Park	Fairbanks	AK	99737	907-895-4990
53	Mountain Gear Shop	3627 Old Steese Highway	Fairbanks	AK	99801	907-780-5823
54	Millie's Sporting Goods	3500 Muldoon Road	Fairbanks	AK	99835	907-747-5678
55	Outside Passage	2636 Lower Mill Road	Fairbanks	AK	99901	907-225-5101
56	Robert's Screenprinting & Engravi	3121 Mayflower Court	Fairbanks	AK	99901	907-225-5261
103	*					
104						

Table 7.2 describes the options available for filtering data.

Table 7.2: AutoFilter options

AutoFilter option	Description
Sort Ascending	Sorts the data in the column in ascending order.
Sort Descending	Sorts the data in the column in descending order.
(All)	Displays all data in the column; this is the default option and the option used to remove a previously applied filter to restore the data so all records are visible.

Table 7.2: AutoFilter options (cont.)

AutoFilter option	Description
(Top 10)	Displays the "top 10" items in a column. Clicking this option in a column that contains numeric data opens the Top 10 AutoFilter dialog box. This dialog box lets you display a specific number (1 to 500) or percentage of values in the column. The default setting selects the top 10 items.
(Custom)	Filters the data using a criterion that you specify. Use this option to find one or more rows that contain values that are equal to, do not equal, are greater than, are greater than or equal to, are less than, are less than or equal to, begin with, do not begin with, end with, do not end with, contain, or do not contain a specific value. You can combine two criteria using the "and" or "or" options. You can also use wildcards to filter data. The asterisk (*) wildcard represents multiple characters and the question mark (?) wildcard represents an individual character. For example, to find all retailers with the word "Outfitter" in their names, you would apply the custom filter "equals *Outfitter*" to the Company Name column. The asterisks at the beginning and end of the word "Outfitter" will find any phrase containing the word "Outfitter." To find all retailers that have a street address in the 100 block of College Road, the custom filter would be "equals 1?? College Road." The two question marks in 1?? find any digits between 100 and 199.
Value	Filters the data for the specified value. All values from the column appear in the menu.

If you need to perform calculations on the filtered data, you can display Total row. The Total row lets you perform the following calculations for data in the Excel list: None, Average, Count, Count Numbers, Max, Min, Sum, Standard Deviation, and Variance. You can display the Total row using the List toolbar, which appears as a floating or docked toolbar when you select an Excel list. (If you do not see the List toolbar when you select the Excel list, click View on the menu bar, point to Toolbars, and then click List.) Figure 7.19 shows the List toolbar with the Toggle Total Row button selected and a Total row added to the Excel list.

7

Level 1

Figure 7.19: Total row added to Excel list

	A	B	C	D	E	F
1	Company Name	Address	City	State	Zip Code	Phone
		2324 Lepak Avenue	Fairbanks	AK	99501	907-279-5101
41	Hansen's	2920 Main Street	Fairbanks	AK	99501	907-562-5242
42	Junket Junction	3425 Mission Street	Fairbanks	AK	99503	907-222-5635
43	Big Frontier Diving	3480 Mountainside Drive	Fairbanks	AK	99503	907-222-5660
44	Big Frontier Diving	1875 Lake Street	Fairbanks	AK	99503	907-277-5070
45	Great Outdoor Clothing Company	1520 Katlian Street	Fairbanks	AK	99507	907-563-5070
46	Great Northern Fish Inc	2633 Long Run Drive	Fairbanks	AK	99576	907-842-5101
47	Paul's Tackle Shop	3500 North Athena Circle	Fairbanks	AK	99603	907-235-5790
48	Street Mercantile	3200 Mi Rich Highway	Fairbanks	AK	99669	907-262-5377
49	John's Alaskan Tackle	1512 Kalakaket Street	Fairbanks	AK	99701	907-479-5011
50	Great Ice Flow Sports	3203 Mill Bay Road	Fairbanks	AK	99705	907-488-5558
51	Queens Sports	1312 Indo Skate Park	Fairbanks	AK	99737	907-895-4990
52	Tundra View Sports	3627 Old Steese Highway	Fairbanks	AK	99801	907-780-5823
53	Mountain Gear Shop	3500 Muldoon Road	Fairbanks	AK	99835	907-747-5678
54	Millie's Sporting Goods	2636 Lower Mill Road	Fairbanks	AK	99901	907-225-5101
55	Outside Passage	3121 Mayflower Court	Fairbanks	AK	99901	907-225-5261
56	Robert's Screenprinting & Engrav					
103	*					16
104	Total					
105						
106						
107						
108						

List ▾ | Σ Toggle Total Row

Total row includes a count   **List toolbar**

You can filter data within filtered data by clicking the list arrow for another column. For example, if you need to select only those retailers in Fairbanks with the zip code 99501, you would click the list arrow for the Zip Code column, and then click 99501 in the menu. Based on the data, two records would be displayed in the Excel list.

To remove a filter from a column and display all of the data in the Excel list again, click the column's list arrow, and then click (All) in the menu.

Adding Data to an Excel List

When data appears in an Excel list, you can insert new rows by typing the data into the blank row at the bottom of the Excel list. You enter existing values into the new row by right-clicking a cell, clicking Pick From Drop-down List on the shortcut menu, and then selecting the value to enter. You can also enter data using the form shown in Figure 7.20.

Figure 7.20: Using a form to work with data in an Excel list

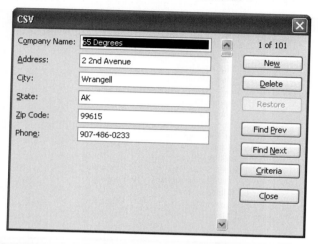

How To

Use a Form to Enter, Find, and Delete Data in an Excel List

1. Click any cell in the Excel list.

2. Click Data on the menu bar, and then click Form. The dialog box shown in Figure 7.20 opens.

3. To add a new record, click the New button, enter the data into the correct text boxes, and then click the Close button.

4. To display a record, click the Find Prev or Find Next button. Or, click the Criteria button and enter the search criterion in the appropriate text box. Use the asterisk (*) character to search for multiple characters or the question mark (?) character to represent a single character. Press the Enter key to display the record(s) matching your criterion. To remove the filter, scroll to the last record selected by the filter, and then click the Clear button. To restore a previously applied filter, click the Restore button.

5. To change data displayed in the form, select and type to replace data. To restore data to its original state, click the Restore button before closing the form.

6. To delete a record, display it in the form, click the Delete button, and then click the OK button.

7. Click the Close button to close the form.

Steps To Success: Level 1

Barbara asks you to organize the data for sportswear retailers into an Excel list. The data is currently stored in a text file and is organized by state. You will begin by creating an Excel workbook and then pasting the data from the text file into a worksheet.

Complete the following:

1. Use Notepad (or another text editor) to open the text file named **Sportswr.txt** in the Chapter 7 folder, select all the data it contains, copy the data to the Clipboard, and then close Notepad.

2. Create a new workbook named **Sportswear Retailers.xls** and save it in the Chapter 7 folder. Paste the data you copied from the text file into a worksheet named Imported Data.

3. Create a list of comma-separated values from the data you pasted by concatenating the company name, street address, city, state/zip code, and phone number. Separate the name, street address, city, state/zip code, and phone number information with commas. Trim each text string in the concatenated value to remove all spaces except for spaces between words.

4. Copy and paste the concatenated information as a list of comma-separated values into a new worksheet named CSV in the Sportswear Retailers.xls workbook. Delete all invalid rows and columns that do not contain the comma-separated values.

5. Convert the comma-separated values into a structured list with the data for the company, street address, city, state, zip code, and phone number appearing in different cells of the worksheet. (*Hint:* Run the Convert Text to Columns Wizard twice to convert all of the data, being careful not to overwrite any existing data in the process. Be certain to remove any extra spaces remaining at the beginning or end of the data.)

6. Correct any errors in the data that were introduced during the conversion.

7. Add a header row with labels to describe the data in each column.

8. Change the data in the worksheet to an Excel list.

9. Sort the data by state, then by city, and then by company in ascending order.

10. Filter the results to display only those companies in Oregon and show the total number of companies in the state.

11. Save and close the Sportswear Retailers.xls workbook.

LEVEL 2

ANALYZING DATA IMPORTED FROM A DATABASE AND ORGANIZING DATA WITH A PIVOTTABLE REPORT

EXCEL 2003 SKILLS TRAINING

- Bring information into Excel from external sources
- Create formulas using the TODAY function
- Import Access files into a worksheet
- Retrieve external data and create queries
- Create a PivotTable report
- Create a PivotChart report
- Create and format a PivotChart report
- Get data from a Web page

IMPORTING DATA FROM A DATABASE INTO EXCEL

The marketing department has been using the Excel list that Barbara created from the distributor's data to organize its efforts of contacting sporting goods retailers to maintain their relationships with TheZone and its products. The marketing department is using Barbara's worksheet as a way to manage a simple database of information in a row-and-column format. Although this worksheet works well for the marketing department, Barbara is concerned about data integrity. She has been pushing for TheZone to use a database to store its data, but many of her colleagues are reluctant to change the existing systems, mostly because they are unfamiliar with how databases can simplify their work and ensure consistent and accurate data. Barbara has proposed the development of a prototype database as a way to demonstrate how TheZone can use a database in conjunction with spreadsheets to store, maintain, and analyze data. Barbara's managers have agreed to her idea and are especially interested in using a database to store information that they can export into Excel for later analysis. They agree that Barbara's proposal would protect the integrity of the data better than relying on just spreadsheets.

Barbara just received some sales data in a Microsoft Access database about sports apparel dealers and sales of TheZone products from the distributor. This database includes the number of orders and total sales of TheZone products for each retailer in the Pacific sales region. The database also includes the dates of each retailer's first and last order with the distributor. Barbara decides to use this database for her prototype system and exports it into Excel. After exporting this data into Excel, Barbara calculates how long a particular retailer has sold TheZone items and the length of time since its last order. This information will help the marketing department focus its efforts so that long-term customers and customers with recent orders are contacted first.

For any business, data is collected on a regular basis. Often, the key to a business's success depends on its ability to manage and organize this data into a usable format. A **database** is a set of related data that is stored in tables. In a database, a **table** is a collection of fields that describe a specific entity. For example, a table might store data about a company's products or its employees. A **field** is a single characteristic of the entity, such as a product ID number or an address. A set of fields that describes one product or person is called a **record**. A database is created by and defined in a **database management system** (**DBMS**), which is a software program that creates and accesses the data in a database. Two examples of DBMSs are Microsoft Access and Oracle. DBMSs impose a great deal of structure on a data set. This structure makes it possible to find specific data very easily, but it can make analysis more difficult. Combining Excel with a database is a powerful combination. The database provides the structure to ensure that the right data is available and protected. The spreadsheet provides the analytical power and flexibility needed by most business people.

Most spreadsheets contain a combination of numeric and nonnumeric data. The nonnumeric data might take the form of labels that describe columns or rows, or it could be in the form of dates and times associated with the data in the spreadsheet. When non-numeric data makes up most of the information in a spreadsheet, you should seriously consider using a database to organize the information. Databases are also used to store numeric data as well as nonnumeric data. Databases have the most advantages over spreadsheets when data is organized into a field/record structure and there is a large quantity of data. For example, in many companies, general ledger accounting data (which is primarily numeric in nature) is sometimes stored in a database and analyzed with a spreadsheet.

The same flexibility that makes Excel so powerful can lead to unintentional data corruption. One of the best ways to analyze text data is to sort it by categories, such as sorting a list of companies by company name. If you don't select all the data before sorting the rows, Excel might sort the company names but not the other data for each company, resulting in a list of alphabetical company names with incorrect address information. Although Excel warns you when you are about to sort data incorrectly, you can choose to ignore the warning and still sort the data incorrectly. This situation cannot happen in a database because all the field data is associated with a particular record.

Best Practice

Combining Spreadsheets and Databases

Importing information from a database table into a spreadsheet has some clear advantages. In a database, the data is protected from accidental changes, yet it is available for export into a spreadsheet for analysis. Database programs are also able to hold much larger and more complex data sets than Excel. Many people use Excel as a "quick and dirty" database because it is easy to enter data that might be better suited for a database into a workbook. Many DBMSs are called **relational database management systems** because the data is stored in tables that are related to each other through a common field in a process called

normalization. By storing data in related tables in a normalized database, you can reduce data redundancy. For example, consider a customer database that stores customer contact information and the details of each customer's purchases. In a database that contains only one table, each time a customer orders a product, a row is created in the table. Customers with multiple purchases might have different information stored about them in each record. In a relational database, the customer information is stored in a Customer table and the customer's purchases are stored in an Orders table. The Customer and Orders tables are linked with information in a common field that appears in both tables, such as a customer ID. In this case, the customer's information is only stored once, which reduces redundancy. Combining spreadsheets and databases is a good idea when you need to secure and protect the data but want to analyze it using a spreadsheet.

Importing an Access Table into Excel

The Access database contains one table with contact information for sports apparel retailers in the Pacific sales region. Barbara opened the database in Access and examined the contents of the Sports Apparel Retailers table. The table contains fields named CompanyName, StreetAddress, City, State, ZipCode, Phone, FirstOrderDate, LastOrderDate, NumberOfOrders, and TotalSales. She imports the data from the Sports Apparel Retailers table into a new Excel workbook named Sports Apparel Retailers.xls, as shown in Figure 7.21. The fields from the tables appear in columns in the worksheet. Each record in the database is one row in the worksheet.

Figure 7.21: Data imported from a database table

Fields from the database table are column headings

	CompanyName	StreetAddress	City
1			
2	Underground Sports	126 South La Brea Avenue	Sunnyvale
3	Churchill's Sportswear	1325 South Main Street	Redondo Beach
4	Summer Times Clothiers	40820 Winchester Road	Mission Viejo
5	Wiseguys Industries	244 East 1st Street	Garden Grove
6	Sport Shoe Shop		Petaluma
7	Latest and Greatest		Los Angeles
8	Ocean Blue Sun Tanning Salon		Sacramento
9	Red White and Blue T Shirt Inc	4906 Dublin Boulevard	Honolulu
10	St Croix Gifts	1664 Babcock Street	Long Beach
11	Fantastic George	13701 Marina Pointe Drive	City Industry
12	The Shoe Store	2801 South Figueroa Street	San Francisco
13	American Claim Company	1063 Island Way	Hilo
14	High Tide Women's Wear of California	2330 Central Way Avenue	Puyallup
15	Homerun Baseball Club	146 South Washington Street	Ventura
16	Sky High Outfitters	6600 Topanga Canyon Boulevard	Santa Monica

External Data

Each row is one record in the table

How To

Import Data Stored in a Database Table into Excel

1. Open the workbook into which you want to import the database data, or open a new workbook.
2. Click Data on the menu bar, point to Import External Data, and then click Import Data. The Select Data Source dialog box opens.
3. Use the Look in list arrow to browse to and select the database from which you will import the data, and then click the Open button. If the database you select contains more than one table, the Select Table dialog box opens. Click the table that contains the data you want to import, and then click the OK button. The Import Data dialog box opens, as shown in Figure 7.22.

Figure 7.22: Import Data dialog box

4. Click the Existing worksheet option button (if necessary), and then click the OK button.

The External Data toolbar shown in Figure 7.21 includes buttons for working with data imported from an external source. (If you don't see this toolbar when you click the imported data set, click View on the menu bar, point to Toolbars, and then click External Data.) The Edit Query button [icon] lets you change the query that selects the data from the database. The Data Range Properties button [icon] lets you change the query definition, data refresh options, and data format and layout. Barbara can use the Refresh Data button [icon] to update the imported data so that it contains the most current information from the database table from which it was imported. In other words, if someone adds or changes records in the Sports Apparel Retailers table in the Apparel database, clicking the Refresh Data button in the worksheet makes those same changes in the worksheet. The Refresh All button [icon] refreshes the query and the data in the worksheet. Barbara imported all of the data in the Sports Apparel Retailers table in the Apparel database into the worksheet. Barbara also wants to demonstrate how to select specific data prior to importing it into Excel so her managers can see how this feature works. To accomplish this goal, Barbara needs to create a query. A **query** is a question that you ask a database. In response to a query, the database displays only those records that meet the criteria you specify in the query.

Using the Query Wizard to Select Data from a Database

Excel includes a program called **Microsoft Query** that lets you create queries to select data from external sources, including Access, and import the query results into a worksheet. A simpler way to use Microsoft Query is to use the **Query Wizard**, which lets you choose your data source and select the database table and fields you want to import into a workbook. The Query Wizard prompts you to define any criteria for the data you want to import by selecting only rows that meet criteria that you specify.

The marketing representative for California needs a list of the retailers located only in California from the database, so Barbara needs to create a query to import only this data into Excel. The representative only wants the records for retailers whose last order date is January 1, 2006 or later. Barbara selects the Sports Apparel Retailers table in the Apparel database as the data source, selects all fields in the table, and then applies a filter so that only those records with CA as the State value and 1/1/2006 as the LastOrderDate value are selected. Barbara also sets the options to sort by city, and then by last order date, in ascending order. She returns the results of her query in a new worksheet, as shown in Figure 7.23.

Figure 7.23: Retailers in California

Records sorted by city and last order date in ascending order

Records selected with last order dates of 1/1/2006 or later

	A	B	C	D	E	F	G	H	
1	CompanyName	StreetAddress	City	State	ZipCode	Phone	FirstOrderDate	LastOrderDate	Nu
2	R&R Sporting	4910 West Rosecrans	Aiea	CA	90015	415-665-3394	12/16/2003 0:00	2/7/2006 0:00	
3	North Shore Surf Shop	3500 South Meridian	Albany	CA	93722	805-238-3424	3/26/1999 0:00	1/12/2006 0:00	
4	One of a Kind Gifts	4071 North Valentine	Alpine	CA	95678	541-967-8891	8/23/2002 0:00	2/13/2006 0:00	
5	Just Beachy	1045 Oakwood Mall	Alpine	CA	93422	760-722-2626	6/10/1996 0:00	2/16/2006 0:00	
6	Mario Brothers Family C	7324 Melrose Avenu				619-282-2650	8/24/1993 0:00	1/4/2006 0:00	
7	Your Factory Stores	110 East 9th Street				707-447-6003	9/11/1994 0:00	2/10/2006 0:00	
8	Paradise Golf Shop	260 Bernal Road				808-875-9399	12/24/1991 0:00	1/10/2006 0:00	
9	Sharp Edge Sportswear	10920 Garfield Avenue	Bainbridge Is	CA	93721	714-357-3485	6/1/2004 0:00	1/2/2006 0:00	
10	Magical Creations Empo	13227 Saticoy Street	Bakersfield	CA	92661	503-288-6299	7/23/2004 0:00	1/4/2006 0:00	
11	101 Value	5491 Philadelphia	Bakersfield	CA	96815	808-877-2337	4/28/2001 0:00	2/6/2006 0:00	
12	O'Neill Sportswear and G	1207 NW 23rd Ave	Bakersfield	CA	92653	949-588-2435	4/3/1998 0:00	2/10/2006 0:00	
13	Wild West Technicians	13268 Jamboree Road	Beaverton	CA	93010	858-560-3173	12/12/2003 0:00	1/8/2006 0:00	
14	Above & Beyond Outfitte	345 Royal Hawn Aven	Beverly Hills	CA	90292	808-484-6976	2/28/2003 0:00	1/20/2006 0:00	
15	Sport N Toy	2216 Fillmore Street	Bothell	CA	95054	909-245-6443	5/20/2003 0:00	1/10/2006 0:00	
16	Outpost for Athletes	444 Hillsdale Mall	Burlingame	CA	92506	925-943-6068	8/6/2002 0:00	1/12/2006 0:00	

External Data

How To

Use the Query Wizard to Import Data from Access

1. Open the worksheet into which you want to import the data.

2. Click Data on the menu bar, point to Import External Data, and then click New Database Query. The Choose Data Source dialog box opens.

3. Click MS Access Database*, verify that the Use the Query Wizard to create/edit queries check box contains a check mark, and then click the OK button. The Select Database dialog box opens.

4. Browse to the Access database, click it to select it, and then click the OK button. The Query Wizard starts.

5. In the Query Wizard – Choose Columns dialog box, click the table that contains the data you want to import, and then click the plus box to the left of the table name to display the columns in the selected table. To add all columns to the query, click the table name, click the Select Column button ▶ to add all columns to your query or select the individual column that you want to include in your query, and then click the Select Column button ▶ to add the field to the Columns in your query list box. When you have selected the columns to include, click the Next button.

6. In the Query Wizard – Filter Data dialog box, click the column to filter and then use the list box to select the appropriate filter for that column. For example, to select only those records with the value CA in the State field, click State in the Column to filter list box, click the State list arrow, and then click equals. Click the list arrow for the second list box, and then click CA. To include other filters in the query, click the list arrow in the second row and define the next filter. Click the And option button to create an And query or click the Or option button to create an Or query. (An And query selects only those records that satisfy both conditions; an Or query selects those records that satisfy the first condition, the second condition, or both conditions.) After you specify a filter for a column, the column name changes to bold in the Column to filter list box. Figure 7.24 shows the filters for the State and LastOrderDate fields. When you have finished creating the filters, click the Next button.

Figure 7.24: Query Wizard – Filter Data dialog box

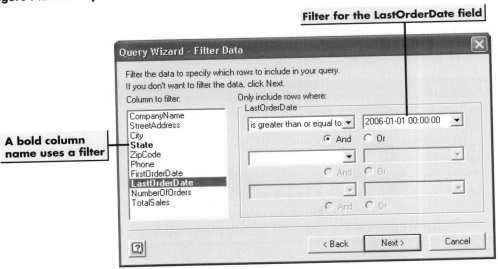

7. In the Query Wizard – Sort Order dialog box, click the Sort by list arrow and select a column on which to filter. The default sort order is Ascending; click the Descending option button to apply a sort in descending order. You can specify up to three sorting options. When you have finished specifying the sort order, click the Next button.

8. In the Query Wizard – Finish dialog box, click the Return Data to Microsoft Office Excel option button, and then click the Finish button. The Import Data dialog box opens.

9. Verify that the Existing worksheet option button is selected, and then click the OK button. The query results are imported into the worksheet.

After using a query to import data, you can update the data by clicking the Refresh Data button on the External Data toolbar. You can also change the query by clicking the Edit Query button on the External Data toolbar, which starts the Query Wizard so you can change the data to select and display in the worksheet.

MAKING CALCULATIONS WITH DATE AND TIME DATA

The data shown in Figure 7.23 includes the date that each retailer in California began ordering TheZone products and the date of the last order by each retailer. Dates are represented by values in Excel. These values are not the same as using numbers in place of months as in the date 9/24/2007. Excel uses serial numbers to represent dates and time. Excel represents a date as the number of days since January 0, 1900: January 1, 1900 is represented as 1, January 2, 1900 is represented as 2, and so on. Excel also uses decimals to represent the time on a particular day. Each day is broken into decimal equivalents. For example, noon on January 1, 1900 is represented by the serial number 1.5; the whole number 1 is one day from January 0, 1900 and the decimal .5 represents noon (halfway through a 24-hour day, or 12 divided by 24). Excel further defines days into hours, minutes, and seconds by dividing the 24 hours in each day accordingly. Using serial numbers makes calculations involving dates and times very easy. To calculate the number of days between the dates in two cells, you just need to subtract one cell from the other.

Best Practice

Formatting Cells with Date and Time Calculations

When you create formulas referencing cells that contain dates and/or times, Excel sometimes formats the result as a date instead of as a number. If you need to calculate the number of days between dates stored in two cells and the result is a date instead of the number of days, select the cell, click Format on the menu bar, click Cells, click the Number tab, and then select the Number category. If you want the result to show days in whole numbers, set the Decimal places list box to 0. If you want to format the result as a serial number that indicates time, set the Decimal places list box to the number of decimal places that you want to display.

The marketing department will use Barbara's data to prioritize the sales calls by geographic area, but it is also interested in prioritizing calls based on the length of time since the retailer last ordered TheZone products and the overall length of time each retailer has carried TheZone products. Barbara uses two functions to determine this information for the marketing department.

For the first request, the marketing department wants to know how many days have elapsed between the current date and the last order date. Barbara first adds today's date in cell M1 using the TODAY function. The **TODAY** function returns the current date's serial number (based on the computer's internal clock). The syntax for the TODAY function is:

=TODAY()

The TODAY function requires no additional arguments, but the opening and closing parentheses are required.

Barbara adds the formula =$M$1-H2 in cell K2 to calculate the number of days between today's date (in cell M1) and the last order date. Because the order time is not important, she reformats the result as a number with zero decimal places. She adds the column heading "Days Since Last Order" in cell K1 and copies the formula in cell K2 down the column. Because Barbara's formula includes the TODAY function, the current date according to the computer's internal clock is always used in the calculation, so the result is different depending on when the calculation occurs. Figure 7.25 shows the new Days Since Last Order column and today's date.

Figure 7.25: Using the TODAY function

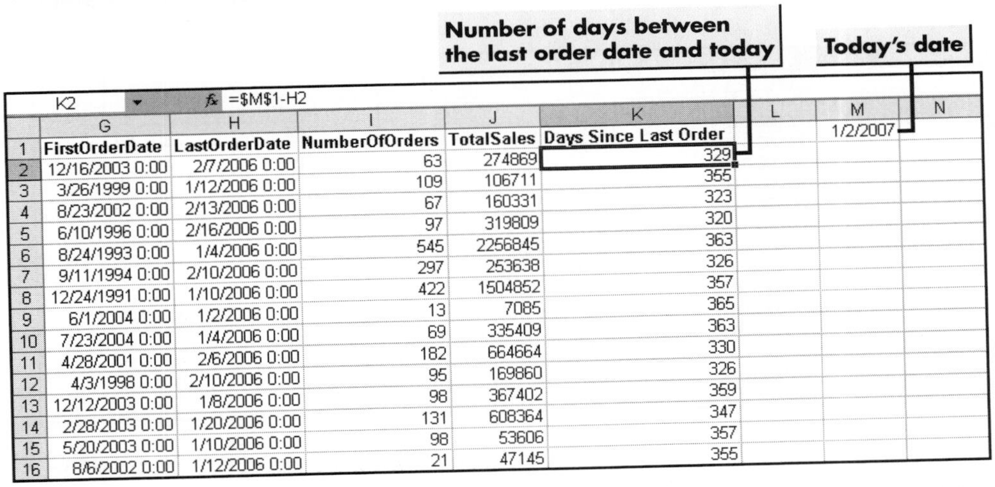

Number of days between the last order date and today | Today's date

	G	H	I	J	K	L	M	N
							1/2/2007	
1	FirstOrderDate	LastOrderDate	NumberOfOrders	TotalSales	Days Since Last Order			
2	12/16/2003 0:00	2/7/2006 0:00	63	274869	329			
3	3/26/1999 0:00	1/12/2006 0:00	109	106711	355			
4	8/23/2002 0:00	2/13/2006 0:00	67	160331	323			
5	6/10/1996 0:00	2/16/2006 0:00	97	319809	320			
6	8/24/1993 0:00	1/4/2006 0:00	545	2256845	363			
7	9/11/1994 0:00	2/10/2006 0:00	297	253638	326			
8	12/24/1991 0:00	1/10/2006 0:00	422	1504852	357			
9	6/1/2004 0:00	1/2/2006 0:00	13	7085	365			
10	7/23/2004 0:00	1/4/2006 0:00	69	335409	363			
11	4/28/2001 0:00	2/6/2006 0:00	182	664664	330			
12	4/3/1998 0:00	2/10/2006 0:00	95	169860	326			
13	12/12/2003 0:00	1/8/2006 0:00	98	367402	359			
14	2/28/2003 0:00	1/20/2006 0:00	131	608364	347			
15	5/20/2003 0:00	1/10/2006 0:00	98	53606	357			
16	8/6/2002 0:00	1/12/2006 0:00	21	47145	355			

Barbara also needs to calculate the overall length of time that each retailer has ordered products from the TheZone. To determine the length of each relationship, Barbara needs to subtract the number of days between today's date and the first order date. As she looks at the values in the FirstOrderDate column, she decides that determining the number of days between today's date and the first order date would yield very high numbers that would not be meaningful to the marketing department. For example, the retailer Just Beachy's first order date is 6/10/1996 and its last order date is 1/12/2006, which results in a length of over 2,400 days between order dates. Barbara decides that results using years would be more meaningful. She uses the **YEARFRAC** function to calculate the number of years between the two dates. The syntax for the YEARFRAC function is as follows:

```
=YEARFRAC(start_date,end_date,basis)
```

In the YEARFRAC function, start_date is the date from which you want to start counting, end_date is the ending date, and basis is the argument that lets you establish the lengths of months and years. Using 1 for the basis calculates months and years with actual values. Using 0 as the basis calculates months using 30 days and years using 360 days. (Some people consider a standard month to be 30 days even though a month can have 28 to 31 days; using a 30-day month results in a year with 360 days. Most years have 365 days, except for leap years, which have 366 days.)

Barbara adds the column heading "Relationship (Years)" in cell L1 and then adds the following formula in cell L2: =YEARFRAC(G2,H2,1). She wants to include fractional years, so she formats cell L2 as a number with two decimal places. Then, she copies the formula to the other cells in column L and the results appear in Figure 7.26.

Figure 7.26: Using the YEARFRAC function

Years between the first order date and the last order date

	G	H	I	J	K	L	M
1	FirstOrderDate	LastOrderDate	NumberOfOrders	TotalSales	Days Since Last Order	Relationship (Years)	1/2/2007
2	12/16/2003 0:00	2/7/2006 0:00	63	274869	329	2.15	
3	3/26/1999 0:00	1/12/2006 0:00	109	106711	355	6.80	
4	8/23/2002 0:00	2/13/2006 0:00	67	160331	323	3.48	
5	6/10/1996 0:00	2/16/2006 0:00	97	319809	320	9.69	
6	8/24/1993 0:00	1/4/2006 0:00	545	2256845	363	12.37	
7	9/11/1994 0:00	2/10/2006 0:00	297	253638	326	11.42	
8	12/24/1991 0:00	1/10/2006 0:00	422	1504852	357	14.05	
9	6/1/2004 0:00	1/2/2006 0:00	13	7085	365	1.59	
10	7/23/2004 0:00	1/4/2006 0:00	69	335409	363	1.45	
11	4/28/2001 0:00	2/6/2006 0:00	182	664664	330	4.78	
12	4/3/1998 0:00	2/10/2006 0:00	95	169860	326	7.86	
13	12/12/2003 0:00	1/8/2006 0:00	98	367402	359	2.08	
14	2/28/2003 0:00	1/20/2006 0:00	131	608364	347	2.89	
15	5/20/2003 0:00	1/10/2006 0:00	98	53606	357	2.64	

If you try using the YEARFUNC function and Excel returns an error, you probably need to install the Analysis ToolPak Add-In, which is a program of supplemental financial, statistical, and engineering analysis tools. Loading an add-in makes its features available in Excel and adds any associated commands to the appropriate menus. To conserve memory and improve performance, you can unload add-ins you seldom use. Unloading an add-in removes its features and commands from the menus in Excel, but the add-in program remains on your computer so you can reload it.

Table 7.3 lists and describes some other commonly used date and time functions.

Table 7.3: Date and time functions

Function	Description
DATE(year,month,day)	Returns the serial number of a particular date
DATEVALUE(date_text)	Converts a date in the form of text to a serial number
DAY(serial_number)	Converts a serial number to a day of the month
DAYS360(start_date,end_date,method)	Calculates the number of days between two dates based on a 360-day year
EDATE(start_date,months)	Returns the serial number of the date that is the indicated number of months before or after start_date
EOMONTH(start_date,months)	Returns the serial number of the last day of the month before or after a specified number of months
HOUR(serial_number)	Converts a serial number to an hour
MINUTE(serial_number)	Converts a serial number to a minute
MONTH(serial_number)	Converts a serial number to a month
NETWORKDAYS(start_date,end_date,holidays)	Returns the number of whole workdays (Monday through Friday, excluding dates identified as holidays) between two dates
NOW( )	Returns the serial number of the current date and time
SECOND(serial_number)	Converts a serial number to a second
TIME(hour,minute,second)	Returns a decimal number for a specific time
TIMEVALUE(time_text)	Returns a decimal number for a specific time that is represented by a text string
TODAY( )	Returns the serial number for today's date
WEEKDAY(serial_number,return_type)	Converts a serial number to a day of the week
WEEKNUM(serial_num,return_type)	Converts a serial number to a number representing where the week falls numerically in a year in which January 1 occurs in the first week of the year
WORKDAY(start_date,days,holidays)	Returns the serial number of the date before or after a specified number of workdays (Monday through Friday, excluding dates identified as holidays)
YEAR(serial_number)	Converts a serial number to a year
YEARFRAC(start_date,end_date,basis)	Returns the number of years between two dates as a fraction

ANALYZING DATA USING A PIVOTTABLE REPORT

Naturally, TheZone wants to keep all of the retailers serviced by the distributor that went out of business, but even with Barbara's worksheets, it will be difficult for the marketing department to contact nearly 2,000 companies. After meeting with the marketing department, Barbara agrees to change her data analysis strategy to identify retailers that have ordered the most products from the TheZone. With this data, the marketing department can locate TheZone's best customers and concentrate its efforts on these businesses first. Barbara needs to determine the state with the most orders and the cities in each state with the highest sales. She needs to organize the data in different ways to produce meaningful reports for the marketing department. To produce these results, Barbara needs to create a PivotTable report.

A **PivotTable report** is an interactive report that lets you summarize and analyze a data set. You can use a PivotTable report to summarize selected fields from a list or data from an external source, such as a database. A unique feature of a PivotTable report is that its organization is somewhat dynamic. The PivotTable report can be "pivoted" to examine the data from various perspectives by rearranging its structure. Unlike any other table, you can change the data contained in a PivotTable report by simply dragging a column to a new location in the PivotTable report. You can transpose the columns and rows as needed for your analysis.

Level 2

Best Practice

Deciding When to Use a PivotTable Report
Pivot tables offer a unique way to analyze data that can come from a variety of sources. After creating a PivotTable report, you can easily rearrange its fields and change its data to analyze data from different perspectives. This ability to "pivot" summaries of the data by rows and columns is what gives this tool its name. Pivot tables are best used to analyze data that can be summarized in multiple ways. One example is sales data that you need to summarize and analyze by month, quarter, and year or by product line and sales region. It is best to use a PivotTable report to summarize data in one place that might require multiple worksheets to analyze the same data on all the different dimensions.

Creating a PivotTable Report

Barbara will use the original data she imported from the Sports Apparel Retailers table in the Apparel database for her PivotTable report. She selects the Retailers worksheet tab to display this data and clicks Data on the menu bar, and then clicks PivotTable and PivotChart Report to start the PivotTable and PivotChart Wizard. In the first step, shown in Figure 7.27, Barbara selects the Microsoft Office Excel list or database option button to indicate the format of the data and the PivotTable option button to create a PivotTable report.

Figure 7.27: PivotTable and PivotChart Wizard – Step 1 of 3 dialog box

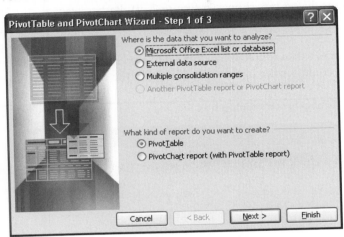

In the second step of the wizard, shown in Figure 7.28, Barbara confirms the range containing the data to use in the PivotTable report. By selecting a cell in the data range that you want to include in the PivotTable report, Excel automatically selects the range.

Figure 7.28: PivotTable and PivotChart Wizard – Step 2 of 3 dialog box

In the third step of the wizard, shown in Figure 7.29, Barbara selects the option to put the PivotTable report in a new worksheet. Because a PivotTable report usually analyzes a large data set, it is usually better to place it in a new worksheet.

Figure 7.29: PivotTable and PivotChart Wizard – Step 3 of 3 dialog box

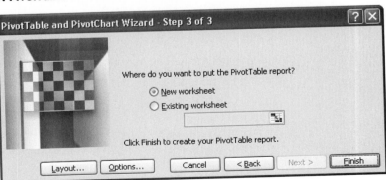

Before clicking the Finish button, Barbara clicks the Options button, which opens the PivotTable Options dialog box shown in Figure 7.30. Barbara can use this dialog box to change the way that data is formatted, organized, and saved in the PivotTable report. For now, Barbara decides to accept the default settings because she knows that she can change them later. If Barbara's data source were external to Excel, the External data options would be enabled so she could set the options for refreshing the data on an automatic schedule.

Figure 7.30: PivotTable Options dialog box

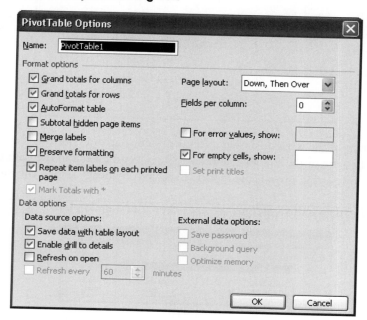

Figure 7.31 shows the PivotTable report in a new worksheet. Notice the PivotTable toolbar and PivotTable Field List. Also, Barbara renames the worksheets that contain data to describe their contents.

Figure 7.31: PivotTable added to worksheet

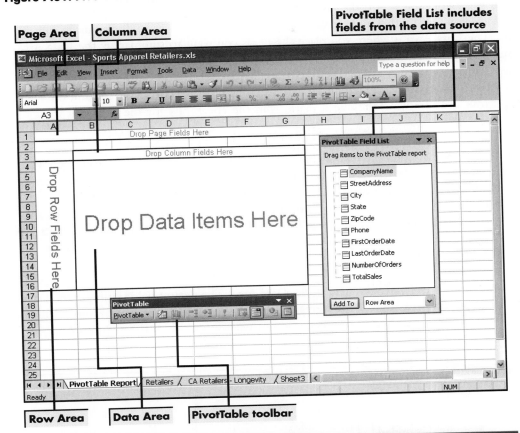

Analyzing Data Using the Row, Column, and Data Areas

When you create a PivotTable report, Excel opens the PivotTable Field List and the PivotTable toolbar shown in Figure 7.31. (If you do not see the PivotTable toolbar, click View on the menu bar, point to Toolbars, and then click PivotTable. If you do not see the PivotTable Field List, click the Show Field List button ▣ on the PivotTable toolbar to display it.) The **PivotTable Field List** contains a list of fields in the data source you selected for the PivotTable report. Because you selected the data in the Retailers worksheet, the columns from that worksheet appear in the PivotTable Field List. To add data to the PivotTable report, you drag the field you want to summarize into one of the four drop areas on the PivotTable report: Drop Page Fields Here (the Page Area), Drop Row Fields Here (the Row Area), Drop Column Fields Here (the Column Area), or Drop Data Items Here (the Data Area). If you drag a field from the PivotTable Field List and place it in the Page Area, you can display data in the PivotTable report grouped by page. Placing a field in the Row Area displays data from that field in rows. Placing a field in the Column Area displays data from that field in columns. Placing a field in the Data Area summarizes data from that field. The cell where each row and column intersects represents a summary of the data on those two dimensions. When you place fields in either the Row Area or Column Area, the PivotTable report displays all values of those fields. Clicking the list arrow for a field lets you select either all field values or individual field values to display using a check box. The Data Area is where you place the fields you want to summarize; the Data Area usually includes field values rather than categories. You can rearrange the fields in a PivotTable report by dragging them to any other location. You can remove a field from the PivotTable report by dragging it out of the PivotTable report or by clicking the Data list arrow and removing the check mark from the check box for the field you want to remove.

Barbara starts setting up the PivotTable report by dragging the State field from the Pivot-Table Field List to the Row Area. When you drag a field and place it over a drop area in the PivotTable report, the drop area is selected. When you drop the field in a drop area, the data from the field appears in the drop area. Another way to add a field to a PivotTable report is to select the field in the PivotTable Field List, click the list arrow at the bottom of the Field List, select the area in which you want to drop the field, and then click the Add To button.

She then drags the Total Sales field to the Data Area. The default field setting in the Data Area is to calculate a sum of the items in this drop area by the categories in the Row Area or Column Area. Because Barbara did not place any fields in the Column Area, the PivotTable report displays the total sales by state, as shown in Figure 7.32.

Figure 7.32: Total sales by state

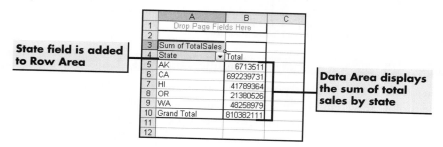

You can change the calculation used in the Data Area by right-clicking a value in the Data Area to open the shortcut menu, and then clicking Field Settings to open the PivotTable Field dialog box shown in Figure 7.33. By clicking a new value in the Summarize by list box, you can perform other calculations on the data, such as Count, Average, Max, Min, and so on. You can also change the default name of the field by typing a new one in the Name text box. Clicking the Number button lets you change the number format of the values. Barbara uses the Number button and the Format Cells dialog box that opens to change the values from the General category to Currency, so the values are displayed as currency.

Figure 7.33: PivotTable Field dialog box

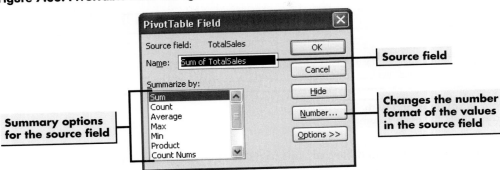

Barbara also wants the PivotTable report to show the number of orders by state. You can place more than one field in the Data Area by dragging another field into the drop area. She drags the NumberOfOrders field from the PivotTable Field List to the Data Area, and then uses the PivotTable Field dialog box to change the calculation to Count and the number format to use a comma separator in values over 1,000 and zero decimal places. The PivotTable report changes to summarize the total sales and number of orders by state, in rows, as shown in Figure 7.34. When you organize the data by row, you can compare the states by the total sales and number of orders. This organization results in multiple data labels that indicate the sum of total sales and the number of orders for each state.

Figure 7.34: Total sales and number of orders by state (rows)

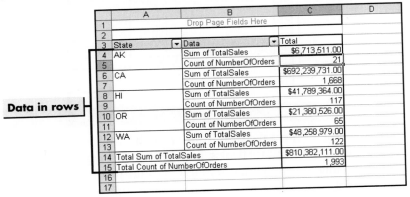

Barbara could have organized the data in columns, as shown in Figure 7.35, by moving the State field to the Column Area and keeping the TotalSales and NumberOfOrders fields in the Data Area. The PivotTable report displays the same information as shown in Figure 7.34, but the data is summarized in columns instead of rows. This organization results in a comparison of the total sales and number of orders by each state.

Figure 7.35: Total sales and number of orders by state (columns with labels)

	A	B	C	D	E	F	G
1				Drop Page Fields Here			
2							
3		State ▼					
4	Data ▼	AK	CA	HI	OR	WA	Grand Total
5	Sum of TotalSales	$6,713,511.00	$692,239,731.00	$41,789,364.00	$21,380,526.00	$48,258,979.00	$810,382,111.00
6	Count of NumberOfOrders	21	1,668	117	65	122	1,993
7							

Data in columns and with data labels for each column

Alternatively, Barbara could have organized the data as shown in Figure 7.36 by moving the State field to the Row Area and keeping the TotalSales and NumberOfOrders fields in the Data Area. This arrangement organizes the data by column and reduces the number of data labels.

Figure 7.36: Total sales and number of orders by state (columns with fewer labels)

	A	B	C	D
1			Drop Page Fields Here	
2				
3	Data ▼	State ▼	Total	
4	Sum of TotalSales	AK	$6,713,511.00	
5		CA	$692,239,731.00	
6		HI	$41,789,364.00	
7		OR	$21,380,526.00	
8		WA	$48,258,979.00	
9	Count of NumberOfOrders	AK	21	
10		CA	1,668	
11		HI	117	
12		OR	65	
13		WA	122	
14	Total Sum of TotalSales		$810,382,111.00	
15	Total Count of NumberOfOrders		1,993	
16				
17				

Data in columns with fewer data labels

Adding Fields to the Page Area

Barbara uses the PivotTable report and begins analyzing the data. She sees that California has the most orders and the highest total sales, followed by Washington, Hawaii, Oregon, and Alaska. Barbara wants to identify the cities in California that have the most retailers. She moves the State field to the Page Area, which organizes the data by the selected state. Then, she places the City field in the Row Area. She changes the PivotTable report to remove the Count of NumberOfOrders field from the Data Area by clicking the Data list arrow, clicking the Count of NumberOfOrders check box to clear it, and then clicking the OK button. Then, she places the CompanyName field in the Data Area, which counts the number of retailers in each city. The data is now sorted alphabetically by city name. Because Barbara wants to identify the cities in California with the most retailers, she clicks the list arrow in the Page Area, clicks CA in the list, and then clicks the OK button. She selects a cell in the Count of CompanyName column, and then clicks the Sort Descending button on the Standard toolbar. Figure 7.37 shows that Los Angeles is the city with the most retailers and the highest sales. The marketing department can use this data to focus its efforts on contacting stores in the top California markets.

Figure 7.37: Cities in California with the highest sales

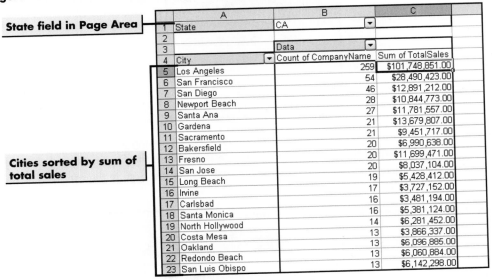

State field in Page Area

Cities sorted by sum of total sales

	A	B	C
1	State	CA ▾	
2			
3		Data ▾	
4	City ▾	Count of CompanyName	Sum of TotalSales
5	Los Angeles	259	$101,748,851.00
6	San Francisco	54	$28,490,423.00
7	San Diego	46	$12,891,212.00
8	Newport Beach	28	$10,844,773.00
9	Santa Ana	27	$11,781,557.00
10	Gardena	21	$13,679,807.00
11	Sacramento	21	$9,451,717.00
12	Bakersfield	20	$6,990,638.00
13	Fresno	20	$11,699,471.00
14	San Jose	20	$8,037,104.00
15	Long Beach	19	$5,428,412.00
16	Irvine	17	$3,727,152.00
17	Carlsbad	16	$3,481,194.00
18	Santa Monica	16	$5,381,124.00
19	North Hollywood	14	$6,281,452.00
20	Costa Mesa	13	$3,866,337.00
21	Oakland	13	$6,096,885.00
22	Redondo Beach	13	$6,060,884.00
23	San Luis Obispo	13	$6,142,298.00

To view the retailers with the most retailers by city in another state, click the State list arrow, select another state, and then sort the Count of CompanyName column in descending order. To view the data for all states, click the State list arrow, and then click (All). When you sort the data in descending order, you see the cities with the most retailers for the region.

Because you are usually analyzing large amounts of data with a PivotTable report, you might need to summarize data into groups. For example, if one of your fields contains date data, you can summarize values into periods, such as months, quarters, or years, to arrange records into groups instead of listing individual dates in the range. You can also summarize data by creating a group of days, such as 0 to 30 days, 31 to 60 days, and so on. You can do the same thing with numeric data.

How To

Group Data in a PivotTable Report
1. Drag the field that contains the values you want to group into the PivotTable report.
2. Right-click the field to open the shortcut menu, point to Group and Show Detail, and then click Group. If the data you are grouping contains numeric values, the Grouping dialog box shown in Figure 7.38 opens. When the Auto grouping feature is enabled, the Starting at value is set to the lowest value in the range and the Ending at value is set to the highest value in the range.

To change the starting or ending value, select the value in the text box, and then type a new value. Set the By value to the range you want to group. In Figure 7.38, the default group is 100.

Figure 7.38: Grouping dialog box for numeric data

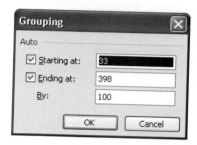

If the data you are grouping contains date values, the Grouping dialog box shown in Figure 7.39 opens. When the Auto grouping feature is enabled, the Starting at value is set to the first date in the range and the Ending value is set to the last date in the range. Use the By list box to select the desired grouping.

Figure 7.39: Grouping dialog box for date data

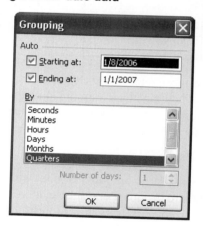

3. Click the OK button to close the Grouping dialog box.

To remove an existing group from a PivotTable report, right-click the field in the Pivot-Table report that contains the group to open the shortcut menu, point to Group and Show Detail, and then click Ungroup.

EVALUATING DATA USING A PIVOTCHART REPORT

Just like its chart counterpart, a **PivotChart report** represents source data as a graphic. The easiest way to create a PivotChart report is to use an existing PivotTable report as the source data. When you create a PivotChart report using existing data from a PivotTable report, you just click the Chart Wizard button on the PivotTable toolbar to add a new worksheet to the workbook that contains the PivotChart report. Unlike a regular chart, you can change the layout and data displayed in a PivotChart report by moving fields in addition to changing the chart type. A PivotChart report includes series, axes, and data markers, just like a regular chart. A PivotChart report also includes a Page field, a Data field, a Series field, a Category field, and Items. The Page field functions like the Page Area in a PivotTable report in that it lets you filter data by specific values in a field. A Data field functions like the Data Area in a PivotTable report in that it is the field in the data source that includes the data to summarize. The Series field provides the series of data for the chart. The Category field is a field that contains the individual categories for the data points in the chart by combining the data in the Row and Column Areas in the PivotTable report. An Item is an individual entry in a field that appears in a series. Barbara created a PivotChart report from the existing PivotTable report. The PivotChart report, which is a bar chart, appears in Figure 7.40.

Figure 7.40: PivotChart report for cities in California

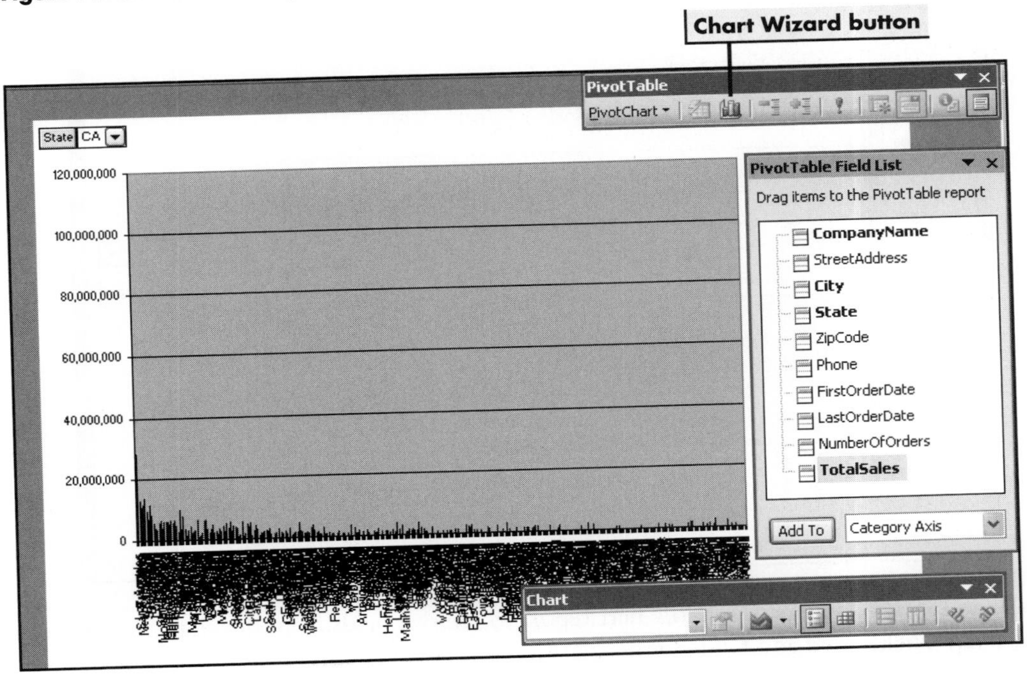

Figure 7.40 shows the Chart toolbar, which contains buttons for changing the appearance of a chart. Most of the options available for regular charts are also available for PivotChart reports. For example, clicking the Chart Type button lets you change the chart type, and clicking an area on the chart and then clicking the Format Data Series button lets you change the properties of the selected chart object.

Create a PivotChart Report Using a PivotTable Report
1. Click the PivotTable report to select it.
2. Click the Chart Wizard button 🔲 on the PivotTable toolbar.

The first thing that Barbara notices about the PivotChart report in Figure 7.40 is that the data for California is too crowded for a meaningful analysis. Because a PivotTable report usually summarizes a large amount of data, you might need to experiment with different chart types or filter the data to find an effective way to present the data visually. Barbara clicks the State list arrow on the chart's Y-axis, clicks HI in the list, and then clicks the OK button. The values in the PivotChart report change to display the sales data in descending order for cities in Hawaii, as shown in Figure 7.41. Because there are fewer cities with sales in Hawaii, the bar chart effectively communicates the information it contains.

Figure 7.41: PivotChart report for cities in Hawaii

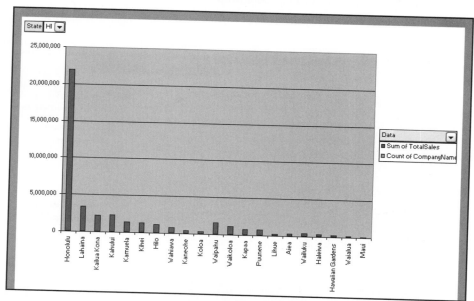

Barbara can also change the PivotChart report to remove fields from the chart, rearrange the chart's fields, and add fields to the chart just like in a PivotTable report.

IMPORTING INFORMATION FROM THE WEB INTO EXCEL

TheZone has been looking for ways to expand its market by working with international distributors. Because some of these distributors provide their estimates in foreign currencies, Barbara spends a lot of time finding resources on the Internet that convert foreign currencies into U.S. dollars. She usually goes to a Web site to get current information on currency exchange rates. Excel 2003 offers a way to retrieve data from Web pages using a Web query. A **Web query** is an automated method for retrieving information from a Web page without having to copy and paste it into an application. Excel includes several external data sources saved as Web queries that you can use to import currency rates, investor indexes, and stock quotes from MSN MoneyCentral Investor. Figure 7.42 shows the Investor Currency Rates in a new workbook. Because this data source is a Web page that MoneyCentral updates on a regular basis, each time Barbara opens the workbook, the data is refreshed. Barbara can use this information to get currency exchange rate information for approximately 50 countries around the world.

Figure 7.42: Currency rates imported from MSN MoneyCentral Investor

	A	B	C	D	E
1	**Currency Rates Provided by MSN MoneyCentral Investor**				
2	Click here to visit MSN MoneyCentral Investor				
3					
4	**Name**	**In US$**	**Per US$**		
5	Argentine Peso	0.3358	2.978		
6	Australian Dollar	0.7231	1.383		
7	Austrian Schilling	0.08935	11.192		
8	Bahraini Dinar	2.6524	0.377		
9	Bolivian Boliviano	0.12518	7.989		
10	Brazilian Real	0.35273	2.835		
11	British Pound	1.7784	0.562		
12	Canadian Dollar	0.79378	1.26		
13	Chilean Peso	0.00166	601.1		
14	Chinese Yuan	0.12068	8.287		
15	Colombian Peso	0.00038	2607		
16	Cyprus Pound	2.1327	0.469		
17	Czech Koruna	0.03906	25.604		
18	Danish Krone	0.16524	6.052		
19	Dutch Guilder	0.55791	1.792		
20	Ecuador Sucre	0.00004	25500		
21	Euro	1.2294	0.813		
22	Finnish Markka	0.20679	4.836		
23	French Franc	0.18742	5.336		

How To

Use a Saved Web Query to Import Data into a Worksheet

1. Open a new workbook or select the cell into which you want to import the data.
2. Click Data on the menu bar, point to Import External Data, and then click Import Data. The Select Data Source dialog box shown in Figure 7.43 opens and displays a list of saved Web queries (your list of Web queries might differ).

Figure 7.43: Select Data Source dialog box

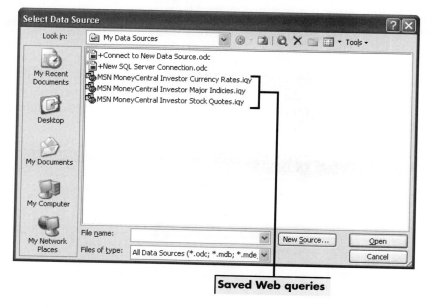

Saved Web queries

3. If necessary, browse to the folder that contains the Web query you want to use.

4. Click the Web query you want to use, and then click the Open button. The Import Data dialog box opens.

5. Click the option button for putting the data in the existing worksheet or a new worksheet, and then click the OK button.

Steps To Success: Level 2

Barbara received some additional data from the distributor that she needs to analyze and give to the marketing department. The data is stored in an Access database. The data includes the company name, address, phone number, first order date, and last order date for each retailer located in the Pacific Northwest. There is a field that identifies the total number of orders placed by each retailer for TheZone products. The distributor's database also includes total sales by month, from January 2005 through March 2006. Some of the records in the database are for sales from retailers in British Columbia, Canada, and the sales amounts are reported in Canadian dollars. Barbara wants to use a Web query to convert the Canadian dollar amounts into U.S. dollars so she can learn how to use a Web query, but also so all of the sales figures will be in U.S. dollars. Because currency exchange rates change daily, Barbara realizes that the conversion amounts will not reflect the actual values at the time of the sales, but this quick conversion will be fine for her current data analysis needs.

7

Complete the following:

1. Create a new workbook and save it as **Pacific Sales.xls** in the Chapter 7 folder.

2. Import the data contained in the Pacific Region table of the **Pacific.mdb** Access database into a worksheet named Pacific Region.

3. Sort the data first by state/province, then by city, and then by company name in ascending order.

4. Use a Web query to import currency conversion rates from the appropriate MSN MoneyCentral Investor Web page into a worksheet named Currency.

5. In the Pacific Region worksheet, create an IF statement in cell Y2 to convert the sales amounts for companies in British Columbia, Canada into U.S dollars. For U.S. companies, display the U.S. dollar amount. (*Hint:* Use the In US$ amount for Canada in the Currency worksheet to convert Canadian dollars to U.S. dollars.) Format the result as currency. Copy the IF statement down column Y and then to the range Z2:AM2333. Copy the column labels from the original financial data into these new columns. Type "(adj.)" at the end of each label to indicate that you have adjusted the data in these columns.

6. Calculate the total sales since January 2005 for each company in a column labeled AdjustedSales. Format the result as currency.

7. Hide the original columns containing financial information to allow the data to be updated from the original database table.

8. Assuming a report date of 4/1/2006, calculate the number of days since each company has placed an order with TheZone in a column named Days Since Last Order. Format the values with zero decimal places.

9. Calculate the number of fractional years that each company has been ordering from TheZone in a column named Relationship (Years). Format the values with two decimal places.

10. Create a PivotTable report from the data in the Pacific Region worksheet in a worksheet named PivotTable Report.

11. Add the AdjustedSales field to the Data Area and format its values as currency.

12. Add the Days Since Last Order field to the Row Area of the PivotTable report. After adding the Days Since Last Order field to the PivotTable report, group records in this field into groups of 100, starting with the value 0.

13. Add the StateProv field to the Column Area, and then add the CompanyName field to the Data Area to count the number of companies in each state.

14. Save and close the Pacific Sales.xls workbook.

LEVEL 3

IMPORTING AND EXPORTING XML DATA

EXCEL 2003 SKILLS TRAINING

* Create an XML Web query
* Export structured data from Excel
* Import XML into a worksheet

Level 3

UNDERSTANDING MARKUP LANGUAGES AND XML

A computer's ability to store data in one medium and reproduce it many times in other media was the foundation for the theory that the information or content of a document could exist separately from the formatting of the document. A **markup language** is the link between the content in a document and the instructions for formatting that content. A markup language uses a set of tags to distinguish different elements in a document and uses attributes to define those elements further. A markup language that you might already be familiar with is **HTML**, or **Hypertext Markup Language**, which is the markup language that creates Web pages (also called HTML documents). In HTML, you embed tags in the document to describe how to format its content. When a Web browser reads an HTML document, it uses the tags to format text according to a set of predefined descriptions of those tags. For example, when a browser reads the <b> and </b> HTML tags in a Web page, the browser formats the text between those tags as bold because the <b> and </b> tags are used to define bold text. Most Web browsers, regardless of the operating system on which they are installed, read and interpret the HTML tags in the same way, making HTML very effective at defining document content for a variety of computers.

The most significant markup language created for text was **Standardized General Markup Language (SGML)**, which was created in 1986 after eight years of development. SGML provides structure for a document by dividing it into elements (pieces), such as title, paragraph, text, name, part number, and so on. The markup language identifies these elements so that any program that interprets SGML can understand them. SGML also uses a **document type definition (DTD)** that identifies all the elements in a document and their structural relationships. The DTD contains information that identifies the tags used in the markup language and defines how they are related to each other. The DTD also describes which tags can be nested in other tags. SGML is a powerful and complex markup language that also allows the definition of other markup languages. HTML is defined as a SGML document type. HTML combines the text markup abilities of SGML with hypertext that links together Web pages. HTML uses predefined markup elements (called tags) to control the appearance of content in a Web page. The tags do not describe the content and are defined by a standards body that is fairly slow to change.

XML is the acronym for **Extensible Markup Language**. XML is a fairly recent innovation created through the efforts of the **World Wide Web Consortium** (**W3C**). The W3C was created in 1994 with the goal of leading the World Wide Web to its full potential. The W3C has approximately 350 member organizations that develop common protocols to promote the Web's evolution and ensure its interoperability. The XML specification is part of that goal. XML was originally developed to meet the needs of large-scale electronic publishing efforts, but it has been playing an increasingly important role in describing and exchanging data.

XML was designed to combine the markup power of SGML with the ease of use of HTML. The result is a language that defines the structure and rules for creating markup elements—in fact, this flexibility is what the term "extensible" in Extensible Markup Language means. In a way, the XML standard just provides the grammatical rules and the alphabet. A user can apply the standard to data in any way that makes sense. XML is increasingly being used as an enterprise data format for the transfer of information between different applications. XML stores information in a nonproprietary data format. Many programs can read XML documents, which makes it possible to read the data using a variety of applications. Most programs store data in a proprietary binary format, which can result in an organization becoming locked into a particular solution. Translating data from one format to another can be a very expensive task.

Barbara is also part of a team that is exploring how to use XML to improve the company's business processes. After a discussion with the team about how spreadsheets and databases create a powerful combination for analyzing data, she fielded a question about how to use XML data in spreadsheets. Barbara agrees to report back to the team about the potential of using XML at TheZone. As part of her research, Barbara will convert some existing data into XML format to learn more about using XML.

XML Documents

XML documents are user-defined documents in which the user develops a DTD that defines the elements contained in a document and descriptions of how those elements are related to each other. Because you can define elements in XML, it makes sense to make them as meaningful as possible. Instead of identifying a paragraph of text in a document as a paragraph, you can define individual types of paragraphs based on the content they will contain. For example, an XML document for TheZone might include elements that store data about a shoe as follows:

```
<shoe>
  <shoe_ID>SH-1987</shoe_ID>
  <shoe_name>Running shoe</shoe_name>
  <description>Men's size 11, white</description>
</shoe>
```

This code sample shows how you can combine data with meta-data. **Meta-data** is data that describes other data. You can think of it as data about data, but don't think too hard about that. XML uses angle brackets < > to separate markup from the data. The end of a particular element is represented by a forward slash </>. In this code example, the meta-data is combined with the content using XML. Because they are nested within the <shoe> and </shoe> elements, the shoe_ID, shoe_name, and description describe one shoe sold by TheZone. XML adds meaning to content by providing a description of the data through user-defined elements and a hierarchical structure that shows the relationship of one data element to another. At first, this system might seem very simple and obvious, but much like a language, the real power isn't in the ability to write and speak—it is in the ability to have others read and understand what you say. The potential of XML to transform business lies in the ability for business partners to share both data and meaning in a nonproprietary format.

Best Practice

Using XML Data in Excel

The improved functionality of working with XML data is one of the most important new features in Excel 2003. Excel 2000 and 2002 only had the ability to save and open spreadsheets that had been saved as XML documents that captured all the information, such as content and formatting. Other forms of XML documents could not be used. XML is quickly becoming a common output format for many enterprise data systems. As a result, working with this data format makes it possible for Excel to act as a front-end system for these larger data systems. For example, an employee might use Excel to manage travel receipts and then use XML to submit the travel claim information in the format required by the company for processing. It is a good idea to use XML data when the data is used by a variety of systems that can read and process data stored in this format.

ANALYZING XML DATA WITH EXCEL

Just like other uses of external data, the first step for analyzing XML data in Excel is to import the data into a worksheet. The import method you use depends on the data. For a simple XML document, you usually will import all of the data elements by importing the entire XML document as a list. For more complex XML documents with many data elements, you might be interested in only a few elements. In this case, you would use the XML Source task pane to map the elements you need to columns in a list. You can also export XML data that is added or edited in Excel as a "well-formed" XML document for distribution that conforms to the XML specification put forward by the World Wide Web Consortium. The term **well-formed** is commonly used in the XML community to describe an XML document that is properly structured and meets established rules and guidelines for how data is described and defined using XML.

Importing XML Data as an XML List

Barbara used Notepad to create a small XML document using data from the Sports Apparel Retailers table in the Apparel database. The XML document defines the data and includes two records. Figure 7.44 shows the XML document that Barbara created when viewed using a Web browser.

Figure 7.44: XML document with two records

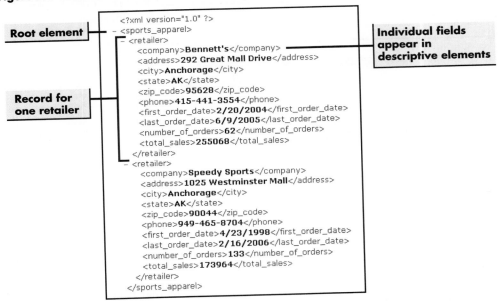

In Barbara's XML document, the <sports_apparel> element is the document's **root element**. An XML document can have only one root element, and all other elements are nested within the root element. She created the <retailer> element to contain the data for one record by nesting it in elements that describe the data. The elements between the <retailer> and </retailer> elements will become the column headings in the Excel list. The hierarchical structure clearly identifies which elements are related.

When you import XML data into a worksheet, Excel can create a schema based on the contents of the file being imported if the XML document does not already contain a schema. Because Barbara's XML document does not contain a schema, Excel creates one for her. A **schema** is a set of validation rules for an XML document. The schema describes the elements in the document and how they are structured or related to each other. You can use a schema to create very complex validation rules by defining the data type and valid values for an element. Schemas are useful for establishing a set of standards as a way for organizations to share data. The schema acts like a dictionary that defines the permissible words and their meanings for a transaction. After importing the XML document into a worksheet, the content appears in the worksheet in an XML list, as shown in Figure 7.45. An **XML list** is similar in appearance and functionality to an Excel list, but the data in an XML list is mapped to XML elements. Each column in an XML list represents an XML element in the XML document.

Figure 7.45: XML list in a worksheet

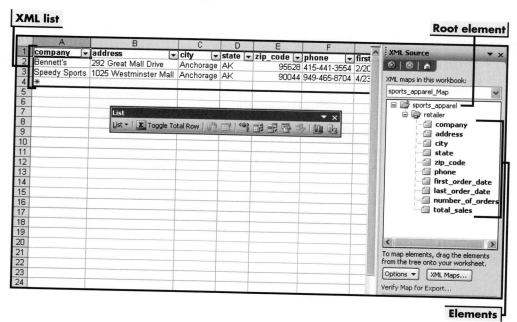

Barbara opened the XML Source task pane to view the schema that Excel generated from the source data in the XML document. When you add a schema to a workbook, Excel generates an **XML map** to create mapped ranges of data and define the relationships between these ranges and the elements in the XML schema. Excel uses the XML map to relate the data to the elements when importing and exporting XML data. A workbook can contain many XML maps, but an XML map can contain only one root element. The sports_apparel XML map shows the hierarchy of the XML document and the elements that contain data.

Import an XML Document as an XML List

1. Open the worksheet into which you want to import the data.
2. Click Data on the menu bar, point to XML, and then click Import. The Import XML dialog box opens.
3. Browse to the folder that contains the XML document you want to import.
4. Click the XML document, and then click the Import button. If the XML document does not refer to a schema, a message box opens to tell you that Excel will create a schema from the source data.
5. Click the OK button to close the message box. The Import Data dialog box opens.
6. Click the option button to import the data in the existing worksheet or in a new worksheet, and then click the OK button to import the data.

The XML data in the XML list shown in Figure 7.45 functions just like the data in an Excel list. You can sort, filter, and analyze the data in the same way. You can add a new row to the XML list by typing values into the blank row at the bottom of the XML list. If you later export this data as XML data, any new rows you added will appear in the correct elements in the XML document that Excel creates. You can add new columns of data to the XML list, but these new columns will not be exported because new columns are not part of the XML map or schema.

Adding an XML Map to a Workbook

Another method for importing XML data into Excel is by using the XML Source task pane. You can import a schema into a workbook or have Excel generate a schema or XML map from an existing XML document without importing any data. After you create the XML map in the workbook, you can use it to import individual data elements as columns in an XML list. You can use an XML map when you are importing a large, complex XML document that contains more elements than you need for your analysis. To import data using an XML map, open the XML Source task pane, and then click the XML Maps button. Figure 7.46 shows the XML Maps dialog box for Barbara's workbook.

Figure 7.46: XML Maps dialog box

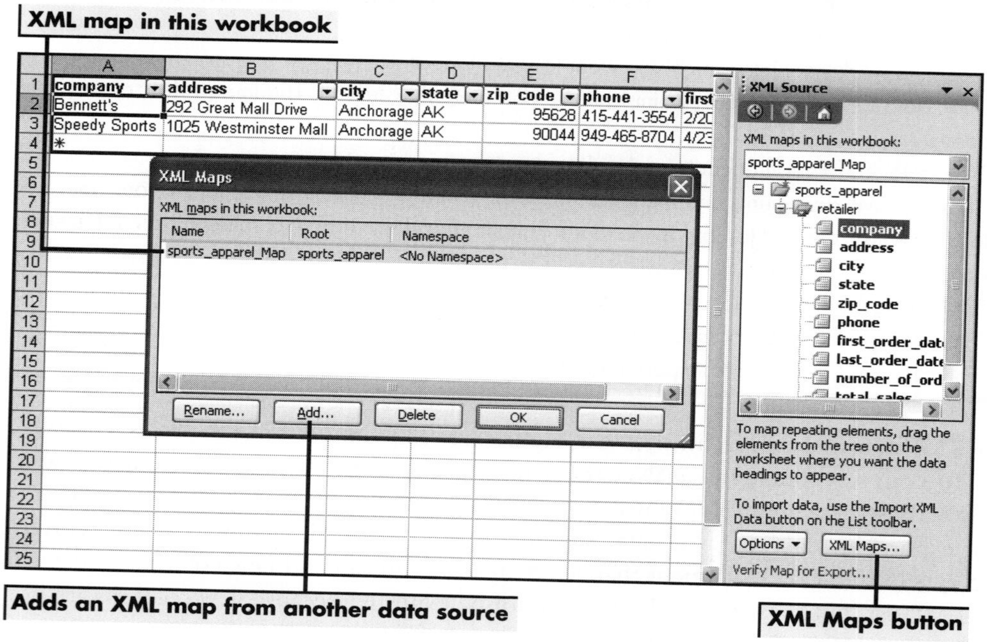

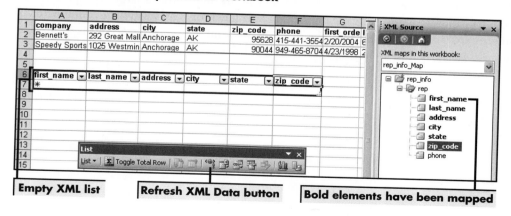

There is only one XML map, named sports_apparel_Map, defined in the workbook. Barbara can add another XML map to the workbook and then individually add the elements from the new XML map into the worksheet. Figure 7.47 shows Barbara's worksheet after adding the rep_info XML map to the workbook. Notice that she added five of the six fields from the rep_info XML map to the worksheet.

Figure 7.47: New XML map added to workbook

How To

Add an XML Map to a Workbook
1. Open the worksheet in which you want to import the data.
2. Click Data on the menu bar, point to XML, and then click XML Source. The XML Source task pane opens.
3. Click the XML Maps button on the XML Source task pane. The XML Maps dialog box opens.
4. Click the Add button. The Select XML Source dialog box opens.
5. Browse to the folder that contains the XML document, click the XML document to select it, and then click the Open button.
6. If necessary, click the OK button in the message box that opens to close it.
7. Click the OK button in the XML Maps dialog box.

Because the data elements are being imported using an XML map, only the element names appear in the worksheet. To import the data from these elements into the worksheet, click the Refresh XML Data button on the List toolbar. Figure 7.48 shows the worksheet after Barbara refreshes the data.

Figure 7.48: XML data added to XML list

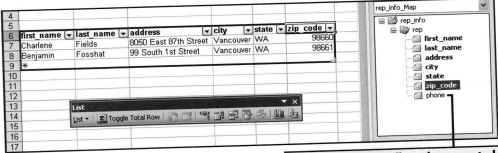

Unmapped field will not be exported

You can remove mapped elements from a worksheet by right-clicking the element you want to remove, pointing to Delete on the shortcut menu, and then clicking Column. However, if you delete an element from the worksheet, you cannot add it back to the original data range. The same thing is true for elements that you do not add to the worksheet before refreshing the data. In Figure 7.48, for example, Barbara cannot add the phone element to the data range because the range has already been mapped.

EXPORTING XML DATA

Excel exports XML lists that comply with the well-formed standard for XML documents. Barbara added two reps to the XML list that she just added to the worksheet. She wants to be certain that the data is included, so she exports it to a new file named Reps1.xml.

Export an XML List to an XML Document
1. Click the XML list to select it.
2. Click the Export XML Data button on the List toolbar. The Export XML dialog box opens.
3. Type a filename in the File name text box, and then click the Export button.

Barbara's XML document is shown in Figure 7.49. Excel only exported the data and elements in the XML list; notice that the phone element is not included in the exported file. You need to be careful when you export an XML list because only the elements in the XML list are exported, and not the elements from the XML map.

Figure 7.49: Exported data in an XML document

```
<?xml version="1.0" encoding="UTF-8" standalone="yes" ?>
- <rep_info xmlns:xsi="http://www.w3.org/2001/XMLSchema-instance">
  - <rep>
      <first_name>Charlene</first_name>
      <last_name>Fields</last_name>
      <address>8050 East 87th Street</address>
      <city>Vancouver</city>
      <state>WA</state>
      <zip_code>98660</zip_code>
    </rep>
  - <rep>
      <first_name>Benjamin</first_name>
      <last_name>Fosshat</last_name>
      <address>99 South 1st Street</address>
      <city>Vancouver</city>
      <state>WA</state>
      <zip_code>98661</zip_code>
    </rep>
  - <rep>
      <first_name>Lisa</first_name>
      <last_name>White</last_name>
      <address>800 Alamandine Ct</address>
      <city>Vancouver</city>
      <state>WA</state>
      <zip_code>98660</zip_code>
    </rep>
  - <rep>
      <first_name>Jonathan</first_name>
      <last_name>Plocher</last_name>
      <address>334 Lido</address>
      <city>Seattle</city>
      <state>WA</state>
      <zip_code>98101</zip_code>
    </rep>
  </rep_info>
```

Data for four reps

One of the most difficult issues with any new data format is deciding which data to convert. XML is a free, nonproprietary format, but the labor used to convert information is not. One of Barbara's concerns is how to convert information that TheZone has already stored in Excel workbooks into well-formed XML documents. She has discovered a lot of information about how to import existing XML documents into Excel, but not much about how to export Excel data to XML. She wants to convert the data stored in the company's Excel workbooks to XML so the entire enterprise can share it. She found a way to use XML maps and Excel lists to do this conversion fairly simply.

Excel list data is organized in rows and columns. Each row defines a record and each column defines a field within a group of records. XML documents are organized in a running tabular form with each element occupying one line. The prospect of writing code that would take the rows in an Excel list, add the appropriate XML element tags, and then copy it to a tabular format doesn't appeal to Barbara. She wants to convert the list of sports apparel retailers stored in an Excel worksheet into an XML list. She begins by opening a new workbook.

Barbara imports the XML map from the Apparel.xml document to load the elements from the Apparel.xml document into the XML Source task pane. Now, Barbara can map all the elements from the XML document into the worksheet at once.

How To

Map Elements from an XML Document to a Worksheet

1. Open a new workbook.
2. Click Data on the menu bar, point to XML, and then click XML Source. The XML Source task pane opens.
3. Click the XML Maps button on the XML Source pane to open the XML Maps dialog box.
4. Click the Add button in the XML Maps dialog box, browse to and select the XML document that contains the elements you want to map, and then click the Open button.
5. If necessary, click the OK button to close the message box that opens, and then click the OK button to close the XML Maps dialog box.
6. Click the cell into which you want to paste the elements, right-click the root element in the XML Source task pane to open the shortcut menu, and then click Map element. The Map XML Elements dialog box opens and indicates the range into which you will paste the elements.
7. Click the OK button to close the Map XML Elements dialog box and to paste the elements into the worksheet.

Now, Barbara's worksheet contains the XML elements in an empty XML list. She can open the Sports Apparel Companies.xls workbook, select all the rows that contain data about retailers, and copy this data to the Clipboard. Then, she can click the first cell in the blank row of the XML list and paste the copied data into the XML list. Figure 7.50 shows the pasted data.

Figure 7.50: XML list of sports apparel retailers

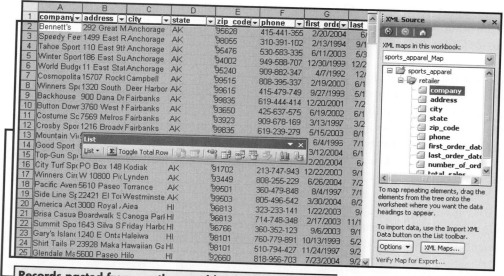

Records pasted from another workbook into an XML list

Now that all of the retailer data is in the XML list, Barbara can export the XML list to an XML document so that all of the records are saved in an XML document with the same structure as the two original records that she used to create the XML map. Barbara clicks the Export XML Data button on the List toolbar, types a filename in the Export XML dialog box, and then clicks the Export button. The data is converted to an XML document that can be used in any application that supports XML data. Barbara plans to use this procedure to convert other data into XML documents.

Steps To Success: Level 3

TheZone often partners with its larger customers on special projects to promote sales of TheZone products. One recently finished promotion was a gift certificate drawing with Above and Beyond Outfitters Inc. Customers from a variety of Above and Beyond stores purchased special TheZone products and filled out information cards for the chance to win certificates ranging in value from $10 to $30. You have a workbook containing the names and addresses of the winners along with the amounts of the gift certificates. You need to convert this information into an XML document that can be used to generate the personalized gift certificates.

Complete the following:

1. Open the **Promo.xls** workbook in the Chapter 7 folder, and then save it as **Above and Beyond Promotion.xls**.

2. Sort the information in ascending order by entry number.

3. Start Notepad, and then create an XML document using the following XML structure. Add the first two records in the workbook to the XML document. When you are finished, save the XML document as **XML-Promo.xml** in the Chapter 7 folder, and then close Notepad.

```xml
<?xml version="1.0" ?>
<promotion-456AB345-5>
  <entry_information>
      <entry_number> </entry_number>
      <last_name> </last_name>
      <first_name> </first_name>
      <address> </address>
      <city> </city>
      <state> </state>
      <zip_code> </zip_code>
      <phone> </phone>
      <amount> </amount>
  </entry_information>
  <entry_information>
      <entry_number> </entry_number>
      <last_name> </last_name>
      <first_name> </first_name>
      <address> </address>
      <city> </city>
      <state> </state>
      <zip_code> </zip_code>
      <phone> </phone>
      <amount> </amount>
  </entry_information>
</promotion-456AB345-5>
```

4. Import the **XML-Promo.xml** document into the workbook as an XML map.

5. On a new worksheet named XML Promo, map the elements from the XML map into the range A1:I1, and then refresh the XML data.

6. Copy rows 4 through 846 from the Gift Certificate Promotion worksheet, and then paste them into the XML list in the XML Promo worksheet.

7. Save the Above and Beyond Promotion.xls workbook, and then export the information in the XML Promo worksheet as an XML document named **Promotion-456AB345-5.xml** in the Chapter 7 folder.

8. Close the Above and Beyond Promotion.xls workbook.

CHAPTER SUMMARY

This chapter presented the different ways to import data from another source into Excel for analysis. In Level 1, you learned how to import data stored in a text file into Excel, and how to use the CONCATENATE, TRIM, RIGHT, and FIND functions to combine multiple text strings into a single text string, to trim unnecessary spaces from a text string, to find and extract characters from a text string, and to find specific characters in a text string. You also learned how to transform delimited data into rows and columns of data that you can sort and filter using the tools available in Excel. Finally, you learned how to create subtotals to analyze data and how to create and work with data stored in an Excel list.

In Level 2, you learned how to import data stored in a database into Excel and about the advantages of using a database to store data that can be exported to Excel for analysis. You used the Query Wizard to select specific records in a database and import them into Excel. You also learned how Excel stores and works with dates and times and used dates in calculations to determine the number of days and years between two dates. You learned how to create and use a PivotTable report to summarize and analyze data stored in a worksheet in a variety of ways. Finally, you used a Web query to import information from the Web into an Excel worksheet so that you can use it in calculations.

In Level 3, you learned about different markup languages, including XML. You saw how to use an existing XML document to import an XML map in a workbook and how to map XML elements into a worksheet. You learned how to import data into an XML list and how to export data to an XML document. For very large data sets, Excel provides a very quick and easy way to import and export XML data that can be used by other applications.

CONCEPTUAL REVIEW

1. List and describe the steps you would take to create a structured list of data from a text file that contains values stored on separate lines.

2. Why should you remove unnecessary spaces from data imported from another source? How do you remove unnecessary spaces from a text string?

3. How do the FIND and SEARCH functions work, and how are they different?

4. What options are available for parsing data when you use the Convert Text To Columns Wizard?

5. What are the advantages and disadvantages of using the Subtotal tool to analyze data?

6. What is the difference between a structured list and an Excel list? How are these two lists different when you sort the data they contain?

7. List and describe the six available options when using the AutoFilter in an Excel list.

8. What is the primary advantage of storing data in a database and importing that data into Excel?

9. Explain the steps you must take to import data stored in an Access database into Excel.

10. What is the Query Wizard and when would you use it?

11. How does Excel store date and time values?

12. What are the arguments for the YEARFRAC function? What are the possible values for calculating months and years using this function?

13. When should you use a PivotTable report to analyze data?

14. List and describe the four areas of a PivotTable report.

15. Not including currency exchange rate data, what other types of Web queries might be useful to a business using Excel for data analysis?

16. List and describe the differences and similarities between HTML and XML.

17. Describe the steps you would take to import XML data as an XML list in Excel.

18. How do you import an XML map into a workbook and map its elements into the worksheet?

19. What advantages exist for businesses to create ways to import, export, and use XML data in its daily operations?

CASE PROBLEMS

Level 1 – Importing and Analyzing Data for Johnson Equipment

Johnson Equipment, the medium-sized laboratory equipment manufacturing company at which you work, is in the process of acquiring Sloan Manufacturing, a smaller equipment manufacturer in the same industry. Because operations between your company and Sloan overlap, you need to merge the data from the new company with similar data for your company. The text file you received from Sloan contains categories, product numbers, and product descriptions, in addition to the on-hand quantity for each product and the number of products produced during each month of the past year. You need to add prefixes to the category names so the data will match the existing data that your company uses. Then, you will use Excel to organize and summarize the data.

Accounting

Complete the following:

1. Use Notepad (or another text editor) to open the text file named **Sloan.txt** from the Chapter 7 folder, select all the data it contains, copy the data to the Clipboard, and then close Notepad.

2. Create a new workbook named **Johnson-Sloan.xls**, and save it in the Chapter 7 folder. Paste the data you copied from the text file into a worksheet named Imported Data.

3. Convert the information in the worksheet into columns.

4. Sort the data by category and then by product number in ascending order.

5. Use the CONCATENATE function to add the appropriate prefix and a dash to each category using the following list. For example, the Analyzer category would begin with 500, followed by a dash and the category name (500-Analyzer).

Category	Prefix
Analyzer	500
Autoclave	501
Balances	503
Bath	505
Biohood	507
Cell Disrupters	509
Cell Harvesters	511
Centrifuges	513
Chromatography	515
Desiccators	517

Category	Prefix
Evaporators	519
Fermentors	521
Furnace	523
Gas Chromatographs	525
Glove Boxes	527
Microscopes	529
Reactors	531
Spectrophotometers	533
Ultrasonic Cleaners	535

7

Chapter Exercises

6. Change the data set into an Excel list.

7. Use the Total row to calculate the number of units on hand and the number of units produced in each month. Then add a new column named Total to the right of the December column that calculates the number of units produced for the year for each part.

8. Display the top 20 items based on the values in the Total column to show the parts with the highest productions by month.

9. Save and close the Johnson-Sloan.xls workbook.

Level 2 – Analyzing Manager Performance at Home Station

Sales

You are a regional manager for Home Station, a national chain of home renovation stores. You are analyzing the weekly sales data for one of the retail stores located in Austin, Texas. The sales data is reported by department and manager. The Austin store manager wants to rotate the department managers in each of the store's departments so each manager becomes more familiar with the entire store's operations. You have been assigned the task of determining the impact of rotating the managers on store sales. You will import the sales data from a database into Excel and then create a PivotTable report to summarize the quarterly sales by department and by manager.

Complete the following:

1. Create a new Excel workbook and save it as **Home Station-Austin.xls** in the Chapter 7 folder.

2. Import the information from the Sales table in the **Sales.mdb** database in the Chapter 7 folder into a worksheet named Sales.

3. Create a PivotTable report using the data in the Sales worksheet and place the PivotTable report in a new worksheet named Austin.

4. Use the PivotTable report to analyze the sales by department. Change the number format of the sales data to currency and sort the sales so that the department with the highest sales appears first. Print the worksheet.

5. Rearrange the fields in the PivotTable report to analyze department sales by quarter. Which department had the highest quarterly sales and in which quarter did it occur? (*Hint:* Use the Date field to summarize the dates by quarter.)

6. Add the Manager field to the PivotTable report to analyze each department's quarterly sales performance by manager. Which manager had the highest sales for each department? In which quarter did the manager's highest sales occur?

7. Rearrange the fields in the PivotTable report to analyze each manager's quarterly sales performance by department. Which department resulted in the highest sales for each manager? In which quarter did the highest sales occur?

8. Which manager should manage each department? Support your recommendations with data from the PivotTable report.

9. Save and close the Home Station-Austin.xls workbook.

Level 3 – Creating a Loan Application and Amortization for CKG Auto

CKG Auto's financial department has asked you to finish developing an Excel workbook that it plans to use to analyze automotive credit application data stored in individual XML documents. The workbook is based on an existing credit analysis spreadsheet. The workbook will be used to calculate loan payment information and create a loan amortization schedule for customers purchasing new and used vehicles from dealerships that provide financing options through CKG Auto. The Smith.xml file contains sample data that you will import into the spreadsheet to test the workbook.

Complete the following:

1. Open the **Credit.xls** file from the Chapter 7 folder, and then save it as **Automotive Credit Application.xls**.

2. Use the XML Source task pane to create an XML map using the **Smith.xml** file in the Chapter 7 folder.

3. Map the elements in the XML Source task pane to the appropriate cells in the worksheet by dragging them from the XML Source task pane and dropping them into the appropriate cells in the worksheet.

4. Use the List toolbar to import the appropriate data from the **Smith.xml** document to fill the blank cells for the Application Information, Loan Details, and Vehicle information sections in the Automotive Credit Application worksheet.

5. Insert the appropriate function and or formula to calculate the monthly car payment in cell B13.

6. Prepare an amortization schedule based on the information imported from the XML document.

7. Save and close the Automotive Credit Application.xls workbook.

Finance

7

Chapter Exercises

Microsoft
PowerPoint

MICROSOFT OFFICE
PowerPoint 2003

MICROSOFT OFFICE
POWERPOINT

MICROSOFT OFFICE
PowerPoint 2003

Using a Design Template and Text Slide Layout to Create a Presentation

PROJECT

1

CASE PERSPECTIVE

Do you use the 168 hours in each week effectively? From attending class, doing homework, attending school events, exercising, eating, watching television, and sleeping, juggling the demands of school and personal lives can be daunting. Odds are that one of every three students will fail a course at one point in their college career due to poor study habits.

The ability to learn effectively is the key to college success. What matters is not how long people study but how well they use their time in the classroom and while preparing for class assignments and tests. Students with good academic skills maximize their time and, consequently, achieve the highest grades on exams and homework assignments. They ultimately earn higher incomes than their less organized peers because good academic practices carry over to the working environment.

Advisers in the Academic Skills Center at your college are aware of this fact and are developing seminars to help students succeed. Their first presentation focuses on getting organized, enhancing listening skills, and taking tests effectively. Dr. Traci Johnson, the dean of the Academic Skills Center, has asked you to help her create a PowerPoint slide show to use at next month's lunchtime study skills session (Figure 1-1 on page PPT 5). In addition, she would like handouts of the slides to distribute to these students.

As you read through this project, you will learn how to use PowerPoint to create, save, and print a slide show that is composed of single- and multi-level bulleted lists.

MICROSOFT OFFICE
PowerPoint 2003

Using a Design Template and Text Slide Layout to Create a Presentation

PROJECT

Objectives

You will have mastered the material in this project when you can:

- Start and customize PowerPoint
- Describe the PowerPoint window
- Select a design template
- Create a title slide and text slides with single- and multi-level bulleted lists
- Change the font size and font style

- Save a presentation
- End a slide show with a black slide
- View a presentation in slide show view
- Quit PowerPoint and then open a presentation
- Display and print a presentation in black and white
- Use the PowerPoint Help system

What Is Microsoft Office PowerPoint 2003?

Microsoft Office PowerPoint 2003 is a complete presentation graphics program that allows you to produce professional-looking presentations (Figure 1-1). A PowerPoint **presentation** also is called a **slide show**.

PowerPoint contains several features to simplify creating a slide show. For example, you can instruct PowerPoint to create a predesigned presentation, and then you can modify the presentation to fulfill your requirements. You quickly can format a slide show using one of the professionally designed presentation design templates. To make your presentation more impressive, you can add tables, charts, pictures, video, sound, and animation effects. Additional PowerPoint features include the following:

- **Word processing**   create bulleted lists, combine words and images, find and replace text, and use multiple fonts and type sizes.
- **Outlining**   develop your presentation using an outline format. You also can import outlines from Microsoft Word or other word processing programs.
- **Charting**   create and insert charts into your presentations. The two chart types are: standard, which includes bar, line, pie, and xy (scatter) charts; and custom, which shows such objects as floating bars and colored lines.
- **Drawing**   form and modify diagrams using shapes such as arcs, arrows, cubes, rectangles, stars, and triangles.
- **Inserting multimedia**   insert artwork and multimedia effects into your slide show. The Microsoft Clip Organizer contains hundreds of media files, including pictures, photos, sounds, and movies.

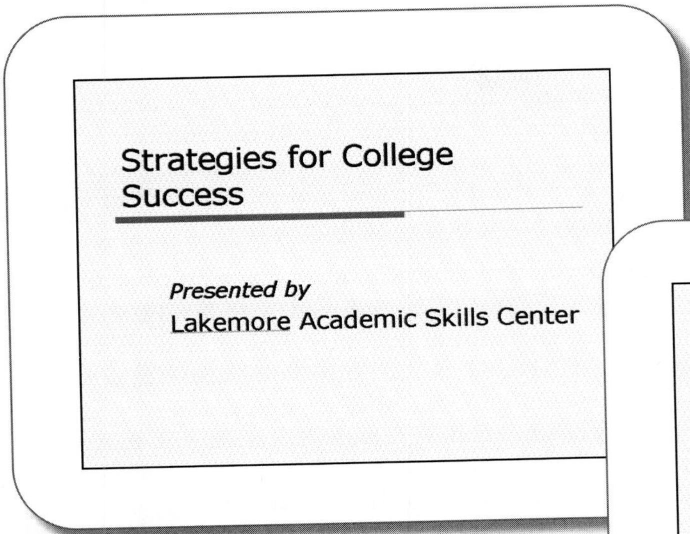

(a) Slide 1 (Title Slide)

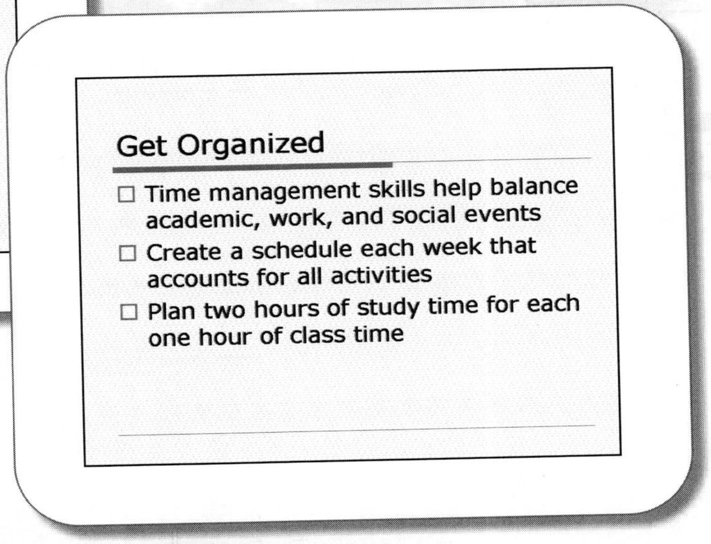

(b) Slide 2 (Single-Level Bulleted List)

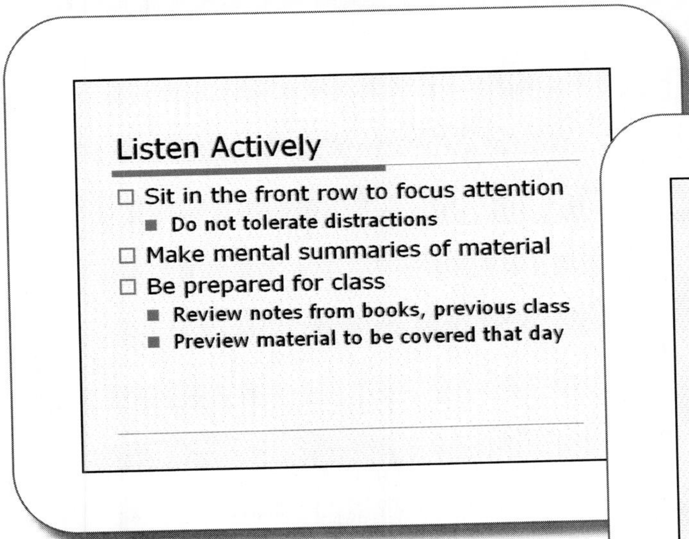

(c) Slide 3 (Multi-Level Bulleted List)

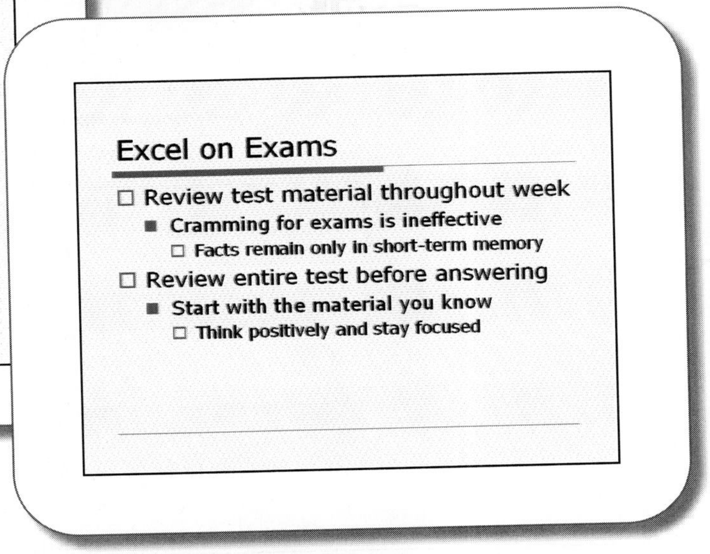

(d) Slide 4 (Multi-Level Bulleted List)

FIGURE 1-1

More About

Portable Projection Devices

New multimedia projectors weigh less than three pounds and can be held in one hand. Some projectors allow users to control the projector wirelessly from 300 feet away using a PDA. For more information about projectors, visit the PowerPoint 2003 More About Web page (scsite.com/ppt2003/more) and then click Projectors.

- **Web support** save presentations or parts of a presentation in HTML format so they can be viewed and manipulated using a browser. You can publish your slide show to the Internet or to an intranet.
- **E-mailing** send your entire slide show as an attachment to an e-mail message.
- **Using Wizards** create a presentation quickly and efficiently by answering prompts for specific content criteria. For example, the **AutoContent Wizard** gives prompts for the type of slide show you are planning, such as communicating serious news or motivating a team, and the type of output, such as an on-screen presentation or black and white overheads.

PowerPoint gives you the flexibility to make presentations using a projection device attached to a personal computer (Figure 1-2a) and using overhead transparencies (Figure 1-2b). In addition, you can take advantage of the World Wide Web and run virtual presentations on the Internet (Figure 1-2c). PowerPoint also can create paper printouts of the individual slides, outlines, and speaker notes.

This latest version of PowerPoint has many new features to make you more productive. It saves the presentation to a CD; uses pens, highlighters, arrows, and pointers for emphasis; and includes a thesaurus and other research tools.

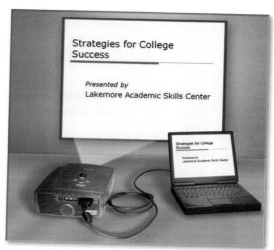

(a) **Projection Device Connected to a Personal Computer**

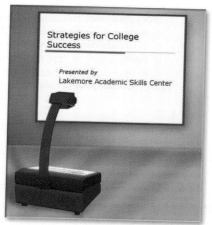

(b) **Overhead Transparencies**

(c) **PowerPoint Presentation on the World Wide Web**

FIGURE 1-2

Project One — Strategies for College Success

PowerPoint allows you to produce slides to use in an academic, business, or other environment. In Project 1, you create the presentation shown in Figures 1-1a through 1-1d. The objective is to produce a presentation, called Strategies for College Success, to be displayed using a projection device. As an introduction to PowerPoint, this project steps you through the most common type of presentation, which is a **text slide** consisting of a bulleted list. A **bulleted list** is a list of paragraphs, each preceded by a bullet. A **bullet** is a symbol such as a heavy dot (•) or other character that precedes text when the text warrants special emphasis.

Starting and Customizing PowerPoint

If you are stepping through this project on a computer and you want your screen to agree with the figures in this book, then you should change your computer's resolution to 800 × 600. To change the resolution on your computer, see Appendix D.

To start PowerPoint, Windows must be running. The quickest way to begin a new presentation is to use the Start button on the **Windows taskbar** at the bottom of the screen. The following steps show how to start PowerPoint and a new presentation.

To Start PowerPoint

1

• **Click the Start button on the Windows taskbar, point to All Programs on the Start menu, point to Microsoft Office on the All Programs submenu, and then point to Microsoft Office PowerPoint 2003 on the Microsoft Office submenu.**

Windows displays the commands on the Start menu above the Start button, the All Programs submenu, and the Microsoft Office submenu (Figure 1-3).

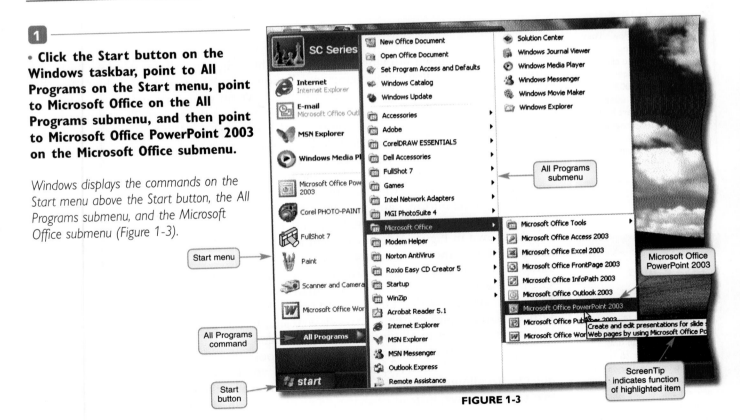

FIGURE 1-3

2

• **Click Microsoft Office PowerPoint 2003.**

PowerPoint starts. While PowerPoint is starting, the mouse pointer changes to the shape of an hourglass. After several seconds, PowerPoint displays a blank presentation titled Presentation1 in the PowerPoint window (Figure 1-4).

3

• **If the PowerPoint window is not maximized, double-click its title bar to maximize it.**

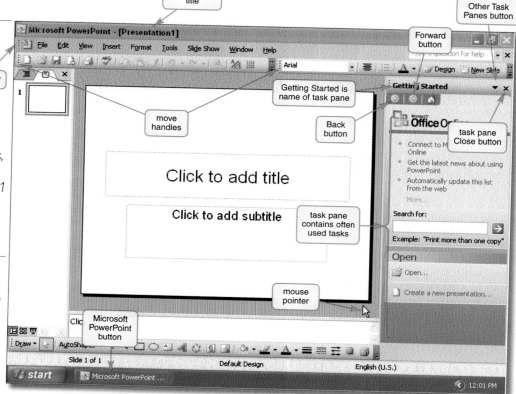

FIGURE 1-4

More About

Task Panes

When you first start PowerPoint, a small window called a task pane may be docked on the right side of the screen. You can drag a task pane title bar to float the pane in your work area or dock it on either the left or right side or the top or bottom of a screen, depending on your personal preference.

The screen shown in Figure 1-4 illustrates how the PowerPoint window looks the first time you start PowerPoint after installation on most computers. If the Office Speech Recognition software is installed and active on your computer, then, when you start PowerPoint, the Language bar is displayed on the screen. The **Language bar** contains buttons that allow you to speak commands and dictate text. It usually is located on the right side of the Windows taskbar next to the notification area, and it changes to include the speech recognition functions available in PowerPoint. In this book, the Language bar is closed because it takes up computer resources, and with the Language bar active, the microphone can be turned on accidentally by clicking the Microphone button, causing your computer to act in an unstable manner. For additional information about the Language bar, see page PPT 16 and Appendix B.

As shown in Figure 1-4, PowerPoint displays a task pane on the right side of the screen. A **task pane** is a separate window that enables users to carry out some PowerPoint tasks more efficiently. When you start PowerPoint, it displays the Getting Started task pane, which is a small window that provides commonly used links and commands that allow you to open files, create new files, or search Office-related topics on the Microsoft Web site. In this book, the Getting Started task pane is hidden to allow the maximum screen size to appear in PowerPoint.

At startup, PowerPoint also displays two toolbars on a single row. A **toolbar** contains buttons, boxes, and menus that allow you to perform frequent tasks quickly. To allow for more efficient use of the buttons, the toolbars should appear on two separate rows, instead of sharing a single row. The following steps show how to close the Language bar, close the Getting Started task pane, and instruct PowerPoint to display the toolbars on two separate rows.

To Customize the PowerPoint Window

1

• **If the Language bar appears, right-click it to display a list of commands.**

The Language bar shortcut menu appears (Figure 1-5).

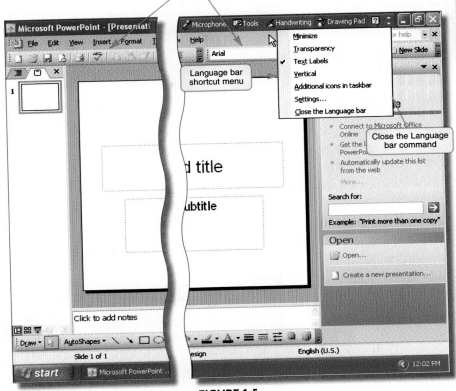

FIGURE 1-5

2

• **Click the Close the Language bar command.**

• **If necessary, click the OK button in the Language Bar dialog box.**

• **Click the Getting Started task pane Close button in the upper-right corner of the task pane.**

• **If the Standard and Formatting toolbars are positioned on the same row, click the Toolbar Options button on the Standard toolbar.**

The Language bar disappears. PowerPoint closes the Getting Started task pane and increases the size of the PowerPoint window. PowerPoint also displays the Toolbar Options list showing the buttons that do not fit on the toolbars when the toolbars are displayed on one row (Figure 1-6).

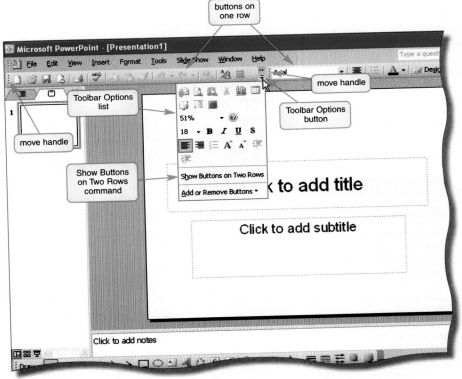

FIGURE 1-6

3

• **Click Show Buttons on Two Rows.**

PowerPoint displays the buttons on two separate rows (Figure 1-7). The Toolbar Options list shown in Figure 1-6 on the previous page is empty because all the buttons are displayed on two rows.

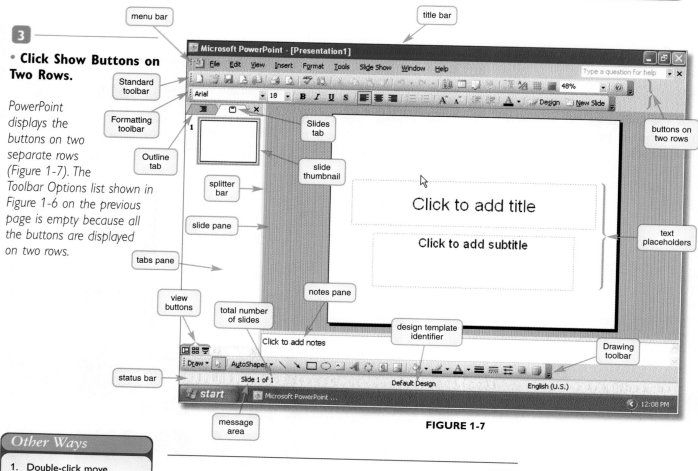

FIGURE 1-7

Other Ways

1. Double-click move handle on toolbar

As you work through creating a presentation, you will find that certain PowerPoint operations result in displaying a task pane. Besides the Getting Started task pane shown in Figure 1-4 on page PPT 8, PowerPoint provides 15 additional task panes: Help, Search Results, Clip Art, Research, Clipboard, New Presentation, Template Help, Shared Workspace, Document Updates, Slide Layout, Slide Design, Slide Design - Color Schemes, Slide Design - Animation Schemes, Custom Animation, and Slide Transition. These task panes are discussed when they are used. You can show or hide a task pane by clicking the Task Pane command on the View menu. You can activate additional task panes by clicking the down arrow to the left of the Close button on the task pane title bar (Figure 1-4) and then selecting a task pane in the list. To switch between task panes that you opened during a session, use the Back and Forward buttons on the left side of the task pane title bar.

The PowerPoint Window

The basic unit of a PowerPoint presentation is a **slide**. A slide contains one or many **objects**, such as a title, text, graphics, tables, charts, and drawings. An object is the building block for a PowerPoint slide. PowerPoint assumes the first slide in a new presentation is the **title slide**. The title slide's purpose is to introduce the presentation to the audience.

More About

Resolution

Resolution refers to the number of pixels, or dots, that can fit into one square inch of a monitor. It is measured, consequently, in dots per inch, which is abbreviated, dpi. PowerPoint's default screen resolution is 72 dpi, and it can be set as high as 1,200 dpi. Use a resolution of 150 dpi if you are going to print handouts of your slides.

In PowerPoint, you have the option of using the PowerPoint default settings or establishing your own. A **default setting** is a particular value for a variable that PowerPoint assigns initially. It controls the placement of objects, the color scheme, the transition between slides, and other slide attributes, and it remains in effect unless you cancel or override it. **Attributes** are the properties or characteristics of an object. For example, if you underline the title of a slide, the title is the object, and the underline is the attribute. When you start PowerPoint, the default **slide layout** is **landscape orientation**, where the slide width is greater than its height. In landscape orientation, the slide size is preset to 10 inches wide and 7.5 inches high. You can change the slide layout to **portrait orientation**, so the slide height is greater than its width, by clicking Page Setup on the File menu. In portrait orientation, the slide width is 7.5 inches, and the height is 10 inches.

When a PowerPoint window is open, its name appears in an icon on the Windows taskbar. The **active application** is the one displaying in the foreground of the desktop. That application's corresponding icon on the Windows taskbar is displayed recessed.

PowerPoint Views

PowerPoint has three main views: normal view, slide sorter view, and slide show view. A **view** is the mode in which the presentation appears on the screen. You may use any or all views when creating a presentation, but you can use only one at a time. You also can select one of these views to be the default view. Change views by clicking one of the view buttons located at the lower-left of the PowerPoint window above the Drawing toolbar (Figure 1-7). The PowerPoint window display varies depending on the view. Some views are graphical while others are textual.

You generally will use normal view and slide sorter view when you are creating a presentation. **Normal view** is composed of three working areas that allow you to work on various aspects of a presentation simultaneously (Figure 1-7). The left side of the screen has a tabs pane that consists of an **Outline tab** and a **Slides tab** that alternate between views of the presentation in an outline of the slide text and a thumbnail, or miniature, view of the slides. You can type the text of the presentation on the Outline tab and easily rearrange bulleted lists, paragraphs, and individual slides. As you type, you can view this text in the **slide pane**, which shows a large view of the current slide on the right side of the window. You also can enter text, graphics, animations, and hyperlinks directly in the slide pane. The **notes pane** at the bottom of the window is an area where you can type notes and additional information. This text can consist of notes to yourself or remarks to share with your audience.

In normal view, you can adjust the width of the slide pane by dragging the **splitter bar** and the height of the notes pane by dragging the pane borders. After you have created at least two slides, **scroll bars**, **scroll arrows**, and **scroll boxes** will be displayed below and to the right of the windows, and you can use them to view different parts of the panes.

Slide sorter view is helpful when you want to see all the slides in the presentation simultaneously. A thumbnail version of each slide is displayed, and you can rearrange their order, add transitions and timings to switch from one slide to the next in a presentation, add and delete slides, and preview animations.

Slide show view fills the entire screen and allows you to see the slide show just as your audience will view it. Transition effects, animation, graphics, movies, and timings are shown as they will appear during an actual presentation.

Table 1-1 identifies the view buttons and provides an explanation of each view.

Table 1-1	View Buttons and Functions	
BUTTON	**BUTTON NAME**	**FUNCTION**
	Normal View	Shows three panes: the tabs pane with either the Outline tab or the Slides tab, the slide pane, and the notes pane.
	Slide Sorter View	Shows thumbnail versions of all slides in a presentation. You then can copy, cut, paste, or otherwise change the slide position to modify the presentation. Slide sorter view also is used to add timings, to select animated transitions, and to preview animations.
	Slide Show View	Shows the slides as an electronic presentation on the full screen of your computer's monitor. Looking much like a slide projector display, this view can show you the effect of transitions, build effects, slide timings, and animations.

More About

The 7 × 7 Rule

All slide shows in the projects and exercises in this textbook follow the 7 x 7 rule. This guideline states that each slide should have a maximum of seven lines, and each of these lines should have a maximum of seven words. This rule requires PowerPoint designers to choose their words carefully and, in turn, helps viewers read the slides easily.

Placeholders, Text Areas, Mouse Pointer, and Scroll Bars

The PowerPoint window contains elements similar to the document windows in other Microsoft Office applications. Other features are unique to PowerPoint. The main elements are the placeholders, text areas, mouse pointer, and scroll bars.

PLACEHOLDERS **Placeholders** are boxes that are displayed when you create a new slide. All layouts except the Blank slide layout contain placeholders. Depending on the particular slide layout selected, placeholders are displayed for the slide title, body text, charts, tables, organization charts, media clips, and clip art. You type titles, body text, and bulleted lists in **text placeholders**; you place graphic elements in chart placeholders, table placeholders, organizational chart placeholders, and clip art placeholders. A placeholder is considered an **object**, which is a single element of a slide.

TEXT AREAS **Text areas** are surrounded by a dotted outline. The title slide in Figure 1-7 on page PPT 10 has two text areas that contain the text placeholders where you will type the main heading, or title, of a new slide and the subtitle, or other object. Other slides in a presentation may use a layout that contains text areas for a title and bulleted lists.

MOUSE POINTER The **mouse pointer** can become one of several different shapes depending on the task you are performing in PowerPoint and the pointer's location on the screen. The different shapes are discussed when they appear.

SCROLL BARS When you add a second slide to a presentation, a **vertical scroll bar** appears on the right side of the slide pane. PowerPoint allows you to use the scroll bar to move forward or backward through the presentation.

The **horizontal scroll bar** also may be displayed. It is located on the bottom of the slide pane and allows you to display a portion of the slide when the entire slide does not fit on the screen.

Status Bar, Menu Bar, Standard Toolbar, Formatting Toolbar, and Drawing Toolbar

The status bar is displayed at the bottom of the screen above the Windows taskbar (Figure 1-7). The menu bar, Standard toolbar, and Formatting toolbar are displayed at the top of the screen just below the title bar. The Drawing toolbar is displayed above the status bar.

STATUS BAR Immediately above the Windows taskbar at the bottom of the screen is the status bar. The **status bar** consists of a message area and a presentation design template identifier (Figure 1-7). Generally, the message area shows the current slide number and the total number of slides in the slide show. For example, in Figure 1-7 the message area shows Slide 1 of 1. Slide 1 is the current slide, and of 1 indicates the slide show contains only one slide. The template identifier shows Default Design, which is the template PowerPoint uses initially.

MENU BAR The **menu bar** is a special toolbar that includes the PowerPoint menu names (Figure 1-8a). Each **menu name** represents a menu of commands that you can use to perform tasks such as retrieving, storing, printing, and manipulating objects in a presentation. When you point to a menu name on the menu bar, the area of the menu bar containing the name changes to a button. To display a menu, such as the Edit menu, click the Edit menu name on the menu bar. A **menu** is a list of commands. If you point to a command on a menu that has an arrow to its right edge, a **submenu** shows another list of commands.

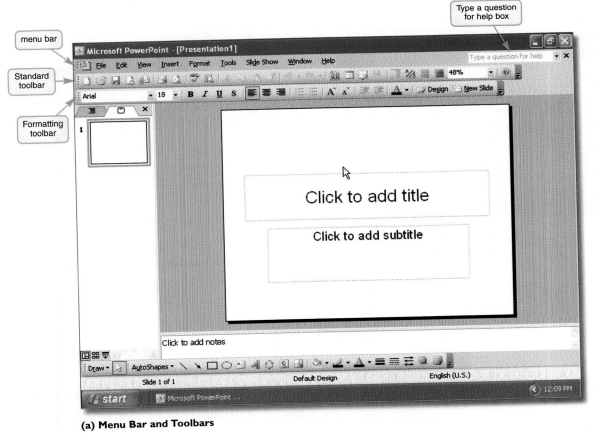

(a) Menu Bar and Toolbars

FIGURE 1-8

When you click a menu name on the menu bar, PowerPoint displays a **short menu** listing the most recently used commands (Figure 1-8b). If you wait a few seconds or click the arrows at the bottom of the short menu, it expands into a full menu. A **full menu** lists all the commands associated with a menu (Figure 1-8c). You also can display a full menu immediately by double-clicking the menu name on the menu bar. In this book, always have PowerPoint show the full menu by using one of the following techniques:

1. Click the menu name on the menu bar and then wait a few seconds.
2. Click the menu name on the menu bar and then click the arrows at the bottom of the short menu.
3. Click the menu name on the menu bar and then point to the arrows at the bottom of the short menu.
4. Double-click the menu name on the menu bar.

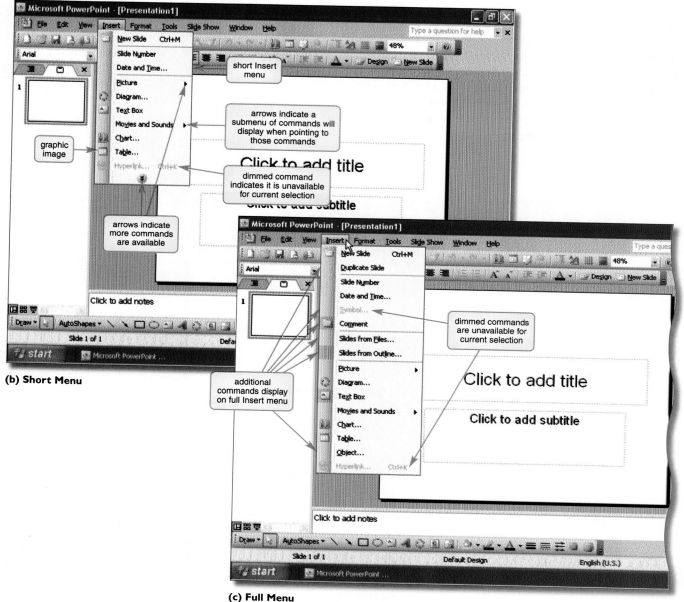

FIGURE 1-8 (continued)

Both short and full menus display some **dimmed commands** that appear gray, or dimmed, instead of black, which indicates they are not available for the current selection. A command with a dark gray shading to the left of it on a full menu is a **hidden command** because it does not appear on a short menu. As you use PowerPoint, it automatically personalizes the short menus for you based on how often you use commands. That is, as you use hidden commands, PowerPoint *unhides* them and places them on the short menu.

The menu bar can change to include other menu names depending on the type of work you are doing in PowerPoint. For example, if you are adding a chart to a slide, Data and Chart menu names are added to the menu bar with commands that reflect charting options.

STANDARD, FORMATTING, AND DRAWING TOOLBARS The **Standard toolbar** (Figure 1-9a), **Formatting toolbar** (Figure 1-9b), and **Drawing toolbar** (Figure 1-9c on the next page) contain buttons and boxes that allow you to perform frequent tasks more quickly than when using the menu bar. For example, to print a slide show, you click the Print button on the Standard toolbar. Each button has an image on the button face that helps you remember the button's function. Also, when you move the mouse pointer over a button or box, the name of the button or box appears below it in a ScreenTip. A **ScreenTip** is a short on-screen note associated with the object to which you are pointing. For examples of ScreenTips, see Figures 1-3 and 1-13 on pages PPT 7 and PPT 19.

Figure 1-9 illustrates the Standard, Formatting, and Drawing toolbars and describes the functions of the buttons. Each of the buttons and boxes will be explained in detail when they are used.

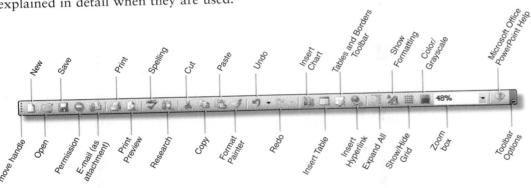

(a) Standard Toolbar

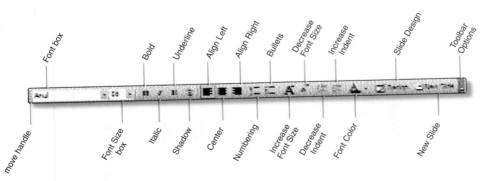

(b) Formatting Toolbar

FIGURE 1-9

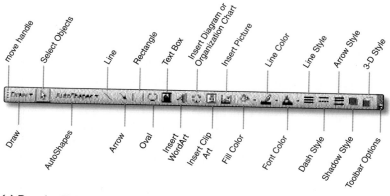

(c) Drawing Toolbar

FIGURE 1-9 (continued)

PowerPoint has several additional toolbars you can display by pointing to Toolbars on the View menu and then clicking the respective name on the Toolbars submenu. You also may display a toolbar by pointing to a toolbar and right-clicking to display a shortcut menu, which lists the available toolbars. A **shortcut menu** contains a list of commands or items that relate to the item to which you are pointing when you right-click.

Speech Recognition

With the **Office Speech Recognition software** installed and a microphone, you can speak the names of toolbar buttons, menus, menu commands, list items, alerts, and dialog box controls, such as OK and Cancel. You also can dictate words to fill the placeholders. To indicate whether you want to speak commands or dictate placeholder entries, you use the Language bar. The Language bar can be in one of four states: (1) **restored**, which means it is displayed somewhere in the PowerPoint window (Figure 1-10a); (2) **minimized**, which means it is displayed on the Windows taskbar (Figure 1-10b); (3) **hidden**, which means you do not see it on the screen but it will be displayed the next time you start your computer; (4) **closed**, which means it is hidden permanently until you enable it. If the Language bar is hidden or closed and you want it to display, then do the following:

1. Right-click an open area on the Windows taskbar at the bottom of the screen.
2. Point to Toolbars and then click Language bar on the Toolbars submenu.

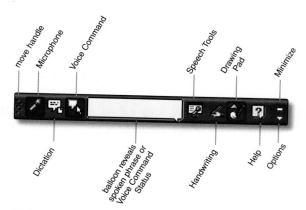

(a) Language Bar Restored

FIGURE 1-10

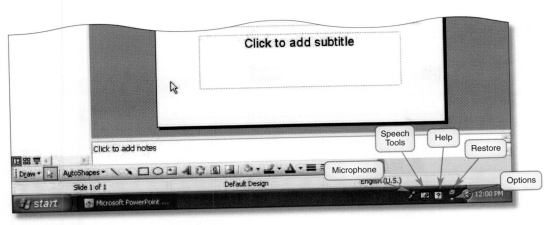

(b) Language Bar Minimized on Windows Taskbar

FIGURE 1-10 *(continued)*

If the Language bar command is dimmed on the Toolbars submenu or if the Speech command is dimmed on the Tools menu, the Office Speech Recognition software is not installed.

In this book, the Language bar does not appear in the figures. If you want to close the Language bar so that your screen is identical to what you see in the book, right-click the Language bar and then click Close the Language bar on the shortcut menu.

Additional information about the speech recognition capabilities of PowerPoint is available in Appendix B.

Choosing a Design Template

A **design template** provides consistency in design and color throughout the entire presentation. It determines the color scheme, font and font size, and layout of a presentation. PowerPoint has three Slide Design task panes that allow you to choose and change the appearance of slides in your presentation. The **Slide Design task pane** shows a variety of styles. You can alter the colors used in the design templates by using the **Slide Design – Color Schemes task pane**. In addition, you can animate elements of your presentation by using the **Slide Design – Animation Schemes task pane**.

In this project, you will select a particular design template by using the Slide Design task pane. The top section of the task pane, labeled Used in This Presentation, shows the template currently used in the slide show. PowerPoint uses the **Default Design** template until you select a different style. When you place your mouse over a template, the name of the template appears. Once a PowerPoint slide show has been created on the computer, the next section of the task pane displayed is the Recently Used templates. This area shows the four templates you have used in your newest slide shows. The Available For Use area shows additional templates. The templates are displayed in alphabetical order in the two columns.

You want to change the template for this presentation from the Default Design to Profile. The steps on the next page apply the Profile design template.

More About

The Default Design Template

Some PowerPoint slide show designers create presentations using the Default Design template. This blank design allows them to concentrate on the words being used to convey the message and does not distract them with colors and various text attributes. Once the text is entered, the designers then select an appropriate design template.

To Choose a Design Template

1

• **Point to the Slide Design button on the Formatting toolbar (Figure 1-11).**

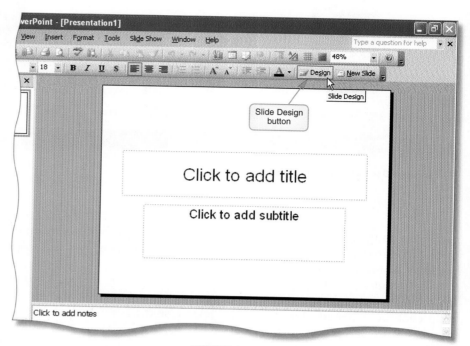

FIGURE 1-11

2

• **Click the Slide Design button and then point to the down scroll arrow in the Apply a design template list.**

The Slide Design task pane appears (Figure 1-12). The Apply a design template list shows thumbnail views of numerous design templates. Your list may look different depending on your computer. The Default Design template is highlighted in the Used in This Presentation area. Other templates display in the Available For Use area and possibly in the Recently Used area. The Close button in the Slide Design task pane can be used to close the task pane if you do not want to apply a new template.

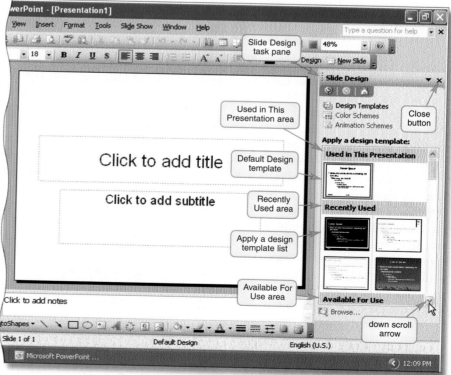

FIGURE 1-12

3

• **Click the down scroll arrow to scroll through the list of design templates until Profile appears in the Available For Use area. Point to the Profile template.**

The Profile template is selected, as indicated by the blue box around the template and the arrow button on the right side (Figure 1-13). PowerPoint provides 45 templates in the Available For Use area. Additional templates are available on the Microsoft Office Online Web site. A ScreenTip shows the template's name. Your system may display the ScreenTip, Profile.pot, which indicates the design template's file extension (.pot).

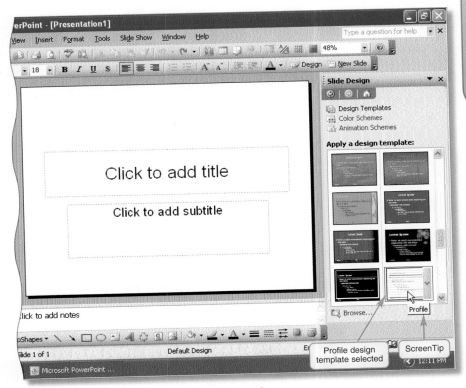

FIGURE 1-13

4

• **Click Profile.**

• **Point to the Close button in the Slide Design task pane.**

The template is applied to Slide 1, as shown in the slide pane and Slides tab (Figure 1-14).

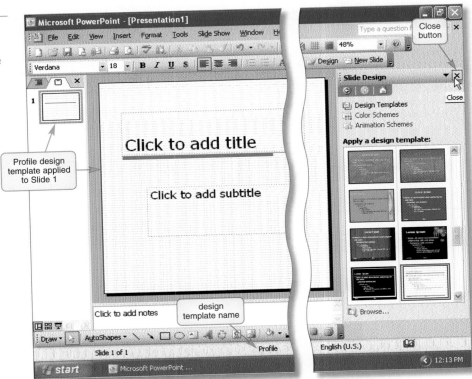

FIGURE 1-14

5

• **Click the Close button.**

Slide 1 is displayed in normal view with the Profile design template (Figure 1-15).

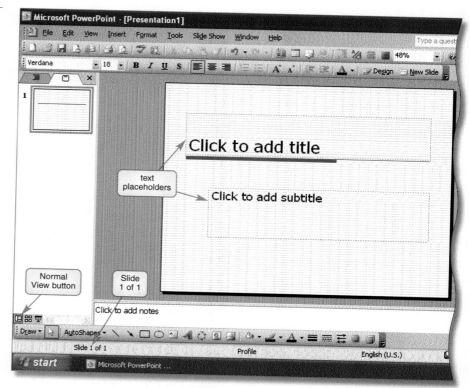

FIGURE 1-15

Creating a Title Slide

With the exception of a blank slide, PowerPoint assumes every new slide has a title. To make creating a presentation easier, any text you type after a new slide appears becomes title text in the title text placeholder.

Entering the Presentation Title

The presentation title for Project 1 is Strategies for College Success. To enter text in your slide, you type on the keyboard or speak into the microphone. As you begin entering text in the title text placeholder, the title text is displayed immediately in the Slide 1 thumbnail in the Slides tab. The following steps create the title slide for this presentation.

To Enter the Presentation Title

1

• **Click the label, Click to add title, located inside the title text placeholder.**

The insertion point is in the title text placeholder (Figure 1-16). The **insertion point** *is a blinking vertical line (|), which indicates where the next character will display. The mouse pointer changes to an I-beam. A* **selection rectangle** *appears around the title text placeholder. The placeholder is selected as indicated by the border and sizing handles displaying on the edges.*

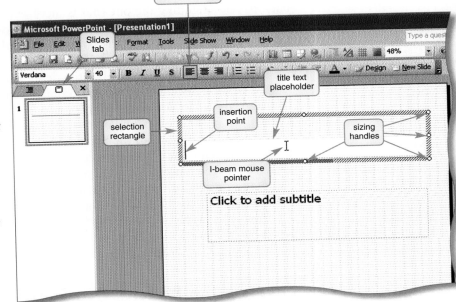

FIGURE 1-16

2

• **Type** Strategies for College Success **in the title text placeholder. Do not press the ENTER key.**

The title text, Strategies for College Success, appears on two lines in the title text placeholder and in the Slides tab (Figure 1-17). The insertion point appears after the final letter s in Success. The title text is displayed aligned left in the placeholder with the default text attributes of the Verdana font and font size 40.

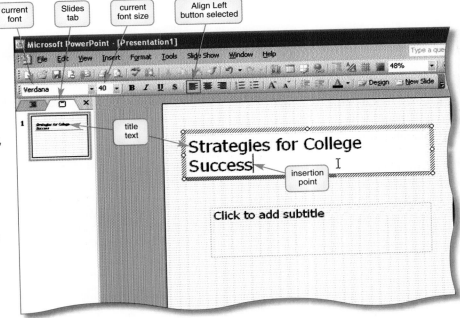

FIGURE 1-17

PowerPoint **line wraps** text that exceeds the width of the placeholder. One of PowerPoint's features is **text AutoFit**. If you are creating a slide and need to squeeze an extra line in the text placeholder, PowerPoint will prompt you to resize the existing text in the placeholder so the spillover text will fit on the slide.

> *Other Ways*
>
> 1. In Dictation mode, say "Strategies for College Success"

Correcting a Mistake When Typing

If you type the wrong letter, press the BACKSPACE key to erase all the characters back to and including the one that is incorrect. If you mistakenly press the ENTER key after typing the title and the insertion point is on the new line, simply press the BACKSPACE key to return the insertion point to the right of the letter s in the word Success.

When you install PowerPoint, the default setting allows you to reverse up to the last 20 changes by clicking the Undo button on the Standard toolbar. The ScreenTip that appears when you point to the Undo button changes to indicate the type of change just made. For example, if you type text in the title text placeholder and then point to the Undo button, the ScreenTip that appears is Undo Typing. For clarity, when referencing the Undo button in this project, the name displaying in the ScreenTip is referenced. Another way to reverse changes is to click the Undo command on the Edit menu. As with the Undo button, the Undo command reflects the last type of change made to the presentation.

You can reapply a change that you reversed with the Undo button by clicking the Redo button on the Standard toolbar. Clicking the Redo button reverses the last undo action. The ScreenTip name reflects the type of reversal last performed.

Entering the Presentation Subtitle

The next step in creating the title slide is to enter the subtitle text into the subtitle text placeholder. Complete the following steps to enter the presentation subtitle.

To Enter the Presentation Subtitle

1

• **Click the label, Click to add subtitle, located inside the subtitle text placeholder.**

The insertion point appears in the subtitle text placeholder (Figure 1-18). The mouse pointer changes to an I-beam, indicating the mouse is in a text placeholder. The selection rectangle indicates the placeholder is selected.

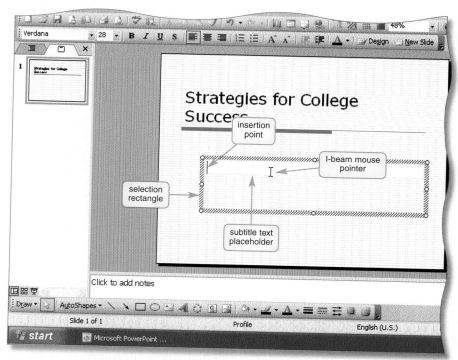

FIGURE 1-18

Q&A

Q: Can I change the capitalization of letters and words?

A: Yes. Simply select the text you want to change, click Change Case on the Format menu, and then click the desired option. For example, you can change all uppercase letters to lowercase letters or capitalize the first letter in each word.

2

- **Type** Presented by **and then press the ENTER key.**

- **Type** Lakemore Academic Skills Center **but do not press the ENTER key.**

The subtitle text appears in the subtitle text placeholder and the Slides tab (Figure 1-19). The insertion point appears after the letter r in Center. A red wavy line appears below the word, Lakemore, to indicate a possible spelling error.

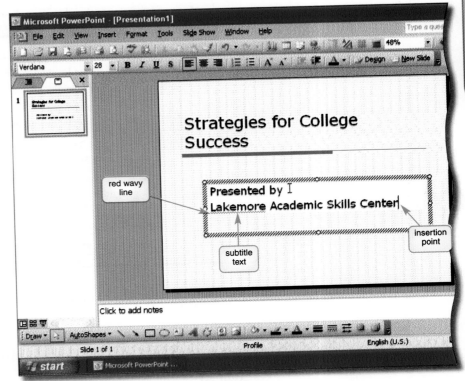

FIGURE 1-19

Other Ways

1. In Dictation mode, say "Presented by, New Line, Lakemore Academic Skills Center"

After pressing the ENTER key in Step 2, PowerPoint created a new line, which is the second paragraph in the placeholder. A **paragraph** is a segment of text with the same format that begins when you press the ENTER key and ends when you press the ENTER key again.

Text Attributes

This presentation uses the Profile design template. Each design template has its own text attributes. A **text attribute** is a characteristic of the text, such as font, font size, font style, or text color. You can adjust text attributes any time before, during, or after you type the text. Recall that a design template determines the color scheme, font and font size, and layout of a presentation. Most of the time, you use the design template's text attributes and color scheme. Occasionally, you may want to change the way a presentation looks, however, and still keep a particular design template. PowerPoint gives you that flexibility. You can use the design template and change the font and the font's color, effects, size, and style. Text may have one or more font styles and effects simultaneously. Table 1-2 on the next page explains the different text attributes available in PowerPoint.

More About

Text Attributes

The Microsoft Web site contains a comprehensive glossary of typography terms. The information includes a diagram illustrating text attributes. For more information, visit the PowerPoint 2003 More About Web page (scsite.com/ppt2003/more) and then click Attributes.

Table 1-2	Design Template Text Attributes
ATTRIBUTE	**DESCRIPTION**
Color	Defines the color of text. Printing text in color requires a color printer or plotter.
Effects	Effects include underline, shadow, emboss, superscript, and subscript. Effects can be applied to most fonts.
Font	Defines the appearance and shape of letters, numbers, and special characters.
Size	Specifies the height of characters on the screen. Character size is gauged by a measurement system called points. A single point is about 1/72 of an inch in height. Thus, a character with a point size of 18 is about 18/72 (or 1/4) of an inch in height.
Style	Font styles include regular, bold, italic, and bold italic.

The next two sections explain how to change the font size and font style attributes.

Changing the Style of Text to Italic

Text font styles include plain, italic, bold, shadowed, and underlined. PowerPoint allows you to use one or more text font styles in a presentation. The following steps add emphasis to the first line of the subtitle text by changing regular text to italic text.

To Change the Text Font Style to Italic

1

• **Triple-click the paragraph, Presented by, in the subtitle text placeholder, and then point to the Italic button on the Formatting toolbar.**

The paragraph, Presented by, is highlighted (Figure 1-20). The Italic button is surrounded by a blue box. You select an entire paragraph quickly by triple-clicking any text within the paragraph.

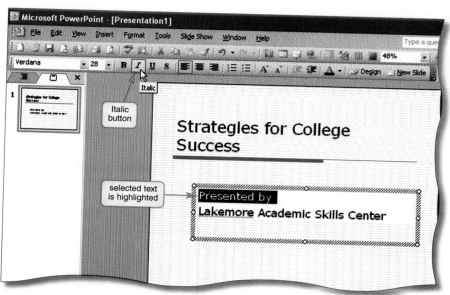

FIGURE 1-20

2

- **Click the Italic button.**

The text is italicized on the slide and the slide thumbnail (Figure 1-21).

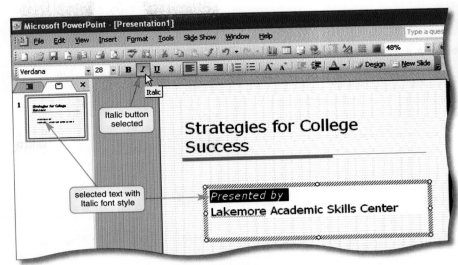

FIGURE 1-21

Other Ways

1. Right-click selected text, click Font on shortcut menu, click Italic in Font style list
2. On Format menu click Font, click Italic in Font style list
3. Press CTRL+I
4. In Voice Command mode, say "Italic"

To remove the italic style from text, select the italicized text and then click the Italic button. As a result, the Italic button is not selected, and the text does not have the italic font style.

Changing the Font Size

The Profile design template default font size is 40 point for title text and 28 point for body text. A point is 1/72 of an inch in height. Thus, a character with a point size of 40 is 40/72 (or 5/9) of an inch in height. Slide 1 requires you to increase the font size for the paragraph, Lakemore Academic Skills Center. The following steps illustrate how to increase the font size.

To Increase Font Size

1

- **Position the mouse pointer in the paragraph, Lakemore Academic Skills Center, and then triple-click.**

PowerPoint selects the entire paragraph (Figure 1-22).

FIGURE 1-22

2

• **Point to the Font Size box arrow on the Formatting toolbar.**

*The ScreenTip shows the words, Font Size (Figure 1-23). The **Font Size box** is surrounded by a box and indicates that the subtitle text is 28 point.*

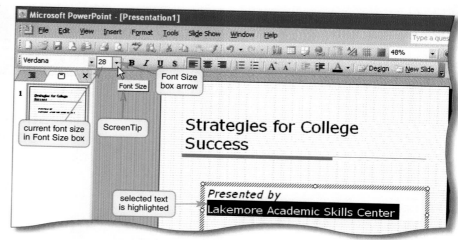

FIGURE 1-23

3

• **Click the Font Size box arrow, click the Font Size box scroll bar, and then point to 32 in the Font Size list.**

When you click the Font Size box, a list of available font sizes is displayed in the Font Size list (Figure 1-24). The font sizes displayed depend on the current font, which is Verdana. Font size 32 is highlighted.

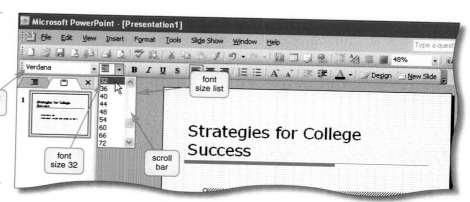

FIGURE 1-24

4

• **Click 32.**

The font size of the subtitle text, Lakemore Academic Skills Center, increases to 32 point (Figure 1-25). The Font Size box on the Formatting toolbar shows 32, indicating the selected text has a font size of 32.

Other Ways

1. Click Increase Font Size button on Formatting toolbar
2. On Format menu click Font, click new font size in Size box, or type font size between 1 and 4000, click OK button
3. Right-click selected text, click Font on shortcut menu, type new font size in Size box, click OK button
4. In Voice Command mode, say "Font Size, [font size]"

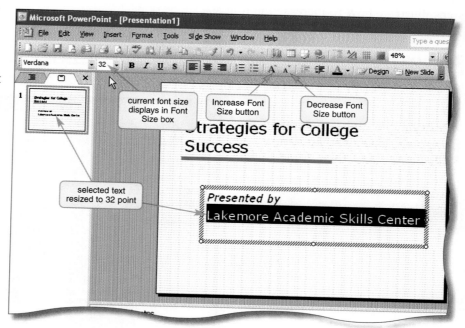

FIGURE 1-25

The Increase Font Size button on the Formatting toolbar (Figure 1-25) increases the font size in preset increments each time you click the button. If you need to decrease the font size, click the Font Size box arrow and then select a size smaller than 32. The Decrease Font Size button on the Formatting toolbar (Figure 1-25) also decreases the font size in preset increments each time you click the button.

Saving the Presentation on a USB Flash Drive

While you are building a presentation, the computer stores it in memory. It is important to save the presentation frequently because the presentation will be lost if the computer is turned off or you lose electrical power. Another reason to save your work is that if you run out of lab time before completing your project, you may finish the project later without starting over. Therefore, always save any presentation you will use later on a USB flash drive or hard disk. A saved presentation is referred to as a **file**. Before you continue with Project 1, save the work completed thus far. The following steps illustrate how to save a presentation on a USB flash drive using the Save button on the Standard toolbar.

Q&A

Q: Does PowerPoint save files automatically?

A: Yes. Every 10 minutes PowerPoint saves a copy of your presentation. To check or change the save interval, click Options on the Tools menu and then click the Save tab. Click the Save AutoRe cover info every check box and then type the specific time in the minutes box.

To Save a Presentation on a USB Flash Drive

1

- **With a USB flash drive connected to one of the computer's USB ports, click the Save button on the Standard toolbar.**

The Save As dialog box is displayed (Figure 1-26). The default folder, My Documents, appears in the Save in box. Strategies for College Success appears highlighted in the File name text box because PowerPoint uses the words in the title text placeholder as the default file name. Presentation appears in the Save as type box. The buttons on the top and on the side are used to select folders and change the appearance of file names and other information.

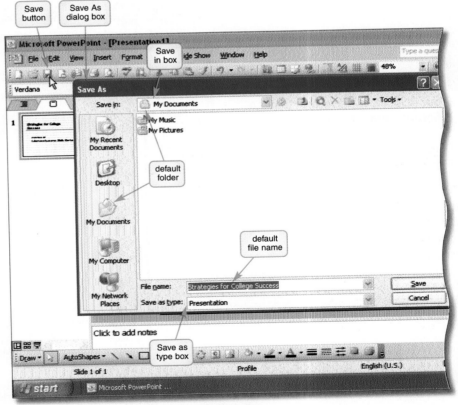

FIGURE 1-26

2

• **Type** College Success **in the File name text box. Do not press the ENTER key after typing the file name.**

• **Click the Save in box arrow.**

The name, College Success, appears in the File name text box (Figure 1-27). A file name can be up to 255 characters and can include spaces. The Save in list shows a list of locations in which to save a presentation. Your list may look different depending on the configuration of your system. Clicking the Cancel button closes the Save As dialog box.

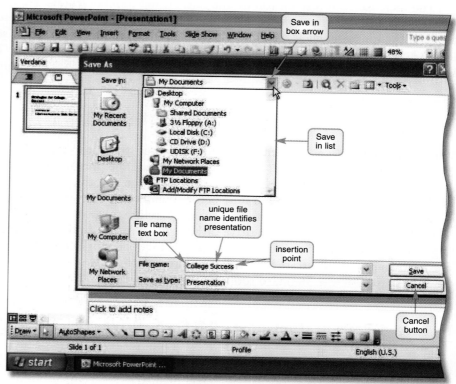

FIGURE 1-27

3

• **Click UDISK (F:) in the Save in list. (Your USB flash drive may have a different name and letter.)**

Drive F becomes the selected drive (Figure 1-28).

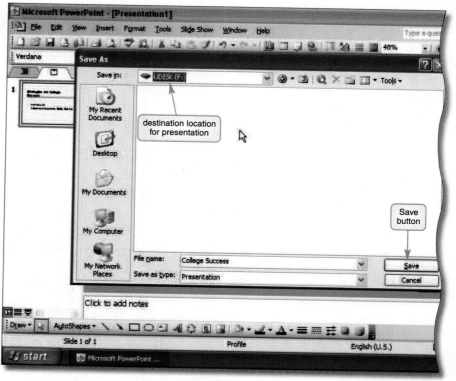

FIGURE 1-28

4

• **Click the Save button in the Save As dialog box.**

PowerPoint saves the presentation on the USB flash drive. The title bar shows the file name used to save the presentation, College Success (Figure 1-29).

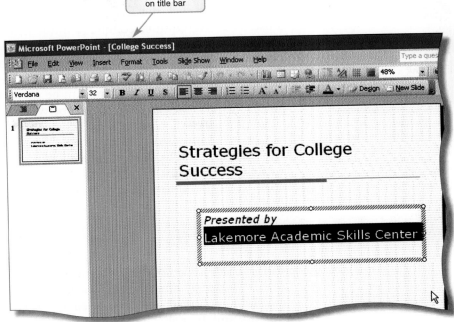

file name displays on title bar

FIGURE 1-29

PowerPoint automatically appends the extension .ppt to the file name, College Success. The **.ppt** extension stands for **P**ower**P**oin**t**. Although the slide show, College Success, is saved on a USB flash drive, it also remains in memory and is displayed on the screen.

It is a good practice to save periodically while you are working on a project. By doing so, you protect yourself from losing all the work you have done since the last time you saved.

The seven buttons at the top and to the right in the Save As dialog box in Figure 1-28 and their functions are summarized in Table 1-3.

Table 1-3 Save As Dialog Box Toolbar Buttons

BUTTON	BUTTON NAME	FUNCTION
	Default File Location	Displays contents of default file location
	Up One Level	Displays contents of folder one level up from current folder
	Search the Web	Starts browser and displays search engine
	Delete	Deletes selected file or folder
	Create New Folder	Creates new folder
	Views	Changes view of files and folders
	Tools	Lists commands to print or modify file names and folders

SAM Training 1-1

To practice the following tasks, launch the SAM Training Companion CD, choose PowerPoint Project 1, and then choose Training 1-1:
• Create presentations from a blank presentation
• Create presentations using Design templates
• Format text in slides

When you click the Tools button in the Save As dialog box, PowerPoint displays a list. The Save Options command in the list allows you to save the presentation automatically at a specified time interval and to reduce the file size. The Security Options command allows you to modify the security level for opening files that may contain harmful computer viruses and to assign a password to limit access to the file. A password is case-sensitive and can be up to 15 characters long. **Case-sensitive** means PowerPoint can differentiate between uppercase and lowercase letters. If you assign a password and then forget the password, you cannot access the file.

The file buttons on the left of the Save As dialog box in Figure 1-28 on page PPT 28 allow you to select frequently used folders. The My Recent Documents button displays a list of shortcuts (pointers) to the most recently used files in a folder titled Recent. You cannot save presentations to the Recent folder.

Adding a New Slide to a Presentation

With the title slide for the presentation created, the next step is to add the first text slide immediately after the title slide. Usually, when you create a presentation, you add slides with text, graphics, or charts. When you add a new slide, PowerPoint uses the Title and Text slide layout. Some placeholders allow you to double-click the placeholder and then access other objects, such as media clips, charts, diagrams, and organization charts.

The following steps add a new Text slide layout with a bulleted list. The default PowerPoint setting will display the Slide Layout task pane each time a new slide is added. Your system may not display this task pane if the setting has been changed.

To Add a New Text Slide with a Bulleted List

1

• **Click the New Slide button on the Formatting toolbar.**

The Slide Layout task pane opens. The Title and Text slide layout is selected. Slide 2 of 2 appears on the status bar (Figure 1-30).

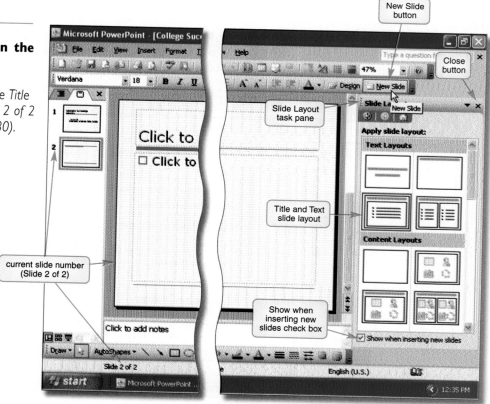

FIGURE 1-30

2

• **If necessary, click the Show when inserting new slides check box to remove the check mark, and then click the Close button on the Slide Layout task pane.**

Slide 2 appears in both the slide pane and Slides tab retaining the attributes of the Profile design template (Figure 1-31). The vertical scroll bar appears in the slide pane. The bullet appears as an outline square.

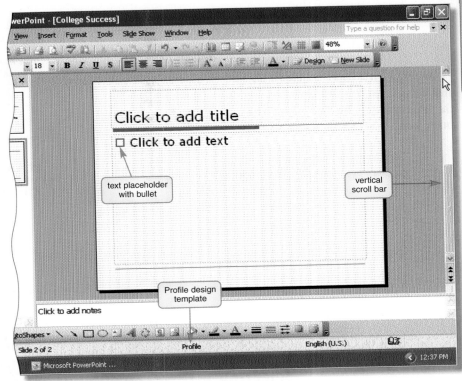

FIGURE 1-31

Slide 2 appears with a title text placeholder and a text placeholder with a bullet. You can change the layout for a slide at any time during the creation of a presentation by clicking Format on the menu bar and then clicking Slide Layout. You also can click View on the menu bar and then click Task Pane. You then can double-click the slide layout of your choice from the Slide Layout task pane.

Creating a Text Slide with a Single-Level Bulleted List

The information in the Slide 2 text placeholder is presented in a bulleted list. All the bullets appear on one level. A **level** is a position within a structure, such as an outline, that indicates the magnitude of importance. PowerPoint allows for five paragraph levels. Each paragraph level has an associated bullet. The bullet font is dependent on the design template.

Entering a Slide Title

PowerPoint assumes every new slide has a title. The title for Slide 2 is Get Organized. The step on the next page shows how to enter this title.

To Enter a Slide Title

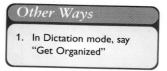

• **Click the title text placeholder
and then type** Get Organized **in
the placeholder. Do not press the
ENTER key.**

*The title, Get Organized, appears in the
title text placeholder and in the Slides tab
(Figure 1-32). The insertion point appears
after the d in Organized. The selection
rectangle indicates the title text placeholder
is selected.*

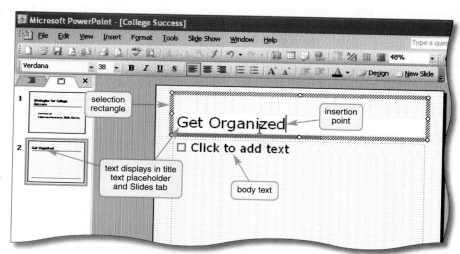

FIGURE 1-32

Selecting a Text Placeholder

Before you can type text into the text placeholder, you first must select it. The
following step selects the text placeholder on Slide 2.

To Select a Text Placeholder

• **Click the bulleted paragraph
labeled, Click to add text.**

*The insertion point appears immediately
to the right of the bullet on Slide 2
(Figure 1-33). The mouse pointer may
change shape if you move it away from
the bullet. The selection rectangle indicates
the text placeholder is selected.*

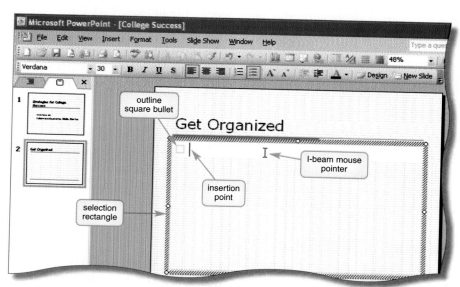

FIGURE 1-33

Typing a Single-Level Bulleted List

As discussed previously, a bulleted list is a list of paragraphs, each of which is preceded by a bullet. A paragraph is a segment of text ended by pressing the ENTER key. The next step is to type the single-level bulleted list, which consists of three entries (Figure 1-1b on page PPT 5). The following steps illustrate how to type a single-level bulleted list.

To Type a Single-Level Bulleted List

1

• **Type** Time management skills help balance academic, work, and social events **and then press the ENTER key.**

The paragraph, Time management skills help balance academic, work, and social events, appears (Figure 1-34). The font size is 30. The insertion point appears after the second bullet. When you press the ENTER key, PowerPoint ends one paragraph and begins a new paragraph. With the Title and Text slide layout, PowerPoint places an outline square bullet in front of the new paragraph.

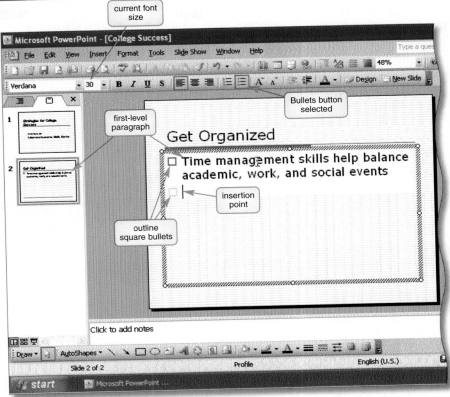

FIGURE 1-34

2

• **Type** Create a schedule each week that accounts for all activities **and then press the ENTER key.**

• **Type** Plan two hours of study time for each one hour of class time **but do not press the ENTER key.**

• **Point to the New Slide button on the Formatting toolbar.**

The insertion point is displayed after the e in time (Figure 1-35). Three new first-level paragraphs are displayed with outline square bullets in both the text placeholder and the Slides tab. When you press the ENTER key, PowerPoint adds a new paragraph at the same level as the previous paragraph.

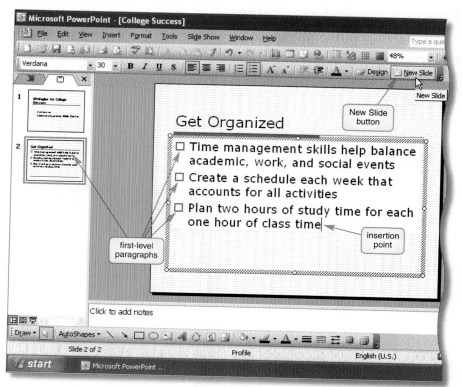

FIGURE 1-35

Notice that you did not press the ENTER key after typing the last paragraph in Step 2. If you press the ENTER key, a new bullet appears after the last entry on this slide. To remove an extra bullet, press the BACKSPACE key.

Creating a Text Slide with a Multi-Level Bulleted List

Slides 3 and 4 in Figure 1-1 on page PPT 5 contain more than one level of bulleted text. A slide that consists of more than one level of bulleted text is called a **multi-level bulleted list slide**. Beginning with the second level, each paragraph indents to the right of the preceding level and is pushed down to a lower level. For example, if you increase the indent of a first-level paragraph, it becomes a second-level paragraph. This lower-level paragraph is a subset of the higher-level paragraph. It usually contains information that supports the topic in the paragraph immediately above it. You increase the indent of a paragraph by clicking the Increase Indent button on the Formatting toolbar.

When you want to raise a paragraph from a lower level to a higher level, you click the Decrease Indent button on the Formatting toolbar.

Creating a text slide with a multi-level bulleted list requires several steps. Initially, you enter a slide title in the title text placeholder. Next, you select the body text placeholder. Then, you type the text for the multi-level bulleted list, increasing and decreasing the indents as needed. The next several sections explain how to add a slide with a multi-level bulleted list.

Adding New Slides and Entering Slide Titles

When you add a new slide to a presentation, PowerPoint keeps the same layout used on the previous slide. PowerPoint assumes every new slide has a title. The title for Slide 3 is Listen Actively. The following steps show how to add a new slide (Slide 3) and enter a title.

To Add a New Slide and Enter a Slide Title

1

• **Click the New Slide button.**

Slide 3 of 3 appears in the slide pane and Slides tab (Figure 1-36).

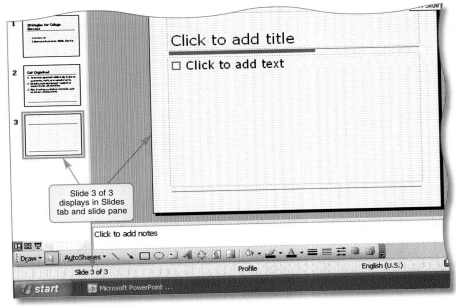

FIGURE 1-36

2

• **Type** Listen Actively **in the title text placeholder. Do not press the ENTER key.**

Slide 3 shows the Title and Text slide layout with the title, Listen Actively, in the title text placeholder and in the Slides tab (Figure 1-37). The insertion point appears after the y in Actively.

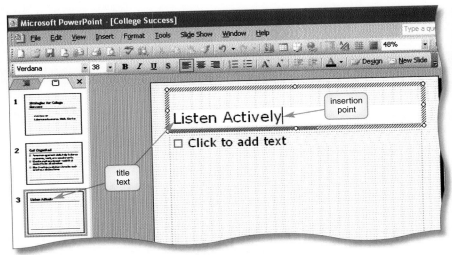

FIGURE 1-37

Slide 3 is added to the presentation with the desired title.

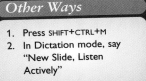

Other Ways

1. Press SHIFT+CTRL+M
2. In Dictation mode, say "New Slide, Listen Actively"

Typing a Multi-Level Bulleted List

The next step is to select the body text placeholder and then type the multi-level bulleted list, which consists of six entries (Figure 1-1c on page PPT 5). The following steps show how to create a list consisting of three levels.

To Type a Multi-Level Bulleted List

- **Click the bulleted paragraph labeled, Click to add text.**

The insertion point appears immediately to the right of the bullet on Slide 3. The mouse pointer may change shape if you move it away from the bullet.

- **Type** Sit in the front row to focus attention **and then press the ENTER key.**
- **Point to the Increase Indent button on the Formatting toolbar.**

The paragraph, Sit in the front row to focus attention, appears (Figure 1-38). The font size is 30. The insertion point appears to the right of the second bullet.

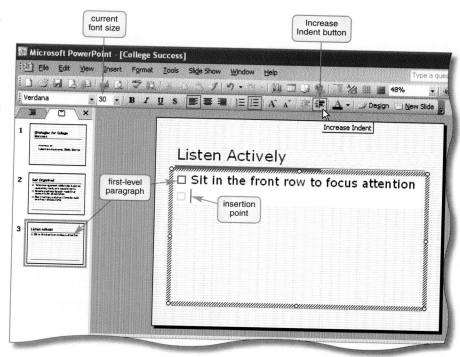

FIGURE 1-38

- **Click the Increase Indent button.**

The second paragraph indents below the first and becomes a second-level paragraph (Figure 1-39). The bullet to the left of the second paragraph changes from an outline square to a solid square, and the font size for the paragraph now is 26. The insertion point appears to the right of the solid square.

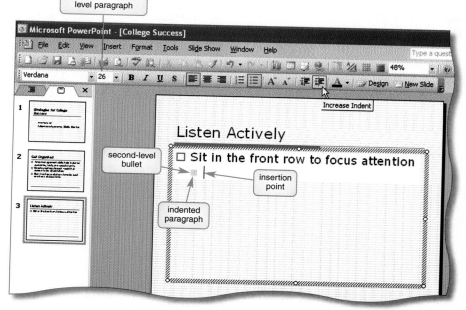

FIGURE 1-39

4

• **Type** Do not tolerate distractions **and then press the ENTER key.**

• **Point to the Decrease Indent button on the Formatting toolbar.**

The first second-level paragraph appears with a solid orange square bullet in both the slide pane and the Slides tab (Figure 1-40). When you press the ENTER key, PowerPoint adds a new paragraph at the same level as the previous paragraph.

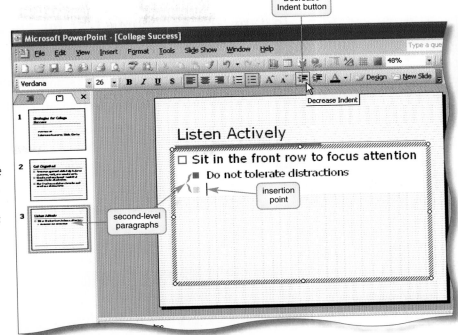

FIGURE 1-40

5

• **Click the Decrease Indent button.**

The second-level paragraph becomes a first-level paragraph (Figure 1-41). The bullet of the new paragraph changes from a solid orange square to an outline square, and the font size for the paragraph is 30. The insertion point appears to the right of the outline square bullet.

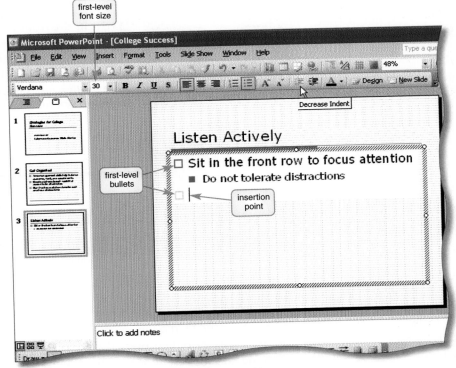

FIGURE 1-41

The steps on the next page complete the text for Slide 3.

Other Ways

1. In Dictation mode, say, "Sit in the front row to focus attention, New Line, Increase Indent, Do not tolerate distractions, New Line, Decrease Indent"

To Type the Remaining Text for Slide 3

1 **Type** Make mental summaries of material **and then press the ENTER key.**

2 **Type** Be prepared for class **and then press the ENTER key.**

3 **Click the Increase Indent button on the Formatting toolbar.**

4 **Type** Review notes from books, previous class **and then press the ENTER key.**

5 **Type** Preview material to be covered that day **but do not press the ENTER key.**

Slide 3 is displayed as shown in Figure 1-42. The insertion point appears after the y in day.

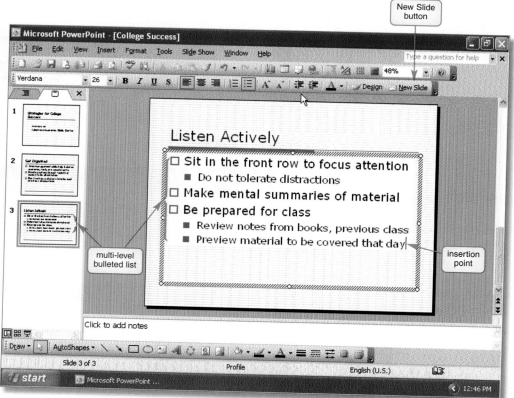

FIGURE 1-42

In Step 4 above, you did not press the ENTER key after typing the last paragraph. If you press the ENTER key, a new bullet appears after the last entry on this slide. To remove an extra bullet, press the BACKSPACE key.

Slide 4 is the last slide in this presentation. It also is a multi-level bulleted list and has three levels. The following steps create Slide 4.

To Create Slide 4

1 **Click the New Slide button on the Formatting toolbar.**

2 **Type** Excel on Exams **in the title text placeholder.**

3 **Press CTRL+ENTER to move the insertion point to the body text placeholder.**

4 **Type** Review test material throughout week **and then press the ENTER key.**

5 **Click the Increase Indent button on the Formatting toolbar. Type** Cramming for exams is ineffective **and then press the ENTER key.**

The title and first two levels of bullets are added to Slide 4 (Figure 1-43).

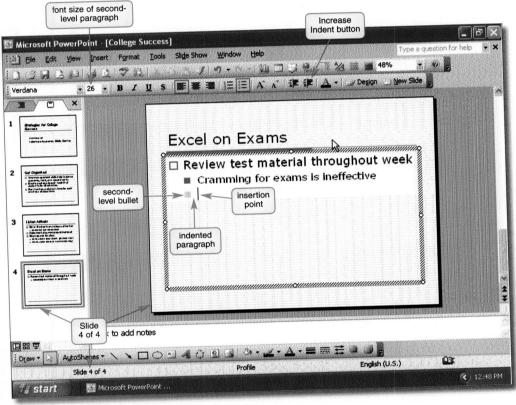

FIGURE 1-43

Creating a Third-Level Paragraph

The next line in Slide 4 is indented an additional level, to the third level. The steps on the next page create an additional level.

To Create a Third-Level Paragraph

1

• **Click the Increase Indent button on the Formatting toolbar.**

The second-level paragraph becomes a third-level paragraph (Figure 1-44). The bullet to the left of the new paragraph changes from a solid square to an outline square, and the font size for the paragraph is 23. The insertion point appears after the outline square bullet.

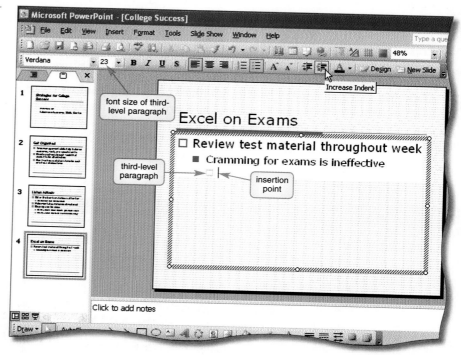

FIGURE 1-44

2

• **Type** Facts remain only in short-term memory **and then press the ENTER key.**

• **Point to the Decrease Indent button on the Formatting toolbar.**

The first third-level paragraph, Facts remain only in short-term memory, is displayed with the bullet for a second third-level paragraph (Figure 1-45).

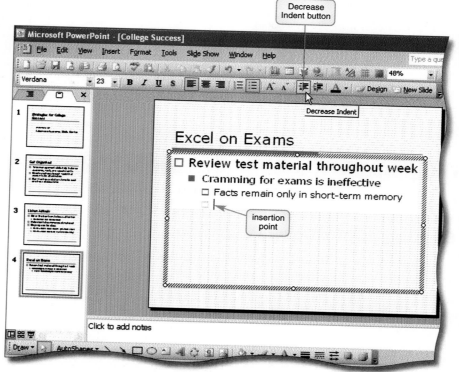

FIGURE 1-45

3

• **Click the Decrease Indent button two times.**

The insertion point appears at the first level (Figure 1-46).

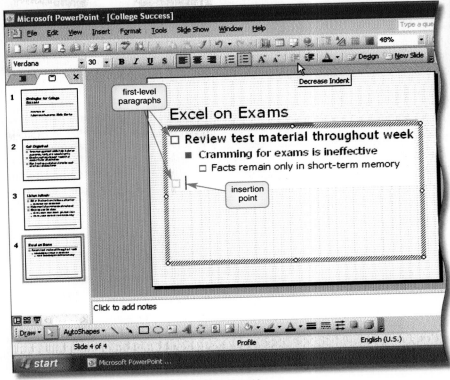

FIGURE 1-46

Other Ways

1. In Dictation mode, say "Tab, Facts remain only in short-term memory, New Line, [type backspace]"

The title text and three levels of paragraphs discussing preparing for exams are complete. The next three paragraphs concern strategies for taking tests. As an alternative to clicking the Increase Indent button, you can press the TAB key. Likewise, instead of clicking the Decrease Indent button, you can press the SHIFT+TAB keys. The following steps illustrate how to type the remaining text for Slide 4.

To Type the Remaining Text for Slide 4

1 **Type** Review entire test before answering **and then press the ENTER key.**

2 **Press the TAB key to increase the indent to the second level.**

3 **Type** Start with the material you know **and then press the ENTER key.**

4 **Press the TAB key to increase the indent to the third level.**

5 **Type** Think positively and stay focused **but do not press the ENTER key.**

The Slide 4 title text and body text are displayed in the slide pane and Slides tabs (Figure 1-47 on the next page). The insertion point appears after the d in focused.

Other Ways

1. In Dictation mode, say "Review entire test before answering, New Line, Tab, Start with the material you know, New Line, Tab, Think positively and stay focused"

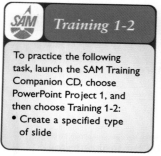

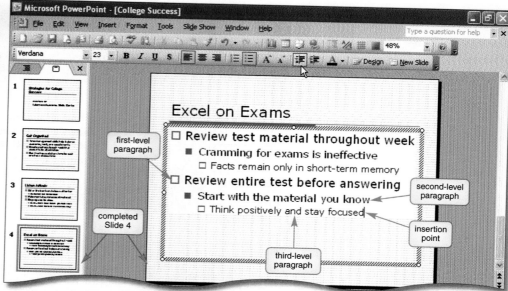

FIGURE 1-47

All the slides are created for the College Success slide show. This presentation consists of a title slide, one text slide with a single-level bulleted list, and two text slides with a multi-level bulleted list.

Ending a Slide Show with a Black Slide

After the last slide in the slide show appears, the default PowerPoint setting is to end the presentation with a black slide. This black slide appears only when the slide show is running and concludes the slide show gracefully so your audience never sees the PowerPoint window. A **black slide** ends all slide shows unless the option setting is deselected. The following steps verify that the End with black slide option is activated.

To End a Slide Show with a Black Slide

1

• **Click Tools on the menu bar and then point to Options (Figure 1-48).**

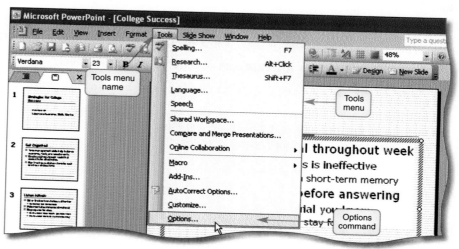

FIGURE 1-48

2

- **Click Options.**

- **If necessary, click the View tab when the Options dialog box appears.**

- **Verify that the End with black slide check box is selected.**

- **If a check mark does not show, click End with black slide.**

- **Point to the OK button.**

The Options dialog box appears (Figure 1-49). The View sheet contains settings for the overall PowerPoint display and for a particular slide show.

3

- **Click the OK button.**

The End with black slide option will cause the slide show to end with a black slide until it is deselected.

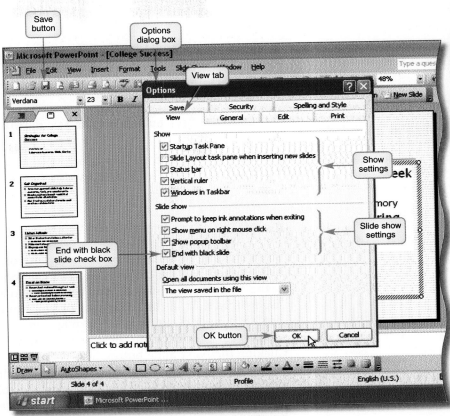

FIGURE 1-49

With all aspects of the presentation complete, it is important to save the additions and changes you have made to the College Success presentation.

Saving a Presentation with the Same File Name

Saving frequently cannot be overemphasized. When you first saved the presentation, you clicked the Save button on the Standard toolbar, and the Save dialog box appeared. When you want to save the changes made to the presentation after your last save, you again click the Save button. This time, however, the Save dialog box does not appear because PowerPoint updates the document called College Success.ppt on the USB flash drive. The steps on the next page illustrate how to save the presentation again.

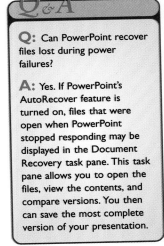
Q & A

Q: Can PowerPoint recover files lost during power failures?

A: Yes. If PowerPoint's AutoRecover feature is turned on, files that were open when PowerPoint stopped responding may be displayed in the Document Recovery task pane. This task pane allows you to open the files, view the contents, and compare versions. You then can save the most complete version of your presentation.

To Save a Presentation with the Same File Name

1 **Be certain your USB flash drive still is connected to one of the computer's USB ports.**

2 **Click the Save button on the Standard toolbar.**

PowerPoint overwrites the old College Success.ppt document on the USB flash drive with the revised presentation document. Slide 4 is displayed in the PowerPoint window.

Moving to Another Slide in Normal View

When creating or editing a presentation in normal view, you often want to display a slide other than the current one. You can move to another slide using several methods. In the Outline tab, you can point to any of the text in a particular slide to display that slide in the slide pane, or you can drag the scroll box on the vertical scroll bar up or down to move through the text in the presentation. In the slide pane, you can click the Previous Slide or Next Slide button on the vertical scroll bar. Clicking the Next Slide button advances to the next slide in the presentation. Clicking the Previous Slide button backs up to the slide preceding the current slide. You also can drag the scroll box on the vertical scroll bar. When you drag the scroll box, the **slide indicator** shows the number and title of the slide you are about to display. Releasing the mouse button shows the slide.

A slide's **Zoom setting** affects the portion of the slide displaying in the slide pane. PowerPoint defaults to a setting of approximately 50 percent so the entire slide is displayed. This percentage depends on the size and type of your monitor. If you want to display a small portion of the current slide, you would zoom in by clicking the **Zoom box arrow** and then clicking the desired magnification. You can display the entire slide in the slide pane by clicking **Fit** in the Zoom list. The Zoom setting affects the action of the vertical and horizontal scroll bars. If Zoom is set so the entire slide is not visible in the slide pane, clicking the up scroll arrow on the vertical scroll bar shows the next portion of the slide, not the previous slide.

Using the Scroll Box on the Slide Pane to Move to Another Slide

Before continuing with Project 1, you want to display the title slide. The following steps show how to move from Slide 4 to Slide 1 using the scroll box on the slide pane vertical scroll bar.

To Use the Scroll Box on the Slide Pane to Move to Another Slide

1

• **Position the mouse pointer on the scroll box.**

• **Press and hold down the mouse button.**

Slide: 4 of 4 Excel on Exams appears in the slide indicator (Figure 1-50). When you click the scroll box, the Slide 4 thumbnail has no gray border in the Slides tab.

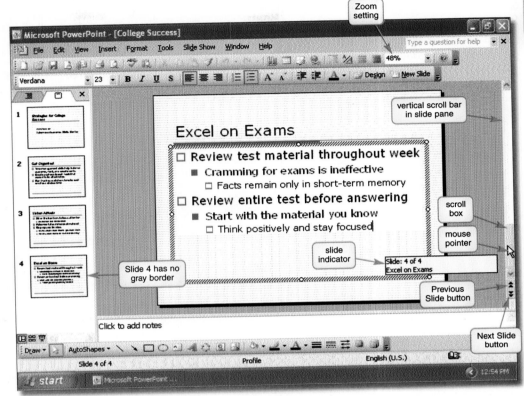

FIGURE 1-50

2

• **Drag the scroll box up the vertical scroll bar until Slide: 1 of 4 Strategies for College Success appears in the slide indicator.**

Slide: 1 of 4 Strategies for College Success appears in the slide indicator (Figure 1-51). Slide 4 still is displayed in the PowerPoint window.

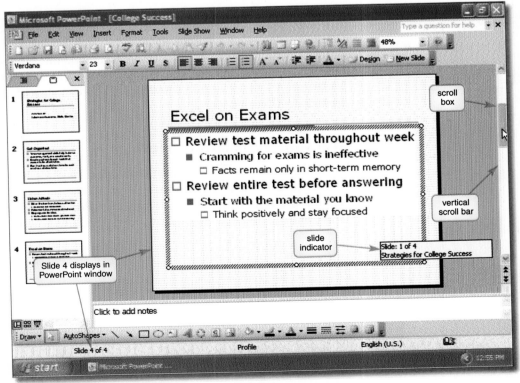

FIGURE 1-51

3

• **Release the mouse button.**

*Slide 1, titled Strategies for College
Success, appears in the PowerPoint window
(Figure 1-52). The Slide 1 thumbnail has a
gray border in the Slides tab, indicating it is
selected.*

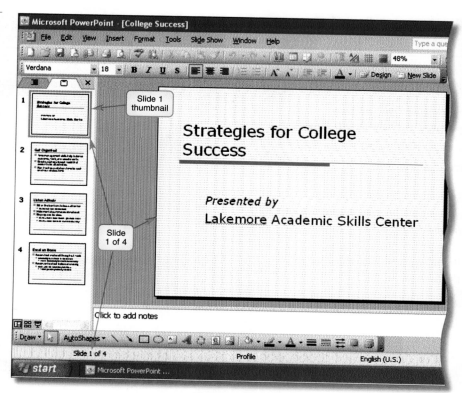

FIGURE 1-52

Viewing the Presentation in Slide Show View

The Slide Show button, located in the lower-left of the PowerPoint window above
the status bar, allows you to show a presentation using a computer. The computer
acts like a slide projector, displaying each slide on a full screen. The full-screen slide
hides the toolbars, menus, and other PowerPoint window elements. When making a
presentation, you use **slide show view**. You can start slide show view from normal
view or slide sorter view.

Starting Slide Show View

Slide show view begins when you click the Slide Show button in the lower-left
of the PowerPoint window above the status bar. PowerPoint then shows the current
slide on the full screen without any of the PowerPoint window objects, such as the
menu bar or toolbars. The following steps show how to start slide show view.

To Start Slide Show View

1

- Point to the Slide Show button in the lower-left corner of the PowerPoint window above the status bar (Figure 1-53).

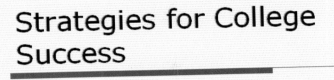

FIGURE 1-53

2

- Click the Slide Show button.

A starting slide show message may display momentarily, and then the title slide fills the screen (Figure 1-54). The PowerPoint window is hidden.

Strategies for College Success

Presented by
Lakemore Academic Skills Center

FIGURE 1-54

Other Ways

1. On View menu click Slide Show
2. Press F5
3. In Voice Command mode, say "View show"

Advancing Through a Slide Show Manually

After you begin slide show view, you can move forward or backward through the slides. PowerPoint allows you to advance through the slides manually or automatically. The steps on the next page illustrate how to move manually through the slides.

To Move Manually Through Slides in a Slide Show

1

• **Click each slide until the Excel on Exams slide (Slide 4) is displayed.**

Slide 4 is displayed (Figure 1-55). Each slide in the presentation shows on the screen, one slide at a time. Each time you click the mouse button, the next slide appears.

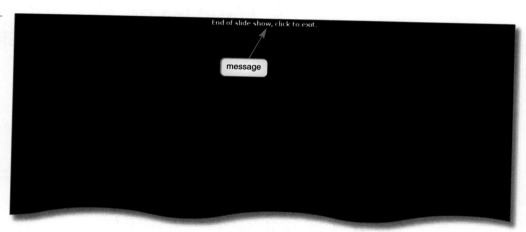

Slide 4 displays in slide show view

Excel on Exams

☐ Review test material throughout week
  ■ Cramming for exams is ineffective
    ☐ Facts remain only in short-term memory
☐ Review entire test before answering
  ■ Start with the material you know
    ☐ Think positively and stay focused

FIGURE 1-55

2

• **Click Slide 4.**

The black slide appears (Figure 1-56). The message at the top of the slide announces the end of the slide show. If you wanted to end the presentation at this point and return to normal view, you would click the black slide.

End of slide show, click to exit.

message

FIGURE 1-56

Using the Popup Menu to Go to a Specific Slide

Slide show view has a shortcut menu, called the Popup menu, that appears when you right-click a slide in slide show view. This menu contains commands to assist you during a slide show. For example, clicking the Next command moves to the next slide. Clicking the Previous command moves to the previous slide. Pointing to the Go to Slide command and then clicking the desired slide allows you to move to any slide in the presentation. The Go to Slide submenu contains a list of the slides in the presentation. You can go to the requested slide by clicking the name of that slide. The following steps illustrate how to go to the title slide (Slide 1) in the College Success presentation.

To Display the Popup Menu and Go to a Specific Slide

1

• **With the black slide displaying in slide show view, right-click the slide.**

• **Point to Go to Slide on the Popup menu, and then point to 1 Strategies for College Success in the Go to Slide submenu.**

The Popup menu appears on the black slide, and the Go to Slide submenu shows a list of slides in the presentation (Figure 1-57). Your screen may look different because the Popup menu appears near the location of the mouse pointer at the time you right-click.

2

• **Click 1 Strategies for College Success.**

The title slide, Strategies for College Success (shown in Figure 1-54 on page PPT 47), is displayed.

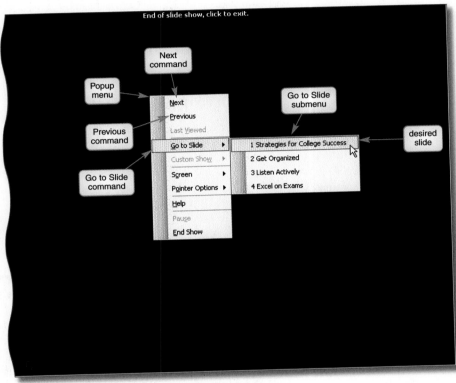

FIGURE 1-57

Additional Popup menu commands allow you to change the mouse pointer to a ballpoint or felt tip pen or highlighter that draws in various colors, make the screen black or white, create speaker notes, and end the slide show. Popup menu commands are discussed as they are used.

Using the Popup Menu to End a Slide Show

The End Show command on the Popup menu ends slide show view and returns to the same view as when you clicked the Slide Show button. The steps on the next page show how to end slide show view and return to normal view.

To Use the Popup Menu to End a Slide Show

1

• **Right-click the title slide and then point to End Show on the Popup menu.**

The Popup menu appears on Slide 1 (Figure 1-58).

2

• **Click End Show.**

• **If the Microsoft Office PowerPoint dialog box appears, click the Yes button.**

PowerPoint ends slide show view and returns to normal view (shown in Figure 1-59 below). Slide 1 is displayed because it is the last slide displayed in slide show view.

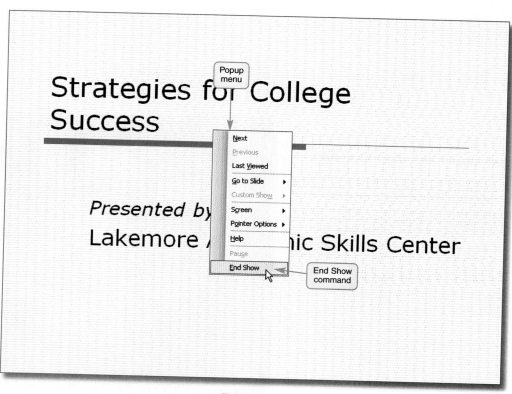

FIGURE 1-58

Other Ways

1. Press ESC (shows slide last viewed in slide show view)
2. In Voice Command mode say "Escape"

Quitting PowerPoint

The College Success presentation now is complete. When you quit PowerPoint, you are prompted to save any changes made to the presentation since the last save. The program then closes all PowerPoint windows, quits, and returns control to the desktop. The following steps quit PowerPoint.

To Quit PowerPoint

1

• **Point to the Close button on the PowerPoint title bar (Figure 1-59).**

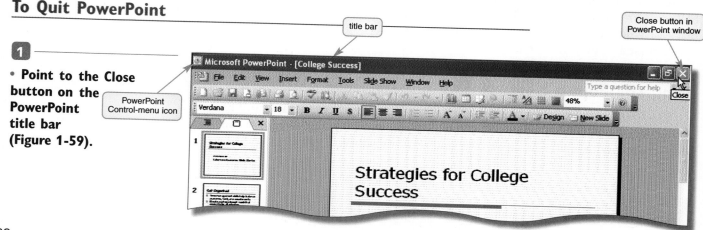

FIGURE 1-59

2

• **Click the Close button.**

PowerPoint closes and the Windows desktop is displayed (Figure 1-60). If you made changes to the presentation since your last save, a Microsoft Office PowerPoint dialog box appears asking if you want to save changes. Clicking the Yes button saves the changes to the presentation before quitting PowerPoint. Clicking the No button quits PowerPoint without saving the changes. Clicking the Cancel button cancels the exit and returns control to the presentation.

desktop

start

FIGURE 1-60

Starting PowerPoint and Opening a Presentation

Once you have created and saved a presentation, you may need to retrieve it from the USB flash drive to make changes. For example, you may want to replace the design template or modify some text. The steps on the next page assume PowerPoint is not running.

To Start PowerPoint and Open an Existing Presentation

1

• With your USB flash drive connected to one of the computer's USB ports, click the Start button on the taskbar, point to All Programs, point to Microsoft Office, and then click Microsoft Office PowerPoint 2003 on the Microsoft Office submenu.

• When the Getting Started task pane opens, point to the Open link in the Open area.

PowerPoint starts. The Getting Started task pane opens (Figure 1-61).

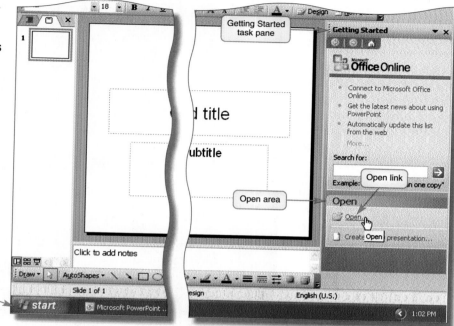

FIGURE 1-61

2

• Click the Open link. Click the Look in box arrow, click UDISK (F:) (your USB flash drive may have a different name and letter), and then double-click College Success.

PowerPoint opens the presentation College Success and shows the first slide in the PowerPoint window (Figure 1-62). The presentation is displayed in normal view because PowerPoint opens a presentation in the same view in which it was saved. The Getting Started task pane disappears.

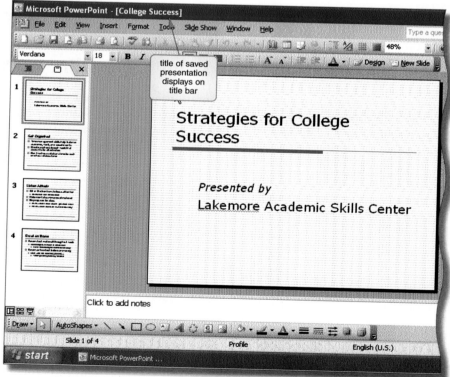

FIGURE 1-62

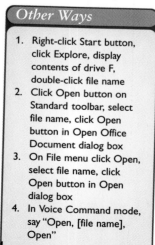

Other Ways

1. Right-click Start button, click Explore, display contents of drive F, double-click file name
2. Click Open button on Standard toolbar, select file name, click Open button in Open Office Document dialog box
3. On File menu click Open, select file name, click Open button in Open dialog box
4. In Voice Command mode, say "Open, [file name], Open"

When you start PowerPoint and open the College Success file, the application name and file name are displayed on a recessed button on the Windows taskbar. When more than one application is open, you can switch between applications by clicking the appropriate application button. If you want to open a presentation other than a recent one, click the Open button on the Standard toolbar or in the Getting Started task pane. Either button lets you navigate to a slide show stored on a disk.

Checking a Presentation for Spelling and Consistency

After you create a presentation, you should check it visually for spelling errors and style consistency. In addition, you can use PowerPoint's Spelling and Style tools to identify possible misspellings and inconsistencies.

Checking a Presentation for Spelling Errors

PowerPoint checks the entire presentation for spelling mistakes using a standard dictionary contained in the Microsoft Office group. This dictionary is shared with the other Microsoft Office applications such as Word and Excel. A **custom dictionary** is available if you want to add special words such as proper names, cities, and acronyms. When checking a presentation for spelling errors, PowerPoint opens the standard dictionary and the custom dictionary file, if one exists. When a word appears in the Spelling dialog box, you perform one of the actions listed in Table 1-4.

Q: Can I rely on the spelling checker?

A: While PowerPoint's Spelling checker is a valuable tool, it is not infallible. You should proofread your presentation carefully by pointing to each word and saying it aloud as you point to it. Be mindful of commonly misused words such as its and it's, through and though, and to and too.

Table 1-4	Summary of Spelling Checker Actions
ACTION	DESCRIPTION
Ignore the word	Click the Ignore button when the word is spelled correctly but not found in the dictionaries. PowerPoint continues checking the rest of the presentation.
Ignore all occurrences of the word	Click the Ignore All button when the word is spelled correctly but not found in the dictionaries. PowerPoint ignores all occurrences of the word and continues checking the rest of the presentation.
Select a different spelling	Click the proper spelling of the word from the list in the Suggestions box. Click the Change button. PowerPoint corrects the word and continues checking the rest of the presentation.
Change all occurrences of the misspelling to a different spelling	Click the proper spelling of the word from the list in the Suggestions box. Click the Change All button. PowerPoint changes all occurrences of the misspelled word and continues checking the rest of the presentation.
Add a word to the custom dictionary	Click the Add button. PowerPoint opens the custom dictionary, adds the word, and continues checking the rest of the presentation.
View alternative spellings	Click the Suggest button. PowerPoint lists suggested spellings. Click the correct word from the Suggestions box or type the proper spelling. Then click the Change button. PowerPoint continues checking the rest of the presentation.
Add spelling error to AutoCorrect list	Click the AutoCorrect button. PowerPoint adds the spelling error and its correction to the AutoCorrect list. Any future misspelling of the word is corrected automatically as you type.
Close	Click the Close button to close the Spelling checker and return to the PowerPoint window.

The standard dictionary contains commonly used English words. It does not, however, contain proper names, abbreviations, technical terms, poetic contractions, or antiquated terms. PowerPoint treats words not found in the dictionaries as misspellings.

Starting the Spelling Checker

The following steps illustrate how to start the Spelling checker and check the entire presentation.

To Start the Spelling Checker

1

• Point to the Spelling button on the Standard toolbar (Figure 1-63).

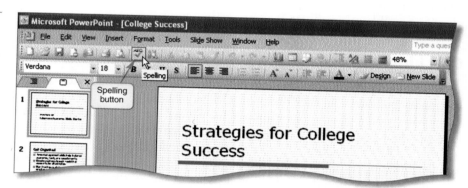

FIGURE 1-63

2

• Click the Spelling button.

• When the Spelling dialog box appears, point to the Ignore button.

PowerPoint starts the Spelling checker and displays the Spelling dialog box (Figure 1-64). The word, Lakemore, appears in the Not in Dictionary box. Depending on the custom dictionary, Lakemore may not be recognized as a misspelled word.

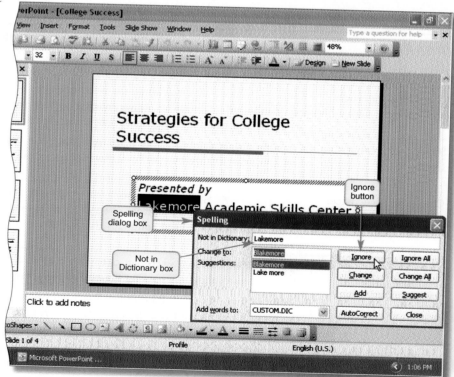

FIGURE 1-64

3

- **Click the Ignore button.**
- **When the Microsoft Office PowerPoint dialog box appears, point to the OK button.**

PowerPoint ignores the word, Lakemore, and continues searching for additional misspelled words. PowerPoint may stop on additional words depending on your typing accuracy. When PowerPoint has checked all slides for misspellings, the Microsoft Office PowerPoint dialog box informs you that the spelling check is complete (Figure 1-65).

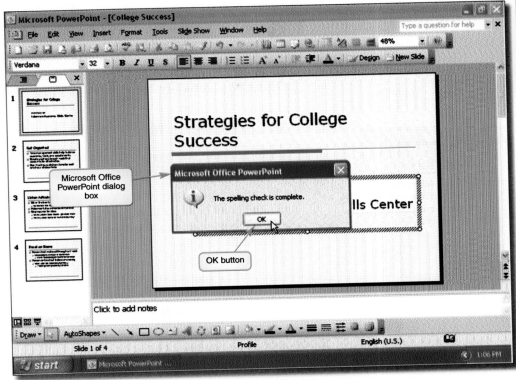

FIGURE 1-65

4

- **Click the OK button.**
- **Click the slide to remove the highlight from the word, Lakemore.**

PowerPoint closes the Spelling checker and returns to the current slide, Slide 1 (Figure 1-66), or to the slide where a possible misspelled word displayed.

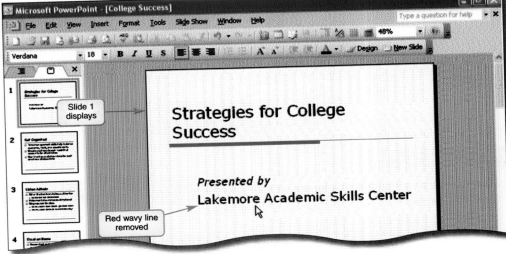

FIGURE 1-66

The red wavy line below the word, Lakemore, is gone because you instructed PowerPoint to ignore that word, which does not appear in the standard dictionary. You also could have added that word to the dictionary so it would not be flagged as a possible misspelled word in subsequent presentations you create using that word.

Other Ways

1. On Tools menu click Spelling
2. Press ALT+T, press S; when finished, press ENTER
3. Press F7
4. In Voice Command mode, say "Spelling"

Correcting Errors

After creating a presentation and running the Spelling checker, you may find that you must make changes. Changes may be required because a slide contains an error, the scope of the presentation shifts, or the style is inconsistent. This section explains the types of errors that commonly occur when creating a presentation.

Types of Corrections Made to Presentations

You generally make three types of corrections to text in a presentation: additions, deletions, and replacements.

- Additions are necessary when you omit text from a slide and need to add it later. You may need to insert text in the form of a sentence, word, or single character. For example, you may want to add the presenter's middle name on the title slide.
- Deletions are required when text on a slide is incorrect or no longer is relevant to the presentation. For example, a slide may look cluttered. Therefore, you may want to remove one of the bulleted paragraphs to add more space.
- Replacements are needed when you want to revise the text in a presentation. For example, you may want to substitute the word, their, for the word, there.

Editing text in PowerPoint basically is the same as editing text in a word processing package. The following sections illustrate the most common changes made to text in a presentation.

Deleting Text

You can delete text using one of three methods. One is to use the BACKSPACE key to remove text just typed. The second is to position the insertion point to the left of the text you wish to delete and then press the DELETE key. The third method is to drag through the text you wish to delete and then press the DELETE key. (Use the third method when deleting large sections of text.)

Replacing Text in an Existing Slide

When you need to correct a word or phrase, you can replace the text by selecting the text to be replaced and then typing the new text. As soon as you press any key on the keyboard, the highlighted text is deleted and the new text is displayed.

PowerPoint inserts text to the left of the insertion point. The text to the right of the insertion point moves to the right (and shifts downward if necessary) to accommodate the added text.

Displaying a Presentation in Black and White

Printing handouts of a presentation allows you to use them to make overhead transparencies. The Color/Grayscale button on the Standard toolbar shows the presentation in black and white before you print. Table 1-5 identifies how PowerPoint objects display in black and white.

Table 1-5 Appearance in Black and White View	
OBJECT	**APPEARANCE IN BLACK AND WHITE VIEW**
Bitmaps	Grayscale
Embossing	Hidden
Fills	Grayscale
Frame	Black
Lines	Black
Object shadows	Grayscale
Pattern fills	Grayscale
Slide backgrounds	White
Text	Black
Text shadows	Hidden

The following steps show how to display the presentation in black and white.

To Display a Presentation in Black and White

1

• **Click the Color/Grayscale button on the Standard toolbar and then point to Pure Black and White in the list.**

The Color/Grayscale list is displayed (Figure 1-67). Pure Black and White alters the slides' appearance so that only black lines display on a white background. Grayscale shows varying degrees of gray.

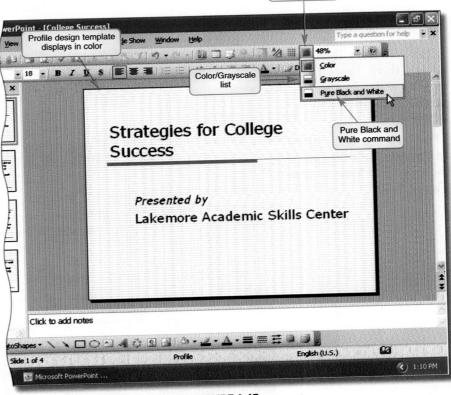

FIGURE 1-67

2

• **Click Pure Black and White.**

Slide 1 is displayed in black and white in the slide pane (Figure 1-68). The four thumbnail slides are displayed in color in the Slides tab. The Grayscale View toolbar appears. The Color/Grayscale button on the Standard toolbar changes from color bars to black and white.

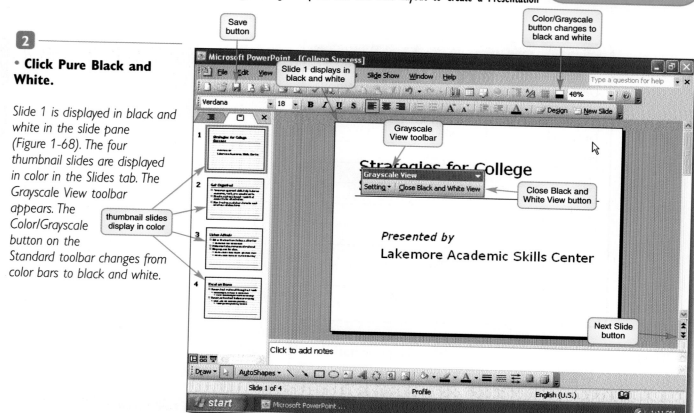

FIGURE 1-68

3

• **Click the Next Slide button three times to view all slides in the presentation in black and white.**

• **Point to the Close Black and White View button on the Grayscale View toolbar (Figure 1-69).**

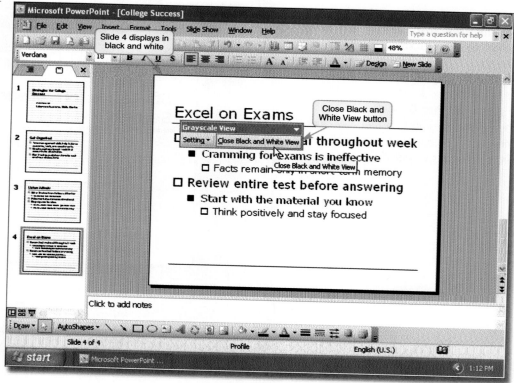

FIGURE 1-69

4

• **Click the Close Black and White View button.**

Slide 4 is displayed with the default Profile color scheme (Figure 1-70).

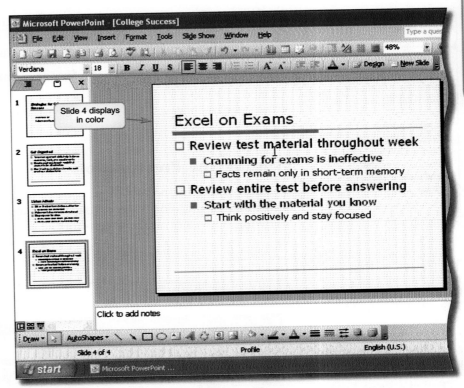

FIGURE 1-70

Other Ways

1. On View menu point to Color/Grayscale and then click Pure Black and White
2. In Voice Command mode, say "View, Color Grayscale, Pure Black and White"

After you view the text objects in the presentation in black and white, you can make any changes that will enhance printouts produced from a black and white printer or photocopier.

Printing a Presentation

After you create a presentation, you often want to print it. A printed version of the presentation is called a **hard copy**, or **printout**. The first printing of the presentation is called a **rough draft**. The rough draft allows you to proofread the presentation to check for errors and readability. After correcting errors, you print the final copy of the presentation.

Saving Before Printing

Before printing a presentation, you should save your work in the event you experience difficulties with the printer. You occasionally may encounter system problems that can be resolved only by restarting the computer. In such an instance, you will need to reopen the presentation. As a precaution, always save the presentation before you print. The steps on the next page save the presentation before printing.

More About

Printing in Black and White

If you have a color printer, you can avoid wasting ink by printing a presentation in black and white. You print in black and white by clicking Color/Grayscale on the View menu and then clicking either Grayscale or Pure Black and White.

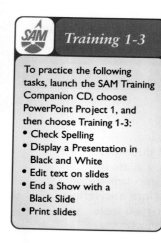

Training 1-3

To practice the following tasks, launch the SAM Training Companion CD, choose PowerPoint Project 1, and then choose Training 1-3:
• Check Spelling
• Display a Presentation in Black and White
• Edit text on slides
• End a Show with a Black Slide
• Print slides

To Save a Presentation Before Printing

1 Verify that the USB flash drive still is connected to one of the USB ports.

2 Click the Save button on the Standard toolbar.

All changes made after your last save now are saved on the USB flash drive.

Printing the Presentation

After saving the presentation, you are ready to print. Clicking the Print button on the Standard toolbar causes PowerPoint to print all slides in the presentation. The following steps illustrate how to print the presentation slides.

To Print a Presentation

1

• **Ready the printer according to the printer instructions.**

• **Click the Print button on the Standard toolbar.**

The printer icon in the tray status area on the Windows taskbar indicates a print job is processing (Figure 1-71). This icon may not display on your system, or it may display on your status bar. After several moments, the slide show begins printing on the printer. When the presentation is finished printing, the printer icon in the tray status area on the Windows taskbar no longer is displayed.

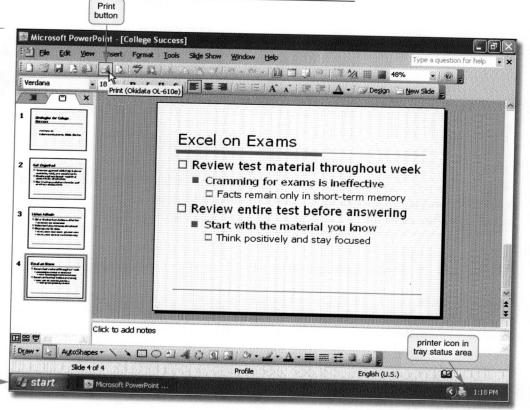

FIGURE 1-71

2

• **When the printer stops, retrieve the printouts of the slides.**

The presentation, College Success, prints on four pages (Figures 1-72a through 1-72d).

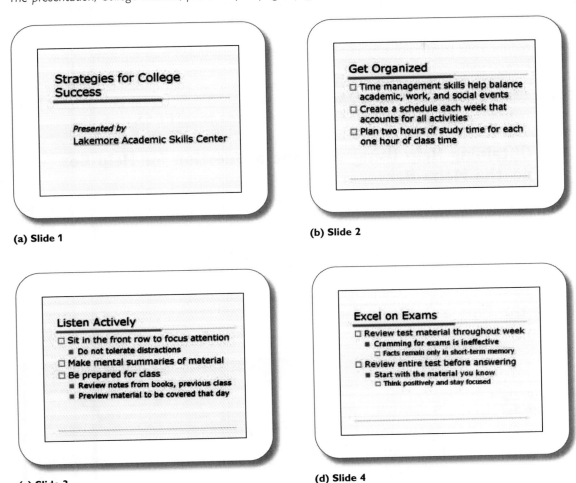

(a) Slide 1

(b) Slide 2

(c) Slide 3

(d) Slide 4

FIGURE 1-72

Other Ways

1. On File menu click Print
2. Press CTRL+P or press CTRL+SHIFT+F12
3. In Voice Command mode, say "Print"

You can click the printer icon next to the clock in the tray status area on the Windows taskbar to obtain information about the presentations printing on your printer and to delete files in the print queue that are waiting to be printed.

Making a Transparency

With the handouts printed, you now can make overhead transparencies using one of several devices. One device is a printer attached to your computer, such as an inkjet printer or a laser printer. Transparencies produced on a printer may be in black and white or color, depending on the printer. Another device is a photocopier. Because each of these devices requires a special transparency film, check the user's manual for the film requirement of your specific device, or ask your instructor.

PowerPoint Help System

You can get answers to PowerPoint questions at any time by using the PowerPoint Help system. You can activate the PowerPoint Help system by using the Type a question for help box on the menu bar, by using the Microsoft PowerPoint Help button on the Standard toolbar, or by clicking Help on the menu bar (Figure 1-73). Used properly, this form of online assistance can increase your productivity and reduce your frustrations by minimizing the time you spend learning how to use PowerPoint.

The following section shows how to get answers to your questions using the Type a question for help box. Additional information on using the PowerPoint Help system is available in Appendix A and Table 1-6 on page PPT 65.

Obtaining Help Using the Type a Question for Help Box on the Menu Bar

The Type a question for help box on the right side of the menu bar lets you type free-form questions such as, *how do I save* or *how do I create a Web page*, or you can type terms such as, *copy*, *save*, or *format*. PowerPoint responds by displaying a list of topics related to what you typed. The following steps show how to use the Type a question for help box to obtain information on formatting bullets.

To Obtain Help Using the Type a Question for Help Box

1

• **Type** bullet **in the Type a question for help box on the right side of the menu bar (Figure 1-73).**

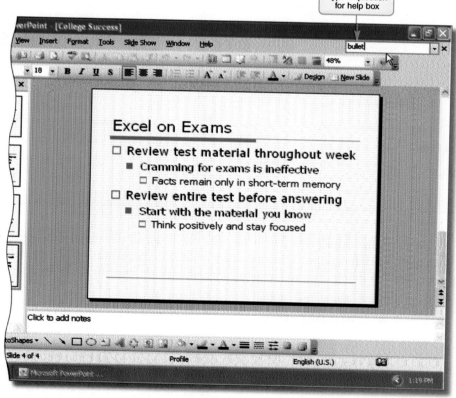

FIGURE 1-73

2

- Press the ENTER key.

- When PowerPoint displays the Search Results task pane, scroll down and then point to the topic, Change the bullet style in a list.

PowerPoint displays the Search Results task pane with a list of topics relating to the term, bullet. PowerPoint found 30 results from Microsoft Office Online. The mouse pointer changes to a hand, which indicates it is pointing to a link (Figure 1-74).

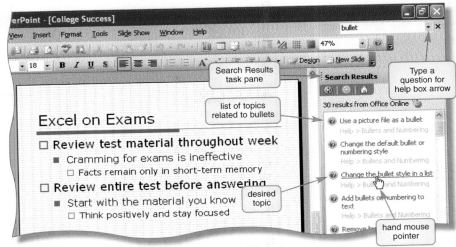

FIGURE 1-74

3

- Click Change the bullet style in a list.

- When the Microsoft Office PowerPoint Help window is displayed, double-click its title bar to maximize it.

A Microsoft Office PowerPoint Help window provides Help information about changing the bullet style in a list (Figure 1-75).

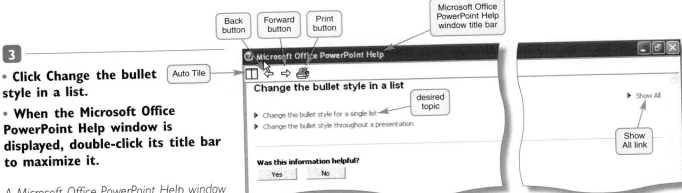

FIGURE 1-75

4

- Click the Show All link.

Directions for changing a bullet style for a single list are displayed. Options include change the bullet character, change the bullet size, and change the bullet color (Figure 1-76).

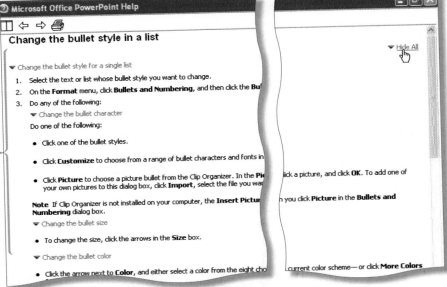

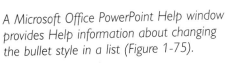

FIGURE 1-76

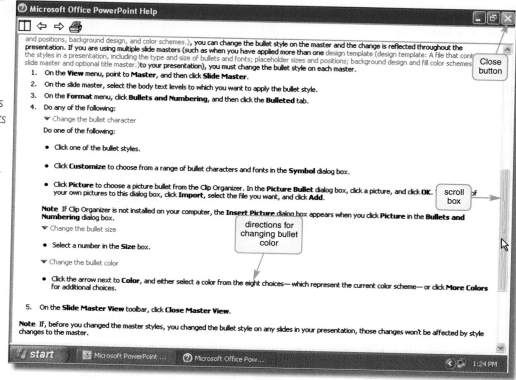

5

• **Drag the scroll box down the vertical scroll bar until Change the bullet color is displayed.**

PowerPoint displays specific details of changing the color of the bullets on a slide (Figure 1-77).

6

• **Click the Close button on the Microsoft Office PowerPoint Help window title bar.**

• **Click the Close button on the Search Results task pane.**

The PowerPoint Help window closes, and the PowerPoint presentation is displayed.

FIGURE 1-77

Use the buttons in the upper-left corner of the Microsoft Office PowerPoint Help window (Figure 1-75 on the previous page) to navigate through the Help system, change the display, and print the contents of the window.

As you enter questions and terms in the Type a question for help box, PowerPoint adds them to its list. Thus, if you click the Type a question for help box arrow (Figure 1-74 on the previous page), PowerPoint will display a list of previously asked questions and terms.

Table 1-6 summarizes the major categories of Help available to you. Because of the way the PowerPoint Help system works, be certain to review the rightmost column of Table 1-6 if you have difficulties activating the desired category of Help. Additional information on using the PowerPoint Help system is available in Appendix A.

Quitting PowerPoint

Project 1 is complete. The final task is to close the presentation and quit PowerPoint. The following steps quit PowerPoint.

To Quit PowerPoint

1 Click the Close button on the title bar.

2 If prompted to save the presentation before quitting PowerPoint, click the Yes button in the Microsoft Office PowerPoint dialog box.

Table 1-6 PowerPoint Help System

TYPE	DESCRIPTION	HOW TO ACTIVATE
Microsoft Office PowerPoint Help	Displays PowerPoint Help task pane. Answers questions or searches for terms that you type in your own words.	Click the Microsoft Office PowerPoint Help button on the Standard toolbar or click Microsoft Office PowerPoint Help on the Help menu.
Office Assistant	Similar to the Type a question for help box. The Office Assistant answers questions that you type in your own words, offers tips, and provides help for a variety of PowerPoint features.	Click the Office Assistant icon. If the Office Assistant does not display, click Show the Office Assistant on the Help menu.
Type a question for help box	Answers questions or searches for terms that you type in your own words.	Type a question or term in the Type a question for help box on the menu bar and then press the ENTER key.
Table of Contents	Groups Help topics by general categories. Use when you know only the general category of the topic in question.	Click the Microsoft Office PowerPoint Help button on the Standard toolbar or click Microsoft Office PowerPoint Help on the Help menu, and then click the Table of Contents link on the PowerPoint Help task pane.
Microsoft Office Online	Used to access technical resources and download free product enhancements on the Web.	Click Microsoft Office Online on the Help menu.
Detect and Repair	Automatically finds and fixes errors in the application.	Click Detect and Repair on the Help menu.

Project Summary

In creating the Strategies for College Success slide show in this project, you gained a broad knowledge of PowerPoint. First, you were introduced to starting PowerPoint and creating a presentation consisting of a title slide and single- and multi-level bulleted lists. You learned about PowerPoint design templates, objects, and attributes.

This project illustrated how to create an interesting introduction to a presentation by changing the text font style to italic and increasing font size on the title slide. Completing these tasks, you saved the presentation. Then, you created three text slides with bulleted lists, two with multi-level bullets, to explain effective academic skills. Next, you learned how to view the presentation in slide show view. Then, you learned how to quit PowerPoint and how to open an existing presentation. You used the Spelling checker to search for spelling errors. You learned how to display the presentation in black and white. You also learned how to print hard copies of the slides in order to make handouts and overhead transparencies. Finally, you learned how to use the PowerPoint Help system to answer your questions.

 If your instructor has chosen to use the full online version of SAM 2003 Assessment and Training, you can go beyond the "just-in-time" training provided on the CD that accompanies this text. Simply log in to your SAM account (http://sam2003.course.com) to launch any assigned training activities or exams that relate to the skills covered in this project.

What You Should Know

Having completed this project, you should be able to perform the tasks below. The tasks are listed in the same order they were presented in this project. For a list of the buttons, menus, toolbars, and commands introduced in this project, see the Quick Reference Summary at the back of this book and refer to the Page Number column.

1. Start PowerPoint (PPT 7)
2. Customize the PowerPoint Window (PPT 9)
3. Choose a Design Template (PPT 18)
4. Enter the Presentation Title (PPT 21)
5. Enter the Presentation Subtitle (PPT 22)
6. Change the Text Font Style to Italic (PPT 24)
7. Increase Font Size (PPT 25)
8. Save a Presentation on a USB Flash Drive (PPT 27)
9. Add a New Text Slide with a Bulleted List (PPT 30)
10. Enter a Slide Title (PPT 32)
11. Select a Text Placeholder (PPT 32)
12. Type a Single-Level Bulleted List (PPT 33)
13. Add a New Slide and Enter a Slide Title (PPT 35)
14. Type a Multi-Level Bulleted List (PPT 36)
15. Type the Remaining Text for Slide 3 (PPT 38)
16. Create Slide 4 (PPT 39)
17. Create a Third-Level Paragraph (PPT 40)
18. Type the Remaining Text for Slide 4 (PPT 41)
19. End a Slide Show with a Black Slide (PPT 42)
20. Save a Presentation with the Same File Name (PPT 44)
21. Use the Scroll Box on the Slide Pane to Move to Another Slide (PPT 45)
22. Start Slide Show View (PPT 47)
23. Move Manually Through Slides in a Slide Show (PPT 48)
24. Display the Popup Menu and Go to a Specific Slide (PPT 49)
25. Use the Popup Menu to End a Slide Show (PPT 50)
26. Quit PowerPoint (PPT 50)
27. Start PowerPoint and Open an Existing Presentation (PPT 52)
28. Start the Spelling Checker (PPT 54)
29. Display a Presentation in Black and White (PPT 57)
30. Save a Presentation Before Printing (PPT 60)
31. Print a Presentation (PPT 60)
32. Obtain Help Using the Type a Question for Help Box (PPT 62)
33. Quit PowerPoint (PPT 64)

Learn It Online

Instructions: To complete the Learn It Online exercises, start your browser, click the Address bar, and then enter the Web address scsite.com/ppt2003/learn. When the PowerPoint 2003 Learn It Online page is displayed, follow the instructions in the exercises below. Each exercise has instructions for printing your results, either for your own records or for submission to your instructor.

1 Project Reinforcement TF, MC, and SA

Below PowerPoint Project 1, click the Project Reinforcement link. Print the quiz by clicking Print on the File menu for each page. Answer each question.

2 Flash Cards

Below PowerPoint Project 1, click the Flash Cards link and read the instructions. Type 20 (or a number specified by your instructor) in the Number of playing cards text box, type your name in the Enter your Name text box, and then click the Flip Card button. When the flash card is displayed, read the question and then click the ANSWER box arrow to select an answer. Flip through Flash Cards. If your score is 15 (75%) correct or greater, click Print on the File menu to print your results. If your score is less than 15 (75%) correct, then redo this exercise by clicking the Replay button.

3 Practice Test

Below PowerPoint Project 1, click the Practice Test link. Answer each question, enter your first and last name at the bottom of the page, and then click the Grade Test button. When the graded practice test is displayed on your screen, click Print on the File menu to print a hard copy. Continue to take practice tests until you score 80% or better.

4 Who Wants To Be a Computer Genius?

Below PowerPoint Project 1, click the Computer Genius link. Read the instructions, enter your first and last name at the bottom of the page, and then click the PLAY button. When your score is displayed, click the PRINT RESULTS link to print a hard copy.

5 Wheel of Terms

Below PowerPoint Project 1, click the Wheel of Terms link. Read the instructions, and then enter your first and last name and your school name. Click the PLAY button. When your score is displayed, right-click the score and then click Print on the shortcut menu to print a hard copy.

6 Crossword Puzzle Challenge

Below PowerPoint Project 1, click the Crossword Puzzle Challenge link. Read the instructions, and then enter your first and last name. Click the SUBMIT button. Work the crossword puzzle. When you are finished, click the Submit button. When the crossword puzzle is redisplayed, click the Print Puzzle button to print a hard copy.

7 Tips and Tricks

Below PowerPoint Project 1, click the Tips and Tricks link. Click a topic that pertains to Project 1. Right-click the information and then click Print on the shortcut menu. Construct a brief example of what the information relates to in PowerPoint to confirm you understand how to use the tip or trick.

8 Newsgroups

Below PowerPoint Project 1, click the Newsgroups link. Click a topic that pertains to Project 1. Print three comments.

9 Expanding Your Horizons

Below PowerPoint Project 1, click the Expanding Your Horizons link. Click a topic that pertains to Project 1. Print the information. Construct a brief example of what the information relates to in PowerPoint to confirm you understand the contents of the article.

10 Search Sleuth

Below PowerPoint Project 1, click the Search Sleuth link. To search for a term that pertains to this project, select a term below the Project 1 title and then use the Google search engine at google.com (or any major search engine) to display and print two Web pages that present information on the term.

11 PowerPoint Online Training

Below PowerPoint Project 1, click the PowerPoint Online Training link. When your browser displays the Microsoft Office Online Web page, click the PowerPoint link. Click one of the PowerPoint courses that covers one or more of the objectives listed at the beginning of the project on page PPT 4. Print the first page of the course before stepping through it.

12 Office Marketplace

Below PowerPoint Project 1, click the Office Marketplace link. When your browser displays the Microsoft Office Online Web page, click the Office Marketplace link. Click a topic that relates to PowerPoint. Print the first page.

Apply Your Knowledge

1 Searching on the World Wide Web

Instructions: Start PowerPoint. Open the presentation Apply 1-1 Internet Searching from the Data Files for Students. See the inside back cover of this book for instructions for downloading the Data Files for Students or see your instructor for information on accessing the files required for this book. The two slides in the presentation give information on tools to search the Web. Make the following changes to the slides so they appear as shown in Figure 1-78.

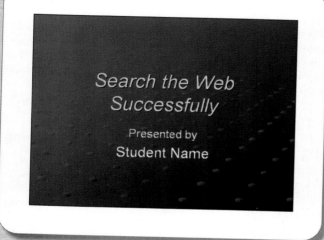

(a) Slide 1 (Title Slide)

(b) Slide 2 (Multi-Level Bulleted List)

FIGURE 1-78

Change the design template to Digital Dots. On the title slide, use your name in place of Student Name and change the font size to 40. Italicize the title text.

On Slide 2, increase the indent of the second and fourth paragraphs, Categorized lists of links arranged by subject and displayed in series of menus, and Requires search text: a word, words, phrase, to second-level paragraphs. Then change the last paragraph, Carefully craft keywords to limit search, to a third-level paragraph.

Display the revised presentation in black and white, and then print the two slides.

Save the presentation using the file name, Apply 1-1 Search Tools. Hand in the hard copy to your instructor.

Note: These labs require you to create presentations based on notes. When you design these slide shows, use the 7 × 7 rule, which states that each line should have a maximum of seven words, and each slide should have a maximum of seven lines.

1 Proper Tire Care Presentation

Problem: Your tires are one of the most important safety features on your car. Regarding tire maintenance, the Rubber Manufacturers Association recommends you "play your PART": Pressure, Alignment, Rotation, Tread. Terry Quinn, the owner of the local tire dealer in your community, is concerned that approximately 10 percent of cars have at least one worn out or bald tire, according to the National Highway Traffic Safety Administration. He has asked you to prepare a short PowerPoint presentation and handouts to educate drivers about how to care for their tires. He hands you the outline shown in Figure 1-79 and asks you to create the presentation shown in Figures 1-80a through 1-80f on the following pages.

I.) Tire Maintenance
Presented by
Terry Quinn

II.) Play Your PART in Tire Maintenance
- Pressure
- Alignment
- Rotation
- Tread

III.) Proper Pressure
- Check monthly when tires are cold
- Information placard has correct pressure
  o Mounted in drivers' door frame or glove box
  o Front and rear pressures may differ
- Use reliable tire pressure gauge
  o Do not rely on air pump gauge

IV.) Alignment Action
- Vehicles can become misaligned over time
  o Bumps, potholes create suspension problems
  o Apply brakes as you approach hole
  o Release just before striking it
- Misalignment causes tires to ride at angle
  o May experience handling problems

V.) Rotation Rules
- Each tire wears out at different rate
  o Rotating keeps wear even
- Should be done every 6,000 – 8,000 miles
- Pattern depends on type of vehicle, tires
  o Consult owner's manual
  o Adjust air pressure after rotation

VI.) Tread Tactics
- Uneven tread wear indicates problems
  o Incorrect balance, underinflation, misalignment
- Shallow tread
  o Should be at least 1/16-inch deep
- Check tread wear indicators
  o When tread is even with bars, replace tire

FIGURE 1-79

(continued)

Proper Tire Care Presentation *(continued)*

Tire Maintenance

Presented by
Terry Quinn

(a) Slide 1

Play Your PART in Tire Maintenance

- Pressure
- Alignment
- Rotation
- Tread

(b) Slide 2

Proper Pressure

- Check monthly when tires are cold
- Information placard has correct pressure
  - Mounted in drivers' door frame or glove box
  - Front and rear pressures may differ
- Use reliable tire pressure gauge
  - Do not rely on air pump gauge

(c) Slide 3

Alignment Action

- Vehicles can become misaligned over time
  - Bumps, potholes create suspension problems
  - Apply brakes as you approach hole
  - Release just before striking it
- Misalignment causes tires to ride at angle
  - May experience handling problems

(d) Slide 4

FIGURE 1-80

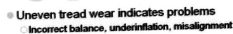

In the Lab

Rotation Rules

- Each tire wears out at different rate
  - Rotating keeps wear even
- Should be done every 6,000 – 8,000 miles
- Pattern depends on type of vehicle, tires
  - Consult owner's manual
  - Adjust air pressure after rotation

(e) Slide 5

Tread Tactics

- Uneven tread wear indicates problems
  - Incorrect balance, underinflation, misalignment
- Shallow tread
  - Should be at least 1/16-inch deep
- Check tread wear indicators
  - When tread is even with bars, replace tire

(f) Slide 6

FIGURE 1-80 (continued)

Instructions: Perform the following tasks.

1. Create a new presentation using the Watermark design template.
2. Using the typed notes illustrated in Figure 1-79 on page PPT 69, create the title slide shown in Figure 1-80a using your name in place of Terry Quinn. Italicize the title paragraph, Tire Maintenance, and increase the font size to 60. Increase the font size of the first paragraph of the subtitle text, Presented by, to 36. Italicize your name, and increase the font size to 40.
3. Using the typed notes in Figure 1-79, create the five text slides with bulleted lists shown in Figures 1-80b through 1-80f.
4. Click the Spelling button on the Standard toolbar. Correct any errors.
5. Drag the scroll box to display Slide 1. Click the Slide Show button to start slide show view. Then click to display each slide.
6. Save the presentation using the file name, Lab 1-1 Tire Maintenance.
7. Display and print the presentation in black and white. Close the presentation. Hand in the hard copy to your instructor.

2 Credit Card Safety Measures Presentation

Problem: The credit union on your campus issues many credit cards to students. Brian Brown, the branch manager, desires to inform these students about using their credit cards safely, especially because the Federal Trade Commission found recently that nearly 30 percent of identity theft was reported by people 18 to 29 years old. He has asked you to help him design a PowerPoint presentation that he can show during student orientation. He has typed information about wise credit habits (Figure 1-81) and has asked you to create the presentation shown in Figures 1-82a through 1-82d.

---

1) Credit Card Safety
Guard Your Card
Brian Brown
Credit Union Manager

2) Check Your Monthly Statements
- Compare receipts with billing statements
  - Evaluate whether all purchases are yours
- Check personal information
- Thieves often make small purchases
  - If not detected, they then charge large amounts
- Shred all documents and receipts

3) Secure Your Cards
- Do not
  - Put credit cards in glove compartment
  - Lend your card to anyone
  - Write your password on your card
  - Write your account number on an envelope
  - Leave receipts lying around

4) Take Security Measures
- Forward mail if you move
- Hold mail if leaving town for extended time
- Record account numbers, expiration dates, and customer service numbers
  - Store in safe location
  - Call immediately when problems arise

FIGURE 1-81

In the Lab

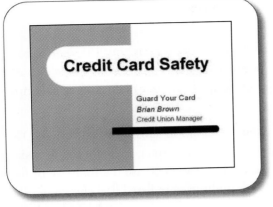

(a) Slide 1 (Title Slide)

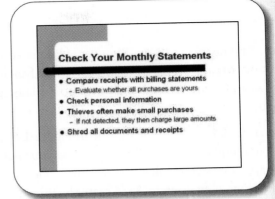

(b) Slide 2

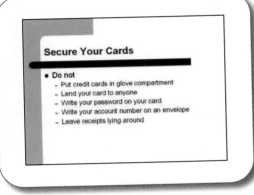

(c) Slide 3

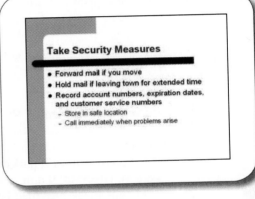

(d) Slide 4

FIGURE 1-82

Instructions: Perform the following tasks.

1. Create a new presentation using the Capsules design template.
2. Using the typed notes illustrated in Figure 1-81, create the title slide shown in Figure 1-82a using your name in place of Brian Brown. Italicize your name. Increase the font size of the title paragraph, Credit Card Safety, to 60. Decrease the font size of the third paragraph of the subtitle text, Credit Union Manager, to 24.
3. Using the typed notes in Figure 1-81, create the three text slides with bulleted lists shown in Figures 1-82b through 1-82d.
4. Click the Spelling button on the Standard toolbar. Correct any errors.
5. Save the presentation using the file name, Lab 1-2 Credit Card.
6. Display the presentation in black and white.
7. Print the black and white presentation. Close the presentation. Hand in the hard copy to your instructor.

3 Bodacious Bikers City Tour Presentation

Problem: The members of the Bodacious Bikers sponsor several activities throughout the year to raise money for community organizations in their city. One of their most popular events is a three-day bicycle tour that winds through major metropolitan cities. Bikers stay at a college campus the first night and at a campground the second night.

Instructions Part 1: Using the outline in Figure 1-83, create the presentation shown in Figure 1-84. Use the Studio design template. On the title slide, type your name in place of Louisa Garcia. Increase the font size of the title paragraph, Bodacious Bikers, to 54, and underline and italicize that text. Increase the font size of the subtitle paragraph, Spring City Tour, to 36. Create the three text slides with multi-level bulleted lists shown in Figures 1-84b through 1-84d.

Correct any spelling mistakes, and then view the slide show. Save the presentation using the file name, Lab 1-3 Part One Spring Bikers. Display and print the presentation in black and white.

1. Bodacious Bikers
Spring City Tour
April 10 – 12
Louisa Garcia, President

2. Day 1
- Meet at Midtown Mall parking lot
  - 8 a.m. check-in; 9 a.m. start
    - Light snack provided before ride starts
- End at Stevens College
- Approximately 62 miles
- Accommodations at Conference Center

3. Day 2
- Leave Stevens College at 9 a.m.
- End at Joseph Bay on Lake Echo
- Approximately 60 miles
- Accommodations at Dunes Campground
  - Tents and sleeping bags provided
  - Barbecue dinner served

4. Day 3
- Leave Joseph Bay at 8:30 a.m.
- Arrive at Midland Mall
- Approximately 55 miles
- Enjoy a celebration dinner
  - Awards ceremony for fundraisers
    - First prize: Cannondale Sport Road Bicycle

FIGURE 1-83

In the Lab

Bodacious Bikers

Spring City Tour
April 10 – 12
Louisa Garcia, President

(a) Slide 1 (Title Slide)

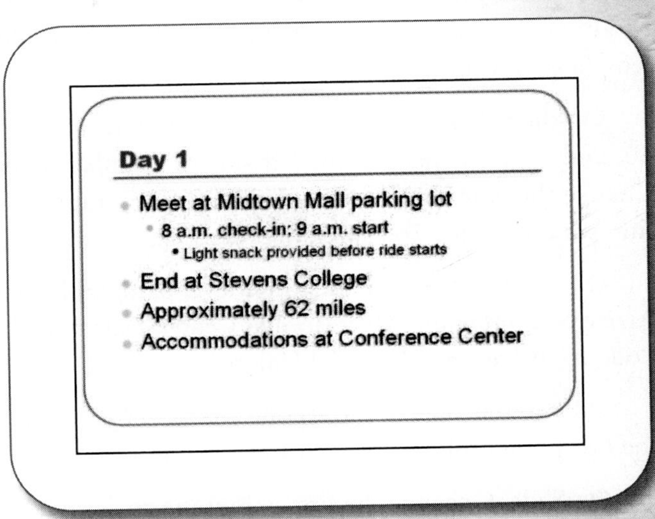

Day 1

- Meet at Midtown Mall parking lot
  - 8 a.m. check-in; 9 a.m. start
    - Light snack provided before ride starts
- End at Stevens College
- Approximately 62 miles
- Accommodations at Conference Center

(b) Slide 2

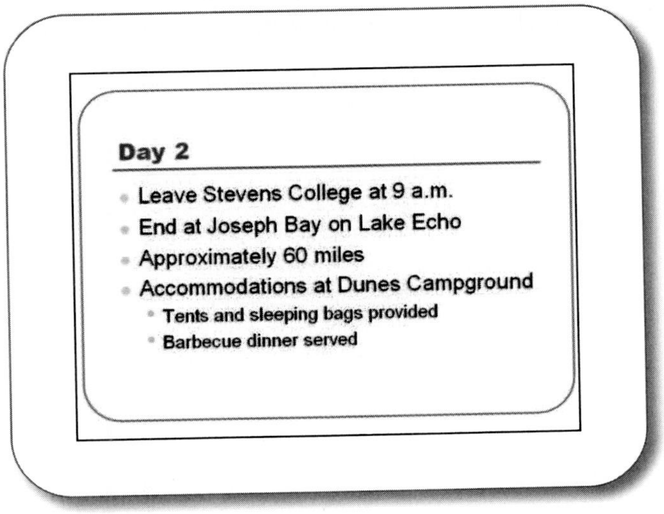

Day 2

- Leave Stevens College at 9 a.m.
- End at Joseph Bay on Lake Echo
- Approximately 60 miles
- Accommodations at Dunes Campground
  - Tents and sleeping bags provided
  - Barbecue dinner served

(c) Slide 3

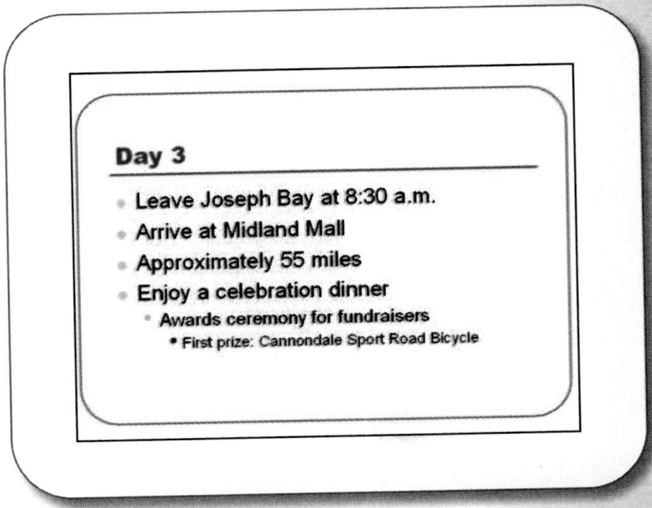

Day 3

- Leave Joseph Bay at 8:30 a.m.
- Arrive at Midland Mall
- Approximately 55 miles
- Enjoy a celebration dinner
  - Awards ceremony for fundraisers
    - First prize: Cannondale Sport Road Bicycle

(d) Slide 4

FIGURE 1-84

(continued)

Bodacious Bikers City Tour Presentation *(continued)*

Instructions Part 2: The Bodacious Bikers want to update their presentation to promote the Fall bicycle tour. Modify the presentation created in Part 1 to create the presentation shown in Figure 1-85. Change the design template to Maple.

On the title slide, remove the underline from the title paragraph, Bodacious Bikers, decrease the font size to 60, and align the text on the left side of the placeholder. Change the first subtitle paragraph to, Fall City Tour. Change the dates in the second subtitle paragraph to, October 9 – 11. Then change your title in the third subtitle paragraph to, Treasurer, and decrease the font size of that paragraph to 28.

On Slide 2, delete the first first-level paragraph regarding the Midtown Mall and replace it with the paragraph, Arrive at Community Recreational Center. Delete the last paragraph on the slide and replace it with the paragraph, Lodging at Stevens Memorial Union.

On Slide 3, change the second first-level paragraph to, End at Twilight Shores on Lake Baker. Then change the last paragraph to, Enjoy a fresh fish dinner.

On Slide 4, change the first paragraph to, Leave Twilight Shores at 9 a.m., and then change the last paragraph to, Grand Prize: Rocky Mountain Ski Trip.

Correct any spelling mistakes, and then view the slide show. Save the presentation using the file name, Lab 1-3 Part Two Fall Bikers. Display and print the presentation in black and white. Close the presentation. Hand in both presentation printouts to your instructor.

In the Lab

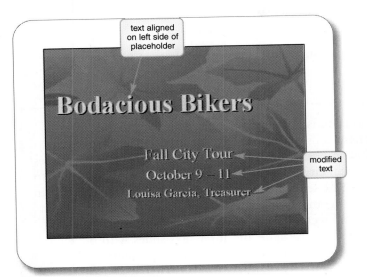

text aligned on left side of placeholder

Bodacious Bikers

Fall City Tour
October 9 – 11
Louisa Garcia, Treasurer

modified text

(a) Slide 1

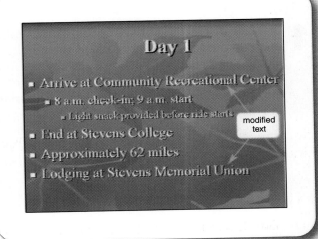

Day 1

- Arrive at Community Recreational Center
  - 8 a.m. check-in; 9 a.m. start
    - Light snack provided before ride starts
- End at Stevens College
- Approximately 62 miles
- Lodging at Stevens Memorial Union

modified text

(b) Slide 2

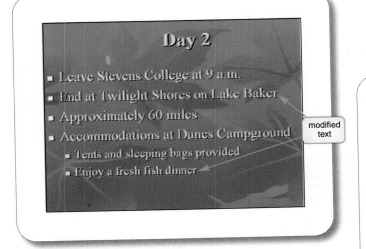

Day 2

- Leave Stevens College at 9 a.m.
- End at Twilight Shores on Lake Baker
- Approximately 60 miles
- Accommodations at Dunes Campground
  - Tents and sleeping bags provided
  - Enjoy a fresh fish dinner

modified text

(c) Slide 3

Day 3

- Leave Twilight Shores at 9 a.m.
- Arrive at Midland Mall
- Approximately 55 miles
- Enjoy a celebration dinner
  - Awards ceremony for fundraisers
    - Grand Prize: Rocky Mountain Ski Trip

modified text

(d) Slide 4

FIGURE 1-85

Cases and Places

The difficulty of these case studies varies: ■ are the least difficult and ■ ■ are more difficult. The last exercise is a group exercise.

Note: Remember to use the 7 × 7 rule as you design the presentations: a maximum of seven words on a line and a maximum of seven lines on one slide.

1 ■ The dispatcher at the Imperial Grove Police Station is noticing an increase in the number of calls made to the emergency 911 telephone number. These calls, unfortunately, are not always emergencies. Community residents have been calling the number to obtain information on everything from the times of movies at the local theatre to the names of the local city trustees. Police Chief Gina Colatta wants to inform homeowners of the importance of using the 911 service correctly. She created the outline shown in Figure 1-86 and asks you to help her prepare an accompanying PowerPoint presentation to show at the local mall and food stores. Using the concepts and techniques introduced in this project, together with Chief Colatta's outline, develop a slide show with a title slide and three text slides with bulleted lists. Print the slides so they can be distributed to residents at the conclusion of the presentation.

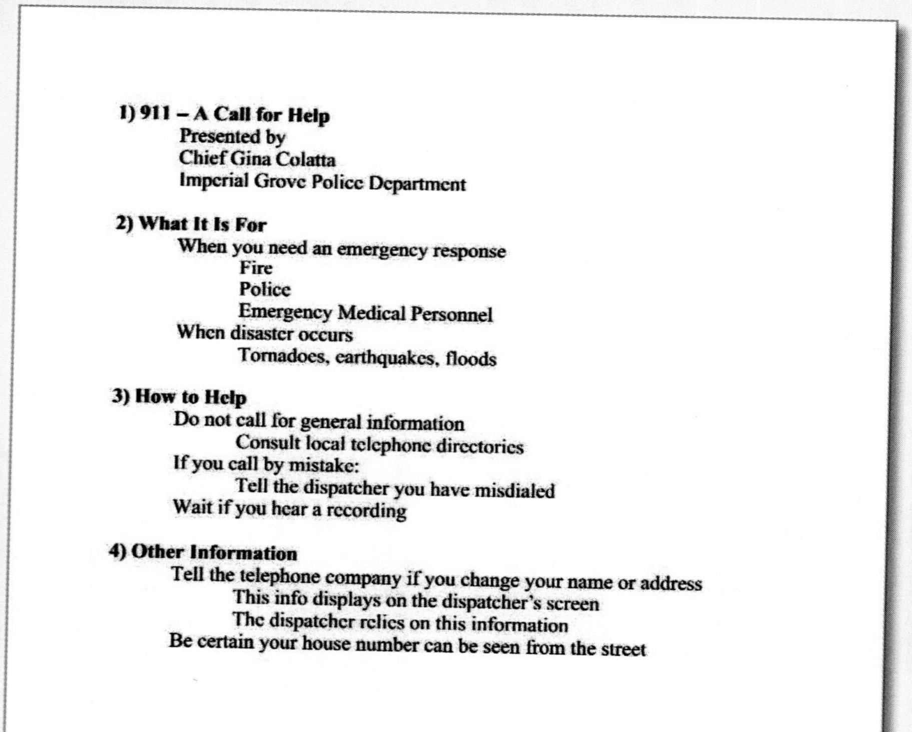

> **1) 911 – A Call for Help**
> Presented by
> Chief Gina Colatta
> Imperial Grove Police Department
>
> **2) What It Is For**
> When you need an emergency response
> Fire
> Police
> Emergency Medical Personnel
> When disaster occurs
> Tornadoes, earthquakes, floods
>
> **3) How to Help**
> Do not call for general information
> Consult local telephone directories
> If you call by mistake:
> Tell the dispatcher you have misdialed
> Wait if you hear a recording
>
> **4) Other Information**
> Tell the telephone company if you change your name or address
> This info displays on the dispatcher's screen
> The dispatcher relies on this information
> Be certain your house number can be seen from the street

FIGURE 1-86

Cases and Places

2 ▪ Your school is planning a job fair to occur during the week of midterm exams. The Placement Office has invited 100 companies and local businesses to promote its current and anticipated job openings. The Placement Office director, Latasha Prince, hands you the outline shown in Figure 1-87 and asks you to prepare a presentation and handouts to promote the event. Use this list to design and create a presentation with a title slide and three text slides with bulleted lists.

1. Brookville College Career Fair
Presented by
Brookville College Placement Office
Latasha Prince, Director

2. Who Is Coming?
National corporations
   Progressive companies looking for high-quality candidates
Local companies
   Full-time and part-time
   - Hundreds of jobs

3. When Is It?
Midterm week
   Monday through Friday
Brookville College Cafeteria
Convenient hours
   9:00 a.m. to 8:00 p.m.

4. How Should I Prepare?
Bring plenty of resumes
   More than 100 companies expected
Dress neatly
View the Placement Office Web site
   Up-to-date information
   Company profiles

FIGURE 1-87

Delivering Professional Presentations with PowerPoint
Sales: Wooing New Customers for Caitlin's Café

"Tell the audience what you are going to tell 'em. Tell 'em it. Then tell 'em what you told 'em."
—Dale Carnegie

LEARNING OBJECTIVES

Level 1

Use the AutoContent Wizard to create a presentation
Modify the design and the slide master
Add objects to slides to add interest and clarity
Prepare and run the presentation

Level 2

Apply an animation scheme to a presentation
Add transitions to slides
Add custom animation to objects on slides
Add sound to the presentation

Level 3

Record narration for a self-running presentation
Set up a presentation to run on its own at a trade show or via the Web
Use the Package for CD feature
Print handouts and speaker notes

TOOLS COVERED IN THIS CHAPTER

Animation Schemes	**Handouts**	**Slide Transitions**
AutoContent Wizard	**Package for CD**	**Speaker Notes**
Custom Animation	**Slide Layouts**	**Summary Slide**
Design Templates	**Slide Shows**	**Voice Narration**

CHAPTER INTRODUCTION

PowerPoint is a practical and potent tool for creating and delivering business presentations that can combine text, graphics, sound, and even video. In this chapter, you will create dynamic PowerPoint presentations that combine essential content with professional design.

In Level 1, you will learn the basic skills for conveying key ideas to your audience, with a special emphasis on presentation planning and design. Not only will you learn to create simple presentations using PowerPoint's ready-made templates, but you will also learn how to customize those presentations using slide designs and varying colors and fonts. In Level 2, you will learn to make your presentation more dynamic by adding multimedia, such as sound and video, and linking files from other programs to be displayed in your slide show. In Level 3, you will learn how to add narration to your slide show and run it in a continuous loop for stand-alone presentations without a speaker.

4

Level 1

CASE SCENARIO

Caitlin Callahan recently hired Grace Brennan as the marketing manager of Caitlin's Cafés. Her first assignment is to promote the café's catering service and on-site banquet rooms to event planners by giving formal business presentations to prospective customers. She wants to emphasize the potential of their catering services for a variety of venues such as weddings, parties, and corporate events. Grace will design professional PowerPoint presentations for potential customers to persuade them to choose Caitlin's Café for all their catering needs.

Sales

LEVEL 1

PLANNING A PRESENTATION

POWERPOINT SKILLS TRAINING

- **Add clip art images to slides**
- **Add graphical bullets**
- **Add slides to presentations**
- **Change the color of a PowerPoint object**
- **Embed fonts in presentations**
- **Insert an AutoShape**
- **Insert embedded Excel charts in slides**
- **Insert Excel charts in slides as linked objects**
- **Locate and download a template**

SAM

DETERMINING YOUR PURPOSE AND AUDIENCE

Before attempting to design an effective and persuasive business presentation, it is essential to identify the *purpose* of the presentation and the *audience* you are trying to target. Consider what message you are trying to relay and who you are trying to appeal to. Your design will depend largely upon the situational context of the presentation. Some of the questions you might ask yourself include the following:

- Is the presentation meant to be formal or familiar?
- What is the age range of the audience members?
- What do they already know about the topic?
- What do I want them to learn?

Designing a successful business presentation involves balancing your own needs with that of your audience. You need to try to anticipate the expectations of your audience while keeping your own message first and foremost in mind.

Grace knows how important it is to consider the unique needs of the customers to whom she will be pitching the catering services and banquet facilities. She has created a general PowerPoint presentation that she can show to potential customers to introduce the restaurant's banquet and catering services. She wants to create a special presentation for one particular client who promises to bring substantial business to Caitlin's Café due to his position in the business community. She starts by analyzing this potential customer's needs.

Understanding Your Audience

Yoshihiko Nakamura, a Japanese businessman in his early forties, runs a midsized hotel in the vicinity of Caitlin's Café. His facilities do not include a restaurant and he is looking for a venue that is close by that he can use on a regular basis when his clients need banquet facilities. Grace has been in contact with Yoshihiko to try to convince him to use Caitlin's Café as his first choice when he needs a restaurant. He mentioned to Grace that he is planning a large party for his son's fifth birthday, and she persuaded him to consider Caitlin's Café as the place to hold the party. If she can convince him to hold the party at the restaurant, she knows that he will be impressed enough to contract Caitlin's Café's Catering services for his hotel functions.

Grace spent some time talking with Yoshihiko and found out that he wants to serve both Japanese and American fare to his guests. He has concerns that the staff of Caitlin's Café might not know enough about Japanese food and culture to provide an authentic Japanese experience for his other guests, which will include family members who will be visiting from Japan. Grace knows that she needs to address these concerns in her presentation.

Knowing the Purpose of Your Presentation

Grace's presentation actually has a dual purpose. First, she needs to convince Yoshihiko that Caitlin's Café can successfully host his son's birthday party and incorporate Japanese and American themes and food. Her second purpose is to lay the groundwork for a contract with the hotel, so she needs to emphasize the ability of Caitlin's Café to adapt to any client. Before she begins to create her presentation, she embarks upon a fact-finding mission about the needs of her target audience. She calls some friends of hers who used to live in Japan, to see if they can provide some insight about Japanese culture. In addition, she visits several Japanese restaurants to learn more about traditional Japanese dishes. She learns the following things:

- The seventh, fifth, and third birthdays are considered to be "special" in Japanese culture, as the odd numbers are considered to be lucky. There is a festival called "Shichi-go-san," meaning seven-five-three, in which parents celebrate and pray for their children's continuing good health. A sweet candy called chitose-ame is often given to children as a treat on this festival day. Because Yoshihiko's son is turning five, this will be a significant birthday for him.
- There are certain rituals that are part of an authentic Japanese dining experience, including that guests usually share several large dishes rather than consuming their own; they also pour one another's drinks rather than having the waiter or waitress refill their beverages. The catering staff, therefore, needs to consider not only what will be served, but also how it should be presented.
- The party is set to take place on December 29, which falls during the Japanese New Year holidays. Traditional Japanese New Year parties include the New Year's dish Osechi-Ryori. Other foods recommended by Grace's friends and confirmed by her visit to the Japanese restaurants, include the following:

  o Sushi
  o Sashimi
  o Gyoza
  o Miso soup
  o Soba noodles
  o Okonomiyaki
  o Edamame

Even though these dishes are not on Caitlin's Café's regular menu, Grace wants to show that her catering team will go the distance to make their guests feel at home. She will want to emphasize in her presentation to Yoshihiko to demonstrate that her catering staff can adapt to any type of event or client.

STRUCTURING A PROFESSIONAL PRESENTATION

Many speakers lack structure to their presentations. It is not uncommon for there to be no introduction, no conclusion, and few transitions between topics. To avoid this mistake, you should state a clear purpose for your presentation and reasons that the audience will want to listen; in other words, provide an introduction to foretell the content of the speech and inspire audience members to listen. Next, you should make sure the middle part of your presentation, often called the body, flows logically from one point to the next, united by reasonable transitions. Finally, at the end of your presentation, summarize the main points of your speech and perhaps offer recommendations or include a call to action. To do all of this, you need to create a plan for your presentation.

Creating a Plan for Your Presentation

Now that Grace better understands the purpose of her presentation and her target audience, she can begin to plan the content of her presentation. At this point, it is a good idea to craft a statement (or several statements) that succinctly describes the purpose of the presentation. Grace has determined that her purpose is threefold. She wants to demonstrate that the staff of Caitlin's Café:

- Can accommodate the needs of any client or event
- Can provide both American and ethnic fare
- Is aware of the needs of its client's guests

Best Practice

Putting Yourself in the Audience's Shoes

When preparing presentations, many speakers focus only on their own needs, the most important of which is to get their point across to the audience. Good speakers, however, put themselves in their audience's shoes. They provide benefits to the audience for listening and provide guideposts for what was just said and what is to yet to come.

In his book *Say it with Presentations**, Gene Zelazny proposes an Audience Bill of Rights that includes the following suggestions for considering the role of the audience:

1. **Respect your audience.** Do not talk down to them. Allow them to contribute to the "intellectual content" of the presentation.
2. **Adhere to a schedule.** Let the audience know ahead of time how long the presentation will take and do not violate this contract. Give breaks during longer presentations so that the audience does not lose focus.
3. **Make content matter.** Let the audience know what you will be covering in your presentation and present the most important information first. Provide adequate support.
4. **Make visuals clear.** Fonts should be large enough to see without straining, even from the back row. Complex charts should be explained.

5. **Be flexible.** Stop, when necessary, to allow for discussion. Do not put the audience off by saying "I'll get to that later."

6. **Deliver with style.** Speak loudly and clearly. Let the audience see your face—not the back of your head. Use humor to help illustrate your point, relieve tension, or establish rapport with the audience.

7. **End emphatically.** The audience should have a clear sense that something meaningful has been accomplished.

*Zelazny, Gene. *Say it with Presentations: How to Design and Deliver Successful Business Presentations*, p. 4-6. New York: McGraw-Hill, 2000.

Managing Your Time During a Presentation

As part of her presentation plan, Grace must decide how long her presentation should be. She must also decide how much time to spend on each section so that the pace of her presentation keeps her audience interested. She has decided that 45 minutes will allow her enough time to present her pitch to potential clients. She wants to allot 5 to 10 minutes at the beginning of her presentation to talk to the client one-on-one to develop a more personal relationship, and she wants to reserve 15 minutes at the end of the presentation to answer any questions that the client might have. Thus, she needs to be sure that the PowerPoint portion of her presentation is approximately 20 minutes long.

Knowing how long she has to present her ideas formally will help her to determine the number of slides she will include and how much time to spend on each one. She does not want to rush through her points, but she doesn't want to run out of time. Grace determines that if she spends only two minutes on each slide, she can have no more than 10 slides in her presentation.

PRESENTATION TIPS

As Grace prepares to create her presentation slides, she recalls a course that she took in the past about how to create and deliver effective presentations. She also recalls both the good and bad PowerPoint presentations she has seen over the years. She knows that to be effective, she must do the following:

- Make sure her slides are legible—she should not use dark-colored fonts on dark backgrounds, and the font size on each slide must be large enough to be visible to all audience members.
- Augment the presentation with graphics and perhaps sound without distracting from the purpose and content; too much text can be tiresome to view, but with an interesting visual, you will help your audience to focus on your ideas.

- Be conservative with sound, animation, and color.
- Use text sparingly—she should follow the 6 × 6 Rule—that is, include no more than six bullet points per slide and no more than six words per bullet point; avoid writing in complete sentences by avoiding articles such as "a" and "the"; and employ images, charts, tables, and other graphics, where possible.

Best Practice

Using Visuals and Stories to Convey Your Message

Research indicates that people think in pictures and remember stories. Consequently, use visuals extensively in your PowerPoint presentations and relate narratives that people will remember when associating the facts of your speech. For example, The U.N. World Food Program reported recently that more than 38 million people in Africa are at risk of starvation. That number, while staggering, might not motivate your audience to do anything about the problem and might not even be remembered in 10 minutes—much less 10 weeks—after your presentation. Conversely, were you to replace some of the text on your slide with a photo of a young, starving child, and then told a story of how *this* child—this 1 in 38 million people—lives on $1 a day and might not live to see her next birthday, the impact of your presentation will be significantly greater. Why? Because people think in pictures and remember stories.

Grace has sat through scores of presentations, many of which were unmemorable because the presenters lacked basic public speaking skills. She knows how important it is to remember that, first and foremost, PowerPoint presentations must be guided by basic public speaking skills. During the actual presentation, she also knows that she must not simply read the content of each slide to the audience. She wants her PowerPoint presentation to augment her speech, not replace it or distract from it. A common mistake that many people make is to simply place large portions of text on slides, which, in effect, serves to replace the speech. This is distracting to the audience, because they often try to read the slides while listening to the spoken words and frequently miss the meaning of both.

When you are presenting information, a good rule of thumb is to "speak in 3s"; that is, when possible, group concepts into three umbrella categories, as research indicates that people remember this coupling better than others. For example, many presentations would benefit from identifying the "past, present, and future" of an organization or the "advantages, disadvantages, and expected outcomes" of a proposed policy change. By grouping concepts as such, the speaker aids the audience in assigning particulars of a speech to one of three categories even if those particulars number in the dozens.

After paring down the text on your slides, including more visuals, stories, and concept grouping, it is imperative to prepare for the actual presentation by rehearsing. Many speakers conclude their presentations much too quickly or ramble on extensively after their allotted time. Both of these faults reflect a lack of rehearsal. By practicing your presentation, you not only get a sense of the time restraint, but also become more confident in your delivery as the words flow better, the concept grouping becomes ingrained, and the content of the slides become familiar so that you don't need to look at the screen extensively.

Best Practice

Anticipating Technological Failure

Despite all the practice in the world, however, you must be prepared for, and even anticipate, technological failure. Many speakers, practiced or unpracticed, arrive to give a presentation and become flustered when technology fails: the computer won't read the removable drive, doesn't have a CD drive, can't connect to the Internet, or is not compatible with the expected operating system or software; or maybe the projector isn't working. An experienced presenter *anticipates* that technology might fail and has backups: the presenter saves the presentation on numerous media and Web space, brings a backup laptop, projector, and overhead slides, and has printed slides to hand out in a worst-case scenario. The comfort and confidence that coincide with having these types of backups is well worth the effort to produce them.

4

Level 1

Best Practice

Delivering Your Presentation: What To Do and What Not To Do

Do	Don't
Speak with confidence and enthusiasm.	Apologize or diminish presentation (don't be facetious).
Vary your pace and volume.	Talk to the screen.
Establish eye contact with audience members.	Fear silence.
Employ strong body language.	Use fillers.
Use effective gestures (but not too many).	Let them see you sweat.

CREATING CONTENT USING THE AUTOCONTENT WIZARD

Now that Grace knows what she wants to include in her presentation, she can begin creating the actual slides. Although she could create a presentation from scratch, she decides to use the AutoContent Wizard to save time. The **AutoContent Wizard** allows you to choose from a variety of presentation templates, complete with a design and suggestions for content. After the presentation is created, Grace will need only to replace the suggested content in each slide with her own content.

To start the AutoContent Wizard, Grace starts PowerPoint, clicks the Create a new presentation link in the Getting Started task pane to open the New Presentation task pane, then clicks the From AutoContent wizard link in the New Presentation task pane. The

AutoContent Wizard starts, and the first screen in the wizard gives a general introduction. Grace clicks the Next button, and the second screen in the wizard appears offering a choice of presentation type, as shown in Figure 4.1. Table 4.1 lists the general categories of presentation types.

Figure 4.1: Presentation type screen in the AutoContent Wizard

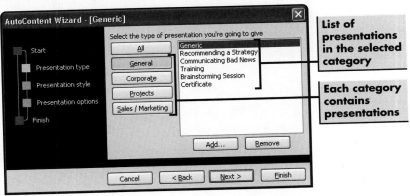

Table 4.1: Categories of presentations available in the AutoContent Wizard

General	Corporate	Projects	Sales/Marketing
• Generic • Recommending a Strategy • Communicating Bad News • Training • Brainstorming Session • Certificate	• Business Plan • Financial Overview • Company Meeting • Employee Orientation • Group Home Page • Company Handbook	• Project Overview • Reporting Progress or Status • Project Post-Mortem	• Selling a Product or Service • Marketing Plan • Product/Services Overview

Grace clicks the Sales/Marketing button, and then clicks Selling a Product or Service because it best describes the type of presentation she plans to create.

She continues moving through the AutoContent Wizard choosing the type of output she wants to use (on-screen presentation), inserts the title of her presentation, and chooses whether to display the date last updated, the current slide number, and any other information at the bottom of each slide. After clicking the Finish button, the AutoContent Wizard closes and a new presentation is created with placeholder content and a design template already applied. Figure 4.2 shows the presentation with the AutoContent.

Figure 4.2: Results of running the AutoContent Wizard

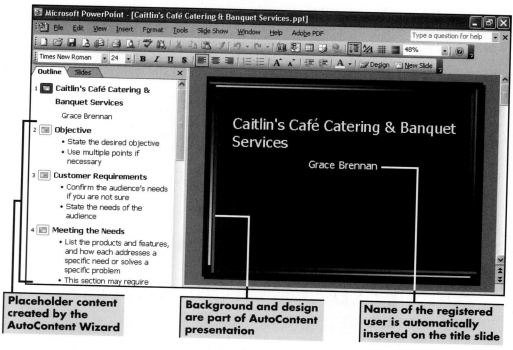

Placeholder content created by the AutoContent Wizard

Background and design are part of AutoContent presentation

Name of the registered user is automatically inserted on the title slide

Grace can now begin to replace the template's content with her own.

CUSTOMIZING A DESIGN TEMPLATE

Over the years, Grace has learned that it is best to use the predefined templates and slide layouts whenever possible. She does not see them as inhibiting her creativity as she knows she can always make subtle changes after the predefined features are applied. In this case, she decides to customize the template in the presentation to more closely coordinate with the theme of her presentation.

Changing the Background

For the slide background, Grace wants something with a Japanese flair. Grace knows that the color red is used in Japan for special occasions, such as birthdays and New Year's celebrations, so she wants to replace the blue, green, and purple color scheme with one that uses the color red. She starts by clicking the Design button on the Standard toolbar to open the Slide Design task pane. She doesn't want to change the design template, just the colors, so she clicks the Color Schemes link to see the color schemes associated with her design template. None of the available schemes contains any red at all, so she decides to customize the template herself. She clicks the Edit Color Schemes link at the bottom of the task pane. The Edit Color Scheme dialog box opens, as shown in Figure 4.3.

Figure 4.3: Edit Color Scheme dialog box

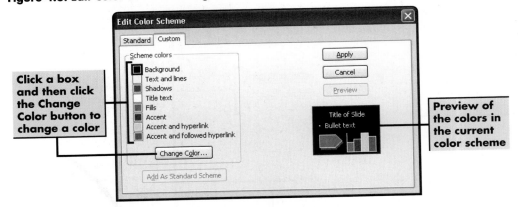

She changes each element in the dialog box to create a new color scheme; she chooses light red for the background and complementary colors in reds, browns, black, and yellow, for the other elements.

How To

Choose a New Color Scheme

1. Click the Design button on the Standard toolbar. The Slide Design task pane opens.
2. Click a predesigned color scheme, or click the Edit Color Schemes link at the bottom of the task pane. The Edit Color Scheme dialog box opens. (See Figure 4.3.)
3. Click a color tile next to an element, and then click the Change Color button. The Color dialog box for that element opens.
4. Click a new color for the element, and then click the OK button.
5. Change the color for each element as desired, and then click the Apply button.

Grace chose a shade of red for the background, but the plain red background looks somewhat unsophisticated, so Grace decides to add a gradient to the background. She right-clicks the slide background, clicks Background on the shortcut menu to open the Background dialog box, clicks the list arrow at the bottom of that dialog box, and then clicks Fill Effects to open the Fill Effects dialog box. Figure 4.4 shows her final choices in the Fill Effects dialog box to get a gradient background. After clicking the OK button to close the Fill Effects dialog box, she clicks the Apply to All button in the Background dialog box to apply her changes to all the slides in the presentation.

Figure 4.4: Adding a gradient in the Fill Effects dialog box

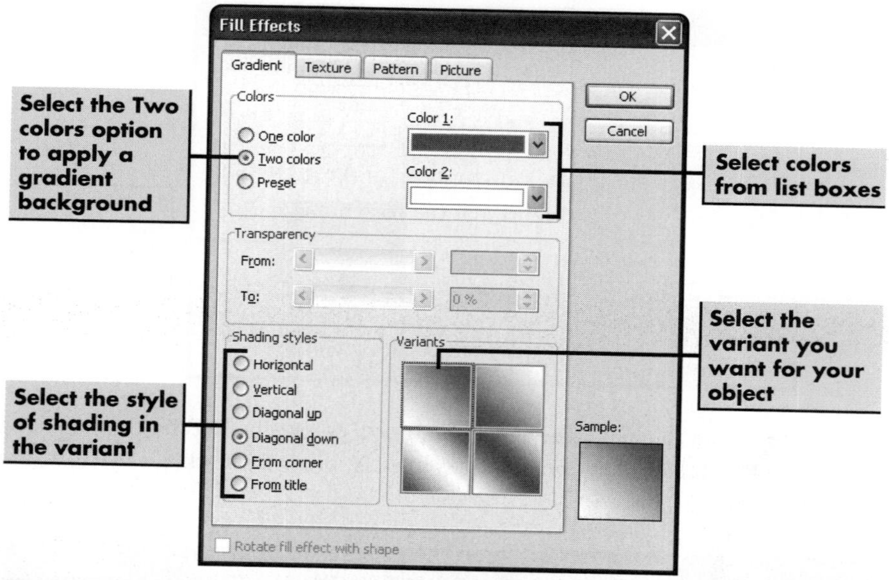
Select the Two colors option to apply a gradient background
Select the style of shading in the variant
Select colors from list boxes
Select the variant you want for your object
Fill Effects
Gradient
Texture
Pattern
Picture
Colors
One color
Two colors
Preset
Color 1:
Color 2:
OK
Cancel
Transparency
From:
To:
0 %
Shading styles
Horizontal
Vertical
Diagonal up
Diagonal down
From corner
From title
Variants
Sample:
Rotate fill effect with shape

Using the Slide Master

Grace wants to make a few more changes to the overall look of the presentation. Rather than spending time making changes to each individual slide, she uses the Slide Master to make uniform changes to the formatting of the entire presentation. The **Slide Master** is a tool that allows her to make changes to just one slide (the master) that will apply to all the slides in the presentation. When you use the Slide Master, you can add elements to the background or change the fonts used in the presentation so that they appear uniformly throughout the presentation. She wants to do the following:

- Customize the bullet points.
- Add clip art to the background to give the presentation a Japanese theme.
- Add the logo for Caitlin's Café to the title slide.

Grace switches to Slide Master view by clicking View on the menu bar, pointing to Master, and then clicking Slide Master. In Slide Master view, only two slide thumbnails appear on the Slides tab to the left; the one on top is the Slide Master, and the one on the bottom is the Title Master. Changes to the Slide Master apply to all the slides in the presentation; changes to the Title Master affect only the first slide in the presentation.

To customize the bullet points, she right-clicks the top-level bullet in the Slide Master, clicks Bullets and Numbering on the shortcut menu to open the Bullets and Numbering dialog box, clicks Picture to open the Picture Bullet dialog box, and then scrolls to look for an image that she likes to replace the bullet in the first level of bulleted text.

To add clip art to every slide in the presentation, she clicks the Insert Clip Art button 🖼 on the Drawing toolbar to open the Clip Art task pane, then she types Japan in the Search for text box. A selection of clip art with the keyword "Japan" associated with it appears in the task pane, some from the collection stored on her computer and, because she is connected to the Internet, some from Office Online. She scrolls through the list, clicks her choice, and then clicks Insert on the menu that appears. Then she drags the sizing handles to resize it to fit on the slide, and she clicks the Crop button 🔲 on the Picture toolbar that appears when the image is inserted, and drags a sizing handle to crop the image.

Next, Grace decides to add the company logo to the Title Master. She clicks the Title Master in the pane on the left, clicks the Insert Picture button 🖼 on the Drawing toolbar to open the Insert Picture dialog box, and then locates the image file of the logo for Caitlin's Café that she has stored on her computer.

How To

Add a Graphic to a Slide or a Master

1. If necessary, switch to Slide Master view, and then click the Slide or Title Master on the Slides tab.
2. Click the Insert Clip Art button 🖼 or the Insert Picture button 🖼 on the Drawing toolbar.
3. If you are inserting clip art, type a keyword on which to search in the Search for text box at the top of the Clip Art task pane (see Figure 4.5), click the Search in list arrow and select the check boxes next to the collections you want to search, click the Results should be list arrow and select the type of media you want to search for, and then click the Go button. Look for the image you want in the images that appear in the task pane, and then click it.

Figure 4.5: Clip Art task pane

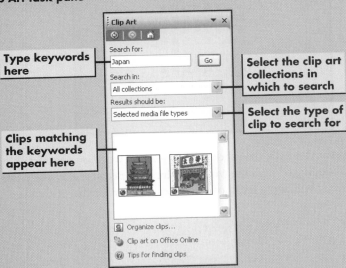

4. If you are inserting an image from a file, click the Look in list arrow and browse for the picture that you want to insert in the Insert Picture dialog box, click it, and then click Insert.

5. Reposition the image by dragging it to where you want it to appear on the slide.

6. Resize the image, if necessary, by dragging a sizing handle.

7. Crop the image by clicking the Crop button [icon] on the Picture toolbar, and then dragging a sizing handle.

When Grace changed the color scheme, the border lines in the graphic on the background picked up the colors she chose for some of the elements. Grace thinks that they stand out too much and wants to make them subtler, so she changes the colors of the border lines so that they are all the same. Because each of the lines is an embedded object, she does this by right-clicking each of the four objects that comprise her border, choosing Format Object on the shortcut menu, and then making her selections from the Format Object dialog box, as shown in Figure 4.6. To give the object some contrast, she clicks the Color list arrow in the Fill section, and then clicks Fill Effects to open the Fill Effects dialog box (see Figure 4.4), and then adds a contrasting gradient.

Figure 4.6: Format Object dialog box

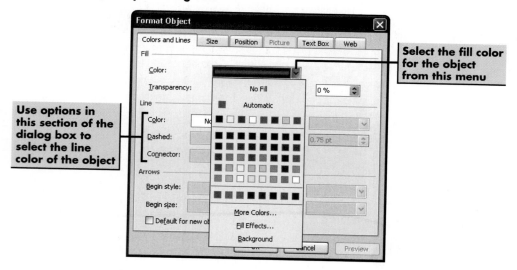

Now that she has customized the title slide, she begins to work on the rest of the slides. Her final Title and Slide Masters are shown in Figure 4.7. Because she made her changes to the Slide Master, they will apply to all of the slides, except for the title slide.

Figure 4.7: Completed Slide and Title Masters

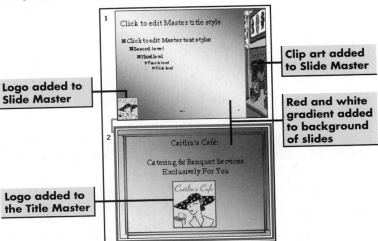

Now that Grace has decided on the overall look for each slide, she is ready to modify the placeholder text that the AutoContent Wizard inserted on the slide.

Best Practice

Choosing Font Colors

When Grace chose the colors for her new color scheme, she made sure that she chose complementary colors. In particular, she made sure that there was enough contrast between the background and the text to ensure legibility for her audience. Colors look different when projected on an LCD projector. Sometimes, the colors fade and there is not enough contrast between the font color and the background to allow the text to be seen clearly. In addition to choosing text colors with enough contrast to stand out on your background, you should also test your presentation using a projector so that you can adjust the colors if necessary.

Best Practice

Using Design Templates

The design templates that are available in PowerPoint have been created by professionals who have a good eye for presentation details, such as font sizes and color combinations. Although it is possible to make an infinite number of changes to the design template, it is best to do so judiciously. Generally speaking, the font sizes that have been chosen for the template designs will be large enough to be viewed by all audience members when projected on a screen. In addition, the color combinations have been chosen to make it easy for the audience to read the text. It is fine to individualize the presentation, but use the template as a guideline for good design principles.

Choosing Fonts to Enhance Your Presentation

The design templates that come with PowerPoint offer a good starting point for presentation designs, but you might want to customize the design to suit your audience, for example, or coordinate with the colors in your company's logo. Grace now considers the font used in her slides. She feels that the Tahoma font in the template is too impersonal and does not reflect the cozy atmosphere of the café. She wants to replace it with a softer font. She chooses the Garamond font because it has stylized edges and yet it is still clearly legible.

Best Practice

Choosing Fonts That Will Display Correctly in Your Presentation

One of the most important things to remember when designing a presentation, and one that is easily overlooked, is to choose a standard font that is installed on computers running Windows. Not all computers have the same fonts installed. It is best to be sure that the fonts you choose will be available on the computer you will be using for your presentation; otherwise, you might be unpleasantly surprised by the way your presentation appears when you show it. Microsoft Windows provides the same standard fonts on all computers that are running the same version of Windows. The fonts common to all versions of Windows are the Microsoft TrueType fonts, which include Arial, Times New Roman, Georgia, Verdana, and Tahoma. These are safe fonts to use if you do not know which version of Windows the computer you will be using for your presentation is using.

If you are not using these standard fonts, and you cannot do your presentation on the same computer on which you created your presentation, find out which version of Windows the computer that you will be using has. Then check the following Web site to see if that version of Windows includes the same fonts that you have chosen for your own presentation:

http://www.microsoft.com/typography/fonts/default.aspx

If it doesn't, you should change the fonts you have chosen to ones that are compatible with the version of Windows that you will be using for the presentation, or, when you save your presentation, you should embed the fonts so that they become part of the presentation.

You should consider the following fundamental points when choosing fonts to use in a PowerPoint presentation:

- Don't sacrifice readability for style. An attractive font is useless if it can't be read by your audience.
- Use fonts that match the tone and purpose of your presentation. If you want to be serious or conservative, avoid overly stylized or silly fonts.
- Be consistent. Limit the number of fonts you use to two or three. Any more than that makes your presentation look cluttered and unprofessional.

- Use the underline, italic, and bold features sparingly. It is effective to highlight a word or phrase for emphasis, but overuse of these features is distracting.
- Do not use any fonts smaller than 18 points. Remember, your audience will be reading your slides from a distance.

It is easy to change the fonts in a presentation. Because Grace wants to change the font used on all the slides in her presentation, she switches to the Slide Master. Both the slide title and the bulleted list are contained in a text box. Because text boxes are objects, you can make the text box active by clicking anywhere in it, and then you can select the text box as a whole by clicking the edge of the text box. Grace selects the title text box, presses and holds the Shift key, and then clicks the body text box. She then changes the font of all the text in the selected objects by using the Font list arrow on the Formatting toolbar.

Changing the title and body text box fonts on the Slide Master does not affect the default font used in PowerPoint objects added to the slides. To replace all of the instances of one font with another font, you use the Replace Font feature. To access this, you click Format on the menu bar, and then click Replace Fonts to open the Replace Font dialog box. You select the font you want to replace and the corresponding replacement font. However, keep in mind that any new slides that you add will use the formatting of the Slide Master, so the Replace Font feature is best used when the presentation is near completion. To make the fonts used in any drawn text boxes or AutoShapes consistent with the Garamond font she used on the Slide Master, Grace intends to replace all instances of the Times New Roman font (the default font for drawn text boxes and AutoShapes in this template) with Garamond when she is finished adding content to her presentation.

Best Practice

Embedding Fonts in a Presentation

If you want to use fonts that might not be installed on the computer that you will use to give your presentation, you can embed the fonts you choose in your presentation. Embedding fonts ensures that the fonts are able to be viewed and edited on computers other than the one on which you composed your presentation. To embed your fonts, when you save the presentation, use the Save As dialog box, click Tools on the toolbar at the top of the dialog box, click Save Options on the menu, and then select the Embed TrueType Fonts check box in the Save Options dialog box, as shown in Figure 4.8. If you do not plan to edit the presentation after it is on the presentation computer, click the Embed Characters In Use option button; if you are sending the presentation to someone else for editing, click the Embed All Characters option button (this option creates a larger file size).

Figure 4.8: Choosing to embed fonts in the Save Options dialog box

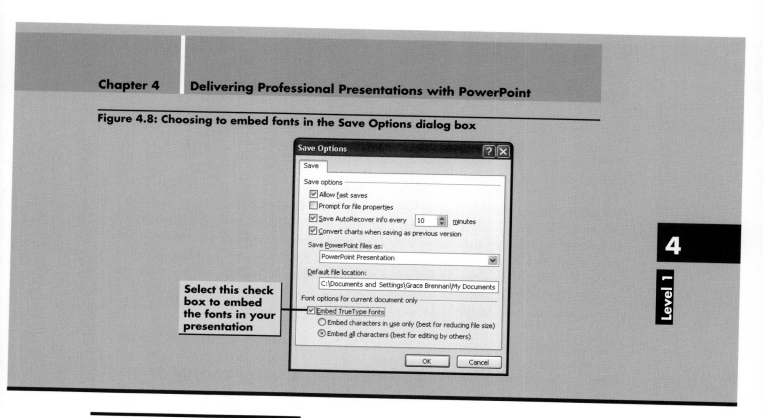

Select this check box to embed the fonts in your presentation

MODIFYING TEXT ON A SLIDE

Because Grace wants to consider the content of the presentation as a whole, she decides to work on the Outline tab as she replaces the text generated by the AutoContent Wizard with her own content. Using the Outline tab to add and edit the text of your presentation allows you to see the presentation as a whole. If you need to work on the design of an individual slide, you can switch to Slide view at any time.

To change the text in the presentation, Grace clicks to the left of each slide title and bullet point that she wants to change to select it, and then types her own content. Working in Outline view makes it easy to add additional bullet points by pressing the Enter key at the end of a line. You also can easily indent a bulleted point to a lower level by pressing the Tab key and promote a bulleted point up one level by pressing the Shift+Tab keys. To move text around, in addition to the standard Cut, Copy, and Paste operations, you can drag a selected text box to a new position on any slide on the Outline tab.

After Grace has included her main points in her presentation, she can add graphics and other special effects.

WORKING WITH SLIDE LAYOUTS

The **layout** is the arrangement of text and images on a PowerPoint slide. As with most functions in PowerPoint, you can manually add all the layout features yourself, such as text boxes, columns, charts, tables, and pictures, and then arrange these objects in different combinations on an individual slide. The predefined slide layouts make it easy to customize your presentation while simultaneously acting as a guide for the elements of professional design.

Grace wants to add a picture of the banquet facilities to one of her slides along with a bulleted list about its features. She chooses one of the slides created by the AutoContent Wizard, clicks Format on the menu bar, and then clicks Slide Layout to open the Slide Layout task pane. She scrolls through the available layouts, and clicks the "Title and Content over Text" layout. Like most of the layouts, this layout has a slide title placeholder and a body text placeholder. This layout also has an object placeholder just below the slide title and above the body text placeholder, as shown in Figure 4.9.

Figure 4.9: Slide Layout task pane

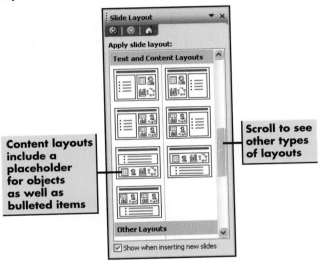

She types the slide title in the title text placeholder. Next, she inserts an image of the banquet facilities by clicking the Insert Picture button in the top placeholder. After adding a picture of the facilities, she clicks in the main text placeholder beneath the picture and types two bullets that describe the facilities.

Embedding and Linking Objects

To make her presentation more convincing, Grace wants to show how other clients have responded to using the restaurant's banquet and catering facilities. She decides to insert the results of a survey that was given to the customers of Caitlin's Café. Rather than simply listing the customer responses, Grace wants to emphasize the high rate of satisfaction that her customers are reporting. This is best done by using a chart, which she includes in the slide show. Graphics are a powerful way to convey ideas and concepts to an audience.

Grace created the chart in a Microsoft Excel workbook and wants to insert the chart into one of her slides. She can embed the chart or link it. An **embedded** object is one that was created in one program and inserted into a file created in another program. The embedded object is static, which means that changes made to the object in its original source file are not reflected in the embedded object. However, by double-clicking on an embedded object, you can make changes to it just as if you were working on it in the original program. A **linked** object is also an object created in one program and inserted into a file created in another program, but a connection between the original file and the linked object is maintained so that any changes that are made to the source file are also reflected in the linked object.

Grace added a new slide by clicking the New Slide button on the toolbar, then clicking the Title Only layout in the Slide Layout task pane. She cannot use the predefined layouts that contain placeholders for graphics because they will not allow her to insert objects already created in other programs. To embed the chart, she clicks Insert on the menu bar, and then clicks Object to open the Insert Object dialog box. From this dialog box, you can choose to insert a new object that you create or one that already exists in a file. This type of object is always embedded. If you choose to insert one from a file, click the Browse button to browse for the file. To link an object that already exists in a file, check the Link check box in the Insert Object dialog box. Grace decides to embed the chart because it will not be updated before she gives this presentation (see Figure 4.10).

Figure 4.10: Insert Object dialog box

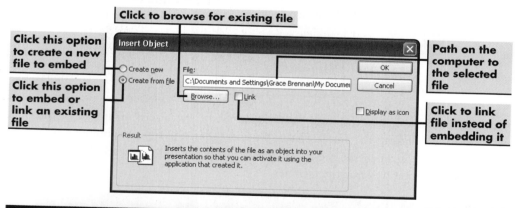

Maintaining Links Between the Source File and PowerPoint Presentation
After you have established a link between your source file and PowerPoint, the link remains unless you move, rename, or delete the source file. Likewise, if you move the target file, you risk breaking your links. If you accidentally break a link, you can reestablish it.

If you move your source file, you can update the link. To do this, right-click the linked object and click Update Link. If PowerPoint can find the source file, the link will be updated; if it can't find the source file, a dialog box opens telling you this, and your only option is to click the OK button. If this happens, you can manually browse for the source file. To do this, click Edit on the menu bar, and then click Links to open the Links dialog box. See Figure 4.11. Select the link you want to update in the list, and then click the Change Source button to browse for the source file.

Figure 4.11: Links dialog box

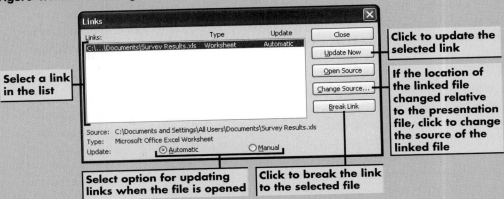

One of the downsides to linking objects is that you have to take special measures if you are going to be showing your presentation on a different computer. Be sure to create a file folder that contains all your presentation files, including those linked to files in other programs, such as charts or audio and video clips, and save that folder on your CD, USB flash drive, or other digital storage, and then manually update the links before your presentation to make sure that it works as you expect.

How To

Embed an Object
1. With the slide in which you want to embed your object in Slide view, click Insert on the menu bar, and then click Object. The Insert Object dialog box opens. (See Figure 4.10.)
2. If you are embedding an object that already exists, click the Create From File option button; if you are creating a new object, click the Create New option button.
3. If you are embedding an object that already exists, click the Browse button, browse for and select the file in which you have created your object, and then click the OK button.
4. If you are creating a new object to embed, select the type of object from the Object type list.
5. Click the OK button in the Insert Object dialog box to paste the embedded object or to start creating the new one in the slide.
6. To modify the embedded object, double-click it to access the object's program from within PowerPoint.

Grace knows that using a chart will help her to emphasize the good track record that their catering service has established. In particular, she wants to highlight the high praise that they have received from clients about their service staff. This is very clear from the chart she has created.

Creating Drawings and Diagrams in PowerPoint

Custom-made drawings and diagrams can be a welcome break from text. In addition, they can help to liberate the presenter from simply reading text and bullet points directly from each slide. Grace has used drawings and diagrams in the past to enhance her presentations because she knows that visuals are often more powerful than words alone. It is important to keep in mind that drawings and diagrams should help to convey a message rather than detract from it.

Grace wants to include a drawing to illustrate the way in which her catering staff will customize their services for their clients' individual events. She has noticed that drawings created in other programs, such as Word, often change after they are inserted into PowerPoint. She has learned from experience that it is best to create drawings and diagrams directly in PowerPoint rather than importing them from other programs. She decides to keep her illustration simple. She will include three arrows with labels. She wants two arrows pointing downward toward a third arrow on a new slide titled "Personalized Plan." Grace creates the new slide and adds the title. She clicks the AutoShapes button on the Drawing toolbar, points to Block Arrows, and then clicks one of the arrow buttons in the top row. She moves the pointer to the slide and drags it to draw an arrow. With the arrow selected, she positions the pointer over the green Rotate handle so it changes to ↻, and then drags the Rotate handle so that the arrow is pointing in the direction she wants. She next clicks the Text Box button ▣ on the Drawing toolbar, and then drags the pointer on the slide to draw a text box above the top, left arrow, and then types "Client Budget" in the text box. Finally, she clicks the text box to select it, clicks the slanted line border of the text box to select the entire object, clicks Format on the menu bar, clicks Font, and then formats the selected text box with a color to match the arrow it is near and a shadow. She then adds two more arrows and text boxes, and then adjusts any object not positioned correctly by clicking it to select it and then dragging an edge of the selected object. Her final slide is shown in Figure 4.12.

Figure 4.12: Drawn arrows added to slide

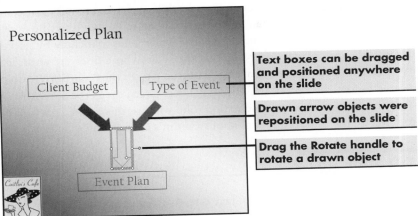

This kind of diagram, while simple, allows Grace to highlight the way that her event coordinators will use these two criteria to create a plan for their customers' events. She can use the diagram as a springboard to speak extemporaneously about the services her restaurant offers.

How To

Create a Drawing

1. Click the AutoShapes button on the Drawing toolbar, point to a shape category, and then click the shape you want to add.
2. Position the pointer on the slide so that it changes to ┼, and then click and drag the pointer until the image attains the desired size and proportion.
3. Drag the green dot to rotate the image, if necessary.
4. Drag the adjustment handle (indicated by the small yellow square) to change the shape of the drawn object without changing its size.
5. Position the pointer on the selected object so that the pointer changes to ⬚, and then drag it to reposition it.
6. Change the color of the object by selecting it, clicking the Fill Color button list arrow ⬚ ▾ on the Drawing toolbar, and then selecting a color. Change the outline color by clicking the Line Color button list arrow ⬚ ▾ on the Drawing toolbar.

CREATING A SUMMARY SLIDE

A summary slide at the beginning of a presentation is an excellent way to give your audience an overview of what you will present, or at the end of a presentation, a summary of what has been presented. It is easy to produce as it is automatically created from the slide titles of each presentation slide.

Grace knows the importance of giving her audience an overview of what is to come and also of what has been presented. She creates a summary slide at the end of her presentation to highlight the most important elements. She does not need to include the title of every slide that appears in her presentation. Rather, she chose which ones to include by selecting only those slides in Slide Sorter view. After selecting the slides whose titles she wants listed in the summary slide, she clicks the Summary Slide button 🖼 on the Slide Sorter toolbar. The slide is inserted before the first of the selected slides. Grace drags the summary slide to reposition it as the last slide in her presentation. She will use this as she concludes her presentation to reiterate the important ideas about Caitlin's Café.

RUNNING THE SLIDE SHOW

Now that she has completed all of her slides, Grace is ready to run her slide show by moving to Slide 1, and then clicking the Slide Show button 🖵 at the bottom of the Slides tab. After you have started a slide show, you can advance from one slide to the next and navigate the presentation in numerous ways. Grace moves from slide to slide by pressing the Space-bar because it is large and easy to find. However, you can navigate through a slide show in several other ways, including clicking the left mouse button, pressing the Enter key, or pressing the Right Arrow key. To see more options for advancing or reversing slides, right-click while running the slide show, and then click Help to display the Slide Show Help dialog box.

When the presentation is complete, Grace wants to have the summary slide on screen so clients can use it as a jumping-off point for questions. She also wants to be able to go to a specific slide that might deal specifically with a client's questions. To do this while the slide show is still running, she can type the slide number and press the Enter key, or she can right-click anywhere on the current slide, point to Go to Slide on the shortcut menu, and then click the slide from the list of all the slides in the slide show.

Grace makes sure to practice her presentation several times to ensure that she can easily navigate from slide to slide. She wants to ensure that she doesn't spend too much time on any particular slide so she rehearses what she will say again and again, getting a feel for how long to spend on each slide. She is well aware of how awkward it can be for the audience when a speaker is unfamiliar with the technology he is using. She wants to be sure that she does not fumble around, trying to locate the correct slide.

After rehearsing several times and making a backup of her presentation on transparencies (in the event that her technology isn't working correctly), Grace feels prepared to deliver her presentation. She ends her slide show by pressing the Esc key, although she knows she could just continue advancing until she reached the black slide that PowerPoint inserts automatically at the end of a slide show to signal that it is over, and then advance one more slide to return to the PowerPoint program window.

Steps To Success: Level 1

Every summer, Milwaukee plays host to a number of ethnic festivals at the lakefront of Lake Michigan, including African World Festival, Arab World Fest, Asian Moon Festival, Bastille Days, Festa Italiana, Irish Fest, Mexican Fiesta, Oktoberfest, Polish Fest, and others. The festivities attract participants throughout the Midwest, the United States, and the world. There is a huge marketing potential for Caitlin's Café as it is within walking distance of the lakefront. The Irish Fest, in particular, is very popular. Grace heard that the steering committee of the Irish Fest is allowing vendors to present proposals to be the primary food provider at the festival. Your job is to help Grace market Caitlin's Café to the steering committees of the Irish Fest by creating a PowerPoint presentation modeled after Grace's presentation.

Complete the following:

1. On paper, determine the purpose of your presentation and your audience.

2. Create a presentation using the AutoContent Wizard, and then save it as **Caitlin's Café Festival Promotion.ppt**.

3. Insert Caitlin's Café logo on all the slides in the presentation. The logo can be found in the file **Caitlin's Cafe logo.bmp** located in the Communications\Chapter 4 folder.

4. Change the color scheme so that it is appropriate for a presentation to the Irish Fest steering committee. Add a gradient to the background.

5. Modify the fonts used to fit the style of the presentation.

6. Add and delete slides from the AutoContent presentation you chose until you have a reasonable outline. Use the information in the Word file **Notes for Festival Promotion.doc** located in the Communications\Chapter 4 folder.

7. Add a new slide titled "Customer Demographics" and embed the chart stored in the Excel file **Demographics.xls** located in the Communications\Chapter 4 folder.

8. Use an AutoShape to draw an arrow pointing to the column with the highest number.

9. Add another AutoShape and list the four festivals with the top attendance inside the AutoShape.

10. Add clip art to some of the slides to add interest. Search for clips matching the keywords "party," "Irish," or "festive."

11. Replace the fonts so that all the fonts match the new fonts you chose on the Slide and Title Masters.

12. Review your presentation to make sure it adheres to professional design standards; for example, remember the 6 × 6 Rule and that visuals are effective in communicating benefits.

13. Create a summary slide and position it as the final slide in the presentation.

14. Run and practice your presentation.

15. Save and close your presentation.

LEVEL 2

ADDING EMPHASIS TO A PRESENTATION

POWERPOINT SKILLS TRAINING

- **Add sound effects to slides**
- **Add streaming audio and video with media player**
- **Apply an animation scheme to an entire presentation**
- **Apply transition effects to a single slide**

USING ANIMATION SCHEMES

Caitlin has been asked to prepare a report to be presented to the head office of Bon Vivant Café Corporation to document the restaurant's successes since they opened. She asked Grace to develop a PowerPoint presentation that will give the head office a better idea of how Caitlin's Café is meeting the needs of its customers. Grace wants her presentation to be vibrant by employing custom animation and adding multimedia, so that her audience can get a better idea of what it is really like to experience a catered event at Caitlin's Café. She wants to provide up-to-the-minute sales and marketing updates. She knows how to create a basic PowerPoint presentation for potential customers, but she feels that this presentation needs to be more dynamic.

Grace has already started creating the presentation. She has entered her content and applied a template with a blue theme. She recalls hearing that blue is a good background color for presentations as it is subtle and is not distracting. Now she is ready to add some special effects to make the presentation come alive. She decides to animate the objects on her slides; that is, have the objects on her slides appear one at a time instead of all at once when the slide appears on screen.

Just about any object that can be placed in a PowerPoint slide can be animated. This includes text boxes, pictures, drawings, diagrams, charts, and transitions. In addition, you can add countless combinations of animations to a slide show presentation. One of the easiest ways to add animation to slides is to apply an animation scheme to a presentation. An **animation scheme** is a preset style of animation that is applied to the title and bullet points within the body text placeholders in a slide. For example, if she applied the Dissolve in animation scheme and then switched to Slide Show view, the slide with all its background elements would appear first, then the slide title would appear gradually, as if a layer above it were dissolving, and then the bulleted points would dissolve in one by one. Different animation schemes apply different combinations of animation to a slide. Animation schemes can affect many of the slide show features. Some change the way that bulleted points are displayed in a particular slide; others can even affect the slide transitions. Animation schemes can be applied to one slide, several slides, or all slides. To make an animation scheme affect all the slides in a presentation, even if you add additional slides after applying the animation scheme, you must apply it to the Slide and Title Masters.

The advantage of using an animation scheme rather than individually customizing objects in your slide is time and consistency. It takes time to animate individual objects, but by applying an animation scheme to several or all of your slides, you can save a considerable amount of time. Moreover, animation schemes give a presentation a certain degree of symmetry. If you apply an animation scheme to all of your slides, you get the same look and feel for every point.

If you want to animate objects on a slide one at time, apply different animations to different objects, or animate objects other than the slide title and bulleted text, you can use custom animation. With **custom animation**, you can animate individual objects, such as pictures or charts, so that they stand out from the rest of the information on a slide.

Grace wants to make each of her bulleted points appear on every slide one at a time. Without using any animation scheme, all the bulleted points within each body placeholder appear at once. Because she wants some degree of uniformity, she decides to use an animation scheme. She knows she wants to apply the animation scheme to all the slides in the presentation, so she clicks Slide Show on the menu bar, and then clicks Animation Schemes to open the Slide Design task pane with the Animation Schemes visible without worrying about selecting any slides first. She browses through the animation scheme choices, occasionally clicking one to see a preview on the current slide, then she decides to apply the "Fade in one by one" scheme. See Figure 4.13. This way, the slide title and each bulleted point will appear to fade in when she advances the slide show, helping her audience to focus on each point as it is presented, rather than reading ahead and becoming distracted. She clicks her choice, and then clicks the Apply to All Slides button at the bottom of the task pane. (This is the same as switching to Slide Master view and applying the animation scheme to the Slide and Title Masters.)

Figure 4.13: Animation scheme selected in the Slide Design task pane

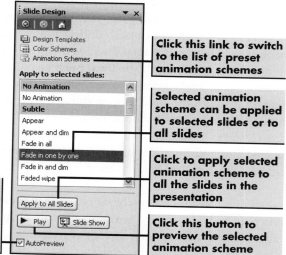

Click this link to switch to the list of preset animation schemes

Selected animation scheme can be applied to selected slides or to all slides

Click to apply selected animation scheme to all the slides in the presentation

Keep this option selected to automatically preview the animation scheme in the current slide in the Slide pane or selected slides in Slide Sorter view

Click this button to preview the selected animation scheme

4

Level 2

How To

Apply an Animation Scheme

1. Select the slides to which you want to apply the animation scheme, if necessary.
2. Click Slide Show on the menu bar, and then click Animation Schemes. The Slide Design task pane opens with the Animation Schemes link selected.
3. Click an animation scheme from the Apply to selected slides list in the task pane to apply it to selected slides.
4. To see a preview of the selected scheme, click the AutoPreview check box to select it, or click the Play button.
5. Click the Apply to All Slides button to apply the scheme to all the slides in the presentation.
6. To apply no animation scheme to slides (in other words, to remove an animation scheme), click No animation near the top of the list of schemes.

Grace views her slide show and likes the overall effect of the animation scheme she has chosen. She decides to apply a slide transition to one of the slides to emphasize it.

CHANGING SLIDE TRANSITIONS

The addition of well-chosen transitions is an excellent way to give presentations a vibrant and professional look and feel. Normally, when moving from one slide to the next, the new slide just appears. By adding transitions, the appearance of the new slide becomes animated. PowerPoint provides a number of options for incorporating transitions into presentations, such as by having the old slide fade or move to the side while the new one appears. As with most of PowerPoint's special effects, Grace knows that it is best not to get too carried away with the possibilities. She has seen presentations in which the speaker has used a different transition for every slide, making the overall feeling disjointed and confusing. By contrast, skilled presenters are careful to choose transitions that are consistent and appropriate for the tone they are trying to achieve.

Grace knows that the executives at Bon Vivant will be most interested in knowing how much revenue the restaurant has generated from their catering and event-planning services. One of her slides includes an Excel chart that displays the revenue generated in the first quarter that their newest location has been open for business. Because they have done rather well, she really wants this slide to stand out. She decides to apply a special slide transition to this slide only to capture the audience's attention and cause them to pay particular attention to the information on that slide.

She switches to that slide in Normal view, clicks Slide Show on the menu bar, then clicks Slide Transition to open the Slide Transition task pane. She scrolls through the list of transitions in the task pane, and then clicks her choice, the Newsflash transition; she chose this because of its stark contrast to the more subtle transitions of the animation scheme. Because she wants to add emphasis to this slide, she includes the sound of a camera click in the transition by clicking the Sound list arrow and selecting Camera. Finally, she looks at the Advance slide section of the task pane. She wants to manually control when each bullet point appears on screen, so she leaves the On mouse click option checked. If she wanted, she could click the Automatically after check box to select it and type in a time in the box, and then the next bullet would appear if she hadn't advanced the slide after that amount of time passes, but she decides not to use this option. Her final selections in the task pane are shown in Figure 4.14.

Figure 4.14: Newsflash transition selected in Slide Transition task pane

Selected transition can be applied to selected slides or to all slides

Select this option to advance the slides automatically after the time set in the text box below

Keep this option selected to automatically preview the transition in the current slide in the Slide pane or selected slides in Slide Sorter view

Click to select a different speed for the transition

Click to add a sound effect to the transition

Select this option to advance the slides manually during a slide show

Click this button to apply the transition to all the slides in the presentation

Click this button to preview the selected animation scheme

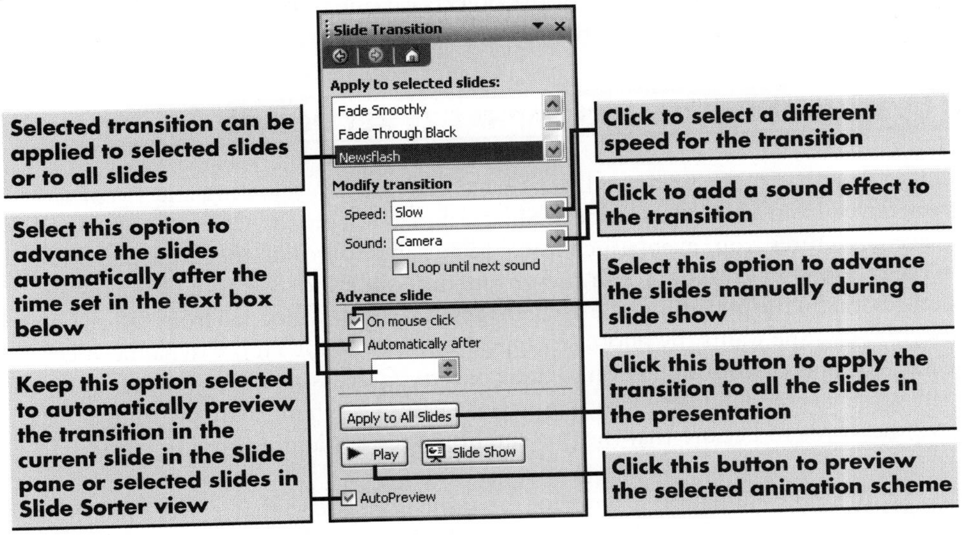

How To

Apply a Slide Transition

1. Select the slides to which you want to apply the transition, if necessary.
2. Click Slide Show on the menu bar, and then click Slide Transition.
3. Click a transition from the Apply to selected slides list in the Slide Transition task pane to apply it to selected slides.
4. Click the Speed list arrow and choose the speed for your transition from the drop-down list (Fast, Medium, or Slow).
5. Click the Sound list arrow and choose a sound effect to add to the transition, if desired.
6. Choose how the transition will occur:

   - **Manually**—Select only the On mouse click check box.
   - **Automatically**—Select only the Automatically after check box and then set a time.
   - **Automatically after a specified length of time if you haven't advanced the slide show by that time**—Select both the On mouse click and the Automatically after check boxes and specify a time.

7. To see a preview of the selected transition, click the AutoPreview check box to select it or click the Play button.
8. Click the Apply to All Slides button to apply the transition to all the slides in the presentation.
9. To apply no transition to slides (in other words, to remove a transition), click No Transition at the top of the list.

Grace previews the new transition by running the slide show. She is pleased with the overall effect; it is subtle, and yet professional as each slide fades seamlessly in to the next. She feels that the unique transition introducing the first quarter sales revenue is effective. Next, she decides that she wants to animate some of the objects on one of the slides in her presentation to emphasize the information in that slide.

USING CUSTOM ANIMATION TO EMPHASIZE KEY POINTS

Grace wants to emphasize the great feedback that Caitlin's Café's Catering and Event services have received from satisfied customers. She created a slide titled "Client Satisfaction" to show several pictures from events such as weddings and corporate meetings that were hosted in the restaurant's banquet room and private outdoor patio. She asked her assistant for the pictures, but in the meantime, she used images that she downloaded from Office Online as placeholders. She wants the photos to appear one by one for a more dynamic effect, so she decides to apply custom animation to these objects. Grace is careful to choose the animation she wants to use deliberately and cautiously. Although there are many things that she *can* do, she wants to be sure that the presentation does not appear busy or cluttered.

First, Grace removes the animation scheme for this particular slide so that it won't interfere with the new custom animation. She then opens the Custom Animation task pane by clicking Slide Show on the menu bar, and then clicking Custom Animation. Grace presses the Ctrl key and clicks each photo on the slide. The Add Effect button becomes available when an object is selected. You can click the Add Effect button to see the four categories of animation styles: Entrance, Emphasis, Exit, and Motion Paths. To see the effects available in a category, point to it, and the five most recently selected animation effects are listed with the option More Effects at the bottom of the list. To see additional effects, click More Effects, and many more effects appear in the Add Effect dialog box. After you apply an animation, you can click the three list arrows below the Add Effect button to change how the animation starts, the direction, and the speed of the animation. Grace adds a Fade entrance animation to each photo and specifies that she wants the animation to occur after the previous event so that the photos appear by fading in, one after another.

After setting all of her animation options, Grace clicks the Play button at the bottom of the task pane to preview the animation. The objects don't appear in the order she planned, so she changes the animation order by clicking one of the objects in the list in the task pane and then clicking the up and down Reorder buttons, as needed, to change the order of appearance for each picture until she achieves the effect she desires. Her final choices are shown in Figure 4.15.

Figure 4.15: Custom animation applied to objects on slide

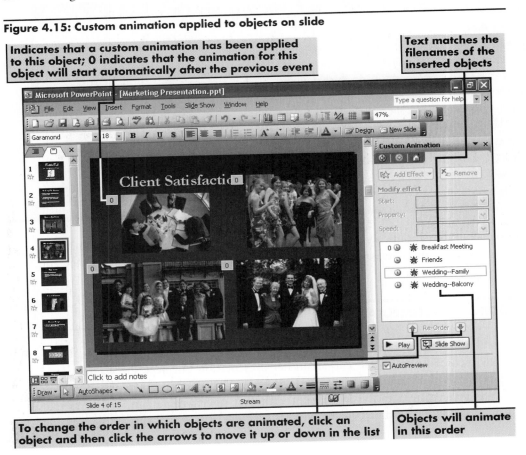

Indicates that a custom animation has been applied to this object; 0 indicates that the animation for this object will start automatically after the previous event

Text matches the filenames of the inserted objects

To change the order in which objects are animated, click an object and then click the arrows to move it up or down in the list

Objects will animate in this order

How To

Add Custom Animation to a Slide

1. Click Slide Show on the menu bar, and then click Custom Animation. The Custom Animation task pane opens.
2. Select the objects you want to animate, click the Add Effect button in the task pane, click one of the animation categories (Entrance, Emphasis, Exit, or Motion Paths), and then click one of the listed effects. If you want to see additional effects, click More Effects to open the Add Effect dialog box. Click an effect in the dialog box, and then click the OK button.
3. Click the Start list arrow, and then choose how you want the animation to begin (on mouse click, with previous event, or after previous event).
4. Click the Direction list arrow, and select the direction of the animation.
5. Click the Speed list arrow, and then click the speed of your animation.
6. Select animated objects in the list in the task pane and then click the up or down Reorder buttons, if necessary.
7. Click the Play button to preview the animation.

Best Practice

Hiding Animated Text

When you want to display a lot of objects on one slide, but you don't want the slide to appear overcrowded, you can hide an object with the click of the mouse and have a new object appear in its place. To do this, animate all of the objects on a slide, and then click one of the objects in the list of animations in the task pane to make a list arrow appear. Click the list arrow, and then click Effect Options on the menu that appears to open a dialog box. The name of the dialog box changes depending on the animation effect chosen. On the Effect tab in the dialog box, click the After Animation list arrow, and then click Hide on Next Mouse Click. With this effect, you can have overlapping objects on a slide, and it won't appear cluttered to your audience because they will see only one at a time. The Hide on Next Mouse Click feature will work with both text and graphic objects, so don't be afraid to be creative!

With an overall animation scheme and specific, carefully chosen transitions and animations, Grace feels that her presentation is still professional, while becoming more interesting and compelling.

INCLUDING MULTIMEDIA

PowerPoint makes it easy to incorporate various forms of media into a presentation. Grace has already included photos and clip art in her presentation but now she wants to add some audio. She thinks that having a sound clip of music playing at the beginning of her presentation will create a mood in keeping with that of her restaurant. She feels that an instrumental piece would be best, to evoke the feeling of actually being in the banquet facilities; she also wants to find a music clip that will match her title slide named "Caitlin's Café: An Auspicious Start." She wants the clip to begin playing as she projects the title slide and waits to begin her presentation.

She clicks Insert on the menu bar, points to Movies and Sounds, and then clicks Sound from Clip Organizer. This opens the Clip Art task pane. She types "music" in the Search for text box, selects the Sounds check box in the Results should be list, makes sure that the Everywhere check box is selected in the Search in text box, and then clicks the Go button to conduct the search on her computer and Office Online. She scrolls through the selections, and listens to those that sound as though they might work by pointing to a clip, clicking the list arrow that appears on the clip, and then clicking Preview/Properties to open the Preview/Properties dialog box. When she finds the one she wants, she clicks it. A dialog box opens asking if she wants to play the sound Automatically or When Clicked. She clicks Automatically so that the music will begin playing upon running her presentation rather than having to click the mouse to have it start.

Grace wants the clip to play as people are getting settled in the audience, waiting for her to begin her presentation. Because the clip is short, Grace wants to loop the sound so that it plays continuously, until she advances the slide and begins. She also does not want the sound icon to appear in her presentation. To make these changes to the sound clip, she right-clicks the sound icon, then clicks Edit Sound Object to open the Sound Options dialog box, as shown in Figure 4.16.

Figure 4.16: Sound Options dialog box

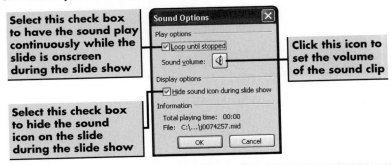

How To

Add a Sound Clip to a Slide
1. In the slide in which you want the sound clip or video clip to play, click Insert on the menu bar, and then point to Movies and Sounds.
2. Click the command corresponding to the location where the sound clip is stored: either the Clip Organizer or a file.

3. If you choose to insert a clip from the Clip Organizer:

    *   Type keywords in the Search for text box in the Clip Art task pane.
    *   Click the Search in list arrow and then click a category to restrict the search to that category, if necessary.
    *   Click the Results should be list arrow, and then select the Sounds check box.
    *   Click the Go button to search the Clip Organizer on your computer.
    *   Point to a clip in the task pane that you want to listen to, click the list arrow on the clip, and then click Preview/Properties to open the Preview/Properties dialog box and listen to the clip. Click the Close button to close the dialog box when you are finished.
    *   Click the clip you want to insert. A sound icon appears in the middle of the slide.

4. If you choose to insert a clip from a file, browse for the clip you want to include in the Insert Sound dialog box, and then click the OK button.

5. In the dialog box that opens asking how you want the clip to start, click the Automatically or When Clicked button. (This dialog box does not open for animated GIFs.)

How To

Edit Sound Playback Options

1. Right-click the sound icon, and then click Edit Sound Object on the shortcut menu to open the Sound Options dialog box.
2. Check the Loop until stopped check box to play the sound continuously.
3. Click the Sound volume icon, drag the slider to adjust the volume of the inserted clip, and then click outside of the slider to close it.
4. Check the Hide sound icon during slide show check box to hide the sound icon during the slide show.
5. Click the OK button.

She is almost done adding the finishing touches to her presentation.

Now that she has finished her presentation, Grace feels good about the work that she has done. She believes that the addition of animation effects, transitions, and music to her presentation will help to bring life to her presentation and to help those at the head office to better understand what it is like to host a party at Caitlin's Café.

Steps To Success: Level 2

Grace reviewed the presentation you created to show the steering committee for the Irish Fest ethnic festivals in Milwaukee. She wants you to add some animation and transitions, and she wants you to see if you can find some appropriate sound and video clips. She wants to include excerpts from it in her presentation to the Bon Vivant Café Corporation as evidence of a high-quality marketing campaign.

Complete the following:

1. Open the presentation named **Caitlin's Café's Festival Promotion.ppt** that you created in Level 1 Steps To Success, and then save it as **Animated Festival Promotion.ppt**.

2. Apply the Faded Zoom animation scheme to all the slides.

3. Apply a custom animation to the embedded chart to draw attention to it.

4. To entertain early arrivals to your presentation, add three slides to the beginning of your presentation. Each one must:

   a. Contain an interesting trivia fact about Irish food or culture.
   b. Stay on the screen for 30 seconds.
   c. Be accompanied by looped jazz music.

5. Apply the Newsflash transition to one of your slides.

6. Save your changes to the presentation, and then close it.

LEVEL 3
DELIVERING A PRESENTATION

POWERPOINT SKILLS TRAINING

- **Add hyperlinks to slides**
- **Add notes**
- **Prepare a presentation for remote delivery using Package for CD**
- **Save a presentation as a Web page (using the Publish option)**
- **Print handouts**
- **Use pens, highlighters, arrows, and pointers for emphasis**

RECORDING NARRATION FOR A SELF-RUNNING PRESENTATION

As part of her marketing plan, Grace wants to showcase Caitlin's Café at the upcoming wedding tradeshow to be held at the Milwaukee Convention Center. She wants to have a kiosk with a self-running PowerPoint presentation that will attract potential customers to her booth to learn more about her restaurant's catering and banquet services. There are several things that she needs to do to her presentation to make it appropriate as a stand-alone display. First, she wants to include narration to give her audience an audio guide because there will be no live speaker. Second, she needs the presentation to run continually, beginning again automatically when it reaches the end. Third, she wants to make her presentation available on the Web, so that potential customers can go back and view the presentation online at their leisure.

Grace also plans to conduct live presentations throughout the day, where she will present Caitlin's Café's Catering services to a small audience. For these occasions, she wants to create speaker notes so that her audience members can follow along with her presentation and she makes notes for the question-and-answer period that will follow. With these things in mind, she begins to customize her presentation for this event.

To create an effective stand-alone presentation, Grace feels that it is important to include narration. She wants to be sure that if she is already engaged in conversation with potential customers, that new visitors to her booth are not left alone waiting for her attention. Including narration will allow her to record the more salient points of the catering and banquet services, giving her presentation the feeling of having a live presenter.

Before she actually begins recording the narration for each of her slides, Grace invests in a high-quality microphone to ensure professional sound. In addition, she writes a script and rehearses it many times. This is a time-consuming process, but the results speak for themselves. Her narration gives the presentation a professional sound and feel. After her script is finished, she is ready to begin recording the narration. She clicks Slide Show on the menu bar, and then clicks Record Narration to open the Record Narration dialog box, as shown in Figure 4.17. She checks the microphone level, and then starts recording. She records a brief explanation of each slide, and then waits 30 seconds or so, depending on the material on the slide, for the reader to view all the written content before advancing to the next slide. After she clicks the black slide at the end of the presentation, she saves the recordings and the slide timings.

Figure 4.17: Record Narration dialog box

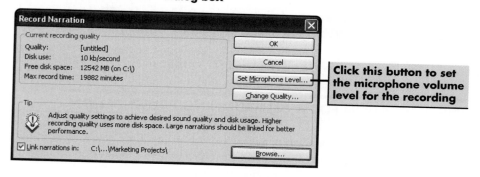

748

Record Voice Narration

1. Go to the first slide in your presentation, click Slide Show on the menu bar, and then click Record Narration. The Record Narration dialog box opens.
2. Click Set Microphone Level. The Microphone Check dialog box opens. Read the text aloud to check the microphone recording level, and then click the OK button.
3. Click the OK button in the Record Narration dialog box to start recording. The slide show starts.
4. Begin narrating.
5. Advance the slide show normally after you have allowed the correct amount of time for each slide to appear on screen.
6. Click the black slide at the end of the presentation. A dialog box opens telling you that the narrations were saved on each slide and asking if you want to save the timings as well. Click the Save or Don't Save button as desired.

After viewing her slide show with the narration, Grace decides that some of the slides speak for themselves and the narration on those slides is distracting, so she decides to remove the narration from those slides. She does this by switching to Normal view, and then deleting the sound icon in the lower-right corner of each slide from which she wants to remove the narration.

RUNNING IN A CONTINUOUS LOOP AT A TRADE SHOW

Now that Grace has added narration to her presentation, she wants to configure the presentation to run continuously. Then she can set it up at a stand-alone computer at the trade show, and customers can stop and view the presentation without needing Grace's help. To set up the slide show to run continuously, she clicks Slide Show on the menu bar, and then clicks Set Up Show to open the Set Up Show dialog box. She clicks Browsed at a Kiosk (full screen) option button. After she does this, the Loop Continuously until 'Esc' check box is automatically checked. She wants the slides to advance automatically according to the timing she set when she recorded her narration, so she checks the Using timings, if present option button. See Figure 4.18.

Figure 4.18: Set Up Show dialog box

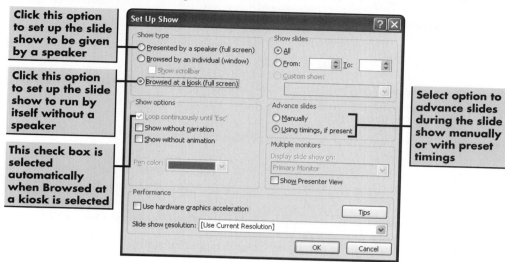

Click this option to set up the slide show to be given by a speaker

Click this option to set up the slide show to run by itself without a speaker

This check box is selected automatically when Browsed at a kiosk is selected

Select option to advance slides during the slide show manually or with preset timings

Grace views the completed slide show and feels that it is very effective as a stand-alone presentation. She decides that it is now ready to be uploaded to the Caitlin's Café Web site. At the wedding show, she plans to place a small card with the presentation URL next to her computer so that people can view it online or forward the presentation to others.

DELIVERING PRESENTATIONS VIA THE WEB

Before publishing her presentation to the Web, Grace looks at the size of the PowerPoint file. It is a good idea to keep files no larger than 100 KB so that people with slow Internet connections can still view the presentation. The easiest way to reduce the file size of a presentation file is to delete multimedia and graphic elements, or at least reduce the size of photo files. Huge file sizes for photos can slow down a presentation tremendously. Grace has only a few pictures in her presentation, but she makes sure to reduce their file sizes before publishing the presentation by editing them in photo editing software. Next, she reviews the slide show and decides to remove more of the narration, leaving only the essential information.

To save the file as a Web page, Grace clicks File on the menu bar, and then clicks Save as Web Page. The Save As dialog box opens with the Save As type automatically set to Single File Web Page. This option creates a file with a .mht extension and saves the entire presentation as one file.

Next, she clicks the Change Title button in the Save As dialog box to change the title of the Web page. This way, it will have a unique title, rather than "PowerPoint Presentation," in case the viewer decides to print the presentation. Finally, she clicks the Publish button in the Save As dialog box so that she can customize the published presentation, including choosing which slides she wants to publish and whether to publish the presentation in a format compatible with older browsers. Her final choices are shown in Figure 4.19.

Figure 4.19: Publish as Web Page dialog box

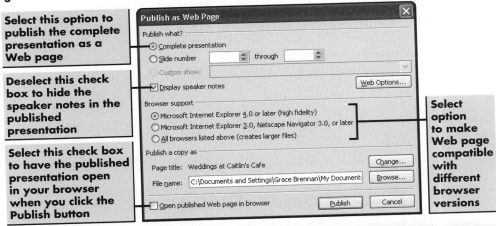

Select this option to publish the complete presentation as a Web page

Deselect this check box to hide the speaker notes in the published presentation

Select this check box to have the published presentation open in your browser when you click the Publish button

Select option to make Web page compatible with different browser versions

How To

Save a Presentation as a Web Page
1. Click File on the menu bar, and then click Save As Web Page. The Save As dialog box opens with Single File Web Page in the Save as type text box, and buttons to click to customize the Web page.
2. Click the Change Title button to open the Set Page Title dialog box, type the page title in the Page title text box, and then click the OK button.
3. Click the Publish button. The Publish as Web Page dialog box opens.
4. To publish only selected slides as a Web page, click the Slide number option button, then type the starting and ending slide numbers in the text boxes.
5. Click an option button under Browser Support to choose whether to support older browsers.
6. Check the Open published Web page in browser check box to open the presentation in your browser.
7. Click the Publish button.

PACKAGING A PRESENTATION ON A CD

Before she leaves for the wedding tradeshow, Grace saves her presentation on a CD and makes several copies to be distributed at the show. This way, visitors to her booth can leave with something tangible to view at their leisure.

In the past, when Grace saved PowerPoint presentations on portable storage drives, she had the unfortunate experience of discovering broken links to her video and audio files and her fonts did not display properly. Once she even recalls spending a tremendous amount of time saving her presentation to a disk to view on another computer, only to find out that the computer she was to use did not have PowerPoint installed on it. The Package for CD option in PowerPoint 2003 takes all the worry out of taking your presentation on the road. Not only does it link all your necessary files and embed all your fonts, but it also includes the PowerPoint Viewer in the event that the computer on which you run your presentation does not have PowerPoint. PowerPoint Viewer is a small program that is packaged with the CD that enables you to run the presentation without the need for the actual PowerPoint program.

Grace clicks File on the menu bar, and then clicks Package for CD. The Package for CD dialog box opens, as shown in Figure 4.20.

Figure 4.20: Package for CD dialog box

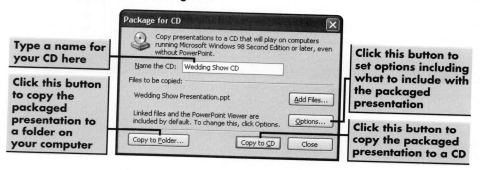

She clicks the Options button to open the Options dialog box. She chooses from the various options by clicking on the Options button. She is sure to check the PowerPoint Viewer box so that the Viewer will be packaged with her presentation. She also checks the Linked Files and Embedded TrueType Fonts check boxes. The Linked Files option ensures that the source files for her charts or any other objects that originated in other programs are included on the CD. This protects against having broken links. The Embedded TrueType Fonts option ensures that her fonts will display correctly on any computer. She does not include a password because she wants to distribute the CDs at the wedding show. See Figure 4.21. Finally, she clicks the Copy to CD button to create the CD.

Figure 4.21: Options dialog box for Package for CD

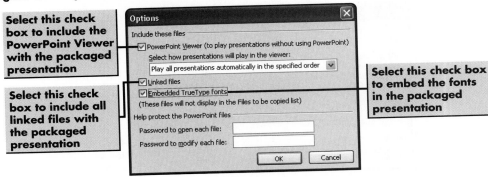

PRINTING HANDOUTS AND NOTES

Handouts and notes are excellent tools to augment your presentation. Handouts can be made quickly and are easy to print out for the audience. When your audience knows that they have a copy of your presentation, they won't feel the need to take notes. As such, they will be more attentive to what you have to say. Notes, by contrast, are excellent tools for the presenter. As you design each slide, you can jot down notes that you can refer to while presenting or even a script that you want to read. Even the process of creating notes is a good way to review the material that you will be presenting.

Printing Handouts

Before Grace leaves for the tradeshow, she wants to make a handout to give to the audience members who attend the scheduled live presentations she will deliver throughout the day. Although she has uploaded her presentation to the Web and provided a Web address for others to access it, she knows that certain people prefer to have hard copies of handouts. She decides to create handouts from her presentation and provide multiple copies for those who attend her presentation. She clicks File on the menu bar, and then clicks Print to open the Print dialog box. From the Print dialog box, she makes sure that she has selected Handouts in the Print what list. She chooses the layout for her handouts, including the number of slides to appear on each page. When she has made all her selections, as shown in Figure 4.22, she clicks OK to print.

Figure 4.22: Print dialog box set to print handouts

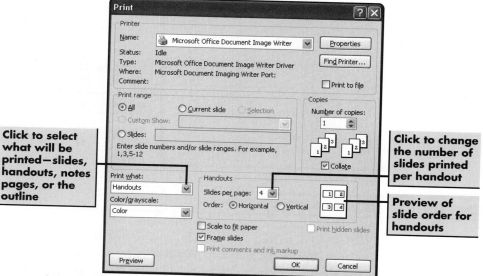

Click to select what will be printed—slides, handouts, notes pages, or the outline

Click to change the number of slides printed per handout

Preview of slide order for handouts

Creating and Using Speaker Notes

Notes are also a useful tool for planning your presentation. It is neither necessary nor desirable to include all the information you want to relay in your slide. However, it is helpful to prepare and rehearse what you will say for each slide in your presentation so that you do not end up reading your slides. Notes are a great way to remind you what you will say. Although it is not recommended that you read from your notes, you might find it helpful to refer to them if you lose your train of thought.

You type notes in the Notes pane below each slide in Normal view. You can preview your notes before printing. You will notice that notes are printed with the slide at the top of the page and the notes beneath the slide. Grace moves through her presentation in Normal view and adds speaker notes on most of her slides. One of her slides is shown in Figure 4.23.

Figure 4.23: Speaker notes added to a slide

Best Practice

Printing and Publishing Speaker Notes

It is unlikely that you will print your notes for your audience, as this would take a lot of paper, given that only one slide is printed on each sheet. Notes are wonderful tools for presenters, whereas handouts are more suited for the audience.

If you publish your presentation for the Web and you have included speaker notes, be aware of the Display Speaker Notes check box in the Publish as Web Page dialog box. If you leave this checked, which is the default, your speaker notes will be displayed for everyone to see. This can be helpful if you write your notes with this in mind. However, if you use the notes feature as a guide for yourself as a speaker, you probably want to omit them from your Web presentation.

CHANGING THE POINTER WHILE RUNNING A PRESENTATION

For her scheduled live presentations at the wedding tradeshow, Grace wants to be able to draw attention to specific parts of her presentation as she is talking. She has seen presenters use laser pointer-pens, but she has found those difficult to follow on a projected screen. Moreover, a laser can look jittery on the screen as the presenter struggles to keep her hand still. Instead, she opts to change the pointer options while running her slide show. She practices how she might use the pointer options as she presents. In one of her slides, she wants the audience to pay particular attention to the words "gourmet menu," "favorites," and "ethnic specialties." To change pointer options, right-click on the screen while the presentation is running, and then point to Pointer Options on the shortcut menu. Figure 4.24 shows one of Grace's slides with highlighted words.

Figure 4.24: Pointer used as a highlighter

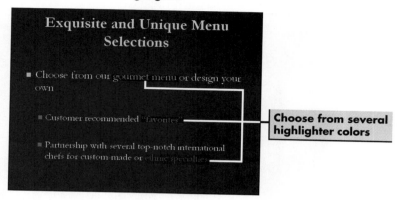

When you have finished running a slide show to which you have added annotation with the pointer, you are prompted to save or discard the marks you made. Grace decides to discard the marks because she wants to be able to draw them when she is actually giving the presentation.

Grace is excited to present Caitlin's Café at the wedding tradeshow because of all her preparation. She has prepared her presentation to be delivered live, on the Web, and as a stand-alone show. She has also packaged the presentation to a CD that includes all her media files, fonts, and even the PowerPoint Viewer, in the event she has to do her presentation on a computer that does not have PowerPoint. She has prepared and rehearsed a script that she has also printed out as notes. And finally, she has created handouts to distribute to her audience. Grace knows that being prepared will help her to be a more persuasive and effective speaker.

Steps To Success: Level 3

Grace asked you to finalize the presentation for the Irish Fest steering committee for Milwaukee's ethnic festivals. The committee has asked Grace to send a self-running presentation so they can evaluate it privately. She asks you to add narration, set up the show to run without needing a presenter, and package the presentation on a CD. Then she wants you to create a file to put on Caitlin's Café Web site. Finally, she wants you to print handouts that she can give to each committee member.

Complete the following:

1. Open the presentation named **Animated Festival Promotion.ppt** that you created in Level 2 Steps To Success, and then save it as **Final Festival Promotion.ppt**.

2. Record narration for the presentation and save it with the timings.

3. Print the presentation as handouts, three slides per page.

4. Add speaker notes to at least three of the slides. Save your changes.

5. Save the presentation for publication on the Web with the filename **Festival Promotion for the Web.mhtl**. Add a meaningful page title, and do not include the speaker notes.

6. Set up the show to be browsed at a kiosk, and loop it continuously.

7. Package the presentation on a CD. Using the CD, run the presentation on another computer to ensure that it runs as expected.

8. Practice delivering the presentation live while using the pen and highlighter options. Change the highlighter color to green and highlight the key points in each slide. Save the marks you made.

CHAPTER SUMMARY

In this chapter, you learned how to plan, create, and customize a persuasive presentation for delivery in a variety of formats. In Level 1, you learned that good presentations take into consideration the needs of both the speaker and the audience. Using the AutoContent Wizard, you learned how to create basic PowerPoint presentations and how to change and customize the overall presentation, using the Slide Master, as well as individual slides. Finally, you learned how to run your presentation. In Level 2, you learned how to add emphasis to your presentation by incorporating multimedia, such as video and audio files. You learned how to employ transitions to create uniformity and to make individual slides stand out. You learned how to embed and link objects from other Microsoft Office programs. In Level 3, you learned how to prepare your presentation for different venues; you can run your PowerPoint presentation as a Web page or a stand-alone presentation. You learned to add narration to individual slides and to create customized notes and handouts from your presentation.

CONCEPTUAL REVIEW

1. When trying to determine the purpose and audience for your presentation, what questions should you ask yourself?

2. Why are visuals important when giving a presentation?

3. What is the 6 × 6 Rule?

4. Name three of the most important design rules that you should keep in mind when creating your presentation.

5. Why is it helpful to use the Slide Master?

6. When including objects created in other programs, when would you want to embed your object and when would it be better to link it?

7. Where in a presentation is the best place to include a summary slide? Why?

8. How are animation schemes different from custom animation and when would you be more likely to use one over the other?

9. When would you use a self-running presentation?

10. What different kinds of audio files can be added to a PowerPoint presentation?

11. List at least two ways that you can update linked objects in a presentation.

12. What are some important things to consider when preparing your presentation for viewing on the Web?

13. In what types of presentations would narration be most effective? Why?

14. What are the risks of not packaging your presentation for CD if you are taking it on the road?

15. What is the difference between speaker notes and handouts?

CASE PROBLEMS

Level 1—Planning a Presentation at Kewaskum Community College

Mary Jo McLaughlin, information systems manager at Kewaskum Community College, is good at computers, but inexperienced at public speaking. She must prepare a presentation detailing the college computer network to the Board of Regents so that they can evaluate the necessity of upgrading the system. She will learn to communicate difficult concepts using simple terms, charts, and tables.

Information Systems

After brainstorming some ideas, she writes down the following points that she wants to convey in her presentation:

- Network usage has become more evenly distributed across academic disciplines over the past 10 years.
- It is not just faculty and students in the sciences who need and use the computer network.
- The cost of maintaining the network is increasing.
- The existing system is vulnerable to computer viruses and hackers.

- The resulting increase in computer crashes and viruses has cost the university countless hours of labor and tens of thousands of dollars.
- The school needs to provide more wireless access points for students with laptops.
- The existing network was designed 10 years ago and is now outdated.
- The cost of a new system will justify the savings gained from not having to constantly fix the ongoing problems.

As her assistant, she asks you to create her presentation.

Complete the following:

1. Create one statement of purpose for the presentation.

2. Create a basic PowerPoint presentation for Mary Jo, using the AutoContent Wizard. Save the presentation as **Kewaskum Computer Upgrade Proposal.ppt**.

3. Add your statement of purpose as a speaker note on Slide 1 of your presentation.

4. Apply a design template to the presentation that reflects the purpose of the presentation.

5. Using the Slide Master, customize the slides by inserting an image or clip art that will appear on every slide. Make sure to resize the picture as necessary.

6. Change at least one type of font to a different one, keeping in mind basic rules for design.

7. Draw an arrow or another object using AutoShapes, to accent one of your slides.

8. Open the file **Kewaskum Community College.xls** from the Communications\ Chapter 4\Case 1 folder and embed the charts from the Excel sheets titled Distribution Chart #1 and Distribution Chart #2.

9. Create a summary slide to either introduce or conclude your presentation.

10. Add other clip art or images from Microsoft Online or from your own collection to enhance the message you are trying to relay.

11. Run the presentation, save your changes, and then close the presentation.

Level 2—Adding Emphasis to a Presentation at Reath, Avsenik, and Stevenson

Accounting

Peter Harrington, an accountant at Reath, Avsenik, and Stevenson, keeps most of his data in Excel. He wants to link his charts and other data in Excel to a PowerPoint presentation and employ animation, multimedia, and clip art to spice up his otherwise dry figures when presenting accounting information to his youthful clients, 20-something founders of a video gaming company. Peter has asked you to improve his presentation.

Complete the following:

1. Open the file **Gaming.ppt** from the Communications\Chapter 4\Case 2 folder, and then save it as **Gaming Revised.ppt**.

2. Change the design theme to better suit the client.

3. Link the charts on the Revenue Gains and Revenue Losses worksheets in the Excel file **Video Revolution Sales.xls** in the Communications\Chapter 4\Case 2 folder to appropriate slides in the presentation.

4. Embed the chart on the Revenue Change Chart worksheet in the Excel file **Video Revolution Sales.xls** to the appropriate slide in the presentation.

5. Apply an appropriate animation scheme to the entire presentation.

6. Create customized animation for slides 2 and 3 that will emphasize the fiscal year's gains and losses.

7. Search for an appropriate music clip to insert in the opening slide. Have the clip play for the first two slides only.

8. Search for and insert clip art that will help to improve the look and feel of the presentation.

9. Apply some custom animation to those images to make the presentation more dynamic.

10. Save your changes and close the presentation.

Level 3—Delivering Presentations for an Online Law School

John Dylan, marketing manager for Brooklyn University, a 100% online law school, travels the country promoting his twenty-first century educational opportunity. He wants to create a PowerPoint presentation to help him convince people to apply to Brooklyn U. He wants to print his speaker notes to help him prepare for the presentations, and he wants handouts to pass out to his audience. In addition, John needs the presentation to be set up so that he can show it at a kiosk delivery when attending job fairs and school fairs. For these situations, he wants to record narration to accompany the kiosk presentations. As the new assistant in the office, John has asked you to prepare his presentation for him.

Marketing

Complete the following:

1. Research online law schools using your favorite search engine, and then create a presentation of at least eight slides to promote the online law school to prospective students. During your research, look for the following information at various schools, and then add content to your presentation based on the information you find:

   - School information
   - Degree programs
   - Curriculum
   - Faculty and lecturers
   - Admissions

2. Create a new presentation using the AutoContent Wizard. Save your presentation as **Law School Promotion.ppt**.

3. Modify the content of your presentation to include the information you found during your research. Modify the design to suit your audience.

4. Insert at least two pieces of clip art.

5. Add animation and transitions as needed.

6. For each slide, add a one- or two-sentence script as a speaker note.

7. Record each slide's script as narration.

8. Set the presentation to be run at a kiosk in a continuous loop.

9. Print handouts for your presentation.

10. Run the presentation, using the highlighter several times, and then save your highlights in the presentation.

11. Package your presentation for CD.

Table 2.3: Three ways to insert objects from one application into another

Method	Procedure	Comments
Copy and Paste	You press Ctrl+C to copy what you want from the source document (such as an Excel workbook), and then use Ctrl+V to paste the content in the destination document (such as a Word document).	The copied object becomes part of the destination document and can be edited in the destination document as necessary.
Embed	Click Insert on the menu bar, and then click Object to open the Object dialog box, where you select the object you want to insert and specify that you want to embed the object rather than link it.	Embedded objects also become part of the destination document. For example, an embedded Excel object becomes part of a Word document or PowerPoint slide. If you modify the object by double-clicking it, Excel or PowerPoint menus and toolbars appear but the object is only updated in the Word document, not the original. Likewise, any changes made to the source object in the other program are not updated in the Word document. Embedding makes the source document larger because the object is included in the total of the document's size.
Link	In Word, click Insert on the menu bar, and then click Object to open the Object dialog box. In other Office programs, click Edit on the menu bar and then click Paste Special.	Linked objects do not become part of the destination document, although they appear to be. When you edit the linked object, the source application opens the linked object and you perform your editing tasks in the source program. If you open the original program and edit the object directly, it is also updated in the Word document. The benefit of linking is that the source document might be "owned" and updated by another user. By linking, you will always have the latest data without having to maintain the source document yourself.

Best Practice

Deciding When to Embed and When to Link

Both embedding and linking allow you to edit an object in its source program. For example, if you want to include material from Excel in a Word or PowerPoint document, you could edit that material whether you embed or link the object. How do you know which method to use? See Table 2.4 for suggestions.

Table 2.4: Choosing to embed or link

When to Embed	When to Link
The source document or portion of a document is small.	The source document is large.
The contents require specialized formatting available in the source program but are relatively small in size.	Contents of the object are video or sound files (they are usually very large).
You might not have access to the original document in the future (you will travel with a portable PC and need to modify the contents).	Both source and destination documents will be readily available (for example, both are stored on a network).
Any modifications you make only need to be made to the embedded object, not the original source.	Someone else owns the source document and you always want the latest updated version of the object.

Microsoft
Access

MICROSOFT OFFICE
ACCESS

MICROSOFT OFFICE
Access 2003

Creating and Using a Database

CASE PERSPECTIVE

Ashton James College (AJC) has a solid reputation in the community, delivers quality computer courses, and has a faculty of highly professional, dedicated instructors. Its graduates are among the top achievers in the state. Recently, at the urging of area businesses that depend on the college-educated workforce, AJC has begun to offer corporate computer training through its Continuing Education department. The programs have proved to be very popular, and the client list is growing rapidly.

AJC employs several trainers to teach these corporate courses. It assigns each client to a specific trainer. The trainer contacts the client to determine the particular course the client requires. The trainer then customizes a program for that particular client. The trainer will schedule all the necessary training sessions.

To ensure that operations run smoothly, Ashton James College needs to maintain data on its trainers and their clients. The AJC administration wants to organize the data in a database, managed by a database management system such as Access. In this way, AJC can keep its data current and accurate while program administrators analyze the data for trends and produce a variety of useful reports. Your task is to help the director of continuing education at Ashton James College, Dr. Robert Gernaey, create and use the database.

As you read through this project, you will learn how to use Access to create a database.

Creating and Using a Database

Objectives

You will have mastered the material in this project when you can:

- Describe databases and database management systems
- Start Access
- Describe the features of the Access desktop
- Create a database
- Create a table and add records
- Close a table
- Close a database and quit Access
- Open a database
- Print the contents of a table
- Create and use a simple query
- Create and use a simple form
- Create and print a custom report
- Design a database to eliminate redundancy

What Is Microsoft Office Access 2003?

Microsoft Office Access 2003 is a powerful database management system (DBMS) that functions in the Windows environment and allows you to create and process data in a database. Some of the key features are:

- **Data entry and update** Access provides easy mechanisms for adding, changing, and deleting data, including the capability of making mass changes in a single operation.
- **Queries (questions)** Access makes it possible to ask complex questions concerning the data in the database and then receive instant answers.
- **Forms** Access allows the user to produce attractive and useful forms for viewing and updating data.
- **Reports** Access report creation tools make it easy to produce sophisticated reports for presenting data.
- **Web support** Access allows you to save objects, reports, and tables in HTML format so they can be viewed using a browser. You also can import and export documents in XML format. Access's capability of creating data access pages allows real-time access to data in the database via the Internet.

What Is New in Access?

This latest version of Access has many new features to make you more productive. You can view information on dependencies between various database objects. You can enable error checking for many common errors in forms and reports. You can add smart tags to fields in tables, queries, forms, or data access pages. Access now has a command to backup a database. Many wizards provide more options for sorting data. You can export to, import from, or link to a Windows SharePoint Services list. Access now offers enhanced XML support.

Project One — Ashton James College Database

Creating, storing, sorting, and retrieving data are important tasks. In their personal lives, many people keep a variety of records such as names, addresses, and telephone numbers of friends and business associates, records of investments, records of expenses for tax purposes, and so on. For effective use of this data, users must have quick access to it. Businesses also must be able to store and access information quickly and easily.

The term **database** describes a collection of data organized in a manner that allows access, retrieval, and use of that data. A **database management system**, such as Access, is a software tool that allows you to use a computer to create a database; add, change, and delete data in the database; sort the data in the database; retrieve data in the database; and create forms and reports using the data in the database.

In Access, a database consists of a collection of tables. Figure 1-1 shows a sample database for Ashton James College, which consists of two tables. The Client table contains information about the clients to which Ashton James College provides services. The college assigns each client to a specific trainer. The Trainer table contains information about the trainers to whom these clients are assigned.

Client table

CLIENT NUMBER	NAME	ADDRESS	CITY	STATE	ZIP CODE	AMOUNT PAID	CURRENT DUE	TRAINER NUMBER
BS27	Blant and Sons	4806 Park	Lake Hammond	TX	76653	$21,876.00	$892.50	42
CE16	Center Services	725 Mitchell	San Julio	TX	78364	$26,512.00	$2,672.00	48
CP27	Calder Plastics	7300 Cedar	Lake Hammond	TX	76653	$8,725.00	$0.00	48
EU28	Elba's Furniture	1445 Hubert	Tallmadge	TX	77231	$4,256.00	$1,202.00	53
FI28	Farrow-Idsen	829 Wooster	Cedar Ridge	TX	79342	$8,287.50	$925.50	42
FL93	Fairland Lawn	143 Pangborn	Lake Hammond	TX	76653	$21,625.00	$0.00	48
HN83	Hurley National	3827 Burgess	Tallmadge	TX	77231	$0.00	$0.00	48
MC28	Morgan-Alyssa	923 Williams	Crumville	TX	76745	$24,761.00	$1,572.00	42
PS82	PRIM Staffing	72 Crestview	San Julio	TX	78364	$11,682.25	$2,827.50	53
TE26	Telton-Edwards	5672 Anderson	Dunston	TX	77893	$8,521.50	$0.00	48

Trainer table

TRAINER NUMBER	LAST NAME	FIRST NAME	ADDRESS	CITY	STATE	ZIP CODE	HOURLY RATE	YTD EARNINGS
42	Perry	Belinda	261 Porter	Burdett	TX	76734	$23.00	$27,620.00
48	Stevens	Michael	3135 Gill	Rockwood	TX	78884	$21.00	$23,567.50
53	Gonzalez	Manuel	265 Maxwell	Camino	TX	76574	$24.00	$29,885.00
67	Danville	Marty	1827 Maple	Dunston	TX	77893	$20.00	$0.00

FIGURE 1-1

More About

Databases in Access 2003

In some DBMSs, every table, query, form, or report is stored in a separate file. This is not the case in Access 2003, in which a database is stored in a single file on disk. The file contains all the tables, queries, forms, reports, and programs created for this database.

The rows in the tables are called **records**. A record contains information about a given person, product, or event. A row in the Client table, for example, contains information about a specific client.

The columns in the tables are called fields. A **field** contains a specific piece of information within a record. In the Client table, for example, the fourth field, City, contains the city where the client is located.

The first field in the Client table is the Client Number. Ashton James College assigns a number to each client. As is common to the way in which many organizations format client numbers, Ashton James College calls it a *number*, although it actually contains letters. The AJC client numbers consist of two uppercase letters followed by a two-digit number.

These numbers are unique; that is, no two clients are assigned the same number. Such a field can be used as a **unique identifier**. This simply means that a given client number will appear only in a single record in the table. Only one record exists, for example, in which the client number is CP27. A unique identifier also is called a **primary key**. Thus, the Client Number field is the primary key for the Client table.

The next seven fields in the Client table are Name, Address, City, State, Zip Code, Amount Paid, and Current Due. The Amount Paid field contains the amount that the client has paid Ashton James College year-to-date (YTD), but before the current period. The Current Due field contains the amount due to AJC for the current period.

For example, client BS27 is Blant and Sons. The address is 4806 Park in Lake Hammond, Texas. The Zip code is 76653. The client has paid $21,876.00 for training services so far this year. The amount due for the current period is $892.50.

AJC assigns each client a single trainer. The last field in the Client table, Trainer Number, gives the number of the client's trainer.

The first field in the Trainer table, Trainer Number, is the number Ashton James College assigns to the trainer. These numbers are unique, so Trainer Number is the primary key of the Trainer table.

The other fields in the Trainer table are Last Name, First Name, Address, City, State, Zip Code, Hourly Rate, and YTD Earnings. The Hourly Rate field gives the trainer's hourly billing rate, and the YTD Earnings field contains the total amount that AJC has paid the trainer for services so far this year.

For example, Trainer 42 is Belinda Perry. Her address is 261 Porter in Burdett, Texas. The Zip code is 76734. Her hourly billing rate is $23.00, and her YTD earnings are $27,620.00.

The trainer number appears in both the Client table and the Trainer table. It relates clients and trainers. For example, in the Client table, you see that the trainer number for client BS27 is 42. To find the name of this trainer, look for the row in the Trainer table that contains 42 in the Trainer Number field. After you have found it, you know the client is assigned to Belinda Perry. To find all the clients assigned to Belinda Perry, however, you must look through the Client table for all the clients that contain 42 in the Trainer Number field. Her clients are BS27 (Blant and Sons), FI28 (Farrow-Idsen), and MC28 (Morgan-Alyssa).

The last trainer in the Trainer table, Marty Danville, has not been assigned any clients yet; therefore, his trainer number, 67, does not appear on any row in the Client table.

Figure 1-1 on page AC 5 shows the data that must be maintained in the database. The first step is to create the database and the tables it contains. In the process, you must define the fields included in the two tables, as well as the type of data each field will contain. Then, you must add the appropriate records to the tables. Finally, you will print the contents of the tables. After you have completed these tasks, you will create a query, a form, and a report.

Starting Access

If you are stepping through this project on a computer, and you want your screen to agree with the figures in this book, then you should change your computer's resolution to 800 × 600. For more information on how to change the resolution on your computer, see Appendix D. To start Access, Windows must be running. The following steps show how to start Access.

To Start Access

1

• **Click the Start button on the Windows taskbar, point to All Programs on the Start menu and then point to Microsoft Office on the All Programs submenu.**

Windows displays the Start menu, the All Programs submenu, and the Microsoft Office submenu (Figure 1-2).

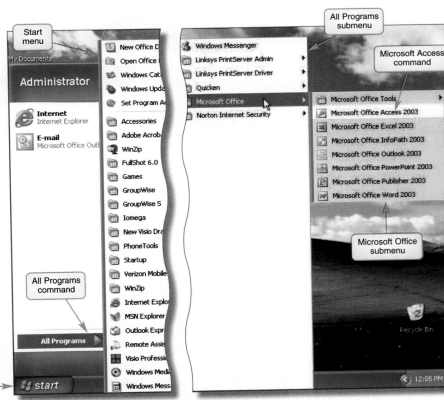

FIGURE 1-2

2

• **Click Microsoft Office Access 2003.**

Access starts. After several seconds, the Access window appears (Figure 1-3).

3

• **If the Access window is not maximized, double-click its title bar to maximize it.**

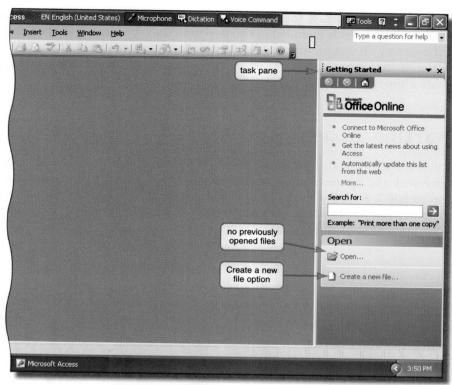

Labels in figure: task pane; no previously opened files; Create a new file option

FIGURE 1-3

The screen in Figure 1-3 illustrates how the Access window looks the first time you start Access after installation on most computers. Access displays a task pane on the right side of the screen at startup. A **task pane** is a separate window that enables users to carry out some Access tasks more efficiently. When you start Access, it displays the Getting Started task pane, which is a small window that provides commonly used links and commands that allow you to open files, create new files, or search Office-related topics on the Microsoft Web site. The task pane is used only to create a new database and then it is closed.

If the Office Speech Recognition software is installed and active on your computer, then when you start Access the Language bar is displayed on the screen. The **Language bar** allows you to speak commands and dictate text. It usually is located on the right side of the Windows taskbar next to the notification area and changes to include the speech recognition functions available in Access. In this book, the Language bar is closed. For additional information about the Language bar, see the next page and Appendix B. The following steps show how to close the Language bar if it appears on the screen.

To Close the Language Bar

1

- **Right-click the Language bar to display a list of commands.**

The Language bar shortcut menu appears (Figure 1-4).

2

- **Click Close the Language bar.**
- **Click the OK button.**

The Language bar disappears.

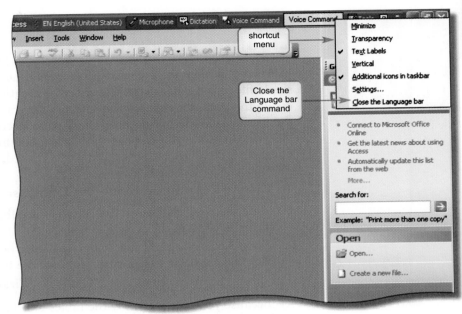

FIGURE 1-4

Speech Recognition

With the **Office Speech Recognition software** installed and a microphone, you can speak the names of toolbar buttons, menus, menu commands, list items, alerts, and dialog box controls, such as OK and Cancel. You also can dictate field entries, such as text and numbers. To indicate whether you want to speak commands or dictate cell entries, you use the Language bar. The Language bar can be in one of three states: (1) **restored**, which means it is displayed somewhere in the Access window (Figure 1-5a); (2) **minimized**, which means it is displayed on the Windows taskbar (Figure 1-5b); or (3) **hidden**, which means you do not see it on the screen. If the Language bar is hidden and you want it to display, then do the following:

1. Right-click an open area on the Windows taskbar at the bottom of the screen.
2. Point to Toolbars and then click Language bar on the Toolbars submenu.

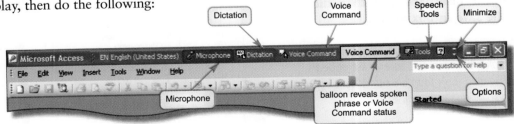

(a) Language Bar in Access Window with Microphone Enabled

(b) Language Bar Minimized on Windows Taskbar

FIGURE 1-5

If the Language bar command is dimmed on the Toolbars submenu or if the Speech command is dimmed on the Tools menu, the Office Speech Recognition software is not installed.

Creating a New Database

In Access, all the tables, reports, form, and queries that you create are stored in a single file called a database. Thus, before creating any of these objects, you first must create the database that will hold them. You can use either the Database Wizard or the Blank database option in the task pane to create a new database. The Database Wizard can guide you by suggesting some commonly used databases. If you choose to create a database using the Database Wizard, you would use the following steps.

To Create a Database Using the Database Wizard

1. Click the New button on the Database toolbar and then click the On my computer link in the New File task pane.
2. When Access displays the Template dialog box, click the Databases tab, and then click the database that is most appropriate for your needs.
3. Follow the instructions in the Database Wizard dialog box to create the database.

Because you already know the tables and fields you want in the Ashton James College database, you would use the Blank database option in the task pane rather than the Database Wizard. The following steps illustrate how to use the Blank database option to create a database on a USB flash drive.

To Create a New Database

1

• **With a USB flash drive connected to one of the computer's USB ports, click the New button on the Database toolbar to display the task pane.**

• **Click the Blank database option in the task pane, and then click the Save in box arrow.**

Access displays the File New Database dialog box and the Save in list appears (Figure 1-6a). Your File name text box may display db1.mdb, rather than db1.

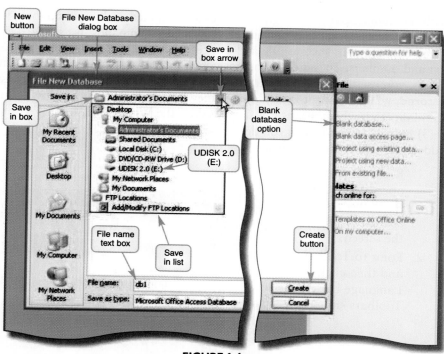

FIGURE 1-6a

2

• **Click UDISK 2.0 (E:). (Your USB flash drive may have a different name and letter.)**

• **Click the File name text box.**

• **Use the BACKSPACE key or the DELETE key to delete db1 and then type** Ashton James College **as the file name.**

The file name is changed to Ashton James College (Figure 1-6b).

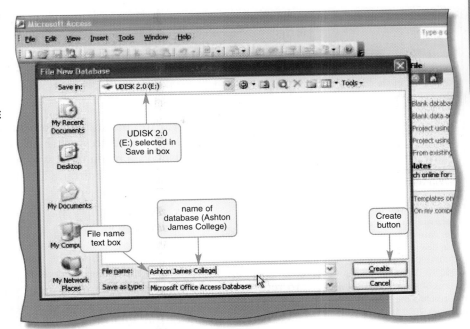

FIGURE 1-6b

3

• **Click the Create button to create the database.**

The Ashton James College database is created. The Ashton James College : Database window appears in the Microsoft Access window (Figure 1-7). The task pane does not appear.

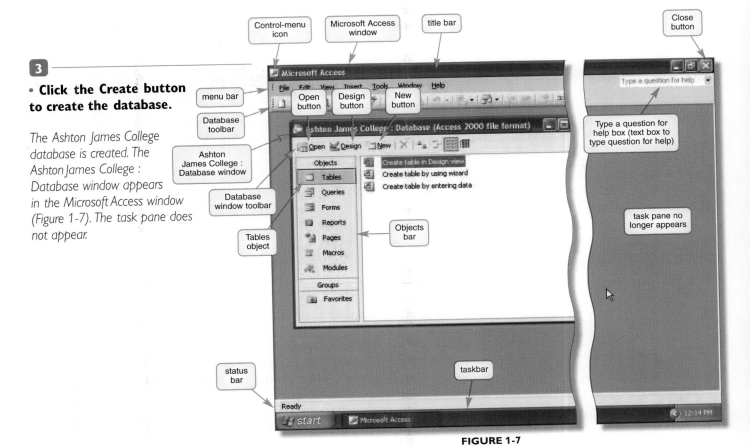

FIGURE 1-7

773

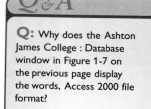

The Access Window

The Access window (Figure 1-7 on the previous page) contains a variety of features that play important roles when you are working with a database.

Title Bar

The **title bar** is the top bar in the Microsoft Access window. It includes the title of the application, Microsoft Access. The icon on the left is the Control-menu icon. Clicking this icon displays a menu from which you can close the Access window. The button on the right is the Close button. Clicking the Close button closes the Access window.

Menu Bar

The **menu bar** is displayed below the title bar. It is a special toolbar that displays the menu names. Each menu name represents a menu of commands that you can use to retrieve, store, print, and manipulate data. When you point to a menu name on the menu bar, the area of the menu bar is displayed as a selected button. Access shades selected buttons in light orange and surrounds them with a blue outline. To display a menu, such as the Edit menu, click the Edit menu name on the menu bar (Figures 1-8a and 1-8b). A **menu** is a list of commands. If you point to a command on the menu with an arrow to its right, a **submenu** is displayed from which you can choose a command.

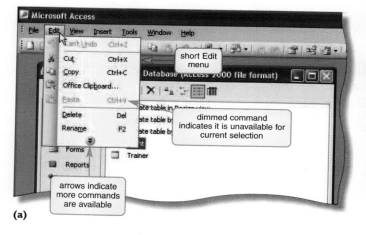

(a)

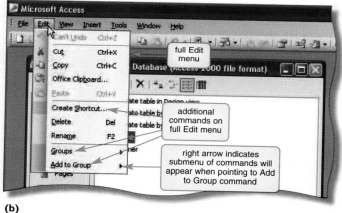

(b)

FIGURE 1-8

When you click a menu name on the menu bar, Access displays a **short menu** listing the most recently used commands (Figure 1-8a). If you wait a few seconds or click the arrows at the bottom of the short menu, the full menu appears. The **full menu** lists all the commands associated with a menu (Figure 1-8b). You also can display a full menu immediately by double-clicking the menu name on the menu bar. In this book, always have Access display the full menu using one of the following techniques.

1. Click the menu name on the menu bar and then wait a few seconds.
2. Click the menu name and then click the arrows at the bottom of the short menu.

3. Click the menu name and then point to the arrows at the bottom of the short menu.
4. Double-click the menu name.

Both short and full menus display some **dimmed commands** that appear gray, or dimmed, instead of black, which indicates they are not available for the current selection. A command with a medium blue shading to the left of it on a full menu is called a **hidden command** because it does not display on a short menu. As you use Access, it automatically personalizes the short menus for you based on how often you use commands. That is, as you use hidden commands, Access *unhides* them and places them on the short menu.

Toolbars

Below the menu bar is a toolbar. A **toolbar** contains buttons that allow you to perform certain tasks more quickly than using the menu bar. Each button contains a picture, or **icon**, depicting its function. When you move the mouse pointer over a button, the name of the button appears below it in a **ScreenTip**. The toolbar shown in Figure 1-7 on page AC 11 is the Database toolbar. The specific toolbar or toolbars that appear will vary, depending on the task on which you are working. Access routinely displays the toolbar or toolbars you will need for the task. If you want to change these or simply to determine what toolbars are available for the given task, consult Appendix D.

Taskbar

The Windows **taskbar** at the bottom of the screen displays the Start button, any active windows, and the current time.

Status Bar

Immediately above the Windows taskbar is the **status bar**. It contains special information that is appropriate for the task on which you are working. Currently, it contains the word, Ready, which means Access is ready to accept commands.

Database Window

The **Database window**, referred to in Figure 1-7 as the Ashton James College : Database window, is a special window that allows you to access easily and rapidly a variety of objects such as tables, queries, forms, and reports. To do so, you will use the various components of the window.

Shortcut Menus

Rather than use toolbars to accomplish a given task, you also can use **shortcut menus**, which are menus that display the actions available for a particular item. To display the shortcut menu for an item, right-click the item; that is, point to the item and then click the right mouse button. Figures 1-9a and 1-9b on the next page illustrate the use of toolbars and shortcut menus to perform the same task, namely to print the contents of the Client table. In the figure, the tables you will create in this project already have been created.

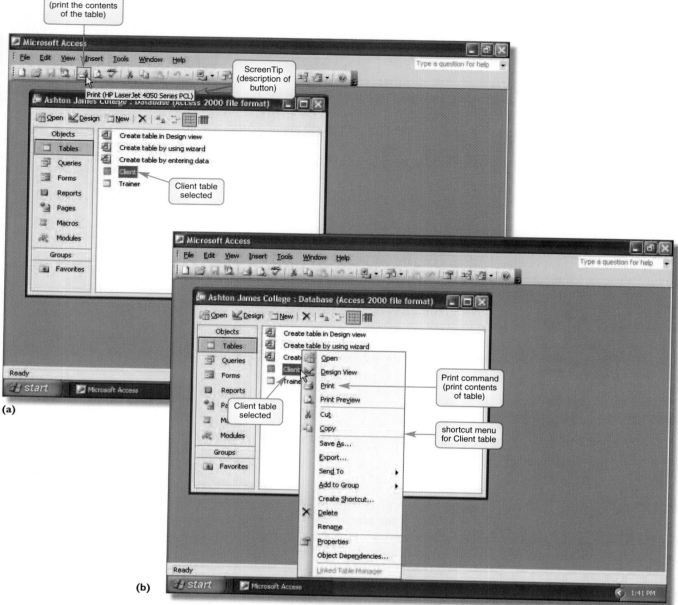

FIGURE 1-9

Before the action illustrated in Figure 1-9a, you would have to select the Client table by clicking it. Then, you would point to the Print button on the toolbar as shown in the figure. When you point to a button on a toolbar, the ScreenTip appears, indicating the purpose of the button, in this case Print. When you click the button, the corresponding action takes place. In this case, Access will print the contents of the Client table.

To use a shortcut menu to perform the same task, you would right-click the Client table, which produces the shortcut menu shown in Figure 1-9b. You then would click the desired command, in this case the Print command, on the shortcut menu. The corresponding action then takes place.

You can use whichever option you prefer. Many professionals who use Access will use a combination. If it is simplest to use the shortcut menu, which often is the case, they will use the shortcut menu. If it is simpler just to click a toolbar button, they will do that. The steps in this text follow this approach; that is, using a combination of both options. The text indicates how to accomplish the task using the other approach, as well. Thus, if the steps use a shortcut menu, the Other Ways box at the end of the steps will indicate how you could accomplish the task using a toolbar button. If the steps use a button, the Other Ways box will indicate how you could accomplish the task with a shortcut menu.

AutoCorrect

Not visible in the Access window, the **AutoCorrect** feature of Access works behind the scenes, correcting common mistakes when you complete a text entry in a cell. AutoCorrect makes three types of corrections for you:

1. Corrects two initial capital letters by changing the second letter to lowercase.
2. Capitalizes the first letter in the names of days.
3. Replaces commonly misspelled words with their correct spelling. For example, it will change the misspelled word *recieve* to *receive* when you complete the entry. AutoCorrect will correct the spelling automatically of more than 400 commonly misspelled words.

Creating a Table

An Access database consists of a collection of tables. After you have created the database, you must create each of the tables within it. In this project, for example, you must create both the Client and Trainer tables shown in Figure 1-1 on page AC 5.

To create a table, you describe the structure of the table to Access by describing the fields within the table. For each field, you indicate the following:

1. **Field name** — Each field in the table must have a unique name. In the Client table (Figure 1-10a and 1-10b on the next page), for example, the field names are Client Number, Name, Address, City, State, Zip Code, Amount Paid, Current Due, and Trainer Number.

More About

AutoCorrect

Using the Office AutoCorrect feature, you can create entries that will replace abbreviations with spelled-out names and phrases automatically. For example, you can create the abbreviated entry *dbms* for *database management system*. Whenever you type dbms followed by a space or punctuation mark, Access automatically replaces dbms with database management system. AutoCorrect works with text in a datasheet or in a form. To specify AutoCorrect rules and exceptions to the rules, click Tools on the menu bar and then click AutoCorrect Options.

More About

Creating a Table: The Table Wizard

Access includes a Table Wizard that guides you by suggesting some commonly used tables and fields. To use the Table Wizard, click Tables on the Objects bar and then click Create table by using wizard. Follow the directions in the Table Wizard dialog boxes. After you create the table, you can modify it at any time by opening the table in Design view.

Structure of Client table

FIELD NAME	DATA TYPE	FIELD SIZE	PRIMARY KEY?	DESCRIPTION
Client Number	Text	4	Yes	Client Number (Primary Key)
Name	Text	20		Client Name
Address	Text	15		Street Address
City	Text	15		City
State	Text	2		State (Two-Character Abbreviation)
Zip Code	Text	5		Zip Code (Five-Character Version)
Amount Paid	Currency			Amount Paid by Client This Year
Current Due	Currency			Current Due from Client This Period
Trainer Number	Text	2		Number of Client's Trainer

FIGURE 1-10a

Client table

CLIENT NUMBER	NAME	ADDRESS	CITY	STATE	ZIP CODE	AMOUNT PAID	CURRENT DUE	TRAINER NUMBER
BS27	Blant and Sons	4806 Park	Lake Hammond	TX	76653	$21,876.00	$892.50	42
CE16	Center Services	725 Mitchell	San Julio	TX	78364	$26,512.00	$2,672.00	48
CP27	Calder Plastics	7300 Cedar	Lake Hammond	TX	76653	$8,725.00	$0.00	48
EU28	Elba's Furniture	1445 Hubert	Tallmadge	TX	77231	$4,256.00	$1,202.00	53
FI28	Farrow-Idsen	829 Wooster	Cedar Ridge	TX	79342	$8,287.50	$925.50	42
FL93	Fairland Lawn	143 Pangborn	Lake Hammond	TX	76653	$21,625.00	$0.00	48
HN83	Hurley National	3827 Burgess	Tallmadge	TX	77231	$0.00	$0.00	48
MC28	Morgan-Alyssa	923 Williams	Crumville	TX	76745	$24,761.00	$1,572.00	42
PS82	PRIM Staffing	72 Crestview	San Julio	TX	78364	$11,682.25	$2,827.50	53
TE26	Telton-Edwards	5672 Anderson	Dunston	TX	77893	$8,521.50	$0.00	48

FIGURE 1-10b

2. **Data type** — Data type indicates to Access the type of data the field will contain. Some fields can contain only numbers. Others, such as Amount Paid and Current Due, can contain numbers and dollar signs. Still others, such as Name and Address, can contain letters.

3. **Description** — Access allows you to enter a detailed description of the field.

You also can assign field widths to text fields (fields whose data type is Text). This indicates the maximum number of characters that can be stored in the field. If you do not assign a width to such a field, Access assumes the width is 50.

You also must indicate which field or fields make up the primary key; that is, the unique identifier, for the table. In the Ashton James College database, the Client Number field is the primary key of the Client table and the Trainer Number field is the primary key of the Trainer table.

The rules for field names are:

1. Names can be up to 64 characters in length.

2. Names can contain letters, digits, and spaces, as well as most of the punctuation symbols.

3. Names cannot contain periods, exclamation points (!), accent graves (`), or square brackets ([ ]).

4. The same name cannot be used for two different fields in the same table.

Each field has a **data type**. This indicates the type of data that can be stored in the field. The data types you will use in this project are:

1. **Text** — The field can contain any characters. A maximum number of 255 characters is allowed in a field whose data type is Text.

2. **Number** — The field can contain only numbers. The numbers either can be positive or negative. Fields are assigned this type so they can be used in arithmetic operations. Fields that contain numbers but will not be used for arithmetic operations usually are assigned a data type of Text. The Trainer Number field, for example, is a text field because the trainer numbers will not be involved in any arithmetic.

3. **Currency** — The field can contain only monetary data. The values will appear with currency symbols, such as dollar signs, commas, decimal points, and with two digits following the decimal point. Like numeric fields, you can use currency fields in arithmetic operations. Access assigns a size to currency fields automatically.

Table 1-1 shows the other data types that are available.

Table 1-1	Additional Data Types
DATA TYPE	**DESCRIPTION**
Memo	Field can store a variable amount of text or combinations of text and numbers where the total number of characters may exceed 255.
Date/Time	Field can store dates and times.
AutoNumber	Field can store a unique sequential number that Access assigns to a record. Access will increment the number by 1 as each new record is added.
Yes/No	Field can store only one of two values. The choices are Yes/No, True/False, or On/Off.
OLE Object	Field can store an OLE object, which is an object linked to or embedded in the table.
Hyperlink	Field can store text that can be used as a hyperlink address.
Lookup Wizard	Field can store a value from another table or from a list of values by using a list box or combo box. Choosing this data type starts the Lookup Wizard, which assists in the creation of the field. The field then is a Lookup field. The data type is set based on the values you selected in the wizard. If the values are text for example, the field is assigned the Text data type.

The field names, data types, field widths, primary key information, and descriptions for the Client table are shown in Figure 1-10a on page AC 15.

With the information in Figures 1-10a and 1-10b, you are ready to begin creating the table. The following steps illustrate how to create a table.

To Create a Table

1

- **Click the New button on the Database window toolbar.**

The New Table dialog box appears (Figure 1-11).

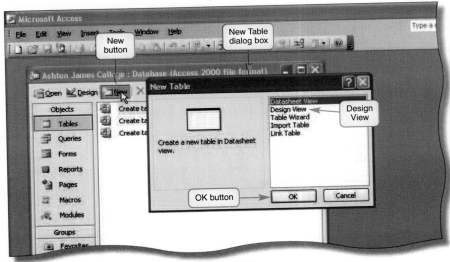

FIGURE 1-11

2

• **Click Design View and then click the OK button.**

The Table1 : Table window appears (Figure 1-12).

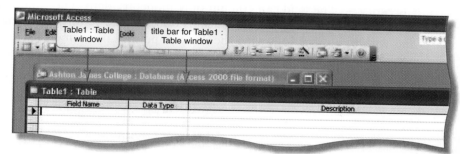

FIGURE 1-12

3

• **Double-click the title bar of the Table1 : Table window to maximize the window.**

Access displays the maximized Table1 : Table window (Figure 1-13).

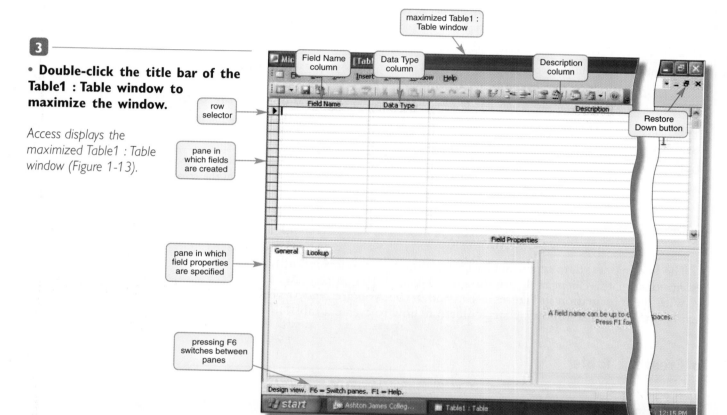

FIGURE 1-13

Other Ways

1. On Insert menu click Table
2. Double-click Create table in Design view
3. Press ALT+N
4. In Voice Command mode, say "Insert, Table"

Defining the Fields

The next step in creating the table is to define the fields by specifying the required details in the Table window, which include entries in the Field Name, Data Type, and Description columns and additional information in the Field Properties pane in the lower portion of the Table window. You press the F6 key to move from the upper **pane** (portion of the screen), the one where you define the fields, to the lower pane, the one where you define field properties. As you define the fields, the **row selector** (Figure 1-13), the small box or bar that, when you click it, selects the entire row, indicates the field you currently are describing. It is positioned on the first field, indicating Access is ready for you to enter the name of the first field in the Field Name column.

The following steps show how to define the fields in the table.

To Define the Fields in a Table

1

- **Type** Client Number **(the name of the first field) in the Field Name column, and then press the TAB key.**

The words, Client Number, appear in the Field Name column and the insertion point advances to the Data Type column, indicating you can enter the data type (Figure 1-14). The word, Text, one of the possible data types, currently appears. The arrow indicates a list of data types is available by clicking the arrow.

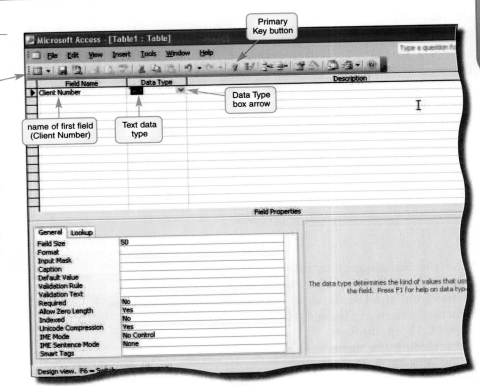

FIGURE 1-14

2

- **Because Text is the correct data type, press the TAB key to move the insertion point to the Description column, type** Client Number (Primary Key) **as the description, and then click the Primary Key button on the Table Design toolbar.**

The Client Number field is the primary key as indicated by the key symbol that appears in the row selector (Figure 1-15). A ScreenTip, which is a description of the button, appears.

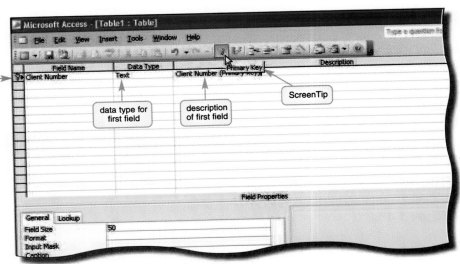

FIGURE 1-15

3

- **Press the F6 key.**

The current entry in the Field Size property box (50) is selected (Figure 1-16).

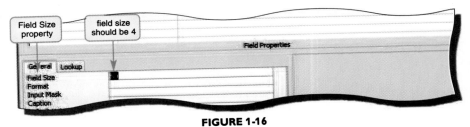

FIGURE 1-16

4

• **Type** 4 **as the size of the Client Number field.**

• **Press the F6 key to return to the Description column for the Client Number field, and then press the TAB key to move to the Field Name column in the second row.**

The insertion point moves to the second row just below the field name Client Number (Figure 1-17).

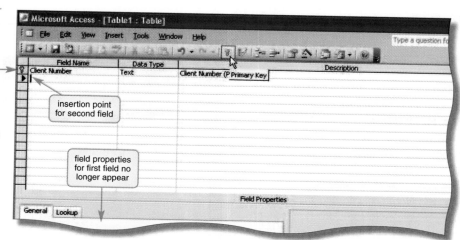

FIGURE 1-17

5

• **Use the techniques illustrated in Steps 1 through 4 to make the entries from the Client table structure shown in Figure 1-10a on page AC 15 up through and including the name of the Amount Paid field.**

• **Click the Data Type box arrow.**

The additional fields are entered (Figure 1-18). A list of available data types appears in the Data Type column for the Amount Paid field.

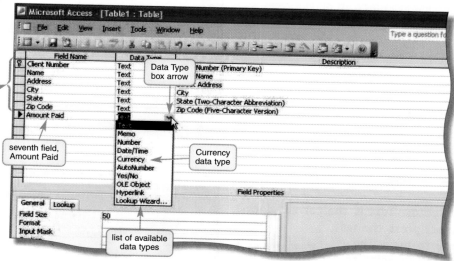

FIGURE 1-18

6

• **Click Currency and then press the TAB key.**

• **Make the remaining entries from the Client table structure shown in Figure 1-10a.**

All the fields are entered (Figure 1-19).

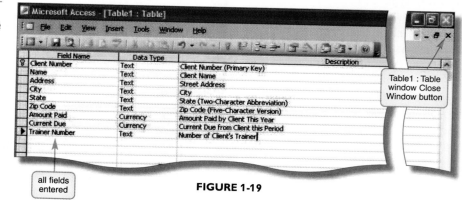

FIGURE 1-19

The description of the table is now complete.

Correcting Errors in the Structure

When creating a table, check the entries carefully to ensure they are correct. If you make a mistake and discover it before you press the TAB key, you can correct the error by repeatedly pressing the BACKSPACE key until the incorrect characters are removed. Then, type the correct characters. If you do not discover a mistake until later, you can click the entry, type the correct value, and then press the ENTER key.

If you accidentally add an extra field to the structure, select the field by clicking the row selector (the leftmost column on the row that contains the field to be deleted). After you have selected the field, press the DELETE key. This will remove the field from the structure.

If you forget a field, select the field that will follow the field you want to add by clicking the row selector, and then press the INSERT key. The remaining fields move down one row, making room for the missing field. Make the entries for the new field in the usual manner.

If you made the wrong field a primary key field, click the correct primary key entry for the field and then click the Primary Key button on the Table Design toolbar. As an alternative to these steps, you may want to start over. To do so, click the Close Window button for the Table1 : Table window and then click the No button in the Microsoft Office Access dialog box. The initial Microsoft Access window is displayed and you can repeat the process you used earlier.

Closing and Saving a Table

The Client table structure now is complete. The final step is to close and save the table within the database. At this time, you should give the table a name.

Table names are from 1 to 64 characters in length and can contain letters, numbers, and spaces. The two table names in this project are Client and Trainer.

The following steps close and save the table.

To Close and Save a Table

More About

Correcting Errors in the Structure

You also can correct errors by using the Undo button on the Table Design toolbar. Access displays a list of the 20 most recent actions you can undo. When you undo an action, you also undo all actions above it in the list. If you later decide you did not want to undo an action, click Redo.

Q&A

Q: Why is the data type for Zip Code Text instead of Number?

A: Zip codes are not used in arithmetic operations. You do not add Zip codes or find an average Zip code, for example.

1

• **Click the Close Window button for the Table1 : Table window (see Figure 1-19). (Be sure not to click the Close button on the Microsoft Access title bar, because this would close Microsoft Access.)**

The Microsoft Office Access dialog box appears (Figure 1-20).

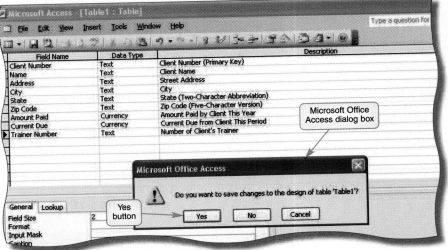

FIGURE 1-20

2

• **Click the Yes button in the Microsoft Office Access dialog box, and then type** Client **as the name of the table.**

The Save As dialog box appears (Figure 1-21). The table name is entered.

3

• **Click the OK button in the Save As dialog box.**

The table is saved. The window containing the table design no longer is displayed.

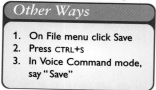

Other Ways

1. On File menu click Save
2. Press CTRL+S
3. In Voice Command mode, say "Save"

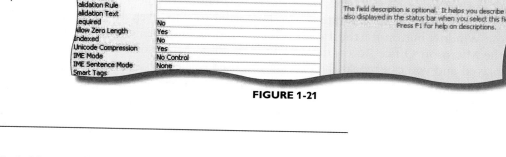

FIGURE 1-21

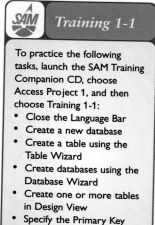

Training 1-1

To practice the following tasks, launch the SAM Training Companion CD, choose Access Project 1, and then choose Training 1-1:
• Close the Language Bar
• Create a new database
• Create a table using the Table Wizard
• Create databases using the Database Wizard
• Create one or more tables in Design View
• Specify the Primary Key
• Start Access
• Use Undo and Redo

Adding Records to a Table

Creating a table by building the structure and saving the table is the first step in a two-step process. The second step is to add records to the table. To add records to a table, the table must be open. When making changes to tables, you work in Datasheet view. In **Datasheet view**, the table is represented as a collection of rows and columns called a **datasheet**. It looks very much like the tables shown in Figure 1-1 on page AC 5.

You often add records in phases. You may, for example, not have enough time to add all the records in one session. To illustrate this process, this project begins by adding the first two records in the Client table (Figure 1-22). The remaining records are added later.

Client table (first 2 records)

CLIENT NUMBER	NAME	ADDRESS	CITY	STATE	ZIP CODE	AMOUNT PAID	CURRENT DUE	TRAINER NUMBER
BS27	Blant and Sons	4806 Park	Lake Hammond	TX	76653	$21,876.00	$892.50	42
CE16	Center Services	725 Mitchell	San Julio	TX	78364	$26,512.00	$2,672.00	48

FIGURE 1-22

The following steps illustrate how to open the Client table and then add records.

To Add Records to a Table

1

• **Right-click the Client table in the Ashton James College : Database window.**

The shortcut menu for the Client table appears (Figure 1-23). The Ashton James College : Database window is maximized because the previous window, the Client : Table window, was maximized. (If you wanted to restore the Database window to its original size, you would click the Restore Window button.)

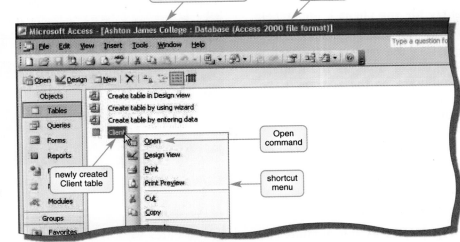

FIGURE 1-23

2

• **Click Open on the shortcut menu.**

*Access displays the Client : Table window (Figure 1-24). The window contains the Datasheet view for the Client table. The **record selector**, the small box or bar that, when clicked, selects the entire record, is positioned on the first record. The status bar at the bottom of the window also indicates that the record selector is positioned on record 1.*

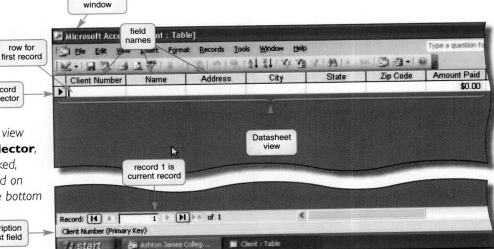

FIGURE 1-24

3

• **Type BS27 as the first client number (see Figure 1-22). Be sure you type the letters in uppercase as shown in the table in Figure 1-22 so they are entered in the database correctly.**

The client number is entered, but the insertion point is still in the Client Number field (Figure 1-25). The pencil icon in the record selector column indicates that the record is being edited but changes to the record are not saved yet. Microsoft Access also creates a row for a new record.

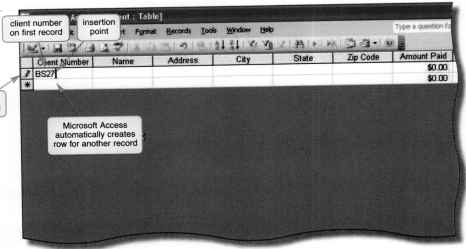

FIGURE 1-25

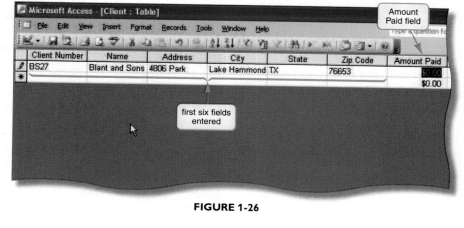

4

- **Press the TAB key to complete the entry for the Client Number field.**

- **Type the following entries, pressing the TAB key after each one:** Blant and Sons **as the name,** 4806 Park **as the address,** Lake Hammond **as the city,** TX **as the state, and** 76653 **as the Zip code.**

The Name, Address, City, State, and Zip Code fields are entered (Figure 1-26).

FIGURE 1-26

5

- **Type** 21876 **as the Amount Paid amount and then press the TAB key. (You do not need to type dollar signs or commas. In addition, because the digits to the right of the decimal point are both zeros, you do not need to type either the decimal point or the zeros.)**

- **Type** 892.50 **as the current due amount and then press the TAB key.**

- **Type** 42 **as the trainer number to complete data entry for the record.**

The fields have shifted to the left (Figure 1-27). The Amount Paid and Current Due values appear with dollar signs and decimal points. The insertion point is positioned in the Trainer Number field.

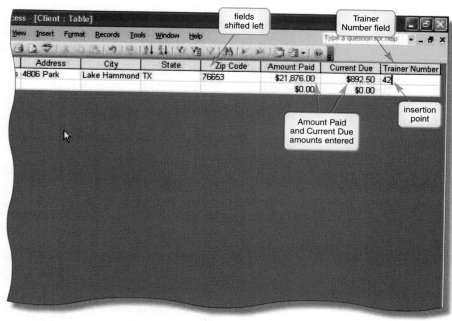

FIGURE 1-27

6

- **Press the TAB key.**

The fields shift back to the right, the record is saved, and the insertion point moves to the client number field on the second row (Figure 1-28).

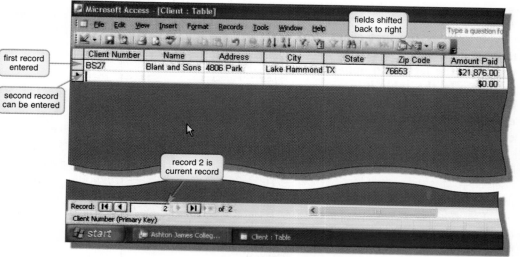

FIGURE 1-28

7

- Use the techniques shown in Steps 3 through 6 to add the data for the second record shown in Figure 1-22 on page AC 22.

The second record is added and the insertion point moves to the Client Number field on the third row (Figure 1-29).

first two records entered in Client table

FIGURE 1-29

As soon as you have entered or modified a record and moved to another record, the original record is saved. This is different from other applications. The rows entered in a spreadsheet, for example, are not saved until the entire spreadsheet is saved.

Correcting Errors in the Data

Check your entries carefully to ensure they are correct. If you make a mistake and discover it before you press the TAB key, correct it by pressing the BACKSPACE key until the incorrect characters are removed and then typing the correct characters.

If you discover an incorrect entry later, correct the error by clicking the incorrect entry and then making the appropriate correction. If the record you must correct is not on the screen, use any technique, such as the UP ARROW and DOWN ARROW keys to move to it. If the field you want to correct is not visible on the screen, use the horizontal scroll bar along the bottom of the screen to shift all the fields until the one you want appears. Then make the correction.

If you add an extra record accidentally, select the record by clicking the record selector that immediately precedes the record. Then, press the DELETE key. This will remove the record from the table. If you forget a record, add it using the same procedure as for all the other records. Access will place it in the correct location in the table automatically.

If you cannot determine how to correct the data, you are, in effect, stuck on the record. Access neither allows you to move to any other record until you have made the correction, nor allows you to close the table. If you encounter this situation, simply press the ESC key. Pressing the ESC key will remove from the screen the record you are trying to add. You then can move to any other record, close the table, or take any other action you desire.

Closing a Table and Database and Quitting Access

It is a good idea to close a table as soon as you have finished working with it. It keeps the screen from getting cluttered and prevents you from making accidental changes to the data in the table. If you no longer will work with the database, you should close the database as well. With the creation of the Client table complete, you also can quit Access at this point.

The steps on the next page close the table and the database and then quit Access.

> *More About*
>
> **Correcting Errors in the Data**
>
> You also can undo changes to a field by clicking the Undo typing button on the Table Datasheet toolbar. If you already have moved to another record and want to delete the record you just added, click Edit on the menu bar and then click Undo Saved Record.

To Close a Table and Database and Quit Access

1

• **Click the Close Window button for the Client : Table window.**

The datasheet for the Client table no longer appears (Figure 1-30).

2

• **Click the Close Window button for the Ashton James College : Database window.**

The Ashton James College : Database window no longer appears.

3

• **Click the Close button for the Microsoft Access window.**

The Microsoft Access window closes and the Windows desktop appears.

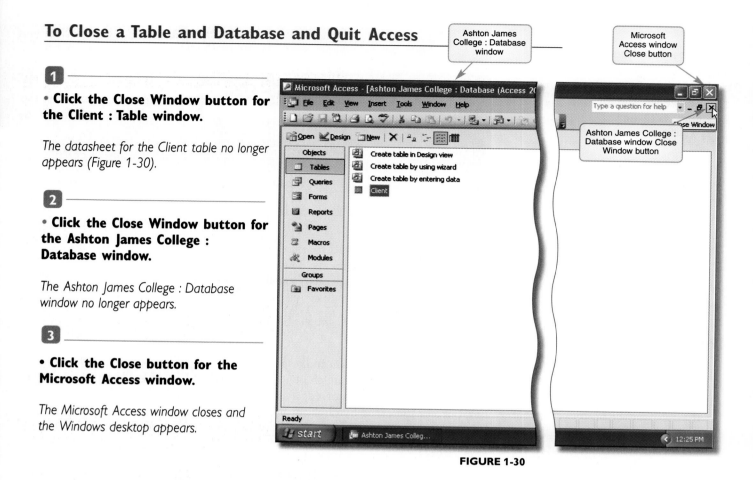

FIGURE 1-30

Opening a Database

To work with any of the tables, reports, or forms in a database, the database must be open. The following steps open the database from within Access.

To Open a Database

1

• **Start Access following the steps on pages AC 7 and AC 8.**

• **If the task pane appears, click its Close button.**

• **Click the Open button on the Database toolbar.**

The Open dialog box appears (Figure 1-31).

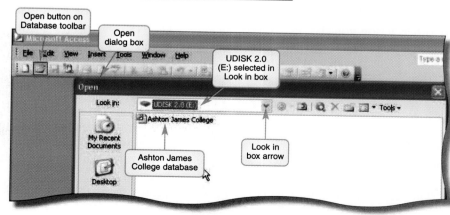

FIGURE 1-31

2

- Be sure UDISK 2.0 (E:) appears in the Look in box. If not, click the Look in box arrow and click UDISK 2.0 (E:). (Your USB flash drive may have a different name and letter.)
- Click Ashton James College.

Access displays the Open dialog box (Figure 1-32). UDISK 2.0 (E:) appears in the Look in box and the databases on the USB flash drive are displayed. (Your list may be different.)

3

- Click the Open button in the Open dialog box.
- If a Security Warning dialog box appears, click the Open button.

The database opens and the Ashton James College : Database window appears.

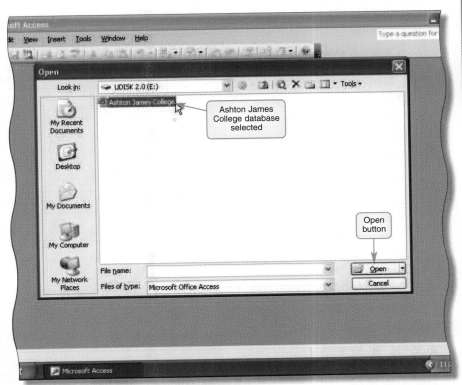

Ashton James College database selected

Open button

FIGURE 1-32

Other Ways

1. On File menu click Open
2. In Getting Started task pane, click name of database
3. Press CTRL + O
4. In Voice Command mode, say "Open"

Adding Additional Records

You can add records to a table that already contains data using a process almost identical to that used to add records to an empty table. The only difference is that you place the insertion point after the last data record before you enter the additional data. To do so, use the **Navigation buttons**, which are buttons used to move within a table, found near the lower-left corner of the screen shown in Figure 1-34 on the next page. The purpose of each of the Navigation buttons is described in Table 1-2.

Table 1-2 Navigation Buttons in Datasheet View	
BUTTON	**PURPOSE**
First Record	Moves to the first record in the table
Previous Record	Moves to the previous record
Next Record	Moves to the next record
Last Record	Moves to the last record in the table
New Record	Moves to the end of the table to a position for entering a new record

Q & A

Q: Why click the New Record button? Could you just click the Client Number on the first open record and then add the record?

A: You could click the Client Number on the first open record, provided that record appears on the screen. With only two records in the table, this is not a problem. Once a table contains more records than will fit on the screen, it is easier to click the New Record button.

The steps on the next page add the remaining records (Figure 1-33 on the next page) to the Client table.

Client table (last 8 records)

CLIENT NUMBER	NAME	ADDRESS	CITY	STATE	ZIP CODE	AMOUNT PAID	CURRENT DUE	TRAINER NUMBER
CP27	Calder Plastics	7300 Cedar	Lake Hammond	TX	76653	$8,725.00	$0.00	48
EU28	Elba's Furniture	1445 Hubert	Tallmadge	TX	77231	$4,256.00	$1,202.00	53
FI28	Farrow-Idsen	829 Wooster	Cedar Ridge	TX	79342	$8,287.50	$925.50	42
FL93	Fairland Lawn	143 Pangborn	Lake Hammond	TX	76653	$21,625.00	$0.00	48
HN83	Hurley National	3827 Burgess	Tallmadge	TX	77231	$0.00	$0.00	48
MC28	Morgan-Alyssa	923 Williams	Crumville	TX	76745	$24,761.00	$1,572.00	42
PS82	PRIM Staffing	72 Crestview	San Julio	TX	78364	$11,682.25	$2,827.50	53
TE26	Telton-Edwards	5672 Anderson	Dunston	TX	77893	$8,521.50	$0.00	48

FIGURE 1-33

To Add Additional Records to a Table

1

- **Right-click the Client table in the Ashton James College : Database window, and then click Open on the shortcut menu.**

- **When the Client table appears, maximize the window by double-clicking its title bar.**

The datasheet appears (Figure 1-34).

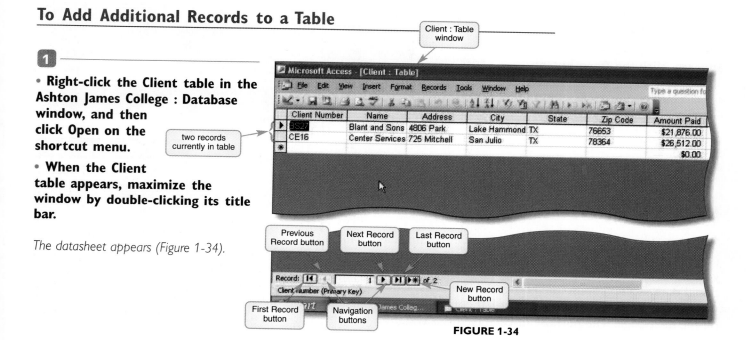

FIGURE 1-34

2

- **Click the New Record button.**

Access places the insertion point in position to enter a new record (Figure 1-35).

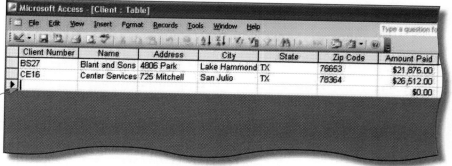

FIGURE 1-35

3

• **Add the records from Figure 1-33 using the same techniques you used to add the first two records.**

The additional records are added (Figure 1-36).

4

• **Click the Close Window button for the datasheet.**

The window containing the table closes and the Ashton James College : Database window appears.

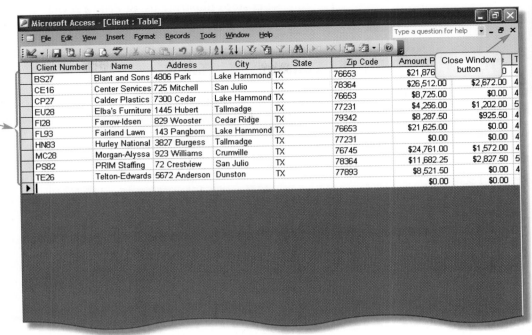

all 10 records entered

FIGURE 1-36

Previewing and Printing the Contents of a Table

When working with a database, you often will need to print a copy of the table contents. Figure 1-37 shows a printed copy of the contents of the Client table. (Yours may look slightly different, depending on your printer.) Because the Client table is wider substantially than the screen, it also will be wider than the normal printed page in portrait orientation. **Portrait orientation** means the printout is across the width of the page. **Landscape orientation** means the printout is across the length of the page. Thus, to print the wide database table, use landscape orientation. If you are printing the contents of a table that fit on the screen, you will not need landscape orientation. A convenient way to change to landscape orientation is to preview what the printed copy will look like by using Print Preview. This allows you to determine whether landscape orientation is necessary and, if it is, to change the orientation easily to landscape. In addition, you also can use Print Preview to determine whether any adjustments are necessary to the page margins.

Training 1-2

To practice the following tasks, launch the SAM Training Companion CD, choose Access Project 1, and then choose Training 1-2:
• Enter records into a datasheet table
• Open an existing database
• Use the New Record button to add a record

Client   9/15/05

Client Number	Name	Address	City	State	Zip Code	Amount Paid	Current Due	Trainer Number
BS27	Blant and Sons	4806 Park	Lake Hammon	TX	76653	$21,876.00	$892.50	42
CE16	Center Service	725 Mitchell	San Julio	TX	78364	$26,512.00	$2,672.00	48
CP27	Calder Plastics	7300 Cedar	Lake Hammon	TX	76653	$8,725.00	$0.00	48
EU28	Elba's Furniture	1445 Hubert	Tallmadge	TX	77231	$4,256.00	$1,202.00	53
FI28	Farrow-Idsen	829 Wooster	Cedar Ridge	TX	79342	$8,287.50	$925.50	42
FL93	Fairland Lawn	143 Pangborn	Lake Hammon	TX	76653	$21,625.00	$0.00	48
HN83	Hurley National	3827 Burgess	Tallmadge	TX	77231	$0.00	$0.00	48
MC28	Morgan-Alyssa	923 Williams	Crumville	TX	76745	$24,761.00	$1,572.00	42
PS82	PRIM Staffing	72 Crestview	San Julio	TX	78364	$11,682.25	$2,827.50	53
TE26	Telton-Edwards	5672 Anderson	Dunston	TX	77893	$8,521.50	$0.00	48

FIGURE 1-37

The following steps illustrate using Print Preview to preview and then print the Client table.

To Preview and Print the Contents of a Table

1

• **Right-click the Client table.**

The shortcut menu for the Client table appears (Figure 1-38).

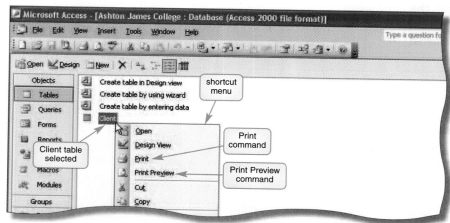

FIGURE 1-38

2

• **Click Print Preview on the shortcut menu.**

• **Point to the approximate position shown in Figure 1-39.**

The preview of the report appears. The mouse pointer shape changes to a magnifying glass, indicating you can magnify a portion of the report.

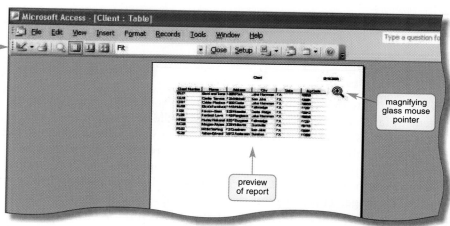

FIGURE 1-39

3

• **Click the magnifying glass mouse pointer in the approximate position shown in Figure 1-39.**

The portion surrounding the mouse pointer is magnified (Figure 1-40). The last field that appears is the Zip Code field. The Amount Paid, Current Due, and Trainer Number fields do not appear. To display the additional fields, you will need to switch to landscape orientation.

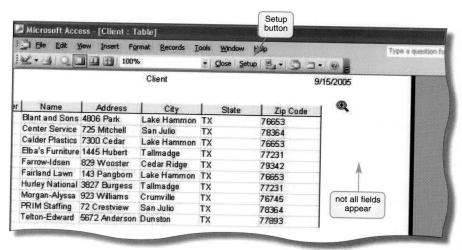

FIGURE 1-40

4

• **Click the Setup button on the Print Preview toolbar.**

Access displays the Page Setup dialog box (Figure 1-41).

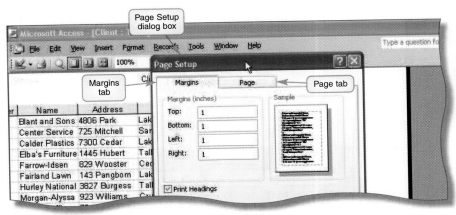

FIGURE 1-41

5

• **Click the Page tab.**

The Page sheet appears (Figure 1-42). The Portrait option button currently is selected. (**Option button** refers to the round button that indicates choices in a dialog box. When the corresponding option is selected, the button contains within it a solid circle. Clicking an option button selects it, and deselects all others.)

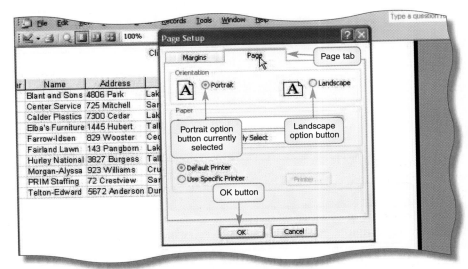

FIGURE 1-42

6

• **Click Landscape, and then click the OK button.**

The orientation is changed to landscape as shown by the report that appears on the screen (Figure 1-43). The last field that is displayed is the Trainer Number field; so all fields currently appear. If they did not, you could decrease the left and right margins; that is, the amount of space left by Access on the left and right edges of the report.

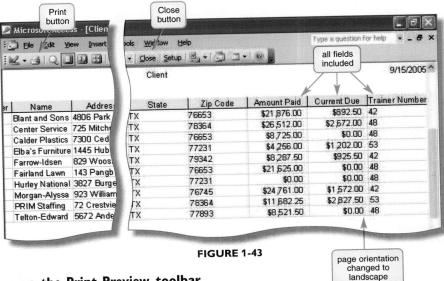

FIGURE 1-43

7

• **Click the Print button to print the report, and then click the Close button on the Print Preview toolbar.**

The report prints. It looks like the report shown in Figure 1-37 on page AC 29. The Print Preview window closes and the Ashton James College : Database window appears.

Creating Additional Tables

A database typically consists of more than one table. The Ashton James College database contains two, the Client table and the Trainer table. You need to repeat the process of creating a table and adding records for each table in the database. In the Ashton James College database, you need to create and add records to the Trainer table. The structure and data for the table are given in Figure 1-44.

Structure of Trainer table

FIELD NAME	DATA TYPE	FIELD SIZE	PRIMARY KEY?	DESCRIPTION
Trainer Number	Text	2	Yes	Trainer Number (Primary Key)
Last Name	Text	10		Last Name of Trainer
First Name	Text	8		First Name of Trainer
Address	Text	15		Street Address
City	Text	15		City
State	Text	2		State (Two-Character Abbreviation)
Zip Code	Text	5		Zip Code (Five-Character Version)
Hourly Rate	Currency			Hourly Rate of Trainer
YTD Earnings	Currency			YTD Earnings of Trainer

Trainer table

TRAINER NUMBER	LAST NAME	FIRST NAME	ADDRESS	CITY	STATE	ZIP CODE	HOURLY RATE	YTD EARNINGS
42	Perry	Belinda	261 Porter	Burdett	TX	76734	$23.00	$27,620.00
48	Stevens	Michael	3135 Gill	Rockwood	TX	78884	$21.00	$23,567.50
53	Gonzalez	Manuel	265 Maxwell	Camino	TX	76574	$24.00	$29,885.00
67	Danville	Marty	1827 Maple	Dunston	TX	77893	$20.00	$0.00

FIGURE 1-44

The following steps show how to create the table.

More About

Printing the Contents of a Table

You can change the margins, paper size, paper source, or the printer that will be used to print the report. To change the margins, select the Margins sheet in the Page Setup dialog box and then enter the appropriate margin size. To change the paper size, paper source, or the printer, select the Page sheet in the Page Setup dialog box, click the appropriate down arrow, and then select the desired option.

To Create an Additional Table

1

- **Make sure the Ashton James College database is open.**

- **Click the New button on the Database window toolbar, click Design View, and then click the OK button.**

- **Enter the data for the fields for the Trainer table from Figure 1-44. Be sure to click the Primary Key button when you enter the Trainer Number field.**

The entries appear (Figure 1-45).

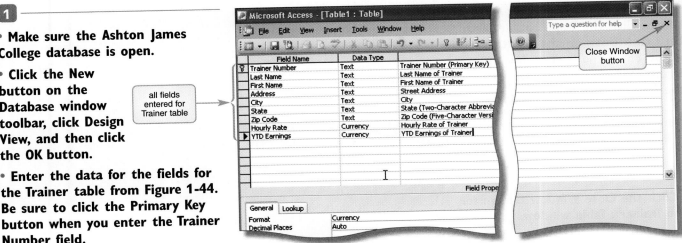

FIGURE 1-45

2

- **Click the Close Window button, click the Yes button in the Microsoft Office Access dialog box when asked if you want to save the changes, and then type** Trainer **as the name of the table.**

The Save As dialog box appears (Figure 1-46). The table name is entered.

3

- **Click the OK button.**

The table is saved in the Ashton James College database. The window containing the table structure no longer appears.

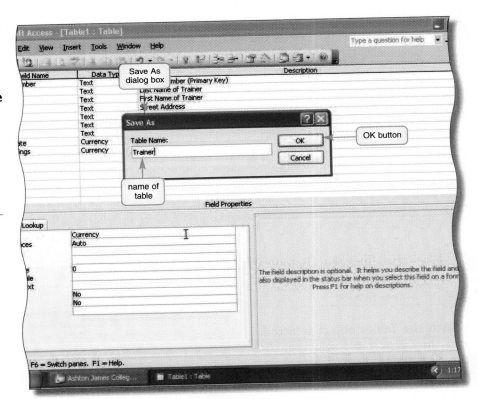

FIGURE 1-46

Adding Records to the Additional Table

Now that you have created the Trainer table, use the steps on the next page to add records to it.

To Add Records to an Additional Table

1

• **Right-click the Trainer table, and then click Open on the shortcut menu. Enter the Trainer data from Figure 1-44 on page AC 32 into the Trainer table.**

The datasheet displays the entered records (Figure 1-47).

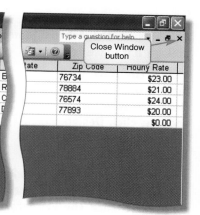

FIGURE 1-47

2

• **Click the Close Window button for the Trainer : Table window.**

Access closes the table and removes the datasheet from the screen.

The records are now in the table.

Using Queries

Queries are simply questions, the answers to which are in the database. Access contains a powerful query feature. Through the use of this feature, you can ask a wide variety of complex questions. For simple requests, however, such as listing the number, name, and trainer number of all clients, you do not need to use the query feature, but instead can use the Simple Query wizard.

The following steps use the Simple Query wizard to create a query to display the number, name, and trainer number of all clients.

To Use the Simple Query Wizard to Create a Query

1

• **With the Tables object selected and the Client table selected, click the New Object button arrow on the Database toolbar.**

A list of objects that can be created is displayed (Figure 1-48).

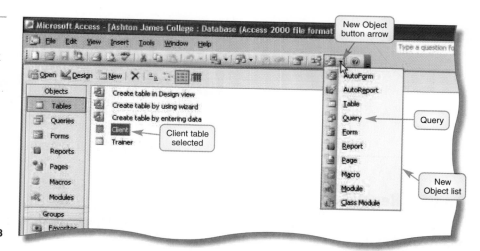

FIGURE 1-48

2

• **Click Query on the New Object list.**

The New Query dialog box appears (Figure 1-49).

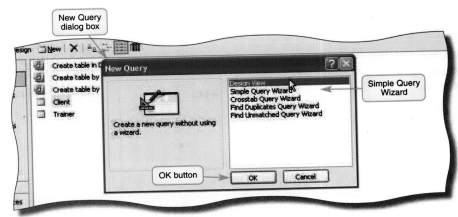

FIGURE 1-49

3

• **Click Simple Query Wizard, and then click the OK button.**

Access displays the Simple Query Wizard dialog box (Figure 1-50). It contains a list of available fields and a list of selected fields. Currently no fields are selected for the query.

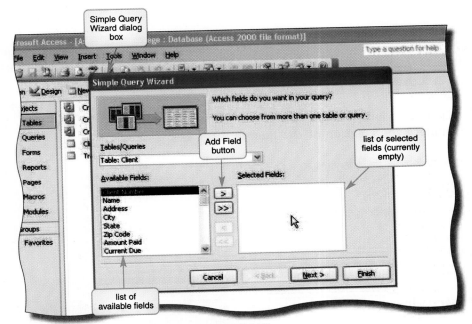

FIGURE 1-50

4

• **Click the Add Field button to add the Client Number field.**

• **Click the Add Field button a second time to add the Name field.**

• **Click the Trainer Number field, and then click the Add Field button to add the Trainer Number field.**

The fields are selected (Figure 1-51).

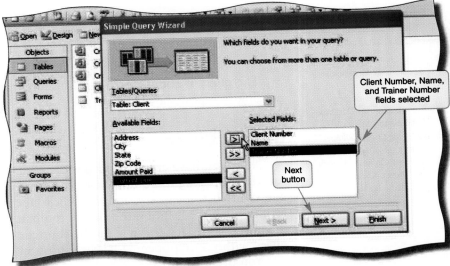

FIGURE 1-51

5

- **Click the Next button, and then type** Client-Trainer Query **as the name for the query.**

The Simple Query Wizard dialog box displays the new query name (Figure 1-52).

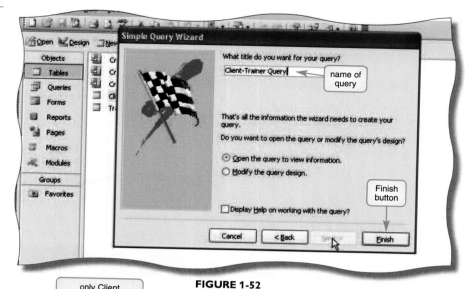

FIGURE 1-52

6

- **Click the Finish button to complete the creation of the query.**

Access displays the query results (Figure 1-53). The results contain all records, but only contain the Client Number, Name, and Trainer Number fields.

7

- **Click the Close Window button for the Client-Trainer Query : Select Query window.**

Access closes the query and the Ashton James College : Database window appears.

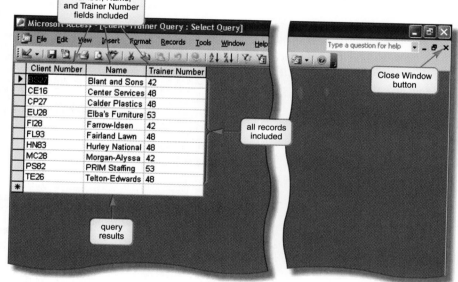

FIGURE 1-53

Other Ways

1. Click Queries object, double-click Create query by using wizard
2. Click Queries object, click New button on Database window toolbar
3. On Insert menu click Query
4. In Voice Command mode, say "Insert, Query"

The query is complete. You can use it at any time you like in the future without needing to repeat the above steps.

Using a Query

After you have created and saved a query, you can use it at any time in the future by opening it. To open a saved query, click the Queries object on the Objects bar, right-click the query, and then click Open on the shortcut menu. To print the results, click the Print button on the toolbar. If you want to change the design of the query, click Design View on the shortcut menu rather than Open. To print the query without first opening it, click Print on the shortcut menu.

You often want to restrict the records that are included. For example, you might only want to include those clients whose trainer number is 42. In such a case, you need to enter the 42 as a **criterion**, which is a condition that the records to be included must satisfy. To do so, you will open the query in Design view, enter the criterion below the appropriate field, and then run the query. The following steps show how to enter a criterion to include only clients of trainer 42 and then run the query.

To Use a Query

1

• **If necessary, click the Queries object. Right-click the Client-Trainer Query.**

The shortcut menu for the Client-Trainer Query is displayed (Figure 1-54).

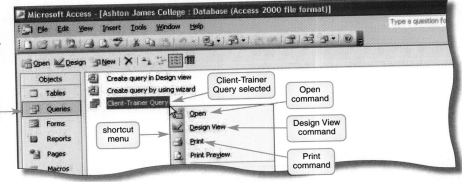

FIGURE 1-54

2

• **Click Design View on the shortcut menu.**

The query appears in Design view (Figure 1-55).

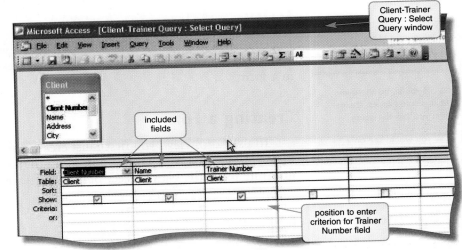

FIGURE 1-55

3

• **Click the Criteria row in the Trainer Number column of the grid, and then type 42 as the criterion.**

The criterion is typed (Figure 1-56).

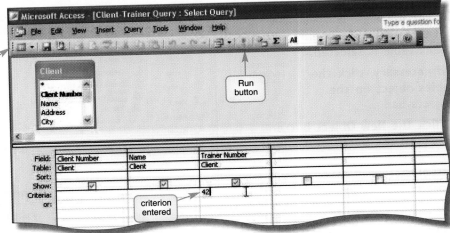

FIGURE 1-56

4

• **Click the Run button on the Query Design toolbar.**

Access displays the results (Figure 1-57). Only the clients of trainer 42 are included.

5

• **Close the window containing the query results by clicking its Close Window button.**

• **When asked if you want to save your changes, click the No button.**

The results no longer appear. The changes to the query are not saved.

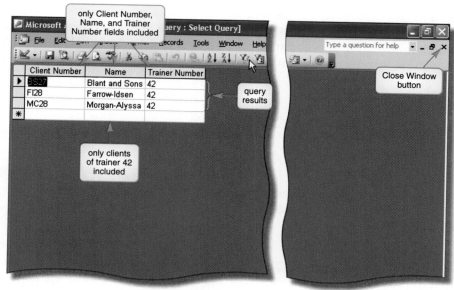

only Client Number, Name, and Trainer Number fields included

Client Number	Name	Trainer Number
8827	Blant and Sons	42
FI28	Farrow-Idsen	42
MC28	Morgan-Alyssa	42

query results

only clients of trainer 42 included

Close Window button

FIGURE 1-57

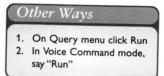

Other Ways

1. On Query menu click Run
2. In Voice Command mode, say "Run"

Q&A

Q: If you saved the query, what would happen the next time you ran the query?

A: You would see only clients of trainer 42.

Using a Form to View Data

In creating tables, you have used Datasheet view; that is, the data on the screen appeared as a table. You also can use **Form view**, in which you see data contained in a form.

Creating a Form

To use Form view, you first must create a form. The simplest way to create a form is to use the New Object button on the Database toolbar. The following steps illustrate using the New Object button to create a form for the Client table.

To Use the New Object Button to Create a Form

1

• **Make sure the Ashton James College database is open, the Database window appears, and the Client table is selected.**

• **If necessary, click the Tables object on the Objects bar.**

• **Click the New Object button arrow on the Database toolbar.**

A list of objects that can be created appears (Figure 1-58).

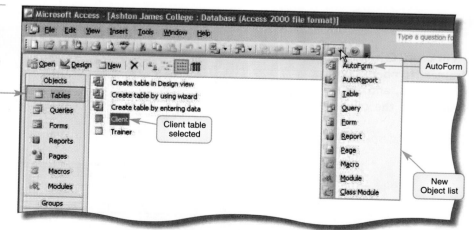

Tables object selected

Client table selected

AutoForm

New Object list

FIGURE 1-58

2

• **Click AutoForm on the New Object list.**

After a brief delay, the form appears (Figure 1-59). If you do not move the mouse pointer after clicking the New Object button, the ScreenTip for the Properties button may appear when the form opens. Access displays the Formatting toolbar when a form is created. (When you close the form, this toolbar no longer appears.)

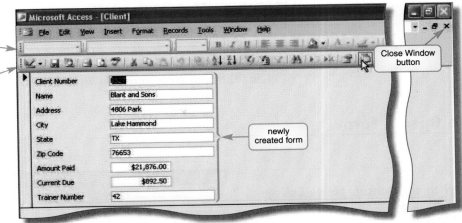

FIGURE 1-59

Closing and Saving the Form

Closing a form is similar to closing a table. The only difference is that you will be asked if you want to save the form unless you previously have saved it. The following steps close the form and save it as Client.

To Close and Save a Form

1

• **Click the Close Window button for the Client window (see Figure 1-59).**

Access displays the Microsoft Office Access dialog box (Figure 1-60).

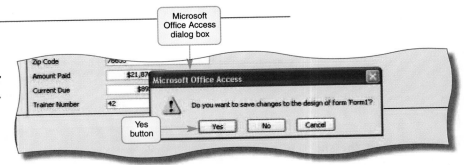

FIGURE 1-60

2

• **Click the Yes button.**

The Save As dialog box appears (Figure 1-61). The name of the table (Client) becomes the name of the form automatically. This name could be changed, if desired.

3

• **Click the OK button.**

The form is saved as part of the database and the form closes. The Ashton James College : Database window is redisplayed.

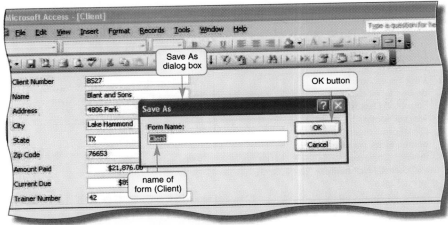

FIGURE 1-61

Opening the Saved Form

After you have saved a form, you can use it at any time in the future by opening it. Opening a form is similar to opening a table. Before opening the form, however, the Forms object, rather than the Tables object, must be selected.

The following steps show how to open the Client form.

To Open a Form

1

• **With the Ashton James College database open and the Database window on the screen, click Forms on the Objects bar, and then right-click the Client form.**

The list of forms appears (Figure 1-62). The shortcut menu for the Client form appears.

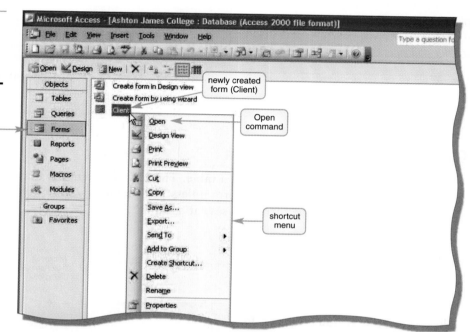

FIGURE 1-62

2

• **Click Open on the shortcut menu.**

The Client form appears (Figure 1-63).

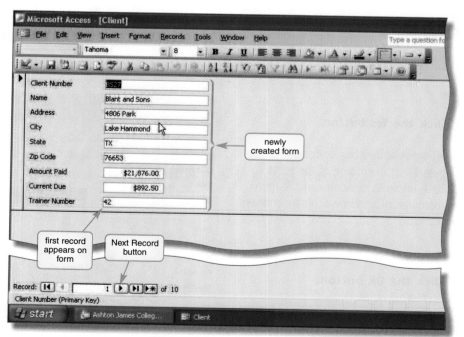

FIGURE 1-63

Using the Form

You can use the form just as you used Datasheet view. You use the Navigation buttons to move between records. You can add new records or change existing ones. To delete the record appearing on the screen, after selecting the record by clicking its record selector, press the DELETE key. Thus, you can perform database operations using either Form view or Datasheet view.

Because you can see only one record at a time in Form view, to see a different record, such as the fifth record, you must use the Navigation buttons to move to it. The following step illustrates moving from record to record in Form view.

To Use a Form

1

- **Click the Next Record button four times.**

Access displays the fifth record on the form (Figure 1-64).

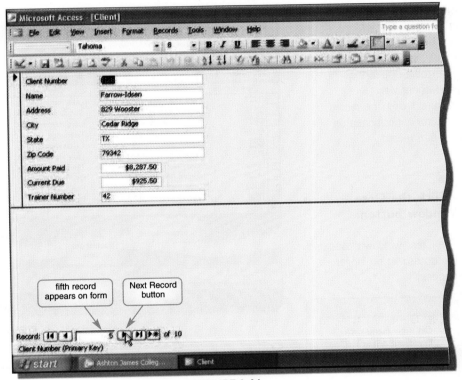

FIGURE 1-64

Switching Between Form View and Datasheet View

In some cases, after you have seen a record in Form view, you will want to switch to Datasheet view to see the collection of records. The steps on the next page show how to switch from Form view to Datasheet view.

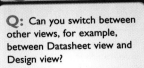

To Switch from Form View to Datasheet View

1

• **Click the View button arrow on the Form View toolbar.**

The list of available views appears (Figure 1-65).

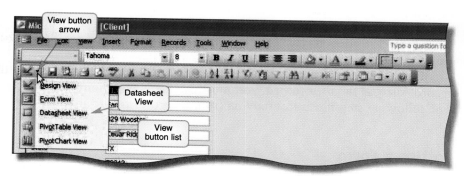

FIGURE 1-65

2

• **Click Datasheet View.**

The table appears in Datasheet view (Figure 1-66). The record selector is positioned on the fifth record.

3

• **Click the Close Window button.**

The Client window closes and the datasheet no longer appears.

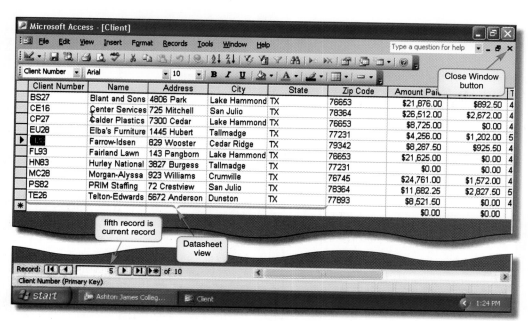

Client Number	Name	Address	City	State	Zip Code	Amount Paid	
BS27	Blant and Sons	4806 Park	Lake Hammond	TX	76653	$21,876.00	$892.50	4
CE16	Center Services	725 Mitchell	San Julio	TX	78364	$26,512.00	$2,672.00	4
CP27	Calder Plastics	7300 Cedar	Lake Hammond	TX	76653	$8,725.00	$0.00	4
EU28	Elba's Furniture	1445 Hubert	Tallmadge	TX	77231	$4,256.00	$1,202.00	4
FI28	Farrow-Idsen	829 Wooster	Cedar Ridge	TX	79342	$8,287.50	$925.50	5
FL93	Fairland Lawn	143 Pangborn	Lake Hammond	TX	76653	$21,625.00	$0.00	4
HN83	Hurley National	3827 Burgess	Tallmadge	TX	77231	$0.00	$0.00	4
MC28	Morgan-Alyssa	923 Williams	Crumville	TX	76745	$24,761.00	$1,572.00	4
PS82	PRIM Staffing	72 Crestview	San Julio	TX	78364	$11,682.25	$2,827.50	5
TE26	Telton-Edwards	5672 Anderson	Dunston	TX	77893	$8,521.50	$0.00	4
*						$0.00	$0.00	

Record: 5 of 10

Client Number (Primary Key)

FIGURE 1-66

Other Ways

1. On View menu click Datasheet View
2. In Voice Command mode, say "View, Datasheet View"

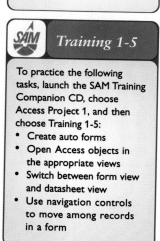

Training 1-5

To practice the following tasks, launch the SAM Training Companion CD, choose Access Project 1, and then choose Training 1-5:
• Create auto forms
• Open Access objects in the appropriate views
• Switch between form view and datasheet view
• Use navigation controls to move among records in a form

Creating a Report

Earlier in this project, you printed a table using the Print button. The report you produced was shown in Figure 1-37 on page AC 29. While this type of report presented the data in an organized manner, the format is very rigid. You cannot select the fields to appear, for example; the report automatically includes all the fields and they appear in precisely the same order as in the table. A way to change the title of the table is not available. Therefore, it will be the same as the name of the table.

In this section, you will create the report shown in Figure 1-67. This report features significant differences from the one in Figure 1-37. The portion at the top of the report in Figure 1-67, called a **page header**, contains a custom title. The contents of this page header appear at the top of each page. The **detail lines**, which are the lines that are printed for each record, contain only those fields you specify and in the order you specify.

Client Amount Report

Client Number	Name	Amount Paid	Current Due
BS27	Blant and Sons	$21,876.00	$892.50
CE16	Center Services	$26,512.00	$2,672.00
CP27	Calder Plastics	$8,725.00	$0.00
EU28	Elba's Furniture	$4,256.00	$1,202.00
FI28	Farrow-Idsen	$8,287.50	$925.50
FL93	Fairland Lawn	$21,625.00	$0.00
HN83	Hurley National	$0.00	$0.00
MC28	Morgan-Alyssa	$24,761.00	$1,572.00
PS82	PRIM Staffing	$11,682.25	$2,827.50
TE26	Telton-Edwards	$8,521.50	$0.00

FIGURE 1-67

The following steps show how to create the report in Figure 1-67.

To Create a Report

1

• **Click Tables on the Objects bar, and then make sure the Client table is selected.**

• **Click the New Object button arrow on the Database toolbar.**

The list of available objects appears (Figure 1-68).

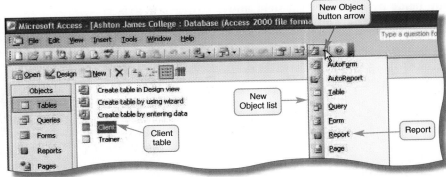

FIGURE 1-68

2

• **Click Report.**

Access displays the New Report dialog box (Figure 1-69).

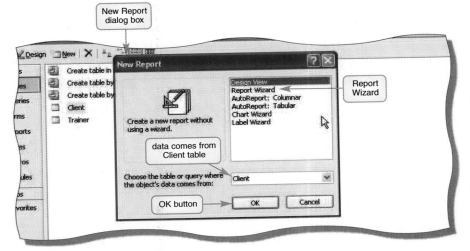

FIGURE 1-69

3

• **Click Report Wizard, and then click the OK button.**

Access displays the Report Wizard dialog box (Figure 1-70). As you click the Next button in this dialog box, a series of options helps you create the report.

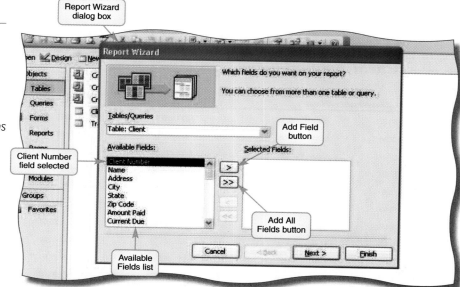

FIGURE 1-70

4

• **Click the Add Field button to add the Client Number field.**

• **Click the Add Field button to add the Name field.**

• **Add the Amount Paid and Current Due fields by clicking each field and then clicking the Add Field button.**

The fields for the report appear in the Selected Fields box (Figure 1-71).

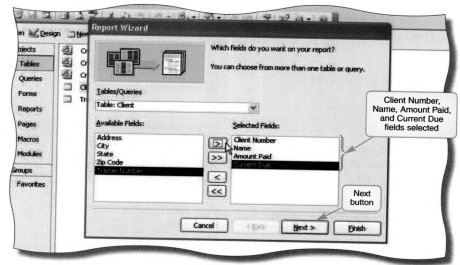

FIGURE 1-71

5

• **Click the Next button.**

The Report Wizard dialog box displays options to specify any grouping that is to take place (Figure 1-72).

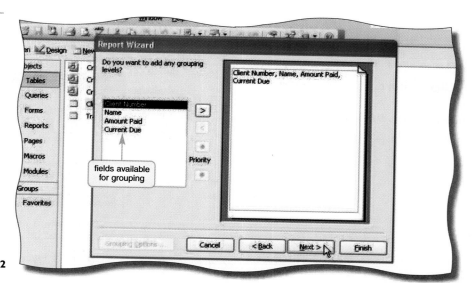

FIGURE 1-72

6

• **Because you will not specify any grouping, click the Next button in the Report Wizard dialog box.**

• **Click the Next button a second time because you will not need to change the sort order for the records.**

The Report Wizard dialog box displays options for changing the layout and orientation of the report (Figure 1-73).

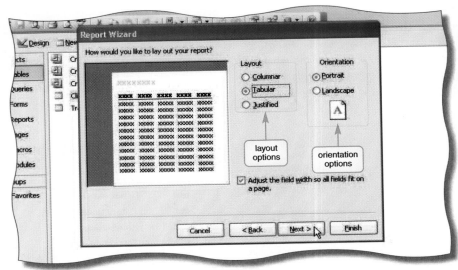

FIGURE 1-73

7

• **Make sure that Tabular is selected as the Layout and Portrait is selected as the Orientation, and then click the Next button.**

The Report Wizard dialog box displays options you can select for the style of the report (Figure 1-74).

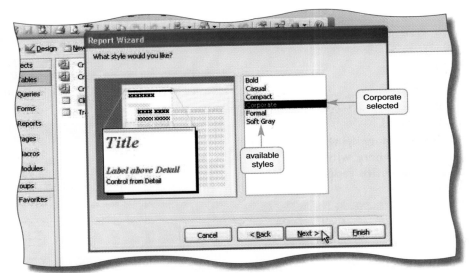

FIGURE 1-74

8

• **Be sure the Corporate style is selected, click the Next button, and then type** Client Amount Report **as the new title.**

The Report Wizard dialog box displays the new title of the report (Figure 1-75).

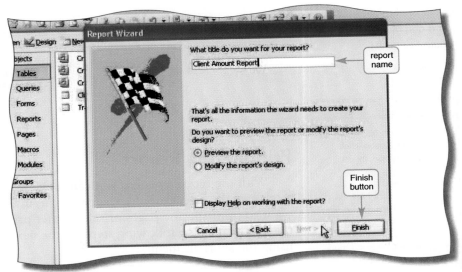

FIGURE 1-75

9

• **Click the Finish button.**

Access displays a preview of the report (Figure 1-76). Your report may look slightly different, depending on your printer.

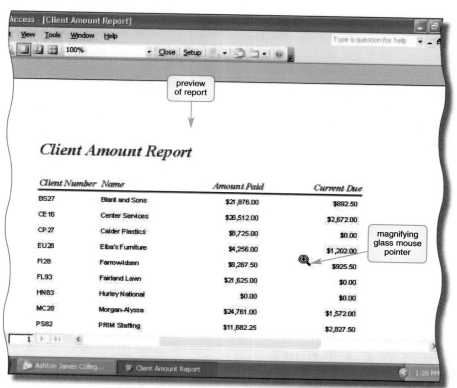

FIGURE 1-76

10

• **Click the magnifying glass mouse pointer anywhere within the report to see the entire report.**

The entire report appears (Figure 1-77).

11

• **Click the Close Window button in the Client Amount Report window.**

The report no longer appears. It has been saved automatically using the name Client Amount Report.

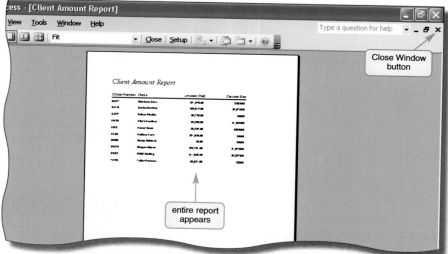

FIGURE 1-77

Other Ways

1. On Objects bar click Reports, double-click Create report by using wizard
2. On Objects bar click Reports, click New on Database window toolbar
3. On Insert menu click Report
4. In Voice Command mode, say "Insert, Report"

Printing the Report

With the report created, you can preview the report to determine if you need to change the orientation or the page margins. You also can print the report. If you want to print specific pages or select other print options, use the Print command on the File menu. The following steps on the next page show how to print a report using the shortcut menu.

To Print a Report

1

- **If necessary, click Reports on the Objects bar in the Database window.**
- **Right-click the Client Amount Report.**

The Client Amount Report is selected and the shortcut menu appears (Figure 1-78).

2

- **Click Print on the shortcut menu.**

The report prints. It should look similar to the one shown in Figure 1-67 on page AC 43.

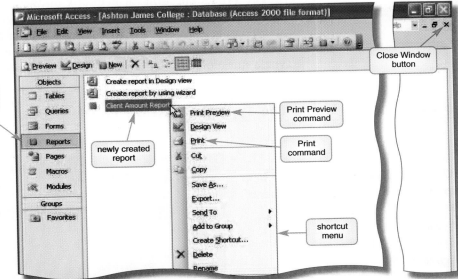

FIGURE 1-78

Closing the Database

After you have finished working with a database, you should close it. The following step closes the database by closing its Database window.

To Close a Database

1 **Click the Close Window button for the Ashton James College : Database window.**

Access Help System

At any time while you are using Access, you can get answers to questions by using the Access Help system. You can activate the Access Help system by using the Type a question for help box on the menu bar, by clicking the Microsoft Access Help button on the toolbar, or by clicking Help on the menu bar (Figure 1-79 on the next page). Used properly, this form of online assistance can increase your productivity and reduce your frustrations by minimizing the time you spend learning how to use Access.

The section on the next page shows how to get answers to your questions using the Type a question for help box. Additional information about using the Access Help system is available in Appendix A.

More About

The Access Help System

The best way to become familiar with the Access Help system is to use it. Appendix A includes detailed information on the Access Help system and exercises that will help you gain confidence in using it.

Obtaining Help Using the Type a Question for Help Box on the Menu Bar

The Type a question for help box on the right side of the menu bar lets you type in free-form questions, such as *how do I save* or *how do I create a Web page* or, you can type in terms, such as *copy*, *save*, or *formatting*. Access responds by displaying a list of topics related to what you entered. The following steps show how to use the Type a question for help box to obtain information on removing a primary key.

To Obtain Help Using the Type a Question for Help Box

1

• **Click the Type a question for help box on the right side of the menu bar.**

• **Type** how do I remove a primary key **in the box (Figure 1-79).**

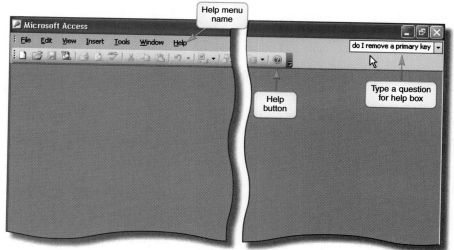

FIGURE 1-79

2

• **Press the ENTER key.**

Access displays the Search Results task pane, which includes a list of topics relating to the question, how do I remove a primary key (Figure 1-80). Your list may be different.

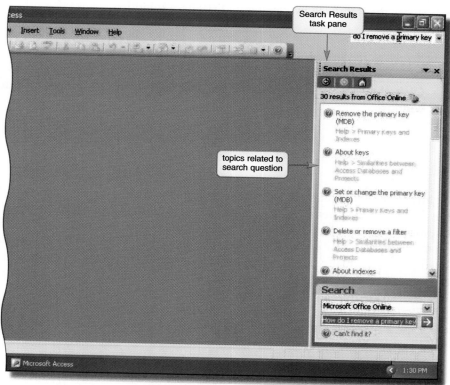

FIGURE 1-80

3

• **Point to the Remove the primary key (MDB) topic.**

The mouse pointer changes to a hand indicating it is pointing to a link (Figure 1-81).

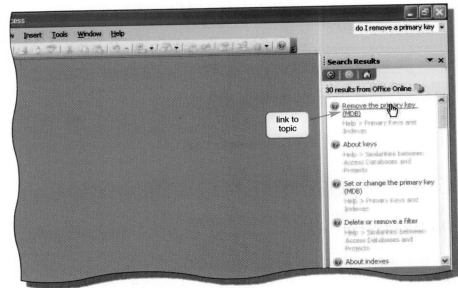

FIGURE 1-81

4

• **Click Remove the primary key (MDB).**

Access displays a Microsoft Office Access Help window that provides Help information about removing the primary key (Figure 1-82). Your window may be in a different position.

5

• **Click the Close button on the Microsoft Office Access Help window title bar.**

The Microsoft Access Help window closes.

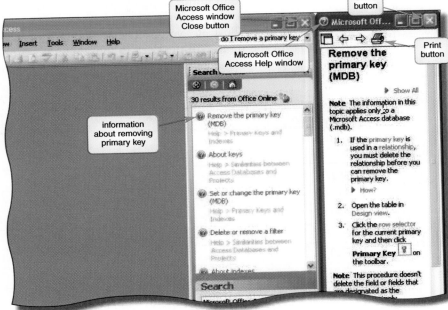

FIGURE 1-82

Use the buttons in the upper-left corner of the Microsoft Office Access Help window (Figure 1-82) to navigate through the Help system, and change the appearance and print the contents of the window.

As you enter questions and terms in the Type a question for help box, Access adds them to its list. Thus, if you click the Type a question for help box arrow, a list of previously asked questions and terms will appear.

Quitting Access

After you close a database, you can open another database, create a new database, or simply quit Access and return to the Windows desktop. The following step quits Access.

To Quit Access

1 Click the Close button in the Microsoft Access window (see Figure 1-82 on the previous page).

More About

Database Design: Design Method

A variety of methods have been developed for designing complex databases given a set of input and output requirements. For more information about database design methods, visit the Access 2003 More About Web page (scsite.com/ac2003/more) and click Database Design.

Designing a Database

Database design refers to the arrangement of data into tables and fields. In the example in this project, the design is specified, but in many cases, you will have to determine the design based on what you want the system to accomplish.

With large, complex databases, the database design process can be extensive. Major sections of advanced database textbooks are devoted to this topic. Often, however, you should be able to design a database effectively by keeping one simple principle in mind: design to remove redundancy. **Redundancy** means storing the same fact in more than one place.

To illustrate, you need to maintain the following information shown in Figure 1-83. In the figure, all the data is contained in a single table. Notice that the data for a given trainer (number, name, address, and so on) occurs on more than one record.

Client table

duplicate trainer names

CLIENT NUMBER	NAME	ADDRESS	...	CURRENT DUE	TRAINER NUMBER	LAST NAME	FIRST NAME	...
BS27	Blant and Sons	4806 Park	...	$892.50	42	Perry	Belinda	...
CE16	Center Services	725 Mitchell	...	$2,672.00	48	Stevens	Michael	...
CP27	Calder Plastics	7300 Cedar	...	$0.00	48	Stevens	Michael	...
EU28	Elba's Furniture	1445 Hubert	...	$1,202.00	53	Gonzalez	Manuel	...
FI28	Farrow-Idsen	829 Wooster	...	$925.50	42	Perry	Belinda	...
FL93	Fairland Lawn	143 Pangborn	...	$0.00	48	Stevens	Michael	...
HN83	Hurley National	3827 Burgess	...	$0.00	48	Stevens	Michael	...
MC28	Morgan-Alyssa	923 Williams	...	$1,572.00	42	Perry	Belinda	...
PS82	PRIM Staffing	72 Crestview	...	$2,827.50	53	Gonzalez	Manuel	...
TE26	Telton-Edwards	5672 Anderson	...	$0.00	48	Stevens	Michael	...

FIGURE 1-83

More About

The Quick Reference

For a table that lists how to complete tasks covered in this book using the mouse, menu, shortcut menu, and keyboard, see the Quick Reference Summary at the back of this book, or visit the Access 2003 Quick Reference Web page (scsite.com/ac2003/qr).

Storing this data on multiple records is an example of redundancy, which causes several problems, including:

1. Redundancy wastes space on the disk. The name of trainer 42 (Belinda Perry), for example, should be stored only once. Storing this fact several times is wasteful.

2. Redundancy makes updating the database more difficult. If, for example, Belinda Perry's name changes, her name would need to be changed in several different places.

3. A possibility of inconsistent data exists. If, for example, you change the name of Belinda Perry on client FI28's record to Belinda Martin, but do not change it on client BS27's record, the data is inconsistent. In both cases, the trainer number is 42, but the names are different.

The solution to the problem is to place the redundant data in a separate table, one in which the data no longer will be redundant. If, for example, you place the data for trainers in a separate table (Figure 1-84), the data for each trainer will appear only once.

trainer data is in separate table

Trainer table

TRAINER NUMBER	LAST NAME	FIRST NAME	ADDRESS	CITY	STATE	ZIP CODE	HOURLY RATE	YTD EARNINGS
42	Perry	Belinda	261 Porter	Burdett	TX	76734	$23.00	$27,620.00
48	Stevens	Michael	3135 Gill	Rockwood	TX	78884	$21.00	$23,567.50
53	Gonzalez	Manuel	265 Maxwell	Camino	TX	76574	$24.00	$29,885.00

Client table

CLIENT NUMBER	NAME	ADDRESS	CITY	STATE	ZIP CODE	AMOUNT PAID	CURRENT DUE	TRAINER NUMBER
BS27	Blant and Sons	4806 Park	Lake Hammond	TX	76653	$21,876.00	$892.50	42
CE16	Center Services	725 Mitchell	San Julio	TX	78364	$26,512.00	$2,672.00	48
CP27	Calder Plastics	7300 Cedar	Lake Hammond	TX	76653	$8,725.00	$0.00	48
EU28	Elba's Furniture	1445 Hubert	Tallmadge	TX	77231	$4,256.00	$1,202.00	53
FI28	Farrow-Idsen	829 Wooster	Cedar Ridge	TX	79342	$8,287.50	$925.50	42
FL93	Fairland Lawn	143 Pangborn	Lake Hammond	TX	76653	$21,625.00	$0.00	48
HN83	Hurley National	3827 Burgess	Tallmadge	TX	77231	$0.00	$0.00	48
MC28	Morgan-Alyssa	923 Williams	Crumville	TX	76745	$24,761.00	$1,572.00	42
PS82	PRIM Staffing	72 Crestview	San Julio	TX	78364	$11,682.25	$2,827.50	53
TE26	Telton-Edwards	5672 Anderson	Dunston	TX	77893	$8,521.50	$0.00	48

FIGURE 1-84

Notice that you need to have the trainer number in both tables. Without it, no way exists to tell which trainer is associated with which client. The remaining trainer data, however, was removed from the Client table and placed in the Trainer table. This new arrangement corrects the problems of redundancy in the following ways:

1. Because the data for each trainer is stored only once, space is not wasted.
2. Changing the name of a trainer is easy. You have only to change one row in the Trainer table.
3. Because the data for a trainer is stored only once, inconsistent data cannot occur.

Designing to omit redundancy will help you to produce good and valid database designs.

Project Summary

In Project 1, you learned about databases and database management systems. You learned how to create a database and how to create the tables within a database. You saw how to define the fields in a table by specifying the characteristics of the fields. You learned how to open a table, how to add records to it, and how to close it. You also printed the contents of a table. You learned how to use the Simple Query wizard to create a query that included columns from a table as well as how to enter a criterion to restrict the rows that were included. You created a form to view data on the screen and also created a custom report. You learned how to use Microsoft Access Help. Finally, you learned how to design a database to eliminate redundancy.

 If your instructor has chosen to use the full online version of SAM 2003 Assessment and Training, you can go beyond the "just-in-time" training provided on the CD that accompanies this text. Simply log in to your SAM account (http://sam2003.course.com) to launch any assigned training activities or exams that relate to the skills covered in this project.

What You Should Know

Having completed this project, you should be able to perform the tasks below. The tasks are listed in the same order they were presented in this project. For a list of the buttons, menus, toolbars, and commands introduced in this project, see the Quick Reference Summary at the back of this book and refer to the Page Number column.

1. Start Access (AC 7)
2. Close the Language Bar (AC 9)
3. Create a New Database (AC 10)
4. Create a Table (AC 17)
5. Define the Fields in a Table (AC 19)
6. Close and Save a Table (AC 21)
7. Add Records to a Table (AC 23)
8. Close a Table and Database and Quit Access (AC 26)
9. Open a Database (AC 26)
10. Add Additional Records to a Table (AC 28)
11. Preview and Print the Contents of a Table (AC 30)
12. Create an Additional Table (AC 33)
13. Add Records to an Additional Table (AC 34)

14. Use the Simple Query Wizard to Create a Query (AC 34)
15. Use a Query (AC 37)
16. Use the New Object Button to Create a Form (AC 38)
17. Close and Save a Form (AC 39)
18. Open a Form (AC 40)
19. Use a Form (AC 41)
20. Switch from Form View to Datasheet View (AC 42)
21. Create a Report (AC 43)
22. Print a Report (AC 47)
23. Close a Database (AC 47)
24. Obtain Help Using the Type a Question for Help Box (AC 48)
25. Quit Access (AC 50)

Learn It Online

Instructions: To complete the Learn It Online exercises, start your browser, click the Address bar, and then enter the Web address scsite.com/ac2003/learn. When the Access 2003 Learn It Online page is displayed, follow the instructions in the exercises below. Each exercise has instructions for printing your results, either for your own records or for submission to your instructor.

1 Project Reinforcement TF, MC, and SA

Below Access Project 1, click the Project Reinforcement link. Print the quiz by clicking Print on the File menu for each page. Answer each question.

2 Flash Cards

Below Access Project 1, click the Flash Cards link and read the instructions. Type 20 (or a number specified by your instructor) in the Number of playing cards text box, type your name in the Enter your Name text box, and then click the Flip Card button. When the flash card is displayed, read the question and then click the ANSWER box arrow to select an answer. Flip through Flash Cards. If your score is 15 (75%) correct or greater, click Print on the File menu to print your results. If your score is less than 15 (75%) correct, then redo this exercise by clicking the Replay button.

3 Practice Test

Below Access Project 1, click the Practice Test link. Answer each question, enter your first and last name at the bottom of the page, and then click the Grade Test button. When the graded practice test is displayed on your screen, click Print on the File menu to print a hard copy. Continue to take practice tests until you score 80% or better.

4 Who Wants To Be a Computer Genius?

Below Access Project 1, click the Computer Genius link. Read the instructions, enter your first and last name at the bottom of the page, and then click the PLAY button. When your score is displayed, click the PRINT RESULTS link to print a hard copy.

5 Wheel of Terms

Below Access Project 1, click the Wheel of Terms link. Read the instructions, and then enter your first and last name and your school name. Click the PLAY button. When your score is displayed, right-click the score and then click Print on the shortcut menu to print a hard copy.

6 Crossword Puzzle Challenge

Below Access Project 1, click the Crossword Puzzle Challenge link. Read the instructions, and then enter your first and last name. Click the SUBMIT button. Work the crossword puzzle. When you are finished, click the Submit button. When the crossword puzzle is redisplayed, click the Print Puzzle button to print a hard copy.

7 Tips and Tricks

Below Access Project 1, click the Tips and Tricks link. Click a topic that pertains to Project 1. Right-click the information and then click Print on the shortcut menu. Construct a brief example of what the information relates to in Access to confirm you understand how to use the tip or trick.

8 Newsgroups

Below Access Project 1, click the Newsgroups link. Click a topic that pertains to Project 1. Print three comments.

9 Expanding Your Horizons

Below Access Project 1, click the Expanding Your Horizons link. Click a topic that pertains to Project 1. Print the information. Construct a brief example of what the information relates to in Access to confirm you understand the contents of the article.

10 Search Sleuth

Below Access Project 1, click the Search Sleuth link. To search for a term that pertains to this project, select a term below the Project 1 title and then use the Google search engine at google.com (or any major search engine) to display and print two Web pages that present information on the term.

11 Access Online Training

Below Access Project 1, click the Access Online Training link. When your browser displays the Microsoft Office Online Web page, click the Access link. Click one of the Access courses that covers one or more of the objectives listed at the beginning of the project on page AC 4. Print the first page of the course before stepping through it.

12 Office Marketplace

Below Access Project 1, click the Office Marketplace link. When your browser displays the Microsoft Office Online Web page, click the Office Marketplace link. Click a topic that relates to Access. Print the first page.

Apply Your Knowledge

1 Changing Data, Creating Queries, and Creating Reports

Instructions: Start Access. Open the database Begon Pest Control from the Data Files for Students. See the inside back cover of this book for instructions for downloading the Data Files for Students or see your instructor for information about accessing the files required in this book.

Begon Pest Control is a company that performs pest control services for commercial businesses. Begon has a database that keeps track of its technicians and customers. The database has two tables. The Customer table contains data on the customers who use the services of Begon. The Technician table contains data on the individuals employed by Begon. The structure and data are shown for the Customer table in Figure 1-85 and for the Technician table in Figure 1-86.

Structure of Customer table

FIELD NAME	DATA TYPE	FIELD SIZE	PRIMARY KEY?	DESCRIPTION
Customer Number	Text	4	Yes	Customer Number (Primary Key)
Name	Text	20		Customer Name
Address	Text	15		Street Address
City	Text	15		City
State	Text	2		State (Two-Character Abbreviation)
Zip Code	Text	5		Zip Code (Five-Character Version)
Balance	Currency			Amount Owed by Customer
Technician Number	Text	3		Number of Customer's Technician

Customer table

CUSTOMER NUMBER	NAME	ADDRESS	CITY	STATE	ZIP CODE	BALANCE	TECHNICIAN NUMBER
AT23	Atlas Repair	220 Beard	Kady	TN	42514	$335.00	203
AZ01	AZ Auto	412 Beechwood	Conradt	TN	42547	$300.00	210
BL35	Blanton Shoes	443 Chedder	Kady	TN	42514	$290.00	210
CJ45	C Joe Diner	87 Fletcher	Carlton	TN	52764	$0.00	214
CM90	Cramden Co.	234 Fairlawn	Conradt	TN	42546	$355.00	203
HI25	Hill Crafts	245 Beard	Kady	TN	42514	$334.00	210
KL50	Klean n Dri	378 Stout	Carlton	TN	52764	$365.00	210
MC10	Moss Carpet	109 Fletcher	Carlton	TN	52764	$398.00	203
PV83	Prime Video	734 Lanton	Conradt	TN	42547	$0.00	214
SE05	Servete Mfg Co.	879 Redfern	Kady	TN	42515	$343.00	210

FIGURE 1-85

Apply Your Knowledge

Structure of Technician table

FIELD NAME	DATA TYPE	FIELD SIZE	PRIMARY KEY?	DESCRIPTION
Technician Number	Text	3	Yes	Technician Number (Primary Key)
Last Name	Text	10		Last Name of Technician
First Name	Text	8		First Name of Technician
Address	Text	15		Street Address
City	Text	15		City
State	Text	2		State (Two-Character Abbreviation)
Zip Code	Text	5		Zip Code (Five-Character Version)
Hourly Rate	Currency			Hourly Pay Rate

Technician table

TECHNICIAN NUMBER	LAST NAME	FIRST NAME	ADDRESS	CITY	STATE	ZIP CODE	HOURLY RATE
203	Estevez	Miguel	467 Clay	Kady	TN	42517	$11.50
210	Hillsdale	Rachel	78 Parkton	Conradt	TN	42547	$11.75
214	Liu	Chou	897 North	Carlton	TN	52764	$11.65
220	Short	Chris	111 Maple	Conradt	TN	42547	$11.50

FIGURE 1-86

Instructions: Perform the following tasks:

1. Open the Customer table and change the Technician Number for customer KL50 to 214.
2. Print the Customer table.
3. Use the Simple Query Wizard to create a new query to display and print the customer number, name, and technician number for records in the Customer table as shown in Figure 1-87 on the next page.
4. Save the query as Customer-Technician Query and then close the query.
5. Open the Customer-Technician Query in Design View and restrict the query results to only those customers whose technician number is 210.
6. Print the query but do not save the changes.
7. Create the report shown in Figure 1-88 on the next page for the Customer table.
8. Print the report.

(continued)

Changing Data, Creating Queries, and Creating Reports *(continued)*

Microsoft Access - [Customer-Technician Query :

File   Edit   View   Insert   Format   Records   Tools

Customer Numb	Name	Technician Num
AT23	Atlas Repair	203
AZ01	AZ Auto	210
BL35	Blanton Shoes	210
CJ45	C Joe Diner	214
CM90	Cramden Co.	203
HI25	Hill Crafts	210
KL50	Klean n Dri	214
MC10	Moss Carpet	203
PV83	Prime Video	214
SE05	Servete Mfg Co.	210

FIGURE 1-87

Customer Amount Report

Customer Number	Name	Balance
AT23	Atlas Repair	$335.00
AZ01	AZ Auto	$300.00
BL35	Blanton Shoes	$290.00
CJ45	C Joe Diner	$0.00
CM90	Cramden Co.	$355.00
HI25	Hill Crafts	$334.00
KL50	Klean n Dri	$365.00
MC10	Moss Carpet	$398.00
PV83	Prime Video	$0.00
SE05	Servete Mfg Co.	$343.00

FIGURE 1-88

1 Creating the Birds2U Database

Problem: Birds2U is a new online retailer. The company specializes in products for bird and nature enthusiasts. The database consists of two tables. The Item table contains information on items available for sale. The Supplier table contains information on the companies that supply the items.

Instructions: Perform the following tasks:

1. Create a new database in which to store all the objects related to the items for sale. Call the database Birds2U.
2. Create the Item table using the structure shown in Figure 1-89. Use the name Item for the table.
3. Add the data shown in Figure 1-89 to the Item table.
4. Print the Item table.

Structure of Item table

FIELD NAME	DATA TYPE	FIELD SIZE	PRIMARY KEY?	DESCRIPTION
Item Code	Text	4	Yes	Item Code (Primary Key)
Description	Text	20		Description of Item
On Hand	Number			Number of Units On Hand
Cost	Currency			Cost of Item
Selling Price	Currency			Selling Price of Item
Supplier Code	Text	2		Code of Item's Supplier

Item table

ITEM CODE	DESCRIPTION	ON HAND	COST	SELLING PRICE	SUPPLIER CODE
BA35	Bat House	14	$43.50	$45.50	21
BB01	Bird Bath	2	$82.10	$86.25	13
BE19	Bee Box	7	$39.80	$42.50	21
BL06	Bluebird House	9	$14.35	$15.99	13
BU24	Butterfly Box	6	$36.10	$37.75	21
GF12	Globe Feeder	12	$14.80	$16.25	05
HF01	Hummingbird Feeder	5	$11.35	$14.25	05
PM05	Purple Martin House	3	$67.10	$69.95	13
SF03	Suet Feeder	7	$8.05	$9.95	05
WF10	Window Feeder	10	$14.25	$15.95	05

FIGURE 1-89

5. Create the Supplier table using the structure shown in Figure 1-90 on the next page. Use the name Supplier for the table.
6. Add the data shown in Figure 1-90 to the Supplier table.
7. Print the Supplier table.
8. Create a form for the Supplier table. Use the name Supplier for the form.
9. Open the form you created and change the address for Supplier Code 17 to 56 Beechtree. Print the Supplier table.
10. Create and print the report shown in Figure 1-91 on the next page for the Item table.

(continued)

In the Lab

Creating the Birds2U Database (continued)

Structure of Supplier table

FIELD NAME	DATA TYPE	FIELD SIZE	PRIMARY KEY?	DESCRIPTION
Supplier Code	Text	2	Yes	Supplier Code (Primary Key)
Name	Text	20		Supplier Name
Address	Text	15		Street Address
City	Text	15		City
State	Text	2		State (Two-Character Abbreviation)
Zip Code	Text	5		Zip Code (Five-Character Version)
Telephone Number	Text	12		Telephone Number (999-999-9999 Version)

Supplier table

SUPPLIER CODE	NAME	ADDRESS	CITY	STATE	ZIP CODE	TELEPHONE NUMBER
05	All Birds Supply	234 Southward	Elgin	AZ	85165	602-555-6756
13	Bird Casa Ltd	38 Junction	Grandber	TX	78628	512-555-3402
17	Lawn Fixtures	56 Beecham	Holligan	CA	95418	707-555-4545
21	Natural Woods	67 Main	Ghostman	MI	49301	610-555-3333

FIGURE 1-90

Inventory Report

Item Code	Description	On Hand	Cost
BA35	Bat House	14	$43.50
BB01	Bird Bath	2	$82.10
BE19	Bee Box	7	$39.80
BL06	Bluebird House	9	$14.35
BU24	Butterfly Box	6	$36.10
GF12	Globe Feeder	12	$14.80
HF01	Hummingbird Feeder	5	$11.35
PM05	Purple Martin House	3	$67.10
SF03	Suet Feeder	7	$8.05
WF10	Window Feeder	10	$14.25

FIGURE 1-91

2 Creating the Babbage Bookkeeping Database

Problem: Babbage Bookkeeping is a local company that provides bookkeeping services to several small businesses in the area. The database consists of two tables. The Client table contains information on the businesses that use Babbage's services. The Bookkeeper table contains information on the bookkeeper assigned to the business.

Instructions: Perform the following tasks:

1. Create a new database in which to store all the objects related to the bookkeeping data. Call the database Babbage Bookkeeping.
2. Create and print the Client table using the structure and data shown in Figure 1-92. Then, create and print the Bookkeeper table using the structure and data shown in Figure 1-93 on the next page.

Structure of Client table

FIELD NAME	DATA TYPE	FIELD SIZE	PRIMARY KEY?	DESCRIPTION
Client Number	Text	3	Yes	Client Number (Primary Key)
Name	Text	20		Name of Client
Address	Text	15		Street Address
City	Text	15		City
Zip Code	Text	5		Zip Code (Five-Character Version)
Balance	Currency			Amount Currently Owed for Services
Bookkeeper Number	Text	2		Number of Client's Bookkeeper

Client table

CLIENT NUMBER	NAME	ADDRESS	CITY	ZIP CODE	BALANCE	BOOKKEEPER NUMBER
A54	Afton Mills	612 Revere	Grant City	58120	$315.50	22
A62	Atlas Suppliers	227 Dandelion	Empeer	58216	$525.00	24
B26	Blake-Scripps	557 Maum	Grant City	58120	$229.50	24
D76	Dege Grocery	446 Linton	Portage	59130	$485.75	34
G56	Grand Cleaners	337 Abelard	Empeer	58216	$265.00	22
H21	Hill Shoes	247 Fulton	Grant City	58121	$228.50	24
J77	Jones Plumbing	75 Getty	Portage	59130	$0.00	24
M26	Mohr Crafts	665 Maum	Empeer	58216	$312.50	22
S56	SeeSaw Ind.	31 Liatris	Portage	59130	$362.50	34
T45	Tate Repair	824 Revere	Grant City	58120	$254.00	24

FIGURE 1-92

(continued)

Creating the Babbage Bookkeeping Database *(continued)*

Structure of Bookkeeper table

FIELD NAME	DATA TYPE	FIELD SIZE	PRIMARY KEY?	DESCRIPTION
Bookkeeper Number	Text	2	Yes	Bookkeeper Number (Primary Key)
Last Name	Text	10		Last Name of Bookkeeper
First Name	Text	8		First Name of Bookkeeper
Address	Text	15		Street Address
City	Text	15		City
Zip Code	Text	5		Zip Code (Five-Character Version)
Hourly Rate	Currency			Hourly Rate
YTD Earnings	Currency			Year-to-Date Earnings

Bookkeeper table

BOOKKEEPER NUMBER	LAST NAME	FIRST NAME	ADDRESS	CITY	ZIP CODE	HOURLY RATE	YTD EARNINGS
22	Lewes	Johanna	26 Cotton	Portage	59130	$14.50	$18,245.00
24	Rodriguez	Mario	79 Marsden	Grant City	58120	$13.50	$17,745.50
34	Wong	Choi	263 Topper	Empeer	58216	$14.00	$16,750.25

FIGURE 1-93

3. Change the Bookkeeper Number for client J77 to 34.
4. Use the Simple Query Wizard to create a new query to display and print the Client Number, Name, and Bookkeeper Number for all clients where the bookkeeper number is 34.
5. Create and print the report shown in Figure 1-94 for the Client table.

Balance Due Report

Client Number	Name	Balance
A54	Afton Mills	$315.50
A62	Atlas Suppliers	$525.00
B26	Blake-Scripps	$229.50
D76	Dege Grocery	$485.75
G56	Grand Cleaners	$265.00
H21	Hill Shoes	$228.50
J77	Jones Plumbing	$0.00
M26	Mohr Crafts	$312.50
S56	SeeSaw Ind.	$362.50
T45	Tate Repair	$254.00

FIGURE 1-94

In the Lab

3 Creating the City Guide Database

Problem: The local chamber of commerce publishes a guide for newcomers. To help finance the guide, the chamber includes advertisements from local businesses. Advertising representatives receive a commission based on the advertising revenues they generate. The database consists of two tables. The Advertiser table contains information on the businesses that advertise in the guide. The Ad Rep table contains information on the advertising representative assigned to the account.

Instructions Part 1: Using the data shown in Figures 1-95 and 1-96 on the next page create the City Guide database, the Advertiser table, and the Ad Rep table. Note that the Ad Rep table uses the number data type. Print the tables. Then, create a form for the Advertiser table.

Structure of Advertiser table

FIELD NAME	DATA TYPE	FIELD SIZE	PRIMARY KEY?	DESCRIPTION
Advertiser Number	Text	4	Yes	Advertiser Number (Primary Key)
Name	Text	20		Name of Advertiser
Address	Text	15		Street Address
Zip Code	Text	5		Zip Code (Five-Character Version)
Telephone Number	Text	8		Telephone Number (999-9999 Version)
Balance	Currency			Amount Currently Owed
Amount Paid	Currency			Amount Paid Year-to-Date
Ad Rep Number	Text	2		Number of Advertising Representative

Data for Advertiser table

ADVERTISER NUMBER	NAME	ADDRESS	ZIP CODE	TELEPHONE NUMBER	BALANCE	AMOUNT PAID	AD REP NUMBER
A228	Adam's Music	47 Berton	19363	555-0909	$90.00	$565.00	26
B103	Barbecue Joint	483 Cantor	19363	555-8990	$185.00	$825.00	29
C048	Chloe's Salon	10 Main	19362	555-2334	$0.00	$375.00	29
C135	Creative Toys	26 Jefferson	19362	555-1357	$130.00	$865.00	32
D217	Dog Groomers	33 Maple	19362	555-2468	$290.00	$515.00	26
G346	Gold's Clothes	196 Lincoln	19364	555-3579	$0.00	$805.00	29
M321	Meat Shoppe	234 Magnolia	19363	555-6802	$215.00	$845.00	29
P124	Palace Theatre	22 Main	19364	555-8024	$65.00	$180.00	26
S111	Suds n Spuds	10 Jefferson	19365	555-5791	$465.00	$530.00	32
W456	Western Wear	345 Oaktree	19363	555-7913	$105.00	$265.00	26

FIGURE 1-95

(continued)

Creating the City Guide Database *(continued)*

Structure for Ad Rep table

FIELD NAME	DATA TYPE	FIELD SIZE	PRIMARY KEY?	DESCRIPTION
Ad Rep Number	Text	2	Yes	Advertising Rep Number (Primary Key)
Last Name	Text	10		Last Name of Advertising Rep
First Name	Text	8		First Name of Advertising Rep
Address	Text	15		Street Address
City	Text	15		City
Zip Code	Text	5		Zip Code (Five-Character Version)
Comm Rate	Number	Double		Commission Rate on Advertising Sales
Commission	Currency			Year-to-Date Total Commissions

Data for Ad Rep table

AD REP NUMBER	LAST NAME	FIRST NAME	ADDRESS	CITY	ZIP CODE	COMM RATE	COMMISSION
26	Febo	Jen	57 Barton	Crescent	19111	0.09	$6,500.00
29	Martinson	Kyle	87 Pearl	Newton	19124	0.08	$6,250.00
32	Rogers	Elena	45 Magret	San Luis	19362	0.09	$7,000.00

FIGURE 1-96

Instructions Part 2: Correct the following error. The ad rep assigned to the Meat Shoppe account should be Elena Rogers. Use the form you created to make the correction, and then print the form showing the corrected record. To print the form, open the form, click File on the menu bar, and then click Print. Click Selected Records(s) as the Print Range. Click the OK button.

Instructions Part 3: Create a query to find which accounts Jen Febo represents. Print the results. Prepare an advertiser status report that lists the advertiser's number, name, balance currently owed, and amount paid to date.

Cases and Places

The difficulty of these case studies varies:
▪ are the least difficult and ▪▪ are more difficult. The last exercise is a group exercise.

1 ▪ To help finance your college education, you formed a small business. You provide dog-walking services to local residents. Dog walkers are paid by the walk for each dog they walk. The business has grown rapidly and you now have several other students working for you. You realize that you need to computerize your business.

Design and create a database to store the data that College Dog Walkers needs to manage its business. Then create the necessary tables and enter the data from the Case 1-1 College Dog Walkers Word document on the Data Files for Students. Print the tables. See the inside back cover of this book for instructions for downloading the Data Files for Students or see your instructor for information on accessing the files required in this book.

2 ▪ The Health and Physical Education department at your college recognized early that personal training would be a growth field. One of your friends graduated from the program and has started a company, InPerson Fitness Company. The company specializes in personal training in the comfort of the customer's home. It designs exercise programs for clients based on each person's health history, abilities, and fitness objectives. The company is expanding rapidly and you have been hired to computerize the business.

Design and create a database to store the data that InPerson Fitness needs to manage its business. Then create the necessary tables and enter the data from the Case 1-2 InPerson Fitness Word document on the Data Files for Students. Print the tables. See the inside back cover of this book for instructions for downloading the Data Files for Students or see your instructor for information on accessing the files required in this book.

3 ▪▪ Regional Books is a local bookstore that specializes in books that are of local interest. These are books that are set in the region or are written by authors who live in the area. The owner has asked you to create and update a database that she can use to keep track of the books she has in stock.

Design and create a database to store the book data. To create the Books table, use the Table Wizard and select the Books table. You do not need to select all the fields the Table Wizard provides and you can rename the fields in the table. (*Hint*: See More About Creating a Table: The Table Wizard on page AC 15.) Enter the data from the Case 1-3 Regional Books Word document on the Data Files for Students. Print the tables. Prepare a sample query and a sample report to illustrate to the owner the types of tasks that can be done with a database management system. See the inside back cover of this book for instructions for downloading the Data Files for Students or see your instructor for information on accessing the files required in this book.

Cases and Places

4 ■■ The Campus Housing office at the local university provides a listing of available off-campus rentals by private owners. The office would like to make this listing available on the campus Web site. The administrator has asked you to create and update a database that can store information about available off-campus housing. The housing list is in the Case 1-4 Campus Housing Word document on the Data Files for Students. A listing that has 0 bedrooms is either an efficiency apartment or a room for rent in a home. Distance indicates the rental unit's distance in miles from the university. Parking signifies whether reserved parking is available with the unit.

Design and create a database to meet the needs of the Campus Housing office. Then create the necessary tables, enter the data from the Case 1-4 Campus Housing Word document on the Data Files for Students. Print the tables. Prepare a sample form, sample query, and sample report to illustrate to the office the types of tasks that can be done with a database management system. See the inside back cover of this book for instructions for downloading the Data Files for Students or see your instructor for information on accessing the files required in this book.

5 ■■ **Working Together** Conducting a job search requires careful preparation. In addition to preparing a resume and cover letter, you will need to research the companies for which you are interested in working and contact these companies to let them know of your interest and qualifications. Microsoft Access can help you manage the job search process. The Database Wizard includes a Contact Management template that can create a database that will help you keep track of your job contacts.

Have each member of your team explore the features of the Database Wizard and determine individually which fields should be included in a Contact Management database. As a group, review your choices and decide on one common design. Prepare a short paper for your instructor that explains why your team chose those particular fields to include in the database.

After agreeing on the database design, assign one member to create the database using the Database Wizard. Every other team member should research a company and add the data to the database. Print the alphabetical contact listing that the Database Wizard creates. Turn in the short paper and the report to your instructor.

Querying a Database Using the Select Query Window

PROJECT

2

CASE PERSPECTIVE

Dr. Gernaey and his colleagues are eager for Ashton James College (AJC) to obtain the benefits they anticipated when they set up the database of client and trainer data. One immediate benefit they expect is the capability of easily asking questions such as the following concerning the data in the database and rapidly getting the answers.

1. What are the name, the amount paid, and the current due of client CP27?

2. Which clients' names begin with Fa?

3. Which clients are located in Lake Hammond?

4. Which clients have a current due of $0.00?

5. Which clients have an amount paid that is more than $20,000.00?

6. Which clients of trainer 48 have an amount paid that is more than $20,000.00?

7. In what cities are all the clients located?

8. How many hours has each trainer worked so far this year?

9. What is the client number and name of each client, and what is the number and name of the trainer to whom each client is assigned?

AJC needs to find information about clients located in a specific city, but they want to enter a different city each time they ask the question. A parameter query would enable this. They also have a special way they want to summarize their data and a crosstab query will present the data in the desired form.

Your task is to assist the administration of AJC in obtaining answers to these and other questions using Access query features.

As you read through this project, you will learn how to query a database and use the Select Query window.

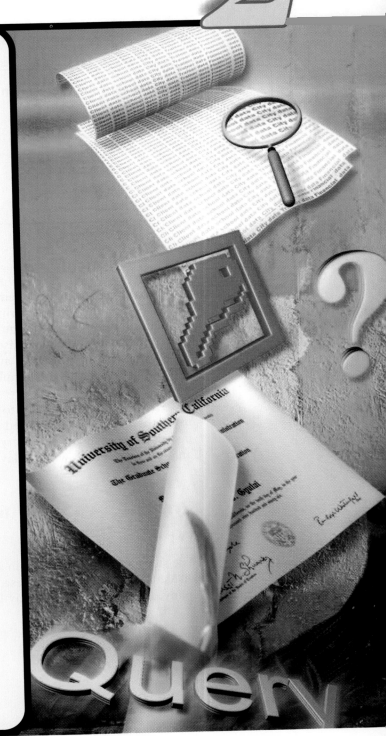

Query

MICROSOFT OFFICE
Access 2003

Querying a Database Using the Select Query Window

Objectives:

You will have mastered the material in this project when you can:

- Create and run queries
- Print query results
- Include fields in the design grid
- Use text and numeric data in criteria
- Create and use parameter queries
- Save a query and use the saved query

- Use compound criteria in queries
- Sort data in queries
- Join tables in queries
- Perform calculations in queries
- Use grouping in queries
- Create crosstab queries

Introduction

A database management system such as Access offers many useful features, among them the capability of answering questions such as those posed by the administration of Ashton James College (Figure 2-1). The answers to these questions, and many more, are found in the database, and Access can find the answers quickly. When you pose a question to Access, or any other database management system, the question is called a query. A **query** is simply a question represented in a way that Access can understand.

Thus, to find the answer to a question, you first create a corresponding query using the techniques illustrated in this project. After you have created the query, you instruct Access to run the query; that is, to perform the steps necessary to obtain the answer. Access then will display the answer in Datasheet view.

Project Two — Querying the Ashton James College Database

The steps in this project obtain answers to the questions posed by the administration of Ashton James College. These include the questions shown in Figure 2-1, as well as many other questions that may be deemed important.

What are the name, the amount paid, and the current due for client CP27?

Which clients' names begin with Fa?

In what cities are all the clients located?

Which clients are located in Lake Hammond?

Which clients of trainer 48 have an amount paid that is more than $20,000.00?

Client table

CLIENT NUMBER	NAME	ADDRESS	CITY	STATE	ZIP CODE	AMOUNT PAID	CURRENT DUE	TRAINER NUMBER
BS27	Blant and Sons	4806 Park	Lake Hammond	TX	76653	$21,876.00	$892.50	42
CE16	Center Services	725 Mitchell	San Julio	TX	78364	$26,512.00	$2,672.00	48
CP27	Calder Plastics	7300 Cedar	Lake Hammond	TX	76653	$8,725.00	$0.00	48
EU28	Elba's Furniture	1445 Hubert	Tallmadge	TX	77231	$4,256.00	$1,202.00	53
FI28	Farrow-Idsen	829 Wooster	Cedar Ridge	TX	79342	$8,287.50	$925.50	42
FL93	Fairland Lawn	143 Pangborn	Lake Hammond	TX	76653	$21,625.00	$0.00	48
HN83	Hurley National	3827 Burgess	Tallmadge	TX	77231	$0.00	$0.00	48
MC28	Morgan-Alyssa	923 Williams	Crumville	TX	76745	$24,761.00	$1,572.00	42
PS82	PRIM Staffing	72 Crestview	San Julio	TX	78364	$11,682.25	$2,827.50	53
TE26	Telton-Edwards	5672 Anderson	Dunston	TX	77893	$8,521.50	$0.00	48

CLIENT NUMBER	NAME	AMOUNT PAID	CURRENT DUE
FI28	Farrow-Idsen	$8,287.50	$925.50
FL93	Fairland Lawn	$21,625.00	$0.00

CLIENT NUMBER	NAME	ADDRESS
BS27	Blant and Sons	4806 Park
CP27	Calder Plastics	7300 Cedar
FL93	Fairland Lawn	143 Pangborn

CLIENT NUMBER	NAME	AMOUNT PAID	CURRENT DUE
CP27	Calder Plastics	$8,725.00	$0.00

CITY
Cedar Ridge
Crumville
Dunston
Lake Hammond
Tallmadge

CLIENT NUMBER	NAME	AMOUNT PAID	CURRENT DUE	TRAINER NUMBER
CE16	Center Services	$26,512.00	$2,672.00	48
FL93	Fairland Lawn	$21,625.00	$0.00	48

FIGURE 2-1

Opening the Database

If you are stepping through this project on a computer, and you want your screen to agree with the figures in this book, then you should change your computer's resolution to 800 × 600. For more information on how to change the resolution on your computer, see Appendix D. Before creating queries, first you must open the database. The following steps summarize the procedure to complete this task, once you have started Access.

To Open a Database

1 Click the Open button on the Database toolbar.

2 If necessary, click the Look in box arrow and then click UDISK 2.0 (E:). (Your USB flash drive may have a different name and letter.) Click Ashton James College, the database created in Project 1. (If you did not complete the steps in Project 1, see your instructor for a copy of the database.)

3 Click the Open button in the Open dialog box. If a Security Warning dialog box appears, click the Open button.

The database opens and the Ashton James College : Database window appears.

Creating and Running Queries

You create a query by making entries in a special window called a **Select Query window**. Once the database is open, the first step in creating a query is to select the table for which you are creating a query in the Database window. Then, you use the New Object button to design the new query in the Select Query window. It typically is easier to work with the Select Query window if it is maximized. Thus, as a standard practice, maximize the Select Query window as soon as you have created it. In addition, it often is useful to resize both panes within the window. This enables you to resize the field list that appears in the upper pane so more fields appear.

The following steps initiate creating a query.

To Create a Query

1

• **Be sure the Ashton James College database is open, the Tables object is selected, and the Client table is selected.**

• **Click the New Object button arrow on the Database toolbar.**

The list of available objects appears (Figure 2-2).

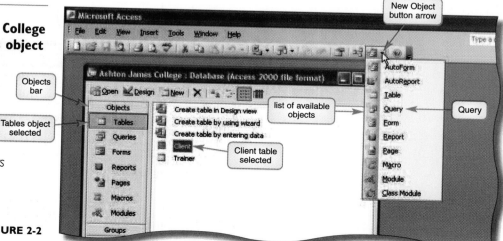

FIGURE 2-2

2

• **Click Query.**

Access displays the New Query dialog box (Figure 2-3).

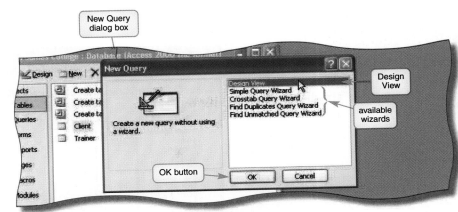

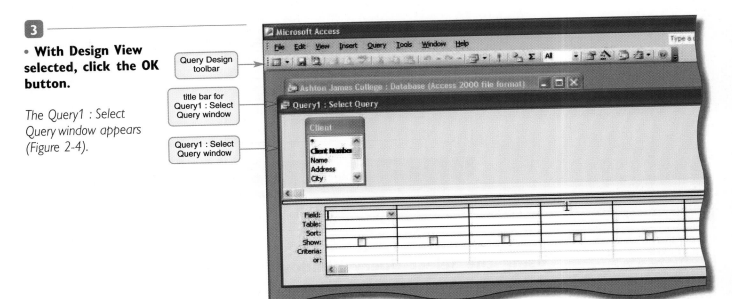

FIGURE 2-3

3

• **With Design View selected, click the OK button.**

The Query1 : Select Query window appears (Figure 2-4).

FIGURE 2-4

4

• **Maximize the Query1 : Select Query window by double-clicking its title bar, and then drag the line separating the two panes to the approximate position shown in Figure 2-5.**

The Query1 : Select Query window is maximized. The upper pane contains a field list for the Client table. The lower pane contains the design grid, which is the area where you specify fields to be included, sort order, and the criteria the records you are looking for must satisfy. The mouse pointer shape indicates you can drag the line.

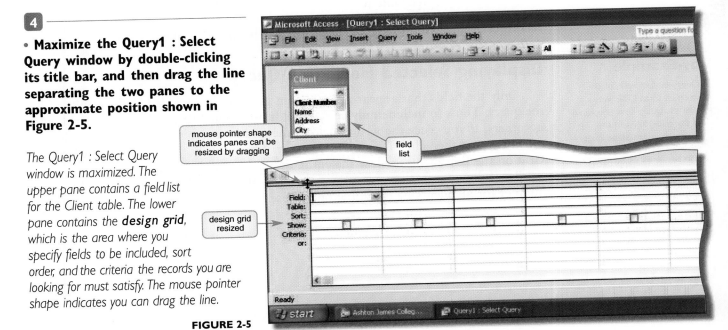

FIGURE 2-5

5

• Drag the lower edge of the field box down far enough so all fields in the Client table are displayed (Figure 2-6).

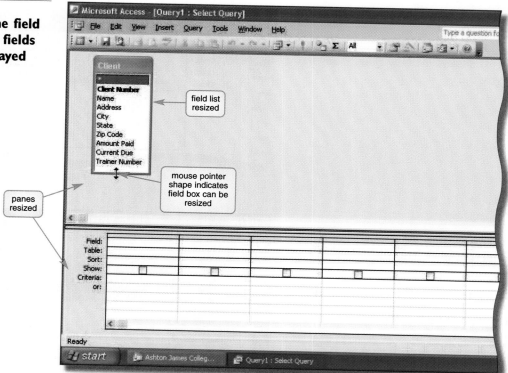

FIGURE 2-6

Using the Select Query Window

Once you have created a new Select Query window, you are ready to create the actual query by making entries in the design grid in the lower pane of the window. You enter the names of the fields you want included in the Field row in the grid. You also can enter criteria, such as the fact that the client number must be a specific number, such as CP27, in the Criteria row of the grid. When you do so, only the record or records that match the criterion will be included in the answer.

Displaying Selected Fields in a Query

Only the fields that appear in the design grid will be included in the results of the query. Thus, to include only certain fields, place only these fields in the grid, and no others. If you place the wrong field in the grid inadvertently, click Edit on the menu bar and then click Delete to remove it. Alternatively, you could click Clear Grid on the Edit menu to clear the entire design grid and then start over.

The following step creates a query to show the client number, name, and trainer number for all clients by including only those fields in the design grid.

To Include Fields in the Design Grid

1

- **If necessary, maximize the Query1 : Select Query window containing the field list for the Client table in the upper pane of the window and an empty design grid in the lower pane.**

- **Double-click the Client Number field in the field list to include it in the query.**

- **Double-click the Name field to include it in the query, and then double-click the Trainer Number field to include it as well.**

The Client Number, Name, and Trainer Number fields are included in the query (Figure 2-7).

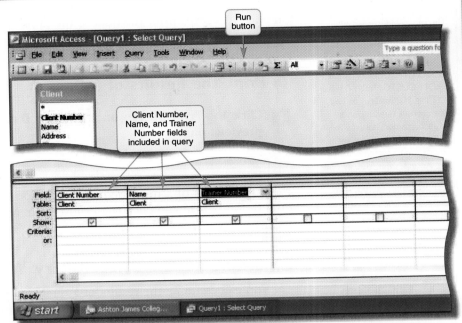

FIGURE 2-7

Other Ways

1. Drag field from field list to design grid
2. Click column in grid, click arrow, click field name

Running a Query

Once you have created the query, you run the query to produce the results using the Run button on the Query Design toolbar. Access performs the steps necessary to obtain and display the answer. The set of records that makes up the answer will be displayed in Datasheet view. Although it looks like a table that is stored on your disk, it really is not. The records are constructed from data in the existing Client table. If you were to change the data in the Client table and then rerun this same query, the results would reflect the changes. The following step runs the query.

To Run the Query

1

- **Click the Run button on the Query Design toolbar (see Figure 2-7).**

The query is executed and the results appear (Figure 2-8).

Other Ways

1. On Query menu click Run
2. In Voice Command mode, say "Run"

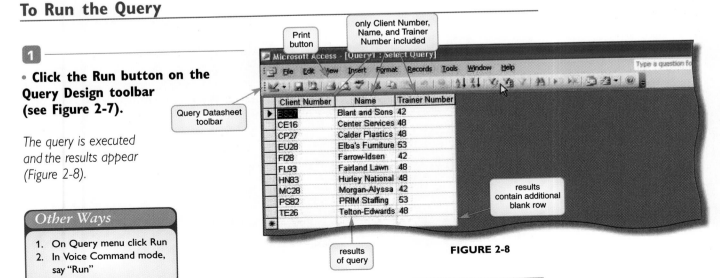

FIGURE 2-8

Printing the Results of a Query

To print the results of a query, use the same techniques you learned in Project 1 on page AC 29 to print the data in the table. The following step prints the current query results.

To Print the Results of a Query

1 **Click the Print button on the Query Datasheet toolbar (see Figure 2-8 on the previous page).**

The results print.

If the results of a query require landscape orientation, switch to landscape orientation before you click the Print button as indicated in Project 1 on page AC 31.

Returning to the Select Query Window

You can examine the results of a query on your screen to see the answer to your question. You can scroll through the records, if necessary, just as you scroll through the records of any other table. You also can print a copy of the table. In any case, once you are finished working with the results, you can return to the Select Query window to ask another question. The following steps illustrate how to return to the Select Query window.

To Return to the Select Query Window

1

• **Click the View button arrow on the Query Datasheet toolbar.**

The Query View list appears (Figure 2-9).

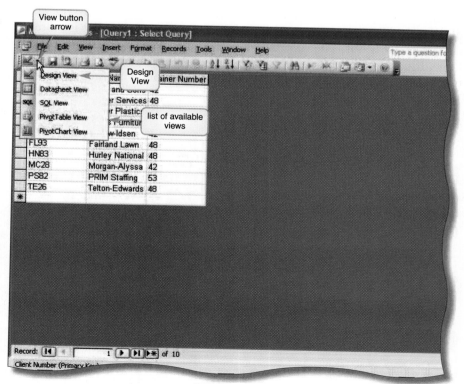

FIGURE 2-9

2

• **Click Design View.**

The Query1 : Select Query window is redisplayed (Figure 2-10).

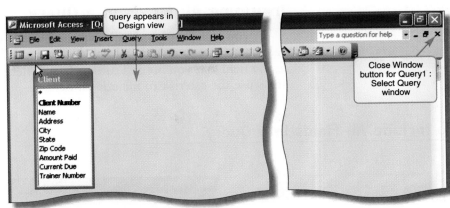

FIGURE 2-10

Other Ways

1. On View menu click Design View
2. In Voice Command mode, say "View, Design View"

Notice that the icon on the View button is the Design View icon. This indicates that the next time you want to display the window in Design view, you need only click the View button.

Closing a Query

To close a query, close the Select Query window. When you do so, Access displays the Microsoft Office Access dialog box asking if you want to save your query for future use. If you think you will need to create the same exact query often, you should save the query. For now, you will not save any queries. You will see how to save them later in the project. The following steps close a query without saving it.

To Close the Query

1

• **Click the Close Window button for the Query1 : Select Query window (see Figure 2-10).**

Access displays the Microsoft Office Access dialog box (Figure 2-11). Clicking the Yes button saves the query and clicking the No button closes the query without saving.

2

• **Click the No button in the Microsoft Office Access dialog box.**

The Query1 : Select Query window closes. The query is not saved.

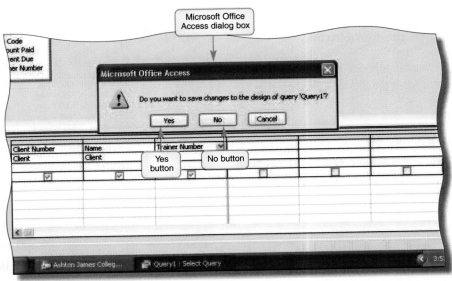

FIGURE 2-11

Other Ways

1. On File menu click Close
2. In Voice Command mode, say "File, Close"

Including All Fields in a Query

If you want to include all fields in a query, you could select each field individually. A simpler way to include all fields is available, however. By selecting the asterisk (*) in the field list, you are indicating that all fields are to be included. The following steps use the asterisk to include all fields.

To Include All Fields in a Query

* **Be sure you have a maximized Query1 : Select Query window with resized upper and lower panes, an expanded field list for the Client table in the upper pane, and an empty design grid in the lower pane. (See Steps 1 through 5 on pages AC 68 through AC 70 to create the query and resize the window.)**

* **Double-click the asterisk at the top of the field list.**

The maximized Query1 : Select Query window displays two resized panes. The table name, Client, followed by a period and an asterisk is added to the design grid, indicating all fields are included (Figure 2-12).

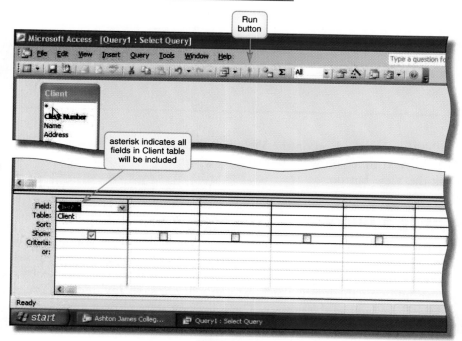

FIGURE 2-12

* **Click the Run button.**

The results appear and all fields in the Client table are included (Figure 2-13).

* **Click the View button on the Query Datasheet toolbar to return to the Query1 : Select Query window.**

The Query1 : Select Query window replaces the datasheet.

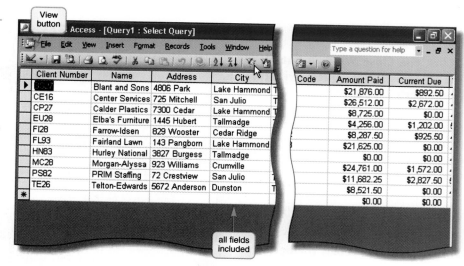

FIGURE 2-13

Other Ways

1. Drag asterisk from field list to design grid
2. Click column in grid, click arrow, click Client.*

Clearing the Design Grid

If you make mistakes as you are creating a query, you can fix each one individually. Alternatively, you simply may want to clear the query; that is, clear out the entries in the design grid and start over. One way to clear out the entries is to close the Select Query window and then start a new query just as you did earlier. A simpler approach, however, is to use the Clear Grid command on the Edit menu. The following steps clear the design grid.

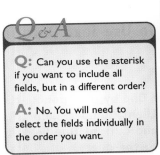

Q: Can you use the asterisk if you want to include all fields, but in a different order?

A: No. You will need to select the fields individually in the order you want.

To Clear the Design Grid

 1

- **Click Edit on the menu bar.**

The Edit menu appears (Figure 2-14).

 2

- **Click Clear Grid.**

Access clears the design grid so you can enter your next query.

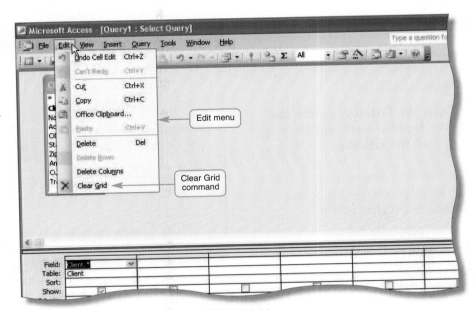

FIGURE 2-14

Entering Criteria

When you use queries, usually you are looking for those records that satisfy some criterion. You might want the name, amount paid, and current due amounts of the client whose number is CP27, for example, or of those clients whose names start with the letters, Fa. To enter criteria, enter them in the Criteria row in the design grid below the field name to which the criterion applies. For example, to indicate that the client number must be CP27, you first must add the Client Number field to the design grid. You then would type CP27 in the Criteria row below the Client Number field.

The next examples illustrate the types of criteria that are available.

Using Text Data in Criteria

To use **text data** (data in a field whose data type is Text) in criteria, simply type the text in the Criteria row below the corresponding field name. The steps on the next page query the Client table and display the client number, name, amount paid, and current due amount of client CP27.

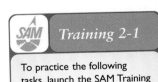

Training 2-1

To practice the following tasks, launch the SAM Training Companion CD, choose Access Project 2, and then choose Training 2-1:
- Clear a query
- Resize panes and field list in Query Design view

To Use Text Data in a Criterion

1

• **One by one, double-click the Client Number, Name, Amount Paid, and Current Due fields to add them to the query.**

The Client Number, Name, Amount Paid, and Current Due fields are added to the design grid (Figure 2-15).

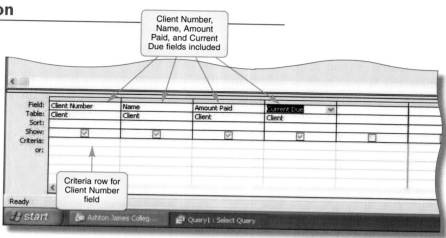

Client Number, Name, Amount Paid, and Current Due fields included

Criteria row for Client Number field

FIGURE 2-15

2

• **Click the Criteria row for the Client Number field and then type** CP27 **as the criterion.**

The criterion is entered (Figure 2-16). When the mouse pointer is in the Criteria box, its shape changes to an I-beam.

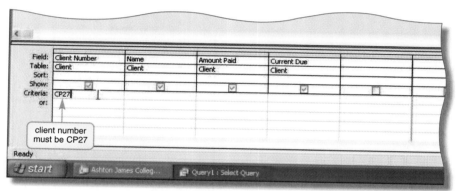

client number must be CP27

FIGURE 2-16

3

• **Click the Run button to run the query.**

The results appear (Figure 2-17). Only client CP27 is included. (The extra blank row contains $0.00 in the Amount Paid and Current Due fields. Unlike text fields, which are left blank, number and currency fields in the extra row contain 0. Because the Amount Paid and Current Due fields are currency fields, the values are displayed as $0.00.)

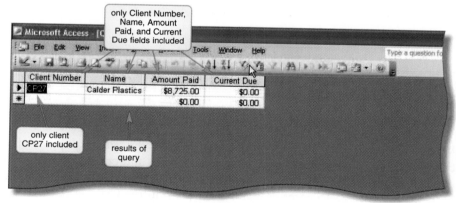

only Client Number, Name, Amount Paid, and Current Due fields included

only client CP27 included

results of query

FIGURE 2-17

Using Wildcards

Two special wildcards are available in Microsoft Access. **Wildcards** are symbols that represent any character or combination of characters. The first of the two wildcards, the **asterisk** (*), represents any collection of characters. Thus Fa* represents the letters, Fa, followed by any collection of characters. The other wildcard symbol is the **question mark** (?), which represents any individual character. Thus t?m represents the letter, T, followed by any single character followed by the letter, m, such as Tim or Tom.

The following steps use a wildcard to find the number, name, and address of those clients whose names begin with Fa. Because you do not know how many characters will follow the Fa, the asterisk is appropriate.

To Use a Wildcard

1

- **Click the View button on the Query Datasheet toolbar to return to the Query1 : Select Query window.**
- **If necessary, click the Criteria row below the Client Number field.**
- **Use the DELETE or BACKSPACE key as necessary to delete the current entry (CP27).**
- **Click the Criteria row below the Name field.**
- **Type Fa* as the criterion.**

The criterion is entered (Figure 2-18).

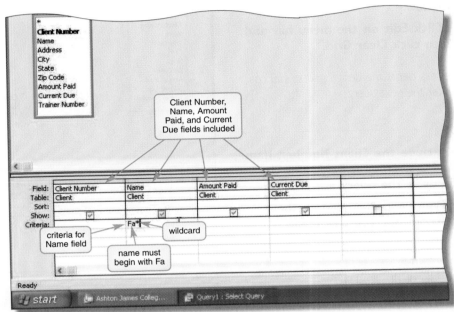

FIGURE 2-18

2

- **Click the Run button to run the query.**
- **If instructed to do so, print the results by clicking the Print button on the Query Datasheet toolbar.**

The results appear (Figure 2-19). Only the clients whose names start with Fa are included.

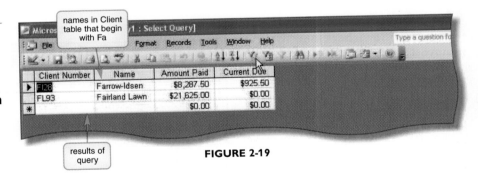

FIGURE 2-19

Criteria for a Field Not in the Result

In some cases, you may have criteria for a particular field that should not appear in the results of the query. For example, you may want to see the client number, name, address, and amount paid for all clients located in Lake Hammond. The criteria involve the City field, which is not one of the fields to be included in the results.

To enter a criterion for the City field, it must be included in the design grid. Normally, this also would mean it would appear in the results. To prevent this from happening, remove the check mark from its Show check box in the Show row of the grid. The steps on the next page illustrate the process by displaying the client number, name, and amount paid for clients located in Lake Hammond.

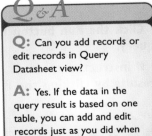

Q: Can you add records or edit records in Query Datasheet view?

A: Yes. If the data in the query result is based on one table, you can add and edit records just as you did when the table was displayed in Table Datasheet view.

To Use Criteria for a Field Not Included in the Results

1

• **Click the View button on the Query Datasheet toolbar to return to the Query1 : Select Query window.**

• **Click Edit on the menu bar and then click Clear Grid.**

Access clears the design grid so you can enter the next query.

2

• **Include the Client Number, Name, Address, Amount Paid, and City fields in the query.**

• **Type** Lake Hammond **as the criterion for the City field.**

The fields are included in the grid, and the criterion for the City field is entered (Figure 2-20).

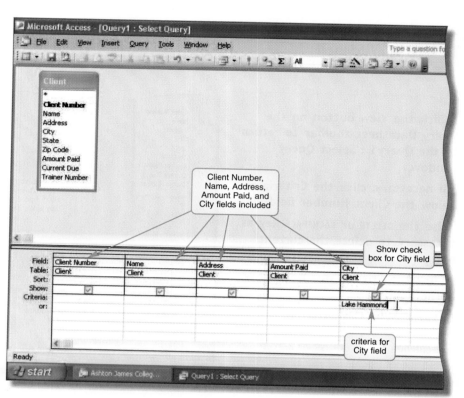

FIGURE 2-20

3

• **Click the Show check box to remove the check mark.**

The check mark is removed from the Show check box for the City field (Figure 2-21), indicating it will not show in the result. Because the City field is a text field, Access has added quotation marks before and after Lake Hammond automatically.

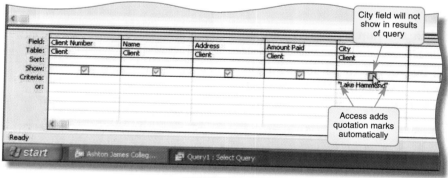

FIGURE 2-21

4

• **Click the Run button to run the query.**

• **If instructed to do so, print the results by clicking the Print button.**

The results appear (Figure 2-22). The City field does not appear. The only clients included are those located in Lake Hammond.

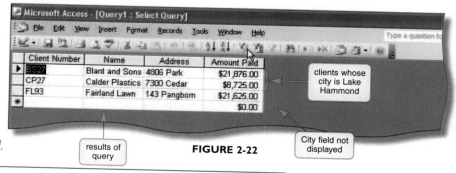

FIGURE 2-22

Creating a Parameter Query

Rather than giving a specific criterion when you first create the query, on occasion, you may want to be able to enter part of the criterion when you run the query and then have the appropriate results appear. For example, to include all the clients located in Tallmadge, you could enter Tallmadge as a criterion in the City field. From that point on, every time you ran the query, only the clients in Tallmadge would appear.

A better way is to allow the user to enter the city at the time the query is run. Thus a user could run the query, enter Tallmadge as the city and then see all the clients in Tallmadge. Later, the user could run the same query, but enter Lake Hammond as the city, and then see all the clients in Lake Hammond. To do this, you create a **parameter query**, which is a query that prompts for input whenever it is run. You enter a parameter, rather than a specific value as the criterion. You create one by enclosing a value in a criterion in square brackets. It is important that the value in the brackets does not match the name of any field. If you enter a field name in square brackets, Access assumes you want that particular field and will not prompt the user for input. For example, you could place [Enter City] as the criterion in the City field.

The following steps create a parameter query that will prompt the user to enter a city, and then display the client number, name, address, and amount paid for all clients located in that city.

To Create and Run a Parameter Query

1

- **Click the View button on the Query Datasheet toolbar to return to the Query1 : Select Query window.**

- **Erase the current criterion in the City column, and then type [Enter City] as the new criterion.**

The criterion is entered (Figure 2-23).

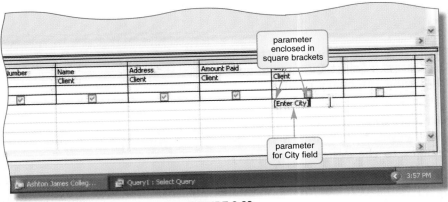

FIGURE 2-23

2

- **Click the Run button to run the query.**

Access displays the Enter Parameter Value dialog box (Figure 2-24). The value (Enter City) previously entered in brackets appears in the dialog box.

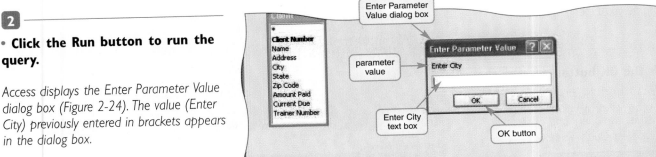

FIGURE 2-24

3

• **Type** Tallmadge **in the Enter City text box and then click the OK button.**

The results appear (Figure 2-25). Only clients whose city is Tallmadge are included. The city name is not displayed in the results.

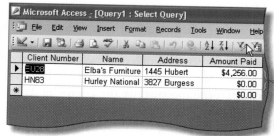
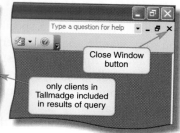

Close Window button

only clients in Tallmadge included in results of query

FIGURE 2-25

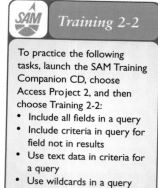

Training 2-2

To practice the following tasks, launch the SAM Training Companion CD, choose Access Project 2, and then choose Training 2-2:
• Include all fields in a query
• Include criteria in query for field not in results
• Use text data in criteria for a query
• Use wildcards in a query

Each time you run this query, you will be asked to enter a city. Only clients in the city you enter will be included in the results.

Saving a Query

In many cases, you will construct a query you will want to use again. By saving the query, you will eliminate the need to repeat all your entries. The following steps illustrate the process by saving the query you just have created and assigning it the name Client-City Query. You can save with either the query design or the query results appearing on the screen.

To Save a Query

1

• **Click the Close Window button for the Query1 : Select Query window containing the query results.**

• **Click the Yes button in the Microsoft Office Access dialog box when asked if you want to save the changes to the design of the query.**

• **Type** Client-City Query **in the Query Name text box.**

The Save As dialog box appears with the query name you typed (Figure 2-26).

2

• **Click the OK button to save the query.**

Access saves the query and closes the Query1 : Select Query window.

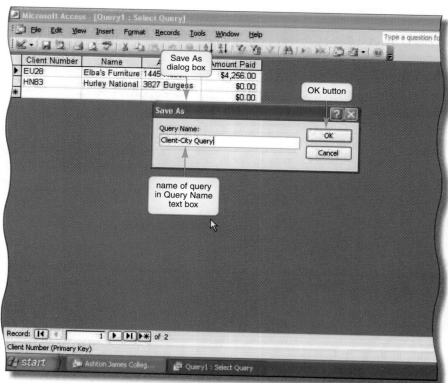

Save As dialog box

OK button

name of query in Query Name text box

FIGURE 2-26

Using a Saved Query

Once you have saved a query, you can use and manipulate it at any time in the future by opening it. When you right-click the query in the Database window, Access displays a shortcut menu containing commands that allow you to open, print, and change the design of the query. You also can print the results by clicking the Print button on the toolbar. If you want to print the query results without first opening the query, you would click Print on the shortcut menu.

The query is run against the current database. Thus, if changes have been made to the data since the last time you ran it, the results of the query may be different. The following steps use the query named Client-City Query.

More About

Saved Queries

Forms and reports can be based on either tables or saved queries. To create a report or form based on a query, click the Query tab, select the query, click the New Object button arrow, and then click the appropriate command (Report or Form). From that point on, the process is the same as for a table.

To Use a Saved Query

1

• **Click Queries on the Objects bar, and then right-click Client-City Query.**

The shortcut menu for Client-City Query appears (Figure 2-27).

2

• **Click Open on the shortcut menu, type** Tallmadge **in the Enter City text box, and then click the OK button.**

The results appear. They look like the results shown in Figure 2-25.

3

• **Click the Close Window button for the Client-City Query : Select Query window containing the query results.**

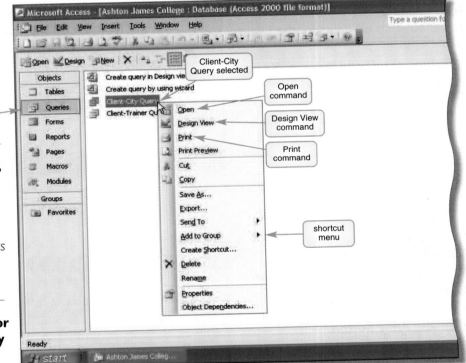

FIGURE 2-27

You can use the query at any time by following the above steps. Each time you do so, you will be prompted to enter a city. Only the clients in that city will be displayed in the results.

Using Numeric Data in Criteria

To enter a number in a criterion, type the number without any dollar signs or commas. The steps on the next page display all clients whose current due amount is $0.00.

To Use a Number in a Criterion

1

- Click the Tables object on the Objects bar and ensure the Client table is selected.

- Click the New Object button arrow on the Database toolbar, click Query, and then click the OK button in the New Query dialog box.

- Drag the line separating the two panes to the approximate position shown in Figure 2-28, and drag the lower edge of the field box down far enough so all fields in the Client table appear.

- Include the Client Number, Name, Amount Paid, and Current Due fields in the query.

- Type 0 as the criterion for the Current Due field. You should not enter a dollar sign or decimal point in the criterion.

The fields are selected and the criterion is entered (Figure 2-28).

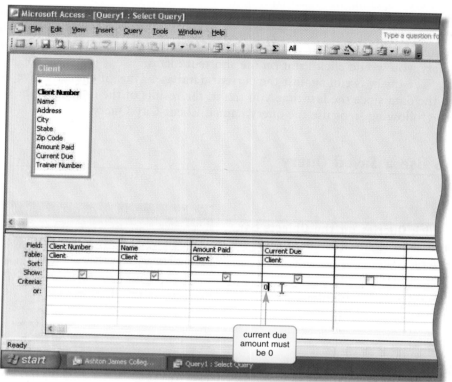

FIGURE 2-28

2

- Click the Run button to run the query.

- If instructed to print the results, click the Print button.

The results appear (Figure 2-29). Only those clients that have a current due amount of $0.00 are included.

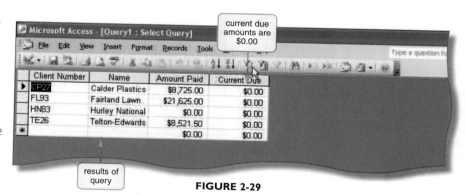

FIGURE 2-29

Using Comparison Operators

Unless you specify otherwise, Access assumes that the criteria you enter involve equality (exact matches). In the last query, for example, you were requesting those clients whose current due amount is equal to 0 (zero). If you want something other than an exact match, you must enter the appropriate **comparison operator**. The comparison operators are > (greater than), < (less than), >= (greater than or equal to), <= (less than or equal to), and NOT (not equal to).

The following steps use the > operator to find all clients whose amount paid is more than $20,000.00.

To Use a Comparison Operator in a Criterion

 1

• **Click the View button on the Query Datasheet toolbar to return to the Query1 : Select Query window.**

• **Erase the 0 in the Current Due column.**

• **Type >20000 as the criterion for the Amount Paid field. Remember that you should not enter a dollar sign, a comma, or decimal point in the criterion.**

The fields are selected and the criterion is entered (Figure 2-30).

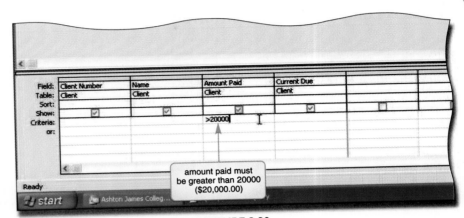

amount paid must be greater than 20000 ($20,000.00)

FIGURE 2-30

2

• **Click the Run button to run the query.**

• **If instructed to print the results, click the Print button.**

The results appear (Figure 2-31). Only those clients who have an amount paid greater than $20,000.00 are included.

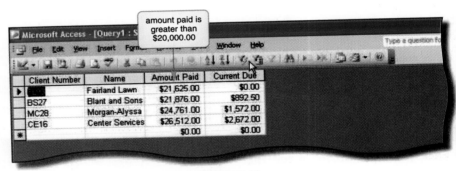

amount paid is greater than $20,000.00

FIGURE 2-31

Using Compound Criteria

Often you will have more than one criterion that the data for which you are searching must satisfy. This type of criterion is called a **compound criterion**. Two types of compound criteria exist.

In an **AND criterion**, each individual criterion must be true in order for the compound criterion to be true. For example, an AND criterion would allow you to find those clients that have an amount paid greater than $20,000.00 and whose trainer is trainer 48.

Conversely, an **OR criterion** is true provided either individual criterion is true. An OR criterion would allow you to find those clients that have an amount paid greater than $20,000.00 or whose trainer is trainer 48. In this case, any client whose amount paid is greater than $20,000.00 would be included in the answer whether or not the client's trainer is trainer 48. Likewise, any client whose trainer is trainer 48 would be included whether or not the client had an amount paid greater than $20,000.00.

Using AND Criteria

To combine criteria with AND, place the criteria on the same line. The following steps use an AND criterion to find those clients whose amount paid is greater than $20,000.00 and whose trainer is trainer 48.

To Use a Compound Criterion Involving AND

1

• **Click the View button on the Query Datasheet toolbar to return to the Query1 : Select Query window.**

• **Include the Trainer Number field in the query.**

• **Type** 48 **as the criterion for the Trainer Number field.**

Criteria have been entered for the Amount Paid and Trainer Number fields (Figure 2-32).

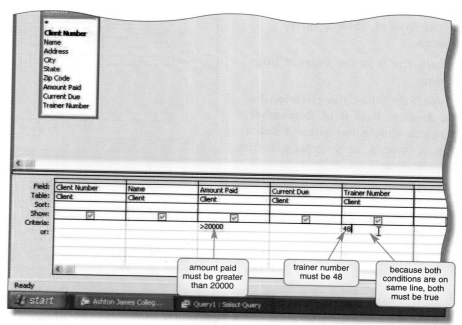

FIGURE 2-32

2

• **Click the Run button to run the query.**

• **If instructed to print the results, click the Print button.**

The results appear (Figure 2-33). Only the clients whose amount paid is greater than $20,000.00 and whose trainer number is 48 are included.

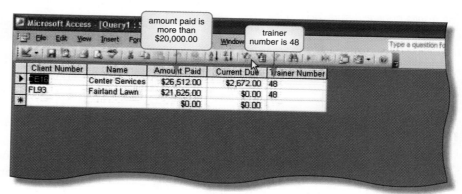

FIGURE 2-33

Using OR Criteria

To combine criteria with OR, the criteria must go on separate lines in the Criteria area of the grid. The following steps use an OR criterion to find those clients whose amount paid is greater than $20,000.00 or whose trainer is trainer 48 (or both).

To Use a Compound Criterion Involving OR

1

• Click the View button on the Query Datasheet toolbar to return to the Query1 : Select Query window.

2

• If necessary, click the Criteria entry for the Trainer Number field and then use the BACKSPACE key or the DELETE key to erase the entry ("48").

• Click the or row (below the Criteria row) for the Trainer Number field and then type 48 as the entry.

The criteria are entered for the Amount Paid and Trainer Number fields on different lines (Figure 2-34).

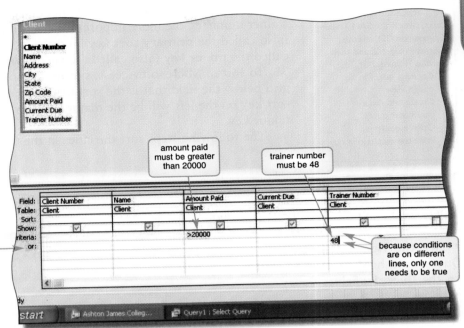

amount paid must be greater than 20000

trainer number must be 48

or row

because conditions are on different lines, only one needs to be true

FIGURE 2-34

3

• Click the Run button to run the query.

• If instructed to print the results, click the Print button.

The results appear (Figure 2-35). Only those clients whose amount paid is greater than $20,000.00 or whose trainer number is 48 are included.

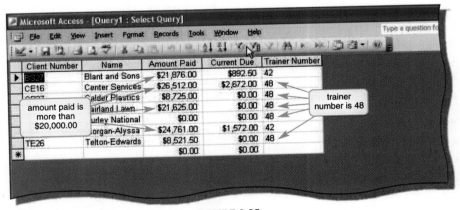

amount paid is more than $20,000.00

trainer number is 48

FIGURE 2-35

Sorting Data in a Query

In some queries, the order in which the records appear really does not matter. All you need be concerned about are the records that appear in the results. It does not matter which one is first or which one is last.

In other queries, however, the order can be very important. You may want to see the cities in which clients are located and would like them arranged alphabetically. Perhaps you want to see the clients listed by trainer number. Further, within all the clients of any given trainer, you might want them to be listed by amount paid.

More About

Sorting Data in a Query

When sorting data in a query, the records in the underlying tables (the tables on which the query is based) are not actually rearranged. Instead, the DBMS will determine the most efficient method of simply displaying the records in the requested order. The records in the underlying tables remain in their original order.

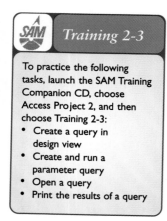

Training 2-3

To practice the following tasks, launch the SAM Training Companion CD, choose Access Project 2, and then choose Training 2-3:
• Create a query in design view
• Create and run a parameter query
• Open a query
• Print the results of a query

To order the records in the answer to a query in a particular way, you **sort** the records. The field or fields on which the records are sorted is called the **sort key**. If you are sorting on more than one field (such as sorting by amount paid within trainer number), the more important field (Trainer Number) is called the **major key** (also called the **primary sort key**) and the less important field (Amount Paid) is called the **minor key** (also called the **secondary sort key**).

To sort in Microsoft Access, specify the sort order in the Sort row of the design grid below the field that is the sort key. If you specify more than one sort key, the sort key on the left will be the major sort key and the one on the right will be the minor key.

The following steps sort the cities in the Client table.

To Sort Data in a Query

1

• **Click the View button on the Query Datasheet toolbar to return to the Query1 : Select Query window.**

• **Click Edit on the menu bar and then click Clear Grid.**

2

• **Include the City field in the design grid.**

• **Click the Sort row below the City field, and then click the Sort row arrow that appears.**

The City field is included (Figure 2-36). A list of available sort orders appears.

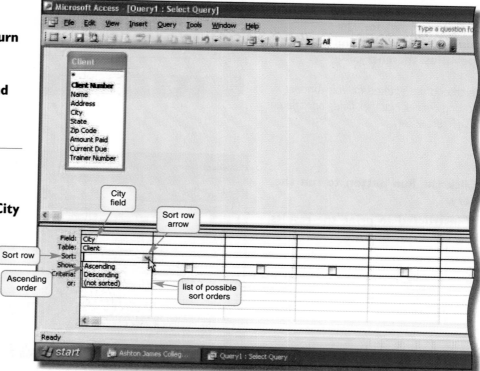

FIGURE 2-36

3

• **Click Ascending.**

Ascending is selected as the order (Figure 2-37).

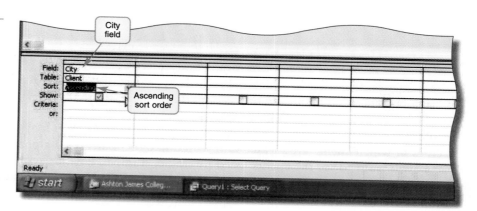

FIGURE 2-37

4

- Click the **Run button** to run the query.

- If instructed to print the results, click the **Print button**.

The results contain the cities from the Client table (Figure 2-38). The cities appear in alphabetical order. Duplicates, also called **identical rows***, are included.*

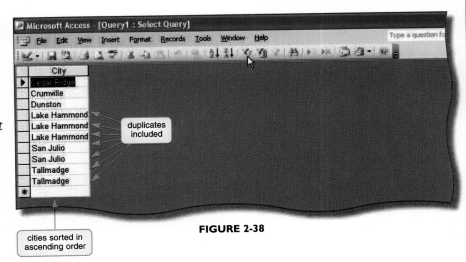

duplicates included

cities sorted in ascending order

FIGURE 2-38

Omitting Duplicates

When you sort data, duplicates normally are included. In Figure 2-38, for example, San Julio appeared twice, Lake Hammond appeared three times, and Tallmadge appeared twice. To sort to eliminate duplicates, use the Properties button on the Query Design toolbar or the Properties command on the shortcut menu to display the item's property sheet. A **property sheet** is a window containing the various properties of the object. To omit duplicates, you will use the property sheet to change the Unique Values property.

The following steps produce a sorted list of the cities in the Client table in which each city is listed only once.

To Omit Duplicates

1

- Click the **View button** on the Query Datasheet toolbar to return to the **Query1 : Select Query** window.

- Click the second field in the design grid (the empty field following City). You must click the second field or you will not get the correct results and will have to repeat this step.

- Click the **Properties button** on the Query Design toolbar.

Access displays the Query Properties sheet (Figure 2-39). (If your sheet looks different, you clicked the wrong place and will have to repeat the step.)

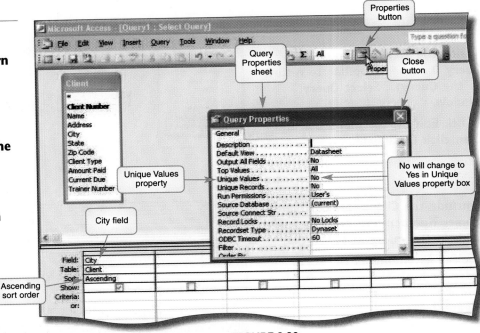

Properties button

Query Properties sheet

Close button

No will change to Yes in Unique Values property box

Unique Values property

City field

Ascending sort order

FIGURE 2-39

2

• Click the Unique Values property box, and then click the arrow that appears to produce a list of available choices for Unique Values.

• Click Yes and then close the Query Properties sheet by clicking its Close button.

• Click the Run button to run the query.

• If instructed to print the results, click the Print button.

The results appear (Figure 2-40). The cities are sorted alphabetically. Each city is included only once.

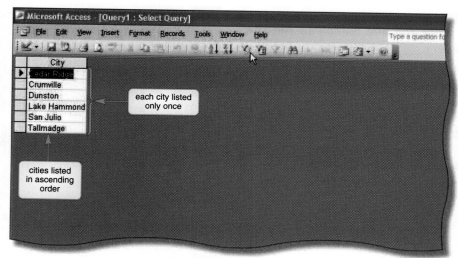

each city listed only once

cities listed in ascending order

FIGURE 2-40

Sorting on Multiple Keys

The next example lists the number, name, trainer number, and amount paid for all clients. The data is to be sorted by amount paid (low to high) within trainer number, which means that the Trainer Number field is the major key and the Amount Paid field is the minor key.

The following steps accomplish this sorting by specifying the Trainer Number and Amount Paid fields as sort keys.

To Sort on Multiple Keys

1

• Click the View button on the Query Datasheet toolbar to return to the Query1 : Select Query window.

• Click Edit on the menu bar and then click Clear Grid.

2

• Include the Client Number, Name, Trainer Number, and Amount Paid fields in the query in this order.

• Select Ascending as the sort order for both the Trainer Number field and the Amount Paid field (Figure 2-41).

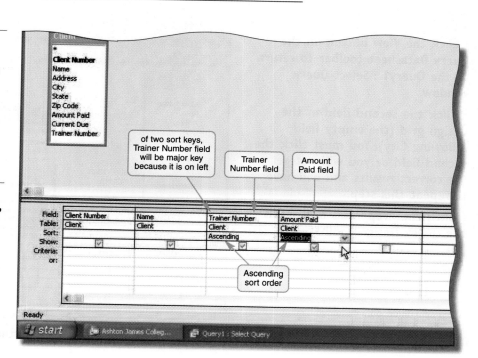

of two sort keys, Trainer Number field will be major key because it is on left

Trainer Number field

Amount Paid field

Ascending sort order

FIGURE 2-41

3

• **Click the Run button to run the query.**

• **If instructed to print the results, click the Print button.**

The results appear (Figure 2-42). The clients are sorted by trainer number. Within the collection of clients having the same trainer, the clients are sorted by amount paid.

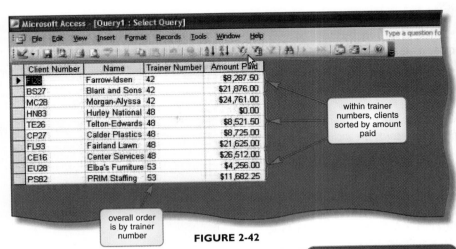

FIGURE 2-42

It is important to remember that the major sort key must appear to the left of the minor sort key in the design grid. If you attempted to sort by amount paid within trainer number, but placed the Amount Paid field to the left of the Trainer Number field, your results would be incorrect.

Creating a Top-Values Query

Rather than show all the results of a query, you may want to show only a specified number of records or a percentage of records. Creating a **top-values query** allows you to quantify the results. When you sort records, you can limit results to those records having the highest (descending sort) or lowest (ascending sort) values. To do so, first create a query that sorts the data in the desired order. Next, use the Top Values box on the Query Design toolbar to change the number of records to be included from All to the desired number. The following steps show the first four records that were included in the results of the previous query.

To Create a Top-Values Query

1

• **Click the View button on the Query Datasheet toolbar to return to the Query1 : Select Query window.**

• **Click the Top Values box on the Query Design toolbar, and then type 4 as the new value.**

The value in the Top Values box is changed from All to 4 (Figure 2-43).

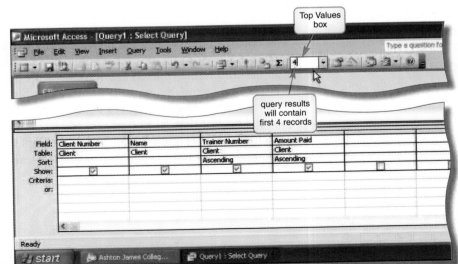

FIGURE 2-43

2

• **Click the Run button to run the query.**

• **If instructed to print the results, click the Print button.**

The results appear (Figure 2-44). Only the first four records are included.

3

• **Close the query by clicking the Close Window button for the Query1 : Select Query window.**

• **When asked if you want to save your changes, click the No button.**

The Query1 : Select Query window closes. The query is not saved.

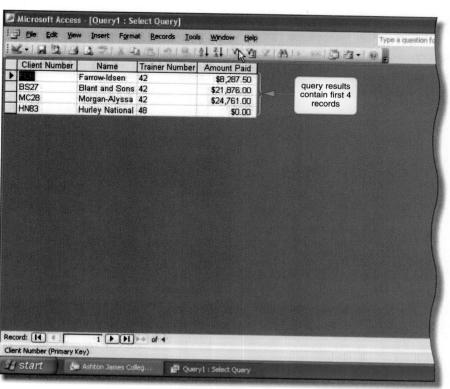

FIGURE 2-44

When you run a top-values query, it is important to change the value in the Top Values box back to All. If you do not change the Top Values value back to all, the previous value will remain in force. Consequently, you may very well not get all the records you should in the next query.

A good practice whenever you use a top-values query is to close the query as soon as you are done. That way, you will begin your next query from scratch, which guarantees that the value is set back to All.

Joining Tables

The Ashton James College database needs to satisfy a query that requires values from the Client table and the Trainer table. Specifically, the query needs to list the number and name of each client along with the number and name of the client's trainer. The client's name is in the Client table, whereas the trainer's name is in the Trainer table. Thus, this query cannot be satisfied using a single table. You need to **join** the tables; that is, to find records in the two tables that have identical values in matching fields (Figure 2-45). In this example, you need to find records in the Client table and the Trainer table that have the same value in the Trainer Number fields.

Give me the number and name of each client along with the number and name of each client's trainer.

Client table

CLIENT NUMBER	NAME	...	TRAINER NUMBER
BS27	Blant and Sons	...	42
CE16	Center Services	...	48
CP27	Calder Plastics	...	48
EU28	Elba's Furniture	...	53
FI28	Farrow-Idsen	...	42
FL93	Fairland Lawn	...	48
HN83	Hurley National	...	48
MC28	Morgan-Alyssa	...	42
PS82	PRIM Staffing	...	53
TE26	Telton-Edwards	...	48

Trainer table

TRAINER NUMBER	LAST NAME	FIRST NAME	...
42	Perry	Belinda	...
48	Stevens	Michael	...
53	Gonzalez	Manuel	...
67	Danville	Marty	...

Join of Client and Trainer table

CLIENT NUMBER	NAME	...	TRAINER NUMBER	LAST NAME	FIRST NAME	...
BS27	Blant and Sons	...	42	Perry	Belinda	...
CE16	Center Services	...	48	Stevens	Michael	...
CP27	Calder Plastics	...	48	Stevens	Michael	...
EU28	Elba's Furniture	...	53	Gonzalez	Manuel	...
FI28	Farrow-Idsen	...	42	Perry	Belinda	...
FL93	Fairland Lawn	...	48	Stevens	Michael	...
HN83	Hurley National	...	48	Stevens	Michael	...
MC28	Morgan-Alyssa	...	42	Perry	Belinda	...
PS82	PRIM Staffing	...	53	Gonzalez	Manuel	...
TE26	Telton-Edwards	...	48	Stevens	Michael	...

FIGURE 2-45

To join tables in Access, first you bring field lists for both tables to the upper pane of the Select Query window. Access will draw a line, called a **join line**, between matching fields in the two tables indicating that the tables are related. You then can select fields from either table. Access will join the tables automatically.

The first step is to select the Trainer table in the Database window and create a new query. Then, add the Client table to the query. A join line will appear connecting the Trainer Number fields in the two field lists. This join line indicates how the tables are related; that is, linked through these matching fields. (If you fail to give the matching fields the same name, Access will not insert the line. You can insert it manually, however, by clicking one of the two matching fields and dragging the mouse pointer to the other matching field.)

The steps on the next page create a new query, add the Client table and then select the appropriate fields.

Q & A

Q: Assuming you want the Trainer Number field to be the major key and the Amount Paid field to be the minor key as in the previous steps, how could you display the Amount Paid field before the Trainer Number field?

A: Include the Trainer Number field, the Amount Paid field, and then the Trainer Number field a second time. Select Ascending as the sort order for the first Trainer Number field and for the Amount Paid field. Remove the check mark from the Show check box for the first Trainer Number field. Thus, the first Trainer Number field will be part of the sort key, but will not appear in the results. The second Trainer Number field will appear in the results after the Amount Paid field.

To Join Tables

1

• **With the Tables object selected and the Trainer table selected, click the New Object button arrow on the Database toolbar.**

• **Click Query, and then click the OK button.**

• **Drag the line separating the two panes to the approximate position shown in Figure 2-46, and then drag the lower edge of the field list box down far enough so all fields in the Trainer table appear.**

• **Click the Show Table button on the Query Design toolbar.**

Access displays the Show Table dialog box (Figure 2-46).

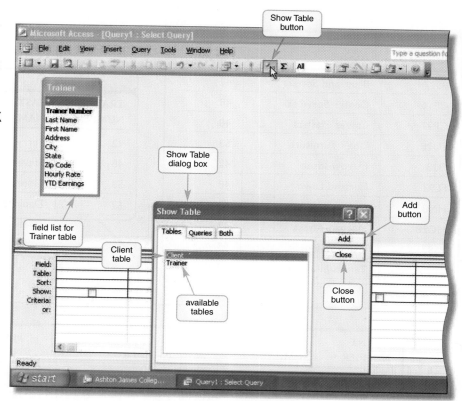

FIGURE 2-46

2

• **Be sure the Client table is selected, and then click the Add button.**

• **Close the Show Table dialog box by clicking the Close button.**

• **Expand the size of the field list so all the fields in the Client table appear.**

The field lists for both tables appear (Figure 2-47). A join line connects the two field lists.

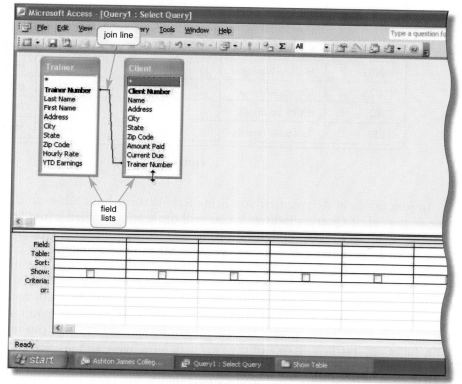

FIGURE 2-47

854

3

- **Include the Trainer Number, Last Name, and First Name fields from the Trainer table as well as the Client Number and Name fields from the Client table.**

- **Select Ascending as the sort order for both the Trainer Number field and the Client Number field.**

The fields from both tables are selected (Figure 2-48).

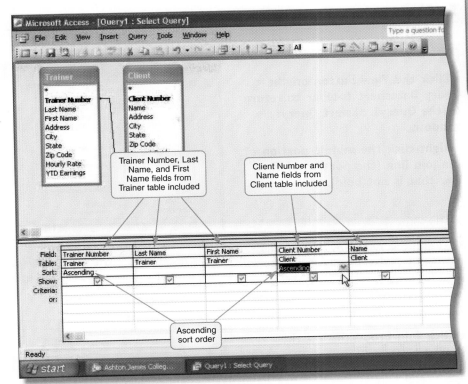

FIGURE 2-48

4

- **Click the Run button to run the query.**

- **If instructed to print the results, click the Print button.**

The results appear (Figure 2-49). They contain data from both the Trainer and Client tables. The records are sorted by trainer number and within trainer number by client number.

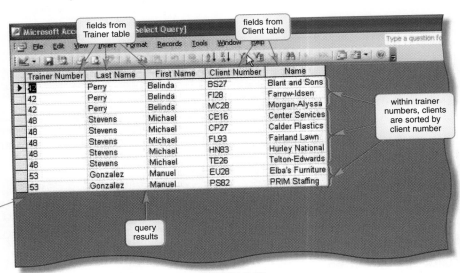

FIGURE 2-49

Other Ways

1. On Query menu click Show Table
2. Right-click any open area in upper pane, click Show Table on shortcut menu
3. In Voice Command mode, say "Show Table"

Changing Join Properties

Normally records that do not match will not appear in the results of a join query. A trainer such as Marty Danville, for whom no clients currently exist, for example, would not appear. To cause such a record to be displayed, you need to change the **join properties**, which are the properties that indicate which records appear in a join, of the query as the steps on the next page illustrate.

To Change Join Properties

1

• **Click the View button on the Query Datasheet toolbar to return to the Query1 : Select Query window.**

• **Right-click the middle portion of the join line (the portion of the line that is not bold).**

The shortcut menu appears (Figure 2-50). (If Join Properties does not appear on your shortcut menu, you did not point to the appropriate portion of the join line. You will need to right-click again.)

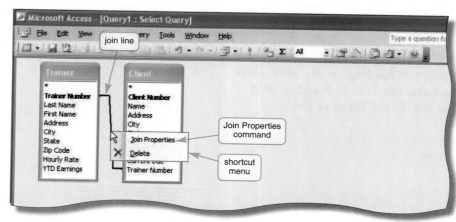

FIGURE 2-50

2

• **Click Join Properties on the shortcut menu.**

Access displays the Join Properties dialog box (Figure 2-51).

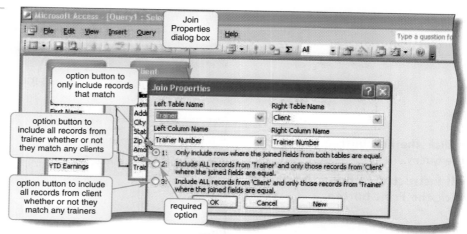

FIGURE 2-51

3

• **Click option button 2 to include all records from the Trainer table regardless of whether or not they match any clients.**

• **Click the OK button.**

• **Run the query by clicking the Run button.**

• **If instructed to print the results, click the Print button.**

The results appear (Figure 2-52).

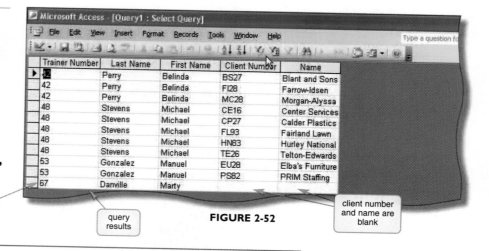

FIGURE 2-52

With the change to the join properties, trainer 67 is included, even though the trainer does not have any clients.

Restricting Records in a Join

Sometimes you will want to join tables, but you will not want to include all possible records. In such cases, you will relate the tables and include fields just as you did before. You also will include criteria. For example, to include the same fields as in the previous query, but only those clients whose amount paid is more than $20,000.00, you will make the same entries as before, but also include >20000 as a criterion for the Amount Paid field.

The following steps modify the query from the previous example to restrict the records that will be included in the join.

To Restrict the Records in a Join

1

- **Click the View button on the Query Datasheet toolbar to return to the Query1 : Select Query window.**

- **Add the Amount Paid field to the query.**

- **Type** >20000 **as the criterion for the Amount Paid field and then click the Show check box for the Amount Paid field to remove the check mark.**

The Amount Paid field appears in the design grid (Figure 2-53). A criterion is entered for the Amount Paid field, and the Show check box is empty, indicating that the field will not appear in the results of the query.

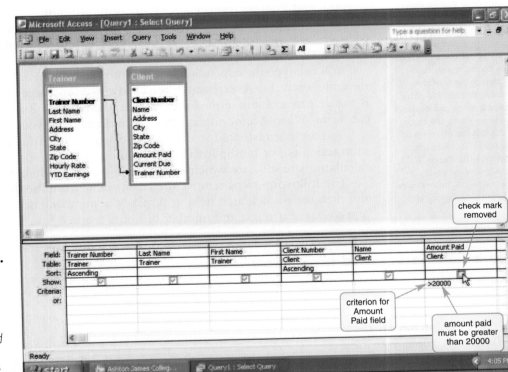

FIGURE 2-53

2

- **Click the Run button to run the query.**

- **If instructed to print the results, click the Print button.**

The results appear (Figure 2-54). Only those clients with an amount paid greater than $20,000.00 are displayed in the result. The Amount Paid field does not appear.

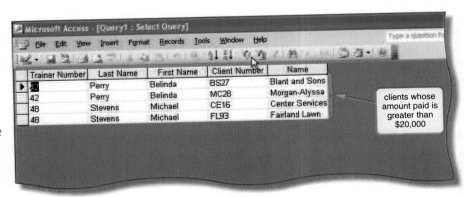

FIGURE 2-54

Calculations

Many types of calculations are available for use in queries. For example, you can add the values in two fields together, or you can calculate the sum or average of the values in one field.

Using Calculated Fields

Suppose that Ashton James College wants to know the number of hours worked by each trainer. This poses a problem because the Trainer table does not include a field for hours worked. You can calculate it, however, because the number of hours worked is equal to the YTD earnings divided by the hourly rate. A field that can be computed from other fields is called a **calculated field**.

To include calculated fields in queries, you enter a name for the calculated field, a colon, and then the expression in one of the columns in the Field row. Any fields included in the expression must be enclosed in square brackets ([ ]). For the number of hours worked, for example, you will type Hours Worked:[YTD Earnings]/[Hourly Rate] as the expression.

You can type the expression directly into the Field row. You will not be able to see the entire entry, however, because the Field row is not large enough. The preferred way is to select the column in the Field row and then use the Zoom command on its shortcut menu. When Access displays the Zoom dialog box, you can enter the expression.

You are not restricted to division in calculations. You can use addition (+), subtraction (-), or multiplication (*). You also can include parentheses in your calculations to indicate which calculations should be done first.

The following steps remove the Client table from the query (it is not needed), and then use a calculated field to display the number, last name, hourly rate, year-to-date earnings, and number of hours worked for all trainers.

To Use a Calculated Field in a Query

1

- **Click the View button on the Query Datasheet toolbar to return to the Query1 : Select Query window.**

- **Right-click any field in the Client table field list.**

- **Click Remove Table on the shortcut menu to remove the Client table from the Query1 : Select Query window.**

- **Click Edit on the menu bar and then click Clear Grid. Include the Trainer Number, Last Name, Hourly Rate, and YTD Earnings.**

- **Right-click the Field row in the first open column in the design grid.**

The shortcut menu appears (Figure 2-55).

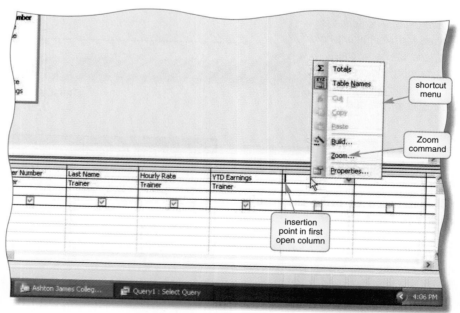

FIGURE 2-55

2

- **Click Zoom on the shortcut menu.**
- **Type** Hours Worked:[YTD Earnings]/[Hourly Rate] **in the Zoom dialog box that appears.**

Access displays the Zoom dialog box (Figure 2-56). The expression you typed appears within the dialog box.

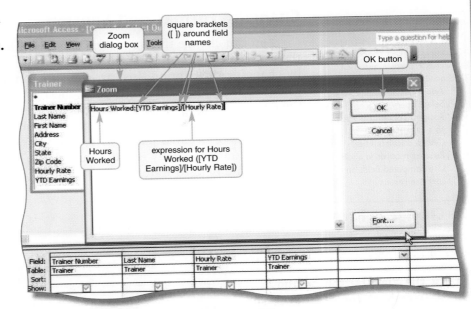

FIGURE 2-56

3

- **Click the OK button.**

A portion of the expression you entered appears in the fifth field in the design grid (Figure 2-57).

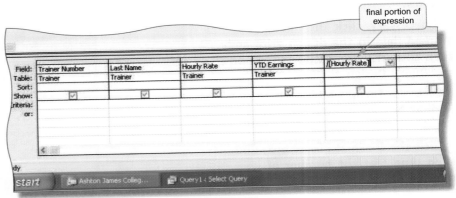

FIGURE 2-57

4

- **Click the Run button to run the query.**
- **If instructed to print the results, click the Print button.**

The results appear (Figure 2-58). Microsoft Access has calculated and displayed the number of hours worked for each trainer.

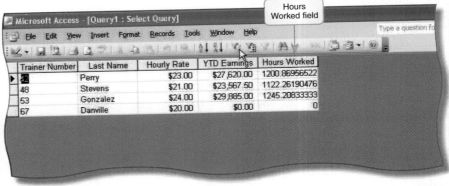

FIGURE 2-58

Other Ways
1. Press SHIFT+F2

Instead of clicking Zoom on the shortcut menu, you can click Build. Access displays the Expression Builder dialog box that provides assistance in creating the expression. If you know the expression you will need, however, usually it is easier to enter it using the Zoom command.

Training 2-5

To practice the following tasks, launch the SAM Training Companion CD, choose Access Project 2, and then choose Training 2-5:
• Add a calculated field to a Select query
• Assign a conditional value to a calcuated field
• Create calculated fields
• Restrict records in a join
• Use computed fields and sort the results

Changing Format and Caption

You can change the way items appear in the results of a query by changing their format. You also can change the heading at the top of a column in the results by changing the caption. Just as when you omitted duplicates, you will make this change by using the field's property sheet. In the property sheet, you can change the desired property, such as the format, the number of decimal places, or the caption. The following steps change the format of Hours Worked to Fixed and the number of decimal places to 1, thus guaranteeing that the number on each row will contain exactly one decimal place. They also change the caption of the Hourly Rate field to Rate.

To Change a Format and a Caption

1

• **Click the View button on the Query Datasheet toolbar to return to the Query1 : Select Query window.**

• **If necessary, click the Hours Worked field in the design grid, and then click the Properties button on the Query Design toolbar.**

• **Click the Format box, click the Format box arrow, and then click Fixed.**

• **Click the Decimal Places box, and then type 1 as the number of decimal places.**

Access displays the Field Properties sheet (Figure 2-59). The format is changed to Fixed and the number of decimal places is set to 1.

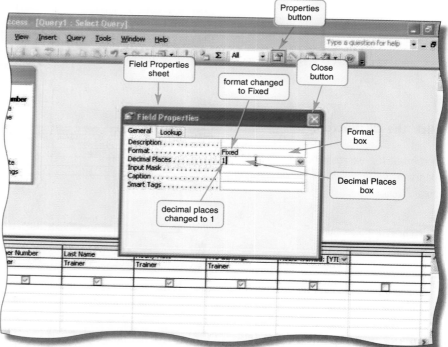

FIGURE 2-59

2

• **Close the Field Properties sheet by clicking its Close button.**

• **Click the Hourly Rate field in the design grid, and then click the Properties button on the Query Design toolbar.**

• **Click the Caption box, and then type Rate as the caption.**

Access displays the Field Properties sheet (Figure 2-60). The caption is changed to Rate.

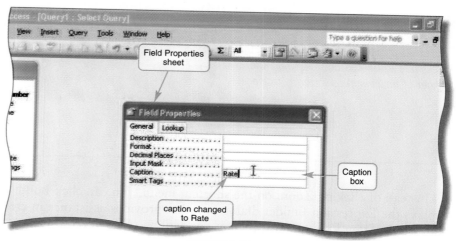

FIGURE 2-60

3

• **Click the Run button to run the query.**

• **If instructed to print the results, click the Print button.**

The results appear (Figure 2-61). The Hourly Rate caption is changed to Rate. The numbers in the Hours Worked column all contain exactly one decimal place.

4

• **Click the Close Window button for the Query1 : Select Query window.**

• **When asked if you want to save your changes, click the No button.**

The Query1 : Select Query window closes. The query is not saved.

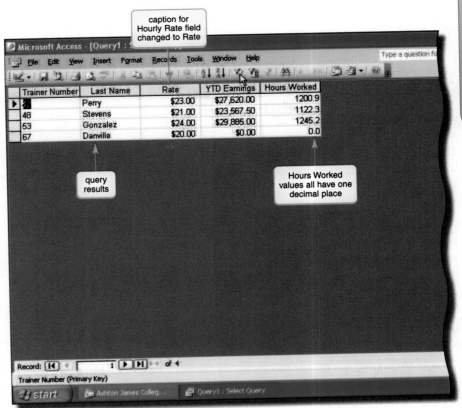

caption for Hourly Rate field changed to Rate

query results

Hours Worked values all have one decimal place

FIGURE 2-61

If you had saved the query, the changes you made to the properties would be saved along with the query.

Calculating Statistics

Microsoft Access supports the built-in statistics: COUNT, SUM, AVG (average), MAX (largest value), MIN (smallest value), STDEV (standard deviation), VAR (variance), FIRST, and LAST. These statistics are called aggregate functions. An **aggregate function** is a function that performs some mathematical function against a group of records. To use any of these aggregate functions in a query, you include it in the Total row in the design grid. The Total row routinely does not appear in the grid. To include it, click the Totals button on the Query Design toolbar.

The steps on the next page create a new query for the Client table and then calculate the average amount paid for all clients.

To Calculate Statistics

1

• **With the Tables object selected and the Client table selected, click the New Object button arrow on the Database toolbar.**

• **Click Query, and then click the OK button.**

• **Drag the line separating the two panes to the approximate position shown in Figure 2-62, and drag the lower edge of the field list box down far enough so all fields in the Client table appear.**

• **Click the Totals button on the Query Design toolbar, and then double-click the Amount Paid field.**

The Total row now is included in the design grid (Figure 2-62). The Amount Paid field is included, and the entry in the Total row is Group By.

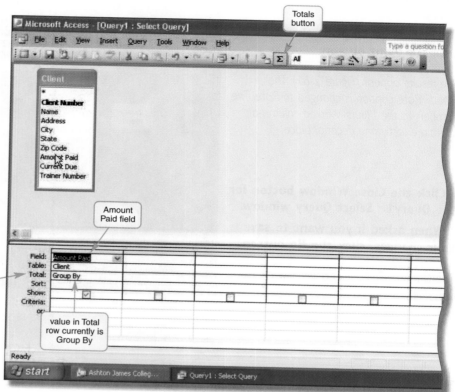

FIGURE 2-62

2

• **Click the Total row in the Amount Paid column, and then click the Total row arrow that appears.**

The list of available options appears (Figure 2-63).

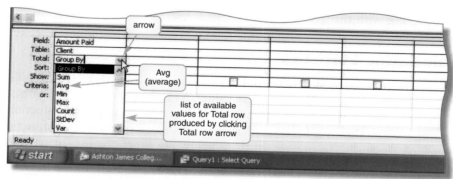

FIGURE 2-63

3

• **Click Avg.**

Avg is selected (Figure 2-64).

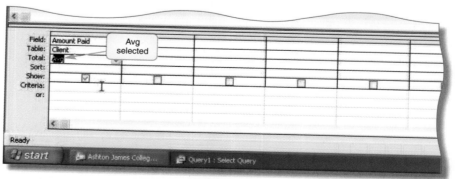

FIGURE 2-64

4

• Click the Run button to run the query.

• If instructed to print the results, click the Print button.

The result appears (Figure 2-65), showing the average amount paid for all clients.

average amount paid by all clients

FIGURE 2-65

Using Criteria in Calculating Statistics

Sometimes calculating statistics for all the records in the table is appropriate. In other cases, however, you will need to calculate the statistics for only those records that satisfy certain criteria. To enter a criterion in a field, first you select Where as the entry in the Total row for the field and then enter the criterion in the Criteria row. The following steps use this technique to calculate the average amount paid for clients of trainer 48.

To Use Criteria in Calculating Statistics

1

• Click the View button on the Query Datasheet toolbar to return to the Query1 : Select Query window.

2

• Include the Trainer Number field in the design grid.

• Produce the list of available options for the Total row entry just as you did when you selected Avg for the Amount Paid field.

• Use the vertical scroll bar to move through the options until the Where option appears.

The list of available options appears (Figure 2-66). The Group By entry in the Trainer Number field may not be highlighted on your screen depending on where you clicked in the Total row.

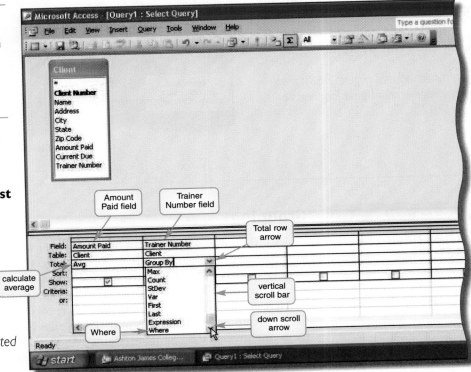

Amount Paid field

Trainer Number field

Total row arrow

calculate average

vertical scroll bar

down scroll arrow

Where

FIGURE 2-66

3

• **Click Where.**

• **Type** 42 **as the criterion for the Trainer Number field.**

Where is selected as the entry in the Total row for the Trainer Number field and 42 is entered in the Criteria row (Figure 2-67).

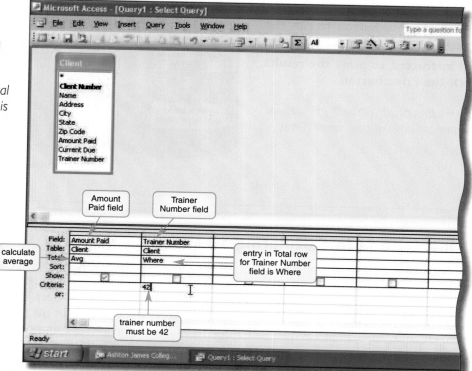

FIGURE 2-67

4

• **Click the Run button to run the query.**

• **If instructed to print the results, click the Print button.**

The results appear (Figure 2-68), giving the average amount paid for clients of trainer 42.

FIGURE 2-68

Grouping

Another way statistics often are used is in combination with grouping; that is, statistics are calculated for groups of records. You may, for example, need to calculate the average amount paid for the clients of each trainer. You will want the average for the clients of trainer 42, the average for clients of trainer 48, and so on.

Grouping means creating groups of records that share some common characteristic. In grouping by Trainer Number, for example, the clients of trainer 42 would form one group, the clients of trainer 48 would be a second, and the clients of trainer 53 form a third group. The calculations then are made for each group. To indicate grouping in Access, select Group By as the entry in the Total row for the field to be used for grouping.

The following steps calculate the average amount paid for clients of each trainer.

To Use Grouping

1

- **Click the View button on the Query Datasheet toolbar to return to the Query1 : Select Query window.**

- **Click Edit on the menu bar and then click Clear Grid.**

- **Include the Trainer Number field.**

- **Include the Amount Paid field, and then click Avg as the calculation in the Total row.**

The Trainer Number and Amount Paid fields are included (Figure 2-69). Group By currently is the entry in the Total row for the Trainer Number field, which is correct; thus, it was not changed.

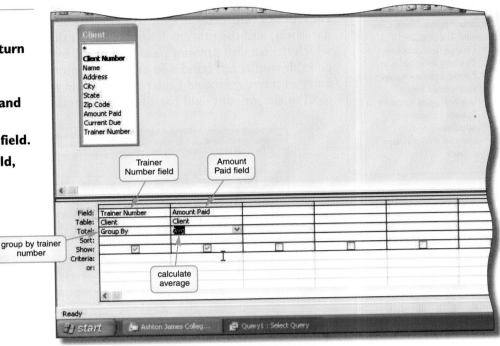

FIGURE 2-69

2

- **Click the Run button to run the query.**

- **If instructed to print the results, click the Print button.**

The results appear (Figure 2-70), showing each trainer's number along with the average amount paid for the clients of that trainer. Because the results are grouped by trainer number, a single row exists for each trainer summarizing all the clients of that trainer.

3

- **Close the query by clicking the Close Window button for the Query1 : Select Query window.**

- **When asked if you want to save your changes, click the No button.**

The Query1 : Select Query window closes. The query is not saved.

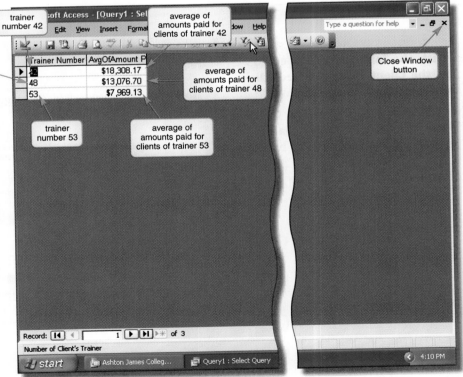

FIGURE 2-70

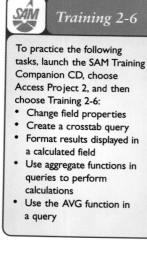

Training 2-6

To practice the following tasks, launch the SAM Training Companion CD, choose Access Project 2, and then choose Training 2-6:
• Change field properties
• Create a crosstab query
• Format results displayed in a calculated field
• Use aggregate functions in queries to perform calculations
• Use the AVG function in a query

Crosstab Queries

Crosstab queries are useful for summarizing data. A **crosstab query** calculates a statistic (for example, sum, average, or count) for data that is grouped by two different types of information. One of the types will appear down the side of the resulting datasheet, and the other will appear across the top. Figure 2-71 shows a crosstab in which the total of amount paid is grouped by both city and trainer number with cities down the left-hand side and trainer numbers across the top. For example, the entry in the row labeled Cedar Ridge and in the column labeled 42 represents the total of the amount paid for all clients of trainer 42 who live in Cedar Ridge.

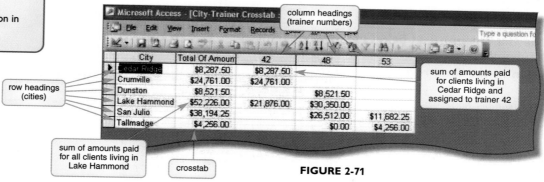

FIGURE 2-71

The following steps use the Crosstab Query wizard to create a crosstab query.

To Create a Crosstab Query

1

• **With the Tables object selected and the Client table selected, click the New Object button arrow.**

• **Click Query, click Crosstab Query Wizard in the New Query dialog box, and then click the OK button.**

Access displays the Crosstab Query Wizard dialog box (Figure 2-72).

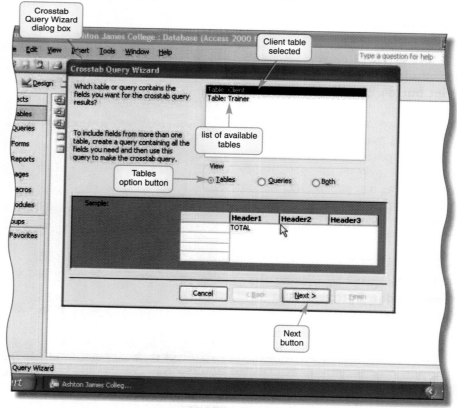

FIGURE 2-72

2

• **With the Tables option button selected and the Client table selected, click the Next button.**

• **Click the City field, and then click the Add Field button.**

The Crosstab Query Wizard dialog box displays options for selecting field values as row headings (Figure 2-73). The City field is selected as the field whose values will provide the row headings.

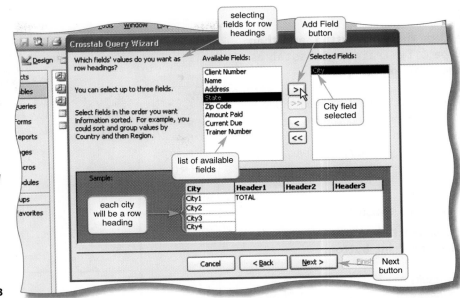

FIGURE 2-73

3

• **Click the Next button, and then click the Trainer Number field.**

The Crosstab Query Wizard dialog box displays options for selecting field values as column headings (Figure 2-74). The Trainer Number field is selected as the field whose values will provide the column headings.

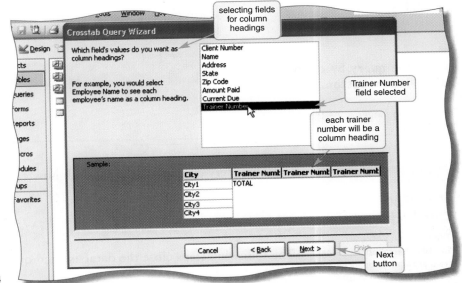

FIGURE 2-74

4

• **Click the Next button, click the Amount Paid field, and then click Sum.**

The Crosstab Query Wizard dialog box displays options for selecting fields for calculations for column and row intersections (Figure 2-75). The Amount Paid field is selected as the field whose value will be calculated for each row and column intersection. Because Sum is the selected function, the calculation will be the total amount paid.

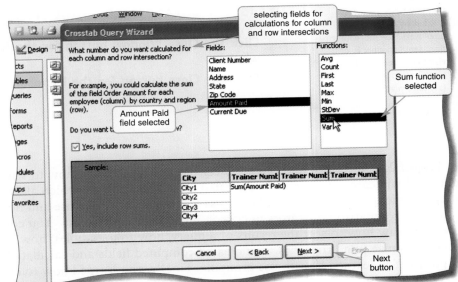

FIGURE 2-75

5

• **Click the Next button, and then type** City-Trainer Crosstab **as the name of the query.**

The Crosstab Query Wizard dialog box displays options for naming and viewing the query and modifying the design (Figure 2-76). The name is entered.

6

• **Click the Finish button.**

• **If instructed to print the results, click the Print button.**

The results now can appear. They look like the results shown in Figure 2-71 on page AC 104.

7

• **Close the query by clicking its Close Window button.**

The query no longer appears.

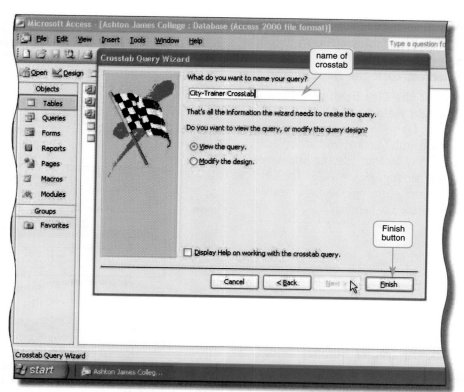

FIGURE 2-76

More About

Microsoft Certification

The Microsoft Office Specialist Certification program provides an opportunity for you to obtain a valuable industry credential — proof that you have the Access 2003 skills required by employers. For more information, see Appendix E, or visit the Access 2003 Certification Web page (scsite.com/ac2003/cert).

The query containing the crosstab now can be run just like any other query.

Closing a Database and Quitting Access

The following steps close the database and quit Access.

To Close a Database and Quit Access

1 Click the Close Window button for the Ashton James College : Database window.

2 Click the Close button for the Microsoft Access window.

Project Summary

In Project 2, you created and ran a variety of queries. You saw how to select fields in a query. You used text data and wildcards in criteria. You created a parameter query, which allowed users to enter a criterion when they run the query. You learned how to save a query for future use and how to use a query you have saved. You also used comparison operators in criteria involving numeric data. You combined criteria with both AND and OR. You saw how to sort the results of a query, how to join tables, how to restrict the records in a join, and how to change join properties. You created computed fields and calculated statistics. You changed formats and captions. You learned how to use grouping. Finally, you learned how to create a crosstab query.

What You Should Know

Having completed this project, you should be able to perform the tasks below. The tasks are listed in the same order they were presented in this project. For a list of the buttons, menus, toolbars, and commands introduced in this project, see the Quick Reference Summary at the back of this book and refer to the Page Number column.

1. Open a Database (AC 68)
2. Create a Query (AC 68)
3. Include Fields in the Design Grid (AC 71)
4. Run the Query (AC 71)
5. Print the Results of a Query (AC 72)
6. Return to the Select Query Window (AC 72)
7. Close the Query (AC 73)
8. Include All Fields in a Query (AC 74)
9. Clear the Design Grid (AC 75)
10. Use Text Data in a Criterion (AC 76)
11. Use a Wildcard (AC 77)
12. Use Criteria for a Field Not Included in the Results (AC 78)
13. Create and Run a Parameter Query (AC 79)
14. Save a Query (AC 80)
15. Use a Saved Query (AC 81)
16. Use a Number in a Criterion (AC 82)
17. Use a Comparison Operator in a Criterion (AC 83)
18. Use a Compound Criterion Involving AND (AC 84)
19. Use a Compound Criterion Involving OR (AC 85)
20. Sort Data in a Query (AC 86)
21. Omit Duplicates (AC 87)
22. Sort on Multiple Keys (AC 88)
23. Create a Top-Values Query (AC 89)
24. Join Tables (AC 92)
25. Change Join Properties (AC 94)
26. Restrict the Records in a Join (AC 95)
27. Use a Calculated Field in a Query (AC 96)
28. Change a Format and a Caption (AC 98)
29. Calculate Statistics (AC 100)
30. Use Criteria in Calculating Statistics (AC 101)
31. Use Grouping (AC 103)
32. Create a Crosstab Query (AC 104)
33. Close a Database and Quit Access (AC 106)

Learn It Online

Instructions: To complete the Learn It Online exercises, start your browser, click the Address bar, and then enter the Web address scsite.com/ac2003/learn. When the Access 2003 Learn It Online page is displayed, follow the instructions in the exercises below. Each exercise has instructions for printing your results, either for your own records or for submission to your instructor.

1 Project Reinforcement TF, MC, and SA

Below Access Project 2, click the Project Reinforcement link. Print the quiz by clicking Print on the File menu for each page. Answer each question.

2 Flash Cards

Below Access Project 2, click the Flash Cards link and read the instructions. Type 20 (or a number specified by your instructor) in the Number of playing cards text box, type your name in the Enter your Name text box, and then click the Flip Card button. When the flash card is displayed, read the question and then click the ANSWER box arrow to select an answer. Flip through Flash Cards. If your score is 15 (75%) correct or greater, click Print on the File menu to print your results. If your score is less than 15 (75%) correct, then redo this exercise by clicking the Replay button.

3 Practice Test

Below Access Project 2, click the Practice Test link. Answer each question, enter your first and last name at the bottom of the page, and then click the Grade Test button. When the graded practice test is displayed on your screen, click Print on the File menu to print a hard copy. Continue to take practice tests until you score 80% or better.

4 Who Wants To Be a Computer Genius?

Below Access Project 2, click the Computer Genius link. Read the instructions, enter your first and last name at the bottom of the page, and then click the PLAY button. When your score is displayed, click the PRINT RESULTS link to print a hard copy.

5 Wheel of Terms

Below Access Project 2, click the Wheel of Terms link. Read the instructions, and then enter your first and last name and your school name. Click the PLAY button. When your score is displayed, right-click the score and then click Print on the shortcut menu to print a hard copy.

6 Crossword Puzzle Challenge

Below Access Project 2, click the Crossword Puzzle Challenge link. Read the instructions, and then enter your first and last name. Click the SUBMIT button. Work the crossword puzzle. When you are finished, click the Submit button. When the crossword puzzle is redisplayed, click the Print Puzzle button to print a hard copy.

7 Tips and Tricks

Below Access Project 2, click the Tips and Tricks link. Click a topic that pertains to Project 2. Right-click the information and then click Print on the shortcut menu. Construct a brief example of what the information relates to in Access to confirm you understand how to use the tip or trick.

8 Newsgroups

Below Access Project 2, click the Newsgroups link. Click a topic that pertains to Project 2. Print three comments.

9 Expanding Your Horizons

Below Access Project 2, click the Expanding Your Horizons link. Click a topic that pertains to Project 2. Print the information. Construct a brief example of what the information relates to in Access to confirm you understand the contents of the article.

10 Search Sleuth

Below Access Project 2, click the Search Sleuth link. To search for a term that pertains to this project, select a term below the Project 2 title and then use the Google search engine at google.com (or any major search engine) to display and print two Web pages that present information on the term.

11 Access Online Training

Below Access Project 2, click the Access Online Training link. When your browser displays the Microsoft Office Online Web page, click the Access link. Click one of the Access courses that covers one or more of the objectives listed at the beginning of the project on page AC 66. Print the first page of the course before stepping through it.

12 Office Marketplace

Below Access Project 2, click the Office Marketplace link. When your browser displays the Microsoft Office Online Web page, click the Office Marketplace link. Click a topic that relates to Access. Print the first page.

Apply Your Knowledge

1 Querying the Begon Pest Control Database

Instructions: Start Access. Open the Begon Pest Control database that you modified in Apply Your Knowledge 1 in Project 1 on page AC 54. (If you did not complete this exercise, see your instructor for a copy of the modified database.) Perform the following tasks:

1. Create a query for the Customer table and add the Name and Address fields to the design grid.
2. Find only those records where the client has an address on Fletcher. Run the query and change the address for the client on 109 Fletcher to 190 Fletcher. Print the results. Return to Design view and clear the grid.
3. Add the Customer Number, Name, City, and Balance fields to the design grid. Sort the records in ascending order by City and descending by Balance. Run the query and print the results. Return to Design view.
4. Modify the query to allow the user to enter a different city each time the query is run. Run the query to find all customers who live in Kady. Print the query results. Save the query as Customer-City Query.
5. Open the Customer-City Query in Design view. Run the query to find all customers who live in Carlton but restrict retrieval to the top two records. Print the results. Close the query without saving it.
6. Create a new query for the Technician table and then join the Technician and Customer tables. Add the Technician Number, First Name and Last Name fields from the Technician table and the Customer Number, and Name fields from the Customer table. Sort the records in ascending order by Technician Number and Customer Number. All technicians should appear in the result even if they currently have no customers. Run the query and print the results.
7. Restrict the records retrieved in task 6 above to only those customers who have a balance greater than $350.00. Run the query and print the results. Close the query without saving it.
8. Create and print the crosstab shown in Figure 2-77. The crosstab groups total of customers' balances by city and technician number.

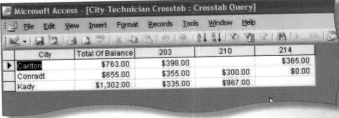

FIGURE 2-77

In the Lab

1 Querying the Birds2U Database

Problem: The management of Birds2U has determined a number of questions it wants the database management system to answer. You must obtain the answers to the questions posed by management.

Instructions: Use the database created in the In the Lab 1 of Project 1 on page AC 57 for this assignment or see your instructor for information on accessing the files required for this book. Perform the following tasks:

1. Open the Birds2U database and create a new query to display and print the Item Code, Description, On Hand, and Cost for all records in the Item table.
2. Display and print the Item Code, Description, Cost, and Supplier Code fields for all products where the Supplier Code is 21.

(continued)

1 Querying the Birds2U Database (continued)

3. Display and print the Item Code and Description fields for all items where the description includes the word House.
4. Display and print the Item Code and Description fields for all items with a selling price less than $15.00.
5. Display and print the Item Code and Description fields for all products that have a cost greater than $50.00.
6. Display and print all fields for those items with a selling price greater than $30.00 and where the number on hand is less than 5.
7. Display and print all fields for those items that have a supplier code of 13 or a cost less than $15.00.
8. Include the Item Code, Description, On Hand, and Cost in the design grid. Change the caption for the On Hand column to In Stock and sort the records in descending order by cost. Run the query and print the results. Run the query again but this time limit retrieval to the top 3 records.
9. Join the Supplier table and the Item table. Display the Supplier Code and Name from the Supplier table and the Item Code, Description, On Hand, and Cost from the Item table. Sort the records in ascending order by Supplier Code and by Item Code. All suppliers should display in the result even if they currently supply no items. Run the query and print the results. Save the query as Suppliers and Items.
10. Restrict the records retrieved in task 9 above to only those products where number on hand is less than 6. Run the query and print the results. Close the query and do not save the changes.
11. Create a new query for the Item table and include the Item Code and Description fields in the design grid. Calculate the sales value (on hand * selling price) for all records in the table. Run the query and print the results.
12. Display and print the average cost of all items.
13. Display and print the average cost of items grouped by supplier code.

2 Querying the Babbage Bookkeeping Database

Problem: Babbage Bookkeeping has determined a number of questions it wants the database management system to answer. You must obtain the answers to the questions posed by the bookkeeping service.

Instructions: Use the database created in the In the Lab 2 of Project 1 on page AC 59 for this assignment or see your instructor for information on accessing the files required for this book. Perform the following tasks:

1. Open the Babbage Bookkeeping database and create a new query for the Client table.
2. Display and print the Name and Balance fields for all clients where the bookkeeper number is 34.
3. Display and print the Client Number, Name, and Balance fields for all clients located in Portage with a balance greater than $300.00.
4. Display and print the Client Number, Name, and Address fields for all clients with an address on Revere.
5. Display and print the cities in descending order. Each city should appear only once.
6. Create a query that will allow the user to enter the city to search when the query is run. The query results should display the Client Number, Name, and Balance. Test the query by searching for those records where the client is located in Empeer. Save the query as Client-City Query.
7. Include the Client Number, Name, and Balance fields in the design grid. Sort the records in descending order by the Balance field. Display and print the top 25% of the records.

8. Display and print the Client Number, Name, and Balance fields for all clients where the bookkeeper number is 22 or 24 and the balance is greater than $300.00. (*Hint:* Use Microsoft Access Help to solve this problem.)

9. Display and print the First Name, Last Name, and Hourly Rate fields from the Bookkeeper table and the Client Number, Name, and Balance fields from the Client table. Sort the records in descending order by bookkeeper's last name and client's name.

10. Create a new query for the Bookkeeper table and include the Bookkeeper Number, First Name, Last Name, and Hourly Rate in the design grid. Calculate the number of hours each bookkeeper has worked (YTD Earnings/ Hourly Rate). Display hours worked as an integer (0 decimal places). Run the query and print the results.

11. Display and print the following statistics: the average balance for all clients; the average balance for clients of bookkeeper 24; and the average balance for each bookkeeper.

12. Create the crosstab shown in Figure 2-78. The crosstab groups total of clients' balances by city and bookkeeper number. Save the crosstab as City-Bookkeeper Crosstab. Print the crosstab.

City	Total Of Balance	22	24	34
Empee	$1,102.50	$577.50	$525.00	
Grant City	$1,027.50	$315.50	$712.00	
Portage	$848.25			$848.25

FIGURE 2-78

3 Querying the City Guide Database

Problem: The chamber of commerce has determined a number of questions it wants the database management system to answer. You must obtain the answers to the questions posed by the chamber.

Instructions: Use the database created in the In the Lab 3 of Project 1 on page AC 61 for this exercise or see your instructor for information on accessing the files required for this book. Print the answers to each question.

Instructions Part 1: Create a new query for the Advertiser table and include the Advertiser Number, Name, Balance, and Amount Paid fields in the design grid. Answer the following questions: (1) Which advertisers' names begin with S? (2) Which advertisers are located on Jefferson? (3) Which advertisers have a current balance of $0.00? (4) Which advertisers have a balance greater than $200.00 and have an amount paid less than $800.00? (5) Which three advertisers have the highest balances? (6) For each advertiser, what is the total of the current balance and the amount paid?

Instructions Part 2: Join the Ad Rep table and the Advertiser table. Include the Ad Rep Number, First Name, and Last Name from the Ad Rep table and the Advertiser Number, Name, and Amount Paid from the Advertiser table in the design grid. Sort the records in ascending order by Ad Rep Number and Advertiser Number. Perform the following: (1) Calculate the commission (comm rate * amount paid) for each ad rep. The commission should display as currency. (2) Restrict retrieval to only those records where the commission is greater than $50.00.

Instructions Part 3: Calculate the following statistics: (1) What is the average balance for advertisers assigned to ad rep 29? (2) What is the total balance of all advertisers? (3) What is the total amount paid for each ad rep?

Cases and Places

The difficulty of these case studies varies:
▪ are the least difficult and ▪▪ are more difficult. The last exercise is a group exercise.

1 ▪ Use the College Dog Walkers database you created in Cases and Places 1 in Project 1 on page AC 63 for this assignment or see your instructor for information on accessing the files required for this book. Perform the following: (a) Display and print the number and name of all customers who live on Easton. (b) Display and print the number, name, telephone number, and balance for all customers who have a balance of at least $40.00. (c) Display and print the number, name, balance, walker first name, and walker last name for all customers. Sort the records in ascending order by walker last name. (d) Display and print the average balance of all customers. (e) Display and print the average balance of customers grouped by walker. (f) Display and print the total balance of all customers.

2 ▪ Use the InPerson Fitness Company database you created in Cases and Places 2 in Project 1 on page AC 63 for this assignment or see your instructor for information on accessing the files required for this book. Perform the following: (a) Display and print the number, client name, and balance for all clients of a particular trainer. The owner should be able to enter a different trainer number each time the query is run. (b) Display and print the number, client name, and total of balance due and amount paid. (c) Display and print the number, client name, and balance of all clients whose amount paid is greater than $400.00. (d) Display and print the trainer number, trainer name, client number, client name, client address, and client telephone number for all clients. Sort the data ascending by trainer number and client number. (e) Display and print the total amount paid and total balance grouped by trainer.

3 ▪▪ Use the Regional Books database you created in Cases and Places 3 in Project 1 on page AC 63 for this assignment or see your instructor for information on accessing the files required for this book. Perform the following: (a) List the book code, title, and on-hand value (units on hand * price) of all books. (b) List the book code, title, and price of all paperback books. (c) List the book code, title, price, and publisher name for all books where there are less than 3 books on hand. (d) Display and print the book code, title, and author for all books. (e) Find the lowest priced book and the highest priced book.

4 ▪▪ Use the Campus Housing database you created in Cases and Places 4 in Project 1 on page AC 64 for this assignment or see your instructor for information on accessing the files required for this book. Display and print the following: (a) List all rental units that are located two miles or less from campus. (b) List all rental units that have parking and allow pets. (c) List all three-bedroom apartments that rent for less than $1,000.00 a month. (d) Find the average rent for two-bedroom apartments. (e) List the owners of all units that are efficiencies or rooms for rent. (f) List the different lease terms in ascending order. Each lease term should display only once.

5 ▪▪ **Working Together** Create an additional query for each of the four databases described in the Cases and Places. Each team must create a parameter query, a top values query, a crosstab query, and an aggregate query. Select the database to use to create each specific query type. Use all four databases, that is, one database per specific query type. Run each of the queries and print the results. Write a one-page paper that lists the queries the team created and explains why the team chose those queries.

Maintaining a Database Using the Design and Update Features of Access

CASE PERSPECTIVE

Dr. Gernaey and his colleagues at Ashton James College have received many benefits from the database they created and loaded, including the ability to ask questions concerning the data in the database. They now face the task of keeping the database up-to-date. As they take on new clients and trainers, they will need to add new records and make changes to existing records.

Access offers many features for maintaining a database that they want to utilize. For example, they must change the structure of the database to categorize the clients by type. They will do this by adding a Client Type field to the Client table. They discovered the Name field was too short to contain the name of one of the clients, so they will enlarge the size of the field. Along with these changes, they want to change the appearance of a datasheet when displaying data.

They would like the ability to make mass updates, that is, to update many records in a single operation. They want rules that make sure users can enter only valid data into the database, and they want to ensure that it is not possible for the database to contain a client who is not associated with a specific trainer. Finally, they want to improve the efficiency of certain types of processing, specifically sorting and retrieving data. Your task is to help the administration accomplish these goals.

As you read through this project, you will learn how to use the Access design and update features to maintain a database.

875

Maintaining a Database Using the Design and Update Features of Access

Objectives

You will have mastered the material in this project when you can:

- Add, change, and delete records
- Search for records
- Filter records
- Update a table design
- Format a datasheet
- Use queries to update records

- Specify validation rules, default values, and formats
- Create and use a Lookup field
- Specify referential integrity
- Use a subdatasheet
- Sort records
- Create indexes

Introduction

Once a database has been created and loaded with data, it must be maintained. **Maintaining the database** means modifying the data to keep it up-to-date, such as adding new records, changing the data for existing records, and deleting records. Updating can include mass updates or mass deletions; that is, updates to, or deletions of, many records at the same time.

In addition to adding, changing, and deleting records, maintenance of a database can involve the need to **restructure the database** periodically; that is, to change the database structure. This can include adding new fields to a table, changing the characteristics of existing fields, and removing existing fields. It also can involve the creation of indexes, which are similar to indexes found in the back of books. Indexes are used to improve the efficiency of certain operations.

Figure 3-1 summarizes some of the various types of activities involved in maintaining a database.

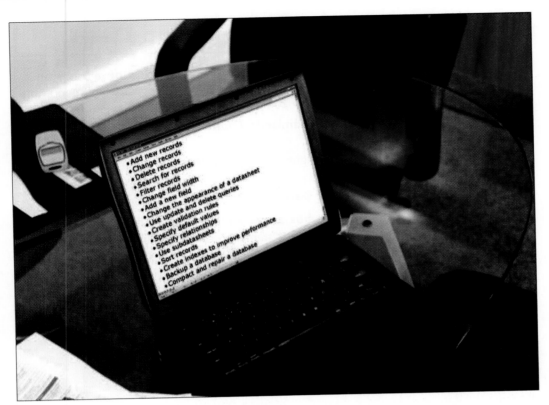

- Add new records
- Change records
- Delete records
- Search for records
- Filter records
- Change field width
- Add a new field
- Change the appearance of a datasheet
- Use update and delete queries
- Use validation rules
- Create default values
- Specify relationships
- Use subdatasheets
- Sort records
- Create indexes to improve performance
- Backup a database
- Compact and repair a database

FIGURE 3-1

Project Three — Maintaining the Ashton James College Database

The steps in this project show how to make changes to the data in the Ashton James College database. They also illustrate how to search for records as well as filter records. The steps restructure the database, that is, make changes that meet the needs of the user, in this case, Ashton James College. This includes adding an additional field as well as increasing the width of one of the existing fields. Other changes modify the structure of the database in a way that prevents users from entering invalid data. Steps are presented to create indexes that reduce the time it takes for some operations, for example, those involving sorting the data.

Opening the Database

If you are stepping through this project on a computer and you want your screen to match the figures in this book, then you should change your computer's resolution to 800 × 600. For more information on how to change the resolution on your computer, see Appendix D. Before carrying out the steps in this project, first you must open the database. The steps on the next page start Access and open the database. The steps assume that the Ashton James College database is located on a USB flash drive. If your database is located anywhere else, you will need to adjust the appropriate steps.

To Open a Database

1 Click the Start button on the Windows taskbar, point to All Programs on the Start menu, point to Microsoft Office on the All Programs submenu, and then click Microsoft Office Access 2003 on the Microsoft Office submenu.

2 If the Access window is not maximized, double-click its title bar to maximize it.

3 If the Language bar appears, right-click it and then click Close the Language bar on the shortcut menu.

4 Click the Open button on the Database toolbar.

5 If necessary, click the Look in box arrow and then click UDISK 2.0 (E:). (Your USB flash drive may have a different name and letter.) Click Ashton James College, the database modified in Project 2. (If you did not complete the steps in Project 2, see your instructor for a copy of the database.)

6 Click the Open button in the Open dialog box. If the Security Warning dialog box appears, click the Open button.

The database opens and the Ashton James College : Database window appears.

Updating Records

Keeping the data in a database up-to-date requires updating records in three ways: adding new records, changing the data in existing records, and deleting existing records.

Adding Records

In Project 1, you added records to a database using Datasheet view; that is, as you were adding records, the records were appearing on the screen in the form of a datasheet, or table. When you need to add additional records, you can use the same techniques.

In Project 1, you used a form to view records. This is called Form view. You also can use **Form view** to update the data in a table. To add new records, change existing records, or delete records, you will use the same techniques you used in Datasheet view. The following steps add a record to the Client table with a form, for example. These steps use the Client form created in Project 1.

To Use a Form to Add Records

1

• **With the Ashton James College database open, click Forms on the Objects bar, and then right-click the Client form.**

The list of forms appears (Figure 3-2). The shortcut menu for the Client form also appears.

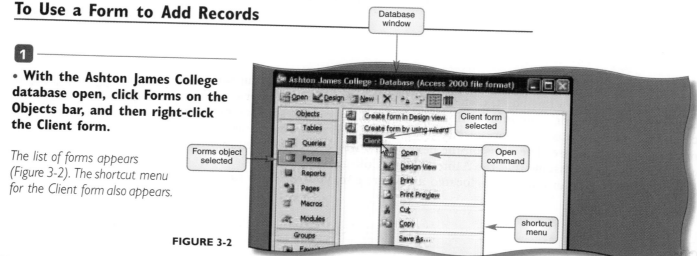

FIGURE 3-2

2

- **Click Open on the shortcut menu.**

The form for the Client table appears (Figure 3-3). Your toolbars may be arranged differently.

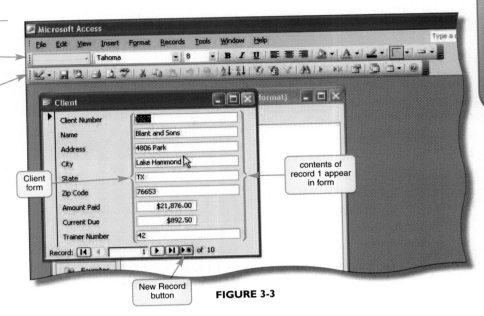

FIGURE 3-3

3

- **Click the New Record button on the Navigation bar, and then type the data for the new record as shown in Figure 3-4. Press the TAB key after typing the data in each field, except after typing the data for the final field (Trainer Number).**

The record appears.

4

- **Press the TAB key.**

The record now is added to the Client table and the contents of the form are erased.

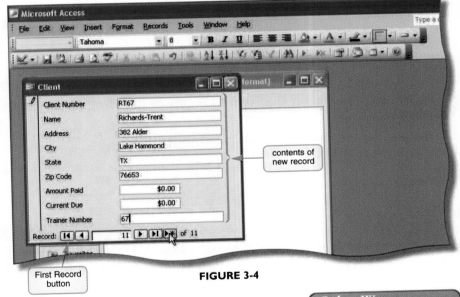

FIGURE 3-4

Other Ways

1. Click New Record button on Form View toolbar
2. On Insert menu click New Record
3. In Voice Command mode, say "Insert, New Record"

Searching for a Record

In the database environment, **searching** means looking for records that satisfy some criteria. Looking for the client whose number is FL93 is an example of searching. The queries in Project 2 also were examples of searching. Access had to locate those records that satisfied the criteria.

A need for searching also exists when using Form view or Datasheet view. To update client FL93, for example, first you need to find the client.

You need a way to be able to go directly to a record just by giving the value in some field. This is the function of the Find button. Before clicking the Find button, select the field for the search.

The steps on the next page show how to search for the client whose number is FL93.

To Search for a Record

1

• Make sure the Client table is open and the form for the Client table is displayed.

• If necessary, click the First Record button to display the first record.

• If the Client Number field currently is not selected, select it by clicking the field name.

The first record appears on the form (Figure 3-5).

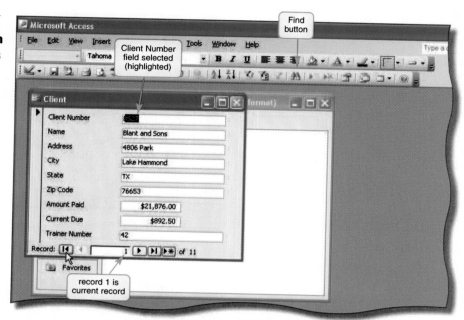

FIGURE 3-5

2

• Click the Find button on the Form View toolbar.

• Type FL93 in the Find What text box and then click the Find Next button.

Access displays the Find and Replace dialog box, locates the record for client FL93, and displays it in the Client form (Figure 3-6). The Find What text box contains the entry, FL93.

3

• Click the Cancel button in the Find and Replace dialog box.

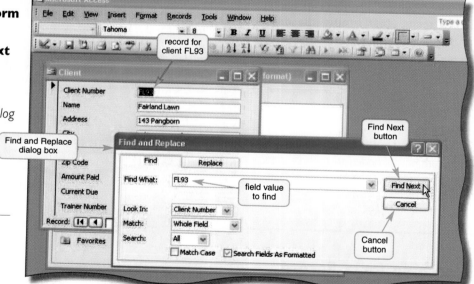

FIGURE 3-6

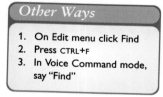

Other Ways

1. On Edit menu click Find
2. Press CTRL+F
3. In Voice Command mode, say "Find"

In some cases, after locating a record that satisfies a criterion, you might need to find the next record that satisfies the same criterion. For example, if you just found the first client whose trainer number is 42, you then may want to find the second such client, then the third, and so on. To do so, repeat the same process. You will not need to retype the value each time, however.

Changing the Contents of a Record

After locating the record to be changed, select the field to be changed by clicking the field. You also can press the TAB key repeatedly. Then make the appropriate changes. (Clicking the field automatically produces an insertion point. If you use the TAB key, you will need to press F2 to produce an insertion point.)

Normally, Access is in **Insert mode**, so the characters typed will be inserted at the appropriate position. To change to **Overtype mode**, press the INSERT key. The letters, OVR, will appear near the bottom right edge of the status bar. To return to Insert mode, press the INSERT key. In Insert mode, if the data in the field completely fills the field, no additional characters can be inserted. In this case, you would need to increase the size of the field before inserting the characters. You will see how to do this later in the project.

The following step uses Form view to change the name of client FL93 to Fairland Lawns by inserting the letter s after Lawn. Sufficient room exists in the field to make this change.

To Update the Contents of a Field

1

• **Click in the Name field text box for client FL93 after the word Lawn, and then type s (the letter s) to change the name.**

The name is changed. The mouse pointer shape is an I-beam (Figure 3-7).

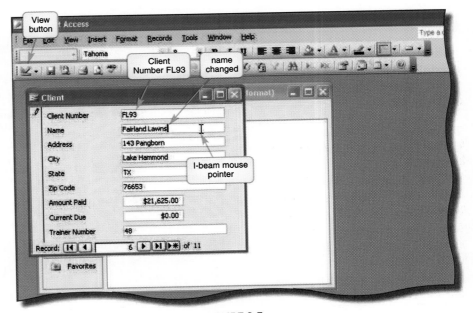

FIGURE 3-7

Once you move to another record or close this table, the change to the name will become permanent.

Switching Between Views

Sometimes, after working in Form view where you can see all fields, but only one record, it is helpful to see several records at a time. To do so, switch to Datasheet view. The steps on the next page switch from Form view to Datasheet view.

To Switch from Form View to Datasheet View

1

• **Click the View button arrow on the Form View toolbar (see Figure 3-7 on the previous page).**

The View button list appears (Figure 3-8).

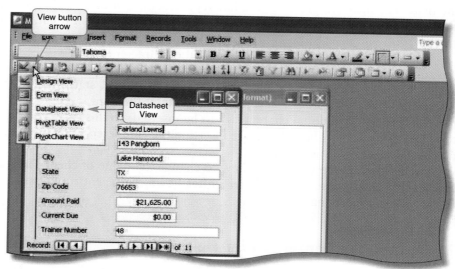

FIGURE 3-8

2

• **Click Datasheet View, and then maximize the window containing the datasheet by double-clicking its title bar.**

The datasheet appears (Figure 3-9). The position in the table is maintained. The current record selector points to client FL93, the client that appeared on the screen in Form view. The Name field, the field in which the insertion point appears, is selected. The new record for client RT67 is currently the last record in the table. When you close the table and open it later, client RT67 will be in its appropriate location.

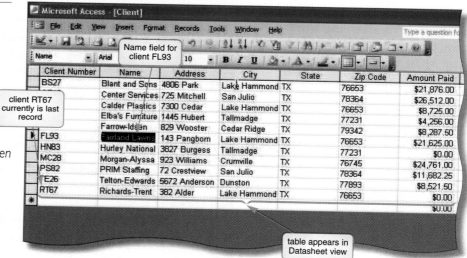

FIGURE 3-9

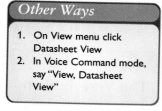

Other Ways

1. On View menu click Datasheet View
2. In Voice Command mode, say "View, Datasheet View"

If you want to return to Form view, use the same process. The only difference is that you click Form View rather than Datasheet View.

Filtering Records

You can use the Find button in either Datasheet view or Form view to locate a record quickly that satisfies some criterion (for example, the client number is FL93). All records appear, however, not just the record or records that satisfy the criterion. To have only the record or records that satisfy the criterion appear, use a **filter**. Three types of filters are available: Filter By Selection, Filter By Form, and Advanced Filter/Sort. You can use a filter in either Datasheet view or Form view.

Using Filter By Selection

The simplest type of filter is called **Filter By Selection**. To use Filter By Selection, you first must give Access an example of the data you want by selecting the data within the table. The following steps use Filter By Selection in Datasheet view to display only the records for clients in San Julio.

To Use Filter By Selection

1

- **Click the City field on the second record.**

The insertion point appears in the City field on the second record (Figure 3-10). The city on this record is San Julio.

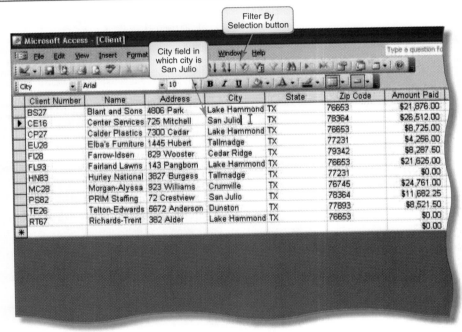

FIGURE 3-10

2

- **Click the Filter By Selection button on the Table Datasheet toolbar (see Figure 3-10).**

- **If instructed to do so, print the results by clicking the Print button on the Table Datasheet toolbar.**

Only the clients located in San Julio appear (Figure 3-11).

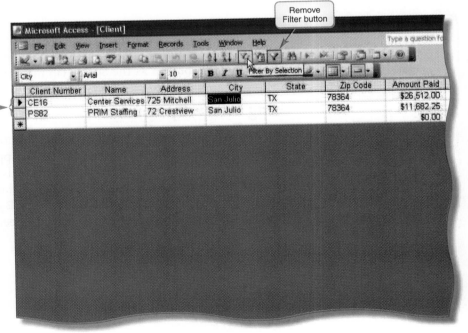

FIGURE 3-11

To redisplay all the records, remove the filter as shown in the following step.

To Remove a Filter

1

• **Click the Remove Filter button on the Table Datasheet toolbar (see Figure 3-11 on the previous page).**

All records appear (Figure 3-12).

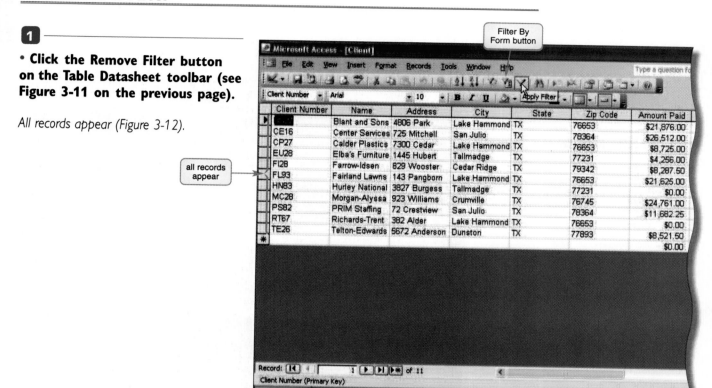

FIGURE 3-12

After you remove the filter, the button changes from the Remove Filter button to the Apply Filter button as the ScreenTip indicates.

Using Filter By Form

Filter By Selection is a quick and easy way to filter by the value in a single field. For more complex criteria, however, it is not appropriate. For example, you could not use Filter By Selection to restrict the records to those for which the city is Lake Hammond and the trainer number is 42. For this type of query, in which you want to specify multiple criteria, you can use **Filter By Form**. The following steps illustrate using this filtering method in Datasheet view.

To Use Filter By Form

1

- Click the **Filter By Form** button on the Table Datasheet toolbar (see Figure 3-12).

- Click the **City** field (San Julio may appear in the field), click the arrow that appears, and then click **Lake Hammond**.

- Click the right scroll arrow so the **Trainer Number** field is on the screen, click the **Trainer Number** field, click the down arrow that appears, and then click **42**.

The form for filtering appears (Figure 3-13). Lake Hammond is selected as the city, and 42 is selected as the trainer number.

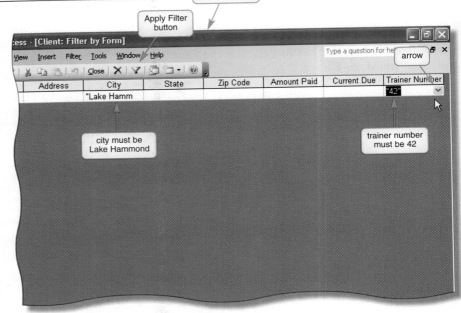

FIGURE 3-13

2

- Click the **Apply Filter** button on the Filter/Sort toolbar.

- If instructed to do so, print the results by clicking the **Print** button on the Table Datasheet toolbar.

The only record included is the record on which the city is Lake Hammond and the trainer number is 42 (Figure 3-14).

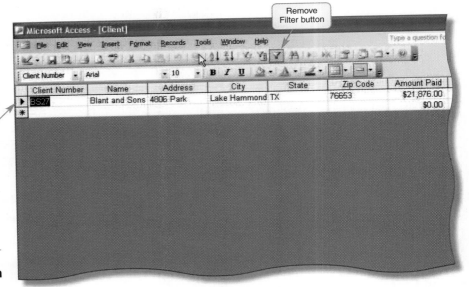

FIGURE 3-14

3

- Click the **Remove Filter** button on the Table Datasheet toolbar.

All records are shown.

Using Advanced Filter/Sort

In some cases, your criteria may be too complex even for Filter By Form. For example, you might want to include any client for which the city is Lake Hammond and the trainer is number 42. You also may want to include any client of trainer 48, no matter where the client is located. Further, you might want to have the results sorted by name. To filter records using complex criteria, you need to use **Advanced Filter/Sort** as illustrated in the steps on the next page.

To Use Advanced Filter/Sort

1

• **Click Records on the menu bar, and then point to Filter.**

The Filter submenu appears (Figure 3-15).

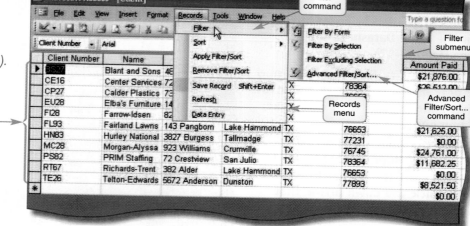

FIGURE 3-15

2

• **Click Advanced Filter/Sort.**

Access displays the ClientFilter1 : Filter window (Figure 3-16). The screen looks just like the screens you used to create queries. The city and trainer number criteria from the previous filter appear. If you were creating a different filter, you could delete these.

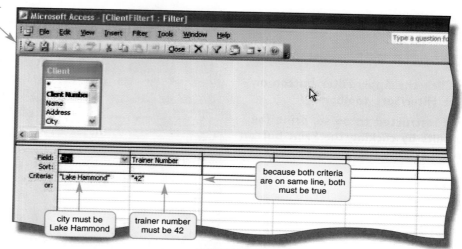

FIGURE 3-16

3

• **Type 48 as the criterion in the second Criteria row (the or row) of the Trainer Number column, double-click the Name field to add the field to the filter, click the Sort row for the Name column, click the arrow that appears, and then click Ascending.**

The additional criteria for the Trainer Number field are entered (Figure 3-17). The data will be sorted on Name in ascending order.

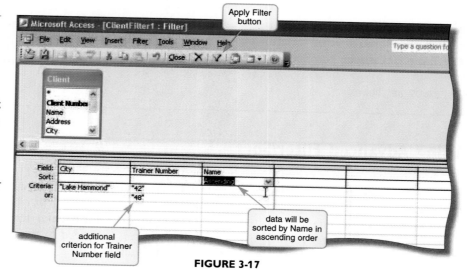

FIGURE 3-17

4

• **Click the Apply Filter button on the Filter/Sort toolbar.**

• **If instructed to do so, print the results by clicking the Print button on the Table Datasheet toolbar.**

The filtered data appears (Figure 3-18). Only the clients who satisfy the criteria in the filter are included. The clients are ordered by name.

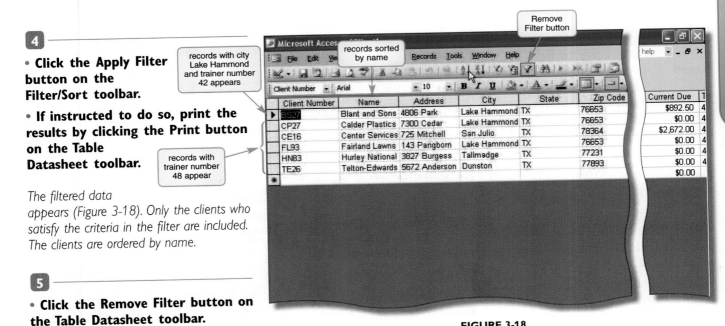

FIGURE 3-18

5

• **Click the Remove Filter button on the Table Datasheet toolbar.**

All records are shown.

Q&A

Q: Can you filter records that have been retrieved as the result of a query?

A: Yes. You can use Filter By Selection, Filter By Form, and Advanced Filter/Sort in the Query Datasheet window just as you did in the Table Datasheet window. You also can use the command in Form view.

Deleting Records

When records no longer are needed, **delete the records** (remove them) from the table. For example, suppose client EU28 no longer is served by Ashton James College and its final payment is made. The record for that client should be deleted. The following steps delete client EU28.

To Delete a Record

1

• **With the datasheet for the Client table on the screen, click the record selector of the record in which the client number is EU28.**

The record is selected (Figure 3-19).

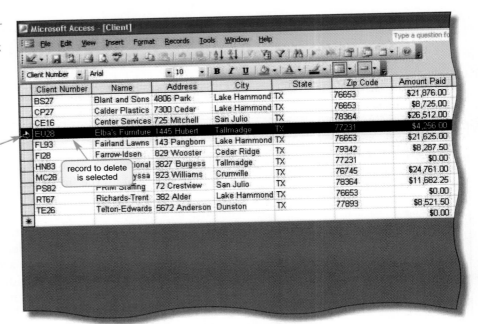

FIGURE 3-19

2

• **Press the DELETE key to delete the record.**

Access displays the Microsoft Office Access dialog box (Figure 3-20). The message indicates that one record will be deleted.

3

• **Click the Yes button to complete the deletion.**

• **If instructed to do so, print the results by clicking the Print button on the Table Datasheet toolbar.**

• **Close the window containing the table by clicking its Close Window button.**

The record is deleted and the table no longer appears.

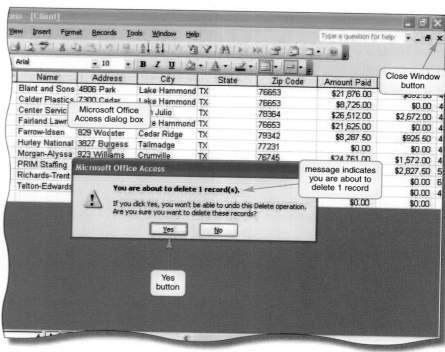

FIGURE 3-20

You can delete records using a form just as you delete records using a datasheet. To do so, first navigate to the record to be deleted. For example, you can use the Navigation buttons or you can locate the desired record using the Find button. The following steps illustrate how to delete a record in Form view after you have located the record to be deleted.

To Delete a Record in Form View

1. Click the Record Selector (the triangle in front of the record) to select the entire record.
2. Press the DELETE key.
3. When Access displays the dialog box asking if you want to delete the record, click the Yes button.

Changing the Structure

When you initially create a database, you define its **structure**; that is, you indicate the names, types, and sizes of all the fields. In many cases, the structure you first define will not continue to be appropriate as you use the database.

Characteristics of a given field may need to change. For example, a client name might be stored incorrectly in the database. In this example, the name Morgan-Alyssa actually should be Morgan-Alyssa Academy. The Name field is not large enough, however, to hold the correct name. To accommodate this change, you need to restructure the database by increasing the width of the Name field.

It may be that a field currently in the table no longer is necessary. If no one ever uses a particular field, it is not needed in the table. Because it is occupying space and serving no useful purpose, it should be removed from the table. You also would need to delete the field from any forms, reports, or queries that include it.

To make any of these changes, you first must open the table in Design view.

Changing the Size of a Field

The following steps change the size of the Name field from 20 to 25 to accommodate the change of name from Morgan-Alyssa to Morgan-Alyssa Academy.

To Change the Size of a Field

1

• **In the Database window, click Tables on the Objects bar, and then right-click Client.**

The shortcut menu for the Client table appears (Figure 3-21).

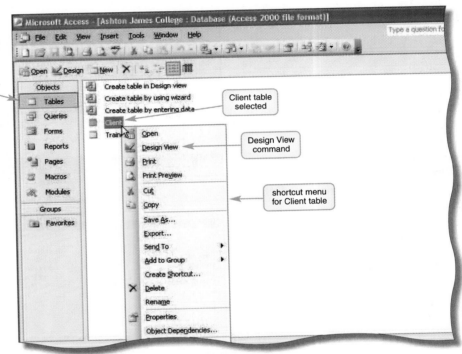

FIGURE 3-21

2

• **Click Design View on the shortcut menu.**

Access displays the Client : Table window (Figure 3-22).

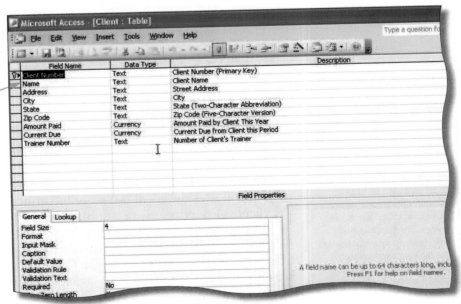

FIGURE 3-22

3

• **Click the row selector for the Name field.**

The Name field is selected (Figure 3-23).

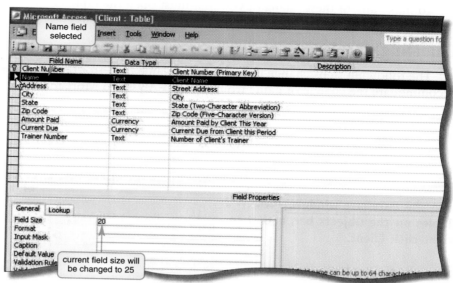

FIGURE 3-23

4

• **Press F6 to select the field size, type 25 as the new size, and then press F6 again.**

The field size is changed (Figure 3-24).

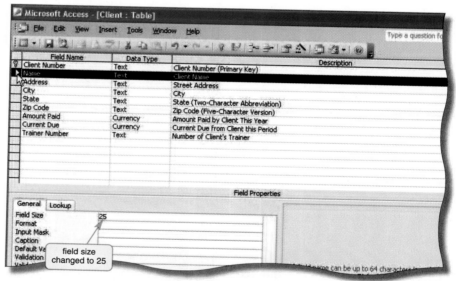

FIGURE 3-24

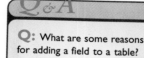

Adding a New Field

The next step is to categorize the clients of the Ashton James College database. To do so, you must add an additional field, Client Type. The possible values for Client Type are EDU (which indicates the client is an educational institution), MAN (which indicates the client is a manufacturing organization), or SER (which indicates the client is a service organization).

To be able to store the client type, the following steps add a new field, called Client Type, to the table. The possible entries in this field are EDU, MAN, and SER. The new field will follow Zip Code in the list of fields; that is, it will be the seventh field in the restructured table. The current seventh field (Amount Paid) will become the eighth field, Current Due will become the ninth field, and so on. The following steps add the field.

To Add a Field to a Table

1

- **Click the row selector for the Amount Paid field, and then press the INSERT key to insert a blank row.**

A blank row appears in the position for the new field (Figure 3-25).

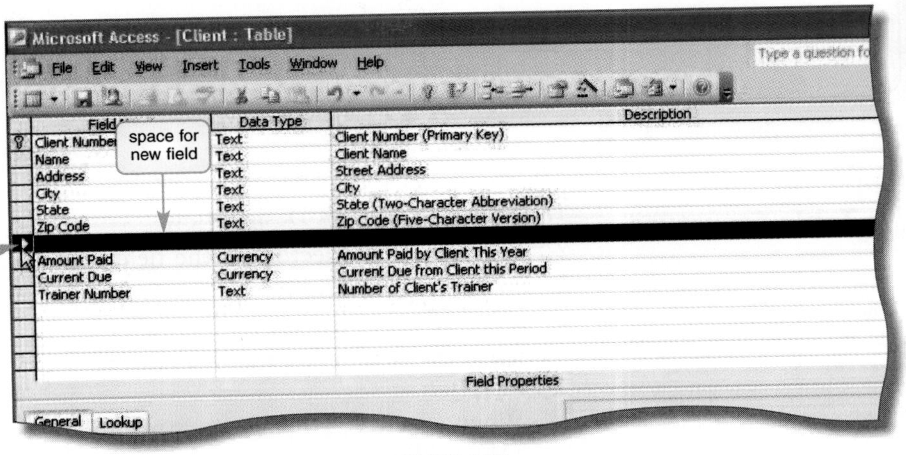

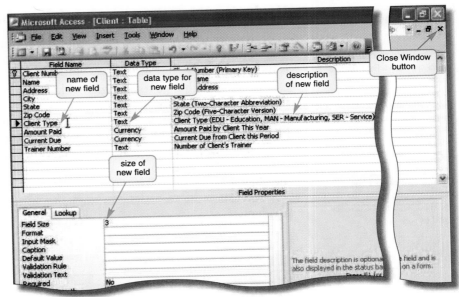

FIGURE 3-25

2

- **Click the Field Name column for the new field.**

- **Type** Client Type **as the field name and then press the TAB key. Select the Text data type by pressing the TAB key.**

- **Type** Client Type (EDU - Education, MAN - Manufacturing, SER - Service) **as the description.**

- **Press F6 to move to the Field Size text box, type** 3 **(the size of the Client Type field), and then press F6 again.**

The entries for the new field are complete (Figure 3-26).

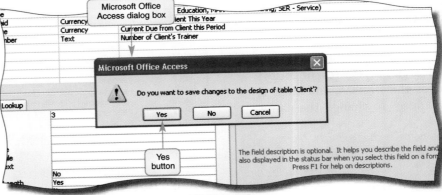

FIGURE 3-26

 3

- **Close the Client : Table window by clicking its Close Window button.**

The Microsoft Office Access dialog box is displayed (Figure 3-27).

 4

Click the Yes button to save the changes.

The changes are saved.

FIGURE 3-27

Other Ways

1. Click Insert Rows button on Table Design toolbar
2. On Insert menu click Rows
3. In Voice Command mode, say "Insert Rows"

More About

Moving a Field in a Table Structure

If you add a field to a table and later realize the field is in the wrong location, you can move the field. To do so, click the row selector for the field twice, and then drag the field to the new location.

More About

Changing Data Types

It is possible to change the data type for a field that already contains data. Before you change a data type, however, you should consider what effect the change will have on other database objects, such as forms, queries, and reports. For example, you could convert a Text field to a Memo field or to a Hyperlink field. You also could convert a Number field to a Currency field or vice versa.

The Client Type field now is included in the table and available for use.

Deleting a Field

If a field in one of your tables no longer is needed; for example, it serves no useful purpose or it may have been included by mistake, you should delete the field. The following steps illustrate how to delete a field.

To Delete a Field

1. Open the table in Design view.
2. Click the row selector for the field to be deleted.
3. Press the DELETE key.
4. When Access displays the dialog box requesting confirmation that you want to delete the field, click the Yes button.

When you save your changes to the table structure, the field will be removed from the table.

Updating the Restructured Database

Changes to the structure are available immediately. The Name field is longer, although it does not appear that way on the screen, and the new Client Type field is included.

To make a change to a single field, such as changing the name from Morgan-Alyssa to Morgan-Alyssa Academy, click the field to be changed, and then make the necessary correction. If the record to be changed is not on the screen, use the Navigation buttons (Next Record, Previous Record) to move to it. If the field to be corrected simply is not visible on the screen, use the horizontal scroll bar along the bottom of the screen to shift all the fields until the correct one appears. Then make the change.

The following step changes the name of Morgan-Alyssa to Morgan-Alyssa Academy.

To Update the Contents of a Field

1

• **Be sure the Client table is selected in the Database window, and then click the Open button on the Database window toolbar.**

• **Click to the right of the final a in Morgan-Alyssa (client MC28), press the SPACEBAR, and then type** Academy **to change the name.**

The name is changed from Morgan-Alyssa to Morgan-Alyssa Academy (Figure 3-28). Only the final portion of the name currently appears.

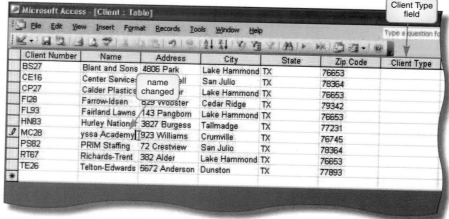

FIGURE 3-28

Changing the Appearance of a Datasheet

You can change the appearance of a datasheet in a variety of ways. You can resize columns and rows. You can change the font, the font size, the font style, and the color. You also can change the color of the gridlines in the datasheet as well as the cell effects.

Q&A

Q: Why would you need to change a data type?

A: You may need to change a data type because you imported data from another tool and Access imported the data type incorrectly. Also, you may find that a data type no longer is appropriate for a field. For example, a Text field can contain a maximum of 255 characters. If the data stored in a Text field exceeds 255 characters, you could change the data type to Memo.

Resizing Columns

The Access default column sizes do not always allow all the data in the field to appear. You can correct this problem by **resizing** the column (changing its size) in the datasheet. In some instances, you actually may want to reduce the size of a column. The State field, for example, is short enough that it does not require all the space on the screen that is allotted to it.

Both types of changes are made the same way. Position the mouse pointer on the right boundary of the column's **field selector** (the line in the column heading immediately to the right of the name of the column to be resized). The mouse pointer will change to a two-headed arrow with a vertical bar. You then can drag the line to resize the column. In addition, you can double-click in the line, in which case Access will determine the **best fit** for the column.

The following steps illustrate the process for resizing the Name column to the size that best fits the data.

To Resize a Column

1

- **Point to the right boundary of the field selector for the Name field.**

The mouse pointer shape changes to a bar with a double-arrow, indicating that the column can be resized (Figure 3-29).

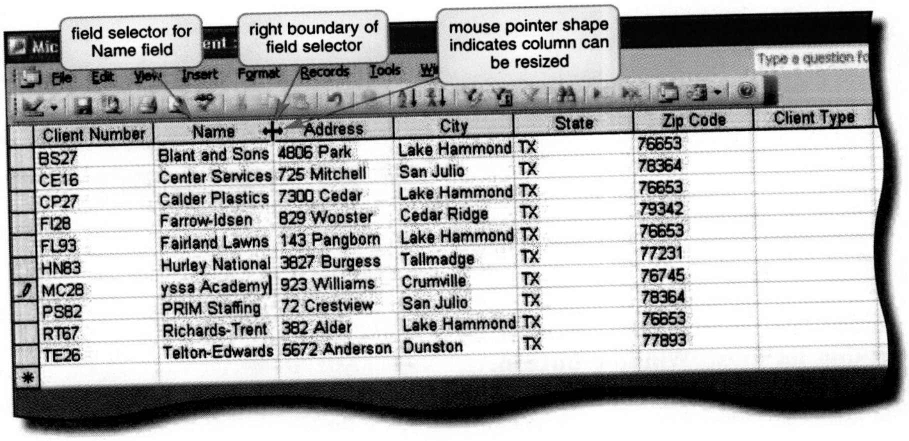

FIGURE 3-29

2

- **Double-click the right boundary of the field selector for the Name field.**

The Name column has been resized (Figure 3-30).

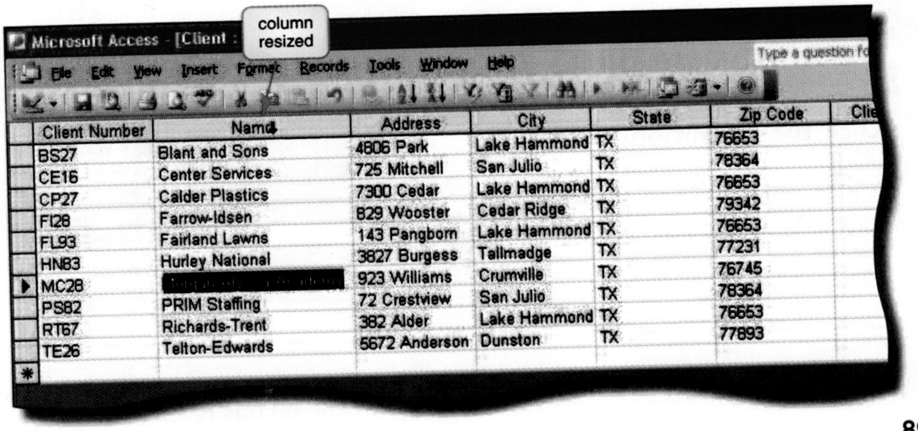

FIGURE 3-30

3

• **Use the same technique to resize the Client Number, Address, City, State, Zip Code, Client Type, and Amount Paid columns to best fit the data.**

The columns have been resized (Figure 3-31).

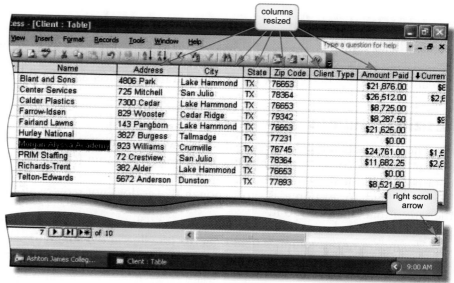

FIGURE 3-31

4

• **If necessary, click the right scroll arrow to display the Current Due and Trainer Number columns, and then resize the columns to best fit the data.**

All the columns have been resized (Figure 3-32).

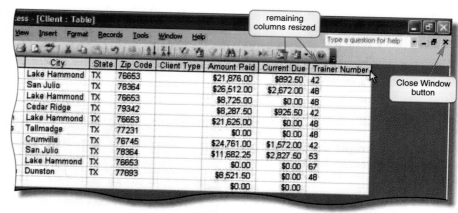

FIGURE 3-32

5

• **Close the Client : Table window by clicking its Close Window button.**

The Microsoft Office Access dialog box is displayed (Figure 3-33). Changing a column width changes the layout, or design, of a table.

6

• **Click the Yes button.**

The next time the datasheet is displayed, the columns will have the new widths.

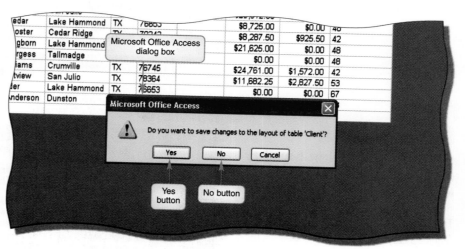

FIGURE 3-33

The change to the layout is saved.

Formatting a Datasheet

In addition to changing the column size, you can format a datasheet in other ways. You can change various aspects of the font, including the font itself, the font style, the size, and the color. You can change the cell effects to make the cells appear raised or sunken, and you can change the gridline color.

The changes to the datasheet will be reflected not only on the screen, but also when you print or preview the datasheet.

In this section, the following steps illustrate how to change the font in the datasheet and the format of the datasheet grid. You then will preview what the datasheet would look like when it is printed. At this point, you can print the datasheet if you so desire. Finally, you will close the datasheet without saving the changes. That way, the next time you view the datasheet, it will appear in its original format.

These steps show how to open the Trainer table in Datasheet view and then change the font.

To Change the Font in a Datasheet

1

- **With the Tables object selected and the Trainer table selected, click the Open button on the Database Window toolbar.**

- **Click Format on the menu bar.**

Access displays the Trainer table in Datasheet view (Figure 3-34). The Format menu appears.

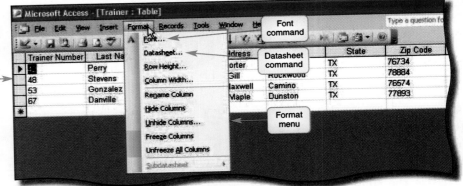

FIGURE 3-34

2

- **Click Font, click Arial Rounded MT Bold in the Font list, and then click 9 in the Size list. (If you do not have Arial Rounded MT Bold available, click another similar font.)**

Access displays the Font dialog box (Figure 3-35). Arial Rounded MT Bold is selected as the font style and 9 is selected as the font size.

3

- **Click the OK button.**

The font is changed.

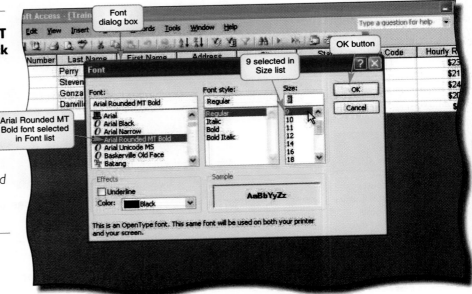

FIGURE 3-35

The following steps change the format of the grid.

To Change the Format of the Datasheet Grid

1

• **Click Format on the menu bar, and then click Datasheet.**

Access displays the Datasheet Formatting dialog box (Figure 3-36).

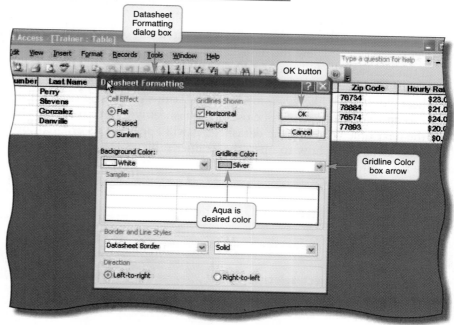

FIGURE 3-36

2

• **Click the Gridline Color box arrow, click Aqua, and then click the OK button.**

• **Resize the columns to best fit the data.**

The gridline color is changed to aqua and the columns have been resized (Figure 3-37).

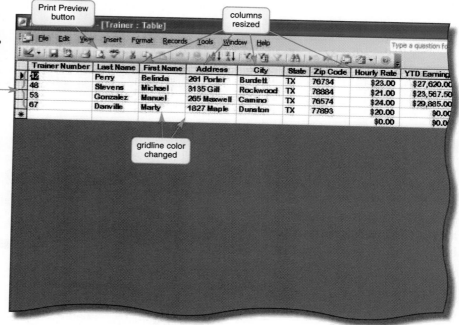

FIGURE 3-37

The following steps use Print Preview to preview the changes to the datasheet.

To Use Print Preview

1

• **Click the Print Preview button on the Table Datasheet toolbar.**

• **If instructed to do so, print the results by clicking the Print button on the Print Preview toolbar.**

Access displays the pre-view window (Figure 3-38). The changes in the datasheet format are reflected in the preview.

2

• **Click the Close button on the Print Preview toolbar.**

The preview no longer appears.

Close button

columns resized

font and font size changed

Trainer Number	Last Name	First Name	Address	City	State	Zip Code	Hourly Rate
42	Perry	Belinda	261 Porter	Burdett	TX	76734	$23.00
48	Stevens	Michael	3135 Gill	Rockwood	TX	78884	$21.00
53	Gonzalez	Manuel	265 Maxwell	Camino	TX	76574	$24.00
67	Danville	Marty	1627 Maple	Dunston	TX	77893	$20.00

Trainer   9/15/2005

gridline color changed

print preview of Trainer table

FIGURE 3-38

To print the datasheet, click the Print button on either the Table Datasheet toolbar or the Print Preview toolbar. The changes to the format are reflected in the printout.

The following steps show how to close the datasheet without saving the changes to the format.

To Close the Datasheet Without Saving the Format Changes

1 Click the Close Window button for the **Trainer : Table** window.

2 Click the **No** button in the **Microsoft Office Access** dialog box when asked if you want to save your changes.

Because the changes are not saved, the next time you open the Trainer table it will appear in the original format (see Figure 3-34 on page AC 133). If you had saved the changes, the changes would be reflected in its appearance.

Mass Changes

In some cases, rather than making individual changes, you will want to make mass changes. That is, you will want to add, change, or delete many records in a single operation. You can do this with queries. An update query allows you to make the same change to all records satisfying some criterion. If you omit the criterion, you will make the same changes to all records in the table. A delete query allows you to delete all the records satisfying some criterion. You can add the results of a query to an existing table by using an append query. You also can add the results to a new table by using a make-table query.

Q: Can you format query results?

A: Yes. You can format the results of a query in Query Datasheet view just as you can in Table Datasheet view. You can resize columns, change various aspects of the font, change cell effects, and change gridline colors.

More About

Action Queries

An action query is a query that makes changes to many records in just one operation. The four types of action queries are: delete, update, append, and make-table.

Using an Update Query

The Client Type field is blank on every record. One approach to entering the information for the field would be to step through the entire table, assigning each record its appropriate value. If most of the clients have the same type, a simpler approach is available.

In the Ashton James College database, for example, most clients are type SER. Initially, you can set all the values to SER. To accomplish this quickly and easily, you can use an **update query**, which is a query that makes the same change to all the records satisfying a criterion. Later, you can change the type for educational institutions and manufacturing organizations.

The process for creating an update query begins the same as the process for creating the queries in Project 2. You select the table for the query and then use the Query Type button to change to an update query. In the design grid, an extra row, Update To, appears. Use this additional row to indicate the way the data will be updated. If a criterion is entered, then only those records that satisfy the criterion will be updated.

The following steps change the value in the Client Type field to SER for all the records. Because all records are to be updated, criteria are not required.

To Use an Update Query to Update All Records

1

• **With the Client table selected, click the New Object button arrow on the Database toolbar and then click Query. With Design View selected in the New Query dialog box, click the OK button.**

• **Be sure the Query1 : Select Query window is maximized.**

• **Resize the upper and lower panes of the window as well as the Client field list so all fields in the Client table field list appear (see Figure 2-6 on page AC 70 in Project 2).**

Click the Query Type button arrow on the Query Design toolbar.

The list of available query types appears (Figure 3-39).

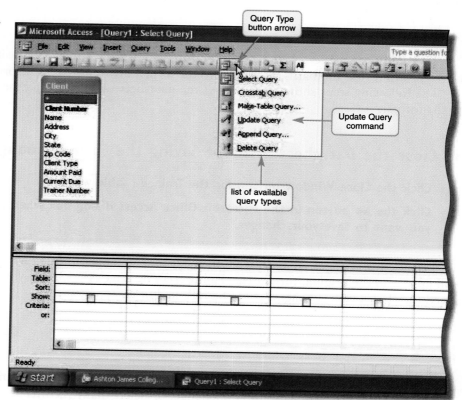

FIGURE 3-39

2

• Click Update Query, double-click the Client Type field to select the field, click the Update To row in the first column of the design grid, and then type SER as the new value.

The Client Type field is selected (Figure 3-40). In an update query, the Update To row appears in the design grid. The value to which the field is to be changed is entered as SER. Because no criteria are entered, the Client Type value on every row will be changed to SER.

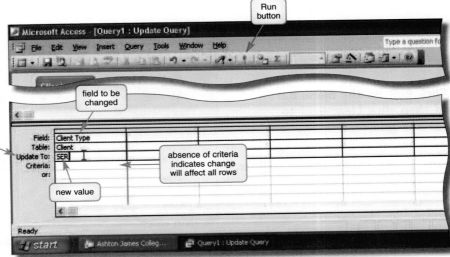

FIGURE 3-40

3

• Click the Run button on the Query Design toolbar.

The Microsoft Office Access dialog box is displayed (Figure 3-41). The message indicates that 10 rows (records) will be updated by the query.

4

• Click the Yes button.

The changes are made.

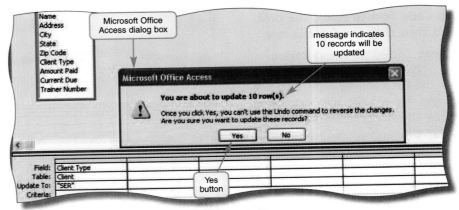

FIGURE 3-41

Other Ways

1. On Query menu click Update Query
2. Right-click any open area in upper pane, point to Query Type on shortcut menu, click Update Query on Query Type submenu
3. In Voice Command mode, say "Query, Update Query"

Using a Delete Query

In some cases, you may need to delete several records at a time. If, for example, all clients in a particular Zip code are to be serviced by another firm, the clients with this Zip code can be deleted from the Ashton James College database. Instead of deleting these clients individually, which could be very time-consuming in a large database, you can delete them in one operation by using a **delete query**, which is a query that will delete all the records satisfying the criteria entered in the query.

You can preview the data to be deleted in a delete query before actually performing the deletion. To do so, click the View button arrow on the Query Design toolbar and then click Datasheet View after you create the query, but before you run it. The records to be deleted then would appear in Datasheet view. To delete the records, click the View button arrow on the Query Datasheet toolbar and then click Design View to return to Design view. Click the Run button on the Query Design toolbar, and then click the Yes button in the Microsoft Office Access dialog box when asked if you want to delete the records.

The steps on the next page use a delete query to delete any client whose Zip code is 77893 without first previewing the data to be deleted. (Only one such client currently exists in the database.)

Q&A

Q: Why should you preview the data before running a delete query?

A: If you inadvertently enter the wrong criterion and do not realize it before you click the Yes button, you will delete the incorrect set of records. Worse yet, you might not even realize that you have done so.

To Use a Delete Query to Delete a Group of Records

1

• **Click Edit on the menu bar and then click Clear Grid to clear the grid.**

• **Click the Query Type button arrow on the Query Design toolbar.**

The list of available query types appears (Figure 3-42).

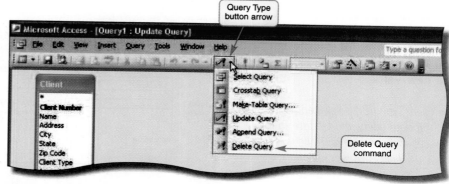

FIGURE 3-42

2

• **Click Delete Query, double-click the Zip Code field to select the field, and then click the Criteria row.**

• **Type** 77893 **as the criterion.**

The criterion is entered in the Zip Code column (Figure 3-43). In a delete query, the Delete row appears in the design grid.

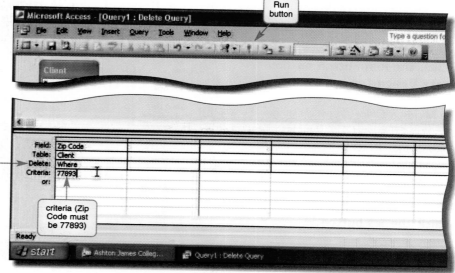

FIGURE 3-43

3

• **Click the Run button on the Query Design toolbar to run the query.**

The Microsoft Office Access dialog box is displayed (Figure 3-44). The message indicates the query will delete 1 row (record).

4

• **Click the Yes button.**

• **Close the Query window. Do not save the query.**

The client with Zip code 77893 has been removed from the table.

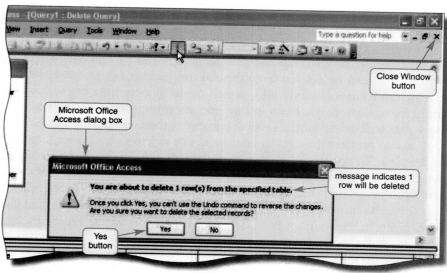

FIGURE 3-44

Using Append and Make-Table Queries

An **append query** adds a group of records from one table to the end of another table. For example, suppose that Ashton James College acquires some new clients and a database containing a table with those clients. To avoid entering all this information manually, you can append it to the Client table in the Ashton James College database using the append query. The following steps illustrate how to create an append query.

To Create an Append Query

1. Create a select query for the table containing the records to append.
2. In the design grid, indicate the fields to include, and then enter any necessary criteria.
3. Run the query to be sure you have specified the correct data, and then return to the design grid.
4. Click the Query Type button arrow on the Query Design toolbar, and then click Append Query.
5. When Access displays the Append Query dialog box, specify the name of the table to receive the new records and its location. Run the query by clicking the OK button.
6. When Access indicates the number of records to be appended, click the OK button.

The records then are added to the indicated table.

In some cases, you might want to add the records to a new table, that is, a table that has not yet been created. If so, use a **make-table query** to add the records to a new table. Access will create this table as part of the process and add the records to it.

Other Ways

1. On Query menu click Delete Query
2. Right-click any open area in upper pane, point to Query Type on shortcut menu, click Delete Query on Query Type submenu
3. In Voice Command mode, say "Query, Delete Query"

Training 3-4

To practice the following tasks, launch the SAM Training Companion CD, choose Access Project 3, and then choose Training 3-4:
• Create and run a Delete query
• Create and run an Update query

Validation Rules

You now have created, loaded, queried, and updated a database. Nothing you have done so far, however, makes sure that users enter only valid data. To ensure the entry of valid data, you create **validation rules**; that is, rules that a user must follow when entering the data. As you will see, Access will prevent users from entering data that does not follow the rules. The steps also specify **validation text**, which is the message that will appear if a user violates the validation rule.

Validation rules can indicate a **required field**, a field in which the user actually must enter data. For example, by making the Name field a required field, a user actually must enter a name (that is, the field cannot be blank). Validation rules can make sure a user's entry lies within a certain **range of values**; for example that the values in the Amount Paid field are between $0.00 and $90,000.00. They can specify a **default value**; that is, a value that Access will display on the screen in a particular field before the user begins adding a record. To make data entry of client numbers more convenient, you also can have lowercase letters appear automatically as uppercase letters. Finally, validation rules can specify a collection of acceptable values; for example, that the only legitimate entries for the Client Type field are EDU, MAN, and SER.

Specifying a Required Field

To specify that a field is to be required, change the value for the Required property from No to Yes. The steps on the next page specify that the Name field is to be a required field.

To Specify a Required Field

1

• **With the Database window open, the Tables object selected, and the Client table selected, click the Design button on the Database Window toolbar.**

• **Select the Name field by clicking its row selector.**

Access displays the Client : Table window (Figure 3-45). The Name field is selected.

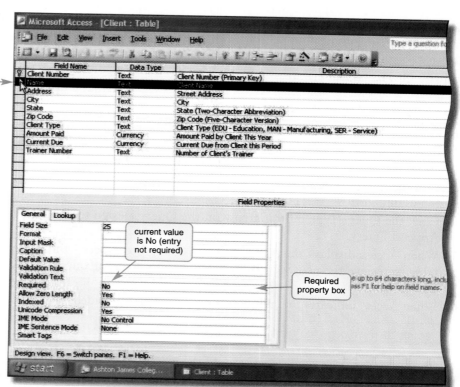

FIGURE 3-45

2

• **Click the Required property box in the Field Properties pane, and then click the down arrow that appears.**

• **Click Yes in the list.**

The value in the Required property box changes to Yes (Figure 3-46). It now is required that the user enter data into the Name field when adding a record.

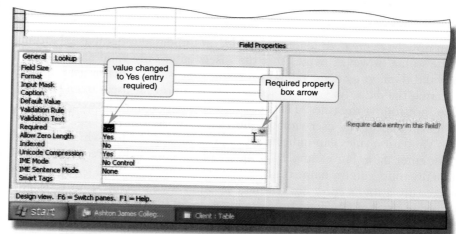

FIGURE 3-46

Specifying a Range

The following step specifies that entries in the Amount Paid field must be between $0.00 and $90,000.00. To indicate this range, the criterion specifies that the amount paid amount must be both >= 0 (greater than or equal to 0) and <= 90000 (less than or equal to 90000).

To Specify a Range

1

• **Select the Amount Paid field by clicking its row selector. Click the Validation Rule property box to produce an insertion point, and then type** >=0 and <=90000 **as the rule.**

• **Click the Validation Text property box to produce an insertion point, and then type** Must be between $0.00 and $90,000.00 **as the text.**

The validation rule and text are entered (Figure 3-47). In the Validation Rule property box, Access automatically changed the lowercase letter, a, to uppercase in the word, and. In the Validation Text property box, you should type all the text, including the dollar signs, decimal points, and comma.

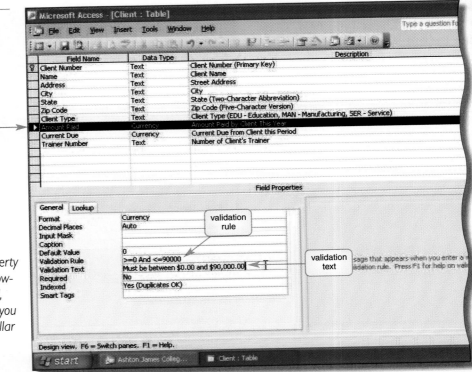

Amount Paid field selected

validation rule

validation text

FIGURE 3-47

Users now will be prohibited from entering an amount paid amount that either is less than $0.00 or greater than $90,000.00 when they add records or change the value in the Amount Paid field.

Specifying a Default Value

To specify a default value, enter the value in the Default Value property box. The step on the next page specifies SER as the default value for the Client Type field. This simply means that if users do not enter a client type, the type will be SER.

To Specify a Default Value

1

• **Select the Client Type field. Click the Default Value property box, and then type =SER as the value.**

The Client Type field is selected. The default value is entered in the Default Value property box (Figure 3-48).

Client Type field selected

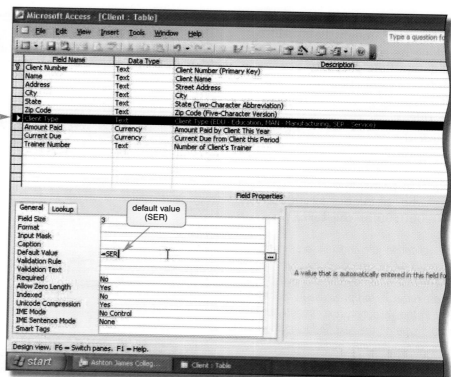

FIGURE 3-48

From this point on, if users do not make an entry in the Client Type field when adding records, Access will set the value equal to SER.

Specifying a Collection of Legal Values

The only **legal values** for the Client Type field are EDU, MAN, and SER. An appropriate validation rule for this field can direct Access to reject any entry other than these three possibilities. The following step specifies the legal values for the Client Type field.

To Specify a Collection of Legal Values

1

- **Make sure the Client Type field is selected.**

- **Click the Validation Rule property box and then type** =EDU or =MAN or =SER **as the validation rule.**

- **Click the Validation Text property box and then type** Must be EDU, MAN, or SER **as the validation text.**

The Client Type field is selected. The validation rule and text have been entered (Figure 3-49). In the Validation Rule property box, Access automatically inserted quotation marks around the EDU, MAN, and SER values and changed the lowercase letter, o, to uppercase in the word, or.

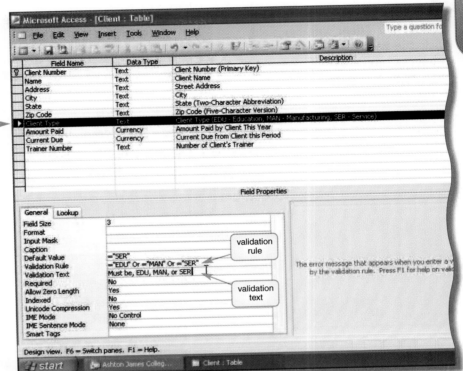

FIGURE 3-49

Users now will be allowed to enter only EDU, MAN, or SER in the Client Type field when they add records or make changes to this field.

Using a Format

To affect the way data appears in a field, you can use a **format**. To use a format with a Text field, you enter a special symbol, called a **format symbol**, in the field's Format property box. The Format property uses different settings for different data types. The following step specifies a format for the Client Number field in the Client table and illustrates the way you enter a format. The format symbol used in the example is >, which causes Access to display lowercase letters automatically as uppercase letters. The format symbol < causes Access to display uppercase letters automatically as lowercase letters.

Relationships and Lookup Wizard Fields

You cannot change the data type for a field that participates in a relationship between two tables. For example, you cannot change the data type for the Trainer Number field in the Client table to Lookup Wizard because a one-to-many relation exists between the Trainer table and the Client table. If you want to change the data type for the Trainer Number field, first you must delete the relationship in the Relationships window, change the data type to Lookup Wizard, and then re-create the relationship.

To Specify a Format

1

• **Select the Client Number field. Click the Format property box and then type > (Figure 3-50).**

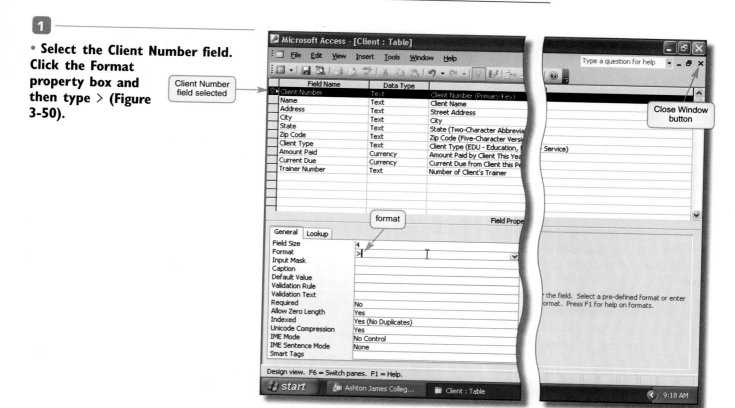

FIGURE 3-50

From this point on, any lowercase letters will appear automatically as uppercase when users add records or change the value in the Client Number field.

Saving Rules, Values, and Formats

The following steps save the validation rules, default values, and formats.

To Save the Validation Rules, Default Values, and Formats

1

• **Click the Close Window button for the Client : Table window to close the window (see Figure 3-50).**

The Microsoft Office Access dialog box is displayed, asking if you want to save your changes (Figure 3-51).

FIGURE 3-51

2

• **Click the Yes button to save the changes.**

The Microsoft Office Access dialog box is displayed (Figure 3-52). This message asks if you want the new rules applied to current records. If this were a database used to run a business or to solve some other critical need, you would click Yes. You would want to be sure that the data already in the database does not violate the rules.

3

• **Click the No button.**

The changes are saved. Existing data is not tested.

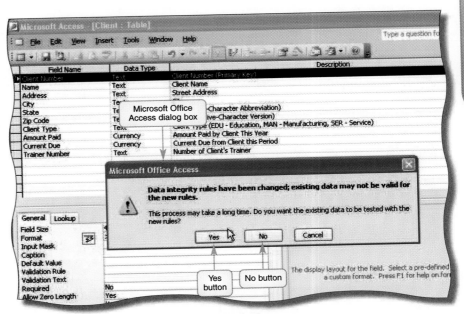

FIGURE 3-52

Updating a Table that Contains Validation Rules

When updating a table that contains validation rules, Access provides assistance in making sure the data entered is valid. It helps in making sure that data is formatted correctly. Access also will not accept invalid data. Entering a number that is out of the required range, for example, or entering a value that is not one of the possible choices, will produce an error message in the form of a dialog box. The database will not be updated until the error is corrected.

If the client number entered contains lowercase letters, such as st21 (Figure 3-53), Access will display the data automatically as ST21 (Figure 3-54).

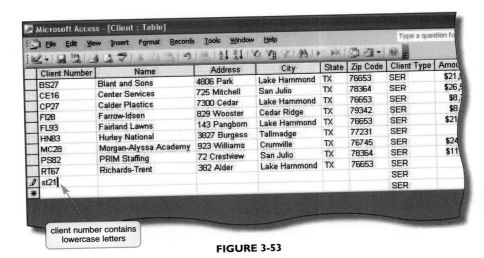

client number contains lowercase letters

FIGURE 3-53

letters automatically appear as uppercase

FIGURE 3-54

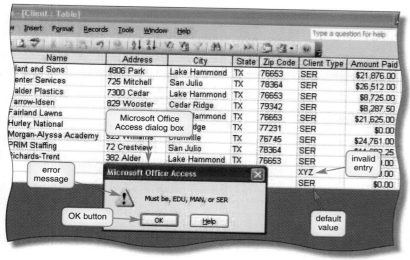

FIGURE 3-55

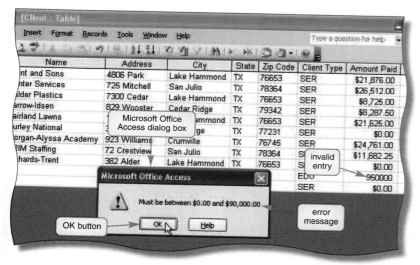

FIGURE 3-56

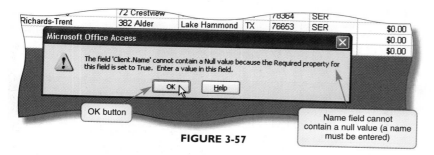

FIGURE 3-57

If the client type is not valid, such as XYZ, Access will display the text message you specified (Figure 3-55) and not allow the data to enter the database.

If the amount paid value is not valid, such as 950000, which is too large, Access also displays the appropriate message (Figure 3-56) and refuses to accept the data.

If a required field contains no data, Access indicates this by displaying an error message as soon as you attempt to leave the record (Figure 3-57). The field must contain a valid entry before Access will move to a different record.

When entering data into a field with a validation rule, you may find that Access displays the error message and you are unable to make the necessary correction. It may be that you cannot remember the validation rule you created or it was created incorrectly. In such a case, you neither can leave the field nor close the table because you have entered data into a field that violates the validation rule.

If this happens, first try again to type an acceptable entry. If this does not work, repeatedly press the BACKSPACE key to erase the contents of the field and then try to leave the field. If you are unsuccessful using this procedure, press the ESC key until the record is removed from the screen. The record will not be added to the database.

Should the need arise to take this drastic action, you probably have a faulty validation rule. Use the techniques of the previous sections to correct the existing validation rules for the field.

Creating a Lookup Field

Currently, the data type for the Client Type field is text. Users must enter a type. The validation rules ensure that they can enter only a valid type, but they do not assist the users in making the entry. To assist them in the data-entry process, you can change the Client Type field to a lookup field. A **Lookup field** allows the user to select from a list of values.

To change a field to a lookup field that selects from a list of values, use the Lookup Wizard data type as shown in the following steps.

To Create a Lookup Field

1

- **If necessary, click the Tables object. Click Client and then click the Design button on the Database Window toolbar.**

- **Click the Data Type column for the Client Type field, and then click the arrow.**

The list of available data types appears (Figure 3-58).

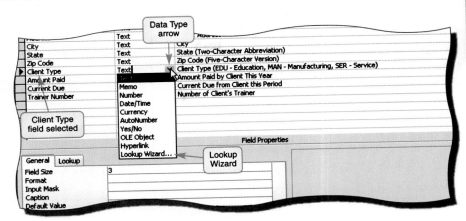

FIGURE 3-58

2

- **Click Lookup Wizard, and then click the "I will type in the values that I want" option button.**

Access displays the Lookup Wizard dialog box with options for creating a lookup column (Figure 3-59).

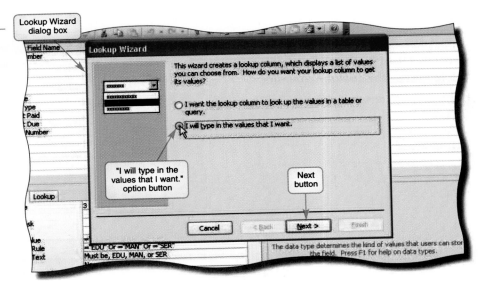

FIGURE 3-59

3

- **Click the Next button.**

The Lookup Wizard dialog box displays options for the number of columns and their values (Figure 3-60). In this screen, you enter the list of values.

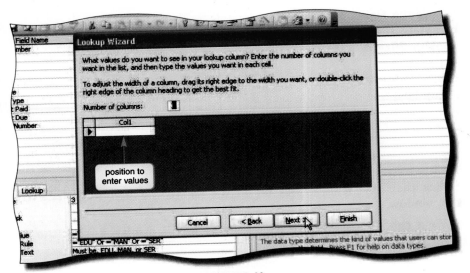

FIGURE 3-60

4

- **Click the first row of the table (below Col1), and then type** EDU **as the value in the first row.**

- **Press the DOWN ARROW key, and then type** MAN **as the value in the second row.**

- **Press the DOWN ARROW key, and then type** SER **as the value in the third row.**

The list of values for the lookup column is entered (Figure 3-61).

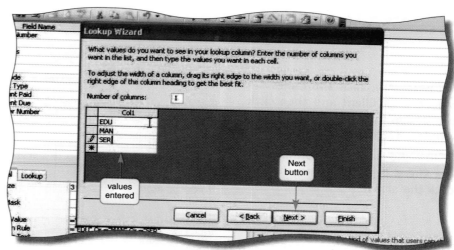

FIGURE 3-61

5

- **Click the Next button.**

- **Ensure Client Type is entered as the label for the lookup column.**

- **The label is entered (Figure 3-62).**

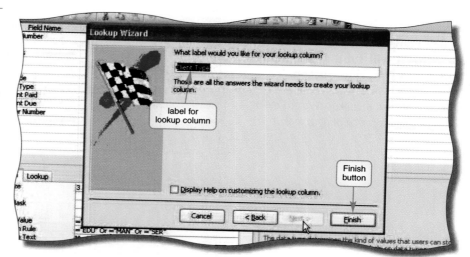

FIGURE 3-62

6

- **Click the Finish button to complete the definition of the Lookup Wizard field.**

Client Type is now a Lookup Wizard field, but the data type still is Text because the values entered in the wizard were entered as text (Figure 3-63).

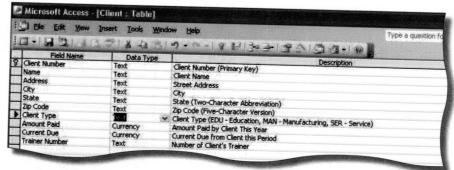

FIGURE 3-63

7

- **Click the Close Window button on the Client : Table window title bar to close the window.**

- **When the Microsoft Office Access dialog box is displayed, click the Yes button to save your changes.**

The Client Type field is now a lookup field and the changes are saved.

Using a Lookup Field

Earlier, you changed all the entries in the Client Type field to SER. Thus, you have created a rule that will ensure that only legitimate values (EDU, MAN, or SER) can be entered in the field. You also made Client Type a Lookup field. You can make changes to a Lookup field by clicking the field to be changed, clicking the arrow that appears in the field, and then selecting the desired value from the list.

The following steps change the Client Type value on the second and sixth records to MAN and on the seventh and ninth records to SER.

More About

Lookup Fields

You also can create a lookup field that looks up the values in a table or query. To do so, click the "I want the lookup column to look up values in a table or query." option button (Figure 3-59 on AC 147) in the Lookup Wizard dialog box.

To Use a Lookup Field

1

- **Make sure the Client table is displayed in Datasheet view.**

- **Click to the right of the SER entry in the Client Type field on the second record.**

An insertion point and down arrow appear in the Client Type field on the second record (Figure 3-64).

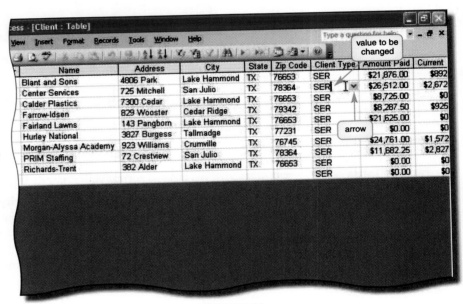

FIGURE 3-64

2

- **Click the down arrow.**

The list of values for the Client Type field appears (Figure 3-65).

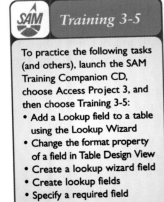
SAM   Training 3-5

To practice the following tasks (and others), launch the SAM Training Companion CD, choose Access Project 3, and then choose Training 3-5:
- Add a Lookup field to a table using the Lookup Wizard
- Change the format property of a field in Table Design View
- Create a lookup wizard field
- Create lookup fields
- Specify a required field

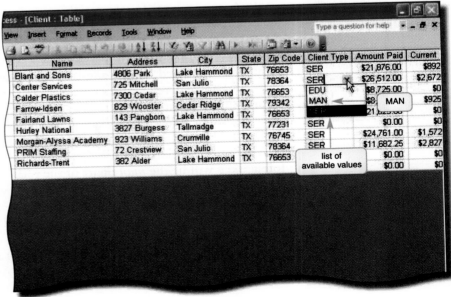

FIGURE 3-65

3

• **Click MAN to change the value.**

• **In a similar fashion, change the SER on the sixth record to MAN, on the seventh record to EDU, and on the ninth record to EDU (Figure 3-66).**

• **If instructed to do so, print the results by clicking the Print button on the Table Datasheet.**

4

• **Close the Client : Table window by clicking its Close Window button.**

The Client Type field changes now are complete.

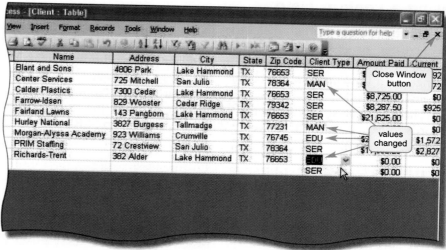

FIGURE 3-66

Referential Integrity

The property that ensures that the value in a foreign key must match that of another table's primary key is called **referential integrity**. A **foreign key** is a field in one table whose values are required to match the *primary key* of another table. In the Client table, the Trainer Number field is a foreign key that must match the primary key of the Trainer table; that is, the trainer number for any client must be a trainer currently in the Trainer table. A client whose trainer number is 92, for example, should not be stored because no such trainer exists.

Specifying Referential Integrity

In Access, to specify referential integrity, you must define a relationship between the tables by using the Relationships command. Access then prohibits any updates to the database that would violate the referential integrity.

The type of relationship between two tables specified by the Relationships command is referred to as a **one-to-many relationship**. This means that *one* record in the first table is related to (matches) *many* records in the second table, but each record in the second table is related to only *one* record in the first. In the Ashton James College database, for example, a one-to-many relationship exists between the Trainer table and the Client table. *One* trainer is associated with *many* clients, but each client is associated with only a single trainer. In general, the table containing the foreign key will be the *many* part of the relationship.

When specifying referential integrity, two ways exist to handle deletions. In the relationship between clients and trainers, for example, deletion of a trainer for whom clients exist, such as trainer number 42, would violate referential integrity. Any clients for trainer number 42 no longer would relate to any trainer in the database. The normal way to avoid this problem is to prohibit such a deletion. The other option is to **cascade the delete**, that is, have Access allow the deletion but then automatically delete any clients related to the deleted trainer.

Two ways also exist to handle the update of the primary key of the Trainer table. In the relationship between trainers and clients, for example, changing the trainer number for trainer 42 to 62 in the Trainer table would cause a problem. Clients are in the Client table on which the trainer number is 42. These clients no longer would relate to any trainer. Again, the normal way of avoiding the problem is to prohibit this type of update. The other option is to **cascade the update**; that is, have Access allow the update but then automatically make the corresponding change for any client whose trainer number was 42. It now will be 62.

The following steps use the Relationships command to specify referential integrity by specifying a relationship between the Trainer and Client tables. The steps also ensure that update will cascade, but that delete will not.

More About

Relationships: Printing Relationships

You can obtain a printed copy of your relationships after you have created them. To do so, first click the Relationships button to display the relationships. Next click File on the menu bar and then click Print Relationships. When Access displays the Print Preview window, click the Print button on the Print Preview toolbar.

To Specify Referential Integrity

1

- **With the Database window displaying, click the Relationships button on the Database toolbar.**

Access displays the Show Table dialog box (Figure 3-67).

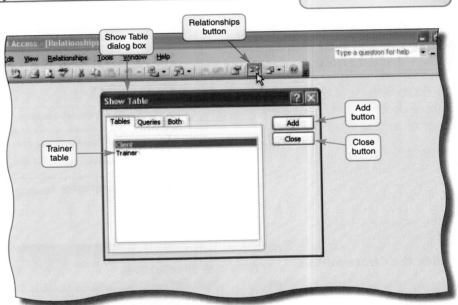

FIGURE 3-67

2

- **Click the Trainer table and then click the Add button. Click the Client table, click the Add button again, and then click the Close button in the Show Table dialog box.**

- **Resize the field lists that appear so all fields are visible.**

Field lists for the Trainer and Client tables appear (Figure 3-68). The lists have been resized so all fields are visible.

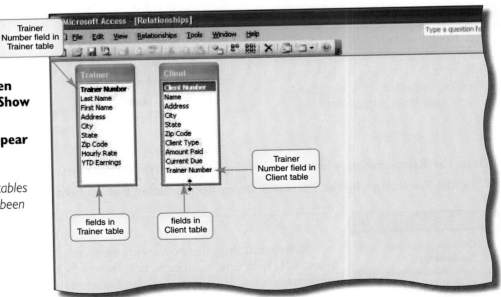

FIGURE 3-68

913

3

• **Drag the Trainer Number field in the Trainer table field list to the Trainer Number field in the Client table field list.**

Access displays the Edit Relationships dialog box (Figure 3-69). The correct fields (the Trainer Number fields) have been identified as the matching fields.

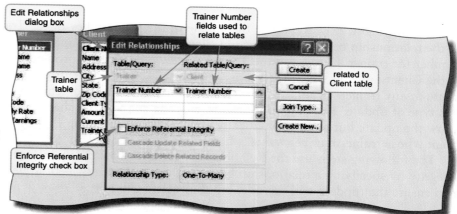

FIGURE 3-69

4

• **Click Enforce Referential Integrity to select it, and then click Cascade Update Related Fields to select it.**

The Enforce Referential Integrity and Cascade Update Related Fields check boxes are selected (Figure 3-70).

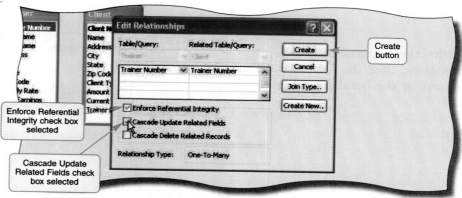

FIGURE 3-70

5

• **Click the Create button.**

*Access creates the relationship and displays it visually with the **relationship line** joining the two Trainer Number fields (Figure 3-71). The number 1 at the top of the relationship line close to the Trainer Number field in the Trainer table indicates that the Trainer table is the one part of the relationship. The infinity symbol at the other end of the relationship line indicates that the Client table is the many part of the relationship.*

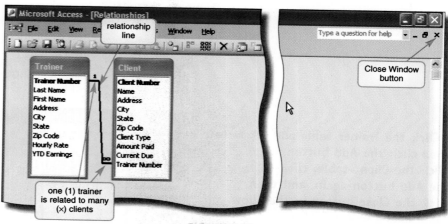

FIGURE 3-71

6

• **Close the Relationships window by clicking its Close Window button.**
• **Click the Yes button in the Microsoft Office Access dialog box to save the relationship you created.**

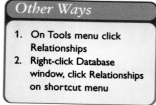

Other Ways

1. On Tools menu click Relationships
2. Right-click Database window, click Relationships on shortcut menu

Referential integrity now exists between the Trainer and Client tables. Access now will reject any number in the Trainer Number field in the Client table that does not match a trainer number in the Trainer table. Attempting to add a client whose

Trainer Number field does not match would result in the error message shown in Figure 3-72.

A deletion of a trainer for whom related clients exist also would be rejected. Attempting to delete trainer 53 from the Trainer table, for example, would result in the message shown in Figure 3-73.

Access would, however, allow the change of a trainer number in the Trainer table. Then it automatically makes the corresponding change to the trainer number for all the trainer's clients. For example, if you changed the trainer number of trainer 42 to 62, the same 62 would appear in the trainer number field for clients.

Using Subdatasheets

Now that the Trainer table is related to the Client table, it is possible to view the clients of a given trainer when you are viewing the datasheet for the Trainer table. The clients for the trainer will appear below the trainer in a **subdatasheet**. The fact that such a subdatasheet is available is indicated by a plus sign that appears in front of the rows in the Trainer table. The following steps display the subdatasheet for trainer 48.

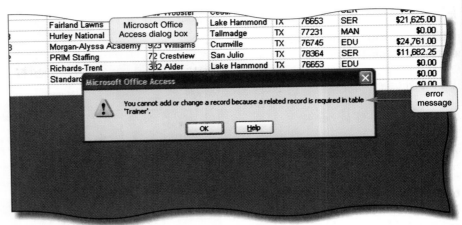

FIGURE 3-72

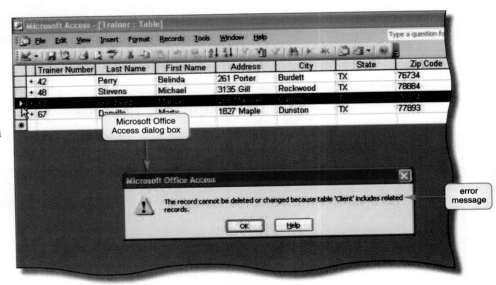

FIGURE 3-73

To Use a Subdatasheet

1

• **With the Database window on the screen, the Tables object selected, and the Trainer table selected, click the Open button on the Database Window toolbar.**

The datasheet for the Trainer table appears (Figure 3-74).

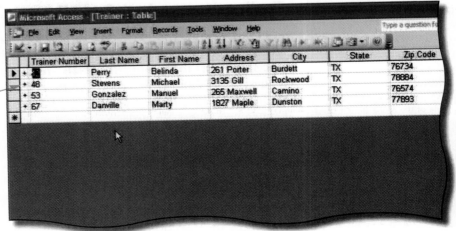

FIGURE 3-74

2

• **Click the plus sign in front of the row for trainer 48.**

The subdatasheet appears (Figure 3-75). It contains only those clients that are assigned to trainer 48.

3

• **Click the minus sign to remove the subdatasheet, and then close the datasheet for the Trainer table by clicking its Close Window button.**

The datasheet no longer appears.

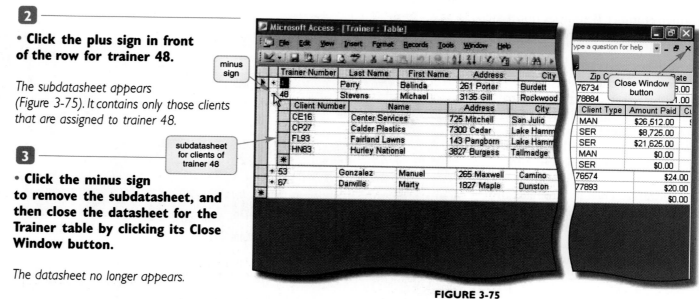

minus sign

subdatasheet for clients of trainer 48

Close Window button

FIGURE 3-75

Q&A

Q: Can I delete a trainer from the Trainer table?

A: If a trainer currently has clients in the Client table, Access will not allow you to delete the trainer. For example, trainer 48 currently has clients in the Client table. If you deleted trainer 48, these clients' trainer numbers would no longer match anyone in the Trainer table.

More About

Referential Integrity

Referential integrity is an essential property for databases, but providing support for it proved to be one of the more difficult tasks facing the developers of relational database management systems. For more information about referential integrity, visit the Access 2003 More About Web page (scsite.com/ac2003/ more) and click Referential Integrity.

Finding Duplicate Records

One reason to include a primary key for a table is to eliminate duplicate records. A possibility still exists, however, that duplicate records can get into your database. Perhaps, a client's name was misspelled and the data entry person assumed it was a new client. The **Find Duplicates Query Wizard** allows you to find duplicate records. The following steps illustrate how to use the Find Duplicates Query Wizard to find duplicate records.

To Find Duplicate Records

1. Select the table that you want to query.
2. Click the New Object button arrow, and then click Query.
3. When Access displays the New Query dialog box, click the Find Duplicates Query Wizard and then click the OK button.
4. Follow the directions in the Find Duplicates Query Wizard dialog boxes.

Finding Unmatched Records

Occasionally, you may want to find records in one table that have no matching records in another table. For example, suppose the clients of Ashton James College placed requests for training materials. You may want to know which clients have no requests. The **Find Unmatched Query Wizard** allows you to find unmatched records. The following steps illustrate how to find unmatched records using the Find Unmatched Query Wizard.

To Find Unmatched Records

1. Click the New Object button arrow, and then click Query.
2. When Access displays the New Query dialog box, click Find Unmatched Query Wizard and then click the OK button.
3. Follow the directions in the Find Unmatched Query Wizard dialog boxes.

Ordering Records

Normally, Access sequences the records in the Client table by client number whenever listing them because the Client Number field is the primary key. You can change this order, if desired.

Using the Sort Ascending Button to Order Records

To change the order in which records appear, use the Sort Ascending or Sort Descending buttons. Either button reorders the records based on the field in which the insertion point is located.

The following steps order the records by city using the Sort Ascending button.

To Use the Sort Ascending Button to Order Records

1

- **With the Database window on the screen, the Tables object selected, and the Client table selected, click the Open button on the Database Window toolbar.**

- **Click the City field on the first record (any other record would do as well).**

An insertion point appears in the City field (Figure 3-76).

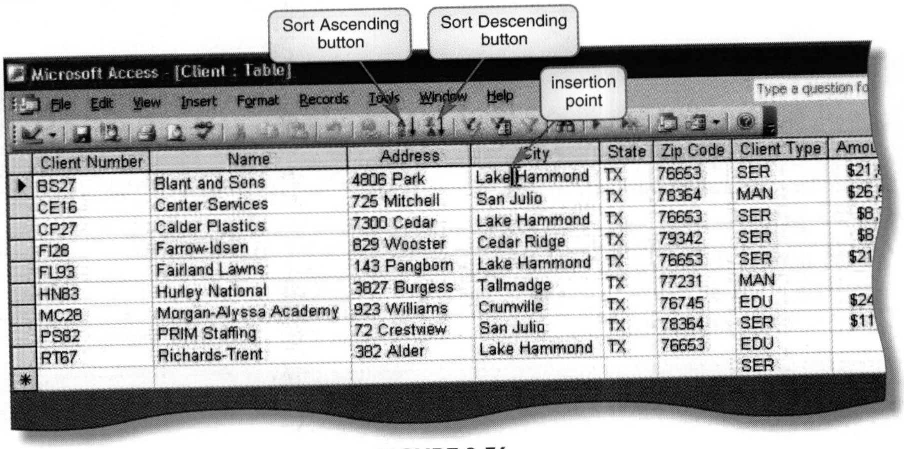

FIGURE 3-76

2

- **Click the Sort Ascending button on the Table Datasheet toolbar.**

- **If instructed to do so, print the table by clicking the Print button on the Table Datasheet toolbar.**

The rows now are ordered by city (Figure 3-77).

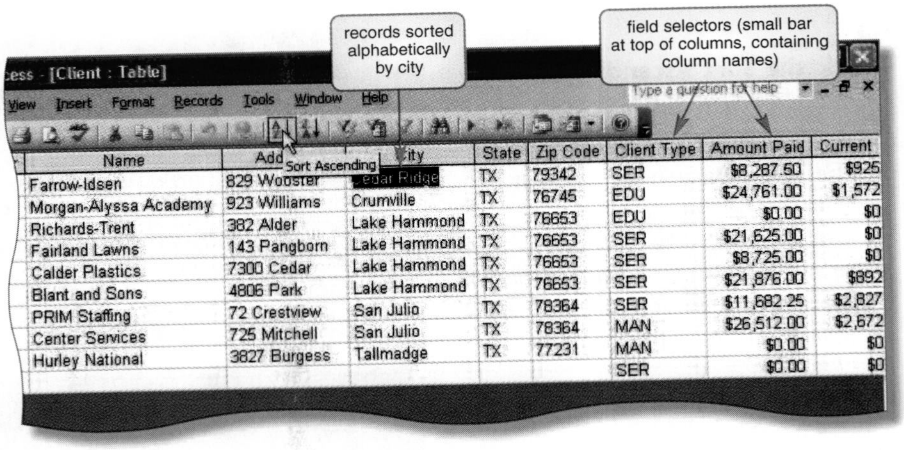

FIGURE 3-77

If you wanted to sort the data in reverse order, you would use the Sort Descending button instead of the Sort Ascending button.

Other Ways

1. On Records menu point to Sort, click Sort Ascending on Sort submenu
2. In Voice Command mode, say "Sort Ascending"

Ordering Records on Multiple Fields

Just as you are able to sort the answer to a query on multiple fields, you also can sort the data that appears in a datasheet on multiple fields. To do so, the major and minor keys must be next to each other in the datasheet with the major key on the left. (If this is not the case, you can drag the columns into the correct position. Instead of dragging, however, usually it will be easier to use a query that has the data sorted in the desired order.)

The following steps order records that have the major and minor keys in the correct position on the combination of the Client Type and Amount Paid fields. To select the fields, use the field selector, which is the small bar at the top of the column that you click to select an entire field in a datasheet.

To Use the Sort Ascending Button to Order Records on Multiple Fields

1

• Click the field selector at the top of the Client Type column to select the entire column (see Figure 3-77 on the previous page).

• Hold down the SHIFT key and then click the field selector for the Amount Paid column.

The Client Type and Amount Paid columns both are selected (Figure 3-78).

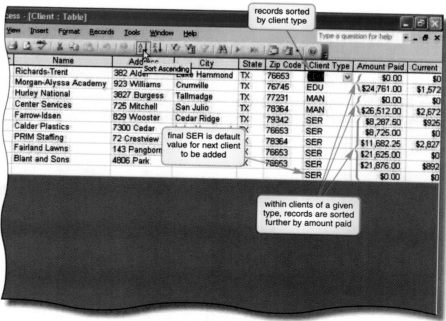

FIGURE 3-78

2

• Click the Sort Ascending button.

• If instructed to do so, print the table by clicking the Print button on the Table Datasheet toolbar.

The rows are ordered by client type (Figure 3-79). Within each group of clients of the same type, the rows are ordered by the amount paid amount.

3

• Close the Client : Table window by clicking its Close Window button.

• Click the No button in the Microsoft Office Access dialog box to abandon the changes.

The next time the table is open, the records will appear in their original order.

FIGURE 3-79

Creating and Using Indexes

You already are familiar with the concept of an index. The index in the back of a book contains important words or phrases together with a list of pages on which the given words or phrases can be found. An **index** for a table is similar. Figure 3-80, for example, shows the Client table along with an index built on client names. In this case, the items of interest are names instead of keywords or phrases as is the case in the back of this book. The field or fields on which the index is built is called the **index key**. Thus, in Figure 3-80, the Name field is the index key. (The structure of an index actually is a little more complicated than the one shown in the figure and is beyond the scope of this book. The concept is the same, however, and the structure shown in the figure illustrates the important concepts.)

Index on Name

NAME	RECORD NUMBER
Blant and Sons	1
Calder Plastics	3
Center Services	2
Fairland Lawns	5
Farrow-Idsen	4
Hurley National	6
Morgan-Alyssa Academy	7
PRIM Staffing	8
Richards-Trent	9

Client Table

RECORD NUMBER	CLIENT NUMBER	NAME	ADDRESS	CITY	STATE	ZIP CODE	...
1	BS27	Blant and Sons	4806 Park	Lake Hammond	TX	76653	...
2	CE16	Center Services	725 Mitchell	San Julio	TX	78364	...
3	CP27	Calder Plastics	7300 Cedar	Lake Hammond	TX	76653	...
4	FI28	Farrow-Idsen	829 Wooster	Cedar Ridge	TX	79342	...
5	FL93	Fairland Lawns	143 Pangborn	Lake Hammond	TX	76653	...
6	HN83	Hurley National	3827 Burgess	Tallmadge	TX	77231	...
7	MC28	Morgan-Alyssa Academy	923 Williams	Crumville	TX	76745	...
8	PS82	PRIM Staffing	72 Crestview	San Julio	TX	78364	...
9	RT67	Richards-Trent	382 Alder	Lake Hammond	TX	76653	...

FIGURE 3-80

Each name occurs in the index along with the number of the record on which the corresponding client is located. Further, the names appear in the index in alphabetical order. If Access were to use this index to find the record on which the name is Farrow-Idsen, for example, it could scan the names in the index rapidly to find Farrow-Idsen. Once it did, it would determine the corresponding record number (4) and then go immediately to record 4 in the Client table, thus finding this client more quickly than if it had to look through the entire Client table one record at a time. Indexes make the process of retrieving records very fast and efficient. (With relatively small tables, the increased efficiency associated with indexes will not be as apparent as in larger tables. In practice, it is common to encounter tables with thousands, tens of thousands, or even hundreds of thousands of records. In such cases, the increase in efficiency is dramatic. In fact, without indexes, many operations in such databases simply would not be practical. They would take too long to complete.)

Because no two clients happen to have the same name, the Record Number column contains only single values. This may not always be the case. Consider the index on the Zip Code field shown in Figure 3-81 on the next page. In this index, the Record Number column contains several values, namely all the records on which the corresponding Zip code appears. The first row, for example, indicates that Zip code 76653 is found on records 1, 3, 5, and 9; the fourth row indicates that Zip code 78364 is found on records 2 and 8. If Access were to use this index to find all clients in Zip code 78364, it could scan the Zip codes in the index rapidly to find

78364. Once it did, it would determine the corresponding record numbers (2 and 8) and then go immediately to these records. It would not have to examine any other records in the Client table.

Index on Zip Code

ZIP CODE	RECORD NUMBER
76653	1, 3, 5, 9
76745	7
77231	6
78364	2, 8
79342	4

Client Table

RECORD NUMBER	CLIENT NUMBER	NAME	ADDRESS	CITY	STATE	ZIP CODE	...
1	BS27	Blant and Sons	4806 Park	Lake Hammond	TX	76653	...
2	CE16	Center Services	725 Mitchell	San Julio	TX	78364	...
3	CP27	Calder Plastics	7300 Cedar	Lake Hammond	TX	76653	...
4	FI28	Farrow-Idsen	829 Wooster	Cedar Ridge	TX	79342	...
5	FL93	Fairland Lawns	143 Pangborn	Lake Hammond	TX	76653	...
6	HN83	Hurley National	3827 Burgess	Tallmadge	TX	77231	...
7	MC28	Morgan-Alyssa Academy	923 Williams	Crumville	TX	76745	...
8	PS82	PRIM Staffing	72 Crestview	San Julio	TX	78364	...
9	RT67	Richards-Trent	382 Alder	Lake Hammond	TX	76653	...

FIGURE 3-81

SAM Training 3-6

To practice the following tasks, launch the SAM Training Companion CD, choose Access Project 3, and then choose Training 3-6:
- Create a database with at least one many-to-many relationship
- Create a one-to-many relationship using the Relationships windows
- Specify a default value
- Specify referential integrity options
- Use subdatasheets

Another benefit of indexes is that they provide an efficient way to order records. That is, if the records are to appear in a certain order, Access can use an index instead of physically having to rearrange the records in the database. Physically rearranging the records in a different order can be a very time-consuming process.

To use the index to order records, use record numbers in the index; that is, simply follow down the Record Number column, listing the corresponding clients. In this index, you would first list the client on record 1 (Blant and Sons), then the client on record 3 (Calder Plastics), then the client on record 2 (Center Services), and so on. The clients would be listed alphabetically by name without actually sorting the table.

To gain the benefits from an index, you first must create one. Access automatically creates an index on the primary key as well as some other special fields. If, as is the case with both the Client and Trainer tables, a table contains a field called Zip Code, for example, Access will create an index for it automatically. You must create any other indexes you feel you need, indicating the field or fields on which the index is to be built.

Although the index key usually will be a single field, it can be a combination of fields. For example, you might want to sort records by amount paid within client type. In other words, the records are ordered by a combination of fields: Client Type and Amount Paid. An index can be used for this purpose by using a combination of fields for the index key. In this case, you must assign a name to the index. It is a good idea to assign a name that represents the combination of fields. For example, an index whose key is the combination of the Client Type and Amount Paid fields might be called TypePaid.

How Does Access Use an Index?

Access creates an index whenever you request that it do so. It takes care of all the work in setting up and maintaining the index. In addition, Access will use the index automatically.

If you request that data be sorted in a particular order and Access determines that an index is available that it can use to make the process efficient, it will do so. If no index is available, it still will sort the data in the order you requested; it will just take longer.

Similarly, if you request that Access locate a particular record that has a certain value in a particular field, Access will use an index if an appropriate one exists. If not, it will have to examine each record until it finds the one you want.

In both cases, the added efficiency provided by an index will not be apparent readily in tables that have only a few records. As you add more records to your tables, however, the difference can be dramatic. Even with only 50 to 100 records, you will notice a difference. You can imagine how dramatic the difference would be in a table with 50,000 records.

When Should You Create an Index?

An index improves efficiency for sorting and finding records. On the other hand, indexes occupy space on your disk. They also require Access to do extra work. Access must keep all the indexes that have been created up-to-date. Thus, both advantages and disadvantages exist to using indexes. Consequently, the decision as to which indexes to create is an important one. The following guidelines should help you in this process.

Create an index on a field (or combination of fields) if one or more of the following conditions are present:

1. The field is the primary key of the table (Access will create this index automatically).
2. The field is the foreign key in a relationship you have created.
3. You frequently will need your data to be sorted on the field.
4. You frequently will need to locate a record based on a value in this field.

Because Access handles 1 automatically, you need only to concern yourself about 2, 3, and 4. If you think you will need to see client data arranged in order of amount paid amounts, for example, you should create an index on the Amount Paid field. If you think you will need to see the data arranged by amount paid within trainer number, you should create an index on the combination of the Trainer Number field and the Amount Paid field. Similarly, if you think you will need to find a client given the client's name, you should create an index on the Name field.

Creating Single-Field Indexes

A **single-field index** is an index whose key is a single field. In this case, the index key is to be the Name field. In creating an index, you need to indicate whether to allow duplicates in the index key; that is, two records that have the same value. For example, in the index for the Name field, if duplicates are not allowed, Access would not allow the addition of a client whose name is the same as the name of a client already in the database. In the index for the Name field, duplicates will be allowed. The steps on the next page create a single-field index.

More About

Changing Table Properties

You can change the properties of a table by opening the table in Design view and then clicking the Properties button on the Table Design toolbar. Access will display the property sheet for the table. To display the records in a table in an order other than primary key order (the default sort order), use the Order By property. For example, to display the Client table automatically in Name order, click the Order By property box, type Client.Name in the property box, close the property sheet, and save the change to the table design. When you open the Client table in Datasheet view, the records will be sorted in Name order.

To Create a Single-Field Index

1

• **With the Database window on the screen, the Tables object selected, and the Client table selected, click the Design button on the Database Window toolbar.**

• **Be sure the Client : Table window is maximized.**

• **Click the row selector to select the Name field.**

• **Click the Indexed property box in the Field Properties pane.**

• **Click the down arrow that appears.**

The Indexed list appears (Figure 3-82). The items in the list are No (no index), Yes (Duplicates OK) (create an index and allow duplicates), and Yes (No Duplicates) (create an index but reject (do not allow) duplicates).

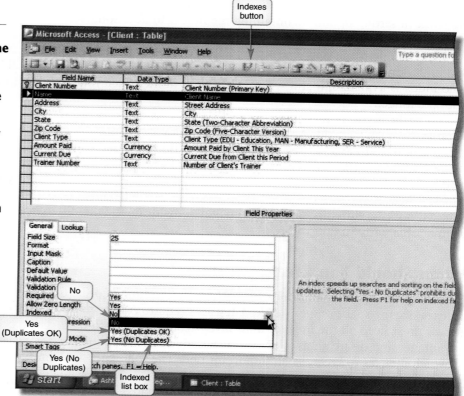

FIGURE 3-82

2

• **Click the Yes (Duplicates OK) item in the list.**

The index on the Name field now will be created and is ready for use as soon as you save your work.

Creating Multiple-Field Indexes

Creating **multiple-field indexes**, that is, indexes whose key is a combination of fields, involves a different process from creating single-field indexes. To create multiple-field indexes, you will use the Indexes button, enter a name for the index, and then enter the combination of fields that make up the index key. The following steps create a multiple-field index with the name TypePaid. The key will be the combination of the Client Type field and the Amount Paid field.

To Create a Multiple-Field Index

1

• **Click the Indexes button on the Table Design toolbar (see Figure 3-82).**

• **Click the blank row (the row following Name) in the Index Name column in the Indexes: Client dialog box.**

• **Type** TypePaid **as the index name, and then press the TAB key.**

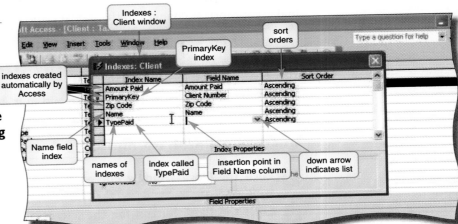

FIGURE 3-83

Access displays the Indexes: Client dialog box. It shows the indexes that already have been created and allows you to create additional indexes (Figure 3-83). The index name has been entered as TypePaid. An insertion point appears in the Field Name column. The index on the Client Number field is the primary index and was created automatically by Access. The index on the Name field is the one just created. Access created other indexes (for example, the Zip Code and Amount Paid fields) automatically. In this dialog box, you can create additional indexes.

2

• **Click the down arrow in the Field Name column to produce a list of fields in the Client table. Select Client Type.**

• **Press the TAB key three times to move to the Field Name column on the following row.**

• **Select the Amount Paid field in the same manner as the Client Type field.**

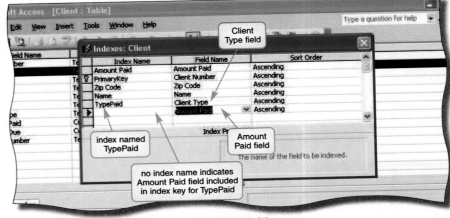

FIGURE 3-84

Client Type and Amount Paid are selected as the two fields for the TypePaid index (Figure 3-84). The absence of an index name on the row containing the Amount Paid field indicates that it is part of the previous index, TypePaid.

3

• **Close the Indexes: Client dialog box by clicking its Close button, and then close the Client : Table window by clicking its Close Window button.**

• **Click the Yes button in the Microsoft Office Access dialog box to save your changes.**

The indexes are created and Access displays the Database window.

<table>
<tr><td colspan="2">Other Ways</td></tr>
<tr><td>1.</td><td>On View menu click Indexes</td></tr>
<tr><td>2.</td><td>In Voice Command mode, say "Indexes"</td></tr>
</table>

The indexes are created. Access will use them automatically whenever possible to improve efficiency of ordering or finding records. Access also will maintain them automatically. That is, whenever the data in the Client table is changed, Access will make appropriate changes in the indexes automatically.

Closing the Database and Quitting Access

The following steps close the database and quit Access.

To Close a Database and Quit Access

1 Click the Close Window button for the Ashton James College : Database window.

2 Click the Close button for the Microsoft Access window.

The database and Access close.

Special Database Operations

The special operations involved in maintaining a database are backup, recovery, compacting a database, and repairing a database.

Backup and Recovery

It is possible to damage or destroy a database. Users can enter data that is incorrect; programs that are updating the database can end abnormally during an update; a hardware problem can occur; and so on. After any such event has occurred, the database may contain invalid data. It even may be totally destroyed.

Obviously, you cannot allow a situation in which data has been damaged or destroyed to go uncorrected. You must somehow return the database to a correct state. This process is called **recovery**; that is, you say that you **recover** the database.

The simplest approach to recovery involves periodically making a copy of the database (called a **backup copy** or a **save copy**). This is referred to as **backing up** the database. If a problem occurs, you correct the problem by copying this backup copy over the actual database, often referred to as the **live database**.

To backup the database that is currently open, you use the Back Up Database command on the File menu. In the process, Access suggests a name that is a combination of the database name and the current date. For example, if you back up the Ashton James College database on April 20, 2005, Access will suggest the name Ashton James College_2005-04-20. You can change this name if you desire, although it is a good idea to use this name. By doing so, it will be easy to distinguish between all the backup copies you have made to determine which is the most recent. In addition, if you discover that a critical problem occurred on April 18, 2005, you may want to go back to the most recent backup before April 18. If, for example, the database was not backed up on April 17 but was backed up on April 16, you would use Ashton James College_2005-04-16.

The following steps back up a database to a file on a hard disk or high-capacity removable disk. You should check with your instructor before completing these steps.

To Backup a Database

1. Open the database to be backed up.
2. Click File on the menu bar, and then click Back Up Database.
3. Selected the desired location in the Save in box. If you do not want the name Access has suggested, enter the desired name in the File name text box.
4. Click the Save button.

Access creates a backup copy with the desired name in the desired location. Should you ever need to recover the database using this backup copy, you can simply copy it over the live version.

Compacting and Repairing a Database

As you add more data to a database, it naturally grows larger. Pictures will increase the size significantly. When you delete objects (for example, records, tables, forms, or pictures), the space previously occupied by the object does not become available for additional objects. Instead, the additional objects are given new space, that is, space that was not already allocated. If you decide to change a picture, for example, the new picture will not occupy the same space as the previous picture, but instead it will be given space of its own.

To remove this wasted space from the database, you must **compact** the database. Compacting the database makes an additional copy of the database, one that contains the same data, but does not contain the wasted space that the original does. The original database will still exist in its unaltered form.

A typical three-step process for compacting a database is as follows:

1. Compact the original database (for example, Ashton James College) and give the compacted database a different name (for example, Ashton James College Compacted).
2. Assuming that the compacting operation completed successfully, delete the original database (Ashton James College).
3. Also assuming that the compacting operation completed successfully, rename the compacted database (Ashton James College Compacted) with the name of the original database (Ashton James College).

Of course, if a problem occurs in the compacting operation, you should continue to use the original database; that is, do not complete Steps 2 and 3.

The operation can be carried out on a floppy disk, provided sufficient space is available. If the database to be compacted occupies more than half the floppy disk, however, Access may not have enough room to create the compacted database. In such a case, you should first copy the database to a hard disk or network drive. (You can use whatever Windows technique you prefer for copying files to do so.) You then can complete the process on the hard disk or network drive.

In addition to compacting the database, the same operation is used to **repair** the database in case of problems. If Microsoft Access reports a problem with the database or if some aspect of the database seems to be behaving in an unpredictable fashion, you should run the Compact and Repair operation to attempt to correct the problem. If Access is unable to repair the database, you will need to revert to your most recent backup copy.

More About

Compacting and Repairing a Database

You can require Access to compact a database automatically whenever the database is closed. To do so, click Tools on the menu bar and then click Options. When Access displays the Options dialog box, click the General tab. Click the Compact on Close check box.

More About

Backup and Recovery

Before making changes to the database, such as the changes made in this project, it is a good idea to make a copy of the database. Then, if a problem occurs that damages either the data in the database or the structure of the database, you can recover the database by copying the backup copy over it.

 Training 3-7

To practice the following tasks, launch the SAM Training Companion CD, choose Access Project 3, and then choose Training 3-7:
• Compact on close
• Create a find duplicate query
• Create a find unmatched query
• Create a single field index
• Create multiple field indices
• Create queries using Wizards
• Order records in datasheet view
• Sort records in a database
• Use database tools to compact a database
• Use the Backup Database command

Q: Is it possible to compact an open database?

A: Yes, to do so, click Tools on the menu bar, point to Database Utilities, and then click Compact and Repair Database on the Database Utilities submenu.

The following steps compact a database and repair any problems after you have copied the database to a hard disk. If you have not copied the database to a hard disk, check with your instructor before completing these steps.

To Compact and Repair a Database

1. Be sure the database is closed. Click Tools on the menu bar, point to Database Utilities, and then click Compact and Repair Database on the Database Utilities submenu.
2. In the Database to Compact From dialog box, select the database to be compacted and then click the Compact button.
3. In the Compact Database Into dialog box, enter a new name for the compacted database and then click the Save button in the Database to Compact From dialog box.
4. Assuming the operation is completed successfully, delete the original database and rename the compacted database as the original name.

The database now is the compacted form of the original.

Project Summary

In Project 3, you learned how to maintain a database. You saw how to use Form view to add records to a table. You learned how to locate and filter records. You saw how to change the contents of records in a table and how to delete records from a table. You restructured a table, both by changing field characteristics and by adding a new field. You saw how to make a variety of changes to the appearance of a datasheet. You learned how to make changes to groups of records and delete a group of records. You created a variety of validation rules that specified a required field, a range, a default value, legal values, and a format. You examined the issues involved in updating a table with validation rules. You also saw how to specify referential integrity. You learned how to view related data by using subdatasheets. You learned how to order records. You saw how to improve performance by creating single-field and multiple-field indexes.

If your instructor has chosen to use the complete SAM Assessment and Training product, you can go beyond the "just-in-time" training provided on the CD accompanying this text. Simply log onto the SAM 2003 site to launch any assigned training activities or exams that relate to the skills covered in this project.

Introduction to Data Management with Microsoft Access 2003

"To succeed in life in today's world, you must have the will and tenacity to finish the job."
—Chin-Ning Chu

LEARNING OBJECTIVES

Introduce the company used in this section
Identify how an organization manages data
Understand the roles of data consumers in an organization
Determine how data is interlinked throughout an organization
Understand the current deficiencies in an organization's data

ABOUT THIS SECTION AND MICROSOFT OFFICE ACCESS 2003

Traditional study of computer applications has mostly involved acquiring skills related to an application's features and functions. Although this approach is important in teaching the mechanics required to perform certain tasks, it does not address *when* a particular tool is most appropriate or *how* it should best be utilized in solving a specific problem.

Although this section focuses on learning how to organize data using Microsoft Office Access 2003, the concepts and tasks presented in this section could apply to other database programs as well. Access is a relational database program in which data is stored in tables that are related to each other using relationships. You will learn about tables and relationships in Chapters 1 and 2, but the idea is important, because these tables can store a great deal of related information in one location and display the information in many ways. Access stores information in one database and lets the user manipulate that information to see as much or as little of it as is desired and in many ways. For example, Access can provide you with a list of employees living in certain cities or a report that shows sales organized and totaled by product category.

What is information and where does it come from? The term "information" can mean many things to different people. For the purpose of this discussion, **information** is defined as data that is organized in some meaningful way. **Data** can be words, images, numbers, or even sounds. Using data to make decisions depends on an organization's ability to collect, organize, and otherwise transform data into information that can be used to support those decisions—a process more commonly referred to as **analysis**. A **data consumer** is a person in an organization who transforms data into information by sorting, filtering, or performing calculations on it to perform this analysis.

The amount of information available can overwhelm many decision makers as they try to determine which sets of data and information are important and which should be ignored. The result is a complex world in which decision makers can no longer rely on intuition and back-of-the-envelope calculations to make effective decisions; they need tools that support decision making and help to solve problems.

CASE SCENARIO

The problems to be solved in this section are presented within the context of the fictional company 4Corners Pharmacy, which is so named because it is located in southwestern Colorado on the border of the four corners connecting the states of Arizona, Colorado, New Mexico, and Utah. This case scenario is used to provide real-world business examples to illustrate the lessons in each chapter; it is not based on real people or events. You will be guided through the solutions to solve realistic business problems for various people working for this company. These "employees" represent a variety of business functions: accounting, finance, human relations, information systems, marketing, operations management, and sales. Context is an important factor to consider when solving the problems in this section. The following background on 4Corners Pharmacy gives you perspective on the situations that you will encounter throughout this section.

The Company

Vincent Ferrino opened 4Corners Pharmacy in 1989. Over the years, Vincent's business evolved from a small "mom and pop" corner drugstore to the busiest pharmacy in the area. Vincent's son, Paul Ferrino, has worked at the pharmacy in different capacities since 1990. After graduating with a degree in pharmacy and becoming licensed by the state of Colorado, Paul worked as a pharmacist in his father's store, and then took two years off to earn an MBA from Thunderbird University in Arizona. When Vincent decided to retire, he sold the store to Paul but continues to work as a part-time pharmacist.

Paul envisions expanding his father's business to take advantage of the growing pharmaceutical industry. Paul was encouraged recently by a study indicating that 44% of Americans take prescription drugs on a regular basis. He sees the trend increasing as more baby-boomers get older and need an increasing number of prescriptions as life expectancy and medical invention increase. Although he was a shrewd and successful businessperson, Vincent ran the day-to-day operations of the business with little help from computers, primarily because he was never trained to use them and never realized the benefits they could offer his business. Consequently, the pharmacy's recordkeeping, although meticulous and professional, is inefficient. Maintaining the growing business using mostly manual systems is becoming more costly as additional people are hired to meet stricter industry regulations regarding the Health Insurance Portability and Accountability Act (HIPAA) and because of state regulations that affect the sale, storage, and dispensing of prescription drugs. Although Paul succeeded in automating some of the pharmacy's data management in Excel workbooks, he knows that a more substantial change is needed to properly maintain and store data about the business.

Key Players

Paul Ferrino—Pharmacist and Owner

Paul began working as a pharmacist at 4Corners Pharmacy in January 1990, and bought the store from his father in May 2006. Paul is the head pharmacist and, as such, he manages a dedicated and capable group of experienced pharmacists, pharmacy technicians, and sales assistants. Paul's vision for the pharmacy is to continue his father's lifelong pledge of providing excellent customer service and "giving back" to the community. Vincent regularly sponsored and underwrote local events for kids and senior citizens, which resulted in several community service awards for Vincent and multiple wins in the "best pharmacy" category by a reader's poll sponsored by the local newspaper. The pharmacy also earned three awards from the local Chamber of Commerce. Although there are other big chain drugstores in the area, Vincent has managed to hang on to generations of customers because of his community involvement and excellent rapport with his customers. Paul is dedicated to continuing his father's traditions.

Donald Linebarger—Information Systems Director

After purchasing the store, Paul's first order of business was hiring someone who could overhaul the pharmacy's manual recordkeeping systems. Don Linebarger worked for many years as a systems analyst for a large business in the area. He was the perfect choice to work at 4Corners Pharmacy because he is capable and experienced, but also because he has been a satisfied customer of 4Corners Pharmacy for many years. After developing the system for 4Corners Pharmacy, Don will train employees to use it, perform system maintenance and make any necessary changes, and maintain all of the records necessary for the business. He will also work to improve relationships with doctors, a source of many of the pharmacy's customers, and to develop greater knowledge of existing customers to anticipate their needs and generate more business.

Maria Garcia—Human Resources Manager

Maria Garcia has been the human resources manager at 4Corners Pharmacy since 2004. She is responsible for interviewing and hiring employees; maintaining data about certifications for pharmacists and pharmacy technicians; monitoring attendance and sick days; and maintaining and administering company benefits, including life and health insurance, 401(k) programs, and bonuses.

Elaine Estes—Store/Operations Manager

Elaine Estes has worked at 4Corners Pharmacy since 1995. During this time, she has been the store's general manager and operations manager. Elaine maintains the inventory of prescription and nonprescription items, places orders for additional stock, and disposes of drugs when they are stocked past their expiration dates. Elaine also supervises the 4Corners Pharmacy staff and reports their achievements and any problems to Maria.

Company Goal: Expand Operations into Other Areas

The strength of 4Corners Pharmacy has always been Vincent's dedication to his customers and his community. Paul wants to continue this tradition by sponsoring local events and ensuring that his customers and their families never have a reason to seek another pharmacy. Paul also wants to open a second store in Colorado by the end of the year, possibly by acquiring an existing business. With the addition of another store on the horizon, Paul needs to ensure that the database created to run 4Corners Pharmacy is easily expanded and adapted as necessary to run the operations at a second location.

How Is Access Used at 4Corners Pharmacy?

Employees at 4Corners Pharmacy will use Access in many ways to assist them with the daily operations of the pharmacy. Specific examples of how a database will improve store operations and customer service are as follows:

- **Accounting**

  As the store manager, Elaine needs reports that detail how much inventory remains for each prescription and nonprescription item in the store. She also needs to know the value of the existing inventory for insurance purposes. Access can compute information about sales and produce it in a report that is current and easy to read.

Accounting

- **Finance**

  Elaine and Paul need to ensure that the pharmacy's bottom line is healthy. As a result, Access must produce reports that detail the pharmacy's sales figures, salary commitments, and similar financial data to determine the financial health of the pharmacy.

Finance

- **Human Resources**

  As the human resources manager, Maria needs to manage all of the data about employees. Some of this data is descriptive, such as the employee's name and address. Other data is sensitive, such as the employee's Social Security number, salary, and information about job performance, and needs to be protected from unauthorized access. Maria can use Access to manage data about employees and ensure that sensitive data is protected from fraud and abuse.

Human Resources

- **Information Systems**

  Don's goal for the new database at 4Corners Pharmacy is to produce a system that meets user needs, stores and manages the correct information, displays it in the correct format, and is easy for employees to use. He will use the tools available in Access to secure, back up, and maintain the database to ensure that it is properly protected from unauthorized access, loss, and failure. Don will also add Web functionality to the system so that customers can use the pharmacy's database to update their information, display a list of their current prescriptions, and obtain general drug information.

Information Systems

- **Marketing**

  As the store's marketing contact, Elaine works with an outside advertising agency to produce the store's weekly advertising inserts in the local newspaper. Elaine can use Access to determine how store items are selling and determine which products to

Marketing

add to the store's advertising. She can also use Access to produce reports about the buying behavior and demographic data for 4Corners Pharmacy customers. Although this data exists within the pharmacy, it is not currently organized in a format that makes it easy to analyze for determining market trends and buying behavior by demographic group.

Management

- **Operations Management**

  Elaine needs a way to know which drugs to order from suppliers and in what quantities. She frequently evaluates the store's inventory for low drug volumes and expired drugs. Customer health is of great importance to the pharmacy. Although no one has ever been injured as a result of pharmacist negligence at 4Corners Pharmacy, increased federal regulations and legal liability issues mandate that pharmacy employees are properly certified and diligently inform customers of dosage instructions, possible side effects, and adverse interactions for each prescription sold. The pharmacy keeps meticulous records about pharmacist certifications, and pharmacists and pharmacy technicians diligently inform their customers about the drugs they dispense, but with the increase in hiring and the possible expansion of the company, Don wants formal processes in place to track these things.

Sales

- **Sales**

  Customers are also data consumers at the pharmacy. They receive data from the pharmacists detailing drug information and potential interactions. Some customers participate in flexible spending accounts (FSAs) that allow them to pay for prescriptions with pre-tax dollars. Participating customers frequently request a list of the prescriptions ordered by their households on a quarterly or annual basis. Access can manage these requests by creating reports of all drugs ordered by a single customer or household.

All of these business areas are related, just as the tables in the database are related. For example, when a customer fills a prescription, it affects different parts of the database as shown in Figure 1.

Figure 1: Data to store in the database at 4Corners Pharmacy

1. Doctor writes a prescription for patient. Doctor and clinic data is stored in the database.

2. Patient presents prescription to pharmacist. Data about pharmacists and other employees is stored in the database.

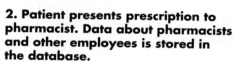

3. Pharmacy staff enters customer, insurance, and prescription data into the database.

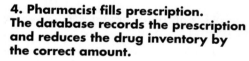

4. Pharmacist fills prescription. The database records the prescription and reduces the drug inventory by the correct amount.

5. Customer picks up prescription and makes payment. The database stores the cost and price of the drug, which are used to generate the profit amount.

The customer requests the prescription, either by presenting a written order from a doctor to a pharmacist or asking for a refill of an existing prescription. The pharmacist adds this request to the system by getting the required information to fill it, including information

932

about the drug, customer, customer's health plan, and so on. The prescription also affects the inventory that is tracked by operations and the profile of buying behavior that is tracked for marketing purposes. Eventually, the prescription affects the pharmacy's financial health by contributing revenue and profit to the store. In Chapter 1, you will learn how 4Corners Pharmacy manages its data and create a plan for storing this data in a database.

MANAGING DATA FOR THE ORGANIZATION

All organizations must deal with how to best collect, store, and manage their data. There are several problems at 4Corners Pharmacy. First, not all data is gathered for managers to make informed business decisions. For example, marketing data is scarce and dispersed throughout the organization. Several departments import and export data to each other and then maintain that data separately, resulting in errors and redundancy of data. The operations department, for example, manages inventory based on data imported from the pharmacists, but this data is not updated on a regular basis, resulting in orders placed too early, too frequently, or not frequently enough. Moreover, redundancy occurs in the customer list as each customer is listed with his own address, despite the fact that several people might live at the same address. Therefore, if one person submits a change of address or phone number, this data is not updated for people living in the same household. This problem leads to erroneous data that might result in undelivered mail sent to customers from 4Corners Pharmacy or the pharmacist not being able to reach a customer because of an incorrect phone number.

The business motivation for gathering all the data used in 4Corners Pharmacy and storing it in one relational database is to save time and money and to prevent errors and redundancy. But why is using a database program such as Access a superior method for organizing data? Why not use Excel to manage this data? After all, it is possible to sort, filter, and manipulate a significant amount of data in an Excel worksheet. There are many benefits to using a relational database to address the data deficiencies at 4Corners Pharmacy. First, the pharmacy produces too much data to effectively store in an Excel workbook. 4Corners Pharmacy gathers data about employees, customers, drugs, health plans, and doctors, each of which is its own unique category and should have its own worksheet. It would be difficult to list all the pharmacy's employees, customers, and prescribing doctors in one Excel worksheet, much less all the drug and health plan data. Excel is limited in the structure of its data; you cannot easily manage all of this data in one workbook, but you can do so in one database. A database might contain dozens of tables, just as an Excel workbook might contain dozens of worksheets. However, through a process of relating tables to each other, you can join together multiple tables in Access if they share common data and then query those tables as though they were one big table, presenting a huge advantage over managing data in multiple worksheets in Excel. For example, 4Corners Pharmacy will use three tables to store and manage data about employees, customers, and doctors; a table to store and manage data about prescriptions that pharmacists fill for customers; and a table to store and manage data about the drugs prescribed, such as the drug's name, dosage, expiration date, cost, and so on. All of these tables have a relationship that connects them to the others, as shown in Figure 2.

Figure 2: Interlinked data at 4Corners Pharmacy

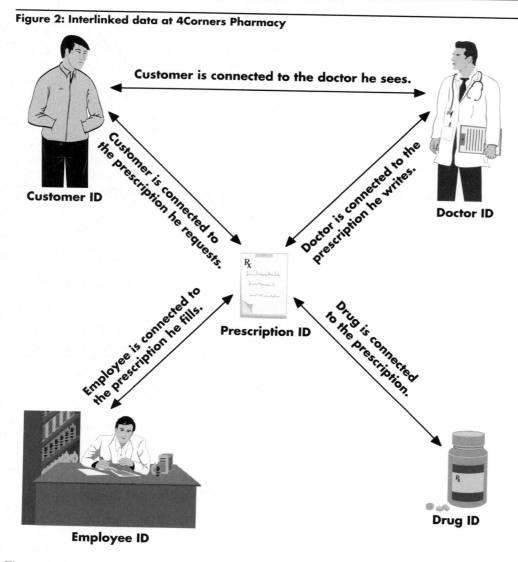

Customer is connected to the doctor he sees.

Customer is connected to the prescription he requests.

Doctor is connected to the prescription he writes.

Employee is connected to the prescription he fills.

Drug is connected to the prescription.

Customer ID

Doctor ID

Prescription ID

Employee ID

Drug ID

Figure 2 shows that a customer fills a prescription written by a doctor for a drug, and then a pharmacist fills the prescription. In the database, the customer's data is stored in a table that stores information about all customers. The prescription table contains data about prescriptions and a reference to the customer table (such as a customer identification number) to indicate the customer who purchased the prescription. The prescription table contains a reference (such as a prescription identification number) to the table that stores data about pharmacists, a reference to which pharmacist filled the prescription, and a reference (such as a drug identification number) to the table that stores data about drugs. Finally, the doctor table contains a reference to the prescription table, indicating which doctor wrote the prescription.

The benefit of designing tables and then creating relationships between them is that you are able to retrieve the data stored in these tables easily and quickly. For example, you can select any prescription and find out which doctor wrote it, which pharmacist filled it, and which customer purchased it. This type of querying simply isn't possible in Excel.

Steps To Success Exercises

As you read each level in a chapter, you will see how business problems are evaluated and solved at 4Corners Pharmacy using a database. At the end of each level, you will complete the exercises in the Steps To Success section to reinforce what you learned in the level. However, to ensure that you have a way to practice everything you learned in each level, the Steps To Success exercises are completed in a separate database for a similar business, Hudson Bay Pharmacy, which has slightly different data needs and requirements. The Hudson Bay Pharmacy is located in Edmonton, Alberta (Canada). This pharmacy has similar needs to those of 4Corners Pharmacy, but because Canada has different requirements for the data it collects about employees and drugs, you will need to develop the database with these needs in mind. You will create this database in the Steps To Success exercises in Level 1 of Chapter 2, and then do all subsequent work for the Steps To Success exercises in your copy of the database. This approach makes it possible for you to develop a database from scratch and practice everything you learned in the chapter in your copy of the database. Because the database has slightly different requirements, you will be faced with decisions and problems that are unique to that database but are not specifically taught in the levels.

SKILLS TRAINING

This section assumes that you are already familiar with some of the more fundamental skills in Access, such as entering records into a datasheet, navigating a datasheet, and creating simple queries and forms. Depending on your skill level and working knowledge of Access, you might want to use the SAM Training product before you begin Chapter 1. (See the Preface section of this book or ask your instructor for more information about SAM.) The following is a list of prerequisite skills for which SAM Training is available; your instructor might have other requirements as well:

- Close Access
- Create a new database
- Create forms using the Form Wizard
- Create queries using wizards
- Delete records from a table using a datasheet
- Edit records from a table using a datasheet
- Enter records into a datasheet table
- Enter records using a form
- Open a form

- Open Access objects in the appropriate views
- Open an existing database
- Order records in Datasheet view
- Preview a report
- Preview the contents of a table
- Print a report
- Print specific pages of a report
- Resize to best fit
- Start Access
- Use Access Help
- Use navigation controls to move among records in a form
- Use navigation controls to move among records in a table
- Use the New Record button to add a record
- Use Undo and Redo
- Work with the Task Pane

In addition to these prerequisite skills, additional SAM skills are listed at the beginning of each level. These skills correspond to the material presented in that level, and give you a chance to practice the "mechanics" before you start applying the skills to solve problems. If you are using SAM Training with this book, it is recommended that you check each list of SAM skills before beginning work on a particular level. In this way, you can take advantage of the SAM Training to come up to speed on any of those skills and be better prepared to move forward in the chapter.

Preparing to Automate Data Management
Information Services: Gathering Data and Planning the Database Design

"You can use all the quantitative data you can get, but you still have to distrust it and use your own intelligence and judgment."
—Alvin Toffler

LEARNING OBJECTIVES

Level 1

Discover and evaluate sources of existing business data

Research sources of missing or incomplete data

Assign data to tables and use field types and sizes to define data

Level 2

Understand relational database objects and concepts

Create table relationships

Understand referential integrity

Level 3

Learn the techniques for normalizing data

Evaluate fields that are used as keys

Test the database design

CHAPTER INTRODUCTION

The first step in planning a database is to gather existing data, determine the desired output, confirm that you have all the fields required to produce that output, and obtain data that you are missing. Existing data within an organization might be stored using paper forms, Microsoft Excel workbooks, Microsoft Word documents, or other applications.

This chapter details the process that you should follow prior to creating a database. The first step, the **discovery phase**, includes gathering all existing data, researching missing and incomplete data, and talking with users about their data output needs. Subsequent steps in the process include putting data into groups, called tables; identifying unique values for each record in those tables; and designing the database to produce the desired output. It is then imperative to test the new database prior to its implementation. Designing the database requires knowledge of database concepts, which are introduced in this chapter. Figure 1.1 illustrates the steps followed in the database design process and highlights the first step, the discovery phase.

Figure 1.1: Database design process: the discovery phase

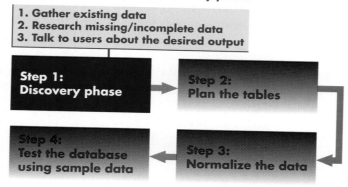

CASE SCENARIO

Creating a database is a significant undertaking that requires careful planning, organization, and management. In many cases, it takes several weeks or even months to identify the data that an organization needs to collect and then determine how managers and employees will enter and use that data to assist them in the organization's day-to-day operations and long-term planning. The 4Corners Pharmacy is an existing business, and you have already learned that Vincent Ferrino's system for managing the prescription, inventory, employee, and other data for the pharmacy is lacking in several respects. Paul Ferrino's vision for the pharmacy, which he now owns, is to convert all of the existing paper and spreadsheet systems to a database. By doing so, Paul will realize many benefits, such as more accurate and consistent data and the ability to track inventory and customer buying habits.

LEVEL 1
EXAMINING EXISTING AND MISSING SOURCES OF DATA

DISCOVERING AND EVALUATING SOURCES OF EXISTING DATA

One of the first tasks of creating a database is to identify the information that the organization needs to manage and organize. This task might take several days to several months and might involve interviewing department heads and other key employees to understand the data they collect and the way they use it. You might find that some departments manage their data in paper files or in computerized records. In larger organizations, data might be stored in different computerized systems. Regardless of the current data storage method, it is important to take the time to understand not only what data is collected, but also how that data is used.

As you collect information from the organization's key players, you might begin to see patterns that indicate how to organize the data. For example, you might see that the organization manages data about customers, employees, and products. Different departments might use this data in different ways and employees might need different levels of access to this data, depending on the departments in which they work and their positions in the company. For example, a manager of an order department needs information about products and customers, but not about employees; a human resources manager needs information about employees, but not about products; a customer service representative needs information about products and orders, but not about employees; and so on. In addition to needing different kinds of data, some employees might need more detailed information than others. An assistant in the human resources department might need a list of employees working in the organization, but only the human resources manager should be able to obtain a list of employees and their salaries.

You can use a **database management system**, or **DBMS**, to manage data. There are several DBMSs, including Oracle, ColdFusion, Microsoft Access, and MySQL. Each of these DBMS programs has specific advantages that benefit different organizations, depending on the kind and amount of data they store. For example, very large organizations will benefit from the power of Oracle or ColdFusion to manage large amounts of data on a network or in a Web site. Smaller organizations might choose to use Access because this DBMS, part of the Microsoft Office suite of programs, is fairly easy to use and quite powerful, but does not require extensive programming knowledge. Some businesses might choose MySQL, an open source program that is available for free. MySQL, however, requires programming expertise in Structured Query Language (SQL), the language used by most DBMSs. You will learn about SQL in Chapter 3.

Because the 4Corners Pharmacy is a small business, the company's information systems director, Don Linebarger, selected Access as the DBMS to manage the pharmacy's database. As the business grows in the future, Don might choose another DBMS, but for now, Access will handle the pharmacy's data management needs.

Before he gets started, Don needs to determine how the pharmacy collects and stores data about prescription transactions, drug inventories, customers, and employees. Don also needs to determine if there are other data needs at the pharmacy that are currently going unfulfilled or about which he is not informed. After extensive consulting with Vincent and Paul Ferrino, Don learns that data is managed in many ways and realizes that entering customer data at 4Corners Pharmacy is a manual and time-consuming process. When new customers visit the pharmacy to fill a prescription, they complete a customer information form by hand. A pharmacy technician enters the information into an Excel workbook. Figure 1.2 shows the pharmacy's customer information form.

Figure 1.2: Customer information form used by 4Corners Pharmacy

CUSTOMER INFORMATION	

Thank you for choosing 4Corners Pharmacy. Please fill out this form so that we can assist you promptly.

Name:	Birth Date:
Address:	
Social Security Number:	
Home Phone Number:	Fax Number:
E-mail Address:	
Gender: Male Female	Marital Status (circle one): Single Married Widowed Divorced
Employer:	Occupation:
Primary Care Physician:	Physician's Phone Number:
Emergency Contact:	Relationship to Patient:
Emergency Contact's Phone Number:	Spouse's Name:
Allergies:	
Prefer child proof caps? Y N	

HEAD OF HOUSEHOLD
(Complete this section only if someone other than the customer is financially responsible.)

Name:	Social Security Number:
Address:	
Home Phone Number:	Work Phone Number:

INSURANCE INFORMATION

Insurance Plan:	
Insurance Plan Phone Number:	Insurance ID Number:
Subscriber's Name:	Subscriber's Employer:

I authorize the release of any medical information necessary to process my claim and payment of benefits to 4Corners Pharmacy.

_____   _____

Signature of Customer/Responsible Party   **Date**

After entering the data from the customer information form into the workbook, the technician stores the form in a filing cabinet in one of 26 file folders arranged by the first letter of the customer's last name. This system makes it difficult to find individual customer information later when forms require an update, such as a change of address, a change in insurance information, or a new drug allergy. Vincent's original objective was to have one row in the worksheet for each customer, as shown in Figure 1.3.

Figure 1.3: Customer data maintained in an Excel workbook

One row for each customer

	A	B	C	D	E	F	G	H
1	SSN (Last 4)	First Name	Last Name	Birthdate	Address	City	State	Zip
2	0424	Gaetano	Feraco	7/4/1946	19504 Lowell Boulevard	Aneth	UT	84510
3	0849	Scott	Prager	8/27/1951	2510 West 108th Avenue	Pleasant View	CO	81331
4	0975	Isabel	Lopez	8/30/1949	6969 South Valmont Road	Montezuma Creek	UT	84534
5	0979	Geoffrey	Baaz	12/31/2001	1233 Myrna Place	Kirtland	NM	87417
6	1064	Sonia	Cardenas	4/12/1968	16455 Warren Avenue	Chinle	AZ	86547
7	1068	Gina	Mercado	6/17/1979	240 South Monaco Parkway	Cortez	CO	81321
8	1168	Ted	Sabus	12/11/1954	460 West Pioneer Road	Dolores	CO	81323
9	1329	Daniel	Cardenas	5/12/2002	16455 Warren Avenue	Chinle	AZ	86547
10	1395	Josefina	Hernandez	6/30/1978	411 Mariposa Street	Flora Vista	NM	87145
11	1422	Chloe	Feraco	6/1/1946	19504 Lowell Boulevard	Aneth	UT	84510
12	1486	Oksana	Lapshina	4/29/1957	5171 Idylwild Creek Road	Yellow Jacket	CO	81335
13	1689	Gloria	Fernandes	5/1/1979	1011 East Bayaud Avenue	Flora Vista	NM	87415
14	2197	Christina	Hargus	2/14/1998	5465 South Nelson Circle	Shiprock	NM	87420
15	2215	Maria	Gabel	8/12/1980	4255 Kittredge Street	Lewis	CO	81327
16	2243	Anders	Aannestad	9/11/1974	1279 Cherokee Avenue	Farmington	NM	87499
17	2253	Steven	Nguyen	10/12/1976	9874 South Main Street	Blanding	UT	84511
18	2797	Jessica	Cortez	8/13/1978	3663 South Sheridan Boulevard	Kayenta	AZ	86033
19	2943	Rose	Baaz	4/12/1970	1233 Myrna Place	Kirtland	NM	87417
20	3623	Kimberley	Schultz	1/16/1969	411 East Cornish Court	Chinle	AZ	86507
21	3659	Adriana	Woltore	4/23/1952	14444 North Tamarac Street	Cortez	CO	81321

4Corners Customers

Don knows from experience that this recordkeeping system is error-prone, as it is possible to store two records for the *same* customer without realizing the mistake. For example, if a customer has a formal name and a nickname or goes by a middle name, it might be possible to store two separate records for the same individual without realizing that these records are for the same person. This problem might also occur if the person who entered the record misspelled a customer's name on one or more occasions. This phenomenon is known as **data duplication**, and it is undesirable because additional space is required in the database to store extra records, which leads to inconsistent and inaccurate data. For example, a pharmacist might indicate that the customer named John W. Jackson has a drug allergy, but the record for J. William Jackson—the same person but with a different version of his name—might not indicate this important fact. This situation might not seem important for billing or correspondence issues, but a serious error occurs when the pharmacist accesses the duplicate customer record that does *not* include the important information about the customer's drug allergy and gives the customer a prescription to which he is allergic. Don's first order of business is to work to avoid data duplication in the database.

In addition to deleting duplicate records for customers, Don also notes that he needs to find a way to group and store the address and phone information for people in the same household, thereby reducing the amount of space required to store this information. This repetition is known as **data redundancy** and is to be avoided. When one member of a household reports a new address or change of insurance that also affects other people in the household, the database must update the records for everyone affected by the change. Figure 1.4 shows the customer data shown in Figure 1.3, but it is sorted alphabetically by last name.

Figure 1.4: Sorted customer data illustrates data duplication and errors

Daniel and Danny Cardenas are the same person

Baaz address listed twice

	A	B	C	D	E	F	G	H
1	SSN (Last 4)	First Name	Last Name	Birthdate	Address	City	State	Zip
2	2243	Anders	Aannestad	9/11/1974	1279 Cherokee Avenue	Farmington	NM	87499
3	8848	Dusty	Alkier	4/5/1940	3046 West 36th Avenue	Aneth	UT	84510
4	0979	Geoffrey	Baaz	12/31/2001	1233 Myrna Place	Kirtland	NM	87417
5	2943	Rose	Baaz	4/12/1970	1233 Myrna Place	Kirtland	NM	87417
6	6282	Byron	Buescher	6/1/1944	4165 Umatilla Avenue	Pleasant View	CO	81331
7	1064	Sonia	Cardenas	4/12/1968	16455 Warren Avenue	Chinle	AZ	86547
8	1329	Daniel	Cardenas	5/12/2002	16455 Warren Avenue	Chinle	AZ	86547
9	1329	Danny	Cardenas	5/12/2002	16455 Warren Avenue	Chinle	AZ	86547
10	4293	Jonathan	Cardenas	8/22/2004	16455 Warren Avenue	Chinle	AZ	86547
11	9189	Albert	Cardenas	10/14/1965	16455 Warren Avenue	Chinle	AZ	86547
12	5229	Dana	Coats	8/16/2002	126 Valley View Road	Shiprock	NM	87420
13	8361	Dallas	Coats	10/31/1972	5541 East Zuni Street	Shiprock	NM	87420
14	9493	Octavia	Coats	6/30/1976	5541 East Zuni Street	Shiprock	NM	87420
15	2797	Jessica	Cortez	8/13/1978	3663 South Sheridan Boulevard	Kayenta	AZ	86033
16	5569	Malena	D'Ambrosio	4/15/1980	10555 East Circle Way	Montezuma Creek	UT	84534
17	0424	Gaetano	Feraco	7/4/1946	19504 Lowell Boulevard	Aneth	UT	84510
18	1422	Chloe	Feraco	6/1/1946	19504 Lowell Boulevard	Aneth	UT	84510
19	1689	Gloria	Fernandes	5/1/1979	1011 East Bayaud Avenue	Flora Vista	NM	87415
20	4484	James	Fernandes	2/18/1977	1011 East Bayaud Avenue	Flora Vista	NM	87415
21	2215	Mario	Gobel	8/12/1990	4255 Kittredge Street	Louis	CO	81227

I◄ ◄ ► ►I \ 4Corners Customers /

Old address for Dana Coats

Don spots several errors when the data is arranged in this different way. For example, Don suspects that Daniel and Danny Cardenas might be the same person. Although it is possible that two similarly named boys live in Chinle, Arizona, a closer look reveals that they share the same date of birth and address. Don imagines that the first record is the boy's formal name and the second is his nickname. Further evidence supports Don's belief: Daniel and Danny share the same last four digits of their Social Security numbers. Don must devise a way to eliminate this repetition while at the same time preserving the customer's prescription history.

Don also notices cases of data redundancy. For example, there are two records for people with the last name Baaz, and both people share the same address. As mentioned earlier, this duplication consumes a great deal of space in the database—it would be more efficient and require less space in the database to store the address for the Baaz family just once.

Don also notices that there are three records for people with the last name Coats. Don scrutinizes these records and suspects that Dallas and Octavia must have informed the pharmacy of an address change at some point, but failed to identify Dana Coats, who is listed as having a different address, as their daughter. No child of Dana's age lives alone, yet her address appears to suggest that she does.

Concerned that other errors might exist in the 4Corners Pharmacy recordkeeping system, Don asks Paul about the method he uses to manage new prescriptions and prescription refills that are brought to the pharmacy by customers or that are phoned in or faxed from doctors' offices. Paul explains that prescriptions are logged in a separate worksheet for each day the pharmacy is open. For each prescription filled by the pharmacy, the worksheet contains one row that includes the customer's first and last names, address, phone number, and insurance information; the prescription number, drug name, instructions, fill date, expiration date, and number of refills authorized by the physician; and the prescribing physician's name, address, clinic affiliation, and phone number. Figure 1.5 shows the worksheet from January 2, 2008.

Figure 1.5: Prescription data managed in an Excel workbook

Anders Aannestad is listed three times

	A	B	N	O	P
1	First Name	Last Name	PrescriptionID	Name	Instructions
2	Anders	Aannestad	2	Myobuterol	1 teaspoon every 4 hours
3	Dusty	Alkier	4	Dseurton	2 pills every 12 hours
4	Dusty	Alkier	5	Clonazepam	2 pills every 6 hours with food
5	Anders	Anestad	72	Syocil	2 pills every 6 hours with food
6	Anders	Annestad	60	Phalastat	3 teaspoons full every 6 hours
7	Daniel	Cardenas	61	Myobuterol	1 teaspoon every 4 hours
8	Octavia	Coats	56	Myobuterol	1 teaspoon every 4 hours
9	Octavia	Coats	70	Tvalaxec	1 teaspoon every 6 hours
10	Christina	Hargus	47	Ampicillin	1 pill every 4 hours
11	Paula	Hargus	55	Montelukast sodium	2 pills daily
12	Isabel	Lopez	10	Phalastat	3 teaspoons full every 6 hours
13	Steven	Nguyen	52	Didanosine	2 pills every 4 hours with food
14	Scott	Prager	19	Cefixime	1 pill every 5 hours with food
15	Jennifer	Ramsey	3	Nvalax	2 pills daily
16	Shannon	Sabus	18	Rivastigmine tartrate	2 pills every 6 hours with food
17	Ted	Sabus	24	Acebutolol hydrochloride	2 pills daily
18	Marisella	Velasquez	33	Quentix	2 pills every 8 hours
19	Marisella	Velasquez	63	Tolbutamide	2 pills every 6 hours
20	Kevin	Wachter	39	Myobuterol	1 teaspoon every 4 hours
21	Adriana	Walters	14	Didanosine	2 pills every 4 hours with food

⏮ ◀ ▶ ⏭ Jan. 2, 2008 Prescriptions

Don sorted the worksheet by last name and in doing so notices that Anders Aannestad is listed three times, with three different spellings of his last name due to typographical errors or illegible penmanship on a written or faxed prescription. Don also realizes that the table is unwieldy because it spans 27 columns and requires hiding columns or frequent scrolling to see the details of a given prescription, such as which doctor prescribed which drug for which customer.

Don hides 11 columns of customer address and insurance information so he can see prescription details. An audit of this customer address and insurance information reveals additional errors. Figure 1.6 shows another view of the prescription worksheet from January 2, 2008, with the customer health plan identification numbers displayed.

Figure 1.6: Prescription data with address and insurance plan errors

	A	B	C	D	E	F	G
1	First Name	Last Name	Address	City	State	Zip	PlanID
2	Anders	Aannestad	1279 Cherokee Avenue	Farmington	NM	87499	498-1112-A
3	Dusty	Alkier	3046 West 36th Avenue	Aneth	UT	84510	A089
4	Dusty	Alkier	3046 West 36th Avenue	Aneth	UT	84510	A098
5	Anders	Anestad	1279 Cherokee Avenue	Farmington	NM	87499	498-1112-A
6	Anders	Annestad	1279 Cherokee Avenue	Farmington	NM	87499	498-1112-A
7	Daniel	Cardenas	16455 Warren Avenue	Chinle	AZ	86547	498-1112-A
8	Octavia	Coats	5541 East Zuni Street	Shiprock	NM	87420	OP-87-A087
9	Octavia	Coats	5541 East Zuin Street	Shiprock	NM	87420	OP-87-A087
10	Christina	Hargus	5465 South Nelson Circle	Shiprock	NM	87420	OP-87-A087
11	Paula	Hargus	5465 South Nelson Circle	Shiprock	NM	87420	OP-87-A087
12	Isabel	Lopez	6969 South Valmont Road	Montezuma Creek	UT	84534	2B8973AC
13	Steven	Nguyen	9874 South Main Street	Blanding	UT	84511	498-1112-A
14	Scott	Prager	2510 West 108th Avenue	Pleasant View	CO	81331	4983
15	Jennifer	Ramsey	4775 Argone Circle	Chinle	AZ	86547	498-1112-A
16	Shannon	Sabus	460 West Pioneer Road	Dolores	CO	81323	4983
17	Ted	Sabus	406 West Pioneer Road	Dolores	CO	81323	4983
18	Marisella	Velasquez	54213 Oak Drive	Kirtland	NM	87417	000H98763-01
19	Marisella	Velasquez	54213 Oak Drive	Kirtland	NM	87417	000H98763-01
20	Kevin	Wachter	2931 East Narcissus Way	Montezuma Creek	UT	84534	A089
21	Adriana	Walters	14444 North Tamarac Street	Cortez	CO	81321	4983

Jan. 2, 2008 Prescriptions

Figure 1.6 shows multiple data-entry errors and some design problems that create redundant data. The address data for each customer is redundant in the Prescriptions worksheet; these addresses already exist in the Customers worksheet shown in Figure 1.4. This problem is compounded when data-entry mistakes are made. In looking at the data shown in Figure 1.6, Don sees that Octavia Coats lives on either Zuni or Zuin Street, that Shannon and Ted Sabus live in house number 460 or 406, and that Dusty Alkier's health insurance is a plan with the identification number A089 or A098.

Don continues examining the Prescriptions worksheet by scrolling and hiding columns as necessary and notes the many mistakes it contains. Figure 1.7 details the last of Don's sleuthing. Marisella Velasquez's doctor is named either Chinn or Chin, and the phone number of Octavia Coats's doctor ends with the digits 1879 or 1897. These problems are probably the result of typographical errors.

Figure 1.7: Prescription data with doctor name and telephone errors

Incorrect phone number for this doctor

	B	N	O	U	V	AA
1	Last Name	PrescriptionID	Name	DoctorLast	ClinicName	DoctorPhone
2	Aannestad	2	Myobuterol	Gramann	Connley Memorial Clinic	(928) 488-1741
3	Alkier	4	Dseurton	Allen	San Juan County Clinic	(505) 884-0542
4	Alkier	5	Clonazepam	Allen	San Juan County Clinic	(505) 884-0542
5	Anestad	72	Syocil	Gramann	Connley Memorial Clinic	(928) 488-1741
6	Annestad	60	Phalastat	Gramann	Connley Memorial Clinic	(928) 488-1741
7	Cardenas	61	Myobuterol	Deleon	Chinle Memorial Clinic	(928) 888-4178
8	Coats	56	Myobuterol	Escalante	Northwest New Mexico Area Clinic	(505) 545-1879
9	Coats	70	Tvalaxec	Escalante	Northwest New Mexico Area Clinic	(505) 545-1897
10	Hargus	47	Ampicillin	Escalante	Northwest New Mexico Area Clinic	(505) 545-1879
11	Hargus	55	Montelukast sodium	Escalante	Northwest New Mexico Area Clinic	(505) 545-1879
12	Lopez	10	Phalastat	Jurski	Blanding City Clinic	(435) 887-1818
13	Nguyen	52	Didanosine	Zamarron	Blanding City Clinic	(435) 887-1818
14	Prager	19	Cefixime	Wilson	Sodt Memorial Clinic	(435) 189-9874
15	Ramsey	3	Nvalax	Loke	University of Northern Arizona Clinic	(928) 449-4174
16	Sabus	18	Rivastigmine tartrate	Trevino	Dolores LaPlata Memorial Clinic	(970) 429-7475
17	Sabus	24	Acebutolol hydrochloride	Huddleston	St. Thomas Clinic	(970) 898-4788
18	Velasquez	33	Quentix	Chinn	San Juan County Clinic	(505) 884-0542
19	Velasquez	63	Tolbutamide	Chin	San Juan County Clinic	(505) 884-0542
20	Wachter	39	Myobuterol	Zamarron	Blanding City Clinic	(435) 887-1818
21	Walter	14	Didanosine	Huddleston	St. Thomas Clinic	(970) 898-4788

Jan. 2, 2008 Prescriptions

Incorrect spelling of this doctor's last name

Don sees some very serious problems with the current process of logging prescriptions using this system. First, there is no method to control the duplication of data. If a customer fills three prescriptions on the same day, there will be three rows in the worksheet—one row for each prescription filled. The name, address, and phone number can vary in each of these three rows because there is no built-in method in a worksheet to prevent this problem from occurring. It is possible to have similar variances in the doctor's name, address, clinic affiliation, and phone number. Second, data is difficult to track and aggregate. For example, because the pharmacy creates new worksheets for each day's prescriptions, pharmacists would need to know the original fill date for a prescription to find out how many refills the doctor authorized. Aggregating data by customer, doctor, or drug would also be difficult.

After finishing his exploration of the current system, Don asks Paul for other changes that he wants to make and data that he wants to store in the future that is lacking in the current system. Paul tells Don that he wants to eliminate the paper registration forms; make it easier to update customer information; have quick access to a customer's prescription history (without searching a paper file); print a list of drug names; create a way to ensure that the person entering the customer's information inquired about the customer's allergies, that the pharmacist explained interactions with other drugs, and that the pharmacist provided counseling about using the drug to the customer; and print a list of doctors and their contact information.

In talking with the pharmacy staff, Don also learns that in the past it has been difficult to generate items for the marketing person, such as mailing labels for customers and doctors, so that the pharmacy can send notices to customers and doctors about events at the pharmacy, such as drug recalls or local health fairs. Don also learns from the pharmacy technicians that some customers have requested year-end reports identifying all of the prescriptions and their total cost for each family member so they can reconcile their insurance statements and produce the total prescription drug costs to use when reconciling their prescription costs with Flexible Spending Accounts (FSAs) provided by their employers. Because the current system has no way to account for this data, this need is going unmet.

After examining the pharmacy's records and discovering all of the problems with data-entry errors and data duplication, Don moves on to look at how Vincent manages the pharmacy's inventory of prescription drugs. He talks with Vincent about his method for tracking the value and number of each item in inventory and the system he uses for reordering out-of-stock items, evaluating items that do not sell well and discontinuing them, and making sure that items on sale are stocked in appropriate quantities before the sale is advertised. Figure 1.8 shows the worksheet that Vincent uses to track prescription drug inventory.

Figure 1.8: Prescription drug inventory data

	A	B	C	D	E	F	G	H	I
1	UPN	Name	Generic	Description	Unit	Dosage	DosageForm	Cost	Price
2	247	Acebutolol hydrochloride		Arthritis	Pill	400	mg	$0.55	$1.10
3	732	Albuterol Sulfate	Yes	Asthma	Pill	2	mg	$0.30	$0.95
4	741	Almotriptan	Yes	Conjunctivitis	Pill	6.25	mg	$0.14	$0.87
5	102	Ampicillin	Yes	Antibiotic	Pill	250	mg	$0.75	$1.45
6	224	Avatocin		Allergies	Pill	100	mg	$0.65	$1.40
7	524	Cefixime	Yes	Antihistamine	Pill	400	mg	$0.95	$1.60
8	398	Clonazepam		Epiliepsy	Pill	4	mcg	$0.65	$1.20
9	452	Diazapam	Yes	Anxiety	Pill	5	mg	$0.45	$1.12
10	878	Didanosine	Yes	Sinus infection	Pill	200	mg	$0.65	$1.12
11	256	Dseurton	Yes	High blood pressure	Pill	175	mg	$0.60	$1.20
12	311	Dyotex		Tonsillitis	Bottle	2	tsp	$0.25	$1.05
13	412	Epronix		Pain	Pill	500	mg	$0.85	$1.50
14	467	Glimepiride	Yes	Diabetes	Pill	2	mg	$0.25	$0.90
15	587	Haloperidol		Diuretic	Pill	6	mcg	$0.70	$1.30
16	644	Hyometadol		Asthma	Bottle	2	tsp	$0.65	$1.35
17	289	Levothyroxine	Yes	Thyroid disorders	Pill	25	mg	$0.70	$1.40
18	642	Montelukast sodium	Yes	Acne	Pill	10	mcg	$0.32	$0.90
19	828	Myobuterol	Yes	Antibiotic	Bottle	1	tsp	$0.55	$1.60
20	711	Nvalax	Yes	Depression	Pill	200	mg	$0.30	$0.90
21	852	Oxaprozin	Yes	Anti-inflammatory	Pill	1200	mg	$0.60	$1.25
22	366	Phalastat		Allergies	Bottle	1	tsp	$0.75	$1.60

Drugs

Because the data in this worksheet isn't connected to the systems that the pharmacists and cashiers use to sell prescription drugs and other items, sales volume cannot be calculated electronically. Indeed, Vincent has always performed a bimonthly hand count of inventory, and then built temporary columns in Excel to determine costs and profits. Don suspects that it would be difficult to use this worksheet to determine how much inventory exists for any given item in the store or prescription drug in the pharmacy, and imagines that it is unlikely that Vincent could accurately account for any product in stock. Thus, not only is it difficult to determine the quantity or volume of drugs in stock and the overall value of the inventory, there is no way to determine which items sell well and which sell poorly. Consequently, Don guesses that reordering occurs only when a pharmacist or other employee notices that a product's inventory is low or nonexistent. Don wants the database to address all of these problems by providing timely and accurate information about sales volume, inventory levels, and drug expiration dates. Furthermore, he wants to incorporate a list of interactions, pregnancy risks, and suppliers of each drug in the inventory, as presently these must be cross-referenced with data found online or in proprietary databases.

Vincent explains to Don that his system has worked fine for the nearly two decades in which he has been in business. However, Don knows that Paul wants to automate all of the business processes that must occur to run the pharmacy. As a pharmacist working for his father's company, Paul knows that Vincent's systems do not work well enough to ensure timely and accurate information. Paul also knows that his father's systems contain many errors.

Don moves to his examination of the employee records by talking with Maria Garcia, who manages all of the pharmacy's employment records, including applications, employee reviews, benefits, certifications, training, and salary and tax-related information. Maria tells Don that as the pharmacy grows, it is becoming increasingly difficult to manage employee records. Currently, she maintains employee data in paper forms and in three programs. As shown in Figure 1.9, Maria uses Microsoft Outlook contacts to maintain employee address and telephone information.

Figure 1.9: Employee contact information in Outlook

Maria uses Excel for tracking key employee dates, such as date of birth, hire date, termination date, and date of the employee's last personnel review. Maria also uses Excel for recording salary data. Because this worksheet contains sensitive information—in addition to salaries the table lists employee Social Security numbers—Maria keeps this file in its own workbook and has protected it with a password that only she knows. Figure 1.10 shows Maria's Excel workbooks.

Figure 1.10: Employee date and salary data in Excel workbooks

	A	B	C	D	E	F
1	First Name	Last Name	Birth Date	Hire Date	End Date	Review Date
2	Brian	Cavillo	8/14/1970	6/14/2005		7/19/2008
3	Richard	Conlee	3/1/1971	1/29/1992		3/17/2008
4	Elaine	Estes	5/1/1969	5/18/1995		1/15/2009
5	Marco	Farello	12/16/1974	11/22/2001		4/18/2008
6	Paul	Ferrino	7/4/1962	1/29/1990		
7	Vincent	Ferrino	4/2/1939	2/15/1989		
8	Joan	Gabel	9/12/1968	1/22/2002	5/31/2004	
9	Maria	Garcia	12/29/1971	10/11/2004		10/3/2008
10	Gregory	Hempstead	2/14/1975	9/12/2005		11/20/2007
11	Shayla	Jackson	9/28/1978	6/14/2000		4/2/2008
12	Cynthia	Jones	10/6/1958	3/14/1993		12/7/2008
13	Tara	Kobrick	7/30/1976	10/15/1999	6/15/2005	
14	Dora	Langston	10/14/1978	6/14/2006		2/20/2008
15	Anthony	Laporte	11/24/1975	4/5/2001		4/16/2008
16	Dominque	Latour	6/20/1977	8/14/2005		10/3/2008
17	Darnell	Lightford	4/5/1977	9/10/2005		7/21/2007
18	Donald	Lineharger	2/28/1968	5/30/2006		11/15/2007

Employees

Employee date data

	A	B	C	D	E
1	First Name	Last Name	SSN	Salary	HourlyRate
2	Brian	Cavillo	711-56-6444		$8.17
3	Richard	Conlee	968-96-3214		$12.00
4	Elaine	Estes	545-98-0000	$50,000.00	
5	Marco	Farello	885-00-7777		$11.00
6	Paul	Ferrino	953-23-3639	$135,000.00	
7	Vincent	Ferrino	998-01-5466	$35,000.00	
8	Joan	Gabel	901-88-3636		$10.75
9	Maria	Garcia	701-05-2465	$65,250.00	
10	Gregory	Hempstead	701-12-2765		$7.40
11	Shayla	Jackson	998-36-4789		$6.88
12	Cynthia	Jones	000-23-3655	$65,000.00	
13	Tara	Kobrick	728-12-3465		$11.00
14	Dora	Langston	718-78-4111		$11.15
15	Anthony	Laporte	727-65-5752		$8.00
16	Dominque	Latour	926-95-4878		$7.70
17	Darnell	Lightford	512-00-8899		$7.50
18	Donald	Lineharger	707-55-7541	$72,000.00	

Salary

Employee salary data

In addition to using Outlook and Excel, Maria keeps several employee records in Word, including a list of bilingual employees at 4Corners Pharmacy. If a bilingual employee is not on duty, pharmacists can refer to this list and call these employees when Spanish-speaking customers request assistance. She also keeps a Word document to track absenteeism. Although absenteeism is not a large problem at 4Corners Pharmacy, Maria is aware that Paul plans to expand the company and documentation should be in place as the employee base grows. Figure 1.11 shows both of these documents.

Figure 1.11: Bilingual employees and absentee report

4Corners Pharmacy Bilingual Employees

Name	Language	Proficiency
Joan Gabel	Spanish	Fluent
Maria Garcia	Spanish	Fluent
Darnell Lightford	Spanish	Fluent

4Corners Pharmacy Absentee Report

Name	Date	Absent/Tardy
Dominque Latour	9/28/07	Tardy
Shayla Jackson	10/15/07	Absent
Gregory Hempstead	11/14/07	Tardy

Maria is also responsible for monitoring staff development, a time-consuming task. Each pharmacist and pharmacy technician must maintain the proper license and certification as mandated by Colorado state law. Maria is responsible for ensuring that employees take the required classes to maintain their certifications. In addition, she must manage the employee performance reviews, which occur every 90 days, six months, or 12 months for employees, depending on their job titles and the number of years they have worked at the pharmacy. She also serves as the pharmacy's benefits coordinator and manages requests for sick days and vacation, extended leaves of absence, pension benefits, and life insurance benefits.

Although Maria's various documents and workbooks seem to manage the information she needs, Don worries that these systems will not work well if the pharmacy grows as expected and adds additional stores and employees. Don sees that Maria could also benefit from storing and managing personnel data in a database.

After talking extensively with Vincent, Paul, and Maria, Don took a few days to talk to other employees in the store to understand and view the data that they use and need to perform their jobs. Upon concluding his discovery phase of the database design process, Don learned many things. First, there are many paper-based and handwritten methods of gathering data at 4Corners Pharmacy that use various forms, faxes, and memos. Second, many employees copy and paste data from one worksheet to another or import and export data from one program to another, thereby creating redundant data. This process occasionally leads to errors. Finally, Don suspects that the pharmacy is not collecting data that it needs to produce reports for outside consultants, such as the value of inventory in the pharmacy for insurance purposes or the value of business capital for local taxing authorities.

Don also sees that some data collected by the customer information form (Figure 1.2), such as insurance information, is never recorded in detail. As the business grows, it will be important to automate all of the processes at the pharmacy. Don knows that a DBMS will serve this function better than hiring a large staff of people to manage the growing data needs of 4Corners Pharmacy and that using a DBMS will make Paul's business run smoother and more efficiently.

Concluding the first part of the discovery phase, Don details his findings to Paul. Table 1.1 lists the expectations of the database as Don understands them.

Table 1.1: Preliminary database expectations for 4Corners Pharmacy

Department	Expectation
Pharmacy	• Eliminate paper forms. • Provide quick access to prescription history. • Print list of drug names. • Ensure pharmacist consulted with customer about dosage instructions, allergies, and interactions. • Print doctor contact information.
Marketing	• Print customer mailing labels. • Print doctor mailing labels. • Use customer data to gather data information on customer buying habits.
Operations	• Track inventory. • Identify poor-selling items.
Human Resources	• Monitor staff development. • Confirm certifications. • Create employee performance reviews.
Customers	• Print a year-end report of all prescriptions purchased by individual or household.
Accounting and Finance	• Determine profit and loss for individual sale items. • Value the store's inventory. • Track the business profit.

Best Practice

Combating "Scope Creep" During the Database Design Process

During the discovery phase of the database design process, it is necessary to interview as many members of the organization as possible to learn about all sources of input and desired output. This process might result in a large "wish list." At 4Corners Pharmacy, Paul asks Don if it is possible to include legal, tax, and investment data in the DBMS. Don informs Paul that while it is *possible* to do this, it would require a great deal more work, be significantly more expensive, and lie outside the scope of the original project, which is creating a database to manage day-to-day store operations. As a result, Paul and Don agree on the scope and deliverables of the project—managing customer and prescription data, managing personnel data, tracking buying behavior, and evaluating inventory. The exact specifications of the project—how much it costs, when it is delivered, and what exact output is expected—will be negotiated after Don concludes the database design process. During the planning stage, it is important to manage expectations early and agree on project specifications, as Don has done. Otherwise, the project can become unmanageable.

Now that Don has identified the existing sources of data and has interviewed many of the employees at the pharmacy, he turns his attention to another important part of the discovery phase—researching sources of missing data.

RESEARCHING SOURCES OF MISSING DATA

Don's efforts have identified the data collected by 4Corners Pharmacy and have given him a chance to evaluate how employees and managers use it. Another important part of the discovery phase is determining data that is missing and identifying the sources you can use to obtain that missing data. This part of the process is often difficult because you must ask the right questions of the right people to get the right answers. In interviews with key employees and managers, it is best to ask questions such as "What else would you like to know about the data?" and similarly worded inquiries. You might find that employees need to know certain things about the data that the current system cannot provide.

In his conversations with employees, Don learned a great deal about the kind of data that the DBMS must collect, organize, and manage. He also learned about data that various departments and employees want to collect but are not collecting presently. For example, Maria needs to obtain certain data about employee training and classes, but has no way to do so. She also wants to have an electronic record of the classes that employees have taken and need to take, a way to determine which employees are bilingual, and scanned images of important employment documents such as the driver's licenses of employees who are authorized to make pharmacy deliveries.

Best Practice

Determining Output

When interviewing members of an organization during the discovery phase of database design, listen closely to their needs. Few people are familiar with database concepts. Consequently, they will speak of needing lists, reports, files, printouts, records, and other terms. Your job is to translate those needs into database deliverables. You will learn database terms later in this chapter, but it is important to remember that no one will direct you to "employ the 'and' logical operator in conjunction with the 'or' logical operator in a select query to list the customers in Colorado who are allergic to aspirin." People don't talk that way. They will say: "I need a printout of every customer who can't take aspirin and who's either been a customer for a long time or who spends a lot of money at the pharmacy. I want to send these customers a free sample of a new aspirin substitute." It becomes your job to translate this information into database commands. You will learn how to work in a database as you complete this book.

ASSIMILATING THE AVAILABLE INFORMATION AND PLANNING THE DATABASE

Databases are not created in a vacuum; it is essential to interview employees, managers, and potential users of the database to learn how data is gathered and stored in an organization and to seek feedback regarding what output and functionality they want to obtain from the database. After gathering this information, you will better understand which users require access to which data, how that data should be stored and formatted, and how to organize the data into logical groups.

Now that Don has completed his interviews with the various managers and key employees at 4Corners Pharmacy, he is ready to start planning the database. His notes include sample documents showing how and which data is currently stored, data that should be collected but currently is not, and information that suggests possible additions and desires from future users of the system. With all of this information, Don has a good understanding of how 4Corners will store, manage, and use the data it collects, so he is ready to move into the next phase of database development—planning the database design.

The first step in database design is to determine the best way to organize the data that you collected in the discovery phase into logical groups of fields. These logical groups of fields are known as entities. An **entity** is a person, place, thing, or idea. In a database, a **field** (or **column**) is a single characteristic of an entity. For example, the fields to describe a customer would be ones such as first name, last name, address, city, state, and so on. When all the fields about an entity are grouped together, they create **record** (or **row**). A **table** (also called a **relation**) is a collection of records that describe one entity. A **database** is a collection of one or more tables.

When a database contains related tables through fields that contain identical data, the database is called a **relational database**. For example, a table that stores customer data might be named Customer and contain a field that stores unique identification numbers for each customer; this field might be named Customer ID. To relate customers to the sales representatives who represent them, the database might also contain a table named Rep that includes information about sales representatives. To relate the Customer and Rep tables to each other so you can determine which representative represents which customers, the Rep table would also contain a field named Customer ID and this field would contain identical values in both tables. You will learn more about tables and relationships later in this chapter.

EVALUATING FIELD VALUES AND ASSIGNING APPROPRIATE DATA TYPES

After identifying the fields that describe the data that will be stored in the tables in the database, the next step is to determine the data type to assign to each field. A database stores data in different ways; a **data type** determines how to store the data in the field.

Some fields store text values, such as a person's name; other fields store numbers, such as zip codes, phone numbers, or dollar amounts. A database might also store objects such as pictures or fields that contain hyperlinks to Internet or file locations. Table 1.2 describes the different data types that you can assign to fields. DBMSs use different names for some data types. In Table 1.2, Access data type names are listed in the first column; when other DBMSs use a different data type name, it is noted in parentheses. For example, the Text data type used in Access is called a Char data type in other DBMSs.

Table 1.2: Common data types and their descriptions

Data Type	Description	Example
Text (Char)	Text or alphanumeric combinations of data and numbers that are not used in calculations	Names, addresses, phone numbers, Social Security numbers, and zip codes
Memo	Long passages of data containing text and alphanumeric characters	Employee review information and detailed product descriptions
Number (Decimal)	Numbers that are used in calculations	Currency values, number ordered, and number of refills
Date/Time (Date)	Dates or date and time combinations	Inventory expiration dates and birth dates
Currency (not available in all DBMSs)	Monetary amounts	Item cost and item price
AutoNumber (not available in all DBMSs)	An automatically generated number that produces unique values for each record	Any number that is necessary to uniquely identify records, such as a customer ID number or product ID number that is not assigned by another method
Yes/No (not available in all DBMSs)	A field value that is limited to yes or no, on or off, and true or false values	Responses to indicate whether child-proof caps are requested or whether the employee is CPR certified (both require yes or no responses)
OLE Object (not available in all DBMSs)	Linked or embedded objects that are created in another program	Photographs, sounds, documents, and video
Hyperlink (not available in all DBMSs)	Text that contains a hyperlink to an Internet or file location	Web pages, e-mail addresses, and files on network or workstation
Lookup Wizard (not available in all DBMSs)	A field that lets you look up data in another table or in a list of values created for the field	Predefined list of drug codes, categories of information, and state abbreviations

How do you determine which data type to assign each field? Doing so depends on what function you want to derive from that data, because each data type has different properties. For example, 4Corners Pharmacy requires name and address data for employees, customers, and doctors. Don will create separate tables for each of these entities. Within each table, he will create fields for first names, last names, street addresses, cities, states, and zip codes. The data stored in each field and its intended use determine what data type to assign to the field.

The Text and Memo Data Types

Don will assign the **Text** data type to the fields that store a person's name, because names are composed of letters, but he will also assign the Text data type to the street address as it is often an alphanumeric combination. A zip code is a number, but this number is not used in calculations—you would never add, subtract, multiply, or divide one customer's zip code by another or use it in any other calculation, so the appropriate data type is Text.

Maria wants to enter comments about disciplinary actions for employees in the database. Don will need to create a field in the Employee table for this and assign it the **Memo** data type as this data type can store long passages of text. You might wonder how much longer the Memo data type is than the Text data type and whether you should assign the Memo data type to all fields requiring textual entries. The Text data type stores a maximum of 255 characters, whereas the Memo data type stores a maximum of 65,535 characters. Maria could write a 15-page evaluation in a Memo field and have plenty of room to spare. So why not assign the Memo data type to every field containing text? A primary goal in designing a database is to keep it small by assigning the data type to each field that is large enough to hold the data required in that field without wasting additional space. Thus, names, addresses, descriptions, and so on generally require the Text data type, whereas notes, comments, and journal entries generally require the Memo data type. Because it is the most commonly assigned data type, the Text data type is the default for all fields created in an Access database.

The Number Data Type

Don will also create a table to store the details for every prescription filled at 4Corners Pharmacy, including the number of prescriptions filled for each customer and the number of refills authorized by the doctor. Don will assign the **Number** data type to these fields because Paul will want to use them to calculate how many prescriptions were filled in a given period or perhaps to calculate the average refill allowance per drug type. The Number data type stores both positive and negative numbers in a field (although the pharmacy probably will not need to store negative numbers) containing up to 15 digits. A simple way to remember the purpose of the Number data type is that it is for numbers that you need to use in calculations. As mentioned earlier, data such as telephone numbers, Social Security numbers, and zip codes, despite their appearance and the fact that most people identify these values as numbers, are not used in calculations and are not assigned the Number data type, but rather the Text data type.

The Currency Data Type

Another important consideration is that monetary values are not assigned the Number data type, as you might expect. Despite the fact that these amounts are numbers and are used in calculations, fields storing monetary data are assigned the **Currency** data type, which by default includes two decimal places and displays values with a dollar sign. Thus, Don will assign the Currency data type to fields that store the costs and prices for drugs and the salaries and wages for employees.

Best Practice

Avoiding Storing Calculated Fields in Tables

Although it is important to assign the Number data type to fields containing values that you will use in calculations, it is important not to include calculated fields in your tables. That is, you must avoid creating fields to store data such as a person's age or GPA, since a person's age is valid for only one year and a person's GPA is good for only one semester. Many amateur database developers include calculated fields such as these in their tables, but soon find themselves having to update fields or correct static values that have changed. To avoid this problem, you should include the raw numbers from which such things as age and GPA are calculated, such as a date of birth or a grade and the credit hours earned, respectively, and calculate an age or GPA when you need to do so. You will learn more about performing calculations on Number fields later in this book.

The Date/Time Data Type

Don will include a field in the Employee and Customer tables to store a person's date of birth. He will assign this field the **Date/Time** data type. By default, fields assigned the Date/Time data type display values in the format mm/dd/yyyy, but they can also include the time in different formats. Dates can be used in calculations if necessary to calculate the number of days between a starting date and an ending date, or to determine a person's age. Just like other data types, Don can change the default formatting of the Date/Time data type to display date and time values in different ways.

The AutoNumber Data Type

The **AutoNumber** data type is unique to Access; it is a number automatically generated by Access that produces unique values for each record. This data type is useful when you need to distinguish two records that share identical information. For example, two prescriptions of the same drug, in the same amount, filled on the same day might be entered into a Prescription table. It would be difficult to tell these prescriptions apart, but if assigned the AutoNumber data type, this unique value created for each record would differentiate them. The AutoNumber field produces values of up to nine digits.

The Yes/No Data Type

The **Yes/No** data type is assigned to those fields requiring a yes/no, true/false, or on/off answer and takes up one character of storage space. Don will assign the Yes/No data type to the field in the Customer table that indicates whether the customer prefers child proof caps on prescription bottles. The Yes/No field will make data entry easy; a user only needs to click the check box to place a check mark in it to represent a "yes" value. Using a check box also saves space, as each field takes only one character of space compared to the 16 characters that would be required to type the words "child proof caps."

The OLE Object Data Type

The **OLE object** data type is used to identify files that are created in another program and then linked or embedded in the database. (OLE is an abbreviation for object linking and embedding.) Don might use this data type if he needs to link an employee's record to a scanned image of the employee driver's license that Maria might have on file for delivery personnel.

The Hyperlink Data Type

The **Hyperlink** data type is assigned to fields that contain hyperlinks to Web pages, e-mail addresses, or files that open in a Web browser, an e-mail client, or another application when clicked. Don can use this data type when creating fields that link to Web sites for health plans or doctors.

The Lookup Wizard Data Type

The **Lookup Wizard** data type creates fields that let you look up data in another table or in a list of values created for the field. Don could use the Lookup Wizard in a Customer table to display the two-letter abbreviations for each state so the user could choose the correct state from a drop-down menu. A lookup field accomplishes two things—it makes data entry easy and ensures that valid data is entered into the field. The user cannot misspell the state and cannot enter more or fewer letters than are available in the drop-down menu. For example, if you have the lookup table store state values, you won't have mistakes such as a user entering the abbreviation for Mississippi as MI when in fact that abbreviation is for Michigan. In addition, you won't have an erroneous entry of DA, which isn't an allowable value because it's not a valid abbreviation for a state. In this case, did the user mean to type DE for Delaware or DC for Washington, DC? Is this a typo that you need to correct or is this abbreviation for something else? Lookup fields are also good for controlling inconsistent data. Without them, users might erroneously enter DA as indicated earlier. Were Don to search later for all customers from Delaware, find customers with state abbreviations of DA, because he would not know to look for them. Thus, a state field is an ideal candidate for a lookup field.

Selecting the Correct Data Type

Choosing the appropriate data type for each field in a table is essential for two reasons. First, it helps store the correct data in the correct format while using the least amount of space. Second, it eases data entry and interactivity with data because choosing certain data types results in user-friendly interactive features, such as drop-down menus, check boxes, and hyperlinks. Choosing the appropriate data type also lets you correctly manipulate the data. For example, if the pharmacy decides to start a customer loyalty program in which the pharmacy rewards longtime customers who spend a set amount at the pharmacy by giving them a coupon to save 10% off their next pharmacy purchase, Don will need a way to calculate the sum of all orders placed by each customer. If the database can calculate the total for each pharmacy order, Don can use it to create yearly or monthly totals by customer. If this field uses the Text data type, these calculations would not be possible because a database cannot perform calculations on text values, even if they contain numbers. If this field uses the Currency data type, then these calculations are possible.

Data types are important not only for manipulating data, but also for entering data into the database. A Memo field accepts a large amount of text—even an essay, if desired—whereas the default Text data type accepts up to 255 characters (a few sentences). For example, Maria might want to include a field in a table that identifies the various training classes and describes the content of the classes. To accomplish this goal, she might need to use a field with the Memo data type to have room to include a complete course description that includes the course objectives, prerequisites, and requirements.

The Yes/No and Lookup Wizard data types ease data entry by controlling what data a user can enter into a field. The Yes/No data type only accepts the values "yes" and "no." This restriction is valuable for answering such questions as "Did the pharmacist ask the customer about her allergies?" In this case, the pharmacist simply clicks the check box to indicate that he asked the question. Either the pharmacist followed or did not follow the procedures—there is no other choice for this field. The Yes/No data type provides a nice audit trail in this case.

What happens when the answer is not always yes or no? What if the answer could be "undetermined," "undecided," or "maybe?" If any of these answers are possible—however rare—then you should not use the Yes/No data type because the allowable responses—yes or no—would be inaccurate.

The Lookup Wizard data type also ensures accurate data, but can be more flexible than the Yes/No data type. For example, if the majority of 4Corners Pharmacy customers reside in the four nearby states of Colorado, Utah, New Mexico, and Arizona, it might be convenient to list those four states in a lookup field that provides a drop-down menu allowing the pharmacist to choose among them. The menu saves a great deal of typing for the pharmacist and ensures that the state abbreviations are entered correctly and in the appropriate format into the State field. For any other values, such as CA for a customer from California, the default is to let a user override the lookup field values by typing the value CA directly into the field. If you need to prohibit a user from overriding the lookup field values—perhaps the pharmacy cannot accept out-of-state patients, for example—you could set the field's properties to forbid new values. You will learn more about data validation and other field properties in Chapter 2.

Assigning the Correct Field Size for Text Fields

As mentioned earlier, it is important to consider field size when assigning data types and to minimize the space reserved for each record by assigning the smallest data type that will store your data. For example, to store the two-letter abbreviation for a state instead of the state's full name, you would need to create a field with the Text data type and a field size of two characters. In this case, the field size not only saves space, but also prohibits someone from entering "Cal," "Cali," "Calif," or "California" instead of "CA" into the field. Any value *except* CA would pose problems later when Don tried to search for customers from CA.

It is important to be conservative when assigning field sizes, but not too conservative. For example, how many spaces should be allowed for a person's last name? Upon first consideration you might choose a field size of 10 or 12 characters and safely store the names "Jefferson" (requiring nine characters) or "O'Callaghan" (requiring 11 characters). But what happens when you try to store the names "Thangsuphanich," "Traiwatanapong," or "Jefferson-O'Callaghan," which requires 21 characters (nine characters in Jefferson, one character for the hyphen, and 11 characters for O'Callaghan)? Storing a last name with 21 characters in a field designed to store 12 characters would result in almost half of the name being truncated, or cut off. On the other hand, you would not want to leave the last name field at the default 50 or at the maximum of 255 characters as these field sizes would waste space and violate a cardinal rule of database design. A good compromise is to define fields that store last names with 30 to 40 characters.

Assigning the Correct Field Size for Number Fields

Just as you must be aware of preserving storage space when assigning the Text data type, you must also be conservative when assigning the Number data type, as there are seven choices for Number field sizes. Table 1.3 describes the different field sizes for fields with the Number data type.

Table 1.3: Field sizes for the Number data type

Field Size	Values Allowed	Decimal Precision	Storage Size
Byte	0 to 255 (excludes fractions)	None	1 byte
Integer	–32,768 to 32,767 (excludes fractions)	None	2 bytes
Long Integer	–2,147,483,648 to 2,147,483,647 (excludes fractions)	None	4 bytes
Single	$-3.402823E^{38}$ to $-1.401298E^{-45}$ for negative values and from $1.401298E^{-45}$ to $3.402823E^{38}$ for positive values	7	4 bytes
Double	$-1.79769313486231E^{308}$ to $-4.94065645841247E^{-324}$ for negative values and from $4.94065645841247E^{-324}$ to $1.79769313486231E^{308}$ for positive values	15	8 bytes

Table 1.3: Field sizes for the Number data type (cont.)

Field Size	Values Allowed	Decimal Precision	Storage Size
Decimal	-10^{28-1} through 10^{28-1}	28	12 bytes
Replication ID	Globally unique identifiers (GUID) are used to identify replicas, replica sets, tables, records, and other objects	N/A	16 bytes

To determine the correct field size, you must evaluate the data stored in a Number field just as you would evaluate the data stored in a Text field. For example, Don might assign the Number data type to a Dependents field in the Customer table and then set the field size to Byte. A Byte field stores only positive numbers up to 255. Because a customer cannot have a negative number of dependents, a fractional number of dependents, or more than 255 dependents, this is the correct field size because it stores the correct data using the least amount of space possible.

It is important to choose the correct data type prior to entering data into a table. Although it is possible to change a field's data type after entering data into a table, you might lose some of the data if you decrease a field size because you might truncate any existing data that requires more space than the revised field size allows.

DIVIDING THE EXISTING AND MISSING DATA INTO TABLES

The discovery phase now over, Don must create the tables to be used in the 4Corners Pharmacy database. Figure 1.12 details the four steps involved in this process.

Figure 1.12: Database design process: planning the tables

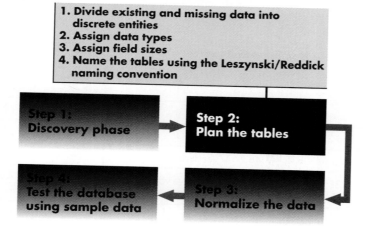

Tables are the single most important component of the database; the other objects in a database could not even exist without being based on tables. A database might have only one table with only one field and only one record in it, such as your first name. Such a database wouldn't be terribly useful, but it would still be a database. Most databases contain multiple tables and hundreds or even thousands of records.

In the discovery phase, Don interviewed 4Corners Pharmacy employees so he could understand the desired database output. Now he needs to divide the existing and missing data into discrete entities, break those entities into smaller fields that describe some attribute, assign data types to these fields, modify the field sizes as necessary, and then name each table according to standard conventions.

Don focuses first on the employee data that Maria collects because it is currently the most fragmented. Recall that Maria keeps personnel records in Outlook, Excel, Word, and on paper, with much of the data, such as the employee's name, appearing in all of these sources. Don lists the data necessary to create the desired output that Maria identified about employees in the discovery phase:

- Name
- Age
- Years with company
- Address
- Position
- Job description
- Pay rate
- Annual review
- Training classes attended
- Other information (such as whether the employee is bilingual and attendance information)
- Prescriptions filled (if the employee is a pharmacist or pharmacy technician)

The amateur database designer might be tempted to list these fields and move on. Don, however, is a seasoned veteran who knows that brainstorming like this is just the first step in creating a table. He must now step back and analyze five things.

1. Don did not include all the data necessary to produce the desired output from his initial discovery phase. Maria needs to print telephone lists of bilingual employees so that if no bilingual pharmacists were on duty and a Spanish-speaking customer required assistance, the staff could call an off-duty colleague to assist with the translation. This telephone list would be impossible to create as Don did not include a phone number in his initial field list. Thus, it is imperative to review the desired output and then ensure that you have the necessary data to produce it. Don expands the list to include one field for telephone number and another field for cell phone number, as most employees have both.

2. Don did not identify a field that he could use as a primary key. A **primary key** is one field (or perhaps a combination of fields) that creates a unique value in each record so you can identify each record in the table. The employees at 4Corners Pharmacy have unique last names, and at first it appears that the last name will uniquely identify each record. However, if a second employee with the last name "Garcia" is hired, there would be no way to use the last name field to distinguish between two employees with that last name. In addition, if Paul opens additional stores, the likelihood of having employees with the same name increases. To create a unique value in each employee's record, Don could expand the list to include the employee's Social Security number. However, because of new privacy laws, Don decides instead to create an Employee ID field, into which he will enter a unique value for each employee, and selects this field as the primary key.

3. The fields Don listed are too broad. Although it is possible to store a person's first and last names in one field (Name), by doing so you would limit what you could do with the data. For example, Maria sends quarterly updates to all employees informing them of how many sick days and holidays they have accrued. Recently learning how to perform a mail merge in Word, Maria wants to customize the contents of the letter to include individualized names. But as listed in Don's brainstorming list, Name is only one field. If Maria used the Name field in the mail merge, the salutation would read "Dear Maria Garcia," which would have an impersonal effect, the exact opposite of Maria's intention of writing the more customary and personal "Dear Maria." Thus, Don decides that the Name field should be broken down into at least two fields to store the first name and last name. Indeed, he could break down the Name field further, including additional fields to store the employee's title, middle name, suffix, and preferred name. For the Employee table, Don includes fields for first name, middle initial, and last name. Following this principle, Don also divides the address into multiple fields (address, city, state, and zip code) and the pay rate into multiple fields (salary and hourly rate).

4. After expanding as many fields as possible into discrete units, Don identifies a fourth problem with the proposed fields in the Employee table: age is a static number. If stored as a whole number, it will become outdated within a year. You will remember from the earlier discussion about data types that age and other calculated fields should never be stored in a table. Rather, good database design includes birth date fields. By storing a person's birth date, you can calculate the person's age by subtracting the birth date from today's date. Don changes the Age field to Date of Birth and then changes the Years with company field, another value that he can calculate, to Start Date and End Date.

5. The fifth and final problem with the proposed fields for the Employee table is that some break the cardinal rule of relational database design—avoiding data redundancy. The Employee table includes fields for job description and training classes attended. Although this data describes employees, these fields belong in two separate tables to prevent data redundancy. For example, 14 employees might attend the same training class. If the training class information appears in the Employee table, Maria would need to add the class to the record for each employee who attended the class, as shown in Figure 1.13.

Figure 1.13: Employee training data

	A	B	C	D
1	**First Name**	**Last Name**	**Class**	**Date**
2	Amy	Urquiza	Adult CPR	6/20/2004
3	Tara	Kobrick	Adult CPR	4/10/2004
4	Joan	Gabel	Adult CPR	2/6/2004
5	Rachel	Thompson	Adult CPR	3/17/2004
6	Tara	Kobrick	Adult CPR Recertification	4/12/2005
7	Louis	Moreno	Adult CPR Recertification	4/1/2006
8	Paul	Ferrino	Adult CPR Recertification	2/5/2007
9	Virginia	Sanchez	Adult CPR Recertification	6/1/2007
10	Virginia	Sanchez	Adult CPR Recertification	6/29/2008
11	Rachel	Thompson	Adult CPR Recertification	3/16/2005
12	Amy	Urquiza	Adult CPR Recertification	6/21/2005
13	Amy	Urquiza	Adult CPR Recertification	3/10/2006
14	Dora	Langston	Adult CPR Recertification	6/15/2006
15	Dora	Langston	Adult CPR Recertification	3/5/2007
16	Vincent	Ferrino	Adult CPR Recertification	2/2/2005
17	Vincent	Ferrino	Adult CPR Recertification	4/2/2007
18	Vincent	Ferrino	Adult CPR Recertification	4/5/2008
19	Marco	Farello	Adult CPR Recertification	2/1/2006
20	Dora	Langston	Child/Infant CPR	6/9/2004
21	Marco	Farello	Child/Infant CPR	1/30/2004

Employee Training

Redundant data: "Adult CPR Recertification" appears 14 times

Typing the same information into each employee's record is a waste of time for Maria and exactly what Don seeks to avoid by designing a relational database. Retyping "Adult CPR Recertification" 14 times is inefficient and could result in inconsistent data. Don is glad that he spotted this redundancy now and knows that this is why the brainstorming component of database design is imperative and often time-consuming, but well worth the effort. By foreseeing this potential redundancy, Don will avoid it by creating a separate table to store data about the class descriptions, cost, provider, and any other pertinent data.

Don also recognizes that the Position field contains repetitive data because multiple employees can share the same job title, so he creates a table to store information about positions held by employees. He also needs a way to identify which employee filled which prescription, so he creates another table to store information about prescriptions.

As you can see, Don's brainstorming about employees resulted in the creation of three additional tables and several more fields. Don will complete this brainstorming process for each table that he creates, making sure to include all necessary fields, identify primary keys, break broad fields into smaller discrete components, avoid calculated fields, and avoid data redundancy. He will create as many tables as necessary to avoid repeating any information in the database. The result of Don's brainstorming is shown in Table 1.4, with the fields for the Employee table and their corresponding data types.

Table 1.4: Field names and data types for the Employee table

Field Name	Data Type
Employee ID	Number
First Name	Text
Middle Initial	Text
Last Name	Text
Social Security Number	Text
Date of Birth	Date/Time
Start Date	Date/Time
End Date	Date/Time
Address	Text
City	Text
State	Text
Zip	Text
Memo	Memo
Phone	Text
Cell	Text
Salary	Currency
Hourly Rate	Currency
Review	Date/Time

The data about training classes attended, job positions, and prescriptions filled, which originally appeared in the Employee table, will become fields in their own tables.

Naming Conventions

After brainstorming the employee fields and grouping them together, Don must name the table. Database tables must have unique names and follow established naming conventions for the DBMS in which they are stored. Some general rules for naming objects (including tables) are as follows:

- Object names cannot exceed 64 characters, although shorter names are preferred.
- Object names cannot include a period, exclamation point, accent grave, or brackets.
- Object names should not include spaces. Most developers capitalize the first letter of each word when a table name includes two words, such as EmployeeTraining.

In general, field names follow the same naming rules. For example, in the Employee table, Don will change the field name First Name (which includes a space) to FirstName.

Most database developers also follow established naming conventions, in which a prefix (also called a tag) precedes the object name to define it further. Instead of naming the table Employee, Don uses the Leszynski/Reddick naming conventions shown in Table 1.5 and names the table tblEmployee.

Table 1.5: Leszynski/Reddick naming conventions for database objects

Database Object	Prefix	Example
Table	tbl	tblEmployee
Query	qry	qryPharmacists
Form	frm	frmCustomer
Report	rpt	rptBilingualPharmacists
Macro	mcr	mcrUpdateClasses
Module	bas	basInventory

Some developers use a prefix to identify the fields in a table, as well, such as changing the field name LastName to txtLastName to identify the field as having the Text data type. Don decides not to use this convention because it will increase the time it takes to type the field names.

Although it will take some time to build all the tables, Paul is encouraged by the benefits that a DBMS will offer the pharmacy. Don interviewed as many key players at 4Corners Pharmacy as possible, gathered the existing data, researched any sources of missing data, and talked to users about desired output. He and Paul agreed on expectations, and then Don began planning the tables by dividing existing and missing data into discrete entities, naming the fields, and assigning data types to these fields.

Steps To Success: Level 1

After concluding the discovery phase of database design, Don began brainstorming about the tables he needs to create and which specific fields within those tables are necessary to capture all data required for the desired output he identified. Don created tblEmployee. He asks you to create the table designs for the remaining tables in the database by grouping the existing and missing data he identified into tables, creating field names and data types, and naming the fields and tables according to the standards he established.

On a piece of paper, complete the following:

1. Plan the tables needed in the 4Corners Pharmacy database using the information Don garnered during the discovery phase.

2. Name each table according to its contents and the Leszynski/Reddick naming conventions.

3. List the fields in each table.

4. Designate data types for each field in each table.

5. Look at the plan you created for the 4Corners Pharmacy and look for any missing or incomplete data. What other changes would you suggest making, and why?

LEVEL 2

UNDERSTANDING AND CREATING TABLE RELATIONSHIPS

UNDERSTANDING RELATIONAL DATABASE OBJECTS

Although tables store the data in a DBMS, users can view the data in tables by opening the table or by creating other objects. The four main objects in a database are tables, queries, forms, and reports.

Tables

You learned in Level 1 that the data in a relational database is stored in one or more tables. You can view the data in a table by opening it and scrolling through its records. However, most of the time you will use one of the three other main database objects—queries, forms, and reports—to display the data from one or more tables in a format that matches your needs.

Queries

A **query** is a question that you ask about the data stored in a database, such as "Which customers live in Colorado?" You could generate a list of customers by scrolling through the records in tblCustomer or by sorting the records alphabetically by state, but with many customers, this process could take a lot of time and is only a temporary rearrangement of the data in the table. If you use a query to find the answer to this question, you can save the query in the database and use it again to list the customers who live in Colorado because the query object searches each record in tblCustomer and lists in the results each one with the value CO (the state abbreviation for Colorado) in the State field. The query results look similar to a table, with fields displayed in columns and records displayed in rows. (This arrangement of data in Access is called a **datasheet**.) There are three different kinds of queries: select queries, action queries, and crosstab queries.

The **select query** is the most commonly used query. As the name suggests, data is selected from the table on which the query is based (also called the **base table** or the **underlying table**), and is displayed in a datasheet. A query can select basic information or very specific information. For example, a select query might select all customers who live in Colorado. A more specific select query might select all customers who live in Colorado, are older than 55, and live in the 81323 zip code. When you run a select query, the query results are dynamic; that is, if every customer living in Colorado moves to another state, the datasheet will display no matching records the next time you run a query that selects customers living in Colorado. On the other hand, if 1,000 new Colorado customers were entered into tblCustomer, running a query that selects customers living in Colorado would display 1,000 new records.

A two-way relationship exists between a table and queries that are based on the table. As you just learned, records are "pulled" from the table upon which a query is based and displayed in a datasheet. You can also use a query to "push" data into the table using the query. For example, if a pharmacist viewing a query that selects customers living in Colorado changes the value in the State field from CO to AZ for a customer, the customer's record is updated in tblCustomer. When he runs the query again, that customer's record will no longer appear in the query results because it no longer satisfies the requirements for being included. If a pharmacist accidentally deletes a record from the query results, that record is also deleted from tblCustomer.

An **action query**, as its name implies, performs an action on the table on which it is based. Some action queries let you select specific records in a table and update them in some way, such as increasing the cost of every drug purchased from a specific supplier by 10%. Other action queries let you select data from one table and append (add) it to another table; you can use this type of query to create a new table or add records to an existing table. You can also use an action query to delete records from a table, such as deleting all customer records from a table when the customer's account has been inactive for a specific length of time.

A **crosstab query** performs calculations on the values in a field and displays the results in a datasheet. A crosstab query might sum the values in a field to create a total or select the maximum or minimum value in a field. You will learn more about queries in Chapter 3.

Forms

A **form** is used to view, add, delete, update, and print records in the database. A form can be based on a table or a query. A form might also have a two-way relationship with a table because changing the data displayed in a form might update the data in the table on which the form is based, depending on how the form was created. Often a form displays many or all the fields from the table on which it is based, and you can enter data into the form to add a record to the table. A form based on tblClinic is shown in Figure 1.14.

Figure 1.14: Form based on a table

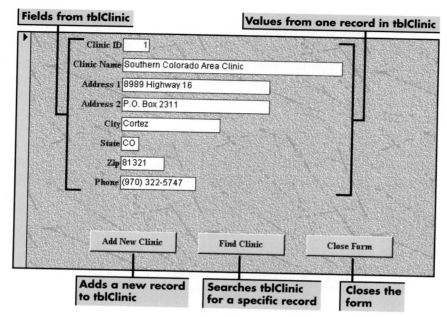

Fields from tblClinic

Values from one record in tblClinic

Adds a new record to tblClinic

Searches tblClinic for a specific record

Closes the form

Don could use the clinic information form he obtained during the discovery phase to create its database counterpart so the pharmacy staff can add a new clinic to the database using the form object. If the clinic's information changes, an employee could update fields as necessary by displaying the form again and using it to find and view the clinic's data, and then make the necessary changes. You will learn more about forms in Chapter 4.

Another benefit of using a form to display data is that the interface is more attractive than the table datasheet, and you can customize a form's appearance with instructions and command buttons. The command buttons shown in Figure 1.14 change the form's function to add a new clinic, find an existing clinic, and close the form. As a result, even the least experienced user of a database feels confident when entering or viewing data. Forms are also used as a type of welcome menu to your database; when used in this capacity, a form is called a switchboard. A **switchboard** is a form that might be displayed when you open a database and provides a controlled method for users to open the objects in a database. Users click buttons to open existing objects, which is more user friendly than using the database interface. You will learn how to create and use a switchboard in Chapter 6.

Reports

A **report** is a formatted presentation of data from a table or query that is created as a printout or to be viewed on screen. A report might contain an employee telephone directory, inventory summaries, or mailing labels. Some reports are simple to create, such as generating telephone lists. Other types of reports, such as inventory summaries, are more complicated because they might display data in ways not available by using other database objects. For example, Don needs to create a report for Paul that details customer expenditures grouped by the city in which the customer lives. Paul will use this information for marketing purposes so he knows where the majority of his customers live. Paul also needs reports showing the pharmacy's daily, monthly, quarterly, and yearly revenues. If Paul opens one or more additional stores, he'll need this same information, but grouped by location.

The data displayed by a report is usually based on a query, although you can also base a report on a table. Reports are dynamic, reflecting the latest data from the object on which they are based. However, unlike forms, you can only view the data in a report; you cannot change the data or use a report to add a new record. The amount of data in a report varies—a report might list the top five best-selling drugs at 4Corners Pharmacy or all customers at the pharmacy who take a certain drug. When a report exceeds more than one page, the user must use the page navigation features to view the pages on screen. Figure 1.15 shows a report that displays the accounts receivable data for customers with outstanding balances.

Figure 1.15: Accounts receivable report

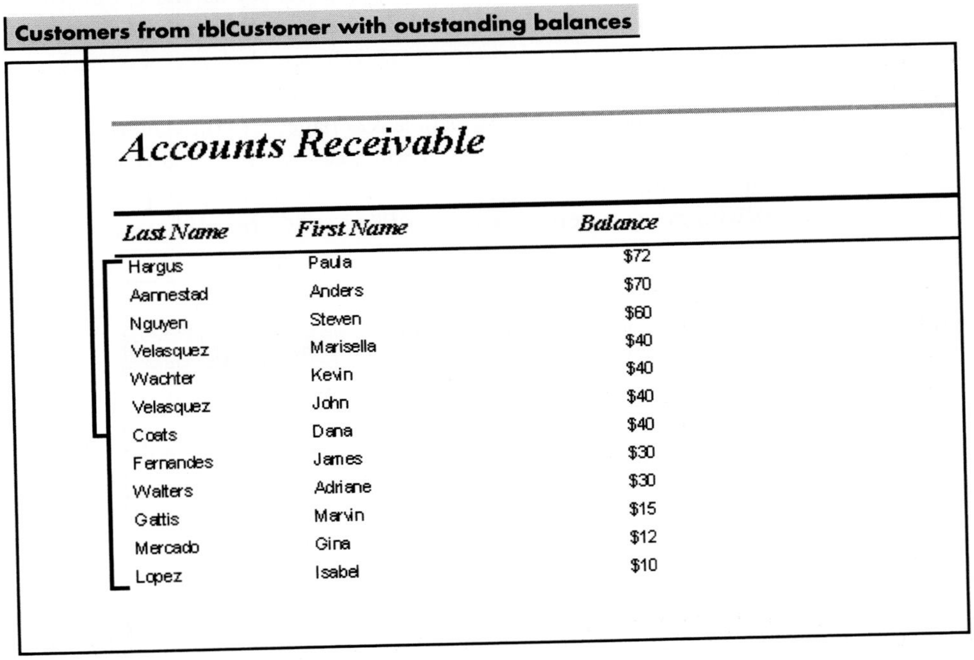

Customers from tblCustomer with outstanding balances

Accounts Receivable

Last Name	First Name	Balance
Hargus	Paula	$72
Aarnestad	Anders	$70
Nguyen	Steven	$60
Velasquez	Marisella	$40
Wachter	Kevin	$40
Velasquez	John	$40
Coats	Dana	$40
Fernandes	James	$30
Walters	Adriane	$30
Gattis	Marvin	$15
Mercado	Gina	$12
Lopez	Isabel	$10

The report shown in Figure 1.15 is based on the query shown in Figure 1.16. As you can see, the data in the report and query are the same, but the report format makes the data easier to read. The report contains a title to identify its contents. You can also add page numbers, headers, and footers to a report. You will learn more about reports in Chapter 5.

Figure 1.16: Query datasheet

tblCustomer Query

First Name	Last Name	SumOfBalance
Paula	Hargus	$72.00
Anders	Aannestad	$70.00
Steven	Nguyen	$60.00
Marisella	Velasquez	$40.00
Kevin	Wachter	$40.00
John	Velasquez	$40.00
Dana	Coats	$40.00
James	Fernandes	$30.00
Adriane	Walters	$30.00
Marvin	Gattis	$15.00
Gina	Mercado	$12.00
Isabel	Lopez	$10.00

Other Database Objects

Most users interact mostly with the tables, queries, forms, and reports in a database, but you might also use three other objects. A **page**, also called a **data access page**, is a Web page that lets you view and interact with data stored in an Access database. A data access page is an HTML document that is stored outside the database, usually in a shared network folder or on a server that is connected to the Internet. All data access pages let you view the data in the object on which the data access page is based; in some cases, you can also add and delete records from the underlying object. Figure 1.17 shows a data access page with information about doctors who have written prescriptions filled at 4Corners Pharmacy.

Figure 1.17: Data access page

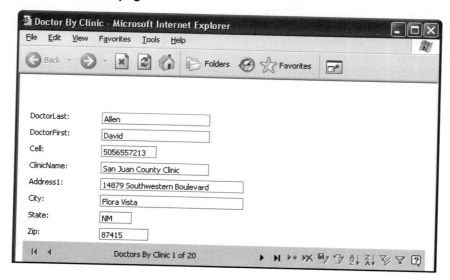

A **macro** is a set of instructions that you specify to automate certain database tasks. A macro might contain instructions to open a specific form or query in the database when you click a command button on a form. A macro can also contain instructions to close an object, find a record, print an object, or close Access. You will learn more about using and creating macros in Chapter 6.

A **module** is another object that contains instructions to automate a database task. Modules are written in **Visual Basic for Applications (VBA)**, the programming language for Microsoft Office programs, including Access. A macro usually automates a simple task, such as opening or closing a form. A module performs more sophisticated actions, such as verifying the data entered into a field before storing it in the database. You will learn more about modules in Chapter 7.

UNDERSTANDING RELATIONAL DATABASE CONCEPTS

The worksheet and other systems used by the pharmacy indicate that Vincent is not familiar with a relational database, but rather with a **flat file database**, a simple database that contains a single table of information. A relational database contains multiple tables to store related information. When most people are faced with a task that requires some kind of data management, they often open Excel and start entering data into a worksheet with columns to define the different fields for each row in the worksheet. Figure 1.18 shows a flat file database that Vincent created using Excel.

Figure 1.18: Flat file database that includes rows for new records

Redundant and inconsistent data for people living in the same household

First Name	Last Name	Address	City	State	Zip	PlanID
Christina	Hargus	5465 South Nelson Circle	Shiprock	NM	87420	OP-87-A087
Paula	Hargus	5465 South Nelson Circle	Shiprock	NM	87420	OP-87-A087
Isabel	Lopez	6969 South Valmont Road	Montezuma Creek	UT	84534	2B8973AC
Steven	Nguyen	9874 South Main Street	Blanding	UT	84511	498-1112-A
Scott	Prager	2510 West 108th Avenue	Pleasant View	CO	81331	4983
Jennifer	Ramsey	4775 Argone Circle	Chinle	AZ	86547	498-1112-A
Shannon	Sabus	460 West Pioneer Road	Dolores	CO	81323	4983
Ted	Sabus	406 West Pioneer Road	Dolores	CO	81323	4983
Marisella	Velasquez	54213 Oak Drive	Kirtland	NM	87417	000H98763-01
Marisella	Velasquez	54213 Oak Drive	Kirtland	NM	87417	000H98763-01
Kevin	Wachter	2931 East Narcissus Way	Montezuma Creek	UT	84534	A089
Adriane	Walters	14444 North Tamarac Street	Cortez	CO	81321	4983
Adriane	Walters	14444 North Tamarac Street	Cortez	CO	81321	4983

Redundant data for the same customer

Figure 1.18 shows a flat file database in which each new prescription was added in a new row in the worksheet. This method creates at least three problems. First, the pharmacist wastes time by entering the name, address, phone number, and data for each prescription the customer fills. Notice that Adriane Walters filled two prescriptions. The pharmacist entered Adriane's name, address, and health plan information into both records, even though this data is the same for both records.

Second, and more important, this process is prone to errors. Notice that Ted and Shannon Sabus, who filled prescriptions on the same day, seem to be related but live in different house numbers, suggesting that one or both of these house numbers contains an error. Such errors are common occurrences in flat file databases because of the amount of data repetition and data redundancy.

Third, what if Adriane or the Sabuses move or change health plans? The pharmacist would need to locate every row in the flat file database containing this data for these customers and change the corresponding data—another waste of time and another opportunity for inconsistent data to occur. You might think that a solution to this problem is to add columns to the worksheet, instead of rows, as shown in Figure 1.19.

Figure 1.19: Flat file database with columns for new prescriptions

First Name	Last Name	PrescriptionID	Name	PrescriptionID	Name	PrescriptionID
Shannon	Sabus	18	Rivastigmine tartrate			
Ted	Sabus	24	Acebutolol hydrochloride			
Marisella	Velasquez	33	Quentix	63	Tolbutamide	
Kevin	Wachter	39	Myobuterol			
Adriane	Walters	14	Didanosine	36	Almotriptan	

This is a clever solution as the name, address, phone number, and health plan data do not repeat. If this design were adopted, 4Corners Pharmacy could track all prescriptions in one worksheet instead of creating a new worksheet daily to detail each day's prescriptions. Although this method will work for some time, the table will become too large after months and years of adding new columns. In addition, Excel limits the number of columns in a worksheet to 256, and it is unlikely that someone would scroll 256 columns to find all prescriptions filled for a customer. Moreover, this system would only work if the customer has the same doctor write all his prescriptions, for each row includes a field for prescribing doctor. If Adriane is prescribed migraine medicine from a general practitioner and eye drops from an ophthalmologist, then the pharmacy could not use this table, or would need to modify it to include a prescribing doctor field for each prescription. This field would contain duplicate data for most customers, thereby defeating the purpose of the new design.

What if you attempt to solve these problems by creating two workbooks to store orders? One workbook would store customer data and the other workbook would store prescription data, as shown in Figure 1.20.

Figure 1.20: Storing customer and prescription data in separate workbooks

First Name	Last Name	Telephone	Date of Birth	Gender	Balance	ChildCap	PlanID	HouseID
Anders	Aannestad	(505) 499-6541	9/11/1974	M	$35.00	FALSE	498-1112-A	9
Dusty	Alkier	(435) 693-1212	4/5/1940	M	$0.00	FALSE	A089	10
Rose	Baaz	(505) 477-8989	4/12/1970	F	$0.00	TRUE	OP-87-A087	3
Geoffrey	Baaz	(505) 477-8989	12/31/2001	M	$0.00	FALSE	4983	18
Byron	Buescher	(970) 119-3474	6/1/1944	M	$0.00	TRUE	498-1112-A	4
Albert	Cardenas	(928) 551-5547	10/14/1965	M	$0.00	TRUE	498-1112-A	4
Sonia	Cardenas	(928) 551-5547	4/12/1968	F	$0.00	TRUE	498-1112-A	4
Daniel	Cardenas	(928) 551-5547	5/12/2002	M	$0.00	TRUE	498-1112-A	4
Jonathan	Cardenas	(928) 551-5547	8/22/2004	M	$0.00	TRUE	OP-87-A087	21
Dallas	Coats	(505) 312-6211	10/31/1972	M	$0.00	TRUE	OP-87-A087	21
Dana	Coats	(505) 312-6211	8/16/2002	F	$20.00	TRUE	OP-87-A087	21
Octavia	Coats	(505) 312-6211	6/30/1976	F	$0.00	FALSE	498-1112-A	17
Jessica	Cortez	(928) 644-1674	8/13/1978	F	$0.00	FALSE	2B8973AC	6
Malena	D'Ambrosio	(435) 444-1233	4/15/1980	F	$0.00	FALSE	000H98763-01	23
Chloe	Feraco	(435) 777-3244	6/1/1946	F	$0.00	FALSE	000H98763-01	23
Gaetano	Feraco	(435) 777-3244	7/4/1946	M	$0.00	FALSE	OP-87-A087	22
James	Fernandes	(505) 988-6547	2/18/1977	M	$30.00	FALSE	OP-87-A087	22
Gloria	Fernandes	(505) 988-6547	5/1/1979	F	$0.00	FALSE	4983	8
William	Gabel	(970) 223-4156	7/4/1980	M	$0.00	FALSE		

Customers

PrescriptionID	UPN	Quantity	Unit	Date	ExpireDate	Refills	AutoRefill	RefillsUsed
1	224	1	mg	9/10/2007	6/10/2008	2	TRUE	0
2	828	1	ml	12/15/2007	12/11/2008	3	FALSE	1
3	711	1	mg	6/21/2008	7/30/2008	5	FALSE	0
4	256	1	mg	1/10/2008	10/24/2008	2	TRUE	0
5	398	1	mg	9/10/2007	9/12/2008	3	TRUE	1
6	121	1	mg	4/26/2008	8/30/2008	4	TRUE	0
7	932	1	ml	1/24/2008	9/22/2008	2	TRUE	1
8	523	1	ml	1/29/2008	6/14/2008	3	FALSE	1
9	311	1	ml	9/24/2007	11/25/2008	4	TRUE	0
10	366	1	ml	3/14/2008	7/26/2008	3	TRUE	0
12	444	1	mg	2/24/2007	1/20/2008	4	TRUE	0
13	642	1	mg	4/12/2007	2/11/2008	3	TRUE	0
14	878	1	mg	5/16/2008	12/12/2008	2	FALSE	0
15	852	1	mg	4/11/2008	11/20/2008	3	TRUE	0
16	654	1	mg	1/22/2007	1/8/2008	3	FALSE	0
17	398	1	mg	4/15/2007	6/11/2008	4	TRUE	1
18	972	1	mg	5/5/2007	6/7/2008	4	TRUE	2
19	524	1	mg	4/28/2007	2/20/2008	4	TRUE	1
20	741	1	mg	6/14/2007	1/2/2008	3	TRUE	1

Prescriptions

Customers are listed only once in the Customers workbook, and all prescriptions filled for those customers are listed in the Prescriptions workbook. There is no longer a need to create daily worksheets to track the prescriptions filled each day. Given that Excel has 65,526 rows, these workbooks could last for some time, and it seems that you have solved the problems caused by using a flat file database. However, there is no indication of which customer purchased which prescription. The only way to distinguish customers is by name, and the workbooks do not share any common fields. Although pharmacists might be able to distinguish customers by name for the time being, what would happen if there were two customers named John Smith? You might suggest that you could distinguish the John Smiths by their addresses. But what if the two people named John Smith are father and son, both sharing the same address, telephone number, and doctor? There would be no way to distinguish the customers and no way to know who ordered which prescriptions, as the workbooks lack a unique identifying value for each customer and prescription.

Professional relational database design requires that every table has a primary key field that stores unique values. To satisfy this requirement, a new column named CustID is added to the Customers workbook. In Figure 1.21, Daniel Cardenas has the CustID 9. No one else has this number, ever had this number, or ever will have this number, except for Daniel Cardenas. It uniquely identifies his record in the table.

Figure 1.21: Customer data with CustID column added

CustID values uniquely identify each customer

CustID	First Name	Last Name	Telephone	Date of Birth	Gender	Balance	ChildCap	PlanID	HouseID
18	Anders	Aannestad	(505) 499-6541	9/11/1974	M	$35.00	FALSE	498-1112-A	9
19	Dusty	Alkier	(435) 693-1212	4/5/1940	M	$0.00	FALSE	A089	10
5	Rose	Baaz	(505) 477-8989	4/12/1970	F	$0.00	TRUE	OP-87-A087	3
6	Geoffrey	Baaz	(505) 477-8989	12/31/2001	M	$0.00	TRUE	OP-87-A087	3
27	Byron	Buescher	(970) 119-3474	6/1/1944	M	$0.00	FALSE	4983	18
7	Albert	Cardenas	(928) 551-5547	10/14/1965	M	$0.00	TRUE	498-1112-A	4
8	Sonia	Cardenas	(928) 551-5547	4/12/1968	F	$0.00	TRUE	498-1112-A	4
9	Daniel	Cardenas	(928) 551-5547	5/12/2002	M	$0.00	TRUE	498-1112-A	4
10	Jonathan	Cardenas	(928) 551-5547	8/22/2004	M	$0.00	TRUE	498-1112-A	4
30	Dallas	Coats	(505) 312-6211	10/31/1972	M	$0.00	TRUE	OP-87-A087	21
31	Dana	Coats	(505) 312-6211	8/16/2002	F	$20.00	TRUE	OP-87-A087	21
32	Octavia	Coats	(505) 312-6211	6/30/1976	F	$0.00	TRUE	OP-87-A087	21
26	Jessica	Cortez	(928) 644-1674	8/13/1978	F	$0.00	FALSE	498-1112-A	17
14	Malena	D'Ambrosio	(435) 444-1233	4/15/1980	F	$0.00	FALSE	2B8973AC	6
35	Chloe	Feraco	(435) 777-3244	6/1/1946	F	$0.00	FALSE	000H98763-01	23
36	Gaetano	Feraco	(435) 777-3244	7/4/1946	M	$0.00	FALSE	000H98763-01	23
33	James	Fernandes	(505) 988-6547	2/18/1977	M	$30.00	FALSE	OP-87-A087	22
34	Gloria	Fernandes	(505) 988-6547	5/1/1979	F	$0.00	FALSE	OP-87-A087	22
16	William	Gabel	(970) 223-4156	7/4/1980	M	$0.00	FALSE	4983	8

Assigning a primary key to the Customers workbook reduces the amount of data repetition and the number of errors. For example, a pharmacist could identify Daniel Cardenas and Danny Cardenas by sorting the records by customer ID number—both records have the CustID 9. Don could then remove the duplicate record, which he discovered in his research of existing data at 4Corners Pharmacy, and implement ways to avoid redundancy prior to entering customer data in order to prevent duplicate records from occurring. Thus, assigning a primary key to the Customers workbook helps pharmacists distinguish customer records, but, even so, problems will remain in the flat file database design because the customer and prescription workbooks do not share any common fields.

Although the Prescriptions workbook includes a PrescriptionID (uniquely identifying each prescription) and the Customers workbook includes a CustID (uniquely identifying each customer), there is no way to know which prescription belongs to which customer, or vice versa. A solution is to add the CustID field to the Prescriptions workbook and assign each prescription to its customer. Figure 1.22 shows the Prescriptions workbook with the CustID field added to it. Now it is possible to associate a customer with his prescriptions using the CustID. For example, CustID 9 was prescribed PrescriptionID 16 on 1/22/2007.

Figure 1.22: Prescription data with CustID column added

CustID 9 (Daniel Cardenas)

PrescriptionID	CustID	UPN	Quantity	Unit	Date	ExpireDate	Refills	AutoRefill	RefillsUsed
1	17	224	1	mg	9/10/2007	6/10/2008	2	TRUE	0
2	18	828	1	ml	12/15/2007	12/11/2008	3	FALSE	1
3	23	711	1	mg	6/21/2008	7/30/2008	5	FALSE	0
4	19	256	1	mg	1/10/2008	10/24/2008	2	TRUE	0
5	19	398	1	mg	9/10/2007	9/12/2008	3	TRUE	1
6	34	121	1	mg	4/26/2008	8/30/2008	4	TRUE	0
7	14	932	1	ml	1/24/2008	9/22/2008	2	TRUE	1
8	16	523	1	ml	1/29/2008	6/14/2008	3	FALSE	1
9	21	311	1	ml	9/24/2007	11/25/2008	4	TRUE	0
10	37	366	1	ml	3/14/2008	7/26/2008	3	TRUE	0
12	1	444	1	mg	2/24/2007	1/20/2008	4	TRUE	0
13	38	642	1	mg	4/12/2007	2/11/2008	3	TRUE	0
14	25	878	1	mg	5/16/2008	12/12/2008	2	FALSE	0
15	27	852	1	mg	4/11/2008	11/20/2008	3	TRUE	0
16	9	654	1	mg	1/22/2007	1/8/2008	3	FALSE	0
17	4	398	1	mg	4/15/2007	6/11/2008	4	TRUE	1
18	3	972	1	mg	5/5/2007	6/7/2008	4	TRUE	2
19	28	524	1	mg	4/28/2007	2/20/2008	4	TRUE	1
20	31	741	1	mg	6/14/2007	1/2/2008	3	TRUE	1

PrescriptionID 16

Sorting the Prescriptions worksheet by CustID, rather than by PrescriptionID, reveals that CustID 9 had two prescriptions filled at 4Corners Pharmacy: Prescription IDs 16 and 61, filled on 1/22/2007 and 3/16/2007, respectively, as shown in Figure 1.23. The CustID field is called a common field in this case because it is appears in the Customers and Prescriptions workbooks. A **common field** is a field that appears in two or more tables and contains identical data to relate the tables. The common field is a primary key in the first table. The common field is called a **foreign key** in the second table.

Figure 1.23: Prescription data sorted by CustID column

PrescriptionID	CustID	UPN	Quantity	Unit	Date	ExpireDate	Refills	AutoRefill	RefillsUsed
12	1	444	1	mg	2/24/2007	1/20/2008	4	TRUE	0
24	1	247	1	mg	1/16/2008	12/18/2008	4	TRUE	0
57	1	102	1	mg	5/2/2008	10/30/2008	3	TRUE	0
40	2	524	1	mg	11/22/2007	6/18/2008	2	TRUE	2
18	3	972	1	mg	5/5/2007	6/7/2008	4	TRUE	0
51	3	644	1	ml	1/17/2008	12/1/2008	3	TRUE	0
17	4	398	1	mg	4/15/2007	6/11/2008	4	TRUE	1
52	4	878	1	mg	6/13/2008	12/12/2008	2	TRUE	0
42	5	452	1	mg	6/14/2007	9/1/2008	3	FALSE	0
64	5	224	1	mg	4/29/2008	10/4/2008	3	TRUE	1
43	6	311	1	ml	7/27/2007	1/21/2008	3	FALSE	0
21	7	587	1	mg	8/12/2007	3/15/2008	3	FALSE	1
35	7	102	1	mg	1/3/2008	12/31/2008	3	TRUE	0
41	8	398	1	mg	5/16/2007	7/11/2008	4	TRUE	0
16	9	654	1	mg	1/22/2007	1/8/2008	3	FALSE	1
61	9	828	1	ml	3/16/2007	4/15/2008	4	TRUE	0
44	10	932	1	ml	9/24/2007	4/16/2008	3	TRUE	0
45	11	732	1	mg	8/14/2007	7/31/2008	4	TRUE	0
55	11	642	1	mg	7/8/2007	1/6/2008	4	TRUE	0

CustID 9 (Daniel Cardenas) filled two prescriptions

975

The solutions to overcoming the limitations of a flat file database are as follows:

- Create separate tables for each entity.
- Assign a primary key to each table, using either a field that already uniquely identifies each record or an AutoNumber field that generates a unique number.
- Include a common field in the related table that identifies which records match.

Figure 1.23 shows that CustID 9 filled two prescriptions with the Prescription IDs 16 and 61. However, there's no easy way to determine the identity of CustID 9. Unless the pharmacist recalls that CustID 9 is Daniel Cardenas, he would have to cross-reference the Customers workbook to identify CustID 9. You cannot overcome this limitation of a flat file database because there is no way to view data from multiple workbooks at the same time. The solution is to create a relational database.

CREATING TABLE RELATIONSHIPS

By now you see the limitations of a flat file database and are familiar with the objects in a relational database and have a good idea of how they interact: tables store the data, queries display subsets of data from the tables in response to a command that asks a question, forms present an interface to enter data into tables and view individual records, and reports produce aesthetically pleasing views and printouts of data pulled from tables or queries. Although a relational database might consist of just one table and several interrelated objects, a database usually consists of at least *two* related tables. You might wonder why you need to create these relationships. You need to create relationships between tables so that you can take advantage of these interrelated objects. Remember that the goal in good database design is to create separate tables for each entity, ensure that each table has a primary key, and use a common field to relate tables. Relational databases overcome the limitations of flat file databases. If you relate two (or more) tables, you can query them as though they are one big table, pulling as much or as little data as you need from each table.

The question then arises: how do the tables know that they are related? They know they are related if they share a common field and you create a join between them. A **join** specifies a relationship between tables and the properties of that relationship. How do you create table relationships? The first step is to decide which type of relationship you need to create: one-to-many, one-to-one, or many-to-many.

One-to-Many Relationships

Most tables have a **one-to-many relationship** (abbreviated as **1:M**), in which one record in the first table matches zero, one, or many records in the related table. For example, one customer can fill zero, one, or many prescriptions at 4Corners Pharmacy; one teacher can have zero, one, or many students; and one realtor can list zero, one, or many homes for sale. In a one-to-many relationship, the **primary table** is on the "one" side of the relationship and the **related table** is on the "many" side of the relationship. For example, at 4Corners Pharmacy, tblCustomer is the "one" table and tblRx is the "many" table because one customer might fill zero, one, or many prescriptions. Figure 1.24 illustrates the one-to-many relationship between customers and prescriptions.

Figure 1.24: One-to-many relationship between customers and prescriptions

| CustID is the primary key in tblCustomer | CustID is the common field that relates the tables | CustID is a foreign key in tblRx |

tblCustomer

CustID	FirstName	LastName
18	Anders	Aannestad
27	Byron	Buescher
113	John	Kohlmetz

tblRx

PrescriptionID	UPN	CustID
60	366	18
2	828	18
123	852	27

In Figure 1.24, CustID 18 (Anders Aannestad) has two prescriptions with the PrescriptionIDs 60 and 2, CustID 27 (Byron Buescher) has one prescription (PrescriptionID 123), and John Kohlmetz, a new customer at 4Corners Pharmacy, has not yet filled a prescription, and, therefore, has no related records in tblRx.

One-to-One Relationships

A **one-to-one relationship** (abbreviated as **1:1**) exists when each record in one table matches exactly one record in the related table. For example, Paul seeks to expand part of his business by selling large quantities of drugs to hospitals. Each hospital has a physical mailing address to use when delivering prescriptions. However, some hospital clients have their accounts payable operations off-site, with separate billing addresses. To store the physical and billing addresses of the hospitals, Don could create one table to store the name and physical address of each hospital and another table to store the billing address for each hospital. These two tables have a one-to-one relationship in which each hospital has one physical address that matches exactly one billing address and one billing address matches exactly one physical address, as shown in Figure 1.25.

Figure 1.25: One-to-one relationship between physical and billing addresses

tblHospital

HospitalID	Name	Address	City	State	Zip
1	County	123 Main	Chinle	AZ	86547
2	St. John's	555 Maple	Blanding	UT	84512
3	Bellview	2121 Chestnut	Farmington	NM	87499

tblHospitalBilling

HospitalID	BillingAddress	City	State	Zip
1	2727 Jefferson	Chinle	AZ	86544
2	8292 Brady	Blanding	UT	84518
3	3230 Bradford	Farmington	NM	87492

HospitalID 1 has exactly one matching record

One-to-one relationships are used infrequently because it is often possible to combine the data in the related tables into one table. Another example of a one-to-one relationship is using two tables to store employee data—one table might contain basic employee data, such as name and address information, and the other table might contain sensitive information, such as psychiatric evaluations. In this case, the sensitive data isn't stored with address information, but kept in a separate table and matched to the primary employee table via a one-to-one relationship.

Many-to-Many Relationships

A **many-to-many relationship** (abbreviated as **M:N**) occurs when each record in the first table matches many records in the second table, and each record in the second table matches many records in the first table. For example, Maria needs to print a class roster for the instructor of the CPR class so employees can sign it to verify their attendance. At the same time, Maria wants to print a report of all the classes that Richard Conlee has attended in the previous year so that she can evaluate Richard's certification status as a pharmacy technician for his next annual review. To be able to print Richard's certification records, Maria needs the database to have a relationship between tblEmployee and tblClass, but what is the nature of that relationship? The classes will go on perfectly fine if Richard never registers for one of them, and Richard will be fine if he never takes a class, thus there is no one-to-many or one-to-one relationship. Maria needs a way to produce the class roster and Richard's attendance report, but these tables are not related. Don can create a third, intermediary table (named tblEmployeeTraining), called a **junction table**, that contains the primary keys from tblEmployee and tblClass. The tblEmployeeTraining table lets you create two one-to-many relationships between the two primary tables (tblEmployee and tblClass) and the related table (tblEmployeeTraining). The tblEmployeeTraining table exists only as a conduit so that data can be retrieved from the primary tables. Figure 1.26 shows this many-to-many relationship. The result is the ability to query both tables as though they are one big table. Now, Maria can display only those classes that Richard or any other employee has taken, and she can display all employees who have taken a specific class, such as Child/Infant CPR.

Figure 1.26: Many-to-many relationship between employees and classes

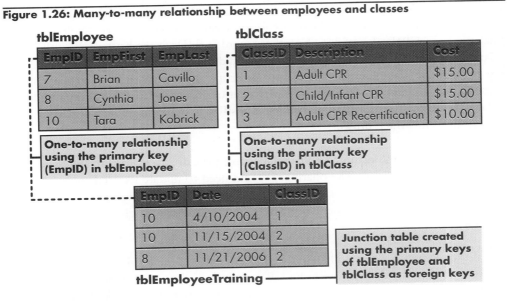

tblEmployee

EmpID	EmpFirst	EmpLast
7	Brian	Cavillo
8	Cynthia	Jones
10	Tara	Kobrick

One-to-many relationship using the primary key (EmpID) in tblEmployee

tblClass

ClassID	Description	Cost
1	Adult CPR	$15.00
2	Child/Infant CPR	$15.00
3	Adult CPR Recertification	$10.00

One-to-many relationship using the primary key (ClassID) in tblClass

EmpID	Date	ClassID
10	4/10/2004	1
10	11/15/2004	2
8	11/21/2006	2

tblEmployeeTraining

Junction table created using the primary keys of tblEmployee and tblClass as foreign keys

UNDERSTANDING REFERENTIAL INTEGRITY

Now that you know the three types of relationships that you can create in a relational database, it is important that you understand how to create them properly. By now you are familiar with the importance of including a primary key in each table to ensure that the table does not contain duplicate records. The database also prohibits users from failing to enter a value in the primary key field because doing so would risk data duplication. How would you differentiate customers if the CustID field contains no value? When a field does not contain a value, either because that value is unknown or inapplicable, it is called a **null value**. Including a primary key field in a table ensures **entity integrity**, a guarantee that there are no duplicate records in a table, that each record is unique, and that no primary key field contains null values.

Entity integrity specifies that the primary key value must not repeat in the primary table; that is, Tara Kobrick is EmpID 10, and no other employee can have that EmpID. However, her EmpID can repeat in the related tblEmployeeTraining table. Indeed, you would expect to see Tara's EmpID number in tblEmployeeTraining because Tara has taken several training classes. This common field, shared by both the primary and related tables, is called the foreign key in the related tblEmployeeTraining table.

Referential integrity is the rule that if the foreign key in one table matches the primary key in a second table, the values in the foreign key must match the values in the primary key. When the database does not enforce referential integrity, certain problems occur that lead to inaccurate and inconsistent data. For example, in tblDrug the primary key is the UPN field, which is a universal drug identifier for prescription drugs. The record for the drug Phalastat has a UPN value of 366. No other record in tblDrug can have a UPN value of 366 because it is this record's primary key value and duplicate values are not allowed in the primary key field. The pharmacy filled three prescriptions for this drug to customers with CustIDs 18, 22, and 37. The one-to-many relationship between tblCustomer and tblRx relates these records to each other, making it possible to determine which customers filled prescriptions for which drugs.

Suppose that the drug manufacturer for Phalastat changes the drug formulation and issues a new UPN code—367—for it. The pharmacy would need to update its database to use the new code. This UPN doesn't exist in tblDrug, so it would be an allowable primary key value because it meets the requirement of being unique. At first, it might seem like this change is possible.

However, if the pharmacy changes Phalastat's UPN value from 366 to 367, then there no longer exists a drug in the database with the UPN value 366. Yet Customers 18, 22, and 37 were prescribed drug 366 and remain in the database with that designation. Were they to seek a refill, or worse yet—become allergic to drug 366—there would be no way to identify which drug they were prescribed. The prescription records would become **orphaned** as the UPN primary key was changed in the primary table, but the corresponding foreign keys in the related table were not. There would no longer be a match between the primary key in the primary table and the foreign keys in the related table, resulting in orphaned records. Enforcing referential integrity prevents this data loss. Figure 1.27 illustrates this referential integrity error.

Figure 1.27: Referential integrity errors

tblDrug

UPN	Name
367	Phalastat
566	Quentix
972	Rivastigmine tartrate

UPN is changed from 366 to 367 in tblDrug

tblRx

PrescriptionID	UPN	CustID
60	366	18
50	366	22
49	366	22
10	366	37

UPN is NOT changed in tblRx, orphaning four records

Customers prescribed the drug with UPN 366 cannot receive refills as there no longer is a drug with UPN 366

tblCustomer

CustID	CustFirst	CustLast
18	Anders	Aannestad
22	Josefina	Hernandez
37	Isabel	Lopez

Another reason to enforce referential integrity is to prevent orphaned related records if the record in the primary table is deleted. For example, identity theft is discovered on occasion at 4Corners Pharmacy; in two cases, a customer used fake identification to obtain restricted prescription drugs. When Paul is informed of such occurrences—usually by the health plan that refuses to pay for such charges—he is obligated to turn over the prescription data to the FBI. After doing so, he no longer wants to retain this data in his database as he cannot collect on the accounts and does not want to keep the record of fictitious customers. Consequently, he is inclined to delete the customer's name, address, and entire record from the database. If he does so, however, the customer's corresponding prescriptions will remain in the database. These prescriptions will become orphaned, appear to belong to no one, and will confuse auditors trying to reconcile the pharmacy's accounts receivable.

A third reason to enforce referential integrity is to make it impossible to add records to a related table that does not have matching records in the primary table. An inexperienced or hurried technician might add prescriptions to tblRx for a new customer that she did not first enter into tblCustomer, resulting in orphaned records in tblRx because it would contain prescriptions that would not belong to a customer.

The results of all three scenarios lead to inconsistent data, which relational databases should be designed to avoid. By enforcing referential integrity, however, you can prohibit changing the primary key of the records in the primary table if matching records exist in the related table, deleting records in the primary table if matching records exist in the related table, and adding records to the related table if no matching record exists in the primary table.

Overriding Referential Integrity

Referential integrity is the rule that makes it possible for a DBMS to prevent records from being orphaned if a user attempts to change a primary key or delete a record in a table that has matching records in another table. But there are times when you might want to override referential integrity to intentionally change a primary key or delete a parent record. Some DBMSs let you change the way that the DBMS handles these types of changes so that changes to the primary key value in a record that has matching records in a related table are also made to the foreign key in the matching records. For example, if a pharmacy technician changes the UPN from 366 to 367 in tblDrug, then records in tblRx would be orphaned because the drug with the UPN 366 no longer exists.

In some DBMSs, including Access, you can choose the option to **cascade updates**, which permits a user to change a primary key value so that the DBMS automatically updates the appropriate foreign key values in the related table. In this case, when the pharmacy changes the UPN value of 366 to 367, the records for the customers with CustIDs 18, 22, and 37 will still indicate that they were prescribed the drug because the DBMS will update the UPN values in the records for these customers by changing it from 366 to 367. Figure 1.28 shows how cascade updates works.

Figure 1.28: Cascade updates

tblDrug

UPN	Name
367	Phalastat
566	Quentix
972	Rivastigmine tartrate

UPN is changed from 366 to 367 in tblDrug

tblRx

PrescriptionID	UPN	CustID
60	367	18
50	367	22
49	367	22
10	367	37

Cascade updates option changes the UPN for matching records in tblRx from 366 to 367

What if the drug manufacturer for the drug Phalastat discontinues it because a risk of heart attack has been identified? In this case, the pharmacy might want to delete the drug from the database to discontinue it. When the pharmacy tries to delete the record from tblDrug with the UPN 366, the DBMS will not permit the deletion because there are related records in tblRx. However, if the DBMS has the **cascade deletes** option enabled, the DBMS will permit the deletion of the record from tblDrug. In addition, the DBMS also deletes the related records from tblRx. Before enabling the cascade deletes option, it is a good idea to verify that you really want to delete all data for this drug and all related data from the database. A better method might be to leave the drug in the database so the customer's prescription records aren't deleted with it. If you delete Phalastat from the database, the database will show that CustIDs 18, 22, and 37 *never* received it. Figure 1.29 shows how the cascade deletes option works.

Figure 1.29: Cascade deletes

tblDrug

UPN	Name
~~366~~	~~Phalastat~~
566	Quentix
972	Rivastigmine tartrate

The record for UPN 366 is deleted from tblDrug

tblRx

PrescriptionID	UPN	CustID
~~60~~	~~366~~	~~18~~
~~50~~	~~366~~	~~22~~
~~49~~	~~366~~	~~22~~
~~10~~	~~366~~	~~37~~

Cascade deletes option deletes all matching records in tblRx

You will learn more about creating relationships and referential integrity in Chapter 2.

Steps To Success: Level 2

You have learned a great deal about database objects, concepts, and table relationships, all requisite knowledge for planning a relational database. Now it is time to consider which database objects are required for the 4Corners Pharmacy database and how to relate the tables.

On a piece of paper, complete the following:

1. Although the 4Corners Pharmacy database might ultimately include additional tables, it will include tables for the following entities: customers, prescriptions, drugs, doctors, clinics, employees, job titles, and training classes. Given these tables, describe five queries, two forms, and three reports that managers at the pharmacy might create and describe how they would use them in the pharmacy's day-to-day operations.

2. What are some examples of flat file databases that you have used? How would a relational database simplify the work you needed to complete?

3. What primary keys might you assign to tables that store data about the following entities: customers, prescriptions, drugs, doctors, clinics, employees, job titles, and training classes? Describe why and how you chose the primary key for each table.

4. Suppose that tblDoctor includes the fields DoctorID, DoctorFirst, DoctorLast, and Phone; and tblClinic includes the fields ClinicID, ClinicName, Address, City, State, Zip, and Phone. Is there a common field? Is there a foreign key? What kind of relationship might you create between these two tables?

5. Paul wants to monitor refills. He wants to use the UPN field to query which drugs are refilled most often. (For example, Paul wants to know how many times the drug Phalastat, with UPN 366, was refilled and by whom.) At the same time, he needs to determine which employees filled a given prescription. (For example, customer

Marvin Gattis was prescribed Hyometadol on 7/7/2007, his doctor authorized five refills, and Mr. Gattis has refilled this prescription three times.) Suppose that tblRx lists every prescription that every customer has filled at 4Corners Pharmacy and contains the following fields: PrescriptionID, UPN, Quantity, Date, Refills, Instructions, CustID, and DoctorID. Also suppose that tblEmployee lists every employee working at 4Corners Pharmacy and contains the following fields: EmpID, FirstName, Last-Name, DOB, SSN, Address, City, State, and Zip. What would you do to create a relationship between these two tables so that Paul can query them to answer his questions? Identify the primary and foreign keys necessary to create this relationship. Would you use the cascade updates and cascade deletes options? Why or why not?

LEVEL 3

IDENTIFYING AND ELIMINATING DATABASE ANOMALIES BY NORMALIZING DATA

NORMALIZING THE TABLES IN THE DATABASE

By now you are familiar with database concepts and how to create tables and relationships between them. You have learned that good database design seeks to avoid data redundancy and inconsistent data. Now you will learn the specific rules for ensuring a good database design using a process called **normalization**. Figure 1.30 details the third step of the database design process and illustrates how normalization fits into the plan.

Figure 1.30: Database design process: normalizing the data

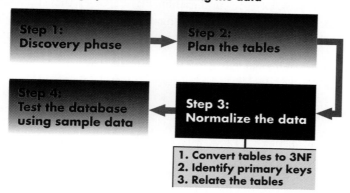

Normalization has three goals. First, normalization reduces the space required to store data by eliminating duplicate data in the database (with the exception of duplicate data in the foreign key fields). Second, normalization reduces inconsistent data in the database by storing data only once, thereby reducing the chance of typographical, spelling, and transposition errors and other inconsistent data that you discovered in the flat file databases you viewed in Level 2. Finally, normalization reduces the chance of deletion, update, and insertion anomalies. The data shown in Figure 1.31 is not normalized (also called **unnormalized data**) and exhibits all three anomalies.

Figure 1.31: Data with anomalies

Deleting Connie Nader's record creates two deletion anomalies because she is the only cashier and the only employee enrolled in the Yoga class; deleting her record also deletes the job title and class information

Adding a new job title or class creates an insertion anomaly because there must first be an employee with that title or taking the class, which is not possible until you add the title or class

EmpID	EmpFirst	EmpLast	SSN	Title	Description	DateAttended
15	Connie	Nader	705-19-1497	Cashier	Yoga	1/23/2007
21	Dora	Langston	718-78-4111	Technician	Nutritional Supplements	9/1/2007
21	Dora	Langston	718-78-4111	Technician	First Aid	6/12/2006
3	Virginia	Sanchez	921-23-3333	Technician	Defibrillator Use	1/25/2005
17	Rachel	Thompson	928-98-4165	Technician	Defibrillator Use	5/2/2004
13	Paul	Ferrino	953-23-3639	Owner	Child/Infant CPR Recertification	6/15/2008
27	Vincent	Ferrino	998-01-5466	Pharmacist	Child/Infant CPR Recertification	5/21/2008
14	Richard	Conlee	968-96-3214	Technician	Child/Infant CPR Recertification	11/15/2006
2	Marco	Farello	885-00-7777	Technician	Child/Infant CPR Recertification	1/15/2006
3	Virginia	Sanchez	921-23-3333	Technician	Child/Infant CPR Recertification	5/15/2006
8	Cynthia	Jones	000-23-3655	Pharmacist	Child/Infant CPR	11/21/2006
2	Marco	Farello	885-00-7777	Technician	Child/Infant CPR	1/30/2004
10	Tara	Kobrick	728-12-3465	Technician	Child/Infant CPR	11/15/2004
21	Dora	Langston	718-78-4111	Technician	Child/Infant CPR	6/9/2004
13	Paul	Ferrino	953-23-3639	Owner	Adult CPR Recertification	2/5/2007
27	Vincent	Ferrino	998-01-5466	Pharmacist	Adult CPR Recertification	2/2/2005
27	Vincent	Ferrino	998-01-5466	Pharmacist	Adult CPR Recertification	4/2/2007
27	Vincent	Ferrino	998-01-5466	Pharmacist	Adult CPR Recertification	4/5/2008
12	Louis	Moreno	666-16-7892	Pharmacist	Adult CPR Recertification	4/1/2006

Changing the Child/Infant CPR class description in the record for Cynthia Jones creates an update anomaly in three other records

A **deletion anomaly** occurs when a user deletes data from a database and unintentionally deletes the only occurrence of that data in the database. In Figure 1.31, Connie Nader is the only cashier at 4Corners Pharmacy and the only employee who took the Yoga class. Deleting her record also deletes the Cashier title and the Yoga class from the database, making it appear as though her title and the Yoga class never existed. An **update anomaly** occurs when, due to redundant data in a database, a user fails to update some records or updates records erroneously. For example, in Figure 1.31, changing the description for the course titled "Child/Infant CPR" in the record for Cynthia Jones leaves inconsistent data in the other records for employees who took this class and creates corrupted data. An **insertion anomaly** occurs when a user cannot add data to a database unless it is preceded by the entry of other data. In Figure 1.31, an insertion anomaly occurs if you try to add a new class. You cannot add a class unless an employee has registered for it, but how is this possible for a new class? As you can see, it is important to avoid creating anomalies in a database; normalization seeks to avoid these problems.

The goal of normalization is to split tables into smaller related tables to avoid creating anomalies. To understand normalization, you must first understand **functional dependency**, because it will help you analyze fields within tables and help you decide if they need to be split into smaller tables. A column in a table is considered functionally dependent on another column if each value in the second column is associated with exactly one value in the first column. Given this definition and after viewing Figure 1.31, it appears that the SSN field is functionally dependent on the EmpID field. Dora Langston's Social Security number (718-78-4111) is associated with exactly one EmpID, 21. It would appear that the Title field, however, is not functionally dependent on the EmpID field because there are multiple records that are associated with the title Technician, for example. Consequently, the Title field becomes a prime candidate for its own table. Your goal should be to use your knowledge of functional dependency to test the columns in the tables that you create, identify columns that are not functionally dependent, and consider moving those columns to their own tables.

Before doing this, however, you must be aware of a partial dependency. In tables in which more than one field is needed to create a primary key, a **partial dependency** occurs when a field is dependent on only part of the primary key. When a primary key uses two or more fields to create unique records in a table, it is called a **composite primary key** (or a **composite key**). Figure 1.32 shows a conceptual diagram of the fields in a proposed tblClassesAttended which indicates which employee took which classes on which dates.

Figure 1.32: tblClassesAttended table design

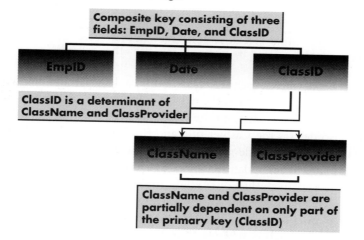

The EmpID field cannot be the table's primary key because an employee can take many classes and, therefore, would have many records in the table. The Date field cannot be the table's primary key because it will contain repeating data if more than one class is taught on the same date or if more than one employee attends the same class on the same date—both of which are likely occurrences. The ClassID field cannot be the table's primary key because it will contain repeating data if more than one employee attends the same class.

Neither the ClassName nor ClassProvider fields can be the table's primary key because they also contain repeating data. Thus, you must create a composite key to create unique values for the records in this table. In some cases a composite key consists of two fields, but this table requires the combination of three fields—EmpID, Date, and ClassID—to create unique records in the table.

Notice the arrows pointing from ClassID to the ClassName and ClassProvider fields. This structure indicates that ClassID is a determinant of the other two fields. A **determinant** is a field or collection of fields whose value determines the value in another field. This determinant relationship between fields is the inverse of dependency, as ClassName and ClassProvider are dependent on ClassID. However, this relationship exhibits a partial dependency, for the two fields are dependent on only part of the composite key. Your goal should be to rid your tables of partial dependencies to avoid anomalies. The solution, again, is to create a separate tblClass table and then create a relationship between tblClass and tblClassesAttended using the common field, ClassID.

Other kinds of keys exist, as well. A **natural key** is a primary key that details an obvious and innate trait of a record. For example, the UPN field in tblDrug is a unique value for each drug sold, and is, therefore, a natural key for the table. Other examples of natural keys include Social Security numbers for people and International Standard Book Numbers (ISBNs) for books. When a natural key exists, it is easy to identify and use as a primary key.

Sometimes, however, a table does not contain a natural key, and no field or combination of fields can be used as a primary key. In these cases, you can create an **artificial key**, a field whose sole purpose is to create a primary key. Artificial keys are usually visible to users. A third type of key field is the surrogate key. A **surrogate key** is a computer-generated primary key that is usually invisible to users.

Best Practice

Choosing a Primary Key

After completing data normalization, you must then assign primary keys to your tables. This is easy to do if a natural key exists, such as a SSN, PIN, or ISBN in your table. If it does not, which field should be the primary key: an artificial key or a composite key? There is no definitive answer, but a best practice is to consider possible negative consequences of creating a composite key. If the composite key comprises more than two fields, as was shown in tblClassesAttended in Figure 1.32, you might want to choose an artificial key, because three fields will be consumed in every table that includes the three-field composite key as a foreign key, wasting significant database space. In addition, primary keys cannot be null. This might prove frustrating if you are trying to enter a record, but lack the values to enter in one or more of the three fields that the composite key comprises. You will not be able to enter a record unless you have all three fields. Consequently, think twice before creating composite keys and consider using artificial keys instead.

Having a good grasp of the fundamental concepts of how fields interact as determinants, dependents, and in composite primary keys is essential to combating anomalies in relational table designs. After you understand these concepts, you are prepared to normalize the tables. Normalization requires a series of steps, each one building on the previous. These steps are called normal forms, or first, second, and third normal forms, sometimes abbreviated as 1NF, 2NF, and 3NF. Three other increasingly more sophisticated normal forms exist, but most database developers agree that they are rarely necessary and might lead to diminished functionality in a database because they make it run slower.

First Normal Form

When a field contains more than one value, it is called a **repeating group**. A table is in **first normal form (1NF)** if it does not contain any repeating groups. Table 1.6 shows a table that violates 1NF rules because the Description field contains more than one value in some cases, creating unnormalized data. Marco Farello, for instance, has taken five classes, all of which reside in the Description field. The repeating groups in this table would make it difficult to filter or query this table to determine which employees have taken which classes.

Table 1.6: Unnormalized data contains repeating groups

EmpID	EmpFirst	EmpLast	SSN	Description	DateAttended	Provider
14	Richard	Conlee	968-96-3214	Child/Infant CPR Recertification	11/15/2006	Red Cross
2	Marco	Farello	885-00-7777	Child/Infant CPR Child/Infant CPR Recertification Adult CPR Recertification	1/30/2004 1/15/2006 2/1/2006	Red Cross Red Cross Red Cross
13	Paul	Ferrino	953-23-3639	Adult CPR Recertification Child/Infant CPR Recertification	2/5/2007 6/15/2008	Red Cross Red Cross
27	Vincent	Ferrino	998-01-5466	Adult CPR Recertification Adult CPR Recertification Adult CPR Recertification Child/Infant CPR Recertification	2/2/2005 4/2/2007 4/5/2008 5/21/2008	Red Cross Red Cross Red Cross Red Cross
1	Joan	Gabel	901-88-3636	Adult CPR	2/6/2004	Red Cross
8	Cynthia	Jones	000-23-3655	Child/Infant CPR	11/21/2006	Red Cross

A seemingly good solution might be to remove the repeating groups and instead create new rows for each class attended, as shown in Table 1.7.

Table 1.7: Unnormalized data contains repeating rows

EmpID	EmpFirst	EmpLast	SSN	Class Description	Date Attended	Provider
14	Richard	Conlee	968-96-3214	Child/Infant CPR Recertification	11/15/2006	Red Cross
2	Marco	Farello	885-00-7777	Child/Infant CPR	1/30/2004	Red Cross
2	Marco	Farello	885-00-7777	Child/Infant CPR Recertification	1/15/2006	Red Cross
2	Marco	Farello	885-00-7777	Adult CPR Recertification	2/1/2006	Red Cross
13	Paul	Ferrino	953-23-3639	Adult CPR Recertification	2/5/2007	Red Cross
13	Paul	Ferrino	953-23-3639	Child/Infant CPR Recertification	6/15/2008	Red Cross
27	Vincent	Ferrino	998-01-5466	Adult CPR Recertification	2/2/2005	Red Cross
27	Vincent	Ferrino	998-01-5466	Adult CPR Recertification	4/2/2007	Red Cross
27	Vincent	Ferrino	998-01-5466	Adult CPR Recertification	4/5/2008	Red Cross
27	Vincent	Ferrino	998-01-5466	Child/Infant CPR Recertification	5/21/2008	Red Cross
1	Joan	Gabel	901-88-3636	Adult CPR	2/6/2004	Red Cross
8	Cynthia	Jones	000-23-3655	Child/Infant CPR	11/21/2006	Red Cross

You already know, however, that repeating data by adding records in this fashion is called data redundancy and is inefficient, wastes space, and can lead to errors. Marco Farello now has three records, all of which repeat his EmpID, EmpFirst, EmpLast, and SSN. Table 1.7 violates normalization rules because of this repetition. What can be done, then, to make this table conform to 1NF? The answer is to create two tables: one for employees and one for classes. Examples of what these tables might look like are shown in Tables 1.8 and 1.9.

Table 1.8: Employee data in 1NF

EmpID	EmpFirst	EmpLast	SSN
1	Joan	Gabel	901-88-3636
2	Marco	Farello	885-00-7777
3	Virginia	Sanchez	921-23-3333
8	Cynthia	Jones	000-23-3655
10	Tara	Kobrick	728-12-3465

Table 1.8: Employee data in 1NF (cont.)

EmpID	EmpFirst	EmpLast	SSN
12	Louis	Moreno	666-16-7892
13	Paul	Ferrino	953-23-3639
14	Richard	Conlee	968-96-3214
15	Connie	Nader	705-19-1497
17	Rachel	Thompson	928-98-4165
19	Amy	Urquiza	728-65-6941
21	Dora	Langston	718-78-4111
27	Vincent	Ferrino	998-01-5466

Table 1.9: Class data in 1NF

ClassID	Description	EmpID	DateAttended	Provider
1	Adult CPR	1	2/6/2004	Red Cross
1	Adult CRP	10	4/10/2004	Red Cross
1	Adult CPR	17	3/17/2004	Red Cross
1	Adult CPR	19	6/20/2004	Red Cross
2	Child/Infant CPR	2	1/30/2004	Red Cross
2	Child/Infant CPR	8	11/21/2006	Red Cross
2	Child/Infant CPR	10	11/15/2004	Red Cross
2	Child/Infant CPR	21	6/9/2004	Red Cross
3	Adult CPR Recertification	2	2/1/2006	Red Cross
3	Adult CPR Recertification	3	6/1/2007	Red Cross
3	Adult CPR Recertification	3	6/29/2008	Red Cross
3	Adult CPR Recertification	10	4/12/2005	Red Cross
3	Adult CPR Recertification	12	4/1/2006	Red Cross
3	Adult CPR Recertification	13	2/5/2007	Red Cross
3	Adult CPR Recertification	17	3/16/2005	Red Cross
3	Adult CPR Recertification	19	6/21/2005	Red Cross
3	Adult CPR Recertification	19	3/10/2006	Red Cross
3	Adult CPR Recertification	21	6/15/2006	Red Cross
3	Adult CPR Recertification	21	3/5/2007	Red Cross

Table 1.9: Class data in 1NF (cont.)

ClassID	Description	EmpID	DateAttended	Provider
3	Adult CPR Recertification	27	2/2/2005	Red Cross
3	Adult CPR Recertification	27	4/2/2007	Red Cross
3	Adult CPR Recertification	27	4/5/2008	Red Cross
4	First Aid	21	6/12/2006	Red Cross
5	Defibrillator Use	3	1/25/2005	Johnston Health Systems
5	Defibrillator Use	17	5/2/2004	Johnston Health Systems
6	Child/Infant CPR Recertification	2	1/15/2006	Red Cross
6	Child/Infant CPR Recertification	3	5/15/2006	Red Cross
6	Child/Infant CPR Recertification	13	6/15/2008	Red Cross
6	Child/Infant CPR Recertification	14	11/15/2006	Red Cross
6	Child/Infant CPR Recertification	27	5/21/2008	Red Cross
7	Nutritional Supplements	21	9/1/2007	Food Co-op
8	Yoga	15	1/23/2007	Yoga Center

The employee training class data now satisfies the requirements for 1NF. This was accomplished by creating two tables—a primary Employee table and a related Class table. These tables share a common field, EmpID, which creates a relationship between them.

Second Normal Form

To ensure that a table is in **second normal form (2NF)**, the table must be in 1NF and must not contain any partial dependencies on the composite primary key. Tables that are in 1NF and contain a primary key with only one field are automatically in 2NF because no other field in the table can be dependent on only a portion of the primary key. The data shown in Table 1.9 violates 2NF rules because the description of the class is dependent not just on the ClassID, but also on the EmpID and DateAttended; the combination of ClassID, EmpID, and DateAttended is the table's composite primary key. If left as is, this table might include inconsistent data, such as the misspelling of "Adult CRP" in the second record. To convert this table to 2NF, it is necessary to break it into two tables: one table listing the classes offered and another table listing the classes taken. Tables 1.10 and 1.11 show these changes.

Chapter 1 | Preparing to Automate Data Management

Table 1.10: ClassesOffered table in 2NF

ClassID	Description	Provider
1	Adult CPR	Red Cross
2	Child/Infant CPR	Red Cross
3	Adult CPR Recertification	Red Cross
4	First Aid	Red Cross
5	Defibrillator Use	Johnston Health Systems
6	Child/Infant CPR Recertification	Red Cross
7	Nutritional Supplements	Food Co-op
8	Yoga	Yoga Center

Table 1.11: ClassesTaken table in 2NF

ClassID	EmpID	Date Attended
1	1	2/6/2004
1	10	4/10/2004
1	17	3/17/2004
1	19	6/20/2004
2	2	1/30/2004
2	8	11/21/2006
2	10	11/15/2004
2	21	6/9/2004
3	2	2/1/2006
3	3	6/1/2007
3	3	6/29/2008
3	10	4/12/2005
3	12	4/1/2006
3	13	2/5/2007
3	17	3/16/2005
3	19	6/21/2005
3	19	3/10/2006
3	21	6/15/2006
3	21	3/5/2007

992

Table 1.11: ClassesTaken table in 2NF (cont.)

ClassID	EmpID	Date Attended
3	27	2/2/2005
3	27	4/2/2007
3	27	4/5/2008
4	21	6/12/2006
5	3	1/25/2005
5	17	5/2/2004
6	2	1/15/2006
6	3	5/15/2006
6	13	6/15/2008
6	14	11/15/2006
6	27	5/21/2008
7	21	9/1/2007
8	15	1/23/2007

The data shown in Tables 1.10 and 1.11 is in 2NF—notice that the ClassesTaken table is a junction table that creates a many-to-many relationship between the ClassesOffered table (Table 1.10) and the Employee table (Table 1.8). As a result, you can query these tables as though they are one big table and do so from two perspectives. You can list all the classes taken by a single employee, or produce a report for a single class, listing all those employees who attended a class on a given day.

Third Normal Form

For a table to be in **third normal form (3NF)**, it must be in 2NF and the only determinants it contains must be candidate keys. A **candidate key** is a field or collection of fields that could function as the primary key, but was not chosen to do so. Table 1.10 is in 2NF, but one problem remains. ClassID is the primary key, but Description and Provider are **nonkey fields**, fields that are not part of the primary key. A **transitive dependency** occurs between two nonkey fields that are both dependent on a third field; tables in 3NF should not have transitive dependencies. The Provider field gives more information about the Description field, so you might think that it is important to keep this field in this table. You might also think that Table 1.10 is pretty small as it is and appears to cause little harm other than having the "Red Cross" provider repeating a few times. The truth is, however, that this table is in jeopardy of a deletion anomaly. The Provider is at the mercy, if you will, of the Class to which it is assigned. If you delete ClassID 5 (Defibrillator Use) from this table, you would also delete Johnston Health Systems from the database. Johnston Health Systems might offer other classes that employees might attend in the future, but if the single present occurrence of the Defibrillator Use class is removed from this database, Johnston Health Systems is also removed. Consequently, to put the data in 3NF, it is necessary to break it, once again, into two smaller tables. The result, as shown in Tables 1.12 and 1.13, is two tables: one solely for class titles and one solely for providers.

Table 1.12: ClassesOffered table in 3NF

ClassID	Description	ProviderID
1	Adult CPR	3
2	Child/Infant CPR	3
3	Adult CPR Recertification	3
4	First Aid	3
5	Defibrillator Use	2
6	Child/Infant CPR Recertification	3
7	Nutritional Supplements	1
8	Yoga	4

Table 1.13: Provider table in 3NF

ProviderID	Provider
1	Food Co-op
2	Johnston Health Systems
3	Red Cross
4	Yoga Center

You can see that data normalization requires creating additional tables so that normalization rules are not violated.

Best Practice

Testing the Database Using Sample Data

After normalizing your data and assigning primary keys, you might think that your work is done in the database design process. Figure 1.33 shows that there is one major step left: testing the database using sample data.

Figure 1.33: Database design process: testing the database

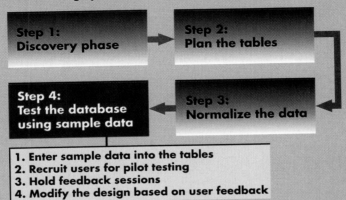

You should, of course, test it yourself, but as Figure 1.33 suggests, the best practice to follow is to recruit pilot testers, hold feedback sessions, modify the design and functionality using the recommendations given during feedback sessions, and *then* unveil the finished database. Getting criticism from third parties is invaluable as the more eyes and hands that scrutinize and investigate your database, the better it will perform after modifications made from the pilot testers.

Steps To Success: Level 3

After learning how Don will normalize the data in the 4Corners Pharmacy database, you have gained a deeper understanding of how to pare down tables so that anomalies do not occur. This process requires ensuring that groups do not repeat in columns, such as avoiding a Dependents field that stores the names of two people. Breaking the data into two tables—HeadOfHousehold and Dependent—satisfies the requirement for 1NF. After doing that, however, it is important to analyze the resultant tables for violations of 2NF. Does data repeat within the same column? For example, in the Dependent table, is the same doctor listed multiple times? Breaking the data into two tables—Dependent and Doctor—satisfies the requirement for 2NF. Converting tables to 3NF is also important and requires diligence to make sure that every column is dependent on the primary key and not on another column.

On a piece of paper, complete the following:

1. Figure 1.34 contains anomalies or potential anomalies.

Figure 1.34: Flat file database with anomalies

PrescriptionID	RefillDate	UPN	Name	CustID	FirstName	LastName	EmpID	EmpFirst	EmpLast	Title
1	12/11/2007	224	Avatocin	17	Maria	Gabel	2	Marco	Farello	Technician
2	4/14/2008	828	Myobuterol	18	Anders	Aannestad	2	Marco	Farello	Technician
2	6/1/2008	828	Myobuterol	18	Anders	Aannestad	8	Cynthia	Jones	Pharmacist
3	7/1/2008	711	Nvalax	23	Jennifer	Ramsey	17	Rachel	Thompson	Technician
4	6/21/2008	256	Dseurton	19	Dusty	Alkier	8	Cynthia	Jones	Pharmacist
5	1/12/2008	398	Clonazepam	19	Dusty	Alkier	2	Marco	Farello	Technician
5	3/11/2008	398	Clonazepam	19	Dusty	Alkier	17	Rachel	Thompson	Technician
6	6/3/2008	121	Tolbutamide	34	Gloria	Fernandes	3	Virginia	Sanchez	Technician
6	8/25/2008	121	Tolbutamide	34	Gloria	Fernandes	17	Rachel	Thompson	Technician
7	5/14/2008	932	Tvalaxec	14	Malena	D'Ambrosio	8	Cynthia	Jones	Pharmacist
8	3/18/2008	523	Xeroflarol	16	William	Gabel	12	Louis	Moreno	Pharmacist
8	6/1/2008	523	Xeroflarol	16	William	Gabel	12	Louis	Moreno	Pharmacist
9	4/14/2008	311	Dyotex	21	Cesar	Lopez	3	Virginia	Sanchez	Technician
9	10/11/2008	311	Dyotex	21	Cesar	Lopez	2	Marco	Farello	Technician
10	3/11/2008	366	Phalastat	37	Isabel	Lopez	2	Marco	Farello	Technician
10	6/21/2008	366	Phalastat	37	Isabel	Lopez	14	Richard	Conlee	Technician
13	11/1/2007	642	Montelukast sodium	38	Oksana	Lapshina	3	Virginia	Sanchez	Technician
13	1/3/2008	642	Montelukast sodium	38	Oksana	Lapshina	12	Louis	Moreno	Pharmacist
14	9/29/2007	878	Didanosine	25	Adriane	Walters	14	Richard	Conlee	Technician
15	6/10/2007	852	Oxaprozin	27	Byron	Buescher	3	Virginia	Sanchez	Technician
16	4/22/2007	654	Warfarin Sodium	9	Daniel	Cardenas	8	Cynthia	Jones	Pharmacist
16	11/13/2007	654	Warfarin Sodium	9	Daniel	Cardenas	8	Cynthia	Jones	Pharmacist
17	11/16/2007	398	Clonazepam	4	Steven	Nguyen	17	Rachel	Thompson	Technician
17	2/14/2008	398	Clonazepam	4	Steven	Nguyen	14	Richard	Conlee	Technician

Ultimately, Paul wants to query this table to answer the following questions:

a. What prescriptions did Marco Farello fill?

b. Which employees processed refills for Anders Aannestad?

c. Which employees processed refills for PrescriptionID 17?

2. Create as many tables as necessary to normalize this data to 3NF.

CHAPTER SUMMARY

This chapter presented some of the fundamental concepts you need to understand when planning an Access database. In Level 1, you learned that the discovery phase of database planning takes a great deal of work and requires researching existing sources of data within an organization, researching sources of missing data, and interviewing users about desired output. The next step is to assimilate your findings by grouping fields into tables, assigning data types to fields, choosing appropriate field sizes, and assigning standardized names to the tables.

Level 2 covered database objects and concepts. You learned that there are seven types of objects in an Access database, four of which—tables, queries, forms, and reports—were discussed at length. Tables hold data, queries display subsets of data in response to a question about the data, forms provide an electronic interface for entering data into tables while at the same time allowing you to view records in the tables, and reports allow you to organize data in a custom or standard format for on-screen display or in a printout. After learning about database objects, you learned about how a flat file database leads to inconsistent and redundant data; the importance of creating primary keys, foreign keys, and common fields in tables; and the process of creating relationships between tables in a relational database, including one-to-many, one-to-one, and many-to-many. You also learned about referential integrity and how it works to prevent deletion, update, and insertion anomalies in the database.

In Level 3, you studied the process of normalizing data, which requires putting tables in first normal form by removing repeating groups, then putting tables in second normal form by eliminating partial dependencies, and then putting tables in third normal form by eliminating transitive dependencies. You also learned that is important to assign primary keys and how to distinguish between natural, artificial, and surrogate keys. Finally, you learned that testing a database before implementation and seeking feedback from a pilot group is the best way to make modifications to a database before implementing the final version.

CONCEPTUAL REVIEW

1. Name and describe the four steps in the database design process.

2. What are data duplication and data redundancy, and how do you work to remove these problems from a database?

3. What is scope creep?

4. What are some of the considerations you must evaluate about the data before assigning it a field data type and size?

5. What is the difference between the Text and Memo data types, and how would you use each one?

6. What is the difference between the Number and Currency data types, and how would you use each one?

7. Should you store calculated fields in a database? Why or why not? If you should not, what data can you store in place of a calculated field?

8. Why and when should you use the Lookup Wizard data type? Give two specific examples not described in the book.

9. What are three general rules about naming objects in a database?

10. What are the four main database objects, and how is each one used?

11. What are the three types of queries you can use, and what does each one accomplish?

12. What are three limitations associated with using flat file databases for data management?

13. What is a primary key? What is a foreign key? How do these keys work together in a database?

14. Which of the following pairs of entities would require a one-to-one, one-to-many, and many-to-many relationship? Describe your answer.

    a. Customers and orders
    b. States and state capitals
    c. College students and classes

15. What is entity integrity? What is referential integrity? Should you enforce referential integrity in a database all the time? Why or why not?

16. Name and describe the three types of anomalies that can occur in a database.

17. What is the goal of normalization? Name and describe the three normal forms.

18. What is a determinant? A partial dependency? A transitive dependency?

CASE PROBLEMS

Case 1—Creating the Database Design for NHD Development Group Inc.

NHD Development Group Inc. builds, leases, and manages shopping centers, convenience stores, and other ventures throughout the country. Last year, NHD purchased several antique malls in the southeastern United States. The antique malls have shown potential for a good financial return over time. Tim Richards is the chief information officer for NHD. Tim's responsibility is to provide information to the board of directors so it can make strategic decisions about future development ventures.

Information Systems

Most of the antique malls do their bookkeeping on paper, and Tim is concerned that the data he needs from the antique malls will not be easy to obtain. Because of the paper-based systems, Tim expects it to be difficult to obtain items such as total sales, total commissions, dealer sales, and staff expenses such as salaries. Tim believes that by creating a specialized database for the antique mall managers to use, he can ensure that the data he needs will be easy for managers to create and maintain. The antique malls will be able to use the database to create the reports he needs so he can easily demonstrate the financial health of the malls to the board.

The antique malls are housed in large buildings that are owned by the parent company, NHD. The buildings are divided into booths that are rented to dealers, who then fill the booths with inventory that is sold to customers. A dealer might be a small company or an individual. It is each dealer's responsibility to manage its own inventory; the mall does not maintain an inventory list for the dealers. As the dealer sells items from its inventory, the mall records the dealer number and the price of each item using the information on the item's price tag. At the end of the month, the mall generates a list of total sales for each dealer, computes the mall's commission, deducts the dealer's rent for booth space, and then issues the dealer a check for the remaining amount.

Tim determined that the database must manage sales, booths in the mall, dealers that rent the booths, and mall employees. At the end of each month, the database must be able to produce a complete list of sales by dealer. In addition, the database must calculate the commission on the sales, subtract the dealer's rent, and determine the profit amount for each dealer.

Some malls also offer classes to their customers. Because the classes provide customers with a reason to return to the mall, NHD will encourage all malls to offer classes. Tim suggests that the database should store information about the classes offered, their instructors, and the customers who enroll in the classes. Instructors are not employees of the mall; rather, they are freelance instructors who are paid from the fees customers pay to take the courses. Customers can sign up for more than one class; payments for course fees are collected at enrollment or on the first day of class. The database needs to manage data about the customers who take these courses, including their name, the course(s) in which they enroll, and the payment of course fees.

Tim has discussed his goals with the board and it has agreed to go forward with developing a database. Tim suggested selecting one mall to serve as a six-month pilot for the project, allowing him to design and test the database before using it elsewhere. Tim selected the Memories Antique Mall in Cleveland, TN, for the pilot project. The mall's manager, Linda Sutherland, has managed the mall for many years and is excited about replacing the mall's manual systems with a database. After meeting with Linda to discuss the database, Tim asks her to provide him with all of the existing documents that she uses to run the mall so he can examine them and use them to better understand the data he needs to collect.

In this chapter, you will begin the discovery and planning phases of creating a database for NHD. You will use the documents that Linda provides to develop a database design. After completing the database design, Tim will review it and provide feedback that you will use to create the database in Chapter 2.

Complete the following:

1. Linda gave you the form shown in Figure 1.35, which the mall uses to collect data about customers who enroll in classes. On paper, design a customer table based on this form. Notice that the form does not contain a place for a customer identification number. Rather, the paper documents are currently filed alphabetically according to the customer's name. You know that you will need an identification number to uniquely identify customers. Be certain to add this field to your table design. Your table design should include field names, data types, field properties (as necessary), and field descriptions.

Figure 1.35: Customer information form

Memories Antique Mall
Customer Information Form

Name: _Angela Sutherland_

Address: _7890 Grandview Dr_

City: _Cleveland_ State: _TN_ Zip: _37364_

Phone: _423-396-1214_

Comments: _____

Do you want to receive our newsletter? Yes ____ No _X_

2. Linda gave you the form shown in Figure 1.36, which she uses to obtain information about dealers. On paper, design a dealer table based on this form. Your table design should include field names, data types, field properties (as necessary), and field descriptions. Be certain that each dealer is uniquely identified.

Figure 1.36: Dealer information form

Memories Antique Mall
Dealer Information Form

Name: _Marcia Tyler_

Address: _9800 Harbor Lane_

City: _Cleveland_ State: _TN_ Zip: _37364_

Phone: _(423) 890-8788_ Cell Phone: _(423) 645-8900_

Tax ID: _34-5690654_

Comments: _Call cell phone first. Up to 15% discount is approved._

3. After meeting with Linda, she tells you that she needs to manage the booths, their sizes, and their monthly rental amounts. She currently keeps this information on a piece of paper that she posts on the bulletin board in her office. Create the booth table using the information in the map shown in Figure 1.37. Linda tells you during your interview with her that she also needs to store data about the booth's location (outside perimeter, inside perimeter, or aisle), its color (green, tan, yellow, or white), which dealer rents the booth (or which booths are vacant), and whether the booth has rafters above it and carpeting.

Figure 1.37: Map of the Memories Antiques Mall

A-16 12x8 $175	A-15 12x8 $175	A-14 12x10 $230	A-13 12x10 $230	A-12 12x18 $310	A-11 12x18 $310	A-10 12x10 $230	A-09 12x10 $230	A-08 12x10 $230	A-07 12x12 $290

A-17 12x8 $175

A-18 12x12 $290

A-19 12x18 $310

A-20 12x18 $310

B-12 8x12 $175 B-11 8x12 $175

B-13 8x12 $175 C-13 8x16 $150

B-14 8x10 $120 C-14 8x20 $200

B-15 8x10 $120 C-15 8x20 $200

B-10 8x10 $120 B-09 8x10 $120

C-12 8x16 $150 C-06 8x8 $90 / C-07 8x8 $90

C-11 8x8 $90 C-08 8x8 $90

C-09 8x8 $90 / Front Counter / C-10 8x8 $90

B-08 8x10 $120 B-07 8x8 $105 B-06 8x8 $105

C-05 8x8 $90 B-05 8x8 $105

C-04 8x8 $90 B-04 8x8 $105

C-03 8x8 $90 B-03 8x10 $120

C-02 8x8 $90 B-02 8x10 $120

C-01 8x8 $90 B-01 8x10 $120

A-06 12x18 $310

A-05 12x12 $290

A-04 12x12 $290

A-03 12x12 $290

A-02 12x18 $310

A-01 12x18 $310

4. Linda uses the spreadsheet shown in Figure 1.38 to collect personal data about the mall's employees.

Figure 1.38: Personal data about employees

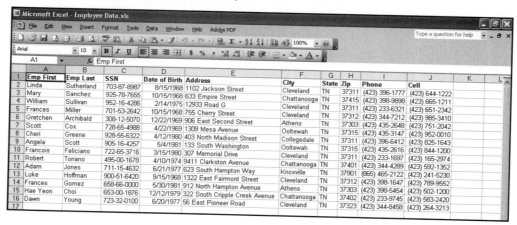

She uses the spreadsheet shown in Figure 1.39 to collect other data about employees, including their hire date, last personnel review date, and salary. Use these spreadsheets to design an employee table. Your table design should include field names, data types, field properties (as necessary), and field descriptions. Be certain that each employee is uniquely identified and that you eliminate redundant data.

Figure 1.39: Employee history and salary data

	Emp First	Emp Last	Start Date	End Date	Position	Memo	Salary	Hourly Rate	Review Date
1									
2	Linda	Sutherland	2/15/2002		Manager		$67,000.00		
3	Mary	Sanchez	6/15/2005		Accounting		$35,500.00		5/31/2008
4	William	Sullivan	5/23/2004		Maintenance			$9.25	3/1/2008
5	Frances	Miller	3/22/2004		Sales			$12.50	4/1/2008
6	Gretchen	Archibald	1/5/2000	5/16/2004	Maintenance			$9.25	
7	Scott	Cox	4/19/2003	4/22/2005	Sales		$35,500.00	$15.50	
8	Cheri	Greene	8/5/2005		Assistant Manager				1/15/2009
9	Angela	Scott	9/22/2005		Sales			$15.00	2/1/2008
10	Francois	Feliciano	7/16/2004		Sales			$16.00	5/1/2008
11	Robert	Toriano	9/16/2004		Administrative Assistant			$15.50	6/1/2008
12	Adam	Jones	10/12/2005		Sales			$15.00	6/1/2008
13	Luke	Hoffman	11/16/2004	2/22/2007	Sales			$15.50	
14	Frances	Gomez	5/31/2006		Administrative Assistant	Speaks fluent Spanish		$12.00	11/1/2008
15	Hae Yeon	Choi	12/15/2007		Administrative Assistant			$13.50	3/1/2009
16	Dawn	Young	1/16/2004		Sales			$15.50	12/15/2008
17									

5. Linda also needs to maintain data about the classes taught at the mall and the instructors who teach these classes. For instructors, she needs to store the instructor's personal information (name, address, phone number, and cell phone number) and the fee that the instructor charges for teaching a class. Design a table that maintains information about instructors. Be certain that each instructor is uniquely identified.

6. Linda needs to maintain information about the classes that instructors teach at the mall. Currently, classes do not have an identification number, and, as such, Linda has a hard time distinguishing different classes with the same class name. For example, the mall offers three "Tattered Treasures" classes, all taught by the same instructor, but the only difference between the classes is the date they occur. Linda wants to distinguish the classes better, and store the class name, cost, classroom in which it is taught, date and time, and the instructor. Classrooms at the mall have a single-digit room number. Recently, the local community college approved some of the mall's classes for continuing education units (CEU) in certain fields, so Linda also needs to indicate whether the classes qualify for credit. Design a table to store this information for Linda.

7. Finally, you need a table that maintains data about class enrollments, including the customer, class, and payment information. Customers can sign up for more than one class. Customers can pay their class fees when they enroll in the class or on the first day of class. Be certain you have a way to indicate the customer's payment status (paid or not paid) for each class.

8. For each table you designed, use a piece of paper to sketch the table design so that you can enter five sample records into it. After creating five records, determine

1

whether you need to make any adjustments in your table designs so that each table is in third normal form. For example, is the job title repeated in the table that stores data about employees? What field will you use as the primary key in each table, or do you need to create a field to use as the primary key? If you need to make any changes to your table designs, do so on your paper and add the necessary documentation to the existing table designs.

9. Review each table design to ensure you have created all of the necessary fields and that they have the correct data type and field size. Be certain that you have designated a primary key field in each table and that your primary key field will contain unique values for each record.

10. Draw arrows to indicate the fields that will form the relationships in the database.

11. If your instructor asks you to turn in your database design, keep a copy for yourself as you will need it to develop the database in subsequent chapters.

Case 2—Creating the Database Design for MovinOn Inc.

MovinOn Inc. is a moving company that provides moving and storage services in Washington, Oregon, and Wyoming. MovinOn provides a truck, driver, and one or more moving assistants to move residential and commercial items from one location to another within the defined coverage area. In addition to moving services, the company provides temporary and long-term storage in its warehouses. MovinOn's customers are commercial and residential. Some of the storage warehouses are climatically controlled for customers who need to store items that are sensitive to extreme temperatures.

Information Systems

The business started in 1990 with a single truck and a single warehouse in Oregon. Due to a very satisfied clientele, the company has grown over the years into a much larger business. Currently, MovinOn has one warehouse in each state it services and is working on a merger with another company that offers similar services in different service areas. When the merger is complete, MovinOn will acquire additional storage warehouses, trucks, and employees and will expand its operations into different states.

David Bowers is the general manager of MovinOn. In the past, David managed the business using a combination of spreadsheets and paper forms. However, with a merger in the company's future, David needs to expand his system to manage data better. David recently hired Robert Iko, an information systems specialist, to recommend and implement a new plan for managing the company's data.

Robert's first task is to understand the current system and its limitations by talking extensively with David about data management and user needs. David explains that the office in each state accepts reservations for moving and storage services by completing a form that includes the customer's name, address, phone number, and the job's details. Jobs that involve trucking items from one location to another or from an outside location to a storage unit in a warehouse are maintained in a filing cabinet that is organized by customer name. Leases for storage space are stored alphabetically in a separate filing cabinet for each warehouse. All of the forms are stored in the on-site offices at the warehouse from which they were purchased. Unfortunately, David admits that forms are often lost or misplaced and sometimes contain inaccurate or missing data. In addition, when a customer requires the services of another warehouse, a MovinOn employee has to copy the customer's record and send it to the second warehouse so that it is on file at the second location. David wants the new system to be capable of sharing data between the three warehouses and any warehouses that the company acquires in the future so that it is easy for the company to share and maintain data.

Each warehouse has its own manager, office staff, and moving assistants. Drivers are contract employees and can work for any warehouse. David wants the new system to manage employee data, including personal information, salary information, and work performance. In addition to managing personnel data, David also wants to use the new system to manage information about drivers, including their personal information and driving records. The system also needs to store information about the trucks and vans that MovinOn owns and operates.

Finally, the system must maintain data about customers who utilize moving and storage services. Some customers might require storage in more than one location. When there is a request for services, the request is recorded on a form. Any request constitutes a "job" in the lingo of the company—a job must include all the pertinent data, including information about the customer, the originating location, the destination location, and the estimated mileage and weight of the load.

Robert gathered a collection of documents during the discovery phase that will help you design the database. You need to be certain that every data item in the existing documents is also represented in the tables in your design. In this chapter, you will begin the discovery and planning phases of creating a database for MovinOn. You will use the documents that Robert provides to develop a database design. After completing the database design, Robert will review it and provide feedback that you will use to create the database in Chapter 2.

Complete the following:

1. Robert gave you the form shown in Figure 1.40, which collects data about employees. In addition to storing the data shown in Figure 1.40, Robert also needs to identify the warehouse in which the employee works. On paper, design an employee table based on this form. The table design for all tables that you create should include field names, data types, field properties (as necessary), and field descriptions. Remember that each table must have a primary key field.

Figure 1.40: Employee information form

mOvinOn Inc.

Employee Information Form

Name: _David Bowers_

Address: _10124 Metropolitan Drive_

City: _Seattle_ State: _WA_ Zip: _98117_

Phone: _(206) 246-5132_ Cell Phone: _(206) 575-4321_

SSN: _154-00-3785_ Date of Birth: _9/12/1958_

(The following information to be filled out by MovinOn human resources manager)

Hire Date: _1/22/1998_ Termination Date: _____

Position: _General Manager_

Annual Salary: _$72,000_ or Hourly Rate: _____

Date of last personnel review: _____

Notes about this employee:

_____

_____

_____

2. The database must manage data about drivers, who are hired on a contract basis. Design a table that stores information about drivers. The table should include the same information stored for employees, except for an indication about the warehouse in which the driver works, in addition to storing the following additional information:

- Drivers are not paid an hourly rate or salary; they are paid based on the number of miles driven for any job. The payment for a job is determined by multiplying the rate per mile by the number of miles for the job.

- MovinOn rates drivers based on their safety records, successful on-time deliveries, and other factors. The company's rating system uses the values A, B, C, D, and F to rate drivers, with A being the highest rating and F being the lowest rating. (You do not need to worry about how MovinOn assigns ratings to drivers; you only need to store the driver's rating.)

3. Design a table that stores data about the trucks and vans owned by MovinOn. Each vehicle has a unique identification number appearing on the vehicle in the format TRK-001 for trucks or VAN-009 for vans. David wants to store the vehicle's license plate number, number of axles, and color.

4. Design a table that stores data about warehouses using the data shown in Figure 1.41. The warehouse identification number is the two-letter state abbreviation in which the warehouse is located followed by a dash and then a number. For example, the warehouse in Wyoming is WY-1.

Figure 1.41: Data about warehouses

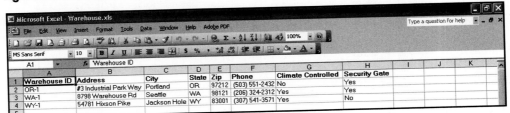

5. Currently, information about storage units is stored in an Excel workbook; a portion of this data is shown in Figure 1.42. Use this information to help you design a table that manages data about the storage units.

1

Figure 1.42: Data about storage units

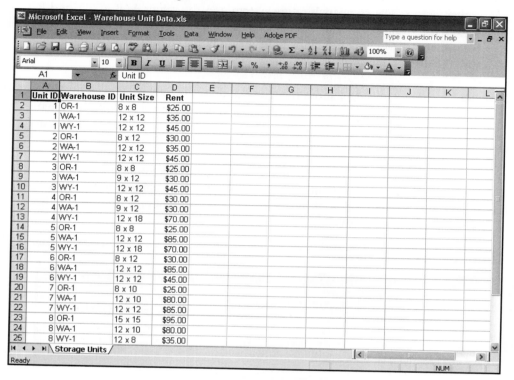

6. You also need to manage data to indicate which customer rents which unit. David wants to store the date the lease started and ended on each unit in each warehouse. For current customers, the ending lease date will be null. Design a table that manages data about unit rentals.

7. You have learned that data pertaining to moving jobs is actually accumulated in two steps. When the customer requests a job, the administrative assistant from the warehouse that will perform the services fills out the form shown in Figure 1.43. This form is considered a "job order."

Figure 1.43: Job order information form

mOvinOn Inc.

Job Order Information Form

Customer: _Piazza Real Estate_

Move Date: _9/5/2008_

Address Moving **FROM**: _1789 Eighth Avenue_

Spokane, WA

Address Moving **TO**: _7899 Grandview Apt #5_

Pullman, WA

Estimated Mileage: _60_ Estimated Weight: _1250 lbs_

Do you need packing service? Yes _X_ No _____

Do you need us to move any heavy items (such as a piano or freezer)?

Yes _X_ No _____

Do you need to store any items? Yes _____ No _X_

8. David needs to store the following data about customers: company name (for commercial customers only), the job contact's name, and the address, city, state, zip code, and phone number. Design a customer table using this information.

9. The administrative assistant uses a scheduling program to manage and assign vehicles and drivers for moving jobs, and then this information is entered into the database. Upon completion of a job, the database must store the details about the job, including the customer, truck or van used, driver, actual mileage, and actual weight. This step is considered to be the "job detail." David wants to store job detail data separately from job order data. Design a table that manages the job detail information.

10. For each table you designed, use a piece of paper to sketch the table design so that you can enter five sample records into it. After creating five records, determine

1

whether you need to make any adjustments in your table designs so that each table is in third normal form. If you need to make any changes to your table designs, do so on your paper and add the necessary documentation to the existing table designs.

11. Review each table design to ensure you have created all of the necessary fields. Be certain that you have designated a primary key field in each table and that your primary key field will contain unique values for each record.

12. Draw arrows to indicate the fields that will form the relationships in the database.

13. If your instructor asks you to turn in your database design, keep a copy for yourself as you will need it to develop your database in subsequent chapters.

Case 3—Creating the Database Design for Hershey College

Information Systems

Hershey College is a small liberal arts college in Hershey, Pennsylvania. Because student enrollment at Hershey College is small, the college participates competitively only in football and basketball. However, the athletic department has been encouraging the college for the past several years to develop an intramural department. The athletic department has conducted research showing that people who exercise regularly have fewer instances of heart disease, osteoporosis, and other illnesses. After receiving a large cash endowment for the development of the intramural department, the college's board of directors agreed to its creation. The board also met with student leadership at the college and by mutual agreement implemented a small activity fee that all students will pay with their tuition to provide funding for the intramural department's activities. The primary goal of the intramural department is to encourage students to participate in sports and activities that promote good health and strong bodies. In addition, many studies have shown that students who are actively involved in sports or other extracurricular activities are less likely to participate in undesirable activities.

The intramural department will offer organized sports leagues for interested students. The department will create schedules for each sport, assign players to teams, provide a coach and a student captain, and manage the team's playing locations. The department will also offer sports equipment that teams can check out and use for practice and games.

Part of the mandate set by the board for the intramural department is to demonstrate that students are using its services by participating on teams and using equipment. The intramural department must provide reports each semester documenting which sports were offered, how many students participated in them, and other information as requested by the board. Admission counselors will also use these reports to show prospective students that there are many opportunities to participate in sports at the college.

The college has appointed Marianna Fuentes as the director of the intramural department. Marianna has hired you to develop and maintain the database that will manage the departmental activities and produce the required reports. Because the intramural department is new, Marianna is not yet certain of the data the department needs to collect and manage. Initially, she wants the database to manage data about each sport offered by the intramural department (including team assignments, coaches, and scheduling), the students who sign up for sports teams, and the equipment.

Because you are the only person responsible for the database, there is a lot of responsibility on your shoulders to provide a database that works well for the department. In this chapter, you will begin the discovery and planning phases of creating a database for the intramural department. You will use the information that Marianna provides to develop a database design. After completing the database design, Marianna will review it and provide feedback that you will use to create the database in Chapter 2.

Complete the following:

1. Marianna decides that the best way to get started planning the database is to prepare a list of all the data items that are needed to support the department. Table 1.14 shows her list, which she asks you to use when planning the database. You will need to identify the data to collect, group fields into tables, normalize the data, and relate the tables.

Table 1.14: Intramural department information needs

Item	Description
Students: We need to store information about students who participate on teams and the sports in which they participate, including the team. Students can sign up for more than one sport.	
ID number	Student and faculty IDs at Hershey are five digits.
Name	First and last names.
Phone	Home phone number, cell phone number.
Waiver	Students must sign a waiver to play on a team; we must have this document on file.
Academic eligibility	Students must be academically eligible to play sports by maintaining a C or better grade point average; we must check eligibility at registration.
Sports	
Name	Sports include basketball, football, ping pong, pool, soccer, softball, swimming, tennis, track, and wrestling.
Coach	Each sport has an assigned coach. We need to know the coach's name, office number (such as JK-18), phone number, and cell phone number. A person can coach one or more teams over one or more seasons.
Minimum and maximum players	Each sport has a designated minimum and maximum number of players.

Table 1.14: Intramural department information needs (cont.)

Item	Description
Begin Date	The date each sport begins.
Notes	A place to record notes about each sport.
Equipment: Teams or coaches check out the equipment they need for their sport's practice sessions. Some sports, such as wrestling, do not have equipment.	
ID number	Equipment is assigned an ID number using a sport abbreviation and a number (BAS = basketball, FTBL = football, PNG = ping pong, POOL = pool table, SOC = soccer, SOF = softball, TEN = tennis, and WRES = wrestling). For example, BAS-1 is a basketball. Some equipment ID numbers indicate a collection of items. For example, BAS-BAG-3 is three basketballs.
Description	A description of the equipment.
Storage building	The building where the equipment is stored, such as SB-1.
Fields: Different courts, fields, and tables are available for practice and games.	
ID number	Courts, fields, and tables are assigned ID numbers. For example, BAS-CRT-1 is a basketball court, SOC-FLD-2 is a soccer field, and POL-TBL-2 is a pool table.
Type	Identify the court, field, or table type (basketball, softball, and so on).
Maintenance Contact	Each court, field, and table has an assigned maintenance person, who manages and resolves problems with the court, field, or location. We will need to know the maintenance person's name, phone number, and office number.
Season	The seasons each field is available for use by a team (some fields are unavailable off-season for maintenance purposes). The seasons are fall and spring; some sports run year-round, in which case the season is "always."
Teams: For each team, we need to know the team number, captain, sport name, location where games are played, and the equipment needed for the game.	

2. For each table you identified, determine the data type to assign to each field, and which fields to use as the primary key.

3. For each table you designed, use a piece of paper to sketch the table design so that you can enter five sample records into it. After creating five records, determine whether you need to make any adjustments in your table designs so that each table is in third normal form. If you need to make any changes to your table designs, do so on your paper and add the necessary documentation to the existing table designs.

4. Use arrows to indicate the relationships between tables and the relationship types. Indicate which fields are involved in the relationship and determine how to maintain data integrity.

5. If your instructor asks you to turn in your database design, keep a copy for yourself as you will need it to develop your database in subsequent chapters.

Building the Database

Information Systems: Creating, Populating, Relating, and Maintaining the Tables in a Database

"It is only the farmer who faithfully plants seeds in the Spring, who reaps a harvest in the Autumn."
—BC Forbes

LEARNING OBJECTIVES

Level 1

Create a database and tables
Work in Design view
Set a field's data type, size, and properties
Use the Input Mask Wizard and the Lookup Wizard
Validate fields

Level 2

Import data into a database
Set a table's primary key
Create foreign keys
Create one-to-many and many-to-many relationships
Use a subdatasheet to view related records in a table

Level 3

Learn about the role of the database administrator
Compact, repair, and back up a database
Document the database design using the Documenter
Secure a database by setting a password, encrypting data, and hiding objects
Create user-level security in a database

TOOLS COVERED IN THIS CHAPTER

Datasheet view

Design view

Documenter

Import Spreadsheet Wizard

Input Mask Wizard

Lookup Wizard

Relationships window

Security Wizard

Subdatasheet

Table Wizard

CHAPTER INTRODUCTION

In Chapter 1, Don Linebarger, the information systems director at 4Corners Pharmacy, interviewed the pharmacy's owner, pharmacists, managers, and key employees to learn more about the data needs of the pharmacy and to understand the existing systems the pharmacy uses to conduct business. Don's work resulted in a plan that identifies the tables he needs to create, the fields to define in those tables, the data types and field sizes needed to store the data, and the relationships between tables. With his plan approved by management, Don is ready to begin building the database using Access.

In this chapter, you will learn different techniques for creating tables, entering data, verifying data, relating tables, documenting the database objects, backing up the database, repairing the database, and securing data.

CASE SCENARIO

Don Linebarger needs to begin work on the database for 4Corners Pharmacy by creating the database in Access and then creating the tables that will store the data the pharmacy needs to track customers, prescriptions, drugs, employees, training classes, health insurance companies, doctors, and clinics. The pharmacy's owner, Paul Ferrino, worked as a cashier, pharmacy technician, and pharmacist in his father's pharmacy before purchasing the pharmacy upon his father's retirement. Vincent Ferrino still works part-time at the pharmacy as a pharmacist. Although Vincent's business was successful for more than two decades, his system for managing data about the pharmacy is obsolete. Paul wants to automate many of the processes at the pharmacy so he can better evaluate and operate the business.

Paul's top priority was hiring Don, who will create the system for the pharmacy, train users, and maintain and expand the system over time.

LEVEL 1

CREATING THE DATABASE TABLES

ACCESS 2003 SKILLS TRAINING

- **Add a field to a table between other fields**
- **Add a field to a table structure**
- **Add a lookup field to a table using the Lookup Wizard**
- **Change field properties**
- **Change the data type**
- **Change the Format property for a field in Table Design view**
- **Create custom input masks**
- **Create one or more tables in Design view**
- **Define Date/Time and Yes/No fields**
- **Define Number and Currency fields**
- **Define Text fields**
- **Delete a field from a table structure**
- **Modify field properties for one or more tables in Table Design view**
- **Move a field in a table structure**
- **Specify a default value**
- **Specify a required value**
- **Specify the primary key**
- **Specify validation text for one or more fields**
- **Use the Input Mask Wizard**

REVIEWING THE DATABASE DESIGN

Throughout the database design process, Don researched and evaluated existing and missing sources of data at the pharmacy. He also interviewed the owner, pharmacists, managers, and key employees to learn about how they plan to use the database so he can better understand the needs of the business. One of Don's most important roles is to make sure that the database he develops stores the pharmacy's data in the correct format and outputs the correct queries, forms, and reports for users.

You learned in Chapter 1 that a relational database is a collection of related tables. As an information systems professional, Don knows the importance of properly planning and designing the database so that it meets users' needs and expectations. Paul already knows that Vincent's system for tracking prescriptions, refills, and customers does not work because it is prone to data-entry errors and inconsistent data. In addition, Paul has limited tools available to him in Excel to search a large worksheet to find related records and other information.

1015

After careful analysis and preparation, Don formulated the database design for Paul's approval. Don reviews the database design with Paul to ensure that it is correct and meets the needs of the pharmacy. To make the design easier to understand, Don begins by presenting some of the table designs to Paul. Figure 2.1 shows the table that stores customer data, including the customer's name, address, phone number, date of birth, gender, balance, preference for child-proof caps, insurance plan, household, and allergies. The table that stores customer information is linked to the table that stores the details about the customer's prescriptions, to the table that stores the details about the customer's health plan, and to the table that stores the details about the customer's household. These links are made by creating foreign keys in the related tables.

Figure 2.1: Data stored about customers

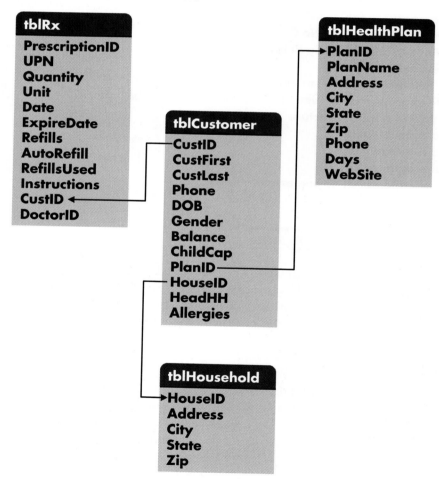

Don used the Leszynski/Reddick guidelines for naming database objects and created four tables: tblCustomer, tblRx, tblHousehold, and tblHealthPlan. When tblCustomer is linked to the related tables tblRx, tblHousehold, and tblHealthPlan, Don can retrieve detailed information about each customer and the prescriptions they have filled, the household to which they belong, and the health plan that covers them. These related tables will also enable him to list all the customers within a household and determine which drugs are being prescribed to which customers.

Figure 2.2 shows the table that stores prescription data, including the prescription's identification number, UPN, quantity ordered, unit of measurement, fill date, expiration date, refills authorized, preference for automatic refills, number of refills used, and the prescribing instructions. In addition, tblRx stores the identification numbers of the customer and the prescribing doctor. The table that stores prescription information is linked to the table that stores the details about the prescribing doctor, to the table that stores details about the customer, to the table that stores details about the drug, and to the table that stores information about refills using foreign keys in the related tables.

Figure 2.2: Data stored about prescriptions

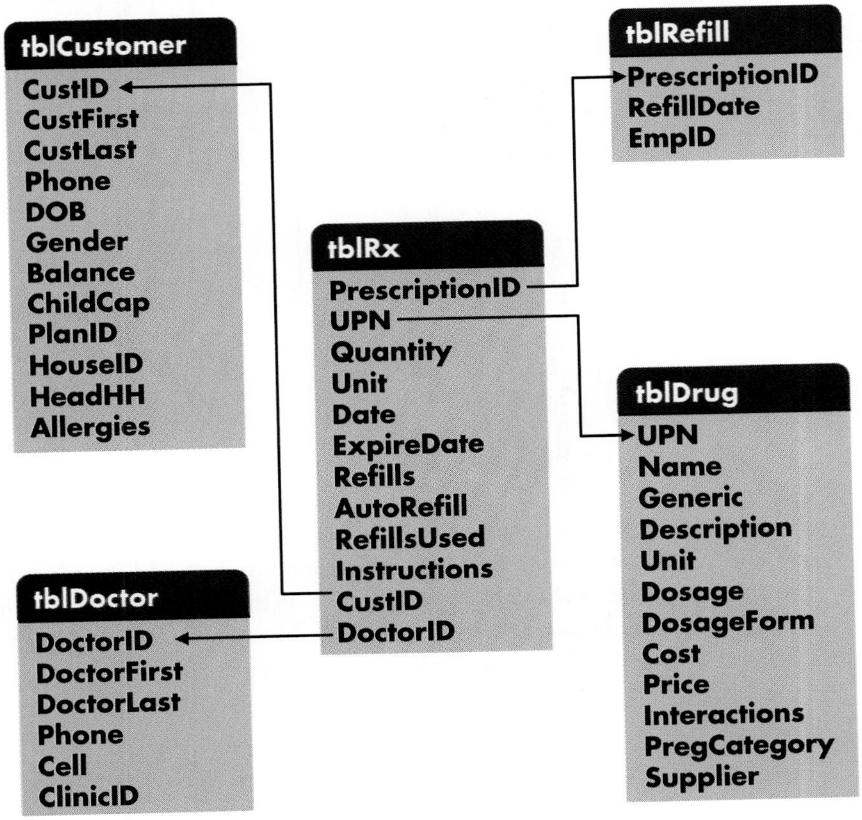

Figure 2.3 shows the table that stores data about employees at the pharmacy, including the employee's identification number, first name, middle initial, last name, Social Security number, date of birth, start date, termination date (if applicable), address, city, state, zip code, job identification number, phone number, cell phone number, salary or hourly rate of compensation, and next personnel review date. In addition, there is a field to store miscellaneous information about the employee, such as being part-time or bilingual. The table that stores employee information is linked to the table that stores the details about the employee's training, to the table that stores information about the refills that the employee has filled, and to the table that identifies the different job titles at the pharmacy.

Figure 2.3: Data stored about employees

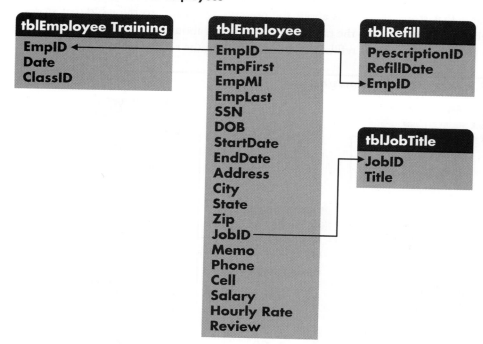

Figure 2.4 shows the table that stores data about doctors, including the doctor's identification number, first and last names, phone number, cell phone number, and the identification number of the clinic at which the doctor works. The table that stores doctor data is linked to the table that stores details about the clinic at which the doctor works and to the table that stores details about prescriptions the doctor has written.

Figure 2.4: Data stored about doctors

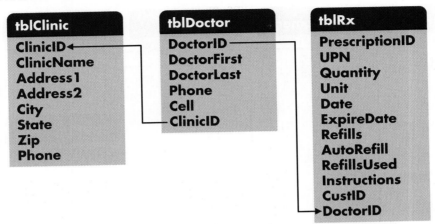

Figure 2.5 shows the table that stores data about the classes that pharmacy employees must take to maintain their professional certifications and other classes of interest. The table stores data about classes, including the class identification number, description, cost, renewal requirement (in years), and provider. In addition, there is a field to indicate whether the class is required. The table that stores data about classes is linked to the table that stores details about the employees who took the classes.

Figure 2.5: Data stored about classes

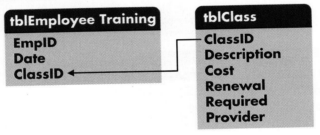

As is customary in the design process, Paul and Don agreed to limit the scope of the new system to managing data about customers, prescriptions, drugs, employees, training classes, doctors, and clinics. As the pharmacy's staff and managers begin using the system, Paul and Don might reevaluate it and add additional functionality, such as managing the inventory of nonprescription items. If Paul opens additional pharmacy locations in the future, he and Don might plan for the system to go on a network so it is possible for employees and managers at each location to share data and other resources across a network.

The entire database design appears in Figure 2.6.

Figure 2.6: Database design for 4Corners Pharmacy

Paul is satisfied that the database will collect and manage the correct data, so he gives his final approval to the design. Don begins by starting Access and creating a new database.

USING THE DATABASE DESIGN TO CREATE THE DATABASE

After receiving Paul's approval on the database design, Don's first task is to create the database in Access. After starting Access, Don clicks the New button ▣ on the Standard toolbar, which opens the New File task pane. Don clicks the Blank database option, types the database name 4Corners in the File name text box of the File New Database dialog box, chooses a file location in which to save the database, and then clicks the Create button. Figure 2.7 shows the 4Corners database in the Database window.

Figure 2.7: 4Corners database in the Database window

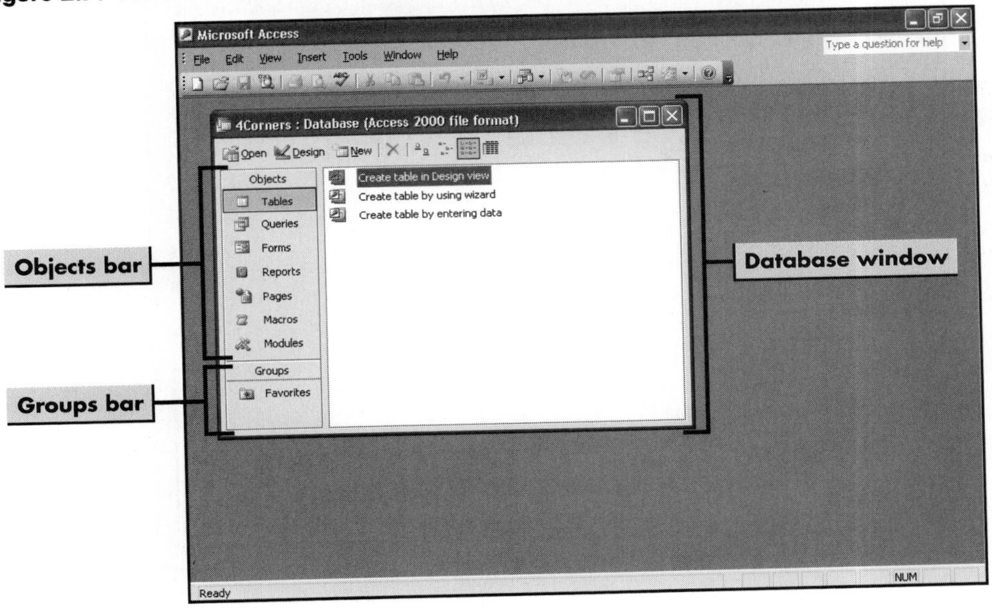

The **Database window** is the main control panel for the database. By clicking the buttons on the **Objects bar**, you can create, open, design, and view all of the objects stored in the database. For example, clicking the Tables button on the Objects bar shows the table objects in the database and shortcuts for creating tables. The **Groups bar** lets you organize database objects and create shortcuts for working with them, making it easier to access the information you need.

Because tables store all of the data in a database, you must create them before any of the other database objects. You can create a table by entering data in Datasheet view, using a wizard, or designing a table in Design view. The method that you select depends on the kind of data that you are ready to organize in a table and your own work preferences. Don will use each of these methods to create the tables in the 4Corners database.

CREATING A TABLE BY ENTERING DATA

The first table that Don creates is the one that stores the details about the different health plans to which customers subscribe. Because he already has a printout with the data for several health plans, he decides to create this table by entering data. Don double-clicks the Create table by entering data option in the Database window to open the datasheet shown in Figure 2.8.

Figure 2.8: Datasheet view

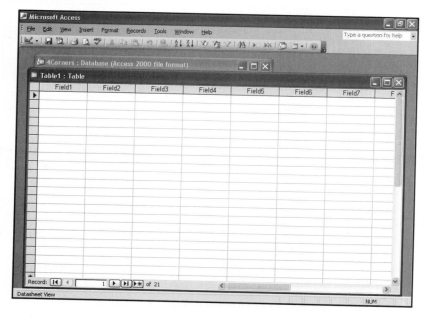

This view of the data in a table is called **Datasheet view**; it shows the table's records in rows and the table's fields in columns. When you are working in a table, the window that opens is called the Table window. The **Table window** indicates the table's name; in this case, the table name is given a default name, Table1, because Don hasn't saved it yet. The table includes default field names, such as Field1 and Field2, because Don hasn't defined the fields yet. When creating a table by entering data, you just start entering the data. Figure 2.9 shows the datasheet after entering the data for six health plans. Don maximized the Table window so he can see more of the datasheet, and he resized the fields so he can see all of the table's fields on the screen at the same time. Some of the records contain a field that does not contain any values because these values are unknown or unavailable.

Figure 2.9: Datasheet with the records for six health plans

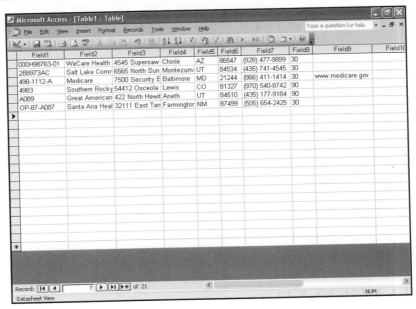

As Don was entering records, Access added a hidden AutoNumber field to the datasheet. Each record that Don entered has a unique value in the hidden _ID field. The datasheet has blank rows for additional records (up to the record with the _ID field value of 21); this is the default datasheet size when creating a table by entering data in Datasheet view.

Now that Don has entered the data for the health plans about which he already has information, he needs to save the table as an object in the 4Corners database and define the fields. Don clicks the Save button on the Table Datasheet toolbar, types tblHealthPlan in the Table Name text box of the Save As dialog box, and then clicks the OK button. Because there is no primary key field in the tblHealthPlan table, a warning box opens and asks if Don wants to create a primary key. Don decides not to create a primary key now, so he clicks the No button. To define the fields in a table, Don changes to Design view by clicking the View button for Design view on the Table Datasheet toolbar. Figure 2.10 shows Design view for tblHealthPlan.

Figure 2.10: Design view for tblHealthPlan

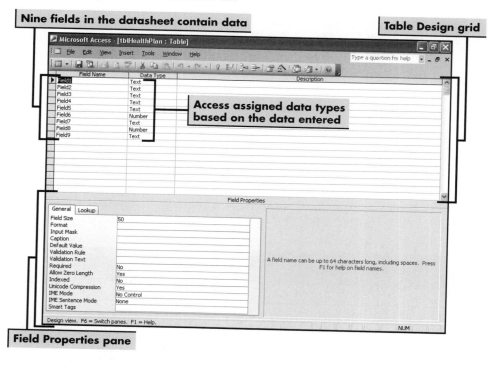

Nine fields in the datasheet contain data

Table Design grid

Access assigned data types based on the data entered

Field Properties pane

WORKING IN TABLE DESIGN VIEW

Don uses **Design view** to define the table's fields and the field properties and rearrange the order of fields as necessary. The top part of Design view is called the **Table Design grid** (or the **design grid**); this area includes the Field Name, Data Type, and Description columns. Each row in the Table Design grid is a field in the table. The bottom part of Design view is called the **Field Properties pane**; this area displays the field properties for the selected field. You can select a field by clicking the field in the Table Design grid. When a field is selected, an arrow appears in the current row. In Figure 2.10, the first field (Field1) is selected.

Next, Don needs to rename the default field names to match the ones in his table design by selecting each field name and typing the new value. Most DBMSs, including Access, have specific rules that you must follow when naming fields and database objects. The following rules apply to naming Access objects:

- Names can contain up to 64 characters.
- Names can contain any combination of letters, numbers, spaces, and special characters, except a period (.), an exclamation point (!), an accent grave (`), and square brackets ([and]).
- Names cannot begin with a space.

In addition to these rules, some organizations establish standards for naming objects and fields. Some organizations might include acronyms or abbreviations in field names to make them shorter. At 4Corners Pharmacy, for example, the field that stores a person's date of birth is abbreviated as "DOB," and field and object names that contain multiple words are capitalized but do not contain any spaces (such as the table name tblHealthPlan or the field name ClinicName).

After changing the default field names, Don defines the data type and field properties for each field. To change the data type, he clicks the right side of the Data Type text box for the field to display a list of all the data types for Access, and then he clicks the desired data type. After selecting a data type, the Field Properties pane changes to display properties associated with the selected data type. Don knows that Text fields can contain a maximum of 255 characters and that there are different field sizes for numeric fields. To save space in the database and improve its performance, Don can use the **Field Size property** to limit the number of characters to store in a Text field or the type of numeric data to store in a Number field.

Best Practice

Setting the Field Size Property for Text and Number Fields Correctly

Choosing the correct Field Size property for a Text or Number field is easy when you have sample data to examine. For Text fields, you can examine the existing data and count the number of characters in the longest field value. For example, the longest address in the sample data might be 29 characters. In this case, you can set the Field Size property for the Address field to 30 or 40 characters to provide enough room for even longer addresses. You can increase the size of a field after designing it, but it is always better to set the field size correctly from the start. If the field size is too small, users might not be able to enter complete data into a field without resizing it in Design view. Depending on the database configuration, users might not be able to make this type of change, in which case the field entry will be incomplete.

Another problem with resizing fields later occurs when the field is involved in one or more relationships. For example, if an EmployeeID number is originally set as a Text field that stores three digits and the company hires 1,000 people, necessitating a four-digit EmployeeID, then the field isn't long enough to store the employee with EmployeeID 1000. If the EmployeeID field is a primary key with a foreign key in a related table, Access prohibits you from changing the field size unless you delete the relationship. In this case, you would need to change the field size in the primary and foreign keys, and then re-create the relationship.

The same problem can occur with Number fields. The values that Access can store in a Number field with the Byte field size are different than the values it can store in a Number field with the Double field size. AutoNumber fields store data using the Long Integer field size. Relationships between fields with the AutoNumber and Number data types must have the same field size, Long Integer, to create the relationship.

When setting field sizes, be certain to consider the data you have from the discovery phase, and then to create a reasonable margin of error to avoid setting the field size so it cannot store values in the future.

Although he can change field options after creating them, Don knows that if the field size is too small, data might be truncated, and if set too long, valuable space might be wasted. The default field size for a Text field is 50 characters; a Text field can store 0 to 255 characters. Don changes the default field size for Text fields to match his table design. For the Days field, which is a Number field, Don changes the field size from the default of Long Integer to Byte as this field will store whole numbers such as 30 and 90.

Adding Descriptions to Fields in Table Design View

Some developers like to use the optional **Description property** for a field to document its contents, such as identifying a field as a primary or foreign key or providing users with instructions about entering values into the field, for example, adding a description of "Must be M or F" in a field that requests a person's gender. When a database is being developed by a team, using the Description property is an important part of documenting the table designs and providing clear instructions for users. Don knows that the Description property is important and adds descriptions to each field in the table to document their contents.

The last thing that Don does is to select the PlanID field and set it as the table's primary key. With the field selected, he clicks the Primary Key button 🔑 on the Table Design toolbar. Access adds a key symbol to the PlanID row to indicate this field as the table's primary key. Figure 2.11 shows the completed table design for tblHealthPlan.

Figure 2.11: Table design for tblHealthPlan

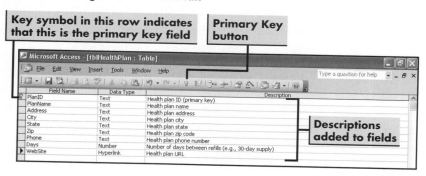

Don finished one table's design and entered data into it. He decides to use another method to create the second table in the database, which will store data about households.

CREATING A TABLE USING THE TABLE WIZARD

The second table that Don will create, tblHousehold, stores the HouseID, address, city, state, and zip code for customers living in the same household (at the same address). Because this table has fields that are commonly used, Don decides to use the Table Wizard to create it. The **Table Wizard** includes sample tables for business and personal needs with fields that you can select and modify to create your own tables. An advantage of using the Table Wizard is that the sample tables and fields already have properties set that might work well in your database or that are easily changed to accommodate your specific data needs. To start the Table Wizard, Don returns to the Tables object in the Database window, and then double-clicks the Create table by using wizard option. The Table Wizard starts, as shown in Figure 2.12.

Figure 2.12: Table Wizard

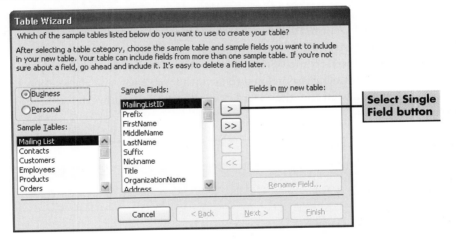

The Business option button is selected by default and displays a list of tables and fields that are commonly used in business situations. Don clicks Customers in the Sample Tables list box. By scrolling the contents of the Sample Fields list box, Don sees that the fields he needs for tblHousehold are included, even though he needs to rename a few of the fields so they match his table design. The first field, CustomerID, is selected by default. To add this field to his new table, Don clicks the Select Single Field button ⟩ to add it to the Fields in my new table list box. Because this field isn't named correctly for his purposes, Don clicks the Rename Field button and types HouseID. He repeats the process to add the BillingAddress, City, StateOrProvince, and PostalCode fields to his new table; the fields are now named Address, City, State, and Zip. He clicks the Next button, and then renames the table to tblHousehold, as shown in Figure 2.13.

Figure 2.13: Naming the table and selecting a primary key

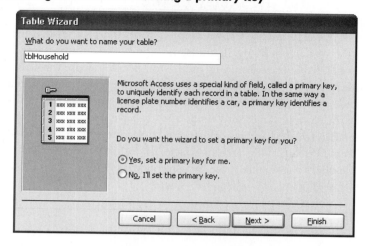

Finally, because household identification numbers are unique, Don will use the HouseID field as the table's primary key. He selects the option to assign a primary key himself, chooses the HouseID field, selects the option to have Access assign consecutive numbers to records, indicates that this table isn't related to any other table yet, and then selects the option to modify the table design after the wizard closes. Figure 2.14 shows the table design for tblHousehold.

Figure 2.14: tblHousehold in Design view

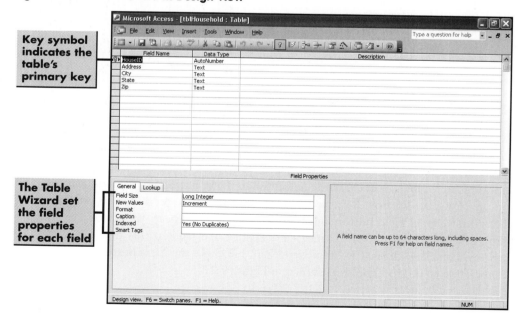

Each field has the correct name and data type and the key symbol in the row for the HouseID field indicates that this field is the table's primary key. Don changes the field size for each field to match his table design and adds field descriptions to document the fields. Don saves the table and clicks the View button for Datasheet view 🔲, and then he enters the pharmacy's household data into the table.

How To

Use the Table Wizard to Create a Table

1. On the Tables object in the Database window, double-click the Create table by using wizard option. The Table Wizard starts.
2. Click the Business or Personal option button to select the category in which the desired table might appear, and then use the Sample Tables and Sample Fields list boxes to find a table that closely meets your needs.
3. Click the sample table to display the sample fields for the selected table.
4. Click a field in the Sample Fields list box to select it, and then click the Select Single Field button ⟩ to add it to the Fields in my new table list box. Repeat this step as necessary to add all of the desired fields to the new table. To add all fields to the Fields in my new table list box, click the Select All Fields button ⟩⟩. To remove a selected field from the Fields in my new table list box, click the Remove Single Field button ⟨ (to remove all fields, click the Remove All Fields button ⟨⟨).
5. To rename a field, select the field in the Fields in my new table list box, click the Rename Field button, and then type a new field name. After selecting and renaming the fields to include in the table, click the Next button.
6. Type the desired table name in the "What do you want to name your table?" text box, click the option button that identifies how you want to set the table's primary key, and then click the Next button. (If you choose to set the primary key yourself, use the next dialog box to identify the primary key field and the type of data it will store, and then click the Next button.)
7. If necessary, define the relationship that the new table has with other tables in the database, and then click the Next button.
8. Select the option to modify the table design (open it in Design view), enter data directly into the table (open it in Datasheet view), or enter data into the table using a form the wizard creates for you (a form), and then click the Finish button.

Creating a table with the Table Wizard is a good method when the table you want to create already exists as a sample table and you can accept the default field properties assigned to the fields created by the wizard or easily change them. Just like any other table, you can use Design view to change the fields and their properties. However, most developers prefer to create a table in Design view because it gives them the most control over the design.

2

CREATING A TABLE IN DESIGN VIEW

The remaining tables that Don needs to create have specific requirements that would make it difficult for him to create them in Datasheet view or by using a wizard. The third way to create a table is in Design view. To create a table in Design view, click the Design button on the Database window, or double-click the Create table in Design view option on the Tables object in the Database window to open the Table window in Design view. Just like when creating a table in Datasheet view, the table's default name is Table1; however, the table has no fields until you define them by entering the field names, data type, and properties.

Don uses Design view to create the next table, which stores data about the classes that employees must take to maintain their professional certifications. He begins by entering the first field name, ClassID, and then he presses the Tab key to move to the Data Type text box. If the ClassID field is the Text data type, Don could press the Tab key to move to the Description text box because Text is the default data type. However, the ClassID field is a Number field, so he must change the data type. Clicking the list arrow for the Data Type text box opens a list of data types, or he can type the first letter of the desired data type to select it. Don types "n" and selects the Number data type, presses the Tab key to move to the Description text box, and then types this field's description. The default field size for the Number data type is Long Integer, and Don accepts the default. Don knows that it is a good idea to use Long Integer as the field size for primary key fields to prevent referential integrity errors later when attempting to relate Number fields to AutoNumber fields. Because this field is the table's primary key, Don clicks the Primary Key button 🔑 on the Table Design toolbar, which adds a key symbol to the left of the field name, indicating that this field is the table's primary key. Don does not need to make any other changes to this field, so he presses the Tab key to move to the Field Name text box for the next field. Don creates the other fields in the table and sets their properties. When he is finished, he saves the table using the name tblClass. Figure 2.15 shows the table design.

Figure 2.15: Table design for tblClass

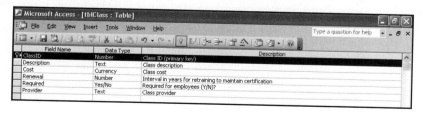

EVALUATING AND TESTING THE TABLE DESIGN

After creating and saving the table design for tblClass, Don switches to Datasheet view, and begins entering the data for this table using the information provided to him by the human resources manager, Maria Garcia. Don enters the value 1 in the ClassID field, presses the Tab key to move to the Description field and types this value, presses the Tab key, and then types 15 in the Cost field. Because the Cost field uses the Currency data type, Access changes the value 15 to $15.00. He presses the Tab key, types 0 in the Renewal field, presses the Tab key and presses the Spacebar to enter a check mark into the Required field, which has the Yes/No data type, and then presses the Tab key and types "Red Cross" in the final field for the first record. To move to the next record, Don can press the Enter key or the Tab key. By moving to the next record, Access saves the record in the table; to cancel the record, Don would press the Esc key. After saving the table for the first time, the only time that Don needs to save the table again is when he makes changes to its design (such as changing a field property in Design view) or to its layout (such as increasing or decreasing a field's width in the datasheet). If you make these kinds of changes to a table and try to close it, Access prompts you to save the table.

Recall from Chapter 1 that data types are necessary to ensure that each field in a table collects the correct values. In theory, you could use the Text data type for any field, but then you would lose the capability to perform calculations on numbers, the flexibility that a Yes/No field provides, the ability to include hyperlinks in a table, and so on.

Now the database contains three tables. Don continues working by creating the table that stores data about customers. He opens the Table window in Design view and enters the field names, data types, and descriptions for each field in the table's design. He also uses the Field Properties pane to set the properties for fields that do not use the default settings. To make his work go faster, he presses the F6 key to move between the design grid and the Field Properties pane. After creating all of the fields and defining their properties, Don selects the CustID field and sets it as the table's primary key, and then saves the table as tblCustomer. Figure 2.16 shows the table's design.

Figure 2.16: Table design for tblCustomer

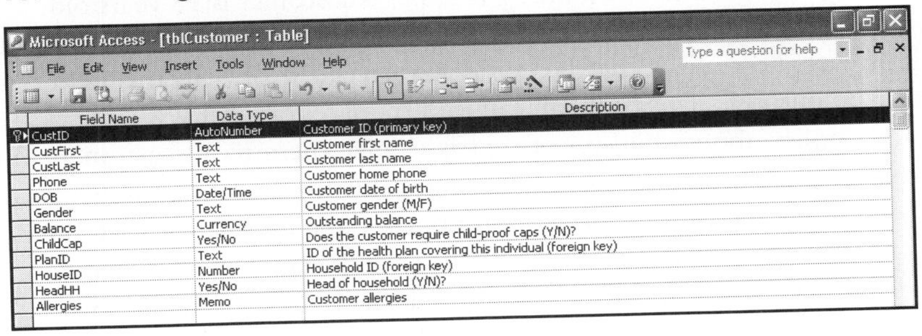

Don changes to Datasheet view and begins entering the data for the first customer, shown in Figure 2.17. (Some of the record has scrolled to the left side of the screen.)

Figure 2.17: tblCustomer with one record entered

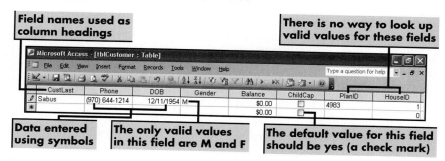

As Don is entering the data, he notices several potential problems:

- The field names are used as the column heading names in the datasheet; for example, "CustFirst" and "CustLast" are the column headings for the fields a pharmacy technician or pharmacist uses to enter the customer's first and last names. Don considers the fact that these field names, although correct, will not be the best ways to identify the information in each field, especially when this data is used in a query, form, or report.

- The Phone field values include telephone numbers. Don entered the phone number using a common format for displaying phone numbers in which the area code appears in parentheses, followed by a space and the seven-digit phone number. He entered the phone number in this way so that it would be displayed with this format each time it appears in a query, form, or report. However, he is concerned that other users won't follow this approach, resulting in inconsistently formatted data. In addition, there is no way to ensure that users enter all 10 digits of the customer's phone number.

- Don entered the DOB (date of birth) field value in a common date format in which the month, date, and year are separated by slash characters. He also entered the year as four digits. This field name is abbreviated, and there is no way to ensure that users enter birth dates in this format, nor is there a way to ensure that users enter four-digit years. If users enter two-digit years, there might be problems later if it becomes necessary to perform calculations with dates, such as determining whether a customer is 18 years old.

- Don entered the uppercase letter "M" in the Gender field to indicate that this customer is a male. However, he realizes that he could have typed q or 9 in this field, either accidentally or on purpose. This problem can lead to inaccurate data.

- The pharmacy's policy about child-proof caps is to give them to all customers unless they specifically request regular caps, so the default value for the ChildCap field should be "yes." To order regular caps for prescription bottles, the user would click the check box or press the Spacebar to remove the check mark and change the value to "no."

- Don entered the plan ID 4983 in the PlanID field to indicate that this customer is insured by Southern Rocky Mountains Health Plan. Knowing that plan ID numbers are often complicated, Don determines that he needs a way to ensure that the plan ID is accurate. For example, a plan ID number might contain commonly mistyped characters, such as reading a zero and typing a capital "O" or reading a lowercase "l" and typing the digit 1. In these cases, the health plan would reject the plan ID number and reject the prescription, causing inconvenience to the customer and taking the pharmacist's time to discover and correct the error.

- Don assigned the HouseID value of 1 to this customer, but realizes that there is no way to determine which HouseIDs correlate with which households without reviewing the data in another table. He needs a way to ensure that the HouseID is correct for all members of a household.

Before entering additional records into tblCustomer, Don considers the potential problems he identified and decides to stop entering records and use the tools available in Design view to set the fields' properties to ensure that the data entered is clearly labeled, accurate, and consistent.

Displaying Descriptive Field Names Using the Caption Property

The first item on Don's list is to ensure that the field names are displayed in clear, simple language so their function is obvious in a table's datasheet and in queries, forms, and reports. Don could edit the field names in Design view, but the naming conventions for field names might prevent him from being able to use the field identifiers that he wants. Instead of changing the field names, Don can use the **Caption property** for a field to change the way the field name is displayed. The Caption property specifies how a field name will appear in different database objects; the default Caption property is the field name for all data types unless you change it. For example, instead of seeing "CustFirst" in a table datasheet, Don wants users to see "First Name." Setting the Caption property properly can turn abbreviated field names into meaningful identifiers that make data entry easier.

How To

Change a Field's Caption Property
1. If necessary, change to Design view, and then select the field that you want to change.
2. Click the Caption text box in the Field Properties pane.
3. Type the caption. See Figure 2.18.

Figure 2.18: Caption property changed for the CustID field

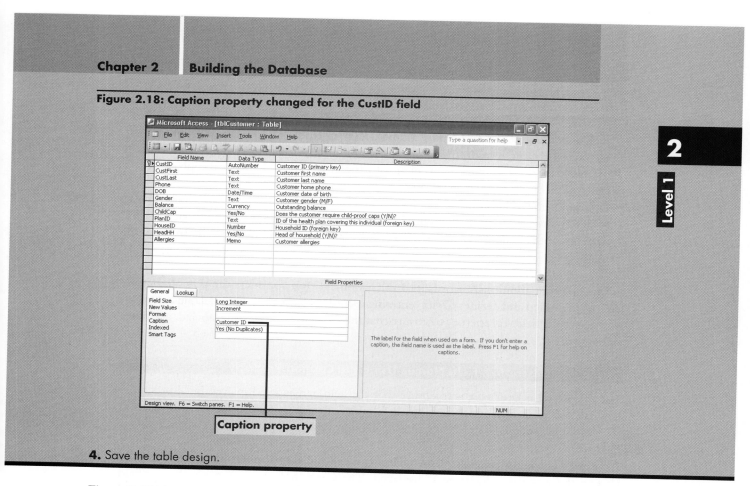

Caption property

4. Save the table design.

Figure 2.19 shows part of the datasheet for tblCustomer after Don changed the Caption property for several of the fields from the default field names to more meaningful descriptions.

Figure 2.19: Datasheet with captions and resized columns

Captions

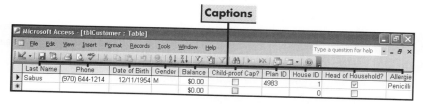

The next item on Don's list is to change the way data is formatted.

Formatting Field Values Using an Input Mask

Don wants the phone number and date of birth for each customer to be formatted the same way; he wants phone numbers in the format (970) 644-1214 and dates of birth in the format 12/11/1954. When Don entered the first record in tblCustomer, he typed the parentheses, space, and dash character in the phone number and the slashes in the date of birth. However, he realizes that other users might not enter these characters correctly, which could result in inconsistently formatted data. In addition, Don knows that by typing the parentheses, space, and dash and slash characters in these fields, these characters must be stored in the database, which requires additional space. The amount of space needed to store these characters in one record isn't significant, but the amount of space required for hundreds or thousands of records is.

In Access, you can control the format of a value by creating an input mask. An **input mask** is a predefined format that you can apply to a field so that its values are displayed using the format you specified. For example, a user might enter a customer's phone number as 9706441214, and this value is stored in tblCustomer. However, when you view the table datasheet or a query, form, or report that includes this value, you see it with the input mask that you defined, such as (970) 644-1214 or 970-644-1214 or 970.644.1214. The input mask supplies these characters, called **literal characters**, but the literal characters are not stored in the database, nor does a user need to type them. An input mask not only works to format data correctly, but it also ensures that all of the necessary data is entered. If a user tries to enter the phone number 6441214 without the area code 970 or 970kajfjfjf, he receives an error message when trying to move to the next field because the input mask only accepts 10-digit numbers. In Access, you can create an input mask for a field by using the **Input Mask Wizard**, which guides you through the necessary steps for creating an input mask and lets you enter sample values to ensure the correct results.

Don changes to Design view for tblCustomer, selects the Phone field in the design grid, and then clicks the Input Mask text box in the Field Properties pane. To create an input mask, Don can type it directly into the Input Mask text box, or he can click the Build button [...] that appears on the right side of the Input Mask text box when he clicks the text box. Because using the Input Mask Wizard is easier, he clicks the [...] button, clicks the Yes button to save the table design, and starts the wizard. Don selects the option to format the phone numbers in the format (970) 644-1214; selects the default placeholder character of an underscore, which appears when the user is entering a value into this field in Datasheet view; and then selects the option so users enter only the value into the field and not the literal characters. Figure 2.20 shows the input mask that the Input Mask Wizard created for the Phone field.

Figure 2.20: Input mask created for the Phone field

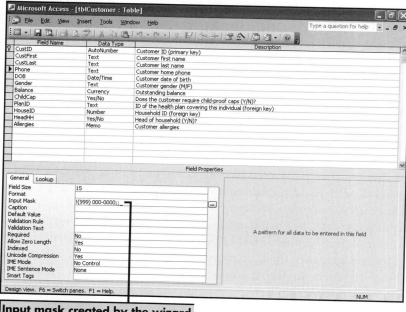

Input mask created by the wizard

Table 2.1 lists some characters that you can use in an input mask and explains their meanings.

Table 2.1: Input mask characters and descriptions

Character	Description
0	Required entry of a digit from 0 to 9
9	Optional entry of a digit from 0 to 9 or a space
L	Letter entry required
?	Letter entry optional
>	Entry that converts all characters following the > to uppercase
!	Entry that causes characters entered into the input mask to fill from right to left rather than from left to right

The input mask shown in Figure 2.20 includes other characters that indicate how to store the input mask in the table, how to display the input mask when a user is entering a value into it, and the identification of literal characters. The two semicolons (;;) near the end of the input mask specify not to store the literal characters in the input mask in the database. Other possible values for storing literal characters are ;1; (do not store literal characters) and ;0; (store the literal characters). Literal characters are generally not stored with the data and are used only to enhance the readability of the information. However, they should be stored if they are an essential part of the data.

The underscore at the end of the input mask specifies to use an underscore when the user is entering a value into the input mask to indicate the current character and total number of characters that the user must enter. Other possible values for the placeholder are #, @, !, $, %, and *. Other characters in the input mask, such as backslashes, quotation marks, and spaces, indicate the literal characters displayed by the input mask.

Because customers can live in multiple states and have different area codes, Don wants to ensure that employees always enter the customer's seven-digit phone number and the three-digit area code. To ensure this data entry, Don changes the 999 in the input mask, which specifies an optional data entry, to 000, which ensures that employees must enter the area code.

How To

Create an Input Mask Using the Input Mask Wizard

1. Click the field in Design view for which you want to create the input mask, click the Input Mask text box in the Field Properties pane, and then click the Build button [...] that appears to the right of the Input Mask text box to start the Input Mask Wizard. See Figure 2.21.

Figure 2.21: Input Mask Wizard

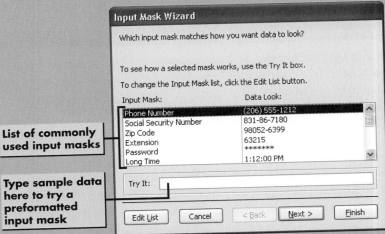

2. Select the input mask that is best suited for the field, use the Try It text box if necessary to test the input mask using your own data, and then click the Next button.
3. If necessary, change the input mask shown in the Input Mask text box and change the placeholder character to use. (*Note:* You do not need to add quotation marks, semicolons, or backslashes to the input mask at this time; Access adds them for you.) If necessary, use the Try It text box to test the revised input mask using your own data, and then click the Next button.
4. If necessary, choose the option that specifies how you want to store literal characters, and then click the Next button.

5. Click the Finish button.

6. Click any other text box in the Field Properties pane to display the completed input mask, and then save the table design.

2

Now users must enter 10 digits in the Phone field; the input mask rejects attempts to store letters, symbols, and incomplete phone numbers. In addition, the input mask does not store the literal characters, which results in the phone numbers being stored using less space in the database.

To ensure that customers' birth dates are formatted consistently and entered properly, Don uses the Input Mask Wizard to create an input mask for the DOB field so that it only accepts digits and displays slashes and four-digit years. The input mask he created for the DOB field is 00/00/0000;;_. This input mask accepts only digits, does not display the literal characters, and ensures that users must enter two-digit months and dates, four-digit years, and complete dates. Because all digits are required, users must enter single-digit month abbreviations and single-digit dates using the leading zero (for example, entering "01" for January and "07" to indicate the 7th day of the month). Requiring input in this manner ensures that all digits are entered into the DOB field for each customer.

Don's next change is to prevent users from entering inaccurate data into the Gender field.

Validating Fields to Ensure Accurate and Consistent Data

Don wants to ensure that the Gender field can contain only the uppercase letter M (for male) or the uppercase letter F (for female). He defined the Gender field using the Text data type and a field size of one character. However, Don notices that a user can type any single character into that field, which could lead to incorrect data.

In Access, you can specify restrictions on the data that users can enter into a field by creating a validation rule. A **validation rule** compares the data entered by the user against one or more valid values that the database developer specified using the Validation Rule property for the field. The **Validation Rule property** specifies the valid values that users can enter into the field. If a user attempts to enter an invalid value, the **Validation Text property** for the field opens a dialog box with a predefined message that explains the valid values. For the Gender field, the only valid values are M and F. Don selects the Gender field's Validation Rule property and enters the validation rule as M or F. When he clicks another property text box, Access changes the validation rule to "M" Or "F" because the values are stored in a Text field and text values must be enclosed within quotation marks. To help users understand the valid values for the Gender field, Don clicks the Validation Text property text box, and then types "Value must be M or F." to specify the valid values. Don also uses the Input Mask property to convert all entries in this field to uppercase by entering the input mask >L. Figure 2.22 shows the completed validation rule, validation text, and input mask for the Gender field. When a user enters an m or f into the Gender field for a customer, Access stores the value as M or F. However, if a user enters any other value, Access opens a dialog box with the message specified in the Validation Text property. The user reads the message, clicks the OK button to close the dialog box, and then can enter a valid value in the Gender field and continue data entry for the customer.

Figure 2.22: Validation rule and validation text entered for the Gender field

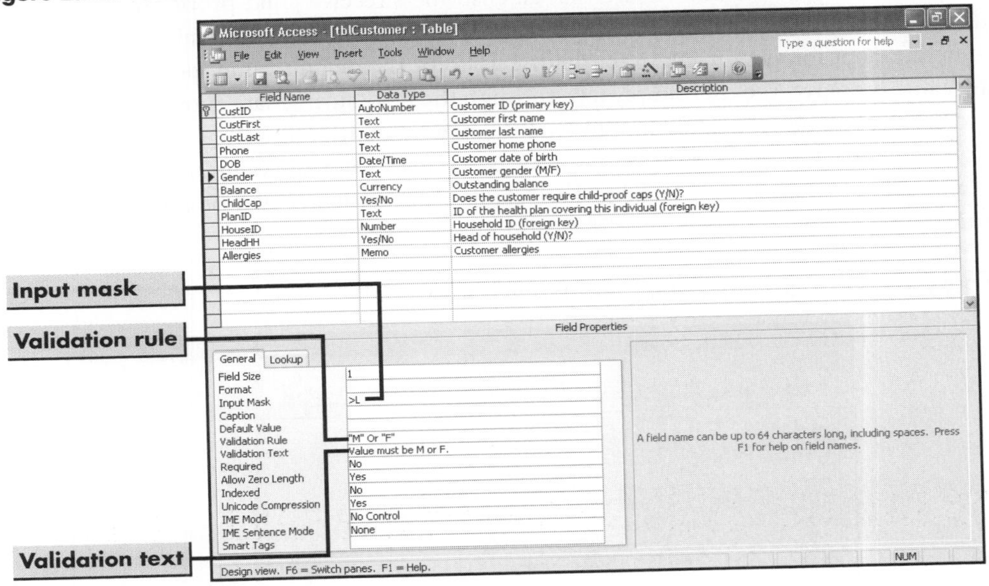

Table 2.2 describes some other validation rules and validation text that you can specify for a field. In the first example, valid values are specified using the In operator and typing valid values within parentheses and separated by commas. The second example uses "Is Not Null" to specify that the field cannot accept null values. The third and fourth examples use comparison operators to specify valid date and numeric values. (You will learn more about operators in Chapter 3.)

Table 2.2: Sample validation rules and validation text

Sample Validation Rule	Sample Validation Text
In('CO', 'AZ', 'NM', 'UT')	The state must be CO, AZ, NM, or UT.
Is Not Null	You must enter a value in this field.
>#01/01/1980#	The date must be later than January 1, 1980.
>=21 And <100	The value must be greater than or equal to 21 and less than 100.

The next item on Don's list is to implement a way to set the default value for using child-proof caps on prescription bottles to "yes."

Automating Data Entry by Using a Default Field Value

According to the pharmacy's policy, all prescriptions are dispensed with child-proof caps unless the customer requests regular caps. This means that the value of the ChildCap field should be set to "Yes" for all prescriptions and changed to "No" only when the client requests a regular cap. By specifying a default value for the ChildCap field, Don can save data-entry time for the user and ensure that all customers receive child-proof caps unless they do not want them. The **Default Value property** enters a default value into any type of field except for an AutoNumber field. To accept the default value specified in the Default Value property, the user simply tabs through the field during data entry. If the user needs to change the default value, he can type the new value. Because the ChildCap field is a Yes/No field, Don needs to specify "Yes" as the field's default value. He clicks the ChildCap field in the design grid, clicks the Default Value property text box in the Field Properties pane, and then types Yes, as shown in Figure 2.23.

Figure 2.23: Default value entered for the ChildCap field

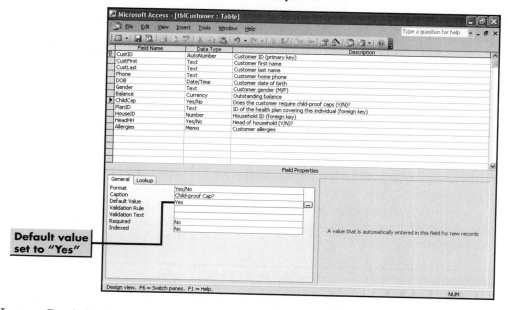

Last on Don's list is to implement a way to ensure that the health plan ID and house ID values for customers are accurate and easy to enter.

Automating Data Entry by Using a Lookup Field

As Don was entering the first record in tblCustomer, he realized that it would be possible for a user to enter a plan ID number for the customer's health plan that is not in tblHealthPlan. He also realized that the user would need a separate method to determine whether the customer belongs to an existing household in the database. Don can solve both of these problems by creating a **lookup field**, which lets the user select a field value from a list of existing field values stored in the database or from a list of values that he specifies when he creates the lookup field. For example, instead of entering the PlanID 4983 for a customer, Don would click this PlanID from a list of PlanIDs stored in tblHealthPlan; instead of entering the HouseID 1, Don would select this household's address by matching it to a list of addresses stored in tblHousehold. Both of these changes to the table design require that the tables on which you will perform the lookup already exist. For example, if the customer resides at a new household that is not yet stored in tblHousehold, the user would need to enter the household information before entering the customer's information so that the household would already exist.

To add a lookup field to a table, you change the field's data type to Lookup Wizard, but the field still stores the data that you specified when you created the field. For the first lookup field, Don selects the PlanID field in the design grid of tblCustomer, clicks the Data Type text box list arrow, and then clicks Lookup Wizard in the menu that opens. The Lookup Wizard starts, as shown in Figure 2.24.

Figure 2.24: Using the Lookup Wizard to specify the lookup column

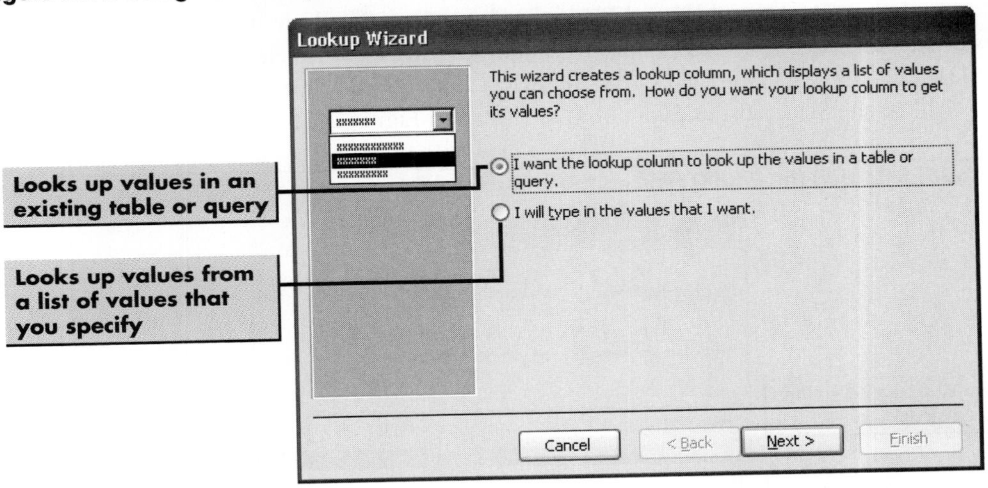

Two types of lookup fields are available. The first type lets you look up field values in another table or query; use this method when the data you want to look up already exists in the database. The second type lets you enter a list of values that you want to permit in the field; use this method when you want to supply a list of valid values for the data entered into the field that are not stored elsewhere in the database.

Don selects the option to look up the data in an existing table or query and clicks the Next button. The database contains three table objects, so he needs to select one of these tables as source of the values he wants to look up. The lookup data for the PlanID field is stored in tblHealthPlan, so he selects this table, as shown in Figure 2.25.

Figure 2.25: Selecting tblHealthPlan as the data source for the lookup field

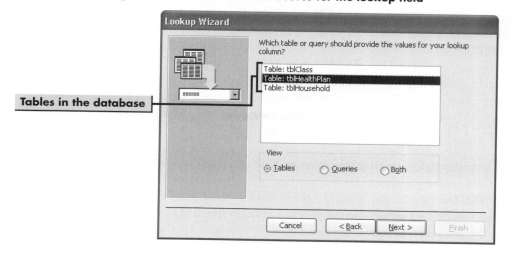

Tables in the database

Don clicks the Next button to display the next dialog box, in which he must select the field or fields in the data source (tblHealthPlan) that he wants to include in the lookup field. Don wants to display the PlanID values in the lookup field, so he selects this field in the Available Fields list box, and then clicks the Select Single Field button ⟨ > ⟩ to move the PlanID field to the Selected Fields list box, as shown in Figure 2.26.

Figure 2.26: Selecting the PlanID field as the lookup field

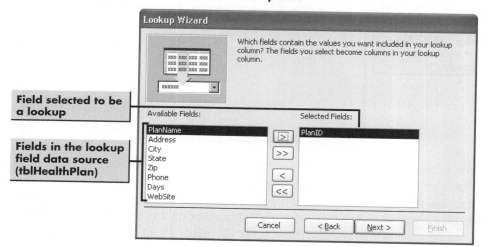

Field selected to be a lookup

Fields in the lookup field data source (tblHealthPlan)

Don could select additional fields to be displayed in the lookup column, but because he only needs to display the PlanID values, he clicks the Next button, which opens the dialog box that lets him sort the values displayed in the lookup field. Selecting a sort order is optional, but as more health plans are added to tblHealthPlan, data entry will be easier if the health plans are sorted in ascending order by PlanID. Don clicks the list arrow for the first list box, and then clicks PlanID to select this field. The button to the right of the first list box displays the label "Ascending," which indicates that the values in the lookup field will be displayed in alphabetical or numerical order. You can also display values in descending order by clicking this button, in which case it displays the label "Descending." Figure 2.27 shows the PlanID field sorted in ascending order.

Figure 2.27: PlanID sorted in ascending order

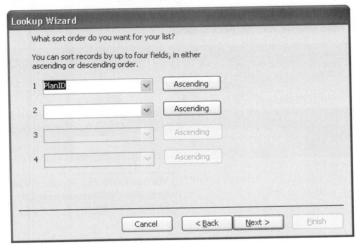

Don clicks the Next button and sees how the lookup field will display existing values in the PlanID field in tblHealthPlan. In some cases, you might need to click and drag the right side of the column to increase or decrease its width so that the data in the lookup field is displayed correctly and completely. The default field size is acceptable, as shown in Figure 2.28, so Don clicks the Next button.

Figure 2.28: Setting the lookup field size

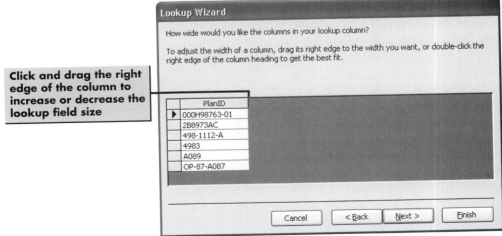

In the final dialog box, you can accept the default label for the lookup field (which is the lookup field's name) or specify a new one. Don clicks the Finish button to accept the default name, PlanID, and the Lookup Wizard closes. A dialog box opens and asks him to save the table design, and then the lookup field is created in tblCustomer. Don changes to Datasheet view for tblCustomer, and then clicks the PlanID field for the first record. The lookup field displays the PlanID values from tblHealthPlan, as shown in Figure 2.29. Now users can select the correct PlanID from this list by clicking it.

Figure 2.29: Lookup field values for the PlanID field

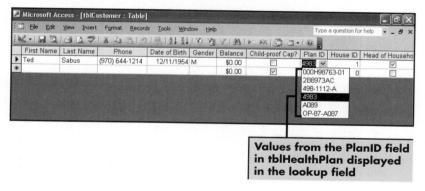

Values from the PlanID field in tblHealthPlan displayed in the lookup field

Don follows the same procedure to create a lookup field for the HouseID field in tblCustomer that displays the HouseID values from tblHousehold. However, in this case, Don wants to display two fields in the lookup field, not just one like in the PlanID field. Displaying only the HouseID field values won't provide enough information for the user entering a record in tblCustomer to determine which household to select because the HouseID stores values in the format 1, 2, 3, and so on. The user needs to enter the HouseID value from tblHousehold into the HouseID field in tblCustomer, but the user determines the correct HouseID based on the complete street address. Because households are unique, displaying the street address will be sufficient information to select the correct household for a new customer. To select more than one field's values in the lookup field, Don adds the HouseID and Address fields to the Selected Fields list box in the Lookup Wizard, as shown in Figure 2.30.

Figure 2.30: HouseID and Address fields added to the Selected Fields list box

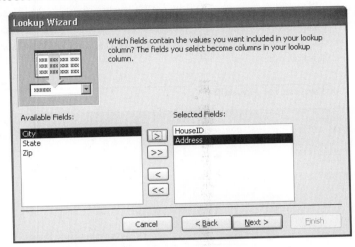

To make values easier to find, Don sorts the lookup field values in ascending order by address, and then removes the check mark from the Hide key column (recommended) check box to display the HouseID and Address values in the lookup field so users entering customer records can select the correct household using either value. Don increases the size of the Address field and decreases the size of the HouseID field so the lookup field will display the complete field values, selects the HouseID as the value to store in the HouseID field in tblCustomer (see Figure 2.31), and then accepts the default lookup field name of HouseID.

Figure 2.31: Selecting the option to store HouseID values in the HouseID field in tblCustomer

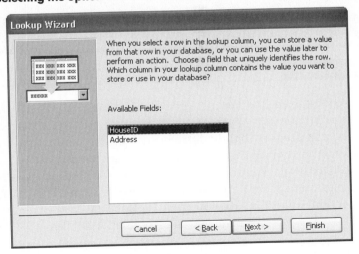

After saving tblCustomer, the lookup field will display data from the HouseID and Address fields stored in tblHousehold. Figure 2.32 shows the lookup field for the HouseID field.

To select a household for the customer, the user clicks the correct one from the list, based on a known HouseID field value or the street address. The values are sorted in ascending order by street address and users can scroll the values using the scroll bar on the lookup field. When the user selects a value in the lookup column, the HouseID value is stored in the HouseID field in tblCustomer.

Figure 2.32: Lookup field values for HouseID

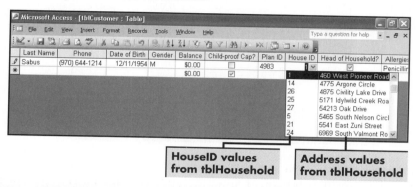

How To

Change or Delete a Lookup Field

1. In the Database window, click the Relationships button [icon] on the Database toolbar. The Relationships window opens.

2. Right-click the join line that connects the lookup field to the table in which you created it.

3. Click Delete on the shortcut menu.

4. Click the Save button [icon] on the Relationship toolbar.

5. Close the Relationships window.

6. Open the table in Design view that contains the field that you want to change to a lookup field, create the lookup field again, and then save the table design.

Steps To Success: Level 1

Don just received a request from Paul Ferrino to develop a database for a new pharmacy that Paul is opening in Edmonton, Alberta, Canada. Because the data collected about customers, employees, and drugs is slightly different in Canada, Don decides to create the databases simultaneously, but separately, so he can account for the individual differences in each version. Don wants you to create the database for Hudson Bay Pharmacy and the following tables using the information you learned in Chapter 1 and Level 1: tblClass, tblCustomer, tblHealthPlan, tblHousehold, tblJobTitle, tblDoctor, tblDrug, tblEmployee, and tblRx. (You will create the tblClinic, tblRefill, and tblEmployeeTraining tables in the Level 2 Steps To Success exercises.) Don provides you with additional information so you will know how to account for the differences in the Canadian version of the database.

Complete the following:

1. Start Access and create a new database named **Hudson.mdb** in the STS folder.

2. Use the information provided in Level 1 of this chapter to create the following tables in the database using any method you choose: tblClass, tblCustomer, tblHealthPlan, and tblHousehold. Be certain that each table includes a primary key and the necessary fields. Also, be certain to set the field properties as necessary to collect the correct data. Fields should include appropriate captions and field descriptions. These tables have the same requirements as the ones in the 4Corners database, with the following exceptions:

   a. Canadian addresses include a street address, city, province, and postal code. Provinces are abbreviated using two uppercase letters. Add properties to the Prov fields so that the data entered by the user is converted to uppercase letters. Also, make sure that users cannot enter digits or any other characters except letters into the Prov field.

   b. Postal codes in Canada have the following format: uppercase letter, number, uppercase letter, space, number, uppercase letter, number (for example, T6H 8U7). Add properties to the PostalCode fields to ensure that data entry into this field is accurate and correctly formatted.

3. Change the PlanID field in tblCustomer to a lookup field that displays the PlanID and PlanName values from tblHealthPlan but stores only the PlanID values. Sort values in ascending order by PlanID and adjust the lookup column widths as necessary to display the values that will be stored in these fields.

4. Change the HouseID field in tblCustomer to a lookup field that displays the HouseID and Address values from tblHousehold but stores only the HouseID values. Sort values in ascending order by Address.

5. Use Datasheet view and the data shown in Table 2.3 to create tblJobTitle. JobIDs are whole numbers and the Title field stores 30 characters. Use the Description property to document each field.

Table 2.3: Data for tblJobTitle

JobID	Title
1	Owner
2	Pharmacist
3	Technician
4	Cashier
5	Manager

6. Examine tblDoctor shown in Figure 2.2, and then start the Table Wizard. Use a template to create tblDoctor. DoctorID numbers are assigned sequentially by Access as you enter records into the table. The tblDoctor table is not related to any other database table yet (you will create relationships in the next level). The fields for the doctor's first name and last name should store 30 characters each. The fields that store phone numbers should store 15 characters each and format values in the following format and require entry of area codes: (###) ###-####. The ClinicID field is a foreign key to tblClinic, which you will create in the next level. (*Hint:* Create this field in Design view, and not with the Table Wizard.) Store ClinicID values as long integers. Use the Description property to document each field and enter appropriate captions to fields that require them.

7. Use Design view and the following information to create tblDrug shown in Figure 2.2. Make sure that the table includes a primary key and the necessary fields. Also, make sure that you set the field properties as necessary to collect the correct data. Fields should include appropriate captions and field descriptions.

- Canadian drugs do not have UPNs. Instead, drugs are uniquely identified using a Drug Identification Number (DIN). The DIN is a unique, eight-digit value that identifies each drug sold in Canada. DINs are not used in calculations.
- Drug names do not exceed 30 characters.
- Generic drugs are indicated by selecting a check box.
- Descriptions are alphanumeric values that might exceed 255 characters. The Description field collects data about the drug, such as counterindications, generic equivalents, and recommended dosages.
- The Unit field stores information about the unit of measure for a drug, such as pill or bottle, and requires 10 characters.
- The Dosage field stores information about the drug's strength and requires 10 characters. The Dosage field is not used in calculations.
- The DosageForm field stores information about the unit of measure for the drug strength, such as mg (for milligrams) or mcg (for micrograms). Dosage abbreviations do not exceed 20 characters.
- The Cost and Price fields store the cost and price, respectively, for one unit of the drug. The Canadian government regulates the prices that pharmacies can charge for drugs so pharmacies cover their overhead costs by charging a separate dispensing fee of $10–$12 per prescription. Dispensing fees are determined by the pharmacy and set individually for each drug.
- The Interactions field stores information about possible drug interactions and possible reactions. This field's data might exceed 255 characters.
- Canada does not track pregnancy risk categories like pharmacies in the United States.
- The Supplier field identifies the drug company or manufacturer from which a drug was purchased. Supplier names do not exceed 50 characters.

8. Use Design view and the following information to create tblEmployee shown in Figure 2.3. Make sure that the table includes a primary key and the necessary fields. Also, make sure that you set the field properties as necessary to collect the correct data. Fields should include appropriate captions and field descriptions.

   - EmpIDs are assigned by the pharmacy using unique numbers. EmpIDs will be used to relate tables in the database.
   - The EmpFirst and EmpLast fields will not exceed 30 characters each. The EmpMI field stores up to two characters.
   - Canada issues Social Insurance numbers (SINs) instead of Social Security numbers. A SIN is a nine-digit number displayed with the following format: ###-###-###.
   - The DOB (date of birth), StartDate, EndDate, and Review fields should store two-digit months and dates and four-digit years in the format ##/##/####.
   - Make sure that the table stores a province (Prov) and postal code (PostalCode) for employees instead of a state and zip code.
   - JobID is a foreign key in tblJobTitle. This field stores values as long integers.
   - The Memo field stores other information about the employee that might exceed 255 characters.
   - The Phone and Cell fields should store 15 characters in the format of (###) ###-####. Area code entry is required.
   - Employees are paid an annual salary or an hourly rate.

9. Use Design view and the following information to create tblRx shown in Figure 2.2. Make sure that the table includes a primary key and the necessary fields. Also, make sure that you set the field properties as necessary to collect the correct data. Fields should include appropriate captions and field descriptions.

   - PrescriptionIDs are assigned by Access as records are added to the table.
   - The DIN is a unique, eight-digit value that identifies each drug sold in Canada. DINs are not used in calculations.
   - The Quantity field stores the amount of medication dispensed and it is a numeric field that might contain decimal places.
   - The Unit field stores information about the unit of measure for a drug, such as pill or bottle, and requires 10 characters.
   - The Date and ExpireDate fields store the date of the prescription and the prescription's expiration date, respectively. Both fields should store two-digit months and dates and four-digit years in the format ##/##/####.
   - The Refills field indicates the number of refills authorized by the prescribing doctor.
   - The AutoRefill field indicates the customer's preference (yes or no) for automatic refills. The default value is not to order auto refills unless requested by the customer.
   - The RefillsUsed field stores the number of refills a customer has used.

- The Instructions field stores medication directions and will not exceed 50 characters.
- The CustID field is a foreign key in tblCustomer and the DoctorID field is a foreign key in tblDoctor. Both fields store numbers.

10. You will enter data into these tables and create the relationships between tables in the next level. Close the **Hudson.mdb** database and Access.

LEVEL 2

POPULATING AND RELATING THE DATABASE TABLES

ACCESS 2003 SKILLS TRAINING

- **Create a database with at least one many-to-many relationship**
- **Create a database with at least one one-to-many relationship**
- **Create a one-to-many relationship using the Relationships window**
- **Enforce referential integrity in a one-to-many relationship**
- **Import a table from another Access database**
- **Import structured data into Access tables**
- **Join a table**
- **Specify a required value**
- **Specify referential integrity options**
- **Use subdatasheets**

CREATING ADDITIONAL TABLES FOR 4CORNERS PHARMACY

While you were working on creating the database and tables for the Hudson Bay Pharmacy, Don created the tblJobTitle, tblDoctor, tblDrug, tblEmployee, and tblRx tables in the 4Corners database. The table designs and properties he used in these tables appear in Tables 2.4 through 2.8.

Table 2.4: Table design for tblJobTitle

Field Name	Data Type	Description	Field Size	Properties
JobID	Number	Job ID (primary key)	Long Integer	Caption: Job ID
Title	Text	Job title (e.g., owner, pharmacist, technician, cashier, manager)	30	

Table 2.5: Table design for tblDoctor

Field Name	Data Type	Description	Field Size	Properties
DoctorID	Number	ID of prescribing doctor (primary key)	Long Integer	Caption: Doctor ID
DoctorFirst	Text	Doctor first name	30	Caption: First Name
DoctorLast	Text	Doctor last name	30	Caption: Last Name
Phone	Text	Doctor phone number	15	Input mask: !\(000") "000\-0000;;_
Cell	Text	Doctor cell phone number	15	Input mask: !\(000") "000\-0000;;_
ClinicID	Number	Clinic ID (foreign key)	Long Integer	Caption: Clinic ID

Table 2.6: Table design for tblDrug

Field Name	Data Type	Description	Field Size	Properties
UPN	Text	Drug ID (primary key)	3	Input mask: 000
Name	Text	Drug name	30	
Generic	Yes/No	Is this the generic (Y/N)?		Caption: Generic?
Description	Memo	Description of drug, counterindications, generic equivalent, and recommended dosage		
Unit	Text	Unit of measure of drug (pill, bottle)	10	
Dosage	Text	Strength of drug (e.g., 30)	10	
DosageForm	Text	Unit of measure	20	Caption: Dosage Form
Cost	Currency	Cost per unit		
Price	Currency	Retail price per unit		
Interactions	Memo	Interactions of drugs and possible reactions		
PregCategory	Text	Pregnancy risks	1	Input mask: >L Caption: Pregnancy Category Validation rule: In ('A','B','C','D','X') Validation text: Invalid pregnancy category. Valid values are A, B, C, D, or X.
Supplier	Text	Name of drug supplier	50	

Table 2.7: Table design for tblEmployee

Field Name	Data Type	Description	Field Size	Properties
EmpID	Number	Employee ID (primary key)	Long Integer	Caption: Employee ID
EmpFirst	Text	Employee first name	30	Caption: First Name
EmpMI	Text	Employee middle initial	2	Caption: Middle Initial
EmpLast	Text	Employee last name	30	Caption: Last Name
SSN	Text	Employee Social Security number	9	Input mask: 000\-00\-0000;;_
DOB	Date/Time	Employee date of birth		Input mask: 00/00/0000;;_ Caption: Date of Birth
StartDate	Date/Time	Employee hire date		Input mask: 00/00/0000;;_ Caption: Start Date
EndDate	Date/Time	Employee termination date		Input mask: 00/00/0000;;_ Caption: End Date
Address	Text	Employee address	30	
City	Text	Employee city	30	
State	Text	Employee state	2	
Zip	Text	Employee zip code	10	
JobID	Number	Employee job ID (foreign key)	Long Integer	Caption: Job ID
Memo	Memo	Other information about the employee		
Phone	Text	Employee home phone	15	Input mask: !\(000") "000\-0000;;_
Cell	Text	Employee cell phone	15	Input mask: !\(000") "000\-0000;;_
Salary	Currency	Employee salary		
HourlyRate	Currency	Employee hourly rate (for non-salaried employees)		Caption: Hourly Rate
Review	Date/Time	Date of next review		Input mask: 00/00/0000;;_

Table 2.8: Table design for tblRx

Field Name	Data Type	Description	Field Size	Properties
PrescriptionID	AutoNumber	Prescription number (primary key)		Caption: Prescription ID
UPN	Text	Drug ID (foreign key)	3	Input mask: 000

Table 2.8: Table design for tblRx (cont.)

Field Name	Data Type	Description	Field Size	Properties
Quantity	Number	Prescription quantity	Long Integer	
Unit	Text	Unit of measure	10	
Date	Date/Time	Date prescription was written		Input mask: 00/00/0000;;_
ExpireDate	Date/Time	Date prescription expires		Input mask: 00/00/0000;;_ Caption: Expire Date
Refills	Number	Number of refills allowed	Integer	Caption: Refills Authorized
AutoRefill	Yes/No	Does customer want auto refills (Y/N)?		Caption: Auto Refill?
RefillsUsed	Number	Number of refills used	Integer	Caption: Refills Used
Instructions	Text	Instructions for prescription	50	
CustID	Number	Customer ID (foreign key)	Long Integer	Caption: Customer ID
DoctorID	Number	Doctor ID (foreign key)	Long Integer	Caption: Doctor ID

POPULATING THE DATABASE TABLES

The 4Corners database now contains nine tables. The next step is to load the tables with data, also known as populating the database. Don could enter records into each table by typing in Datasheet view. However, because much of the data he needs to load is stored in sources found during the discovery phase, Don can import this data into the tables. There are several ways to import data into a database. Don will use two of them, which include copying and pasting records from another database table and importing data from an Excel workbook.

Copying Records from One Table to Another

Before he hired Don, Paul started working on a database and entered his customer data into a Customer table. Don knows that he can import Paul's existing data into tblCustomer as long as the structures of the two tables are identical. Two tables have identical structures if they have the same number of fields and those fields have the same data types and field sizes. For example, you cannot copy the contents of a Text field with a field size of 50 into a Text field with a field size of 10, nor can you copy a Number field with the Long Integer field size into a Number field with the Byte field size. Similarly, you cannot copy Text fields into Number fields, and so on.

If tblCustomer did not already exist in the 4Corners database, Don could import Paul's table design and the data it contains in one step. When you import a table from another database, instead of just the records it contains, you have the option of importing the table's structure (called the table definition) or the table definition and the data stored in the table. You can also choose to import the relationships for the imported table.

How To

2

Level 2

Import an Existing Table into an Access Database

1. Open the database into which you will import the existing table.

2. Click File on the menu bar, point to Get External Data, and then click Import. The Import dialog box opens.

3. Use the Look in list arrow to browse to and select the database that contains the table that you want to import, and then click the Import button. The Import Objects dialog box opens.

4. Click the table that you want to import. If you want to import more than one table, press and hold the Ctrl key, click each table to import, and then release the Ctrl key.

5. Click the Options button. The Import Objects dialog box expands to include options for importing tables.

6. To import the tables and their relationships, select the Relationships check box in the Import section.

7. To import the table definition and data, click the Definition and Data option button; to import only the table definition, click the Definition Only option button.

8. Click the OK button.

Because tblCustomer already exists in the 4Corners database, Don just needs to import the data stored in Paul's table, and not the table definition. Don opens Paul's Customer.mdb database, opens the Customer table in Datasheet view, and then confirms that the structures of the two tables are exactly the same. Then he selects all of the records except for the one with CustomerID 1 because he already entered this record into the table. Don clicks the Copy button 📋 on the Table Datasheet toolbar, closes the Customer database, clicks the Yes button to keep the data he copied on the Clipboard, and then opens tblCustomer in the 4Corners database in Datasheet view. He clicks the second record in the datasheet, clicks Edit on the menu bar, and then clicks Paste Append. Don was expecting the data to appear in the tblCustomer datasheet, but instead he receives a message that the values aren't appropriate for the input mask. Don clicks the OK button in the dialog box, and then clicks the No button to cancel importing the records from the Customer database. Don opens the Customer table in the Customer database again and examines the data. He realizes that some of the values in the DOB field have only a single digit in the month value, such as the digit 4 for April instead of the digits 04. Because the input mask on the DOB field in tblCustomer requires entry of a two-digit month and date, Don must delete the input mask from the DOB field, temporarily, to be able to copy and paste the customer records. He changes to Design view for tblCustomer, selects and deletes the input mask for the DOB field, and then saves the table and changes back to Datasheet view. He clicks the second record again, and then tries to paste the copied records. This time, he is successful. A message indicates that he is going to paste 40 records, which is correct, so he clicks the Yes button. The records now appear in tblCustomer, as shown in Figure 2.33.

Figure 2.33: Imported worksheet data

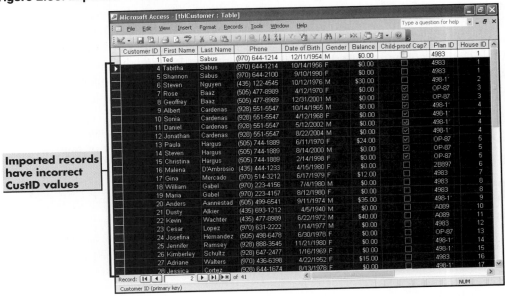

Imported records have incorrect CustID values

Don immediately sees a problem. In Paul's Customer table, the records were added to the table using sequential values with CustIDs 1 through 41. Don's examination of the data he imported shows that the records with CustIDs 2 and 3 were imported with the CustIDs 4 and 5, and the remaining records were renumbered after that. Don realizes that the AutoNumber records 2 and 3 were used when he tried to import the data and received an error message about the input mask. Once an AutoNumber record number is used, it becomes unavailable in the table, even if you delete the record. Right now, Don cannot add back or renumber the records to use CustIDs 2 and 3. Because the CustID is used as a foreign key in another table in the database, this problem will result in two orphaned records in the related table and data integrity errors on every record except the first record because the wrong customer number will exist in the related records. Don must correct this problem before continuing, or the data will not be correct.

To correct errors with AutoNumber field record numbers that should be incremented sequentially, you must delete the AutoNumber field from the table, and then add it back. If the CustID field was related to other tables in the database, Don would need to use the Relationships window to delete the relationship before he could delete the field. Because the CustID field is not yet used in any relationships, he can delete the field without making any changes in the Relationships window. Don right-clicks the CustID field in Design view, and then clicks Delete Rows on the shortcut menu. A message box opens and asks if he wants to permanently delete the selected field and its data, and he clicks the Yes button. Because CustID is the table's primary key, another message box opens asking Don to confirm the deletion, and he again clicks the Yes button. The CustID field is deleted from the table design.

To add the CustID field back to the table design, Don right-clicks the CustFirst field in the design grid, and then clicks Insert Rows on the shortcut menu. He types CustID as the field name, selects AutoNumber as the data type, and types Customer ID (primary key) as the field description. With the field selected, he clicks the Primary Key button 🔑 on the Table Design toolbar to make this field the table's primary key, and then saves the table design. When he changes to Datasheet view, the numbers are listed in sequential order from 1 to 41, which matches the original numbering in Paul's Customer table.

Don returns to Design view, adds the input mask back to the DOB field, and saves the table design. The tblCustomer table is now populated with data that will not cause any referential integrity problems later.

Best Practice

Importing Records with AutoNumber Fields into a Table

When you import data from another database into a table that contains an AutoNumber field, you should be aware of two potential problems.

First, when you use an AutoNumber field to create primary key values in a table, Access uses each incremented value only once. For example, if you delete a record with the value 11 in an AutoNumber field, record 11 is deleted permanently from the table. To the user, record 11 does not exist after you delete it, and there is no way to reenter a record with that AutoNumber value. However, if you import data into another table that also contains an AutoNumber field, Access creates a record 11 in the new table because AutoNumber 11 is an available record number in the *new* table. This difference can cause problems when the AutoNumber field has matching foreign key values with referential integrity enforced in the relationship. In this case, record 11 does *not* exist in the primary table. However, when you import the data into a new table, record 11 *does* exist, and all subsequently imported records are renumbered. If you try to relate data using the AutoNumber field, the foreign key values in the related table might not match.

Second, after importing data into a new or existing table, you cannot change a field's data type to AutoNumber because Access will not create AutoNumber values in a table that contains data. You can use a Number data type and the Long Integer data type to relate the field to an AutoNumber field, but you cannot create AutoNumber values in a table that contains imported or other existing data. If your table design includes an AutoNumber field, create the table structure prior to importing data into it so you can keep the AutoNumber field.

Importing Data from an Excel Workbook

In some cases, you might need to import data stored in an Excel workbook into a table. If you have not yet created the table in the database, you can import the data and create the table at the same time. In the discovery phase, Don received some Excel files from Paul containing data that he needs to store in the database. One of those files, Clinic.xls, contains data about the clinics that employ the doctors who write prescriptions for 4Corners Pharmacy customers. Don decides to create tblClinic by importing the data from the Excel file.

When you import data stored in an Excel workbook into a database, you need to review the contents of the workbook to understand how it is arranged. In most worksheets, the first row of data contains column headings that define the data in each column. If the column heading names comply with the rules for naming fields in Access, Access uses them as field names when you import the data. Figure 2.34 shows the Clinic.xls workbook in Excel. Paul inserted column headings that are valid Access field names, so these column headings will become the field names in tblClinic. If Don wanted to change any existing column headings to different names or to make them comply with the field naming rules in Access, he would make these changes in the worksheet before importing the data into Access.

Figure 2.34: Clinic worksheet data in Excel

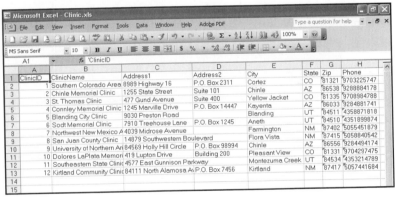

If the worksheet does not contain any column headings, or if the existing column headings violate Access field naming rules, Access assigns generic field names.

Access can import most data from a worksheet, with a few exceptions. It cannot import graphics, such as chart objects. Cells that contain formulas are imported as numbers, without the formulas, and hyperlinks are imported as text data. Access automatically assigns a data type to each column of data it imports by evaluating the data in the first 25 rows of the worksheet. For example, if the data in a column contains text values, Access assigns the Text data type to the field.

Access imports data in columns exactly as they are arranged in the worksheet. If you want to arrange the fields in a different way, you can rearrange the columns in the worksheet to meet your requirements. For example, the worksheet might list a customer's last name first. If you want the database to organize the fields so that the customer's first name comes first, you would need to move the FirstName column in the worksheet so it appears to the left of the LastName column. However, after importing the data, you can always rearrange the fields in the design grid of Table Design view like you would for any other table.

You can use Access to import specific data saved in a workbook. In most cases, you will import the data stored in a single worksheet, but you can also import named ranges of data. For example, if you only want to import the records in the range A2:H3 of the Clinic worksheet, you could specify a name for this range in the worksheet and specify it when you import the data, and Access would import the column headings as field names and the data in rows 2 and 3 and columns A through H of the worksheet.

After examining the worksheet, Don determines that it is properly organized with appropriate field names. He closes the workbook, clicks File on the menu bar in the Access Database window, points to Get External Data, and then clicks Import. The Import dialog box opens. Don selects the folder or drive that contains the workbook, changes the Files of type list arrow to display Microsoft Excel files, and then double-clicks Clinic.xls to select it and to start the Import Spreadsheet Wizard shown in Figure 2.35.

Figure 2.35: Import Spreadsheet Wizard

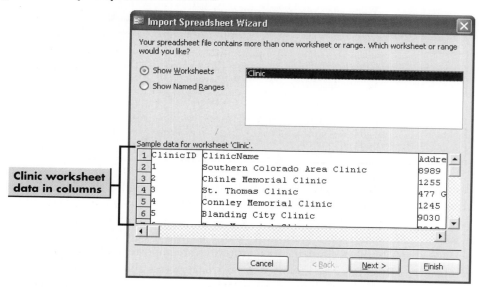

Don wants to import the data stored in the Clinic worksheet, which is the selected option. (If the workbook contained other worksheets, they would be listed in the list box.) If Don wants to select a named range in the worksheet, he would click the Show Named Ranges option button to display the ranges. Don clicks the Next button to accept these settings, and the second dialog box opens, as shown in Figure 2.36.

Figure 2.36: Identifying column headings in the worksheet

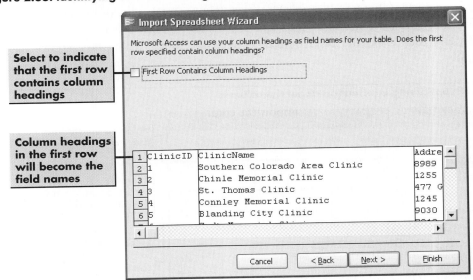

In this dialog box, you specify whether the first row of the worksheet contains column headings. Don selects the First Row Contains Column Headings check box to select it, indicating that the data in the first row should become the field names in the imported table. He clicks the Next button, which opens the third dialog box, shown in Figure 2.37.

Figure 2.37: Choosing the location for the imported data

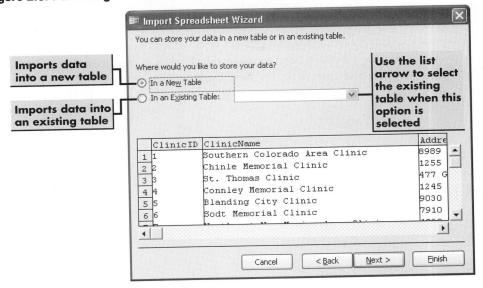

In this dialog box, you must choose the location to store the imported data. You can store it in a new table (the default option) or in an existing database table, in which case you must specify the table name. Don accepts the default option to store the data in a new table, and then clicks the Next button to open the fourth dialog box, shown in Figure 2.38.

Figure 2.38: Specifying information about the columns

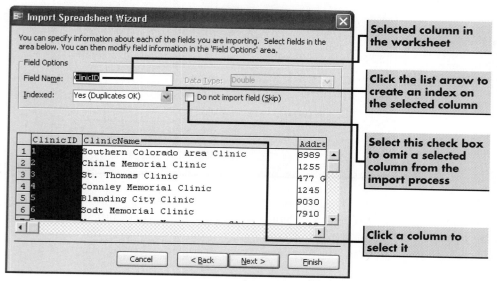

In this dialog box, you can change the default field names and indexing requirements for each field by selecting the field in the table. (Use the scroll bars to examine fields to the right and below the default values.) If the worksheet from which you are importing data is set up correctly, you usually will not need to make any changes in this dialog box. Don accepts the default settings, and then clicks the Next button to open the fifth dialog box, shown in Figure 2.39.

Figure 2.39: Setting a primary key field

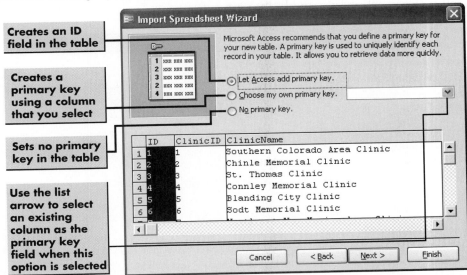

In this dialog box, you can choose a primary key field from the existing worksheet columns, let Access select a primary key (by adding an AutoNumber field to the imported table), or specify that the data contains no primary key. The default option adds an ID field to the table design. Because the worksheet already contains unique values in the ClinicID field, Don clicks the Choose my own primary key option button, and then selects ClinicID using the list box to the right of this option button. He clicks the Next button to open the final dialog box, changes the table name to tblClinic, and then clicks the Finish button. Access creates tblClinic in the 4Corners database and loads it with data. Don clicks the OK button to close the dialog box that opens to tell him that the data was imported, and then the Import Spreadsheet Wizard closes.

Don could use tblClinic as it contains a valid table structure and data. However, the table design that Access created from the imported data most likely does not match the exact table design that Don prepared for this table. To finish creating the table, Don opens tblClinic in Design view so he can verify the field properties for each field in the table and make any necessary changes. The first field, ClinicID, has the Number data type, which is correct. All of the other fields are Text fields, but Access set their field sizes to 255 characters. Because Don knows that the Text field sizes are too long, he changes the field sizes to match his table design. In addition, he adds field descriptions to all fields, captions to the ClinicID, ClinicName, Address1, and Address2 fields, and an input mask to the Phone field. If the table needs to contain any foreign keys, Don would need to add those fields to the table design. He saves the table and closes it. Because he decreased the field sizes for all of the Text fields, a dialog box opens and warns him about potential data loss in one or more fields. Don clicks the Yes button to finish saving the table, knowing that none of the existing data will be truncated by the new field sizes.

Don uses the Import Spreadsheet Wizard to import the existing data into tblDoctor, tblDrug, tblEmployee, tblJobTitle, and tblRx.

How To

Import Spreadsheet Data into an Existing Table

1. Create and save the table in Access, and then close it.

2. Examine the source data and make sure that the columns are arranged in the same order as the fields in the table, make any necessary changes, and then close the spreadsheet file.

3. In the Access Database window, click File on the menu bar, point to Get External Data, and then click Import. The Import dialog box opens.

4. Browse to the folder or drive that contains the file to import, change the Files of type list arrow to find the source data, select the source file, and then click the Import button. The Import Spreadsheet Wizard opens.

5. If necessary, select the worksheet or named range that contains the data to import, and then click the Next button.

6. If necessary, click the First Row Contains Column Headings check box to indicate that the first row in the source file contains headings, and then click the Next button.

7. Click the In an Existing Table option button, click the list arrow, click the table into which to import the data, and then click the Next button.

8. Click the Finish button.

9. Click the OK button to close the wizard.

WORKING WITH PRIMARY AND FOREIGN KEYS

Don's table designs include primary key fields that will contain values that uniquely identify each record in the tables. The table designs also include foreign key fields as necessary to join tables to each other to create the relationships in the database. A primary key and its foreign key counterparts must have the same data type and field size and the fields must contain identical values—you cannot relate fields that have different data types, field sizes, and values. Also, if referential integrity is set, a primary key value must exist before entering a corresponding record. For example, you must enter a new household into tblHousehold before you can add a new customer who lives in that household to tblCustomer.

The primary objective of creating a primary key field in a table is to prevent users from entering duplicate records into the table, but it also has other advantages. When a field has no value—a value that is unknown or unavailable or just missing—it is called a **null value**. A user cannot enter a null value into a primary key field because the primary key field is *required* for data entry and *cannot* store a null value. For example, if a user enters a drug into tblDrug but does not specify a UPN field value, Access has no way to uniquely identify each record in tblDrug. However, in some cases, you might want nonprimary key fields to store null values. For example, in tblDrug, the PregCategory field indicates the risk of using the drug during pregnancy; "A" indicates safe usage and "X" indicates a strong likelihood that the drug will cause birth defects. Most drug manufacturers assess their products for risk during pregnancy, but some drugs have unknown drug risks. In this case, the pharmacist doesn't enter a value in the PregCategory field—the risk is simply unknown.

You don't need to specify that primary key values are required in a table; this occurs automatically by setting a field as a table's primary key. By default, nonprimary key fields can store null values. You can, however, use the **Required property** for a nonprimary key field to ensure that users enter a value into the field. For example, Don could set the CustFirst and CustLast fields in tblCustomer so that users must enter values into these fields to add a customer's record to the table. To set the Required property, select the field in Design view and then change its value in the Required property text box from "No" to "Yes" (without the quotation marks). You must be careful about requiring data entry into a field, however. What if you require data entry in the Address field, but the customer has just moved and doesn't yet have an address to give? If you require data entry in the Address field, you cannot enter the customer's information in tblCustomer.

The primary key field also works to make data retrieval faster. When you specify a field as a table's primary key, Access creates an index for the primary key field. An index in a database is similar to an index that you find in a published book. When you need to find a specific topic in a book, you can find the topic in the book's index and obtain a list of the page numbers on which the topic appears so you can find them quickly. In a database, an **index** is a list maintained by the database (but hidden from users) that associates the field values in the indexed field with the records that contain the field values. You might think of a database index as a small table containing values from a table and record numbers that reference those values. An index does not contain an entire record—it only contains the field from the record and a pointer to the record number.

As the pharmacy grows, more records will be added to the tables and additional tables might be added to the database structure. As the number of records and the complexity of the database increases, the efficiency of the database will decrease. Don knows that employees will use certain tables and fields more often than others. For example, the pharmacy staff will use tblCustomer on a regular basis to manage data about the pharmacy's customers. In the first year alone, tblCustomer might grow in size to include thousands of records. Don also knows that the data in tblCustomer will be used many times by other tables, queries, and reports. Don decides to change the table structure to increase the performance of tblCustomer, which, in turn, will increase the speed of the entire database.

Creating an Index

Don anticipates that the pharmacy staff might need to search tblCustomer frequently to find customers by using their last names. To increase the speed at which Access searches tblCustomer, Don can create an index on the CustLast field. To create an index in a table, open the table in Design view, select the field to index, and then click the Indexed property. You can create an index for any field, except for fields with the Memo, Hyperlink, and OLE

Object data types. When you click the Indexed property for a field, three options appear in a menu, as shown in Figure 2.40.

Figure 2.40: Creating an index for a nonprimary key field

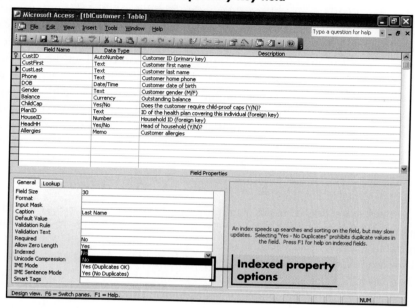

The first option, which is the default option for nonprimary key fields, is "No." The No option means that there is no index for the field. The second option, "Yes (Duplicates OK)," creates an index for the field that accepts and stores duplicate values. Because it is likely that some customers of the pharmacy will have the same last names, using the Yes (Duplicates OK) option permits users to enter duplicate last names into this field. The third option is "Yes (No Duplicates)," which is the default option for primary key fields. You can set this option for nonprimary key fields to control data entry. For example, because U.S. citizens have unique Social Security numbers, two employees in tblEmployee cannot have duplicate Social Security numbers. By setting the SSN field to Yes (No Duplicates), Access prevents duplicate values from being stored in the SSN field.

To view the indexes created in a table, click the Indexes button 📊 on the Table Design toolbar. Figure 2.41 shows the Indexes window for tblCustomer. There are five indexes in this table—two for CustID (the table's primary key), one each for the HouseID and PlanID fields, which are foreign keys, and the one Don just set for the CustLast field. You can add indexes to the Indexes window by typing an index name, field name, and the sort order. You can delete an index by right-clicking the index name, and then clicking Delete Rows on the shortcut menu.

Figure 2.41: Indexes window for tblCustomer

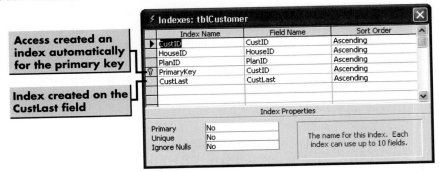

Don can create indexes for as many fields as necessary to optimize searches in the database. When you create an index, the records are indexed when you save the table. The index is updated automatically as records are added, deleted, or changed in the table. If you specify a sort order for an index (the default sort order is ascending), the records are sorted as well. In a small database, you might not notice the time and computer resources required to sort records using an index. However, as the database grows, the indexes might slow down the database and make searching take longer. Another disadvantage of creating an index on a nonprimary key field is that it increases the size of the database and slows down the database because it must update the index as users add, change, and delete records. To overcome these drawbacks, you can add indexes as needed when improved performance is necessary, and delete indexes to increase speed and reduce file size. For example, Don could add an index prior to running a query or report and then remove the index to reduce the size of the database and to improve efficiency when updating.

CREATING ONE-TO-MANY RELATIONSHIPS BETWEEN TABLES

In Chapter 1, you learned how to relate tables in a database using primary key and foreign key fields. In Access, you define table relationships in the Relationships window or when you create a lookup field that searches the records in another table. To open the Relationships window, click the Relationships button [×] on the Database toolbar in the Database window. Figure 2.42 shows the Relationships window for the 4Corners database.

Figure 2.42: Relationships window

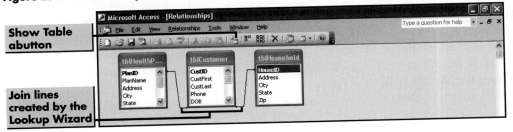

The Relationships window contains the field lists for three tables—tblHealthPlan, tblCustomer, and tblHousehold. Don can use the mouse pointer to resize the field lists to display all of the fields in each table. He can also drag the field lists to new positions to better illustrate the relationships. Because Don created lookup fields in tblCustomer to look up fields in tblHealthPlan and tblHousehold, there are two existing relationships in the database. These relationships appear as join lines that connect the tables to each other. The other tables in the database do not appear in the Relationships window because they do not contain any lookup fields and also because Don has not added them to the window yet.

You learned in Chapter 1 that a relationship has certain properties associated with it. The relationship has a certain type, such as one-to-many, one-to-one, or many-to-many, and certain attributes that specify how to manage changes when records are updated or deleted. To view the properties for a relationship, you can right-click the join line, and then click Edit Relationship on the shortcut menu. Don right-clicks the join line between tblHealthPlan and tblCustomer and opens the Edit Relationships dialog box shown in Figure 2.43.

Figure 2.43: Edit Relationships dialog box

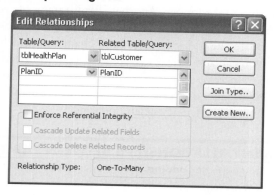

The Edit Relationships dialog box shows the relationship between the primary table tblHealthPlan and the related table tblCustomer, which resulted when Don created the lookup field for PlanID. The relationship type, one-to-many, indicates that one PlanID in the primary table is related to zero, one, or many PlanIDs in the related table (tblCustomer). Don enforces this rule by clicking the Enforce Referential Integrity check box to add a check mark to it. Because a PlanID value in tblHealthPlan might change as a result of a new plan number from an insurance company, Don needs to make sure that changes to the PlanIDs in tblHealthPlan are updated in the related records, so he clicks the Cascade Update Related Fields check box to select it. Don does not, however, want to delete all related records if a PlanID is deleted from tblHealthPlan, so he does not select the Cascade Delete Related Fields check box. After making these changes, Don clicks the OK button to make the changes, and then he clicks the Save button 🖫 on the Relationship toolbar to save the changes in the database. The Relationships window shows a one-to-many relationship between the PlanID field in tblHealthPlan to the PlanID field in tblCustomer. A "1" appears on the "one" side of the relationship and an infinity symbol appears on the "many" side of the relationship. Don edits the relationship created by the lookup field between tblHousehold and tblCustomer to enforce referential integrity and cascade updates as well. The Relationships window appears in Figure 2.44.

Figure 2.44: Relationships window after creating two 1:M relationships

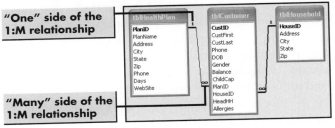

Now Don needs to add the remaining tables to the Relationships window and create the relationships between the appropriate tables using his database design. He clicks the Show Table button on the Relationship toolbar to open the Show Table dialog box, clicks tblClass in the Tables list, and then clicks the Add button. The tblClass table is added to the Relationships window. He repeats this process to add tblClinic, tblDoctor, tblDrug, tblEmployee, tblJobTitle, and tblRx to the Relationships window, and then clicks the Close button to close the Show Table dialog box. He resizes the field lists to display all fields in each new table and rearranges the field lists so that related tables are next to each other, as shown in Figure 2.45, to make it easier to create the relationships. Notice that the primary key fields in each table appear in bold type, making it easy to identify the primary key in each table.

Figure 2.45: Relationships window after adding, resizing, and repositioning the database tables

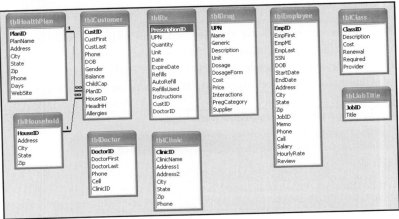

Now Don can start creating the relationships between tables. The first one that Don creates is the one-to-many relationship between tblDoctor and tblRx. A primary key field and the corresponding foreign key field are not required to have the same field name, but the values in the primary key and foreign key fields must match exactly to create the relationship. You can create the relationships by dragging the primary key field from the primary table to the foreign key field in the related table. When you release the mouse button, the Edit Relationships dialog box opens, into which you specify the relationship properties. Don drags the DoctorID field from tblDoctor to the DoctorID field in tblRx, and then releases the mouse button. The Edit Relationships dialog box opens, and he clicks the check boxes to enforce referential integrity and cascade update related fields. After clicking the Create button, the one-to-many relationship between doctors and prescriptions is created. Don also creates the one-to-many relationships between the tblJobTitle and tblEmployee tables, between the tblDrug and tblRx tables, and between the tblCustomer and tblRx tables and then selects the options to enforce referential integrity and cascade update related fields. The Relationships window now looks like Figure 2.46.

Figure 2.46: Relationships window after creating 1:M relationships

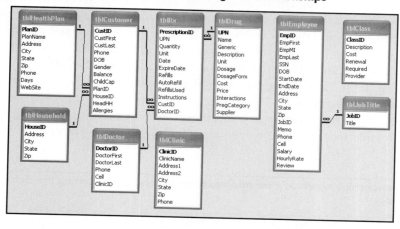

Don sees that he has not yet related the tblClinic and tblDoctor tables. He drags the ClinicID field from tblClinic to the ClinicID field in tblDoctor, and selects the options to enforce referential integrity and to cascade updates. This time, however, instead of creating the one-to-many relationship, Don sees the error message shown in Figure 2.47.

Figure 2.47: Error message about mismatched data types

Don knows that this error message indicates that he is trying to join tables with fields that do not have the same data type or field size. He clicks the OK button to close the message box, clicks the Cancel button to close the Edit Relationships dialog box, and then saves the Relationships window and closes it. He opens tblClinic in Design view and sees that the primary key field, ClinicID, has the Number data type and the Double field size. He then remembers how this problem occurred—when he created the table by importing data, Access assigned this field a data type and field size based on the data he imported. He accepted the default field size, Double, and saved the table. However, the ClinicID field in tblDoctor uses the Long Integer field size. The different field sizes caused the error message, so Don changes the field size of ClinicID field in tblClinic to Long Integer, saves tblClinic, clicks Yes in the message box informing him that some data might be lost, and then returns to the Relationships window. This time, he is able to create the one-to-many relationship between tblClinic and tblDoctor, as shown in Figure 2.48.

Figure 2.48: Relationships window with 1:M relationships created

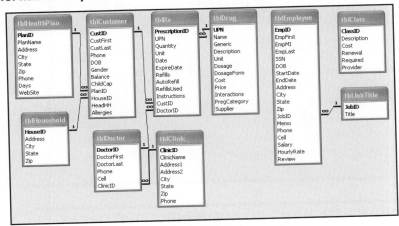

Don looks at the Relationships window and sees that he has no way to relate employees to the classes they take, because there are no common fields between tblEmployee and tblClass. To create this relationship, he needs to create another table in the database that he can use to create a many-to-many relationship.

Best Practice

Troubleshooting Referential Integrity Errors
Relating tables in the Relationships window is usually a smooth process, but you might encounter a few potential problems, especially when you have imported existing table designs and data into your database.

Figure 2.47 showed the error message that opens when the values in the primary key and foreign key fields do not match. This error usually means that you are attempting to relate fields with dissimilar data types or field sizes. This error is common when relating Number and Text fields with different field sizes. If you get this error, open the primary table and the related table in Design view and then compare the primary key and foreign key fields, and change one or both fields so the data types and field sizes match.

Figure 2.49 shows another error that you might see when attempting to relate tables in the Relationships window. In this case, Access cannot create the relationship because it would create orphaned records in the primary or related table.

Figure 2.49: Error message about referential integrity violation

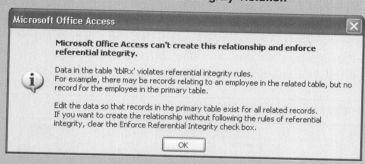

If you receive this error message, it is more difficult to correct the problem because you must compare the primary key values in the primary table to the foreign key values in the related table and identify values in the first table that do not match the second table. To enforce referential integrity and create the relationship, there must be a primary key value in the primary table for every foreign key value in the related table. Correcting this error usually involves adding a missing record to the primary table that matches an existing record in the related table.

CREATING A MANY-TO-MANY RELATIONSHIP BETWEEN TABLES

Don's database design includes creating tblEmployeeTraining, which is a junction table to create the many-to-many relationship between employees and classes. Don creates this table in Design view, as shown in Figure 2.50. Notice that the primary key of tblEmployeeTraining is the combination of all three fields in the table.

Figure 2.50: Table design for tblEmployeeTraining

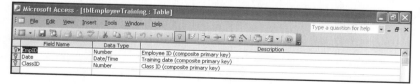

How To

Create a Composite Primary Key

1. In Design view, click in the row for the first field that will become the composite key.

2. Press and hold the Ctrl key, and then click the second field that will become the composite key. If necessary, continue holding the Ctrl key and click any other fields that will become the composite key.

3. When all fields in the composite key are selected, release the Ctrl key.

4. Click the Primary Key button 🔑 on the Table Design toolbar.

5. Save the table.

An employee can take any class on any date—the combination of the EmpID, Date, and ClassID creates a unique record in this table. Don adds tblEmployeeTraining to the Relationships window, and rearranges the field lists so he can see all of the fields in each table and so that related tables are arranged next to each other. To create the many-to-many relationship between employees and classes, he starts by creating the one-to-many relationship between tblClass and tblEmployeeTraining and enforces referential integrity and cascades updates. Then he creates the one-to-many relationship between tblEmployee and tblEmployeeTraining. The result is a many-to-many relationship between employees and classes, as shown in Figure 2.51.

Figure 2.51: Relationships window after creating an M:N relationship

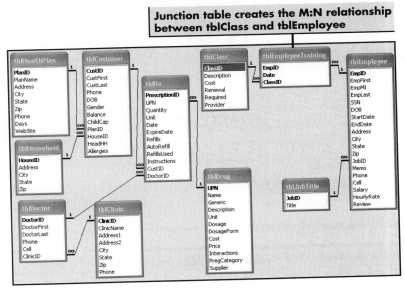

Don needs to add one more table to the database, tblRefill, which will store data about prescription refills, the customers who request them, and the employees who fill them. He returns to Design view and creates tblRefill, as shown in Figure 2.52.

Figure 2.52: Table design for tblRefill

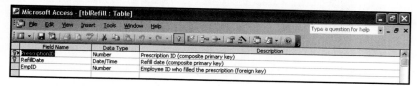

After creating and saving tblRefill, Don adds it to the Relationships window and creates the one-to-many relationship between tblRx and tblRefill and the one-to-many relationship between tblEmployee and tblRefill. Now there is a many-to-many relationship between employees and prescriptions. The final Relationships window appears in Figure 2.53.

Figure 2.53: Completed Relationships window

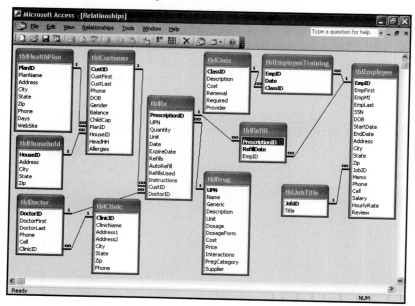

Now that Don has created all of the relationships in the database, he imports the existing data he has from the discovery phase into tblEmployeeTraining and tblRefill. The database is now fully populated.

USING A SUBDATASHEET TO VIEW RELATED RECORDS

After importing data into a database, it is a good idea to open each table in Datasheet view and check the data for any problems. Don checks each table, including tblHousehold, by opening it in Datasheet view. Because of the relationship Don created between the tblHousehold and tblCustomer tables, a plus box ⊞ appears to the left of the HouseID value in each record. He clicks the plus box in the first record, which opens the subdatasheet shown in Figure 2.54.

Figure 2.54: Customer data shown in a subdatasheet

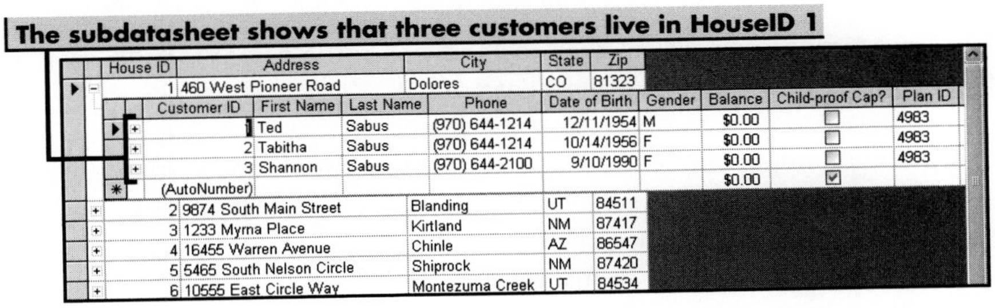

The subdatasheet shows that three customers live in HouseID 1

House ID	Address		City	State	Zip					
1	460 West Pioneer Road		Dolores	CO	81323					
	Customer ID	First Name	Last Name	Phone	Date of Birth	Gender	Balance	Child-proof Cap?	Plan ID	
	1	Ted	Sabus	(970) 644-1214	12/11/1954	M	$0.00	☐	4983	
	2	Tabitha	Sabus	(970) 644-1214	10/14/1956	F	$0.00	☐	4983	
	3	Shannon	Sabus	(970) 644-2100	9/10/1990	F	$0.00	☐	4983	
	(AutoNumber)						$0.00	☑		
2	9874 South Main Street		Blanding	UT	84511					
3	1233 Myrna Place		Kirtland	NM	87417					
4	16455 Warren Avenue		Chinle	AZ	86547					
5	5465 South Nelson Circle		Shiprock	NM	87420					
6	10555 East Circle Way		Montezuma Creek	UT	84534					

When Don clicks the plus box for a record in a table that has a one-to-many relationship, the **subdatasheet** displays records from the related table. In Figure 2.54, Don uses the subdatasheet to see that the customers living in HouseID 1 are Ted, Tabitha, and Shannon Sabus. You can display and hide the subdatasheet for any record in the primary table by clicking the plus box. In addition, you can use the subdatasheet to make changes to the related records, and the subdatasheet will display those changes. The changes are also made in the related table.

Steps To Success: Level 2

In the Steps To Success for Level 1, you created the database for Hudson Bay Pharmacy and created the table designs for nine tables: tblClass, tblCustomer, tblDoctor, tblDrug, tblEmployee, tblHealthPlan, tblHousehold, tblJobTitle, and tblRx. The only table that contains data at this point is tblJobTitle. Don asks you to create the remaining tables in the database (tblClinic, tblEmployeeTraining, and tblRefill) and to populate the database with data using various sources that he has provided to you. You will also need to relate the appropriate tables to each other.

Complete the following:

1. Start Access and open the **Hudson.mdb** database from the STS folder.

2. Populate the existing database tables as follows. The files you need are saved in the Chapter 2 folder.

    a. Use the file **hbpClass.xls** to populate tblClass.

    b. Use the file **hbpCust.xls** to populate tblCustomer.

    c. Use the file **hbpHhold.xls** to populate tblHousehold.

    d. Use the file **hbpHPlan.xls** to populate tblHealthPlan.

e. Use the file **hbpRx.xls** to populate tblRx.

f. Use the file **hbpDrug.xls** to populate tblDrug.

g. Use the file **hbpEmp.xls** to populate tblEmployee.

h. Copy and paste the records in the Doctor table in the **hbpDoc.mdb** database into tblDoctor in the **Hudson.mdb** database.

3. Create tblClinic by importing data from the file **hbpClin.xls**. Be certain the table meets the following requirements:

- The ClinicID field is the table's primary key.
- The ClinicName cannot exceed 50 characters.
- The Address1, Address2, and City fields cannot exceed 40 characters.
- The default value for the Prov field is "AB" and all values entered into this field must be uppercase and two characters in length.
- Values in the PostalCode field must appear in the following format: uppercase letter, number, uppercase letter, space, number, uppercase letter, number (for example, T6H 8U7).
- The Phone field stores 15 characters, displays values in the format of (###) ###-####, and area code entry is required.
- All fields must have appropriate captions and field descriptions.

4. Create tblEmployeeTraining using the following information:

- The EmpID and ClassID fields store numbers with no decimal places and are foreign keys.
- The Date field stores the date of the training session. Display the date using the format ##/##/####.
- Set the composite primary key, add captions to appropriate fields, and add appropriate field descriptions to all fields.
- Use the **hbpEmpTr.xls** file to populate the table.

5. Create tblRefill using the following information:

- The PrescriptionID and the EmpID fields store numbers with no decimal places and are foreign keys.
- The RefillDate field stores the date the prescription was refilled. Display the date using the format ##/##/####.
- Set the composite primary key, add captions to appropriate fields, and add appropriate field descriptions to all fields.
- Use the **hbpRef.xls** file to populate the table.

6. Create an index on the CustLast field in tblCustomer and on the Name field in tblDrug.

7. Create the appropriate relationships in the database.

8. Close the **Hudson.mdb** database and Access.

LEVEL 3

MAINTAINING AND SECURING A DATABASE

ACCESS 2003 SKILLS TRAINING

- **Add permissions to databases**
- **Compact on close**
- **Create a single field index**
- **Create multiple field indexes**
- **Open a database in exclusive mode**
- **Remove a password**
- **Set database encryption**
- **Set passwords for databases**
- **Use database tools to compact a database**
- **Use the Documenter**

THE DATABASE ADMINISTRATOR ROLE

The 4Corners database now contains 12 related tables that store the data needed to dispense prescriptions to customers of the pharmacy. Don populated the tables with the existing data he gathered during the discovery phase. It might be tempting to think that the database is "finished" at this point, but it is not. Don knows that there are other tasks he needs to complete before bringing the database online for users. These tasks include securing the database, backing up and restoring the database, archiving data, and compacting and repairing the database. He also needs to document the database design for himself and other database users. Collectively, these tasks are known as maintaining a database. Most organizations assign these tasks to **database administration**, also known as **DBA**. In many organizations, DBA is a group that is responsible for designing, maintaining, and securing the database. In other organizations, DBA is an individual who is charged with these tasks; sometimes, this individual is called the **database administrator**. At 4Corners Pharmacy, Don is the database administrator. The database administrator sets the security and other features of a database in addition to setting options for individual users and groups of users.

When you open an Access database, the default option is to open it so that it is available to other users should they choose to open the same database at the same time. To change the way you open a database, click the Open button 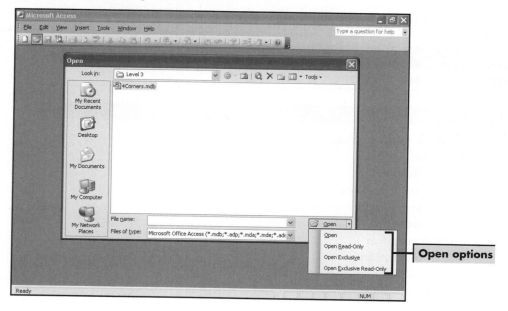 on the Database toolbar, and then click the list arrow for the Open button in the Open dialog box, as shown in Figure 2.55.

Figure 2.55: Open dialog box in Access

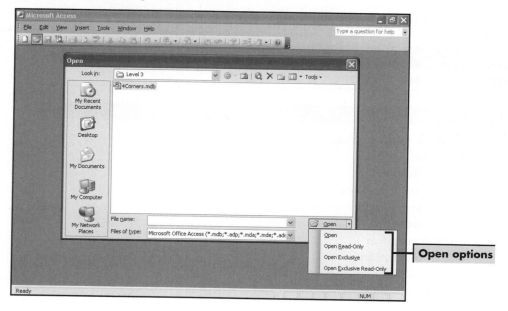

You can open an Access database in four ways:

- **Open mode** allows multiple users to open and use the database at the same time. This is the default option for opening a database.
- **Open Read-Only mode** allows multiple users to open a database, but they cannot write any information to the database, such as adding or changing records or creating new objects. Users are limited to viewing existing data only.
- **Open Exclusive mode** opens the database so that all users except for the current user are locked out from opening and using the database at the same time. A database administrator uses this option to open the database prior to setting a password or database security.
- **Open Exclusive Read-Only mode** opens the database so that all users except for the current user are locked out, but the current user can only view the data in the database.

As the database administrator, Don must open the database with exclusive access prior to performing database maintenance and security tasks to prevent other users from accessing the database while he performs this work. Don knows that there are no other users accessing the database, so he can perform some of these tasks now. He begins by opening the database in exclusive mode.

Open a Database in Exclusive Mode

1. Start Access, and then click the Open button 🗁 on the Database toolbar. The Open dialog box opens.
2. Use the Look in list arrow to browse to and select the database you want to open.
3. Click the list arrow for the Open button.
4. Click Open Exclusive.

With all other users locked out from the 4Corners database, Don can maintain the database and set the security options. First, he will compact, repair, and back up the database.

COMPACTING AND REPAIRING A DATABASE

As users work in a database by adding and deleting records and objects, the size of the database increases and decreases. However, the space created by deleting a record or object is not automatically recovered for use by records and objects that users add to the database. Just like any other computer file, a database becomes large with blocks of unused space. These unused areas can ultimately increase the database size and make it inefficient. The process of recovering unused space in a database is known as compacting the database. When you **compact** a database, the data and objects in the database are reorganized and unused spaces are reassigned and deleted. The end result is usually a database with a decreased file size and improved efficiency.

Don has two options for compacting the database. He can do it manually by clicking Tools on the menu bar in the Database window, pointing to Database Utilities, and then clicking Compact and Repair Database. Access closes the database, compacts it, and also repairs the database. When Access finishes the compact and repair utilities, it reopens the database. Don can also set the database to compact the database each time it closes by clicking Tools on the menu bar in the Database window, clicking Options, and then clicking the General tab, as shown in Figure 2.56.

Figure 2.56: Setting the Compact on Close option

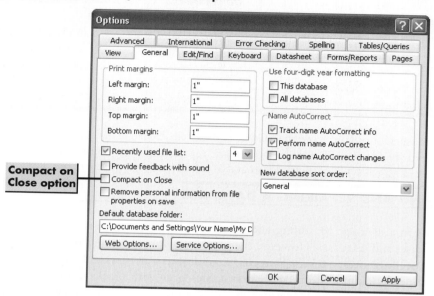

To compact the database when it closes, Don clicks the Compact on Close check box to select it. After clicking the OK button, Access compacts the database each time it is closed. However, setting the Compact on Close option does not also repair the database. Don selects the Compact on Close option, but also decides to run the Compact and Repair utility periodically to repair any problems in the database. He can also use the Compact and Repair utility any time that there is a problem in the database. Don notices that the 4Corners database was just over one megabyte in size before he compacted it manually. After compacting, the database size decreased to 432 KB, which is less than half the original size.

Don's next task is to back up the database so he has another copy of it in case of damage or loss.

Best Practice

Compacting a Database Before Backing Up a Database

Even if you have been compacting a database on a regular basis, either by running the Compact and Repair Database utility or by setting the Compact on Close option, it is a good idea to compact the database immediately prior to performing a backup. When you back up a database, any unused areas become a part of the backup file. By compacting the database first, you might reduce the size of the backup file because these unused spaces are not included in it.

BACKING UP A DATABASE

Now that Don has compacted the database, he wants to create a backup copy. **Backing up** a database creates a copy of the database that you can restore in the event of a loss. A loss might be a power failure or hard disk crash, a user who maliciously or accidentally deletes database objects, or any other situation that affects the records and objects in the database. Most database administrators perform regular database backups for each day the database is used. A good rule of thumb is to schedule database backups based on the amount of data loss that you can manage. If you cannot manage reentering all of the transactions completed in a week's time, you should schedule backups more frequently than once a week. It is not uncommon for an organization to back up a database nightly, after all users have completed their work. Don will schedule a backup of the 4Corners database at midnight each night, so that the most data the pharmacy ever risks losing is the data for one day.

After creating a backup copy of the database, it is important to store the copy in a fireproof location, preferably at a location outside the pharmacy. In most cases, a backup is created on external media, such as a CD, DVD, or external hard drive. Many organizations store multiple backup copies of their databases indexed by date at alternate facilities. For such an organization, a fire might destroy the entire building, but the organization does not lose its business data as well.

To back up the database, Don clicks Tools on the menu bar in the Database window, points to Database Utilities, and then clicks Back Up Database. The default backup database name is the original database name, followed by the current date. You can accept this default filename or create a new one. Clicking the Save button closes the database and begins the backup. Depending on the size of the database, it might take anywhere from a few minutes to several hours to complete the task. When the backup utility is complete, Access reopens the database.

The backup copy of the database is a copy that you can open just like any other Access database. In the event of loss in the master copy of the database, Don could install the backup copy. In this case, he would need to identify any changes that were made between the time of the loss in the original database and the time he installed the backup copy because the backup might not contain all of the data he needs to restore.

The next task Don wants to complete is to document the database objects so he has a record of each table, including the fields in the table and their properties.

DOCUMENTING THE DATABASE DESIGN

After finishing the initial database design, it is a good idea to document the design so you have it for future reference. In Access, the **Documenter** tool produces a report of every object or just selected objects in a database. Don wants to document all of his table designs. Because tables are the only objects in the current database, he will select the option to document every object when he runs the Documenter. To run the Documenter, Don clicks Tools on the menu bar, points to Analyze, and then clicks Documenter. The Documenter dialog box shown in Figure 2.57 opens.

Figure 2.57: Documenter dialog box

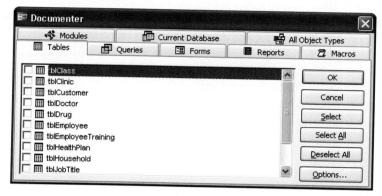

The tabs at the top of the Documenter dialog box let you sort objects by type. The All Object Types tab includes all objects in the current database. Selecting the Current Database tab lets you document the properties of objects or the relationships of objects that you select. Because the database contains only tables, Don clicks the Select All button on the Tables tab, which adds a check mark to each table's check box. Clicking the Options button opens the Print Table Definition dialog box shown in Figure 2.58.

Figure 2.58: Print Table Definition dialog box

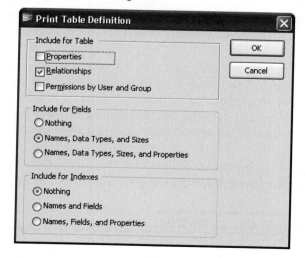

The options in the Print Table Definition dialog box let you specify what to document for each table. You can include table properties, relationships, and permissions; names, data types, field sizes, and field properties for fields; and names, fields, and properties for indexes. Don wants to include the table relationships and names, data types, and field sizes for fields, so he selects these options. When he clicks the OK button in the Documenter dialog box, Access creates an Object Definition report. The first page of this report appears in Figure 2.59.

Figure 2.59: Page 1 of the Object Definition report

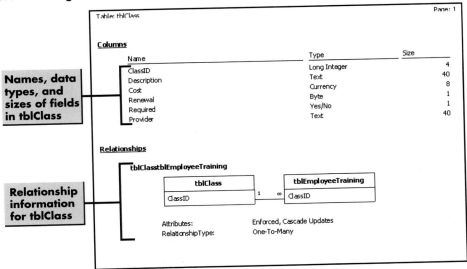

Don can use the Print button ![Print icon] on the Print Preview toolbar to print the report so he can file it away in a safe place. He can also use the Export command on the File menu to save the report as a file. If he needs to run this report again, he would need to run the Documenter again and select the desired options.

SECURING A DATABASE FROM UNAUTHORIZED USE

Even though Don will create regular backup copies of the database, it is still very important to plan for and prevent data loss in the first place. One of Don's most important tasks is to protect the database from unintentional or malicious damage. Access includes several tools that let you control access to a database. In most cases, the database administrator must open the database with exclusive access prior to setting some of the features that protect the database. These tools are setting a database password, encrypting the database, and hiding the database objects.

Using a Password to Protect a Database

Don knows that it is his job to protect the pharmacy's data, but a bigger responsibility is for the pharmacy to protect its customers' and employees' data. The 4Corners database stores personal information about customers and employees, such as Social Security numbers, phone and address information, salary data, and prescription information. The potential exists for an employee to use information in the database inappropriately or for a hacker to gain access to the database and use it in an identity theft scheme. Don knows that the pharmacy is responsible for maintaining and protecting private information and that customers must feel confident that the pharmacy is taking steps to protect their data from fraud and abuse.

The easiest way to secure a database from unauthorized use is to set a password. A **password** is a collection of characters that a user types to gain access to a file. When a database administrator sets a database password, users cannot open the database file in Access unless they provide the correct password. As long as the database administrator and users who know the password protect it from being known by unauthorized users, the password can adequately protect the database.

Don might want to set a password for the 4Corners database. The database is already open in exclusive mode, so he clicks Tools on the menu bar of the Database window, points to Security, and then clicks Set Database Password. The Set Database Password dialog box shown in Figure 2.60 opens.

Figure 2.60: Set Database Password dialog box

To set a database password, Don would type a password in the Password text box, press the Tab key, and then type the same password in the Verify text box. When he clicks the OK button, Access requests the password from the next user who attempts to open the database. If the user fails to provide the correct password in the Password Required dialog box that opens, Access does not open the database. Don can give the password to users as necessary to provide them with the ability to open the database. At this time, Don decides not to set a password until he brings the database online for employee use. The password will prevent customers and vendors who are in the store from being able to access the database. He is confident that the password will protect the pharmacy's data.

Best Practice

Choosing a Strong Password
When creating a password for a database, it is important to select a password that is easy to remember so it is easy to use. However, some users choose passwords that are easy to remember but are also very easy for another person to guess, such as the name of a

pet, child, or spouse or a date of birth or anniversary. Security experts suggest that users create **strong passwords**, which are character strings that contain at least seven characters consisting of combinations of uppercase and lowercase letters, numbers, and symbols. Random collections of characters are much harder to guess or break because the combination of characters is not a word. In any program that requests a password, choose a strong password in favor of one that is a simple word. Even if your password is 5&uJK#8, you will learn it quickly if you type it frequently.

Encrypting a Database to Prevent Unauthorized Use

Don knows that a password will provide users with the access to the database that they need and prevent unauthorized users from accessing it. However, the password won't protect the database in the event that someone steals the file and tries to open it with a program other than Access. Although an Access database is designed to be opened by the Access program, it is possible to open the database using other programs. For example, if you attempt to open an Access database in Microsoft Word, the resulting document would be difficult to read but it still might be possible to decipher some of the information stored in the database file.

One way to stop programs other than Access from opening a database file is to encrypt or encode the database. **Encrypting** a database (also known as **encoding** a database) converts the data in the database into a format that is readable only by Access. If a user tries to open the database with a word-processing program, the data will be scrambled and unintelligible. Although encrypting the database prevents other programs from opening it, the encryption is transparent to users who open the database using Access.

Don knows that it is a good idea to encrypt the database, especially when it is stored on a network, to prevent other programs from being able to access it. With the database open in exclusive mode, he clicks Tools on the menu bar, points to Security, and then clicks Encode/Decode Database. Access closes the 4Corners database, and then opens the Encode Database As dialog box. Don can use the 4Corners.mdb filename for the encrypted version of the database, in which case Access will encrypt the file and save it by overwriting the existing file. He could also choose an alternate filename for the encrypted version so that the two copies are separate. Don decides to encrypt the 4Corners database, so he clicks the database filename, and then clicks the Save button. A message box asks if he wants to replace the existing file, and he clicks the Yes button. After a few seconds, Access opens the encrypted version of the 4Corners database. The database still functions the same, although data will be encrypted as users add and update records and objects. Sometimes Access requires a lot of processing time to encrypt data as users update the database. If Don experiences performance issues as a result of the encryption, he might choose to **decrypt** (or **decode**) the database, which cancels the encryption. While the database is encrypted, if someone tries to open this file with any program besides Access, the data will be unintelligible.

Hiding Database Objects from Users

Don designed the 4Corners database so that all objects in a database are accessible to all users through the Database window. As the database administrator, Don is skilled at manipulating database objects for the benefit of users. Casual users who do not have Don's experience can damage the database by unintentionally altering an object's design or by deleting an object entirely. Another simple technique to add some security to the database is to hide objects from being displayed in the Database window. These objects are still part of the database and interact with other objects but are not visible to the casual user. The advantage of hiding objects is that the user will not be able to accidentally or intentionally damage the database. Unfortunately, revealing a hidden object is not difficult and a user who knows Access or how to use the Access Help system could learn how to reveal hidden objects.

Don might protect the data in tblEmployee, which contains employees' Social Security numbers and salary information, from being viewed by the store's staff. To hide tblEmployee, Don selects it in the Database window, and then clicks the Properties button ⬚ on the Database toolbar. The Properties dialog box for the object opens. Figure 2.61 shows the Properties dialog box for tblEmployee.

Figure 2.61: Properties dialog box for tblEmployee

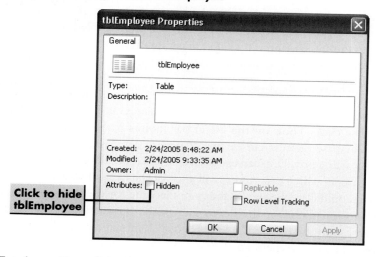

To hide tblEmployee, Don clicks the Hidden check box to select it. When he clicks the OK button, tblEmployee will not appear on the Tables object in the Database window. Maria Garcia, the pharmacy's human resources manager, will need to access this table. Don can show her how to reveal hidden objects by clicking Tools on the menu bar in the Database window, clicking Options, and then clicking the View tab in the Options dialog box. If Maria clicks the Hidden objects check box to select it, tblEmployee will be visible in the Database window again. Figure 2.62 shows tblEmployee after showing hidden objects.

Level 3

2

Figure 2.62: Database window after revealing hidden objects

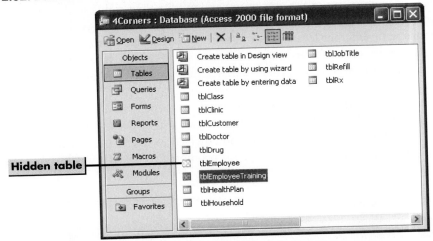

Hidden database objects remain visible unless you remove the check mark from the Hidden objects check box in the Options dialog box. To permanently restore a hidden object, open the Properties dialog box for the object, and then clear the Hidden check box.

Don decides not to hide database objects because Access has better and more secure techniques for hiding objects from users. In Chapter 6, you will learn more about hiding objects from users.

USER-LEVEL SECURITY

The methods that Don has explored thus far protect the database before it is opened and used. He also needs to protect the database while it is in use. The ideal way to protect the database is to create user-level security. **User-level security** establishes specific levels of access to the database objects for individual groups of users. Security is accomplished by setting **permissions** that specify the level of access for each user and group of users. Permissions are granted by the database administrator so that users and groups of users can create the objects, delete and change existing objects, and so on. A user's level of security depends on the access the user needs to perform his job. For example, a cashier requires a different level of access to a database than a person in a management position.

User-level security is implemented by defining groups of users, assigning permissions to groups, and then assigning individuals to those groups. Individuals access the database using passwords assigned to them by the database administrator. Access uses a **workgroup information file** to define user groups, usernames, and user passwords. The database administrator usually assigns users to groups based on their job function so that each user is granted access to the parts of the database that they need to carry out their job functions.

By default, two groups are in the workgroup information file: administrators and users. Don can alter the permissions of the user group and modify their rights so that they have viewing access to objects and have the ability to change specific settings. He can define different groups with different levels of permissions so one group can access a particular set of objects and another group can access a different set of objects. If Don requires more control over a group of users, he can create a new group and then add users to it.

To define user-level security in a database, Don needs to reopen the database with shared access and then run the Security Wizard. To start this wizard, he clicks Tools on the menu bar in the Database window, points to Security, and then clicks User-Level Security Wizard. When he runs this wizard for the first time, he is prompted to create a workgroup information file, as shown in Figure 2.63.

Figure 2.63: Security Wizard

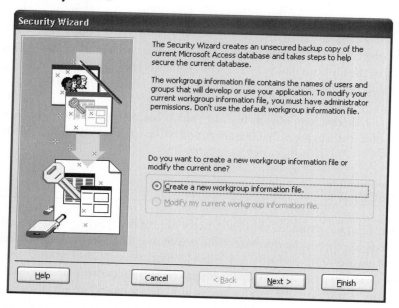

On subsequent uses, Don can modify the workgroup information file. After clicking the Next button, the Security Wizard displays the next dialog box (see Figure 2.64), which Don uses to set the name and workgroup ID for the workgroup information file. The **workgroup ID (WID)** is a unique character string of 4 to 20 characters that identifies the workgroup.

Figure 2.64: Defining the workgroup ID

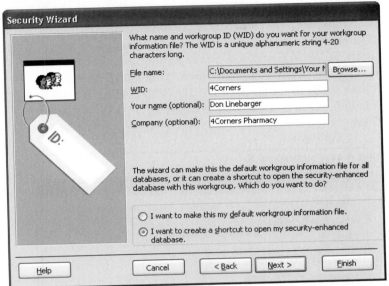

Don clicks the Next button to open the dialog box in which he chooses which database objects to secure. By default, all current and future database objects will be secured, which means that users will need permission to access any object in the database. You can exclude objects from security, but this approach is not recommended. Don accepts the default settings and clicks the Next button to open the dialog box shown in Figure 2.65.

Figure 2.65: Setting permissions for a group

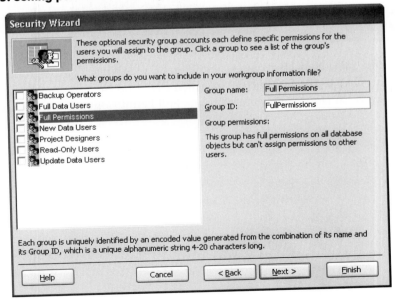

In this dialog box, you set the group name and ID for each group that you want to create. As the database administrator, Don needs full permissions to the database, so he creates a group to have full permissions. He clicks the Next button, chooses the option to skip granting the Users group some permissions, and the next dialog box opens, in which Don can start adding users to the WID. Access automatically adds the administrator of the computer (in Don's case, the administrator is named "Your Name") to the WID. Don sets his password, and then needs to set his **personal ID (PID)**, which is a 4 to 20 character string value that identifies Don as a user. He changes his PID to 4CPAdministrator, as shown in Figure 2.66.

Figure 2.66: Defining a user's personal ID

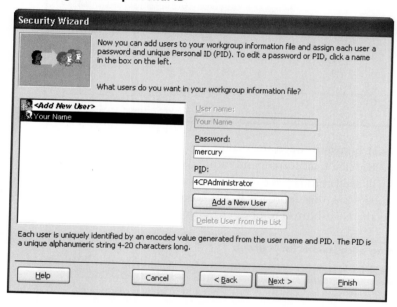

Now Don clicks the Add a New User button, and then he adds himself to the group. Don clicks the Add This User to the List button, and then clicks the Next button to open the next dialog box, in which Don assigns himself to the Full Permissions groups, as shown in Figure 2.67.

Figure 2.67: Assigning users to groups

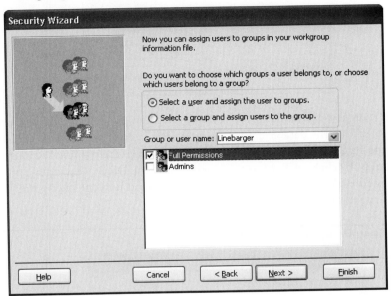

Before closing the Security Wizard, Don needs to specify the filename and location for the backup copy of the unsecured database that Access will create before enhancing the current database with user-level security. He accepts the default name, 4Corners.bak, and stores it in the same folder as the database. When he clicks the Finish button, Access generates a report that identifies the settings used to create users and groups in the WID. Don needs to print and keep this information because it will be important if he needs to re-create the WID. Don prints a copy of the report and also follows the on-screen instructions to save it as a snapshot, and then closes the wizard. The message box shown in Figure 2.68 opens with information about the database.

Figure 2.68: Message box after adding user-level security to a database

After clicking the OK button, Access closes. To reopen the database, Don must use the shortcut that Access created on the Windows desktop. After double-clicking the shortcut, Access starts and opens the Logon dialog box shown in Figure 2.69.

Figure 2.69: Logon dialog box

Because Don is the database administrator, he needs to assign the appropriate permissions to employees who will use the database. By logging on to the database as the administrator (instead of with the account he created for himself), Don can create new user accounts and assign users to groups by clicking Tools on the menu bar in the Database window, pointing to Security, and then clicking User and Group Accounts. Don uses the dialog box shown in Figure 2.70 to make these changes.

Figure 2.70: User and Group Accounts dialog box

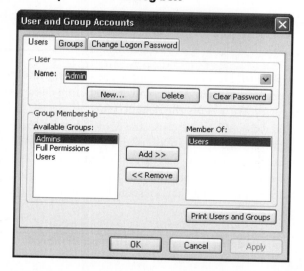

If Don needs to create new groups, he can run the Security Wizard again and choose the option to modify the current workgroup information file and create new users and groups. Don will create user accounts and groups with different levels of access to the database so that some employees can view data, others can update data, and some have full access and can create and delete objects. The user-level security will ensure that users must log on to the database and the permissions granted to these users will grant and restrict access to the database as needed so they can complete their work at the pharmacy.

Steps To Success: Level 3

With the tables created, Don wants to protect the database and improve its operation.

1. Start Access and open the **Hudson.mdb** database in exclusive mode from the STS folder.

2. Run the Compact and Repair utility, and then set the option to compact the database when you close it.

3. Create a backup copy of the Hudson database and save it using the default filename in the STS folder.

4. Document the designs for all tables in the database. Include the table relationships and the field names, data types, and field sizes in the report. Export the report as a Rich Text Format file using the default filename and save it in the STS folder.

5. Suggest three strong passwords that you could use to secure the Hudson database, but do not set any passwords.

6. Create an encrypted copy of the Hudson database, using the filename **HudsonEncrypted.mdb** and saving it in the STS folder.

7. Describe a situation in which you might need to hide a table in the Hudson database (but do not actually hide the table).

8. Use the information in tblJobTitle to describe how you would assign users in specific positions at the pharmacy to groups and describe the kind of access to the database needed by each group. (Do not set user-level security in the Hudson database.)

9. Close the **Hudson.mdb** database and Access.

CHAPTER SUMMARY

This chapter presented the different ways to transform a database design into a collection of related tables in an Access database. In Level 1, you learned how to use Datasheet view, Design view, and the Table Wizard to create tables. You also learned how to create fields in a table, how to set their data types, and how to set properties that format data and ensure its accuracy. These properties included setting a field's caption, formatting values using an input mask, validating fields to ensure accurate and consistent data, and entering a default value in a field. You also learned how to create a lookup field to automate data entry in a field.

In Level 2, you learned how to populate the tables in the database by importing data from another Access database and from an Excel workbook. Importing existing data into a database saves data-entry time and reduces the risk of incorrect data, but it also is subject to problems. You learned how to troubleshoot problems, such as importing data with mismatched data types and nonmatching values into a related table's foreign key field when there are no matching values in the primary table's primary key field. You also learned how to create relationships in a database, how to create an index on a nonprimary key field, how to set a field's properties to require data entry, and how to create a composite primary key. Finally, you learned how to view related records using a subdatasheet.

In Level 3, you examined the role of the database administrator and his duties of securing and maintaining a database. The database administrator provides database maintenance, including compacting and repairing a database, scheduling and storing database backups, and documenting the database design. The database administrator is also charged with securing the database by setting a password, encrypting the database, hiding database objects, and setting user-level security for groups of users.

CONCEPTUAL REVIEW

1. Describe the three methods presented in this chapter for creating a table in Access.

2. What are the rules for naming objects in Access?

3. Write the input mask to control data entry in a field so that users can enter only three uppercase letters followed by three digits.

4. How do you validate a field and inform users of the validation rule?

5. Give three examples not presented in this chapter of how you might use a lookup field to control data entry into a table.

6. Describe how to import data from an Excel workbook into an existing table.

7. Can you set a primary key field so it accepts null values? Why or why not?

8. Can you set a nonprimary key field to accept null values? If so, give three examples not presented in this chapter of fields that might contain null values.

9. Name one advantage and one disadvantage for setting a field's Required property to Yes.

10. What are the three values for the Indexed property? Give one example not presented in this chapter of how you might use each value for a field in a table that stores data about employees.

11. How do you create a many-to-many relationship between two tables in Access?

12. What is a subdatasheet? Can you change the values in the records displayed by the subdatasheet?

13. What is DBA?

14. Describe the four ways to open an Access database.

15. What happens to a database's size and content when you compact it?

16. What is the Documenter?

17. How does encrypting a database provide security?

18. Describe the process for installing user-level security to an Access database.

CASE PROBLEMS

Case 1—Creating the Database for NHD Development Group Inc.

Information
Systems

In Chapter 1, you created the database design for NHD Development Group to use at the Memories Antiques Mall in Cleveland, TN. Tim Richards, the company's chief information officer, reviewed your database design and worked to finalize it before you use Access to create the database. Figure 2.71 shows the database design that Tim approved.

Figure 2.71: Database design for NHD

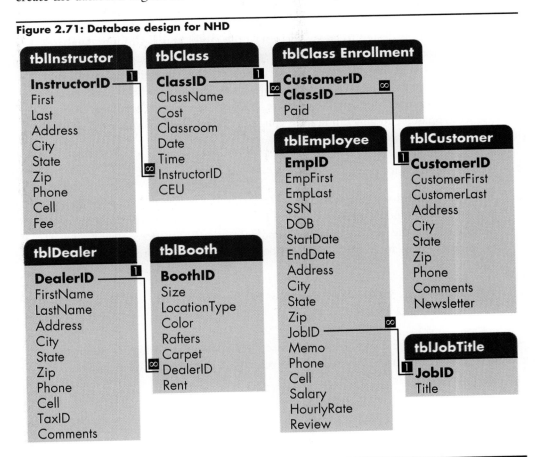

Tim is satisfied that the design shown in Figure 2.71 will satisfy all of the user requirements and output the data he needs to manage the mall. With the design approved, you can begin developing the database.

Complete the following:

1. Compare the database design you developed in Chapter 1 with the one shown in Figure 2.71. If necessary, change your database and table designs to match the ones shown in the figure. If you determine that you need to add or change fields in your table designs, be certain to carefully consider and then set the properties that will support the data being stored in those fields.

2. Start Access and create a new database named **Antiques.mdb** in the Case 1 folder.

3. While Tim was working with your design, he learned that the mall's manager, Linda Sutherland, already built the portion of the database related to classes. All the tables pertaining to classes are stored in the **Classes.mdb** database in the Chapter 2\Case 1 folder. Import these tables and the data they contain, but not their relationships, into the Antiques database.

4. Follow your database design to create the rest of the tables in the Antiques database using any method you choose. Be certain to specify the field names, data types, field descriptions, and field sizes as you create each table. Create validation rules and validation text, input masks, field captions, default values, and lookup fields as necessary to ensure that users enter consistent, complete, and accurate data in the tables. During the discovery phase, Tim and Linda gave you some important information that you must consider in your table designs:

   a. Tax ID numbers for dealers are unique.

   b. The valid booth locations at the mall are Inside Perimeter, Outside Perimeter, and Aisle. (On Linda's map—see Figure 1.37 in Chapter 1—booths that line the outside edge of the mall are outside perimeter booths, booths across from outside perimeter booths are inside perimeter booths, and booths on the inside rows are aisle booths.)

   c. Valid booth sizes are 8×8, 8×10, 8×12, 8×16, 8×20, 12×8, 12×10, 12×12, and 12×18.

5. After creating all of the tables in the database, create the relationships between the tables, as shown in Figure 2.71. Enforce referential integrity in each relationship and cascade updates.

6. Now that you have all the tables set up, you can import the existing data Tim and Linda provided during the discovery phase into your tables. Prior to importing this data, open the files and carefully review the data to identify and correct any compatibility errors between your table and the imported data. If you encounter errors, make the appropriate adjustments in your database. Populate the existing database tables as follows. The file you need is saved in the Chapter 2\Case 1 folder.

   a. Use Table 2.9 to enter data into tblJobTitle.

Table 2.9: Data for tblJobTitle

JobID	Title
1	Manager
2	Assistant Manager
3	Sales
4	Maintenance
5	Accounting
6	Administrative Assistant

   b. The **Memories.xls** workbook contains separate worksheets that include data for booths, dealers, and employees. Import the data into the appropriate tables in the Antiques database. You need to resolve any compatibility issues that arise when you import this data.

7. Check all your tables for accuracy and ensure that all your relationships have been established according to the design shown in Figure 2.71.

8. Set the option to compact the database when you close it.

9. Close the **Antiques.mdb** database and Access.

Case 2—Creating the Database for MovinOn Inc.

**Information
Systems**

In Chapter 1, you created the database design for MovinOn Inc. The database will be used to manage data about the company and its operations. David Powers, the company's general manager, and Robert Iko, the company's information systems specialist, reviewed your database design and worked to finalize it. Figure 2.72 shows the database design that David and Robert approved.

Figure 2.72: Database design for MovinOn

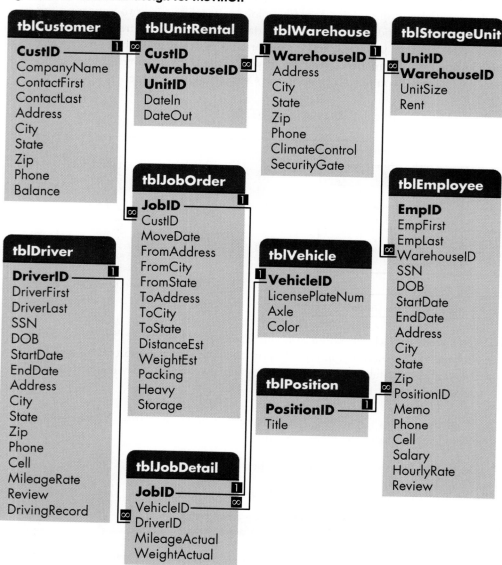

David and Robert are satisfied that the design shown in Figure 2.72 will satisfy all of the user requirements and output the data needed to manage the business. With the design approved, you can begin developing the database.

Complete the following:

1. Compare the database design you developed in Chapter 1 with the one shown in Figure 2.72. If necessary, change your database and table designs to match the ones shown in the figure. If you determine that you need to add or change fields in your table designs, be certain to carefully consider and then set the properties that will support the data being stored in those fields.

2. Start Access and create a new database named **MovinOn.mdb** in the Case 2 folder.

3. Use the database design shown in Figure 2.72 as a guide to help you develop the database. Be certain to specify the field names, data types, field descriptions, and field sizes as you create each table. Create validation rules and validation text, input masks, field captions, default values, and lookup fields as necessary to ensure that users enter consistent, complete, and accurate data in the tables. During the discovery phase, David and Robert gave you some important information that you must consider in your table designs:

   a. Driving records for drivers are rated using the following values: A, B, C, D, or F. Users should input these values from a list.

   b. Users should be able to select the warehouse in which an employee works and the employee's position from a list of values.

   c. In tblJobDetail, the user should select the JobID, VehicleID, and DriverID from a list of values.

   d. In tblJobOrder and tblUnitRental, the user should select the CustID from a list of values.

   e. In tblStorageUnit, the user should select the WarehouseID from a list of values.

4. Check your database carefully to ensure that you have created all the tables, that you have created all the fields and set their properties, and that you have created all the necessary relationships.

5. Use the data shown in Table 2.10 to populate tblPosition.

Table 2.10: Data for tblPosition

PositionID	Title
1	General Manager
2	Warehouse Manager
3	Administrative Assistant
4	Accountant
5	Maintenance
6	Moving Assistant
7	Information Systems

6. Use the data shown in Table 2.11 to populate tblWarehouse.

Table 2.11: Data for tblWarehouse

Warehouse ID	Address	City	State	Zip	Phone	Climate Controlled?	Security Gate?
OR-1	#3 Industrial Park Way	Portland	OR	97212	(503) 551-2432	No	Yes
WA-1	8798 Warehouse Rd	Seattle	WA	98121	(206) 324-2312	Yes	Yes
WY-1	54781 Hixson Pike	Jackson Hole	WY	83001	(307) 541-3571	Yes	No

7. Populate the tables in your database using the data stored in the **MovinOn.xls** and **Job.mdb** files in the Chapter 2\Case 2 folder. Before importing the data, review each worksheet in the file and confirm that your table designs are set up correctly.

8. Set the option to compact the database when you close it.

9. Close the **MovinOn.mdb** database and Access.

Case 3—Creating the Database for Hershey College

Information Systems

In Chapter 1, you created the initial database design for the new intramural department at Hershey College. The department's manager, Marianna Fuentes, provided you with a list of data needs that you used to create the database design. Figure 2.73 shows the database design that Marianna approved.

Figure 2.73: Database design for Hershey College

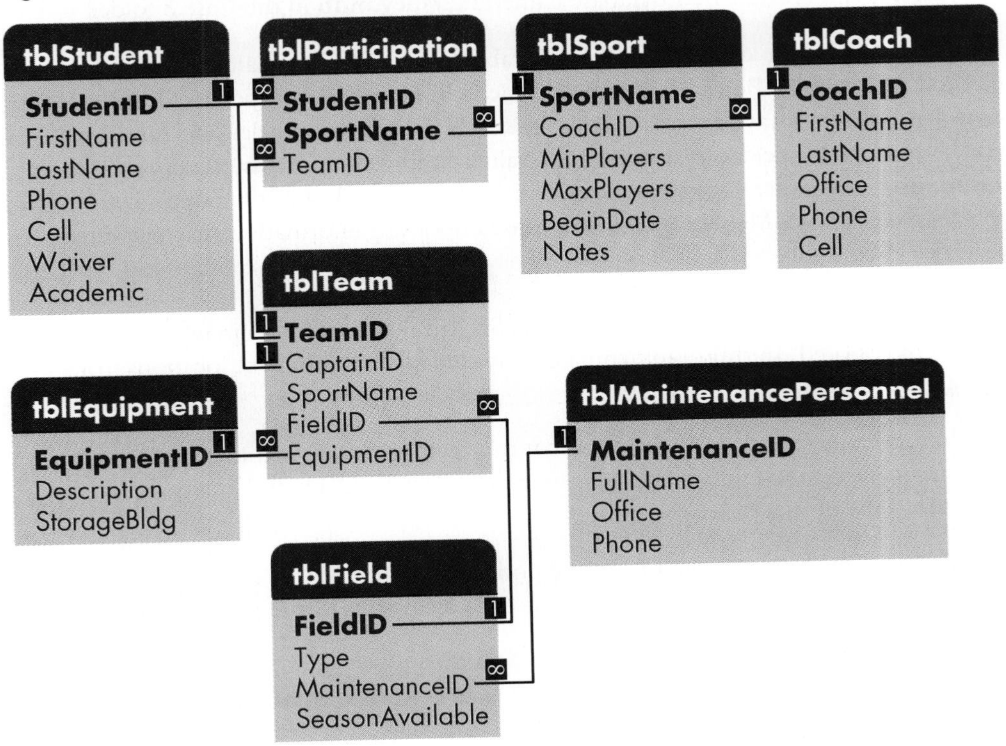

tblStudent
StudentID
FirstName
LastName
Phone
Cell
Waiver
Academic

tblParticipation
StudentID
SportName
TeamID

tblSport
SportName
CoachID
MinPlayers
MaxPlayers
BeginDate
Notes

tblCoach
CoachID
FirstName
LastName
Office
Phone
Cell

tblTeam
TeamID
CaptainID
SportName
FieldID
EquipmentID

tblEquipment
EquipmentID
Description
StorageBldg

tblMaintenancePersonnel
MaintenanceID
FullName
Office
Phone

tblField
FieldID
Type
MaintenanceID
SeasonAvailable

Marianna is satisfied that the design shown in Figure 2.73 will satisfy all of the user requirements and output the data needed to manage the department. With the design approved, you can begin developing the database.

Complete the following:

1. Compare the database design you developed in Chapter 1 with the one shown in Figure 2.73. If necessary, change your database and table designs to match the ones shown in the figure. If you determine that you need to add or change fields in your table designs, be certain to carefully consider and then set the properties that will support the data being stored in those fields.

2. Start Access and create a new database named **Hershey.mdb** in the Case 3 folder.

3. Follow your database design to create the tables in the Hershey database using any method you choose. Be certain to specify the field names, data types, field descriptions, and field sizes as you create each table. Create validation rules and validation text, input masks, field captions, default values, and lookup fields as necessary to ensure that users enter consistent, complete, and accurate data in the tables. During the discovery phase, Marianna gave you some important information that you must consider in your table designs:

   a. There are four storage buildings (SB-1, SB-2, SB-3, and SB-4) in which equipment is stored. In tblEquipment, a user should select equipment locations from a list of values.

   b. In tblTeam, you need to specify the court or field and equipment assigned to the team. Set up the table so that the user can select FieldIDs and EquipmentIDs from a list of values.

   c. Team captains are assigned from the pool of students. Set up the Captain field so that students are selected from a list of valid students. Store the StudentID in the Captain field.

   d. In tblSport, the user should select the CoachID from a list of values.

4. Create the relationships between all the tables, as shown in Figure 2.73. Enforce referential integrity in each relationship and cascade updates.

5. Now that you have all the tables set up, you can import the existing data you found during the discovery phase into your tables. Prior to importing this data, open the files and carefully review the data to identify and correct any compatibility errors between your table and the imported data. If you encounter errors, make the appropriate adjustments in your database. Populate the existing database tables as follows. The files are saved in the Chapter 2\Case 3 folder.

   a. The **IMDept.xls** workbook contains a collection of worksheets. Import this data into the appropriate table in your database. Be certain to check for errors and make any adjustments that are warranted.

b. The **College.mdb** database contains the records for tblField, tblTeam, and tblParticipation.

c. Use Table 2.12 to enter the data into tblSport.

Table 2.12: Data for tblSport

Sport Name	Coach ID	Minimum Players	Maximum Players	Begin Date	Notes
Basketball	18999	5	10	11/1/2008	
Football	79798	11	22	9/1/2008	
Ping Pong	18990	1		11/15/2008	
Pool	18990	1		11/15/2008	
Soccer	17893	11	22	4/18/2008	
Softball	18797	9	20	3/15/2008	
Swimming	78979	1		9/1/2008	
Tennis	78979	1		9/1/2008	
Track	79879	1		3/18/2008	
Wrestling	82374	1		11/1/2008	

6. Run the Compact and Repair utility, and then set the option to compact the database when you close it.

7. Create a backup copy of the Hershey database and save it using the default filename in the Case 3 folder.

8. Document the designs for all tables in the database. Include the table relationships and the field names, data types, and field sizes in the report. Export the report as a Rich Text Format file using the default filename and save it in the Case 3 folder.

9. What security measures do you feel are necessary for this database? Is there a good reason to invoke a password for the database? Why or why not? Keep in mind that a college must always protect the privacy of its students. Suggest three strong passwords that you could use to secure the Hershey database.

10. Create an encrypted copy of the Hershey database, using the filename **HersheyEncrypted.mdb** and saving it in the Case 3 folder.

11. Describe a situation in which you might need to hide a table in the Hershey database (but do not actually hide the table).

12. Describe how you would create groups of users in the intramural department and the kind of access to the database needed by each group. (Do not set user-level security in the Hershey database.)

13. Close the **Hershey.mdb** database and Access.

Analyzing Data for Effective Decision Making

Human Resources: Managing Employees at 4Corners Pharmacy

> *"The human problems which I deal with every day—concerning employees as well as customers—are the problems that fascinate me, that seem important to me."*
> —Hortense Odlum

LEARNING OBJECTIVES

Level 1

Filter and sort data to make it more meaningful
Create simple queries to answer business questions
Develop queries using comparison criteria and wildcards
Display and print query results

Level 2

Design queries that compare data from more than one table
Refine table relationships by specifying the join type
Perform calculations in queries
Customize queries and their results

Level 3

Calculate and restructure data to improve analysis
Examine and create advanced types of queries
Make decisions in a query using the immediate IF (IIF) function
Develop queries using SQL

TOOLS COVERED IN THIS CHAPTER

Action queries (update, append, delete, crosstab, and make-table)
Aggregate functions (Avg, Max, Min, Sum)
Calculated field
Comparison and logical operators
Crosstab query
Filter by Form and Filter by Selection
Find duplicates query
Find unmatched records query

Immediate IF (IIF) function
Parameter query
Query Design view
Select query
Simple Query Wizard
SQL commands (AS, FROM, GROUP BY, HAVING, ORDER BY, SELECT, WHERE)
Top Values query
Wildcard characters

CHAPTER INTRODUCTION

As you add data to a database, it can become increasingly difficult to find the information you need. This chapter begins by showing you how to filter data in a Microsoft Office Access 2003 database so you can retrieve and examine only the records you need. You will also learn how to sort data to rearrange records in a specified order. Next, the chapter focuses on queries, which provide quick answers to business questions such as which employees earn the highest pay rate, which employees have completed their occupational training requirements, and whether a company should continue to reimburse employees for job-related training. In Level 1, you will learn how to perform simple select queries, which specify only the fields and records Access should select. Level 2 explains how to increase the complexity of queries by using multiple tables and adding options to prepare data for forms and reports. It also explores how to make your queries interactive. Level 3 covers advanced types of queries such as those that update and add records to a table, and explains how to use the Immediate IF function to make decisions in a query and Structured Query Language (SQL) to retrieve data from an Access database.

CASE SCENARIO

Maria Garcia is the human resources manager for 4Corners Pharmacy. Her responsibilities involve hiring and firing employees and making sure they complete the necessary employment paperwork. In addition, she manages employee training, schedules periodic job reviews, and helps analyze compensation and other employee information.

Human
Resources

Most of the training sessions that employees of 4Corners Pharmacy attend involve mandatory certification for cardiopulmonary resuscitation (CPR) and the use of defibrillators. Maria needs a way to make sure all employees attend required classes and receive annual certification as necessary.

Until now, Maria has maintained employee and training information on printed forms that she stores in a filing cabinet. However, it is often inconvenient and time consuming to access and update these forms, especially to answer management questions that require her to analyze data. Maria plans to automate the records by using the 4Corners.mdb database to track employee and training information.

LEVEL 1
ORGANIZING AND RETRIEVING INFORMATION FROM A DATABASE

ACCESS 2003 SKILLS TRAINING

- Build summary queries
- Clear a query
- Create a query in Design view
- Create select queries using the Simple Query Wizard
- Filter datasheet by form
- Filter datasheet by selection
- Print the results of a query
- Sort a query on multiple fields in Design view
- Sort records in a database
- Use date and memo fields in a query
- Use filter by form
- Use text data in criteria for a query
- Use wildcards in a query

FILTERING AND SORTING DATA

Paul Ferrino, the owner of 4Corners Pharmacy, periodically reviews the wages he pays to his employees so he can budget for upcoming pay raises. He has recently increased the salaries of the two pharmacists at 4Corners, but he needs to check the hourly rates he pays to the other employees. He asks Maria to list the wages for pharmacy technicians and cashiers, ranked from highest to lowest so he can quickly see the full range of pay for nonsalaried employees.

Four tables in the 4Corners.mdb database contain employee information that Maria needs to perform her management tasks. These tables and their relationships are shown in Figure 3.1 and are described in the following list.

Figure 3.1: Relationships in the 4Corners Pharmacy database

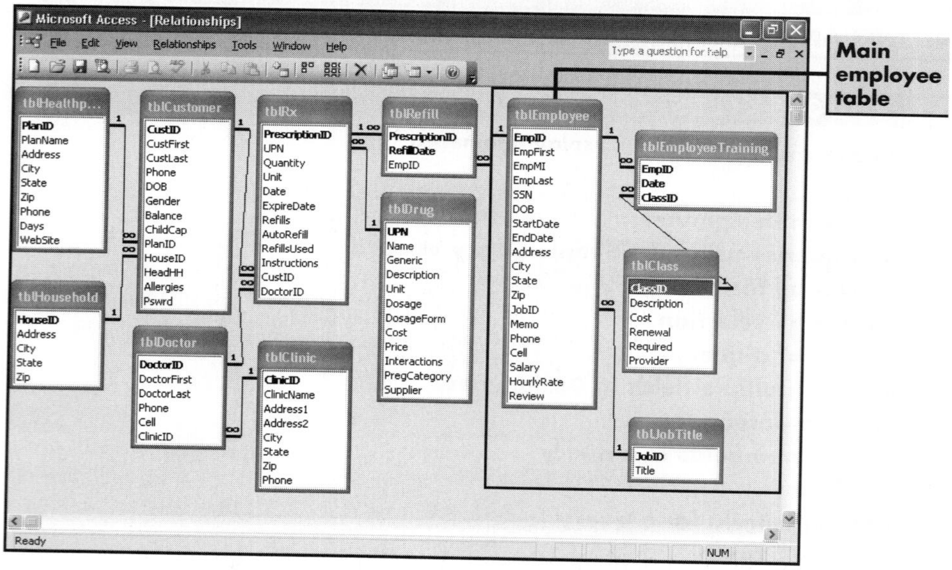

- **tblEmployee**—This table contains information about employees, including identifying information such as their ID number, name, and Social Security number, contact information such as their address and phone numbers, and employment information such as their starting date, salary or hourly rate, and job ID.
- **tblJobTitle**—This table lists the five job categories at 4Corners Pharmacy by ID number: 1—Owner, 2—Pharmacist, 3—Technician, 4—Cashier, and 5—Manager.
- **tblEmployeeTraining**—This table tracks the training classes that employees attend.
- **tblClass**—This table lists the classes employees can attend to receive required certifications or other professional training.

Maria thinks she can find the information she needs by using a filter and then sorting the results. A **filter** restricts data in a single table to create a temporary subset of records. A filter allows you to see only certain records in a table based on criteria you specify. **Sorting** records means organizing them in a particular order or sequence. You can sort records in a table regardless of whether it's filtered.

Filtering by Selection

Two tools that Access provides for filtering data are Filter by Selection and Filter by Form. **Filter by Selection** lets you select a particular field in a datasheet and then display only data that matches the contents of that field. When you filter by selection, you specify only one criterion for the filter.

Maria first wants to review employment information for pharmacy technicians only. She opens the tblEmployee table, which currently contains 24 records, and clicks the first

JobID field that contains a "3." (Recall that technicians have a JobID of 3.) Then she clicks the Filter by Selection button ▼ on the Table Datasheet toolbar. Access filters the data by selecting only those records with a "3" in the JobID field, and then displays the filtered results—eight employment records for the pharmacy technicians only. See Figure 3.2.

Figure 3.2: Using Filter by Selection to display a temporary subset of records

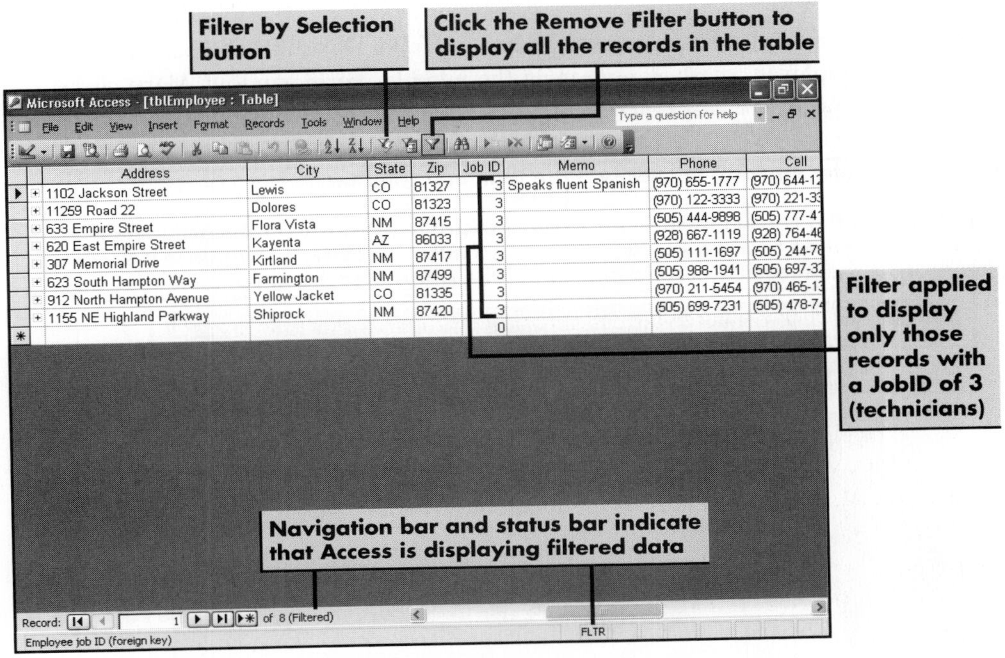

Now Maria can focus on the employment information for technicians, including their hourly rate of pay. After she prints this datasheet, she could remove the filter for displaying technician records and apply a different filter for displaying cashier records. However, she can use a different tool to display the hourly pay rates for technicians and cashiers at the same time. To accomplish that goal, she must use Filter by Form.

Filtering by Form

Whereas you specify only one criterion when you use Filter by Selection, you can specify two or more criteria with **Filter by Form**. In addition, Filter by Selection filters for records that exactly match the criterion, such as those that contain "3" in the JobID field, while Filter by Form can filter for comparative data, such as those records in which the HourlyRate field value is greater than or equal to $8.00. To enter comparative data, you use comparison operators, such as >= for greater than or equal to. You specify these criteria in a blank version of the datasheet by entering or selecting the data in one or more fields that you want to match. Access displays only those records that contain the data you selected.

Maria wants to view hourly pay rates for employees whose records contain a "3" (for technicians) or "4" (for cashiers) in the JobID field. Because she needs to specify more than one criterion, she will use the Filter by Form tool. Before doing so, however, she notes that a filter is still applied to tblEmployee because FLTR appears in the status bar (shown earlier in Figure 3.2). Maria redisplays all the records in tblEmployee by clicking the Remove Filter button [⧩] on the Table Datasheet toolbar.

Next, she clicks the Filter by Form button [⧩] on the Table Datasheet toolbar. A blank version of the tblEmployee datasheet appears in the Filter by Form window. Maria clicks the JobID field to specify the first criterion for displaying records. See Figure 3.3.

Figure 3.3: Using Filter by Form to specify more than one criterion

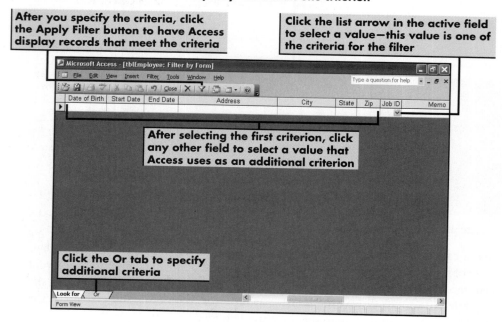

To specify the first criterion, she clicks the list arrow in the JobID field to display all of its values, and then clicks 3 (for technician). This means that Access will display records in tblEmployee that contain a "3" in the JobID field. If Maria wanted to display a list of technicians who live in Colorado, she could also click the list arrow in the State field and then click CO. This type of criteria is called **AND criteria**—it selects records that contain *all* specified values.

However, Maria wants to view records that contain a "3" (technicians) or "4" (cashiers) in the JobID field. This type of criteria is called **OR criteria**—it selects records that contain *any* of the specified values. To enter an OR criterion, Maria clicks the Or tab. Another version of the blank tblEmployee datasheet appears in the Filter by Form window. She clicks the list arrow in the JobID field, and then clicks 4. When she clicks the Apply Filter button [Y] on the Filter/Sort toolbar, Access displays the records that satisfy any of her criteria—records that contain a "3" or a "4" in the JobID field. This is the list that Maria wants—information about the current 4Corners technicians and cashiers, including their rate of pay.

Now that Maria has filtered the tblEmployee datasheet, she needs to sort the records to rank the hourly rates of pay for technicians and cashiers.

Sorting Data to Increase Information Content

Recall that sorting records means organizing them in a particular order or sequence. Table 3.1 describes how Access sorts different types of data.

Table 3.1: Sorting types of data

Data Type	Ascending Sort Order	Descending Sort Order
Text	Alphabetic order from A to Z	Reverse alphabetic order from Z to A
Numbers and Currency	From lowest to highest	From highest to lowest
Date/Time	From earliest to latest	From latest to earliest
Yes/No	Yes values appear first	No values appear first

Sorting the data in a table or datasheet organizes the data and increases its information value. When you create a table and designate one or more fields as the primary key, Access sorts the records based on the primary key values. To change the order, you can sort the records. For example, you could sort a list of customers by state or a list of vendors in alphabetic order.

When you sort records, you select a sort field, the one Access uses first to reorder the records. For example, if you are sorting an employer list, LastName might be the sort field. You can select more than one sort field, such as when you want to sort records first by last name and then by first name. To sort on multiple fields, you must move the fields in Datasheet view, if necessary, so that they are adjacent. The leftmost field becomes the **primary sort field**, meaning that Access sorts the records by this field first. For example, you could move a LastName field to the left of a FirstName field in an employee table, select both columns, and then sort in ascending order. Access would list the records in alphabetical order by last name. If two or more employees have the same last name, Access would list those employee records in alphabetic order according to their first name.

Now that Maria has filtered tblEmployee to show records only for technicians and cashiers, she can sort the records in descending order by the HourlyRate field so that the employee with the highest hourly wage appears first and the one with the lowest wage appears last. To do so, she clicks in an HourlyRate field, and then clicks the Sort Descending button [Z↓] on the Table Datasheet toolbar.

Although it took Maria several steps, she produced the results she needs. She prints the sorted datasheet, clicks the Remove Filter button ▼ on the Table Datasheet toolbar to turn off the filter, and then closes tblEmployee. However, she suspects there must be an easier way to produce the same results, and decides to explore queries, which can also retrieve only selected records from a table.

USING QUERIES TO ANSWER BUSINESS QUESTIONS

If you need a quick way to restrict the data displayed in one table, the Filter by Selection and Filter by Form tools are appropriate. However, recall that a filter creates a *temporary* subset of records in a single table. Although you can save a filter, if you want to reuse the filter criteria or need data from two or more tables, the easiest approach is to create a query. A **query** is a database object that stores criteria for selecting records from one or more tables based on conditions you specify. You can save a query and use it again when you want to see the results of its criteria. Queries are often used as the basis for forms and reports and they can add, update, and delete records in tables. A special kind of query can even create a table based on criteria you supply.

Although queries and filters both display records based on specified criteria, a query is more powerful than a filter. Besides saving the criteria and letting you select records from more than one table, you can also use a query to display only some of the fields in a table. (When you use a filter, you must display all of the fields.) In addition, you can create fields in a query that perform calculations, such as sums and averages.

The following list summarizes the capabilities of Access queries:

- Display selected fields and records from a table.
- Sort records on one or multiple fields.
- Perform calculations.
- Generate data for forms, reports, and other queries.
- Update data in the tables of a database.
- Find and display data from two or more tables.
- Create new tables.
- Delete records in a table based on one or more criteria.

The most common type of query is called a **select query**. Select queries allow you to ask a question based on one or more tables in a database. Access responds by displaying a datasheet containing the set of records that answers your question. You can select only the fields you want in your result. To analyze the data that you retrieve, you can also use a select query to group records and calculate sums, counts, averages, and other kinds of totals. When you save a query, you are saving the criteria that select the records you want to display. Each time you open, or run, the query, it retrieves the records that meet the criteria you specified and displays them in a **recordset**, a datasheet that contains the results of a query. Running a typical select query does not affect the records and fields in the underlying tables; it only selects records to make your data more useful.

Maria determines that she can use a select query to provide the list of hourly wages for the 4Corners technicians and cashiers that Paul Ferrino requested. Because she is still getting acquainted with the 4Corners database, the easiest way for her to create a select query is to use the Simple Query Wizard.

Using the Simple Query Wizard to Create a Query

Access provides a number of query wizards, which guide you through the steps of creating a query. The Simple Query Wizard presents a list of tables and queries in your database and the fields that they contain. You select the fields you want from one or more tables, and the wizard creates and displays the results. For example, if an employee table contains 20 fields of information, including name, address, phone number, and Social Security number, you can use the Simple Query Wizard to create a phone list that contains only the name and phone number for each employee. Although the Simple Query Wizard provides a quick way to retrieve selected records, it does have some limitations. Table 3.2 lists the advantages and limitations of the Simple Query Wizard.

Table 3.2: Advantages and limitations of the Simple Query Wizard

You Can Use the Simple Query Wizard to:	You Cannot Use the Simple Query Wizard to:
Display selected fields and records from one or more tables and queries	Update data, create tables, or delete records
Produce summary data if one or more of the selected fields are of the numeric or currency data type	Add selection criteria
Include a count of the records	Choose the sort order of the query
Specify summary grouping by day, month, quarter, or year if one or more of your fields is a Date/Time field	Change the order of the fields in a query; fields appear in the order they are added to the Selected Fields list in the first wizard dialog box

To start the Simple Query Wizard, Maria clicks the Queries button on the Objects bar in the Database window, and then double-clicks the Create query by using wizard option. The Simple Query Wizard dialog box opens, which Maria can use to select the fields she wants to display in the query results. All of the fields she needs are included in tblEmployee, so she clicks the Tables/Queries list arrow, and then clicks tblEmployee. See Figure 3.4.

Figure 3.4: The Simple Query Wizard dialog box

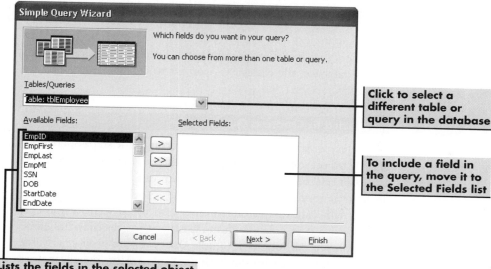

Lists the fields in the selected object

To make the results easy to read, Maria decides to list only the employee's name, job ID, and hourly rate. She double-clicks the EmpLast, EmpFirst, JobID, and HourlyRate fields in that order to move them to the Selected Fields list. These are the fields Access will include in the query results. Then she clicks the Next button to open the next dialog box in the wizard, which asks if she wants to create a detail or summary query. A detail query shows every selected field of every record. A summary query groups records and can calculate the sum, average, minimum, or maximum value in each selected field. It can also provide a count of the records in a table. Maria wants to show every field of every record, so she selects the Detail option button.

When Maria clicks the Next button, the next dialog box in the wizard opens, where she can enter a name for the query. She types qryHourlyRate as the name, and then clicks the Finish button. Access displays the results—a list of 4Corners employees showing only the employee name, job ID, and hourly pay rate.

Best Practice

Using Prefixes in Database Object Names
When prompted to save a query, be certain to use the "qry" prefix in the query name. Naming objects with a prefix that identifies the object type is particularly important with queries because it distinguishes those objects from tables. (A query recordset looks exactly like a table datasheet.) The query wizards, however, usually suggest using a table name as the start of the query name, even if the table name uses the "tbl" prefix. Using the "qry" prefix helps you distinguish queries from tables, which is especially helpful when you are using one or the other as the basis for a new form or report.

How To

Create a Detail Query with the Simple Query Wizard

1. To create a detail query with the Simple Query Wizard, click Queries on the Objects bar in the Database window, and then double-click the Create query by using wizard option.

2. Click the Tables/Queries list arrow and then select the table or query you want to use as the basis for the query. From the Available Fields list, select the fields you want to include in the query. Use the Select Single Field button ⟨ > ⟩ to select the fields one by one; use the Select All Fields button ⟨ >> ⟩ to select them all at once. If you want to include fields from more than one table or query, click the Tables/Queries list arrow again, select another table or query, and then select the fields you want to include. Click the Next button. If a selected field contains a numeric value, the next dialog box asks if you want a detail or summary query.

3. Click the Detail option button to show all the records. Click the Next button.

4. Name the query using the "qry" prefix, and then click the Finish button.

Maria can now achieve the results she wants by sorting the results of the query. She selects the JobID and HourlyRate fields and then clicks the Sort Descending button ⟨ Z↓A ⟩ on the Query Datasheet toolbar to sort the records first by JobID and then by HourlyRate. The records with a JobID of 5 appear first, followed by the records with a JobID of 4, sorted from highest to lowest by HourlyRate. The records with a JobID of 3 appear next, also sorted from highest to lowest by HourlyRate. The records with no HourlyRate value appear at the top and bottom of the list because employees with a JobID of 5 are managers and receive a salary. Similarly, employees with a JobID of 2 are pharmacists, and JobID 1 is the owner; they all receive salaries, not hourly wages. See Figure 3.5.

Figure 3.5: The sorted results of the qryHourlyRate query

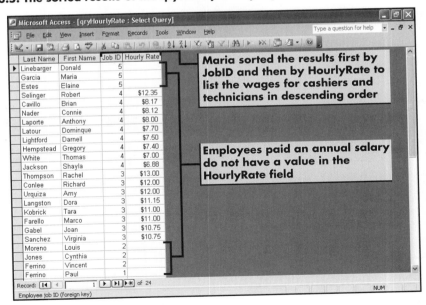

Although using the Detail option with the Simple Query Wizard displays all the employee records, even for employees other than technicians and cashiers, creating a query allows Maria to increase the information content of the results by displaying only relevant fields and sorting the records. She shows the query results to Paul Ferrino, noting that the records at the top and bottom of the list are for salaried employees. Paul looks over the list, mentioning that he appreciates the sort order so that he can quickly analyze the range of pay for nonsalaried employees. He wonders if she could provide this information in a more accessible format, listing only the highest and lowest hourly pay rates. Including the average pay rate would also help him analyze the wages. Maria decides to explore the summary option in the Simple Query Wizard to produce the results Paul requests.

Including Summary Statistics in a Query for Data Analysis

Recall that a summary query groups records and can calculate the sum, average, minimum, or maximum value in each selected field. It can also count the records in a table or query.

Maria starts the Simple Query Wizard again so she can use it to create a summary query. In the first dialog box (shown earlier in Figure 3.4), she clicks the Tables/Queries list arrow and then selects qryHourlyRate. She can create the new query by modifying qryHourlyRate and then saving it with a different name. Instead of listing the employee name and job ID for each record, she only wants to summarize the hourly pay rate data. She double-clicks HourlyRate so it becomes the only field in the Selected Fields list. When she clicks the Next button, the next dialog box asks if she wants to create a detail or summary query. This time, she chooses to create a summary query, and clicks the Summary Options button to select the statistics she wants Access to calculate for the HourlyRate field. See Figure 3.6.

Figure 3.6: Creating a summary query with the Simple Query Wizard

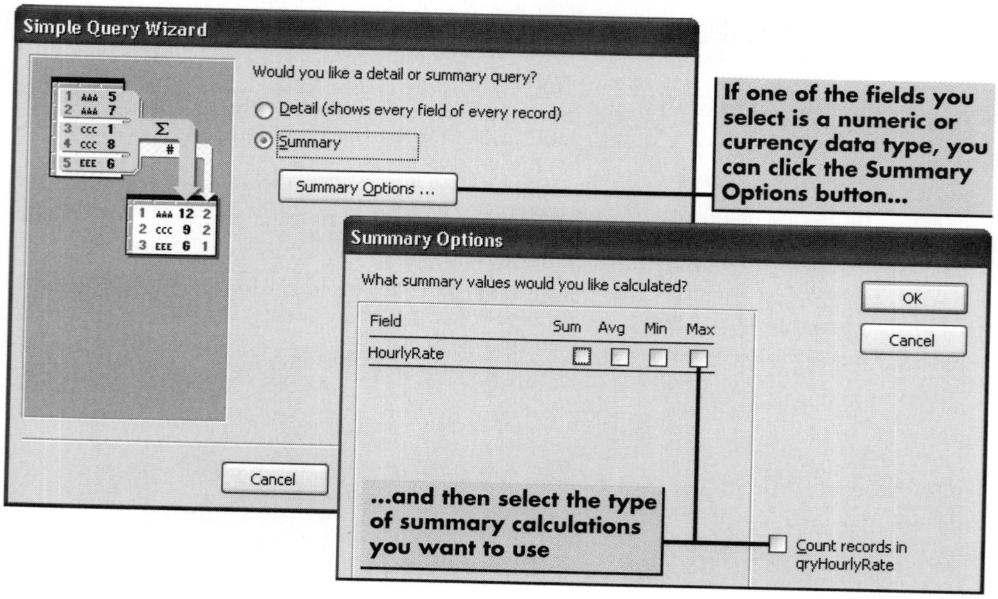

Maria selects the Avg, Min, and Max options because Paul wants to analyze the pharmacy's pay structure by examining the average, lowest, and highest hourly wages, and then completes the wizard, naming the new query qryHourlyRateSummary. The results, shown in Figure 3.7, include the average, minimum, and maximum calculations for the values in the HourlyRate field.

Figure 3.7: Summary statistics in the qryHourlyRateSummary query

How To

Create a Summary Query with the Simple Query Wizard

1. To create a summary query with the Simple Query Wizard, click Queries on the Objects bar in the Database window, and then double-click the Create query by using wizard option.

2. Click the Tables/Queries list arrow and then select the table or query you want to use as the basis for the query. From the Available Fields list, select the fields you want to include in the query. Use the Select Single Field button [>] to select the fields one by one; use the Select All Fields button [>>] to select them all at once. If you want to include fields from more than one table or query, click the Tables/Queries list arrow again, select another table or query, and then select the fields you want to include. Click the Next button. If a selected field contains a numeric value, the next dialog box asks if you want a detail or summary query.

3. Click the Summary option button, and then click the Summary Options button to open the Summary Options dialog box.

4. Click the check boxes for the summary values you want to calculate on each field that contains numeric data. Click the Count records in check box to count records in the table or query that contains numeric data. Click the OK button and then click the Next button.

5. Name the query using the "qry" prefix, and then click the Finish button.

As she examines the results, Maria becomes concerned about the average value, recalling that in the records for salaried employees, the HourlyRate field is blank. She is not sure if qryHourlyRateSummary is using these blank fields as zero or null values. (Recall that nulls have no value.) The average is calculated by summing all the values in the HourlyRate field and then dividing that by the number of records (24, as shown earlier in Figure 3.5). However, the calculation should include only those fields that are not blank—these fields belong to records for technicians and cashiers, the employees who receive hourly wages. Therefore, the average should be calculated by summing only the nonblank values in the HourlyRate field and then dividing that by the number of records for employees who receive hourly wages (17). If the HourlyRate field contains zero instead of null values, the AvgOfHourlyRate fields in qryHourlyRateSummary will not reflect the average pay rate for employees who receive hourly wages—it will erroneously include the zero values for salaried employees. Maria wants to make sure that the query does not include the records for salaried employees, and realizes she needs to create a query using a method that allows her more options than the Simple Query Wizard. She needs to use selection criteria to display only records for technicians and cashiers, and then calculate summary statistics using those records. To accomplish this, she must work in Query Design view.

Best Practice

Verifying Calculation Results
After Access calculates a value, examine the results to make sure the value makes sense in the context of the data. Many database developers use a calculator to check the results by hand to make sure the calculations they use in queries are working correctly. For this reason, most developers prefer to test their queries and other objects with only a few sample records and simple data so they can easily determine whether their results are correct.

Creating a Query in Design View

Recall from Table 3.1 that the Simple Query Wizard does not allow you to use selection criteria when creating a query, set the sort order of the results, or change the order of the fields displayed in the results. If you need to perform any of these tasks, create a query in Design view instead of using a wizard. In Design view, you can still create queries that accomplish the same goals as the Simple Query Wizard, such as displaying selected fields and records from one or more tables and calculating summary statistics.

When you create a query in Design view, you work in a window similar to the one shown in Figure 3.8

Figure 3.8: The Select Query window in Design view

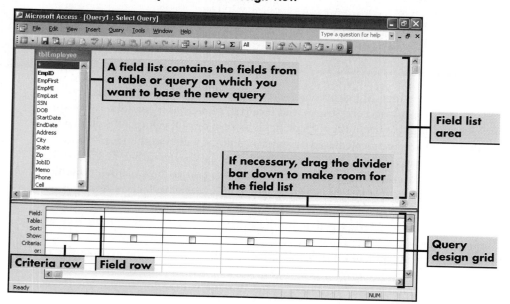

The Select Query window in Design view has two sections: an area for field lists at the top of the window and the design grid below it. You add the tables you need for the query to the top part of the window; they appear as field lists. You can resize the field lists as necessary to display all the fields and the complete field names. You add the fields you want in the query to the design grid by dragging the field from the field list to the design grid or by double-clicking the field name.

For each field you add to the design grid, you can specify criteria by typing an expression in the Criteria row. For example, to select only employees with a JobID of 3, type 3 in the Criteria row for the JobID field. Typing the value you are looking for as a criterion is why Access calls its query approach **query by example (QBE)**.

Table 3.3 describes the tools and features of query Design view.

Table 3.3: Query Design view tools

Feature or Tool	Description
Field list	Contains the fields for a selected table or query.
Design grid	Provides a grid for the fields and record selection criteria you want to use in the query.
Field row	Displays the field name in the design grid.
Table row	Displays the name of the table that contains the current field.
Sort row	Specifies ascending or descending sort order for the field. Sorting is from left to right. Fields do not need to be next to each other to be included in the sort.
Show row	When the Show box is checked, displays the field in the results. When the Show box is unchecked, the query uses the field to establish criteria, but does not display the field in the results.
Criteria row	Specifies the criteria for including or eliminating the record for the field. When one or more criteria are specified in this row, all criteria must be true for the query to display a record in the results.
or row	Specifies OR criteria for including or eliminating the record for the field. When one or more criteria are specified in this row and the Criteria row, any criteria can be true for the query to display a record in the results.
Datasheet view button	Click to display the query results.
Query Type button	Click the list arrow to select the type of query you want to run.
Run button	Click to run the query and display the results.
Show Table button	Click to select tables and add them to the field list area.
Totals button Σ	Click to add a Total row to the design grid and perform calculations with the values in a field.

Maria is ready to design a query that will display the names of 4Corners technicians and cashiers only, their job IDs, and their hourly pay rates. The query will also sort the list in descending order first by the JobID field and then by HourlyRate.

To create this query, Maria double-clicks the Create query in Design view option in the Database window. The Select Query window opens in Design view and then the Show Table dialog box opens, listing the tables in the 4Corners database. All of the fields Maria needs are in the tblEmployee table, so she double-clicks tblEmployee to display its field list in the field list area, and then she clicks the Close button to close the Show Table dialog box.

Next, she adds the four fields she needs to the design grid. In the tblEmployee field list, she double-clicks EmpLast, EmpFirst, JobID, and HourlyRate in that order to add them to the design grid.

Her next task is to specify the criteria for displaying records only for technicians and cashiers. To do so, she must use multiple criteria, as she did when she used Filter by Form.

Creating Queries with Multiple Criteria

Most queries involve more than one criterion. You can represent AND criteria—multiple conditions that must all be true—by entering the conditions in the same Criteria row in the query design grid. For a record to be included in the results of the query, it must meet all criteria specified in the Criteria row. For example, if you want to display information about cashiers who live in Colorado, you enter "3" in the Criteria row for the JobID field and "CO" in the Criteria row for the State field.

To specify OR criteria—conditions that allow more than one alternative condition to be true—you use the "or" row of the query design grid. If the conditions apply to the same field, you enter the first condition in the Criteria row for the field, and then enter each additional condition in an "or" row for that field. The query selects records that meet all the criteria in the Criteria row, or those that meet all of the criteria in an "or" row. For example, if you want to display information about employees who live in Arizona or New Mexico, you can enter "AZ" in the Criteria row and "NM" in the "or" row for the State field. You can also type all the conditions separated by the Or operator in the same Criteria cell, as in "AZ" Or "NM".

If the conditions apply to different fields, you also enter the first condition in the Criteria row for one field, and then enter each additional condition in an "or" row for the other fields. For example, if you want to display information about employees who live in Colorado or Phoenix, you can enter "CO" in the Criteria row for the State field and "Phoenix" in the "or" row for the City field.

Best Practice

Understanding Or Criteria

In querying, "or means more." A query with criteria in more than one row of the query design grid is likely to return more results than the more restrictive AND criteria, in which two or more conditions must be true.

Now, Maria can specify the criteria for displaying records only for technicians and cashiers. Because she wants to display records that include 3 or 4 in the JobID field, she will use OR criteria. Recall that Maria could do this earlier when she used Filter by Form, but not when she used the Simple Query Wizard. She clicks in the Criteria row of the JobID field and then types 3 to set the criteria for displaying records only for cashiers. To include an OR criterion, she clicks in the "or" row of the JobID field and then types 4 to set the criterion for also displaying technician records. See Figure 3.9.

Figure 3.9: Setting criteria for the query in Design view

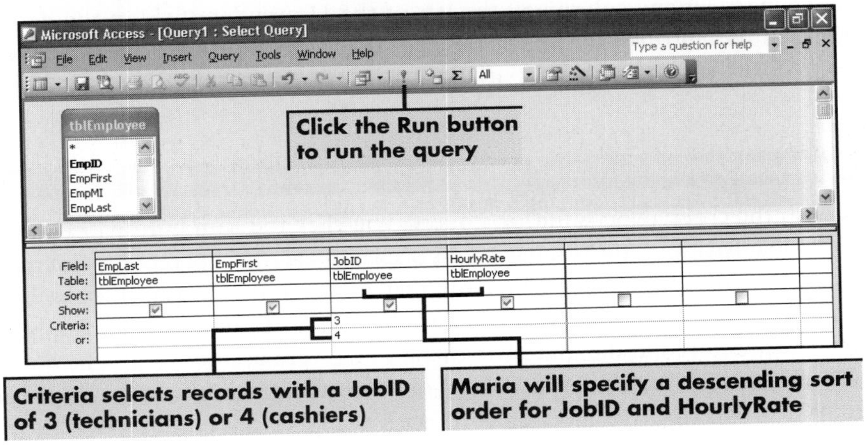

Maria's only remaining task is to sort the records the query displays so that the records for cashiers appear first, sorted from highest to lowest by hourly pay rate. Then she wants the records for technicians to appear, also sorted from highest to lowest by hourly pay rate.

Specifying Sort Order in Queries

Query results appear in the same order as the data from the underlying tables unless you specify a sort order when you design the query. Sort order is determined from left to right, so the primary sort field must appear to the left of any other sort field on the grid. You might want to sort on one or more additional fields to determine the order of records that all have the same primary sort order value. Fields do not need to be next to each other to be included in a sort within a query. You can choose ascending or descending sort order.

For example, to sort employee records alphabetically by name, you could place the EmpLast field to the left of the EmpFirst field in the query design grid. If you specify an ascending sort order for both fields, Access sorts the records in alphabetic order by last name. If two employees have the same last name, Access sorts those records according to the names in the EmpFirst field. For example, if one employee is named Arthur Johnson and another is named Tyrone Johnson, Access sorts Arthur before Tyrone.

The main reason to specify a sort order for a query is that it is saved as part of the design with the other query settings. After you run a query, you might decide to sort the data in one or more columns as you examine the data in Datasheet view. This sort order is not saved as part of the query design. Recall also that multiple columns must be adjacent to sort on more than one field in Datasheet view. In Design view, you can sort on more than one field even if they are not adjacent—the sort order is determined by their left-to-right placement in the design grid.

To sort the records first by JobID and then by HourlyRate, Maria must make sure that the JobID field appears in any column to the left of the HourlyRate field in the design grid. Maria clicks in the Sort row of the JobID field, clicks the list arrow, and then clicks Descending. She does the same for the HourlyRate field. She reviews her selections before she runs the query.

Running a Query

After you establish the criteria you want for a query, you click the Run button 🔘 on the Query Design toolbar to display the results. Access displays a datasheet of records that meet the criteria you specified in the design grid. Note that although the datasheet looks like a set of records in a table, and you can often enter and change data from the query datasheet, the data is still actually stored in the underlying tables that were used to create the query. When you save a query, you save only the design, not the values from the tables displayed in the results. When you run the query again, Access reapplies the criteria saved in the design grid to the data in the underlying tables to produce the query results. If the data in the query fields has changed, these changes appear when you rerun the query.

Maria saves the query as qryHourlyRateAnalysis. She is ready to run her query, so she clicks the Run button 🔘 on the Query Design toolbar. Access runs the query and displays the results in Datasheet view. See Figure 3.10.

Figure 3.10: Results of the query in Datasheet view

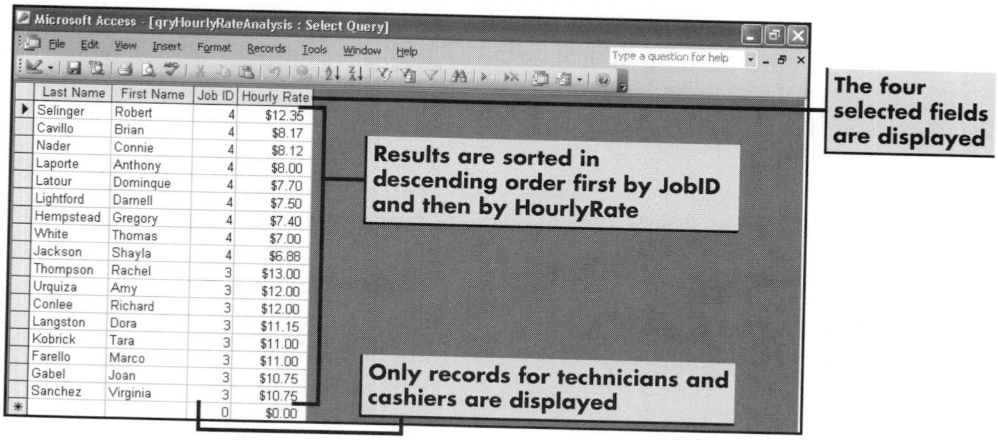

Best Practice

Referring to Query Results

Results from a query are not new tables. The original tables and queries used to create the query do not change when you run a select query. A query recordset contains "columns" and "rows" because they are not necessarily records or fields in any table. As you will see later, you can create a new column with a calculated value that does not appear in the underlying tables in the database.

Best Practice

Working with Query Datasheets

Avoid entering or editing data in the query results. It is generally considered best practice to enter data directly into a table (or form, as you will see in Chapter 4) to make sure you enter data for all fields, not only those in the query results.

Under certain conditions, you can edit the values in the query datasheet to update the records in the underlying tables. Access lets you update table records from a query datasheet if the query is based on only one table or on tables that have a one-to-one relationship (which is rare), or if the query results contain a Memo, Hyperlink, or OLE Object field. Editing records from query results saves you a few steps if you need to correct a typographical error, for example, because you don't need to close the query datasheet and then open the table datasheet to make a change.

Access might also let you update table records from a query datasheet if the query is based on two or more tables that have a one-to-many relationship. Fields you cannot update include the primary key field for the table on the "one" side of the relationship, unless you've enabled cascading updates when you set referential integrity for the relationship.

You can add records using the query datasheet only if you include a primary key or foreign key field in the query. One exception is a summary query—because it displays calculations based on the contents of the underlying tables, you cannot enter or change the data itself. If you try to enter a record or change data in a query that does not include a primary or foreign key for the underlying tables, you will receive an error message similar to the one shown in Figure 3.11, which indicates a data integrity error.

Figure 3.11: Entering or changing data in the datasheet of query results

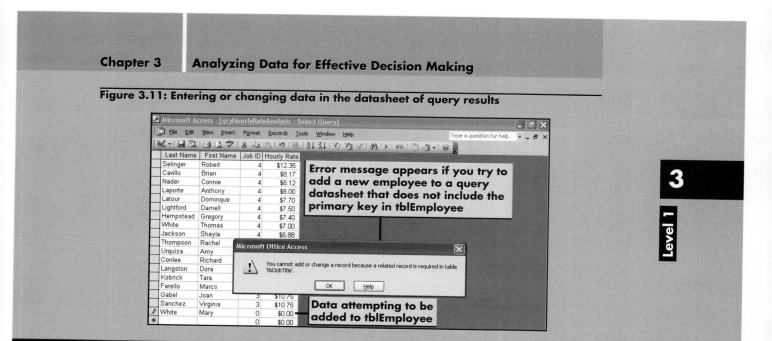

Now that Maria knows how to work in Design view, she can modify the qryHourlyRateSummary query so it uses only hourly pay rates for technicians and cashiers in its average calculation. She opens the query in Design view, adds the JobID field to the design grid, and enters the same criteria she used to select records only for technicians and cashiers in qryHourlyRateSummary—she enters 3 in the Criteria row of the JobID field and 4 in the "or" row.

If Maria runs the query now, she will probably receive an error—the three fields that calculate the average, minimum, and maximum values summarize the values in all the selected employee records, while the JobID field selects each employee record that matches the criteria. Access can't run a query that shows summary values in one row of the query results, and then uses two or more rows to display detail information. To solve this problem, Maria can use the JobID field in the query design grid to specify criteria, but not show the JobID field in the query results. She can remove the check mark from the Show box in the JobID field to indicate that it should not appear in the query results. Figure 3.12 shows the modified query design for qryHourlyRateSummary and the results, which verify that the original query calculated the average hourly rate correctly.

Figure 3.12: Revised qryHourlyRateSummary that calculates statistics for technicians and cashiers only

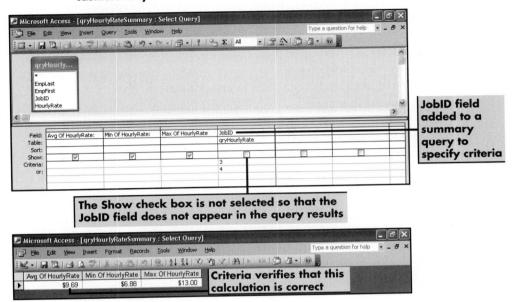

Maria has another problem she wants to work on next. Paul asked Maria to look into the possibility of scheduling at least one employee in the pharmacy who is fluent in Spanish for all shifts. She thinks she can create a query that uses broader criteria than the exact match criteria she's used so far to help with Paul's scheduling request.

ENHANCING QUERY CRITERIA TO IMPROVE DATA ANALYSIS

When you specify the criteria for a query, you are setting conditions that determine which records Access should display in the query results. Recall that to define a condition for a query, you enter the criterion in the Criteria row of the query design grid. If you enter a value, Access displays records that have an exact match of that value in the appropriate field. For example, when Maria entered 3 in the Criteria row of the JobID field, Access selected records in tblEmployee with the value 3 in the JobID field. Specifying a single criterion that Access must match exactly means you can pinpoint the records you want to select. However, suppose you want to select records for employees who earn between $8.00 and $9.00 per hour. If you know that the wages range from $8.00 to $9.00 in $.10 increments, for example, you could specify "8.00" as the first criteria, "8.10" as the next OR criteria, "8.20" as the next OR criteria, and so on, up to "8.90." Specifying 10 OR criteria is inefficient and can slow the query if the data source contains many records. In addition, this method of specifying multiple OR criteria is only possible if you are already familiar with the data in the database. If you don't know all the wage values, the criteria you specify will only retrieve some of the appropriate records. Instead of specifying exact criteria in such a case, you can expand the criteria by using wildcards or comparison operators.

Using Wildcards for Inexact Query Matches

Suppose you want to use a criterion such as a name, but do not know the spelling, or want to display records with values that match a pattern, such as phone numbers that all begin with a certain area code. In these cases, you cannot specify an exact match. Instead, you can use a **wildcard character**, a placeholder that stands for one or more characters. Use wildcard characters in query criteria when you know only part of the criteria, want to search for a value based on some of its characters, or want to match a pattern. Table 3.4 summarizes the wildcards you can use in queries.

Table 3.4: Wildcard characters used in queries

Symbol	Purpose	Example
*	Match any number of characters	Ab* to locate any word starting with Ab
?	Match any single alphabetic character	J?n finds Jan, Jon, and Jen
#	Match any single digit in a numeric field	(970) ###-#### finds phone numbers that have 970 area codes 1/##/08 finds dates during January 2008
[ ]	Match any single character listed within the brackets	J[eo]n finds Jen and Jon but not Jan
!	Match any character not within the brackets	J[!eo] finds Jan but not Jen or Jon
-	Match any one of a range of characters within the brackets; letters must be in ascending order	A[d-p] finds aft, ant, and apt, but not act and art

As you enter data in Memo fields, try to use the same keywords throughout the memos so that you can easily retrieve records later. Be certain to use wildcards when you specify the keyword as a query criterion to select records that contain characters before and after the keyword. For example, to discover how many employees speak Spanish at 4Corners Pharmacy, Maria could type *Spanish* in the Criteria row of the Memo field. The asterisk (*) wildcard character on either side of the criterion means Access selects records that contain text or other values before and after "Spanish" in the Memo field, such as those that include "Speaks Spanish fluently" and "Knows some Spanish." If Maria specifies Spanish without the asterisks, Access selects records that contain only the word Spanish in the Memo field.

Wildcards can help you match a pattern. For example, if you want to display the employees who started working in 2004, you could use */*/2004 or *2004 as the criterion in the StartDate field. Wildcards can also help you overcome data-entry errors. For example, if want to retrieve records for employees who live in Dolores, Colorado, which is often misspelled as Delores, you could specify D?lores as the criterion in the City field. In these ways, using wildcards can make your queries more powerful, allowing you to retrieve data without using criteria that demand an exact match.

Access inserts the word "Like" for criteria with wildcards, quotation marks around text, and pound signs around dates you enter, as in Like "*Spanish*" or Like #12/*/2008#.

Maria is ready to turn to Paul's scheduling request. Because many of the pharmacy's clientele speak Spanish, he wants to schedule at least one Spanish-speaking employee for each shift. If an employee speaks Spanish (or any other language besides English), it is noted in the Memo field of tblEmployee. Because this field has a Memo data type, which allows for lengthy text or combinations of text and numbers, it is often best to use wildcards in criteria that involve Memo fields.

To create this query, Maria double-clicks the Create query in Design view option in the Database window. The Select Query window opens in Design view, followed by the Show Table dialog box. All the fields she needs are in tblEmployee, so she double-clicks tblEmployee to display its field list, and then closes the Show Table dialog box. She adds the EmpLast, EmpFirst, JobID, and Memo fields to the design grid by double-clicking each one in that order. She selects EmpLast before EmpFirst because she plans to sort the records alphabetically by last name; the sort order will then be clear to anyone viewing the query results. She types *Spanish* in the Criteria row for the Memo field. The asterisks are necessary so that Access selects records that contain Spanish anywhere in the field. When she presses the Enter key, she notices that Access adds the word Like and inserts quotation marks around Spanish. See Figure 3.13.

Figure 3.13: Entering a query criterion using wildcards

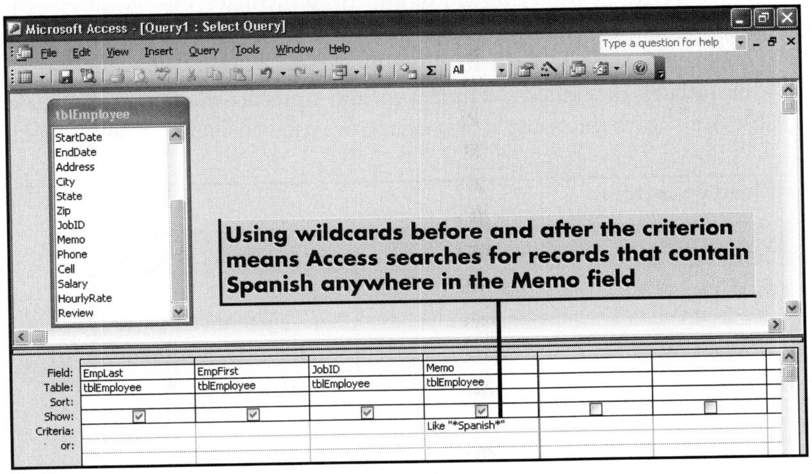

Maria saves the query as qrySpeakSpanish, runs the query, and finds three employees who speak Spanish, noting that none of them are pharmacists and that one no longer works at 4Corners. See Figure 3.14. She plans to talk to Paul Ferrino about hiring more Spanish-speaking employees; she cannot currently meet the goal of scheduling a Spanish-speaking employee for each shift. Because queries do not save the data, but rather the design, criteria, and sort order, Maria can use this query in the future to periodically update the list.

Figure 3.14: Results of a wildcard search for Spanish-speaking employees

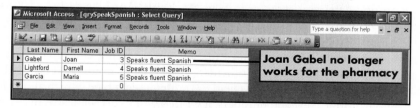

She notices that Joan Gabel is listed as an employee who speaks Spanish. However, Joan no longer works at 4Corners. Maria needs to solve the problem of maintaining data about employees who no longer work for the pharmacy. In the 4Corners database, she included records for past employees so she wouldn't lose the data about them. Eventually, the pharmacy will discard or archive printed information about previous employees, and the database will contain only current records. Maria needs a way to exclude the past employees from her queries.

Using Comparison Operators to Refine Query Criteria

In addition to entering a criterion that exactly matches a single value or using wildcards to match a pattern, you can use criteria that match a range of values. In this case, you use **comparison operators**, which compare the value in a field with a range of values in a criterion. If the value is within the range, data from the record is included. For example, you might want to know if an employee was hired after a particular date, such as June 1, 2007. Using a date as the criterion would only display those employees hired on that date. Instead, you can use a comparison operator to specify a range of dates, such as >= #6/1/2007# in the StartDate field to display employees who started working on June 1, 2007 or later. (Recall that Access requires pound signs around date values used in query criteria.) Table 3.5 shows the comparison operators used to specify a range of values.

Table 3.5: Comparison operators

Operator	Description	Examples
<	Less than	<500 <#1/1/2008#
<=	Less than or equal to	<=500 <=#12/31/2007#
=	Equal to	=500 ="CO"
>=	Greater than or equal to	>=500 >=12.75
>	Greater than	>500 >#12/31/2007#
<>	Not equal to	<>500 <>"CO"

Table 3.5: Comparison operators (cont.)

Operator	Description	Examples
BetweenAnd	Include values within the specified range (inclusive); always use with dates	Between #1/01/2007# And #1/31/2007# Between 5000 And 10000
In	Include values within the specified list	In("CO","AZ")
Is	Include records in which the field contains a null, not null, true, or false value, as specified	Is Null, Is Not Null Is True, Is False
Like	Include values matching the specified pattern	Like "*Spanish*"

When Maria queries the 4Corners database for employee information, she needs to use a comparison operator in the criteria so that the query excludes employees who no longer work for 4Corners Pharmacy. These are employees whose records include a value in the EndDate field. For example, Joan Gabel stopped working for 4Corners in 2004. The EndDate field in her employee record contains the date value 5/31/2004, the last date of her employment. Maria considers using the Not comparison operator because it excludes records that contain a specified value. However, if she uses Not #5/31/2004# as the criterion in the EndDate field, the query excludes only Joan Gabel's record, and not those of other past employees. She could use the In operator with Not to list the EndDate values of all the past employees, as in Not In(#5/31/2004#,#6/15/2005#), but that requires her to find and possibly update these values each time she runs the query.

Maria reexamines the fields in the tblEmployee field list, trying to find a fresh approach to solve her problem. Instead of excluding employees with a value in the EndDate field, perhaps she could focus on selecting only those employees who do not have a value in the EndDate field. Instead of a value, the EndDate field for current employees is blank, or null. She could use the Is operator with null, as in Is Null, in the EndDate field to select current employees only.

Best Practice

Understanding Null Fields

Access has a special character called a null that indicates a field contains no value, or is blank. Nulls are different from a space or zero character, and can be used in expressions to check whether a field contains a value. To do so, you can use *Is Null* or *Is Not Null* as a criterion. Is Null selects records in which the specified field does not contain a value. Is Not Null selects records in which the specified field contains any type of value.

Maria modifies qrySpeakSpanish by adding the EndDate field to the design grid. Then she enters Is Null as its criterion to select only those records in which the EndDate field is blank, effectively eliminating former employees from the query results. She also clears the Show check box for the EndDate field because she does not want to display this field in the query results. She saves the modified query, and then runs it. Figure 3.15 shows the design and results of this query.

Figure 3.15: Only EndDate fields with null values are displayed

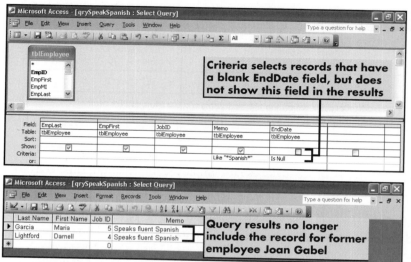

Now that Maria has refined her query for displaying current Spanish-speaking employees, she can turn her attention to solving a different problem. Paul Ferrino wants to reward long-term employees because he knows that they increase the efficiency, consistency, and quality of the pharmacy and its services. He also knows that hiring and training employees can be a drain on profits, and employee turnover can erode morale. He is considering presenting substantial bonuses to each employee who has worked at the pharmacy for more than five years. In addition, he has asked Maria to schedule a celebration later this year to acknowledge these employees and their contributions to the pharmacy. Maria needs to produce a list of employees who have worked at 4Corners Pharmacy for at least five years, or since January 1, 2003.

To produce this list, Maria can create a query that includes the StartDate field and uses the less than or equal to comparison operator (<=) to select records in which the start date is January 1, 2003 or earlier.

Because she needs to use the same tblEmployee field list as in qrySpeakSpanish, which is still open in Datasheet view, Maria switches to Design view and **clears the grid** to start with the same field list but a blank grid. To do this, she clicks Edit on the menu bar, and then clicks Clear Grid. She adds the EmpLast, EmpFirst, StartDate, and EndDate fields, and uses <=#1/1/2003# as the criterion in the StartDate field. She also decides to sort the records in ascending order by the values in the StartDate field so she and Paul can easily see who has worked for the pharmacy the longest. Finally, Maria uses the Is Null criterion in the EndDate field and removes the check from the Show box so this field does not appear in the query results. She saves the query as qryStartDate, and then runs it. Figure 3.16 shows the design and results of this query.

Figure 3.16: Using comparison operators with dates

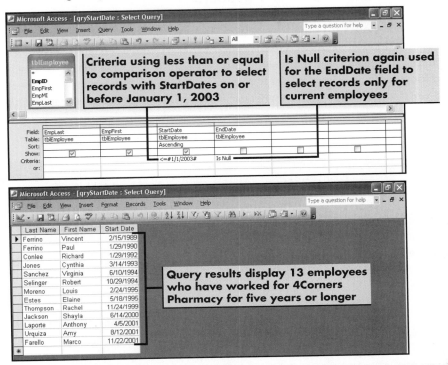

Best Practice

Clearing the Design Grid to Create or Modify a Query

When you are working with a query in Design view, you can clear the design grid by clicking Edit on the menu bar and then clicking Clear Grid. You can then create a query using the field lists that are already open in the field list area. Be certain to save the new query with a different name by clicking File on the menu bar and then clicking Save As so you don't overwrite the original query. You might also clear the grid when you don't plan to save the current query, but want to continue working in Design view, or the query is not producing the results you expect and want to try different criteria.

Before continuing her work with queries, Maria decides to print the results of all the queries she's created so far so that she can show them to Paul later.

VERIFYING AND PRINTING QUERY RESULTS

Before you distribute a query to others or use it as the basis for decisions, verify its results. Use your business knowledge to determine whether the results adequately answer the question you intended to answer. For example, if you want to list all the employees who have worked for your company for at least five years, but the query displays those who were hired within the last five years, you probably used the wrong comparison operator in the query criteria, such as the greater than operator (>) instead of the less than or equal to operator (<=).

Best Practice

Correcting Errors in Queries

If your query does not return any results, it might have a number of problems. Perhaps the underlying tables do not contain any matching data. Perhaps you have entered the criteria incorrectly. If you run a complex query that does not return any results when you know it should, revise the query so it specifies only one condition, and then run the query. If that works, add another condition and run the query again. As you build your query, you will probably see which additional condition is causing the problem.

If you receive an error similar to "Can't evaluate expression," look for a typographical error in the query criteria. An error similar to "Type mismatch" probably indicates that you have tried to perform mathematical operations on a Text or Date/Time data type value. An error similar to "Enter Parameter Value" usually indicates that you have misspelled a field name or have modified the table structure without changing the query to reflect the changes.

After you verify the query results, you can print the query datasheet. Although Access users usually print query results in the form of a report, which is more attractive and accessible than a datasheet, printing a query datasheet can help you and others review the query results and verify its accuracy or answer a quick question. It is good practice to check the format of the datasheet in Print Preview before printing so you can modify column widths and orientation for best results.

Modifying Query Datasheets

Access provides a number of formatting options to help you improve the appearance of a query or table datasheet. You set these formatting options when you are working in Datasheet view. (They are not available in Design view.) Table 3.6 describes the most common options you can use to format datasheets you print or view. You can open most of the dialog boxes noted in Table 3.6 by clicking Format on the menu bar and then clicking the appropriate option. You can also use tools on the Formatting (Datasheet) toolbar to achieve the same results.

Table 3.6: Formatting options for query and table datasheets

Format Option	Effect	Access Tool to Use
Font	Change font, font style, and size	Font dialog box
Datasheet	Change cell effects to flat, sunken, or raised Change background and gridline colors Show or hide gridlines	Datasheet Formatting dialog box
Row Height	Set row height	Row Height dialog box
Column Width	Set column width or click the Best Fit button	Column Width dialog box
Hide Columns	Hide a column	Hide Columns command on the Format menu
Unhide Columns	Unhide a column	Unhide Columns dialog box
Freeze Columns	Set columns to display and print even if you scroll to the right	Freeze Columns command on the Format menu
Unfreeze All Columns	Unfreeze columns previously frozen	Unfreeze All Columns command on the Format menu
Subdatasheet	Expand, collapse, or remove subdatasheets	Subdatasheet command on the Format menu

Note that you can resize the column widths in any datasheet by double-clicking the line between field names to resize the columns to their best fit. If you have too many columns or they are too wide to fit on a single page in portrait orientation, you can use the Page Setup dialog box to change the page orientation to landscape.

Maria formats qryStartDate by increasing the size of the font and resizing the columns so that each is wide enough to display all the data it contains. She clicks the Print Preview button 🔍 on the Query Datasheet toolbar to view the effects of her changes. To print the results, she clicks the Print button 🖨 on the Query Datasheet toolbar.

Steps To Success: Level 1

Kim Siemers, human resources manager at Hudson Bay Pharmacy, is ready to use the Hudson database to extract information that will help her manage employees. She asks for your help in filtering table data and creating queries, especially those that use criteria to select the information they need. As you create and save the new queries, be certain to use the "qry" prefix as part of the naming convention. Also consult your instructor for instructions about submitting your results.

Note: To complete the following steps, you must have completed the Steps to Success for Levels 1 and 2 in Chapter 2.

Complete the following:

1. Start Access and open the **Hudson.mdb** database from the STS folder.

2. Kim needs quick answers to three questions. First, she needs to know how many pharmacists are listed in the tblEmployee table. Filter the data in the tblEmployee table to answer Kim's question. How many records are displayed?

3. Next, Kim wants to know how many records in tblEmployee are for pharmacists, owners, or managers. Refilter the data in tblEmployee to answer Kim's second question. How many records are displayed?

4. Finally, Kim wants to know who was the first employee hired by Hudson Bay Pharmacy, and who was the most recent. Organize the data in tblEmployee so that you can easily answer Kim's question. Who was the first employee hired by the pharmacy? Who was the most recent?

5. To help Kim call employees when she needs a substitute, create an alphabetical phone list of Hudson Bay employees and their phone numbers. Save the query as qryEmpPhoneList.

6. Kim is planning to meet with Joan Gabel, the owner of Hudson Bay Pharmacy, to review the wages paid to employees so they can budget for upcoming pay raises. Kim wants to check the hourly rates paid to employees. List the wages for employees who are paid according to their hourly rate, ranked from highest to lowest to display the full range of pay for current, nonsalaried employees. Also include information that clearly identifies each employee. Save the query as qryHourlyRate.

7. Kim mentions that a summary of the hourly rate information would also be helpful as she prepares for her meeting. List only the highest, lowest, and average pay rates for nonsalaried employees. Make sure that the average calculation does not include zero values for salaried employees. Save the query as qryHourlyRateAnalysis.

8. Kim wants to schedule employees so that at least one who speaks Spanish is working each shift. Produce a list of current employees at Hudson Bay Pharmacy who speak Spanish. Save the query as qrySpeakSpanish.

9. To prepare for employee reviews, Kim asks you to produce a list of all employees who have been reprimanded at least once. (*Hint*: Look for keywords in the Memo field.) Save the query as qryReprimand.

10. Kim has analyzed employment data and discovered that those who have been working for one to three years are most likely to accept employment elsewhere. Kim asks you to identify employees who started working between January 1, 2005 and January 1, 2007, ranked so the most recent start date is first. Save the query as qryStartDate.

11. Format one of the queries you created for Hudson Bay Pharmacy to make it easier to read, and then print one page of the results.

12. Close the **Hudson.mdb** database and Access.

LEVEL 2

CREATING MORE COMPLEX QUERIES

ACCESS 2003 SKILLS TRAINING

- **Add a calculated field to a select query**
- **Add a table to the Design view query grid**
- **Build summary queries**
- **Change join properties**
- **Create a find duplicate query**
- **Create a find unmatched query**
- **Create a query in Design view**
- **Create a top values query**
- **Create and run a parameter query**
- **Create calculated fields**
- **Create queries using wizards**
- **Create queries with AND conditions**
- **Create queries with OR conditions**
- **Include criteria in query for field not in results**
- **Use aggregate functions in queries to perform calculations**
- **Use computed fields and sort the results**
- **Use the AVG function in a query**

EVALUATING DATA USING SPECIAL TYPES OF QUERIES

In addition to the Simple Query Wizard, Access provides other query wizards that help you evaluate and verify the data stored in a database. For example, you can use the Find Duplicates Query Wizard to retrieve duplicate records in a table, which is especially useful if the table contains data for a mailing list or if you have imported records from another source. Table 3.7 lists query wizards other than the Simple Query Wizard and describes their purpose.

Table 3.7: Wizards for specialized queries

Query Type	Purpose	Example
Find Duplicates	Locate duplicate records in a table or query	Identify the same employee who is entered multiple times with different IDs
Find Unmatched	Locate records with no related records in a second table or query	Identify employees who have not taken any training classes

In this section, you will learn how to use query wizards to answer complex business questions, analyze data, and maintain the integrity of your database.

Now that Maria Garcia is familiar with the 4Corners database, she wants to use it to automate many of her human resources tasks. First, she wants to help employees determine how they can share rides to work. To conserve gasoline and other vehicle maintenance costs, employees have asked Maria to help them coordinate car pools. Parking near the pharmacy is limited, so Paul Ferrino is also encouraging employees to organize car pools. Employees who live in the same city can contact each other and share a ride to work. Maria's next task is to create a car pool list identifying those employees who live in the same city.

Using Queries to Find Duplicate Records

One select query wizard that Access offers besides the Simple Query Wizard is the **Find Duplicates Query Wizard**, which searches for duplicate values in the fields you select. For example, you might have accidentally entered the same employee or customer name twice with two different IDs. Newly transferred data from a spreadsheet or other source to an Access table also often contains duplicate information, as does a database that was not set up correctly. In these cases, you can use the Find Duplicates Query Wizard to identify duplicate records. Be certain to examine the records the wizard identifies to determine that they indeed contain duplicate data. You can then edit the data in the table as necessary.

Besides using the Find Duplicates Query Wizard to identify and then repair data errors, you can also use the wizard to improve business operations. For example, you can find customers who live in the same city so you can coordinate sales calls, identify vendors who supply the same products or services so you can compare costs, or find employees enrolled in the same training session so you can notify them about a schedule change.

The Find Duplicates Query Wizard is designed to identify records that contain the same information in a particular field, even if you don't know all or part of the duplicated values. If a table of employee data contains five records with "Springfield" and three records with "Ashton" in the City field, the wizard selects all eight records. To select records containing the same value that you specify, however, set criteria to select those records. For example, if you want to retrieve the records for employees who live in Springfield, use "Springfield" as the criterion in the City field. The query then selects five employee records.

Maria wants to identify employees who live in the same city so they can create car pools and share rides to work. Because 4Corners Pharmacy is located in southwestern Colorado on the border of the four states of Arizona, Colorado, New Mexico, and Utah, employees live in many surrounding cities. Maria can use the Find Duplicates Query Wizard to create a list of employees who live in the same city. She can post this list so that employees can form car pools.

To accomplish this task, Maria starts the Find Duplicates Query Wizard by clicking the Queries button on the Objects bar in the Database window, clicking the New button on the Database window toolbar, and then double-clicking Find Duplicates Query Wizard. The first dialog box in the wizard opens, shown in Figure 3.17.

Figure 3.17: First dialog box in Find Duplicates Query Wizard

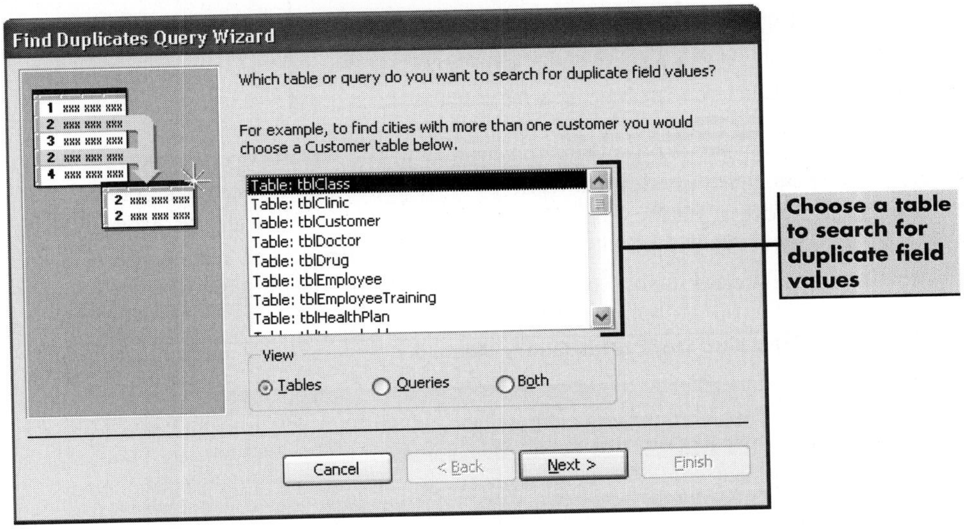

Because the tblEmployee table contains employee addresses, she clicks tblEmployee and then clicks the Next button.

The next wizard dialog box asks her to identify the fields that might contain duplicate information. Maria double-clicks City and State in the Available fields box to add them to the Duplicate-value fields box. She includes State because cities with the same name might be located in more than one state. See Figure 3.18.

Figure 3.18: Select field or fields that might contain duplicate information

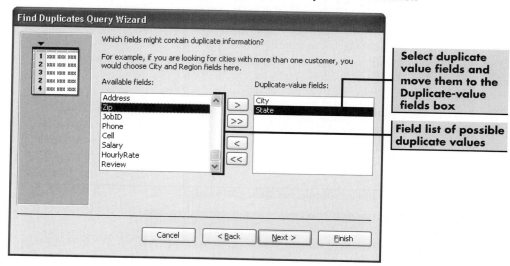

When she clicks the Next button, the third dialog box in the wizard opens, asking if she wants the query to show fields in addition to those with duplicate values. Maria selects the EmpFirst, EmpLast, Address, Phone, and Cell fields so the list will have all the information employees need to share rides, and then clicks the Next button. She names the query qryDuplicateCities, and clicks Finish. The results are shown in Figure 3.19.

Figure 3.19: Results of the Find Duplicates Query Wizard

City	State	Last Name	First Name	Address	Phone	Cell
Aneth	UT	White	Thomas	322 South Cripple Creek Avenue	(435) 167-9745	(435) 134-9462
Aneth	UT	Selinger	Robert	9411 Clarkston Avenue	(435) 243-4289	(435) 474-3497
Dolores	CO	Ferrino	Paul	133 South Washington	(970) 344-2616	(970) 445-2974
Dolores	CO	Ferrino	Vincent	1109 Siesta Shores Drive	(970) 348-5466	
Dolores	CO	Linebarger	Donald	1998 SE First Avenue	(970) 357-5546	(970) 487-6522
Dolores	CO	Farello	Marco	11259 Road 22	(970) 122-3333	(970) 221-3333
Flora Vista	NM	Sanchez	Virginia	633 Empire Street	(505) 444-9898	(505) 777-4125
Flora Vista	NM	Moreno	Louis	403 North Madison Street	(505) 599-6412	(505) 621-4477
Kayenta	AZ	Kobrick	Tara	620 East Empire Street	(928) 667-1119	(928) 764-4632
Kayenta	AZ	Laporte	Anthony	620 East Empire Street	(928) 667-1119	(928) 764-5211
Kayenta	AZ	Nader	Connie	1645 Johnny Cake Ridge Road	(928) 477-3145	(928) 397-6869
Lewis	CO	Estes	Elaine	801 Airport Road	(970) 541-8765	(970) 555-7655
Lewis	CO	Gabel	Joan	1102 Jackson Street	(970) 655-1777	(970) 644-1222
Lewis	CO	Latour	Dominque	56 East Pioneer Road	(970) 147-8458	(970) 239-6487
Pleasant View	CO	Jones	Cynthia	755 Cherry Street	(970) 344-7212	(970) 445-1498
Pleasant View	CO	Garcia	Maria	707 Cherry Street	(970) 344-8241	(970) 447-5465
Shiprock	NM	Langston	Dora	1155 NE Highland Parkway	(505) 699-7231	(505) 478-7411
Shiprock	NM	Lightford	Darnell	1309 Mesa Avenue	(505) 744-3147	(505) 775-1678

Only employees with the same city and state are listed

Avoiding Duplicate Records

If you expect duplicates to be a problem, the best way to solve the problem is to use good database design. For example, the 4Corners database allows only one person to be listed as the head of household in the HeadHH field in tblCustomer, and addresses are listed only once in a separate table named tblHousehold. The tblCustomer and tblHousehold tables share a common field, HouseID, which allows the two tables to be used in queries. By setting a criterion that HeadHH must be Yes, the problem of duplicates is eliminated by good design.

You could use the same technique with employees, but it would be difficult to designate one employee as head of the household. Although some employees might form a household, many might be roommates only. Most mailings to employees need to be sent individually for privacy reasons as well.

Using Queries to Find Unmatched Records

Another useful query wizard is the Find Unmatched Query Wizard. This type of select query compares the records in two specified tables or recordsets, and finds all the records in one table or query that have no related records in a second table or query. For example, you could find all customers who have not ordered any products, or vendors who provide services you no longer use. Identifying these unmatched records means you can then contact inactive customers to solicit business or delete records for vendors who no longer serve your needs. Note that the Find Unmatched Query Wizard requires that the two tables being compared have a common field.

At 4Corners Pharmacy, Paul Ferrino has set a store policy that all employees must maintain certifications in adult, infant, and child CPR and in defibrillator use. One of Maria's new responsibilities is to monitor training to make sure employees are enrolling in the required certification classes. This information is stored in the tblEmployeeTraining table. However, Maria is concerned that some employees might not have completed any training, and would therefore not have a record in tblEmployeeTraining. To identify these employees, she can use the Find Unmatched Query Wizard.

To start the query, Maria clicks Queries on the Objects bar of the Database window. She clicks the New button and then double-clicks Find Unmatched Query Wizard. The first dialog box opens, as shown in Figure 3.20.

Figure 3.20: Find Unmatched Query Wizard opening dialog box

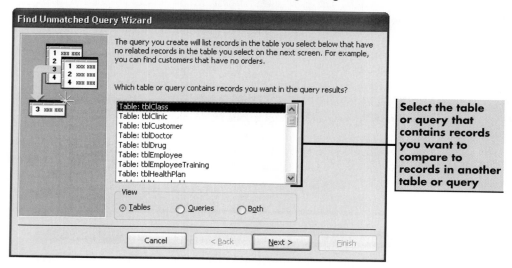

Maria wants to produce the names of employees who have not enrolled in any training classes. She therefore selects tblEmployee because it contains the employee records, which include employee names. She clicks the Next button, and the dialog box shown in Figure 3.21 opens.

Figure 3.21: Selecting the related table to compare records

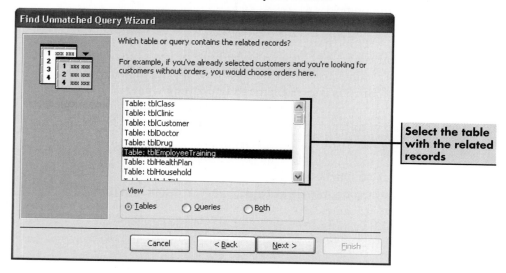

Maria selects tblEmployeeTraining and clicks the Next button because she suspects that this table might not contain records for all the employees in tblEmployee. She knows that both tables must have a common field so that the query can compare the records; tblEmployee and tblEmployeeTraining share the common field EmpID. See Figure 3.22.

Figure 3.22: Identifying the field to relate the two tables or queries

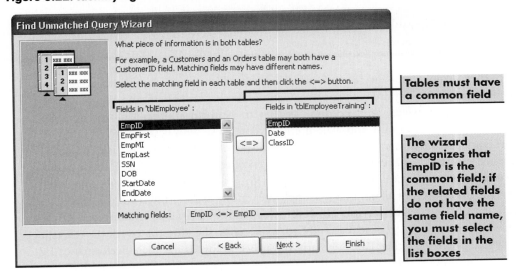

She clicks the Next button, and the next dialog box asks what other fields she wants to see in the query results. She decides to include EmpLast and EmpFirst in the results so she can easily identify the employees. Then she clicks the Next button, saves the query as qryNoTraining, and clicks the Finish button. The results are shown in Figure 3.23.

Figure 3.23: Results of the Find Unmatched Query Wizard

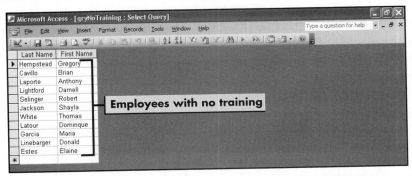

How To

Create a Query Using the Find Unmatched Query Wizard

1. Click Queries on the Objects bar in the Database window.
2. Click the New button and then double-click Find Unmatched Query Wizard.
3. Double-click to select the table or query that has the records you want in your query results. Click the Next button.
4. Double-click to select the table or query with the related records. Click the Next button.

5. If necessary, click the matching field in each table. Access identifies the common field if the fields have the same name in each table. Click the Next button.

6. Double-click the fields you want to display in the query results, and then click the Next button.

7. Name the query and then click the Finish button.

Maria finds 11 employees who have no matching records, meaning these employees need to schedule certification training as soon as possible. As she writes a note to remind herself to notify these employees, Paul Ferrino asks her to perform another task for him. He wants to identify the five best nonsalaried employees, those who have been rewarded for extraordinary customer service or other contributions to the pharmacy. He is considering developing a program that encourages employee excellence, and he might start by recognizing these five employees. Maria considers how to provide this information. She could pull out the file folders for all nonsalaried employees and scan the printed employee reviews to find citations for special service. However, this would be time consuming and error-prone; she would have to read carefully to make sure she doesn't overlook relevant information. She recalls that Paul regularly rewards employees for their performance by increasing their wages. Maria can use the 4Corners database to identify the top five wage earners—these are the same employees who provide the best service to the pharmacy.

Limiting the Records in the Query Results

Sometimes, showing all the data in a query provides more detail than you need, especially if the query selects many records that match your criteria. Limiting the results to only a few records often aids analysis. For example, schools need to identify students in the top 5% of their class. A bookstore might want to list the top 10 best-selling books, while a national business might want to increase advertising in the three regions with the fewest sales. To limit the number of records in the query results, you can create a Top Values query, which sorts and then filters records to display the specified number of records that contain the top or bottom values. You can apply the Top Values limitation to any query by using the Top Values list box on the Query Design toolbar. You indicate the number of records you want the query to display by entering or selecting an integer, such as 10 (to display the top or bottom 10 records), or a percentage, such as 25% (to display the top or bottom 25% of records). To indicate whether you want to select records with the top or bottom values, set a sort order for the field—Descending to display the records with the highest values, or Ascending to display the records with the smallest values.

Maria wants to identify the top five current wage earners at 4Corners Pharmacy. She creates a query in Design view using the EmpFirst, EmpLast, HourlyRate, and EndDate fields from tblEmployee. She uses the Is Null criterion in the EndDate field to select records only for current employees, and then removes the check mark from the Show box so the End-Date field doesn't appear in the results. Then she clicks in the Sort row of the HourlyRate field and specifies a Descending sort order. To limit the records to the top five values in that field, she clicks the arrow on the Top Values list box [All ▼] and then clicks 5. She saves the query as qryTop5HourlyRates, and then runs the query. Figure 3.24 shows the design and results of qryTop5HourlyRates.

Figure 3.24: Top Values query design and results

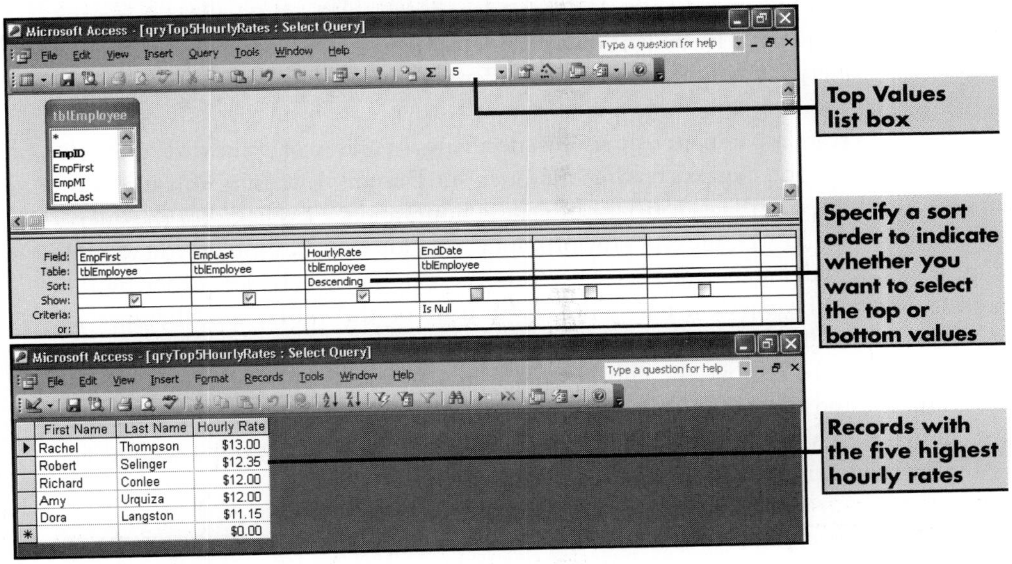

Maria can give the results of qryTop5HourlyRates to Paul to support his plans for an employee excellence program. Before she can return to the problem of tracking employee certification training, a pharmacy technician calls to say he can't work later today because of illness. Maria needs to find another pharmacy technician who can work for him. Instead of pulling out an employee phone list and searching for technicians as she's done before, Maria decides to create a query that will help her schedule employees when someone calls in sick or otherwise misses work. She'd like a way to generate a list of employees in a job category so she can quickly call others with the same job and find a substitute. She can create a query that selects employee information, including name and phone number, and uses the job ID as the criterion for selection. The problem she faces, however, is that the job ID will change depending on who is missing work. If a cashier calls in sick, for example, Maria needs to run the query using 4 as the criterion. If she needs a substitute for a pharmacy technician, she'll use 3 as the criterion. She needs to create a query that requests the criterion before it runs—then she can enter 3 or 4 as appropriate, and generate a list of employees in a particular job category.

Using Parameter Values in Queries

When you need to run a query multiple times with changes to the criteria, you can enter a **parameter value**. Parameter values are a phrase, usually in the form of a question or instruction, enclosed in square brackets, such as [Enter a job ID:] or [What job category do you want to select?]. The parameter value serves as a prompt to the user to enter a value.

To create a parameter query, you enter a parameter value as the criterion for a field, such as the JobID field. When you run the query, it opens a dialog box displaying the prompt you specified and allowing you to enter a value. For example, the dialog box might display "What job category do you want to select?" and provide a text box in which you can enter 3 or 4. When you click OK or press Enter, the query continues. Your response is then used as a criterion for the query. The benefit of a parameter query is that it is interactive—you can run the same query many times and specify different values each time.

Maria decides to create a parameter query by specifying a parameter value in the JobID field of tblEmployee. She begins creating the query in Design view using tblEmployee. She chooses EmpLast, EmpFirst, JobID, EndDate, Phone, and Cell as fields for the query. In the Criteria row for JobID, she types the prompt [What job classification do you want?], including the required square brackets. She sorts the data in alphabetical order by last name, and removes the check mark in the Show box for the JobID field because all employees in the results will have the same JobID. She remembers to include the EndDate criterion Is Null and to remove the check mark in its Show box. She saves the query as qrySubstituteList, and then runs it to make sure the Enter Parameter Value dialog box appears. Figure 3.25 shows the design of qrySubstituteList, the dialog box that appears when running the query, and the results.

Figure 3.25: Parameter query to allow user input when the query is run

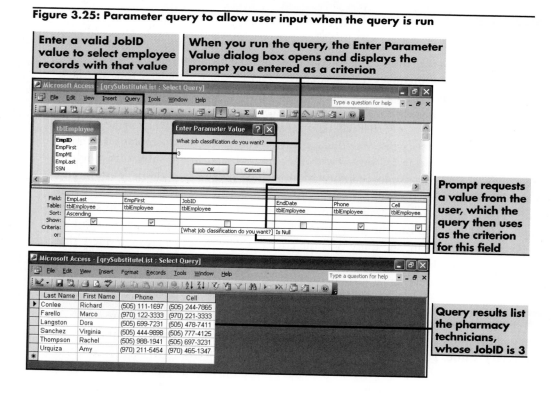

When Maria runs the query from the Database window, first the Enter Parameter Value dialog box appears, in which she can enter the job ID of the job for which she needs a substitute. When she clicks the OK button, the results will display a list of employees in that job category.

When you enter the parameter value prompt as a criterion in Design view, Access assumes you want users to enter a value with the default data type, which is Text. If the required value is of a different data type, you can use the Query Parameters dialog box to specify the parameter's data type. Because many parameter queries work without specifying the data type, you should try the query first without specifying the data type to see if it runs correctly.

How To

Specify the Parameter's Data Type

1. Open a query in Design view. In the Criteria row for the field whose criterion will change each time the query runs, type the prompt you want to appear in the Enter Parameter Value dialog box. Be certain to type the prompt within square brackets.
2. Copy the text of the parameter prompt without including the square brackets. (Select the text and then press Ctrl+C to copy it.)
3. Click Query on the menu bar and then click Parameters. The Query Parameters dialog box opens.
4. Click in the first open line of the Query Parameters dialog box, and then press Ctrl+V to paste the prompt. You can also type the prompt instead.
5. Click in the corresponding Data Type text box, click the list arrow, and then click the appropriate data type. See Figure 3.26.

Figure 3.26: Changing the data type of a parameter value

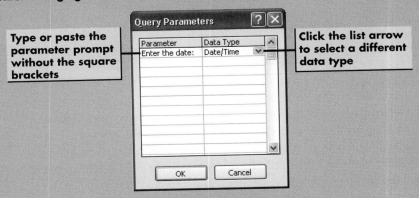

Type or paste the parameter prompt without the square brackets

Click the list arrow to select a different data type

6. Click the OK button.

Best Practice

Testing a Parameter Query
As you create a parameter query, test it by using fixed criteria and then add the parameter prompts. You can then switch between the Design view and Datasheet view without stopping to enter one or more parameters. After you have tested the query, replace the fixed criteria with the prompt for the Enter Parameter Value dialog box.

Maria now has time to revisit the training issues for the pharmacy's employees. She needs to know which employees need to attend training classes to keep their certifications up to date. To investigate this problem fully, she needs to analyze data from tblEmployee and tblEmployeeTraining.

ANALYZING DATA FROM MORE THAN ONE TABLE

Often, data from more than one table is required to answer a question. In fact, the most powerful advantage of creating queries is that they let you combine records from two or more tables to display only the information you need. For example, Maria needs data from both tblEmployee and tblEmployeeTraining to answer questions about employee certification training. Although you can use the Simple Query Wizard to select fields from more than one table or query, you must work in Design view to specify criteria for selecting records from multiple tables. Figure 3.27 shows the field lists for two tables in Design view for a select query.

Figure 3.27: Join line for related tables in Query Design view

Notice that a line connects the EmpID fields in the two tables. Recall that this line represents the relationship between the primary key in tblEmployee and a foreign key in tblEmployeeTraining that you created when you established referential integrity in Chapter 2. If tables are related, you can select fields from those tables and use them together in queries. The lines between tables link the primary key, the field designated with a "1," in a table called the **primary table** to the foreign key, the field designated with an infinity symbol (∞), in a table called a **related table.** The primary table is on the "one" side of the relationship, and the related table with the foreign key is on the "many" side of the relationship. For example, in tblEmployee, the EmpID field is the primary key. Each employee has only one ID and only one record in tblEmployee, but can take many classes.

By including the EmpID in the tblEmployeeTraining table, the two tables are linked by EmpID, and fields from both tables can therefore be used in a query. This linking of tables using their primary and foreign keys is called a **join** of the tables.

If you have not already established a relationship between two tables, Access creates a join under the following conditions: each table shares a field with the same or compatible data type and one of the join fields is a primary key. In this case, Access does not display the "1" and "many" symbols because referential integrity is not enforced.

If the tables you want to use in a query do not include fields that can be joined, you must add one or more extra tables or queries to link the tables that contain the data you want to use. For example, suppose Maria needs to display a list of classes taken by pharmacists only, and wants to include the ClassID and Date fields from tblEmployeeTraining and use the JobID field from tblJobTitle to set the criterion. The tblEmployeeTraining and tblJobTitle tables are not related and do not share any common fields. She must add a table to the query that is related to tblEmployeeTraining and tblJobTitle, which is tblEmployee. Then tblEmployee serves as a bridge between the two unrelated tables so that Maria can produce a list of classes taken by pharmacists.

Note that if your query includes related tables, the values you specify in criteria for fields from the related tables are case sensitive—they must match the case of the values in the underlying table.

Maria wants to start investigating employee training by producing a list of employees who have taken certification classes, including the date and class ID. To do so, she needs fields from two tables: tblEmployee and tblEmployeeTraining. She starts creating a query in Design view, selecting the field lists for tblEmployee and tblEmployeeTraining. To the query design grid, she adds the EmpLast and EmpFirst fields from tblEmployee and the Date and ClassID fields from tblEmployeeTraining. She notes that the tables have a one-to-many relationship, and that they are linked by the common EmpID field. Maria saves the query as qryEmployeeClasses, and then runs it. The results list employees who have attended training classes. Because some employees have taken more than one class, they are listed more than once. See Figure 3.28.

Figure 3.28: Query using fields from two tables

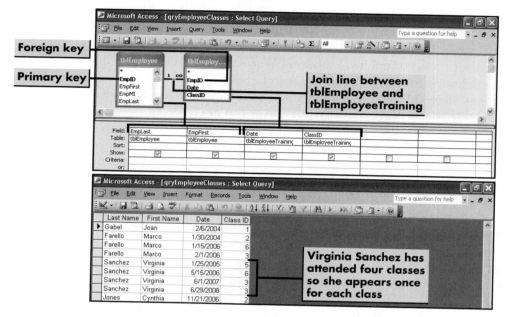

Maria can use this list herself, but she needs a similar list that includes the class description instead of the class ID. She'll post this list on the employee bulletin board as a reminder about the certification classes. Now that she's created qryEmployeeClasses, she can save time by using it as the basis for a new query that lists class descriptions. The qryEmployeeClasses query already has fields from tblEmployee and tblEmployeeTraining, including ClassID. However, neither table contains the Description field, which provides a description or title of each class. Because only tblClass contains that field, she needs to include the tblClass table in the new query to list class descriptions instead of class IDs.

You can use queries as the source of the underlying data for another query in place of one or more tables. For example, you might want to restrict the records you select by using a Top Values query or you might have already saved a query with the fields and criteria you want as the start for a new query. When you use the Show Table dialog box to select the objects to query, you can click the Query tab or the Both tab to choose queries as well as tables for field lists. Queries do not have primary keys or defined relationships the way tables do, but a line connects a field in a query used as a field list if the field names are the same in the other table or query.

Maria starts creating a query in Design view. When the Show Table dialog box opens, she clicks the Both tab to show tables and queries, and then adds qryEmployeeClasses and tblClass to the query. Because she wants to list employee names, the date they attended a class, and the class description, she double-clicks EmpLast, EmpFirst, and Date in the qryEmployeeClasses field list and Description in the tblClass field list to add these fields to the query design grid, and sorts the EmpLast field in ascending order. She saves the query as qryEmployeeClassesDescription, and then runs it. The results now include the descriptions of the classes instead of the ClassIDs, which is more meaningful to the employees who will view the list. See Figure 3.29.

Figure 3.29: Joining a query and a table

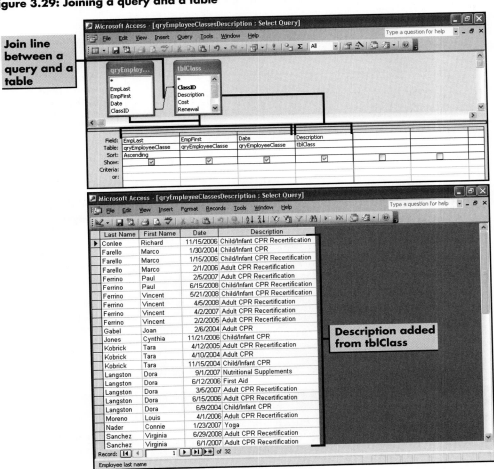

Note that when you create queries based on more than one object, you should not use any table or query that does not have a common field with at least one of the other tables or queries. If the tables in a query are not joined to one another, Access cannot associate one record with another, so it displays every combination of records between the two tables. The data from a query created with unrelated tables therefore contains many extra records, often producing nonsensical results. For example, suppose Maria tried to produce a list of employee names and class descriptions by including EmpLast and EmpFirst from tblEmployee and Description from tblClass. The tblEmployee and tblClass tables are not related and contain no common fields. When Maria runs the query, Access would simply list the 24 current employees in the EmpLast and EmpFirst columns of the results, and the descriptions for all eight classes contained in tblClass in the Description column. The results would contain 192 rows of information, or 8 × 24—each employee name listed eight times for each class, regardless of whether the employee attended the class. See Figure 3.30.

Figure 3.30: Unrelated tables show no join line and give meaningless results when queried

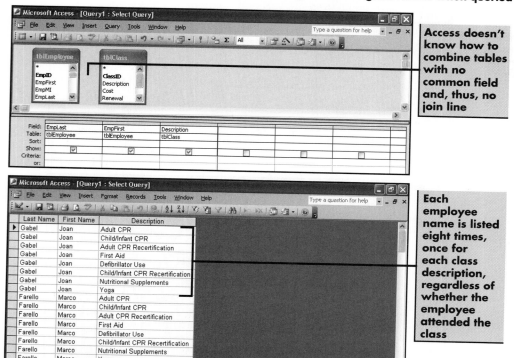

Access doesn't know how to combine tables with no common field and, thus, no join line

Each employee name is listed eight times, once for each class description, regardless of whether the employee attended the class

Best Practice

Verifying that Your Query Results Make Sense

When you examine the results of a query, be certain to verify that they make sense for your data and your business. One quick check is to note the number of rows in the query datasheet. Queries created using unrelated tables often contain many more rows than you expect. If you combine a large customer list of 100 customers, for example, with many purchases for each customer, you expect hundreds of rows in the results. However, if you list customers who live in a few specified cities, you expect the list to contain fewer than 100 customers. As a general rule, when the query results include a high number of rows, check to make sure the field lists have join lines and that the results seem plausible.

As Maria examines the results of qryEmployeeClassesDescription, she realizes it would provide more information if she could include the employees who have not attended any training classes—these are the employees who need to schedule training as soon as possible.

She already used the Find Unmatched Query Wizard to create qryNoTraining, which identifies employees who have not attended any training classes. Ideally, the list she posts on the employee bulletin board will include these employees and those who have attended training—some might need to update their certification. She decides to find out if she can refine the query to list all employees and their training information, even if they have not attended a class.

Refining Relationships with Appropriate Join Types

Tables with a relationship (and a common field) can be joined in two ways, and each affects the records a query selects. The most common type of relationship for select queries is an **inner join**. This type of join displays all records in one table that have corresponding values in the common field in another table. Usually, this joins the records of the primary table to the records of a related table (one with a foreign key). Records must match before they are displayed in the query results. For example, in the 4Corners database, the tblEmployee table is on the "one" side of a one-to-many relationship with the tblEmployeeTraining table. The primary key for tblEmployee is EmpID. In the tblEmployeeTraining table, EmpID is a foreign key. When these tables are related with an inner join, a query displays only those records that have a matching EmpID value—all the records in tblEmployee that have a matching record in tblEmployeeTraining, or all the employees who have attended training classes.

If you want to display all the records of one table regardless of whether a corresponding record is stored in a related table, use an **outer join**. For example, an employee record in tblEmployee might not have a corresponding record in tblEmployeeTraining because not every employee has attended a training class. An outer join query using tblEmployee and tblEmployeeTraining would list all employees regardless of whether they have attended a training class. This type of outer join applies when you want to show all the records from the primary table and only data that matches in the related table. Another type of outer join shows all the records from the related table and only data that matches in the primary table. Figure 3.31 shows an inner join, while Figures 3.32 and 3.33 show the two types of outer joins.

Figure 3.31: Inner join

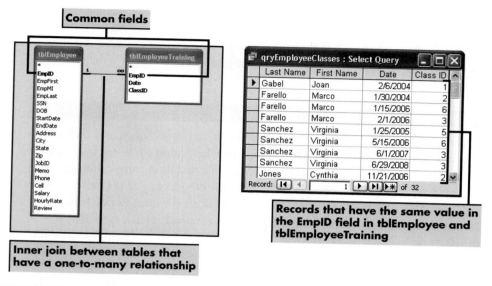

Common fields

Inner join between tables that have a one-to-many relationship

Records that have the same value in the EmpID field in tblEmployee and tblEmployeeTraining

Figure 3.32: Left outer join

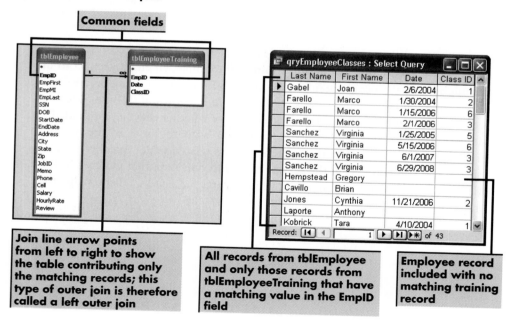

Common fields

Join line arrow points from left to right to show the table contributing only the matching records; this type of outer join is therefore called a left outer join

All records from tblEmployee and only those records from tblEmployeeTraining that have a matching value in the EmpID field

Employee record included with no matching training record

Figure 3.33: Right outer join

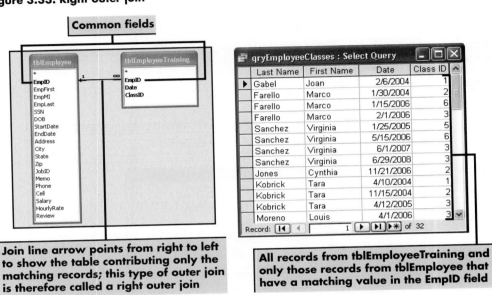

Common fields

Join line arrow points from right to left to show the table contributing only the matching records; this type of outer join is therefore called a right outer join

All records from tblEmployeeTraining and only those records from tblEmployee that have a matching value in the EmpID field

The two types of outer joins are often designated as left or right, depending on the placement of the field lists in Design view for the query and whether you want the one on the right or the left to show all its records. Left outer joins include all of the records from the table on the left, even if there are no matching values for records in the table on the right. Right outer joins include all of the records from the table on the right, even if there are no matching values for records in the table on the left. Changing the position of the field lists in the query reverses the right/left designation for the join.

To produce a list of all employees and their training information, even if they have not attended a class, Maria needs fields from tblEmployee and tblEmployeeTraining, the same fields she used to create qryEmployeeClasses. She opens qryEmployeeClasses in Design view so she can modify it, and saves it as qryAllEmployeeClasses. By default, this query uses an inner join between tblEmployee and tblEmployeeTraining. To change the join type, she double-clicks the join line. The Join Properties dialog box opens, shown in Figure 3.34.

Figure 3.34: Using the Join Properties dialog box to change the join type

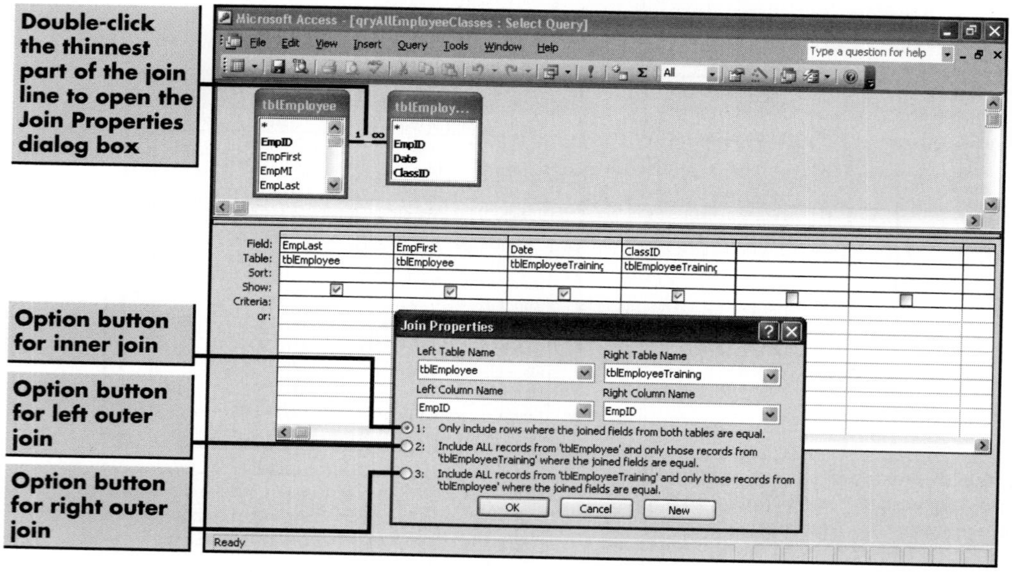

Double-click the thinnest part of the join line to open the Join Properties dialog box

Option button for inner join

Option button for left outer join

Option button for right outer join

The first option, "Only include rows where the joined fields from both tables are equal" is for an inner join. The second option, "Include ALL records from 'tblEmployee' and only those records from 'tblEmployeeTraining' where the joined fields are equal" is exactly what Maria wants. This type of outer join selects all the records from tblEmployee, even if there are no matching records in tblEmployeeTraining. In other words, it lists all the employees and the classes they've taken; if an employee has not attended a class, this outer join query lists the employee name, but leaves the Date and ClassID fields blank. The third option, "Include ALL records from 'tblEmployeeTraining' and only those records from 'tblEmployee' where the joined fields are equal" would select all the records from tblEmployeeTraining, even if there are no matching records in tblEmployee. If a class were scheduled, for example, but no employees were recorded as attending it, the results would include the Date and ClassID of that class, but no data in the EmpLast and EmpFirst fields.

Maria clicks the option button for the second option to create a left outer join, runs the query, and then saves it using the same name. The results are shown earlier in Figure 3.32.

This query, however, has the same problem as qryEmployeeClasses—it lists classes by ID number, not by the more meaningful description. Maria wants to display the Description column in the query results, not the ClassID column. Recall that tblClass contains the Description field, not tblEmployeeTraining. If she starts creating a query and uses fields from tblEmployee and tblClass, the query will not produce the results she wants because the tables are not related—they contain no common field. That means a query cannot retrieve records from these two tables as if they were one larger table, and will not produce meaningful results. Instead, she can use a third table to link tblEmployee and tblClass. The tblEmployeeTraining table is linked to tblEmployee by the common EmpID field, and is also linked to tblClass by the common ClassID field. She starts creating a query in Design view, adds the field lists for tblEmployee, tblEmployeeTraining, and tblClass to the query window, and then adds the EmpLast, EmpFirst, and Description fields to the design grid so she can list all employees and any classes they have attended. She decides to sort the records in ascending order by last name.

By default, the tables are related using inner joins. She double-clicks the join line between tblEmployee and tblEmployeeTraining to open the Join Properties dialog box, and then reviews the options for joining the two tables:

- Option 1 for an inner join is selected by default. It only includes records that contain the same value in the common field that links the tables.
- Option 2 is for an outer join that selects all records from the tblEmployee table and only those records from tblEmployeeTraining that contain matching EmpID fields.
- Option 3 is for an outer join that selects all records from the tblEmployeeTraining table and only those records from tblEmployee that contain matching EmpID fields.

Given that she wants to list all employees in the query results, she selects Option 2 to include all records from tblEmployee. The join line now includes an arrowhead pointing from tblEmployee to tblEmployeeTraining. She tries running the query, but receives an error message indicating that the query contains an ambiguous outer join. She also needs to specify the properties for the join line between tblEmployeeTraining and tblClass.

She double-clicks the join line between tblEmployeeTraining and tblClass, rereads the options in the Join Properties dialog box, and realizes that she needs to select Option 3 to include all records from tblEmployeeTraining and only those records from tblClass that contain matching ClassID fields. The join line includes an arrowhead pointing from tblEmployeeTraining to tblClass. She saves the query as qryEmployeeTraining, and then runs it. The query with outer joins produces the results she wants, shown in Figure 3.35.

Figure 3.35: Maria finally has the results she wants—all employees and descriptions of classes

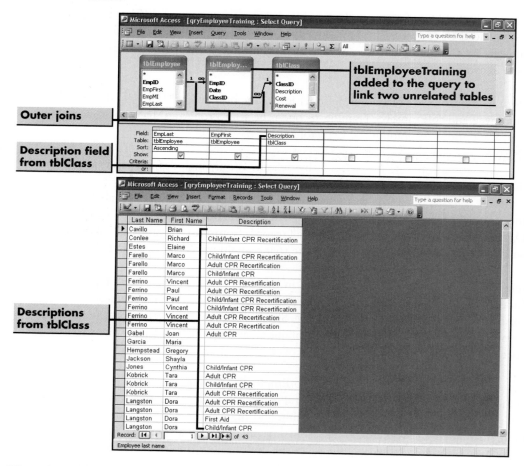

Now that Maria has produced the list she wants, she needs to review the classes that employees have attended. 4Corners requires a few classes, such as Defibrillator Use and CPR, and she wants to determine how many employees are complying with the policy. All required classes must be completed annually. Until now, it has been difficult for Maria to track compliance with the certification policy—employees postpone classes when they are busy, and she suspects that many certifications have lapsed.

Using Logical Operators to Specify Multiple Conditions

Some queries require one or more **logical operators**, which are used to test values that can only be true or false. You have already used the logical AND and OR in filters and queries when you want to combine criteria by comparing conditions. Figure 3.36 shows how the logical AND and OR operators work in the query design grid.

Figure 3.36: Using the logical operators AND and OR in query selection criteria

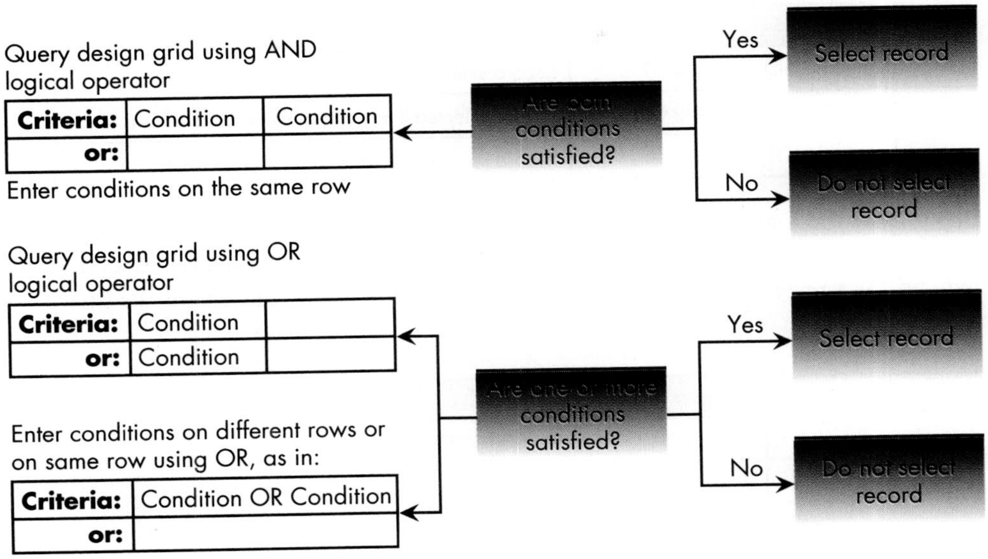

Recall that if you place conditions in separate fields in the same Criteria row of the design grid, all conditions in that row must be met to select a record. For example, if you want to select pharmacy technicians (JobID 3) who live in Colorado, enter "3" in the Criteria row for the JobID field, and "CO" in the Criteria row for the State field. You can combine the AND logical operator with the Like comparison operator to set conditions for the same field. For example, if you want to identify all the employees who are scheduled for a review in October 2008, enter the following condition in the Criteria row for the Review field: Like "10*" And Like "*2008".

If you place conditions in different Criteria rows in the query design grid, at least one of the conditions must be met to select a record. If the conditions apply to the same field, you can enter each condition separated by OR in the Criteria row. For example, if you want to select employees who live in Colorado or those who live in Utah, enter the following condition in the Criteria row for the State field: "CO" OR "UT".

The **NOT** logical operator excludes values that don't meet the criterion. For example, if you enter NOT 3 in the Criteria row for the JobID field, the query results show all employees except for pharmacy technicians. The NOT logical operator is often combined with the In comparison operator, as in NOT In("CO","UT"), which selects employees who do not live in Colorado or Utah. (Table 3.5 describes the comparison operators, including In and Like.)

Table 3.8 lists the logical operators you can use in an Access query and the results they return.

Table 3.8: Logical operators

Operator	Description	Examples	Results
AND	Logical AND	A AND B	Record selected only if both criteria are true
OR	Inclusive OR	A OR B	Record selected if any one of the rows of criteria is true
NOT	Logical NOT	NOT A	Record selected if it does not meet the condition

You can combine the logical and comparison operators to retrieve the records you need. For example, if you want to identify all the technicians and cashiers (JobIDs 3 and 4) who are scheduled for a review in October 2008, enter the following conditions in the query design grid:

	JobID	Review
Criteria:	3	Like "10*" And Like "*2008"
or:	4	Like "10*" And Like "*2008"

The qryEmployeeTraining query produces a list that includes employees and the classes they've attended and employees who have not attended any classes. Maria wants to base a new query on qryEmployeeTraining to check to see if employees taking required classes are up to date on their certifications in Adult CPR, Child/Infant CPR, and Defibrillator Use. Each type of certification needs to be renewed at different intervals, so she needs to set the criteria carefully to produce the results she needs.

Maria decides to save qryEmployeeTraining as qryUpToDate and then modify it in Design view. The query already includes field lists for tblEmployee, tblEmployeeTraining, and tblClass, with outer joins specified so that all employees are listed in the results, even if they have not attended a class. The EmpLast and EmpFirst fields from tblEmployee and the Description field from tblClass already appear in the query design grid. To determine whether an employee's certification is up to date, she needs the Date field from tblEmployeeTraining. To determine whether a particular class is required for certification, she needs to include the Required field from tblClass. She also decides to include ClassID from tblClass to make setting up the criteria easier—all she will have to do is specify the ID of the class rather than the long description. She adds the three fields—Date, Required, and ClassID—to the design grid. She clears the Show check boxes for ClassID and Required because she doesn't need to see the contents of these fields in the results.

Next, she will specify the criteria for selecting information about only the classes required for certification. Pharmacy employees must take the five classes listed in Table 3.9.

Table 3.9: Required classes for pharmacy employees

ClassID	Description	Renewal in Years
1	Adult CPR	0
2	Child/Infant CPR	0
3	Adult CPR Recertification	1
5	Defibrillator Use	1
6	Child/Infant CPR Recertification	1

The first two classes—Adult CPR and Child/Infant CPR—are the comprehensive classes employees take to receive CPR certification for the first time. Employees complete these comprehensive classes only once, and do not need to renew them. Instead, they need to complete classes with IDs 3 and 6, which are refresher courses for recertification. ClassID 5 provides certification for defibrillator use, and must be taken every year.

First, Maria adds a criterion to determine which employees are current in their Adult CPR certification. These employees would have completed the Adult CPR or the Adult CPR Recertification classes (ClassIDs 1 or 3) in the past year. She can use the logical operator OR to select employees who have completed ClassID 1 or 3, so she types "1 Or 3" in the Criteria row for the ClassID field.

To narrow the criteria and select only those employees who have taken these courses in the past year, Maria can use the Between...And comparison operator, which you use to specify two Date fields. She needs to specify the time period from January 1, 2008 to December 31, 2008, so she types "Between #1/1/2008# And #12/31/2008#" in the Criteria row for the Date field. (Recall that you use pound signs on either side of date values entered as criteria.)

Finally, she enters "Yes" as the criterion for the Required field to make sure the class is required. She runs qryUpToDate to test the results. See Figure 3.37.

Figure 3.37: Multiple criteria for listing employees who are up to date in their Adult CPR certification

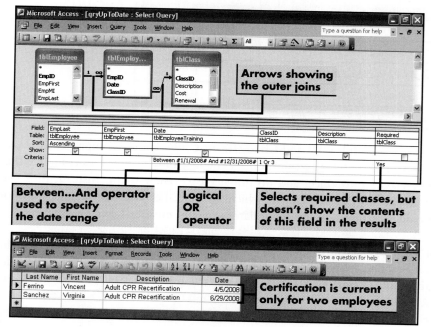

The results show that only two employees are currently certified in Adult CPR. Because these results seem accurate, Maria can continue adding criteria to the query for the other classes, starting with Child/Infant CPR. She knows that data on a second criteria row means that as long as all criteria on either line are true, records that satisfy one or the other line of criteria will be included. She types "2 Or 6" as the second criterion for the ClassID field to identify employees who have current Child/Infant CPR certification. Now, the results will include any employee who has completed Adult or Child/Infant CPR classes.

She also needs to specify the time period for the second ClassID criterion. If she doesn't, the results will include employees who have completed Adult CPR certification this year and those who have completed Child/Infant CPR certification at any time. To select only employees who have completed Child/Infant CPR in the past year, she copies the Between #1/1/2008# And #12/31/2008# criterion from the first criteria row to the second. She also enters "Yes" as the second criterion for the Required field. The three conditions on the second criteria row are three AND conditions—a record must contain all of the criteria to appear in the query results. She enters the third criteria for the Defibrillator Use class— Between #1/1/2008# And #12/31/2008# as the criterion for the Date field, "5" as the criterion for the ClassID field, and "Yes" as the criterion for the Required field. Maria saves the query with the same name—qryUpToDate—and then runs it. See Figure 3.38.

Figure 3.38: Results of modified qryUpToDate query with two rows of criteria

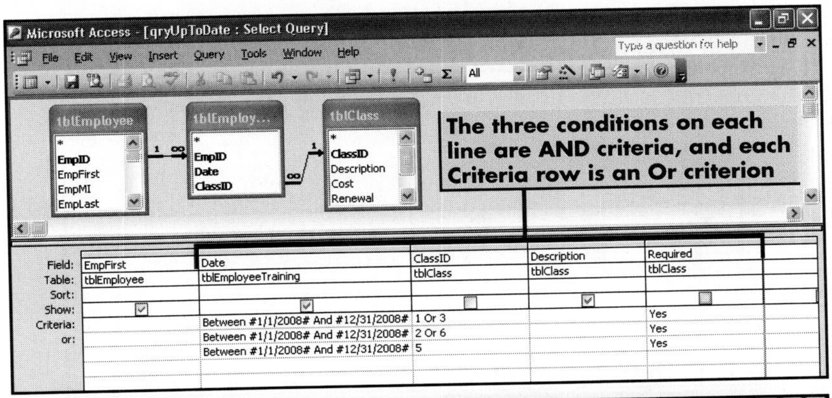

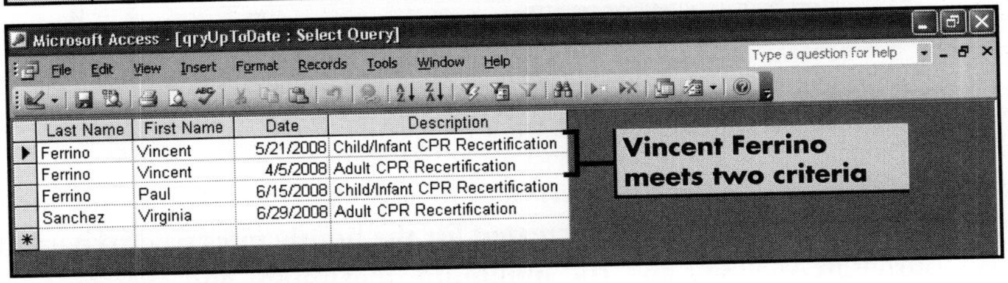

The results now include four records, but only Vincent Ferrino is completely up to date on CPR certifications. Even he needs to take the Defibrillator Use class again. As she suspected, employees have been postponing certification classes, and many no longer have current CPR certifications.

As she examines qryUpToDate in Design and Datasheet view, Maria realizes that using specific dates in the Date field criteria can cause problems. The query shows who has up-to-date certifications now, but if employees complete their requirements in the next three months, the query won't reflect that information. To allow her to enter a range of dates when she runs the query instead of changing the criteria in Design view each time she runs the query, she can change the fixed dates to parameter values. She replaces the fixed dates in the Date field with prompts for beginning and ending dates, so that Between #1/1/2008# And #12/31/2008# becomes Between [Beginning date?] And [Ending date?]. When she runs the query, it stops to ask for beginning and ending dates and waits for user input. This will make the query much more flexible in the future. See Figure 3.39.

Figure 3.39: Prompts for parameter values instead of fixed dates

When the query runs, the first prompt appears; when you enter a valid value and press OK, the second prompt appears

Parameter prompts instead of fixed dates

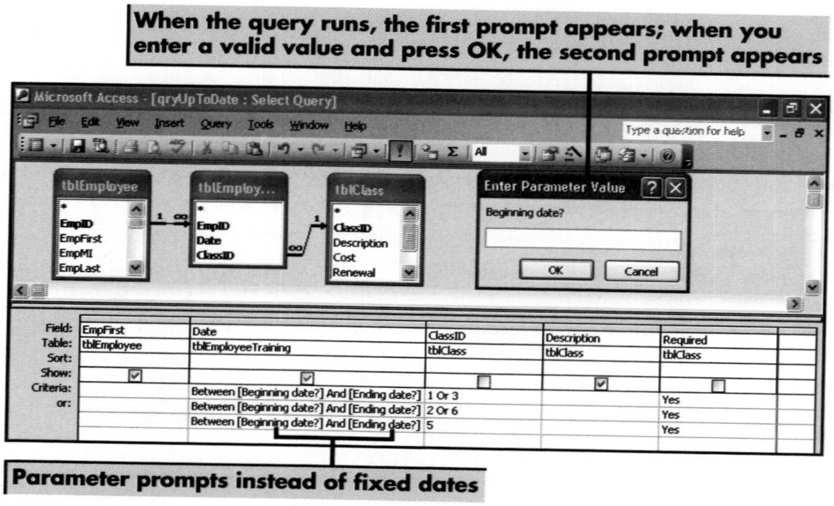

As she finishes qryUpToDate, Paul Ferrino returns and asks Maria to take another look at the hourly rate analysis. The two queries she created list the hourly rates paid to part-time employees (qryHourlyRateAnalysis) and the minimum, maximum, and average hourly rates (qryHourlyRateSummary). Paul wants to improve these results so they list these statistics by job ID, not by employee name. He also wants to know how many years each employee has worked at 4Corners Pharmacy—he is reviewing plans for retirement accounts and needs to set eligibility rules if he decides to offer a plan.

PERFORMING CALCULATIONS WITH QUERIES

So far, you have worked with queries that retrieve and sort records based on criteria. More complex queries often need to include statistical information or calculations based on fields in the query. For example, you can calculate the sum or average of the values in one field, multiply the values in two fields, or calculate the date three months from the current date. Any information that can be derived from fields in a table or query should be calculated in a query rather than included as data in a table. For example, if you want to know the age of an employee or customer, calculate the age in a query rather than include the age as a field in a table. Over time, the age would become obsolete;calculating it each time you need it ensures that the age is current.

The types of calculations you can perform in a query fall into two categories: predefined and custom calculations. Predefined calculations, also called totals, compute amounts for groups of records or for all the records combined in the query. The amounts predefined calculations compute are sum, average, count, minimum, maximum, standard deviation, and variance. You select one totals calculation for each field you want to calculate.

A custom calculation performs numeric, date, and text computations on each record using data from one or more fields. For example, you can multiply each value in one field by 100. To complete a custom calculation, you need to create a calculated field in the query design grid.

When you display the results of a calculation in a field, the results aren't actually stored in the underlying table. Instead, Access performs the calculation each time you run the query so that the results are always based on the most current data in the database.

Calculating Statistical Information

Recall that you can use the Summary options in the Simple Query Wizard to calculate statistical information such as totals and averages in query results. You can also use Design view to set up these calculations. To do so, you use **aggregate functions**, which are arithmetic and statistical operations you apply to records that meet a query's selection criteria. You can group, or aggregate, the records so that your results are for records in each group that meet the selection criteria. Table 3.10 lists the aggregate functions you can use in Access.

Table 3.10: Aggregate functions

Aggregate Function	Operation
Avg	Average of the field values for records meeting the criteria within each group
Count	Number of records meeting the criteria in each group
Max	Highest field value for selected records in each group
Min	Lowest field value for selected records in each group
Sum	Total of the field values for the selected records
StDev	Standard deviation for the selected records
Var	Statistical variance for the selected records
First	Returns the value from the first row encountered in the group; results may be unpredictable because the result depends on the physical sequence of the stored data
Last	Returns the value for the last row encountered for the group; results may be unpredictable because the result depends on the physical sequence of the stored data
Expression	Allows you to create an expression to use as criteria for selecting records
Where	Indicates column has criteria in selecting records

You can calculate all types of totals by using the Total row in the query design grid. You add this row to the grid by clicking the Totals button Σ on the Query Design toolbar. You can then click the Totals list arrow in a field to select an aggregate function for the calculation you want to perform on the field. To show the calculation results for a particular field, you select Group By in the Total row. For example, because Maria wants to calculate statistics for each job ID, she can group the records on the JobID field.

Maria needs to calculate the minimum, maximum, and average hourly rates for each job ID. She creates a query in Design view, adding the JobID and HourlyRate fields from the tblEmployee table to the query design grid and setting criteria to display only records for technicians and cashiers. Because she wants to calculate three types of statistics on the HourlyRate field, she adds that field to the design grid two more times. Then she clicks the Totals button Σ on the Query Design toolbar to specify the aggregate functions and group options she wants to use—Max for the first HourlyRate field, Min for the second, and Avg for the third.. She names the query qryMaxMinAvgHourlyRate, and then runs it. See Figure 3.40.

Figure 3.40: Using aggregate functions in a query

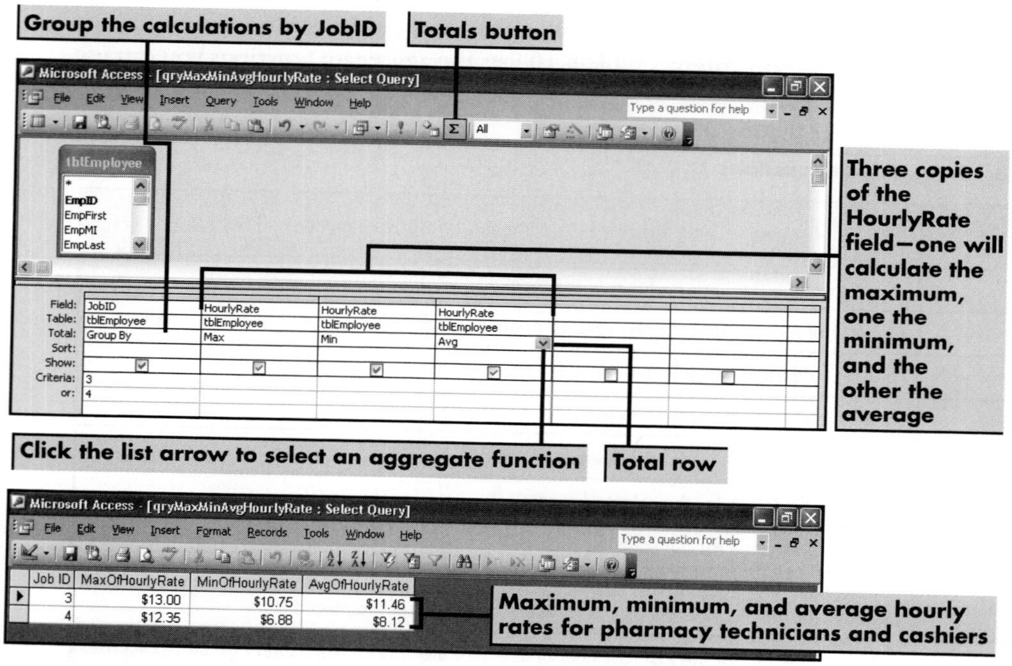

As hourly rates change, Maria can run this query again to recalculate the statistics and produce updated results for Paul.

Next, Maria can determine how long each employee has worked at 4Corners Pharmacy. She knows that she can calculate the number of days of service by subtracting the current date from the value in the StartDate field. Then she can convert the number of days to years. The aggregate functions do not perform this type of calculation. Instead, she needs to create a calculated field in a query.

Creating Calculated Fields in a Query

You can use a query to perform a calculation for immediate use or to include the calculation later when you create a report or form based on the query. You specify the calculation by defining an expression that contains a combination of database fields, constants, and operators. An **expression** is an arithmetic formula used to make the calculation. You can use the standard arithmetic operators (+, -, *, and /) in the expression. If an expression is complex, use parentheses to indicate which operation should be performed first. Access follows the order of operations precedence: multiplication and division before addition and subtraction. If the precedence is equal, Access works from left to right. For example, if you use 5 + 6 * 100, the result is 605. If you use (5 + 6) * 100, the result is 1100. It's a good idea to check your formula with a calculator to make sure it is working correctly.

To perform a calculation in a query, you add a field to the query design grid called a **calculated field**. Where you would normally insert the field name from a table or query, you type an expression. For example, suppose you want to calculate the wages employees earn if all hourly rate employees receive a 10% bonus. In the query design grid, you could enter an expression in a blank field such as the following:

```
Wage with Bonus: ([HourlyRate]* 1.10)
```

In this expression, Wage with Bonus is the name you specify for the field. Field names in the expression are enclosed in square brackets. The calculation ([HourlyRate]*.10) computes the bonus as 10% of the value in the HourlyRate field. This bonus is added to the value in the HourlyRate field to calculate the total wages including bonus. When the query is run, the expression uses values from the records that meet the criteria you specify to make the calculation.

To type a complete expression, you often need more space than is provided by the field box in the query design grid. In this case, you can open the Zoom dialog box, which provides a large text box for entering expressions or other values.

Some database developers use the **Expression Builder** when they need to build complex expressions or when they are not familiar with the field, table, and query names in the database. This database tool, shown in Figure 3.41, allows you to work with lists of objects such as tables and queries as well as constants, functions, and common operators to help you construct the expression for your calculation. You can click a field name or operator and then paste it into the expression you are building. You type any constant values that need to be part of the expression.

Figure 3.41: Using the Expression Builder to create an expression for a calculated field

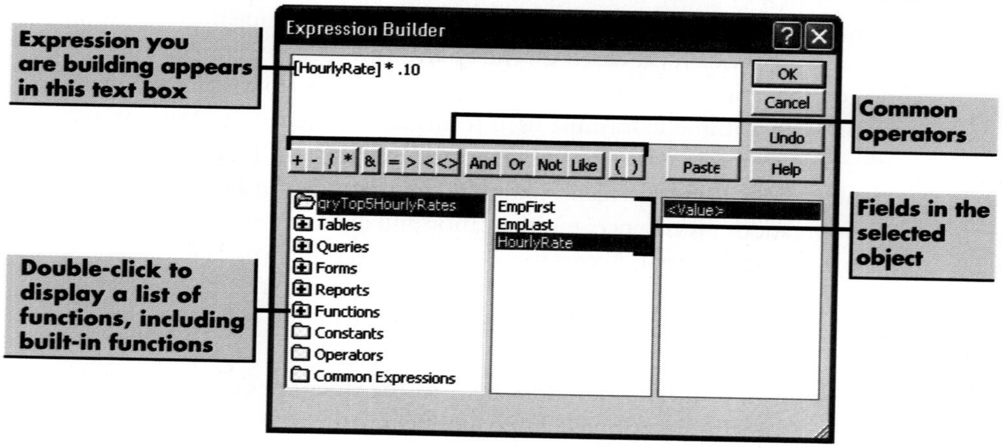

Maria needs to calculate how long each employee has worked for 4Corners Pharmacy. Paul will use this information as he reviews retirement account plans and sets eligibility rules. Maria needs to calculate the years of service each employee has provided 4Corners, and decides to use a calculated field in a query to do so. In the calculation, she needs to subtract the value in the StartDate field from today's date. She could create a parameter query that prompts her to enter today's date and then uses that value in the calculation. However, that means she would enter today's date 24 times, which seems unnecessarily repetitive. Instead, she can use the Date function to retrieve today's date.

When you are creating expressions, you can use a **function** to perform a standard calculation and return a value. The Date function is a built-in function, meaning it is provided with Access, and has the following form: **Date()**. To use today's date in an expression, type Date() instead of a fixed date value. The calculation then stays current no matter when you run the query. The Date function can also be used in query criteria.

Maria creates a query in Design view, using the EmpLast, EmpFirst, and StartDate fields from tblEmployee. Even former employees might be eligible for the retirement plan, so Maria does not include the EndDate field and criteria to eliminate former employees from the query results. To make room for typing an expression and create a calculated field, she right-clicks the Field row in the first empty column, and then clicks Zoom on the shortcut menu to open the Zoom dialog box. She types "Years of Service:" as the name for the calculated field. The expression should subtract the value in the StartDate field from today's date to calculate the number of days of service. Then the expression should divide that result by 365 to calculate the years of service. Rather than using a fixed date for today's date, she will substitute Date() so that Access retrieves this value each time the query runs. She types the following expression into the Zoom box:

```
Years of Service: (Date() - [StartDate]) / 365
```

"Years of Service" is the name that will appear as the datasheet column heading. The colon (:) separates the name from the calculated expression. The first part of the expression—Date()—is the Access function for calculating today's date. Next comes the subtraction operator followed by [StartDate], which is the name of the StartDate field enclosed in square brackets. You use square brackets around field names to distinguish them from function names or other types of values. Including Date() – [StartDate] in parentheses means that Access subtracts the value in the StartDate field from today's date before performing the second part of the calculation, which is to divide that value by 365, the approximate number of days in a year. (This number is approximate because it doesn't account for leap years.) Dividing by 365 converts the days to years.

She clicks the OK button to close the Zoom dialog box, saves the query as qryYearsOfService, and then runs it. The results calculate the approximate years of service, but display a number with many digits after the decimal point. See Figure 3.42.

Figure 3.42: Using a calculated field in a query

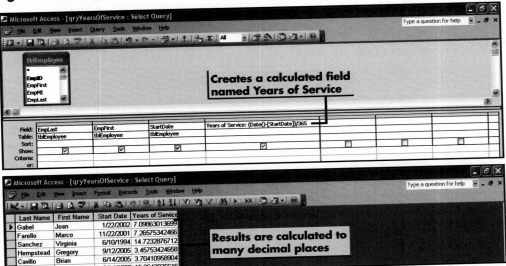

To change the format and number of decimal places for the calculated field, Maria switches to Design view, right-clicks the Years of Service field, and then clicks Properties on the shortcut menu to display the list of properties for the field. Table 3.11 describes the properties you can set for fields in a query.

Table 3.11: Field properties

Property	Description
Description	Provide information about the field.
Format	Specify how numbers, dates, times, and text are displayed and printed. You can select a predefined format, which varies according to data type, or create a custom format.
Decimal Places	Specify the number of decimal places Access uses to display numbers.
Input Mask	Specify an input mask to simplify data entry and control the values users can enter in a field as you do when designing a table.
Caption	Enter the text that appears as a column heading for the field in query Datasheet view.
Smart Tags	Assign an available Smart Tag to the field.

Maria uses the Format and Decimal Places properties to specify the format of the field values. She selects Standard as the Format and 1 for Decimal Places. She closes the property list, sets a descending sort order for the calculated field to better interpret the results, and then saves and runs the query again. She resizes each column in the resulting datasheet to its best fit. See Figure 3.43. (Your results will vary depending on the current date.)

Figure 3.43: Formatting a calculated field

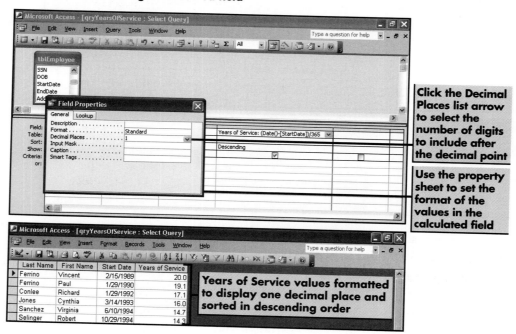

Including approximate results is appropriate for Paul's purpose now—he is only reviewing retirement plans and needs to know how many people would be eligible. Considering that Paul might need precise values after he selects a plan, Maria consults the database developer, Donald Linebarger, to see if he can suggest a more accurate way to calculate the date. He gives Maria the following expression, which accounts for leap years when it calculates years of service and has the advantage of formatting the result, and explains the parts of the expression.

```
Years of Service: DateDiff("yyyy",[tblEmployee]!
     [StartDate],Now())+ Int(Format(Now(),"mmdd")
          <Format([tblEmployee]![StartDate],"mmdd"))
```

- **Years of Service**—Specifies the name of the calculated field.
- **DateDiff("yyyy",[tblEmployee]![StartDate],Now())**—The DateDiff function calculates the difference between two date values, which are defined as arguments within parentheses following the function name. The arguments are separated by commas. The "yyyy" argument specifies the interval of time between the two date values as years. The [tblEmployee]![StartDate] argument defines the first date as the value in the StartDate field of tblEmployee. The Now() argument retrieves the current date and time as stored in your computer system. In other words, this DateDiff function calculates the number of years between the value in StartDate and today, taking leap years into account.
- **Int(Format(Now(),"mmdd")<Format([tblEmployee]![StartDate],"mmdd"))**— This part of the expression verifies that the results are shown as whole numbers. The Int function removes any fractional part of the result, and returns only the integer part.

Maria copies the formula into the Years of Service field, and then runs the query to test it. The dates are in whole numbers and, Donald assures her, it also takes leap years into account. She doesn't save qryYearsOfService with the new formula because she doesn't need it yet, but she does note the expression so she can use it later.

As she looks over the results of qryYearsOfService, she considers fine-tuning the results to display employee names as full names instead of as separate last name and first name values. Doing so will make the printed datasheet more appealing and easy to use for Paul. Furthermore, if Paul decides to institute a retirement plan, she will need to develop a report based on qryYearsOfService, in which a full name will be even more well received.

Best Practice

Using Calculated Fields

Values that can be derived from other fields generally should not be stored as separate fields in a database. For example, in a product orders table, rather than store quantity ordered, unit price, and total price in three fields, use a calculated field to derive the total price from the quantity and unit price (Quantity*UnitPrice, for example). Age data would become outdated if you entered it directly. If you plan to use a calculation in a form or report, you should create a query to perform the calculation and then use the query as the basis for the form or report.

Concatenating in Queries

When you create field names for a table, you usually want to store data in separate fields for common values such as first name, last name, city, state, and zip code. Sorting or querying on a field containing a last name value is faster than on a field containing first and last name. However, when using the data in a mailing label or report, you might want to present these common values together to save space and improve readability. In the same way that you can add two or more numbers to obtain a result, you can also add text data, such as first name and last name, to display the full name. To do this, you create a calculated field that combines the values in other fields. Combining the contents of two or more fields is called **concatenation**.

You use the concatenation operator (&) for concatenating, not the plus sign (+), or addition operator, which is reserved for adding numbers. Specify spaces that naturally fall between words or other characters by enclosing the spaces in quotation marks. For example, you could use the following expression to concatenate the EmpFirst and EmpLast fields, displaying the first name and last name separated by a space:

`[EmpFirst]& "" & [EmpLast]`

Maria wants to combine the contents of the EmpFirst and EmpLast fields in qryYearsOfService so that a single field displays the first and last name. She opens qryYearsOfService in Design view, deletes the contents of the EmpLast field so that the column is blank, and then deletes the EmpFirst field. In the first column, she types the following expression to specify "Name" as the field name and displays the first name and last name separated by a space:

`Name: [EmpFirst]& " " & [EmpLast]`

She saves her changes and runs the query. Figure 3.44 shows the final design and results of qryYearsOfService.

Figure 3.44: Concatenated field for employee names

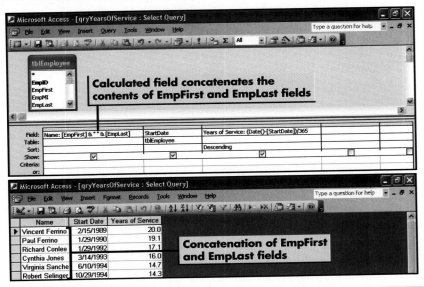

Steps To Success: Level 2

Hudson Bay Pharmacy is ready to create more complex queries to analyze employee data. Kim Siemers is the human resources manager for Hudson Bay, and asks for your help in creating queries that extract the employee information she needs from their database. As you create and save the new queries, be certain to use the "qry" prefix as part of the naming convention. Also consult your instructor for instructions about submitting your results.

Complete the following:

1. Start Access and open the **Hudson.mdb** database from the STS folder.

2. Kim wants to identify employees who live in the same neighborhood in Edmonton so they can create car pools and share rides to work. In Edmonton, the postal codes roughly correspond to neighborhood. Prepare a list of employees who live in the same neighborhood so that Kim can create a list of employees who can share rides to work. Name the query qryDuplicatePostalCodes.

3. A new policy at Hudson Bay Pharmacy is that all employees must acquire and maintain certifications in adult, infant, and child CPR and in using defibrillators. Kim asks you to identify employees who have not completed any certification training. Save the query as qryNoTraining.

4. Kim also needs to list all employees and the classes they have taken. The results should include current employees who have not attended training as well as those who have. Save the query as qryEmployeeTraining.

5. Kim also needs to identify employees whose CPR or defibrillator certification has expired, depending on the time period she specifies. Show all employees whose Adult CPR, Child/Infant CPR, or Defibrillator Use certification has expired in any specified time period. Save the query as qryUpToDate.

6. Joan Gabel, owner of Hudson Bay Pharmacy, wants to identify the five current non-salaried employees who are earning the highest wages per hour. These are the five employees who have been working for the pharmacy the longest or who have regularly received raises for their work. List the top five wage earners of all the current non-salaried employees. Save the query as qryTop5HourlyRates.

7. To prepare for employee reviews, Kim needs to calculate the minimum, maximum, and average hourly rates for each job category. Provide this information for her, saving the query as qryMaxMinAvgHourlyRate.

8. Joan is considering offering life insurance as an employee benefit, and needs to know the current age of all employees. Provide this information for her. Be certain to provide an appropriate name for the column with the result and to show the ages in descending order. Include the job title and format the results so that they include one decimal place. Also show the first name and last name together. Save the query as qryEmployeeAge.

9. Kim asks you to provide one other statistical analysis. Show the average age of employees by job title. Save this query as qryAvgEmployeeAge.

10. Close the **Hudson.mdb** database and Access.

LEVEL 3

EXPLORING ADVANCED QUERIES AND QUERIES WRITTEN IN STRUCTURED QUERY LANGUAGE

ACCESS 2003 SKILLS TRAINING

- **Create a crosstab query**
- **Create a make-table query**
- **Create a new SQL query**
- **Create a query in Design view**
- **Create and run a delete query**
- **Create and run an update query**
- **Include all fields in an SQL query**
- **Sort an SQL query**

ANALYZING QUERY CALCULATIONS

In this level, you will learn about more advanced queries. You will learn how to use the Crosstab Wizard to create a crosstab query, one of the most useful queries for preparing data for further analysis. You will also learn how to create action queries, which are those that change or move many records in one operation. There are four types of action queries: append, update, delete, and make-table. You use these types of queries to add records to one table from another, change values in a field based on criteria, delete records based on criteria, or make a new table. You will also learn how to use the IIF function to make decisions in a query and to write queries in Structured Query Language (SQL), which is the language Access uses to query, update, and manage its databases.

Crosstab queries are a special type of Totals query that performs aggregate function calculations on the values of one database field and allows you to determine exactly how your summary data appears in the results. You use crosstab queries to calculate and restructure data so that you can analyze it more easily. Crosstab queries calculate a sum, average, count, or other type of total for data that is grouped by two types of information—one as a column on the left of a datasheet and another as a row across the top. You might think of a crosstab query rotating the data to present repeating fields as columns so your data appears in a spreadsheet-like format. Figure 3.45 compares a select query and a crosstab query.

Figure 3.45: Comparing a select and crosstab query

Year	Class	Total Cost
2004	Adult CPR	$60.00
2004	Child/Infant CPR	$45.00
2004	Defibrillator Use	$25.00
2005	Defibrillator Use	$25.00
2006	Child/Infant CPR	$15.00
2006	First Aid	$15.00

This select query only groups the totals vertically by year and class, resulting in more records

Class	2004	2005	2006	Total Cost
Adult CPR	$60.00			$60.00
Child/Infant CPR	$45.00		$15.00	$60.00
Defibrillator Use	$25.00	$25.00		$50.00
First Aid			$15.00	$15.00

This crosstab query displays the same information, but groups it both horizontally and vertically so the results are easier to analyze

Create a crosstab query when you want to take advantage of one of the following benefits:

- You can display a large amount of summary data in columns that are similar to a spreadsheet. The results can be easily exported for further analysis in a program such as Microsoft Office Excel 2003.
- You can view the summary data in a datasheet that is ideal for creating charts automatically using the Chart Wizard.
- You can easily design queries to include multiple levels of detail.

Crosstab queries work especially well with **time-series data**, which is data that shows performance over time for periods such as years, quarters, or months.

Creating a Crosstab Query

You create a crosstab query using a wizard to guide you through the steps, or on your own in Design view. If you want to work in Design view, it's best to start with a select query that includes numeric values or summary calculations. You can then create a crosstab query manually by clicking Query on the menu bar and then clicking Crosstab Query. This method adds a Crosstab row to the design grid. Each field in a crosstab query can have one of four settings: Row Heading, Column Heading, Value, or Not Shown. Table 3.12 explains the four settings, which also helps you answer the questions the Crosstab Query Wizard asks.

Table 3.12: Crosstab field settings

Crosstab Field Setting	Explanation
Row Heading	You must have at least one row heading, and you can specify more than one field as a row heading. Each row heading must be a grouped value or expression, with the expression containing one or more of the aggregate functions (such as Count, Min, Max, or Sum). The row heading fields form the first column on the left side of the crosstab.
Column Heading	Only one field can be defined as the column heading, and this must also be a grouped or totaled value. These values become the headings of the columns across the crosstab datasheet.
Value	Only one field is designated as the value. This field must be a totaled value or expression that contains one of the aggregate functions. The value field appears in the cells that are the intersections of each row heading value and each column heading value.
Not Shown	You can use other fields to limit the results. If you include a field in the query design grid, and then click the (Not Shown) option in the Crosstab cell and Group By in the Total cell, Access groups on the field as a Row Heading, but doesn't display the row in the query's results.

Although you can create crosstab queries manually, if you want Access to guide you through the steps and show samples of how the crosstab results will look based on your selections, use the Crosstab Query Wizard instead.

Although the Crosstab Query Wizard can generate a crosstab query from a single table, a single table usually doesn't contain the data necessary for the Crosstab Wizard. For instance, you might want to analyze employee training costs over time. You can retrieve cost data from tblClass, but you need tblEmployeeTraining to include the dates of the training. To prepare the data for the Crosstab Query Wizard, you often need to create a query first. This query should contain data that you want to include as the rows, column headings, and values in the crosstab query. For example, each row might be a class that employees might take, the column headings the dates grouped by years, and the values the sum of the class costs per year.

A few years ago, Maria met with Paul Ferrino, and they decided that all health-related training would be reimbursed by 4Corners Pharmacy. The policy has been in effect since 2004. In preparation for the training budget, Maria wants to analyze the annual cost of training to determine whether Paul wants to continue the policy. She could create a Totals query that would calculate the total cost of training, but that would not display the cost per year. She decides to create a crosstab query to help with this analysis.

Maria starts by creating a select query with only the fields she needs in the crosstab query—Description and Cost from tblClass and Date from tblEmployeeTraining. She does not need any fields from tblEmployee because she is only interested in summary data for the costs by year for classes. She saves this query as qryTrainingCostAndDate.

She then starts the Crosstab Query Wizard and selects qryTrainingCostAndDate as the basis for the Crosstab query. See Figure 3.46.

Figure 3.46: First dialog box of the Crosstab Query Wizard

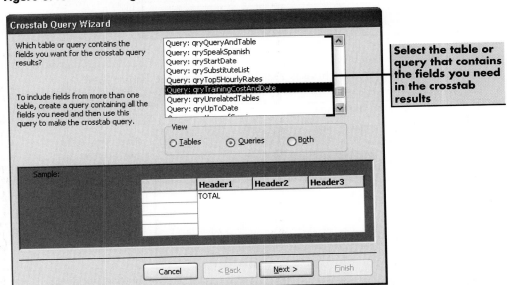

For the row headings, she selects Description because she wants to see the costs for each class. See Figure 3.47.

Figure 3.47: Select only one field for row headings

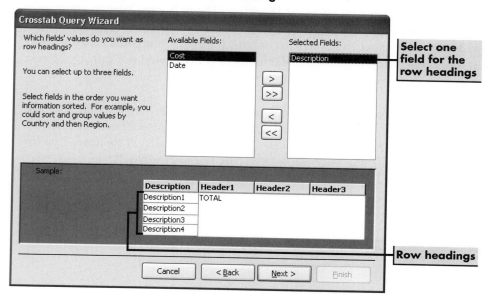

Maria wants to analyze the data by year, so she chooses Date for column headings. Because she is interested in annual cost, she chooses Year as the interval. See Figure 3.48

Figure 3.48: Select the column headings

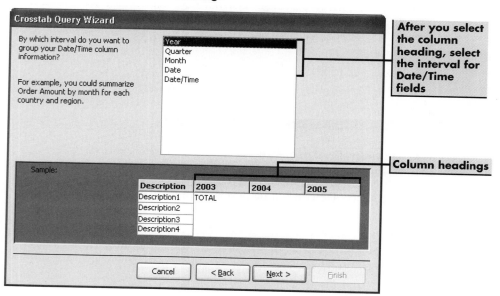

She wants the total cost for classes as the value, so she chooses Cost as the field and Sum as the function. See Figure 3.49.

Figure 3.49: Select the value to calculate

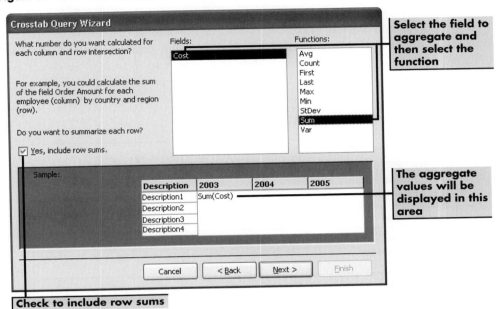

Select the field to aggregate and then select the function

The aggregate values will be displayed in this area

Check to include row sums

She names the query qryClassCostAnalysis and then runs it. See Figure 3.50. The results clearly compare the total annual costs of training classes and the annual costs per class.

Figure 3.50: Results of a crosstab query

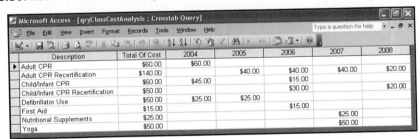

Description	Total Of Cost	2004	2005	2006	2007	2008
Adult CPR	$60.00	$60.00				
Adult CPR Recertification	$140.00		$40.00	$40.00	$40.00	$20.00
Child/Infant CPR	$60.00	$45.00		$15.00		
Child/Infant CPR Recertification	$50.00			$30.00		$20.00
Defibrillator Use	$50.00	$25.00	$25.00			
First Aid	$15.00			$15.00		
Nutritional Supplements	$25.00				$25.00	
Yoga	$50.00				$50.00	

Maria next needs to remove obsolete data from the database. She is interested in removing records for classes employees have completed and for which their certification has already been updated. In addition, she must currently remember to exclude previous employees when she is querying the 4Corners database, and wants to archive those employee records in a table separate from tblEmployee. Rather than manually deleting out-of-date class records and reentering previous employee data in a new table, she plans to use action queries to automate these tasks.

MODIFYING DATA USING QUERIES

In addition to the select and crosstab queries, Access provides a number of query types that perform an action on the data in a database: the update, append, delete, and make-table queries. These **action queries** let you modify data in a table, add records to or delete records from a table, or create a new table based on expressions you enter and criteria you set. Table 3.13 lists the purpose of each type of action query and provides an example of how it might be used.

Table 3.13: Access action queries

Query Type	Purpose	Example
Append	Add records from one table to another table with the same structure based on a criteria	Add records of employees no longer with the pharmacy to a separate employee history table to archive the records while removing them from a table of current employees
Delete	Delete records from a table based on a criterion	Delete the employees from the current employee table after the records of past employees have been appended to an employee history table
Make-table	Create a table from the results of a query	Create the history table of past employees the first time you decide to remove past employees from tblEmployee
Update	Change the contents of a field based on a criterion	Change values for hourly wage of all hourly employees to reflect a negotiated raise in a job category

Best Practice

Backing Up Your Database Before Using Action Queries

Because action queries permanently change the data in a database, you should always back up the database before performing an action query. To do so, open the database you want to back up, click Tools on the menu bar, point to Database Utilities, and then click Back Up Database. If you are working in a network environment that allows multiple users to work in the database simultaneously, the other users should close the database while you create the backup.

Maria wants to delete old classes for employees after the certification time has expired. She needs to set criteria that select only obsolete class records in tblEmployeeTraining, and then wants Access to delete the records. While discussing her problem with Donald Linebarger, database developer, he suggests that she archive the obsolete data in a new table before she deletes it from tblEmployeeTraining. If she later needs the data for another query or report, she can retrieve it from the archived table. He suggests the general procedure shown in Figure 3.51 for archiving obsolete data.

Figure 3.51: Process for archiving data

Back up the database first—this is a must.

↓

Create a select query to set up the criteria for selecting the obsolete records. Test it to make sure it selects the correct records. Then convert it to a make-table action query to create a table to store the obsolete records. Run the query to create the new table. You don't need to save this query because you only need it once to create the table.

↓

Modify the new table to add a primary key. This prevents you from adding duplicate records in the future.

↓

Create a select query that will select obsolete records and then test it. Convert it to an append action query and save it without running it. Use the query when you want to move obsolete records to another table. Use parameters to make it more general, if necessary. Save and run this query on a regular basis or as needed.

↓

Regularly check the history table to make sure the records have been successfully appended before the next step.

↓

Create a delete action query to delete the obsolete records from the original table. Run this query only after the append query as needed.

Archiving Data with Make-Table Queries

As its name suggests, a **make-table query** creates a table from some or all of the fields and records in an existing table or query. When you create a new table based on an existing one, Access does not delete the selected fields and records from the existing table. Keep in mind that the new table reflects the data as it appeared when you created the table; changes you subsequently make to the original table are not reflected in the new table.

When you use a make-table query, you usually create a select query first that contains the necessary fields and selection criteria, and then run the query to make sure the results contain the data you want. When you are sure that the query is working properly, you can change the query type to make-table. When you run the make-table query, Access creates a table containing the table structure and records that meet the criteria you established. Access asks for a new table name and adds this table to the list of available tables in the database. Be sure to change the default name of any table created with a make-table query to include the tbl prefix.

Best Practice

Using Make-Table Queries

Make-table queries are often used to create **history tables** for accounting applications. These tables contain records that need to be saved or archived, but are no longer needed in the tables used for current activities in the database. Make-table queries are also frequently used by developers who inherit poorly designed tables in a database. The developer can choose those fields that should be part of new and well-designed tables as the fields in the make-table queries. If necessary, fields from multiple tables can be combined in a query first, and then the new table can be created from the fields in the query. This way, the developer doesn't need to reenter data, but the data from the tables and queries used in the make-table queries remain in the database until they are removed manually or with a Delete query.

You can also use a make-table query to create a table to export to other Access databases. For example, you could create a table that contains several fields from tblEmployee, and then export that table to a database used by the accounting or payroll personnel.

Maria backs up the database before beginning the tasks that Donald outlined. She plans her next task—creating a select query—by considering the goals of her query and the criteria she should use. She wants to select the following classes in which employees earn certification: Adult CPR (class ID 1), Child/Infant CPR (class ID 2), Adult CPR Recertification (class ID 3), or Child/Infant CPR Recertification (class ID 6). In addition to classes 1, 2, 3, or 6, Maria wants to select all of the classes attended on or before January 1, 2005 because certification achieved in these classes is now out of date. She briefly considers setting parameters so that she can specify the date each time she runs the query. However, she realizes that she does not need to save the make-table query—after she runs it to create a table of obsolete employee training records, she can add subsequent obsolete records to it using an append query, not a make-table query.

Maria creates a select query that contains all of the fields in tblEmployeeTraining. She adds all the fields by double-clicking the field list title bar, and then dragging the selection to the design grid. She types <=#1/1/2005# in the Criteria row for the Date field and then types In(1,2,3,6) as the criteria for the ClassID field. Before converting the query to a make-table query, she runs the query to make sure it selects the correct data—it selects seven records from tblEmployeeTraining, all containing obsolete data.

To convert the select query to a make-table query, she returns to Design view, clicks the list arrow on the Query Type button 🖼 on the Query Design toolbar, and then clicks Make-Table Query. The Make Table dialog box opens, in which Maria enters tblEmployeeTrainingHistory as the name of the new table, and specifies that Access should save it in the current database.

She clicks the OK button, and then clicks the Run button 🔳 on the Query Design toolbar to run the query. Access displays a message indicating that she is about to paste seven rows into a new table. She clicks the Yes button to confirm that she wants to create the table. To verify that the query created the table as she planned, she closes the make-table query without saving it, opens tblEmployeeTrainingHistory in Datasheet view, and sees the seven records for obsolete classes as she expected. However, when she opens the table in Design view, she notices that the new table doesn't have a primary key. She also notices that the captions are missing, as are other property settings for the fields.

Best Practice

Modifying Tables Created with Make-Table Queries

When you use a make-table query to create a new table, only the field name and data type are included in the new table. You lose other property settings, such as captions, formats, and decimal places. Furthermore, the new table doesnt inherit the primary key from the original table. If you plan to use the data for reports or queries in the future, you should add a primary key and correct any important field properties such as default formats for Date/Time fields. Adding the primary key also prevents you from adding duplicate rows.

Maria creates the composite primary keys for the new table and adds captions to match the old table. She also opens tblEmployeeTraining and notes that the seven obsolete records are still stored in tblEmployeeTraining. She will have to delete these records later. Her next step is to create an append query to continue to archive obsolete training records in tblEmployeeTrainingHistory.

Adding Records to Tables with Append Queries

An **append query** is another type of action query that allows you to select records from one or more tables by setting criteria and then add those records to the end of another table. The selected records also remain in the original tables. Because the table to which you add records must already exist (as opposed to a make-table action query that creates a table), you can define field properties and primary keys in advance. You can also use an append query to bring data from another source into your database, even if some of the fields in one table don't exist in the other table. For example, the tblEmployee table has 19 fields. If you import a table named tblPersonnel, for example, and it includes only 10 fields that match the 19 in tblEmployee, you could use an append query to add the data from tblPersonnel in the fields that match those in tblEmployee and ignore the others.

Maria remembers that she needs to add obsolete records for the Defibrillator Use class to tblEmployeeTrainingHistory. She can create an append query for adding obsolete training records from tblEmployeeTraining to tblEmployeeTrainingHistory. Again, she considers the goals of her query and the criteria she should use. As with the make-table query, she can use all of the fields in tblEmployeeTraining and similar criteria. However, because she will continue to use this query, she can use parameter values that prompt for the Date and ClassID field values. For the Date field, she uses the following criterion:

```
<=[Enter the date before which certification is out of date:]
```

If she were entering a fixed criterion for the ClassID field, she would enter "In(1,2,3,5,6)" to select the required certification classes. To convert this criterion to a parameter prompt, she can still use the In comparison operator and substitute a parameter value for each ClassID value, as follows:

```
In([Enter the ID of the first certification class:],
    [Enter the ID of the second certification class:],
        [Enter the ID of the third certification class:],
            [Enter the ID of the fourth certification
                class:], [Enter the ID of the fifth
                    certification class:])
```

This criterion will work even if she wants to select fewer than five classes—she can specify "5," for example, and then click the OK button on the Enter Parameter Value dialog box without entering a value the next four times it opens.

When she runs the select query, a dialog box opens and prompts her for the date. After she enters 1/1/2006 to test the query, five other dialog boxes open and prompt her for the five class IDs. When she is sure her query returns the results she wants, she saves it as qryAppendObsoleteClasses. She then converts it to an append query by clicking the list arrow on the Query Type button 🔲 on the Query Design toolbar and then clicking Append Query. The Append dialog box opens, in which Maria enters tblEmployeeTrainingHistory as the name of the table to which she wants to append the data, and specifies that this table is in the current database. See Figure 3.52.

Figure 3.52: Creating an append query

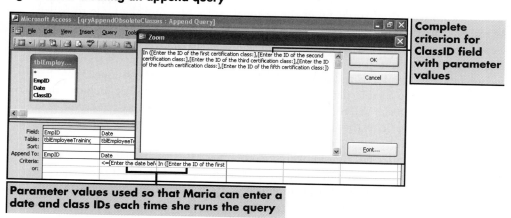

Complete criterion for ClassID field with parameter values

Parameter values used so that Maria can enter a date and class IDs each time she runs the query

She clicks the OK button, saves the query, and then runs it, entering 1/1/2005 as the date criterion and 5 as the class ID so that Access adds the obsolete Defibrillator Use class record to tblEmployeeTrainingHistory. Next, she needs to delete the obsolete records from tblEmployeeTraining because they are now archived in tblEmployeeTrainingHistory.

Removing Records from Tables with Delete Queries

A **delete query** removes information from a table based on the criteria you specify. As with other action queries, you create a select query first to specify the criteria, test it, and then convert the select query to a delete query. When you run the query, all records meeting your criteria are permanently removed from the table. You usually run a delete query after you use an append query to add those same records to a history table and have verified that you appended the correct records before you delete them in the original table.

Because a delete query permanently removes records from a table, be certain to back up the database and preview the data before you convert the select query to a delete query and run the query. Also, if your query uses only the primary table of two tables in a one-to-many relationship, and you've set up cascading deletes for that relationship, running a delete query might delete records in related tables, even if you do not include them in the query. In other words, with cascading deletes, deleting records from the "one" table also deletes records from the "many" table.

Now that Maria has created the tblEmployeeTrainingHistory table and checked to make sure it contains the obsolete training data, she can delete those records from tblEmployeeTraining. First, she backs up the database. She then creates a select query and sets up criteria to remove the obsolete records. Again, she uses the same parameter values she used in the append query, qryAppendObsoleteClasses, so she can enter the oldest date and the class IDs when she runs the query. She tests the query first to make sure it selects the right records. Next, she clicks the list arrow on the Query Type button ⊞ on the Query Design toolbar, and then clicks Delete Query to convert the select query to a delete query. She saves the query as qryDeleteObsoleteClasses and then runs it, entering 1/1/2005 as the date and class IDs 1, 2, 3, 5, and 6. Access asks her to confirm that she wants to delete the records. When she clicks the Yes button, Access permanently deletes the eight obsolete records from tblEmployeeTraining.

Now that Maria has archived outdated employee training records, she wants to use the same process to create a history table containing records for previous employees. Recall that she included previous employees in tblEmployee because she didn't want to lose their data, but needed to enter criteria to eliminate former employees from query results that listed information about current employees.

She creates and runs a make-table query to store records for former employees in a new table named tblEmployeeHistory. However, when she creates a delete query and tries to delete these records from tblEmployee, a message appears indicating that Access cannot delete the records due to key violations. In other words, she cannot delete the former employees from tblEmployee because that table is maintaining relationships with other tables. When Don Linebarger designed the database, he did not set cascading updates or deletes for employees. The tblEmployeeTraining and tblRefill tables include the EmpID field, which is a foreign key to tblEmployee. If the relationships in these tables allowed cascading deletes, deleting records for previous employees in tblEmployee would also delete the refill records for prescriptions that the previous employees refilled, which is inappropriate. Maria has already created queries that include the Is Null criterion in the EndDate field of tblEmployee, and she must remember to set this criterion in other queries so the results do not include previous employees.

Maria meets with Paul Ferrino to review all of the hourly rate analyses. Paul has been reviewing the results, and decides to give all technicians a 3% raise effective immediately. Maria could calculate the new hourly rates by hand and then update the table, but she can use an update query instead to automatically change the HourlyRate value for pharmacy technicians.

Updating Data with an Update Query

An **update query** changes the values of data in one or more existing tables. It is very useful when you must change the values of a field or fields in many records, such as raising salaries by 3% for all employees within a particular job category. Rather than change each value by editing the individual records, you can create an expression to update all the values based on a criterion you set.

How To

Create an Update Query

1. Back up the database before creating and running an action query.
2. Create a select query that includes only the field or fields you want to update and any fields necessary to determine the criteria for the update.
3. Enter the criteria and run the query to verify that the results contain the appropriate records and values and that the criteria are correct.
4. Click the Query Type button 🖅 on the Query Design toolbar, and then click Update Query to convert the select query to an update query.
5. In the Update To row for the fields you want to update, enter the expression or value you want to use to change the fields. If necessary, right-click the cell and then click Zoom on the shortcut menu to use the Zoom dialog box to enter the expression.
6. Run the query. Accept the modifications by clicking the Yes button.

Maria needs to change the values in the HourlyRate field for pharmacy technicians so they reflect the 3% raise Paul Ferrino has approved. She needs to update the records in the tblEmployee table to reflect these pay increases, and knows that an update query is the easiest way to change a number of records at the same time based on criteria. First, she backs up the 4Corners database to protect its data before performing an action query. She also notes a few wage rates for technicians so she can check the results with her calculator. For example, Virginia Sanchez currently earns $10.75 per hour. Three percent of $10.75 is about $.32, so Virginia's salary after the raise should be $11.07.

In the 4Corners database, Maria creates a query in Design view using tblEmployee and its JobID, EndDate, and HourlyRate fields. She specifies "3" as the criterion for JobID to select only pharmacy technicians, and Is Null as the criterion for EndDate so that the query selects only current employees. She also unchecks the Show box so the EndDate field does not appear in the results.

After she runs this query to make sure it selects only current pharmacy technicians, she clicks the Query Type button 🖳 on the Query Design toolbar and then clicks Update Query to convert the select query to an update query. A new row named Update To appears in the design grid, in which Maria enters the following expression to increase the technicians' HourlyRate by 3%:

[HourlyRate]*1.03

When she clicks the Run button 🔳 on the Query Design toolbar, a warning appears, reminding her that action queries are not reversible. See Figure 3.53.

Figure 3.53: Creating and running an update query

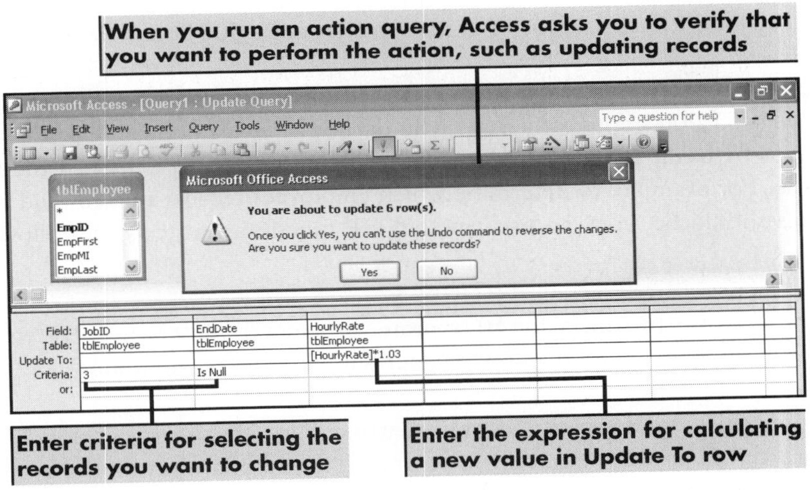

She clicks the Yes button to update the records. Maria closes the update query without saving it, checks the new rate for Virginia Sanchez, and verifies that she now makes $11.07 per hour—a 3% raise. She doesn't save the query because she doesn't want to run it by accident and give the technicians another 3% raise.

Paul also wants to encourage employees to maintain their employment at 4Corners—low turnover saves the pharmacy training time and costs and is strongly associated with excellent service. He has decided to award a $500 bonus to employees who have worked at 4Corners for at least five years, and a $1,000 bonus to employees who have worked at least 10 years. How can Maria set up criteria that display a $1,000 bonus for some records that meet one condition and a $500 bonus for other records that meet a different condition? To do so, she needs an expression that assigns one of two values to a field based on a condition, one that, in effect, makes a decision and takes different actions depending on the outcome.

MAKING DECISIONS IN QUERIES

One of the most powerful tools available in programming languages is the ability to make a decision based on more than one condition. You do so using an IF statement, a programming statement that tests a condition and takes one action if the condition is true and another action if the condition is false. In Access, you can use the IIF function, also called an Immediate IF, Instant IF, and Inline IF, to perform the same task. The format for an IIF function statement is as follows:

IIF(*condition to test, what to do if true, what to do if false*)

For example, to determine which employees receive a $1,000 bonus, you can use an IIF function that tests the following condition:

IIF(you've worked for the pharmacy for 10 or more years, get $1,000 bonus, get no bonus)

You can interpret this expression as "If you've worked for the pharmacy for 10 or more years, you receive a $1,000 bonus; otherwise, you do not receive a bonus." You can also nest IIF functions by using a second IIF statement to test another condition if the first condition is false. For example, to determine which employees receive a bonus and how much the bonus should be, you can use a nested IIF function that tests the following conditions:

IIF(you've worked for the pharmacy for 10 or more years, get $1,000 bonus, IIF(you've worked for the pharmacy for more than 5 years, get $500 bonus, get no bonus))

You can interpret this expression as "If you've worked for the pharmacy for 10 or more years, you receive a $1,000 bonus; if you've worked for the pharmacy for five or more years, you receive a $500 bonus; otherwise, you do not receive a bonus."

You can use an IIF function to return a value or text. Enclose the text in quotation marks. For example, the following IIF statement checks to see if the value in the OrderAmt field is greater than 1,000. If it is, it displays "Large." If the value is not greater than 1,000, it displays "Small."

IIF(OrderAmt > 1000, "Large", "Small")

How To

Use the Immediate IF Function in Expressions

1. Create or open a query in Design view.

2. In a calculated field, as criteria, or in the Update To row of an update query, enter an expression beginning with IIF.

3. Within parentheses, enter the condition to test, the action to take if the condition is true, and the action to take if the condition is false.

4. As you type the expression, remember that each left parenthesis must have a right parenthesis to match. If you have one IIF, you need one set of parentheses. If you nest IIF statements, count the IIFs and make sure the parentheses on the right match the number of IIFs.

5. Test your results by clicking the Datasheet view button 🔳.

Maria plans the expression that assigns a bonus to an employee depending on their years of service. She can use this expression in a query that includes a calculated field for determining an employee's years of service to 4Corners Pharmacy. The first condition selects employees who have worked for the pharmacy for 10 or more years and assigns a $1,000 bonus to those employees. The IIF statement for this part of the expression is as follows:

IIF([Years of Service]>=10,1000,

This statement can be interpreted as "If the value in the Years of Service field is greater than or equal to 10, return the value 1,000." After the second comma in that statement, Maria inserts an expression that the query should perform if the first condition is false—in other words, if the value in the Years of Service field is not greater than or equal to 10. The second condition is as follows:

IIF([Years of Service]>=5,500,

This statement can be interpreted as "If the value in the Years of Service field is greater than or equal to 5, return the value 500." After the second comma in that statement, Maria inserts an expression that the query should perform if the first and second condition are false—in other words, if the value in the Years of Service field is not greater than or equal to 5: **0))**

This part of the expression returns the value 0 if the first and second conditions are false—if employees have worked at 4Corners Pharmacy for less than five years. The two parentheses complete the first and second condition. Maria will include the complete expression in a new calculated field named Bonus. The complete entry is as follows:

Bonus: IIF([Years of Service]>=10,1000,IIF([Years of Service]>=5,500,0))

Maria is ready to create the query that includes employees who are eligible for a bonus and lists the bonus they should receive. In Design view, she opens qryYearsOfService, the query she created earlier to calculate years of service for each employee. She saves the new query as qryBonus, and adds a calculated field named Bonus to the query. She then enters the IIF statement, shown in Figure 3.54.

Figure 3.54: Using an Immediate IF in an expression

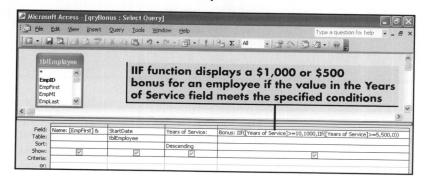

When she runs the query, the results include many employees who are not eligible for bonuses and two who no longer work for 4Corners. She realizes that she only wants to display employees who are eligible for bonuses, so she adds the criterion >5 to the Years of Service field. Then she adds the EndDate field to the query design grid, enters Is Null as the criterion, and unchecks the Show box. Figure 3.55 shows the results—current employees who are eligible for a bonus.

Figure 3.55: Employees who are eligible to receive a $500 or $1,000 bonus

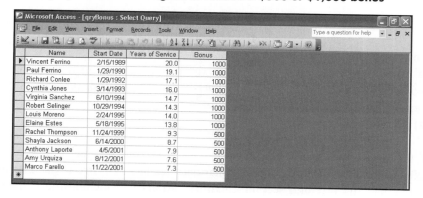

CUSTOMIZING QUERIES USING STRUCTURED QUERY LANGUAGE

Access was designed as a database management system (DBMS) for small businesses or departments within large businesses, not a DBMS for large, enterprise systems that must run at high performance levels. Creating basic database objects such as queries, forms, and reports is easy for Access users, as you have discovered, but users of enterprise DBMSs generally do not have the same access to database objects. Their interaction is usually to query the enterprise system and import the data to a program such as Access for further analysis. To do so, they must use a common query language that their DBMS and Access can both interpret.

Structured Query Language (SQL—usually pronounced "sequel" but more properly pronounced "ess-cue-ell") is the common query language of most DBMSs, including Access. You can use SQL to query, update, and manage relational databases such as Access. When you create a query in query Design view, Access translates the entries and criteria into SQL statements. You can view these statements by switching from Design view to SQL view. Parts of the SQL statements are the same as the entries you make in query Design view. For example, when you use a field name in a calculation, you enclose it in square brackets in Design view or SQL view. The two views are similar enough that some SQL developers use the query design grid in Access to develop the basic SQL code before adding specialized features.

For example, Figure 3.56 shows the qryHourlyRate query in Design view and SQL view. Recall that this query lists all nonsalaried employees and their hourly pay rates.

Figure 3.56: qryHourlyRate in Design view and SQL view

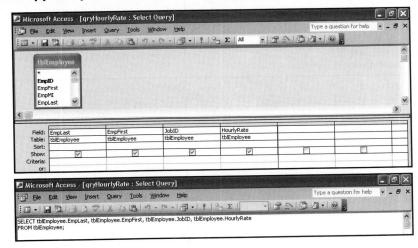

The SELECT statement defines what data the query should retrieve from the database and how it should present the data. For example, SELECT tblEmployee.EmpLast indicates that the query should select data from the EmpLast field in the tblEmployee table. The FROM statement defines the database objects that contain this data. For example, FROM tblEmployee indicates that all the data is stored in tblEmployee. SELECT and FROM are keywords in SQL; they have special meaning in SQL. To make it easy to identify the keywords in SQL code, Access displays them in all uppercase letters. An SQL statement usually begins with a keyword, which serves to define a command or clause in the expression.

Exploring the Components of an SQL Query

Table 3.14 lists the common keywords you can use to construct SQL statements. SQL code isn't required to follow a particular format, but Access and most developers place each statement on a separate line to make the SQL code easy to read. All of the wildcards, comparison operators, and logical operators you learned about in this chapter are also available in SQL.

Table 3.14: Common SQL keywords

SQL Term	What Follows the Term	Example
SELECT	List the fields you want to display. They will appear in the results in the order you list them. Note that field names with no spaces or special symbols do not require square brackets around them, but it is good practice to use the square brackets for consistency. Separate the field names with commas.	SELECT tblEmployee.EmpLast Display the EmpLast field from tblEmployee
FROM	List the table or tables involved in the query. Separate the table names with commas, and use square brackets around table names that include a space or special symbol.	FROM tblEmployee Use the tblEmployee table in the query
WHERE	List the criteria that apply. If more than one table has a field with the same name, you need to "qualify" your conditions with the name of the table followed by a period.	WHERE ((tblEmployee.JobID)=3) AND ((tblEmployee.EndDate) Is Null)) Select records in which the value in the JobID field of tblEmployee is 3 and the value in the EndDate field is null
GROUP BY	Group records with identical values in the specified fields into a single record, usually to calculate summary statistics.	GROUP BY tblEmployee.JobID Group the results by records in the JobID field
HAVING	List the conditions for selecting grouped records, connected by AND, OR, or NOT.	HAVING ((tblEmployee.JobID)=3 Or (tblEmployee.JobID)=4)) Select records that have the value 3 or 4 in the JobID field of tblEmployee
ORDER BY	Specify sorting specifications; for descending order, insert DESC after a sort field.	ORDER BY tblEmployee.EmpLast Sort the records by the EmpLast field in tblEmployee
AS	Use with calculated columns to specify the name of the resulting calculation.	[EmpFirst] & " " & [EmpLast] AS Name Concatenate the contents of the EmpFirst and EmpLast fields and display the results as the Name field
; (semicolon)	Use to end every SQL command, because it is required in some versions of SQL.	N/A

Maria wants to explore SQL view in case she needs to modify queries to include more flexibility or power than Design view can offer. One task Paul asked her to complete is to create a query similar to qryTop5HourlyRates that displays the top three salaries paid to employees. She can open qryTop5HourlyRates in SQL view and then modify it so that it selects the three records that have the highest values in the Salary field instead of the five records that have the highest values in the HourlyRate field.

Maria opens qryTop5HourlyRates in Design view, clicks the list arrow on the View button 🔲 on the Query Design toolbar, and then clicks SQL View. The query appears in SQL view. See Figure 3.57.

Figure 3.57: SQL view of qryTop5HourlyRates

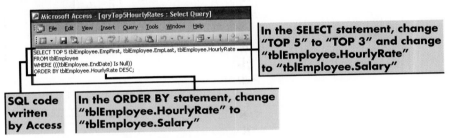

Maria takes some time to interpret the SQL statements in this view:

- **SELECT TOP 5 tblEmployee.EmpFirst, tblEmployee.EmpLast, tblEmployee.HourlyRate**—Display the EmpFirst, EmpLast, and HourlyRate fields from tblEmployee, and select the top five records in the field specified in the ORDER BY clause.
- **FROM tblEmployee**—Use only the tblEmployee table in the query.
- **WHERE ((tblEmployee.EndDate) Is Null))**—Select only those records in which the value in the EndDate field is null.
- **ORDER BY tblEmployee.HourlyRate DESC;**—Sort the results in descending order by the values in the HourlyRate field, and then end the query.

To change this query to select the records with the top three values in the Salary field, Maria changes "TOP 5" in the SELECT statement to "TOP 3." She also changes "tblEmployee.HourlyRate" in the SELECT statement to "tblEmployee.Salary." She doesn't need to change the FROM statement because she still wants to select records only from the tblEmployee table, nor does she need to change the WHERE statement—she only wants to display salaries of current employees. However, she does need to change the ORDER BY statement so that it sorts records by the Salary field instead of HourlyRate. That change also means the query selects the three records with the highest values in the Salary field. She completes these changes, saves the query as qryTop3Salaries, and switches to Design view, which reflects the changes she made in SQL view. Finally, she runs the query to view the results. See Figure 3.58.

Figure 3.58: Three views of qryTop3Salaries

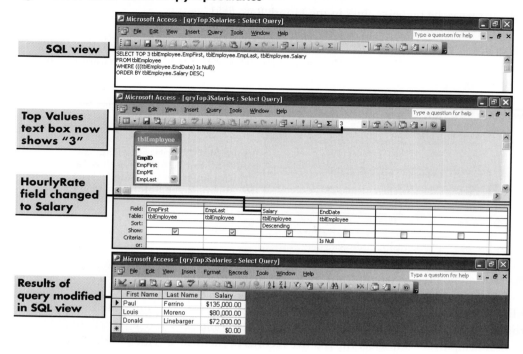

As you create or modify SQL statements in SQL view, Access makes corresponding changes in the query design grid in Design view. After you create a query in SQL view, you can modify it in Design view. Access reformats your SQL code so it looks like an Access-generated SQL command. Access SQL code always uses the qualified field names even if you only have one table in your query, not all fields will be enclosed in square brackets, and there might be extra parentheses in the criteria. While you are learning how to create SQL queries, you can change from SQL view to Design view to Datasheet view to gauge the effect of your SQL statements in the other views.

Steps To Success: Level 3

Kim Siemers, human resources manager for Hudson Bay Pharmacy, needs to analyze statistical data for the pharmacy and to archive obsolete records. She asks for your help creating crosstab queries and action queries that modify the data in the Hudson database. As you create and save the new queries, be certain to use the "qry" prefix as part of the naming convention. Also consult your instructor for instructions about submitting your results.

Complete the following:

1. Start Access and open the **Hudson.mdb** database from the STS folder.

2. Kim is preparing the human resources budget for Hudson Bay Pharmacy, and needs to analyze the annual cost of training to determine how much to budget for training classes. She asks you to provide summary data for the costs by year for classes. The results you create should clearly compare the total annual costs of training classes and the annual costs per class. Save the query as qryClassCostAnalysis.

3. Kim needs to remove obsolete data from the Hudson database. First, she asks you to identify all employees who no longer work for Hudson Bay Pharmacy. She then wants you to create a new history table with that data. Name the history table tblEmpHistory. Save the query as qryEmpHistory.

4. Kim also wants to remove records for classes employees have completed and for which their certification has already been updated. She asks you to select classes in which employees earn certification—Adult CPR, Adult CPR Recertification, Child/Infant CPR, and Child/Infant CPR Recertification—and that they attended before January 1, 2007 because certification achieved in these classes is now out of date in Canada. Create a history table that contains this data, and name the table tblEmployeeTrainingHistory. Name the query qryEmployeeTrainingHistory.

5. Kim checked your results, and realizes that tblEmployeeTrainingHistory should also include obsolete data for Defibrillator Use classes. Add the obsolete training records for Defibrillator Use classes to tblEmployeeTrainingHistory. Because Kim will continue to use this query for other classes as they become outdated, set up the query so that it prompts her for the necessary criteria before running. Defibrillator Use certifications before 1/1/08 are no longer valid. Save the query as qryObsoleteClasses.

6. Verify that tblEmployeeTrainingHistory includes all the obsolete classes. Delete the now archived records from tblEmployeeTraining. As with qryObsoleteClasses, Kim will continue to use this query to remove obsolete records after they've been archived. Set up the query so that it prompts her for the necessary criteria before running. Save the query as qryDeleteClasses. Make sure the total number of records you deleted is the same as the number of records in tblEmployeeTrainingHistory.

7. Kim recently met with Joan Gabel, owner of Hudson Bay Pharmacy, who authorized a 5% raise for all current pharmacy technicians. Update the employee records for pharmacy technicians so that their pay rate includes this 5% raise. Save the query as qryTechnicianRaise.

8. Kim also says that current employees are eligible for participation in a 401(k) retirement plan after one year. Identify each employee by full name and show whether they

are eligible for the plan with a column stating "Eligible" or "Not Eligible" in the results. Save the query as qryRetirement.

9. Kim is meeting with Joan later today, and needs to report which salaried employees earn the top three salaries. Create a query in SQL view that lists all employees who earn the top three salaries. Be certain to separate the SQL terms to make it more readable. Save the query as qryTop3Salaries.

10. Close the **Hudson.mdb** database and Access.

CHAPTER SUMMARY

In this chapter, you learned how to retrieve data from a database so that you can examine only the information you need. Level 1 showed you how to filter data by form and by selection to create a temporary subset of records, and how to sort data to rearrange records in a specified order. Level 1 also introduced queries, explaining how to create select queries using the Simple Query Wizard, including those that provide summary statistics, or Design view, which is necessary when you need to use multiple criteria. In addition to multiple criteria, queries you create in Design view can include wildcards and comparison operators.

Level 2 focused on more complex queries and specialized query wizards. You learned how to create special types of queries that find duplicate records or unmatched records. You also learned how to create Top Value queries that limit the records in query results and parameter queries that pause before running so that users can enter values that the query uses as criteria. In addition, Level 2 explored refining relationships with appropriate join types and using logical operators to specify multiple conditions. It also explained how to perform calculations in a query by using aggregate functions and by creating calculated fields.

Level 3 covered advanced types of queries, including crosstab queries, which present data to facilitate statistical analysis. In addition, it showed you how to create action queries, including those that create tables, and add, update, or delete records in a table. Level 3 also explained how to create a calculated field with an Immediate IF function that makes decisions in a query. Finally, Level 3 introduced Structured Query Language (SQL), the language Access uses to query its databases.

CONCEPTUAL REVIEW

1. When is it appropriate to use Filter by Selection and Filter by Form?

2. What restrictions does the Simple Query Wizard have for creating queries?

3. Why is it important to use the naming prefix "qry" for all saved queries?

4. Why is it not a good idea to add records to a table from a query datasheet?

5. What is the difference between entering multiple criteria for a query on one line of the design grid versus entering criteria on two or more lines?

6. What query wizards are available other than the Simple Query Wizard? For what do you use these types of queries?

7. What is the purpose of an outer join?

8. What role does "null" play in a field?

9. When should you use the Expression Builder?

10. What is a history table and why would a database designer include one or more in the design?

11. What is the difference between a query written in the query design grid and one written directly in SQL?

12. Describe a situation in which the IIF function would be appropriate.

13. What is the difference between an update query and an append query?

14. Why do many people run a delete query after running a make-table or append query?

15. Name an advantage that crosstab queries offer that other types of queries do not.

CASE PROBLEMS

Case 1—Managing Customer Information for NHD Development Group Inc.

Marketing

After creating the tables and relationships for the Antiques database, you meet with Tim Richards, the chief information officer for the NHD Development Group, and Linda Sutherland, the manager of the antique mall. As you review the database, Linda makes a few requests. When she tracked sales for a month, she found that repeat customers accounted for 60% of her revenue. She therefore wants to use the Antiques database to increase marketing efforts to her current customer base. First, she wants to extract information about her customers, such as a list that organizes customers by city and another that provides customer names and phone numbers. She also needs to retrieve information about the antique and restoration classes the mall offers to determine which customers enroll in the classes. Then she could provide information in the classes about items that might interest those customers. She asks for your help filtering data and creating queries that extract the information she needs.

Complete the following:

1. Open the **Antiques.mdb** database from the Case 1 folder.

2. Many of the mall's customers live in Cleveland or Collegedale, Tennessee, and Linda is debating whether to place an ad in their community newspapers or to send postcards advising these customers about upcoming sales. If she sends more than 50 postcards, mailing costs will exceed advertising rates.

   Show Linda a quick way she can produce a temporary list of customers who live in Cleveland or Collegedale, with all the customers in Cleveland listed first. Is it more economical to send these customers postcards or to advertise in the community newspapers?

3. To increase repeat business, Linda wants to call customers and let them know when new collectibles arrive at the mall. She wants to produce a list of her customers and their phone numbers. To track the customers effectively, this telephone list should also include the customer's ID number.

   a. Create a list that includes the ID numbers, last names, first names, and phone numbers of all the customers.

   b. Because Linda expects to refer to this list by customer name, sort the list by last name.

   c. Save the query as qryPhoneList.

4. Linda is planning to create a brochure for the mall, and wants to highlight the number of booths within the mall. She wants to advertise that the mall has fifteen 8×8 booths, five 12×10 booths, and so on. Because Linda has recently reworked the booth divisions and expects to make additional changes in the future, she wants to list how many booths of each size the mall currently has. Name the query qryBoothSize.

5. Linda wants to promote the classes that will be offered in February. She will be placing an ad in the local newspaper, and wants to include the class list in the ad. She asks you to create a list of all the February classes sorted by date and by time. Be sure the list includes information readers are most interested in, such as the name of the class, the date and time, and the class fee. Name the query qryFebruaryClasses.

6. When Linda reviews the list of February classes, she thinks that the dates would be more meaningful if they spelled out the day of the week, using a format such as "Saturday, February 5, 2005." Linda asks you to modify the class list to display long dates. (*Hint:* In Design view, right-click the date field, click Properties, click the Format property's list arrow, and then click Long Date.)

7. Linda also needs a list of classes that she can use in the mall when customers and others inquire about the classes. When people call for information about the classes, they often want to know when the classes will be held. Linda also wants to use this list to call enrollees in case of a cancellation. Linda considers a person officially enrolled only when they have paid for the class.

   a. Create a list that includes the class ID and other information that callers want to know about the classes. Test your results.

   b. Modify the list so that it also includes information Linda needs to call customers and determine whether a customer is enrolled in a class. To help her find the information she needs, sort the list first by class and then by whether the customer has paid.

   c. Save the query as qryClassListing.

8. To manage the classes and instructors, Linda needs a summary of class enrollment. In addition to the names of the class and instructor, she needs to know the number of students enrolled in each class and the total of the class fees that have been paid. Save this query as qryClassEnrollment.

9. Unless at least five people are enrolled in a class, the class will be canceled. However, Linda wants to review the list of classes that are likely to be canceled to see if she can encourage some of her customers to take these classes. Modify qryClassEnrollment to include only those classes that have fewer than five customers enrolled. Save this query as qryClassDeletions.

10. Linda explains that the primary reason she offers the classes is to have people visit the mall. She has observed that most people come early for the classes and wander around the mall before the class begins. The classes are, therefore, part of her marketing strategy for the mall and she wants to protect this endeavor. One problem she wants to solve is that customers sometimes sign up for classes, but do not attend them. If class attendance is low, instructors have moved their classes to a different antiques mall. Classes with high fees seem to have the lowest attendance. Linda asks you to create a list that shows customers who have signed up for classes with a fee greater than $25 but have not paid. Provide information Linda needs so she can call the customers and request their payment, and sort the list so she can easily find customers by name. Name the qryUnpaidClassesOver25.

11. Linda often receives calls asking whether any of the dealers carry military memorabilia. She asks you to create a list of the dealers who sell such items. She will use this list to call dealers and to find other information about the memorabilia, such as discounts offered. Name this query qryMilitaryMemorabilia.

12. Close the **Antiques.mdb** database and Access.

Case 2—Retrieving Employee Information for MovinOn Inc.

Now that you have worked with Robert Iko at the MovinOn moving and storage company to develop the design for the MovinOn database, he explains that their most pressing task is to serve the needs of the human resources department. Darnell Colmenero is an administrative assistant responsible for many human resources tasks, and asks for your help extracting information from the MovinOn database. Although an outside company processes payroll for MovinOn, Darnell and others maintain complete employment information and strive to meet management's goal of recruiting and retaining skilled, qualified employees who are well trained in customer service. Having employees working in three warehouses in three states has made it difficult to track employee information, and the potential merger and expansion means that human resources must take advantage of the MovinOn database to maintain and retrieve employee information. Darnell asks for your help in filtering data and creating queries that provide the information that he needs.

Complete the following:

1. Open the **MovinOn.mdb** database from the Case 2 folder.

2. The truck drivers for MovinOn are a special type of employee, and their data is stored in a table separate from the rest of the employees because of driving certification requirements. Drivers are certified to drive trucks with a specified number of axles, and MovinOn must be certain that a driver is certified to drive a particular truck.

   a. When Darnell meets with David Bower, the general manager, he learns that only drivers who have a driving record of "A" or "B" are allowed to drive the large trucks (those with four axles or more). He asks you to identify the drivers qualified to drive the four-axle trucks. Because he will use the list you create to call drivers when he needs a substitute, include the phone numbers and driving record for each driver. Save the query as qry4AxleDrivers.

   b. Darnell also learns that he must immediately review drivers who have a driving record lower than "A" or "B." Those drivers who have a record of "C" will be put on notice, and those with a record "D" or "F" can be terminated immediately. List the drivers with these low driving records, and sort the list so that Darnell can easily determine the driving record of each driver. Because he can enroll long-term drivers in a training program, he also needs to know when each driver started working for MovinOn and whether the driver is still employed. Save the query as qryDriversWithLowRecords.

   c. If drivers have been terminated because of their driving record, Darnell wants to include them in an additional list. Create this list for Darnell, and include all relevant employment information. Save this query as qryDriversForTermination.

3. Darnell is completing a small business certification form for the U.S. Department of Labor, and needs quick answers to some basic questions about employees. Answer the following questions:

   a. In what states do the MovinOn employees reside?

   b. How many employees live in each state?

   c. Who is the oldest employee? Who is the youngest?

   d. Who makes the highest salary?

   e. Who is paid by salary? Who is paid by hourly rate?

   f. Who is paid the lowest hourly rate?

   g. Are there any positions for which there are no employees?

   h. How many types of jobs are offered at MovinOn? How many people are employed in each type of job?

4. When MovinOn hires employees, Darnell must process the employees by informing them about company policies and making sure they complete required printed forms. Darnell sometimes spends an entire day with a new employee. He wants to know when he was able to process more than one new employee in a day—he can then look over the forms and his training notes to discover how he can work more efficiently. He asks you to produce a list of employees who were processed on the same day. Because he files the forms he wants to review by Social Security number, include this information in the list. Name the query qryDuplicateStartDates.

5. David Bowers is considering providing bonuses to long-term employees. Darnell asks you to list the 10 employees who have worked for MovinOn the longest. Name the query qryLongestEmployment.

6. To prepare for a payroll, Darnell must provide a list of employees that includes their salary or hourly pay rate. The list must also include Social Security numbers and employee IDs so that an outside firm can properly process the payroll. Produce an employee list that provides this information, and sort it so that it's easy to find an employee by name. For those employees who are on a salary, the list should show their monthly wage. Save the query as qryPayroll.

7. Darnell sometimes needs to contact the warehouse managers, accountants, administrative assistants, and other employees at the warehouse where they work. Create a contact list that he can use to phone employees, and that contains enough information to identify employees, their positions, and their warehouses along with the warehouse phone number. Because Darnell might eventually use this list as the basis for a report, the employee's name should appear as one full name, with the last name first. Save the query as qryEmployeeContact.

8. When you show qryEmployeeContact to Darnell, he realizes that it would be more helpful if he could specify a particular warehouse before producing the list, and then see the contact information only for the employees who work in that warehouse. Create a query that meets these needs, saving it as qryEmployeeContactByWarehouse. Test this query with valid and invalid warehouse information.

9. MovinOn knows that having a workforce of long-term employees improves customer service and avoids the high expense of training new employees. Darnell wants to know if one warehouse is more effective at retaining employees than another. He asks you to do the following:

   a. Create an employee list that calculates the number of years each employee has worked for MovinOn.

   b. Organize the list by job title within each warehouse.

   c. Save the query as qryEmployeeLongevity.

10. MovinOn wants to offer hourly pay rates that are competitive with other moving companies in the Pacific Northwest. To identify nonsalaried employees who might be eligible for a raise in pay, Darnell asks you to do the following:

    a. Identify employees at each warehouse who earn less than $12.00 per hour. Do not include salaried employees in the list.

    b. Let users specify a particular warehouse, and then see information only for the employees who work in that warehouse.

    c. Save the query as qryEmployeeLowWage.

11. Darnell learns that the manager of the Oregon warehouse has decided to give his hourly employees a 10% raise. He asks you to list all the employees who work in the Oregon warehouse, and show the old rate along with the new rate after a 10% increase to their hourly pay rate. The increase applies only to hourly employees. Save the query as qryOregonRateIncrease.

12. Close the **MovinOn.mdb** database and Access.

Case 3—Managing Equipment and Preparing for Games in the Hershey College Intramural Department

Operations Management

Recall that you are working on a database for the intramural department at Hershey College, under the direction of Marianna Fuentes. The department is preparing for its first semester of operation and needs to set up teams for each sport, manage the equipment and fields for each sport, keep track of coaches and team captains, and allow students to sign up for the sports offerings.

Marianna has interviewed the rest of the intramural staff to determine the data needs of the department. She has prepared a list of those needs. Your next task is to create lists that meet the operational needs of the department. For each list, Marianna asks you to name the columns so that it is clear what each column contains.

Complete the following:

1. Open the **Hershey.mdb** database from the Case 3 folder.

2. Review the tables that you created in Chapter 2. Keep in mind that you will use the existing data to test the database. When the database has been fully designed, the department staff will enter real data in place of the test data you have provided.

3. The intramural staff often needs to contact students who have enrolled in an intramural sport. Create a phone list the staff can use. Marianna states that they usually use the cell phone number to contact students, but they want to have both the land line and the cell phone numbers on the contact list. The list should be ordered so that it is easy to find a student by name. Name the query qryStudentContact.

4. Because the intramural department staff members serve as coaches in addition to their other responsibilities, the staff needs to schedule their time carefully. In particular, they need to monitor people who coach more than one sport. Marianna asks you to list coaches who are assigned to more than one sport and to identify the sports to which each coach is assigned. Name the query qryCoachesWithMultipleSports.

5. Before students can participate in a sport, they must provide a liability waiver and academic approval form. One staff member is assigned to calling students who are missing a required form. Marianna asks you to create a list, including all phone numbers, of students who are missing one or both of the required forms. The list should also identify the missing form. Name the query qryMissingApprovals.

6. For the next staff meeting, the department needs a list of coaching assignments. Coaches often want a quick reference to their sport, the maximum and minimum numbers of players on each team, and the date the teams start playing. Name the query qryCoachingAssignments.

7. The staff also needs to know how many sports each coach is assigned to coach for each quarter of the year. They ask you to provide this information in the form of a spreadsheet, with the coaches' names appearing for the rows of the table and the quarters appearing as the columns. The rest of the information indicates the number of sports each coach is assigned to in each quarter. Name the query qryCoachingPerQuarter.

8. Recall that students must sign a waiver of liability and maintain academic approval before they can play an intramural sport. The department wants to have a list showing students and these two ratings. If a student has submitted a signed waiver and academic approval forms, indicate that they are approved to play. If the student has not submitted both forms, indicate that they are not approved to play. Organize the list so that those with approval are grouped at the beginning. Save the query as qryApprovalStatus.

9. In some cases, students who have academic approval but not a signed liability form can play intramural sports. However, students who do not have academic approval cannot participate in intramural sports. At the beginning of each semester, the department receives a list of students who are not approved to play sports. The staff records that information in the student table. They also want to remove from the table the students who do not have academic approval. Marianna asks you to identify students who do not have academic approval, isolate them in a separate table, and then remove them from the student table, which should contain only those students who have been academically approved. Name the queries qryUnapprovedStudents and qryDeleteUnapprovedStudents as appropriate.

10. All of the students who have signed up to play a sport have been assigned to a team. Provide a list of teams and the students assigned to those teams. Name the query qryTeamAssignments.

11. The staff also needs a way to track students in the future in case someone signs up for a sport and is not assigned to a team. Provide a way for the staff to track these students. Name the query qryStudentWithoutTeam.

12. To manage the teams, the coaches need a list of teams and their student captains. The captain names for this list are most useful as full names, with the last name appearing first. Name the query qryTeamCaptainAssignments.

13. If a sports field is available in the spring, it is also available in the summer. In other words, a field that is recorded as available only in the spring is actually available in the spring and summer, and a field that is recorded as available in the fall and spring is actually available in the fall, spring, and summer. Marianna wants to know if you can easily update the data to reflect this information. Name the query qrySeasonChange.

14. Provide at least two additional lists that would be helpful to the intramural staff. Create at least one by modifying an existing query in SQL view.

15. Close the **Hershey.mdb** database and Access.

Microsoft Word

Managing Everyday Communications with Microsoft Word

Operations Management: Communicating with Customers and Businesses

"The art of effective listening is essential to clear communication, and clear communication is necessary to management success."
—James Cash Penney

LEARNING OBJECTIVES

Level 1

Create a business document using a template
E-mail business prospects
Create a business letter
Send a mass mailing

Level 2

Create a newsletter using a template
Customize a template
Design a brochure
Create a table

Level 3

Design and create a form
Test and disseminate a form
Control formatting and editing changes in a document
Manage information rights in a document

TOOLS COVERED IN THIS CHAPTER

E-mail
Forms
Information Rights Management
Permissions
Mail merge
Templates
Tables

CHAPTER INTRODUCTION

Microsoft Word provides a number of tools for communicating professionally in business. Most people are able to type letters or simple reports in Word, but many are unaware of the features that exist to make doing these things easier, faster, and professionally formatted. In addition, some people new to business employ writing styles that lack the crispness and clarity desired in the field. Word is a word-processing program that produces **documents**, including letters, memos, flyers, brochures, newsletters, certificates, surveys, and other types of text-based expressions.

This chapter presents the tools necessary to produce many of these documents as well as tips and tricks for writing professionally for business audiences. You will learn how to use templates to write flyers, memos, newsletters, brochures, and certificates. In addition, you will learn to create form letters and e-mail using the Mail Merge Wizard, which allows you to personalize correspondence sent to many people. Furthermore, you will learn to design surveys using Word forms as well as new features in Word 2003, such as Information Rights Management and controlling editing and formatting changes.

CASE SCENARIO

Operations Management

Caitlin Callahan owns a successful small chain of restaurants in the upper Midwest called Caitlin's Café. She contacted Bon Vivant several years ago to see if they would buy her out, but at the time the vice president of franchise operations was not interested. As Alicia Fernandez, the new vice president of franchise operations, goes through her predecessor's files, however, she comes across Caitlin's old proposal, and decides to take another look. Caitlin's Café is trendier than Bon Vivant and a little more upscale. In addition, Caitlin's Café provides catering for weddings and offers a back room for small functions. Alicia thinks that if Caitlin can show evidence of a successful business model, then Bon Vivant might be interested in purchasing the chain and franchising the model.

Caitlin is in the midst of preparing for the Grand Opening of her tenth restaurant, which will be located in Milwaukee, Wisconsin. At Alicia's request, she starts sending correspondence to Bon Vivant as part of her efforts to convince them that her chain is worth their investment. Caitlin's first order of business is to create flyers announcing the Grand Opening. She plans to have the flyers delivered around the neighborhood as well as stuffed in the Milwaukee newspapers. The flyer will request feedback from prospective customers regarding their tastes in cuisine and entertainment, which will be rewarded, if provided, with a chance to win a free dinner. As requested by Alicia, she will write a memo to Bon Vivant corporate headquarters informing them of her promotion and attach the marketing piece.

LEVEL 1

IDENTIFYING PROSPECTIVE CUSTOMERS

WORD SKILLS TRAINING

- **Complete an entire mail merge process for form letters**
- **Create a document from a template**
- **Insert Clip Art**
- **Position a graphic**

SAM

CREATING BUSINESS DOCUMENTS USING TEMPLATES

In her first marketing effort, Caitlin wants to identify prospective customers by encouraging feedback to her advertisements, so she decides to offer free dinners and beverage samples to prospective customers who respond to her marketing flyer. By doing this, Caitlin will be able to collect useful data about customer preferences in cuisine and entertainment, as well as establish a mailing list for subsequent targeted marketing pieces. The first step, then, in identifying prospective customers so that she can begin to build goodwill and business relationships with the community is to produce an alluring flyer that promotes the café and entices serious customers to respond to her marketing inquiries. Caitlin could begin designing her marketing flyer from scratch, but she knows that templates exist that contain professional designs that she can then modify.

Using a Template from Office Online to Create a Flyer

Word templates are professionally designed documents that you can use as a basis for your own documents. They contain formatting, design, and often placeholder text that you can edit, replace, or delete as you wish. To access the New Document task pane, you click File on the menu bar, and then click New. As Figure 3.1 depicts, the New Document task pane gives you access to templates, some of which are installed with Office and stored on your computer, and many more that are accessible on Office Online, a Web site offered by Microsoft. Templates are available in many categories, including letters, résumés, meeting agendas, scholarly theses, and so forth.

Figure 3.1: Accessing Word templates from the New Document task pane

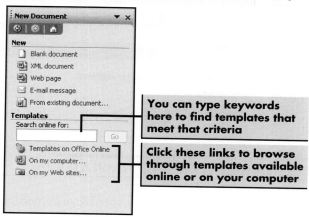

You can type keywords here to find templates that meet that criteria

Click these links to browse through templates available online or on your computer

To find an appropriate template for her flyer, Caitlin types "event flyer" in the Search online for text box in the New Document task pane, and then clicks the Go button. Because her computer is connected to the Internet, flyer samples from Office Online appear in the Search Results task pane. To preview them, she clicks one to open the Template Preview dialog box, and then uses the Previous and Next links at the bottom of the dialog box to see what they look like. Caitlin chooses the one shown in Figure 3.2, titled Event flyer (4-up). She downloads it to her computer, and it opens in a new document window.

Figure 3.2: Template Preview dialog box

Title of template appears here

Category in which template is located on Office Online

Click to scroll through previews of templates

Click to download current template

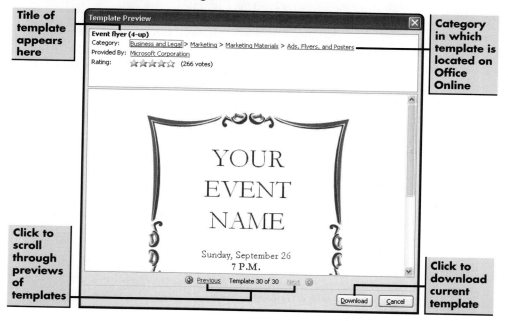

Caitlin edits the text in the flyer to include the café's name and address, the announcement of the Grand Opening, and the clever marketing prompt: "The first 50 customers to RSVP to caitlin@caitlinscafe.com will receive a complimentary dinner!" The finished flyer is shown in Figure 3.3.

Figure 3.3: Caitlin's flyer based on the Event Flyer (4-up) template

Caitlin knows that hundreds of thousands of people will receive this ad and that hundreds, or perhaps, thousands will respond in hope of a free dinner. She estimates the wholesale cost for fifty dinners to be $1,000, which she considers a marketing expense. She will, of course, be creating goodwill with those 50 customers, but also will respond to the others who RSVP with offers of free beverages or invitations for VIP admission to entertainment held at the café, thereby enticing them to visit. In responding to both parties, Caitlin will request permission to add their names to her preferred customer database so that she can send them a monthly newsletter that she is planning.

Caitlin is pleased with her flyer and marketing plan, and she is ready to send it to Alicia at Bon Vivant.

Using a Template to Create a Memo

Prospective franchisees of the Bon Vivant Corporation are instructed to attach proposed flyers, brochures, newsletters, and other homemade marketing materials to memos explaining the purpose of the campaign, identifying the target audience, and explaining the rationale for the piece. Caitlin knows that templates exist in Word for creating memos and decides to use one to create hers.

Caitlin again opens the New Document task pane, but this time, instead of searching online, she clicks the On my computer link in the task pane to open the Templates dialog box. This dialog box contains templates organized into categories on tabs, such as Letters & Faxes and Reports. She clicks the Memos tab, which is shown in Figure 3.4.

Figure 3.4: Memos tab in the Templates dialog box

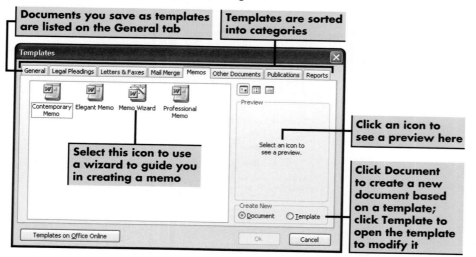

She clicks each of the icons to see what the template looks like in the Preview pane, and then chooses the Elegant Memo. To open a new document based on the template, she makes sure the Document option button is selected under Create New, and then clicks OK. The memo opens as a new, untitled document with placeholder text. She clicks in the placeholder field next to TO: in the memo header, types Alicia's name, and then adds her own name, subject, and date in their respective fields. Caitlin then replaces all of the text in the body of the memo with the content of her memo, as shown in Figure 3.5. Notice in Figure 3.5 Caitlin's use of bold formatting, numbered lists, and detailed contact information, which guides the reader's eye and indicates clearly how to contact Caitlin. Caitlin still needs to delete the placeholder text in the CC field as no one will be copied on this memo.

Figure 3.5: Caitlin's memo based on the Elegant Memo template

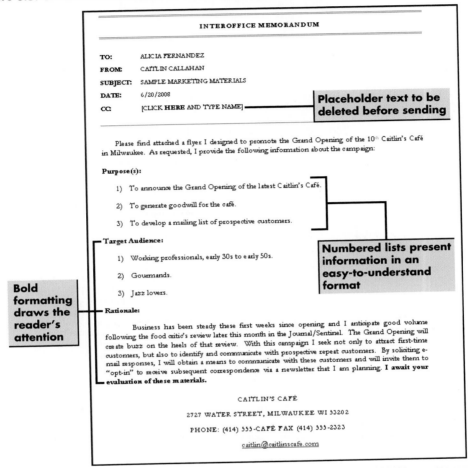

Placeholder text to be deleted before sending

Numbered lists present information in an easy-to-understand format

Bold formatting draws the reader's attention

Best Practice

Writing Professionally in Business

Business writing in general, and memo writing in particular, requires crispness and clarity. Time is money to businesspeople who prefer communications that get right to the point. Business memos, therefore, should be no more than one page and often include the elements listed in Table 3.1.

Table 3.1: Business memo writing tips

Element	Best Practice
To, From, and CC fields	Write out full names; avoid using first names only.
Subject	Explain the purpose of the correspondence. Caitlin's "Sample Marketing Materials" accomplishes this perfectly because the reader knows what the memo contains.
Introduction	Provide a brief overview of memo contents. Caitlin's statement "As requested, I provide the following information about the campaign" is brief, professional, and explains that the memo is written in accordance to corporate request and sets up the body of the memo.
Bold headings	Use bold headings to signify separate parts of the body of the memo. Notice that Caitlin did this for purpose, target audience, and rationale, highlighting the elements requested by corporate headquarters.
Numbered lists	Use numbered and bulleted lists frequently in business communication as they are easy to comprehend quickly. In the lists, use words, phrases, or sentence fragments as the items listed rather than full sentences as they, also, are easier to comprehend quickly.
Conclusion	Direct the reader to do something at the end of the memo. The conclusion of Caitlin's memo explains the rationale for her request and ends with "I await your evaluation...," formatted in bold. The formatting grabs the reader's attention and the wording instructs the reader to do something. In this case, Alicia must reply to Caitlin's request for evaluation of her marketing campaign.
Footer	Include contact information. Make sure that the reader knows how to reply to your memo. Caitlin provided four ways for Alicia to respond: postal address, phone number, fax number, and an e-mail address. She will include a Web site address in future correspondence after she has launched her Web site.

Saving and Managing Templates

When you use a template to create a new document, the title bar indicates that the open file is a new Word document, not the template itself. Likewise, when you download a template from Office Online, a new document based on the template is opened in the Word window. If you modify an existing memo by right-clicking its icon in the Templates dialog box and choosing Open, the template itself opens, ready for you to modify, not a document based on a template. The proof of this is in the title bar as evidenced in Figure 3.6.

Figure 3.6: Template opened as a new document and as a template

This template was opened as a new document as indicated by the new document name in the title bar

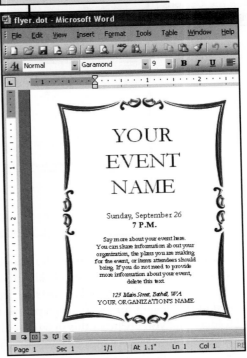

This template was opened as a template as indicated by the filename in the title bar

When you find a template online that you want to use repeatedly, you should save the template to your hard disk—not just a document based on that template. In addition, if you create a document whose format you will use many times, you can save that as a template as well. To save a document as a template, you click File on the menu bar, click Save As, click the Save as type list arrow, and then click Document Template (*.dot). The Save in folder automatically changes to the Templates folder, usually located in C:\Documents and Settings*username*\Application Data\Microsoft\Templates. Templates that are saved to this default location appear on the General tab in the Templates dialog box that opens when you click the On my computer link in the New Document task pane.

You can confirm the default storage location for Word templates by opening a Word document, clicking Tools on the menu bar, and then clicking Options to open the Options dialog box. Click the File Locations tab and note the path next to User templates, as shown in Figure 3.7.

Figure 3.7: Determining the location of the default templates folder

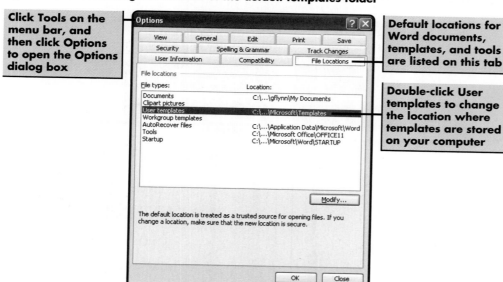

You can change the default location by double-clicking this entry in the list to open the Modify Location dialog box, and then clicking the Look in list arrow to navigate to a new location. The folder you designate becomes the new default location for templates. Templates stored in the default folder are displayed on the General tab of the Templates dialog box. Subfolders that you create in this default folder appear as new tabs on the Templates dialog box after you save templates in them. It is important to note that new tabs do *not* appear in the Templates dialog box until you save templates in them. Any template that you save from Office Online is saved in the default folder and appears on the General tab of the Templates dialog box unless you intentionally save it elsewhere. If you want to add templates to existing tabs, you must create subfolders with the same name as the existing tabs, for example, Reports, Memos, Publications, and so forth, within the default templates folder.

Caitlin knows that using templates saves a great deal of time. Consequently, she has created her own tab in the Templates dialog box titled Caitlin's Café, as shown in Figure 3.8, and has saved skeletal templates of the flyer and memo she created.

Figure 3.8: Tab added to Templates dialog box

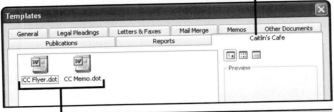

Templates that Caitlin created and saved in the folder "Caitlin's Cafe" in the Templates folder on her hard drive

How To

Save a Document as a Template

1. With the document open, click File on the menu bar, and then click Save As. The Save As dialog box opens.
2. Click the Save as type list arrow, and then click Document Template (*.dot). The Save in location changes to the default location for templates.
3. Type a meaningful name for the template, and then click the Save button. The template is now listed on the General tab of the Templates dialog box.

How To

Organize Templates

1. With a document open, click Tools on the menu bar, and then click Options. The Options dialog box opens.
2. Click the File Locations tab, and then double-click User templates in the list. The Modify Location dialog box opens with the default location where your templates are stored shown in the Look in list box.
3. If you want, click the Look in list arrow, and then navigate to a new default location for templates you save.
4. To create new tabs in the Templates dialog box, create subfolders in the default location. These will appear as tabs in the Templates dialog box after you save templates in them.

(*Note:* If a template that came installed with Office is deleted or erroneously edited, most users can retrieve the original by going to C:\Program Files\Microsoft Office\Templates\1033.)

E-MAILING BUSINESS PROSPECTS

Just as Word templates make document design more professional and efficient, e-mail messages composed in Word might appear more professional and be sent more efficiently than those composed in other programs. A number of features in Word allow for e-mail composition and transmission. One way to do so is to create a document in Word, click File on the menu bar, and then click Send To. From the list of options, you can choose Mail Recipient (as Attachment), which opens your e-mail client, if configured, and attaches the document to a blank e-mail message. This is much quicker than opening your e-mail program, starting a new e-mail message, and then adding an attachment. You can also send the body of your Word document as the e-mail message itself—not as an attachment—with one click of a button. If you need to send a message to many people, it can be more efficient to use mail merge, a process that merges names, addresses, and other information from one file with a document in another file so that each person is addressed individually—not generically and not carbon copied.

Sending Individual E-Mails from Within Word

After receiving positive feedback from Bon Vivant headquarters about her flyer, Caitlin has it professionally rendered and pays a marketing fee to the local newspapers to have it delivered among the circulars on the Sunday and Wednesday before the Grand Opening. In addition, she employs a few people to distribute them to 1,000 residences in the affluent neighborhoods nearby. Having produced the marketing content herself rather than employing a professional desktop publisher, Caitlin has a marketing budget surplus, and so she buys radio ads the week before the Grand Opening announcing the event and encouraging listeners to RSVP by e-mail to caitlin@caitlinscafe.com to be eligible for one of the 50 free dinners that she is offering.

As a result of these marketing efforts, Caitlin begins receiving e-mail from customers seeking the free dinner. She composes a congratulatory message in a Word document to send to the first 50 people who contact her. Caitlin could send her document to each of the first 50 respondents individually. By clicking the E-mail button 🖹 on the Standard toolbar in the Word window, you turn the Word document into an e-mail message with the Subject field pre-populated with the name of the Word file. An Introduction field appears below the Subject field in e-mail messages created from a Word document. You can use this field to explain the Word document you are sending (if the document is not the message itself).

Best Practice

Checking the Spelling and Proofreading

You must check the spelling of any document that you disseminate, but most surely for e-mail as sending error-filled e-mail is unprofessional and reflects negatively on your company and on you. In addition to checking the spelling of your work, to communicate professionally in business, you must also proofread your work before sending to avoid letting typographical errors slip through that the spell-checking process does not detect. For example, Caitlin is a great speller, but a poor typist. Invariably, she types the word "form" when she intends the word "from." The Spelling and Grammar checker does not pick up this error because "form" is a perfectly correct word. Make it a practice to always meticulously check the spelling of any correspondence you send and then proofread it before sending. By doing so, you will ensure that you represent yourself professionally in all of your business communications.

Sending a Mass E-Mailing to Numerous Prospects

Caitlin's flyer was a marketing success and she quickly becomes inundated with responses. She realizes that even if she personally answers the first 50 who will win the dinners, there is no way that she can respond to the hundreds of messages that are pouring in every day. If she sends one message to everyone who responds, she will encounter several other problems. Have you ever had to send an e-mail message to several people? Typically, you do this by adding multiple e-mail addresses to the Cc field. The problem with doing so is that much of the real estate at the top of the message is wasted displaying e-mail addresses and the recipient might need to scroll for some time just to read the message. In addition, exposing many e-mail addresses in this way can compromise the recipients' privacy as any one of the recipients might disseminate the message, copy the recipient list, or annoyingly click the Reply to All button. Some of these problems can be avoided by putting the addresses in the Bcc field instead of the Cc field, but even after doing so each recipient still receives a generic e-mail, impersonally addressed. Caitlin decides to employ a Word feature that allows her to send multiple e-mail messages, each customized and protective of recipients' privacy.

To send mass e-mailings to her potential customers, Caitlin decides to use a process called **mail merge**, a way to create custom documents, usually mailings, that combine standard text and individualized text to create customized documents. The benefit of creating a mail merge is that you eliminate copying and pasting when customizing mailings to more than one recipient. Rather, you create one message, insert the greeting line, and then each person receives a personalized e-mail containing the exact same body.

First, Caitlin directs an assistant to create a **data source**, which is a file that contains the records that you want merged. Often, this is a list of recipients that contains names, titles, e-mail addresses, and other contact information. The data source can be kept in documents, databases, spreadsheets, or in electronic address books. To create Caitlin's data source, the assistant enters prospective customers' contact information into an Excel spreadsheet, and places each type of data in a different column. In addition to customer contact information, Caitlin asks her assistant to include two additional columns: one to indicate whether the customer is one of the 50 winners and another to indicate whether the customer has been sent an invitation to the Grand Opening. Caitlin's data source is shown in Figure 3.9.

Figure 3.9: Customer data in an Excel worksheet

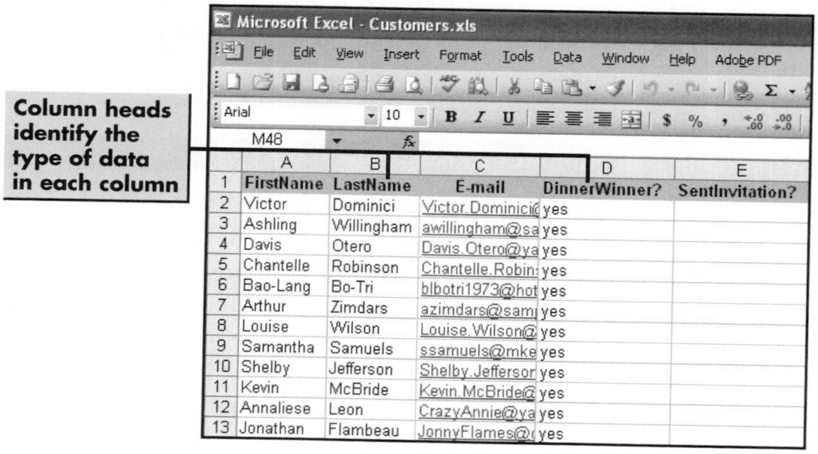

Column heads identify the type of data in each column

Best Practice

Choosing a Data Source Program

Data sources can be created in a number of programs. The simplest data source might be a list of names and addresses in a Word document. Each column of data should include a heading that clearly identifies the type of data beneath it, for example, First Name, Zip Code, Amount Due, and so forth. Data sources created in Word, however, can become difficult to manage as the list grows. If you use the data source only for mailings, then electronic address books (such as your Outlook contacts) are ideal to use, for Word knows what type of data resides in each field automatically because the fields are already named. For larger data sources, many people use spreadsheet or database programs because it is easier to manage more complex and greater volume of data in them.

Caitlin's next step is to create a **main document**, the document that will be sent to each recipient. The main document includes **merge fields**, fields that will be replaced by customized data for each recipient. Caitlin is first interested in e-mailing the group of 50 that won the free dinner. She begins the mail merge process by clicking Tools on the menu bar, pointing to Letters and Mailings, and then clicking Mail Merge to open the Mail Merge Wizard in the Mail Merge task pane, as shown in Figure 3.10.

Figure 3.10: First step in the Mail Merge task pane

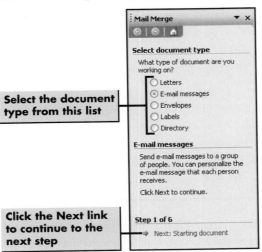

Select the document type from this list

Click the Next link to continue to the next step

The first of six steps in the Mail Merge Wizard is to select the document type. Caitlin chooses the E-mail messages option button, and then clicks the Next link at the bottom of the task pane. The task pane changes to show the second step of the process, in which you need to select the starting document that will be your main document. You can base the main document on an existing document or on a template, but unless the e-mail contains standard boilerplate text that you have saved, often you will choose to use the current document as your starting document and create an e-mail message from scratch. Caitlin has already created her e-mail message in the current document, so she leaves the Use the current document option button selected, and then clicks the Next link.

Step 3 requires you to attach a data source to the main document. The options include choosing your Outlook contacts folder or even typing a new list from scratch. As Caitlin has her contact information in an Excel spreadsheet, the data source that her assistant created, she leaves the default Use an existing list option button selected, and then clicks the Browse link to locate her customer spreadsheet. The Select Data Source dialog box opens with the My Data Sources folder in the My Documents folder listed in the Look in text box. This is where Word anticipates that your data sources are stored and where they will be saved by default if you choose to type a new list during the mail merge process. You needn't store your data source in this folder, but you might want to if the file is used primarily for mail merging. Caitlin finds and opens the Excel file her assistant created. Data sources kept in Excel, Access, or Outlook can be found in one of many worksheets, tables (or queries), or folders, respectively. As a result, you must choose the one that contains the appropriate data source. Because Caitlin is using an Excel file, the Select Table dialog box opens so that she can select the correct worksheet in the Excel workbook file. After connecting the data source and the main document, the Mail Merge Recipients dialog box opens. Caitlin notices that the table is not sorted in any logical way; rather, the records appear in the order that they were entered into the data source, as shown in Figure 3.11.

Figure 3.11: Mail Merge Recipients dialog box

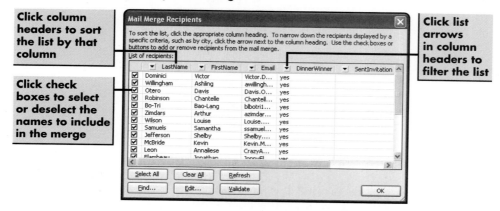

Click column headers to sort the list by that column

Click check boxes to select or deselect the names to include in the merge

Click list arrows in column headers to filter the list

If she continues with the Mail Merge Wizard at this point, the messages would be created in the order the data appears in the Mail Merge Recipients dialog box. Caitlin reasons that this will make it difficult to monitor for quality control issues, such as checking an alphabetical list to see if anyone was missed. To sort the list by last name, she clicks the gray column heading titled LastName.

The Mail Merge Recipients dialog box also allows you to select as many or as few of the names listed in the customer table as you want. By default, all names are selected and will receive the mass mailing. You can deselect names individually or you can filter the list to display only those names that meet specific criteria, for example, those who won the contest. To filter the list to include only the contest winners, Caitlin clicks the black list arrow to the right of the DinnerWinner? column heading and selects yes. She then clicks the OK button to close the dialog box, and then moves to the fourth step by clicking the Next link in the Mail Merge task pane.

After selecting the recipients of a mail merge, which connects the data source to the main document, your next step is to write your e-mail message, if necessary, and insert merge fields by using Step 4 in the Mail Merge Wizard, as shown in Figure 3.12.

Figure 3.12: Step 4 in the Mail Merge task pane

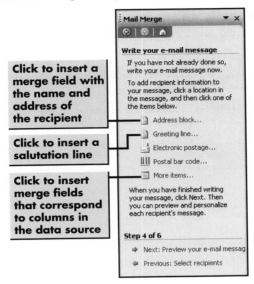

Click to insert a merge field with the name and address of the recipient

Click to insert a salutation line

Click to insert merge fields that correspond to columns in the data source

Caitlin already wrote the e-mail message congratulating the winners, but she needs to add the merge fields. After positioning the insertion point in the document at the point she wants to insert the greeting line, she clicks the Greeting line link in the task pane. The Greeting Line dialog box opens, as shown in Figure 3.13, so that Caitlin can choose the format of the salutation.

Figure 3.13: Greeting Line dialog box

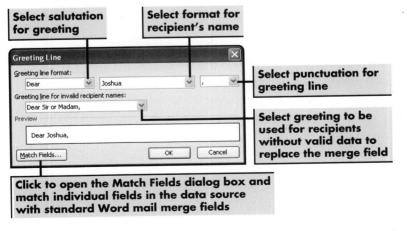

Select salutation for greeting

Select format for recipient's name

Select punctuation for greeting line

Select greeting to be used for recipients without valid data to replace the merge field

Click to open the Match Fields dialog box and match individual fields in the data source with standard Word mail merge fields

She chooses a less formal salutation, for example "Dear Joshua," rather than "Dear Mr. Randall:". As shown in Figure 3.14, the merge field is set off by double arrows, called chevrons, and contains the name of the merge field, for example GreetingLine. This will be replaced with individual names when the merge is complete.

Figure 3.14: Caitlin's e-mail message

> **Chevrons indicate this is a merge field**
>
> «GreetingLine»
>
> Congratulations on winning 1 of the first 50 dinners that will be served at Milwaukee's newest and finest restaurant on Water Street!
>
> Please join us for the Grand Opening of Caitlin's Café on Saturday, September 20, 2008 at 7:00 p.m. and bring this confirmation with you to receive your complimentary dinner.
>
> By the way, we are starting a monthly newsletter that will inform you of seasonal cuisine and the latest entertainment available at Caitlin's Café as well as share with you some of our great recipes. If you would like to receive the newsletter, please respond to this e-mail.
>
> Sincerely,
>
> Caitlin Callahan
> Owner
> Caitlin's Café
> 2727 Water Street, Milwaukee, WI 53202
> Phone: (414) 555-café Fax (414) 555-2323
> caitlin@caitlinscafe.com

Before sending a mail merged e-mail message or letter, it is important to see what the merged e-mail or letter will look like. To do this, Caitlin moves to Step 5 in the Mail Merge task pane, Preview your e-mail messages, as shown in Figure 3.15. She clicks the right-pointing arrow button >> in the task pane to see how each recipient is addressed. Notice that each recipient's first name and a comma replaces the Greeting Line merge field, as expected.

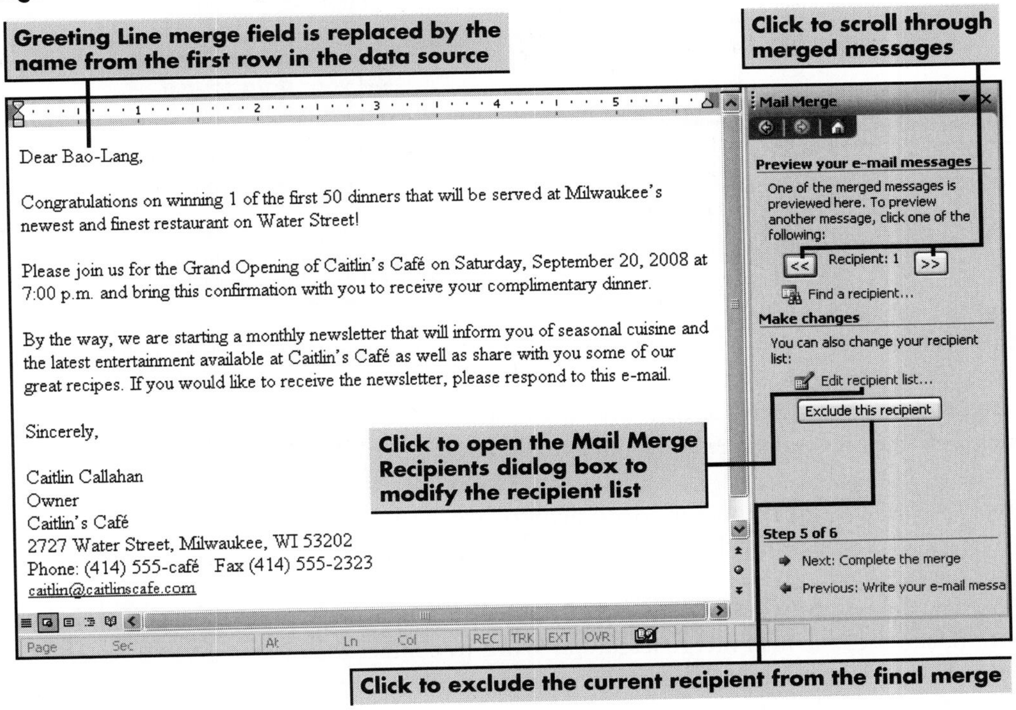

Figure 3.15: Previewing merged messages

Greeting Line merge field is replaced by the name from the first row in the data source

Click to scroll through merged messages

Dear Bao-Lang,

Congratulations on winning 1 of the first 50 dinners that will be served at Milwaukee's newest and finest restaurant on Water Street!

Please join us for the Grand Opening of Caitlin's Café on Saturday, September 20, 2008 at 7:00 p.m. and bring this confirmation with you to receive your complimentary dinner.

By the way, we are starting a monthly newsletter that will inform you of seasonal cuisine and the latest entertainment available at Caitlin's Café as well as share with you some of our great recipes. If you would like to receive the newsletter, please respond to this e-mail.

Sincerely,

Caitlin Callahan
Owner
Caitlin's Café
2727 Water Street, Milwaukee, WI 53202
Phone: (414) 555-café Fax (414) 555-2323
caitlin@caitlinscafe.com

Mail Merge

Preview your e-mail messages

One of the merged messages is previewed here. To preview another message, click one of the following:

<< Recipient: 1 >>

Find a recipient...

Make changes

You can also change your recipient list:

Edit recipient list...

Exclude this recipient

Step 5 of 6

→ Next: Complete the merge
← Previous: Write your e-mail messa

Click to open the Mail Merge Recipients dialog box to modify the recipient list

Click to exclude the current recipient from the final merge

Step 6 in the Mail Merge task pane, Complete the merge, is the final step and arguably the most important. It is your last chance to review the document. Check the spelling in your e-mail and proofread it for any typographical or grammatical errors. You can edit the text as needed and can always return to previous steps if you need to modify the merged fields, recipient list, or anything else that you deem necessary to make the e-mail more professional in its content or appearance. When you are satisfied, click the Electronic Mail link in the task pane to complete the merge. In the resultant Merge to E-mail dialog box, shown in Figure 3.16, the Email field is picked up from the data source in the To field. If Email does not appear in the To: line, you will need to click the list arrow and select the field from your data source in which e-mail addresses are stored. Add a subject for the e-mail message, and choose an appropriate e-mail format, HTML, Plain text, or Attachment. Usually, you will choose HTML instead of Plain text because you lose all of your formatting if you choose Plain text. Also, if you choose Plain text or Attachment and you use Outlook, a dialog box opens warning you that a program is trying to access your e-mail addresses. This message is intended to prevent viruses from accessing your Address Book without your knowledge by alerting you to the fact that Word is interacting with Outlook. Given that you intentionally want this to happen, the message is obtrusive because it reappears for every recipient and requires you to authorize them individually. That defeats the purpose of using mail merge for large e-mail correspondence.

Figure 3.16: Merge to E-mail dialog box

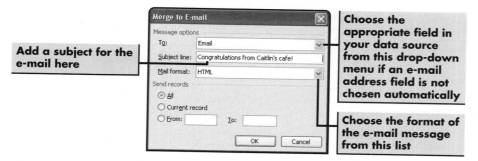

Add a subject for the e-mail here

Choose the appropriate field in your data source from this drop-down menu if an e-mail address field is not chosen automatically

Choose the format of the e-mail message from this list

3

Level 1

Click the OK button in the Merge to E-mail dialog box to close it and send the e-mail messages. Individual e-mails are sent using the e-mail client program installed on your computer to as many recipients as you chose in the Select Recipient dialog box. Each e-mail contains the same message in the body, but the salutation is personalized for each recipient.

At this point, you can save the merged document to save the final document with the merge fields and the data source attached to the document.

After Caitlin contacts the winners of the 50 free dinners that she promised in her marketing promotion, she uses the mail merge feature in Word to contact the more than 800 other prospective customers who responded. To some, she offers free breakfast beverages, to others a discounted lunch, and to others a free appetizer with dinner, hoping to attract customers throughout the day during the week of the Grand Opening.

Best Practice

Sending Mass E-Mailings

Sending unsolicited mass e-mailing is called spamming and is not only unappreciated, but can also be illegal. Make sure you use the mail merge feature to send e-mail only to those expecting or wanting the correspondence. You should be aware, however, that even if your intended recipients are desirous of your e-mail, some e-mail filters might block it if thought to be spam. Generally speaking, you can avoid such filtering if e-mail is sent in batches of 50 or fewer.

How To

Send a Mass E-Mailing via Mail Merge
1. With a blank document or the main document open, click Tools on the menu bar, click Letters and Mailings, and then click Mail Merge to open the Mail Merge task pane.
2. Click the E-mail messages option button in the Select document type section of the task pane, and then click the Next link at the bottom of the task pane to go to the second step.

3. Click the desired option button from the Select starting document section of the task pane, and then click the Next link at the bottom of the task pane to go to the third step.

4. Click the desired option in the Select recipients section of the task pane, and then click the link to browse for or create a recipient list.

5. Select as many or as few recipients as you wish from the resultant Mail Merge Recipients dialog box. Click the column headers to sort the columns, if desired, click the list arrow to filter the list, if desired, and then click the OK button to close the Mail Merge Recipients dialog box.

6. Click the Next link in the task pane to go to the fourth step, click the Greeting line link in the task pane, choose the desired options in the Greeting Line dialog box, and then click the OK button to close the Greeting Line dialog box.

7. Type the body of your e-mail, if necessary, check the spelling and grammar, confirm professionalism in tone and content, save the document with the merge field inserted, if desired, and then click the Next link at the bottom of the task pane to go to the fifth step.

8. Click the right double-arrow button >> to scroll through the merged messages, and then click the Next link to go to the sixth step.

9. Click the Electronic mail link in the task pane. In the resultant Merge to E-mail dialog box, confirm that the To: line includes the field from your data source that contains recipients' e-mail addresses, add a subject line, and choose a mail format.

10. Click the OK button to send the e-mail messages.

11. Save the merged document, if desired.

SENDING INDIVIDUAL BUSINESS LETTERS

Caitlin is pleased with the response to her marketing efforts, but knows that the promotion will need to continue after the buzz wears off after the Grand Opening is over. Consequently, Caitlin plans a marketing program called the VIP Business Club that involves giving incentives to local businesses with 50 or more employees to have breakfast meetings or lunches at Caitlin's Café. In exchange for guaranteed business, Caitlin will offer 10% off group orders for 10 or more people. Caitlin knows that such a program would appear innovative to the Bon Vivant Corporation and help her chances in being acquired by that company so she begins a letter to Alicia Fernandez explaining the details of the incentive program. To make sure that her letter is addressed and spaced professionally, she uses a Word template for creating her letter, and to make creating the letter even easier, she uses the Letter Wizard. To start the Letter Wizard, Caitlin clicks Tools on the menu bar, points to Letters and Mailings, and then clicks Letter Wizard.

The Letter Wizard asks for input regarding the style of the letter, the formality of it, the recipient address information, and the sender return address information. On the Letter Format tab of the Letter Wizard, Caitlin selects the Date line check box and chooses the full date format; she chooses Professional letter as the template from the Choose a page design list; and she keeps the default option of Full block style in the Choose a letter style

3

list. These are preferred business settings, though you are free to use or experiment with the other options. Notice in Figure 3.17 that there is a place to indicate that you have letterhead and to set the margins appropriately.

Figure 3.17: Letter Wizard dialog box

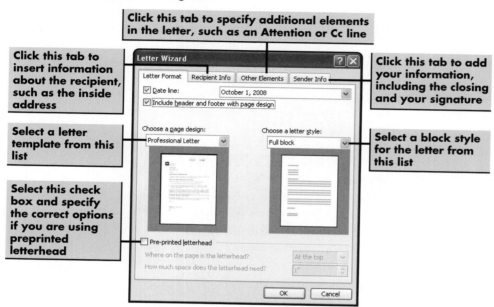

After choosing these letter format options, you can add your recipient's name and address to the Recipient Info tab and evaluate the options available on the Other Elements tab, which includes such things as options for including an Attention or Cc line. Then, click the Sender Info tab of the Letter Wizard to add your return address information. "Best Regards" or something equally formal is generally preferred in the complimentary close. Finally, click OK in the Letter Wizard dialog box to produce a pre-populated letter that includes your return address, date line, inside address, salutation, complimentary close, signature, and signature identification, as well as a prompt to replace the existing body: "Type your text here." Figure 3.18 details Caitlin's letter to Alicia that she produced with the Letter Wizard.

Figure 3.18: Letter produced by the Letter Wizard

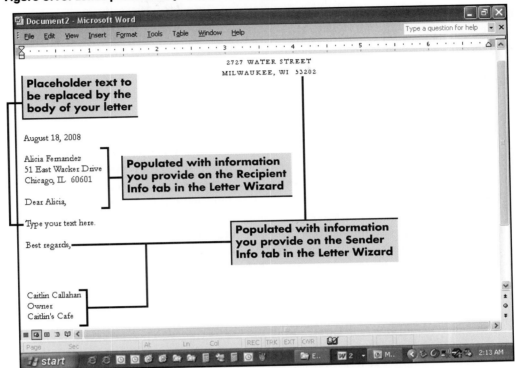

You can, of course, modify any of the text pre-populated by the Letter Wizard. You can also right-click on the salutation or the complimentary close to choose alternate versions of each. Using Word's Letter Wizard is useful as the sender and return address is remembered for use in future correspondence.

Best Practice

Designing Professional Business Letters

You can design business letters in many ways and you should adopt the style preferred by your company. However, in the absence of a preferred design you must be aware of standard business letter design. Eight basic elements are required in business letters: letterhead (or heading), date line, inside address, salutation, body, complimentary close, signature, and signature identification.

In addition, other elements can also be included, for example, filename, subject line, attention line, initials of author and typist, indication of attachments or enclosures, distribution (cc, bcc), and postscript. If the letter requires a second page or more, the header on subsequent pages should include the sender's name, the date, and the page number.

Sending a Mass Mailing Using the Post Office

Sending mass print mailings in Word requires the same six-step process as sending mass e-mail messages, but it usually requires greater sophistication in usage, including such things as matching fields of oddly named fields in data sources, inserting multiple merged fields in the body of the letter, and ensuring that formatting is not stripped from currency fields in the data source.

Caitlin sends her letter to Alicia, who is impressed with the marketing concept. Caitlin then does market research to identify local companies with more than 50 employees and goes about cold-calling them to discern their interest in participating in her VIP Business Club. In addition, being entrepreneurially inclined, everywhere that she goes, Caitlin introduces herself, her café, and her VIP Business Club, and asks interested parties to give her their business cards so that she can contact them with more information. Upon receipt of each card, Caitlin discreetly writes on them the location where she met the person and the particulars of their conversation. She feels that obtaining such information will help her customize further communication with each prospective customer, thereby demonstrating the goodwill and attention to customer service that she wants Caitlin's Café to become famous for. She enters prospective VIP Business Club customers into the Excel spreadsheet depicted in Figure 3.19.

Figure 3.19: Caitlin's data source in Excel

Field names are picked up by Word during a mail merge

	A	B	C	D	E	F	G
1	Company	Contact's First Name	Contact's Last Name	Method of Introduction	Where Met?	Meeting Needs	Catering Budget
2	Kinsale & Dunkirk Law Firm	David	Els	speaking with	on the phone	staff meetings	$ 1,000
3	Midwest Realtors	Sandra	Jackson	meeting	at Caitlin's Cafe	employee recognition	$ 500
4	21st century Designs	Tyler	Woo	being introduced to	at the gym	client breakfasts	$ 1,500
5	City Hall	Gunnar	Nygaard	speaking with	at the supermarket	employee recognition	$ 350
6	Skyline Hotel	Peggy	Ward	meeting	at the mall	staff meetings	$ 1,200
7	Convention Center	Patricia	Rodriguez	meeting	in the park	client luncheons	$ 2,500
8	Milwaukee College	Etienne	LaFollette	meeting	at the Lakefront	staff meetings	$ 1,000
9	Milwaukee Bucks	Darnell	Jones	meeting	at the Brewers	employee recognition	$ 350
10	Wisconsin Medical College	Aleeysha	Andreeson	being introduced to	at the Packers game	staff breakfasts	$ 800
11	Davis, Hatchet, & Cullins	Oscar	Cullins	speaking with	the other day	client luncheons	$ 1,600

Notice in Figure 3.19 that the fields containing the first and last names of the prospective VIP clients are labeled Contact's First Name and Contact's Last Name. This is not standard; such fields are normally called simply First Name and Last Name, respectively, or something similar. When you insert a Greeting line or Address block merge field, Word attempts to match the fields in your data source with its built-in fields. If you name the fields in your data source in a manner similar to the way Word names its fields—for example, LastName or Surname—then Word can match each field and insert the correct data. If, however, the fields in your data source are named in such a way that Word cannot easily match the fields—for example, if you named the field containing the recipients' street addresses "Street" instead of "Address"—you need to tell Word which field matches its built-in fields. Consequently, Caitlin will need to take steps to overcome this when she creates the merge.

Caitlin wants to follow up with her prospective VIP Business Club customers by sending them letters encouraging their enrollment. Caitlin knows that Word's mail merge feature allows her to produce one letter that contains the basic information that she wants to relay to all prospective customers, while at the same time giving her the freedom to personalize not only the address and salutation, but also some particulars in the body. Caitlin starts the Mail Merge Wizard to begin writing her letter.

In the first step of the Mail Merge Wizard, Caitlin leaves the default selection, Letters, as the document type, and then clicks the Next link to go to the second step of the wizard. She could create a letter from scratch, but she realizes that the letter that she sent to Alicia contains all the formatting and return address information that she wants, so Caitlin clicks the Start from existing document option button in the task pane, and then clicks the Open link to browse for her letter to Alicia. After clicking the Next link to get to the third step of the wizard, Caitlin browses for the Excel file from which she will select the recipients of this letter. In the resultant Mail Merge Recipients dialog box, Caitlin clicks the column header to sort the prospective customers by company name, and confirms that they are all selected. In the fourth step of the Mail Merge Wizard, she revises her letter to Alicia and inserts the merge fields. First, she needs to identify the oddly named fields in her data source so that the Mail Merge Wizard will know when to use the data in those columns. She does this by clicking the More items link in the task pane, and then clicking the Match Fields button in the resultant Insert Merge Field dialog box. The Match Fields dialog box opens. She clicks the list arrow next to the Last Name field, and selects the corresponding field in her data source, titled Contact's Last Name, as shown in Figure 3.20. She then repeats this for the First Name field.

Figure 3.20: Match Fields dialog box

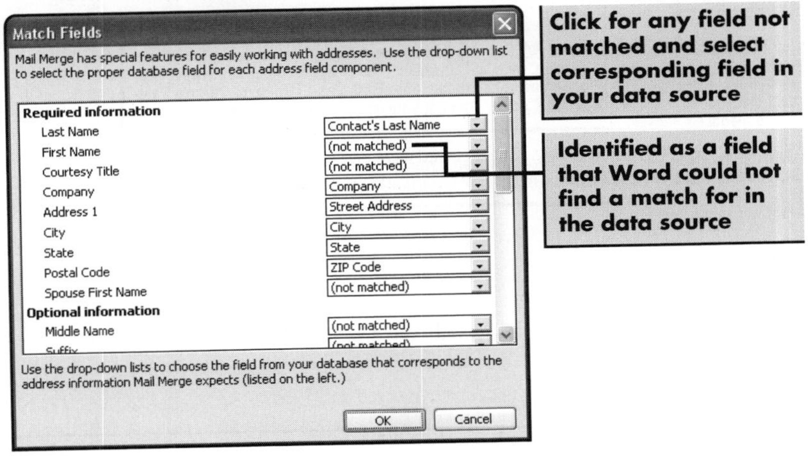

Caitlin clicks the OK button in the Merge Fields dialog box, and then clicks the Cancel button in the Insert Merge Field dialog box. She then adds the inside address to the letter. This will be unique for each recipient, and as such, will be a merge field. Caitlin selects the existing inside address, that of Alicia Fernandez, replaces it by clicking the Address block link in the task pane, and then accepts the default options in the Insert Address Block dialog box. Had she not taken the previous steps to match her data source fields, the address block would be devoid of names in the merged document.

Her next step is to highlight the salutation in the letter to Alicia and click the Greeting line link in the task pane. She accepts the defaults in the Greeting Line dialog box as well.

Next, Caitlin highlights the existing body of the letter, and begins writing her VIP Business Club pitch. The pitch is identical for all prospective VIP Business Club customers except for the following particulars: how Caitlin met them, where they met, what the prospective customer indicated as a potential need, and how much each prospective customer has budgeted for monthly catering expenses. Caitlin types a prototype of the letter and highlights in yellow those items that need to be replaced with merge fields. Caitlin selects the first phrase to be replaced, "meeting" and clicks the More items link in the task pane. In the Insert Merge Field dialog box, Caitlin selects Method of Introduction as that is the name of the field she created in Excel that stores the information about how she met this person. Caitlin repeats these steps to replace the other highlighted text in the body of her letter with the appropriate fields from the Insert Merge Field dialog box. The completed letter with the merge fields inserted is shown in Figure 3.21.

Figure 3.21: Prototype mail merge letter

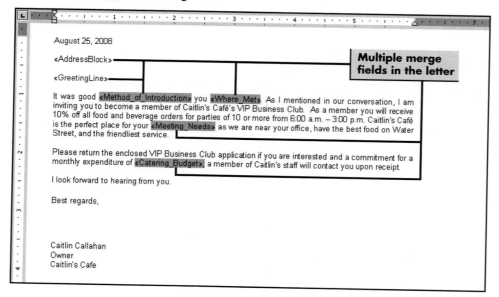

Caitlin moves to the fifth step in the Mail Merge Wizard, and then previews several of the letters to make sure that the merge executed correctly. Although she is pleased that she has successfully matched her oddly named fields with those that the wizard was expecting, that she included multiple merged fields in her letter, and that the spacing and punctuation looks good, she is not pleased with the fact that the Currency formatting was stripped from the data in the Catering_Budget field, as is evident in Figure 3.22.

Figure 3.22: Loss of formatting in merged field

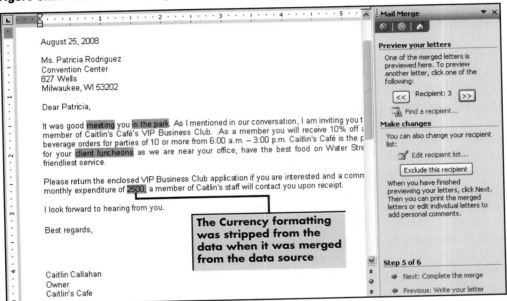

You can restore this formatting by clicking the Previous link twice to return to the third step of the Mail Merge Wizard. You then need to change an option in Word so that you are asked to confirm your data source when you attach it to the main document. To do this, you click Tools on the menu bar, and then click Options to open the Options dialog box. Click the General tab, and then click the Confirm conversion at Open check box to select it. This step is necessary just once; all subsequent mail merges will then prompt you appropriately when opening your data source.

Now Caitlin must reselect her data source by clicking the Select a different list link in the task pane. After she selects the Excel file, she is prompted to confirm her data source, which she does by selecting MS Excel Worksheets via DDE (*.xls), as shown in Figure 3.23.

Figure 3.23: Confirm Data Source dialog box

The DDE option enables Dynamic Data Exchange, which is a communication system that allows two programs to share data. In the case of a mail merge, not only is the raw data exchanged, but so too is numerical formatting, for example currency symbols, dates, and percentages. To remember this, you should memorize DDE (Dynamic Data Exchange) when using Excel as your data source, as the choice in the mail merge process is not intuitive. Similarly, should you use an Access database as your data source for mail merges, select the DDE process for Access when prompted to confirm your data source.

This time, when Caitlin previews the letters, the Currency formatting is in place in the Catering_Budget field. In the sixth step of the wizard, she runs the Spelling and Grammar checker, proofreads for typographical errors, and then eliminates the yellow highlighting she had added as a visual marker for her mail merge fields.

Caitlin wants to add a postscript to only one letter. She clicks the Edit individual letters link in the task pane. The Merge to New Document dialog box opens. This dialog box provides another chance to merge the main document with only specific data from the data source. Caitlin selects the All option button and then clicks the OK button. The data source and the main document are merged into a new document titled Letters1. Caitlin searches that document for the letter addressed to Tyler Woo, as she knows Tyler from her gym and wants to add a postscript to just his letter. Finding it, Caitlin writes "P.S. Come in for a visit, Tyler; I owe you a cappuccino!" at the bottom of the letter. Tyler had beaten her in a recent racquetball match. Then Caitlin saves the merged document, and prints the letters.

How To

Match Fields in a Mail Merge

1. In the fourth step of the Mail Merge Wizard, click the More items link in the task pane. The Insert Merge Field dialog box opens.
2. Click the Match Fields button. The Match Fields dialog box opens.
3. Click the drop-down list arrow for any field listed as "(not matched)" that you know you have data for in your data source, and select the corresponding field in your data source.
4. Click the OK button to close the Match Fields dialog box, and then click the Cancel button to close the Insert Merge Field dialog box.

How To

Combat Format Stripping in a Mail Merge

1. Click Tools on the menu bar, and then click Options. The Options dialog box opens.
2. Click the General tab, and then select the Confirm conversion at Open check box. (This is a one-time step; all subsequent mail merges will prompt you appropriately thereafter.)
3. In Step 3 of the Mail Merge Wizard, click the Browse link or the Select a different list link. The Confirm Data Source dialog box opens.

4. Select MS Excel Worksheets via DDE (*.xls) if you are using Excel as your data source; select MS Access Databases via DDE (*.mdb), (*.mde) if you are using Access as your data source.

5. Click the OK button, and then continue with the steps in the Mail Merge Wizard.

Steps To Success: Level 1

Caitlin sends monthly invoices to her VIP Business Club members. Some members have not paid their membership fees in several months, and she asks you to send e-mails or letters reminding them that their account is past due. She wants you to send a friendly, but firm, e-mail message to those members whose accounts are past due but who owe less than $1,000, and she wants you to create a professional letter to be sent to those members whose accounts are past due and who owe more than $1,000.

Complete the following:

1. Open the Excel file **VIP Invoices.xls** located in the Communications\Chapter 3 folder. Save it as **VIP Invoices with E-mail Addresses.xls**.

2. Add your own e-mail address to the E-Mail Address field for each of the three VIP Business Club clients who owe between $500 and $1,000. Save and close the file.

3. Create a new mail merge document that will produce e-mail messages to go to the three people who owe at least $500 but than less than $1,000. Write an e-mail that thanks them for their membership but firmly reminds them their membership dues are past due.

4. Select only the three recipients of the e-mail in the Mail Merge Recipients dialog box.

5. Check the spelling and proofread the e-mail.

6. Add a subject line and choose HTML format in the Merge to E-mail dialog box.

7. Send the e-mail (all of which are sent to your e-mail address as per your actions in Step 2).

8. Save the Word document as **Reminder E-mail.doc**, and then close the document.

9. Use the Letter Wizard to write a professional business letter to the members of the VIP Business Club who owe more than $1,000 that thanks them for their patronage, but states firmly that the invoice amount is overdue and must be paid promptly or else the VIP Business Club membership will be revoked. Make sure you include all eight elements of a professional business letter. Also, include a field within the body of the letter that will be replaced by the exact amount owed by each member.

10. Use the mail merge process to produce the letters. Use the same file, **VIP Invoices.xls**, located in the Communications\Chapter 3 folder, as the data source.

11. Sort the data source so that Caitlin can easily flip through the finished letters and make sure all the members are included, and then filter the list so that only those members owing more than $1,000 will receive the letter.

12. Match fields as needed.

13. Complete the mail merge, and then add a customized postscript to Oscar Cullins thanking him for a recent business referral.

14. Save the merged document as **Revoke Letter.doc**, and then close the documents.

3

Level 2

LEVEL 2

RETAINING EXISTING CUSTOMERS

WORD SKILLS TRAINING

- Create a watermark
- Create tables
- Insert graphics in documents
- Modify table formats by merging table cells
- Resize a graphic
- Revise a column layout
- Use Format Painter

SAM

CREATING NEWSLETTERS

One of the keys to maintaining a successful business is to develop good relationships with your customers, for without customers, you do not have a business. "Studies show that increasing your customer retention by as little as five percent can bump up profits by at least 20—and up to as much as 80—percent" (Stone).* Therefore, as the manager of her new café, Caitlin knows the importance of maintaining positive and ongoing communication with her existing customers.

Caitlin plans to market her restaurant aggressively for the first year by continually offering incentives to her customers for visiting. She also wants to inform them as new dishes are added to the menu and give them money-saving coupons for the new dishes to entice

*Stone, Adam. Retaining customers requires constant contact. ECommerce-Guide. http://www.ecommerce-guide.com/article.php/3461841 (accessed August 31, 2005).

them to return. As such, she develops a plan to establish ongoing communication with her customers. She decides that one of the best ways to let others know about the recent happenings at Caitlin's Café is to create and distribute a monthly newsletter. She begins to plan the first monthly newsletter in which she wants to give her customers an overview of the new products and services that her restaurant has to offer.

It is important that a newsletter is actually read by customers and not discarded as junk mail. Consider all of the flyers and newsletters that you receive from local businesses in your own neighborhood. The problem with many of these publications is that they do not have anything interesting to relate to the customer. A successful newsletter is a publication that is both informative and enjoyable to read, one that customers actually look forward to receiving. Trader Joe's, a small national chain, publishes a successful newsletter, which is devoted to describing the grocery store's unique and often exotic comestibles. The newsletter makes readers feel as though they are getting the inside scoop about the new products. The prose is skillfully written and goes beyond basic descriptions of the products. Every product has a story; the newsletter's writers describe how each product was selected and why, sometimes suggesting that their buyers traveled far and wide to bring each special find to their customers. It is not only informative, but entertaining as well. Caitlin decides to use this type of newsletter as a model for her own.

Newsletters can be e-mailed or mailed to customers, according to their preference. In addition, they can be posted on a Web site for all to see. Caitlin plans to design one to be mailed and will create e-mail and Web versions at a later date.

Planning a Newsletter

Before undertaking the design of the newsletter, it is important to know what content you will include. This will help you to make good decisions about the design. Consider the following things:

- Who is your target audience?
- What is the goal of your newsletter?
- How will you personalize the newsletter for your audience?

The target audience is important because it will affect the choices you make as you design your document. Caitlin knows from the data she collected when she was doing the market research to open her restaurant that the majority of her patrons will most likely be upper middle-class professionals in their mid 30s to mid 50s. She feels that a classic design for her newsletter that uses subtle colors and traditional fonts will most likely appeal to this demographic. By contrast, if she were targeting a younger audience, she would be inclined to choose a more contemporary design theme with brighter colors and more casual fonts.

Identifying the goal of the newsletter is important because purposeful correspondence is more effective than just mass mailing reminders to customers about the existence of

3

the restaurant. She wants to convey the sense that there is always something new at Caitlin's Café by highlighting new dishes from different regions of the world as well as by emphasizing the classic American fare that will always be on the menu. In addition, she wants to provide incentives, such as excellent entertainment and valuable coupons, to encourage new and existing customers to patronize her restaurant. Her first newsletter aims to provide potential customers with an idea of what it is like to dine at Caitlin's Café. She will feature highlights of new, exotic, and classic menu items, give recipes that people can try to replicate at home, and provide photos of happy restaurant patrons dancing and dining.

The content that you decide to include is of utmost importance in designing your newsletter. Some customers will be attracted to the money-saving features, such as coupons, which are particularly helpful for attracting first-time customers. Regular customers might enjoy a "Reader's Response" section where they can submit questions and have both their inquiries and responses published. Because Caitlin's Café features weekly entertainment, she wants to include reviews of selected musicians and bands so that her customers can see the type of atmosphere that her restaurant promotes. Whatever content you decide to include in your newsletter, make sure it is important not only to you, but also to your customers.

Best Practice

Giving Your Audience a Reason to Read Your Newsletter

You can increase the likelihood that your newsletter will be both read and appreciated by your target audience in many ways. One way is to include unique content that your audience can only find in *your* newsletter. The following are some examples that Caitlin is considering:

- **Recipes**—Publish a recipe for an entrée, sauce, or dessert that is served only at her restaurant.
- **Entertainment**—Highlight the musical lineup that will be performing at her restaurant this month.
- **Specials**—Feature an entrée she wants to promote by providing a mouth-watering description and an alluring price.
- **Coupons**—Give offers published only in the newsletter that provide special savings (such as "buy one entrée get second one at half price" deals).
- **Staff recommendations**—Highlight a member of her staff, replete with his or her picture, and that staff member's personal food recommendations.
- **Customer of the Month**—Feature customers who complete a customer satisfaction survey by giving them a prize and publishing their profiles in the newsletter.

The more interesting the newsletter, the more likely your customers will make a point of reading it from beginning to end. Strive to highlight those things that separate you from the competition.

Customizing a Template to Create a Newsletter

The design of a newsletter is as important as the content. It should not only be informative, but pleasing to the eye. Here are a few guidelines to consider when designing your newsletter:

- Use a consistent format. After you have developed a newsletter or customized an existing template, use the finished newsletter as a new template for your future newsletters. This will help to increase audience recognition and eliminate time-consuming and unnecessary formatting.
- Keep the format simple—two to three columns is ideal.
- Avoid overwhelming your newsletter with text. Too much text can discourage readers from reading the entire newsletter; instead, break up text with graphics.
- Limit the number of different font types you use to two or three. More than that makes the newsletter look crowded and unprofessional.
- Allow some white space to contrast the important details. Too much text is overwhelming to the eyes.
- Include a table of contents to guide readers to the sections that they are most interested in (be sure to have some "regulars" that they will keep coming back for).
- Include some pictures and/or clip art but do not go overboard. Too many graphics can make a newsletter look amateur. Moreover, gratuitous pictures detract from the message. Choose all your content judiciously.

The thought of designing a newsletter from scratch might seem daunting. The good news is that there is little reason to do so because many preexisting templates are available on Microsoft Office Online. To find one, Caitlin types "newsletter" in the Search online for text box in the New Document task pane, and then starts her search. Even if you want a unique and personal newsletter, it is a good idea to use a preexisting template so that you will not have to spend time formatting the margins and columns. You can modify the format after you have a basic template structure that suits your needs.

Caitlin finds a newsletter template that has a layout that appeals to her because of its tailored look and classic fonts. The template, named "Holiday newsletter (with Santa's sleigh and reindeer)" obviously needs some customizing as she doesn't want to use the winter holiday theme, as shown in Figure 3.24.

Figure 3.24: Newsletter template

She sets about customizing the newsletter by making the following changes:

1. She removes each holiday graphic (the silhouette of Santa and his reindeer and each of the snowflakes) by clicking each image to select it, and then pressing the Delete key.

2. She changes the title of the newsletter from "Our Family Newsletter" to "Caitlin's Café Monthly Newsletter."

3. She deletes the family picture and replaces it with the Caitlin's Café logo by clicking Insert on the menu bar, pointing to Picture, clicking From File, and then locating and double-clicking the graphic in the Insert Picture dialog box.

4. She adds clip art of food and beverages to the top of the colored box on the left. To do this, she places the insertion point inside the top box, clicks Insert on the menu bar, points to Picture, and then clicks Clip Art to open the Clip Art task pane. To locate the clip art she wants, she types "food" in the Search for text box in the task pane, clicks the Search in list arrow, makes sure the Everywhere check box is selected, clicks the Results should be list arrow, selects only the Clip Art check box, and then clicks the Go button. She also tries searching for clip art with the keyword "beverage." She finds an appropriate piece of clip art, and then clicks it to insert it at the insertion point in the document.

Changing Object Colors in a Document

The colored box on the left of the newsletter is actually two drawn rectangles filled with color. Caitlin wants to change the color of these boxes to match the restaurant's color scheme. She clicks in the lower-right corner of the maroon box at the top, outside of the graphic, and a selection box with slanted lines appears around the box, which means the object is active. Next, she opens the Drawing toolbar by right-clicking one of the toolbars, and then clicking Drawing. She clicks the Fill Color list arrow 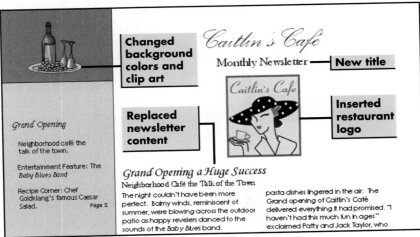, and then clicks the Brown color tile. The top box changes to brown. Next, she clicks the lower box, clicks the Fill Color list arrow, and then clicks More Fill Colors to open the Colors dialog box. She clicks a light tan color tile, and then clicks the OK button. The bottom box is now light tan.

After making changes to the design of the newsletter, she begins replacing the template's content with her own. She replaces the text in the bottom of the colored box on the left with a table of contents to help readers navigate through the newsletter, and she selects the text in the article on the first page and types her article about the Grand Opening. She formats the table of contents and the headline of the article, as well as the newsletter title in navy blue. Figure 3.25 shows page one of her newly customized newsletter.

Figure 3.25: Customized template

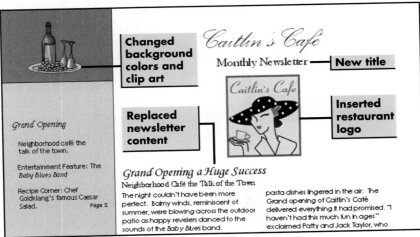

The newsletter, although using the basic design and formatting of the template, takes on a completely new look, one that is much more appropriate to Caitlin's intended audience.

Creating and Linking Text Boxes

Newsletter templates use text boxes to organize text into different areas in the document. A **text box** is an object that contains text. To create a text box, you click Insert on the menu bar, click Text Box, and then drag the pointer until the text box is the desired size.

You move a text box as you would any object by clicking in one to select it and then dragging it by its edge to any place in your document. **Linked text boxes** are often used in newsletters to allow a story to continue from one section or page in the newsletter to another section or page. This way, it is possible to introduce several different stories or features on the first page and continue them at different locations within the newsletters. If you want to create your own linked text boxes, you can do this using the Text Box toolbar which automatically appears when you create a text box. First, create two text boxes, click in the first text box, and then click the Create Text Box Link button [⚭] on the Text Box toolbar. Next, position the pointer in the empty text box you want to link to so that the pointer changes to ✇⁊, and then click. The text boxes automatically link so that excess text flows from the first text box to the next.

3

Level 2

Best Practice

Changing Text Boxes Within a Newsletter Template
Templates are a quick way to create professional looking newsletters. The templates that are included in Microsoft Office are created by professional designers and, generally speaking, they are better than what the average person might create on her own. However, there might be instances in which it is necessary to make some modifications to the template. Because newsletters use text boxes to hold their content, you might want to resize the text box to better suit your purposes. This is easily done by clicking on the perimeter of the text box to highlight it. Place your mouse pointer on the lower-right corner of the text box until it is highlighted and the sizing handle appears. Drag the box up, down, or sideways until it is the size that you want.

Caitlin enjoys brainstorming for the content of the newsletter and encourages staff members to contribute. When the newsletter is finished, she intends to mail it to all those customers who opted to receive it when responding to her Grand Opening correspondence, to all VIP Business Club members, and to all customers who request one in the restaurant. In addition, she will place a stack of them in the lobby of the café and is investigating the cost of mailing them to targeted audiences. She might even create an electronic version that she could e-mail to larger audiences, replete with hyperlinks to her future Web site and other sites of interest, but likes the look and feel of the paper version and has not yet created a Web site to make this feasible.

How To

Insert Clip Art
1. Click Insert on the menu bar, point to Picture, and then click Clip Art. The Clip Art task pane opens.
2. Type a keyword in the Search for text box in the task pane.
3. Click the Search in list arrow, and then select the check boxes next to the places you want to search.

4. Click the Results should be list arrow, and then select the check boxes next to the type of clip you want to search for.
5. Click the Go button. Clips that match your keyword appear in the task pane.
6. Click the clip you want to insert at the insertion point in the document.

CREATING A BROCHURE

Several customers have come into Caitlin's Café requesting food for take-out. Caitlin wants to create a take-out menu so that customers can decide what to order before coming to her restaurant and call ahead with their orders. She decides to create one in the style of a brochure that will list all the menu items and their prices as well as important information about the restaurant, such as the address, phone number, and hours of operation. The finished menu can then be distributed throughout the neighborhood as additional advertising, as well as be made available at the cash register at the front of the restaurant.

Caitlin decides to use a simple brochure template stored in the Templates folder on her computer. She opens the Templates dialog box, and then opens a new document based on the Brochure template on the Publications tab. This brochure template has a threefold design. The advantage of a threefold design is that it allows for more variety in that there are six different faces on which you can put text. However, the smaller area necessitates a smaller font that can compromise readability. Caitlin thinks a twofold design for her menu will be easier to read, so she changes the number of the columns in the brochure from three to two. She clicks Edit on the menu bar, and then clicks Select All to select all of the text in the document. Next she clicks Format on the menu bar, and then clicks Columns to open the Columns dialog box. She clicks Two in the Presets section of the dialog box, clicks the Apply to list arrow, and then clicks Whole Document to apply the two columns to the whole document.

Now that she has two columns, Caitlin begins adding content to the brochure. She begins by editing the right column, as this will be the first page of the brochure. She replaces all the content that will appear on the front page of the brochure with one large text box. She changes the background color of the text box to light pink and gives the text box a dark blue border. She types a title for the menu, and then inserts the restaurant's logo below the title. She also adds the address, phone and fax numbers, and hours of operation to this first page. See Figure 3.26.

Figure 3.26: The first page of the take-out menu

Caitlin continues to add content to remaining pages of the brochure. Although her brochure is quite different from the original, the template was useful in determining the margins for her document so that when folded in half, the text would be evenly placed on the page.

USING TABLES

On the second page, Caitlin creates a table to hold the menu items and their corresponding prices in the left column. The table is organized in rows and columns, and the intersection of these columns and rows is a **cell**. Just as in Excel, the upper-left cell in a table is identified as cell A1 (the first column, A, intersecting the first row, 1). Below A1 is cell A2, then cell A3, and so forth. Adding and deleting rows and columns can be done in several ways. Caitlin does this by clicking Table on the menu bar, pointing to Insert, and then clicking Table to open the Insert Table dialog box. In this dialog box, you modify the number in the Number of columns and the Number of rows text boxes to create a table with the proportions you specify.

Caitlin adjusts the proportions of the table to better fit her intended content. She drags the column border between the columns to the right to make the first column much wider than the second column. Now the description of each menu item will fit in the left column and the right column is narrower because it only needs to hold the price of each item. She clicks in each cell and types each item and its corresponding price into each row until the appetizer menu is complete. She finds that she needs one more row in her table, so with the insertion point in the last cell in the table, she clicks the Insert Table button list arrow ▣▾ on the Tables and Borders toolbar, and then clicks Insert Rows Below. In cell A1, she types "Appetizers" and then merges cells A1 and B1 so that the table title spans both columns. To do this, she opened the Tables and Borders toolbar, dragged to select cell A1 and B1, and then clicked the Merge Cells button [image] on the Tables toolbar. She creates a table for entrées in the right column on the second page of the brochure.

Next, Caitlin formats the Appetizers table. She selects the Appetizers cell, and formats the text so it is blue and in italic. She then changes the font size of "Appetizers" to 18-point. She then selects all of the cells in the table except the Appetizers cell, and fills them with white by clicking the Shading Color button [image] on the Tables and Borders toolbar, and then clicking the White color tile. Finally, she clicks the Table Move Handle [image] to select the entire table, removes the cell border lines by clicking the Outside Border button list arrow [image] on the Tables and Borders toolbar, and then clicks the No Border button [image] on the menu.

Because she wants each page of her menu to look the same, Caitlin uses the Format Painter to copy the formatting of the text in the Appetizer table to that of the Entrées table. This way, she does not need to make changes repeatedly to the new text. The final menu, shown in Figure 3.27, shows the result of using the Format Painter to apply the formatting in the Appetizer table to the content of the Entrées table.

Figure 3.27: Final menu

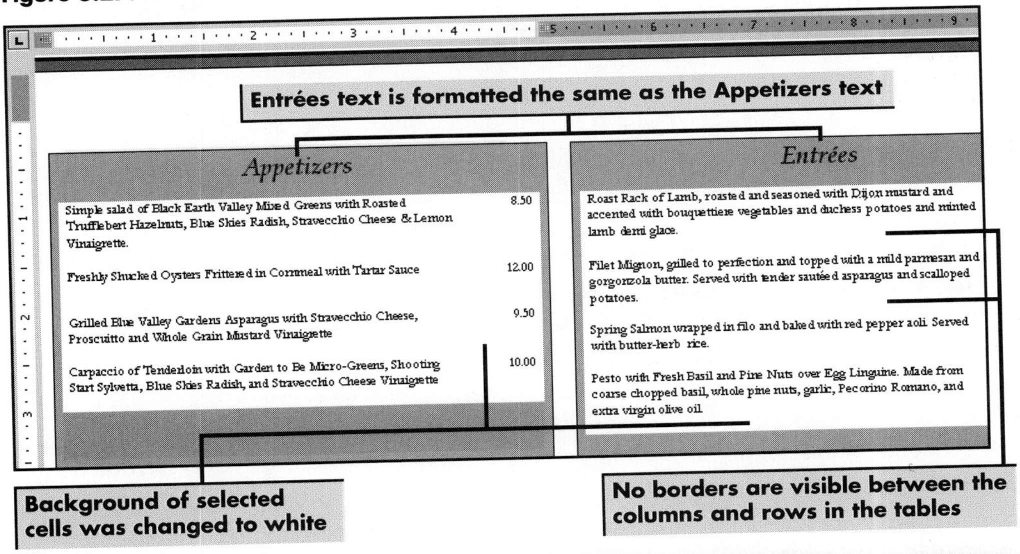

How To

Modify a Table
To move a table within a text box:
1. Click the upper-left corner of the table so that the Table Move Handle [image] appears.
2. Drag the Table Move Handle to reposition the table.

To adjust the size of a table:

1. Resize a column by dragging the right column boundary of the column you want to resize.
2. Add new rows by clicking the Insert Table button list arrow 🔲▾ on the Tables and Borders toolbar, and then clicking one of the Insert commands.

To merge cells within a table:

1. Highlight the cells that you want to merge.
2. Click the Merge Cells button 🔳 on the Tables and Borders toolbar.

Best Practice

Using the Format Painter

The Format Painter is useful when you want to apply a series of formatting settings from one selection of text to another. Imagine for a moment that you have changed one of the headings of your document so that the font type, size, and color are different from that of the rest of the document. To make the same changes to another selection of text would require you to again go through three steps. The Format Painter eliminates extra steps by allowing you to apply all of these settings to a new selection of text in only one step. To apply the Format Painter, do the following:

1. Select the text that has the formatting you want to copy.
2. Click the Format Painter button 🖌 on the Standard toolbar.
3. Drag to select the text whose format you want to change.

If you want to apply this same formatting to several different text selections, double-click the Format Painter button after you've selected the text whose formatting you want to copy. This keeps the Format Painter active as you apply the formatting to your different text selections. To turn it off, just click the Format Painter button again or press the Esc key.

Best Practice

Creating a Watermark

Caitlin could add a watermark of the restaurant logo to the final page of her menu. A **watermark** is a faded graphic that subtly appears behind the text of a document. Watermarks are useful if you want to include a graphic in your document, such as a company logo, but you do not want it to detract from the text. Because watermarks are faded and in the background, they give documents a professional look and feel without taking over valuable real estate on the page.

To create a watermark, click Format on the menu bar, point to Background, and then click Printed Watermark. In the Printed Watermark dialog box that opens, click the Picture watermark option button. Next, click the Select Picture button and browse for the graphic that you want to insert as a watermark, select it, and then click the Insert button. Click the Washout check box to select it, and then click the OK button.

If you want to make changes to your Watermark, click View on the menu bar, and then click Header and Footer. In this view, you can move and resize the watermark. Click the Close button on the Header and Footer toolbar when you are finished.

Steps To Success: Level 2

Caitlin has begun to design her newsletter, but she needs to add more content to the second page. She asks you to change the design of the second page to match the first and add the additional content. She also needs to add a beverage and dessert section to her take-out menus and she has asked you to take on this task as well.

Complete the following:

1. Open the file **Newsletter.doc** in the Communications\Chapter 3 folder, and then save it as **Revised Newsletter.doc**.

2. Using the photos and text provided in the Communications\Chapter 3 folder, finish Caitlin's newsletter doing the following things:

   a. Change the default colors on the second page to match the customized design on the first page.
   b. On page 2, replace the picture of the puppy with clip art of a salad. Copy the Caesar salad recipe from the file **Newsletter Contents.doc** in the Communications\Chapter 3 folder, and then paste it into the body of the newsletter adjacent to the picture of the salad below Caitlin's answer to the question in the Ask Caitlin section.
   c. Paste the article about the Baby Blues Band from the **Newsletter Contents.doc** file onto page 1 of the newsletter. Resize the text boxes and change the font size of the text, as necessary, to fit the story into the newsletter.
   d. Create a text box at the bottom of page 2 of the newsletter and insert the restaurant coupon found in the graphic file **Coupon.bmp** located in the Communications\Chapter 3 folder.
   e. Add clip art depicting a band or band members at the bottom of page 1 to the left of the article you pasted about the Baby Blues Band. Replace the image at the bottom of page 2 with clip art of people dancing.
   f. Update the table of contents, if necessary, and delete any old information from the previous newsletter.

3. Save and close the newsletter.

4. Open the file **Menu Brochure.doc**, located in the Communications\Chapter 3 folder. Save it as **Draft of Spring Menu.doc**.

5. In the menu contents section, add three rows to the beverages menu list and add the following: Assorted Soft Drinks—$3.00, Café Latté, Espresso, and Cappuccino—$4.00; Fruit Smoothies—$4.00.

6. Under the last item in the Entrées menu, add four rows. In the first row, merge the cells to make room for a new menu title.

7. Type DESSERTS in the new row with the merged cells and change the background color of the cell to match the pink background of the rest of the menu. Change the background color of the last three rows to white.

8. To add content to the Dessert menu, add three items of your own choosing to each of the three remaining rows.

9. Use the Format Painter to make the type color and size identical to the other menu titles.

10. Format the tables as necessary to ensure that the menu is consistent in its design.

11. Save and close the document.

CASE PROBLEMS

Level 1—Communicating with Customers at Engeleiter Mortgage

You are currently employed at a small mortgage company, Engeleiter Mortgage, as a sales manager. As part of your job, you need to send notices to current customers who are late making their mortgages payments; in addition, you need to solicit new business by encouraging new customers to refinance with Engeleiter. Your office maintains two databases, one with the names and addresses of customers who presently hold mortgages with the company and one of prospective customers. You decide to use mail merge to create and send letters to the people in the databases.

Complete the following:

Sales

1. Open the file **Customers.xls** from the Communications\Chapter 3\Case 1 folder. This file contains loan information for existing customers.

2. Create a letter using the Letter Wizard that details each customer's monthly mortgage statement. Employ titles, communicate professionally, be formal in tone of correspondence, and include merge fields to indicate the following:

   a. Amount of unpaid principal balance
   b. Interest rate
   c. Current monthly payment
   d. Due date of payment
   e. Amount of late fee (to be added to current monthly payment if paid after due date)

3. Filter the data source and merge the letter with only those people who have mortgages in California. (Make sure that formatting is not stripped for currency or date fields.)

4. Save the merged document as **Existing Engeleiter Customers.doc**, and then close the document.

5. Using the entire, unfiltered list, create an e-mail merge that encourages existing customers to refer their friends to Engeleiter Mortgage.

6. Do not send the e-mail. Save the main document as **Referrals.doc**, and then close the document.

Capstone
Projects

Project 1
Analyzing Vendor Data and Profitability
Sales: Best Fresh Grocery Chain Vendor Analysis of Randall Dairy

LEARNING OBJECTIVES

Extract sales data from a database

Transfer and verify the data in a spreadsheet

Evaluate the sales data

Examine alternative profit scenarios

Complete a financial analysis

Format a workbook

Present the results of an analysis to management

Sales

1

PROBLEM DESCRIPTION

The grocery store chain Best Fresh wants to analyze its relationship with one of its small but popular dairy vendors, Randall Dairy. The purpose of this analysis is to understand how much Randall Dairy product Best Fresh sells, the type of service Best Fresh receives, and the revenues generated from these sales. Best Fresh has noticed that products from this dairy sell very well within the local Indiana region where they are available. Customers have stated that the products are fresher than other dairy products and that they like the idea of supporting local industry. Consequently, Best Fresh wants to analyze its business dealings with Randall Dairy thoroughly and determine whether to expand this relationship.

You are currently working at the Best Fresh corporate office as a marketing analyst and have been assigned the job of retrieving and analyzing the Randall Dairy data. Currently, each Best Fresh store has its own method of gathering vendor data, making it time consuming to obtain and combine the information. Because Randall Dairy is interested in expanding its relationship with Best Fresh, Scott Vandenberg, the general manager at Randall Dairy, will allow you to use a copy of part of Randall Dairy's Microsoft Access database—specifically data for deliveries in May 2008. Using this partial database will make your job easier and let you complete your analysis more quickly. You anticipate this is a one-time request because Best Fresh's new corporate database is now in the final stages of development, and after this system is online, you can use the complete Best Fresh database as necessary.

The first part of your assignment is to retrieve the specific sales information you need from the Randall Dairy database. You will then transfer the data into a Microsoft Excel spreadsheet to complete several analyses, which will help you identify the Randall Dairy products sold in Best Fresh stores, in what quantities, and the amount of time these products can be offered before their expiration dates. Your manager expects you to present your findings at the monthly purchasing meeting.

REQUIRED FILES

To complete this project, you need the following files from the Capstone_Projects\Project1 folder:

- BestFresh.jpg
- BestFresh104.txt
- BestFresh107.txt
- BestFresh117.txt
- BestFresh126.txt
- Randall.mdb

EXTRACTING SALES DATA

When you examine the Randall Dairy database, Randall.mdb, you find that it contains the tables shown in Figure 1.1 and described in the following list, where primary keys are underlined.

Figure 1.1: Randall Dairy database tables

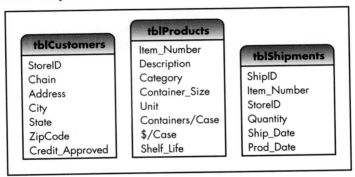

- **tblCustomers**—This table contains the details of each store to which Randall ships, including store identification number (storeID), associated store chain, address, city, state, zip code, and credit approval status, which is Yes (credit granted) or No (credit not granted).
- **tblProducts**—This table lists detailed information on each product sold, including the item identification number (ItemNumber), description, category, container size, unit (unit of measurement for the container, such as ounces or pounds), number of containers per case, wholesale case price ($/case), and item shelf life (the number of days to expiration from production).
- **tblShipments**—This table provides the details of each shipment made, including a shipment identification number (ShipID), item number, store ID number, quantity of cases shipped, ship date, and production date.

Your first task is to analyze each shipment from Randall Dairy to a Best Fresh store during May 2008. You also need to report your findings to your manager by completing each of the following tasks.

1. Copy the file **Randall.mdb** from the Capstone_Projects\Project1 folder to a work folder, renaming the file **RandallStudy.mdb**.

2. Because this is a copy of a partial database, you need to set up the appropriate table relationships.

3. Modify the field captions as necessary so that the data is easy to read in Datasheet view and in reports.

4. Using the query tool, create a summary that combines the detailed sales information for each shipment. Include only items shipped from Randall Dairy to the Best Fresh supermarket chain during May 2008. For each of these shipments, list the following:

- Shipment ID number
- Store ID number
- Store zip code
- Item number
- Shipment quantity
- Item description
- Item category

- Item container unit
- Item container size
- Number of containers per case
- Item price ($/case)
- Date produced
- Date shipped
- Item shelf life

5. Save the query (or queries) you used to obtain this data so this information can be extracted again easily later. Name a query with this combined information **qryBestFreshShipmentsByItem**.

6. Prepare an Access report based on the data you just extracted using the following guidelines:

- For each separate shipment, list the item number, item description, store number, quantity shipped, items per case, and price per case.
- Group the report data by item number, listing the total cases shipped. Sort the data within each group by store number.
- Format your report using a suitable format, orientation, and design. Preview the report to verify the results.
- Name the report **rptBestFreshShipmentsByItem**.
- Print the report to a Microsoft Document Image file and save it as **BestFreshShipmentsByItem.mdi**. (*Hint*: In the Print dialog box, select the Microsoft Office Document Image Writer as the printer and provide a file location and filename.)

TRANSFERRING AND VERIFYING THE DATA

Your next task is to transfer the data you extracted in qryBestFreshShipmentByItem into an Excel workbook for further analysis to identify the Randall Dairy products sold in Best Fresh stores, the quantities, and the amount of time these products can be offered before their expiration dates.

1. Save your extracted data to an Excel worksheet named **RShipments**, and name the workbook file **RandallDairyAnalysis.xls**.

2. To verify the data, you have decided to match the shipment data from Randall Dairy to the shipment data kept by each of the Best Fresh stores. Each Best Fresh store maintains a list of receipts from Randall Dairy, which include the shipment number and shipment status (A—Acceptable condition, I—Incorrect products or quantity, D—Damaged). These lists are adequate for matching shipment receipts, but do not contain details such as item numbers or costs. Match the items from Randall's data to a combined list of the Best Fresh store data by completing the following steps:

   - Combine the shipment data for each of the four Best Fresh stores onto a separate worksheet named **BFShipData** in your Excel workbook. Structure the data into the columns shown in Table 1.1.

Table 1.1: Column headings for combining Best Fresh data

Ship#	Item#	Quantity	Ship Date	Shipment Status

   - The files containing shipment data for each store have been saved in a delimited text format. Each store file is named as **BestFresh###.txt**, where the # symbols are replaced by the store number, as in BestFresh104.txt.
   - Copy this data into the BFShipData worksheet and modify the data as needed to align columns in a consistent format.

3. Add a column to the RShipments worksheet to automatically look up the corresponding Best Fresh shipment status based on the shipment number. Shipment numbers that do not match should display #N/A for the status.

4. On the RShipments worksheet, instruct Excel to highlight any damaged shipments by shading the row. This formatting should change as necessary when the corresponding data is later updated.

5. Filter the data to show only those shipments that match from both lists and that are not an incorrect product or quantity. These are the shipments that Randall Dairy sent to Best Fresh stores and that each store accepted.

6. Copy the filtered data into a new worksheet named **Analysis**.

EVALUATING THE SALES DATA

Now you have successfully compiled the data on acceptable shipments Best Fresh received from Randall Dairy. On the Analysis worksheet, you are ready to analyze the service Best Fresh receives from Randall Dairy, determine the wholesale and modified wholesale values of the dairy shipments received, and calculate store revenues and profits based on the number of cases shipped, the cost per case, and the category markups. Because you might need to reuse these analyses for data from different time periods or from other vendors, be sure that you use worksheet formulas that automatically update your values.

1. **Service Analysis**—Because dairy products have varying but short shelf lives, the product must be shipped to the stores promptly. You can measure the quality of the service Randall Dairy provides by calculating the amount of time Best Fresh has to sell Randall Dairy products. This interval from when Best Fresh receives a shipment to the last day it can sell a dairy product is a product's remaining shelf life. On the Analysis worksheet, in a column adjacent to the existing data, determine the remaining shelf life status for each shipment as follows:

   - *Excellent:* If the shipment arrival is at least seven days before the product expiration date (production date + number of days of shelf life) it has an "Excellent" remaining shelf life.
   - *Satisfactory:* If the shipment arrival is less than seven days before expiration but at least four days before expiration, it has a "Satisfactory" remaining shelf life.
   - *Unsatisfactory:* If the shipment has less than four days before expiration, it has an "Unsatisfactory" remaining shelf life.

   Assume that the arrival date and ship date are the same because all of the stores selling Randall Dairy products are within a two-hour drive.

2. **Supplier Comparison**—On a separate worksheet named **Comparison**, enter the data listed in Table 1.2 and compare the percentage of Excellent, Satisfactory, and Unsatisfactory shipments from Randall Dairy to those from other dairy suppliers listed in the table. Percentages are calculated as the number of shipments in a specific category divided by the number of total shipments. Table 1.2 also shows the average profit margin percentages, which will be calculated later in step 9.

Table 1.2: Comparing the status of dairy shipments

Dairy Vendor	Shipments Excellent (%)	Shipments Satisfactory (%)	Shipments Unsatisfactory (%)	Profit Margin (%)
Elsie Inc.	77%	18%	5%	22%
Stouts Farms	65%	34%	1%	28%
Willow Foods	49%	49%	2%	23%
Randall Dairy	?	?	?	?

On this Comparison worksheet, use several cells highlighted in yellow to summarize your findings and state your recommendations regarding the current service levels of Randall Dairy to the Best Fresh grocery chain compared to the other dairy vendors.

3. **Wholesale Value of Shipments**—In an adjacent column on the Analysis worksheet, calculate the wholesale value of each shipment based on the number of cases shipped and the cost per case. Calculate the total value of all shipments Randall Dairy made to Best Fresh during May that are included in this analysis.

4. **Display Data Graphically**—On a separate worksheet named **WSValue**, create a chart showing the relative percentage breakdown of wholesale shipment values by store and another chart comparing the wholesale value percentages by item. Format your charts so that they are easy to read and understand and include appropriate headings.

5. **Modified Wholesale Value**—In an adjacent column on the Analysis worksheet, calculate an alternative wholesale value of each shipment and for total shipments based on the following criteria:

    - Apply the full wholesale value to shipments in the Excellent category.
    - Apply a 15% discount to shipments in the Satisfactory category.
    - Apply a 75% discount to shipments in the Unsatisfactory category.

    Be sure to list these values somewhere in the workbook, so they can be easily modified, if necessary. Include a comment in the column title cell documenting how you completed this calculation and referencing where you placed these input values or performed any intermediate calculations. (*Hint*: To insert a comment, right-click the cell and then click Insert Comment.)

6. **Forecast Store Revenues**—In an adjacent column on the Analysis worksheet, forecast store revenues from these shipments based on the pricing structure listed in Table 1.3. To calculate store revenues, use the quantity sold times the modified selling price plus markup. Round the values to the nearest cent. Explicitly list these values on a separate worksheet and then use cell references in your formulas so you can easily modify these values. Include a comment in the column heading cell documenting how you completed this calculation and referencing where you placed these input values or performed any intermediate calculations.

Table 1.3: Pricing structure for shipments

Category	Description	Container Size	Markup over Modified Wholesale Price
C, LFC, SC, LFSC	Cottage cheese and sour cream	< 16 oz.	60%
C, LFC, SC, LFSC	Cottage cheese and sour cream	>= 16 oz.	40%
M, 2M, 1M, SM	Milk	< 1 gallon	50%

Table 1.3: Pricing structure for shipments (cont.)

Category	Description	Container Size	Markup over Modified Wholesale Price
M, 2M, 1M, SM	Milk	>= 1 gallon	35%
HC, USB, B	Cream and butter	All sizes	75%

Hints: Product categories are defined in the Randall database. Forecasting revenues might be easier if you group the categories. For example, assign the value 1 to any item in category C, LFC, SC, or LFSC, or a value 2 if an item is in category M, 2M, 1M, or SM. You can add extra columns to the worksheet as necessary. After you group the categories, test for a value (such as 1) and size (such as <16 oz) to assign a markup value.

7. **Expected Profit**—In an adjacent column on the Analysis worksheet, calculate the expected profit defined as follows:

Expected profit = revenues − modified wholesale value − store overhead

Store overhead is calculated as $.10 per container. (*Hint*: The number of containers per case varies by item number.) Again, be sure this value is explicitly listed in your workbook and include a comment in the column heading cell documenting how you completed this calculation and referencing where you placed these input values or performed any intermediate calculations.

8. **Item Category Summary**—In a separate worksheet named **Summary**, create a summary by item category (such as C, LFC, and SC), including the following:

   • The modified wholesale value of these shipments, revenues, and expected profits.
   • Totals for each of these values for all categories combined. Be sure these totals correspond to the appropriate values on the Analysis worksheet.
   • On the same worksheet, a stacked column chart that displays the wholesale value, revenue, and profit data by category.

9. **Profit Margin Comparison**—Evaluate the overall profit margin of Randall Dairy's products (profits/revenues) as they compare to other Best Fresh dairy vendors. Profit is the calculation of revenues from sales minus wholesale costs and other overhead expenses. This profit is then divided by revenue to arrive at the profit margin percentage. Other comparison data was displayed in Table 1.2. Complete the table on the Comparison worksheet and highlight the profit margin value in light blue so it is easy to find. Below the data, enter your conclusions regarding Randall Dairy's competitiveness and highlight your conclusions in the same color.

EXAMINING ALTERNATIVE PROFIT SCENARIOS

Before expanding the sales of Randall Dairy products, management wants to explore the revenue and profit implications by modifying various cost elements.

1. On the Summary worksheet of the **RandallDairyAnalysis.xls** workbook, report the new profit expected if the markup for all Randall Dairy milk products—M, 2M, 1M, SM—is increased to 55% regardless of container size. Report this new profit in a *separate* cell below the category profit summary. Highlight the cell in blue with white text so that the new profit is easy to find. Enter a label to the left of this value marked Alternate Markup 1. Except for this reported value on the Summary worksheet, restore the original markup values, profits, and other values in the workbook.

2. Copy the Analysis worksheet (including formulas) to a new worksheet named **Analysis2**. Change the revenue calculation to equal the modified wholesale value plus 55%, representing a 55% markup on all items regardless of category or size. Explicitly list this markup value (55%) in a cell inserted above the revenue column. Determine the new profit with this simplified markup.

3. Using this same Analysis2 worksheet, determine what this simple markup percentage would have to be to obtain a total profit of $1,000 instead of the current profit obtained using a 55% markup. Record this markup percentage in a cell on the Summary worksheet, just below your Alternate 1 value, highlighted in dark green with white text. Enter a label to the left of this value marked Alternate Markup 2. If necessary, restore the original markup of 55% on the Analysis2 worksheet.

COMPLETING THE FINANCIAL ANALYSIS

Best Fresh knows that products from Randall Dairy sell so well that customers are willing to pay a premium for them, even though the wholesale costs of the products are comparable to the national brands. Based on your analysis, Best Fresh might want to expand its relationship with Randall Dairy. To greatly increase this business, however, Randall Dairy needs to expand its operations. This expansion will require additional capital investment, and as a small dairy, Randall's access to low-interest loans and the capital markets is limited.

To fund the expansion, Best Fresh is considering borrowing $200,000 at a favorable interest rate, and then lending that amount to Randall Dairy at no interest over the next three years. Randall Dairy will pay the principal portion of any loan Best Fresh obtains, and Best Fresh will pay the interest. In exchange for this loan, Randall Dairy guarantees it will first offer all additional capacity product to Best Fresh at wholesale prices at or below the competitive prices of the three national brands. This capital investment will allow Randall

Dairy to increase its shipments to Best Fresh tenfold. You need to analyze the effects of the loan. Complete your analyses on a new worksheet named **Financial** as follows:

1. Assume that in a typical month Best Fresh makes a profit of $10,000 from the sale of dairy products. By investing with Randall Dairy, Best Fresh expects to increase this profit by 5%. Calculate the total additional profit expected each month and over the three-year period. (Do not factor in any interest.) Label these values "Additional monthly profit" and "Additional profit 3 years."

2. If Best Fresh borrows the requested amount ($200,000) from their bank at 3.5% interest compounded monthly, what is the monthly payment required to pay back the loan, assuming it will be completely paid off at the end of three years? Label this value "Monthly loan payment." Be sure to explicitly list your input values so they can be easily modified.

3. Create an amortization table detailing the interest and principal portion of each payment for the proposed loan over the next three years. Summarize the total value of the interest payments made over the three-year period. Label this value "Total interest expense."

4. Compare the value of interest payments over this three-year period to the additional profits expected from selling Randall Dairy products over the same three years. In an adjacent cell, discuss if paying the interest on this loan so that Randall Dairy can increase production is profitable for Best Fresh. Highlight your calculations and discussion in yellow.

Formatting the Workbook

To prepare your workbook for review before the upcoming management meeting, make sure your workbook contains the following:

- Worksheets that are clearly labeled and identified with colored tabs
- Worksheet headings that are centered and merged over the relevant data
- Column headings that are clearly labeled and sized, with text wrapped as necessary
- Number values that are consistently displayed, using the appropriate number of decimal places or date value formats, for example

PRESENTING THE RESULTS OF THE ANALYSIS TO MANAGEMENT

The final task in your analysis is to prepare your findings for management. Because you expect to deliver this information in a formal meeting, your manager recommends that you create a PowerPoint presentation.

To explain your findings for each of the analyses you have prepared, create a PowerPoint presentation named **RandallDairyAnalysis.ppt**. The presentation should also give your overall recommendation whether to continue Best Fresh's relationship with Randall Dairy as it is or to expand it. Because this presentation is important to management, and also a good opportunity for you to shine, your manager advises you to include the following elements:

- A title page including your name as the author and the current date
- The company logo on each slide (provided in the file **BestFresh.jpg**)
- A consistent, appropriate, and easy-to-read design for all slides
- At least two slide animations or transition effects to emphasize critical points of your presentation and enhance its delivery
- At least two charts or tables that you've prepared in your analysis to illustrate your conclusions
- (Optional) If possible, a saved presentation for Web delivery posted to an appropriate Web site

COMPLETED WORK

Submit the following files when you have completed this project:

1. The **RandallStudy.mdb** database, including the queries and reports you created

2. The Access report that you saved as a document image named **BestFreshShipments ByItem.mdi**

3. The **RandallDairyAnalysis.xls** workbook that contains all of the worksheets you have used in your analysis, including the ones explicitly specified (the workbook may contain additional worksheets as needed):

   - BFShipData
   - RShipments
   - Analysis
   - Comparison
   - WSValue
   - Summary
   - Analysis2
   - Financial

4. The **RandallDairyAnalysis.ppt** file containing your presentation to management

Project 3
Developing Retirement Strategies for Clients
Finance: Grey & Shamrock Investment Advisors

Forecast monthly contributions based on desired monthly retirement income
Forecast monthly retirement income based on monthly contributions
Select an investment strategy
Analyze a client's existing portfolio

PROBLEM DESCRIPTION

Finance

You have finally completed your investment advisor certification and have decided to form an investment advisory group with several other colleagues. The market is full of advisors who either work for large investment firms or are associated with financial institutions. Many reap their profits from sales commissions regardless of whether these sales are in the best long-term interest of their clients. Your group has conducted some market research and discovered that there is a market niche for investment advisors whose revenues are based solely on an hourly consulting fee.

Your role in this new firm is to specialize in mutual funds for retirement investments. In general, you plan your advising strategy as follows:

- Review a client's retirement goals and set a strategy to meet those goals in terms of their ultimate retirement income and the level of risk appropriate for their age and preferences.
- Analyze a client's current portfolio, reviewing whether their current investments meet these goals and evaluating the overall performance of their current investments.
- Recommend that clients modify their current portfolios or begin new portfolios to meet these goals.

Because you will be charging an hourly advisory fee, to be competitive you know that you need efficient tools to help in these analyses. To this end, you have decided to develop several spreadsheet tools using some sample data. These tools should allow you to easily substitute different client data and immediately recalculate the required values.

REQUIRED FILES

To complete this project, you need the following files from the Capstone_Projects\Project3 folder:

- GreySham.jpg
- GS.mdb
- PotentialClients.txt

FORECASTING MONTHLY CONTRIBUTIONS BASED ON DESIRED MONTHLY RETIREMENT INCOME

Frequently, clients have a reasonable idea of the income they want to have upon their retirement, yet do not understand the savings commitment they need to make to ensure this level of income. Consider the following examples of Client 1 and Client 2:

- **Client 1**—Cheryl and Roger Chamberlain want to retire in 35 years and only want to withdraw the income generated from their investments, maintaining the capital for their heirs. They want to assume a 6% annual rate of return prior to retirement and a 4% rate of return upon retirement. Their goal is to have a monthly income from these investments of $2,500 after taxes, assuming they pay an average of 20% in taxes. Except for monthly contributions, which they will begin now, Cheryl and Roger have no additional funds to invest.
- **Client 2**—Roberto Salvatore wants to retire in 15 years and has already saved $400,000 toward his retirement. He wants to have a monthly income of $3,500 after taxes of 22%, excluding his Social Security benefits. Based on his prior investment experience, he wants to assume a 5% return on his investments for the next 15 years, and a 3% rate of return after he retires. Because he has no children, he wants to withdraw both interest and principal in the form of an annuity. However, to be cautious, he does not want to run out of money until he reaches 110 years of age. He therefore assumes an expected number of retired years of 45.

On a new worksheet, clients should be able to calculate the *monthly investment* required from now until their retirement to reach a specific retirement income, excluding Social Security benefits. To calculate this required monthly investment, clients should be able to input the following:

- **Desired monthly income after taxes**—The amount of monthly income after taxes at retirement, excluding Social Security benefits.
- **Average tax rate**—The average tax rate clients expect to pay upon retirement. This rate is an estimate of a client's expected combined average federal, state, and local tax rates.
- **Current value of additional retirement funds**—The current value of any additional retirement funds that clients have already invested toward retirement.
- **Number of years**—The expected number of years until retirement.
- **Annual rate of return before retirement**—The expected annual rate of return prior to retirement to be selected in consultation with the client. Historically, the stock market has yielded returns between 4%–8% per year for a 20-year period depending on the specific period and the level of risk. Assume that all income generated from these investments will be reinvested and that all taxes are deferred until the money is withdrawn at retirement. Because contributions will be made monthly, assume monthly compounding of these investments.

- **Postretirement annual rate of return**—After clients retire, they will move the funds within their investment accounts to interest-bearing investments. For purposes of your calculations, assume that this rate is guaranteed and will not vary from year to year.
- **Withdrawal option**—The user should also be able to specify a withdrawal option as follows:

  Option 1: After clients retire, they will withdraw the full value of the investment returns each month. In this case, the principal will be preserved for their heirs. Thus, their monthly income is simply the postretirement investment amount times their simple monthly rate of interest less taxes owed.

  Option 2: Clients withdraw an annuity, a specific amount of money including investment interest plus a portion of the principal such that their investments will be worth $0 at the end of their expected life. Taxes will then need to be deducted from the annuity payment to calculate monthly income. The number of years they expect to live after retirement should also be an input variable for this option.

To set up this analysis, complete the following tasks:

1. Set up a single worksheet to calculate the required monthly investment in a workbook named **RetirementCalculations.xls**. Name your worksheet **MethodA**.

2. Enter your data inputs, and clearly identify them by highlighting the input area in light blue. Be careful to document what each value represents with appropriate labels.

3. Below your data inputs, set up an area for the data outputs. You might also want to leave an area between the inputs and outputs labeled Intermediate Calculations, inserting rows as needed. Calculate the data outputs as detailed here. Figure 3.1 contains an illustration of the steps you will need to take to work backward from a desired monthly retirement income to obtain a required monthly contribution the investor will need to make.

Figure 3.1: Calculating the required monthly investment

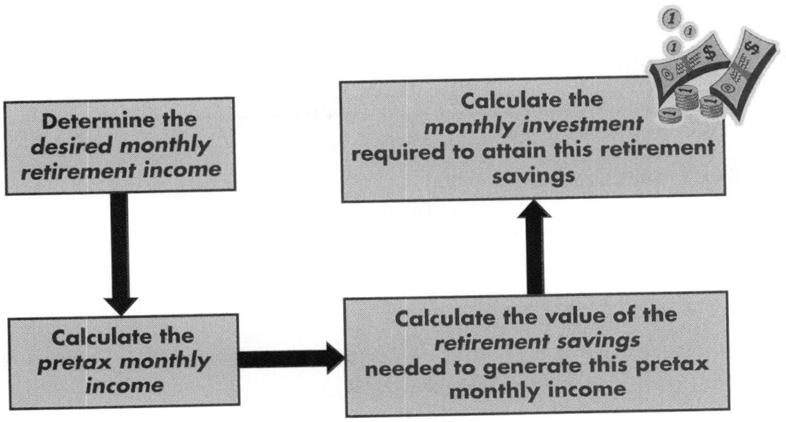

- First calculate the amount of money that clients need to withdraw from their retirement account each month so that after taxes the clients will have their desired monthly income. Highlight the label and value in black with white text to clearly identify it.

- Calculate the total value of the clients' investments at retirement so they will be able to withdraw this desired monthly amount. Be sure to take into account whether the client only wants to use the income from the investment or to create an annuity type of payout where both investment income and principal are being withdrawn each month. Your formula should be able to calculate this amount automatically using the option as an input. Highlight the label and value in plum with white text to clearly identify it.

- Calculate the monthly investment contribution that will be required to reach this specified retirement investment value, taking into account the client's assumptions regarding their preretirement average annual rate of return on their investments and the number of years until their retirement. Highlight the label and value in blue with white text to clearly identify it.

- Calculate the value of these investments at the *end* of their expected retirement. Again, this will depend upon which option the client selected. Highlight the label and value in dark green with white text to clearly identify it.

4. Perform the following sensitivity analyses so that you can show clients how their monthly contribution would change with different inputs selected.

- Below the data outputs, enter the monthly investment required if a client selects the alternative payout option. For example, if a client originally selects Option 1, enter the results of using Option 2 as the alternative payout option. This formula should automatically calculate this value regardless of which option was originally selected. If the number of years they expect to live after retirement is not specified, use a default value of 30. Clearly label this alternative monthly investment value and highlight it so that it is easy to distinguish.

- In an area to the right of your data, create a table that calculates the monthly investment required, assuming preretirement rates of return varying from 4% to 8% in 0.5% increments. Table 3.1 illustrates a possible table structure.

Table 3.1: Sensitivity analysis structure

Interest Rate	Required Monthly Contribution
4.0%	
4.5%	
5.0%	

Based on this data, create a chart that shows the functional relationship between the preretirement interest rate and their required monthly contributions. Be sure that all values update if a client later enters any data inputs other than preretirement interest rate. Monthly investments should be represented as positive values on this table. Clearly label and identify this analysis on the worksheet.

- Create a second sensitivity analysis similar to the first one, but vary the number of years until retirement in increments of 5 years from 5 to 45 years. Create a chart that illustrates the relationship between the number of years until retirement and the client's required monthly contributions. Place this analysis in an area adjacent to the rate sensitivity analysis on the same worksheet. Be sure that all values update if a client later enters any data inputs other than number of years to retirement. Monthly investments should be represented as positive values. Clearly label and identify the analysis.

5. Make sure the worksheet is easy to read and well documented with each of the variables explicitly listed. Include a heading for the worksheet and for each of the worksheet sections (inputs/outputs), tables, and charts.

6. Use the worksheet to test the two different client profiles originally proposed. Save the file with Client 1's data in the original file, and save Client 2's data to a second file named **RetirementCalculations_Client2.xls**.

7. Present the results of Client 2's calculations in a PowerPoint presentation. Include both the client's assumptions and the output values calculated. Demonstrate to your client how altering specific variables will change the required monthly investment. Name the presentation **RetirementAnalysis_Client2.ppt**. Include in your presentation the following elements:

- A title slide with your company name and your name and credentials.
- A slide design for the entire presentation that is consistent, appropriate, and attractive and includes the company name and logo. The Grey & Shamrock logo is provided in the **GreySham.jpg** file.
- At least one chart and one table. All charts and tables should be *linked* to the Excel file so that they will automatically update if any of the data is later modified.
- At least one other drawing or clip art element.
- At least one transition effect and one animation effect.

FORECASTING MONTHLY RETIREMENT INCOME BASED ON MONTHLY CONTRIBUTIONS

Some clients are limited in the amount of money they can afford or are allowed to contribute tax free toward their retirement. These clients want to see how a given monthly contribution and return rate will affect values of their monthly income upon retirement. Many of these clients also anticipate that in future years they can make additional contributions. Therefore, you want to include up to three different monthly payments for three different investment stages leading up to their retirement. Some clients even want to modify their investment strategy and, thus, the expected rate of returns for each of these three investment stages. Consider the following example involving Client 3, Mandy Atkins, as illustrated in Figure 3.2.

Figure 3.2: Mandy Atkins' investment strategy from now until retirement in year 30

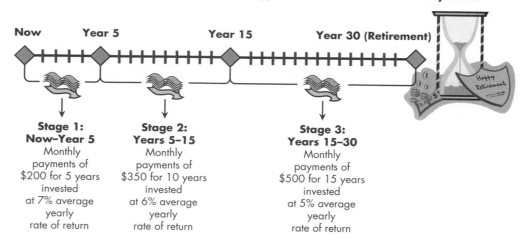

- **Investment stage 1**—During the next five years, Mandy will be able to afford $200 per month and wants to aggressively invest this money. You will therefore assume a 7% average yearly rate of return.
- **Investment stage 2**—During the next 10 years (years 5 to 15) of her investment plan, Mandy anticipates increasing her monthly contribution to $350, assuming a 6% average yearly rate of return. These assumptions reflect a somewhat aggressive investment strategy, though not as aggressive as during the first five years.
- **Investment stage 3**—During the next 15 years (years 15 to 30), Mandy anticipates making monthly contributions of $500; at the end of this period, she will retire. At this point, Mandy prefers more stability in her investments and expects annual return rates of about 5% per year.

Mandy wants to take both income and principal from the investment in equal monthly installments over a 40-year retirement period. She expects to invest this money during retirement in fairly safe financial instruments that yield an average of 3.5% annual interest compounded monthly. Mandy estimates she will have an average tax rate of 15% on her income during retirement. In addition, Mandy already has $8,500 saved toward retirement.

In a new worksheet, clients should be able to calculate the expected monthly retirement income based on the client's payment scheme and assumed rates of return. The user should be able to input the following:

- **Desired monthly contribution, rate of return, and duration of these contributions—** The amounts for each of the three consecutive investment stages.
- **Average tax rate**—The amount clients expect to pay upon retirement.
- **Current value of additional retirement funds**—The current value of any additional funds that have already been invested toward retirement.
- **Postretirement annual rate of return**—The rate of return clients expect to receive during retirement. After clients retire, they will move the funds within their investment accounts to interest-bearing investments. For the purposes of your calculations, assume that this rate is guaranteed and will not vary from year to year.
- **Withdrawal option**—A withdrawal option (Option 1 or 2) that the user can specify in the same manner as in Method A.

To set up this analysis, complete the following tasks:

1. Set up another worksheet in the **RetirementCalculations.xls** workbook to perform this calculation. Name your worksheet **MethodB**.

2. Enter your data inputs and highlight this area in light blue. Be careful to document what each value represents with appropriate labels.

3. Below your data inputs, set up an area for the data outputs. Again, as necessary in a separate area, between your data inputs and outputs, list any intermediate calculations (clearly labeled) that might be needed. For data outputs, include the following:

   - Calculate the total value of the client's investments at retirement based on their specified investment scheme. Remember to account for these investment period groups until the time of retirement even if these payments only last 5 years and were 25 years prior to retirement. Also remember to include any funds that have previously been set aside for retirement. Highlight the label and value in light green with black text to clearly identify it on the worksheet.
   - Calculate the expected monthly income after taxes that the client can expect based on their selected postretirement rate of return, average tax rate, and withdrawal option. Round this value to the nearest cent. Highlight the label and value in yellow with black text to clearly identify it on the worksheet.
   - Calculate the value of these investments at the end of their expected retirement. Again, this will depend upon which option the client selected. Highlight the label and value in pink with black text to clearly identify it on the worksheet.

4. For comparison purposes, in an area below the outputs, calculate the monthly income after taxes using the withdrawal option the client did not select. Clearly label and highlight this calculation.

5. Format this worksheet so it is easy to read and is well documented with each of the variables explicitly listed. Use the data given for Client 3 (Mandy Atkins) at the beginning of this section to test your calculations and then save your file.

SELECTING AN INVESTMENT STRATEGY

Each client who seeks advice usually must consider not only how much they need to invest but also what strategy will best fit their investing needs given the number of remaining years they have until retirement and their willingness to assume risk. You have developed some rules of thumb shown in Table 3.2 to help guide clients as to possible portfolio breakdowns based on years to retirement and acceptable risk. The breakdowns in Table 3.2 show the percent of stock assets recommended for a given level of risk, assuming that the remaining percentage will be invested in bonds.

Table 3.2: Calculating years to retirement based on acceptable risk

# Years to Retirement	Conservative Investment Risk	Moderate Investment Risk	Aggressive Investment Risk
Under 5 years	0%	10%	25%
At least 5 years but less than 10 years	20%	40%	60%
10 years and over	60%	80%	100%
Note that these values do not constitute investment advice and are completely fictitious.			

One task you will be working on in the office is to follow up on sales leads. You have a list of potential customers who answered a previous e-mail, expressed interest via the Web site, or telephoned the office. You now want to set up an automated worksheet that will display the appropriate percentages for each potential client on this list and embed this information into a letter to send to them.

1. On a separate worksheet named **InvestStrategy** in your **RetirementCalculations.xls** workbook, set up a reference table with the values shown in Table 3.2. You need to use this list to automatically look up your recommendation.

2. Import the list of potential clients, including their names, addresses, ages, and risk preferences from the tab-delimited text file **PotentialClients.txt** into an area on the InvestStategy worksheet below your reference table.

3. Create a column adjacent to your imported data to display the recommended percentage of stock for this customer. Assume a retirement age of 65. Set up the retirement age value so that it can be easily modified on your worksheet. Create a named range, ClientData, that includes only this client data and stock percentage recommendation. This named range will be useful later when referring to this data.

4. Do some research on the Web to understand diversification of a stock portfolio. You can use sites provided by major fund services, such as Morningstar, Value Line, and T. Rowe Price; search sites, such as Yahoo Finance; or search engines to find appropriate sites. You might want to understand the concept of style box (Morningstar) or another similar methodology that ranks funds and stocks according to the size of the company (for example, small cap, mid-cap, and large cap) and its growth potential (for example, value, core/blend, and growth). The smaller the firm and higher the growth potential, usually the riskier and more volatile the stock or fund.

5. Create a mailing that will explain to each customer their recommended strategy for investing. Include the following data and style elements:

   - The letter should be well written and easy to read, including a header with your company name and logo. Use the **GreySham.jpg** file for the logo. Create a footer that contains your company's address, phone number, fax number, and Web address. (Be creative.)
   - Individualize the letter to include the potential client's name and address in the top portion of the document. Include in the body of the letter each client's age, risk preference, and resulting stock percentage recommendation. (*Note*: If you have difficulty merging the values in percentage formats, try setting up these values as text in Excel, such as '60%' instead of 60%, into your lookup table.)
   - Also include in the letter a clear explanation of how to invest in stocks and mutual funds containing stocks. Based on your research, explain what an investor should look for to diversify their investments. If you quote any specific Web site or investment advisor, be sure to reference the Web site or author in your letter.
   - End your letter explaining why professional advice and guidance can make investing for retirement easier and help to ensure a more secure future.

6. Save the letter with your merged fields to a file named **MergedPotentialClientLetters.doc**.

7. Create a brochure that can be included with your letter in this mailing, telling the clients a little about your company. Use the drawing tools to include a diagram explaining your three-step retirement planning process (this was outlined in the Project Description). To keep it simple, you might want to use an existing template. Be sure to include your company logo (**GreySham.jpg**) and contact information so potential clients can easily reach you. Name the file **GSBrochure**.

ANALYZING A CLIENT'S EXISTING PORTFOLIO

Grey & Shamrock already has a list of active clients with significant investment holdings in mutual funds. The firm informally maintains information on these holdings in an Access database. Much of the data was gathered before Grey & Shamrock was formed, so the information only provides a starting point for working with these customers. One of these active clients, Joseph Bingham, has scheduled an appointment with you to discuss his retirement goals. You want to extract Joseph's information currently in the database and prepare an analysis of his holdings. You have also noticed that the database structure and definitions are not completed, so you will also perform these tasks before extracting the data you need.

The database GS.mdb contains the tables and fields shown in Figure 3.3 and described in the following list.

Figure 3.3: Grey & Shamrock client database

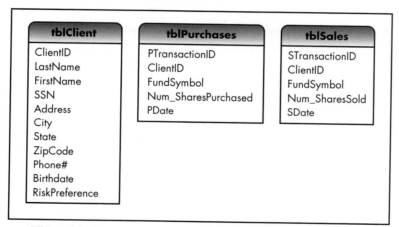

- **tblClient**—This table lists client information. Each client is uniquely identified by a client ID. Client data includes the client's last name, first name, Social Security number (SSN), address, city, state, zip code, phone number, birth date, and risk preference.
- **tblPurchases**—This table lists stock and fund purchases made by clients. Each transaction is uniquely identified by a transaction ID number, PTransactionID. Transaction details include the purchaser's client ID, a fund symbol denoting the code used by investment firms for this stock or mutual fund, the number of shares purchased (Num_SharesPurchased), and the purchase date (PDate).
- **tblSales**—This table lists stock and fund sales made by clients. Each transaction is uniquely identified by a transaction ID number, STransactionID. Transaction details include the seller's client ID, a fund symbol denoting the code used by investment firms for this stock or mutual fund, the number of shares sold (Num_SharesSold), and the selling date (SDate).

To prepare an analysis of Joseph Bingham's retirement holdings, complete the following tasks:

1. Copy the **GS.mdb** file from the Capstone_Projects\Project3 folder to a work folder. Rename the file **GSData.mdb**.

2. Because this database is not yet complete, you need to edit the table designs to specify the primary key fields and then set up the appropriate relationships.

3. Modify the table properties to contain appropriate field sizes and modify field captions as needed, so they are clear and easy to read in Datasheet view and in reports.

4. Set up input masks for the SSN (Social Security number) and ZipCode fields.

5. Create a list of the current portfolio holdings (number of shares) for client 1015 (Joseph Bingham) by fund symbol. Include a subtotal of purchases by fund, a subtotal of sales by fund, and total shares currently owned by fund (purchases minus sales). Name the query with this list qryClient1015Summary. If intermediate queries are required, identify them appropriately.

6. In a separate query, extract this client's full name, phone number, birth date, and risk preferences. Name the query qryClient1015Data.

7. Copy the data from your queries to a new worksheet named **Holdings** in a new workbook named **Client1015.xls**. Transfer both the client's personal information and a summary of his holdings.

8. In a column adjacent to the client's personal data, calculate the age of this client in years based on today's date. Round the age down to the nearest whole year.

9. Research the status of each of these holdings and then enter the appropriate data elements. Record these values on the table you extracted from the database, including the following data:

   - The current price per share.
   - The number of stars it contains on its Morningstar Rating.
   - A description of the type of fund: stocks, bonds, or a combination. If stocks, indicate which style (for example, Large Cap Value or Small Cap Growth).

10. In an adjacent column, calculate the current value of each investment. Below this column, calculate the total value of this client's portfolio.

11. In another adjacent column, determine for each mutual fund whether you recommend to "Sell," "Hold," or do "Additional Analysis." You will recommend holding all funds that have a four- or five-star rating. You will recommend selling all funds with a one- or two-star rating. You will recommend additional analyses on funds given three-star ratings.

12. Based on what you know about balancing portfolios, age, and risk preferences compared to percentages in stocks and diversification of stocks, analyze this client's portfolio. Place this analysis below the data and clearly label and highlight your analysis and conclusions.

13. Research investment sites on the Web (such as Morningstar, Fidelity, or Yahoo Finance) or look for articles on mutual fund recommendations. Find a few funds that will fill in the gaps (bond funds, small cap stock funds, large cap stock funds, and so on) for this client. Your choices should have high ratings. List these recommendations, including fund name, fund symbol, price per share, five-year annual return (if available), and fund profile (stocks, bonds, small cap, blend, and so on). Place these recommendations below your previous analysis, clearly labeling and highlighting your recommendations.

COMPLETED WORK

Submit the following files when you have completed this project:

1. **RetirementCalculations.xls**, including the following worksheets (additional worksheets may be included as needed):

- MethodA
- MethodB
- InvestStrategy

2. **RetirementCalculations_Client2.xls**

3. **RetirementAnalysis_Client2.ppt**

4. **MergedPotentialClientLetters.doc**

5. **GSBrochure** (file extension depends on the program used)

6. **GSData.mdb**, including necessary queries

7. **Client1015.xls**, including the Holdings worksheet

Glossary

A

absolute address The complete URL, including the full pathname from the root directory and the name of the page you are linking. A link to a Web page on another Web site must be referenced by its entire URL, which includes http:// and the rest of the Web address.

absolute cell referencing A cell reference that does not change when copied to another location in the workbook. To indicate that a cell reference is absolute, a $ symbol is used preceding the column reference, row reference, or both of a cell address, for example, $B$2.

action query A special type of query that performs actions on a table, such as changing the contents of a field, adding records from one table to another table, deleting records from a table, or making a new table based on criteria.

aggregate functions The arithmetic and statistical operations such as Avg, Sum, Min, Max, StDev, and Var. You can apply aggregate functions to groups of data to calculate results for each group.

algorithm The rules that govern how a function works. An algorithm is a systematic set of procedures that the computer always steps through to calculate the results of a function.

amortization table A schedule detailing the payments of a financial transaction and the remaining principal in each period.

analysis The process of collecting, organizing, and transforming data into information that can be used to support decision making.

AND criteria The conditions that must all be true for Access to select a record.

AND function The function that determines if a list of Boolean values are all TRUE. If such is the case, a TRUE value is returned.

annual percentage rate (APR) The percentage rate actually charged, taking into account any additional borrower fees.

animation scheme A preset style of animation in PowerPoint that is applied to the title and bullet points within the body text placeholders in a slide to make them appear on screen in ways that make it look like they are moving.

annual percentage yield (APY) The equivalent interest rate based on simple interest, including the effects of compounding.

append query A type of query that selects records from one or more tables and then adds those records to the end of another table.

archive A file containing one or more files in compressed format for more efficient storage and transfer or for long-term storage.

area chart A chart that displays trends over time or by category. Values are indicated by the filled areas below the lines.

argument The function input(s). For example, the ROUND function contains two arguments—a value and the number of decimal places, as follows: =ROUND(2.22, 0).

artificial key A primary key that is created when no natural key exists.

aspect ratio The ratio between the height and width of a graphic. Keeping the ratio constant as you vary the size of a graphic helps to prevent distortion of the graphic.

attributes Values or settings you can specify for the contents of a tag, such as the height and width of a picture or its alignment.

AutoContent Wizard A set of dialog boxes in PowerPoint that allows you to choose from a variety of prebuilt PowerPoint presentations, complete with a design and suggestions for content.

AutoFormat A predefined design you can apply to a form or report.

AutoNumber The Access data type that generates a unique number in a field to produce unique values for each record in a table.

AutoReport Wizard A Report Wizard that creates a report displaying all the fields and records in a single table or query.

B

back up The process of creating a copy of a database that can be restored in the event of a loss.

backup set A file in which you define what files to back up and where.

balloon payment A final payment (additional amount) due at the end of a loan term.

base table (underlying table) The table on which a query, form, report, or data access page is based.

blog An online journal often written by an individual; might contain opinions and news content sponsored by companies.

Boolean value A TRUE or FALSE value.

bot A small program that follows the links on Web pages already in the database of a search tool to locate new or updated Web pages.

browser A program that provides a common interface for accessing and reading Web pages.

bubble chart A chart that compares sets of three values. Values are indicated by the size of the bubbles (filled circles).

business plan A document that describes a business, its objectives, strategies, market, and financial projections.

C

calculated field A field in a query, form, or report containing an expression that is calculated from the data.

calculated value The value that is the result of an Excel formula.

candidate key A field or collection of fields that could function as a table's primary key, but that was not chosen to do so.

Caption property A field property that determines how the field name is displayed in database objects.

cascade deletes An option that allows Access to delete related records in related tables when the primary record in the primary table is deleted.

cascade updates An option that allows Access to update the appropriate foreign key values in related tables when a primary key value in the primary table is updated.

cash flow The money flow into and out of a financial entity.

cell In a table or a worksheet, the intersection of columns and rows. The upper-left cell in a table is identified as cell A1 (the first column, A, intersecting the first row, 1), and then below A1 is cell A2, then cell A3, and so forth.

cell range The two references separated by a colon that designate a range of cells. Ranges are often used in function arguments to define the cells to be operated on. Depending upon the operation, ranges can be one-dimensional, along a row or column; two-dimensional, a block of rows and columns; or even span multiple worksheets. Examples include A1:A10, A1:Z1, A1:Z10.

chart title The descriptive text that identifies the chart's contents.

check box form field A field in a Word form that inserts a check box in the form; the check box can be checked or left unchecked to indicate that something has been accomplished or is yet to be done.

CHOOSE function The function that returns a value *or a range* for up to 29 different values.

cleansing The step in which any data corruption is identified and corrected, if possible. Corrupt data is missing some element or is incorrect in some way. Corruption can be caused by data loss due computer problems, but is often caused by human error.

column chart A chart that compares values across categories in a vertical orientation. Values are indicated by the height of the columns.

common field A field that appears in two or more tables and contains identical data that is used to relate the tables. The common field is called a primary key in the primary table and a foreign key in the related table.

compact To reorganize the data and objects in a database by reassigning and deleting unused space. Compacting a database usually reduces its file size.

composite primary key (composite key) A primary key composed of two or more fields.

compound interest The interest that is calculated by including any previously earned/owed interest.

compressed (zipped) folder A folder that reduces the size of the files it contains.

concatenation The process of combining the contents of two or more fields, such as a first and last name, into one string.

conditional formatting The process of applying formatting features such as color, bold, and font size based on whether the values in a report or form meet criteria that you specify.

container elements An HTML element that requires a beginning and ending tag so it can contain data. The text between the beginning and ending tag is affected by the element. For example, <b> and </b> are container elements and anything between the tags is interpreted as bold text.

control A small object such as a text box, button, or label that lets users interact with a database object.

COUNT function The function that counts the number of numeric and/or Boolean values in a range. Text values and empty cells are ignored.

crosstab query A type of totals query that performs aggregate function calculations on the values of one database field and allows you to determine how your summary data appears in the results.

CUMIPMT function The function that calculates the accumulated value of the interest portion of the period payments of a financial transaction between two specified periods.

CUMPRINC function The function that calculates the accumulated value of the principal portion of the period payments of a financial transaction between two specified periods.

Currency The Access data type that formats numeric values with a dollar sign and two decimal places.

Currency Style The cell formatting style that displays a numeric value with a left-aligned dollar sign, thousands commas, and two decimal places. For example, the value 2000 is displayed as $2,000.00 in a cell. Currency Style can be set from the toolbar button containing a $.

custom One of the options selected when splitting data points between charts in a pie of pie or bar of pie chart type. With this option, you can drag individual pie segments between the two charts so you can include exactly the segments you want in the main pie chart and the second plot.

custom animation A feature in PowerPoint that allows you to animate objects on a slide one at time, apply different animations to different objects, or animate objects other than the slide title and bulleted text.

custom report A report that requires data from more than one table, includes calculated fields, uses summary statistics, or requires parameter input when the report is opened or printed.

D

data Raw information, including words, images, numbers, or sounds.

data access page A dynamic Web page that you can open with a Web browser and use to view or change the data stored in the database object on which the data access page is based.

data consumer The person who transforms data into information by sorting, filtering, or performing calculations with it.

data duplication The process of creating repeated records in a database, which leads to wasted space and inconsistent and inaccurate data.

data gathering The process of identifying sources and obtaining data.

data points The points in a data series at which the X-axis and Y-axis values intersect.

data redundancy An undesirable effect of storing repeated data in fields in a table that wastes space and results in inconsistent and inaccurate data. Data redundancy is often avoided by creating additional tables.

data series The related data points that are plotted on the chart; each data series on a chart has a unique color or pattern and is identified in the chart legend.

data set A group of related data.

data source A file used in a mail merge that contains the records that you want merged. Often, this is a list of recipients that contains names, titles, e-mail addresses, and other contact information. The data source can be kept in documents, databases, spreadsheets, or in electronic address books.

data type A field property that determines how to store the data in the field.

database A collection of one or more tables.

database administration (DBA) The group that is responsible for designing, maintaining, and securing a database.

database administrator The person who designs, maintains, and secures a database.

database management system (DBMS) A system that creates and defines a database; a software program that creates and accesses the data in a database.

Database window The main control panel for an Access database.

datasheet A view of data that displays fields in columns and records in rows.

Datasheet view An Access view that displays the records in a table or query in rows and fields in columns.

Date function A VBA function that returns the current computer system date.

Date/Time The Access data type that stores dates or date and time combinations.

decision making The process of choosing among various options.

decision support system (DSS) A type of information system that helps decision-makers model business scenarios, especially through what-if analysis.

decrypt (decode) The process of canceling the encryption of data in a database.

deep Web The parts of the World Wide Web that are inaccessible to search engines and users without passwords. Much of the deep Web is located behind firewalls in libraries or intranets with restricted access to those who subscribe or have passwords.

Default Value property A field property that enters a default value into a field; can be used for all field types except AutoNumber.

deletion anomaly The problem that occurs when a user deletes data from a database and unintentionally deletes the only occurrence of that data in the database.

demote A term used in Outline view in Word and PowerPoint that means to reduce the level of a heading.

deprecate To gradually phase out a feature. HTML tags that will become obsolete in future versions of HTML are said to be deprecated.

depreciation A process of allocating the cost of an asset less its salvage value over its useful life.

Description property A property of a field used to document its contents.

design grid (Table Design grid) The top pane in Table Design view that includes the Field Name, Data Type, and Description columns; each row in the Table Design grid represents a field in the table.

Design view The window that lets you define the fields and properties for a table, query, form, report, or data access page.

destination document The document in which you want to insert an object from another source document.

Detail The main section in a form or report that displays data from the underlying data source.

detailed report A report that lists each row of data from a table or query.

Details view A view available in the My Computer or Windows Explorer window that displays files as a list of filenames with small icons and detailed information about your files, including name, type, size, and date modified.

determinant A field or collection of fields whose value determines the value in another field.

discount rate Also known as the hurdle rate or rate of return; the rate at which cash flows are discounted. Usually, this rate reflects current interest rates and the relative risk of the cash flows being evaluated.

discovery phase The first step in planning a database, which includes gathering all existing data, researching missing and incomplete data, and talking with users about their data output needs.

document A file produced by Word that has a .doc extension; examples include letters, memos, flyers, brochures, newsletters, certificates, surveys, and other types of text-based expressions.

document type definition (DTD) Another term for an XML schema that describes the structure of the data and the rules the data must follow.

Documenter An Access tool that produces a report of selected objects in a database and their relationships.

down payment An amount of money paid up front in a financial transaction that is not part of the loan amount.

drop-down form field A field in a Word form that inserts a drop-down menu in the form; options can be chosen for a list when the list arrow on the drop-down menu is clicked.

E

embed To insert an object created in one program into a file created in another program in such a way that you can make changes to the object in the destination file using the commands of the source program.

encrypt (encode) A process that converts data in a database into a format that is readable only by Access.

entity integrity A guarantee that there are no duplicate records in a table, that each record is unique, and that no primary key field contains null values.

Excel list A flat-file database management area of an Excel spreadsheet that allows sorting and filtering of data as a unit.

executable file A program whose contents can be loaded into memory and executed.

expression An arithmetic formula that performs a calculation in a query, form, or report.

Expression Builder A tool to assist in developing complicated expressions for calculated fields that shows the fields, functions, and other objects available in Access.

extensible The ability to be extended. XML is extensible because it lets you create new tags rather than rely on a set of predefined tags to describe data.

Extensible Markup Language (XML) A platform-independent standard for marking up data to indicate its structure and to focus on the meaning or content of the data rather than its appearance.

extract To remove a compressed file and create an uncompressed copy of the file in a folder you specify.

F

FALSE The Boolean value False, as differentiated from the text label "False."

feed The content of an RSS update. These are plaintext files with extensible tags to describe the content.

field (column) A single characteristic of an entity in a database. For example, fields that describe a customer might include first name, last name, address, city, and state.

Field Properties pane The lower pane of Table Design view that displays the field properties for the selected field.

Field Size property A property of a field that limits the number of characters to store in a Text field or the type of numeric data to store in a Number field.

file path The standard notation that indicates a file's location on your computer by listing the folders and subfolders in which the file is contained.

file system The operating system files and data structures that keep track of folders and files on a disk.

File Transfer Protocol (FTP) An Internet protocol that allows you to transfer files between computers, including HTML documents to Web servers. FTP is the way documents are loaded onto Web sites and is also used to download software from the Web.

filtering The step that involves removing data that is not useful or necessary for the analysis.

Filter by Form An Access feature that lets you specify two or more criteria when filtering records.

Filter by Selection An Access feature that lets you select a field in a datasheet and then display only data that matches the contents of that field.

filter One or more conditions that restrict data in a single table to create a temporary subset of records.

first normal form (1NF) A database table that does not contain any repeating groups.

fixed-width file format A file format for importing and exporting data that relies on spaces to separate data elements.

flat file database A simple database that contains a single table of information.

footer The portion of a Word document that is used for page numbering and other information that you want to appear at the bottom of the page.

foreign key The common field in the related table between two tables that share a relationship.

form In Word, a document that contains interactive fields and allow users to enter information, choose from drop-down lists, and check boxes indicating preferences, among other things. In Access, the database object you can create and customize to maintain, view, and print records. In Excel, a workbook you can use to collect information for calculations, analysis, or financial documents.

form field A field in a Word document that allows interactivity, makes it easier to fill in the form, and helps the form designer control the type of data entered by a user.

form field options The options that allow you to set restrictions on a form field.

form field shading The gray highlighting in a form field in a Word form so that you can identify the form field visually.

form footer The lower part of a form. It displays information that always appears on a form but at the bottom of the screen in Form view and the bottom of the last page when the form is printed.

form header The upper part of a form. It usually contains static text, graphic images, and other controls on the first page of a form.

formula An equation written in Excel syntax that performs a calculation. Formulas always begin with an equal sign (=) and can contain combinations of operators, operands, and functions, for example, =2+B2*SUM(A1:A5).

Freeze Panes A tool available to divide the worksheet into separate vertical and/or horizontal sections. The top and/or left section are "frozen" in place, always remaining in view while the bottom and right sections can be scrolled.

function In Excel, a predefined formula that performs a calculation. Functions begin with an equal sign, followed by the function name and a list of arguments enclosed in parentheses. The arguments must be in a specified order. An example of the SUM function used in a formula is as follows:=SUM(A1:A10).

function (Function procedure) In a programming language, a function performs operations, returns a value, accepts input values, and can be used in expressions.

functional dependency A column in a table is considered functionally dependent on another column if each value in the second column is associated with exactly one value in the first column.

G

Goal Seek A tool that determines the value of a single input to obtain a specified output.

grid The gray background on a form or report that displays dots and grid lines to help with aligning controls.

group footer A section of a report that is printed at the end of each group of records. Often used to print summary information such as subtotals for a group.

group header A section of a report that is printed at the beginning of each group of records. Often used to print the group name.

grouped report A report that organizes one or more records into categories, usually to subtotal the data for each category. The groups are based on the values in one or more fields.

Groups bar The part of the Database window that can be used to organize database objects and create shortcuts for working with them.

H

header The portion of a Word document that is used for page numbering and other information that you want to appear at the top of the page.

history table A table of data containing archived records.

hit An individual Web page that contains the terms used as keywords in a search expression.

HLOOKUP function The function that looks up a value stored in the first row of a horizontal lookup table and retrieves data stored in the same column of a subsequent row.

hurdle rate Also known as the discount rate or rate of return; the rate at which cash flows are discounted. Usually, this rate reflects current interest rates and the relative risk of the cash flows being evaluated.

hyperlink The linking object you click to open another Web page. The hyperlink can be text or a graphic.

Hyperlink (data type) The Access data type that displays text that contains a hyperlink to an Internet or file location.

hypertext transfer protocol (HTTP) The protocol used by the World Wide Web to link Web pages on servers around the world.

I

Icons view A view available in the My Computer or Windows Explorer window that displays files as icons with a filename.

IF function The logical function that evaluates a logical test (True or False) and applies different outcomes depending upon if the logical test evaluates to True (value_if_true) or to False (value_if_false).

index To identify the text, links, and other content of a Web page and storing this information in a database that allows searching by keyword or other criteria.

INDEX function The function that retrieves data from multidimensional tables. information Data that is organized in some meaningful way.

information Data that is organized in some meaningful way.

input mask A property of a field that applies a predefined format to field values.

Input Mask Wizard An Access wizard that guides you through the steps of creating an input mask and lets you enter sample values to ensure the correct results.

inputs The values and text labels that are directly entered into cells.

insertion anomaly The problem that occurs when a user cannot add data to a database unless other data has already been entered.

interest A user fee paid for use of money, usually charged by the lender as a percent of the value borrowed over a specified period of time.

internal rate of return (IRR) The rate at which a set of cash flows has an NPV of $0.

Internet All of the networks around the world that share information with each other using a common protocol for communicating.

intranet A privately maintained computer network that can be accessed only by employees or other authorized persons.

IPMT function The function that calculates the value of the interest portion of a loan payment based on the original loan amount, periodic interest rate, and payment number.

IRM (Information Rights Management) A process that allows authors of Excel, Outlook, PowerPoint, and Word files to control how the recipient interacts with the document; for example, the author can prevent other users from forwarding, printing, or taking screen shots of the file.

J

junction table An intermediary table created to produce a many-to-many relationship between two tables that do not share a one-to-one or one-to-many relationship.

K

key data The data you want to look up when using a lookup function.

keywords The terms in a search expression that are used by search tools to locate Web pages containing those terms.

knowledge workers The people who work with and develop knowledge. Data and information are their raw material. Knowledge workers use this raw material to analyze a particular situation and evaluate a course of action.

known file type A file whose extension is associated with a program on your computer.

L

layout The arrangement of text, images, art, and multimedia on an Office document.

legend A box that identifies the patterns or colors assigned to the data series in a chart.

line chart A chart that displays trends over time or by category. Values are indicated by the height of the lines.

link To insert a file or other object into a destination file and maintain a connection to the source file; any changes made to the source file will be reflected in the destination file.

linked text boxes The text boxes that are virtually bound together to allow text to automatically continue from one section or page to another.

list range The area of an Excel map that includes columns that will contain the data.

List view A view available in the My Computer or Windows Explorer window that displays files as a list of filenames with small icons.

literal character A character that enhances the readability of data but is not necessarily stored as part of the data, such as a dash in a phone number.

Lookup field A field that provides a list of valid values for another field, either using the contents of another field or values in a list.

LOOKUP function The function that looks up the greatest value that does not exceed a specified value anywhere in a table or range, whether it is organized in a vertical or horizontal orientation.

lookup table A data list that categorizes values you want to retrieve.

Lookup Wizard The Access wizard that allows you to set field properties to look up data in another table or in a list of values created for the field.

M

mail merge The process of creating custom documents from a combination of standard text in a main document and individualized text from a data source.

mailing labels report A type of multicolumn report used to print names and addresses in a format suited for sending mail through the postal service. Labels can also be used for other purposes such as name badges.

main document A Word document used in a mail merge that contains fixed text that will remain in each merged document and merge fields that perform as placeholders to be replaced by customized data for each record or recipient from the data source.

many-to-many relationship (M:N) A relationship between tables in which each record in the first table matches many records in the second table, and each record in the second table matches many records in the first table.

map An area on an Excel spreadsheet that has information about how XML data should be imported. Data imported into an Excel map area doesn't need to be reformatted each time new data is imported.

markup The electronic comments, additions, and corrections that you add to a document.

master document A special type of Word document that acts as a container for other Word documents and data, including embedded or linked content from other applications.

MATCH function The function that returns the relative position (such as 1, 2, or 3) of an item in a list.

mean The arithmetic average of a data set.

median The middle value of a data set in which there are an equal number of values both higher and lower than the median.

Memo The Access data type that stores long passages of alphanumeric data.

merge field A placeholder in a mail merge that is replaced by customized data for each record or recipient from the data source.

metasearch engine A search tool that superficially searches multiple search engines at once and returns limited results.

mixed reference A cell reference that has both a relative and absolute component—for example, $B2 when copied always keeps column B (absolute component) but varies the row.B$2 when copied varies the column but not the row.

mode The most common arithmetic value found in a data set.

module (Access) An object that contains instructions to automate a database task, such as verifying the data entered into a field before storing it in the database.

move handle The larger handle in a control's upper-left corner that you use to move the control.

moving average The term that is used when the average is recalculated each period over a set number of previous periods in a chart. For example, a 30-day moving average calculates the average for the last 30 days—moving the average along the chart. Varying degrees of smoothing are achieved by changing the length of the moving average.

multiple-column report A report that displays information in several columns, such as a telephone listing or mailing labels.

N

natural key A primary key that details an obvious and innate trait of a record, such as an ISBN code for a book.

negative cash flow The monies paid from a person/institution; cash that is paid out.

nest To close HTML or XML tags in the reverse order in which they are opened.

nesting The process of placing one formula inside another formula. For example, =ROUND (AVERAGE(B2:B10), 0) nests an AVERAGE function within a ROUND function of a formula. The AVERAGE function will be evaluated and then the results will be used as the first argument of the ROUND function.

Net Present Value (NPV) A method of discounting cash flows to the present value based on a selected discount rate. A positive NPV for a cash flow indicates that an investment will add value to the investor.

newsgroup An online bulletin board system that has thousands of groups hosted all over the world by individuals or organizations interested in a particular topic; to access messages in a newsgroup, you need to use a newsreader.

nonkey field A field in a table that is not part of a table's primary key.

normal distribution A data set that has an equal number of values, equally spaced both above and below the median value.

normalization A process that reduces the chance of deletion, update, and insertion anomalies in a database.

NOT function The function that changes the Boolean value TRUE to FALSE and the Boolean value FALSE to TRUE.

Null value A field value that is unknown, unavailable, or missing.

Number The Access data type that stores numbers that are used in calculations.

numeric picture symbol A symbol that indicates how a number is displayed in a Word form.

numeric values Numbers such as integers and real numbers—1, 2, 3.3, 6.75, and so on.

O

object A term used to describe a graphic or other content in a file that can be manipulated as a whole.

Objects bar The part of the Database window that contains buttons to access objects so they can be created, opened, designed, and viewed.

OLE object The Access data type that identifies files that were created in another program and then linked to or embedded in the database.

one-to-many relationship (1:M) A relationship between tables in which one record in the first table matches zero, one, or many records in the related table.

one-to-one relationship (1:1) A relationship between tables in which each record in one table matches exactly one record in the related table.

Open Exclusive mode A method of opening an Access database that locks out all users except for the current user from opening and using the database at the same time.

Open Exclusive Read-Only mode A method of opening an Access database that locks out all users except for the current user, but the current user can only view the data in the database.

Open mode A method of opening an Access database that lets multiple users open and use the database at the same time; it is the default option for opening a database.

Open Read-Only mode A method of opening an Access database that lets multiple users open the database, but users cannot write any information to the database and are limited to viewing existing data only.

optimize To place keywords and phrases that a searcher might use to find the information on a Web page in a strategic location on the Web page in an effort to maximize the Web page's relevance for a search tool.

OR criteria The criteria that select records that match any of the specified values.

OR function The function that determines if at least one item from a list of Boolean values is TRUE. If such is the case, a TRUE value is returned.

orphaned The term used to describe a record whose matching record in a primary or related table has been deleted.

output The information generated as a result of data inputs and formulas.

Outline view A view that shows the structure of a document or slide show by using hierarchical headings so that you can easily organize and lay out the document or slide show. You need to work in Outline view when working with master documents.

P

Package for CD A feature in PowerPoint that allows you to save your presentation to a CD while maintaining links, embedding fonts, and providing a viewer that enables you to run the presentation on computers that do not have PowerPoint.

page footer A section of a report or form that appears at the end of every printed page.

page header A section of a report or form that appears at the top of every printed page.

parameter value A prompt used in a query to allow user input when the query is run. The value the user enters is then used as the criterion for that field.

parse To split data that is exported in fixed-width file format into its individual data elements.

partial dependency The situation in which a field is dependent on only part of a composite primary key.

password A collection of characters that a user types to gain access to a file.

payback period The number of periods (years) it will take to pay back an original investment.

percent value One of the options selected when splitting data points between charts in a pie of pie or bar of pie chart type. This option allows you to select a cut-off point by percentage, rather than value, and assign all the percentages below that point to the second plot.

permission The rules that specify the level of access in a database for a user or group of users.

personal ID (PID) In a database that uses user-level security, a string value with 4 to 20 characters that identifies a user.

pharming A type of computer scam in which code is installed on your computer that misdirects you to a fraudulent Web site without your knowledge or consent.

phishing A type of computer scam in which scam artists send authentic-looking e-mail to people purporting to be from a real organization and asking the recipient to reply by e-mail or click a link to a spoofed Web site and verify account information, such as passwords, credit card numbers, and Social Security numbers so that the scam artist can use this information for illegal identity theft.

pie chart A chart that compares the contribution each value in a single numeric data series makes to the whole, or 100%. Values are indicated by the size of the pie slices.

pixels The picture elements that make up the points of light on a computer screen. The higher the number of pixels, the higher the resolution of an image and the higher the quality of the image.

platform independent A characteristic of XML that allows data to be transferred from one type of computer and operating system to another. For example, data on a mainframe computer using a proprietary operating system can be transferred to a Windows XP computer.

PMT function The function that calculates the periodic payment of a financial transaction. This payment is assumed to be paid in equal periodic installments. The PMT function contains arguments for the periodic rate, number of periods (nper), present value (pv), and future value (fv) of the financial transaction.

position One of the options selected when splitting data points between charts in a pie of pie or bar of pie chart type. Data is directed to the secondary chart based on the relative position in the range.

positive cash flow The monies paid to a person/ institution; cash that is received.

PPMT function The function that calculates the value of the principal portion of a loan payment based on the original loan amount, periodic interest rate, and payment number.

preprocessing The process of manipulating data into the needed format.

primary sort field The field used to sort the records first, which must appear to the left of any other field. Additional fields used to further sort the records must appear to the right of the primary sort field.

primary table In a one-to-many relationship, the table that is on the "one" side of the relationship.

principal The value of a loan or investment.

problem A term that can be considered in two ways: as a question to be answered or as an obstacle or difficulty that prevents you from reaching some goal.

prolog The beginning part of an XML document that contains identifying information about the version of XML, the coding used for the data, and the document type.

promote A term used in Outline view in Word and PowerPoint that means to increase the level of a heading.

protect forms To prevent users of a Word form from changing the form fields while allowing them to complete the form.

protocol A set of rules used by the Internet for communication.

Q

query A database object that stores criteria for selecting records from one or more tables based on conditions you specify.

query by example (QBE) Creating a query by entering the values you want to use as criteria for selecting records.

R

radar chart A chart that displays changes in values relative to a center point and is named for their resemblance to the plots on radar screens as they scan a 360-degree circle. Values radiate from the center of the chart in a way that can be compared to radar screen plots, showing the distance of an object from the radar in the center. The categories are represented by lines that radiate out from the center.

RAND function The function that generates a random number (real number) between 0 and 1.

RANDBETWEEN function The function that generates a random integer between two values.

RANK function The function that gives the relative position of a value in a data set.

rate of return Also known as the hurdle rate or discount rate; the rate at which cash flows are discounted. Usually, this rate reflects current interest rates and the relative risk of the cash flows being evaluated.

RATE function The function that calculates the periodic interest rate of a financial transaction. The RATE function contains arguments for the number of periods (nper), periodic payment amount (pmt), present value (pv), and future value (fv) of the financial transaction.

Really Simple Syndication (RSS) An XML standard for providing updates such as news headlines and calendar updates to a Web site. It requires special software to view the results.

record (row) Collectively, the values in each field in a table for a single entity.

record source The underlying table or query object that provides the fields and data in a form.

recordset (query) A datasheet that contains the results of a query.

Reference and Lookup functions A category of functions that can look up or reference data stored in a table.

referential integrity A rule that if the foreign key in one table matches the primary key in a second table, the values in the foreign key must match the values in the primary key. When the database does not enforce referential integrity, certain problems occur that lead to inaccurate and inconsistent data.

registered file A file whose extension is associated with a program on your computer.

related table In a one-to-many relationship, the table that is on the "many" side of the relationship.

relational database A database that contains tables related through fields that contain identical data, also known as common fields.

relational expression A formula containing a relational operator that compares two values and returns a Boolean logical value (TRUE/FALSE).

relational operator An operator that compares two values:
- >>Greater than
- >=Greater than or equal to
- <<Less than
- <<=Less than or equal to
- =Equal to
- <>Not equal to

relative address In a hyperlink, a partial path that indicates the location of the linked page relative to the current page.

relative cell referencing A cell reference that, when copied from one location to another, automatically changes relative to the location to which it is being moved. For example, if a formula containing relative cell references is being copied one row down and two columns to the right, the formula adjusts each cell reference by one row down and two columns to the right.

repeating group In an incorrectly designed database table, a field that contains more than one value.

Replace Font A feature in PowerPoint that allows you to replace all the occurrences of one font with another font.

report A database object that presents the information from one or more database tables or queries in a printed format.

report footer A section of a report that is printed once at the end of the report. The report footer appears last in the report design but is printed before the final page footer.

report header A section of a report that is printed once at the beginning of the report. The report header is printed before the page header.

Report Wizard A wizard that guides you through the steps of creating a report based on one or more tables or queries by asking you questions about the record sources, fields, layout, and format you want to use.

Required property The property of a nonprimary key field that requires users to enter a value in the field.

result pages The list of Web sites that contain the keywords in a search expression.

ROI (Return on Investment) The ratio of profits to initial investment.

root element The element that contains all the other elements of an XML document. The tags are <dataroot> and </dataroot>. This is similar to the <html> and </html> tags that contain all of the other HTML tags.

root directory The top of the file system hierarchy in which Windows stores folders and important files that it needs when you turn on the computer.

S

Search Companion A Windows XP tool that helps you find files on your system.

search criteria The text or properties of the files or information you want to find.

search engine A search tool that searches a database of Web sites compiled by bots.

search expression A word or combination of words and phrases that are used by a search tool to locate Web pages containing the keywords in the search expression.

second normal form (2NF) A database table that is in first normal form and that does not contain any partial dependencies on the composite primary key.

sections The smaller parts of a document created so that headers and footers and other style options can vary from section to section.

select query A query that selects data from one or more tables according to specified criteria, and displays the data in a datasheet.

self-describing The characteristic of tags in an XML file that describe what the document contains rather than the format or style of the document.

shortcut A file that contains the full path to a file, folder, drive, or other object, which creates a direct link to that object.

sizing handle A small square that appears on the corners and edges of a selected control and that lets you resize the control.

Slide Master The place where PowerPoint stores design information about a presentation that is applied to every slide in the presentation, including fonts, placeholders, background design, color schemes, bullet styles, graphics placed on the background, and header and footer text.

SMALL function The function that displays the n the smallest element of a data set.

sort To arrange records in a table or query in a particular order or sequence.

source document The file that contains the original content you want to insert into another document.

spoof To create a Web site that looks like it belongs to another company but is designed to capture personal information from individuals that can be used for illegal identity theft.

stale data The data that is no longer current and shouldn't be used for decision making in an Excel map area.

standard deviation A measure of how widely a data set varies from the arithmetic mean.

static A document or Web page that does not allow data entry or recalculation. It contrasts with an interactive or dynamic document, which does allow user input.

statistics A subset of mathematics that is applied to understanding observed data.

straight line depreciation A method of depreciation that allocates depreciation evenly over a specified time period. The depreciable value is the original cost (Cost) less the salvage value (Salvage) at the end of its useful life (Life).

structural elements A type of container element used to specify the basic sections of an HTML document.

Structured Query Language (SQL) The common query language of most DBMSs, including Access. A query created in SQL can run in most database programs.

stylesheet Usually a separate document that defines how data should look. Because it is separate from the actual data, it doesn't affect the content of the data. XML documents may have different stylesheets for use with different application programs.

subdocument A Word document linked to a master document. Any content that is modified in the subdocument is automatically updated in the master document the next time it is opened.

subfolder A folder contained in another folder.

subject directory A search tool on the WWW that categorizes sites using human editors.

subreport A report that appears within another report and is usually used to display related data.

SUM function The function that adds a continuous or non continuous list of cell references, constants, and/or cell ranges, for example, =SUM(A1:A10, B7, 3).

summary report A type of grouped report that calculates totals for each group and a grand total for the entire report, and doesn't necessarily include details.

surrogate key A computer-generated primary key that is usually invisible to users.

switchboard A special kind of form that appears when you open a database and lists options for working with tables, forms, queries, and reports.

syntax The specific format of a function, including the function name and the order of the arguments in the function.

T

table (entity, relation) A collection of fields that describe one entity, such as a person, place, thing, or idea.

Table Wizard An Access wizard that includes sample tables for business and personal needs with fields that you can select and modify to create your own tables.

tags The text enclosed in angle brackets <> that tells a browser how to interpret and display the contents of the tags.

Text Box toolbar A toolbar in Word that allows the user to perform actions on a text box, including the creation and deletion of links between text boxes, text box navigation, and the changing of the text direction within text boxes.

text form field A field in a Word form that inserts a text box in the form that accepts numbers, spaces, symbols, or text, and can be designed to perform calculations.

text label The textual information that appears in a worksheet.

third normal form (3NF) A table that is in second normal form and the only determinants it contains are candidate keys.

Thumbnails view A view available in the My Computer or Windows Explorer window that displays files as miniature images of the file contents.

Tiles view A view available in the My Computer or Windows Explorer window that displays files as large icons with a filename and other details.

tiling The practice of taking a small graphic image and repeating it multiple times to make it appear as though it is one large graphic. Background images are often created using tiling.

time-series data The data that shows performance over time for periods such as years, quarters, or months.

Track Changes A feature in Word, PowerPoint, and Excel that keeps track of all modifications to a document. These changes include additions, deletions, and comments.

transitive dependency The situation that occurs between two nonkey fields that are both dependent on a third field; tables in third normal form should not have transitive dependencies.

trendline The line in a chart that graphically illustrates trends in the data using a statistical technique known as regression.

TRUE The Boolean value True, as differentiated from the text label "True."

two-dimensional table A lookup table in which data is stored at the intersection of a column and row.

U

unbound form An Access form with no record source, such as one containing instructions to help users navigate through a database.

unnormalized data Data that contains deletion, update, or insertion anomalies.

update anomaly The problem that occurs when, due to redundant data in a database, a user fails to update some records or updates records erroneously.

user-level security A type of database security that establishes specific levels of access to the database objects for individual groups of users.

V

validation rule A rule that compares the data entered into a field by a user against one or more valid values that the database developer specified.

Validation Rule property A property of a field that specifies the valid values that a user can enter into the field.

Validation Text property A property of a field that displays a predefined message if a user enters an invalid value into the field.

value One of the options selected when splitting data points between charts in a pie of pie or bar of pie chart type. This option allows you to select a cut-off point that assigns all the values below that point to the second plot.

Visual Basic for Applications (VBA) The programming language for Microsoft Office programs, including Access.

VLOOKUP function The function that looks up a value stored in the first column of a vertical lookup table and retrieves data stored in the same row of a subsequent column.

W

watermark A faded graphic or text that appears behind the text of a document.

Web Layout view A view in Word that shows how a document will look if saved as a Web page. There are no page breaks in Web layout view and the document expands or contracts in width to fit the size of the screen.

Web pages The documents on servers located around the world that are collected into Web sites and accessible using a browser.

Web sites A set of interconnected documents called Web pages that are stored on computers around the world.

well-formed A term used to describe XML documents that follow the rules for XML syntax.

what-if analysis The process of changing values to see how those changes affect the outcome of formulas in an Excel worksheet.

Wiki site A Web site that anyone can modify by contributing content and editing the content of others.

wildcard character A placeholder that stands for one or more characters. Common wildcards are the asterisk (matches any number of characters), question mark (matches any single alphabetic character), and pound sign (matches any single digit in a numeric field).

workbook An Excel file that contains one or more worksheets.

workgroup ID (WID) In a database that uses user-level security, the unique character string of 4 to 20 characters that identifies a workgroup.

workgroup information file In a database that uses user-level security, the file that defines user groups, usernames, and user passwords.

worksheet An Excel spreadsheet; a single two-dimensional sheet organized into rows (identified by row numbers 1, 2 ...n) and columns (identified by column letters A, B ...Z, AB ....). An Excel 2003 worksheet contains a maximum of 256 columns (IV) and 65, 536 rows.

World Wide Web (WWW) A subset of the Internet consisting of computers that use the hypertext transfer protocol (HTTP) to link together documents called Web pages on servers around the world.

X

X-axis The horizontal axis on which categories are plotted in a chart.

X-axis labels The labels that identify the categories plotted on the X-axis.

XML schema A file created when you export data in XML format that contains the structure for the data and the rules the data must follow.

Y

Y-axis The vertical axis on which data values are plotted in a chart.

Y-axis labels The labels that identify the data values plotted on the Y-axis.

Yes/No The Access data type that stores one of two values, such as yes or no, true or false, or on or off.